THE **LAWYER'S GUIDE** TO THE **FORENSIC SCIENCES**

THE LAWYER'S GUIDE TO THE FORENSIC SCIENCES

EDITED BY CAITLIN PAKOSH

IRWIN LAW

The Lawyer's Guide to the Forensic Sciences

Published in 2016 by
Irwin Law Inc.
14 Duncan Street
Suite 206
Toronto, ON
M5H 3G8
www.irwinlaw.com

ISBN: 978-1-55221-412-1
e-book ISBN: 978-1-55221-413-8

Library and Archives Canada Cataloguing in Publication

The lawyer's guide to the forensic sciences / edited by Caitlin Pakosh.

Includes bibliographical references and index.
Issued in print and electronic formats.
ISBN 978-1-55221-412-1 (paperback).—ISBN 978-1-55221-413-8 (pdf)

1. Forensic sciences—Canada. 2. Evidence, Expert—Canada. I. Pakosh, Caitlin, editor II. Title: Forensic sciences.

HV8073.L39 2016 363.250971 C2016-904942-6
C2016-904943-4

Canada

Ontario
Ontario Media Development Corporation
Société de développement de l'industrie des médias de l'Ontario

Printed and bound by CPI Group (UK) Ltd, Croydon, CR0 4YY
1 2 3 4 5 20 19 18 17 16

Summary Table of Contents

Detailed Table of Contents

List of Illustrations

TABLES

Foreword

This is an important book. It will be of vital importance to all those engaged in the pursuit of criminal justice.

It is the product of two realities. The first is that science is becoming ever-more important to the justice system, particularly to the criminal justice system. As science evolves, it is able to address, and attempt to explain, an ever-growing array of human activity. This makes it increasingly valuable—indeed, in many instances, essential—in resolving many of our most intractable legal problems.

Take the death of an infant in suspicious circumstances: always a deeply troubling event for families, for communities, and for the justice system itself. Often there are only two sources of evidence to throw light on what happened—the identity of the person who had care of the infant at the time of death; and the science of pediatric forensic pathology to address the possible cause of death. Without this science, the law cannot do justice or bring closure to the society it serves.

The second reality is that the justice system has much to learn about how to better engage with, and properly utilize, the science it needs. A number of the public inquiries and forensic science reports reviewed in this text demonstrate that graphically. They make clear the tragic costs of outcomes reached by a justice system acting on scientific evidence that it understands too little to perceive its own weaknesses.

It is in the context of these two realities that this book takes on the ambitious task of improving the understanding of forensic science by the legal community and, as a consequence, improving the quality of justice delivered by our law, particularly our criminal law.

The range of subjects addressed in this book is very impressive. It begins with the systemic issues that every lawyer must grapple with: how to identify the proper expert; how to effectively communicate with the expert; and how to best prepare and effectively present the expert's scientific opinion to a forum of non-scientists.

These chapters are followed by a description of the various public inquiries and reports that have conducted post-mortems on scientific evidence gone wrong, at great cost to wrongly convicted individuals, and to public confidence in the justice system. This provides graphic evidence of past mistakes made because of faulty science, and the need for the criminal justice system to do better.

The core of the book then elucidates how this can be done. The sciences that are essential to adjudicate so many cases are explained in clear language that is easily understood even by lawyers who went to law school because they could not do science. Blood spatter analysis, fingerprint and ballistic evidence, forensic biology, DNA evidence, and forensic pathology are only a few examples of the array of science used in the courts that are addressed, chapter by chapter.

The utility of this book is only enhanced by the credentials of the contributing authors. They range from senior academics to leading legal practitioners to experienced police officers. Each is a worthy exponent of his or her particular science. All also have a close familiarity with the justice system. Collectively, their erudition and experience gives the text real intellectual heft. Its quality is impossible to miss.

In summary, this is a book whose time has come. Science, in all its manifestations, is being called on with ever-greater frequency in our courts. This makes it absolutely essential that lawyers and judges have a growing comfort level with science and the tools with which to assess its reliability. Just outcomes depend on it. The good news is that this book arrives at a moment when lawyers and judges have a growing recognition of this need to do better with scientific evidence, coupled with a growing desire to achieve that goal.

This book points the way. The justice system will be the better for it.

The Honourable Justice Stephen T. Goudge

Preface

This book all started with an idea: criminal lawyers should be scientifically literate and armed with sufficient knowledge of the forensic sciences in order to critically evaluate them. The idea was a good one and, for that reason, was not new. In fact, as a forensic science graduate-turned-lawyer, I quickly came to appreciate the extensive history surrounding this recommendation for improved scientific literacy in the criminal bar. Public inquiries, the judiciary, and lawyers themselves recognized a need for the legal community to learn more about science. Working on wrongful conviction cases, it was clear to me that being scientifically literate and having an understanding of the evolution of the forensic sciences was not only advantageous, but necessary. Justice could only be achieved through education. Speakers at conferences I attended made me feel confident that that belief was true. They joked about the uncomfortable reality that lawyers, who specifically went into the law to avoid science and numbers, would not be able to escape learning about science for long. For that reason, I initially assumed that there would be a number of resources available to help guide lawyers through the forensic sciences. I was surprised by what I found.

In wanting to develop my own specialization in the intersection between forensic sciences and the law, I discovered that there was a paucity of recent Canadian resources directed at lawyers that addressed the forensic sciences. The recommendations made by so many others before me remained in place, repeated and recognized, but not fully realized. The most recent books I could find were from 1999, notably Gary Chayko and Edward

Gulliver's *Forensic Science in Canada*, 2d ed. (Toronto: Canada Law Book, 1999) and Frederick A. Jaffe's *A Guide to Pathological Evidence for Lawyers and Police Officers*, 4th ed. (Toronto: Carswell, 1999). These books were excellent at the time but too old to be relied upon today and, like the books, I was in sore need of an update in the forensic sciences. Alan D. Gold's 2009 book (originally published in 2003), *Expert Evidence in Criminal Law*, 2d ed. (Toronto: Irwin Law, 2009), was helpful for its critical analysis of the sciences in the courtroom, and I read a number of other legal books addressing expert evidence (Glenn Anderson's *Expert Evidence*, 3d ed. [Toronto: LexisNexis, 2014], is an excellent resource). Separate from the legal analysis, I still needed more information about the forensic sciences standing alone. I attended conferences, seminars, and continuing professional development courses, avidly learning as much as I could and realizing that there was no clear, overarching educational strategy in place to teach lawyers about the forensic sciences. Learning about science from legal judgments was difficult and confusing. Since the scientific evidence in some cases had become outdated, relying on caselaw to learn about science was helpful from a historical perspective, but often a risk to apply to current cases.

In June 2014, I thought of putting this guide together to fill the gap in the available literature. I had envisioned this guide being different from other legal texts because I didn't intend it to be a legal book at all. I didn't want it to be another book on expert evidence—that had already been done, and done well. Instead, I wanted this guide to be a science book for lawyers, written by experts, with just enough legal context to provide lawyers with ideas on why knowledge in that area might be important to their cases. Ironically, the voice of the scientific community seemed to be absent in so many legal publications I read about the forensic sciences. And many of the publications addressing the intersection between forensic sciences and the law were not geared towards the Canadian perspective and experience. I hesitated in spearheading a project like this because I was painfully aware of my limited experience and knew full well that far more experienced, senior counsel should put a book like this together. That awareness and insecurity, however, was paired with an understanding of the urgent need to have a resource like this available for the legal community. Time had come and gone, and we were still without a book that was recent, science-centric, and Canadian. Waiting would simply maintain the status quo. Excited but cringing with worry, I decided to jump in and get to work. Looking back now, my excitement was at least half ignorance and I'm grateful for it. If I knew then what I know now, the book may have never been made. I completely underestimated the amount of effort, time, and heart it would take to turn this book into a reality. It has been, however, one of the most rewarding journeys I have ever embarked upon.

The first two experts I approached were Dr. Cecilia Hageman, a forensic biologist, and Dr. Tracy Rogers, a forensic anthropologist and one of my former professors. Both Cecilia and Tracy were excited about the project and signed on immediately, advising me to draw up an outline for the book (at the time, I called it a handbook and didn't see it being any bigger than 250 pages). I told them I would have the outline to them in two weeks. In true and totally prepared form, Tracy sent me an email slightly before the two-week mark asking if I had completed the book outline. It was summertime—of course I had nothing done. I told her I would get it to her by the end of the week. I spent my nights after work constructing the skeleton for what would become a monster of a project. By the end of the week, both Tracy and Cecilia were provided with the outline for the book, and in the ensuing weeks they provided me with feedback on how to improve the outline, making the book better as a whole from its very foundations. I owe both of them my gratitude, as they were instrumental in critically evaluating the structure of the book, giving me the feedback I needed to polish it into a standardized framework that I could confidently present to other experts for the purpose of enticing them to contribute.

The next step? Getting help, and lots of it. I was, of course, not an expert in any of the forensic sciences, so I needed the help of people who were—ideally, Canadian experts who were recognized as being at the top of their fields and who were well-equipped to provide the legal community with education about their specific forensic disciplines. I had a good sense of which forensic sciences would be most needed by lawyers (forensic pathology and fingerprinting, to name just two). Initially, I had about eight chapters in mind, which meant that each contributor would only have to write thirty pages to make a handbook of 250 pages. I set about researching who might be appropriate to approach about contributing to the handbook. This took some time, as I wanted to know as much as I could about the potential experts before approaching them. I also felt it was necessary to be familiar with each discipline before speaking with them so I could convey intelligently what exactly I wanted (admittedly, needed) them to write for this book. Some forensic disciplines I was more familiar with than others. Once the preliminary research was done, I took the time where I could to ask other lawyers about the expert I intended to approach.

With so much already invested, I started cold calling (and cold emailing) to invite experts to contribute to the book. Each time, I was worried that I would be met with a strong "no," but the response was in fact the exact opposite. I was shocked, relieved, and exhilarated at how well-received the idea was by the contributors. Top experts were signing on happily, often suggesting ideas of their own that simply made the book better. Dr. Gail Anderson, for example, asked me if the book would include forensic botany. After asking her for an explanation of what forensic botany even was (a question Irwin Law would ask of me later), she referred me to Dr. Rolf Mathewes, who signed on to write a chapter. The book was gaining momentum and with each expert who signed on, the next "ask" became easier. Very quickly, our little group became a team and the "handbook" I envisioned transformed into a "guide." (I thought at that point the book would be about 700 pages . . . I only learned near the very end of the project that it would be about 1,000 pages.)

On James Wigmore's recommendation, I approached the president of Irwin Law, Jeff Miller, with the idea for the book and the names of the experts who had agreed to contribute. Beyond the outline, nothing had been written. I met with Jeff and his team, who believed in the idea and agreed to publish the book. Being bright-eyed and optimistic with how smoothly the project was coming together, I initially agreed to complete the book in a year. Needless to say, the team at Irwin Law proved to be exceptionally patient.

Over the next two years, our team diligently worked away at completing each portion of the book, which had since grown to twenty-three chapters. Time passed and we all had to juggle our personal and professional lives on top of our commitment to finish the book. I had the pleasure of getting to know each contributor a little better over the course of this project and had a number of moments where I was struck with the high calibre of the contributors—not just as authorities in their field, but as individuals. I learned a great deal about each discipline throughout the project and am grateful to each contributor for taking the time to teach me about their work and perspective as we tried to polish each chapter to its final form. Before long, the book was by and large complete (with editing and re-editing occurring throughout, in concert with the input of each contributor). It was summertime again, June 2016—two years after I scrambled to write an outline—and this time, everything was done.

I can sincerely say that I am proud of what our team accomplished. In all of us having to edit and re-edit the contributions to this book, contributors often expressed contentment with what they produced, but matched that feeling with a critical evaluation of what more they wanted to do. There is always more to do and there will always be more to do. This book is, at the very least, a good beginning. I hope it will serve the legal community well as a basic overview into the forensic sciences and its critical analysis, acting as a touchstone resource on the subject that lawyers can mark up as they work through their own cases.

From my experience in working on this book, I can see that both the scientific and legal communities are interested in improving dialogue and better understanding each other. Working together may not always come naturally, particularly given the adversarial system in criminal law, but education and collaboration is necessary to work within our appropriate roles in the criminal justice system. With an improved understanding of the forensic sciences, the legal community will be better equipped to critically analyze them. Whenever forensic evidence is entered in court, its reliability must be explored and its limitations understood. Legal arguments must be compelling but accurate to the evidence, and forensic scientists must be careful to testify within the scope of their expertise, relying on an evidence-based approach to science. The end goal: to ensure that the criminal justice system operates as fairly and reasonably as possible, upholding the administration of justice while preventing wrongful convictions.

Acknowledgements

The success of this guide has been the result of the dedication of so many people. I am grateful to each one of you.

Without the forensic experts who contributed to this book, the idea of creating a book by forensic experts for criminal lawyers would have never gotten off the ground. I was pleasantly surprised by the scientific community's excitement about creating a book like this, and over the two years we spent putting it together, I had the privilege to work with a team of not only exceptional experts, but wonderful people. Thank you for inspiring me to work early mornings, late nights, and weekends to do my part in seeing this project to completion. To the Irwin Law team and its president, Jeff Miller, thank you for taking a chance on this project in the first place and for believing it could be done when all I came to you with was an idea. Lesley Steeve and Alisa Posesorski, thank you for all the long hours you spent polishing up this book and for guiding me through my own responsibilities as editor. Your attention to detail and patience throughout this process have been sincerely appreciated. Lesley, your sense of humour made reading and rereading the same content over and over again much more fun than it would have been otherwise.

Beyond all the professionals who helped to put this book together, I owe a great deal to everyone in my personal life who put up with me essentially working two jobs over the past two years. I know it was not easy and that the journey has been a long one. To my parents, Russ and Maureen, thank you for giving me the love and support that I needed to grow into the person I am today. Without it, I would not have had the confidence to even think about taking on a project like this, let alone spearheading it. Both of you have been excellent role models and I am proud to be your daughter. To Mimi, thank you for being a wonderful grandmother and confidant, and for sharing all your memories with me. I hope to age like you have—with goodness, grace, and grit (just the right balance to be kind, clever, and tough). To David, thank you for loving me unconditionally and for being my biological best friend. As your older sister, I am so happy to have had the opportunity to watch you grow into the strong and compassionate man you have become and will continue to be. To Cullum, I am stronger as a person because of you and I hope the future brings you happiness and success. To Roman, thank you for loving me through all my stubbornness, for taking the time to convince me to take breaks (no matter how many times I needed to be reminded), and for supporting me on those occasions when I felt completely overwhelmed by the weight of this project. The hugs always helped. To my friends, thank you for keeping me smiling, laughing, and appreciating that the best moments in my life happen outside of work.

DEDICATION

To my family and friends. Thank you for teaching me to laugh first, learn second, and love always. — CMP

CHAPTER 1

The Need for Scientific Literacy in the Legal Community

Caitlin Pakosh

> A criminal case is not the ideal forum for resolving difficult scientific questions. But, if such questions spring from a recognized body of scientific knowledge that bear [*sic*] upon the reliability of important pieces of evidence, whether Crown or Defence, it is no solution to ignore the controversy and shield the jury from difficulties. We do not aid the search for truth by pretending there is no dispute or depriving the defence of the opportunity to challenge the reliability of evidence through presentation of legitimate scientific evidence.[1]
>
> — Rosenberg J.A.

Theoretically, science and the law intersect in the courtroom in the pursuit of truth. This traditional view of truth-seeking, however, is marred by the limitations and realities of the criminal justice system. Science evolves rapidly in a community of competing opinions and ever-changing interpretations. Forensic science—science applied to the legal context—has undergone dramatic changes in recent years, owing to widespread support for an evidence-based approach, an approach grounded in objectivity and experimentation rather than subjectivity and experience. Law, in contrast to the open-ended process of scientific inquiry, embraces finality and seeks to administer justice in a manner that ensures a trial court's decision can be relied upon by those affected by the process. To that end, in the words

1 *R. v. B.M*, [1998] O.J. No. 4359 at para. 79 (C.A.).

of Charron J.A. (as she then was): "The appellate process cannot become or even appear to become a never-closing revolving door through which appellants come and go whenever they propose to argue a new ground of appeal."[2] The adversarial process has its own inequalities that act as a barrier to the truth, not the least of which is a resource and access to evidence imbalance between the Crown and the defence.[3] Therefore, in reality, science and the law intersect in the courtroom to pursue truth, but not without significant tension that may never be fully resolved.

The court in *Daubert v. Merrell Dow Pharmaceuticals* best summarized the core of the tension between science and the law: "Scientific conclusions are subject to perpetual revision. Law, on the other hand, must resolve disputes finally and quickly."[4] The most immediate, practical way to mitigate such tension in the courtroom is through education, well before the laying of any criminal charge. The purpose of this guide is to do exactly that—to educate lawyers about the evolution and current status of multiple disciplines within the forensic sciences in the criminal law context, specific to the Canadian legal system and written by Canadian experts. This guide is macroscopic in view to provide practising criminal lawyers, defence and Crown alike, with an overview of each discipline in a concise format that facilitates further case-specific research. Its goal is to: (1) improve the scientific literacy of criminal lawyers, (2) reinvigorate dialogue and improve collaboration between the forensic and legal communities in Canada, and (3) contribute to the effective functioning of a fair and reasonable criminal justice system.

The need for scientific literacy in the legal community is not a new idea, but the path to developing a comprehensive educational strategy has been less than clear. The importance of science education is evident in countless cases, particularly in the wrongful conviction cases that lead to public inquiries. As observed by Commissioner Patrick J. LeSage, Q.C., in his *Report of the Commission of Inquiry into Certain Aspects of the Trial and Conviction of James Driskell*:

> Several of the panellists noted that in the years since the Morin Report, there has been growing recognition of the importance of ensuring that

---

2 *R. v. Hamilton; R. v. Rhingo*, [1997] O.J. No. 1110 at para 34 (C.A.). Justice Charron was later appointed to the Supreme Court of Canada in 2004 and retired in 2011.

3 Keith A. Findley, "Adversarial Inquisitions: Rethinking the Search for Truth" (2012) 56 *New York Law School Law Review* 911.

4 *Daubert v. Merrell Dow Pharmaceuticals, Inc.*, 509 U.S. 579 (1993).

> judges and juries understand the underlying scientific basis for a stated conclusion, including all of the associated limitations and uncertainties.[5]

In addition to the importance of educating the legal community about the limitations and uncertainties in science, many forensic disciplines have recently been criticized for lacking an underlying scientific basis altogether—arguably necessitating a more in-depth approach to scientific legal education than previously appreciated. In 2009, the National Academy of Sciences (NAS), on the authority of the United States Congress, released a groundbreaking report that strongly criticized the scientific foundation of many forensic disciplines and recommended an overhaul of the approach to the forensic sciences in the United States. To this end, the National Commission on Forensic Science, co-chaired by the Department of Justice (DOJ) and National Institute of Standards and Technology (NIST), was formed in 2013 to enhance the practice and reliability of the forensic sciences.[6] As a result of this process, the development of forensic science standards and guidelines has transitioned from the traditional Scientific Working Groups (SWGs) to the Organization of Scientific Area Committees (OSACs) to reach consensus on documentation standards and guidelines, as well as to ensure that each forensic discipline has a sufficient scientific basis.[7]

Importantly, the NAS committee recognized the importance of educating lawyers and judges to ensure the reliability of forensic evidence offered at trial, highlighting that any admissibility checklist for scientific testimony is imperfect:

> In addition, lawyers and judges often have insufficient training and background in scientific methodology, and they often fail to fully comprehend the approaches employed by different forensic science disciplines and the reliability of forensic science evidence that is offered in trial. Such training is essential, because any checklist for the admissibility of scientific or technical testimony is imperfect. Conformance with items

---

5 The Honourable Patrick LeSage, Q.C., Commissioner, "Report of the Commission of Inquiry into Certain Aspects of the Trial and Conviction of James Driskell" (Winnipeg: The Commission, 2007) at 166.

6 The United States Department of Justice, "National Commission on Forensic Science," online www.justice.gov/ncfs.

7 National Institute of Standards and Technology (NIST), "Organization of Scientific Area Committees" (20 May 2015), online: www.nist.gov/forensics/osac/index.cfm.

> on a checklist can suggest that testimony is reliable, but it does not guarantee it.
>
> . . .
>
> Law schools should enhance this connection by offering courses in the forensic science disciplines, by offering credit for forensic science courses taken in other colleges, and by developing joint degree programs. And judges need to be better educated in forensic science methodologies and practices.[8]

In Canada, some university programs offer a limited selection of law-related courses to forensic science students and forensic science-related courses to law students but unlike the United States, a joint degree program does not exist. Such a program would prepare new forensic scientists and lawyers for a future working within the criminal justice system. Working scientists and lawyers must learn about the intersection of these disciplines through their own case experiences, continuing education programs, and self-directed research projects. Considering the fast-paced evolution of science, and the law's difficulty in keeping pace with scientific developments, it is potentially dangerous for criminal lawyers to construct "rules of thumb" about science by simply reading case law or accepting the expert opinions they encounter in criminal proceedings.

To avoid the creation of inaccurate "rules of thumb," educational materials have been developed to make on-the-job learning about the basics of science easier for the busy lawyer or judge. For example, following the recommendations of the *Inquiry into Pediatric Forensic Pathology in Ontario* (the Goudge Inquiry), the National Judicial Institute (NJI) published the *Science Manual for Canadian Judges*, "to provide judges with tools to better understand expert evidence and to assess the validity of purportedly scientific evidence presented to them."[9] The manual is commendable in its breadth and detail. It covers, among other topics, a number of issues relevant to understanding scientific evidence, including the scientific method, statistics, and ethics. The manual is an excellent resource for judges and counsel alike, but it does not educate the reader on the forensic disciplines themselves, particularly with respect to recent criticisms. This guide is in-

---

8 Committee on Identifying the Needs of the Forensic Sciences Community, National Research Council, *Strengthening Forensic Science in the United States: A Path Forward* (Washington, DC: National Academies Press, 2009) at 27.

9 National Judicial Institute, *Science Manual for Canadian Judges*, online: www.nji-inm.ca/index.cfm/publications.

tended to fill that gap. Canadian lawyers may also find the *Reference Manual on Scientific Evidence*,[10] developed in the United States by the National Research Council, valuable as it addresses specific forensic disciplines.

Importantly, the *Science Manual for Canadian Judges* highlights three areas of similarity between science and the law:

1) An assessment of the weight of the evidence results in a binary (i.e., true/false, yes/no) decision.
   a) *Science*: A provisional conclusion is reached that the hypothesis being tested is or is not true.
   b) *Law*: The court finds in favour of either the prosecution/plaintiff or the accused/defendant.
2) Both fields start with a standing exculpatory predisposition that is overturned only when contradictory evidence exceeds a defined standard of proof.
   a) *Science*: The standing predisposition is that the null hypothesis—an assumption that the experimental observations are produced by chance, rather than a factor that is not random—is presumed to be true. The standard is to reject the null hypothesis only if there is at least 95 percent certainty, statistically speaking, that the null hypothesis is false. The standing predisposition is therefore that any factor is not causative unless the evidence shows otherwise.
   b) *Law*: In criminal law, the standing predisposition is that the accused is presumed innocent. The standard of proof is "beyond a reasonable doubt." The standing predisposition is therefore that the accused is not guilty unless the evidence shows otherwise.
3) The standing predisposition and its standard of proof is set as a normative decision based on the consequences that may occur if an inference is made in error.
   a) *Science*: It is better to reject a true hypothesis than to accept a false hypothesis. Accepting a false hypothesis would be a greater impediment to scientific progress.
   b) *Law*: It is better to free the guilty than to convict the innocent. Convicting the innocent is a greater injustice.[11]

---

10 National Research Council, *Reference Manual on Scientific Evidence*, 3d ed. (Washington, DC: National Academy Press, 2011).

11 Scott Findlay and Nathalie Chalifour, "Chapter 2: Science and the Scientific Method" National Judicial Institute in *Science Manual for Canadian Judges* (2013) at 40–41, online: www.nji-inm.ca/index.cfm/publications.

The similarities between science and the law may be used to make the unfamiliar familiar but, as observed by Justice Ian Binnie, the legal and scientific cultures only *seem* to have a great deal in common.[12] The differences between the two disciplines are most easily observed when considering forensic errors—errors in testing, technique, or testimony—and the corresponding increased likelihood of wrongful convictions in cases where forensic errors exist.[13] The tragic human costs of miscarriages of justice are difficult to calculate and represent a triple failure of the justice system: a person is unjustly convicted, the true perpetrator remains free, and the victim's family must face the reality that the person convicted for the crime is not the true perpetrator.[14]

According to the Innocence Project, based in New York City, unvalidated or improper forensics is the second leading contributing cause of wrongful convictions (47 percent), after eyewitness misidentification (72 percent).[15] The Innocence Project defines unvalidated or improper forensics as:

- the use of forensic disciplines or techniques that have not been tested to establish their validity and reliability;
- testimony about forensic evidence that presents inaccurate statistics, gives statements of probability or frequency (whether numerical or non-numerical) in the absence of valid empirical data, interprets non-probative evidence as inculpatory, or concludes/suggests that evidence is uniquely connected to the defendant without empirical data to support such testimony; or
- misconduct, either by fabricating inculpatory data or failing to disclose exculpatory data.[16]

---

12 Ian Binnie, "Science in the Courtroom: The Mouse That Roared" (2007) 56 *University of New Brunswick Law Journal* 307 at 308 [Binnie].

13 Jon B. Gould et al., *Predicting Erroneous Convictions: A Social Science Approach to Miscarriages of Justice* (Rockville, MD: National Criminal Justice Reference Service, 2012) at xiii–xxii [Gould et al.]. Professor Gould is a lawyer and social scientist at American University in the Department of Justice, Law & Criminology.

14 Bruce A. MacFarlane, "Convicting the Innocent: A Triple Failure of the Justice System" (2006) 31:1 *Manitoba Law Journal* 403 at 480.

15 Innocence Project, "The Causes of Wrongful Conviction," online: www.innocenceproject.org/causes-wrongful-conviction. The percentages do not add up to 100 percent because wrongful convictions may have more than one contributing factor.

16 Innocence Project, "Wrongful Convictions Involving Unvalidated or Improper Forensic Science that Were Later Overturned through DNA Testing," online: www.innocenceproject.org/causes-wrongful-conviction/DNA_Exonerations_Forensic_Science.pdf.

A 2012 study funded by the United States Department of Justice concluded that forensic errors may determine the outcome of a case and that such errors occur most often during the interpretation and testimony stage, rather than during testing[17]—in short, forensic errors occur most frequently at the intersection of the legal and scientific cultures. Forensic errors assist in predicting erroneous convictions,[18] where forensic errors are associated with a 14 percent increase in the chance that an erroneous conviction will occur.[19] Gould et al. recommended better forensic education for prosecutors, particularly since erroneous convictions were associated with weak prosecutions (i.e., weak case facts or weak evidence against the accused), but noted that judges and defence lawyers also appeared to lack training and education in forensic science.[20]

Although this guide focuses on delivering on long-standing recommendations for legal education about science, it is important to recognize that education is only one aspect of the growing support for large-scale systemic reform to the criminal justice system's treatment of expert evidence. This demand for change is grounded in the view that the present adversarial system fails to safeguard against the use of invalid forensic scientific testimony at trial. In one study examining wrongful convictions involving invalid forensic science testimony, it was found that the defence often lacks the expertise and resources needed to challenge such evidence and, when judges are made aware of such issues, they rarely remedy the error.[21] Justice Ian Binnie recommended a number of changes to make courts more "science friendly," including, among other recommendations, modifying the adversarial system by providing basic science seminars outside the courtroom that are relevant to the specific matter in dispute, improving pre-trial case management, appointing scientific *amicus curiae*, and modifying the rules of procedure.[22]

More recently, Gary Edmond and Kent Roach recommended a radical change to the admissibility of expert evidence in court: recognizing a differing admissibility threshold for expert evidence called by the defence and

17 Gould et al., above note 13 at xiii–xxii.

18 *Ibid.* at 76. In this study, the term "erroneous convictions" refers to cases involving "a factually innocent defendant who was indicted by a state for a violent felony against a person and was subsequently relieved of all legal responsibility for the crime" (p. xv).

19 *Ibid.* at 70.

20 *Ibid.* at 78, 83, and 99.

21 Brandon L. Garrett & Peter J. Neufeld, "Invalid Forensic Science Testimony and Wrongful Convictions" (2009) 95 *Virginia Law Review* 1 at 96–97.

22 Binnie, above note 12 at 15–17.

the prosecution. Edmond and Roach argue that expert evidence tendered by the defence should need to meet only a basic threshold of reliability, while expert evidence tendered by the Crown should meet a higher "demonstrable reliability" (i.e., evidence of reliability) standard. The Edmond-Roach proposal represents a contextual approach to admissibility that takes into account "criminal-justice values"[23] and aims to "foster an exclusionary ethos."[24] A contextual approach would demand that incriminating expert opinions without evidence of reliability would be excluded from evidence, independent of any assessment that may have been otherwise made by the jury.[25]

Edmond and Roach also argue that such an approach would address the validity of the forensic science in question and its contribution to wrongful convictions, while also relieving some responsibility from the inconsistently applied traditional safeguards of the criminal justice system.[26] The following were considered to be traditional safeguards of the adversarial system: "prosecutorial restraint, cross-examination, opposing experts, judicial instructions, the participation of lay jurors, and appellate review."[27] The Edmond-Roach proposal, perhaps not surprisingly, ignited heated dialogue.[28] How the legal system should best handle expert evidence is a complex question and it is unlikely that consensus will be reached in the immediate future, if ever. This question is well beyond the scope of this guide.

This guide focuses on the comparatively more manageable goal of educating the legal community about science. Both the scientific and legal communities should shoulder the responsibility for ensuring that scientific testimony offered at trial is valid, accurate, and reliable. By working together and engaging in continual dialogue, the criminal justice system can be strengthened through collaboration. A failure to collaborate will re-

---

23 Gary Edmond & Kent Roach, "A Contextual Approach to the Admissibility of the State's Forensic Science and Medical Evidence" (2011) 61 *University of Toronto Law Journal* 343 at 384. On page 345, these values are described to include: "the presumption of innocence, the need for the state to prove guilt beyond a reasonable doubt, and the goal of preventing the conviction of the innocent."

24 *Ibid.* at 405.

25 *Ibid.*

26 *Ibid.* at 347.

27 *Ibid.*

28 Ken Chasse, "Comment: 'Junk Science' by Way of a Higher Burden of Proof" (2012) 16:3 *Canadian Criminal Law Review* 323. Gary Edmond & Kent Roach, "Comment: A Reply to Chasse's "'Junk Science' by Way of a Higher Burden of Proof" (2012) 16:3 *Canadian Criminal Law Review* 357.

flect a failure on the part of both communities to learn from past mistakes, particularly with the knowledge that flawed or misleading scientific evidence has contributed to wrongful convictions. To maintain the legitimacy and reputation of the administration of justice in Canada, the scientific and legal communities must work together to critically evaluate Canadian systems of forensic science service delivery to ensure that the science is indeed "good," that it meets standards of quality, reliability, and transparency. Where a person's liberty is at stake, procedural fairness and the principles of fundamental justice should dictate that only good science inform the decisions of the Court and impact the future of the individual.

CHAPTER 2

Forensic Experts in the Criminal Justice System*

Caitlin Pakosh

A. INTRODUCTION

On 17 June 2015, a collaborative discussion among the contributors of this book took place to address the use of forensic experts in the criminal justice system. Contributors who could not attend the discussion provided their thoughts to the editor either over the phone or in writing.

Four primary issues were discussed: (1) identifying and retaining a "good" expert; (2) ensuring effective communication in the lawyer-expert relationship; (3) ensuring counsel and the court understand and correctly interpret the expert evidence; and (4) developing recommendations to improve collaboration between the scientific and legal communities.

B. DISCUSSION

1) Identifying and Retaining a "Good" Expert

a) What Is a "Good" Expert?

Defence and prosecution strategies may influence what each side considers to be a "good" expert since the expert that each side wants is the one

* Written by Caitlin Pakosh, this chapter is intended to reflect the content of the collaborative discussion mentioned in section A. Meeting minutes were taken by Katherine Linton, Juris Doctor (J.D.) candidate at the Bora Laskin Faculty of Law at Lakehead University. The space for the meeting was kindly provided by Innocence Canada.

who helps them illustrate their overarching argument. The role and duty of the defence in adversarial proceedings, for example, is to advance every argument that the lawyer thinks will help the client's case.[1] The defence may therefore seek an expert who can clearly and concisely challenge the scientific evidence presented by the prosecution. Either side may retain or subpoena an expert that they believe will help them "win" the case. The use of an inexperienced, biased, or otherwise compromised expert may be viewed by the opposing side as a sign of desperation.

Regardless of the lawyers' strategies, the role of the trier of fact is to weigh the evidence presented at trial. So, in addition to being sufficiently accredited or certified, a "good" expert seeks to assist the court in understanding the issues before it by presenting one piece of the "evidence puzzle." The trier of fact will then assess the expert's testimony in light of the totality of the evidence. The testimony of the expert should be based on empirical evidence and, particularly when the expert is testifying for the Crown, a problematic or insufficient evidentiary base should be quickly identified and challenged by defence counsel. Otherwise, such an expert may contribute to a finding of guilt that is unsupported by scientific evidence.

The context of the case should be explained to the expert to ensure an understanding of the circumstances of the case, and how the scientific evidence fits into the picture of the case as a whole. Experts, however, should not get emotionally involved in the case. Such emotions lead to bias that may negatively impact both their findings and the findings of the court. Lawyers should ask each expert they work with how much information they need to develop an appropriate context for the case. Depending on the discipline, the expert may wish to know everything about the case or as little as possible (to avoid bias).

b) What Issues Should Lawyers Be Aware of When Retaining or Subpoenaing an Expert?

There are certain issues or "red flags" that lawyers should be aware of before finalizing their decision to retain or subpoena a particular expert.

1 Law Society of Upper Canada, "Relationship to the Administration of Justice" in *Rules of Professional Conduct* (2014), online: www.lsuc.on.ca/WorkArea/DownloadAsset.aspx?id=2147499501.

Lawyers should ensure that their expert meets, at a minimum, the following checklist before relying upon a particular expert for assistance:

- *Accreditation and quality assurance.* Experts should come from an accredited lab and/or should meet any accreditation or certification requirements of their profession. Forensic accredited facilities have quality assurance programs to ensure their employees meet a certain level of quality.
- *Continuing education.* Experts should be able to provide a history of their efforts to keep their training up to date.
- *Membership in oversight organizations and relevant academies or associations.* Experts should belong to organizations that have quality assurance and ethical standards that permit membership to be revoked if best practices are breached.

In addition to ensuring an expert has proper credentials, lawyers considering retaining a particular expert should speak to other lawyers who have used or observed the expert while testifying. If practical, obtain transcripts of past testimony to assess the expert. This will assist in determining any existing biases or behaviour on the stand that the lawyer may consider relevant to the decision to retain or subpoena.

c) What Issues Should Experts Be Aware of When Being Retained or Subpoenaed by a Lawyer?

A good expert who understands the importance of context will be wary of a lawyer who provides only a small amount of information about a case. Although this may be done to guard against bias, it may also be done—consciously or unconsciously—to present the case to the expert in a manner most favourable to the legal argument. Whatever the intention, a lawyer who censors the details of the case may leave the expert in the unfortunate position of learning important details in court. If new details are presented to the expert while testifying, the expert may need to modify or retract the original opinion, which may change the tone of the case before the court.

It is difficult for an expert to detect whether a lawyer is advising them of all the necessary details of a case. The expert simply cannot know what they do not know. It is the lawyer's responsibility to assist the expert by providing the necessary context. In DNA cases, for example, it is important that the expert be advised of all of the relationships of the parties involved in the case to determine whether there may be an innocent explanation for DNA transfer.

On the other hand, the expert may prefer not knowing the whole story of the case as that may create bias. The lawyer and the expert should come to an understanding on how to address the problem effectively before the expert begins assessing the case. The information required for the expert to have sufficient context to assess the case varies by discipline. For example, a forensic pathologist may wish to know as little as possible about a case in order to arrive at an independent conclusion with respect to the cause and manner of death. Police theories or witness accounts may bias such conclusions if presented to the forensic pathologist in advance of their assessment.

Experienced lawyers will typically disclose an appropriate amount of information to the expert, but less experienced lawyers may bring too much or too little. An expert should be aware that some lawyers, particularly novice lawyers, may not be able to verbalize exactly why they need an expert. The expert should ask, "Why do you need my expertise?" This will help the lawyer place the required expertise in the context of the case as a whole and help them focus on information relevant to the expert's assessment. The "good" expert will contact the lawyer if more information is necessary.

d) Tunnel Vision: An Issue Relevant to Both the Legal and the Scientific Communities

"Tunnel vision" was first defined in the Canadian legal context by Commissioner Fred Kaufman in his report *The Commission on Proceedings Involving Guy Paul Morin* as "the single-minded and overly narrow focus on a particular investigative or prosecutorial theory, so as to unreasonably colour the evaluation of information received and one's conduct in response to that information."[2]

The legal and scientific communities must maintain an awareness of the effects of tunnel vision. Specifically, that information pointing to a particular person—the accused—may contribute to bias that is difficult to overcome. It is vital that lawyers and experts communicate well when determining how much context is required by the expert to assess the case—such contextual information may inadvertently bias the expert's

---

2 Ontario, Ministry of the Attorney General, *Report of the Kaufman Commission on Proceedings Involving Guy Paul Morin* (Toronto: Queen's Printer for Ontario, 1998) Recommendation 74, online: www.attorneygeneral.jus.gov.on.ca/english/about/pubs/morin/morin_recom.pdf.

findings. At the same time, however, experts must be mindful of the effect of tunnel vision on lawyers and the fact that some lawyers may wish—consciously or unconsciously—for the experts to modify their findings to better support a legal argument.

Sometimes, a lawyer may want an expert to make a specific statement that would help their theory of the case. The lawyer's role does not permit pressuring experts to modify their findings to suit the case the lawyer wants to present, but lawyers may ask many different experts for their opinion until they find one that says the "right thing" for their case. When presented with such a situation, experts must stand their ground and not become the puppet of a lawyer who seeks to fit the expert's opinion into their legal theory.

The discussion group recommended the disclosure of "expert shopping" for both sides of the adversarial process, not just the Crown, as such disclosure would likely reduce the practice. A further discussion in the future would be required to explore how such a change would necessitate alterations to the rules of privilege.

Lawyers must be mindful that their role in criminal proceedings may lead them to view the expert's evidence with tunnel vision. Even where they do not put pressure on an expert to change the findings, they may not properly understand the expert's evidence because of their existing bias in favour of or against the accused. Where a lawyer is not understanding the expert's findings because they do not fit into the theory of the case, the expert will have to be patient and be willing to repeat the findings until its significance becomes as clear as possible to the lawyer.

2) Ensuring Effective Communication in the Lawyer-Expert Relationship

Frequency is key to ensuring effective communication in the lawyer-expert relationship: more contact equates to a stronger working relationship. This seems obvious but, for a variety of reasons, lawyers and experts often do not communicate frequently; in some cases, experts may be faced with desperate phone calls to retain them shortly before an opinion is needed in court. Infrequent contact and last minute retainers can strain the lawyer-expert relationship while frequent contact and ample lead time can improve results in court.

The following tips should assist a lawyer in building a stronger relationship with an expert, regardless of whether the expert is engaged by the lawyer:

- *Meet face-to-face.* Meeting with an expert face-to-face is good practice as it builds the relationship and ensures that both professionals understand each other as best as possible. If a face-to-face meeting is not possible, use any other means of communication that allows frequent contact. Although lawyers like to use the phone in an effort to discuss the case "off-record," experts typically record the details of their phone conversations, so there is no clear benefit to choosing the phone over in-person meetings. Both will be disclosable. Similarly, avoiding email does not guard against the creation of a paper trail of lawyer-expert communication. In short, frequent communication is best to ensure that both the lawyer and the expert understand the expert's role in the case, but all communication, regardless of the form it takes, will be recorded in some manner.
- *Speak with all experts prior to trial, even if they are being called by the opposing side.* If the expert is a government employee that will be called by the Crown, defence lawyers can and should speak to the expert prior to trial to get a full explanation of their opinion. Defence lawyers often avoid doing this for any number of possible reasons: they may not know such a meeting is appropriate or possible, they may fear that the questions asked by the expert will be relayed to the Crown, or they may wish to shield the expert from clues exposing their cross-examination strategy. Lawyers should not learn at trial that they misunderstand the expert's opinion. Pretrial meetings help protect against such a damaging development to an accused person's case and reduce the amount of time spent on cross-examination. This meeting with the expert should take place well before the day of the trial.

3) Ensuring Counsel and the Court Understand and Correctly Interpret the Expert Evidence

The role of the expert when testifying in court is to be an unbiased educator informing the court of their opinion and the underlying facts and reasoning that form the basis of the opinion, in a comprehensive, clear manner. It is, however, possible for lawyers and the court to misunderstand and incorrectly interpret the expert evidence.

The following actions should be taken by the expert to improve the chances that they will be correctly interpreted:

- *Meet with lawyers prior to trial.* As discussed above, pre-trial meetings between the expert and lawyer will hopefully reduce misunderstandings of the expert's evidence.
- *Be objective and provide thorough reasoning for findings, while discussing any associated limitations.* Do not be an advocate! The role of the expert is that of an unbiased educator. It is not the role of the expert to try to sway the trier of fact to reach a particular verdict. The only advocacy role the expert may play is with respect to advocating for their science by thoroughly explaining their findings, their reasoning, and the limitations of their evidence. An expert should assume the trier of fact is intelligent but has limited or no knowledge of the expert's discipline. An unbiased, well-reasoned, and qualified opinion will be given more weight than a biased, ill-reasoned, dogmatic opinion.
- *Anticipate that the counsel, the judge, and the jury may have misconceptions of the scientific discipline.* The expert's role as educator necessarily involves anticipating misconceptions of their discipline. Although much has been written about the "CSI Effect"—juries misunderstanding the realities of forensic science because of popular television programming—it is unclear how much of an effect popular media has on Canadian juries. Some studies in the United States have questioned whether the CSI Effect even exists. That being said, however, juries often *want* forensic evidence. Experts must contend with the common misconception that scientific evidence is a stronger form of evidence. Experts need to address any common misconceptions of their discipline and provide education about the realities of their discipline as applied to the specific case at issue.
- *Be familiar with the case and the courtroom.* The expert should arrive at court understanding which facts are important to the particular circumstances of the case. Time and detail should be spent on relevant issues and the expert should be prepared to present their testimony to suit the needs of the court. For example, if the continuity of a blood sample is at issue, the alcohol toxicology expert should be prepared to discuss the continuity of the sample before addressing the findings with respect to blood alcohol concentration. The expert should know how to provide proper explanations in court and understand the high stakes involved in any criminal matter.

Education about the legal system should occur as early in a scientific career as possible. Experts should attend entire legal proceedings as spectators to understand how the process works and gain perspective into how an expert's evidence fits in the case. The expert should also attend programs that include the opportunity to "practice" testifying. For example, trial advocacy courses for lawyers that use expert witnesses in mock trials and expert witness testimony workshops.

When experts do testify, they should evaluate themselves by obtaining a copy of their own testimony and reviewing it. A peer review of the expert's testimony may also be a valuable source of feedback.

- *Use appropriate, accurate terminology.* Explain technical terms to avoid misunderstandings or misleading the court. Experts should allow for all possible conclusions that could flow from their findings and provide an explanation of the limitations of their evidence whenever they testify. They should describe why certain propositions were either accepted or rejected. Terms should be explained and terms likely to mislead the court should be avoided entirely. For instance, the terms "match" and "consistent with" have been largely abandoned by many disciplines because of their potential to mislead the trier of fact.

  If statistics are being used to describe a conclusion, the expert's testimony often becomes far more complex and likely to mislead. The expert should consider whether statistics are the best way to describe the conclusions and, if so, should use analogies where it is possible to make them accurate and appropriate. The expert should explain how these numbers came to be, stating the parameters and the chance of coincidence. Both the expert and the lawyers should be aware of the interpretation difficulties that are likely to arise when considering scientific jargon such as "hypothesis testing" and "falsifiability." Lawyers should be wary of logical errors they may commit when interpreting scientific evidence, such as the prosecutor's fallacy.[3] An awareness of common logical errors can hopefully reduce the incidence of them when it comes time to address the jury during closing submissions.

  If numbers are being used to express a measurement conclusion, the expert should always provide a range—not just one number—

3 For more information about the prosecutor's fallacy, see Chapter 22.

and judges should be aware that the provision of one final number is less reliable and less appropriate than the provision of a range.

- *Be concise when testifying.* Answer the question directly and do not be afraid to provide a simple "yes" or "no" answer when appropriate. Answering questions in this manner is particularly difficult for experts who are still learning the skill of testifying in court. Counsel will ask further follow-up questions if necessary.

  Scientific evidence is complex and it is important to be precise. There is a difference, however, between being precise and being verbose. Experts should be as concise as possible when explaining their findings. The explanation should address the limitations of the evidence, but should not delve into a limitless pit of theories and possibilities. To be both concise and accurate, speak to the specific case before the court and answer questions from counsel directly, rather than providing a roundabout explanation that muddies the core of the question. Only discuss the specifics of any applicable statistics if asked by counsel.
- *Stay within the scope of your area of expertise.* A well-thought-out hypothetical question or analogy could be an effective cross-examination tool when exploring an expert's evidence in court, but experts should be careful to avoid being dragged into testifying on an area beyond their expertise; an expert should stay within the limits of their qualifications. Novice experts should be particularly wary of this cross-examination tool. The best answer will make clear what assumptions are being made in the hypothetical or analogy and should be clear on whether or not those assumptions can be applied to the particular circumstances of the case. The expert should be able to identify why and where a hypothetical is strained when compared to the case before the court.
- *Be open about the limitations of an opinion.* When testifying, experts should provide their opinion to the court using appropriate qualifications to ensure that the expert is seen by the judge as fair, balanced, and considerate of all possibilities. Dogmatic statements that certain results "always" or "never" happen are not scientific as there is always potential for random error, statistically speaking.
- *Be aware of the specific requirements of the case.* Experienced experts will have developed a tool set or mental script that they rely on going into every trial, but they must remain cognizant that every case is different. Their presentation must be customized. Experts should

prepare well in advance of trial to ensure they are familiar with the details of the case in order to assist the court as well as possible. They should also be familiar with the literature relevant to the case. There is no one-size-fits-all opinion and the expert must be able to help the lawyers, judge, and jury navigate the complexities of a scientific opinion in the context of the individual case before the court.

- *Use visual aids wherever helpful.* Depending on the subject matter and the nature of the question in issue, visual aids such as PowerPoint slides, diagrams, and photos may be a help or a hindrance. Visual aids may provide the benefit of making a complex idea easier to understand and can be made an exhibit, becoming part of the record.

  Experts should use their judgment and consult with the lawyer they are working with to determine whether visual aids should be used. Visual aids were once widely used when presenting DNA evidence, but now that there is a popular understanding of DNA such visual aids are typically not used during testimony. Similarly, when testifying about psychology, explanatory examples are often more helpful than visual aids.

  In other disciplines, such as forensic pathology, it may be easiest for the expert to use a visual aid for a variety of reasons. For example, a diagram may be the easiest way to show the location of an injury on the human body. Photos, taken with a clear scale, may provide visual information helping a jury understand how the forensic pathologist arrived at his or her conclusions. Photos, however, are for educational purposes only and care should be taken that they are not inflammatory. The advent of CT (computed tomography) scanning for forensic pathology purposes at the Centre of Forensic Sciences[4] may also prove helpful going into the future.
- *Avoid drawing conclusions on insufficient data.* Unless there is strong data to state that one conclusion is "more likely" than another, the expert should not comment on what is "more likely" as this opinion amounts to speculation. Although experience may provide the expert with insight into the question, experience does not determine what is in the realm of possibility.

4 Ontario, Centre of Forensic Sciences, Ministry of Community Safety & Correctional Services, online: www.mcscs.jus.gov.on.ca/english/centre_forensic/CFS_intro.html.

In short, the expert should provide the best possible answers to questions, with the understanding that a perceived misunderstanding may reflect the strategy of counsel rather than a true misunderstanding. For example, in closing addresses, the Crown and defence summaries of an expert's evidence are often very different. It is the role of the lawyers to determine how the evidence should be applied to their legal arguments, while the expert's involvement in the courtroom is narrowly confined to providing testimony.

4) Developing Recommendations to Improve Collaboration between the Scientific and Legal Communities

The scientific and legal communities should collaborate to learn how to better work with each other to promote a fair and balanced criminal justice system. Improved collaboration is only possible with education. The following recommendations can build upon existing collaborations:

- *Scientists should tailor scientific publications to the legal community.* Scientists are typically concerned about publishing journal articles that will enhance the scientific literature. A shift in thinking is necessary for those disciplines that have forensic application. Instead of publishing exclusively in scientific journals, scientists should seek to simplify the material and publish their findings in legal journals as well. This will increase the legal community's consumption of scientific knowledge in a format that is familiar and applicable to their work. Articles, updates, and books should be directly developed by scientists for the legal community. Scientists and lawyers should collaborate more frequently to create such products. Scientists should also help lawyers determine what's new in the scientific realm as it applies to the criminal justice system. Change is constant and lawyers need to be aware of such changes.
- *Mock trials and trial advocacy courses should involve scientists.* Mock trials help to ensure experts are courtroom-familiar and have important contextual knowledge to rely upon when testifying during a real trial. Practicing in a "safe" environment will give experts the confidence and legal understanding they need to ensure they are expressing their opinion fairly and accurately. Mock trial participation by scientists is similarly valuable for the lawyers involved as it gives them a chance to apply their advocacy skills to expert

opinion evidence. Scientists and lawyers of varying experience and expertise, including students and young professionals, should be involved to make the experience as diverse, challenging, and educational as possible.

- *Universities should encourage joint projects, training, and education among science and law faculties.* Students in science and law should be encouraged to collaborate, conduct joint-projects, and benefit from training and education directed at the intersection of science and the law. This will enhance student experience and education in both fields. Such collaborations will also create relationships that may enhance the collegiality between the scientific and legal communities.
- *Inter-community conferences and seminars should occur more frequently.* Although there are some legal conferences that invite the attendance of experts, the frequency and diversity of such events should be increased going into the future. Conferences should reach out beyond the professionals who are already aware of the importance of collaborating with the scientific community. Experts should be provided with a balanced view of the criminal justice system by interacting with both Crown and defence lawyers. Making expert knowledge available to both the Crown and the defence could reduce the current inequality of access to educational information.
- *The scientific and legal communities should both shoulder the responsibility for improving collaboration and engaging in continual dialogue.* By communicating with each other regularly, both communities will be able to better adapt their best practices and services according to each other's needs, benefitting the operation of the criminal justice system as a whole. Experts and lawyers should both understand the limits of their knowledge and build upon gaps as required by their role in the criminal justice system.

C. CONCLUSION

Collaboration and education are crucial to addressing and perhaps even resolving systemic problems at the intersection of science and the law. Both experts and lawyers, with their distinct roles within the criminal justice system, should shoulder the responsibility of continuing dialogue between their respective communities.

The legal community must do more to educate themselves about science to better understand the limitations of an expert's opinion evidence, particularly when taking into account the high stakes involved in any criminal trial. Although science may not be involved in many criminal trials, it is important that lawyers be prepared to both present and challenge legal arguments resting on a scientific opinion when such cases do come across their desks.

Experts must be prepared to present their findings in a clear and concise manner, recognizing the limitations of their evidence in the circumstances of the case before the court. Although the expert speaks to only one aspect of the total evidence presented at court, scientific evidence is often viewed by the trier of fact as particularly strong so experts must be careful not to overstate an opinion or speak beyond the scope of their expertise.

Frequent communication between lawyer and expert is key to establishing a strong working relationship and a clear line of questioning during trial. With improved collaboration and education, the tension between science and the law may be tempered, to the benefit of the criminal justice system as a whole.

CHAPTER 3

Expert Evidence: Judge as Gatekeeper

Richard D. Schneider

A. INTRODUCTION

The objective of any trial, in a very general sense, is to determine "what happened?" at some earlier point in time. To facilitate that goal, individuals who are believed to have some knowledge of the event are called to court to answer questions. These individuals are prospective witnesses at the trial. Generally, witnesses are limited to recounting and testifying as to what they actually heard, saw, smelled, and felt. From all admissible information, the trier of fact (either a judge sitting alone or a jury) will determine what happened—the facts. Opinions, or factual inferences, from witnesses as to what transpired are, generally, not permitted except in special circumstances.[1] Generally, it is for the trier of fact to form opinions and draw inferences, not for the witness. However, the "expert" witness may be permitted to give opinion evidence based on provided or assumed facts because of the expert's recognized expertise acquired through education, research, training, work, or other relevant experience. Therefore, "lay person" witnesses are direct observers whereas "expert" witnesses may be indirect "inferors."

Expert opinion evidence can be an essential link to the "truth," but it presents with its own inherent dangers. As many have observed before,

1 *R. v. Graat*, [1982] 2 S.C.R. 819. There are, however, situations where a lay person may be permitted to give an opinion. For example, a lay person may provide an opinion addressing an individual's degree of impairment at a particular point in time.

there is a great danger that, unless very carefully scrutinized and supervised, the aura of the expert will cause the expert's opinion to have a disproportionate and unwarranted impact upon the jury, including that its impact will go beyond the expert's expertise and/or the limited area upon which it was expected to shine a light. For example, Sopinka J. cautioned:

> Dressed up in scientific language which the jury does not easily understand and submitted through a witness of impressive antecedents, this evidence is apt to be accepted by the jury as being virtually infallible and as having more weight than it deserves.
>
> . . .
>
> There is also a concern inherent in the application of this criterion that experts not be permitted to usurp the functions of the trier of fact. Too liberal an approach could result in a trial's becoming nothing more than a contest of experts with the trier of fact acting as referee in deciding which expert to accept.[2]

One can understand why even expert opinion evidence is presumptively inadmissible. At the same time, there are many cases that could not be resolved properly without the assistance of the expert. So, when deciding whether to allow expert testimony in any given case, careful scrutiny is imperative. The judge is the "gatekeeper" who will decide what opinion evidence will be permitted and what will not. It is for the judge to decide:

1) Whether to open the gate,
2) When the gate should be opened,
3) For whom the gate should be opened, and
4) How wide the gate should be opened.

While the judge decides whether or not to open the gate and receive the opinion evidence, it is the trier of fact who determines whether to accept or reject the opinion. What weight to give the opinion evidence is similarly exclusively within the realm of the trier of fact. We must be careful to not permit our process to devolve into trial by expert.

B. FOCUS

Prior to deciding admissibility, the first step for the court is to clearly delineate the permitted scope of the expert's opinion. Focus is essential.

---

2 *R. v. Mohan*, [1994] 2 S.C.R. 9 at 21 and 24 [*Mohan*].

That is, if admissible, what issue(s) will the expert be permitted to opine upon? Often, these matters can be sorted out by agreement at a pre-trial conference. But a common error, as Doherty J.A. notes in *R. v. Abbey*,[3] is for the court to open the door for an expert witness and then permit the expert to weigh in on a boundary-less array of issues. All participants must be careful to keep the testimony within the limits of the expert's expertise and within the range of issues for which expert opinion is appropriate. The gatekeeper must determine with respect to the case in hand, on what specific issues will an opinion be permitted? Where will expert testimony shine a light? As Doherty J.A. emphasizes, the judge must identify "with exactitude the scope of the proposed opinion that may be admissible."[4] These determinations will be made by the trial judge at the conclusion of a *voir dire* and in the absence of the jury (if there is one). The trial judge will decide: (1) whether all or part of the proposed expert opinion will be admitted,[5] (2) whether the range of the tendered opinion will be modified, and (3) whether the manner in which the opinion is expressed will be altered to adjust its focus or to render it more digestible for a jury.

As a gatekeeper with the power to control the trial process, the judge may also direct which witnesses should be called, in what order, and other procedural issues to make the process optimally efficient. As Rosenberg J. put it:[6]

> [I]t is no longer possible to view the trial judge as little more than a referee who must sit passively while counsel call the case in any fashion they please . . . . It would undermine the administration of justice if a trial judge had no power to intervene at an appropriate time and, like this trial judge, after hearing submissions, make directions necessary to ensure that the trial proceeds in an orderly manner.
>
> . . .
>
> It is neither necessary nor possible to exhaustively define its [trial management power] content or its limits. But it at least includes the power to place reasonable limits on oral submissions, to direct that submissions be made in writing, to require proof before embarking on a lengthy *voir dire*, to defer rulings, to direct the manner in which a *voir*

---

3 *R. v. Abbey*, 2009 ONCA 624 [*Abbey*].

4 It may be, for instance, that the expert is found to have expertise in respect of a, b, c, and d, but the expertise is only necessary in respect of a and c. See, for example, *R. v. Palombi*, [2004] O.J. No. 3030 (S.C.J.).

5 See, for example, *R. v. Pham*, 2013 ONSC 4903.

6 *R. v. Felderhof*, [2003] O.J. No. 4819 at paras. 40 and 57 (C.A.).

dire is conducted, especially whether to do so on the basis of testimony or in some other form, and exceptionally to direct the order in which evidence is called.

The power of the trial judge to control the trial process applies equally to statutory courts or tribunals[7] and extends to employing "aggressive prophylactic measures" as unusual circumstances present themselves.[8] With this, the trial judge or adjudicator may intervene to place limits on the number of expert witnesses that may be called in respect of a particular issue.

Hopefully, the days are dwindling where each side in a dispute stacks up as many experts as they can find to advance their theory of the case.[9] The protestation that "my client is entitled to make full answer and defence" should not become a licence to stack up redundant witnesses. Counsel are advised to carefully select and prepare the best expert they can retain and have that expert deliver an opinion that will be of assistance to the court. Tactically, this approach has the benefit of undermining a common objective in the cross-examination—"splitting" the experts to undermine their authority and perceived reliability. With one coherent voice, this vulnerability is obviated.

C. PROCESS

1) The Judge's Role as Evidentiary "Gatekeeper" Has Evolved Considerably Over the Past Two Centuries

In the early years of our modern system, there were virtually no filters placed upon the admission of expert testimony. A good example of this comes from the celebrated trial of Daniel M'Naghten in 1843.[10] M'Naghten was charged with the murder of Edward Drummond (believing him to

---

7 See, for example, *R. v. 974649 Ontario Inc.*, 2001 SCC 81.

8 See, for example, *R. v. Covington*, 1999 CanLII 3247 (Ont. C.A.).

9 *Canada Evidence Act*, R.S.C. 1985, c. C-5, s. 7 reads in full, "Where, in any trial or other proceeding, criminal or civil, it is intended by the prosecution or the defence, or by any party, to examine as witnesses professional or other experts entitled according to the law or practice to give opinion evidence, not more than five of such witnesses may be called on either side without the leave of the court or judge or person presiding." It is submitted that this provision should not be read to permit redundant witnesses or opinions that are not necessary.

10 *Queen v. M'Naghten* (1843), 10 Clark & F. 200, 2 Eng. Rep. 718 (H.L.).

have been the Prime Minister, Sir Robert Peel) and his defence was insanity. Psychiatric evidence was called. Mr. Clarkson, on behalf of the defence, introduced to the court Dr. A. Morison, a physician at St. Luke's Hospital, also affiliated with Bethlem Hospital and the Surrey Asylum:

CLARKSON: I believe, Dr. Morison, that you were one of the gentlemen who saw the prisoner in conjunction with Drs. Monro, Sutherland, and Bright?

DR. MORISON: I was.

CLARKSON: You have been in court during the whole of the day?

DR. MORISON: I have.

CLARKSON: Were you not present during the whole of the examination of the prisoner in Newgate?

DR. MORISON: I was.

CLARKSON: Did you arrive at any conclusion as to the prisoner's state of mind?

DR. MORISON: I did.

CLARKSON: Please do state to the court what your impression was?

DR. MORISON: That M'Naghten was insane.

CLARKSON: After having heard the evidence adduced today in court, has your opinion undergone any alteration?

DR. MORISON: I am still of the same opinion, that the prisoner was insane at the time he committed the act with which he is charged.

CLARKSON: The prisoner's morbid delusions consisted in his fancying himself subject to a system of persecutions?

DR. MORISON: Yes, that was the peculiar cause of his insanity.

CLARKSON: What effect had this delusion upon his mind?

DR. MORISON: It deprived the prisoner of all restraint over his actions.

CLARKSON: Do you speak with any doubt upon the point?

DR. MORISON: Not the slightest.

This trial was of the very highest level of sophistication. It engaged leading counsel of the day. The matter received daily scrutiny by both the national and international press. It is nonetheless clear that gatekeeping was not something the court turned its mind to at that time. Notice that:

1) There is no attempt to "qualify" the witness.
2) We don't know how long the witness has been a physician or where he was trained.

3) We don't know what training he has in psychiatry.
4) We don't know whether he has any "forensic" training.
5) We don't know how and under what circumstances he examined M'Naghten.
6) We don't know what information was provided to the witness.
7) We don't know anything about M'Naghten's diagnosis, how long he has held the diagnosis, his psychiatric history, or whether he is even presently fit to stand trial.
8) We don't know how his "insanity" fits with a defence (M'Naghten intended to kill someone else but mistook the victim for that person).[11]
9) We don't know precisely what form the delusion took.
10) We don't know how the witness came to his "conclusion."

One could ask many other questions of this witness. Logically, in a trial where insanity is the defence, psychiatric evidence will be relevant. And, while it is typical for a court to receive such evidence in a trial of this sort, there is nothing on the face of the record to show that the evidence of Dr. Morison was "necessary."

2) The Development of Detailed Guidelines for Admissibility of Expert Opinion Evidence

From these early days, the court gradually took on a "gatekeeping" role with respect to the admissibility of expert evidence, but it was often executed in a rather perfunctory manner and limited to establishing that an expert indeed had the purported expertise with respect to a particular subject matter. The court would typically define the issues in respect of which the expert would be permitted to testify based on the expert's expertise rather than on what was necessary for the trier of fact.[12]

Since that time, the trend has been to expand the gatekeeping role and restrict the admissibility criteria. Over the last twenty years, the courts have imposed a more formal analytic structure upon the exercise of discretion with respect to the admissibility of expert evidence. The admissi-

11 The matter was referred, post-trial, to the House of Lords who articulated the so-called M'Naghten Rules regarding insanity.

12 See, for example, G.M. Chayko, E.D. Gulliver, & D.V. Macdougall. "Qualifying the Expert" in *Forensic Evidence in Canada* (Aurora, ON: Canada Law Book, 1991) at 19.

bility of expert evidence is currently weighed against four criteria (the "*Mohan* criteria"):[13]

1) Relevance
2) Necessity in assisting the trier of fact
3) The absence of any exclusionary rule
4) A properly qualified expert

In *R. v. Abbey*,[14] Doherty J.A. sets out a useful post-*Mohan* approach to the gatekeeping necessarily involved when admitting expert evidence. Justice Doherty does not depart from the *Mohan* criteria, but builds upon the structure with some sequencing shifts in his analysis. He suggests a two-step process, both of which must be met for the testimony to be admissible (if the basic pre-conditions of the first step are not met, then the second step is not addressed):

1) Basic pre-conditions
   a) The proposed opinion must relate to a subject matter that is properly the subject of expert opinion evidence;
   b) The witness must be qualified to give the opinion;
   c) The proposed opinion must not run afoul of any exclusionary rule; and
   d) The proposed opinion must be logically relevant to a material issue.
2) Gatekeeping (including a cost-benefit analysis)

Justice Doherty makes a distinction between his use of the word "relevant" and that of the Court in *Mohan*, where relevance is also identified as a pre-condition to admissibility. Relevance may mean simply that the evidence renders a fact in issue more or less likely—the evidence is logically probative. Relevance may also take notice of the probative value of the evidence as against any prejudice resulting from its admission. This is the so-called cost-benefit analysis. Justice Doherty refers to the cost-benefit analysis as legal relevance, whereas the former is known as logical relevance. To be legally relevant, the evidence must be logically relevant and its probative value must outweigh its prejudicial impact. The court in *Abbey* used the term "relevance" to mean legal relevance.[15]

---

13 *Mohan*, above note 2.
14 *Abbey*, above note 3 at para. 76.
15 *Ibid.* at para. 84.

In the two-step process above, logical relevance is a basic pre-condition. Only after logical relevance is established, along with the other basic pre-conditions, will the probative value of the evidence be considered. Commonly, this cost-benefit step is referred to as the evaluation of probative value versus prejudicial effect. A consideration of the reliability of the proffered evidence will be part of the assessment of probative value. This is especially so for the more particular consideration of "new scientific evidence." When expert evidence is based upon a "novel scientific theory" an elevated level of scrutiny is applied.[16] The threshold for the determination of admissibility is "on a balance of probabilities." Justice Doherty suggests the following as questions that may be used to inform the reliability issue:

1) To what extent is the field in which the opinion is offered a recognized discipline, profession, or area of specialized training?
2) To what extent is the work within that field subject to quality assurance measures and appropriate independent review by others in the field?
3) What are the particular expert's qualifications with that discipline, profession, or area of specialized training?
4) To the extent that the opinion rests on data accumulated through various means such as interviews, is the data accurately recorded, stored and available?
5) To what extent are the reasoning processes underlying the opinion and the methods used to gather the relevant information clearly explained by the witness and susceptible to critical examination by a jury?
6) To what extent has the expert arrived at his or her opinion using methodologies accepted by those working in the particular field in which the opinion is advanced?

---

16 As indicated by Sopinka J. in *Mohan*, *ibid.* at 25. Where the expert evidence relies upon "novel scientific theory," a concern arises with respect to the scientific reliability and an elevated standard of scrutiny is applied. Criteria such as those cited in *Daubert v. Merrell Dow Pharmaceuticals, Inc.*, 509 U.S. 579 (1993) (cited with approval in *R. v. J.-L.J.*, 2000 SCC 51 [*J.-L.J.*]) guide the determination of admissibility:

1) Can the theory or technique be proved or disproved? (A theory or technique is not scientific if it cannot be falsified or is not testable.)
2) Has the theory or technique been subject to peer review and publication? (The methodology must be exposed to examination by other experts.)
3) What is the known or potential rate of error of the theory or technique?
4) Is the theory or technique "generally accepted" in the relevant scientific community?

7) To what extent do the accepted methodologies promote and enhance the reliability of the information gathered and relied upon by the expert?
8) To what extent has the witness, in advancing the opinion, honoured the boundaries and limits of the discipline from which his or her expertise arises?
9) To what extent is the proffered opinion based on data and other information gathered independently of the specific case or, more broadly, the litigation process?[17]

In the gatekeeping assessment of costs versus benefits, costs will include the expenditure of time in hearing the evidence, the potential for confusion rather than clarity, and inappropriate weighting and the consequent suasion of the evidence based upon the expert's *gravitas*. These considerations are described by Binnie J.:

> In the course of *Mohan* and other judgments, the Court has emphasized that the trial judge should take seriously the role of "gatekeeper." The admissibility of the expert should be scrutinized at the time it is proffered, and not allowed too easy an entry on the basis that all of the frailties could go at the end of the day to weight rather than admissibility.[18]

Finally, Doherty J.A. would move the *Mohan* requirement of "necessity" into the secondary cost-benefit phase of the gatekeeping analysis. The fact finding process might be able to tolerate greater costs where the expert's evidence is essential. Conversely, where the expert's evidence is of little or no benefit, the process will tolerate little or no cost and it will likely be excluded.[19] Where the jury can assess the evidence and resolve the issue in dispute without the assistance of an expert, the expert's evidence is not necessary.[20]

---

17 *Abbey*, above note 3 at para. 119.

18 *J.-L.J.*, above note 16 at para. 28.

19 It may be that alternatives such as enhanced jury instructions could provide the jury with the necessary tools to interpret the evidence without the necessity of an expert. See, for example, *R. v. Pearce*, 2014 MBCA 70 at para 72 (citing *R. v. D.D.*, 2000 SCC 43 at para 67). "A jury instruction, in preference to expert opinion, where practicable, has advantages. It saves time and expense. But of greater importance, it is given by an impartial judicial officer, and any risk of superfluous or prejudicial content is eliminated."

20 See, for example, *R. v. Stobbe*, 2012 MBQB 78.

The issue of expertise in the *Mohan/Abbey* analyses is not limited to an "up-front" process that happens as the evidence in question is being introduced to the court. As Moldaver J. indicates:

> It is not enough to simply consider the *Mohan* criteria at the outset of the expert's testimony and make an initial ruling as to the admissibility of the evidence. The trial judge must do his or her best to ensure that, throughout the expert's testimony, the testimony remains within the proper boundaries of expert evidence.[21]

Most recently, the Supreme Court of Canada has weighed in on the matter of the court's gatekeeping function.[22] The Court endorsed the approach taken in *Mohan* and provided the following structure to the analysis, which does not appear to be at odds with the approach taken by the court in *Abbey*.

A two-step inquiry is taken to determine the admissibility of expert opinion evidence. First, the party tendering the expert evidence must establish that the threshold requirements have been met (i.e., the *Mohan* requirements: relevance, necessity, absence of an exclusionary rule, and a properly qualified expert). Failure to meet these criteria results in exclusion. The second part of the analysis is to determine whether admitting the evidence is sufficiently beneficial to the trial process despite its potential harm or prejudice. Expert witnesses have a duty to provide fair, objective, non-partisan opinions. The expert opinion must be independent and not influenced by the nature of the retainer or a desired outcome of the proceedings. Concerns related to the expert's willingness or ability to comply with the duty to the court are best addressed through the "qualified expert" criterion of the *Mohan* test. Failure to meet the threshold on this criterion results in exclusion of the evidence. Only after the threshold is met are residual concerns regarding the expert's actual compliance with the criterion considered.

This super-added requirement is not designed or expected to protract proceedings significantly. Once the qualified expert criterion has been disposed of with the normal inquiry, absent any challenge, the evidence will be received by the court. Where realistically challenged, the proponent of the evidence will bear the burden of establishing admissibility, but exclusion at this phase of the analysis should occur in only the clearest of

---

21 *R. v. Sekhon*, 2014 SCC 15 at para. 46.

22 *White Burgess Langille Inman v. Abbott and Haliburton Co.*, 2015 SCC 23.

cases. Anything less will be considered in the cost-benefit analysis. Apparent bias is not relevant to the inquiry of whether the witness is "unwilling or unable." At this step, the court will be concerned only with actual unwillingness or inability of the expert to carry out the duty to provide fair, non-partisan, objective assistance.

D. NOVEL SCIENTIFIC EVIDENCE

As mentioned above, where the expert will be relying upon a novel science "special scrutiny" is required. As indicated by the Court in *Mohan*:

> In summary, therefore, it appears from the foregoing that expert evidence which advances a novel scientific theory or technique is subjected to special scrutiny to determine whether it meets a basic threshold of reliability and whether it is essential in the sense that the trier of fact will be unable to come to a satisfactory conclusion without the assistance of the expert.[23]

It stands to reason that as the level of debate or uncertainty surrounding a theory or technique increases, so must the level of scrutiny applied to the prospective evidence. Conversely, where the theory or technique is familiar, well tested, and accepted, the concern is less elevated. As distilled from the caselaw by Paciocco and Stuesser, where the science or theory is "novel," three particular requirements are imposed:

1) The opinion evidence must be "essential in the sense that the trier of fact will be unable to come to a satisfactory conclusion without the assistance of the expert";
2) The reliability must face a "special scrutiny"; and
3) "[T]he closer the evidence [to which the novel scientific technique pertains] approaches an opinion on the ultimate issue, the stricter the application," and where the evidence relates directly to the ultimate issue, "very careful scrutiny" is required.[24]

"Novel science" has not been authoritatively defined, so there is the question of when this more intense examination will be indicated. Courts have attempted a definition but to date there is no satisfactory guidance.[25]

---

23 *Mohan*, above note 2 at 25.

24 D.M. Paciocco & L. Stuesser. *The Law of Evidence*, 7th ed (Toronto: Irwin Law, 2015) at 226.

25 See, for example: *R. v. Trochym*, 2007 SCC 6 at para. 133. Bastarache J. suggests that, "a scientific technique or knowledge will be considered 'novel' in two situations—

Novelty is an inherently elusive and context-specific concept. A theory or technique might be truly novel, or it may be novel to the courts while well-known and established within the scientific community. It is likely that where the court is unfamiliar with the proposed evidence, it will be treated as novel and therefore attract an elevated level of scrutiny regardless of its status within the scientific community.[26] Another problem with the novelty inquiry is that it does not lend itself to a discrete "yes or no" conclusion. A proffered theory or technique will often be neither completely new nor fully commonplace. Inevitably, the courts will apply a sliding scale level of scrutiny depending on where the theory or technique falls between these two extremes.

E. COUNSEL

Counsel should approach the issue of admissibility with all of the above in mind and be prepared to respond to questions from the bench as to why, for example, an expert's opinion is necessary to resolve a particular issue. Once past that hurdle, counsel should be prepared to demonstrate that their expert is indeed an expert in a particular field and that the expert's field of expertise can appropriately shine a light on a carefully defined issue in dispute.

Counsel should equip their expert with all available "facts" that the expert should assume to be true in forming the opinion. Here it is critical that counsel provide the expert with "the good, the bad, and the ugly." It is well-known that an expert's opinion is only as strong as the factual foundation upon which it rests. A factual foundation that is too skimpy, too ambiguous, or is lopsided (that is, with a bias, whether intended or not) will not support an effective opinion.

A skimpy foundation does not have enough facts to connect the dots and form an opinion. An ambiguous foundation has considerable uncertainty as to what the facts might be—that is, what the trier of fact will

---

when it is new, or when the application of recognized scientific knowledge or technique is new."

26 The "Daubert Tracker" tracks a variety of disciplines in a forensic context and reports cases in which they have been considered. It is limited to American decisions, but will no doubt be of interest to the Canadian bench and bar. It is available online at www.dauberttracker.com.

find to be fact.[27] In a situation of this sort, it would be appropriate for counsel to present the expert with a list of "facts" the expert can assume to be true—a hypothetical. This should be based upon counsel's best assessment of what the trier of fact will ultimately find to be fact. As witnesses testify and the picture becomes more vivid, the hypothetical can be adjusted prior to the expert actually testifying. If an objection is raised that the expert is basing the opinion on facts not in evidence, counsel can answer that the expert is being asked to respond to a hypothetical. In cross-examination, the opposite tactic can be employed—"Doctor, how would your opinion change if you were to assume the following (different facts) to be true?" Finally, a lopsided foundation is incomplete or biased. This may result from counsel incompletely providing facts to the expert or, worse, biasing the facts by providing only facts thought sympathetic to the client. There is nothing more devastating to an expert's opinion than having opposing counsel put to the expert: "Doctor, would your opinion differ had you known 'X'?"

Surprises are almost always a bad thing for the expert. It is imperative that counsel provide the expert with all relevant information available about the client (while being cautious regarding potentially biasing evidence that goes beyond what is necessary for the expert's opinion). In that way, the expert will have the ability to reconcile difficult or inconsistent facts and include that discussion in his report prior to testifying. There are almost always alternative interpretations available. Some of the evidence will be consistent with the theory of the defence, while some of it will not. The expert's responsibility to the court is to acknowledge other interpretations but to indicate, if possible, why, as between the various explanations, their conclusion is to be preferred as more likely. There is no advantage to providing your expert with a sanitized version of events. This is a recipe for disaster.

F. JUDGES

Expert evidence can be enormously helpful to the trier of fact, but helpful is not good enough. It can also, for the reasons discussed above, have an exaggerated impact that interferes with the fundamental role of the

27 Of course, if the factual picture is particularly unclear there will more than not be doubt as to what transpired and an acquittal will result without the calling of a defence.

trier of fact. Expert evidence should be used sparingly, surgically, and only when necessary.[28] When deciding whether to allow an expert to give opinion evidence, the following guidance should be applied:

1) The expert evidence must be necessary, not merely helpful, or desirable, to resolve a key question.
2) The expert must have expertise pertaining to the question you have determined expertise is necessary to resolve.
3) The range of subject matter for the opinion should be crisply defined.
4) The judge should remain vigilant throughout the expert testimony to ensure that the opinion is confined to the subject matter as defined.

G. CONCLUSION

Expert opinions can enable a court to decide matters that would otherwise be insoluble. Expert opinions can provide the trier of fact with knowledge that can break through a fact-finding impasse. But despite the importance of expert opinions to the resolution of many cases, courts must manage the expert opinion vigilantly, and use it sparingly and only when necessary. To ensure the opinion serves its proper function and does not usurp the role of the trier of fact through exaggerated influence or otherwise unduly sway the court's conclusions, certain safeguards must be in place. Providers of expert opinion must be scrutinized to ensure that they are indeed qualified to offer the opinions sought. They must be willing and able to provide a fair, non-partisan, and objective opinion. The trier of fact must carefully examine the factual foundation upon which any expert opinion rests. And, finally, the opinion must be independent and impartial. Only then can the opinion evidence be safely introduced into court and into the record.

---

28 Expert evidence may not be necessary in cases where there is no forensic evidence. The judge will therefore be tasked with providing an appropriate jury instruction addressing how the absence of evidence of a forensic link between the accused and the complainant should factor into a jury's assessment of reasonable doubt in a circumstantial case. See, for example, *R. v. Hassanzada*, 2016 ONCA 284.

CHAPTER 4

Presenting Scientific Evidence in the Courtroom

Vincenzo Rondinelli

A. INTRODUCTION

The Honourable Fred Kaufman concluded his report involving the wrongful conviction of Guy Paul Morin by stating, "An innocent person was convicted of a heinous crime he did not commit. Science helped convict him. Science exonerated him."[1] Therein lies the conundrum of science in the criminal justice system. "Good" science may assist in catching criminals and exonerating the wrongfully convicted, while "bad" science may imprison the innocent, but distinguishing between "good" and "bad" science is not a simple or clear task. Part of the problem may be attributed to Canada's adversarial justice system, where trial practice can be a tug-of-war between logic and rhetoric. Logic seeks to find the truth, whereas rhetoric seduces the listener to accept the claims of a partisan actor.

Scientific evidence presents unique challenges for lawyers, judges, and juries. Yet, due to the complexity of criminal prosecutions, the presentation of scientific evidence is sometimes necessary. Should an expert witness make it past the gatekeeping judge,[2] it will be up to counsel calling the witness to help convey the evidence to the jury in an understandable and memorable manner. Opposing counsel will have a different task. They will attempt to expose the deficiencies in the expert opinion to keep the

1 The Honourable Fred Kaufman, C.M., Q.C., *Report of the Kaufman Commission on Proceedings Involving Guy Paul Morin* (Toronto: Queen's Printer, 1998) ch. VI at 1.

2 See Chapter 3.

jurors from being influenced by testimony at odds with their theory of the case.

Lawyers have long cherished their oratory talents as a primary skill for success in a courtroom. However, the complexities associated with the forensic sciences cannot be meaningfully presented to a jury by words alone. Visual demonstrations should be used to increase comprehension, with care to avoid overuse that may inflame the prejudices of the jurors. The rarely used practice of jurors asking the expert witness their own questions to clarify confusing aspects of the scientific evidence can be beneficial and should be more accepted by courts.

B. SEEING IS BELIEVING

Humans tend to be visual learners. Studies have found that most people learn and understand much better when they are both shown and told than they do when they are only told.[3] Teaching someone how to tie a necktie through words alone is no easy feat. But talking through a visual demonstration will greatly increase the chances that the technique will be learned.

Incorporating flowcharts, computer animations, or PowerPoint in the presentation of scientific evidence can go a long way in helping a judge or jury understand and remember the expert's testimony. It should not be expected however, that the judge or jury will completely grasp the scientific evidence being presented. The expert has years of experience in learning and training, while a jury has only hours or days to consider complex methodologies and concepts. Hence, the lawyer's primary objective should be to focus the expert opinion on the evidence most relevant to the main issue at trial. For example, if DNA transfer is a live issue, then the focus should be on the likelihood of transfer in the circumstances of the case. Factors increasing or decreasing the risk of transfer should be kept distinct from the primary point.

Once the expert's evidence is boiled down to its essence, counsel should make efforts to reinforce this pivotal information to the judge or jury. In doing so, counsel must keep in mind the limitations of the human memory. There is immediate memory (e.g., remembering some in-

3 See R.M. Felder & L.K. Silverman, "Learning and Teaching Styles in Engineering Education" (1988) 78(7) *Engineering Education* 674; M. Cobo, "A Strategic Approach to Demonstrative Exhibits and Effective Jury Presentations" (1990) 3 *Practising Law Institute/Litigation* 359.

formation just recited), short-term memory (e.g., remembering the same information an hour later), and long-term memory (e.g., remembering the information a month later). Repetition generally increases the chance of recall. As such, the more important a particular point in evidence is to a party's case, the more it should be repeated to the judge or jury.

It is also important to note that, while humans may be visual learners, they are also emotional beings. Some visuals—such as graphic autopsy photographs—may lead jurors to decide with their hearts, rather than their minds. It has long been established that if a photograph is not relevant to any issue at trial and serves only to inflame the jury, it should not be admitted.[4] Examples of a photograph's potential relevance were provided by Chadwick J. in *R. v. Schaefler*:

> 1) [T]o illustrate the facts on which experts base their opinion and to illustrate the steps by which they arrive at their opinions;
> 2) to illustrate minutiae of objects described in the testimony of a witness; e.g., to show the nature and the extent of the wounds;
> 3) to corroborate testimony and provide a picture of the evidence and to assist the jury in determining its accuracy and weight;
> 4) to link the injuries of the deceased to the murder weapon;
> 5) to provide assistance as to the issues of intent and whether the murder was planned and deliberate;
> 6) to help the jury determine the truth of the theories put forth by the crown or defence; e.g., as to which accused committed the crime; as to whether the crime was committed in self-defence.[5]

Graphic photographs of a deceased have been admitted where the photographs were highly probative. In *R. v. Kendall*, the main issue at trial was which of two accused had committed the murder. In explaining its decision to admit the photographic evidence, the Ontario Court of Appeal noted that the photographs of the deceased and the blood-spattered bathtub area had probative value. The nature of the wounds and blood spray as depicted in the photographs may have been helpful in conjunction with the oral testimony in determining which of the two accused was telling the truth.[6] Autopsy pictures, however, have been excluded in cases where there

---

4 See *R. v. Wade* (1994), 89 C.C.C. (3d) 39 (Ont. C.A.), var'd (1995), 98 C.C.C. (3d) 97 (S.C.C.); *R. v. O'Donnell* (1936), 65 C.C.C. 299 (Ont. C.A.); *R. v. Dilabbio*, [1965] 4 C.C.C. 295 (Ont. C.A.).

5 *R. v. Schaefler*, [1993] O.J. No. 71 at para. 24 (Gen. Div.).

6 *R. v. Kendall*, [1987] O.J. No. 388 (C.A.).

was no dispute concerning the deceased's wounds or the photographs would be of only marginal assistance to the jury.[7]

C. DEFLATING THE INFLATED *CURRICULUM VITAE*

Proposed experts rarely fail to meet the threshold of admissibility. However, a carefully prepared attack on the expert's qualifications in front of a judge or jury may sufficiently undermine the opinion.

Employers typically view resumes with a healthy dose of skepticism due to some applicants' penchant for embellishment. Lawyers should proceed with similar caution when presented with an expert's *curriculum vitae*. The longer the *curriculum vitae*, the more ammunition a lawyer can collect to prepare for cross-examination. The battle will require much pre-trial preparation. Once counsel receives the expert's *curriculum vitae*, counsel should verify it carefully. Investigation should include obtaining and reading each of the expert's listed publications, researching the various organizations with which the expert claims affiliation, researching the courses and certificates completed by the expert, and obtaining as much information as possible on cases where the expert has testified (e.g., judgments, transcripts, newspaper articles, etc.).

With this information in hand, cross-examination should focus on highlighting the exaggerations and deficiencies in the expert's qualifications. For example, with respect to publications, experts should be asked about their authorial involvement. Were they the main contributor? A proofreader? Was authorship a courtesy credit for providing constructive feedback to the primary author? Did the expert's affiliations require testing or other professional verification for membership? Or is paying dues sufficient to maintain membership status? Further probing should be made of the courses completed and certificates obtained by the expert. How demanding was the curriculum? How long did the course or certificate take to complete? Months? Days? An afternoon?

Depending on how wide the expert has purported to cast his or her expertise net, counsel may be able to resort to an effective "alphabet cross" to demonstrate that the expert is "a jack-of-all-trades and an expert in none." Rubinowitz and Torgan provide an example of such questioning:

> Q: Sir, you have testified in Automobile accident cases, true?

---

7 *R. v. Currie*, [2000] O.J. No. 392 at paras. 18–19 (S.C.J.).

Q: You testified in Bus accident cases?
Q: You testified in [Crane] accident cases?
Q: You testified in Dumpster cases?
Q: You testified in Elevator cases?
Q: So let's see, we're up to "F". You've testified in French train cases?
Q: You've testified in Gas explosion cases?[8]

In keeping with the importance of visual learning as discussed above, counsel may wish to have the *curriculum vitae* shown on a projector screen and marked up with a red marker as the witness is cross-examined. By the end of the exercise, the red-filled screen should hopefully provide the jurors with high school flashbacks of error-plagued assignments, which, in turn, may result in rejecting the opinion.

D. REMEMBER THE BASICS: THE RULE IN *BROWNE v. DUNN*

It is not uncommon to have opposing experts give opposing opinions on various issues under examination. If a party wants to maximize the weight a trier of fact will accord its expert's evidence, it should ensure that its expert's theory is put to the opposing expert. This advice is illustrated by Lord Herschel, stating in *Browne v. Dunn*:

> My Lords, I have always understood that if you intend to impeach a witness you are bound, whilst he is in the box, to give him an opportunity of making any explanation which is open to him; and, as it seems to me, that is not only the rule of professional practice in the conduct of a case, but is essential to fair play and fair dealing with witnesses.[9]

Although this principle has become known as a rule, the rule is not absolute. Indeed, the Ontario Court of Appeal has observed that the rule "is not some ossified, inflexible rule of universal and unremitting application . . . ."[10] Compliance with the rule does not require that "every scrap of [contradictory] evidence" be put to the opposing expert, but it would be prudent to confront an opposing expert on matters of substance that a party intends to impeach through its own expert.[11] Importantly, failure to cross-examine

8 B. Rubinowitz & E. Torgan, "Exposing Expert Witness' Bias During Cross: Collateral Attack" *New York Law Journal* (23 December 2013).

9 *Browne v. Dunn*, [1893] 6 R. 67 at 70 (H.L.).

10 *R. v. Quansah*, 2015 ONCA 237 at para. 89.

11 *Ibid.* at para. 81.

an expert on a specific issue later raised by one's own expert may disentitle the trier of fact from placing any weight on that specific point.

E. ANY QUESTIONS?

The practice of allowing jurors to ask questions of witnesses has been gaining momentum in the United States.[12] While this practice has been judicially endorsed in Canada,[13] the Ontario Court of Appeal has observed that the practice is permitted very rarely.[14] The reservation against allowing jurors to ask questions of experts is well placed,[15] but there may be some value in allowing jurors to question DNA expert witnesses. A trial judge has long been entitled to ask questions of witnesses for the purposes of clarification and amplification,[16] and since jurors sit as the triers of fact in a jury trial, there appears to be no rational reason to deny jurors a similar discretion to pose questions to expert witnesses.

Forensic DNA experts have become almost commonplace in jury trials involving serious crimes against the person. These experts give evidence on complex subjects such as human genetics, statistics, and microbiology—topics clearly beyond the realm of jurors' everyday experiences. Expectations that jurors will understand, let alone remember, complex evidence and properly weigh such evidence are a legal fiction. Jury studies in the United States have consistently demonstrated that jurors struggle mightily with DNA and statistical evidence in criminal trials.[17] Clearly then, the

---

12 See *State v. Doleszny*, 844 A.2d 773 (Vt. 2004) [*Doleszny*]; *People v. Milligan*, 77 P.3d 771 at 779 (Colo. App. 2003); *Lance v. State*, 560 S.E.2d 663 at 676 (Ga. 2002); *Trotter v. State*, 733 N.E.2d 527 at 531 (Ind. Ct. App. 2000); *United States v. Richardson*, 233 F.3d 1285 at 1288–91 (11th Cir. 2000); *United States v. Collins*, 226 F.3d 457 at 464–65 (6th Cir. 2000).

13 See *R. v. Andrade* (1985), 18 C.C.C. (3d) 41 at 59–60 (Ont. C.A.); *R. v. Druken*, 2002 NFCA 23 at paras. 79–82; *R. v. Gagnon* (1992), 74 C.C.C. (3d) 385 at 389 (Que. C.A.) [*Gagnon*].

14 *R. v. A.G.*, 2015 ONCA 159 at para. 66 [*A.G.*].

15 As the Ontario Court of Appeal observed in *A.G.*, *ibid.* at para. 64,

> [t]he dangers of permitting a jury to ask questions of a witness are obvious. In addition to potentially eliciting inadmissible evidence, such questioning may run contrary to trial counsel's strategy and an objection by counsel to a question may trigger conflict with the jury or create the impression that important evidence is being hidden. Moreover, there is a risk that a jury empowered to ask questions will move from being judges of the facts to being advocates . . . .

16 See *R. v. Osolin* (1993), 86 C.C.C. (3d) 481 at 542–43 (S.C.C.); *R. v. Valley* (1986), 26 C.C.C. (3d) 207 at 230–32 (Ont. C.A.).

17 See S. Lindsey, R. Hertwig, & G. Gigerenzer, "Communicating Statistical DNA Evidence" (2003) 43 *Jurimetrics: The Journal of Law, Science, and Technology* 147; J.

current system could benefit from some innovative reform to help juries better understand DNA evidence.

In *R. v. Gagnon*, the Quebec Court of Appeal suggested the following procedure be followed where jury questions are permitted:

> In our legal tradition, questions from the jury are not prohibited but certain precautions are necessary: (1) the judge must at the outset indicate to the jury that the very dynamics of an adversarial trial require that the parties have freedom to manoeuvre in their strategy and their examinations; (2) that it is preferable, as a result, that a jury wait until the parties have completed their examinations before asking their questions; (3) that the judge must rule on the legality of these questions; therefore, he must filter these questions; and (4) that the jury's questions cannot be transformed into an examination by a third party.[18]

Such a carefully controlled process would limit jury questions to those seeking clarification and further explanation and would not unduly disrupt or prolong proceedings. In turn, a better-informed jury can lead to a more attentive jury that carefully discharges its decision-making duty.

F. CONCLUSION

Forensic science has evolved to become a significant crime-fighting tool. It has also proven to be indispensible in uncovering wrongful convictions. But forensic science plays a precarious role in a criminal trial. Although expert opinion evidence is tendered to advance the search for truth, counsel should be prepared to expose an expert's deficiencies to prevent undue reliance on their opinions.

Schklar & S.S. Diamond, "Juror Reactions to DNA Evidence: Errors and Expectancies" (1999) 23 *Law and Human Behavior* 159; J.J. Koehler, "Error and Exaggeration in the Presentation of DNA Evidence at Trial" (1993) 34 *Jurimetrics: The Journal of Law, Science, and Technology* 21.

18 *Gagnon*, above note 13 at 389. A similar procedure is followed in American courts. As set out in *Doleszny*, above note 12 at 786–87:

> The procedure should follow that employed in this case: (1) the jurors must submit the proposed questions to the judge and be made part of the record; (2) the judge must disclose the proposed questions to the parties and give them the opportunity to object or request the question be narrowed or rephrased; and (3) the judge must rule on each proposed question on the record, allowing, rejecting or modifying the question. The procedures should be explained to the parties and jurors at the commencement of the trial.

CHAPTER 5

Critically Examining the Forensic Sciences: Inquiries and Reports

Sarah Harland-Logan

A. INTRODUCTION

The 2012 Hart House Report, addressing the state of the forensic sciences in Canada, concluded by observing that "a just peace cannot rest on a foundation of bad science."[1] *The Lawyer's Guide to the Forensic Sciences* presents dozens of case examples in which expert forensic testimony, supported by a solid foundation of good science, has played a crucial role in ensuring that justice is achieved.[2] A fair and full treatment of this topic,

1 Michael S. Pollanen et al., eds., "Forensic Science in Canada: A Report of Multidisciplinary Discussion" (4–5 May 2012) at 104 [Hart House Report], online: www.forensics.utoronto.ca/Assets/LMPF+Digital+Assets/Forensic+Science+in+Canada.pdf. In this discussion, Pollanen et al. invoke s. 91 of the *Constitution Act, 1867* (UK), 30 & 31 Vic., c. 3, s. 91, reprinted in R.S.C. 1985, Appendix II, No. 5, as follows: "we Canadians hold that peace, order and good government are our most fundamental values. Establishing and maintaining a just peace is thus *the* core mission of government, and a just peace cannot rest on a foundation of bad science" [emphasis in original].

2 A number of the inquiries surveyed in this chapter attest to the power of forensic science to facilitate the pursuit of justice and the correction of wrongful convictions: see, for example, Ontario, Ministry of the Attorney General, "The Scope and Nature of the Inquiry" in *Report of the Kaufman Commission on Proceedings Involving Guy Paul Morin* (Toronto: Ministry of the Attorney General, 1998) [*Morin Report* ch. I] at 1, 78, & 79, online: www.attorneygeneral.jus.gov.on.ca/english/about/pubs/morin/morin_ch1.pdf; The Honourable Patrick LeSage, Q.C., Commissioner, *Report of the Commission of Inquiry into Certain Aspects of the Trial and Conviction of James Driskell* (Winnipeg: The Commission, 2007) [*Driskell Inquiry Report*] at 1, 155, and 158, online: www.driskellinquiry.ca/pdf/final_report_jan2007.pdf. Both Morin and Driskell were

however, must survey not only these successes but also the tragic errors to which flawed forensic science has contributed. These errors have resulted in wrongful convictions, denying justice to the accused, the victim, and the true perpetrator.

Both the legal and the scientific communities must learn from these costly mistakes—and rectify the systemic failings that allowed them to happen—to ensure that forensic scientific testimony facilitates, rather than obstructs, the pursuit of justice. This chapter summarizes the findings of a dozen significant judicial inquiries and systemic reviews conducted within the past two decades that examine the practice of one or more forensic sciences in the criminal justice context. While some of these analyses were made in response to specific miscarriages of justice, others seek a proactive response to recent changes in a rapidly evolving scientific landscape.

Science, like the law, constantly evolves. Certain shortcomings within each specialty become evident only in hindsight. By examining and critically analyzing forensic expert testimony and its underlying science, lawyers can help prevent future miscarriages of justice. By presenting expert testimony that carefully delineates both their findings and their limitations, forensic scientists can assist the trier of fact in making appropriate use of forensic evidence. Members of the scientific and legal communities must work together to critically evaluate Canadian systems of forensic science service delivery to ensure that the science meets standards of quality, transparency, and accountability.

B. THE RATUSHNY SELF DEFENCE REVIEW

The Supreme Court of Canada's decision in *R. v. Lavallee*[3] heralded a new understanding of battered women in the context of self-defence law. In *Lavallee*, forensic psychiatric expert evidence on battered woman syndrome was admitted to dispel myths pertaining to intimate partner violence and "to assist the jury in determining whether the appellant had a reasonable apprehension of death or grievous bodily harm and believed on reasonable grounds that she had no alternative but to shoot."[4] Dr. Fred Shane conducted a psychiatric assessment of the appellant—who had

exonerated by the results of DNA testing, a revolutionary technology that had not been available at the time of trial.

3 *R. v. Lavallee*, [1990] 1 S.C.R. 852.

4 *Ibid.* at para. 61.

killed her abusive partner—and concluded that she had been "terrorized" by her partner "to the point of feeling trapped, vulnerable, worthless and unable to escape the relationship despite the violence."[5] The appellant's life was in danger as a result of this "continuing pattern of abuse," and "the appellant's shooting of the deceased was a final desperate act by a woman who sincerely believed that she would be killed that night."[6] The Supreme Court of Canada found that there was "ample" evidence (including, but not limited to, this expert opinion evidence) to support its conclusion that "[t]he fact that [the appellant] . . . may have exhibited aggressive behaviour on occasion or tried (unsuccessfully) to leave does not detract from a finding of systematic and relentless abuse" by her partner.[7] The Court restored the appellant's acquittal.[8]

The Court's acquittal in *Lavallee* brought with it a concern that self-defence may have been overlooked by defence attorneys in at least some murder cases where the defendant was a woman in an abusive relationship. Further, the adequacy of Canada's criminal and sentencing laws in these circumstances was brought into question.[9] In response, the Honourable Lynn Ratushny[10] was appointed to conduct a self-defence review, which sought to determine whether there were Canadian women "convicted of homicide who may have acted in self defence."[11] The review included:

> [C]ases of women under sentence in federal and provincial institutions who apply for a remedy and who are serving a sentence for homicide in circumstances in which the killing allegedly took place to prevent the deceased from inflicting serious bodily harm or death.[12]

Applications to participate in the self-defence review were sent to all 236 women serving a sentence for homicide in Canada. Ninety-eight women responded.[13] Justice Ratushny evaluated each woman's conviction and sentence in view of a series of standards focusing on the issue of self-defence

---

5 *Ibid.* at para. 9. These quotations are in the words of the court (rather than the expert).
6 *Ibid.* The quotations are in the words of the court.
7 *Ibid.* at para. 61.
8 *Ibid.* at para. 78.
9 Justice Lynn Ratushny, *Self Defence Review: Final Report* (Ottawa: Justice Canada, 1997) at 11.
10 *Ibid.* Justice Ratushny was a judge of the Ontario Court of Justice (Provincial Division) at the time.
11 *Ibid.* at 17.
12 *Ibid.* at 11.
13 *Ibid.* at 15.

as it applies to abused and battered women.[14] In her final report, submitted in July 1997, Ratushny J. recommended remedies for seven cases. Specifically, she recommended three pardons, three remissions of sentence, and one new appeal.[15] Only one of these recommendations was accepted, and not a single woman was released from prison as a result of the review.[16]

C. THE MORIN INQUIRY

1) The Investigation

Nine-year-old Christine Jessop disappeared during the afternoon of 3 October 1984, sometime after the school bus dropped her off. By early evening, her family became alarmed and called police, who commenced a search that proved fruitless.[17] Christine's body was found nearly three months later. She had been stabbed and sexually assaulted.[18] The Durham Regional Police Service commenced a murder investigation.[19] It later became apparent that the search of the crime scene was plagued with errors, both inadvertent and deliberate.[20]

Guy Paul Morin, Christine Jessop's neighbour,[21] first came to police attention in February 1985, when the Jessops mentioned in a police interview that he "was a 'weird-type guy' and a clarinet player."[22] As a result of these comments, police began to think of Morin as a suspect prior to interviewing him.[23] During the first police interview, Morin made some

---

14 *Ibid.* at 15–19.

15 *Ibid.* at 7, 15, 19, & 20.

16 Kim Pate, "Justice for Battered Women—Denied, Delayed . . . Diminished: Jails Are Not the Shelters Battered Women Need" (28 September 1997) at 2, online: Canadian Association of Elizabeth Fry Societies www.caefs.ca/wp-content/uploads/2013/04/Justice-for-Battered-Women.pdf.

17 Ontario, Ministry of the Attorney General, "Executive Summary" in *Report of the Kaufman Commission on Proceedings Involving Guy Paul Morin* (Toronto: Queen's Printer for Ontario, 1998) [*Morin Inquiry Report* Executive Summary] at 3 and 24, online: www.attorneygeneral.jus.gov.on.ca/english/about/pubs/morin/morin_esumm.pdf.

18 *Ibid.* at 3.

19 *Ibid.*

20 See *ibid.* at 16–18. The chief identification officer was later charged with perjury and attempting to obstruct justice; he had lied under oath about aspects of the investigation and had kept two notebooks "containing a number of divergent entries for the same events" (at 17).

21 *Ibid.* at 3.

22 *Ibid.* at 20.

23 *Ibid.* at 20 & 21.

remarks that the officers found odd.[24] Although none of Morin's remarks constituted "hard evidence" or an admission, police prematurely focused the investigation on him.[25]

The officers' suspicions were seemingly supported by forensic hair and fibre evidence evaluated at the Centre of Forensic Sciences (CFS) in Toronto, which played a key role in the decision to arrest Morin.[26] Forensic analysis of a single hair "found embedded in skin tissue adhering to . . . [Christine's] necklace"[27] revealed that the hair did not belong to her but was instead microscopically similar to Morin's, meaning that the hair could have come from him.[28] In addition, three hairs taken from Morin's car were found to be microscopically dissimilar to his hair but similar to Christine's.[29] CFS analysts also found that several fibres removed from Morin's car and living room "could have come from the same source" as fibres found on Christine's effects.[30]

2) Morin's Trials and Appeals

Morin was arrested on 22 April 1985.[31] At his first trial, commencing in January 1986, the Crown relied on forensic hair and fibre evidence, Morin's alleged confession to a cellmate, and evidence purportedly demonstrating his opportunity to commit the crime and consciousness of guilt. The defence presented alibi evidence.[32] Morin was acquitted; however, the Crown appealed his acquittal and the Ontario Court of Appeal ordered a new trial.[33] At Morin's second trial, commencing in May 1990,[34] the jury heard from a number of witnesses who had not testified at the first trial but now

---

24 *Ibid.* at 21.

25 *Ibid.* at 21 & 22.

26 *Ibid.* at 4 and 21; Ontario, Ministry of the Attorney General, *Report of the Kaufman Commission on Proceedings Involving Guy Paul Morin* (Toronto: Queen's Printer for Ontario, 1998) ch. II, Sections A–M [*Morin Inquiry Report* ch. II(A–M)] at 83, online: www.attorneygeneral.jus.gov.on.ca/english/about/pubs/morin/morin_ch2am.pdf.

27 *Morin Inquiry Report* Executive Summary, above note 17 at 4.

28 *Ibid.*

29 *Ibid.* at 5.

30 *Morin Inquiry Report* ch. II(A–M), above note 26 at 92 & 93.

31 *Morin Inquiry Report* Executive Summary, above note 17 at 26.

32 *Morin Inquiry Report* ch. I, above note 2 at 69 & 70.

33 *Ibid.* at 71. The Crown appealed on the grounds that the trial judge made two errors in instructing the jury. The Supreme Court of Canada upheld the Ontario Court of Appeal's decision.

34 *Ibid.* at 73 and 77.

claimed to have evidence supporting Morin's consciousness of guilt.[35] This time, the jury found him guilty of first-degree murder.[36]

Morin appealed his conviction. Shortly before his appeal was to be heard, DNA typing definitively excluded him as the perpetrator. The DNA taken from the semen found on Christine's underpants did not match Morin's DNA.[37] On 23 January 1995, approximately a decade after his arrest, Morin's conviction was set aside and an acquittal was entered.[38]

3) Findings and Recommendations of the Morin Inquiry Regarding Faulty Forensic Evidence

On 26 June 1996, the Honourable Fred Kaufman, Q.C., was appointed commissioner of the public inquiry into the causes of Morin's wrongful conviction.[39] The public hearings, beginning on 10 February 1997, spanned 146 days and included testimony from 120 witnesses.[40] The Kaufman Commission made 119 recommendations for systemic change to the Ontario criminal justice system.[41] A complete survey of the findings is beyond the scope of this review, which will focus on the faulty forensic evidence uncovered at the inquiry.

The hair and fibre evidence relied on by the prosecution played a crucial role in Morin's wrongful conviction; indeed, Crown counsel at his second trial regarded this evidence as "some of the most significant evidence incriminating [him]."[42] Commissioner Kaufman, however, concluded that, despite its apparent weight, this evidence was "essentially . . . valueless. Properly understood, it had little or no probative value in demonstrating Mr. Morin's guilt."[43] CFS forensic examiners repeatedly overstated the relevance of this evidence and downplayed its limitations, both to police officers during the investigation and in their courtroom testimony.[44]

---

35 *Morin Inquiry Report* Executive Summary, above note 17 at 26–34.

36 *Morin Inquiry Report* ch. I, above note 2 at 78.

37 *Ibid.* at 78 & 79.

38 *Ibid.* at 79. On 24 January 1997, Morin was awarded $1.25 million in compensation for his wrongful conviction: Dawn Anderson & Barrie Anderson, "The Case of Guy Paul Morin" in *Manufacturing Guilt: Wrongful Convictions in Canada*, 2d ed. (Halifax: Fernwood, 2009) at 80.

39 *Morin Inquiry Report* ch. I, above note 2 at 1 & 2.

40 *Morin Inquiry Report* Executive Summary, above note 17 at 2.

41 *Ibid.* at 2.

42 *Morin Inquiry Report* ch. II(A–M), above note 26 at 1.

43 *Ibid.*

44 *Ibid.* at 99, 100, and 117; *Morin Inquiry Report* Executive Summary, above note 17 at 6–8; Ontario, Ministry of the Attorney General, "Forensic Evidence and the Centre

a) Hair Evidence

Commissioner Kaufman concluded that the hair comparison evidence had little or no probative value. It supported "nothing more than a conclusion that . . . Morin, together with countless others, could not be excluded as the donor of the necklace hair."[45] Similarly, Christine could not be excluded as the donor of the hairs found in Morin's car.[46] This evidence was improperly understood from its first entry into the investigation, in April 1985, when two officers (Detective Fitzpatrick and Inspector Shephard) brought Morin's hair samples to Ms. Stephanie Nyznyk, one of the CFS examiners. Nyznyk performed a preliminary comparison of the hairs and informed the officers that they were "*consistent with* having originated from the same source"[47] as the necklace hair.[48] Detective Fitzpatrick understood this to mean that there was a match—all of the hairs were from the same person.[49] Commissioner Kaufman found that Nyznyk knowingly overstated the probative value of this hair comparison analysis. She lost her objectivity early in the investigation and sought to advance the interests of the prosecution. Moreover, she lacked an adequate understanding of the science.[50] Had Nyznyk adequately communicated the limitations of her evidence to the police, Morin might "not have been arrested when he was—if, indeed, ever."[51]

---

of Forensic Sciences" in *Report of the Kaufman Commission on Proceedings Involving Guy Paul Morin* (Toronto: Queen's Printer for Ontario, 1998) [*Morin Inquiry Report* ch. II(V)] at 249, online: www.attorneygeneral.jus.gov.on.ca/english/about/pubs/morin/morin_ch2v.pdf.

45 *Morin Inquiry Report* ch. II(A–M), above note 26 at 109.

46 *Ibid.* at 109 & 110; *Morin Inquiry Report* Executive Summary, above note 17 at 5.

47 *Morin Inquiry Report* ch. II(A–M), above note 26 at 96 [emphasis in original]. Note that Commissioner Kaufman accepted the officers' evidence over Ms. Nyznyk's where the two differed, as he found her to be an unreliable witness (*ibid.* at 99).

48 *Ibid.* at 96 and 100; *Morin Inquiry Report* Executive Summary, above note 17 at 4.

49 *Morin Inquiry Report* ch. II(A–M), above note 26 at 97. Ms. Nyznyk also stated that the hair found in Morin's car might have come from Christine (*ibid.* at 98) and made various observations as to fibres found in Morin's car (see "(b) Fibre Evidence," below).

50 *Ibid.* at 100.

51 *Ibid.* at 91. (See also further discussion at 101.) Commissioner Kaufman found that the inadequacies in Nyznyk's description of her findings were compounded by the fact that "oral communication of complicated and subtle findings and, more important, the limitations upon those findings, may lead to gross misunderstanding" even where the scientist adequately expresses her opinion (*ibid.* at 100). He recommended: that only written forensic opinions be acted upon in the future (*Morin Inquiry Report* ch. II(V), above note 44: see Recommendation 6 at 329); that CFS establish a policy governing the form and content of these reports; and that the re-

Nyznyk and a colleague, Mr. Norman Erickson, testified at Morin's second trial.[52] While Erickson fairly presented the limitations of the hair evidence, Nyznyk wrongly gave the impression that it was highly unlikely that all of the hair similarities that she noted were due to coincidence.[53] Further, Nyznyk did not adequately communicate the limitations of her evidence to the prosecution, which then misused the hair comparison evidence (unintentionally) in the closing address.[54]

In light of these findings, Commissioner Kaufman made the following recommendation:

> Trial judges should undertake a more critical analysis of the admissibility of hair comparison evidence as circumstantial evidence of guilt. *Evidence that shows only that an accused cannot be excluded as the donor of an unknown hair* (or only that an accused may or may not have been the donor) *is unlikely to have sufficient probative value to justify its reception at a criminal trial* as circumstantial evidence of guilt.[55]

Commissioner Kaufman observed that in the vast majority of cases, the probative value of hair comparison evidence is extremely limited, since it "merely permits the trier of fact to infer that the accused is one of a limitless class of persons who cannot be excluded as the perpetrator based upon this analysis."[56] Moreover, its prejudicial effect can be significant, due to the aura of infallibility that may colour jurors' perception of expert scientific evidence.[57] Commissioner Kaufman made the following recommendation, referencing *R. v. Terceira*:[58]

> Where hair and fibre comparison evidence or other scientific evidence is tendered as evidence of guilt, *the trial judge would be well advised to instruct the jury not to be overwhelmed by any aura of scientific authority*

---

ports include both the forensic examiner's conclusions and the limitations of those conclusions (*ibid.*, Recommendation 7 at 331 & 332).

52 *Morin Inquiry Report* Executive Summary, above note 17 at 4; *Morin Inquiry Report* ch. II(A–M), above note 26 at 84.

53 *Morin Inquiry Report* ch. II(A–M), *ibid.* at 91 and 116. Erickson also testified as to the results of his examination of Christine's classmates' hair samples: two of her classmates could have been donors of the hair as well (at 91 and 139).

54 *Ibid.*

55 *Ibid.* at 312, see Recommendation 2 [emphasis added].

56 *Ibid.* at 313.

57 *Ibid.* at 316 and 320.

58 *R. v. Terceira* (1998), 123 C.C.C. (3d) 1 (Ont. C.A.). See discussion of *Terceira* in Chapter 12: Forensic Biology and DNA.

> *or infallibility associated with the evidence* and to clearly articulate for the jury the limitations upon the findings made by the experts. . . . [I]t is of particular importance that the trial judge ensure that counsel, when addressing the jury, do not misuse the evidence, but present it to the Court with no more and no less than its legitimate force and effect.[59]

It is now well understood that hair microscopy evidence can speak only to general, class characteristics; it cannot be used to individualize one person as the donor of a given hair. In view of this limitation (and especially with the development of DNA testing), hair microscopy evidence is more appropriately used for the purpose of exclusion.[60] In 2013, for instance, the Supreme Court of Canada overturned Leighton Hay's wrongful convictions for first-degree murder and attempted murder on the basis of new hair comparison evidence that excluded him as a suspect. The Court ordered a new trial[61] and, in 2014, the charges against Hay were withdrawn. He had spent over twelve years in prison.[62]

b) Fibre Evidence

Commissioner Kaufman found that the fibre comparison evidence "yielded nothing more than a conclusion that the fibre similarities could be attributed to direct contact, environmental contamination, or random oc-

---

59 *Morin Inquiry Report* ch. II(V), above note 44 at 329, see Recommendation 2 [emphasis added].

60 See, e.g., "E. The Manitoba Forensic Evidence Review Committee," "F. The Driskell Inquiry," " L. Microscopic Hair Comparison Analysis Review," "M. The Motherisk Hair Analysis Independent Review," below.

61 See *R. v. Hay*, 2013 SCC 61. At trial, the Crown tendered hair clippings found in Hay's bathroom garbage and electric razor to support its theory that Hay had shaved his head after participating in a Toronto nightclub shooting (paras. 1 and 14). It relied on this evidence to explain the discrepancy between Hay's appearance at the time of his arrest and the eyewitness description of the perpetrator and to suggest that Hay had attempted to change his appearance to conceal his role in the shooting (paras. 3 and 29). The Crown did not call any experts to testify as to the origin of the hair (para. 28). On appeal, Hay adduced fresh evidence from two forensic hair experts who testified that the hair in question did not originate from Hay's scalp; rather, it was facial hair (paras. 3 and 58–61). The Crown also adduced fresh evidence from two hair experts. They agreed with the defence experts' conclusion that there was "no evidence to support the proposition that the hair clippings represented a head shave" (para. 62). The Supreme Court admitted the fresh evidence, quashed Hay's conviction, and ordered a new trial (para. 78).

62 "Leighton Hay, Wrongfully Convicted of Murder in 2002, Walks Free" *CBC News* (28 November 2014), online: www.cbc.ca/news/canada/toronto/leighton-hay-wrongfully-convicted-of-murder-in-2002-walks-free-1.2853578.

currence."[63] There was no evidence favouring the prosecution's theory of direct contact between Morin and Christine over other possibilities; indeed, the evidence may have been more supportive of the defence theory that no direct contact occurred.[64] Like the hair comparison evidence, however, the fibre comparison evidence was improperly presented at every stage. During Nyznyk's initial meeting with Detective Fitzpatrick and Inspector Shephard, she stated that dyed red animal hair fibres and red plastic chips found in Morin's car were from the same source as fibres and plastic chips found on the victim, and that goldish-beige fibres found on Christine were consistent with the types of fibres used in car interiors.[65] Nyznyk told the officers that she believed that Christine had been in Morin's car.[66]

Both Nyznyk and Erickson overstated the probative value of the fibre evidence at Morin's second trial, testifying that the fibre similarities constituted significant evidence suggestive of direct contact between Morin and Christine.[67] Moreover, they failed to disclose that the fibre evidence had been contaminated within CFS, which might or might not have tainted the findings. They knew of this contamination prior to the first trial yet withheld this knowledge from police, Crown and defence counsel, and the court.[68] In addition, Erickson did not disclose the defence-friendly results of further fibre examination that he had conducted prior to the second trial.[69] Finally, Erickson provided the prosecution with a study on fibre transference that in fact was of limited relevance (at best) to the *Morin* case; however, Erickson and Nyznyk "did not adequately communicate the study's lack of significance to the prosecutors or to the Court," leading to its misuse by the prosecution.[70]

Observing that "[s]imilar issues (to hair analysis) are raised in connection with fibre comparison evidence,"[71] Commissioner Kaufman made the following recommendation:

> *Evidence of forensic fibre comparisons may or may not have sufficient probative value to justify its reception at a criminal trial* as circumstantial evidence

63 *Morin Inquiry Report* ch. II(A–M), above note 26 at 110.
64 *Ibid.*
65 *Ibid.* at 92, 98, and 102.
66 *Ibid.* at 100.
67 *Ibid.* at 93–95 and 117.
68 *Ibid.* at 94 & 95.
69 *Ibid.* at 95.
70 *Ibid.* at 95, 96, and 119.
71 *Morin Inquiry Report* ch. II(V), above note 44 at 325.

> of the accused's guilt. However, *the limitations upon the inferences to be reliably drawn from forensic fibre comparisons need be better appreciated* by judges, police, Crown and defence counsel. This requires better education of all parties, improved communication of forensic evidence and its limitations in and out of court, in written reports and orally.[72]

Commissioner Kaufman's expectation was that there would be "a greater number of cases where fibre comparison evidence," as compared to hair evidence, would possess "sufficient probative value to justify its reception as circumstantial evidence of guilt."[73] He noted, however, that while similarities between fibres may be the result of direct contact between the accused and the victim, there are other possibilities.[74] He concluded that further scientific research in this field would be needed to more reliably identify cases where the inference of direct contact could be safely drawn, and expressed the need for particular caution in cases, such as Morin's, where the fibre comparison evidence was "based upon only a handful of fibres."[75]

c) "Indications of Blood" Evidence

A third CFS forensic analyst, Mr. White, testified that he had found indications of blood in Morin's car.[76] Due to the limited quantity of the substance in question, he was able to perform only a "presumptive test"—that is, one that could not by itself reliably identify the substance as blood.[77] Mr. White appropriately presented these findings at trial, explaining that the substance might or might not be human blood.[78] However, the Crown referred to the "indications of blood" as "blood" and, later, as "traces of blood," in his closing address.[79] Commissioner Kaufman found that the "indications of blood" evidence ought to have been excluded, since it was

---

72 *Ibid.*, see Recommendation 3 [emphasis added].

73 *Ibid.*

74 *Ibid.*

75 *Ibid.* at 326.

76 Ontario, Ministry of the Attorney General, "Forensic Evidence and the Centre of Forensic Sciences" in *Report of the Kaufman Commission on Proceedings Involving Guy Paul Morin* (Toronto: Queen's Printer for Ontario, 1998) [*Morin Inquiry Report* ch. II(N–U)] at 236, online: www.attorneygeneral.jus.gov.on.ca/english/about/pubs/morin/morin_ch2nu.pdf.

77 *Ibid.* at 236 & 237.

78 *Morin Inquiry Report* ch. II(V), above note 44 at 328.

79 *Morin Inquiry Report* ch. II(N–U), above note 76 at 241. Commissioner Kaufman observed that one of the dangers posed by presumptive test evidence is this "potential for participants in the criminal justice system to allow the evidence to take on a meaning beyond that which is actually expressed by the scientist."

not probative of Christine's alleged presence in the car.[80] He concluded that "evidence of a preliminary test, such as an 'indication of blood,' does not have sufficient probative value to justify its reception at a criminal trial as circumstantial evidence of guilt."[81]

d) Other Recommendations

Commissioner Kaufman made a number of other recommendations,[82] of which the following are particularly salient:

- Recommendation 12, that expert witnesses ensure that misinterpretations of their testimony are expeditiously brought to counsel's attention and corrected.[83]
- Recommendations 8–10, that CFS promote the use of forensic terminology that enhances understanding and discourage potentially misleading terms such as "match" and "consistent with."[84]
- Recommendation 11, that CFS employees follow the scientific method, i.e., "work to vigorously challenge or disprove a hypothesis, rather than to prove one."[85]
- Recommendations 13–15, that CFS establish a policy requiring its employees to document their work;[86] their contacts with police, counsel, and non-CFS experts;[87] and instances of in-house contamination.[88]

D. THE INQUIRY REGARDING THOMAS SOPHONOW

1) Faulty Eyewitness Testimony in Thomas Sophonow's Convictions

Thomas Sophonow was tried three times for a murder that he could not have committed.[89] Despite possessing an irrefutable alibi, Sophonow was

---

80 *Morin Inquiry Report* ch. II(V), above note 44 at 328.

81 *Ibid.* at 327, see Recommendation 4.

82 See *ibid.* at 357–402 for the remaining forensic evidence recommendations not addressed below.

83 *Ibid.* at 349.

84 *Ibid.* at 338, 339, and 344.

85 *Ibid.* at 346. The hypothesis in this case was that the hair, fibre, and blood evidence connected Morin to Christine (at 348 & 349).

86 *Ibid.* at 354.

87 *Ibid.* at 352.

88 *Ibid.* at 355.

89 The Honourable Peter Cory, Commissioner, *The Inquiry regarding Thomas Sophonow* (5 November 2001) [*Sophonow Inquiry Report*], online: Government of Manitoba digitalcollection.gov.mb.ca/awweb/pdfopener?smd=1&did=12713&md=1 at 35, 36, and 94.

charged with the murder of sixteen-year-old Barbara Stoppel, who was strangled in December 1981 in the donut shop where she worked. Following an initial mistrial, Sophonow was twice convicted. After the first conviction, the Court of Appeal overturned the verdict and directed a new trial; after the second conviction, it acquitted him.[90] In June 2000, the Winnipeg Police Service formally announced that Sophonow was innocent. The Attorney General of Manitoba apologized to Sophonow for his having endured "three trials and two appeals, and . . . 45 months in jail for an offence he did not commit."[91] A Commission of Inquiry, led by retired Supreme Court Justice Peter Cory, was established to review the circumstances that led to Sophonow's wrongful convictions.[92] Sophonow was subsequently awarded $2.3 million in compensation for this miscarriage of justice.[93]

Commissioner Cory's report, released on 5 November 2001, found that faulty eyewitness testimony played a crucial role in Sophonow's convictions.[94] A number of people who saw Barbara Stoppel's killer mistakenly identified Sophonow as the perpetrator; Commissioner Cory found that these errors resulted both from the inherently malleable nature of memory and from poorly conducted identification procedures.[95] The evidence of several witnesses evolved significantly between the investigation and the first trial.[96] Noted memory and eyewitness identification expert Dr. Elizabeth Loftus[97] found that "many problems [were] . . . apparent in the evidence of the identification witnesses in this case."[98]

a) John Doerksen

Eyewitness John Doerksen attended a line-up that included Sophonow, but was unable to identify him (or anyone else) as the killer.[99] Two days

---

90 *Ibid.* at 35, 36, 94, and 99.

91 *Ibid.* at 35.

92 *Ibid.* at 35, 37, & 38; Manitoba Government, News Release "Sophonow Inquiry Report Released" (5 November 2001), online: www.gov.mb.ca/chc/press/top/2001/11/2001-11-05-05.html [Sophonow News Release].

93 Canadian Press, "Wrongfully Convicted People Who Received Compensation" *The Globe and Mail* (7 July 2008), online: www.theglobeandmail.com/news/national/wrongfully-convicted-people-who-received-compensation/article25579997.

94 "Sophonow News Release," above note 92; *Sophonow Inquiry Report*, above note 89 at 64 and 73.

95 For further discussion on memory, see Chapter 21.

96 *Sophonow Inquiry Report*, above note 89 at 58–73.

97 *Ibid.* at 61 and 67.

98 *Ibid.* at 69.

99 *Ibid.* at 58.

later, however, he coincidentally encountered Sophonow, by which time he had also seen Sophonow's face in the newspaper; on this occasion, Doerksen did identify him. By the time of the preliminary hearing, Doerksen was certain that Sophonow was the killer.[100]

Dr. Loftus testified that as time passes, our memories "become more and more susceptible to post-event information," which, if false or misleading, can in turn create a false memory.[101] She found that Doerksen's increasing certainty could be attributed to the impact of post-event information on his memory.[102] Dr. Loftus also testified that, contrary to popular opinion, there is "a very weak relationship" between a witness's confidence level and his or her accuracy.[103]

b) Lorraine and Norman Janower

Each of these witnesses was shown a photo lineup that was "startlingly unfair."[104] Sophonow's photograph stood out from the others, as it was the only one that had a border and appeared to have been taken outside. Upon viewing the photos, both Janowers tentatively indicated that Sophonow stood out to them for some reason.[105] In addition, Norman Janower viewed a live lineup, in which Sophonow again stood out unfairly (he was the tallest participant).[106] Mr. Janower tentatively identified Sophonow ("from what I see I'd say #7").[107] He then asked the sergeant in the room with him "if he had picked out the 'right guy.'"[108] The sergeant confirmed that he had selected the suspect. Mr. Janower became certain of his identification by the time of the preliminary hearing; indeed he retained this certainty even after Sophonow's exoneration. Commissioner Cory found that the conversation after the lineup "reinforced Mr. Janower's identification

---

100 *Ibid.* at 59. Commissioner Cory noted several further troubling features of Doerksen's evidence: he had significant vision limitations; he developed a friendship with the victim's family; and he testified while intoxicated during both trials.

101 *Ibid.* at 67.

102 *Ibid.* at 73. Post-event information also played an important role in other eyewitnesses' evolving confidence levels, as below (see 70 & 71).

103 *Ibid.* at 68.

104 *Ibid.* at 61.

105 *Ibid.* at 61 & 62. Specifically, Lorraine Janower stated that "[i]f anything he's like this. There's something about this guy, of all of them he'd be the closest" (at 61), while Norman Janower stated that "[t]his guy, I know him from somewhere. I don't know why. I couldn't be sure with the pictures" (at 62).

106 *Ibid.* at 71.

107 *Ibid.* at 62.

108 *Ibid.*

with the result that it then became certain while before it was tentative at best."[109]

Dr. Loftus found that Sophonow's photograph "might just as well have carried a notation saying, 'here I am.'"[110] Categorizing live lineups and photo arrays as forms of multiple-choice testing, she testified that "[i]f a suspect stands out in some obvious way, it is an unfair multiple choice test," as though the correct answer were underlined or in boldface.[111] Dr. Loftus emphasized that once a witness' memory has been contaminated by an unfair testing procedure, the damage cannot be undone.[112] She also found that, as likely occurred with Mr. Janower, "often the main reason for someone's change in testimony is . . . receiving or being supplied with new information from police officers."[113]

c) Mildred King

Eyewitness Mildred King was initially unable to make any identification upon viewing a live lineup. The officer then asked her if she was positive, to which she replied, "yes." However, she requested to see the men again, and then made a very tentative statement identifying Sophonow: "No, I can't swear. Number 7 was the closest from . . . the right side view."[114] As with the other witnesses, by the time of the preliminary inquiry, Mrs. King was positive that Thomas Sophonow was the perpetrator.[115]

2) Recommendations

The *Inquiry Regarding Thomas Sophonow* set out findings and recommendations on a number of topics, most of which do not apply to the forensic sciences. However, Commissioner Cory issued several findings regarding eyewitness identification evidence.[116] Regarding live lineups, he rec-

---

109 *Ibid.*
110 *Ibid.* at 61.
111 *Ibid.* at 67.
112 *Ibid.*
113 *Ibid.* at 71.
114 *Ibid.* at 64.
115 *Ibid.*
116 *Ibid.* at 17 & 18. Most, though not all, of these recommendations were reiterated in the recent report of the Committee on Scientific Approaches to Understanding and Maximizing the Validity and Reliability of Eyewitness Identification in Law Enforcement and the Courts, *Identifying the Culprit: Assessing Eyewitness Identification* (Washington, DC: National Academies Press, 2014) [*Assessing Eyewitness Identification*]. See discussion below in "K. Identifying the Culprit: Assessing Eyewitness Identification."

ommended the use of a double-blinded procedure (i.e., the officer in the room with the witness "should have no knowledge of the case or whether the suspect is contained in the lineup").[117] Further, the officer "should advise the witness that he does not know if the suspect is in the lineup or, if he is, who he is,"[118] emphasizing that the suspect may not be present. The lineup should include at least ten persons; the "fillers" (non-suspects) should resemble, as closely as possible, the description of the perpetrator provided by eyewitnesses, or, failing that, the suspect.[119] If the witness makes an identification, the officer should ask the witness to state his or her degree of certainty as to that identification. The lineup proceedings should be recorded, and all statements made by the eyewitness (notably including any confidence statements) should be "recorded verbatim and signed by the witness."[120] Following the lineup, the officer should escort the witness away from the premises, so as to "eliminate any possibility of contamination of that witness by other officers, particularly those involved in the investigation."[121]

Commissioner Cory made similar recommendations regarding the use of photo pack lineups, finding that these too should be double-blinded (and the officer should confirm his lack of knowledge as to the suspect's presence or absence), be recorded (including verbatim, signed documentation of the witness's comments), and include a minimum of ten subjects, who ought to bear the closest possible resemblance to the eyewitness's description, or, failing that, to the suspect. He found that "[t]he photo pack must be presented sequentially and not as a package."[122] The photo array should be presented to each witness separately, and the officer should refrain from making comments regarding the witness's identification (or lack thereof).[123] Additionally, prior to presenting the photo pack, "the officer should advise the witness that it is just as important to clear the innocent as it is to identify the suspect."[124]

Commissioner Cory also made several recommendations regarding how to conduct a trial so as to safeguard against the inherent dangers of eyewitness evidence. He recommended that the court admit properly

117 *Sophonow Inquiry Report*, above note 89 at 17.
118 *Ibid.*
119 *Ibid.*
120 *Ibid.*
121 *Ibid.*
122 *Ibid.*
123 *Ibid.* at 17 and 63.
124 *Ibid.* at 17.

qualified expert evidence on this topic, since jury exposure to the scientific underpinnings of this field would help the accused person to receive a fair trial. For instance, the expert may aid in dispelling the myth that the degree of certainty of an eyewitness identification correlates with its accuracy,[125] and the court should caution the jury in regard to eyewitness evidence that has progressed from tentative to certain. Further, the trial judge must provide "strong and clear directions . . . emphasizing the frailties of eyewitness identification."[126] The trial judge should also inform the jury that "the vast majority of wrongful convictions have arisen as a result of faulty eyewitness identification," and that these tragic mistakes have been "made by honest, right-thinking eyewitnesses."[127]

E. THE MANITOBA FORENSIC EVIDENCE REVIEW COMMITTEE

The Manitoba Forensic Evidence Review Committee was established on 23 April 2003, shortly after DNA evidence demonstrated the innocence of James Driskell, who had been convicted of first-degree murder in part due to flawed hair microscopy evidence presented at his trial.[128] The committee's mandate was to seek out additional miscarriages of justice resulting from hair microscopy evidence by conducting a fifteen-year retrospective review of Manitoba homicide cases in which it was relied on to secure a conviction. The committee limited its mandate to those cases where the accused pled not guilty, was convicted, appealed to the Manitoba Court of Appeal asserting factual innocence, and had his appeal dismissed.[129] The committee identified two unrelated first-degree murder convictions of relevance to its mandate: the cases of *R. v. Unger* and *R. v. Sanderson.*[130] In both cases, experts testified at trial that the hair evidence found at the crime scene was "consistent with" the known scalp hair samples voluntarily supplied by the defendant.[131]

125 *Ibid.* Commissioner Cory described Mr. Janower's evidence as "a classic example of misplaced but absolute confidence."

126 *Ibid.* at 18.

127 *Ibid.*

128 Manitoba Justice, *Forensic Evidence Review Committee: Final Report* by Richard A. Saull et al. (19 August 2004) [*FERC Report*] at 3, online: www.gov.mb.ca/justice/publications/forensic/pubs/finalreportaug2004.pdf; *Driskell Inquiry Report*, above note 2 at 1 and 155. (See "F. The Driskell Inquiry," below, for further discussion of James Driskell's case.)

129 *FERC Report*, above note 128 at 3.

130 *Ibid.* at 6, referencing *R. v. Unger*, [1993] M.J. No. 363 (C.A.); *R. v. Sanderson* (1999), 134 Man. R. (2d) 191 (C.A.) [*Sanderson*].

131 *FERC Report*, above note 128 at 10–13 and 16.

Kyle Unger was convicted of the sexual assault and murder of a sixteen-year-old girl who had attended the same rock festival as did Unger and his co-accused (Houlahan) in 1990.[132] Unger's hair sample was found to be microscopically comparable with hair samples taken from the victim's sweatshirt, which was recovered from the crime scene.[133] At trial, the hair and fibre expert, James Cadieux, testified that he could not determine how long the hair might have been on the victim's sweater—important information considering that Unger had spoken to the victim on the night of the murder.[134] Multiple police searches of Unger's home and car did not yield hair or fibre evidence belonging to the victim.[135]

Robert Sanderson was convicted of a triple homicide in 1996, in which the victims had been repeatedly shot and stabbed.[136] Sanderson's hair sample was found to be microscopically consistent with the hair retrieved from the right foot of one of the victims. The hair expert, again James Cadieux, testified that it was possible that Sanderson could have shed hair onto someone or something which then transferred the hair to the deceased. In short, even accepting that the hair was Sanderson's (the defence argued that there was no clear evidence to support this contention), it was unclear how the hair had come to be at the crime scene.[137]

In 2004, the mtDNA (mitochondrial DNA) testing conducted as part of the Forensic Evidence Review proved that the incriminating hairs did not

---

132 *FERC Report, ibid.* at 8. Unger was arrested on 29 June 1990, but the Crown entered a stay of proceedings following the preliminary hearing. However, police later learned that Unger had allegedly made inculpatory statements to his former cellmate (at 8, 9, and 12). In the course of the ensuing undercover operation—a Mr. Big sting—Unger confessed to the crime (at 8 and 10): Bruce A. MacFarlane, Q.C., "Wrongful Convictions: Is It Proper for the Crown to Root Around, Looking for Miscarriages of Justice?" (2012) 36 *Manitoba Law Journal* 1 at 18. He was rearrested on 25 June 1991, and convicted, along with Houlahan, on 29 February 1992 (*FERC Report*, above note 128 at 8). Unger's appeal was dismissed on 7 July 1993. His leave to appeal to the Supreme Court of Canada was dismissed on 2 December 1993 (at 9).

133 *FERC Report, ibid.* at 12 & 13.

134 *Ibid.* at 11 and 16.

135 *Ibid.* at 12.

136 *Sanderson*, above note 130 at paras 1, 4, and 7. Three co-accused, including Sanderson, were jointly charged with first-degree murder; all three were convicted on 26 June 1997 (*FERC Report*, above note 128 at 14). The Manitoba Court of Appeal dismissed Sanderson's appeal on 19 March 1999 (*Sanderson*, above note 130). The Supreme Court of Canada dismissed his application for leave to appeal on 16 September 1999 (*FERC Report*, above note 128 at 14).

137 *Ibid.* at 16.

belong to Unger and Sanderson (nor to any of their maternal relatives).[138] Although the Crown had relied on other evidence in addition to the hair microscopy results in securing the convictions,[139] the committee recommended that the cases be referred to the Manitoba Department of Justice to determine the impact, if any, of the hair evidence on each finding of guilt.[140]

In October 2005, Manitoba Justice announced that the case against Sanderson remained strong, despite the fact that the hair found at the crime scene was not his. Since there was no "obvious miscarriage of justice,"[141] Manitoba Justice did not recommend the case for ministerial review under section 696.1 of the *Criminal Code*. Although Manitoba Justice promised its co-operation in the event that Sanderson chose to pursue this process, a section 696.1 application was never filed.[142]

In Unger's case, however, Innocence Canada (formerly known as the Association in Defence of the Wrongly Convicted [AIDWYC]) filed a section 696.1 application. After spending fourteen years in prison, Unger was granted bail pending the decision of the Federal Minister of Justice, who subsequently ordered a new trial. On 23 October 2009, the Crown advised the court that it would not be proceeding with the retrial, and Unger was acquitted.[143] In 2011, he filed a $14.5 million lawsuit seeking compensation

---

138 *Ibid.* at 20.

139 *Ibid.* at 9, 10, 12, 14, 15, and 17. In Unger's case, other inculpatory evidence included the co-accused's assertion that Unger was the main aggressor (at 12); the inculpatory statement that Unger allegedly made to his cellmate (at 9); and his confession, obtained in the course of a Mr. Big sting (at 10). In Sanderson's case, other inculpatory evidence included the testimony of two witnesses (at 14 & 15); compositionally similar vehicle oil found near the crime scene and in Sanderson's car (at 15); trace amounts of blood from one of the victims on a seatbelt in Sanderson's car (at 15); blood from two of the victims found on a baseball bat located in the car's trunk (at 15); and Sanderson's own statement that the car might have been involved in the crime, but that he had lent it to someone whom he refused to identify, in accordance with Los Bravos' "Code of Silence" (at 17).

140 *Ibid.* at 20. In light of these findings, the Committee's mandate was renewed on 15 September 2004 to address possible miscarriages of justice resulting from hair microscopy evidence in sexual assault, robbery, and other cases (Manitoba Justice, *Forensic Evidence Review Committee #2: Final Report* by Richard A. Saull et al. (13 September 2005) at 3, online: www.gov.mb.ca/justice/publications/forensic/pubs/finalreportsep2005.pdf). Despite an extensive search, no cases met the Committee's criteria and no further action was taken. In its report (published on 13 September 2005), however, the Committee recognized the importance of this review process in maintaining public confidence in the administration of justice (*FERC Report*, above note 128 at 6 & 7).

141 MacFarlane, above note 132 at 23.

142 *Ibid.*; *Criminal Code*, R.S.C. 1985, c. C-46, s. 696.1.

143 MacFarlane, above note 132 at 17 & 18.

for his wrongful conviction. The federal Attorney General's office filed a statement of defence in 2013. The lawsuit remains outstanding.[144]

F. THE DRISKELL INQUIRY[145]

1) Background

In November 1989, James Driskell and Perry Harder were charged with several offences related to their operation of a "chop shop,"[146] where police discovered thousands of dollars' worth of stolen property. Harder accepted a plea deal but, on 21 June 1990, he failed to attend court as agreed and a bench warrant was issued for his arrest. The Crown requested an adjournment to deal with the charges against Driskell, but the request was denied and the charges were dropped.[147]

Three months later, Harder's body was found in a shallow grave. He had been shot twice in the chest.[148] Driskell was arrested and charged with first-degree murder.[149] The prosecution's theory was that Driskell had killed Harder to prevent Harder from testifying against him.[150] The Crown relied heavily on the testimony of two witnesses (Zanidean and Gumieny)—both criminal associates of Driskell's with lengthy, serious records—who claimed that Driskell had told them that he planned to kill Harder and had proposed possible methods, one of which involved trans-

144 *Ibid.* at 18; Steve Lambert, "Unger Sues for Wrongful Conviction in Murder of Manitoba Teen" *Globe and Mail* (21 September 2011), online: www.theglobeandmail.com/news/national/kyle-unger-sues-for-wrongful-conviction-in-murder-of-manitoba-teen/article4256694; The Canadian Press, "Feds Deny Liability in Kyle Unger Wrongful Conviction" *CBC News* (27 August 2013), online: www.cbc.ca/news/canada/manitoba/feds-deny-liability-in-kyle-unger-wrongful-conviction-1.1339338. Unger alleged that he had been wrongfully convicted based on the faulty hair microscopy science and the false confession extracted from him in the course of a flawed Mr. Big sting. The federal attorney general argued that Unger bears partial responsibility for his conviction because of his repeated admissions to committing the murder, and that both the Crown and the RCMP acted in good faith throughout the investigations. The attorney general defended the use of hair microscopy in Unger's case as the analysis was conducted using established scientific methods of the time.

145 *Driskell Inquiry Report*, above note 2.

146 *Ibid.* at 1, 6, & 7.

147 *Ibid.* at 7 & 8.

148 *Ibid.* at 8.

149 *Ibid.* at 1.

150 *Ibid.* at 6 and 8.

porting him in Driskell's van.[151] Zanidean was offered immunity from prosecution on an arson charge in exchange for his testimony and both men received payments to testify—important credibility-impacting information that was not disclosed to Driskell.[152]

This dubious testimony appeared, however, to be supported by forensic hair microscopy evidence. Police searched the van that Driskell had owned at the time and obtained thirty-four human hairs from it. These were provided to Tod Christianson, a hair and fibre analyst at the RCMP Forensic Laboratory in Winnipeg, who compared them to hairs taken from Harder's gravesite that were thought to have come from his scalp.[153] Christianson concluded that three of the hairs retrieved from Driskell's van were microscopically similar to the gravesite hairs.[154] At Driskell's trial, Christianson testified that these three hairs were "consistent with the hair samples from the gravesite,"[155] and that it was highly likely that they belonged to Harder.[156]

Driskell was convicted on 14 June 1991. He received a life sentence with no eligibility for parole for twenty-five years.[157] Driskell appealed his conviction to the Manitoba Court of Appeal, which held that there was "absolutely no merit" to his arguments.[158] He spent thirteen years in prison,[159] remaining there until mitochondrial DNA (mtDNA) testing exonerated him. The mtDNA testing revealed that the three hairs taken from Driskell's van that were presented at his trial as very likely belonging to Harder were in fact from three different individuals, none of whom were Harder.[160] On 28 November 2003, Driskell was released on bail, pending a ministerial review of his conviction. Following this review, Driskell's conviction was set aside and a new trial was ordered. The Manitoba Attorney General entered a Stay of Proceedings on 2 March 2005.[161] Driskell was subsequently awarded $4 million in compensation for his wrongful conviction.[162]

---

151 *Ibid.* at 6; *R. v. Driskell*, 2004 MBQB 3 at paras. 22, 26, and 35 [*Driskell*].
152 *Driskell Inquiry Report*, above note 2 at 98, 100, & 101; *Driskell*, *ibid.* at paras. 27, 29, & 30.
153 *Driskell Inquiry Report*, above note 2 at 146 & 147.
154 *Ibid.* at 147.
155 *Ibid.* at 149.
156 *Ibid.* at 59 and 158.
157 *Ibid.* at 1.
158 *R. v. Driskell*, [1992] M.J. No. 589 (C.A.).
159 *Driskell Inquiry Report*, above note 2 at 1.
160 *Ibid.* at 155 and 158.
161 *Ibid.* at 1.
162 The Canadian Press, "Wrongly Convicted James Driskell Offered $4M Deal" *CTV News* (20 September 2008), online: www.ctvnews.ca/wrongly-convicted-james-driskell-offered-4m-deal-1.326680; "Driskell Insurance Claim Settled" *Winnipeg*

On 7 December 2005,[163] Commissioner Patrick J. LeSage was appointed to lead the public inquiry into the systemic failures that contributed to Driskell's wrongful conviction.[164] The inquiry, which commenced on 18 July 2006,[165] found that a number of factors contributed to this miscarriage of justice, principally the Crown's "failure to disclose information to Driskell with respect to matters that were relevant and extremely cogent regarding the credibility"[166] of Zanidean and Gumieny. This chapter addresses only those findings pertaining to forensic science.

2) Findings Regarding the Driskell Hair Examination and Evidence

a) Hair Examination Standards and Practices

Commissioner LeSage first noted that there were two possible explanations for the discrepancy between Christianson's conclusions and the results of the DNA testing. Either the three hairs were not in fact microscopically similar or the hairs were similar, but their similarity was coincidental. Since the hairs were destroyed in the mtDNA testing process, it was not possible to determine which explanation was correct.[167] Commissioner LeSage found that Christianson had sufficient training and qualifications to conduct hair microscopy examinations and that his methods and techniques were generally in accordance with the accepted forensic laboratory standards of the time.[168] Commissioner LeSage noted, however, that Christianson's report, though drafted in accordance with RCMP Forensic Laboratory Services (FLS) policy, was briefer than what would have been the standard in many forensic facilities at the time.[169] Significantly, the report omitted the total number of hairs that Christianson examined—important information, since "the likelihood of a coincidental microscopic 'consistency' cannot properly be assessed"[170] without

Free Press (19 January 2011), online: www.winnipegfreepress.com/breakingnews/Driskell-114196669.html. Driskell's mother received $25,000.

163 Order in Council dated 7 December 2005, referred to as Appendix "A" to the *Driskell Inquiry Report*, above note 2, cited at 1.

164 *Driskell Inquiry Report*, *ibid.* at 1 & 2.

165 "In Depth: James Driskell" *CBC News* (18 July 2006), online: www.cbc.ca/news2/background/driskell.

166 *Driskell Inquiry Report*, above note 2 at 6.

167 *Ibid.* at 158.

168 *Ibid.* at 159.

169 *Ibid.*

170 *Ibid.* at 160.

it. In addition, FLS policy did not require Christianson's conclusions to be reviewed by another examiner, though the highly subjective nature of microscopic hair comparisons was well-known at the time.[171]

Commissioner LeSage also identified RCMP FLS policies that were in accordance with the norms of the day but deficient in hindsight. For instance, Christianson followed RCMP FLS note-taking policy in not making "detailed notes of the characteristics of the three questioned hairs he concluded were microscopically 'consistent with' the known hairs,"[172] making it impossible to conduct a meaningful review of his conclusions. In addition, FLS hair comparisons at the time were not conducted "blind";[173] that is, the hair examiner generally "knew if the police were expecting to find a hair 'match,'" raising the spectre of confirmation bias.[174]

b) Christianson's Trial Testimony

Commissioner LeSage found that Christianson's trial testimony was "in most respects typical of how hair microscopy evidence was presented in the early 1990s."[175] However, he expressed concern that Christianson's opinion nonetheless may not have been scientifically justifiable and that the jury may not have properly understood the limited probative value of the hair microscopy evidence.[176] Commissioner LeSage observed that:

> [L]ike other hair examiners at that time, . . . [Christianson] did not explain in any significant detail why he concluded . . . [that the observed] similarity was unlikely to be coincidental, nor did he set out the relevant factors that the jury should consider to appropriately assess the scientific validity of this belief. He may not have fully appreciated that what he had been taught about the rarity of coincidental matches was largely conjectural and lacked a solid foundation.[177]

Moreover, Christianson did not explain to the jury that the chance of a coincidental hair match increases with the number of hair samples surveyed, nor did he indicate that he had examined thirty-four human hairs

---

171 *Ibid.* at 160 & 161.

172 *Ibid.* at 162. There is no indication in the inquiry as to why the FLS might have adopted this problematic policy.

173 *Ibid.* at 161 & 162.

174 *Ibid.* at 163.

175 *Ibid.* at 165.

176 *Ibid.* at 165, 166, 169, and 173.

177 *Ibid.* at 166.

from the van, of which only three "matched" the gravesite hairs. Instead, he relied on potentially misleading analogies to jurors' experiences of the low likelihood of their encountering individuals with indistinguishable faces or hairstyles. Thus, the jury did not possess the information required to meaningfully address the question of the likelihood that the three hair matches were coincidental.[178]

Commissioner LeSage also noted that, in accordance with FLS policy at the time, Christianson used the term "consistent with" to describe his results. FLS did not then have the benefit of the Morin inquiry's critique of this terminology.[179] Commissioner LeSage adopted this critique,[180] noting that the principal danger posed by the term "consistent with" is that the trier of fact "may misinterpret a statement meant by a witness to suggest only a weak association, as indicating a much closer connection."[181]

3) Systemic Recommendations

Commissioner LeSage recommended that "microscopic hair comparison evidence . . . be received with great caution and, when received, jurors should be warned of the inherent frailties of such evidence."[182] He agreed with Commissioner Kaufman's conclusion that, generally speaking, hair microscopy evidence has very little probative value and can have significant prejudicial effect.[183] He found that the increasing availability of DNA testing—which had largely eclipsed hair microscopy evidence as a method of identification by the time of the Driskell inquiry—made it "increasingly questionable to justify exposing criminal defendants to the prejudicial dangers identified by Commissioner Kaufman."[184] Moreover, "the number of DNA exonerations in cases involving hair microscopy evidence [had] . . . tipp[ed] . . . the balance of probative value versus prejudicial effect further towards exclusion"[185] since the Morin inquiry. Commissioner LeSage also agreed with Commissioner Kaufman that, when admitted, hair microscopy evidence should be "expressed in 'exclusionary' rather than 'inclusionary'

178 *Ibid.* at 167 & 168.
179 *Ibid.* at 164; see "C. The Morin Inquiry," above.
180 *Ibid.* at 164.
181 *Ibid.* at 165. Christianson, however, "was trying to indicate a strong association."
182 *Ibid.* at 181.
183 *Ibid.* at 178.
184 *Ibid.* at 180.
185 *Ibid.* at 179.

terms (i.e., framed as a statement that the source of the known hairs cannot be excluded as the source of the questioned hairs)."[186]

G. THE GOUDGE INQUIRY

1) Background

The Goudge Inquiry was commissioned in response to a series of wrongful convictions and other adverse outcomes related to clinical pathologist Dr. Charles Smith's problematic testimony in criminal pediatric death cases between 1991 and 2001.[187] The inquiry aimed "to determine what went so badly wrong in the practice and oversight of pediatric forensic pathology in Ontario, especially as it relates to the criminal justice system,"[188] and "to make recommendations to restore and enhance the public confidence in pediatric forensic pathology."[189]

Dr. Charles Smith was employed as a pedriatric pathologist at the Hospital for Sick Children (SickKids), in Toronto, from 1981 to 2005. Dr. Smith had no formal training in forensic pathology, nor was he certified to practice in this field. Nevertheless, he began to work on criminally suspicious pediatric death cases in the late 1980s and "soon came to dominate pediatric forensic pathology in Ontario." He provided decisive testimony in many cases.[190]

As Dr. Smith's reputation grew, so too did concerns regarding his competence. Beginning in 1991, and continuing onwards, "coroners, police officers, and Crown counsel [raised] . . . a litany of concerns about Dr. Smith's work practices,"[191] including his testimony.[192] These concerns went unaddressed for several years.[193] The Chief Coroner for Ontario called for a full review into Dr. Smith's work on criminally suspicious cases in 2005, after fourteen years of warnings. The review was conducted by five eminent forensic pathologists.[194] In nine of the forty-five cases treated in the

---

186 *Ibid.* at 172.

187 Ontario, Ministry of the Attorney General, "Executive Summary" in *Inquiry into Pediatric Forensic Pathology in Ontario* by the Honourable Stephen T. Goudge, Commissioner [Goudge Inquiry Report] vol. 1 at 6–8, online: www.attorneygeneral.jus.gov.on.ca/inquiries/goudge/report/v1_en_pdf/Vol_1_Eng_ES.pdf.

188 *Ibid.* at 5.

189 *Ibid.* at 6. See also discussion at 7 & 8.

190 *Ibid.* at 6. See discussion at 13 as well as Chapter 18: Forensic Pathology.

191 *Ibid.* at 24.

192 *Ibid.* at 6 and 20–34.

193 *Ibid.* at 6 & 7.

194 *Ibid.* at 7.

Chief Coroner's review, "the reviewers did not agree with significant facts that appeared in either Dr. Smith's report or his testimony";[195] moreover, "[i]n 20 of the 45 cases, the reviewers took issue with Dr. Smith's opinion in either his report or his testimony, or both. In 12 of those 20 cases, there had been findings of guilt by the courts."[196] The Goudge Inquiry was commissioned on 25 April 2007, six days after the release of these results.[197] In 2011, Dr. Smith was stripped of his medical licence.

2) Findings of the Goudge Inquiry

In his report, released on 1 October 2008, Commissioner Goudge identified "a wide range of failings in the practice of pediatric forensic pathology in Ontario from 1981 to 2001."[198] Dr. Smith's errors exemplified "grave systemic problems" in this field.[199]

a) Educational Background[200]

Commissioner Goudge addressed a number of problematic aspects of Smith's training and practice. He observed that Dr. Smith was "a pediatric pathologist, not a forensic pathologist," and was neither trained nor certified in the latter field.[201] Dr. Smith failed to rectify these deficiencies despite his increasing interest and prominence in the field of pediatric forensic pathology.[202] By the time of the inquiry, Dr. Smith himself believed that his background was "woefully inadequate" and had contributed significantly to his errors.[203] This deficiency was compounded by his tendency to work in isolation rather than consulting with his colleagues.[204] Commissioner Goudge found that Dr. Smith "violated a cardinal rule of scientific expertise" by failing to appreciate, and confine himself within, the limits of his knowledge.[205]

---

195 *Ibid.*

196 *Ibid.* [internal citations omitted].

197 *Ibid.* Canadian Press, "Disgraced Pathologist Charles Smith Stripped of Medical Licence" *The Globe and Mail* (1 February 2011), online: http://fw.to/Sxc7XNF.

198 *Ibid.* at 11.

199 *Ibid.*

200 *Ibid.*

201 *Ibid.*

202 *Ibid.* at 13.

203 *Ibid.*

204 *Ibid.* at 14.

205 *Ibid.*

This said, Dr. Smith's forensic pathology background was not unusual for the time. Indeed "almost all the coroner's autopsies in Ontario" during this period "were performed by fee-for-service pathologists who had neither training nor certification in forensic pathology."[206] Commissioner Goudge found, however, that while "every forensic pathologist needs to be a competent clinical pathologist, the opposite is not true."[207] Forensic pathologists must be familiar with the requirements of the legal process, which include an emphasis "on identifying forensically significant findings such as injury, collecting potentially relevant evidence, and maintaining its continuity, none of which arise in clinical pathology." These findings must be documented in a manner that meets the needs of justice system participants, and must be conveyed in court using fair, objective, and clear language.[208] Commissioner Goudge found that "forensic pathologists, rather than pediatric pathologists, should take the lead in criminally suspicious pediatric cases."[209]

b) Autopsy Practice[210]

Commissioner Goudge identified a number of deficiencies in Dr. Smith's autopsy practice that "contributed to misdiagnoses with significant consequences":[211] (1) he seldom attended the death scene; (2) at times, he failed to obtain all the relevant information, and only the relevant information, prior to commencing the autopsy (with the result that "scientific conclusions [were] skewed by unscientific considerations"[212]); (3) he failed to account for contradictory evidence and new information in formulating his opinion; and (4) his documentation was careless and uneven. In particular, Commissioner Goudge criticized Dr. Smith's post-mortem examination reports, which typically provided only findings and bald conclusions, with no reasoning process or scientific literature to support them.[213] These reports were, "at best, of little use to the criminal justice system and, at worst, misleading."[214] Moreover, in many cases the opinions that they provided were simply wrong. Commissioner Goudge found that Dr. Smith's

206 *Ibid.* at 11.
207 *Ibid.* at 9.
208 *Ibid.*
209 *Ibid.* at 41.
210 *Ibid.* at 14.
211 *Ibid.*
212 *Ibid.*
213 *Ibid.*
214 *Ibid.* at 14 & 15.

deficient reporting practices reflected serious systemic problems, though he was not certain as to the precise frequency with which these problematic practices were employed.[215]

c) Interaction with the Criminal Justice System[216]

Commissioner Goudge found that Dr. Smith's interactions with Crown counsel, police, and coroners reflected additional systemic problems, one of which was a lack of timeliness in producing post-mortem reports.[217] Commissioner Goudge found that Dr. Smith repeatedly ignored requests for his reports, sometimes only producing reports after a subpoena or court order had been obtained.[218]

Dr. Smith was not mindful of the expert's independent, objective role in the criminal justice system.[219] He believed that his role was to support the Crown. Dr. Smith made excessively categorical statements to police in a number of criminal investigations, which may have skewed the investigation toward a specific suspect.[220] At court, he failed to remain impartial and to testify in a clear, balanced, and scientifically substantiated manner. He offered "erroneous or unscientific opinions" in a manner that "ranged from confusing to dogmatic."[221] Further, Dr. Smith sometimes misled the court as to the limits of his expertise and testified on matters that were not within them. He speculated, prejudicially, on topics not pertaining to pathology findings; he failed to acknowledge the existence of scientific controversies; he made inappropriate references to his own parenting experiences and unjustified criticisms of other experts; he used unscientific terminology;[222] and he lied under oath.[223] Commissioner Goudge concluded that, while the primary responsibility for these failings rested with

---

215 *Ibid.* at 15.

216 *Ibid.*

217 *Ibid.*

218 *Ibid.*

219 *Ibid.* at 15 & 16. See also discussion at 19.

220 *Ibid.* at 16.

221 *Ibid.* These problems with Dr. Smith's testimony were compounded by his failure to prepare adequately for his court appearances. Rather than reviewing his case file prior to testifying, he would merely reread his post-mortem examination report. Commissioner Goudge found that this insufficient preparation created difficulties, since an expert's opinion is only of assistance to the court where he or she has "a complete understanding of the case and the basis of the . . . opinion" (at 17).

222 *Ibid.* at 18.

223 *Ibid.* at 17 & 18.

Dr. Smith, the burden must be shared by counsel, the courts, and the Office of the Chief Coroner for Ontario (OCCO).[224]

d) Systemic Failures of Oversight[225]

Commissioner Goudge found that, as a result of insufficiencies in the legislative and regulatory framework and in their application by those responsible, Dr. Smith's work was inadequately supervised.[226] In particular, Commissioner Goudge cited the *Coroners Act*, which "provide[d] . . . no foundation for effective oversight of forensic pathology in Ontario."[227]

3) Recommendations[228]

Commissioner Goudge made 169 recommendations to address the systemic problems that he identified and to restore public confidence in the practice of pediatric forensic pathology.[229]

a) Institutional Framework

Commissioner Goudge found that Smith had achieved his status as a leading expert in the field "in large part because there was no one who had the training, experience, and expertise to take him on,"[230] and called for the creation of "a truly professionalized Ontario forensic pathology service."[231] Commissioner Goudge determined that this service would need to be built on four cornerstones: (1) legislative change; (2) a commitment to providing education, training, and certification in forensic pathology; (3) a commitment to recruiting and retaining qualified practitioners; and (4) the provision of adequate financial resources to achieve these goals (finding that the forensic pathology system had been undervalued and underfunded for decades).[232]

Commissioner Goudge recommended that the *Coroners Act* be amended to provide a stronger legislative framework for the organization and supervision of Ontario forensic pathologists.[233] In particular, he recommended

224 *Ibid.* at 19 & 20.
225 *Ibid.* at 20.
226 *Ibid.* at 20–34.
227 *Ibid.* at 21 & 22; *Coroners Act*, R.S.O. 1990, c. C.37.
228 *Ibid.* at 34.
229 *Ibid.*
230 *Ibid.*
231 *Ibid.* at 35.
232 *Ibid.* at 35 and 38.
233 *Ibid.* at 35 & 36.

the creation of an Ontario Forensic Pathology Service (OFPS) as a distinct service within the OCCO to be responsible for providing and supervising forensic pathology services;[234] a new, independent governance structure to oversee the OCCO;[235] and a registry of approved forensic pathologists.[236] The Ontario legislature has since adopted each of these recommendations.[237]

Commissioner Goudge also found that the development of a professionalized forensic pathology service in Canada had been "seriously hampered by the fact that there [were] . . . no domestic postgraduate training programs in the science."[238] He called on the Royal College of Physicians and Surgeons of Canada (Royal College) to provide such a program. He emphasized the need for this training to include education about the requirements of forensic pathologists' role as experts in the criminal justice system.[239] The Royal College now offers a one-year residency program in forensic pathology at the University of Toronto.[240]

b) Best Practices[241]

Commissioner Goudge found that it is equally vital that "forensic pathologists be highly skilled scientists [and] . . . that they be able to communicate their opinions effectively to the criminal justice system."[242] He identified two sets of basic principles that ought to guide forensic pathologists in performing autopsies and giving expert opinions.

i) Autopsy Work

Commissioner Goudge called on forensic pathologists to guard against confirmation bias by "thinking truth." They should adopt an independent, objective, evidence-based approach to the autopsy that follows the pathology evidence to whatever outcome it indicates. They should seek to avoid

---

234 *Ibid.* at 36.

235 *Ibid.* at 39.

236 *Ibid.* at 43.

237 *Coroners Act*, R.S.O. 1990, c. C.37, ss. 6–8.1; Ontario, Ministry of Community Safety and Correctional Services, "Ontario Forensic Pathology Service," online: www.mcscs.jus.gov.on.ca/english/DeathInvestigations/Pathology/pathology_main.html; Ontario, News Release, "Ontario Acts on Goudge Recommendations" (23 October 2008), online: news.ontario.ca/archive/en/2008/10/23/Ontario-Acts-On-Goudge-Recommendations.html.

238 Goudge Inquiry Report, above note 187 at 36.

239 *Ibid.* at 37.

240 Hart House Report, above note 1 at 17.

241 Goudge Inquiry Report, above note 187 at 43.

242 *Ibid.* at 45.

"thinking dirty"[243] (i.e., "approaching every sudden and unexpected child death with a high index of suspicion"[244]). He also recommended that forensic pathologists remain independent of the coroner, police, and counsel in discharging their duties; document their autopsy work with sufficient care to ensure its transparency and ability to be reviewed or challenged; and maintain a commitment to quality and teamwork.[245]

ii) Expert Opinion

Commissioner Goudge recommended that forensic pathologists pay particular attention to the following aspects of their testimony, with a view to avoiding misunderstandings: (1) whether the substance and/or language of the opinion "is susceptible to varied meanings or otherwise does not elucidate the pathology issues at stake";[246] (2) whether the expert's level of confidence or certainty is accurately expressed; (3) whether the opinion addresses relevant alternative explanations or scientific controversies, where applicable; (4) whether the opinion falls outside the boundaries of the pathologist's expertise, or is based on exogenous non-pathology information or on other expert opinions; and (5) whether the opinion includes the facts and reasoning processes on which the expert relied.[247]

c) Responsibilities of Other Justice System Participants[248]

Commissioner Goudge observed that, in addition to the expert, "other participants in the criminal justice system have important roles to play in protecting the public against the introduction of flawed or misunderstood pediatric forensic pathology into the system."[249] For instance, he noted the importance of having officers with specialized training and expertise conduct criminally suspicious pediatric death investigations; he emphasized the need for defence counsel to remain mindful of their duty of competence and refrain from taking on criminal cases pertaining to the death of a child unless they possess the requisite skill set; and he called on Crown and defence counsel to properly prepare forensic pathology experts prior to calling them to the stand.[250] However, it is the court that "must bear

243 *Ibid.* at 43.
244 *Ibid.* at 33.
245 *Ibid.* at 44.
246 *Ibid.* at 45.
247 *Ibid.*
248 *Ibid.* at 46.
249 *Ibid.*
250 *Ibid.* at 46 & 47.

the heavy burden of being the ultimate gatekeeper in protecting the system from unreliable expert evidence."[251] Commissioner Goudge listed a number of factors that might assist the court in assessing the admissibility of expert scientific evidence, including the reliability of the witness and/or the scientific theory or technique on which the opinion is based, whether the expert has considered alternative explanations for his or her findings, and whether the opinion will be expressed appropriately.[252] In addition, the court must ensure that experts remain within the limits of their expertise.[253]

H. STRENGTHENING FORENSIC SCIENCE IN THE UNITED STATES: A PATH FORWARD

1) Introduction

In 2009, the Committee on Identifying the Needs of the Forensic Sciences Community, a subgroup of the U.S. National Academy of Sciences (NAS), released a report assessing the state of the forensic sciences in the United States.[254] It aimed "to chart an agenda for progress in the forensic science community and its scientific disciplines"[255] and observed that further advancement of the forensic sciences would enable law enforcement "to identify perpetrators with higher reliability"[256] while reducing the rate of wrongful convictions and, therefore, "the risk that true offenders [will] continue to commit crimes."[257]

This report was ground-breaking in its critical view of the quality of forensic evidence relied upon in criminal cases[258] and of the high degree of decentralization of the forensic sciences in the United States.[259] Its conclusion

251 *Ibid.* at 47.

252 *Ibid.* at 47 & 48.

253 *Ibid.* at 48.

254 National Research Council Committee on Identifying the Needs of the Forensic Sciences Community, *Strengthening Forensic Science in the United States: A Path Forward* (Washington, DC: National Academies Press, 2009) at xix [2009 NAS Report], online: www.ncjrs.gov/pdffiles1/nij/grants/228091.pdf. The U.S. Congress commissioned this report in 2005 (at 1). The history of the report's formulation and scope is set out in detail at 1–4.

255 *Ibid.* at xix.

256 *Ibid.* at 4.

257 *Ibid.* at 5. The report also identified improvements to U.S. Homeland Security as a key potential benefit. See also 20 and 279–86.

258 *Ibid.* at 9, 12, and 86.

259 *Ibid.* at xix, 5, 6, 15, & 16.

was that the country's forensic science system had "serious problems that can only be addressed by a national commitment to overhaul the current structure that supports the forensic science community."[260] In addition to its thirteen recommendations (which are principally relevant to the U.S. context),[261] the report provided a thorough overview of the scientific basis for a number of forensic disciplines.

2) Shortcomings in Forensic Science

The 2009 NAS Report found that "[t]he law's greatest dilemma in its heavy reliance on forensic evidence . . . concerns the question of whether—and to what extent—there is science in any given forensic science discipline."[262] The committee observed that the term "forensic science" includes a wide range of different disciplines, each with its own methodologies and standards,[263] and found that forensic scientists in a number of disciplines had "yet to establish the validity of their approach or the accuracy of their conclusions."[264] The report cautioned against courts certifying certain forensic sciences and techniques as reliable before they have been properly verified by the scientific community, since the adversarial system "is not suited to the task of finding 'scientific truth'."[265] This is especially true as most lawyers and judges do not have the scientific background required to perform an informed evaluation of proffered forensic evidence.[266]

The report called for an influx of resources to support research[267] to correct the "notable dearth of peer-reviewed, published studies establishing the scientific bases and validity of many forensic methods."[268] In particular, the committee noted the frequent absence of adequate measures of accuracy and certainty, finding that additional research is needed to enable forensic scientists to estimate these values,[269] and that more rigorous protocols must be developed for performing subjective interpreta-

260 *Ibid.* at xx.
261 *Ibid.* at xx and 19–33.
262 *Ibid.* at 9.
263 *Ibid.* at 6 & 7.
264 *Ibid.* at 53.
265 *Ibid.* at 12.
266 *Ibid.*
267 *Ibid.* at 53, 184, 185, and 187.
268 *Ibid.* at 8.
269 *Ibid.* at 184, 186, 188, & 189.

tions.[270] The report also recommended that forensic science laboratories be "independent of or autonomous within" law enforcement agencies,[271] enabling them to decrease the risk of bias, as well as to set their own case management priorities.[272]

In terms of presentation, the report recommended that forensic scientists compose complete and thorough laboratory reports, including their materials and methods, results, and conclusions. Reports and testimony should be presented so that non-scientists can understand them.[273] Both must include "clear characterizations of the limitations of the analyses, including associated probabilities where possible."[274] The committee also called for consistency in the use of forensic terminology to describe degrees of confidence, observing that terms such as "match," "consistent with," "identical," and "cannot be excluded" are used inconsistently despite their potentially profound impact on how the trier of fact perceives the evidence.[275] The committee found that this imprecision stemmed in part from the dearth of forensic science research and commensurate difficulties in precisely interpreting forensic findings.[276]

3) Overviews of Specific Forensic Sciences

The report sets out the principles, methods, strengths, and shortcomings of several forensic scientific disciplines.[277] Its findings are briefly summarized below.

---

270 *Ibid.* at 188. Specifically, the committee recommended that the following types of forensic science research be performed: "[s]tudies to establish the strengths and limitations of each procedure, sources of bias and variation, quantification of uncertainties created by these sources, measures of performance, procedural steps in the process of analyzing the forensic evidence, and methods for continual monitoring and improving the steps in that process."

271 *Ibid.* at 184.

272 *Ibid.* at 183–85 and 188.

273 *Ibid.* at 186.

274 *Ibid.*

275 *Ibid.* at 185.

276 *Ibid.* at 186.

277 *Ibid.* at 127. See also Chapter 9, addressing the state of forensic pathology in the U.S. institutional context as of 2009 (241–68). Of particular note, see 256–58, addressing the shortage of forensic pathologists and its implications; and 261–63, addressing research needs in this field. (Both topics are also salient in the Canadian context: see below, "J. Forensic Science in Canada: A Report of Multidisciplinary Discussion (the Hart House Report).")

a) DNA Analysis[278]

DNA analysis is scientifically sound and possesses great probative power.[279] It is the only forensic science that can be used reliably to individualize a sample (i.e., match a sample to a specific individual or source).[280]

b) Toxicology[281]

Forensic toxicology is a mature forensic scientific discipline. It employs well-established analytical chemistry methods, the limitations of which are well understood. The standards of analysis and reporting set out by the Scientific Working Group for the Analysis of Seized Drugs (SWG-DRUG) are in widespread use in the United States and internationally.[282]

c) Friction Ridge Analysis[283]

Friction ridge analysis, which consists of "experience-based comparisons of the impressions left by the ridge structures of volar surfaces"[284] (i.e., finger, palm, and sole prints), has proved to be a valuable forensic tool.[285] The technique used to perform friction ridge analysis, known as ACE-V (analysis, comparison, evaluation, and verification),[286] is necessarily subjective since many factors can affect the quality of a print and introduce variability (unlike in DNA analysis, it is impossible to create a set list of features to be compared).[287] The results of a friction ridge analysis may vary between examiners.[288] Despite these limitations, "it seems plausible that a careful comparison of two impressions can accurately discern whether or not they had a common source."[289] As of 2009, however, there was "limited information about the accuracy and reliability of friction ridge analyses."[290] The committee identified a need for further research on print variability, in terms of both "features across a population" and "re-

---

278 *Ibid.* at 128.

279 *Ibid.* at 128 and 133.

280 *Ibid.* at 7. However, techniques that cannot be safely used for individualization can "still provide useful information about questions of classification" (at 8).

281 *Ibid.* at 133.

282 *Ibid.* at 134 & 135.

283 *Ibid.* at 136.

284 *Ibid.*

285 *Ibid.* at 142.

286 *Ibid.* at 137.

287 *Ibid.* at 137 and 139.

288 *Ibid.* at 139 and 142.

289 *Ibid.* at 142.

290 *Ibid.*

peated impressions left by the same finger,"[291] to provide a solid basis for examiners' intuitive, experientially based opinions as well as a framework for statistical modeling.[292] In addition, print examiners should keep better records for each step of the ACE-V process, allowing for the analysis to be reconstructed as needed.[293]

d) Shoeprint and Tire Track Analysis[294]

Shoes and tires leave prints that have identifiable class characteristics resulting from their manufacturing processes and individual characteristics arising from wear and tear as the item is used.[295] As of 2009, however, there was "no consensus regarding the number of individual characteristics needed to make a positive identification."[296] Further, there were insufficient population studies analyzing "the variability of class or individual characteristics or about the validity or reliability of the method"[297] to allow an assessment of "the number of characteristics that must match in order to have any particular degree of confidence about the source of the impression."[298] The committee found that further research was needed to rectify these deficiencies.[299] An encouraging sign was that, as of 2009, SWGTREAD ("a group of footwear and tire track examiners formed by the FBI"[300]) was moving toward standardizing the language used in these disciplines.[301]

e) Toolmark and Firearms Identification[302]

Toolmarks are made when a tool comes into contact with a comparatively softer object (e.g., dents left by a crowbar, a notch from a screwdriver, or

291 *Ibid.* at 144.
292 *Ibid.* at 144 & 145.
293 *Ibid.* at 143.
294 *Ibid.* at 145.
295 *Ibid.* at 146 & 147.
296 *Ibid.*
297 *Ibid.*
298 *Ibid.*
299 *Ibid.* at 150.
300 *Ibid.* at 148.
301 *Ibid.* at 148–50. SWGTREAD has since continued this work, publishing its "Standard for Terminology Used for Forensic Footwear and Tire Impression Evidence" and "Range of Conclusions Standard for Footwear and Tire Impression Examinations" in March 2013 (online: SWGTREAD, www.swgtread.org/images/documents/standards/published/swgtread_15_terminology_evidence_201303.pdf and www.swgtread.org/images/documents/standards/published/swgtread_10_conclusions_range_201303.pdf).
302 2009 NAS Report, above note 254 at 150.

scratches on a bullet left by a firearm's internal mechanism), and are determined largely via the process used to manufacture the tool, but sometimes also through usual wear and tear.[303] The theory underpinning this discipline is that each such tool has individually identifying characteristics that are visible at the microscopic level.[304] One "fundamental problem with toolmark and firearms analysis is the lack of a precisely defined process."[305] The source of this problem is insufficient understanding[306] of "the degree of similarity that can be found between marks made by different tools and the variability in marks made by an individual tool."[307] Class characteristics can be helpful in including or excluding some tools as being able or unable to have left a distinctive mark.[308] Individualizing marks might be distinctive enough to suggest a specific source in some cases, though additional research is needed "to make the process of individualization more precise and repeatable."[309]

f) Hair Evidence[310]

Hair comparison evidence is of limited probative value and cannot be used to uniquely identify a specific person, but it can be used for exclusion purposes.[311] There is "no scientific support for the use of hair comparisons for individualization," absent confirmatory DNA testing.[312]

g) Fibre Evidence[313]

Fibres can be subjected to the same type of microscopic examination performed in hair analysis. They can also be examined using more scientifically reliable analytical chemistry techniques.[314] However, fibre analysis is

---

303 *Ibid.*
304 *Ibid.*
305 *Ibid.* at 155.
306 *Ibid.* at 154 & 155.
307 *Ibid.* at 155.
308 *Ibid.* at 154.
309 *Ibid.*
310 *Ibid.* at 155.
311 *Ibid.* at 156 and 161. (See also "C. The Morin Inquiry," "E. The Manitoba Forensic Evidence Review Committee," "F. The Driskell Inquiry" (above), and "L. Microscopic Hair Comparison Analysis Review" (below).)
312 *Ibid.* at 161. Animal hair comparison can prove useful in certain circumstances such as in cases of animal poaching, but often it is limited to identifying the type of animal, rather than the specific breed or individual animal (at 156).
313 *Ibid.* at 161.
314 *Ibid.*

limited to identifying a specific fibre class (e.g., a type of garment, carpet, or furniture) rather than a unique source.[315] The Fibre Subgroup of the Scientific Working Group on Materials Analysis (SWGMAT) has set out guidelines for determining "the number and quality of characteristics that must correspond in order to conclude that two fibres came from the same manufacturing batch."[316] However, though the reliance of fibre analysis on well-established chemistry means that it is theoretically possible to determine the degree of uncertainty associated with these analyses, as of 2009 such research had yet to be performed.[317]

h) Forensic Document Examination[318]

Forensic (or "questioned") document examination (i.e., comparing and analysing handwritten or printed documents and the instruments used to produce them) encompasses several different types of analysis.[319] The committee found that "the scientific basis for handwriting comparisons needs to be strengthened,"[320] because there has been insufficient research to "quantify the reliability and replicability of the practices used by trained document examiners."[321] By contrast, the "[a]nalysis of inks and papers, being based on well-understood chemistry, presumably rests on a firmer scientific foundation."[322]

i) Paint and Coatings Evidence[323]

As with fibre evidence, the chemical analysis of paints and coatings rests on a solid scientific foundation.[324] In several studies, over 97 percent of paint samples surveyed were successfully differentiated.[325] However, the discipline had yet to define "precise criteria for determining whether two samples come from a common source class."[326]

---

315 *Ibid.* at 161 and 163.
316 *Ibid.* at 162 & 163.
317 *Ibid.* at 163.
318 *Ibid.*
319 *Ibid.* at 163 & 164.
320 *Ibid.* at 166.
321 *Ibid.* at 167. See further discussion on this topic in Chapter 14.
322 *Ibid.* at 167.
323 *Ibid.*
324 *Ibid.* at 170.
325 *Ibid.*
326 *Ibid.*

j) Explosives and Fire Debris Evidence[327]

The forensic analysis of explosives is well supported by established principles of chemistry[328] and explosives examiners usually have an extensive scientific background.[329] By contrast, the committee was critical of forensic fire science, finding that:

> [M]uch more research is needed on the natural variability of burn patterns and damage characteristics and how they are affected by the presence of various accelerants. Despite the paucity of research, some arson investigators continue to make determinations about whether or not a particular fire was set. However . . . many of the rules of thumb that are typically assumed to indicate that an accelerant was used . . . have been shown not to be true. Experiments should be designed to put arson investigations on a more solid scientific footing.[330]

k) Forensic Odontology[331]

Forensic odontology includes several distinct subfields. The most controversial is bite-mark comparison analysis,[332] where there is "considerable dispute about the value and reliability of the collected data for interpretation."[333] There is a notable lack of consensus in regards to "the accuracy of human skin as a reliable registration material for bite marks, the uniqueness of human dentition, the techniques used for analysis, and the role of examiner bias."[334] As with many other comparison techniques, bite-mark comparison analysis has greater value as an exclusionary factor than as an inclusionary one.[335] Further research is required "to identify the circumstances within which the methods of forensic odontology can provide probative value."[336]

---

327 *Ibid.*
328 *Ibid.* at 172.
329 *Ibid.* at 170–72.
330 *Ibid.* at 173.
331 *Ibid.*
332 *Ibid.* at 173 and 176. By contrast, the committee observed that "the identification of human remains by their dental characteristics is well established in the forensic science disciplines" (at 173).
333 *Ibid.* at 176.
334 *Ibid.*
335 *Ibid.*
336 *Ibid.*

l) Bloodstain Pattern Analysis[337]

Noting that "many sources of variability arise with the production of bloodstain patterns,"[338] the committee found that some, but not all, aspects of bloodstain pattern analysis are supported by scientific research.[339] In many cases, the interpretation of a complex bloodstain pattern is difficult to impossible.[340] Overall, "the opinions of bloodstain pattern analysts are more subjective than scientific"[341] and are often affected by prosecution- or defence-friendly bias.[342] In view of the enormous[343] uncertainties associated with these analyses, the committee recommended that great care be taken in terms of how they are presented in court.[344]

m) Digital and Multimedia Evidence[345]

The analysis of digital evidence has matured rapidly in response to today's fast-evolving technological milieu.[346] Noting the origin of this discipline in police departments rather than forensic laboratories, the committee found that:

> Three holdover challenges remain: (1) the digital evidence community does not have an agreed certification program or list of qualifications for digital forensic examiners; (2) some agencies still treat the examination of digital evidence as an investigative rather than a forensic activity; and (3) there is wide variability in and uncertainty about the education, experience, and training of those practicing this discipline.[347]

---

337 *Ibid.* at 177.
338 *Ibid.*
339 *Ibid.* For instance, "[o]ne can tell . . . if the blood spattered quickly or slowly," but the damage caused by bullets to soft tissue and the specific spatter pattern are highly variable, requiring the expert to conduct many experiments to make reliable causal inferences (at 178 & 179).
340 *Ibid.* at 177 & 178.
341 *Ibid.* at 178.
342 *Ibid.*
343 *Ibid.* at 179.
344 *Ibid.*
345 *Ibid.*
346 *Ibid.* at 180. Today, "almost every crime could have digital evidence associated with it."
347 *Ibid.* at 181.

I. LATENT PRINT EXAMINATION AND HUMAN FACTORS

1) Introduction

In December 2008, the Office of Investigative and Forensic Sciences (OIFS), a branch of the U.S. National Institute of Justice (NIJ), convened an expert working group on human factors in latent print analysis to "conduct . . . a scientific assessment of the effects of human factors on forensic latent print analysis."[348] The working group's report, released in February 2012, set out the part played by human factors in latent print analyses,[349] sources of error and uncertainty in these analyses, and recommendations for best practices and future research.[350]

The working group observed that "[l]atent print analysis provides perhaps the single most common type of forensic science evidence . . . [and] is critical to the successful operation of the criminal justice system."[351] Fingerprint analysis has been "a valuable method of personal identification in forensic science and criminal investigations for more than 100 years."[352] However, human error can affect the results of latent print analysis, as highlighted by a number of high-profile cases.[353] The working group found that "[b]y identifying and managing the human factors issues relevant to latent print analysis, the latent print community [could] . . . enhance the quality and accuracy of its contributions to the justice system."[354] It also noted that many of its recommendations, particularly those regarding "cognitive bias,

---

348 U.S. Department of Commerce Expert Working Group on Human Factors in Latent Print Analysis, *Latent Print Examination and Human Factors: Improving the Practice through a Systems Approach* (Washington DC: National Institute of Standards and Technology, 2012) [*Latent Print Examination and Human Factors*] at vii, online: www.nist.gov/oles/upload/latent.pdf.

349 *Ibid.* at vi. Latent prints are "unintentional reproductions of the arrangement of ridges on the skin made by the transfer of materials (such as amino acids, proteins, polypeptides, and salts) to a surface. Palms and the soles of feet also have friction ridge skin that can leave latent prints. The examination of a latent print consists of a series of steps involving a comparison of the latent print to a known (or exemplar) print." (vi).

350 *Ibid.* at vii.

351 *Ibid.* at 206.

352 *Ibid.* at vi.

353 *Ibid.* See, for example, another landmark inquiry addressing the role of latent print analysis in the criminal justice system: Sir Anthony Campbell, *The Fingerprint Inquiry Report* (Edinburgh: APS Group Scotland, 2011) (on behalf of The Fingerprint Inquiry), online: www.webarchive.org.uk/wayback/archive/20150428160106/http://www.thefingerprintinquiryscotland.org.uk/inquiry/files/TheFingerprintInquiryReport_High_res.pdf.

354 *Latent Print Examination and Human Factors*, above note 348 at ix.

standardization of procedures, documentation of examinations, working conditions, error detection and correction, and accuracy in testimony," also apply to other forensic science disciplines.[355]

2) Recommendations

a) Performing Analysis, Comparison, Evaluation, and Verification[356]

The procedure by which a fingerprint examiner compares a latent print to a known, or exemplar, print is known as performing analysis, comparison, evaluation, and verification (ACE-V).[357] While ACE-V sets out a logical sequence of steps to perform, it does not "provide substantive guidance about standards to be applied within each step."[358] Following the ACE-V process does not ensure that the examiners' results will be accurate or reproducible,[359] as it is inherently subjective, requiring examiners to apply their training and experience in exercising their judgment.[360] The working group emphasized that this inherent subjectivity is not a "criticism of the technique," but the examiner should be mindful "that issues related to human factors can be especially salient to the outcome."[361]

i) Subjectivity, Bias, and Transparency

The working group recommended that, to increase the transparency of the application of the ACE-V process, the examiner should contemporaneously document the examination in sufficient detail "to permit another examiner

---

355 *Ibid.*

356 *Ibid.* at 197.

357 *Ibid.* at 1 & 2. Specifically, the components of ACE-V are as follows:

> *Analysis* refers to an initial information-gathering phase in which the examiner studies the unknown print to assess the quality and quantity of discriminating detail present. . . . *Comparison* is the side-by-side observation of . . . the two prints to determine the agreement or disagreement in the details. In the *Evaluation* phase, the examiner assesses the agreement or disagreement of the information observed during Analysis and Comparison and forms a conclusion. *Verification* in some agencies is a review of an examiner's conclusions with knowledge of those conclusions; in other agencies, it is an independent re-examination by a second examiner who does not know the outcome of the first examination. [Emphasis in original.]

358 *Ibid.* at 9.

359 *Ibid.* The Working Group referred to the findings of the National Research Council in its seminal 2009 report on the forensic sciences in America: see 2009 NAS Report, above note 254

360 *Ibid.* at 8.

361 *Ibid.* at 9.

to assess the accuracy and validity of the initial examiner's assessment of the evidence."[362] In particular, any changes to the examiner's original observations of the latent print that were made after viewing the known print "should be specifically documented as having occurred after comparison had begun."[363] Such modifications "should be viewed with caution," in case the examiner was unduly influenced by the known print and was led to perceive "a similarity that does not exist."[364] In addition, latent print analysis facilities should minimize exposure to potentially biasing information by implementing procedures to shield examiners from case-specific facts that are not relevant to their task.[365] Further, agencies should seek to enhance the transparency of their analyses by creating guidelines as to what constitutes a suitable or sufficient print for analysis at various stages of the process.[366]

ii) Individualization

The working group observed that "latent print examinations can produce very powerful evidence regarding the possible association between a suspect and the source of a print."[367] However, a fingerprint identification cannot be considered an individualization. It cannot be "identified to one finger of a specific individual to exclude every other potential source in the universe."[368] This traditional view of the strength of fingerprint evidence is not supported by empirical evidence or statistical modelling. The working group recommended that:

> [E]xaminers should not claim to be able to exclude every other finger in the world as a potential source. Rather, an identification decision suggests a substantial enough similarity that, based on the examiner's training and experience, the examiner believes that the two impressions originated from a common source. Whether any other finger in the entire world might also be able to leave an impression with a comparable amount of similarity is not fully known, and the examiner's testimony should not suggest otherwise.[369]

362 *Ibid.* at 198, see Recommendation 3.1.
363 *Ibid.* at 43, see Recommendation 3.2.
364 *Ibid.*
365 *Ibid.* at 44, see Recommendation 3.3.
366 *Ibid.* at 198 & 199, see Recommendation 3.4.
367 *Ibid.* at 197.
368 *Ibid.*
369 *Ibid.*, see Recommendation 3.7.

iii) Automated Fingerprint Databases

Today's print examiners often compare latent prints to known prints generated by automated fingerprint identification system (AFIS) searches. The working group noted that some nonmatching prints selected from a large database may be "far more similar to the latent print than examiners are accustomed to seeing from non-matching sources." Examiners "whose idea of the necessary amount of information for a match comes from a non-database world may not be taking into account the possibility of incidental similarity that a large database carries with it."[370] Examiners "must recognize the possibility and dangers of incidental similarity" when comparing latent prints to known prints retrieved from AFIS searches, and make commensurate adjustments to their criteria and certainty threshold for finding that there is a match.[371]

b) Reports and Testimony

The working group found that in view of the needs of police, counsel, and courts, expert latent print examiners' reports should be written in a manner such that the findings and their limitations can be understood by non-experts.[372] These reports should define technical terms, describe the procedures used by the expert in the analysis, state the conclusions and the methods used to arrive at them, set out any important limitations to the conclusions, and state whether or not a verification was made and whether there were conflicting opinions among examiners.[373] Forensic service providers should review a sample of their examiners' work at least annually.[374]

To assist latent print analysts in providing appropriate testimony, the working group recommended that:

> Forensic service providers . . . adopt codes of ethics that require testifying in a nonpartisan manner; answering questions from both the prosecution and the defense directly, accurately, and fully; and providing appropriate scientific information before, during, and after trial.[375]

Counsel should confer with the expert prior to conducting the examination-in-chief. At this meeting, the expert can clarify "the nature and

---

370 *Ibid.* at 199.
371 *Ibid.*, see Recommendation 3.6.
372 *Ibid.*, see Recommendation 5.1.
373 *Ibid.* at 200, see Recommendation 5.2.
374 *Ibid.* at 201, see Recommendation 6.4.
375 *Ibid.* at 200, see Recommendation 6.2.

limits of the testimony that the evidentiary material warrants and can work with the lawyer to present this information fully, fairly, and clearly."[376] Topics to be addressed include "the presentation of technical information in lay terms, the organization of the direct examination, possible cross-examination, and the possible use of visual aids."[377] Experts should be familiar with the scientific literature pertaining to error rates and should be able to describe the steps taken to reduce the risk of error.[378]

c) Education, Training, and Workplace Culture

The working group made the following recommendations:

- All forensic service providers should be accredited and all employees should become certified through an accredited program.[379]
- All forensic service providers should maintain systematic training programs that include "education in the scientific method, reading and understanding relevant scientific literature, communication skills, and methods for logically developing conclusions."[380]
- All employees should participate in formal mentoring programs and continuing education.[381]

To identify and address sources of error, forensic service providers should use an error-tracking system, establish case review policies and procedures, and strive for a workplace culture in which openness about errors "is part of an effective system to detect deviations from desired practices and incorrect judgments in latent print casework."[382]

d) Research Needs

The working group found that additional research is needed on many topics pertaining to latent print analysis. In particular, it noted "a critical need for a focused program of research into the interpretive process that is at the heart of ACE-V."[383] Research identifying the most reliable print features for comparison purposes and enabling the reduction of variation

---

376 *Ibid.*
377 *Ibid.*, see Recommendation 6.1.
378 *Ibid.* at 201, see Recommendation 6.3.
379 *Ibid.* at 201 & 202, see Recommendations 9.3 and 8.7.
380 *Ibid.* at 202, see Recommendation 8.1.
381 *Ibid.*, see Recommendations 8.3 and 8.7.
382 *Ibid.* at 201, see Recommendations 9.1, 9.2, and 9.4.
383 *Ibid.* at 203.

in feature selection between examiners would be helpful. The working group also noted a lack of research on the topic of utility (or "sufficiency") assessments in the context of latent print analysis. It ascribed this shortcoming, in part, to the lack of a clearly defined metric for assessing print utility.[384] To rectify this deficit, the working group recommended the development of a research program with the following aims:

a. Develop measures and metrics relevant to the analysis of latent prints;
b. Use such metrics to assess the reproducibility, reliability, and validity of various interpretive stages of latent print analysis; and
c. Identify key factors related to variations in performance of latent print examiners during the interpretation process.[385]

The working group recommended that a concerted effort be made to automate, at least partially, the initial quality assessment step of the latent print analysis.[386] It also observed that the weighting process by which examiners determine the value of a particular feature when determining whether there is a match "is mainly based upon subjective, experience-based judgments of the probability associated with . . . [its] occurrence."[387] The working group recommended that the U.S. government "create large, anonymous databases of exemplars and latent prints [to] . . . facilitate the validation of probabilistic models and other statistical research."[388]

---

384 *Ibid.* at 204–6. See also (i) "Subjectivity, Bias, and Transparency," above, regarding utility assessments. Note that this deficit is particularly troubling given that, in the Working Group's experience, "[t]he initial quality assessment of the latent print is often the weak link in the analytical process, as examiners are susceptible to making one of two types of errors. In the first type of error, the examiner prematurely discards a print that should be deemed suitable for further analysis and comparison, possibly resulting in a missed identification. In the second type of error, the examiner continues to evaluate a latent print that ought to be deemed unsuitable for further processing. This outcome results in wasted time and might even contribute to an erroneous identification" (at 205–6).

385 *Ibid.* at 204, see Recommendation 3.9.

386 *Ibid.* at 206, see Recommendation 4.4.

387 *Ibid.* at 204.

388 *Ibid.* at 205, see Recommendation 4.2.

J. FORENSIC SCIENCE IN CANADA: A REPORT OF MULTIDISCIPLINARY DISCUSSION (THE HART HOUSE REPORT)

1) Overview

In May 2012, the Centre for Forensic Science and Medicine (CFSM)[389] at the University of Toronto published the Hart House Report, reviewing the state of forensic science in Canada and making recommendations for its improvement.[390] In the preface to this report, Dr. Michael Pollanen observed that:

> Forensic science in Canada is at a critical juncture. Both public and judicial confidence in our practice have been eroded by several high-profile inquiries into damage wrought by faulty forensic evidence, and must be rebuilt. Furthermore, members of the forensic science community are themselves demanding better scientific practices and an increased emphasis on building academic foundations for forensic work.[391]

The Hart House Report, which focused on the institutional infrastructure of nine leading forensic scientific disciplines in Canada (rather than on their underlying scientific foundation), presented a more optimistic picture of Canadian forensic sciences than did its American counterpart, the 2009 NAS Report.[392] It found, however, "an urgent need for greater investment in research, training and graduate education,"[393] which are currently hampered by a chronic funding shortage, a lack of national standardization, and limited integration with academic institutions.[394]

---

389 The CFSM is an interdisciplinary initiative established in 2008 that is "dedicated to the advancement of teaching and research in the forensic disciplines at the crossroads of medicine, the law and social sciences" (Hart House Report, above note 1 at 17).

390 *Ibid.* at 10.

391 *Ibid.* at 3.

392 *Ibid.* at 1 & 2; see the 2009 NAS Report, above note 254.

393 *Ibid.* at 2.

394 *Ibid.* at 10. Unlike the 2009 NAS Report, the Hart House Report did not "recommend the creation of new agencies" or "advocate for specific systemic reforms"; nor did it provide direction to courts as to how to apply its findings. The Hart House Report thus provides limited direct assistance to lawyers and judges seeking to rectify potential problems regarding the use that they make of forensic science evidence. From this standpoint, the most valuable aspect of the report may be "Appendix F," which charts current controversies in each of the nine disciplines surveyed (at 111 & 112).

2) Conclusions and Recommendations

After its field-specific review, the Hart House Report set out a series of conclusions and recommendations aimed at improving the practice of forensic science in Canada.[395] It found that insufficient forensic scientific research was being conducted in Canada, due in large part to the absence of (1) a national granting agency dedicated to funding such research, and (2) "a culture of research in Canada's forensic science community."[396] The report recommended that a research culture be fostered through, *inter alia*, an infusion of grant funding into the forensic sciences, greater collaboration between universities and forensic science institutions, and development of university forensic research programs.[397] In addition, the report found that most forensic disciplines currently lack adequate regulatory and credentialing infrastructure.[398] To ameliorate this problem, it recommended, *inter alia*, the development of professional certification programs and accreditation standards, the adoption of international standards and practices for use in Canada, and the creation of "a systemic response to error . . . [a]fter each adverse event."[399]

The report also recommended quality assurance measures, including the development of field-specific workload standards and "[f]unding models that emphasize full-time personnel" specifically trained in a given discipline "over fee-for-service providers."[400] Of particular interest to practitioners, it called for "[m]ultidisciplinary cross-training . . . between scientists, police, lawyers and judges,"[401] and for judges to "receive continuing education in forensic science, forensic pathology and forensic psychiatry, including basic training in 'scientific literacy.'"[402]

---

395 *Ibid.* at 100–4.

396 *Ibid.* at 101.

397 *Ibid.* at 102.

398 *Ibid.* at 101.

399 *Ibid.* at 103. The report "note[d] with regret that, at present, the public inquiry is the primary mechanism for remediation after a miscarriage of justice occurs, if the error is detected at all."

400 *Ibid.* at 104.

401 *Ibid.* at 102.

402 *Ibid.* at 103.

3) Discussion of Nine Key Disciplines

a) Forensic Pathology[403]

Forensic pathology, "the application of pathology to legal issues involving deaths that society has an interest in examining for the good of public health,"[404] has "made enormous strides in the last decade."[405] In 2003, the Royal College of Physicians and Surgeons of Canada "recognized forensic pathology as a medical subspecialty."[406] It now offers a one-year residency program in forensic pathology.[407] The report commented favourably on the establishment, in 2008, of the Centre for Forensic Science and Medicine,[408] "the only active forensic pathology research centre in Canada."[409] The report did, however, identify several barriers to Canadian forensic pathology research, including unsustainable workloads and the unavailability of research grant funding.[410]

National forensic pathology practice standards are lacking, particularly in regard to peer review.[411] There are no Canadian guidelines pertaining to the final work product of the death-investigation system, which provides the trier of fact with the "opinion on cause and manner of death."[412] Furthermore, despite "an increasing recognition that high-quality forensic pathology services require the employment of full-time, qualified forensic pathologists working collaboratively in institutional settings,"[413] many homicide and suspicious death autopsies are still performed by "hospital-based, fee-for-service pathologists [who] . . . often work in inadequate facilities"[414] and by non-forensic pathologists who "may have variable degrees of training and skill in the nuances of

---

403 *Ibid.* at 11–20.

404 *Ibid.* at 11. Such deaths include those that are sudden or unexpected, not due to natural causes, and where the deceased was in custody at the time of death.

405 *Ibid.* at 20.

406 *Ibid.* at 17. This step was long overdue given that the equivalent U.S. and U.K. certifying bodies have recognized it for decades.

407 *Ibid.* This program is offered at the University of Toronto, Toronto, ON.

408 *Ibid.*

409 *Ibid.* at 18–19. It is also the only institution "with the mandate and the expertise to provide continuing education for forensic pathologists" (at 18).

410 *Ibid.* Heavy workloads result from the inadequate number and uneven geographical distribution of forensic pathologists in Canada (at 16). Fortunately, "more forensic pathologists are now being hired in Canada, much to the public's benefit" (at 15).

411 *Ibid.* at 20; see also discussion at 14.

412 *Ibid.* at 14.

413 *Ibid.* at 15.

414 *Ibid.*

medicolegal practice."[415] This unacceptable practice has diminished but has not yet been eliminated.[416]

b) Forensic Anthropology[417]

Forensic anthropology is the study of non-visually identifiable human remains—remains in an advanced state of decomposition.[418] The report identified a number of deficiencies in the institutional infrastructure that undermine the development and practice of forensic anthropology in Canada. There is no national professional body, certification, or accreditation process for Canadian forensic anthropologists.[419] There are no Canadian graduate degrees or training programs offered for this field.[420] Canadian forensic anthropologists have a wide range of educational and training backgrounds, and some have limited practical experience.[421] The dearth of Canadian forensic anthropology research is attributable to a lack of funding opportunities and university interest[422] in hiring people to teach and conduct research solely in this field.[423] With these shortcomings and the inconsistent quality of forensic anthropology facilities between provinces, the availability and use of forensic anthropology services vary widely.[424] In many parts of the country, such services are provided by police, pathologists, or coroners.[425] The report made three recommendations:

> Firstly, the federal government [must] . . . provide research funding to solidify the foundations of our opinions. Secondly, universities should take the discipline seriously, recognizing it as an academic area and hiring appropriately trained faculty. Finally, the provincial government

---

415 *Ibid.* at 16.

416 *Ibid.*

417 *Ibid.* at 21–30.

418 *Ibid.* at 22.

419 *Ibid.* at 21, 23, 25, & 26.

420 *Ibid.* at 21.

421 *Ibid.* at 24. Happily, "Ontario is in the process of formalizing service-level agreements with consulting forensic anthropologists, with a view to standardizing the level of education and experience required to practice" in this province.

422 *Ibid.* at 21, 27 & 28.

423 *Ibid.* at 27.

424 *Ibid.* at 21 and 23.

425 *Ibid.* at 24. "These services include the determination of animal versus human bones, the proper recording, recovery and interpretation of human remains from outdoor environments and graves, and the determination of whether human remains are of recent forensic interest or are historical. Some jurisdictions continue to employ police for the interpretation of injuries and tool marks on bone."

forensic and death-investigation services should use properly trained experts in all cases where forensic anthropology can assist.[426]

c) Forensic Odontology[427]

Forensic odontology involves the interpretation of dental evidence from crime scenes to identify remains or determine the cause of bitemarks.[428] The Royal College of Dentists of Canada has not yet recognized this discipline.[429] There is no certification process for Canadian forensic odontologists,[430] although a handful of practitioners have been certified by the American Board of Forensic Odontology (ABFO).[431] Typically, forensic odontology practitioners are general dentists or specialists from other disciplines who have taken short continuing education courses in this field in the United States and perform forensic services after hours.[432] In addition, the research and development infrastructure in this field is not funded.[433] However, the report also noted some encouraging signs of progress, including active leadership and mentorship by a core group of ABFO-certified forensic dentists,[434] field growth over the past forty-five years,[435] a growing interest in forensic odontology among younger dental practitioners,[436] and a well-developed and well-trained group of forensic odontologists in British Columbia, Ontario, and Quebec.[437]

d) Forensic Nursing[438]

"Forensic nursing is the integration of forensic-science knowledge and principles with nursing knowledge in the clinical investigation of trauma and the recovery of medical evidence."[439]

Forensic nurses provide direct service to victims, offenders, and witnesses.[440] The report found that forensic nursing in Canada is "very much

426 *Ibid.* at 30.
427 *Ibid.* at 31–40.
428 *Ibid.* at 31.
429 *Ibid.*
430 *Ibid.* at 33 and 37–40.
431 *Ibid.* at 32, 33, and 37.
432 *Ibid.* at 32.
433 *Ibid.* at 31.
434 *Ibid.* at 32, 39, & 40.
435 *Ibid.* at 40.
436 *Ibid.* at 31.
437 *Ibid.* at 33.
438 *Ibid.* at 41–52.
439 *Ibid.* at 41.
440 *Ibid.*

in its infancy"[441] and there is little formal recognition or regulation in the field.[442] Encouragingly, the Canadian Nurses' Association (CNA) has recognized forensic nursing as an emerging specialty. It began collaborating with the Forensic Nurses Society of Canada (FNSC) in 2007, a promising step with "the potential to develop certification and standardization for forensic nurses across Canada."[443] In addition, there have been several exciting developments in Canadian forensic nursing research.[444] The report recommended the creation of a national strategy on forensic nursing research to better coordinate and develop the scientific foundation of these efforts.[445]

e) Forensic Entomology[446]

Forensic entomology is the study of insects within a legal context,[447] a rapidly evolving discipline that has made significant progress in the past two decades.[448] Practitioners can attain certification through the American Board of Forensic Entomology (ABFE), a step that is increasingly viewed as required in the Canadian forensic entomology community.[449] However, a number of factors prevent Canadian forensic entomology from attaining its full potential.[450] Prominent among these are a severe shortage of certified forensic

---

441 *Ibid.* at 42.

442 *Ibid.* at 41. As a result, many Canadian forensic nurses, particularly Sexual Assault Nurse Examiners (SANEs), "are using the Standards and Practices as described by the International Association of Forensic Nurses. Professional standards in other areas are less well defined" (at 45; see also 48). An exception to this general absence of a forensic nursing regulatory framework is the Canadian Federation of Mental Health Nurses, an associate group of the Canadian Nurses' Association "that represents the national voice of psychiatric and mental health nursing in Canada," which has provided national credentialing for psychiatric and mental health nurses since 1995 (at 45).

443 *Ibid.* at 44.

444 *Ibid.* at 41 and 49–51. Ontario nurses have produced numerous publications on the role of SANEs and on specific clinical issues (at 49); nurses are well represented at the Centre for Forensic Behavioural Sciences and Justice Studies (University of Saskatchewan, Saskatoon, SK) and participate in leadership roles in various projects; and "several excellent forensic nursing researchers . . . have greatly contributed in this effort on both the national and global fronts" (at 50–51).

445 *Ibid.* at 51.

446 *Ibid.* at 53–60.

447 *Ibid.* at 54.

448 *Ibid.* at 53 and 59.

449 *Ibid.* at 55, 56, 59, & 60. Though the ABFE has not developed a set of best practices, forensic entomologists generally accept those of the European Association of Forensic Entomology (at 55). In addition, forensic entomologists can join "a professional association (the North American Forensic Entomology Association—NAFEA) formed for the exchange of research and case analyses" (at 59–60).

450 *Ibid.* at 53.

entomologists and a widespread lack of understanding of the uses of insect evidence in death investigations.[451] In addition, Canadian forensic entomologists are contracted on a fee-for-service basis.[452] As a result of these factors, forensic entomologists are often called into a case long after the crime scene examination and autopsy are over, resulting in an incomplete collection of the insect evidence.[453] Non-forensic entomologists perform a significant percentage of the entomology evidence work in Canada.[454] Further, the lack of forensic entomology research funding makes it difficult for Canadian universities to recruit both qualified practitioners and graduate students.[455]

f) Forensic Physical Sciences[456]

Forensic physical sciences is an umbrella term used in the report to include forensic identification (FI, the analysis of pattern-based evidence such as fingerprints, footprints, and tire tracks), firearms identification, and bloodstain pattern analysis (BPA).[457] FI and BPA analysts are most often police officers, while firearm examiners are typically civilian scientists.[458] There are no national standards governing forensic physical sciences experts; instead, they are guided by agency-specific policies and guidelines.[459] Practitioners in each of these disciplines generally must complete an in-house training program.[460] Several external organizations set out nonbinding best practice guidelines that analysts are encouraged to follow.[461]

The report found that further research is needed to support the forensic physical sciences in Canada.[462] The available research funding is insufficient to support graduate-level work.[463] Most research projects are internally funded by police services and laboratories. The report also found that "[a] major barrier to research in the FI area and the advancement of this discipline in Canada is that practitioners are only able to

---

451 *Ibid.* at 56.
452 *Ibid.* at 54.
453 *Ibid.*, see also discussion at 56.
454 *Ibid.* at 56.
455 *Ibid.* at 57, 58, and 60.
456 *Ibid.* at 61–71.
457 *Ibid.* at 61 & 62.
458 *Ibid.* at 65 & 66.
459 *Ibid.* at 64. Ontario, however, began requiring that its FI personnel receive provincial certification in 2009 (at 68).
460 *Ibid.* at 67 & 68.
461 *Ibid.* at 64.
462 *Ibid.* at 70.
463 *Ibid.*

conduct research when caseloads permit";[464] meanwhile, the practitioners may have little research experience.[465]

g) Forensic Toxicology[466]

Forensic toxicology is the application of toxicology to the legal context.[467] Canadian forensic toxicologists are not required to belong to any professional organization, nor are there set professional standards to which they must adhere.[468] No formal training in this discipline is available in Canada, and little internationally.[469] The report found "an overall lack of consistency in quality systems and testing models in Canada's toxicology-related services"[470] and identified a need for national-level oversight "to ensure the same high quality and completeness in testing from all laboratories . . . or to at least ensure transparency and a fulsome accounting of limitations."[471] These deficiencies contribute to a shortage of trusted experts available to testify in court, which can lead to miscarriages of justice.[472] The report recommended that the government provide sufficient funding to enable a national body (e.g., the Scientific Working Group in Toxicology) to make national-level recommendations[473] regarding how to standardize toxicology testing across Canada.

In addition, the report found that there is little opportunity for Canadian forensic toxicologists "to pursue the type of independent academic research needed to advance the discipline."[474] Practitioners are often too busy managing large caseloads and preparing testimony to focus on research, a problem that is compounded by a severe funding shortage.[475]

h) Forensic Biology[476]

Forensic biology "establish[es] associations between biological samples submitted as evidence . . . and the individuals from whom they could have

---

464 *Ibid.* at 69. The RCMP, however, "has two full-time research scientists working in forensic identification."

465 *Ibid.*

466 *Ibid.* at 72–79.

467 *Ibid.* at 72.

468 *Ibid.* at 74.

469 *Ibid.* at 75.

470 *Ibid.* at 74.

471 *Ibid.* at 75.

472 *Ibid.*

473 *Ibid.* at 78.

474 *Ibid.* at 76.

475 *Ibid.* at 76 and 78.

476 *Ibid.* at 80–90.

originated."[477] For the past two decades, it has relied on DNA profiling.[478] Currently, three public-sector laboratories conduct almost all human forensic DNA testing in Canada.[479] The report found that "the Canadian system delivers high-quality forensic biology services in support of official investigations,"[480] generating results with high probative power.[481] Though "there are no mandatory legislated professional standards for forensic biology laboratories in Canada," these laboratories follow "well-defined and consistent guidelines and standards creating . . . stringent checks and balances."[482] In addition, public-sector forensic biology laboratories have succeeded in recruiting well-qualified scientists.[483] However, the report found that Canadian laboratories have produced little published research in this field; rather, "advancements in forensic biology in Canada are largely dependent on research completed in other countries."[484] In addition, Canadian forensic biologists have limited opportunities for continuing education. The report found that Canada is at risk of falling behind in the field without a well-developed infrastructure to support it.[485]

i) Forensic Psychiatry[486]

Forensic psychiatry is the practice of psychiatry as it relates to the legal system.[487] It incorporates several practice areas and settings.[488] Today, a sufficient number of forensic psychiatrists are practicing in Canada.[489] A

---

477 *Ibid.* at 81.
478 *Ibid.*
479 *Ibid.* at 84.
480 *Ibid.* at 80.
481 *Ibid.* at 90.
482 *Ibid.* at 85. The Scientific Working Group on DNA Analysis Methods (at 82) has published best-practice guidelines since 1989, covering "subjects such as validation, training and data interpretation" (at 85); and the U.S. National Research Council published a landmark report in 1996, entitled "The Evaluation of Forensic DNA Evidence," which "established the framework for the application of population genetics and statistics in the field of forensic DNA analysis, and established broad consensus among forensic scientists and academics" (at 85). Further, Canada's major forensic biology laboratories are "accredited to the ISO 17025 standards" (at 86), a framework "considered by many to be the best mechanism for ensuring adherence to professional standards" (at 88).
483 *Ibid.* at 86.
484 *Ibid.* at 89.
485 *Ibid.* at 88.
486 *Ibid.* at 91–99.
487 *Ibid.* at 91.
488 *Ibid.* at 91–93.
489 *Ibid.* at 91.

recent and significant positive step for Canadian forensic psychiatry is the Royal College of Physicians and Surgeons' 2012 launch of a forensic psychiatry residency program, offered at the University of Toronto.[490] However, a number of challenges remain for the Canadian forensic psychiatric community.[491] The nature and quality of forensic psychiatric work continues to vary widely.[492] Practice standards and guidelines have not been developed "for many of the key tasks performed specifically in forensic work, including assessment of fitness to stand trial, assessment of criminal responsibility, or risk assessment and management."[493] The Forensic Directors Group[494] has undertaken to develop these much-needed practice guidelines, but this ambitious project "is not particularly well-resourced, and the process has been slow."[495] There are several barriers to forensic psychiatric research in Canada, including the overall national dearth of forensic science research funding, the segregation of forensic psychiatric practice from other practices, the seductive higher pay grade available in clinical practice as compared to academia, and the dissemination of the applicable research through numerous different journals and organizations.[496]

K. IDENTIFYING THE CULPRIT: ASSESSING EYEWITNESS IDENTIFICATION

1) Introduction

In 2013, the U.S. National Academy of Sciences appointed a committee to assess current scientific research relating to eyewitness identification, identify topics requiring further research, and recommend best practices for criminal justice system personnel seeking to make use of this type of evidence.[497]

Eyewitness identification is a powerful but imperfect tool: the protean nature of human vision, memory, and confidence can interact with law enforcement policies and procedures to produce "mistaken identifications

---

490 *Ibid.* at 96 and 99.

491 *Ibid* at 91.

492 *Ibid.* at 93 and 95. This is especially true in the following areas: clinical sexological assessment; urban areas; and correctional, particularly remand, facilities.

493 *Ibid.* at 94.

494 *Ibid.* The Group "comprise[s] . . . the medical and administrative directors of the designated facilities in the province of Ontario."

495 *Ibid.*

496 *Ibid.* at 97 & 98.

497 *Assessing Eyewitness Identification*, above note 116 at 2, 11, & 12. For further discussion of the fallibility of memory in the criminal justice context, see Chapter 21.

with significant consequences."[498] Moreover, the advent of DNA testing has "dramatically highlighted" the limitations of eyewitness testimony: "at least one mistaken eyewitness identification was [made] . . . in almost three-quarters of DNA exonerations,"[499] often with complete confidence. As the committee observed, "[a]t its core, eyewitness identification relies on brain systems for visual perception and memory."[500] Neither of these systems is infallible.[501]

2) Visual Processing

Human vision does not capture a complete and accurate picture of events.[502] Many factors can influence visual perception. Some of these factors are readily apparent—the viewing conditions, visual deficits (e.g., myopia or colour blindness),[503] the distance of the object or event viewed,[504] and the angle at which the object or event was observed.[505] More surprising is that "[t]he way an observer experiences a visual scene . . . is commonly influenced as much by expectations from prior experience with the world as it is by the precise patterns of light cast upon the retina."[506] The sensory input that our eyes and brain receive "is often noisy, incomplete and ambiguous," necessitating reliance on our "memories of what is *likely* to be out there, given the context, [which] are called on to fill in the blanks."[507] As a result, the accuracy of the observer's perception of the scene correlates with its degree of correspondence to his expectations.[508] The committee concluded that, given "this inherent dependence of perception on prior experiences and context[,] . . . accurate eyewitness identification may be difficult to achieve."[509]

In addition, "visual perception is categorical," meaning that we simplify perceptual processing by treating all members of a common class (such as faces with specific characteristics) as identical.[510] Humans categorize

498 *Ibid.* at 119.
499 *Ibid.* at 11.
500 *Ibid.* at 14.
501 *Ibid.* at 15.
502 *Ibid.*
503 *Ibid.* at 50.
504 *Ibid.* at 92.
505 *Ibid.* at 56.
506 *Ibid.* at 57.
507 *Ibid.* [emphasis in original].
508 *Ibid.*
509 *Ibid.* at 57 & 58.
510 *Ibid.* at 58.

faces by gender, race, and age, as well as by subtler markers such as hair colour and facial structure. As a result, an eyewitness may not perceive (and thus will not encode into memory) the particularizing details required to make an identification.[511] A suspect in a lineup whose facial features fall into the same broad category as those of the perpetrator may thus be misperceived as the perpetrator.[512]

Limited attentional focus can also problematize eyewitness identification.[513] Since it is impossible to process all of the visual information that we receive at any given time, competing interests can readily catch the attention and distract the viewer.[514] A witness to a crime must "select" what to focus on, typically during a brief time window, and often is also experiencing anxiety and fear.[515] "[A]ttention is compellingly drawn to emotionally laden [visual] stimuli" (for instance, a gun or knife, the "weapon focus") that often do not contain information relevant to suspect identification.[516] In addition, high stress can significantly impair a witness' ability to perceive key facial characteristics.[517]

3) Memory Formation and Storage

Memory, like vision, is influenced by an array of factors:

> The contents [of our memory] cannot be treated as a veridical permanent record, like photographs stored in a safe. On the contrary, the fidelity of our memories for real events may be compromised by many factors at all stages of processing, from encoding through storage, to the final stages of retrieval. Without awareness, we regularly encode events in a biased manner and subsequently forget, reconstruct, update, and distort the things we believe to be true.[518]

---

511 *Ibid.* at 58 & 59. Note also that witnesses are better able to remember faces with age and racial characteristics similar to their own (93, 96, & 97).

512 *Ibid.* at 66.

513 *Ibid.* at 53.

514 *Ibid.* at 54.

515 *Ibid.* at 53. Note that "[e]yewitness identification researchers have long believed that exposure duration (for example, time spent observing a perpetrator's face during a crime) is correlated with greater accuracy of eyewitness identification" (at 97; see discussion at 97 & 98).

516 *Ibid.* at 55. See also discussion at 93 & 94.

517 *Ibid.* at 94. See also discussion at 94 and 96.

518 *Ibid.* at 60.

Fabricated content can be incorporated into memories, changing one's recollection of an event, while the actual source of this new content is forgotten.[519] Since memories evolve over time, a witness' interactions with family, friends, members of the media, and justice system participants can significantly alter the memory of facial and other details of the crime. For instance, "[a]n eyewitness might learn from the police . . . that a potential suspect has a moustache and then attribute that knowledge to the witnessed events," with potentially disastrous consequences.[520] The accuracy of eyewitness identification evidence is likely to decline over time. The committee found that this "conclusion . . . calls into question the validity of in-court identifications and their appropriateness as statements of fact."[521]

While emotionally impactful events tend to be recalled more vividly (and with higher confidence[522]), such memories are just as prone to error as are memories of less impactful events.[523] Further, police indications that the witness has "picked the right guy" from a lineup can increase confidence in the identification.[524] As a result, "self-reported confidence at the time of trial is not a reliable predictor of eyewitness accuracy."[525]

4) Recommendations

The committee compiled a list of recommendations aimed at translating the findings summarized above into a set of best practices to maximize the reliability of eyewitness identification evidence.[526] The first five recommendations set out best practices for law enforcement personnel.[527] The committee recommended that police receive training "on vision and memory and the variables that affect them, on practices for minimizing contamination, and on effective eyewitness identification protocols."[528] These protocols should include double-blind identification procedures in which "the test administrator does not know the composition of the

519 *Ibid.* at 63 and 66.
520 *Ibid.* at 66 & 67.
521 *Ibid.* at 65.
522 *Ibid.* at 64 & 65.
523 *Ibid.* at 64.
524 *Ibid.* at 92.
525 *Ibid.* at 108.
526 *Ibid.* at 105–19.
527 *Ibid.* at 105.
528 *Ibid.* at 106, see Recommendation 1.

photo array or lineup"[529] (to minimize the risk of suggesting the "right" answer to the witness and thus biasing the outcome[530]) and a consistent set of instructions, to be presented to eyewitnesses prior to every photo array or lineup, stating that "the perpetrator may or may not be [included] ... and that the criminal investigation will continue regardless of whether the witness selects a suspect."[531] The committee also recommended that police "document the witness' level of confidence verbatim at the time when she or he first identifies a suspect,"[532] refrain from providing feedback that might affect this confidence level,[533] and record photo arrays and lineups.[534]

The committee's next four recommendations set out ways to "strengthen the value of eyewitness identification evidence in court."[535] Finding that judges have a positive obligation to ensure that proffered eyewitness testimony is reliable, the committee recommended that the court "make basic inquiries"[536] as to how the evidence was obtained and, if necessary, conduct a pretrial hearing to determine its admissibility.[537] The committee also recommended that jurors be provided with "detailed information about any earlier identification,"[538] including the witness' confidence level at that time, on each occasion that an eyewitness identifies a suspect in court,[539] and that jury instructions be used to convey the relevant principles of eyewitness identification.[540] Further, the committee recommended that "judges have the discretion to allow expert testimony on relevant precepts of eyewitness memory and identifications." Since "many scientifically established aspects of eyewitness memory are counterintuitive and may defy expectations, ... [j]urors will likely need assistance in understanding the factors that may affect the accuracy of an identification."[541]

---

529 *Ibid.*
530 *Ibid.* at 106 & 107, see Recommendation 2.
531 *Ibid.* at 107, see Recommendation 3.
532 *Ibid.* at 108.
533 *Ibid.*, see Recommendation 4.
534 *Ibid.*, see Recommendation 5.
535 *Ibid.* at 109.
536 *Ibid.*
537 *Ibid.* at 109 & 110, see Recommendation 6.
538 *Ibid.* at 111.
539 *Ibid.* at 110 & 111, see Recommendation 7.
540 *Ibid.* at 112, see Recommendation 9. The Committee also recommended that model jury instructions be formulated on this topic.
541 *Ibid.* at 111, see Recommendation 8.

Finally, the committee recommended that further research be conducted on a number of topics.[542] It identified a particular need for research to determine other system variables (i.e., "conditions such as the procedures followed to obtain identifications"[543]) and estimator variables (i.e., "conditions associated with the actual crime"[544]) that might influence an eyewitness' performance.[545] The committee found that no definitive conclusions could yet be drawn regarding the comparative efficacy of sequential versus simultaneous lineup procedures, and recommended that law enforcement exercise caution when considering changes to existing lineup procedures until further research has addressed this question.[546]

L. MICROSCOPIC HAIR COMPARISON ANALYSIS REVIEW

In July 2013, the U.S. Federal Bureau of Investigation (FBI), in conjunction with the Department of Justice (DOJ) and with the assistance of the National Association of Criminal Defense Lawyers (NACDL), the Innocence Project, and pro bono partner Winston & Strawn LLP, commenced a review of the microscopic hair comparison evidence provided by FBI laboratory examiners.[547] The review includes criminal cases prior to the year 2000, "when

---

542 *Ibid.* at 113. The committee found that "much remains unsettled in many areas of eyewitness identification research" (at 100) and recommended the creation of a national program (see Recommendation 10 at 113) that would support research on a range of topics including, *inter alia*: "the variables that affect the accuracy, precision, and reliability of eyewitness identifications" (at 116); "best practices for probing witness memory with the least potential for bias or contamination" and for assessing witnesses' confidence levels (at 116); "photo array composition and procedures" (at 116 & 117); "innovative technologies that might increase the reliability of eyewitness testimony" (at 117); and "the most effective means of informing jurors how to consider the factors that affect the strengths and weaknesses of eyewitness identification evidence" (at 117).

543 *Ibid.* at 1.

544 *Ibid.*

545 *Ibid.* at 119, see Recommendation 11 at 117.

546 *Ibid.* at 118.

547 Federal Bureau of Investigation, Laboratory Services, "FBI/DOJ Microscopic Hair Comparison Analysis Review" [FBI/DOJ Review], online: www.fbi.gov/about-us/lab/scientific-analysis/fbi-doj-microscopic-hair-comparison-analysis-review; Federal Bureau of Investigation, News Release, "FBI Testimony on Microscopic Hair Analysis Contained Errors in at least 90 Percent of Cases in Ongoing Review" (20 April 2015) [FBI Testimony], online: www.fbi.gov/news/pressrel/press-releases/fbi-testimony-on-microscopic-hair-analysis-contained-errors-in-at-least-90-percent-of-cases-in-ongoing-review; Norman L. Reimer, "The Hair Microscopy Review Project: An Historic Breakthrough for Law Enforcement and A Daunting Challenge for the Defense Bar" (July 2013) *The Champion* 16, online: www.nacdl.org/champion.aspx?id=29488. On 25

mitochondrial DNA testing on hair became routine at the FBI,"[548] and is to extend back until at least the early 1980s.[549] The FBI and DOJ commenced this review in the wake of the 2009 National Academy of Sciences report, which was critical of hair microscopy evidence,[550] and the exoneration of three people who were wrongfully convicted at least in part due to FBI hair examiners' flawed testimony.[551] The purpose of this review is to ensure that FBI hair comparison analysis testimony met accepted scientific standards, and, where it did not, to take remedial action if appropriate.[552]

The scope of this review includes both federal and state court cases[553] in which inculpatory hair microscopy evidence was presented that met the following criteria:

1. The defendant was convicted;
2. DNA analysis was **not** conducted on the evidentiary hair;
3. The case was submitted to the FBI Laboratory and the analysis occurred prior to December 31, 1999; and
4. The FBI provided the contributing law enforcement agency a Laboratory report regarding the results of the microscopic hair comparison.[554]

The review is predicated on the principle that, while hair microscopy evidence can reliably exclude an individual as the donor of the hair sample(s) in question, "it cannot support any statement as to the likelihood of a match."[555] With this touchstone in mind, the review seeks to identify three types of errors: (1) "[t]he examiner stated or implied that the evidentiary hair could be associated with a specific individual to the exclusion of all others";[556] (2) the examiner provided a statistical weight, probability, or likelihood that the hair sample in question came from a given source; and (3) the examiner bolstered the conclusion that the hair sample(s) came

---

February 2016, it was reported that the Justice Department will expand the review to include testimony from FBI units that examined pattern-based evidence: see Spencer S. Hsu, "Justice Dept. to Expand Review of FBI Forensic Techniques beyond Hair Unit" (25 February 2016), online: The Washington Post http://wpo.st/RIsO1.

548 FBI Testimony, *ibid.*

549 *Ibid.*; Reimer, above note 547.

550 Reimer, *ibid.*; see the 2009 NAS Report, above note 254.

551 Reimer, *ibid.*

552 FBI/DOJ Review, above note 547.

553 FBI Testimony, above note 547.

554 FBI/DOJ Review, above note 547 [emphasis in original].

555 Reimer, above note 547.

556 *Ibid.*

from a given source by citing "the number of cases or hair analyses worked in the lab and the number of samples from different individuals that could not be distinguished."[557]

As of March 2015, the FBI had reviewed approximately 500 of the nearly 3,000 cases identified in which FBI hair examiners may have given testimony or submitted laboratory reports.[558] Analysis of these cases yielded the following results:

> In the 268 cases where examiners provided testimony used to inculpate a defendant at trial, erroneous statements were made in 257 (96 percent) of the cases. Defendants in at least 35 of these cases received the death penalty and errors were identified in 33 (94 percent) of those cases. Nine of these defendants have already been executed and five died of other causes while on death row. . . . All but two of 28 FBI examiners provided testimony that contained erroneous statements or authored lab reports with such statements.[559]

Peter Neufeld, co-director of the Innocence Project, decried this "epic miscarriage of justice" in which FBI analysts "committed widespread, systematic error, grossly exaggerating the significance of their data under oath[,] . . . unfairly bolstering the prosecutions' case."[560] He called on lawmakers to "demand research and national standards to prevent the exaggeration of results in reports and in testimony by crime lab analysts."[561] Norman L. Reimer, executive director of NACDL, observed that while it would take many months to determine how many people were wrongfully convicted due to prosecutorial reliance on this flawed but highly persuasive evidence, the number would be high.[562]

The DOJ and FBI have committed to "[c]onducting an independent investigation of the FBI Laboratory protocols, practices, and procedures" to determine how this miscarriage of justice occurred "and why it was allowed to continue for so long."[563] In addition, the DOJ and FBI will seek to identify any further measures that could be taken to enhance the re-

---

557 *Ibid.* ("[O]ver the last 12 years, I personally have looked at hairs from about 10,000 different people, and over that time, I've only had two occasions out of the 10,000 people where I had hairs from two different people that I could not separate them.")

558 FBI Testimony, above note 547.

559 *Ibid.*

560 *Ibid.*

561 *Ibid.*

562 *Ibid.*

563 *Ibid.*

view process, and will encourage the states to conduct their own reviews of hair microscopy cases, including testimony from state and local hair examiners trained by the FBI. The DOJ is also working with its partners to locate and notify counsel who defended the cases reviewed, while NACDL is working to offer all affected defendants access to pro bono counsel to review the new evidence and challenge convictions where appropriate.[564]

M. THE MOTHERISK HAIR ANALYSIS INDEPENDENT REVIEW

1) Background

In October 2014, the Ontario Court of Appeal quashed two of Tamara Broomfield's convictions on a set of counts alleging that she had abused her young son. Convictions for aggravated assault and administering a noxious substance had been supported by the evidence of two experts from the Motherisk Drug Testing Laboratory (MDTL) at the Hospital for Sick Children (SickKids), who had conducted a toxicological analysis of her son's hair and concluded that Broomfield had administered substantial amounts of cocaine to her son over a fourteen-month period. On appeal, defence counsel submitted fresh evidence questioning the expert's methodology and results.[565] The court found that the trial judge had been "unaware of the genuine controversy . . . about the use of the testing methods relied upon by the Crown expert"[566] and determined that the convictions founded on this evidence could not be sustained.[567]

2) Results of the Independent Review

As a result of this decision, the Ontario government initiated an independent review of the Motherisk hair-strand drug testing program in November 2014. Retired Justice of the Ontario Court of Appeal Susan Lang was

---

564 *Ibid.*

565 *R. v. Broomfield*, 2014 ONCA 725 at paras. 1, 6–8, and 12–16 [*Broomfield*]; Ontario, Ministry of the Attorney General, "Ontario Initiates Review of Motherisk Hair Analysis" (28 November 2014), online: news.ontario.ca/mag/en/2014/11/ontario-initiates-review-of-motherisk-hair-analysis.html [Motherisk News Release]; The Honourable Susan E. Lang, Independent Reviewer, Report of the Motherisk Hair Analysis Independent Review (15 December 2015) [Motherisk Report] at 224–27, online: www.m-hair.ca.

566 *Broomfield*, *ibid.* at para. 12.

567 *Ibid.* at paras. 13 & 14.

appointed to serve as Independent Reviewer.[568] In her final report, provided to the Attorney General on 15 December 2015, Lang J. observed that MDTL "held itself out as a leader in the field of hair testing for drugs of abuse," testing "hair samples from more than 16,000 individuals at the request of Ontario child protection agencies" between 2005 and 2015.[569] Justice Lang also identified six criminal cases resulting in a conviction, including *Broomfield*, in which the Crown put forth MDTL evidence.[570]

Justice Lang made the following findings regarding MDTL's hair testing program:

1. The hair-strand drug and alcohol testing used by MDTL between 2005 and 2015 was inadequate and unreliable for use in child protection and criminal proceedings.
2. Between 2005 and 2015, MDTL operated in a manner that did not meet internationally recognized forensic standards.
3. The Hospital for Sick Children did not provide meaningful oversight over MDTL.
4. The use of MDTL hair-testing evidence in child protection and criminal proceedings has serious implications for the fairness of those proceedings and warrants an additional review.[571]

Justice Lang's report documents an array of alarming deficiencies in MDTL's analytical, interpretation, and communication practices that contributed to the inadequacy and unreliability of its hair-strand drug and alcohol testing.

a) Lack of Qualifications to Provide Forensic Services

MDTL was founded as a research laboratory.[572] None of its leaders "had any formal training or experience in forensic toxicology"; indeed, neither MDTL nor SickKids "appear[ed] to have appreciated that the Laboratory was engaged in forensic work and that it was required to meet forensic standards."[573] As a result, the laboratory's "testing and operations fell woefully short of internationally recognized forensic standards."[574]

---

568 Motherisk News Release, above note 565; "Motherisk Hair Analysis Independent Review," online: www.m-hair.ca/about-the-review, and "Independent Reviewer: The Honourable Susan Lang," online: www.m-hair.ca/independent-reviewer.

569 Motherisk Report, above note 565 at 1.

570 *Ibid.* at 17.

571 *Ibid.* at 4.

572 *Ibid.* at 2.

573 *Ibid.* at 5.

574 *Ibid.*; see also 12 & 13.

b) Inadequacy and Unreliability of Test Results

Justice Lang found that from 2005 to 2010, "MDTL's analytical practices for drugs of abuse suffered from two fatal flaws."[575] First, during this period, MDTL "relied on the unconfirmed results of . . . a preliminary screening test . . . both qualitatively (to distinguish positive hair samples from negative ones) and quantitatively (to calculate the drug concentration in the sample)."[576] This practice was unacceptable and, in the latter case, unheard of.[577] Second, "the Laboratory had no written standard operating procedures for the hair tests it carried out, thereby calling into question the reliability and standardization of all its testing procedures."[578] Though MDTL made improvements to its practices and procedures during the 2010–2015 period, a number of problems remained, including: relying on a flawed gas chromatography-mass spectroscopy procedure; continued reliance on unconfirmed preliminary tests in some contexts; and failure to wash hair samples and to maintain appropriate chains of custody.[579]

MDTL's alcohol hair-testing methods were also inadequate, principally in that: (1) they, too, relied on a flawed gas chromatography-mass spectroscopy procedure; and (2) MDTL misapplied cut-offs used to determine whether a test was positive or negative.[580]

c) Deficient Interpretation and Communication Practices

Justice Lang found that MDTL's interpretation and communication practices "were inadequate and further undermined the reliability of the [Laboratory's] results."[581] MDTL created "concentration ranges" purporting to indicate the concentration of drugs in a given hair sample—an unacceptable practice, since the ranges did not account for inter-subject variation

575 *Ibid.* at 5.

576 *Ibid.* at 6. The preliminary screening test was an enzyme-linked immunosorbent assay (ELISA); Lang J. noted that "[t]he requirement to carry out a confirmation test on any preliminary positive results from . . . ELISA, was highlighted in the literature and in all internationally recognized hair-testing standards well before 2005. Indeed, the Immunalysis kits that MDTL used included an explicit warning for the user about the preliminary nature of the ELISA results" (*ibid.*).

577 *Ibid.* at 6 & 7.

578 *Ibid.* at 6. Justice Lang also identified a number of other procedural flaws during this period, including: a lack of contemporaneous documentation and record keeping; a lack of oversight of the laboratory technician who conducted the hair tests; failure to wash hair samples before analysis; and inadequate chain-of-custody procedures (at 7 & 8).

579 *Ibid.* at 8.

580 *Ibid.* at 8, 54, & 55.

581 *Ibid.* at 9.

and were derived from unconfirmed preliminary test results—and relied on them to derive unsupported conclusions regarding individuals' drug use habits.[582] In addition, MDTL did not adequately communicate its test results for a number of reasons, including: (1) the staff members' lack of forensic toxicology expertise, and (2) MDTL's practices of providing test result interpretation by telephone rather than in writing, and of regularly sending test results to customers without providing any interpretation at all.[583]

d) Failures of Oversight and Accountability

Justice Lang found that no one at SickKids "charged with overseeing MDTL provided any meaningful oversight."[584] As a result, "MDTL slipped through the cracks."[585] MDTL did not participate in an accreditation assessment until 2011, and, though it did achieve clinical laboratory accreditation, it was never accredited as a forensic laboratory (these are typically assessed to a more stringent standard).[586] Moreover, although MDTL participated in proficiency testing offered by the Society of Hair Testing—and relied on its test results in support of its flawed analytical methods—Lang J. found that from 2001 to 2009, "MDTL frequently submitted quantitative results that had been produced by another laboratory or results that were inconsistent with its own data."[587]

e) Troubling Parallels

Justice Lang's findings evoke troubling parallels to the Goudge Inquiry Report released in 2008; her "conclusion that SickKids failed to exercise meaningful oversight over MDTL's work must be considered in the context of the Hospital's experience with Dr. Charles Smith."[588] The Goudge Inquiry Report "highlighted the dangers associated with having a laboratory

---

582 *Ibid.* Ranges included, e.g., "trace," "medium," or "very high." "Inter-subject variation" means that "two people who use the same amount of a drug are not expected to have the same concentration of drug in their hair because of differences such as in metabolism and hair characteristics" (*ibid.*).

583 *Ibid.* at 10.

584 *Ibid.* at 13.

585 *Ibid.* at 14.

586 *Ibid.* at 12, 178–80, and 182–83. In fact, SickKids specifically chose not to include MDTL in the Ontario Laboratory Accreditation midterm self-assessment completed by its clinical laboratories in 2008 "because it recognized that accreditation would likely not be achieved" (at 13).

587 *Ibid.* at 11.

588 *Ibid.* at 14; see "G. The Goudge Inquiry," above.

within the institution that routinely provided a forensic service yet was led by individuals who lacked any forensic training" or real oversight.[589] These lessons ought to have been applied to the MDTL; they were not.[590]

3) Recommendations and Next Steps

Justice Lang recommended establishing a Second Review into individual cases affected by MDTL's flawed testing.[591] On 15 January 2016, the Honourable Justice Judith C. Beaman was appointed to lead an independent commission that will identify persons whose cases may have been affected by MDTL's hair testing program between 1990 and 2005; inform them of Lang J.'s findings; and offer support, including legal advice, alternative dispute resolution, and counselling services. Justice Beaman will seek to conclude her mandate within two years.[592]

Justice Lang recommended that child protection agencies ensure that MDTL test results are not relied upon in any current or future proceeding, and identify and reassess cases involving MDTL hair testing that still remain open or in which a child removed from his or her family has not yet been adopted.[593] On 5 March 2015, SickKids suspended MDTL's operations. On 17 April 2015, SickKids announced that it would not be reinstating the laboratory's non-research-related activities.[594] Shortly thereafter, on 22 April 2015, the Ontario Ministry of Children and Youth Services directed the province's Children's Aid Societies to no longer use or rely on hair

---

589 *Ibid.* at 14.

590 *Ibid.* at 21.

591 *Ibid.* at 17, and see 3 & 4. Such a review was not within Justice Lang's mandate.

592 Ontario, Ministry of the Attorney General, "Ontario Launches Commission to Support People Impacted by Motherisk Tests" (15 January 2016), online: news.ontario.ca/mag/en/2016/01/ontario-launches-commission-to-support-people-impacted-by-motherisk-tests.html; Ontario, Ministry of the Attorney General, "Order in Council" (15 January 2016), online: news.ontario.ca/mag/en/2016/01/order-in-council-1.html.

593 Motherisk Report, above note 565 at 18. Justice Lang observed that, "[i]f an affected child has been placed for adoption . . . in part because of flawed evidence from MDTL, the . . . range of remedies is legislatively limited." She suggested that the Commissioner of the second review "consult broadly with affected persons, including youth . . . to develop approaches to resolution based on the best interests of the child" (at 19).

594 Hospital for Sick Children, "Motherisk News: Operations of Motherisk Drug Testing Lab Closed" (17 April 2015), online: SickKids, www.motherisk.org/women/commonDetail.jsp?content_id=1100.

strand testing results in the provision of child protection services.[595] Upon the Motherisk Report's publication, the Ontario Association of Children's Aid Societies announced that it would follow all of Lang J.'s recommendations.[596] As of February 2016, hundreds of ongoing adoption cases involving MDTL test results had been put on hold pending review.[597]

Justice Lang also found that flawed MDTL evidence was often introduced on consent and without meeting the *Mohan* requirements for expert opinion evidence.[598] She recommended that counsel and the judiciary participate in continuing legal education regarding expert scientific evidence, and noted that counsel should take care to properly qualify experts and to understand and properly delineate the scope of their expertise.[599]

Justice Lang's mandate did not include consideration of monetary compensation.[600] On 22 December 2015, a class action lawsuit against SickKids and MDTL's director and manager was commenced on behalf of all persons who received a positive MDTL hair test result between 2005 and 2015 and their close relatives.[601]

---

595 Ontario, Ministry of Children and Youth Services, "Timeline of Events Related to the Independent Review of the Motherisk Hair Analysis Program" (17 December 2015), online: news.ontario.ca/mcys/en/2015/12/timeline-of-events-related-to-the-independent-review-of-the-motherisk-hair-analysis-program.html.

596 Ontario Association of Children's Aid Societies, "The Ontario Association of Children's Aid Societies responds to the Final Report of the Motherisk Hair Analysis Independent Review" (17 December 2015), online: www.oacas.org/2015/12/the-ontario-association-of-childrens-aid-societies-responds-to-the-final-report-of-the-motherisk-hair-analysis-independent-review.

597 Mike Crawley, "Hundreds of Ontario Adoptions on Hold Amid Motherisk Drug-Test Scandal" CBC News (1 February 2016), online: www.cbc.ca/news/canada/toronto/ontario-adoption-motherisk-1.3426386.

598 Motherisk Report, above note 565 at 16.

599 *Ibid.* at 20. Justice Lang further observed that "[c]ounsel should be vigilant to ensure that justice is not undermined by the use of flawed forensic evidence. The recommendations of the Goudge Report continue to provide valuable insights on these issues" (*ibid.*).

600 *Ibid.*

601 Statement of Claim (Notice of Action Issued on 22 December 2015), *Yvonne Marchand v. The Hospital for Sick Children, Gideon Koren and Joey Gareri* (Court File No.: CV-15-54325900CP, 20 January 2016), online: Koskie Minsky LLP kmlaw.ca/wp-content/uploads/2016/01/IssuedSOC_20Jan15.pdf. At the time of publication, the Province of Ontario was to be added to the claim following the expiration of the notice period pursuant to the *Proceedings Against the Crown Act*, R.S.O. 1990, c. P.27 (*ibid.*).

CHAPTER 6

Bloodstain Pattern Analysis

Patrick Laturnus

LEGAL CONTEXT: CAITLIN PAKOSH

A. OVERVIEW OF THE DISCIPLINE: BLOODSTAIN PATTERN ANALYSIS

In the courtroom, packed with strategy and detail, there is great value placed on physical evidence—in a sea of conflicting expert opinions and complex legal jargon, physical evidence is perceptible, tangible. Bloodstains are such evidence and, when the origins of a bloodstain can be faithfully and scientifically explained, bloodstain pattern analysis can offer key information about a case.

Bloodstain pattern analysis is the study of the shapes, sizes, and locations of bloodstains in an effort to interpret the physical events that gave rise to their origin. If bloodstains are observed on a wall, for example, it is possible to understand how they were created and where they came from based on the shape, size, and location of the stains in relation to each other and to the wall.[1] This type of analysis can be useful when applied to any bloodletting event but, in the criminal context, it is particularly informative in cases such as a physical assault and murder.

Bloodstain pattern analysis (BPA) evidence has been accepted as expert testimony in Canadian courts since the 1878 case of *R. v. McPherson and Burke*. On 26 July 1878, Ellen Bennett was raped and murdered. Dr. William Hodgson Ellis, a professor at the School of Technology, testified at the trial in Whitby, Ontario. In addition to the identification of blood, Dr. Hodgson

1 The surface on which the bloodstain is present is known as the substrate.

Ellis testified to the significance of the number, size, and position of bloodstains on the trousers of the accused. The beginning of BPA as it is known today, however, can be traced to a 25 January 1977 second-degree murder conviction, where Herb MacDonnell testified as a bloodstain analyst at the trial of *R. v. Sparrow*.[2] At this time, analysts received training based on experiments and they began to exchange ideas that would advance the discipline towards a more science-based approach. Subsequently, BPA became recognized in the court system and trained individuals began to qualify as experts.

When there is a bloodletting crime, the initial crime scene investigator will assess the value of the evidence and call in a qualified analyst if required. In Canada, these analysts are typically police officers with the necessary training and experience. Just how the analysis is conducted has changed over time. In the early days and up to the 1990s, much of the opinion evidence was based on the experience of the analyst. With training and experience, the differences between one bloodstain pattern and another seemed obvious. The analyst could testify with confidence to the meaning of the patterns and describe what events might have happened to create the observed bloodstain pattern. For example, the observation of an impact pattern indicates the location of the blood source being struck, while a passive blood trail could show the direction that the blood source was moving.

As this discipline evolved over time, analysts have moved towards the scientific method of analysis. Although experience still plays a key role in bloodstain pattern analysis, the analyst must now be able to explain the underlying science when offering an opinion. Through the use of new technology and a more in-depth study of physics, bloodstain analysts are better able to understand and explain the bloodstain patterns they have observed and analyzed, particularly when compared to the early days of the discipline.

B. THE SCIENCE OF BLOODSTAIN PATTERN ANALYSIS

1) Basic Principles of Bloodstain Pattern Analysis: Key Terms and Concepts

Bloodstain pattern analysis will provide information about bloodletting events, but the validity of the discipline is based in its foundation in scientific principles. The complexities inherent in assessing bloodstains, relying upon both science and experience, practically make this discipline a science in its own right. The scientific terms used to describe an expert's

2 For the appeal decision, see (1979), 55 C.C.C. (2d) 443 (Ont. C.A.).

understanding of the evidence bridge the physical reality of bloodletting scenes with the abstract nature of scientific theories. Science explains why the evidence found in a bloodstain pattern is predictable and reproducible. Two particular concepts, "surface tension" and "directionality" underpin why and how an analyst will form certain conclusions. The scientific principles most relevant to BPA are adopted from the disciplines of mathematics, biology, and physics.

a) Surface Tension

When a liquid is exposed to air, the molecules within it hold on tightly to each other. In doing so, the liquid becomes spherical because the liquid naturally tends to minimize its surface area. This results in a "skin" forming on the surface of the sphere. Surface tension allows certain species of insects to walk on water. Of importance to BPA, surface tension also causes blood to quickly form a sphere when exposed to air. That sphere will travel intact through the air until it impacts a substrate. The resulting bloodstain will provide evidence of its origin (i.e., "the three-dimensional location from which spatter originated").[3]

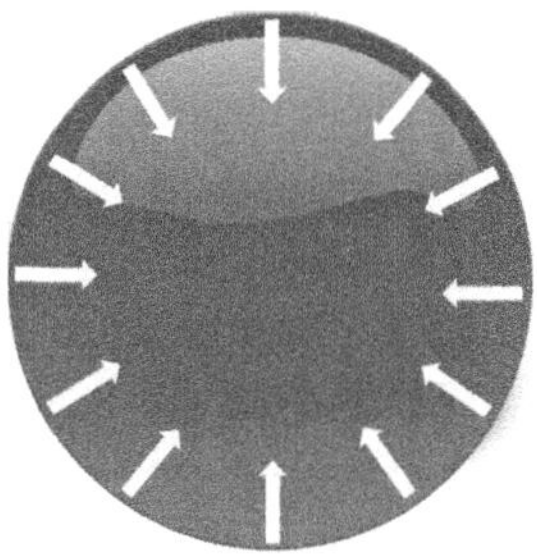

FIGURE 6.1. This diagram depicts how the sphere is formed in flight due to surface tension. The arrows show the direction of air pressure as the droplet falls.

b) Directionality

When a blood droplet strikes a surface, it will result in a bloodstain. By observing the characteristics of that bloodstain, it is possible to determine what direction it was moving at the time of deposition. Typically, the narrow or pointed end of the bloodstain will point in the direction that it was moving. If, for example, the bloodstain is pointed on its right side but rounded on its left, then the bloodstain was moving from left to right, and vice versa.

3 Scientific Working Group on Bloodstain Pattern Analysis (SWGSTAIN), "Recommended Terminology," online: SWGSTAIN www.swgstain.org/resources.

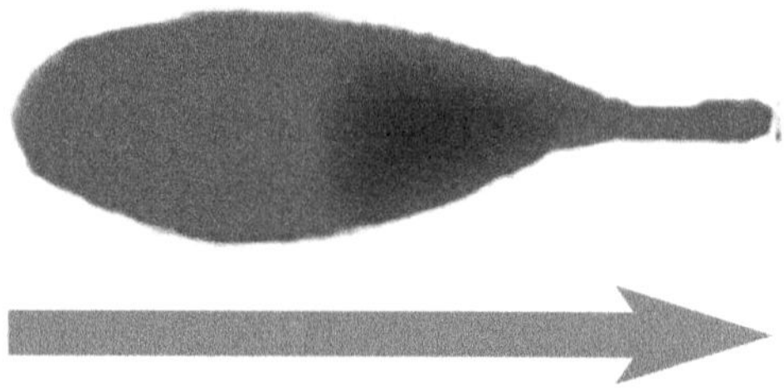

FIGURE 6.2. This diagram depicts how a bloodstain pattern may indicate the direction the blood source was moving at the time of deposition.

This information is crucial to reconstructing the events that occurred at a scene under analysis. For example, directionality analysis is important when determining an area of origin for the impact pattern, or when visualizing which direction a blood source (i.e., a person) may have been moving at the time of the bloodletting event. In all cases, the determination of directionality must be kept in context. It is possible to visualize what direction a droplet was moving even if it does not show a clear point, but instead shows one side with more spines than the other side. The spines indicate the direction of travel, as found in some drip trail patterns (i.e., "a bloodstain pattern resulting from the movement of a source of drip stains between two points").[4]

Before an analyst can provide reliable opinion evidence, certain exceptions and limitations to these rules must be considered. For example, if bloodstains are distorted by the underlying substrate, which may be rough or uneven (ex., concrete, carpet, clothing, etc.), then they cannot be used to determine directionality. Circular stains show no direction and indicate that the blood droplet landed at a 90 degree angle (or "straight on"). Similarly, if a blood droplet is a perfect ellipse, then it will not show any direction.

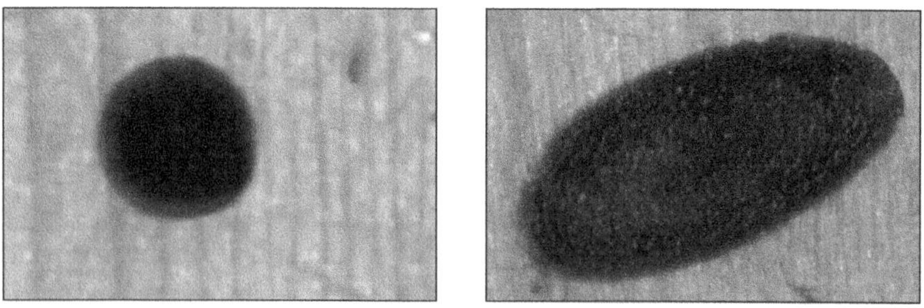

FIGURE 6.3. The circular bloodstain (L) and the elliptical bloodstain (R) do not provide information about the direction the blood source was moving at the moment of impact.

4 *Ibid.*

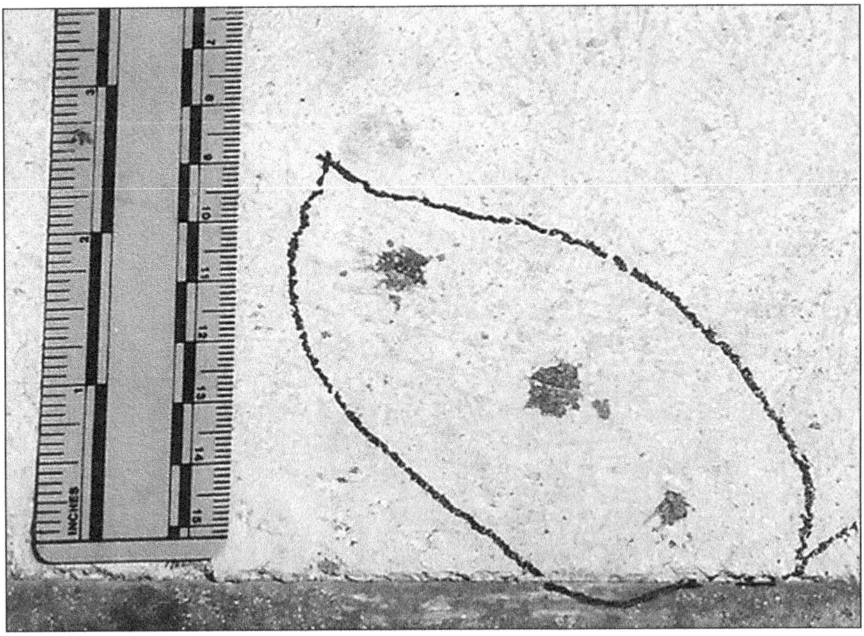

FIGURE 6.4. Bloodstains deposited on a concrete surface.

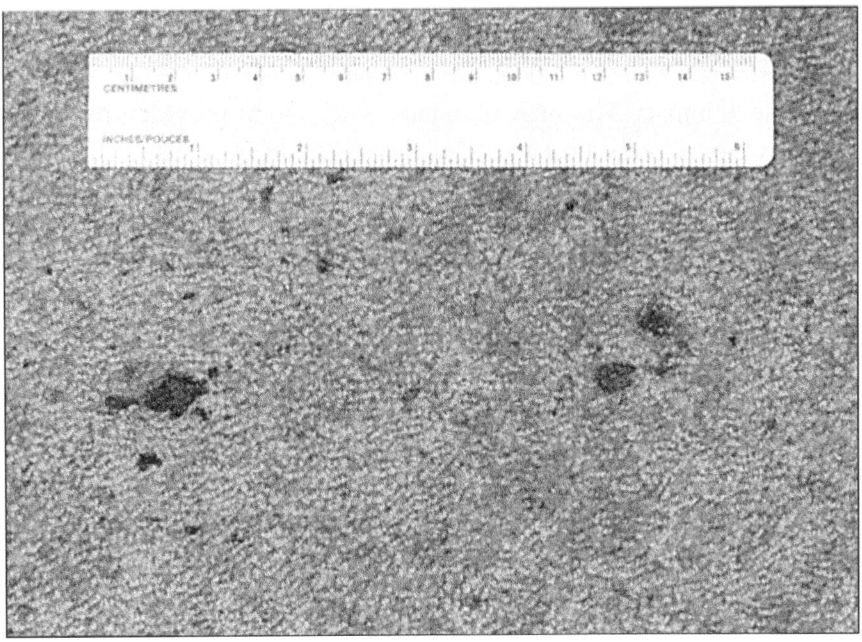

FIGURE 6.5. Bloodstains deposited on a carpeted surface.

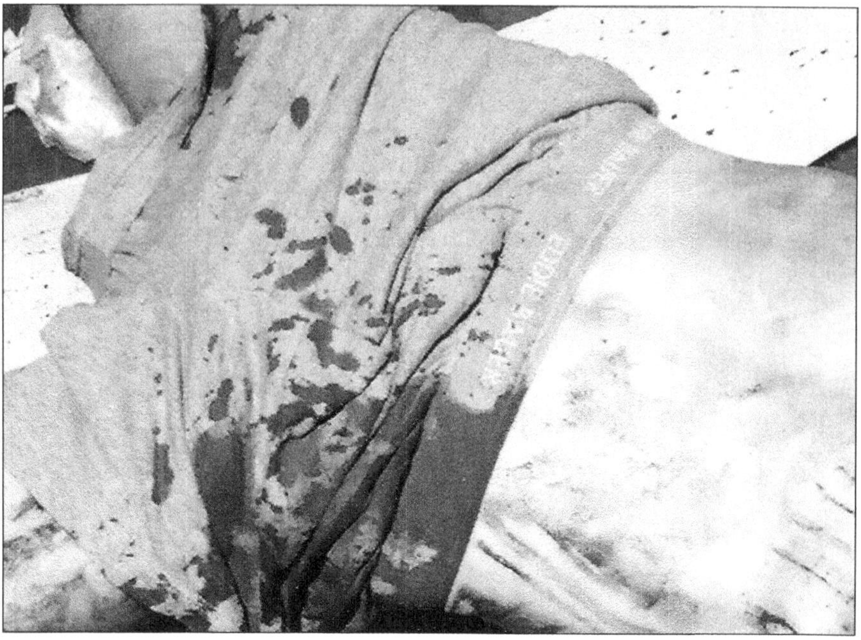

FIGURE 6.6. Bloodstains deposited on clothing.

c) Angle of Impact

To determine where the bloodstain originated, an analyst must calculate the angle of impact. The angle of impact is defined by the Scientific Working Group on Bloodstain Pattern Analysis (SWGSTAIN) as "[t]he acute angle (alpha), relative to the plane of a target, at which a blood drop strikes the target."[5] After calculating the angle of impact for several bloodstains, it is then possible to determine an area of origin for an impact pattern.

As previously mentioned, one of the relevant scientific disciplines in bloodstain pattern analysis is mathematics. To determine the angle of impact for a specific bloodstain, an analyst must measure the elliptical shape found in a bloodstain. The angle of impact is determined through trigonometry: the sine of the angle of impact $=W \div L$, where "W" is the width of the ellipse and "L" the length. For example, if $W=1.5$ cm and $L=3.0$ cm, then the sine of the angle of impact is $1.5 \text{ cm} \div 3.0 \text{ cm} = 0.5$ cm. Using a trigonometric table to obtain the angle with a sine of 0.5 cm, it is determined that the droplet struck the surface at a 30 degree angle.

---

5 *Ibid.*

The angle at which a droplet strikes will depend on its location relative to the target surface. The closer the blood source is to the target surface, the smaller (the more acute) the angle. For example, if a blood droplet strikes a surface at a 10 degree angle, then its long and narrow appearance reflects that it was much closer to the blood source (i.e., a person) compared to small and wide droplets (e.g., those striking a surface at a 40 degree angle). These results are not affected by the velocity of the bloodstain.

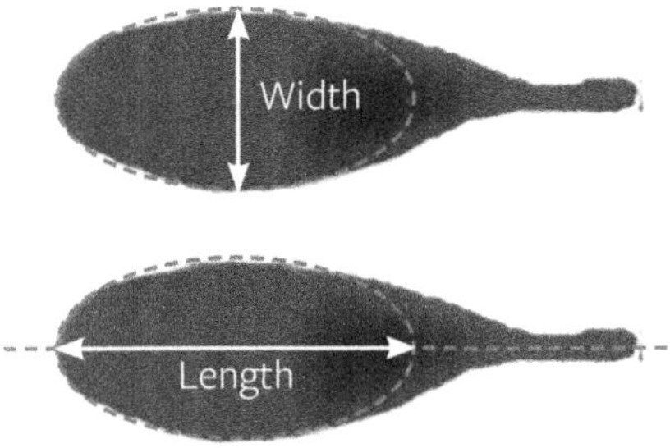

Width = 1.5 cm

Length = 3.0 cm

1.5 cm ÷ 3.0 cm = 0.5 cm

Trigonometric Table			
Angle	Sine	Cosine	Tangent
29	0.484810	0.874620	0.554309
30	**0.500000**	0.866025	0.577350
31	0.515038	0.857167	0.600861
32	0.529919	0.848048	0.624869

FIGURE 6.7. This figure depicts the angle of impact calculation. As the trigonometric table indicates, the sine of 0.5 is 30, indicating a 30 degree angle of impact.

10 degrees | 30 degrees | 40 degrees | 90 degrees

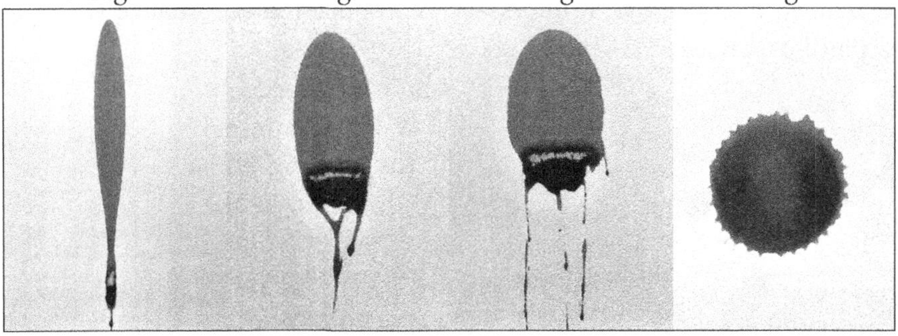

FIGURE 6.8. This figure depicts the inverse relationship between the length of the droplet and the angle to the blood source; the longer the droplet, the closer it was to the blood source.

d) Area of Convergence and Area of Origin

The area of convergence is "[t]he area containing the intersections generated by lines drawn through the long axes of individual stains that indicates in *two dimensions* the location of the blood source."[6] If a blood source (i.e., a person) is near a wall when struck, then the blood will fly out and strike the wall. Certain individual stains will show the direction that the stains were moving through the air (and, therefore, indicate the direction of the blow). They can also be used to show the area of convergence of the blow. The analyst will draw a line through the length of the stain and extend it downward. As each stain is analyzed, several lines will be drawn. Ultimately, these lines will converge and illustrate the area of convergence at which the blow was struck.

The area of origin is "[t]he *three-dimensional* location from which spatter originated."[7] Where there are stains of sufficient number and quality, each stain can be measured for its angle of impact and, when the angle of impact is determined for each stain, lines can be drawn to illustrate the three-dimensional area of origin. Most Canadian bloodstain pattern analysts will use a computer program during the analysis of the impact pattern. This program reduces line-drawing requirements and will automatically conduct the necessary calculations.

The number and quality of the bloodstains determine whether the analyst will measure the two-dimensional area of convergence or the three-dimensional area of origin. Both are useful in crime scene reconstruction. If the analyst can only determine location and direction, then the analyst will visualize the two-dimensional area of convergence. If there are a sufficient number of quality stains to allow for the calculation of the angle of impact, then the analyst will calculate the three-dimensional area of origin. These measurements and observations can easily be explained in court and, if necessary, reproduced in accordance with the scientific method.

6 *Ibid.* [emphasis added].

7 *Ibid.* [emphasis added].

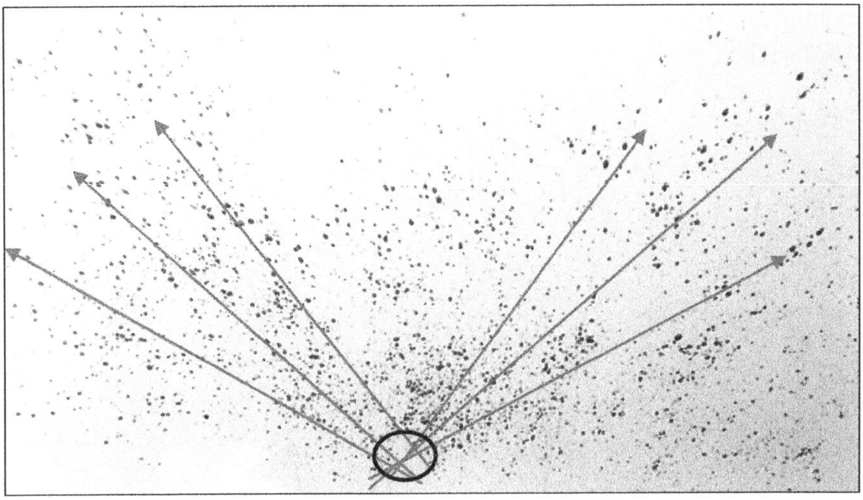

FIGURE 6.9. This figure depicts a two-dimensional analysis of an impact pattern to determine the area of convergence. By drawing lines through the centre of several bloodstains, a view of the area of convergence of these bloodstains can be seen.

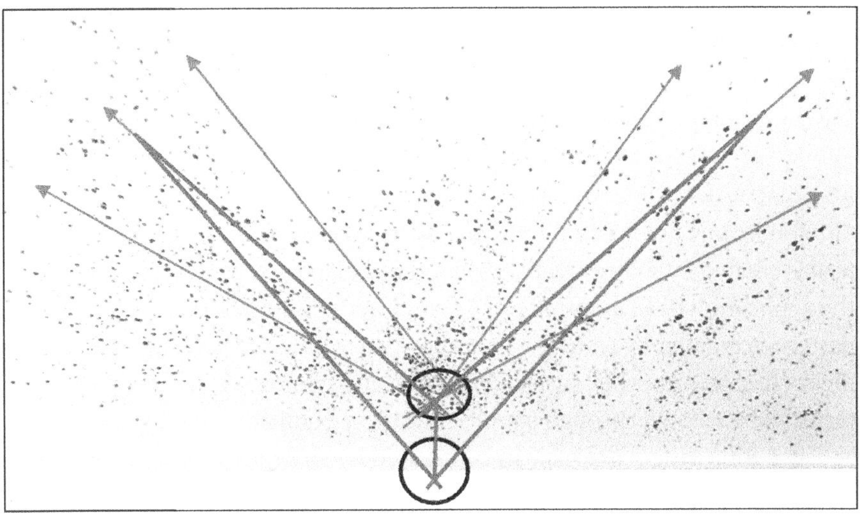

FIGURE 6.10. This figure depicts a three-dimensional analysis of an impact pattern. By applying trigonometric functions to each bloodstain, an area of origin can be visualized.

e) Amount of Force versus Size of Bloodstain

When a blow is struck, the amount of force applied to a given quantity of blood will directly affect the size of the resulting bloodstain. It is an inverse relationship—the greater the force, the smaller the bloodstain. For example, the bloodstains resulting from a gunshot wound would be much smaller than the bloodstains resulting from a kick.

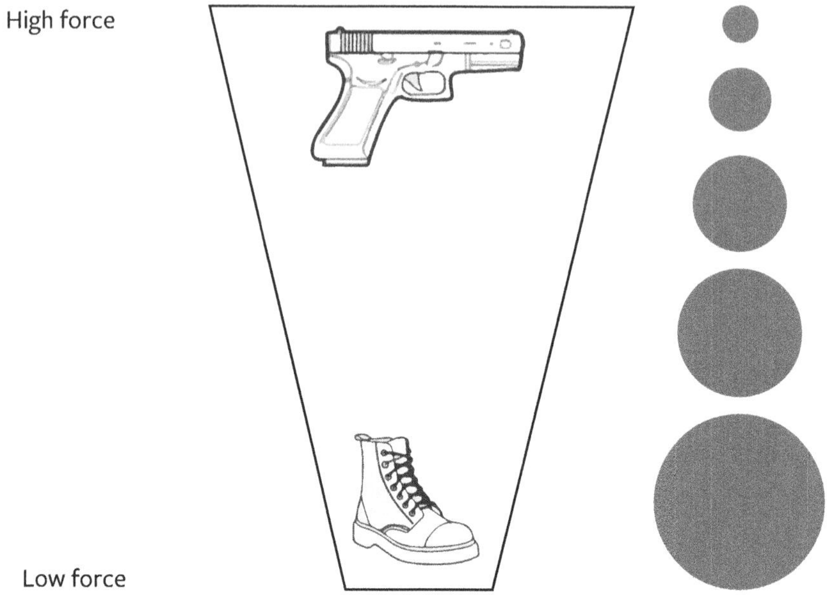

FIGURE 6.11. This figure depicts the inverse relationship between the amount of force and the size of the resulting bloodstain: the lower the force, the larger the bloodstain.

f) Spatter versus Transfer

All bloodstains are created by either spatter or transfer. If a bloodstain pattern is created by spatter, then the blood was dispersed through the air due to the application of an external force to a source of liquid blood. If a bloodstain pattern is created by transfer, then there was contact between a blood-bearing surface and another surface, by touch and without force.[8] A transfer pattern can be created through simple contact or contact with movement.

The following patterns can be created by spatter:

1) *Cast-off pattern*: "A bloodstain pattern resulting from blood drops released from an object due to its motion."[9] When a bloodied object is swung through the air, the blood will travel to the end of that object and be "cast-off" of it. Cast-off patterns are often linear (i.e., a straight line of spatter) and the droplets are similar in size.

8 *Ibid.*
9 *Ibid.*

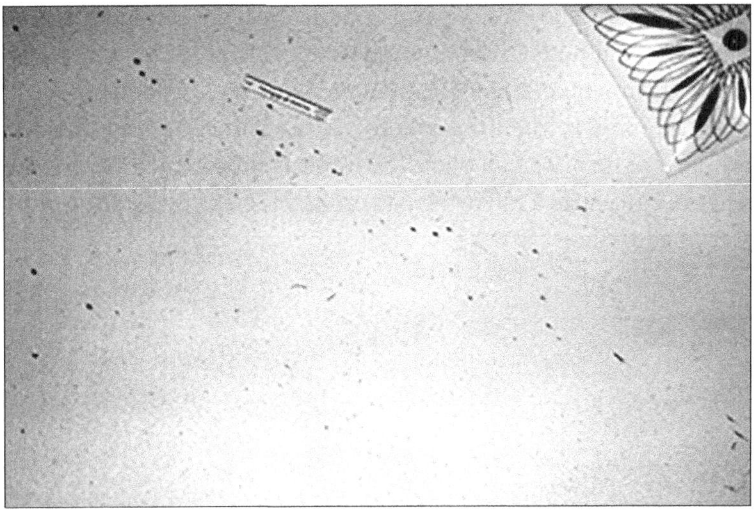

FIGURE 6.12. When a bloodied object is swung through the air, the blood will travel to the end of that object and then be "cast off" of it. Cast-off patterns are often linear and the droplets are similar in size.

2) *Projected pattern*: "A bloodstain pattern resulting from the ejection of a volume of blood under pressure."[10] For example, if an artery is breached, then the blood will be ejected under pressure, resulting in large volume stains.

FIGURE 6.13. In this example, an artery was breached, causing the blood to be ejected, resulting in large volume stains.

10 *Ibid.*

3) *Drip pattern*: "A bloodstain pattern resulting from a liquid that dripped into another liquid, at least one of which was blood."[11] For example, a drip pattern would result if a person is not moving and allows blood droplets to fall to the floor due to gravity alone. The droplets can accumulate to form a small pool. The force of additional droplets striking the pool can cause a radiating pattern that is spoke-like in appearance.

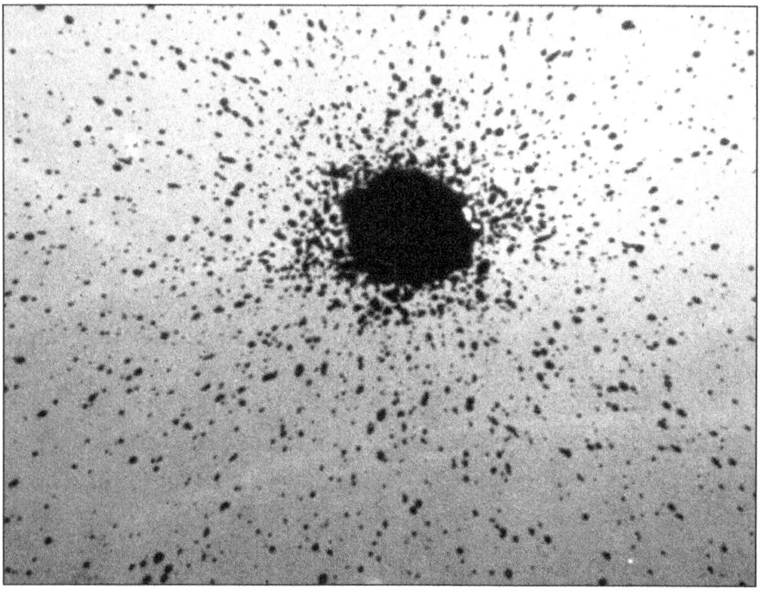

FIGURE 6.14. In this example, blood droplets fell to the floor due to gravity alone. The resulting pattern was caused when the droplets formed a small pool and the force of additional droplets striking the pool caused the radiating pattern. This example shows that the blood source was not moving at the time.

4) *Drip trail*: "A bloodstain pattern resulting from the movement of a source of drip stains between two points."[12] A drip trail would result if a person is moving and allowing blood droplets to fall to the floor due to gravity. The resulting pattern shows bloodstains that have directionality, allowing the analyst to determine the direction the blood source would have been moving.

11 *Ibid.*
12 *Ibid.*

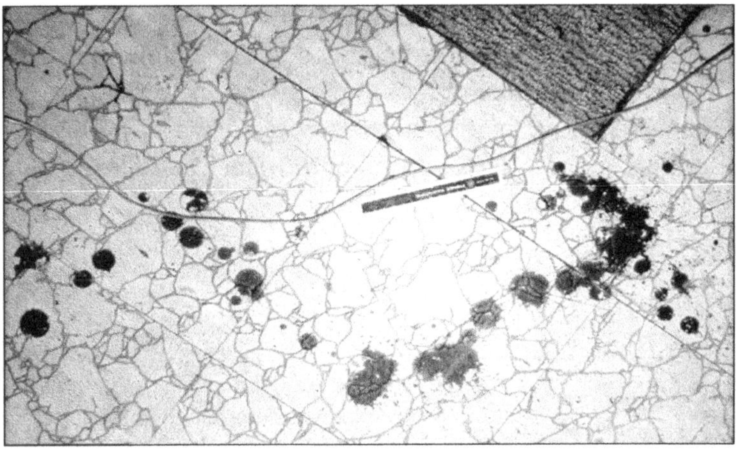

FIGURE 6.15. In this example, blood droplets fell to the floor due to gravity while moving. The resulting pattern shows bloodstains that have directionality, allowing the analyst to determine what direction the blood source would have been moving.

5) *Splash pattern*: "A bloodstain pattern resulting from a volume of liquid blood that falls or spills onto a surface."[13]

FIGURE 6.16. In this example, the blood source was near a wall when a volume of blood was released and hit the floor. Note the difference in radiating spatter from the drip pattern (Figure 6.14) to this pattern.

The following patterns can be created by transfer:

---

13 *Ibid.*

1) *Swipe pattern*: This pattern results from blood being transferred from a bloody surface in motion to another surface, exhibiting characteristics indicative of the relative motion between the two surfaces.[14] For example, "streaking" marks may be generated by bloody fingers moving across a surface. The direction of movement may be determined through analysis.

FIGURE 6.17. In this example, a hand can be seen in the pattern. Through analysis of the swipe pattern, it was determined that the "streaking" marks are all generated from the fingers of a hand moving right to left.

2) *Wipe pattern*: "An altered bloodstain pattern resulting from an object moving through a pre-existing wet bloodstain."[15] For example, if a series of circular wet bloodstains exist on a surface and then an object is "wiped" through these stains, the wipe pattern will be seen. In addition, there may be additional stains that have not been disturbed. The direction of movement may be determined through analysis.

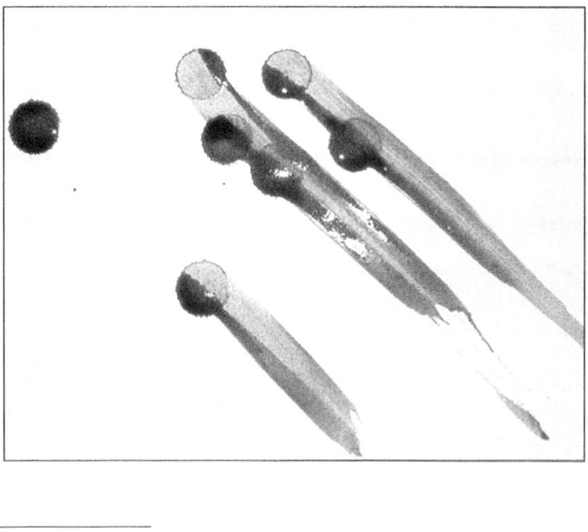

FIGURE 6.18. In this example, a series of circular bloodstains can be seen. Through analysis, it was determined that the outside edge of several stains were visible. In this case, an object was "wiped" through these pre-existing stains causing streaking from left to right.

14 *Ibid.*
15 *Ibid.*

A bloodstain pattern analyst may be able to make determinations that are useful for event reconstruction surrounding a bloodletting incident, including:

1) Identifying the bloody object that caused the transfer stain, possibly allowing for a determination to be made with respect to the blood source's position within the scene. For example, if transfer stains from a bra strap and a person's head hairs are present in a stain on the floor, it may be reasonable to infer that the person (i.e., the blood source) was, at one point, lying on the floor. Most often, however, there will be insufficient detail to make such determinations.

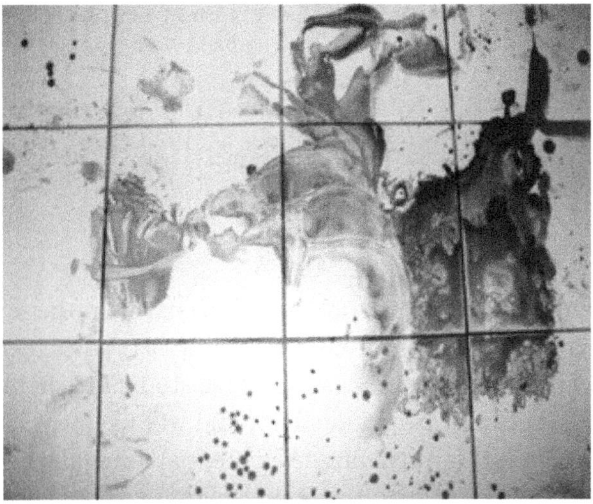

FIGURE 6.19. In this example, a bra strap was identified at the centre of the photo. In addition, hair transfer can be seen at the lower left. This photo is an example of how a transfer pattern can place a blood source in a position within the crime scene.

2) Determining the sequence of events at the scene of the bloodletting incident. Based on physical evidence, it may be possible to determine when a bloodstain had been altered in relation to the occurrence of other events at the scene. The analyst may be able to report that a particular bloodstain came first and another bloodstain came after. If multiple blood sources or bleeders are involved, DNA analysis will assist the BPA analyst in determining the sequence of events with respect to who bled when in relation to each other.

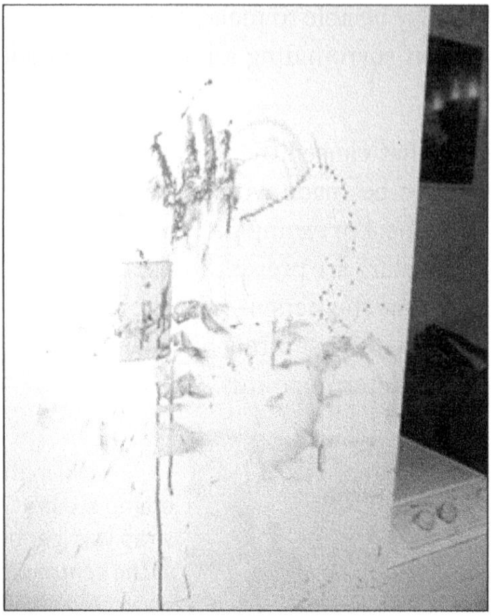

FIGURE 6.20. In this example, a cast-off pattern can be seen on the right side of the photo. Analysis of that pattern shows that an object moved through the cast-off in an upward direction. By following the movement it appears that the object was a hand; therefore, the cast-off was present before the hand went through it.

2) Methods and Protocol for Bloodstain Pattern Analysis

In Canada, bloodstain pattern analysts are found primarily in the police service, but they can also be with a forensic laboratory. Forensic identification officers (i.e., crime scene investigators) have studied basic bloodstain pattern analysis, but they are not analysts and will need to call on the services of an analyst if they recognize the potential for evidence at a bloodletting scene. These scenes are often homicides but any bloodletting scene, including assaults and apparent suicides, may require analysis by a qualified bloodstain analyst.

Most Canadian analysts undergo an understudy training period with qualified and experienced analysts. The training analyst (known as a bloodstain pattern understudy) will be exposed to actual bloodletting scenes while working under the mentorship of a qualified analyst. Advanced courses will also be taken. After the completion of the understudy training period, analysts will be encouraged to stay abreast of current developments in the field through membership in relevant associations, such as the International Association of Bloodstain Pattern Analysts (IABPA).[16]

An analysis begins when the BPA analyst receives a call to attend a scene or, in some cases, to provide an analysis from photographs. In all

16 Online: www.iabpa.org.

cases, the analyst will strive to limit any bias by obtaining only basic facts surrounding a particular case including, but not limited to:

1) The location and environmental condition of the scene.
2) A list of persons who had access to the scene and their involvement, such as first responders and medical personnel.
3) Information on other bloodletting events that may have occurred prior to this event.
4) A count of the total number of bleeders at the scene.
5) Information relative to any items removed or seized as evidence.
6) The source of the photographs: were they taken by a crime scene investigator or a bloodstain analyst, or both?

Opinions expressed by police investigators are disclosed to the BPA analyst only after the initial bloodstain pattern analysis has been completed. The analyst can share certain details of the scene analysis with investigators, such as the implication of cast-off patterns, providing the analyst's opinion and interpretation are qualified as preliminary pending in-depth analysis.

Upon arrival at the scene, the bloodstain analyst will conduct a "walkthrough." This procedure allows for an independent look at the evidence and provides an opportunity to begin to organize the collection of data. After the walkthrough, the analyst will identify, isolate, and mark the patterns, typically with a series of letters or numbers.

Photographs will be taken that cover the entire scene. Although the crime scene officer will have taken photographs, the bloodstain analyst will take additional photographs intended to capture the crime scene from an analytical perspective to assist subsequent measurement and analysis, as well as to capture any evidence that may not have been readily apparent. In addition, the analyst will begin to consider how the evidence can best be explained. This will involve taking photographs from the appropriate angle and keeping all patterns in context to provide an accurate interpretation of the scene.

The analyst begins by focusing on an individual bloodstain. Individual stains will be considered as part of a pattern. The pattern will be considered in the context of its location within the scene. This process is similar to the forensic photography method of close-up, midrange, and overall photographs.

After careful consideration and complete documentation of the scene, the analyst will begin to study the data collected. Notes are taken in preparation for a report, but the report will not be written until all necessary information has been received. In particular, DNA reports will not only verify the substance being analyzed as blood, but will also provide crucial information as to the number of bleeders. With the totality of the available information assessed in the context of the scene, it may be possible to determine the sequence of events.

a) Photographs in Bloodstain Pattern Analysis

Bloodstain pattern analysis is a visual medium and ideally the analyst will be physically present at the scene. There are subtle nuances to observe, a few isolated bloodstains in a corner, a faint wipe of blood, or an awkwardly located pattern. The dynamics of a bloodletting scene are often controlled by physical limitations and nuances that are easily missed if the analyst does not attend the scene in person. One of the most limiting factors in the discipline is poor-quality crime scene photographs. Good quality photographs will provide opportunities for helpful information, particularly where the analyst did not have the opportunity to attend the scene (as is often the case when an analyst is called by the defence). Poor quality photographs should lead the analyst to determine that there is insufficient detail to form an opinion concerning the event that may have caused the pattern observed.

In Canada, crime scene officers, who determine when it is necessary to call in an analyst, are trained in photography and in the significance of bloodstain patterns. In most cases, they will provide quality photographs that can be used by a qualified analyst to achieve an acceptable analysis. Analysts will often refer in their opinions to photographs taken by the crime scene officer in addition to their own.

In cases where a bloodstain analyst has been called into an investigation without having the benefit of attending the crime scene, the analyst doing the review will be limited to the data collected and the photographs of the scene. The strength of the analysis will necessarily depend on the quality of the data collected. Analysts in this situation should request all photographs and reports related to the case. Ideally, the crime scene data would be complete, with photographs taken by a bloodstain analyst. They should analyze the data according to the same standards and principles as they would use at the scene itself. In particular, analysts should aim to limit bias by first receiving basic information about the case,[17] then con-

17 For a description of the elements of "basic information," see Section C(1) in this chapter.

ducting a thorough review of all photographs. Then observations, notes, and initial opinions should be written prior to reading any relevant reports.

Improvements in analysis techniques have created the opportunity to uncover helpful additional information or fresh evidence in "cold cases" from a review of the photographs and data collected at the time. It is also possible that this review can provide information that identifies errors in judgment made by previous experts. For instance, it is now understood that similar spatter patterns may have been created by different events. For example, if a person has blood in their mouth or nose, then blows that blood out, the resulting pattern may be mistaken for an impact pattern.

3) The Evolution of Bloodstain Pattern Analysis

There is a strong element of common sense in BPA. For example, a mother, upon walking into her kitchen and seeing some utensils on the counter, a bit of blood nearby and drops of blood between the kitchen and the bathroom, might reasonably conclude that her child has cut himself while making something to eat. This is common sense, likely reinforced by life experience.

People have been following trails of blood from time immemorial, but today this age-old practice has developed into a forensic discipline aimed at answering specific questions. Did the blood trail show directionality? How large were the bloodstains? How frequent were they? Did they stop at any time? Whose blood was it? Although this initial knowledge base was grounded in scientific facts related to Newton's laws, biology, physics, and mathematics, little effort was spent on scientific study. Consequently, the measure of a bloodstain analyst's skill was often through their quality of training and breadth of experience.

During the 1970s, research expanded into the evaluation of bloodstains found at crime scenes. Experiments were conducted and patterns were identified. Observable differences and classifications could be delineated. For example, an impact pattern could be distinguished from a cast-off pattern. Analysts discovered that bloodstain patterns were reproducible and predictable, allowing analysts to report observations accurately and to testify with confidence.

A comparison of texts explaining impact patterns shows the evolution of the discipline over time. Prior to 2001, impact patterns were typically attributed to low, medium, or high velocity forces. These velocity determinations were based on the size of the bloodstains. Some textbooks still use that terminology; however, the discipline has evolved to a greater, more nuanced understanding of impact patterns. Today, it is understood that similarities exist in different patterns created by different forces. Where once it was thought that the small stains visible in a pattern were created by a high velocity force, today it is understood that the stains may also be the result of the instrument used or the volume of blood present. It is more accurate to refer to impact patterns as spatter resulting from a force (or an object) striking exposed blood, rather than in terms of velocity level. The size of a bloodstain is not information that lends itself to a definitive conclusion on its own.

There have been significant advancements in the discipline of bloodstain pattern analysis and the approach to all aspects of the field has greatly improved. Analysts are more acutely aware of the limitations of the discipline and take steps to provide an accurate and unbiased report. In an effort to quantify error rates and the effect of contextual bias on the conclusions of experienced BPA analysts, a 2014 grant study for the National Institute of Justice has, for the first time, produced baseline measures of reliability for the pattern recognition method used in bloodstain pattern analysis. These new measures focus on method reliability, instead of analyst competency.[18] The study consisted of over 730 bloodstain patterns being analyzed by a panel of experienced bloodstain pattern analysts, where:

> The type of pattern, extent of available pattern, the nature of the substrate and the type of contextual information were varied in a balanced experiment designed to determine the effect of these variables on pattern classification accuracy.[19]

Lawyers and analysts should familiarize themselves with the details of this study. In addition to quantifying the varying levels of accurate identifications between surface types and spatter patterns,[20] the report explains that some patterns were more reliably classified than others. Possible explanations were advanced, but the ultimate reason for differing levels of reliability in successfully classifying pattern types remains unclear.[21]

---

18 Terry Laber et al., *Reliability Assessment of Current Methods in Bloodstain Pattern Analysis* (Laurel, MD: National Institute of Justice, 2014), online: www.ncjrs.gov/pdffiles1/nij/grants/247180.pdf.

19 *Ibid.* at 2.

20 For instance, 13.1 percent of patterns identified on a rigid surface were determined incorrect. When the pattern was on a fabric surface, the rate of incorrect identifications jumped to 23.4 percent.

21 Laber et al., above note 18 at 68.

C. THE ROLE OF THE BLOODSTAIN PATTERN ANALYST IN CRIMINAL CASES

Experts who are called to testify can best serve the court by providing complete and unbiased opinions that relate only to the scope of their expertise. As they analyze the evidence, they will keep in mind that, ultimately, their opinion will be delivered in court. Their preparation must include presenting and explaining the evidence in an understandable, yet accurate, manner.

The investigating BPA analyst becomes involved when the initial crime scene investigator discovers bloodletting evidence. Their role begins with providing opinions to the police investigators prior to the laying of any charges. The opinion can be significant in supporting or undermining a suspect's explanation of events. The police may also want to use the BPA evidence as a tool during the interview process. For instance, where a homicide suspect claims that the death was a result of suicide, bloodstain pattern analysis will be very useful in determining whether the physical evidence is consistent with this explanation.

The BPA analyst working with the defence becomes involved much later. When there is significant blood evidence, even if the report appears complete, the defence may want an independent review. It is always possible that patterns were missed or errors made. Although the defence can interview the investigating BPA analyst, it may be wise to have questions answered and observations made by an independent analyst. A defence lawyer may gain confidence in addressing the evidence by asking even the most fundamental questions, leading to a better understanding of the bloodstain pattern reports.

1) The Significance of the Bloodstain Pattern Expert at Trial: Common Questions

Every case is unique. No matter how experienced the analyst, there is always some new twist on the physical evidence. That being said, however, there are some basic questions commonly asked of, and answered by, the BPA expert at trial:

1) *Given an impact pattern, where was the blow struck?*

   Provided a sufficient number of spatter stains, this question can be answered with a great deal of accuracy using mathematics for a three-dimensional area of origin or simple pattern analysis for a two-dimensional area of convergence.

2) *What was the minimum number of blows evident by the bloodstain patterns?*

Typically, at least one blow must be struck to get blood flowing and, therefore, the impact pattern will typically be created by the second blow. If the blood source does not move, it will not be possible to count the number of impact patterns (i.e., blows). When the blood source does move and is struck again, that would be counted as a second impact pattern. So there would typically be at least one more blow than there are impact patterns.

3) *What movement occurred by the persons involved in the bloodletting?*

Evidence of passive blood trails will provide information on the movement of a blood source (i.e., a person or persons). In addition, when a bloodied object comes into contact with a non-bloodied surface and then moves, it will leave a swipe pattern. If an existing blood pattern is altered, the swipe pattern will also show movement.

4) *What direction was a person moving while shedding blood?*

When a blood source is moving and is not in contact with the floor, it will leave a series of bloodstains known as a blood trail. The stains within that series of bloodstains will show directionality and give evidence of which direction the person was moving.

5) *Was there evidence of more than two people at the scene?*

In all cases, blood samples must be taken for DNA analysis. It may be that only one person was bleeding, however, it is quite possible that both the assailant and the victim were blood sources. Physical evidence, such as fingerprints and footwear, will provide valuable information. A void is an interruption in an otherwise continuous bloodstain pattern and may indicate the presence of a third person.

6) *Was there evidence of an object being involved during the bloodletting?*

When a bloodied object comes in contact with a non-bloodied surface, a transfer pattern will result. The transfer pattern may provide evidence supporting a determination of the type of object used during the bloodletting event.

7) *What was the position of the blood source during the bloodletting?*

With the proper quality data, impact pattern analysis can determine the precise location of a blood source. In addition, other patterns, such as drip patterns (blood dripping into itself), will indicate the position of the blood source.

8) *Was an artery cut?*

> When an artery is cut and the heart continues to beat, it will cause blood to "gush" out of the wound. It is possible to distinguish this pattern by the large volume stains that result.

While testifying, a bloodstain analyst must be prepared to answer questions on any given scenario. Bloodletting is often a very dynamic situation. Given specific patterns, the bloodstain analyst will determine the most likely course of events. Should an alternate theory exist, the analyst must be ready to put that theory in context and determine if it is viable or not.

2) Canadian Standards in Bloodstain Pattern Analysis

All Canadian bloodstain pattern analysts receive similar training, whether they are part of a national, provincial, or municipal police service.[22] This common background has contributed to the development of standards that will be followed by all members of the profession. The conclusions of the bloodstain pattern analyst will be in the form of a formal report. All photographs, notes, and raw data must be peer reviewed and made available as part of full disclosure. This report will often tie the physical evidence together to assist the court in developing a full understanding of a complicated crime scene. It is expected that each police service will have standard operating guidelines to ensure a credible work product.

D. A CASE STUDY

Paramedics responded to a call regarding an apparent heart attack victim. On arrival, the husband advised that his wife had collapsed and that she was now lying on their bed. The paramedics found her body on its side, with blood covering her mouth and nose. The husband answered questions regarding the blood by explaining that, when she fell, she struck a night table. Due to the unusual circumstances, police were called. They observed some blood evidence that may or may not have been associated with a fall. A bloodstain pattern analyst was called and attended the scene.

All bloodstains were confined to the bedroom. Although the body of the deceased had already been removed, her location was verified with a soak pattern where her head had been. In addition, several transfer stains were found on the bedding and further analysis discovered spatter on the wall

22 See Section B(2) in this chapter.

at the head of the bed and on a wall to the right side of the bed. The bloodstain pattern analyst recorded the transfer stains and concluded that these stains indicated movement of a blood source. The movement could have been caused either before or after the paramedics attended.

The spatter in this case was attributed to an impact. When the husband was questioned by police, he maintained that the spatter must have occurred when his wife collapsed and hit her face on the night stand. Further analysis confirmed a minimum of one blow, calculated to be in the position where the pillow on the right side of the bed was located.

This case went to preliminary hearing. The analyst explained the theory of bloodstain pattern analysis and went on to describe the precise area of origin of the blow, which was not consistent with the woman having struck her head on the night stand. After a short break, the defendant changed his plea and admitted guilt to manslaughter.

E. CONCLUSION

As a discipline, bloodstain pattern analysis continues to advance with continued research and improved techniques. As a crime scene analysis tool, it is no longer acceptable to overlook bloodstain pattern evidence. When investigators are met with a bloodletting scene, they will call upon the services of a bloodstain pattern analyst. Sometimes, what seems obvious is not, what seems trivial is crucial, and what seems beyond the reach of analysis is not.

One of the important goals of a qualified analyst is to educate. Analysts work to ensure that police services recognize the value of their evidence. Many analysts seek to instruct and thereby increase their ability to articulate the fundamental aspects of their discipline. As a community, analysts recognize that teaching provides a great way to learn.

Moving forward, it is important to inform those involved in the legal system of the value of bloodstain pattern evidence. Lawyers, whether Crown or defence, have a responsibility to study and understand scientific evidence. Without some knowledge of bloodstain pattern analysis, lawyers will be limited in their ability to question and cross-examine BPA experts. The Canadian system provides for well-qualified analysts; however, it is incumbent on the legal community to have a working knowledge of the discipline so that they will be better equipped to distinguish between experts with sufficient qualification and those without.

Each case provides a new set of circumstances and bloodstain pattern analysis has limitations. Not every case has sufficient detail to allow conclusions to be confidently drawn and analysts should be careful to avoid trying to prove their worth through speculation or over-stating the evidence. Every conclusion provided by the analyst must be supported by the evidence of the case as well as by scientific principles. The days of saying that the assailant was a tall, left-handed, angry man are over.

F. THE LEGAL CONTEXT

> Understanding how a particular bloodstain pattern occurred can be critical physical evidence, because it may help investigators understand the events of the crime. Bloodstain patterns occur in a multitude of crime types—homicide, sexual battery, burglary, hit-and-run accidents—and are commonly present. Bloodstain pattern analysis is employed in crime reconstruction or event reconstruction when a part of the crime scene requires interpretation of these patterns.
>
> However, many sources of variability arise with the production of bloodstain patterns, and their interpretation is not nearly as straightforward as the process implies . . . .[23]

According to the 2009 National Academy of Sciences (NAS) Report, bloodstain pattern analysis (BPA) opinions "are [generally] more subjective than scientific"[24] and targeted expert requests from both the prosecution and the defence can result in contextual bias. While aspects of BPA are supported by scientific studies, some experts provide opinions that go well beyond what can be scientifically supported.[25] With respect to BPA expert training and education, the report characterized the favouring of experience over basic scientific principles as "misguided, given the importance of rigorous and objective hypothesis testing and the complex nature of fluid dynamics."[26] Recent research following the 2009 NAS Report has addressed the need to strengthen the relationship between bloodstain pattern analysis and fluid dynamics,[27] and has also aimed to provide the

---

23 National Research Council, *Strengthening Forensic Science in the United States: A Path Forward* (Washington, DC: National Academies Press, 2009) at 177, online: www.ncjrs.gov/pdffiles1/nij/grants/228091.pdf.

24 *Ibid.* at 178.

25 *Ibid.* at 178–79.

26 *Ibid.* at 178.

27 See, for example, Daniel Attinger et al., "Fluid Dynamics Topics in Bloodstain Pattern Analysis: Comparative Review and Research Opportunities" (2013) 231 *Forensic Science International* 375.

BPA expert community with potentially promising tools to quantitatively differentiate between different types of bloodstains.[28]

Five years before the publication of the 2009 NAS Report, the defence argument in the *voir dire* of *R. v. Luciano*[29] foreshadowed concerns identified by the report when considering the qualification of a police officer as an expert witness in BPA. The defence argued that the officer was not a properly qualified expert, he did not follow proper collection and recording procedures, he lacked scientific training, his evidence was subjective and impressionistic, and the witness' service as a police officer impaired his impartiality as an expert.[30] The court found that the officer's evidence met the *Mohan* admissibility criteria[31] for expert evidence and that the officer was qualified to present BPA expert evidence.[32] The court stated outright: "This is not junk science."[33]

Taken together, the *Luciano voir dire* and the subsequent 2009 NAS Report support the idea that courts should accept bloodstain pattern analysis as an admissible form of expert evidence so long as the expert opinion is based on both the examiner's experience and a scientific foundation. Unfortunately, the exact methodology used by experts is not readily discernable by reviewing reported judgments. What can be discerned, however, is that blood droplet size, directionality, and velocity seem to be commonly used to arrive at "consistent with" conclusions—a term that has historically drawn a great deal of criticism. Alan Gold, for example, argues in his book on scientific expert evidence in criminal law that: "[e]vidence would be better given in terms of 'no discernible difference' or 'not inconsistent with'" to avoid overstating the confidence of the conclusion.[34]

Active and retired police officers are most commonly called to testify as experts in bloodstain pattern analysis, but forensic biologists trained in the discipline have also given such evidence in Canada.[35] To enhance

---

28 See, for example, Yuen Cho et al., "Quantitative Bloodstain Analysis: Differentiation of Contact Transfer Patterns Versus Spatter Patterns on Fabric via Microscopic Inspection" (2015) 249 *Forensic Science International* 233.

29 [2004] O.T.C. 1002 (S.C.J.) [*Luciano*].

30 *Ibid.* at para. 7.

31 See Chapter 3, Section C(2).

32 *Luciano*, above note 29 at paras. 21–23 and 30.

33 *Ibid.* at para. 30.

34 Alan D. Gold, *Expert Evidence in Criminal Law: The Scientific Approach*, 2d ed. (Toronto: Irwin Law, 2009) at 227.

35 See, for example, *R. v. Landell*, 2005 ONCJ 414.

the understanding of events surrounding the bloodletting incident, DNA analysis assists in determining the number of individuals present and the identity of the bleeders at various locations at the scene.

Although forensic pathologists and BPA experts may provide evidence in the same proceeding, the court found in *R. v. MacDonald*[36] that it is outside the scope of a proposed BPA expert's training and experience (a police officer in this case) to provide an opinion about the potential cause of a person's injuries or wounds; such evidence is therefore inadmissible.[37] In arriving at her decision, Anne S. Derrick J. cited *R. v. Smith*,[38] a case where a forensic identification expert testified to a trail of blood at the scene, but evidence of wound causation was admitted through the testimony of forensic pathologists.[39] Similarly, forensic pathologists can testify to arterial blood being under pressure in living persons and to this blood leaving the body with significant velocity upon the severing of the artery, but should not testify to whether this velocity is sufficient to cause the spatter seen in relation to the decedent's possible body position at the time. Such evidence should be given by a bloodstain pattern analysis expert.[40]

Similar to other disciplines in the forensic sciences, bloodstain pattern analysis evidence forms only one aspect of a larger body of evidence. In the context of this larger body of evidence, bloodstain pattern analysis evidence interacts with other types of evidence with the effect of:

1) Substantiating or refuting alibis, confessions, or differing accounts of events surrounding the bloodletting event;
2) Connecting items with the bloodletting event, including supporting the conclusion that a particular item was used as a weapon;
3) Sequencing the order of events that occurred at the scene where bloodletting occurred, with the help of DNA analysis;
4) Determining the position of the victim when the bloodletting injury occurred and evaluating the movements of the victim, in life and after death; and
5) Comparing the bloodstaining at the scene to the injuries described at autopsy.

---

36 2013 NSPC 109 [*MacDonald*].
37 *Ibid.* at paras. 73–74, 83 and 86.
38 2010 BCCA 35 [*Smith*].
39 *MacDonald,* above note 36 at para. 85. *Smith, ibid.* at paras. 14–23.
40 *R. v. Taylor*, 2001 BCSC 1025 at para. 15.

1) Criminal Cases Involving BPA Expert Evidence

In the trial judgment of *R. v. Langlet*,[41] Arnold-Bailey J. convicted Langlet of first-degree murder for the 2000 shooting death of Shayne Preece, who had been shot five times at close range, including three shots to the head. His body was discovered in the Jeep in which he was shot.[42] Although this case involved a variety of complex evidence, the Crown's case rested largely on the confessions Langlet made during the course of a Mr. Big sting in 2010. Without these inculpatory statements, Arnold-Bailey J. found that the Crown's case would not have passed the substantial likelihood of conviction test.[43] The defence did not call any witnesses except Langlet, who testified in his own defence and pointed to Matthew DaSilva as the true shooter. DaSilva had worked for Langlet on a drug line and, in 2009, approached police with the information that led them to conduct the undercover investigation targeting Langlet, during which time DaSilva was a paid agent for police.[44] The court found that DaSilva was with Langlet on the night of the murder.[45]

John Mellis was qualified as an expert in bloodstain pattern analysis and crime scene examination. He was called by the Crown.[46] Mellis could not comment on the sequencing of the shots because both the head of the deceased and the weapon could have been moving throughout the incident.[47] Justice Arnold-Bailey made the following findings based on the BPA evidence:

> Mr. Mellis impressed the Court as a highly skilled professional. Neither his expertise nor his analysis and conclusions regarding the blood stains in the interior of the Jeep were challenged. It is noteworthy that he carried out his investigations independent of the photographs or observations of [the primary investigator] Supt. Bouchard or the findings of [the forensic pathologist] Dr. Charlesworth, although he was advised of the location of the tooth fragments.

---

41 2013 BCSC 2274 [*Langlet*].

42 *Ibid.* at paras. 1 and 463.

43 *Ibid.* at para. 429. Justice E.A. Arnold-Bailey went on to say, "In the event that the Supreme Court of Canada were to decide that the Mr. Big technique was not permitted generally or set guidelines as to when such evidence ought not to be admitted that encompassed the circumstances of the present case, then Mr. Langlet would be entitled to an acquittal." (*Ibid.*) Subsequent to *R. v. Langlet*, the Supreme Court of Canada ruled in *R. v. Hart*, 2014 SCC 52, that confessions obtained during the course of Mr. Big stings are presumptively inadmissible unless the framework the court set out is met.

44 *Langlet*, *ibid.* at paras. 2–6.

45 *Ibid.* at para. 460.

46 See *ibid.* at paras. 122–31 for a thorough review of his evidence.

47 *Ibid.* at para. 129.

> I accept Mr. Mellis's evidence that based on the blood stains and brain material located inside the Jeep, there were indications of four shots being fired. On that evidence I find that the driver's door was closed at the time shots were fired and the driver's side rear door was open when some of the shots were fired in the rear of the Jeep. The passenger side rear door was closed. The deceased was shot once, possibly twice in the head in the central area near the driver's headrest when the deceased was in close proximity to the top right side of the driver's seat. While the deceased was in the back seat he probably sustained multiple shots, but at least one, with the direction of travel for the blood stains being primarily left to right, but not necessarily through the open rear driver's side door. Mr. Mellis's final opinion regarding the [shooter's] arm needing to be "about five feet long" [to reach into the vehicle, angle the gun, and fire it] and that nothing is impossible was, I find, a glib and inaccurate statement that I do not accept.[48]

The bloodstain pattern analysis evidence contributed to corroborating Langlet's confession that he shot Preece "in the face, in the head,"[49] that Preece was sitting in the passenger seat,[50] that he shot Preece a couple of times before Preece "squirmed into the back,"[51] and that he had shot Preece as Preece moved inside the car by reaching his hand into the Jeep's open window.[52]

In the case of the "Surrey Six"—an execution-style shooting of six men—Cody Rae Haevischer and Matthew James Johnston were charged with six counts of first-degree murder and one count of conspiracy to commit murder.[53] Both men were found guilty as charged.[54] The case itself is complex and, among other evidence, involved the testimony of a bloodstain pattern analyst whose evidence about the lack of the victims' movement at the scene ultimately supported the finding that the men were shot while lying on the floor defenceless.[55]

The first-degree murder trial of *R. v. Newman*[56] involved bloodstain pattern evidence that also spoke to the movements of the deceased and, with DNA analysis evidence, provided support for Ehrcke J. to reject Michael Newman's

48 *Ibid.* at paras. 130–31.
49 *Ibid.* at para. 450.
50 *Ibid.* at para. 441.
51 *Ibid.* at paras. 440 and 452.
52 *Ibid.* at para. 453.
53 *R. v. Haevischer,* 2014 BCSC 1863 at paras. 1–2.
54 *Ibid.* at para. 728.
55 *Ibid.* at paras. 41–42.
56 2013 BCSC 592. The conclusions of the BPA expert can be found at para. 95.

testimony that a struggle did not occur between Newman and the deceased, Marc Rozen.[57] Interestingly, the trial judge's finding that Rozen was confined at least three times rested in large part on the BPA evidence.[58] The semi-circular stains on the deadbolt knob on the front door were, according to the BPA expert, representative of a turning motion and, along with the presence of expirated blood from the nose or mouth next to the front door,[59] satisfied the trial judge that Rozen's attempt to leave the apartment through the front door was prevented by Newman.[60] The BPA evidence of a blood-soaked cushion and a bloodstain on the front of a chair found overturned at the scene, considered with the autopsy evidence, satisfied the trial judge that Rozen was again confined, as he was forced to sit in the chair while bleeding onto the chair and its cushions from stab wounds to his inner thighs.[61] Other evidence addressed the downward trajectory of the close-range shot to the back of Rozen's head, supporting the judge's third finding that Rozen was unlawfully confined when shot.[62] The trial judge found that the Crown proved all of the elements of first-degree murder and, accordingly, convicted Newman.[63] On appeal, the court substituted a second-degree murder conviction on the basis that only the first incident of confinement could be supported by the evidence and the confinement was coextensive with the acts causing death. Justice of Appeal Smith dissented and concluded that the first-degree conviction should be upheld because the confinement "was not integral to or consumed by the act of shooting Mr. Rozen in the back of the head."[64] The Supreme Court of Canada reinstated the first-degree murder conviction.[65]

Although BPA evidence may assist in determining the movements of the victim near the time of bloodletting and in supporting the identification of a weapon, the findings of a bloodstain pattern analyst may be consistent with more than one explanation. In some cases, it is not possible to determine the sequence of events at a scene.[66] For example, in the second-degree murder trial of *R. v. Hurtado*,[67] the bloodstain pattern expert called by the

57 *Ibid.* at paras. 267–68, 292 and 304–307.
58 *Ibid.* at para. 347.
59 *Ibid.* at para. 92.
60 *Ibid.* at para. 347.
61 *Ibid.* at para. 348.
62 *Ibid.* at para. 349.
63 *Ibid.* at para. 351.
64 *R. v. Newman*, 2015 BCCA 237 at para. 112.
65 *R. v. Newman*, 2016 SCC 7.
66 See, for example, *R. v. Florence*, 2014 BCCA 288 at para. 72.
67 2009 BCSC 1891.

Crown agreed that any number of scenarios beyond the one suggested by the Crown could explain the bloodstain pattern evidence present in the cell in which Victor Hurtado, an inmate, beat his cellmate, Mr. Parker, to the point where he later died.[68] Hurtado's defence relied primarily on self-defence. Based on the available evidence, Silverman J. found the following facts: the deceased struck the first blow,[69] Hurtado struck the deceased "no less than two and possibly as many as five" times,[70] at least some of those blows involved the use of chairs inside the cell, and the victim could have been continuing to struggle after sustaining head injuries.[71] These findings were based, in part, on the BPA evidence relating to the chairs:

> The bloodstain expert found two chairs stacked one on top of the other in the cell. They are heavy, approximately ten pounds each. He described, through photographs, the finding of blood stains in various places around the cell and on the chairs. On the chairs, he described hair transfer stains and opined that there were at least two of them, suggesting that Mr. Parker's head, with an open blood source either on the chair or on the hair, came into contact with that chair on two occasions. There are blood stains indicating manual handling of the arms of the chairs, and there are stains consistent with the rapid movement of the chairs with blood on them on at least two occasions.
>
> The bloodstain expert expressed the opinion that the chair had been used for at least two medium-velocity impacts delivered to a passive blood source. That passive blood source was already bleeding at the time of the impacts, at or very near to the floor level, and at the time of the impacts was not moving or, if moving, moving very little.[72]

Based upon the available evidence heard by the trial judge, Hurtado was found guilty of manslaughter but not guilty of second-degree murder.[73]

The case of *R. v. Bhullar*[74] serves as an interesting example of disclosure and subjectivity issues relating to bloodstain pattern analysis evidence. Bhullar was convicted of the second-degree murder of his adopted nephew, who was stabbed to death in 2004.[75] Approximately a week after the victim

68 *Ibid.* at para. 32.
69 *Ibid.* at para. 60.
70 *Ibid.*
71 *Ibid.*
72 *Ibid.* at paras. 25–26.
73 *Ibid.* at para. 82.
74 2011 BCCA 395 [*Bhullar*].
75 *Ibid.* at para. 4.

was found dead in the family home, the police executed a search warrant of Bhullar's workplace, a hair salon. The police found a plastic bag concealed in the ceiling that contained a pair of bloodied blue jeans and a red fleece jacket appearing to have diluted bloodstains.[76] The blood on the jeans matched the deceased's DNA. Further, the night before the discovery of the deceased, Bhullar was seen on surveillance video wearing a jacket similar to the one in the bag.[77] The issue before the jury at trial with respect to this evidence was determining whether the clothes were Bhullar's, who had testified that the clothes were not his.[78] A police officer provided opinion evidence about the bloodstain patterns apparent at the family home and on the clothing, opining that the diluted stains on the jacket were consistent with washing. Bhullar was convicted of second-degree murder.

The defence appealed Bhullar's conviction on two grounds, where one of the grounds requested the ordering of a new trial since the Crown failed to disclose the concerns of a senior RCMP officer who called into question the reliability of the opinion evidence that the diluted stains were consistent with washing:[79]

> The second ground of appeal arises out of the evidence of a police officer who provided expert evidence with respect to various bloodstains that were found at the residence and on the clothing that was located in the bag at the salon. His expert report noted that the fleece jacket had a number of diluted blood stains on it, and gave the opinion that this was "consistent with washing the garment."
>
> Prior to the trial in this case, as a result of unsatisfactory expert evidence with respect to blood spatter in another case, the R.C.M.P. conducted a review of a number of its files including this one. The senior officer who conducted the review was concerned about the conclusion that the fleece jacket had been washed. He noted that while there were stains on the jacket that appeared to be diluted, there was also a stain that did not share that characteristic. In the result, he was of the view that the conclusion that the jacket had been washed was "far too subjective." He considered that there were many other possible explanations for the dilution of the stains and that the conclusion should be removed from the report.
>
> Unfortunately, the senior officer's concerns do not appear to have been conveyed to the officer who gave the evidence, or to the Crown. As

76 *Ibid.* at para. 8.
77 *Ibid.* at para. 9.
78 *Ibid.* at para. 53.
79 *Ibid.* at para. 2.

a result, the questionable conclusion remained in the report, and the defence was unaware until after the trial that concerns with respect to that conclusion had been identified.[80]

The defence argued that the disclosure failure violated the Crown's *Stinchcombe*[81] disclosure obligations, rendering the trial unfair.[82] The Crown conceded that the inadvertent disclosure error violated Bhullar's *Charter* right to disclosure.[83] Justice Groberman considered the error as one of the "imperfections in the process"[84] of this case but found it did not put the verdict into doubt for two reasons: (1) the evidence of the officer who took the clothing out of the bag supported the expert opinion evidence that the jacket was washed since he noticed the jacket was damp and had a "detergenty sort of smell to it";[85] and (2) evidence relating to an attempt to wash the jacket would not have assisted the jury in determining the issue before it; specifically, whether the clothing indeed belonged to the appellant.[86] Justice Groberman recognized that, in other cases, evidence of washing bloodstains from clothing may be powerful but, in this case, such evidence "was of marginal relevance."[87]

With respect to the RCMP internal investigation mentioned by the court in *Bhullar*, it seems that the court is likely referring to the internal investigation into the bloodstain pattern analysis work of retired Staff Sgt. Ross Spenard, who was accused of lying in 2009 when he provided BPA evidence in the murder trial of *R. v. Charlie Rae Lincoln*.[88] During the trial, other experts found that his report in the case was "not scientifically sound"; the jury was directed to ignore all of Spenard's evidence, which was characterized by Justice Truscott as being "completely tainted and without any value whatsoever." Justice Truscott also stated that this is "the perfect example of a person who clearly lied under oath, and violated his oath to tell the truth."[89] The Crown's filing of a complaint in 2009

80 *Ibid.* at paras. 43–45.
81 *R. v. Stinchcombe*, [1991] 3 S.C.R. 326.
82 *Bhullar*, above note 74 at para. 46.
83 *Ibid.* at para. 47.
84 *Ibid.* at para. 3.
85 *Ibid.* at paras. 51–52.
86 *Ibid.* at para. 53.
87 *Ibid.* at para. 55.
88 "Retired RCMP Expert Charged with Perjury during Murder Trial" *The Globe and Mail* (11 January 2011), online: www.theglobeandmail.com/news/british-columbia/retired-rcmp-expert-charged-with-perjury-during-murder-trial/article561348.
89 Kim Bolan, "Retired RCMP Officer Faces Perjury Charge over Murder Trial Testimony" *The Vancouver Sun* (11 January 2011), online: www.vancouversun.com/touch/

with the Vancouver Police Department initiated a criminal investigation, which resulted in Spenard being charged with perjury in 2011.[90] The RCMP review of all of Spenard's files revealed "no significant concerns."[91] In 2011, Spenard pled guilty to perjury and received a nine-month conditional sentence.[92]

Defence lawyers seeking to capitalize on the 2009 NAS Report's conclusions by arguing that a BPA expert retained by the Crown may be presenting subjective and biased evidence must be prepared for the Crown to raise the same argument, requiring the defence to similarly disclose the case materials provided to the expert. In the case of *R. v. Wiens*,[93] the Crown sought an order to compel the disclosure of material that the defence expert relied upon to form his opinion.[94] This was done after the defence challenged the opinion evidence of the expert called by the Crown, but prior to cross-examination of the expert. The defence argued that the expert's knowledge of the investigative theory (that Wiens placed a knife in the deceased's hand after death to bolster his self-defence claim) improperly influenced the expert. The expert called by the Crown had found that it was unlikely that the deceased had a knife in her hand prior to death.[95] This finding was in direct opposition to that of the expert called by the defence, who concluded that no evidence existed to support the theory that a knife was placed in the deceased's hand after death.[96] In response to the Crown seeking a disclosure order, the defence argued that the materials provided to the expert they called were subject to solicitor–client privilege.[97] Justice Barrow found that disclosing the materials to

---

Retired+RCMP+officer+faces+perjury+charge+over+murder+trial+testimony/4092939/story.html?rel=4167390.

90 "The Case of Roberta Marlene Lincoln" *CBC News*, online: www.cbc.ca/missingandmurdered/mmiw/profile/roberta-marlene-lincoln.

91 Wendy Stueck, "Former RCMP Officer Is Charged with Perjury" *The Globe and Mail* (11 January 2011), online: www.theglobeandmail.com/news/british-columbia/former-rcmp-officer-is-charged-with-perjury/article561420.

92 Keith Fraser, "Rare perjury charge sticks to retired RCMP trial expert" *Vancouver Province* (26 July 2011), online: www.bcpolicecomplaints.org/rcmp_staff_sgt_ross_spenard_lies_under_oath.html.

93 2013 BCSC 1539.

94 *Ibid.* at para. 1.

95 *Ibid.* at para. 3.

96 *Ibid.* at para. 5.

97 *Ibid.* at para. 14.

the Crown was necessary and, although he redacted portions of the documents, the balance of the materials was ordered to be disclosed,[98] stating:

> There is a further reason which, in my view, justifies compelling disclosure of this material. The witness [called by the defence] testified about the possibility of bias infecting an expert's opinion if the expert is provided with "preconceived theories" about the case before reaching his or her opinion. It is a reasonable inference to be drawn from his evidence that the opinions advanced by the Crown's bloodstain splatter expert, having been formed after she knew of the police theory of the case, were infected by that very bias. It seems to me that it would be unfair if the defence expert was provided with "preconceived theories," which he read before reaching his opinion, and yet that information would be withheld from the jury. In addition, the Crown would be unable to explore one of the factual underpinnings of his opinion and unable to question him regarding the very circumstances that formed the basis of one of his criticisms of the Crown expert. Thus, either as a matter of general principle or on the basis of the more narrow circumstances which obtain in this case, in my view, disclosure of the synopsis is not precluded on the basis of solicitor-client privilege or work privilege.
>
> . . .
>
> Finally, and of note, the portions of the synopsis that I did order disclosed contained a summary of the accused's version of the events from the moment of the infliction of the gunshot wound until the deceased came to rest on the floor of the master bedroom. That version of events has a number of similarities to the eventual opinion offered by Mr. Slemko [the expert called by the defence]. The jury was aware of that version of events because they had heard it from the accused who testified. What they did not know was whether Mr. Slemko was aware of that version of the events prior to formulating his opinions. It seems to me that the jury was entitled to be aware of that circumstance in order that they might fairly evaluate his evidence.[99]

2) Summary

The above cases represent only a sliver of how BPA expert evidence has been relied upon in court. Although the depth of the scientific underpinnings

---

98 *Ibid.* at para. 1.
99 *Ibid.* at paras. 15 and 18.

of the conclusions reached through bloodstain pattern analysis is not clear in many of the decisions discussed above, the caselaw does at least illustrate how this type of evidence can be useful in reconstructing events at the scene of a bloodletting incident. Further, the caselaw shows a developing concern among Canadian lawyers—Crown and defence alike—that this type of evidence can indeed be influenced by subjectivity and bias. As ongoing research focuses on developing quantitative tools for this discipline, it is hoped that counsel will similarly expand upon their own advocacy skills to critically analyze the discipline as it invariably becomes more complex and scientifically grounded.

CHAPTER 7

Digital Evidence

Steven L. Rogers

LEGAL CONTEXT: DANIEL M. SCANLAN

A. OVERVIEW OF THE DISCIPLINE: DIGITAL EVIDENCE

The use of computers to commit a criminal offence or to aid in the commission of an offence is not new, having been first addressed by changes to the *Criminal Code*[1] and the *Canada Evidence Act*[2] in 1983.[3] Initially, the response of Canadian law enforcement to the increase in offences involving computers was challenged by the lack of commercially available forensic software. Canadian law enforcement agencies responded to the problem using whatever knowledge, skill, and software was available to them. The most critical issue and challenging aspect of performing a computer forensic analysis was the inability to properly preserve the evidence to enable the subsequent analysis. The mere act of reviewing the data may alter it.

In the mid-1980s, Canadian law enforcement authorities created the first centralized computer forensics laboratory at the RCMP "P" Directorate in Ottawa and, with civilian member Gord Hama, developed their own suite of forensics software. This software was known by various names, including "Hama Utils," "RCMP Utilities," and "Gord's Utilities." Through this work, Hama became recognized as the leading pioneer in

1 *Criminal Code*, R.S.C. 1985, c. C-46.

2 *Canada Evidence Act*, R.S.C. 1985, c. C-5.

3 Marilyn Pilon & Monique Hébert, *Computer Crime* (Ottawa: Parliamentary Research Branch, Library of Parliament, 1984, revised 1991), online: publications.gc.ca/collections/collection_2008/lop-bdp/bp/bp87-e.pdf.

the development of forensic utilities for digital forensics. At the suggestion of other members of the RCMP, the RCMP Utilities were eventually offered as "take aways" for domestic and international law enforcement agencies during computer forensics training sessions at the Canadian Police College. The utilities were initially shared with the United States, the United Kingdom, Australia, and New Zealand. Later, they were shared across Europe and South America, as well as other countries. To maintain its position as a leader in computer forensics and cybercrime training, the Canadian Police College established the Technological Crime Learning Institute, which continues to provide a variety of Computer Forensic courses, teaching forensic techniques as well as the use of commercial forensic software to the Canadian and international policing community.

One of the first commercially available disk duplication software programs, Safeback, was developed in 1990 by Sydex in the United States.[4] Other commercially available forensic software began to evolve and, in the early 1990s, Andrew Rosen, ASR Data Acquisition and Analysis, and others began the development of Expert Witness.[5] Rosen, among others, subsequently provided computer forensics training at the Canadian Police College that included how to use the Expert Witness forensic software.

In the mid-1990s, the computer forensic software EnCase by Guidance Software became commercially available and was quickly embroiled in litigation with ASR Data.[6] Although ASR Data continues to provide forensic software and related services to law enforcement and private investigators, Guidance Software rose to become the world leader in the field.

Early computer forensic investigations typically included the examination of comparatively small hard drives,[7] usually still inside the computer,[8] and removable storage devices such as diskettes, floppy disks, jazz,

---

4 George Mohay et al., *Computer and Intrusion Forensics* (Norwood: Artech House, 2003) at 115–16. See also Mark Pollitt, "A History of Digital Forensics" in Kam-Pui Chow & Sujeet Shenoi, eds., *Advances in Digital Forensics VI: Sixth IFIP WG 11.9 International Conference on Digital Forensics, Hong Kong, China, January 4–6, 2010, Revised Selected Papers* (New York: Springer-Verlag Berlin Heidelberg, 2010) 3 at 7, online: www.springer.com/us/book/9783642155055.

5 ASR Data Acquisition & Analysis, online: www.asrdata.com/about-us.

6 *ASR Data Acquisition & Analysis LLC v. Guidance Software Inc.*, AAA Case No. 72 117 01269 98 (L.A. American Arbitration Association Commercial Tribunal 1999), online: www.asrdata.com/wp-content/themes/asr/pdf/ruling.pdf.

7 As compared to the capacity of today's hard drives and often referred to as "memory" but more accurately described as permanent storage or non-volatile memory.

8 Often referred to as the CPU by the public and legal community, which is not correct. The CPU is the central processing unit—essentially, the brains of the computer.

Bernoulli, and zip disks.[9] These removable storage devices, although still encountered during investigations, have since been replaced by more advanced technologies such as USB drives, which serve the same removable storage purpose but are significantly faster, easier to use, and have much greater storage capacity.

After the attacks on the World Trade Center in 2001, Mark Pollitt of the FBI contacted Tom Pownall of the RCMP and requested an update to the RCMP Utilities to assist them with the analysis of data seized after the attacks, since the current commercially available software was not able to meet their needs. An update was shipped to the FBI about four days later. In the following years, development of the RCMP Utilities was discontinued and they were replaced by commercially available software with advanced capabilities. In the mid-1990s, the RCMP began to decentralize Computer Forensic services. One of the first regional laboratories was established at "O" Division headquarters in London, Ontario. Other policing partners, such as the Hamilton Police Service, the Toronto Police Service, the Ontario Provincial Police, and the Waterloo Regional Police attended the RCMP lab in London to observe operations and, in some cases, to mentor the RCMP forensics investigators.

Law enforcement in the United States also responded to the emerging need for computer forensic software:

> [S]ome of the key individuals were Mike Anderson, Danny Mares and Andy Fried from the IRS; Ron Peters and Jack Lewis from the U.S. Secret Service; Jim Christy and Karen Matthews from the Department of Defense; [and] Tom Seipert, Roland Lascola and Sandy Mapstone from local U.S. law enforcement agencies.[10]

Cross border law enforcement meetings eventually led the Canadian and U.S. law enforcement communities to realize they were undertaking the same challenge with forensic software development and they began to share utilities.

Today, continued advancement in computer, storage, and mobile technologies, including those driving the Internet (i.e., e-commerce, discussion forums, social media, online email, and file storage services), have changed the way we think about remote data storage by introducing the term cloud

9 Jazz disks and Bernoulli disks are similar to floppy disks, but larger and with greater storage capacity.

10 Pollitt, "A History of Digital Forensics," above note 4 at 6.

storage. These ever-changing advancements challenge computer forensic investigators to stay ahead of rapidly evolving technology in a global environment that increasingly relies upon computing devices in the course of daily life. For this reason, digital evidence may be helpful to the court in a variety of cases, including those involving charges related to drugs, proceeds of crime, fraud, murder, and counterfeit.

B. THE SCIENCE OF DIGITAL FORENSICS

The term "digital forensics" is used interchangeably with computer forensics, although digital forensics is becoming more widely used because it is more descriptive of the evidence being examined.[11] Digital forensics can be defined as the methodical acquisition, authentication, reconstruction, and examination of digital media using computer software, hardware, and analytical techniques for the purpose of presenting digital evidence in a judicial or quasi-judicial proceeding. This definition, highlighting the forensic examiners' role of presenting non-partisan *viva voce* evidence replaces earlier definitions that may have promoted a forensic examination with a predetermined assumption of guilt.[12] The role of the forensic examiner expert witness is to provide assistance to the court based on the available evidence, not to advocate for either the Crown or the defence.

The science of digital evidence can be described as consisting of two basic components: (1) preservation, and (2) analysis. In preparation for conducting their work, forensic investigators must consider the complexities encompassed in the basic components of the case, such as the unique set of circumstances surrounding the offence alleged, the method of its execution, and the environment in which it was committed. Each of these will impact the preservation and analysis of the data.

The preservation and analysis of digital evidence reflects a scientific approach—a structured, methodical, repeatable approach—to solving a digital question. Specifically, "who is responsible for performing some digital action on the subject media and what is the resulting output?" The scientific process used to solve this question evolved from individual

---

11 In the age of online data storage, including cloud computing, digital evidence does not necessarily exist within a computer. A related field is "IT Forensics," which focuses on a networked environment and deals with a current or previous breach of network security.

12 Eoghan Casey, *Digital Evidence and Computer Crime* (San Diego: Academic Press, 2000) at 1.

investigative efforts to organizational efforts. For example, the Association of Chief Police Officers (ACPO) Computer Crime Working Group produced the first practice guidelines for searching, seizing, and examining computer evidence.[13] The *Good Practice Guide for Computer-Based Electronic Evidence* is now in its fourth version and is accessible online.[14] The United States Department of Homeland Security, the United States Secret Service, the International Association of Chiefs of Police Advisory Committee for Police Investigative Operations, and the U.S. National Institute of Justice have also produced documents addressing the best practices of seizing and analyzing electronic evidence.[15,16]

Digital evidence is sometimes described as "physical evidence,"[17] but it should not be confused with something physical that can be touched.[18] Indeed, the *Canada Evidence Act* does not use the words "physical" or "digital" to describe computer-based evidence, opting instead for the term "electronic." In a publication by the U.S. National Institute of Justice on Electronic Crime Scene Investigation, digital evidence is identified as "latent, like fingerprints or DNA evidence."[19]

1) The Anatomy of Digital Evidence

The various forms of digital evidence can generally be classified as binary information (data). The process or technology of storing data is complex, beyond the scope of this book, and of no evidentiary value in the legal

---

13 Mark Pollitt, "Report on Digital Evidence" (Paper delivered at the 13th INTERPOL Forensic Science Symposium, Lyon, France, 16–19 October 2001) at 2, online: citeseerx.ist.psu.edu/viewdoc/download?doi=10.1.1.304.8748&rep=rep1&type=pdf.

14 Association of Chief Police Officers, "Good Practice Guide for Computer-Based Electronic Evidence," online: www.cps.gov.uk/legal/assets/uploads/files/ACPO_guidelines_computer_evidence%5B1%5D.pdf.

15 International Association of Chiefs of Police Advisory Committee Working Group, "Best Practices for Seizing Electronic Evidence, Version 2.0," online: www.hsdl.org/?view&did=1828; National Institute of Justice, "Electronic Crime Scene Investigation: A Guide for First Responders, Second Edition," (April 2008), online: www.ncjrs.gov/pdffiles1/nij/219941.pdf [NIJ, "E-CSI Guide for First Responders"].

16 National Institute of Justice, "Forensic Examination of Digital Evidence: A Guide to Law Enforcement" (April 2004), online: www.ncjrs.gov/pdffiles1/nij/199408.pdf.

17 Casey, above note 12 at 4.

18 Unless the digital evidence has been printed to paper.

19 NIJ, "E-CSI Guide for First Responders," above note 15 at ix.

profession,[20] but includes technology types such as non-volatile[21] NAND,[22] or NOR flash[23] memory found in solid state drives,[24] as well as electromagnetic storage used on hard drives. There is also volatile random access memory,[25] found in many computing devices, including laptops, work stations, and servers.

Since computers can only understand numbers (specifically, binary code, 1s and 0s), the numbers need to be stored in a form that computer applications can understand and then translate to display in a human-readable format. The data that is written to a storage device will follow a common character coding format, such as ASCII or Unicode. A series of eight digits, or bits, is called a "byte." A byte is the smallest collection of bits that will display on-screen in a human-readable format. In human-readable format, a byte will display as a single character or digit.

There are two basic sources of data on a storage device: (1) a program or application, such as Microsoft Word; and (2) the output generated by that application. The application may become digital evidence but, more often, it is the output from the application that becomes digital evidence. For instance, in an investigation into child pornography, the forensics investigator may discover the software application µTorrent installed on the computer hard drive. It is not an offence to possess a copy of µTorrent, but it is evidence of the ability to access and distribute child pornography since µTorrent is a software application for peer-to-peer file sharing, which is used to distribute large amounts of data over the Internet. Further investigation is required to determine whether child pornography was actually made available. The copy of µTorrent may contain evidence of these actions.

---

20 This statement is from the author's point of view, which may change over time.

21 The term "non-volatile" means that the data is not lost when power is removed from the storage device. Conversely, data in "volatile" storage is lost when power is removed.

22 Developed by Toshiba in 1987. See, generally, Toshiba's website for further information, online: flash25.toshiba.com.

23 Developed by Intel in 1988. Intel, News Release, "Intel Discloses New NOR Flash Memory Technologies, Sets Stage for 2005" (2 March 2005), online: www.intel.com/pressroom/archive/releases/2005/20050302net_a.htm.

24 Neal Ekker, Tom Coughlin, & Jim Handy, "Solid State Storage 101: An Introduction to Solid State Storage" (January 2009), online: www.snia.org/sites/default/files/SSS%20101%20Wht%20Paper%20Final.pdf.

25 "RAM," designed and built at the University of Manchester in 1948. In 1951, RAM was developed into a RAM chip by Jay Wright Forrester. See, generally, Gregory McNamee, "The Invention of Memory (Random Access Memory, That Is)" (11 May 2011), *Encyclopædia Brittanica Blog*, online: blogs.britannica.com/2011/05/invention-memory-random-access-memory.

There are three basic types of data output from applications: (1) user-created content, which is content that a user creates and saves as their "work product"; (2) application-generated content, which is content that an application generates automatically, sometimes unknown to the user, and which may contain user-created content; and (3) system-generated content, which is similar to application-generated content in that the user has little control over what output the system generates. The output generated by users, applications, and systems can be complex and takes on many different forms and functions. For example, it may be a simple string of user-generated text in an email message or it may be an application-generated encoded date and time stamp of when someone visited a website, or it may be a password protected, encrypted file containing many additional records. The objective of the digital forensics investigator is to discover what is hidden and to make the complex simple so that it can be understood by other investigators and members of the court.

Digital evidence cannot be "seen" without the use of computer software[26] and it cannot be physically delivered to someone as a string of bytes without first placing those bytes onto a storage device that is used as the medium of storage and transport.[27] Non-volatile storage devices include laptop hard drives, USB drives, camera SD cards, and DVD discs. Since volatile memory, known as random access memory or RAM, is lost when the computer is turned off, preservation must take place while the computer is still running. Forensic software to capture RAM has been developed in the last several years, providing the forensic examiner with a new source of digital evidence. Important information can be extracted from volatile memory, such as passwords, documents, and pictures. It will also provide the forensic examiner with a list of running processes, which may assist with determining if a virus or other malware was running at the time the RAM was preserved.

To read the digital evidence, a storage device must be connected to a computer so that it can be read and interpreted by a software designed to display it in a human-readable format. The storage device is physical evidence that can be seen, touched, and recorded for continuity of evidence purposes. Although the storage device (and the computer in which it is

---

26 Digital evidence does not necessarily have to be extracted with forensic software.

27 Transport here refers to physical transport of the storage device. Electronic transport of data would take place over cable or wire. Data electronically transported would be captured on a storage device for later analysis.

found) is sometimes referred to as the "digital evidence," it is only the medium that stores the digital evidence.

The identification, preservation, acquisition, analysis, and reporting of digital evidence has been in existence for decades. Banks and other businesses traditionally disclosed digital evidence by producing the output to paper and attaching an affidavit attesting to its authenticity.[28] The *Criminal Code of Canada* contemplates the acceptance of digital evidence in the form of printed output as "best evidence" during the execution of search warrants,[29] giving law enforcement a means of seizing evidence without having to seize the storage device or copy its entire contents. Although banks and other approved businesses continue to provide digital evidence in the form of printed output with an affidavit attesting to its authenticity attached, forensic investigators in law enforcement and private investigation agencies are much less inclined to print the digital evidence seized under judicial authorization. Important digital evidence, such as file attributes and metadata, is lost when digital evidence is printed to paper.[30]

The review of digital evidence cannot be rushed. It is simply not possible to perform an adequate on-site examination[31] of digital evidence seized with judicial authorization, in part because it cannot be assumed that all questions about the documents and data are known in advance. Establishing "the integrity of the electronic documents system by or in which the electronic document was recorded or stored"[32] is generally very difficult to achieve during the course of executing a search warrant, especially if there are multiple storage devices or other complicating factors.[33] Many questions could arise concerning a document's creation date, author, or location found. It may also be important to address whether the document has been copied or modified. The answers to these questions would be lost if the storage device is not seized. The digital evidence examiner will need time to properly research and record the information about each document and this may not be possible on-site.

---

28 *Canada Evidence Act*, above note 2, s. 30(1).

29 *Criminal Code*, above note 1, s. 487(2.1).

30 Metadata is data about data. For example, metadata may be the date, time, and GPS coordinates of a photograph, which are contained within the digital photograph they describe. This evidence can be preserved through separate effort.

31 See Section B(3), below in this chapter, for an explanation of the process of on-site review of computer data.

32 *Canada Evidence Act*, above note 2, s. 31.2(1)(a).

33 Other complicating factors may include multiple users of a single system, open access to a system, and use of anti-forensic tools.

2) The Identification of Digital Evidence

The identification of digital evidence typically applies to situations involving: (1) seizures with judicial authorization, (2) street checks, (3) random Canada Border Services Agency (CBSA) checks, (4) prisoner processing, and (5) voluntary productions of evidence. During the execution of a search warrant, the initial step in the identification process usually involves the common practice of making a drawing of the floor plan of the premises and then a map of the storage devices that are easily identifiable. In all cases, it is the investigator's responsibility to record the specifics of where the storage devices were located.

The identification of storage devices or other sources of digital evidence can be challenging. Identifying a 3.5″ hard drive may be simple, but identifying all available bluetooth and USB devices as possible sources of digital evidence is not. Once identified, a decision must be made whether to triage the computer or storage device on-site, or to seize it for examination at a later date.

During the execution of a search warrant, it is common to first identify computers that are still operating. A decision will need to be made on the likelihood of remote access being obtained and the potential for destructive activity being undertaken by the individual under investigation or a third party. If the computer is a stand-alone system with no access to a network (by connecting to a router or a smartphone hotspot or having a smartphone connected to the computer), then there is no danger of remote access and the system can remain running[34] until such time as investigators can give it their full attention. If the assessment is that the computer is at risk of remote access, removal of the source of the remote access is required. Typically, this would mean disconnecting it from a wired network or turning off the wireless network connection. Shutting down the computer may also be necessary. Once remote access has been prevented, disabled, or terminated, there is no further danger to the data from remote access intrusion.

Another potential source of destruction of data is the helpful home owner, defendant, or bystander who just wants to check their email one last time or just wants to help with shutting the computer off. It is a long-standing protocol to deny anyone access to a computer, especially during the execution of a search warrant or Anton Piller order; however, it

34 Other factors specific to the investigation could impact the decision to permit a computer to remain running.

is not possible to know everything about all computers, storage devices, networks, applications, and programs. The *Criminal Code* contemplated this shortcoming and provides law enforcement with a mechanism to receive assistance: the preservation demand.[35] Although this provision of the *Criminal Code* is not limited to digital evidence, a production order may be of benefit to the forensic investigator where the data of interest resides on a complex network not easily accessed by the investigator. Additionally, computer systems that cannot be taken "off line" for examination may require the assistance of a network administrator to identify and copy the data of interest.

3) Triaging a Computer

Triaging a computer or storage device involves conducting a preliminary review of the digital evidence with the objective of identifying the presence or absence of content relevant to the investigation underway. Usually, this is completed on the strength of judicial authorization or with the consent of the owner. A triage, however, is not always performed and, when it is, the process is not exhaustive or comprehensive. The specific circumstances of the investigative environment, the type of investigation, the type of evidence sought, the computing devices found, and the specific requirements of any judicial authorization all play a role in determining the need, ability, and legal capacity to triage a computer. An examination might include searching the device's Internet history and reviewing image files, videos, and user-created text files (e.g., Microsoft Word documents, Excel spreadsheets, and Adobe PDF documents). The nature of the alleged crime will indicate the types of documents that will be a focus of the search.

If the computer is running, then it is typically left running and the investigator explores its contents using the resources available, such as the computer's operating system and installed programs, connected printers, and external data sources (ex., cloud storage, online e-mail, etc.). A triage review of a live system will change or add evidentiary artifacts to the computer's storage device. It is the responsibility of the investigator to keep notes of his activity so that the state of the computer's hard drive at the conclusion of triage can be reconciled with the findings of the investigator during triage.

---

35 *Criminal Code*, above note 1, s. 487.012.

Typically, it is necessary for the investigator to "plug in" their own USB drive or use their own CD/DVD to run forensic or other software known to be safe for the purpose of performing a more efficient and effective triage on a live system. This process may include the acquisition of a copy of the volatile RAM that will be lost once the computer is turned off. It is possible that commonly used programs on the computer under examination have been renamed and replaced with programs that will perform malicious activity. For instance, a common "war story" is that the shutdown command may actually wipe the hard drive. It is possible for this to happen, but there is also the danger that the authorized user may run the malicious program accidentally, thereby wiping their own data. Today, encryption technology is more likely to be employed to protect the user's data.

Typically, the investigator will not boot up (i.e., not start) a computer for the purpose of conducting the triage. Instead, the investigator will attempt to remove the storage device and connect it to a write blocker,[36] which is then connected to a trusted computer system for preliminary examination.[37] Forensic software on the trusted system will be used to conduct a cursory search for evidence of various type(s) within the framework of the investigative requirements. While this approach is typical for removable media, such as a USB drive, an alternative method is to connect the device to a software[38] write-protected USB port on the trusted computer system or to insert the USB device into a trusted system that does not automatically mount[39] the file system.

If no relevant digital evidence is found, the investigator may conclude that the computer or storage device has not been used for illicit purposes. However, depending on the type of investigation, the specific circumstances of the judicial authorization, and the length of time taken to conduct the triage, the computer or storage device may still be seized for a more

---

36 A write blocker is a piece of hardware or software that prevents new data from being written to a storage device.

37 A "trusted system" is a computer system that is controlled by the investigator, has a known configuration and operating behaviour, is clean of viruses, and has the necessary forensic software installed to copy the data from the source media.

38 The Windows registry, a database that is an integral component of the Windows operating system, can be changed to prevent or block any new data from being written to the USB device.

39 To mount a file system, for the purposes of this book, is to open it so that it can be read. The file system has to be "open" or "mounted" before data can be written to the device.

thorough examination at a later date. The absence of identifying digital evidence during the triage does not mean there is no evidence. Additionally, if there are too many storage devices to triage in a reasonable period of time, they may simply be seized for later examination. In the case of an Anton Piller order, it is common to copy all storage devices on-site, rather than to conduct triage. Thereafter, the copies are removed to the security of the Independent Supervising Solicitor for later access by the plaintiff or the plaintiff's representative in the form of a forensic investigator.

Computers and storage devices are not always subjected to triage. For example, if the computer or storage device needs to be examined for evidence of DNA or fingerprints, it may be seized and processed for digital evidence at a later date. The most volatile evidence, such as DNA or fingerprints, is typically processed first.

4) The Acquisition of Digital Evidence

A forensic copy of a storage device may be obtained either on-site ("in the field") or at the office ("in the lab"). In either case, the same general issues surrounding the copy process will arise. Resolution of those issues, however, is usually much easier in the lab or office since the investigator will have access to more resources, including time, personnel, power (electricity), and hardware and software resources. The storage device identified as the media to be copied will often be referred to as the "source media," and the storage device to which the data is being copied will often be referred to as the "destination drive."[40]

There are a number of methods of obtaining the forensic copy, each with its own advantages and disadvantages. The three basic methods of obtaining a forensic copy of data are: (1) removal/connection of the subject media to a trusted system; (2) booting (i.e., starting) the subject computer with a trusted boot disk;[41] and (3) obtaining the data while the subject computer is running.

Obtaining a forensic copy of the data from the subject media requires the use of forensic software. The most commonly used forensic acquisition software are: EnCase by Guidance Software, FTK Imager by Access Data, X-Ways Imager by X-Ways Software Technology AG, SMART by ASR

---

40 The destination drive is usually of larger capacity than the source media, but it can be smaller if compression is used during the acquisition or copy process.

41 This may include floppy diskettes, CDs, DVDs, or USB drives that contain an operating system to run the subject computer.

Data Acquisition & Analysis LLC, and the open source software, DD.[42] Each of these software packages will output the forensic copy to an "evidence container." The evidence container is one or more files (sometimes referred to as segments) that contain the data from the source media and that must be read by forensic software to enable human interpretation of the forensic evidence. Historically, the data acquired from a subject media were split into one or more evidence containers of a size that would permit archiving to a long-term storage media, typically a CD or DVD. Today, large capacity hard drives that are faster, easier to retrieve, and easier to store have eliminated this requirement.

The first disc duplication software, such as the RCMP Utilities and Safeback, did not include methods of validating the authenticity and integrity of the forensic copy. In other words, there was no way to prove that the copy of data was exactly the same as the original and contained all the data available on the disk. Today, forensic duplication software provides a method of validating the forensic copy against the source data and of verifying the continued integrity of the forensic copy. Forensic acquisition software varies in terms of the structure of the evidence container, the user interface, and the ease of use.

Among the most commonly used forensic duplication software are EnCase, FTK Imager, and DD. Using EnCase as an example, the duplication software will acquire a forensic copy of the source media to an evidence container that has two different formats: (1) the E01 file format that is also referred to as the Expert Witness file format, and (2) the Ex01 file format. EnCase has provided a method of validating that the source data is the same as the forensic copy since at least version 3. Validation is accomplished by passing the entire contents of the source data through a mathematical algorithm called an MD5 hash, a SHA1 hash, or a SHA256 hash that results in a single alphanumeric value that represents the entirety of the source data. EnCase also includes a method to validate the integrity of the forensic copy against itself by comparing the hash value calculated at the time of the acquisition with the calculated hash value of the copy to ensure that there have been no changes to the data.

With the evolving dynamics of digital forensics and disk technology came the need to perform validation testing on the tools and processes being used to conduct digital forensics investigations. The U.S. National

---

42 "DD" stands for "disc to disc" and is not officially forensic, but variants such as DcflDD (Defense Computer Forensics Lab) have been enhanced for forensic purposes.

Institute of Standards and Technology (NIST) has been performing validation testing on digital forensics acquisition software since at least August 2002[43] and in June 2003, EnCase 3.20 was validated. NIST continues to perform tool testing through the Computer Forensics Tool Testing Program.[44]

a) Removal/Connection of the Subject Media to a Trusted System

The traditional method of obtaining a forensic copy of a storage device is by removing it from its original computer chassis and connecting it to a trusted system. This process can sometimes be a challenging undertaking, especially in the field when under pressure to "get the job done," without damaging the storage device.[45] When the acquisition is performed on-site, the digital forensics investigator's work often requires more time to complete than that of other members of an investigating team. A number of factors may increase the difficulty of an on-site acquisition, including the discovery of computers not familiar to the forensics investigator, inadequate supply of tools, or an unfamiliar hardware connection.

Usually the source media from the subject computer will be connected to a trusted system with a write blocker. One of the most common write blockers is the Tableau write blocker. The Tableau is a piece of hardware that is connected to the source media on one side and, on the other side, to the investigator's trusted system. A forensic copy is then obtained using forensic software. The write blocker will prevent any changes from taking place on the source media, thereby preserving the integrity of the original data.

Two alternatives to using a hardware write blocker are (1) using a hardware "write lock" on the source media itself, or (2) using a software write blocker. These methods require that the source media be connected or inserted into the trusted system, but it would not first be connected to a hardware write blocker. It is also possible to prevent changes to the data on the source media by utilizing a trusted system that cannot read the file system of the source media or that does not automatically "mount"[46] the file system of the source media.

---

43 National Institute of Standards and Technology, "Computer Forensics Tool Testing Program: Disk Imaging," online: www.cftt.nist.gov/disk_imaging.htm.

44 National Institute of Standards and Technology, "Computer Forensics Tool Testing Project Web Site," online: www.cftt.nist.gov/index.html.

45 Typically, this is only an issue when executing a civil search warrant, when the movements of defendants and other occupants are not restricted.

46 To mount a file system, for the purposes of this chapter, is to open it so that it can be read.

There are a number of reasons why the subject media would not be removed from the subject computer, including:

1) It is not possible to dismantle the subject computer without risk of damage.
2) The forensic investigator does not have the required tools to complete the dismantle process.
3) The source media is of a type, such as some solid state drives, that cannot be removed from the subject computer.
4) The use of TPM module[47] or other BIOS passwords that "tie" the hard drive to its computer, making it virtually impossible to obtain a copy of the digital evidence by removing the source media from the subject computer.
5) The forensic investigator does not have the correct connectivity from the source media to the trusted system.
6) The source media is part of a complex array of hard drives.
7) The source media is part of a complex network that is not practical to dismantle.

b) Booting the Subject Computer System with a Trusted Boot Device

If the source media cannot be removed or for any reason the decision is made to acquire the data from the subject computer system without removing the source media, the option exists to boot (start) the subject computer with a trusted boot disk. The trusted boot disk would contain an operating system used to run the subject computer and typically would contain utilities for triaging the data and obtaining a forensic copy. In addition to the trusted boot disk, the investigator would also have to attach a destination drive to the subject computer to store the evidence file(s).

c) Obtaining the Data while the Subject System Is Running

The forensic acquisition process may be complicated by the complexity of networked environments, the restrictions on physical access to the subject media, the requirement for "up time," the use of encryption technology, or the need to obtain a copy of RAM. It may be impractical or impossible to obtain a forensic copy of the entire storage device or of the particular data of interest once the computer is turned off. In those cases, the data will need to be copied while the subject computer is running. The data will be

---

47 Microsoft, "Trusted Platform Module Technology Overview" (5 December 2012), online: technet.microsoft.com/en-us/library/jj131725.aspx.

copied either in its entirety (if possible) or as a collection of selected records. A selection of records may include, for example, the entire contents of a user's profile or a user's network share. As usual, this forensic copy would still be directed as output to a destination drive.

A complicating factor during the acquisition phase is the use of encryption technology. In the absence of the key to mount the file/container and decrypt the data, the forensic investigator should attempt to obtain a copy of the data live, while the file/containers are open. As noted in Section B(3), above, RAM is erased upon computer shut down, so obtaining a copy is usually the first action taken on a running computer.[48] Typically, no analysis is conducted on RAM at this stage of the investigation; it is secured for later analysis.

5) The Analysis

Analyzing and interpreting digital evidence is a complex, multi-faceted, and time-consuming process. The forensic investigator may encounter a number of challenges, including encryption and passwords, anti-forensics activity such as file and disc wiping utilities, generic or open multi-user computing environments,[49] legacy systems, and proprietary data formats, to name a few. Before beginning the analysis, the investigator will typically create a "working copy" of the data to conduct the analysis on, preserving the original forensic copy in the event of corruption or loss of the working copy. This practice is especially important when the investigator may lose access to the source media and be left unable to create an additional forensic copy.

The most commonly used commercial, off-the-shelf, multi-function forensic software are EnCase Forensic (Guidance Software), Forensic Toolkit (Access Data), Device Seizure (Paraben), Forensic Explorer (GetData), SMART (ASR Data), and X-Ways Forensic. Software used primarily for the examination of Internet artifacts includes Net Analysis (Digital Detective), Internet Evidence Finder (Magnet Forensics), and Internet Examiner Toolkit (SiQuest). Additionally, there are myriad open source (i.e., free) and commercial tools available, typically as single-function util-

48 This is not to be construed as a "must do first" process as every digital investigation will have its own unique set of circumstances that will impact the decisions made at the time.

49 A computing environment consisting of one computer and many users, with no password or common password in use.

ities, that can be very useful. The most commonly used open source forensic software includes Helix and Sleuth Kit.

Each of these software packages will "read" the forensic evidence container, validate the continued integrity of the forensic copy, and present the data in readable format. Formats vary, with some displaying a logical hierarchy of files and folders similar to the Windows Explorer view, others an email view displaying the hierarchy of the email database (if used). There are also reporting formats that display file metadata and Internet history. Each software package has its strengths and weaknesses. It is not uncommon for a computer forensic investigator to use more than one program, along with any number of other utilities or software packages that provide single or multi-function analysis support. It would be uncommon for today's digital forensics investigator to have only one utility in their toolkit.

Once the forensic investigator has created a working copy of the data, it is common practice, but not a requirement, to conduct a signature analysis[50] and a hash analysis.[51] These processes can, depending on the size of the dataset and the number of hard drives, take many hours to complete. Data is often processed through forensic software to build a search index and "break out" the components of compound files[52] for indexing and analysis.

The analysis may proceed by any of several different methods, including:

1) A simple review of file attributes.[53]
2) As noted in Section B(3), above, reviewing the directory structure and locating files stored in default storage locations, for example, My Documents and Downloads.

---

50 A signature analysis matches a file extension, such as .DOC or .XLS, with the file's signature. Typically, the signature is the first several bytes of the file, not visible in the native application but recognizable with a suitable utility.

51 A hash analysis applies a mathematical algorithm to a file or document, creating an alpha-numeric output that can be compared to the output of other files or documents, to identify ones that are the same.

52 A compound file is a single discreet file that is made up of many parts. For example, an Outlook PST email database is a single discreet file but can contain many thousands of individual email messages.

53 File attributes are stored externally to the file and include information such as the date the document was created, the date it was last modified, whether the document is hidden or in a system file. File attributes are often confused with metadata, which are stored internally to the file. Not all files contain metadata.

3) Reviewing the easily identifiable list of applications installed on the system (e.g., Program Files/Program File(x86) on a Windows operating system or Applications on newer Apple computers) provides the forensic investigator with preliminary insight into the computing environment of users of the system.
4) Checking gallery view, where graphic files such as photographs are displayed in a "grid" for quick review.

The analysis typically has the objective to establish: (1) control over the data; (2) ownership of the data; (3) production of the data; and (4) distribution of the data. These objectives are not limited in scope to specific cases, but instead apply across incident types including fraud, proceeds of crime, child pornography, and murder.

Encryption technology is a complicating factor during the analysis phase. There are three basic types of encryption, including:

1) file encryption, where one or more files are individually encrypted;
2) container encryption, where one or more files found within the boundaries of a container are encrypted (containers can be of various sizes; for example, a 2-GB container may store many files); and
3) whole disc encryption, where access to any of the data on the source media is inaccessible until the disc is mounted.

Each of these types of encryption can be implemented on a single source media and can use different technologies. Any one of them can bring the analysis to a halt for the specific data that has been encrypted.

In addition to data from the source media, the forensic investigator may have RAM to analyze. Data stored in RAM can identify such information as running processes, files associated with programs, identification of hidden and inactive processes,[54] TCP network connections, and portions of the text of documents or passwords in plain text.

6) The Presentation of Results: Report Writing

There is no one method of presenting the results of the analysis and there is a certain degree of personal choice in how a report is formatted. The specific instructions received from counsel, the policies and procedures of any particular investigative unit, the costs associated with analysis (primarily

54 Hidden and inactive processes may shed light on any installed virus or malware applications.

a concern of the defence and private investigators), along with the format, content, and quantity of evidence exposed, will affect the presentation of the analysis, the objectives, and the depth of the reporting.

The following is a non-exhaustive list of items that may be seen in a report:

1) A written case overview, often called a synopsis.
2) A subject-specific evidentiary brief.
3) Identification of the specific details of each storage device or source media analyzed.
4) Pictures of each storage device analyzed.
5) An explanation of the instructions received, if any.
6) Lists or reports of relevant data and their sources.
7) Additional sources of information considered during the course of the analysis, and the source of that information.
8) Copies of pictures, word documents, or other related documents or records, and the source of these documents and records.
9) Pie charts, scatter graphs, or other graphic depictions of various data relationships and attributes.
10) Details of the specific analysis undertaken and the conclusions drawn from that analysis.
11) The results of key word searches.
12) Any known limitations of the analysis.

Reports may also include an overview of the specific details of each subject media, such as the make, model, and serial number; when it was put into service; the current state of warranty; the type of file system that is used; or the number of objects[55] that are available for review.

In criminal investigations, there is usually at least one person who knows what activity, whether an offence or not, was undertaken on the subject computer—the accused. But law enforcement rarely receives much assistance from the accused and a private investigator or forensic examiner retained by defence counsel is often not granted access to the accused. This limitation may lead the investigators to look for evidence to support their side's theory of the case, which may impact the discovery of alternative theories or a more extensive analysis of the data.

---

55 Different forensic software will display data differently and manage the file objects differently. The purpose of this number would be to give the reviewer a sense of the amount of data under examination.

Regardless of the "team" retaining the forensic investigator, the overall objective should be a complete and accurate presentation of the evidence revealed by the data in a form that can be interpreted and understood by lay readers. The forensic examiners' ultimate responsibility is to the court, and to present their evidence as best they can to enable findings of fact. As aptly stated in a recent continuing professional development program, "The days of the hired gun are over."[56]

7) Cellphone, Smartphone, and Tablet Forensics

Cellphones, smartphones, and tablets (i.e., mobile devices) are often a significant source of information and forensic software continue to evolve to meet the challenges these devices present. Mobile devices require the same structured approach to preservation, acquisition, examination, analysis, and reporting of digital evidence that is required of other forms of digital evidence. Mobile devices and cell phone networks are also evolving rapidly. As a result, policies and procedures implemented today may change tomorrow.

Mobile devices provide an array of feature-rich services, including voice communication, email, social networking, video, aircraft navigation, and games, to name a few. The number of applications[57] available for download from the leading service providers is significant,[58] but not all of them will impact a digital investigation. It is the role of the forensic software provider to identify the apps most likely to impact a digital investigation and then modify their own software to support them.

The construction or design of mobile devices is comparable across systems. They have similar basic features, such as a "microprocessor, read only memory (ROM), random access memory (RAM), a radio module, a digital signal processor, a microphone and speaker, a variety of hardware keys and interfaces, and a liquid crystal display (LCD)."[59] Using storage

---

56 Marie Henein, "Ethics and Professional Responsibility Issues with Expert Evidence" (Notes taken at the Expert Forensic Evidence in Criminal Proceedings Conference, Osgoode Hall Law School Professional Development, Toronto, 16 January 2015) [unpublished, on file with author and video recorded by Osgoode Hall Law School].

57 Applications are software, often third party, that can be downloaded from the Internet onto a mobile device to perform a particular function. "Application" is commonly abbreviated to "app."

58 Statista, "Number of Apps Available in Leading App Stores as of July 2015," online: www.statista.com/statistics/276623/number-of-apps-available-in-leading-app-stores.

59 US Department of Commerce, National Institute of Standards and Technology, "Guidelines on Mobile Device Forensics, NIST Special Publication 800-101: Revision 1" by

and memory technology similar to a "regular" computer, mobile devices have the operating system and software applications stored permanently in either NAND or NOR memory, while the operating system and applications run in RAM. Mobile devices can have significant onboard permanent storage capacity for downloading and installing the seemingly endless number of applications available today, as well as for storing personal data. Removable storage may also be used. Despite these similarities to each other and to traditional computers, mobile devices are different across the marketplace, with different manufacturers offering different models, functions, sizes, applications, operating systems, etc. It is the challenge of the forensic investigator to assess the mobile device and to determine the most effective, forensically sound process available to complete the preservation and analysis of the data.

For a mobile device to work on the cellular mobile network, it requires a method to authenticate the user/device. The two most dominant cellular networks are Code Division Multiple Access (CDMA) and Global System for Mobile Communications (GSM). Two other common cellular networks include Time Division Multiple Access (TDMA) and Integrated Digital Enhanced Network (iDEN). The hardware and software used to authenticate the user/device to the cellular network is either contained on a small removable card, commonly referred to as a SIM card, or incorporated directly within the mobile device. Either method of authentication should be considered during the forensic investigation process as contacts, call information, and SMS messages may be present. Additionally, in the case of searches under judicial authorization, the service provider has possession of subscriber details, call detail records (commonly referred to as CDRs), and other related data that may be of assistance during an investigation.

The complexities associated with the forensic acquisition of mobile devices is beyond the scope of this book but, in general, data from mobile devices can be acquired through five methods, presented in increasing order of complexity, cost, and risk of data or hardware destruction (levels (1) and (2) are the most common):

1) *Manual Extraction*: Manual extraction uses the hardware and software, including the menu system on the mobile device, to "step through"

Rick Ayers, Sam Brothers, & Wayne Jansen (May 2014) at 3, online: nvlpubs.nist.gov/nistpubs/SpecialPublications/NIST.SP.800-101r1.pdf.

the various applications, settings, and user-collected data, obtaining photographs as the investigation progresses. This process is still common when forensic software cannot be used to acquire a copy of the data, for such reasons as incompatibility or damaged connection ports. This process will not capture deleted content.

2) *Logical Extraction*: A logical extraction is the process of copying the contents of the mobile phone's file system. In other words, it copies the data that remains accessible to the normal operation of the mobile device and is present in the file system. The logical extraction of data may include deleted content.
3) *Hex Dump/JTAG*: A hex dump/JTAG extraction output is similar to a traditional physical acquisition of a hard drive from a computer; the entire contents of the phone are copied, including all space not currently used for the daily operations of the mobile device.
4) *Chip-Off*: A chip-off extraction is the process of physically removing the flash memory from the mobile device and extracting the contents into a bin file. The output from this process more closely resembles the physical acquisition of a hard drive in traditional forensics, but is significantly more complex and carries with it a much higher risk of permanent damage to hardware and data.
5) *Micro Read*: A micro read extraction requires the use of an electron microscope to manually read the data and record the results. The author is not aware of any law enforcement or private investigators currently providing this service.

One difference between the acquisition of a mobile device and the traditional acquisition of a hard drive is the validation process. Copying a hard drive allows for the verification of the copy to be matched against the source data through an MD5 or SHA verification. The acquisition of a mobile device cannot easily be verified in this manner as the contents of the mobile device are constantly changing through non-user system activity unless it is turned completely off. However, the hash value comparison of individual files generally remains consistent across acquisitions.

Mobile phones are susceptible to remote access, including phone locking and data destruction. An agency can undertake significant effort at significant expense to prevent mobile devices from receiving or sending cell signals using various enclosures, such as Faraday Bags, or specially built rooms, such as Faraday Cages, to block cellular network signals. Additionally, law enforcement agencies have cellular network signal blocking hardware at their disposal (private industry does not). These methods are still used if it is absolutely essential to prevent communication in or out of the phone prior to forensic acquisition of the data. However, if the phone is already on when seized and there is no password (or the password is provided), the phone can be quickly put into "airplane mode," thereby disabling all wireless communications to or from the device.

Most of today's mobile devices also contain removable media, such as a microSD card. There is nothing particularly special about a microSD card used in mobile devices compared to an SD card used in a digital camera. In both cases, the card is processed like any other source media that is a removable storage device.

The software available for the acquisition and analysis of mobile device data includes Oxygen, XRY/XACT, Cellebrite, FTK MPE+, EnCase, Device Seizure, and Internet Evidence Finder. Each of these forensic software packages also provides for the review of the data acquired. Some of the forensic software, such as Internet Evidence Finder and EnCase, have the ability to read various formats of mobile device backups and present that evidence in their own proprietary interface.

At least some of the currently available forensics software for mobile devices seem to have significant limitations when used on iPhones newer than the iPhone 4. Cellebrite, Oxygen, XRY, and Paraben are unable to perform physical acquisitions on the new iOS devices. Cellebrite and Oxygen have "Advanced Logical Extraction" capabilities on some devices and each of the service providers has a few capabilities that the others do not. However, the majority of the service providers, including Oxygen, Cellebrite, and XRY, generally have similar capabilities and limitations.[60]

8) Internet and Cloud Forensics

There are two basic types of data available on the Internet that require preservation: public and private. The process to preserve these two types of data can be generally categorized as Internet and Cloud Forensics.

Preservation of data that is publicly available, often referred to as "open source intelligence," is performed in a manner that enables the forensics investigator to speak to the method, process, and integrity of the

60 National Institute of Standards and Technology, "Search for Forensic Tools by Functionality," online: toolcatalog.nist.gov/populated_taxonomy/index.php, presents a review of some of the currently available mobile device forensic software capabilities.

data preserved. There are a number of sources of publicly available Internet content such as web pages, forum content, news groups, IRC chat rooms, and peer-to-peer networks. Preservation of the publicly available Internet content is different from "hard drive" or mobile device forensics in that a forensics investigator does not have physical possession of the media on which the Internet content resides and another digital forensics investigator on a different date and time may or may not be able to replicate the publicly available content. For example, a publicly available web page or forum content can be "here today and gone tomorrow," making it necessary for the investigator to be able to speak to the integrity of the preservation techniques.

Preserving the contents of a web page, such as Facebook, Twitter, or an online news source, is typically undertaken by printing it to PDF or taking a screen shot of what is displayed on the investigator's computer monitor. Neither of these methods will preserve a copy of the underlying programming or meta data used to display the page contents. More advanced tools will archive a copy of the entire website into a database, including the underlying files that support the visual elements of the web pages, and automatically perform a hash analysis on the file contents for integrity purposes. The database provides restricted view-only access to the archived webpages.

It is important to keep in mind that many of today's most popular websites, such as Twitter and Facebook, do not easily render to a PDF, skewing the display of the page or completely missing content that is otherwise available for review on the live website. For instance, responding tweets can become very long and are contained within a scrollable "text box" on the Twitter website. Without taking corrective action, printing this view to PDF will capture only what is visible at the beginning of the Twitter discussion. Social media web pages also store user data that can only be accessed by logging into the user account or through issuance of a search warrant on the service provider.

Preserving forum content presents additional challenges. The underlying data structure of a forum is a database whose content is delivered to the end user as a number of individual posts formed into a "thread."[61] Some forums will be open to all who visit, while others will require the forensics investigator to register at the forum and to possibly purchase

---

61 The various structures of forum databases and the functionality of forums is beyond the scope of this book.

a higher level of access, most often referred to as premium or VIP access. Other forums are closed to public registration (invitation-only forums, for instance) and require a more tenacious or innovative investigator to obtain user credentials.

Private data on the cloud exists on a server controlled by a third-party service provider that is not physically accessible to the investigator. As such, it is not removable under the usual practices described in Section B(4)(a), above. Without the ability to exert full control over the storage device, the investigator is limited to preserving only what can be seen online, with two caveats:

1) If the investigator has permission to log in as the owner and has full owner access to the online account, then additional information can be preserved that would otherwise not be accessible; and
2) If the online service provider is served with judicial authorization or is otherwise required to preserve all data related to a specific account, then that additional information could be available.

It is not possible to list with any level of depth the various pieces of information that could be available to the account owner or to specify what additional information the service provider could deliver that would go beyond what is available to the account owner. Integral knowledge of the data being stored and its structure is known only to the service provider. Having said that, some information from the service provider might include:

1) the IP address used by the account owner when logging into the account;
2) the name, address, and phone number contained in the account owner's profile;
3) a copy of deleted content; and
4) content that is not publicly available or is otherwise not shared on the Internet.

Sources of content classified as cloud forensics[62] include:

1) file storage, such as Dropbox, OneDrive, Box, and GoogleDocs;
2) web-based email services, such as Yahoo, Gmail, Outlook, and Hushmail; and

62 This list includes only some of the most popular cloud services on the Internet today. The total number of sources available is too large to be listed here.

3) social media, such as Twitter, Facebook, Tumblr, Instagram, and MySpace.[63]

Some forensic software service providers, such as Cellebrite and Oxygen, have introduced a process to retrieve private cloud data as an additional feature of their software offerings. Any of these offerings will require authentication to the service storing the data and, as such, the data can be preserved without the use of third party software.

C. THE ROLE OF THE DIGITAL EVIDENCE EXPERT IN CRIMINAL CASES

The standard for the admission of expert evidence under *R. v. Mohan*[64] requires four criteria to be met: (1) necessity in assisting the trier of fact; (2) relevance; (3) a qualified expert; and (4) the absence of an applicable exclusionary rule. Recent clarification by the Supreme Court of Canada on the role of the witness giving expert evidence will tighten established admissibility standards.[65] The digital forensic expert who conducts a forensic analysis of digital evidence and testifies at a criminal proceeding must provide the court with "fair, non-partisan and objective assistance," regardless of who is paying their fees or wages.[66] The additional clarity on the role of the expert witness solidifies the expectation that the overall objective of the expert witness is to provide evidence of the truths told by the data.

This is a welcomed development since even the most seasoned expert witness can give evidence that is not helpful to the court's fact-finding mission. Sometimes this is the result of client instructions that limit the extent of the expert's search for digital evidence. The scope of the instructions provided to an expert by a client or lawyer may allow the court to draw adverse inferences that weaken the legal position of the party that required the expert evidence in the first place. If a particular digital evidence search is not done, for example because a plaintiff does not ask the expert to conduct such a search, then the court may draw the conclusion

63 While not all social media service providers require users to create a verified account, the general concept of social media is that a user account is required so that comments and postings may be attributed to a particular human subscriber.

64 *R. v. Mohan*, [1994] 2 S.C.R. 9.

65 Cristin Schmitz, "SCC Tightens Rules on Expert Evidence Admissibility" *The Lawyers Weekly* (15 May 2015), online: www.hhllp.ca/assets/files/pdf/Matthew%20Gourlay.pdf.

66 *White Burgess Langille Inman v. Abbott and Haliburton Co.*, 2015 SCC 23 at para. 50.

that the legal team was "more interested in creating a spoliation case rather than finding evidence to help them."[67]

The forensic examiner is an advocate for the truth as told by the data and should always keep an open mind toward different interpretations of the data or novel approaches to its presentation. Expert opinion witnesses should be able to support or refute different interpretations of the data based on their knowledge, skill, and review of the data. An expert should undertake an unbiased approach when responding to a lawyer's question, regardless of the lawyer's "side." It is not the role of the expert to "make a case look good."[68]

D. A CASE STUDY

1) The Investigation

A user on a peer-to-peer network is identified as "making available" pictures categorized as child pornography. An investigation is initiated that results in:

1) many pictures categorized as child pornography, made available for download;
2) identification of the IP address sharing the offensive content;
3) identification of the subscriber of the IP address; and
4) execution of a search warrant at the subscriber's address.

During the execution of the search warrant, there were three residents living in the home and one resident implicated the subscriber as the offender. A number of pieces of media and computers were seized and analyzed.

2) The Analysis

The analysis of data consisted entirely in the identification and multileveled classification of offending content. There was no analysis that specifically identified the offender.

---

67 *Nova Growth Corp. et al v. Andrzej Roman Kepinski et al*, 2014 ONSC 2763 at para. 318.

68 Inquiry into Pediatric Forensic Pathology in Ontario, "Report of the Inquiry into Pediatric Forensic Pathology in Ontario," by The Honourable Stephen T. Goudge, Commissioner (Toronto: Inquiry into Pediatric Forensic Pathology in Ontario, 2008) at 179.

3) The Disclosure

Disclosure was very minimal, consisting of an overview of the investigation and PDF reports listing offending content. There was no content, narrative, analysis, or reporting that specifically identified the offender other than the offender having been the subscriber to the IP address.

4) The Review and Comment

The review of police disclosure by defence counsel often results in a request for additional details and documentation. The legal obligation of the Crown to provide disclosure to the defence is well founded in law, but the disclosure process can still result in disagreements of process and content. The defence must fearlessly advocate for their client—the accused—while the Crown must act fairly to maintain the integrity and reputation of the administration of justice. Crown attorneys should also be cognizant of and guard against factors that may lead to wrongful convictions.

When the police use their in-house expert and/or the defence counsel hires their own expert, the lines of communication for the resolution of requests for additional disclosure or data, and agreement on the resulting analysis, need to be streamlined to:

1) aid in more efficient and effective identification of common ground and discrepancies;
2) reduce the overall cost of the prosecution by streamlining presentation of evidence;
3) reduce the cost to the defence for their analysis through receipt of a more fulsome disclosure package;
4) reduce the burden on the courts through earlier guilty pleas or prompt withdrawal of poorly established charges; and
5) solidify the practice that expert witnesses owe a duty to the court.

The defence and the Crown possess confidential information that requires protection. Enabling a forum for dialogue between forensic experts in advance of preliminary hearing or trial is not meant to circumvent or breach that confidentiality. It is meant to reduce the chances of wrongful conviction while, at the same time, enhance the probability of convicting those who should be properly convicted.

In this case study, additional disclosure was requested in the form of spreadsheets, instead of PDF documents, to enable the defence expert to more quickly and efficiently review and analyze the sources of offending content that, incidentally, were voluminous. The request was denied by the Crown, stating that it is not the practice of the local Crown's office to provide such disclosure. The defence request had nothing to do with a particular disclosure practice in a given jurisdiction and it had nothing to do with disclosing protected or sensitive information. The disclosure request was intended to enable a more efficient analysis of the data, a more timely response to defence inquiries of their expert, and, potentially, a quicker resolution to the alleged offences.

The police analysis consisted of classifying the offending content in the usual categories. Those categories include known offensive content, "new" offensive content, suspected offensive content, and additional categories of non-offending content. The police analysis and disclosure could have been significantly more effective had it:

1) not included references to non-offending content or explained its relevance;
2) provided for the analysis of each individual device and how it relates to the case against the accused;
3) included analysis that interlinked media (the digital evidence), if such linkage exists;
4) provided for the analysis of devices that had been backed up to source media; and
5) provided identification of the devices NOT analyzed.

Overall, forensic experts on either side of a prosecution must learn to co-operate and the courts must embrace this concept by establishing rules on which to build a foundation of trust and integrity for the benefit of all parties.

E. CONCLUSION

Multi-function forensic software has increased in popularity over the past decade and today plays a significant role in enabling the identification of evidentiary artifacts from digital evidence. At the same time, the volume of data to be analyzed has grown exponentially, and the proper analysis and reporting of that data takes organization, structure, focus, technical skill, and time.

Every digital forensics investigation will have some component of evidence that is unique, but there are usually significant similarities as well.

The similarities can help facilitate a more swift analysis, but uncommon digital elements can grind the analysis to a halt, placing greater demands on the digital investigator by requiring significant research and testing to complete the examination.

The commercialization of forensic software has had a two-pronged effect on the discipline of digital forensics. First, it opened the door to myriad "experts." Second, it identified the need for peer review of digital forensic principles and practices. Experts need to be assessed on their own unique set of skills, regardless of whether they work for the Crown or for a private investigation company. Experts, lawyers, and law enforcement all have a responsibility to work together to pursue the truth—an unbiased, accurate account of the events surrounding an alleged offence. One or more lives may stand in the balance.

F. LEGAL CONTEXT

> First, police officers enter your home, take possession of your computer, and carry it off for examination in a place unknown and inaccessible to you. There, without supervision or constraint, they scour the entire contents of your hard drive: your emails sent and received; accompanying attachments; your personal notes and correspondence; your meetings and appointments; your medical and financial records; and all other saved documents that you have downloaded, copied, scanned, or created. The police scrutinize as well the electronic roadmap of your cybernetic peregrinations, where you have been and what you appear to have seen on the Internet—generally by design, but sometimes by accident.[69]

While made in the context of considering the adequacy of information used to obtain a search warrant, this oft-quoted paragraph from the majority reasons in *R. v. Morelli*,[70] highlights the two major issues in cases involving digital forensics: the implications to privacy and the massive volume of data potentially requiring interpretation.

Leading digital forensics evidence is essentially the art of deriving scientifically supportable inferences from data to permit a court to infer the actions, mental state, and communications of a human being who has been using an electronic device. Any modern device will hold and have access to an enormous quantity of data, much of which is systemically

---

69 *R. v. Morelli*, 2010 SCC 8 at para. 3.

70 *Ibid.*

machine generated, some machine generated as a result of human actions, and some generated directly by users of the device. In addition to the portion relevant to an investigation, a device will usually contain data that will have nothing to do with the case. Devices will archive the most intimate details of a person's life, including their web-surfing, communications, social media participation, images, videos, and associated cloud data. Such personal data may have no apparent relevance to the case, but will aid in identifying the user of the computer at the time of the relevant events being investigated. The task facing the forensic examiner and counsel seeking to use any findings is to sift through the results for the relevant, and then communicate these to the trier of fact in understandable language, often across a significant demographic or cultural divide.

1) The Nature of Digital Forensics

There are no governing bodies in the area of digital forensics that accredit digital forensic experts to a known standard before practice and testimony is permitted. While individual organizations such as the RCMP have a standardized understudy training program, other police forces and private experts will have a more *ad hoc* combination of training and experience. There are several organizations seeking to create a standardized certification process, but to date none have been implemented.

Unlike some areas of expert evidence, digital forensics entails far less opinion evidence and is principally concerned with describing digital artefacts to the court along with any appropriate scientific inferences about those artefacts. For example, the presence of a video on a device is not a matter of opinion. The scientific inference from the expert that may be drawn from its presence is that a human being loaded the video into device storage at a certain time. There might be further artefacts indicating that, at the same time the video was loaded, a social media account was in use, requiring a user name and a password. The expert might then be able to give evidence that the user of the computer entered the name and password into the computer and then made use of the social media account for a period of time chronologically corresponding to the events of interest. A body of data from several sources that are typically specific to a single individual may be found to be in temporal proximity to the data at issue. None of this is opinion evidence. It then remains for the court to decide whether to draw the final inference as to whether it is shown that the individual on trial used the computer in the manner alleged.

Since the court is only concerned with the actions of human beings in relation to a device, the expert must be able to distinguish between artefacts that are the result of machine functions from those resulting from human action. Machine artefacts result from the automated functioning of the machine and any software it uses. An example of a purely human-generated artefact would be the human-generated content of an email chain. Less clear are artefacts generated by the device as a result of a person's actions, but not created by the person. For instance, as a result of a human using a web browser to search the Internet, software generates and stores a record of the locations visited. The crucial step for counsel is to ensure the expert explains exactly what is occurring on the device to permit the court to draw accurate inferences about who the user was and what they were doing. All of this must be accomplished without treading on the role of the court and offending the ultimate issue rule.

In many cases, a "virtual machine" will aid the explanation of the examiner's findings. A virtual machine permits the examiner to use a copy of the data from the seized device and recreate how the device would have appeared and functioned at the time it was seized. Using what is often referred to as "VM" software, the examiner can display to the court how the device would have appeared to the user, showing what was visible, what was accessible, and what steps were required to be performed to access the data in issue. While VM software does not offer evidence as to what steps the user actually took, it does often assist the court in evaluating the veracity of a user as to what was visible or accessible to them.

Due to the changing nature of devices and how they are used, the role of the digital examiner is ever-shifting. Many digital artefacts are generated as a result of a device's interaction with other computers over networks like the Internet. To determine what the user was doing, it may be necessary to present artefacts from the accused's device, along with records kept by third parties such as social networking services or other web services. Data may be stored remotely so that the device contains only artefacts indicating where and when the data was stored externally.

In certain cases, expert testimony as to the functioning of social networking sites will be required. This may be within the expertise of some digital examiners or a separate expert may be required to ensure this evidence is admissible and able to be given weight.[71] To ensure the integrity of the proposed evidence, counsel will need to ensure that the expert they

---

71 See *R. v. Moazami*, 2013 BCSC 2398; *R. v. Eaton*, 2013 ONSC 3133.

propose to call is in fact an expert in the relevant area. There is no such thing as a generic "computer expert" knowledgeable in all areas of technology. To make sense of some digital evidence, the court may require not just the expertise of a digital examiner, but also experts in the functionality of relevant websites and the databases that underlie them.

2) Devices

The descriptive term "computer forensics" is often applied to many devices that do not fit the usual definition of a computer. Tablets, mobile communication devices, gaming consoles, on-board automotive entertainment and communication consoles, printers, Blu-ray players, and cameras all contain "computerized electronics" that may yield useful artefacts, but are not themselves computers. Over time, this list will obviously become longer. A modern mobile phone is a fully capable computing device, as was recognized some time ago by the Ontario Court of Appeal in *R. v. Woodward*.[72] The *Criminal Code*[73] definitions regarding computers and data have undergone a recent update that reflects the ubiquitous presence of data and computing functions in a large range of devices.[74] The definitions focus on the functionality of the data and processing capabilities of the technology instead of the device itself; that is, they are defined by what they do, not what they are. Similarly, the *Canada Evidence Act*[75] was amended to reflect the requirements of digital evidence and modify some rules of evidence to accommodate the requirements of digital evidence.

Mobile devices and their functionality change frequently and impose a considerable additional burden on digital examiners that is not present in most other disciplines. While all experts must maintain currency in their field to maintain credibility for their evidence, digital examiners are faced with a constant stream of new devices, new operating systems, new applications, and new Internet services. The software used to examine them must also be constantly updated to permit full examination.

---

72 2011 ONCA 610 at paras. 25–30.

73 Above note 1.

74 *Protecting Canadians from Online Crime Act*, S.C. 2014, c. 31. This legislation amended ss. 164.1, 320.1, 342.1, 342.2, 430, 487.011–487.02 of the *Criminal Code* to use the term "computer data." The amended definition in s. 342.1 amends several other definitions contained in that section, which are used throughout the *Criminal Code*.

75 Above note 2. See Section F(5), below in this chapter, for a fuller discussion of the treatment of digital evidence in the *Act*.

3) Technical Progression and Forensics

Over time, technical advances in digital devices create changes to both the methods of forensic recovery and the nature of the artefacts recovered. Initially, most artefacts were recovered from the data storage of the device, typically the hard drive. Changes in design over time then saw a significant increase in the amount of random access memory commonly installed. Increased RAM permits faster operation of the device and allows more applications to remain open simultaneously. The increased use of RAM poses some challenges to forensic examiners and police. When, as with volatile RAM, data is only available until the computer is switched off, the need for "live capture" increases and on-site attendance by forensic examiners is required. Greater care must be taken by non-forensic investigators to appropriately document and minimize their actions so as to minimally alter the data prior to forensic analysis, facilitating accurate reconstruction by the expert.

The considerable increase in network speed for wireless devices has led to further changes. As network speed increases, there is less need to store data on the device itself as it can be quickly retrieved from Internet storage. This permits the designers of devices and software to use on-board data storage and RAM for increasingly sophisticated and numerous applications. The effect on forensics is that examination of the device sometimes produces not the data itself, but an indication of where the data is stored. Many services also offer "cloud" backup for all data on a mobile device.

Some services have created whole new categories of available evidence. GPS and other location services installed on a mobile device often provide a timeline as to where the device was and when. Services also seek to locate the device physically to target local advertising at the user. A heavily used mobile device has the potential to act as an events and lifestyle "flight recorder."

Encryption is more readily available than previously and much more difficult, sometimes impossible, to defeat. Encryption is offered not only for data stored on devices, but also on cloud storage and on network communications. When used properly, it can defeat the ability of a forensic examiner to locate relevant evidence.

4) The Rise of the Cloud

Cloud storage simply means locating programs or data on remote server computers, which may be located anywhere. For individuals, cloud storage permits access to large amounts of data storage capacity not found on a personal computing device, as well as instant data backup in case of device loss or replacement. Businesses can perform functions that normally require networks, databases, or other infrastructure without the need for extensive networking software or technical personnel. Depending on how the cloud space owners configure their servers, a person's data may be in multiple locations. When a device is seized by police, it is technically possible to access cloud data using the device itself or a police computer. This type of search may be permitted under the terms of the warrant or under section 487(2.1) of the *Criminal Code*. For forensic examiners, techniques for seizing cloud data are likely to become more common as use of the cloud expands.

Cloud computing raises new challenges for digital forensics investigators. When data of interest is stored on the cloud, police will not have physical access to the storage medium. In that case, standard forensic processes for copying and authentication are not possible. Continuity of artefacts and metadata may not be possible. The times when an artefact was saved, accessed, or changed often cannot be reconstructed for remotely seized data in the same way that it can be when police have possession of the storage device. While cloud-derived artefacts in conjunction with data seized from a device in police possession might provide compelling evidence of an accused's activities, cloud artefacts alone may be less persuasive.

5) The *Canada Evidence Act*

The *Canada Evidence Act* was amended in 2000 to permit more efficient use of digital evidence and to amend the application of some rules of evidence to better reflect the unique characteristics of digital evidence. Rules created to govern the veracity of information and obligations recorded on parchment do not function as intended when applied to data. These provisions permit the efficient authentication of data found by digital examiners, in some instances even by the digital examiners themselves.

> *Authentication of Electronic Documents*
>
> 31.1 Any person seeking to admit an electronic document as evidence has the burden of proving its authenticity by evidence capable of supporting a finding that the electronic document is that which it is purported to be.

Application of best evidence rule—electronic documents

31.2 (1) The best evidence rule in respect of an electronic document is satisfied

(a) on proof of the integrity of the electronic documents system by or in which the electronic document was recorded or stored; or
(b) if an evidentiary presumption established under Section 31.4 applies.

Printouts

(2) Despite subsection (1), in the absence of evidence to the contrary, an electronic document in the form of a printout satisfies the best evidence rule if the printout has been manifestly or consistently acted on, relied on or used as a record of the information recorded or stored in the printout.

Presumption of integrity

31.3 For the purposes of subsection 31.2(1), in the absence of evidence to the contrary, the integrity of an electronic documents system by or in which an electronic document is recorded or stored is proven

(a) by evidence capable of supporting a finding that at all material times the computer system or other similar device used by the electronic documents system was operating properly or, if it was not, the fact of its not operating properly did not affect the integrity of the electronic document and there are no other reasonable grounds to doubt the integrity of the electronic documents system;
(b) if it is established that the electronic document was recorded or stored by a party who is adverse in interest to the party seeking to introduce it; or
(c) if it is established that the electronic document was recorded or stored in the usual and ordinary course of business by a person who is not a party and who did not record or store it under the control of the party seeking to introduce it.

Standards may be considered

31.5 For the purpose of determining under any rule of law whether an electronic document is admissible, evidence may be presented in respect of any standard, procedure, usage or practice concerning the manner in which electronic documents are to be recorded or stored, having regard to the type of business, enterprise or endeavor that used, recorded or stored the electronic document and the nature and purpose of the electronic document.

These provisions have been judicially considered, and courts may even permit the admission of evidence under these rules by non-technical witnesses.[76] Affidavit evidence from an employee of a web service may be admitted.[77] As technology progresses, examiners are going to need to rely on and explain evidence they themselves did not retrieve, but which is necessary to permit the court to draw accurate inferences. Of note is the recent amendment to the *Criminal Code*[78] mandating that all documents, digital or otherwise, taken pursuant to a production order are considered originals under the *Canada Evidence Act*. Legal practitioners will need to rely on these provisions to permit that data to be entered as evidence.

6) Privacy Limits on Forensics

A review of the law of search and seizure relating to digital devices is beyond the scope of this section, but it is necessary to discuss the impact of this rapidly changing body of law on the work of digital examiners. Judicial recognition of the immense body of private information contained on digital devices has led to significant scrutiny of how police conduct searches in relation to such devices. Several general propositions have emerged that govern the conduct of digital examiners:

1) Digital devices containing private data will almost always carry some expectation of privacy and this expectation will often extend to a person's data on a third party's device;[79]
2) The use of a computer for online activity carries an expectation of privacy, including the concept of online anonymity;[80]
3) All searches of digital devices (with a minor exception for mobile devices incidental to arrest) must be specifically authorized and are not implied in a search warrant;[81]
4) Examiners may search a device only within the parameters of the warrant and for evidence of the offences listed, otherwise a secondary warrant is required;[82] and

---

76 *R. v. Soh*, 2014 NBQB 20; *R. v. Ghotra* (16 March 2015), Toronto 13/497 (Ont. S.C.J.).

77 *R. v. Oster*, 2013 ONCJ 38. See also *R. v. Adams*, 2009 NSPC 15; *R. v. Marini*, [2006] O.J. No. 4057 (S.C.J.); *R. v. Bishop*, 2007 ONCJ 441; *R. v. Nardi*, 2012 BCPC 318; *R. v. R*, 2012 BCCA 416; *R. v. Rowe*, 2012 ONSC 2600.

78 *Criminal Code*, above note 1, s. 487.0192(6).

79 See *R. v. Cole*, 2012 SCC 53; *R. v. Fearon*, 2014 SCC 77; *R. v. Bredo*, 2014 BCSC 2054.

80 See *R. v. Spencer*, 2014 SCC 43.

81 See *R. v. Vu*, 2013 SCC 60.

82 *R. v. Jones*, 2011 ONCA 632 [*Jones*].

5) Once a device is validly seized, no separate judicial permission to do forensics is required.[83]

How the scope of the search is restricted by the terms of the warrant is of particular concern to digital examiners. As was noted in *Jones*,[84] the concept of "plain view" when examining a computer for data is quite restricted. The software used to examine a device is essentially a very sophisticated search engine capable of finding stored data, as well as data that has been deleted. It can be used to search for file types, to construct an Internet history, and to look for search terms used. Technical limitations prevent software from filtering out what is not covered under the terms of the warrant or limiting a search to relevant portions data. It is up to the examiner viewing the search results to determine if the artefacts located are responsive to terms of the warrant.

The terms of the warrant may be very specific, such as permission to search for images, or they may be general, like permission to search for evidence of use and possession of the device. In each instance, the digital examiner needs to be conscious of whether the judicial authorization permitting their work authorizes the seizure of the artefacts they locate. Secondary warrants and limits on the examination of devices are now a fact of life for police examiners.

7) Conclusion

There are a number of legal, technical, and practical challenges facing experts in the field of digital forensics. In criminal court, most experts will be police officers or civilian employees of the police forces. Private experts rarely give evidence in criminal trials and possess widely varying levels of expertise and training. Counsel seeking to call or respond to digital evidence will need to be aware of the varying qualifications and experience of digital examiners. Some level of understanding of the technology and the nature of the digital artefacts in issue is also required to effectively lead or cross-examine a digital forensics expert. Without such technical understanding, communicating the required technical inferences to the court becomes very difficult and the court's truth seeking function is impaired.

83 *R. v. Ballendine*, 2011 BCCA 221; *Jones*, *ibid.* at paras. 37–44.

84 *Ibid.* at paras. 53–74.

CHAPTER 8

Fingerprint Analysis

Wade Knaap[*]

LEGAL CONTEXT: CAITLIN PAKOSH

A. OVERVIEW OF THE DISCIPLINE: FINGERPRINT ANALYSIS

The use of fingerprints for personal identification in Canada dates back over 100 years. General acceptance and reliability have been secured in the criminal justice system, but a common perception of fingerprint infallibility is also anchored in the attitude of the general population. The increased presence of biometric security features on door-locking systems, smartphones, and laptops demonstrate the effectiveness and specificity of fingerprint identification or individualization in applications unrelated to the criminal realm.

This chapter is intended to provide the reader with a basic understanding of fingerprints and the identification process. The topics and content have been selected to coincide with expectations placed upon the fingerprint expert by the Canadian criminal justice system. These include a brief explanation of the history and origins of fingerprint identification; the formation, structure, and persistence of skin; the identification process; the

* Jessica Piekny, HBSc, assisted Wade Knaap in conducting research, identifying important issues to address, and editing this chapter. In concert with Mr. Knaap, Ms. Piekny also provided valuable feedback to Caitlin Pakosh in refining this chapter's legal context section. Refer to the "Acknowledgements" section. The author would also like to thank Sergeant John Aitkenhead, Forensic Identification Services, Ontario Provincial Police, and Brandy Mora, Latent Print Development Unit, NYPD, for taking the time to review this chapter.

development and preservation of fingerprint evidence; court presentation; judicial issues; and caselaw.

1) The History of Fingerprint Identification

As mentioned, fingerprint identification has been an accepted means of identification in Canada for over 100 years, but its origin dates back for centuries. Ancient China, India, and Japan all recognized the usefulness of fingerprints for identification purposes as a means of authenticating contracts, verifying ownership on artisan pottery work, providing proof of ownership, or simply for personal identification use.[1]

By the late nineteenth century, interest in fingerprinting for identification use and its potential application for criminal justice systems began to gain interest. Other identification techniques used at the time, such as Bertillonage (i.e., anthropometry, which involves the use of anatomical measurements, such as arm length and head circumference among others, and physical characteristics such as eye and hair colour), were being criticized for inaccuracy and the inability to individualize.[2] British fingerprint pioneers working abroad, particularly in India, gained knowledge of fingerprint identification and relayed that information back home.

In 1893, the Home Office secretary in England decided to appoint a committee under Charles Troup of the Home Office to look into the following areas:

- The current method of registering and identifying habitual criminals in England
- The anthropometric system (i.e., body measurements and physical characteristics)
- The suggested system of identification by means of a record of finger-print marks
- Report on which system, Bertillonage or fingerprint identification, should be used, and how this system would be implemented

The committee heard testimony and received demonstrations from Sir Francis Galton, a research pioneer on the topic of fingerprint identification.

---

1 Colin Beavan, *Fingerprints: Murder and the Race to Uncover the Science of Identity* (London: Fourth Estate, 2002).

2 Richard Saferstein, *Criminalistics: An Introduction to Forensic Science*, 11th ed. (New York: Pearson Education, 2014).

Following this extensive inquiry, the committee recommended adding fingerprints to the files of Scotland Yard, but as a supplementary identification means to that of Bertillonage.[3]

Shortly thereafter, Sir Edward Henry, a British official who was appointed Inspector General of Police for Bengal Province in India, assigned Hem Chandra Bose and Azizul Haque, two Indian employees of the Calcutta Anthropo-metric Bureau (before it became the Fingerprint Bureau), to begin work on designing a classification system that could be used for a searchable database of fingerprints. Henry was skeptical of the accuracy of the anthropometric system and was sure that fingerprint identification was superior. It is believed that the inability to search fingerprints on a database of known suspects was crucial to the Troup Committee rejecting fingerprints as the primary means of identification in Great Britain.[4] It was introduced and accepted in British India as the primary means of identification, owing to Henry's classification system.

By 1900, Sir Henry was asked to testify before a subsequent committee that was examining options for the identification of criminals. The Belper Committee heard testimony from Henry and recommended that the British government implement the Henry classification system that had been adopted in India.[5]

In 1904, during the World's Fair in St. Louis, Missouri, a series of events took place that resulted in fingerprint identification coming to Canada. Edward Foster, a police constable with the Dominion of Canada Police, was on assignment at the fair, guarding a display of Canadian gold. Coincidentally, the International Association of Chiefs of Police (IACP) was meeting in St. Louis. Sergeant John Ferrier of Scotland Yard was invited to present to the IACP regarding the concept of fingerprint identification for the criminal justice system. Foster attended the presentation and recognized the usefulness of fingerprint identification. He subsequently brought the idea back to Canada and was tasked with implementing a database. In 1911, the national database of criminal fingerprints was established in Canada.[6]

---

3 Simon A. Cole, *Suspect Identities: A History of Fingerprinting and Criminal Identification* (Cambridge, MA: Harvard University Press, 2001).

4 Beavan, above note 1.

5 Timothy Thompson & Sue Black, eds., *Forensic Human Identification: An Introduction* (Boca Raton, FL: CRC Press, 2007).

6 William Beahen & Stan Horrall, *Red Coats on the Prairies: The North-West Mounted Police* (Regina: Centax Books, 1998).

2) Ridgeology

Ridgeology is a term that was coined by retired RCMP Staff Sergeant David Ashbaugh, who is considered a world authority on fingerprint identification. David Ashbaugh defined fingerprint identification as, "[t]he study of the uniqueness of friction ridge structures and their use for personal identification."[7] Ashbaugh conducted research and authored a book in 1999 titled *Quantitative-Qualitative Friction Ridge Analysis: An Introduction to Basic and Advanced Ridgeology*. This text is widely accepted as one of the most comprehensive books on the topic of fingerprints and has been the foundation for fingerprint practitioner education and instructional content throughout the world since its publication.

a) Anatomy

Human skin is the largest organs in the body. Providing exterior protection and an outer shell for the skeletal structure and internal organs, skin performs several functions, including sensory input and waste elimination. Friction skin is easily differentiated from the skin found on other areas of the body due to its patterned appearance. The friction skin (i.e., friction ridge) is, "[a] raised portion of the epidermis on the palmar or plantar skin consisting of one or more connected ridge units of friction skin."[8] The pattern formation of friction skin appears similar to a ploughed field, with ridges (hills) being elevated, and rows and furrows (valleys) being the recessed areas between the ridge patterns. Friction skin is localized to two areas—the palmar (the palms and underside of fingers) and the plantar (soles of feet and underside of toes) surfaces.

Culminating from years of independent research into skin structure and pattern formation, the commonly accepted reason for primates having friction skin is to assist with grip.[9] By design, the hills and valleys on the body's palmar and plantar surfaces provide friction or grip, making it easier for the hands to pick up small items, and providing traction while walking barefooted. Friction skin accounts for approximately 5 percent of total surface skin area.

---

7 David R. Ashbaugh, *Quantitative-Qualitative Friction Ridge Analysis: An Introduction to Basic and Advanced Ridgeology* (Boca Raton, FL: CRC Press, 1999).

8 "Scientific Working Group on Friction Ridge Analysis, Study and Technology" (SWGFAST), *Glossary*, "friction ridge" online: www.swgfast.org/documents/glossary/030909_Glossary-Consolidated_ver_1.pdf [SWGFAST glossary].

9 Burtis C. Bridges, *Practical Fingerprinting* (New York: Funk & Wagnalls, 1942).

b) What is a Fingerprint?

In Canada, the term "fingerprint" commonly refers to both the friction skin pattern formation found on human skin, as well as the impression or mark left on a surface after having had contact with this type of skin.

The fingerprint impression or mark is a replication or transference of the patterned skin. It can be likened to a stamp and ink pad. A stamp has elevated and recessed areas. The stamp is placed into the cushioned inkpad to accumulate ink on the elevated surfaces. As the stamp is then placed onto another surface, most often paper, the accumulated ink is transferred onto the surface replicating the detail of the elevated areas on the ink stamp. Friction skin has similar properties to an ink stamp in that an accumulation of fingerprint secretions appearing on the raised area of a fingerprint impression will transfer onto another surface upon contact, replicating the pattern and detail from these areas.

c) The Four Premises of Friction Ridge Identification

To appreciate the usefulness of friction ridge skin for personal identification, it is important to understand the premises on which it is founded. Ashbaugh describes four premises or statements of fact regarding friction ridge identification:

1) Friction ridges develop on the fetus in their definitive form prior to birth.
2) Friction ridges are persistent throughout life except for permanent scarring, disease, or decomposition after death.
3) Friction ridge paths and the details in small areas of friction ridges are unique and never repeated.
4) Overall, friction ridge patterns vary within limits, which allow for classification.[10]

These four tenets are the basis for the viability of friction ridge identification. This will be discussed further in the chapter.

Based on these premises, it is necessary to establish an understanding of the development, structure, persistency, and permanence of friction skin.

---

10 Ashbaugh, above note 7.

d) Biology

Friction skin (friction ridges) starts to develop at approximately twelve weeks of fetal growth. Friction ridges complete their development window at or around seventeen weeks.[11] Although these development time frames may vary slightly, at the seventeenth week of fetal growth, pattern formation is complete and remains unaltered throughout gestation, throughout life, and after death. As stated above, friction skin is only affected by explainable differences such as scarring, disease, post-mortem putrefaction, or decomposition. The size of the impression will obviously enlarge as the individual ages from infant to adult, and may be subject to size difference with weight gain and loss. However, these events have no influence on the pattern formation—only on the size.

Friction ridge formations are, in reality, individual single ridge units or ridge dots forming independently of one another and in a random fashion. These formations can stand independently or in series with other single ridge units, thus creating a longer ridge structure.[12] A friction ridge unit is defined as, "a single section of friction ridge containing one pore."[13] Sweat pores are visible along the top of the friction ridge.

Friction skin comprises two main layers, the dermis and epidermis.[14] The dermis (i.e., the dermal layer) is described as a thick foundation layer. The epidermis (i.e., the epidermal layer) is a thin surface or outer layer that is attached atop the dermis by a double row of dermal papillae, or little skin pegs. The epidermis comprises several sub-layers of skin. Each of the sub-layers referenced below is in descending order from the outer surface inward, with the basal layer being the bottom (innermost) layer of the epidermis, adjacent to the dermis:[15]

- Stratum corneum (horny)
- Stratum lucidum (hyalin/hyaline)
- Stratum granulosum (granular)
- Stratum spinosum (spinous)
- Stratum basal/basale (basal)

---

11 *Ibid.*

12 *Ibid.*

13 "Friction ridge unit" as defined in SWGFAST glossary, above note 9.

14 Bridges, above note 8.

15 Ashbaugh, above note 7.

e) Damaging Effects

The layers of friction skin are important not only to explain friction ridge growth, but also to explain the damaging effects of injury.

The basal (i.e., the stratum basal) is often referred to as the generating layer. It is within this layer that epidermal cell rejuvenation occurs. Cells created in the basal layer will migrate upward through the other four layers of the epidermis to the surface where eventually they are sloughed off as dead skin cells. This process takes approximately one month to complete.

Damage or injury sustained and limited to the epidermis, excluding the basal layer, may heal without any indication and to a pre-injury condition. If an injury damages the basal layer or penetrates the dermis, then permanent damage may occur.[16] This damage may include visible scarring and irreversible alteration to friction ridge formations in the damaged area. Alteration to the ridge formations could appear misaligned from that of pre-injury ridge formation, or as a break in continuous ridge flow due to scarring tissue. Such damage, referenced in the four premises of friction ridge identification, represents an explainable difference to the persistence of the affected friction ridge formations.

B. THE SCIENCE OF FINGERPRINT ANALYSIS

1) Pattern Formation

Development of friction ridge formations is influenced by a variety of factors. As described in the four premises above regarding friction ridge identification, overall friction ridge patterns vary within limits, which allows for classification.

It is generally accepted within the friction ridge identification community that there are three umbrella pattern types from which numerous sub-patterns exist. The overall patterns are:

- Arch pattern
- Loop pattern
- Whorl pattern

---

16 Alice Maceo, "Anatomy and Physiology of Adult Friction Ridge Skin" in Alan McRoberts, ed., *Fingerprint Sourcebook* (Washington, DC: U.S. Department of Justice, Office of Justice Programs, National Institute of Justice, 2011) ch 2, online: permanent.access.gpo.gov/gpo18039/225320.pdf [McRoberts].

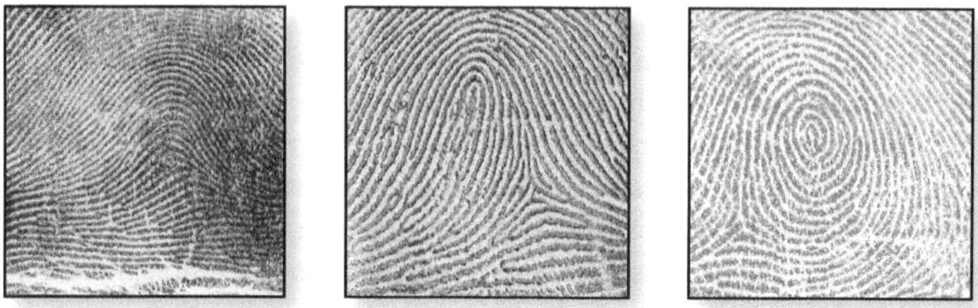

Arch Pattern Loop Pattern Whorl Pattern

FIGURE 8.1. Figure of fingerprint patterns (arch, loop, and whorl). Images created by the author.

These patterns are universal and every person will have one or more of these patterns on their fingertips. Only one pattern (excluding extremely rare "accidental patterns") can be found on each finger, however, individuals can have any combination of these patterns shared on different fingers across both hands. For example, some people will exclusively have all of one pattern, whereas other individuals may have two or more patterns appearing randomly on different digits.

There is a correlation between the location, shape, and size of the volar pads and friction ridge patterns.[17] Volar pads develop *in utero* on the surfaces of the palms, fingers, and feet. These pads are raised surfaces that present the beginnings of friction ridge features as the fetus continues to grow. The characteristics of an individual's volar pads—acted on by pressure (internal and external) and tension during fetal development—will impact upon the type of friction ridge features that develop prior to birth. Pressure or tension on the volar pad during fetal development is indicated by how pronounced or bulbous the volar pad is during the formation of ridges. Varying degrees of pressure may influence which overall pattern type is created. Furthermore, the physical shape and location of the volar pad may have an effect on the ensuing pattern. This is prevalent in the loop pattern, specifically the directionality of the recurving ridges (i.e., which way the loop appears—left or right direction). A more "bulbous" or rounded pad is equated to a high pad, while a less "bulbous" or rounded pad is equated to a low pad. The bulb is like a blister or localized pressure point. Combinations of these internal pressures and the physical shape/

17 Kasey Wertheim & Alice Maceo, "The Critical Stage of Friction Ridge and Pattern Formation" (2002) 52 *Journal of Forensic Identification* 35.

location of the volar pad is essentially what determines overall fingerprint pattern formation.

TABLE 8.1. Table depicting the interrelationship between the location, shape, and size of the volar pads and friction ridge pattern.

Fingerprint Pattern	Internal Pressure during Fetal Development	Physical Shape and Location of the Volar Pad
Arch	Minimal/Low	Low pad
Loop	Medium	Medium pad
Whorl	High	High pad

Research has shown that familial tendencies (i.e., genetics) will also be a factor in determining friction ridge pattern formation. There is an opportunity to pass overall pattern design from parent to child.[18]

2) Fingerprint Pattern Types

As mentioned, three overall pattern types categorize the spectrum of all people. Within the umbrella of arch, loop, and whorl patterns, exists sub-patterns. The following is a list of the patterns and their respective definitions.

a) Arch Pattern

Arch: Plain
A pattern type in which the friction ridges enter on one side of the impression, and flow or tend to flow, out the other side with a rise or wave in the centre.

Arch: Tented
A pattern type that possesses an angle, an up-thrust, or two of the three basic characteristics of the loop.

b) Loop Pattern

A pattern type in which one or more friction ridges enter upon one side, recurve, touch, or pass an imaginary line between delta (defined as, "[t]hat point on a ridge at or nearest to the point of divergence of two type lines, and located at or directly in front of the point of divergence") and core

18 Ashbaugh, above note 7.

(defined as, "[t]he approximate center of a pattern")[19] and flow out, or tend to flow out, on the same side the friction ridges entered. Types include: left slant loops, in which the pattern flows to the left in the impression; right slant loops, in which the pattern flows to the right in the impression; radial loops, in which the pattern flows in the direction of the radius bone of the forearm (i.e., toward the thumb); and ulnar loops, in which the pattern flows in the direction of the ulna bone of the forearm (i.e., toward the little finger).

c) Whorl Pattern

Whorl: Plain
A type of fingerprint pattern which consists of one or more ridges that make, or tend to make, a complete circuit, with two deltas, between which, when an imaginary line is drawn, at least one recurving ridge within the inner pattern area is cut or touched.

Whorl: Accidental
A pattern type consisting of the combination of two different types of patterns (excluding the plain arch), with two or more deltas; or a pattern type that possesses some of the requirements for two or more different types of patterns; or a pattern type that conforms to none of the definitions of a pattern.

Whorl: Central Pocket Loop
A pattern type that has two deltas and at least one friction ridge that makes, or tends to make, one complete circuit, which may be spiral, oval, circular, or any variant of a circle. An imaginary line drawn between the two deltas must not touch or cross any recurving friction ridges within the inner pattern area.

Whorl: Double Loop
A pattern type that consists of two separate loop formations with two separate and distinct sets of shoulders (the shoulders of a loop "are the points at which the recurving ridge definitely turns inward or curves")[20] and two deltas.

---

19 "Delta" and "core" as defined in SWGFAST glossary, above note 9.

20 Federal Bureau of Investigation, *The Science of Fingerprints: Classification and Uses* (FBI, 2006) online: http://www.gutenberg.org/files/19022/19022-h/19022-h.htm.

d) The Frequency of Pattern Types

Statistically, overall pattern types and their respective frequency within the general population are as follows:

- Arch pattern: 10%
- Loop pattern: 60 %
- Whorl pattern: 30%

3) Features within the Fingerprint Impression

Aside from overall pattern types, other descriptors are present within the impression. Two areas of importance are the core and delta(s).

- *Core*: The approximate centre of the impression
- *Delta*: The point on a ridge at or nearest to the point of divergence of two type lines, and located at or directly in front of the point of divergence

The point of divergence is described as the point where the separation of two friction ridges, that have been running parallel or nearly parallel, occurs. Additional features known as friction ridge path characteristics, termed "minutiae" or "Galton Details," are utilized in the identification process.

a) Friction Ridge Path Characteristics (Minutiae or Galton Details)

The term *friction ridge path characteristic* is used to describe a feature of the friction ridge; commonly referred to as minutia(e), Galton detail, point, feature, ridge formation, or ridge morphology. This chapter will focus on the five most commonly referenced major ridge path characteristics.

1) *Ridge unit* (*Ridge dot*): An isolated ridge unit whose length approximates its width in size. Contains one pore.
2) *Short ridge* (*Island*): A single friction ridge beginning, travelling a short distance, and ending.
3) *Ridge ending* (*Ending ridge*): A single friction ridge that terminates within the friction ridge structure.
4) *Bifurcation* (*Dividing ridge*): The point at which one friction ridge divides into two friction ridges.
5) *Enclosure* (*Lake*): A single friction ridge that bifurcates and rejoins after a short course and continues as a single friction ridge.[21]

21 Francis Galton, *Fingerprints* (London: McMillan, 1892).

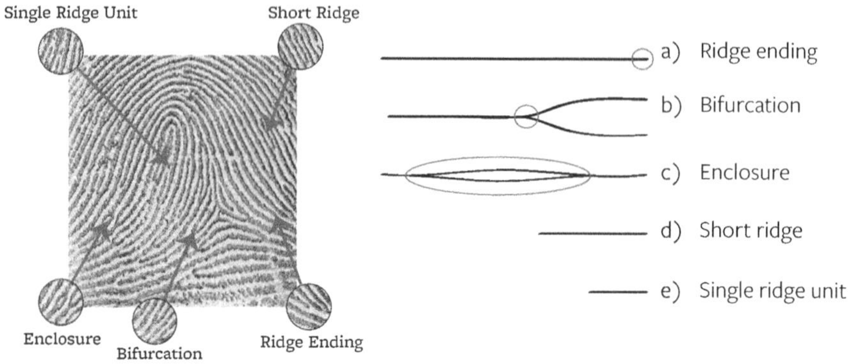

FIGURE 8.2. Figures depicting friction ridge path characteristics. Images created by the author.

4) Fingerprint Composition

In most instances, a fingerprint deposit is a combination from different sources, including naturally secreted materials such as sweat, sebum, or lipids, and foreign materials picked up through daily contact with items and surfaces.

There are three sources of natural secretion on the human body: eccrine glands, sebaceous glands, and apocrine glands. However, only two are considered significant for fingerprint identification purposes: the eccrine and sebaceous glands. Apocrine sweat is not normally a consideration as these glands are primarily found in the underarm and genital areas.[22]

Eccrine sweat glands are located over the entire body and are the only sweat glands located on the palmar and plantar surfaces. Sweat pores located along the peak areas of friction ridge skin secrete eccrine sweat. Although eccrine sweat is the only secretion emanating from the palmar surface and a primary contributor to a fingerprint deposit, it is not the only ingredient. Eccrine sweat is a composition of water and solid materials. Water accounts for approximately 98.5%–99.5% of its structure, with solids being a minimal 0.5%–1.5%. Solid materials include inorganic salts and organic substances.[23] With water being the primary composition of the fingerprint matrix, it may evaporate over time as the moisture content diminishes.

---

22 Michael Bissonnette, Wade Knaap, & Shari L. Forbes, "Steam Development of Latent Fingerprints on Thermal Paper" (2010) 60 *Journal of Forensic Identification* 619.

23 Bridges, above note 8.

Sebaceous glands are found on areas of the body associated with hair follicles. Sebum is secreted from these glands and is comprised mainly of saturated fats, waxes, and squalene. Although sebum is not produced on palmar and plantar surfaces, it readily migrates and is accumulated there as we touch areas of our bodies where it is excreted.[24]

Foreign material, being the third component of a fingerprint deposit, can be any substance that is not manufactured by the body. Although not an exclusive list, the following are commonly found: blood, paint, automotive lubricants, industrial grease, oil, or cooking or food residue. Examples such as these are collected on the palmar area and transferred to the substrate as part of the fingerprint deposit. Even when water evaporates from the fingerprint deposit, generally, the minute amount of other components remains suitable and of sufficient quantity for fingerprint enhancement or development techniques.

Several common factors can affect the composition of fingerprint secretions and the concentration of certain components:

- *Rate and duration of sweating*: Bodily waste materials are vacated through sweat. Excessive and prolonged perspiring can dilute the concentration of solids within the sweat.
- *Dietary habits*: Certain food intake or absence thereof can change the composition of fingerprint secretions and the concentration of its components since dietary intake will influence secretion content and will fluctuate within the individual as well as from person to person.
- *Age*: The concentration of solids within the sweat tends to lessen as we get older.
- *Gender*: Females generally have lower concentrations of solids within sweat than males.
- *Physical health*: General physical health or fitness, as physical conditioning or general health, may influence the quantity of sweat, which relates to the rate and duration of sweating.
- *Physical exertion*: Physical activity will potentially increase or promote sweating.
- *Stress*: Elevated stress or anxiety has been shown to cause an increase in concentration of solids.[25] When people make the conscious decision to commit, or are engaged in the commission of an offence, their stress and anxiety often escalates, resulting in increased sweating

24 Bissonnette, Knaap, & Forbes, above note 22.

25 Max Houck, ed., *Forensic Chemistry* (San Diego, CA: Academic Press, 2015).

and concentration of solid materials. Though such reactions are autonomic, these reactions will differ from person to person.

5) Types of Fingerprint Impressions (Chance Impressions)

The terminology to describe fingerprint impressions will vary slightly, but the following terms are generally accepted:

- *Latent (invisible) impression*: The most commonly encountered fingerprint impression at crime scenes. This type of impression is invisible to the naked eye and requires some form of development technique to render it visible. These development techniques can include fingerprint powder, chemical treatment, or light source. Oblique or grazed lighting techniques can assist in visualizing a latent impression prior to the application of any development technique.
- *Patent (visible) impression*: Patent impressions are visible to the naked eye and require minimal or no development. They are generally composed of a combination of natural bodily secretions and foreign material. Frequently the foreign material is blood, dirt, ink, or grease.
- *Plastic or mold impression*: These are three-dimensional (3D) impressions, created by depressing the finger into soft material. Common occurrences of this type of impression are in chocolate, cheese, putty, caulking, or chewing gum.[26]

For the most part, crime scene fingerprints will be latent deposits (i.e., invisible impressions deposited onto the surface of an item by touch). There are occasions where the reverse occurs, known as take-away impressions, when surface contact is made, but instead of a deposit occurring, something is removed from the surface. This most often occurs with surfaces that are covered with a layer of dust (e.g., computer monitor screens, television screens), and the material is removed from the surface once it is touched. Moisture on the friction skin attracts the dust layer. As the hand is removed from the surface, the dust adheres to the friction skin, creating a void on the surface. The resulting detail is reversed, in that the dust-free area of the impression is replicating the friction ridges, and the remaining dust, the furrows.

---

26 Ross Gardner, *Practical Crime Scene Processing and Investigation*, 2d ed. (Boca Raton, FL: CRC Press, 2012).

6) Surface Suitability for Fingerprint Development

The question is frequently asked, "Can you get a fingerprint from that surface?" Surface suitability is only one factor in determining the success rate of finding and developing a latent fingerprint impression. Surface or substrate suitability can be defined as an environment where "fingerprints can be found on any surface with sufficient size and surface continuity to disclose the necessary ridge characteristics in sequence."[27] This infers that there is no limitation on the suitability of a surface, providing it is large enough and smooth enough to support sufficient friction ridge information to enable the identification process.

In reality however, there are limits on the suitability of a surface to retain an impression, and the ability of the surface or substrate to retain an impression is an important consideration for a forensic investigator in determining whether or not a fingerprint examination will be conducted. Reasons or justifications for not initiating an examination, or explaining poor results can include, but are not limited to:

- The surface was too textured or rough and is therefore unable to sustain continuous agreement of friction ridge structures.
- The surface was contaminated with something that impeded or prohibited examination, for example, if the surface were coated in oil.
- The surface was too small and, as a result, there was insufficient area to support the necessary quantity of minutiae to enable the examiner to draw conclusions.
- The unsafe environment in which the examination would be conducted prevents the examiner from entering. This may be the case if, for example, the scene is structurally unsound.

The previously mentioned reasons or justifications can be applied, being subjective conclusions as determined by the forensic investigator. Based on the knowledge, skills, and abilities of the investigator, the investigator may form the subjective conclusion that a substrate may not be suitable for examination. Past experiences and success rates while examining similar surfaces may factor into this analysis, allowing the investigator to determine if there is justification for processing an item or not. Determining surface suitability is a key responsibility of the fingerprint

27 Wade Knaap, ed., *Toronto Police Scenes of Crime Officer Manual* (2011) [unpublished; copy in author's possession, and the document is still in use with the Toronto Police for training purposes].

examiner. It can be suggested that the only meaningful assessment of surface suitability is to attempt to develop a test impression in an area least likely handled by others. If a latent fingerprint impression can be developed, then the surface is suitable. This is not to suggest that forensic investigators should ignore other considerations, and certainly the addition of unrelated fingerprint impressions to an exhibit can create issues of their own. Forensic investigators require the latitude to determine suitability on their own accord, considering the aforementioned.

7) The Lifespan of a Fingerprint Impression

It is common for the following question to be asked of the fingerprint examiner: "How long can a latent fingerprint impression remain on a surface?" This is a theoretical question, absent context, and not specific to a particular latent fingerprint impression. Undisturbed, is there an expectation of how long a latent impression can survive on any given surface?

The answer is NO.

With current knowledge and technology, there is no way to determine how long a latent fingerprint impression can remain on a surface; however, there are reports of impressions surviving extended periods of time, provided they are left undisturbed.

Three variables that will impact the lifespan of a latent fingerprint impression are:

1) *The person*: As discussed earlier, the composition, quantity, and quality of a fingerprint impression (its matrix) will vary from person to person.
2) *The surface or substrate*: Surface continuity, also known as the texture of the surface, may impact on the ability for a fingerprint impression to be reproduced. If the surface is too rough, then continuity of the impression will not be supported, thus limiting or negating its use. Furthermore, some surfaces are more conducive to retaining fingerprint detail than others. The surface itself or contaminates on the surface, such as oil, may react negatively with the impression, which may result in alterations to or degradation of the impression over time.
3) *The environment*: Fingerprint impressions are delicate by their nature. Due to their composition, environmental conditions can significantly affect the sustainability of an impression. Excessive heat, cold, or exposure to precipitation (e.g., snow, rain) may degrade or obliterate an

impression. If the impression/item was submerged in water, this may also hinder the resulting quality.

a) The Age of a Fingerprint

Another common enquiry regarding fingerprints is: "Can you tell me when that fingerprint impression was placed there?" This question has specificity to a particular fingerprint impression, unlike the general question regarding the lifespan of a fingerprint, which was more theoretical and non-specific.

The answer is NO. However, since this is a general response, it bodes further explanation. There may be occasions when the age of a fingerprint may be narrowed or precisely accounted for through corroborative or supportive evidence and testimony.

Examples of when the age of a specific fingerprint may be narrowed include instances when:

- The fingerprint is deposited onto a time and/or date stamped item, such as a newspaper or point of sale receipt. It may not be feasible to isolate the specific date or time, but the impression was deposited sometime between the creation of the item and the time of discovery or seizure.
- Eyewitness accounts observe the suspect touch a surface.
- The suspect admits to handling an item or touching a surface on a specific date or time.
- Video surveillance shows direct contact onto an item or surface.

8) Surface Considerations

When determining which development technique to use, the forensic investigator weighs a variety of factors. Many accepted development techniques currently used are intended for specific surface types, while others are acceptable for a variety. Arguably, the first consideration should be whether the substrate is porous or non-porous. Non-porous or impervious surfaces will retain friction ridge detail on the surface only, while porous surfaces will permit penetration. When this absorption occurs, it becomes necessary to explore other development options.

The most common porous substrate encountered by forensic investigators is paper. Fraudulent or forged documents, point of sale receipts, death threats, debt lists, non-polymer currencies (real and counterfeit), and other criminal or non-criminal writings frequently require forensic examination.

Amino acids are often present in latent fingerprint impressions and are targeted using chemical development techniques.[28] Reagents are specifically formulated to react with amino acids on or in porous surfaces—1,8 – Diazafluoren – 9 – one (DFO); Ninhydrin; and 1,2 – Indandione – Zinc Chloride are used for this purpose. For a full explanation of various reagents and methods used to process latent fingerprint impressions, see the Appendix in this chapter.

For instances where paper exhibits have been saturated or exposed to an excessive quantity of water, amino acid reagents will no longer work. Amino acids are water-soluble and will dissipate quickly. An accepted alternative for processing evidence of this kind is to utilize chemistry that is suited for fats (lipids), as they will not be affected by water.

Many standard development techniques are available for non-porous surfaces and will be discussed in depth later. For a detailed explanation of many of these techniques, refer to the Appendix.

9) Fingerprint Examination

In fingerprint identification, the individualizing strength of the identification is grounded in the fingerprint's uniqueness. Class characteristics are general characteristics that define a category of items or objects, but alone are not sufficient to define individuality. Individual characteristics are exceptional characteristics that may establish the uniqueness of an object.[29]

As with other forensic disciplines, the fingerprint examiner is tasked with conducting an examination between a questioned and known source. "Questioned fingerprint impression" is a term used to describe the crime scene or unknown impression; "known source" references a fingerprint impression that is known to belong to or has identified a certain individual. For example, a known source may be represented in a fingerprint taken voluntarily from an individual for comparison purposes.

There are a variety of other ways in which an examiner may be provided a known source fingerprint to be used for analysis. These may include, but are not limited to the following:

---

28 Myrian Nafte & Brian Dalrymple, *Crime and Measurement: Methods in Forensic Investigation* (Durham, NC: Carolina Academic Press, 2011).

29 Harold Tuthill, *Individualization: Principles and Procedures in Criminalistics* (Salem, OR: Lightning Powder, 1994).

- A name is provided through investigative leads (i.e., subject is known to police).
- A search is completed on the Automated Fingerprint Identification System (AFIS) of the crime scene impression.
- A sample is discarded from a person of interest, in the public domain.
- A search is completed on AFIS of individuals charged and fingerprinted under authority of the *Identification of Criminals Act*, R.S.C. 1985, c. I-1.

AFIS is a searchable database of persons who have been lawfully fingerprinted under authority of the *Identification of Criminals Act*. In Canada, AFIS is managed by the Royal Canadian Mounted Police (Canadian Criminal Real Time Identification Services—CCRTIS) in Ottawa. Federal, provincial, regional, and municipal police services have access to AFIS through local network user groups. Although some police agencies still use traditional ink and paper for fingerprinting, many are now using digital-electronic scanning devices for this purpose. Digital images of fingerprint impressions can be instantaneously and securely transmitted between police agencies. Although AFIS technologies have replaced single-fingerprint-card file systems of years past, it should be noted that AFIS is simply a searchable database—an investigative tool. It has two basic storage components, one being a fingerprint record of all persons who have been charged in compliance with the *Identification of Criminals Act*, the other being crime scene impressions that have not been identified. As fingerprint impressions are recovered from the crime scene, they are uploaded onto AFIS. Likewise, offender fingerprints are uploaded. A search may link "scene to scene" impressions or "suspect to scene."

AFIS is not relied upon to confirm or exclude identity. It is simply used to narrow the potential search down to fingerprints with similar features (e.g., pattern type and minutiae). Identifications remain the task of qualified fingerprint examiners and are subsequently and independently verified by another qualified examiner. AFIS will provide respondents that have similar spatially related features. The operator will examine each respondent and determine if it is an identification or not.[30]

30 Gardner, above note 26.

a) Quantitative-Qualitative Analysis: Forming an Opinion of Individualization

Considering the concept of identification or individualization is based on a quantitative-qualitative analysis, the examiner must weigh the amount of information present, combined with the quality of that information, when formulating an opinion.

Individualization is the determination by an examiner that there is sufficient quality and quantity of detail in agreement to conclude that two friction ridge impressions originated from the same source.[31] A subjective decision based on objective criteria, individualization, or identification is a conclusion the examiner can arrive at based on the sufficiency and agreement of friction ridge formations within the unknown and known sources. It is the opinion of the examiner that it is "a practical improbability that agreement would exist with another fingerprint impression."[32] If the examiner has doubt about the authenticity of the identification, then an opinion of individualization cannot be formed.

The identification process at one time relied on an accumulated number of points, or points of comparison, but this is no longer the case. Fingerprint examiners would compare the questioned and known fingerprint, tallying the number of points (e.g., ridge path characteristics, deviations, or events) within the two impressions that had spatial similarities or were in agreement. Once a predetermined "threshold number" was reached, the examiner would declare a confirmed identification. It was, and still is, often asked of the expert examiner by Crown and defence counsel, "How many points did you find?" or "How many points do you require to make an identification?"

---

31 Scientific Working Group on Friction Ridge Analysis, Study and Technology (SWGFAST), Document #10, *Standards for Examining Friction Ridge Impressions and Resulting Conclusions (Latent/Tenprint)*, online: www.swgfast.org/documents/examinations-conclusions/130427_Examinations-Conclusions_2.0.pdf [SWGFAST].

32 This is a circulating phrase that is commonly used to express an examiner's opinion that the latent print comparison analysis has been positively identified to a common source. Note, however, that there are many different, acceptable ways to articulate this threshold of sufficiency and this is just one common way to phrase it. For other examples explaining sufficiency and potential wording options for examiner opinions, refer to John R. Vanderkolk, "Examination Process" in McRoberts, above note 16, ch 9 at 17 and 19 [Vanderkolk]. At 17: "In North America, the prevailing threshold of sufficiency is the examiner's determination that sufficient quantity and quality of detail exists in the prints being compared." At 19: "Sufficient details agree and support a determination that the prints came from the same source."

In the early 1970s, the International Association for Identification (IAI) assembled a standardization committee from their ranks to examine the identification doctrine as it applied to fingerprints, conducting a three-year study that was presented in 1973 at the IAI's fifty-eighth annual conference in Jackson, Wyoming. At that time, the following statement was officially endorsed and adopted by all North American friction ridge identification specialists:

> No valid basis exists at this time for requiring that a pre-determined minimum of friction ridge characteristics must be present in two impressions in order to establish positive identification. The foregoing reference to friction ridge characteristics applies equally to fingerprints, palm prints, toe prints and sole prints of the human body.[33]

This position was reaffirmed at the International Symposium on Fingerprint Detection and Identification in Ne'urim, Israel, held from 26 June to 30 June 1995, where the following resolution was agreed to:

> No scientific basis exists for requiring that a pre-determined minimum number of friction ridge features must be present in two impressions in order to establish positive identification.[34]

Fundamentally, the identification process was revamped, adopting the concept of ridgeology. Although examiners continue to look at friction ridge characteristics, deviations, or events, there is a plethora of information within the impression that was not previously considered or articulated. The identification process is now a holistic approach, examining the entire impression and all information that is present. Additionally, the examiner can consider edgeoscopy,[35] poroscopy,[36] and other minutiae not limited to the spatial relationships of ridge path deviations.

---

33 International Association for Identification, *Report of the Standardization Committee* (1973).

34 J. Almog & E. Springer, eds., *Proceedings of the International Symposium on Fingerprint Detection and Identification*, Ne'urim Declaration, Symposium Report (1995) 45:5 *Journal of Forensic Identification* at 489 and 580–81. See also Joseph Polski et al., "The Report of the International Association for Identification Standardization II Committee" (2011) online: www.ncjrs.gov/pdffiles1/nij/grants/233980.pdf.

35 Edgeoscopy is a method of identification through the examination of the unique details and characteristics found along the edges of individual fingerprint ridges.

36 Poroscopy is a method of personal identification through the comparison of the impressions of sweat pores, present on friction ridges of palmar and plantar surfaces. The method was discovered and developed by Edmond Locard in 1912.

"Friction ridge identification is established through the agreement of friction ridge formations, in sequence, having sufficient uniqueness to individualize"[37] is an accurate paraphrase of the philosophy of friction ridge identification as it exists today. This statement can be broken down into four elements: (1) Friction ridge formations (2) in sequence (3) having sufficient uniqueness (4) to individualize.[38]

i) Friction ridge formations

As referenced earlier in this chapter, friction ridge formations are the formations found on friction ridge skin. These are caused through differential growth of ridge units during fetal development and can include major ridge deviations, areas of open fields, intrinsic friction ridge shapes, and relative pore locations.

ii) Sequence

Sequence means, "the act or fact of coming one after the other,"[39] and is synonymous with "systematic." When sequence is maintained, the total available friction ridge area is analyzed and compared systematically. The weight placed on each area of the friction ridge structure when systematically compared is an accumulative process.

iii) Having sufficient uniqueness

Sufficiency is the product of the quality and quantity of the objective data under observation (e.g., friction ridge, crease, scar features). It is a subjective determination. Examiner knowledge, skill, and ability, in concert with the clarity of the print and detail present within it, will factor into the decision of whether sufficient unique detail exists.

The decision of sufficiency is an opinion formed by the examiner, based on friction ridge formations found in agreement during comparison. The validity of the opinion is coupled with an ability to defend that opinion, and both are founded in one's personal knowledge and experience. If the examiner has doubt of whether there is sufficient detail present to individualize, then an opinion of individualization cannot be formed.[40]

---

37 Ashbaugh, above note 7 at 85.

38 *Ibid.*

39 *Ibid.* at 99.

40 *Ibid.*

iv) To Individualize (Identify)

There are *only* three conclusions a qualified fingerprint examiner can arrive at:

1) *Identification*: Agreement exists between the unknown and known source. The determination by an examiner that there is sufficient quality and quantity of detail in agreement to conclude that two areas of friction ridge impressions did originate from the same source.
2) *Exclusion*: Agreement does not exist between the unknown and known source. The determination by an examiner that there is sufficient quality and quantity of detail in disagreement to conclude that two areas of friction ridge impressions did not originate from the same source.
3) *Inconclusive*: The determination by an examiner that there is neither sufficient agreement to individualize nor sufficient disagreement to exclude.

b) Levels of Friction Ridge Detail

In an effort to aid in both understanding and describing the variance in the clarity and detail present in a fingerprint impression, Ashbaugh categorized and defined three levels of detail with specificity. One or more level(s) of detail may be present in a fingerprint impression. As the examination is a quantitative-qualitative analysis, the available detail is weighted accordingly. These descriptors can assist identification specialists when communicating their observations of the impression to colleagues or the court.[41]

An identification is not made using Level 1 detail as its details are more general (i.e., class characteristics) and not unique enough to allow for individualization. Examiners will instead most commonly rely on Level 2 detail to arrive at an identification conclusion as this level of detail shows the unique minutiae of the fingerprint impression. Level 3 detail can also be used, however, these details are not always visible in an impression and, as a result, are not required to make an identification. If Level 3 detail is present, these details would contribute to the individualizing characteristics of the impression.

---

41 *Ibid.* at 94–105.

- *Level 1*: Overall ridge path flow—includes digit orientation, pattern type, and focal points (i.e., core, delta(s), scars, creases) within the impression.

  Identification cannot be established based on Level 1 detail alone, however, it can be used for exclusionary purposes.
- *Level 2*: Ridge path characteristics are visible. Includes the ability to follow continuous friction ridge paths and to observe deviations (i.e., type, location, direction, spatial relationships).

  Identification can be established based on Level 2 detail—the most commonly utilized level of detail during the individualization stage.
- *Level 3*: Friction ridge dimensional attributes, intrinsic shapes, size and shape of pores and ridges (i.e., poroscopy and edgeoscopy).

  Both identification and exclusion decisions can be supported at this level of information.[42]

c) Digit Determination

An important aspect to consider during the examination of crime scene impressions is to determine which digit(s) are present. The examiner should determine if the digits are representative of being deposited as one touch simultaneously (as a cluster impression; more than one digit of the same hand) versus individual touches of each digit. The examiner must determine if, anatomically, it is feasible for the digits to have been deposited as "one touch," given the orientation of the deposit, or if it is consistent with one deposit from multiple digits from the same hand. This may be of importance in recognizing deposits occurring at one time, or subsequent applications. Anatomical aspects may assist in establishing which digit(s), and from which hand, the deposit was made.

i) Ulnar and Radial Loops

As previously addressed, loop patterns account for approximately 60 percent of all fingerprint impressions. A large majority of these have an ulnar slope, that is, the opening of the loop toward the little finger.[43]

In ulnar loops, the ridge enters the pattern area, recurves 180°, and exits on the little finger side (nearest the ulna bone in the forearm). In radial loops, the ridge enters the pattern area, recurves 180°, and exits on

42 Vanderkolk, above note 32, online: permanent.access.gpo.gov/gpo18039/225320.pdf.

43 Bridges, above note 8.

the thumb side.[44] Given the recurrence of ulnar loop pattern formations, it may be of assistance to the examiner in determining the likelihood from which hand the impression originated.

Another consideration of digit determination is to differentiate between a thumb and finger. The physical shape and size of the thumb in comparison to fingers is notable. Thumbs tend to be larger with a distinctive shape to the impression. Other anatomical trends relating to the thumb suggest the core area is lower than the centre point of the impression (the distance between core and tip of digit) with a higher quantity of ridges within that area.[45]

Information obtained from digit determination and orientation can be useful in establishing how an item was handled. This could be crucial in ascertaining if the grasp was offensively or defensively motivated. The court may also draw inferences from such information. As an example, let's say that a broken beer bottle bears developed latent fingerprint impressions. The orientation and location of the impression is vital in forming an opinion on whether the bottle was clutched in a normal drinking fashion or held by the neck, suggesting its use as a weapon.

d) The ACE-V Method

The scientific method that applies to all types of forensic science, including friction ridge identification, is ACE-V (Analysis, Comparison, Evaluation, and Verification).[46]

i) Analysis

It is imperative that the examiner begins the identification process by first studying or analyzing the unknown or questioned fingerprint impression before proceeding to the known source. This ensures that the examiner is only acknowledging minutiae within the questioned impression and not, even unknowingly or on a subconscious level, observing artifacts in the questioned impression that do not exist. This phenomenon can occur if

---

44 Nafte & Dalrymple, above note 28.

45 *Ibid.*

46 R.A. Huber, "Expert Witness" (1959–1960) 2 *Criminal Law Quarterly* 276. See, generally, Michelle Triplett & Lauren Cooney, "The Etiology of ACE-V and its Proper Use: An Exploration of the Relationship between ACE-V and the Scientific Method of Hypothesis Testing" (2006) 56 *Journal of Forensic Identification* 345. See also Peter E. Peterson et al., "Latent Prints: A Perspective on the State of the Science" (2009) 11:4 *Forensic Science Communications*, online: www.fbi.gov/about-us/lab/forensic-science-communications/fsc/oct2009/Zbackup/Review/2009_10_review01_old.htm.

the examiner is predisposed to information in the known impression and envisions that detail in the unknown. In the analysis phase, the examiner is also determining if the impression is sufficient for comparison, what the potential source may be, and whether any distortion issues are present.

ii) Comparison

Once the analysis is complete, a comparison between the unknown and known fingerprint impression begins. During this stage, the examiner will systematically compare both the known and unknown impressions, looking for similarities and differences. These observations are noted, mentally and/or via written bench notes. Unexplainable differences will result in an exclusion.

iii) Evaluation

This is the third step of the ACE-V method, wherein an examiner assesses the value of the details observed during the analysis and the comparison steps to reach a conclusion. As noted, the examiner arrives at one of three possible conclusions: (1) identification; (2) exclusion; or (3) inconclusive (insufficient) detail.[47]

iv) Verification

This is the independent application of the ACE process, as utilized by a subsequent examiner, to either support or refute the conclusions of the original examiner; this process may be conducted as blind verification. Verification may be followed by some level of review as specified by agency policy.[48]

Although a component of the ACE-V methodology, verification stands alone. It is arguably not part of the identification process, but a confirmation of findings as per sound scientific practices.

---

47 Scientific Working Group on Friction Ridge Analysis, Study and Technology (SWGFAST), Document #19, *Standard Terminology of Friction Ridge Examination (Latent/Tenprint)*, online: www.swgfast.org/documents/terminology/121124_Standard-Terminology_4.0.pdf.

48 Referenced from SWGFAST, *ibid*. Verification policy differs from agency to agency. All examiners and their respective agencies subscribe to some form of verification, but how it is conducted isn't mandated. Suffice to say that it must be an independent review or assessment and without bias.

10) The Presentation of Friction Ridge Evidence in the Courtroom

a) Court Challenges: False Identifications

It is imperative to all sciences, including fingerprint identification, that continued research and knowledge is pursued. It is also vitally important to learn from past mistakes. Such is the case with two well-publicized cases where false identifications were discovered.

i) The Case of Brandon Mayfield

On 11 March 2004, in Madrid, Spain, a group of terrorists detonated bombs on several commuter trains, killing over 200 people and injuring over 1,400. From this crime scene, the Spanish National Police (SNP) recovered multiple latent fingerprints, including a print on a bag of detonators.

These prints were sent to INTERPOL for identification. INTERPOL contacted the FBI to assist in this task. The prints given to the FBI laboratory were run through the Integrated Automated Fingerprint Identification System (IAFIS), which identified a list of potential sources for the print. The FBI laboratory then identified latent fingerprint number 17 to a United States citizen, Brandon Mayfield, an individual given as a potential source by IAFIS. A second examiner and the chief of the unit then verified this print.

Once identified, Brandon Mayfield became the centre of the investigation. Mayfield was under twenty-four-hour surveillance and was shown to have links to some suspected terrorists, but no connection to the bombing could be found. The FBI then took further steps to continue their surveillance of Mayfield.

On 13 April, the SNP notified the FBI that they did not agree with the identification made of latent fingerprint 17. After a meeting with the FBI, the SNP agreed to look again at the print.

On 6 May, due to increasing pressure from the media to provide information on a suspect, the FBI arrested Brandon Mayfield as a material witness and executed search warrants on his home and office. In court, Mayfield denied that the fingerprint found on the bag of detonators belonged to him, but he was incarcerated due to the fingerprint identification.

On 19 May, the SNP notified the FBI that they had identified the latent print to Ouhnane Daoud. All prints can be seen in Figure 8.3.

A B C

FIGURE 8.3. Fingerprints compared in the Mayfield case. (A) The recovered latent print, (B) Mayfield's known print, and (C) Daoud's known print.[49]

With this new information, Mayfield was released and the charges against him were dismissed on 24 May. However, by this point, Mayfield had already been identified as a terrorist by the media. In addition, as a lawyer, Mayfield's career was in jeopardy as many believed him to be a terrorist.

After the proceedings of this case, the FBI conducted a full review of their fingerprint analysis processes. Items that were acknowledged to have caused the misidentification included errors by examiners during the examination procedure, the similarities between the latent print and Mayfield's known print, and the pressure to identify a suspect in such a high-profile case. As shown in Figure 8.3, the prints were similar in characteristics, and examiners overlooked differences due to the pressure to find the terrorist. The FBI went on to restructure their analysis process and create a new proficiency test that was more difficult than the previous one. The changes made to the process ensured a more objective analysis, creating a more scientific process. In addition, examiners no longer state that fingerprints are absolutely identified to an individual, as there is still room for human error in the process.

ii) The Case of Shirley McKie

On 6 March 1998, a successful and respectable police officer of the Strathclyde Police in Scotland, Detective Constable Shirley McKie, was accused of leaving a fingerprint within a homicide crime scene from 8 January 1997.

49 Images reprinted with the permission of Ed German, CLPE, FFS, "Problem Idents" (2014), online: onin.com/fp/problemidents.html.

Fingerprint examiners had identified a thumbprint in a bathroom doorframe, located within the victim's house, to McKie; a house that McKie testified she had not entered. Figure 8.4 shows the latent print on the left and the known print on the right.

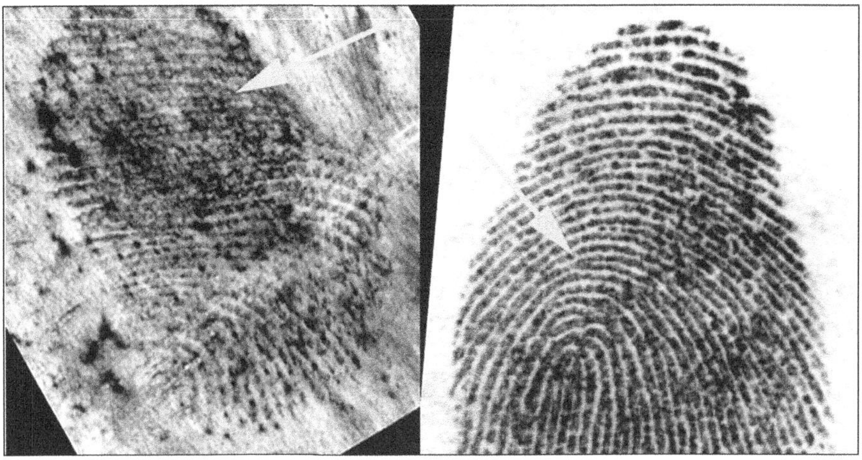

FIGURE 8.4. Four latent fingerprint examiners determined that the latent print at the scene belonged to the police officer.[50]

Upon arrest, police monitored McKie while using the bathroom and taking a shower. At the station, she was paraded in handcuffs in front of colleagues and superiors and referred to as a prisoner. Once inside the charge bar, she was strip-searched by two officers. These actions were excessive in nature and carried out in malice to embarrass McKie in front of colleagues.

McKie was charged with perjury after she testified that she was never inside the residence where the homicide occurred. In McKie's perjury trial, two American experts testified that Shirley McKie was not the source of the print. Due to this evidence, the judge acquitted her at trial, issuing her an apology.

Although this should have put the issue to rest, the Scottish Criminal Records Office (SCRO) refused to admit the misidentification and continued to stand by their original finding. Many recommendations were made as corrective actions for the miscarriage of justice, however, none alleviated the continued actions of the police and SCRO, as well as their belief that the print was sourced from Shirley McKie.

---

50 *Ibid.*

In 2000, due to increased media attention and pressure from the government, the Scottish authorities held an investigation that concluded that Shirley McKie did not make the print. In addition, the original accused and convicted, David Asbury, was freed, as another fingerprint in the case was also deemed erroneous. A member of the Scottish Parliament invited experts from around the world in the fingerprint community to analyze the print. As a result of this invitation, 171 experts from eighteen countries all agreed that the print was not sourced from Shirley McKie.

To this day, the SCRO has still not admitted to having made a misidentification; it claims that fingerprint identification is purely opinion and that its opinion differs from others within the fingerprint community. Although fingerprint analysis is not entirely objective, by utilizing a proper scientific method, errors made by subjectivity can be mitigated and greatly reduced. Recommendations have been made to the SCRO to improve training, education, and the process for analysis to avoid similar issues.

McKie received a settlement of £750,000 as compensatory damages relating to the false identification and subsequent perjury charge.

C. THE ROLE OF THE FINGERPRINT EXAMINER IN CRIMINAL CASES

Categorizing the role of fingerprint examiners is a difficult task as their duties and responsibilities vary not only from one agency to the next, but within their own employ. Many law enforcement agencies will have a blend of civilian members and sworn officer examiners, while others may assign roles with specificity. In some jurisdictions, civilian fingerprint examiners are limited to office functions, such as the uploading of crime scene and known offender fingerprint impressions to the AFIS database, searching prints, and confirming respondent results. Although skilled in fingerprint analysis, they may or may not be permitted to attend court and offer opinion evidence, subject to their agencies' operating protocols.

Forensic identification officers are primarily sworn police officers whose duties may incorporate those of their civilian counterparts; however, the forensic identification officer is also mandated to attend and examine crime scenes, including functions relating to the location, development, documentation, and preservation of fingerprint evidence. Furthermore, forensic identification officers are trained fingerprint examiners and have a responsibility to conduct unbiased comparative analysis between sources of friction ridge skin (e.g., crime scene impression and exemplar).

The results can be beneficial to a criminal investigation by providing circumstantial evidence, insight, or an investigative lead. Forensic identification officers are frequently called upon to provide expert opinion evidence pertaining to fingerprint evidence within the criminal justice system. In that context, it is not the duty of the expert to assess or weigh the evidence. Instead, experts should only present their findings to the court in a neutral fashion, not advocating for one verdict or another.

D. CONCLUSION

For over 100 years, friction ridge identification has been upheld as a viable means of identification. Throughout this time, there have been challenges on varying aspects of the science and its methodologies. Friction ridge identification continues to be one of the most well-established and respected means of personal identification.

E. LEGAL CONTEXT

> Fingerprints, palmprints, and impressions of bare soles have been widely recognized and accepted as a reliable means to identify a person. A reproduction of the friction ridge arrangements on a fingerprint, palmprint, or footprint may be left on an object when it is touched. This permits the impression to be used for personal identification of individuals in criminal investigations. Thus, the forensic science of fingerprints, palmprints, and footprints is utilized by law enforcement agencies in support of their investigations to positively identify the perpetrator of a crime. This forensic science is also used for exculpatory or elimination purposes.
>
> . . .
>
> Any expert trained to competency in forensic friction ridge impression examinations will certainly admit that, in addition to its scientific underpinnings, the task at hand also requires specialized technical knowledge if one is to achieve a reliable conclusion.[51]

Fingerprint identification evidence has one of the longest and most consistent histories of success among the forensic science disciplines. It represented the gold standard of forensic science before the advent of DNA analysis, which was originally termed "DNA fingerprinting" to borrow from

51 Andre A. Moenssens & Stephen B. Meagher, "Fingerprints and the Law" in McRoberts, above note 16, ch 13 at 319 and 321.

the trusted status of fingerprint analysis.[52] Historically, the 1892 Rojas case in Argentina is credited with being the first murder in the world to be solved using fingerprint evidence. Francisca Rojas's two children were murdered. She incurred a throat wound herself and accused a man as the perpetrator, advancing the motive that he was jealous that she loved another and refused to marry him. The man did not confess, despite being severely beaten by authorities. A bloody thumbprint found at the scene matched Rojas and, when confronted with the match, she confessed to the murders.[53]

By comparison, the United States has relied on fingerprints as a means of criminal record identification since 1903, while Canada has relied on fingerprints as "the primary method of identification for law enforcement purposes" since 1908.[54] In 1911, Edward Foster, an inspector with the Dominion Police in Ottawa, testified as one of four fingerprint experts in the American case of *People v. Jennings*.[55] It was "the first American appellate case regarding the admissibility of fingerprint expert testimony."[56] The appellate court found that fingerprint evidence had a scientific basis and was a reliable manner of identification appropriate to expert testimony.[57]

Traditionally, fingerprint identification rests on the premise that fingerprints are unique, on both a microscopic and macroscopic level, as a result of factors in embryonic development that regulate the physical shape and appearance (i.e., the morphology) of friction ridges,[58] therefore allowing individualization (i.e., attributing the fingerprint to one, and only one, source or person).

In recent years, however, the scientific validity of traditional fingerprint analysis has been strongly criticized, drawing attention to the fact that fingerprint analysis is not infallible or irrefutable, as it was once purported

---

52 National Research Council Committee on Identifying the Needs of the Forensic Sciences Community, *Strengthening Forensic Science in the United States: A Path Forward* (Washington, DC: National Academies Press, 2009) at 104, online: National Criminal Justice Reference Service www.ncjrs.gov/pdffiles1/nij/grants/228091.pdf [2009 NAS Report].

53 Jeffery G. Barnes, "History" in McRoberts, above note 16, ch 1 at 15–16 [Barnes].

54 *Ibid.*; *R. v. Beare*; *R. v. Higgins*, [1988] 2 S.C.R. 387 at para. 20 [*Beare*; *Higgins*]. In the U.S., the practice of criminal record keeping using fingerprints began in the state of New York. The first use of fingerprints in a systemic manner in the U.S. was in 1902 at the New York Civil Service Commission.

55 252 Ill. 534, 96 N.E. 1077 (1911).

56 Barnes, above note 53, ch 1 at 17–18.

57 *Ibid.*

58 Henry J. Swofford, "Individualization Using Friction Skin Impressions: Scientifically Reliable, Legally Valid" (2012) 62 *Journal of Forensic Identification* 62 at 66.

to be, and that the logical underpinnings assuming accuracy were flawed. It is now known that claims of infallibility and zero error rates with respect to fingerprint analysis are unjustified and scientifically implausible.[59] In part, this reflects an enhanced understanding of the application of the underlying science to latent print examinations, as affected by a wide range of human factors, including training, experience, bias, cognitive influences, and fatigue, to name a few.[60] With respect to the admission of fingerprint identification evidence in the courtroom, Professor Simon Cole argues that this type of evidence has been grandfathered into American courtrooms from Great Britain as a result of the "fingerprint examiner's fallacy," which he describes as a logical reasoning error, where courts have admitted fingerprint evidence on the basis that the unique nature of fingerprints vouches for the accuracy of the identification process itself. In short, Cole argues that fingerprint uniqueness is independent of an assessment of the accuracy of the identification process.[61]

With respect to the science underlying friction ridge analysis,[62] the criticisms from the National Academy of Sciences (NAS) 2009 report in the United States have included that:[63]

1) The traditional ACE-V methodology, which has been described in forensic literature as early as 1959,[64] is subjective,[65] does not guard against bias, does not guarantee the same results between examiners,

---

59 2009 NAS Report, above note 52 at 142.

60 See, generally, Expert Working Group on Human Factors in Latent Print Analysis, *Latent Print Examination and Human Factors: Improving the Practice through a Systems Approach* (U.S. Department of Commerce, National Institute of Standards and Technology (NIST), 2012), online: NIST www.nist.gov/oles/upload/latent.pdf [*Latent Print Examination and Human Factors*].

61 Simon A. Cole, "Grandfathering Evidence: Fingerprint Admissibility Rulings from Jennings to Llera Plaza and Back Again" (2004) 41 *American Criminal Law Review* 1189 at 1198–199. Note that Cole also explains that fingerprint uniqueness "is impossible to prove, [but] is easy to believe."

62 Friction ridge analysis includes the analysis of the ridge patterns found on both the hands and feet. Together, a collection of friction ridges forms an impression.

63 2009 NAS Report, above note 52 at 136–45.

64 *Ibid.* at 137.

65 *Latent Print Examination and Human Factors*, above note 60. At 9, the report states: "Of course, the mere existence of subjective elements does not make the process unreliable or invalid. Humans can perform many tasks involving subjective judgments quite accurately and consistently. . . . Thus, the mere presence of subjectivity is not a valid criticism of the technique, but it does mean that issues related to human factors can be especially salient to the outcome."

and "does not imply that one is proceeding in a scientific manner or producing reliable results."[66]

2) Contextual bias[67] may affect the results of the analyses, potentially resulting in erroneous fingerprint identifications, as in the case of Brandon Mayfield.
3) Differences between impressions are too easily explained by common sense and "acceptable distortion" based on experience, rather than a scientific foundation, in the interest of making an identification.

Some members of the fingerprint community have viewed the 2009 NAS Report as commendable but inaccurate. For example, Wayne G. Plumtree—the assistant director of the Los Angeles County Sheriff's Department Crime Lab—recommended that "an evidentiary hearing should minimize the weight placed upon the NAS report."[68] Plumtree argued that the NAS committee failed to properly review the latent print discipline as it failed to consider the entirety of the fingerprint community. Instead, the committee focused on a minority of examiners who may have been improperly trained or supervised, and therefore Plumtree believes that many of the issues identified by the committee are not serious since they do not apply to the discipline as a whole.[69] He criticized the report for understating the value of latent prints for forensic purposes, by drawing on the existence of AFIS as evidence of the "high discriminating power of fingerprints."[70] Plumtree suggested that a future report will be issued to correct errors in the existing report.[71]

In response to the 2009 NAS Report, the Honourable Patrick J. Leahy wrote a letter detailing the position of the International Association for Identification (IAI). The IAI agreed with the 2009 NAS Report that further research for independent validation of the comparative analyses conducted by its members is needed, but took the position that "finger-

---

66 2009 NAS Report, above note 52 at 142.

67 See, generally, Peter A.F. Fraser-Mackenzie, Itiel E. Dror, & Kasey Wertheim, "Cognitive and Contextual Influences in Determination of Latent Fingerprint Suitability for Identification Judgments" (2013) 53 *Science and Justice* 144.

68 Wayne G. Plumtree, "A Perspective of the Appropriate Weight to be Given to the National Academy of Sciences' Report on Forensics in Evidentiary Hearings: The Significance of Continued Court Acceptance of Fingerprint Evidence" (2013) 42 *Southwestern Law Review* 605 at 657. The article was published shortly before Mr. Plumtree's retirement.

69 *Ibid.* at 656–57.

70 *Ibid.* at 649–54.

71 *Ibid.* at 659.

print examinations conducted and continuing to be conducted across this country are reliable when conducted by individuals, trained to competency, using scientific and professionally accepted practices and procedures following accepted standards."[72] The IAI provided specific insights to each recommendation made in the 2009 NAS Report stating, in part, that

> Issues of "contextual bias" on the part of forensic examiners are based on poorly structured research and limited testing among the relevant population. None of the existing research involved test subjects who were pre-qualified through skill based testing. It is a great stretch to believe that a professional analyst would risk their integrity and jeopardize the rights and freedoms of the innocent to satisfy some desire to be "accepted" by clients and client agencies.
>
> A mistake often made by critics is to lump acts of fraud, intentional misinformation, with acts of error in calculating the impact on the criminal justice system and society in general. This lumping only serves to confuse the true causes of problematic analyses and does not serve the effort to correct deficiencies.[73]

In accordance with the NAS recommendation to create a national (American) entity for the forensic sciences (which was supported as a concept by the IAI), the National Commission on Forensic Science, co-chaired by the Department of Justice (DOJ) and National Institute of Standards and Technology (NIST), was formed in 2013 to enhance the practice and reliability of the forensic sciences.[74] As a result, the Scientific Working Group on Friction Ridge Analysis, Study and Technology (SWGFAST), the body tasked with creating standards and guidelines for the discipline, was disbanded in 2014. SWGFAST operations were transferred to the Organization of Scientific Area Committees (OSAC) Friction Ridge Subcommittee (FRS) but the existing standards and guidelines by SWGFAST continue to be in effect until the OSAC FRS makes new documents available.[75]

It is important to note that, since the 2009 NAS Report, additional research has been done to estimate the discriminating value of friction ridge

---

72 The Honourable Patrick J. Leahy, "International Association for Identification Letter in Response to the 2009 NAS Report" at 2 (18 March 2009) online: www.theiai.org/current_affairs/nas_response_leahy_20090318.pdf.

73 *Ibid.* at 3.

74 The United States Department of Justice, "National Commission on Forensic Science," online: www.justice.gov/ncfs.

75 SWGFAST, above note 31.

features (i.e., minutiae)[76] using statistical models and reference databases, similar to DNA methods. This research operates on the premise that an entire fingerprint is indeed unique but, since latent prints are usually not representative of an entire fingerprint, the question arises: what is the likelihood or probability that a similar set of minutiae from a specific region of any given fingerprint exists in the world? That is, do regions differ in their similarity? These tools, as well as other studies addressing fingerprint analyses, are expected to improve the transparency of examiner conclusions; to help establish examiner error rates; and to better understand examiner certainty assessments of minutiae points (feature selection) and decision-making with respect to the weight of such features in arriving at an identification. The limitations of these studies, however, must be fully understood before generalizing study conclusions to identifications made in criminal cases, considering the level of variability present in real-world practice. To fairly present the data used to arrive at a conclusion, the examiner should testify to error rates in the discipline and counsel should explore the examiner's reasoning as well as the limitations of the identification process and limitations of the present error rate research.[77]

In Canada, the statutory instruments that govern fingerprinting in the criminal context are the *Criminal Code*[78] and the *Identification of Criminals Act*.[79]

---

76 See, for example, the quote from Stephen J. Taylor et al., *Application of Spatial Statistics to Latent Print Identifications: Towards Improved Forensic Science Methodologies* (Monmouth, OR: Division of Natural Sciences and Mathematics, Western Oregon University, 2012) at 78, online: www.ncjrs.gov/pdffiles1/nij/grants/240590.pdf [report funded by U.S. Department of Justice]. See also Bradford T. Ulery et al., "Measuring What Latent Fingerprint Examiners Consider Sufficient Information for Individualization Determinations" (2014), online: PLoS One www.ncbi.nlm.nih.gov/pmc/articles/PMC4221158; Bradford T. Ulery et al., "Accuracy and Reliability of Forensic Latent Fingerprint Decisions" (2011) 108 *Proceedings of the National Academy of Sciences of the United States of America* 7733, online: www.ncbi.nlm.nih.gov/pmc/articles/PMC3093498; C. Neumann, "Quantifying the Weight of Evidence from a Forensic Fingerprint Comparison: A New Paradigm" (2012) 175 *Journal of the Royal Statistical Society*: Series A1.

77 Personal correspondence with Glenn Langenburg, June 2016. See also, J.J. Koehler, "Fingerprint Error Rates and Proficiency Tests: What They Are and Why They Matter" (2008) 59 *Hasting Law Journal* 1077.

78 *Criminal Code*, R.S.C. 1985, c. C-46. For example, section 487.06(3) relates to taking fingerprints from a person providing an authorized bodily sample for the purpose of the *DNA Identification Act*. Section 487.092(1) relates to a justice's power to order a warrant authorizing the collection of impressions of the body. Section 667 relates to proof of previous conviction. See also Forms 44 and 45 (section 667) and Form 6 (sections 493, 508, and 512). Note that various sections of the *Criminal Code* refer to the *Identification of Criminals Act*.

79 *Identification of Criminals Act*, R.S.C. 1985, c. I-1.

Section 2(1) of the latter statute sets out that persons in lawful custody and charged or convicted with an indictable offence may be fingerprinted, photographed, or subject to other measurements having the object of identifying persons. The Supreme Court of Canada held in *R. v. Beare; R. v. Higgins* that fingerprinting a charged person who has not yet been convicted is constitutional.[80]

Voir dire proceedings that consider the admissibility of fingerprint evidence often focus on arguments involving the *Canadian Charter of Rights and Freedoms*,[81] such as sections 7, 8, and 24(2), as well as impression warrants, rather than the underlying science.[82] Similarly, fingerprint identification evidence has been held to be unreliable in certain cases because of serious concerns over the expert evidence itself, as opposed to the underlying science. In *R. v. J.J.*, for example, the court found the expert opinion of the forensic identification officer to be unreliable, owing to a number of problems with respect to his evidence, including failing to disclose his report before trial; twice incorrectly referencing the print in his identification report; testifying in a manner reflecting that he had not carefully reviewed the basis for his opinion; relying solely on his training rather than scientific literature to support his opinion; twice misidentifying digits; refusing to acknowledge other methods of identification; and failing to disclose that he used a known print from another arrest rather than the arrest involving the present charge.[83]

Typically, forensic identification officers trained in fingerprint analysis testify to their methodology and conclusions in court as expert witnesses. Specifically, these experts will speak to their collection, preservation, processing, identification, and interpretation of the fingerprint at issue. The case of *R. v. Gambilla*, an importation and possession for trafficking cocaine case, serves as a detailed example in caselaw that explains how fingerprint comparisons are conducted, but also features the fingerprint identification expert fairly conceding that such comparisons are not an exact science and that aspects of the analysis reflect the subjective views of the analyst.[84]

---

80 *Beare; Higgins*, above note 54.

81 *The Constitution Act, 1982*, being Schedule B to the *Canada Act 1982* (UK), 1982, c 11.

82 See, for example, *R. v. A.S.S.*, 2013 BCPC 373, where the fingerprints, taken pursuant to a warrant, were excluded.

83 *R. v. J.J.*, 2012 ONCJ 133 at paras. 6–26. For an online resource addressing this case, fingerprints, and the science and the law of various other forensic disciplines, see Mack's Criminal Law, "Fingerprints: The Law," online: www.mackscriminallaw.com/fingerprints-law. Many of the cases covered in this chapter have also been addressed in *Mack's Criminal Law* blog.

84 2015 ABQB 160. See specifically the court's discussion of the expert evidence of Corporal Heidi Godden from paras. 141–70.

Fingerprint identification evidence is useful in a variety of cases, particularly those involving property, theft, and drug offences.[85] Often times, arguments in court centre on the inferences that can be reasonably drawn from fingerprint evidence, rather than the identification itself. The discussion below involves cases where the only issue was identity, and addresses whether the presence of fingerprints can be used to reasonably infer: (1) drug possession; (2) that the fingerprint may not have been left during the offence, based on the totality of the evidence; and (3) that the fingerprint was left during the offence, based on the totality of the evidence.

1) Inference of Possession: Dependent on All the Circumstances and Evidence

In *R. v. Lepage*,[86] the Supreme Court of Canada considered whether drug possession could be inferred based on the presence of fingerprints on a plastic Ziploc bag containing paper sheets with 682 "hits" of LSD. Lepage's fingerprints were on the bag and the bag was found under the couch on which he and his girlfriend were sitting when police executed a search warrant. His fingerprints were not found on the paper itself. Two other people lived in the home; one—Thelland—was jointly charged and took responsibility for the drugs, and then recanted. Lepage did not testify in his own defence at trial and Thelland, who had by then been acquitted by the same trial judge in a severed trial proceeding, testified against Lepage. The trial judge convicted Lepage of possessing LSD for the purpose of trafficking, and for breaching recognizance.

Writing for the majority of the Supreme Court of Canada, Sopinka J. stated that drawing the inference of possession based on the presence of fingerprints is "not subject to a hard and fast rule" and is instead "a question of fact which depends on all of the circumstances of the case and all of the evidence adduced."[87] There was no evidence that Lepage innocently handled the bag. The court found that the fingerprints on the bag containing LSD was highly probative of possession and this evidence was supported by where the bag was found, as well as Thelland's testimony, rendering the conviction reasonable.

---

85 See, for example, the following U.K. study: John W. Bond, "The Value of Fingerprint Evidence in Detecting Crime" (2009) 11 *International Journal of Police Science & Management* 77.

86 [1995] 1 S.C.R. 654 [*Lepage*].

87 *Ibid.* at para. 25.

2) Inference: Fingerprint May *Not* Have Been Left during the Offence

> The probative value of fingerprint evidence depends on the totality of the evidence. Fingerprint evidence will almost always afford cogent evidence that the person whose fingerprint is left on the object touched that object. However, the ability of the fingerprint evidence to connect an accused to the crime charged will depend on whether there is other evidence capable of establishing that the accused touched the object at the relevant time and place so as to connect the accused to the crime.[88]

In the case of *R. v. Mars*,[89] the appellant successfully appealed convictions (arising from a robbery) where the single issue was identity. Only the appellant's fingerprint on a pizza box connected him to the crime; the pizza box was part of a ruse to enter the victims' apartment. A police officer testified to the identification, explaining that he could not determine the age of the fingerprint nor state when the print was placed on the box. The officer further stated that a fingerprint could remain on a surface like a pizza box for years, depending on environmental factors.[90] The eyewitness identification evidence was inconsistent with the appellant.[91]

The trial judge convicted Mars because he was satisfied beyond a reasonable doubt that Mars was involved in the home invasion, even though he could not conclude beyond a reasonable doubt that Mars was the person holding the pizza box when the victim opened the door.[92] The trial judge stated, "Fingerprint evidence, because each person's prints are unique, found at a crime scene is highly inculpatory evidence."[93] The convictions were, in the words of Doherty J.A., "based entirely on the inculpatory *potential* of the fingerprint evidence."[94]

The mere presence of an accused person's fingerprints at a crime scene cannot be assumed to be highly inculpatory evidence as the probative value of fingerprint evidence depends on the totality of the evidence.[95] Justice Doherty held that the convictions were unreasonable, finding that the trial judge made two errors.[96] The first error was based on the trial

---

88 2006 CanLII 3460 at para. 19 (Ont. C.A.) [*Mars*].
89 *Ibid.*
90 *Ibid.* at para. 14.
91 *Ibid.* at para. 1.
92 *Ibid.* at para. 16.
93 *Ibid.* at para. 18.
94 *Ibid.* at para. 4 [emphasis added].
95 *Ibid.* at paras. 19 and 24.
96 *Ibid.* at paras. 1–2.

judge's above-stated and erroneous conclusion that fingerprint evidence is highly inculpatory.[97] Justice Doherty explained that the reasonableness of the verdict turns on whether the inference can be reasonably drawn that the appellant touched the pizza box in connection with the robbery, requiring the court to rely on evidence other than the fingerprint itself to speak to *when* the fingerprint was placed on the box.[98] Since there was no evidence assisting in the determination of when the fingerprint was placed on the pizza box, the trial judge's conclusion that Mars placed his fingerprint on the pizza box at the time of the robbery could not be reasonably drawn.[99] Citing *R. v. Lepage*,[100] Doherty J.A. found that the failure of the appellant to "advance an 'innocent' explanation cannot add weight to the Crown's case so as to justify drawing what would otherwise be an unreasonable inference of guilt."[101] The second error was in relation to the trial judge's understating the exculpatory nature of the eyewitness identification evidence.[102] As a result of the above errors, the conviction was found to be unreasonable and an acquittal was entered.[103]

It is interesting to note that although experts cannot determine when a fingerprint was deposited, caselaw shows that some experts testify to a print being fresh, recent, or likely deposited within a certain time period. It is unclear from the caselaw how such general opinions are reconciled with the inability to determine when a fingerprint has been deposited, making it confusing to learn about this aspect of the discipline through caselaw alone. The age of a fingerprint should not be stated in an analyst's reported findings because it is not scientifically justified and, when providing opinion evidence, an analyst should not stray into making unsupported claims of a print's age. A fingerprint's age, however, can be narrowed or precisely accounted for through corroborative or supportive evidence and testimony.[104]

R. v. D.D.T.,[105] an appeal from convictions for breaking and entering and committing theft under the *Youth Criminal Justice Act*, followed *Mars*. Com-

97 *Ibid.* at paras. 18 and 24.
98 *Ibid.* at para. 20.
99 *Ibid.* at para. 21.
100 *Lepage*, above note 86.
101 *Mars*, above note 88 at para. 23.
102 *Ibid.* at paras. 25–28.
103 *Ibid.* at para. 28.
104 Personal correspondence with Wade Knaap, October 2015. See Section B(7)(a), above in this chapter, for a discussion on information that may be used to substantiate the age of a print.
105 2009 ONCA 918.

puter equipment and a refrigerator were stolen from a Children's Aid Society in 2006, where the point of entry was through the windows at the rear of the building.[106] Justice Epstein entered an acquittal upon determining that the appellant's fingerprints, which were found on window panes removed from the point of entry, could not reasonably support the inference that the appellant touched the windows during the break-in without other evidence. By testifying to the location of the fingerprints on the windows, the investigating officer provided the only relevant evidence addressing the circumstances surrounding the placement of the appellant's finger on the window.[107] Further, "the investigating police officer confirmed that he could not tell how long the prints had been on the windows."[108]

The court described a two-stage process for the appellate review of a verdict's reasonableness in cases where fingerprints are the only means of identification evidence: (1) examine the "reasonableness of the inference that the fingerprints were placed on the object with connection to the crime, at the relevant time and place"; and (2) examine "the soundness of the conclusion that the totality of the evidence and reasonable inferences available to the trial judge were sufficient to prove the appellant's guilt beyond a reasonable doubt."[109] The location where the fingerprints were discovered on the glass was ambiguous; although "a lot of" prints were lifted by the officer from the edge of the windows (suggesting the prints belonged to the perpetrator who removed the windows to gain access to the building), "some" prints were lifted from the centre of the windows.[110]

3) Inference: Fingerprint Left during the Offence

In the appellate judgment of *R. v. Samuels*,[111] the convictions were upheld because of evidence beyond fingerprints that supported a finding of guilt. Samuels was convicted of several criminal offences related to the armed robbery of a home.[112] At trial, each member of the robbed family gave different descriptions of the perpetrators, with one family member testifying that one robber touched a car two doors down from the robbed house while fleeing.[113]

106 *Ibid.* at para. 4.
107 *Ibid.* at para. 27.
108 *Ibid.* at para. 28.
109 *Ibid.* at para. 15.
110 *Ibid.* at paras. 32–33.
111 2009 ONCA 719.
112 *Ibid.* at para. 1.
113 *Ibid.* at paras. 6–7.

The main evidence against Samuels at trial was a palm print and fingerprint on the front windshield of a car parked two houses down from the robbed house. The expert called by the Crown testified to the fingerprint matching Samuels and that the impressions reflected movement from the driver's side of the car towards the passenger's side of the car. The expert stated it was not possible to determine when the prints were placed on the car.[114]

The Crown relied upon other evidence to implicate the accused: the car owner testified that the car was not damaged when he had gone to bed that evening (it was dented after the robbery), and a police officer testified that a muddy footprint leading up to the car, as well as the dent on the car, appeared to be fresh.[115] The Crown further relied upon evidence of prior association between the identified shooter and Samuels.[116] Since other evidence supported the reasonable inference that the palm- and fingerprint were deposited on the windshield when the robber was fleeing the scene, Armstrong J.A. held that the verdicts were reasonable and dismissed the appeal.[117]

In *R. v. Rajalinkham*[118] (an appeal from assault causing bodily harm and related convictions), the main issue before the court was whether the convictions could be safely based on evidence that the appellant's palm print was on the outside of the victim's car.[119] The print was directly above the car's smashed window and the expert, who could not date the print, stated he would be surprised if the print had been present for more than two weeks. The expert further opined that the print's position would be "'anatomically awkward' for it to have been left by a person simply leaning against the car." The print on the car was left using more pressure than that used by the appellant to provide the known print for investigation.[120] The Court of Appeal held that the trial judge was, "entitled to his conclusion that this circumstantial evidence was consistent with guilt and inconsistent with any other rational conclusion."[121]

★ ★ ★

The recent criticisms concerning fingerprint identification can make it tempting for judges to step beyond their proper neutral role in an effort

114 *Ibid.* at para. 9.
115 *Ibid.* at para. 10.
116 *Ibid.* at para. 11.
117 *Ibid.* at paras. 17–24.
118 [2005] O.J. No. 2240 (C.A.).
119 *Ibid.* at paras. 1–2.
120 *Ibid.* at para. 5. This quote is in the words of the court.
121 *Ibid.* at para. 7.

to fully consider the controversies in the discipline. For example, in *R. v. Bornyk* (a Crown appeal from an acquittal of one count of breaking and entering) the key inculpatory evidence at trial was a fingerprint found in the home matching Bornyk's prints; the trial judge acquitted Bornyk on the basis of "troubling aspects" of the expert evidence, citing forensic science articles in his Reasons for Judgment that were not in evidence.[122] The articles were raised by the trial judge himself at the conclusion of the trial, when he reserved judgment and requested further submissions from the Crown and defence. Submissions were provided without objection from either side and the expert was not recalled.

The Court of Appeal agreed with the two grounds of appeal raised by the Crown—that the trial judge had erred in two ways, by: (1) "relying upon independently researched literature that was not properly introduced by either party, not tested in evidence, and not put to the fingerprint witness"; and (2) "engaging in his own unguided comparison of the latent print and known print."[123] In doing so, the trial judge acted as "advocate, witness and judge," compromising the appearance of judicial independence and the fairness of the trial.[124] Whether the difference between the latent and known prints observed by the trial judge is forensically significant is speculation, as it was unassisted by an expert witness in fingerprint analysis.[125] Adopting such an approach opens the door to misunderstanding and misapplying the information in the articles, assuming they are even authoritative in the fingerprint analysis field and applicable to the procedures in this case.[126] The appeal was allowed, the verdict was set aside, and a new trial was ordered.[127] Recent studies have indeed shown expert fingerprint identifications to be more accurate than those made by laypersons, which is attributed to the trained skill and ability of fingerprint examiners. To put it plainly, it is unacceptable for laypersons, including members of the judiciary (even with the best intentions), to make an identification[128] unassisted by a fingerprint examiner.

122 2015 BCCA 28 at paras. 1–4.

123 *Ibid.* at para. 6.

124 *Ibid.* at para. 11.

125 *Ibid.* at para. 19.

126 *Ibid.* at para. 14.

127 *Ibid.* at para. 20.

128 See J.M. Tangen, M.B. Thompson, & D.J. McCarthy, "Identifying Fingerprint Expertise" (2011) 22 *Psychological Science* 995; G. Langenburg, "A Critical Analysis and Review of the ACE-V Process" (2012), online: University of Lausanne Ph.D. Thesis www.unil.ch/files/live//sites/esc/files/shared/Langenburg_Thesis_Critical_Analysis_

Fingerprint identification evidence has been the subject of recent criticisms, but both its critics and supporters seem to agree that fingerprints can be attributed to a common source (i.e., an individual person). Current research, dialogue, and controversy focuses on the meaning and strength of examiner "certainty" in the absence of statistics, as well as the effect of impression quality and human factors when considering the accuracy of the identification decision. In order for criminal lawyers—whether Crown or defence—to be adequately prepared to address fingerprint identification evidence in court, the criticisms and controversies surrounding this discipline must be understood as best as possible to effectively address legal arguments that support or question the validity of fingerprint identification evidence. Similarly, the role of the expert to assist the court requires a full discussion of the identification process and the limitations of this type of evidence, where the expert will ultimately provide an opinion addressing the fingerprint at issue in the specific circumstances of the case. The trier of fact must then weigh the evidence as appropriate in the context of the case as a whole. Most commonly, the matter at issue is not the identification itself, but what inference can be drawn from it.

F. APPENDIX: FINGERPRINT DEVELOPMENT TECHNIQUES (NON-POROUS SURFACES)[129]

1) Fingerprint Powders and Powder Selection

Fingerprint powders are composed of a combination of materials that have been found, by experimentation and practical application, to adhere well to a latent impression. The four most commonly used types of powder (listed below) are applied to the latent fingerprint impression and adhere to the deposit. Powder selection is usually determined to provide contrast of the impression from the substrate, or may just be user preference. The following powders are listed in order from most to least commonly used.

- *Granular Powder*: Applied with a fibreglass filament fingerprint brush or natural hair (squirrel or camel) brush. Granular powder comes in a variety of colours and consists of powdered chemical compounds.

---

of_ACE-V_2012.pdf; and T. Busey et al., "Consistency and Variability Among Latent Print Examiners as Revealed by Eye Tracking Methodologies" (2011) 61 *Journal of Forensic Identification* 60.

129 Note that this Appendix addresses only examples of common practices and is not an exclusive or limiting list.

- *Magnetic Powder*: Applied with a magnetic applicator (called a mag wand) and available in a variety of colours. The magnetic applicator is a forensic instrument, shaped like a pen with a magnet affixed to the tip. The powder is manufactured to work in conjunction with the wand and comprises combined granular powder and iron filings. The iron component enables the suspension powder to be magnetised. The instrument is used like a paintbrush with the suspended ball of fingerprint powder being used similarly to that of the bristles of a brush.
- *Fluorescent Powder*: Applied with a soft feather duster-style forensic brush. This powder should be applied sparingly and visualized with a forensic light source and viewing goggles. This powder is generally used on multicoloured surfaces where a single coloured powder is unsatisfactory for contrast with the substrate. The fluorescing latent fingerprint impression will increase in contrast from the background.
- *Metallic Powder*: Applied with a fibreglass filament fingerprint brush or natural hair (squirrel or camel) brush. Finely ground metal compounds (aluminum, copper, and/or bronze) in a variety of colours. This powder is not used frequently due to the potential health risk to the user.

2) Lifting and Preserving the Impression

Fingerprint impressions developed using these powdering techniques can be labelled with a scale and identifiers, photographed, then lifted and preserved with fingerprint tape and placed onto a backing card.

3) Alternate Lifting Techniques

As mentioned above, in most instances the substrate continuity will be acceptable to lift the impression with fingerprint tape; however, when the surface is textured, other options are available and may be preferred.

- *Gelatin Lifters*: A thin rubber-like membrane that is available in a variety of colours to provide contrast to the developed impression. The lifter has a protective acetate film that, when removed, exposes an adhesive surface. As the gel lifter is applied to the developed impression and then removed, the impression adheres to the adhesive. It can be best preserved by reapplying the clear acetate protective film to the membrane.

- *Polyvinylsiloxanes*: Liquid casting material (e.g., Accutrans® or ReproRubber®) is stored in a dual barrel cartridge (hardener and resin) that is applied with a dispensing gun. The liquid is spread over the developed impression and allowed to cure. Once dry, the material becomes rubber-like and can be removed from the surface, indelibly lifting and securing the impression on the cast.
- *Mikrosil®*: Forensic casting material that is similar in appearance and usability to polyvinylsiloxane; however, it is stored in toothpaste-style tubes. The hardener and resin must be dispensed separately and mixed homogenously. The liquid is then applied to the impression and allowed to cure. Once dry, the material becomes rubber-like and can be removed from the surface, indelibly lifting and securing the impression on the cast.
- *The Knaap Process*: The application of dental stone, a gypsum casting material used in the dental industry. Dental stone slurry is applied to the surface bearing the developed latent fingerprint impression. Once cured, the developed impression is transferred and indelibly secured into the surface of the dental stone cast.
- *Specialty Tape*: Fingerprint tape manufacturers sell specialty tapes as an alternative to regular fingerprint tape. These tapes can be thicker, more pliable and/or stretchable, enabling fingerprints found on difficult or textured surfaces to be lifted more efficiently.

4) Optional Processing Techniques (Non-porous Surfaces)

Cyanoacrylate: Superglue® and KrazyGlue® are cyanoacrylate products. Commercially made processing cabinets are available and use the same principles as an improvised chamber: an item for examination is placed into a cabinet or chamber that is sealable; a quantity of cyanoacrylate is placed on a heat source within the chamber; as the glue heats, it gives off gaseous vapours that will inherently adhere to and polymerize the latent fingerprint impression, effectively turning the fingerprint to glue. The cyanoacrylate process achieves better results by increasing the humidity level within the chamber. This polymerization process will result in a visibly white fingerprint impression. Increased contrast from the substrate can be obtained by applying a fluorescent dye staining (e.g., Rhodamine 6G, Ardrox®, brilliant or basic yellow) onto the impression and visualizing it with a forensic light source and viewing goggles.

Iodine Fuming, camphor smoke, and vacuum metal deposition processes are examples of other commonly used techniques for non-porous surfaces. Many other acceptable processes are also being used and should be explored by the reader.

5) Fingerprint Development Techniques (Porous Surfaces)

- *Iodine Fuming*: Vaporized iodine crystals can be directed onto an area of examination, developing latent impressions. This is a non-destructive technique; however, it is used less frequently due to health risks to the examiner.
- *Amino Acid Reagents*: As mentioned earlier in the chapter, porous surfaces (e.g., paper) require chemical development techniques to visualize latent fingerprint impressions. It should be noted that some success may be achieved by using fingerprint powder techniques on paper; however, chemical processing should be considered as the preferred option.

  The following is a list of amino acid reagents used on paper items:

  - » 1.8 Diazafluoren-9-One (DFO)
  - » Ninhydrin
  - » 1,2 Indanedione Zn/Cl

  Amino acids are water-soluble and are ineffective on previously wetted paper items (e.g., submersed in water or exposed to excessive precipitation). Lipids or fats within the fingerprint secretion are not affected in the same way as amino acids, and other processing options that target them are available.

  The following are common chemistries for paper items that have been previously wetted:

  - » *Fat/Lipid Reagents:*
    - o Physical Developer
    - o Oil Red O

CHAPTER 9

Firearms and Ballistics

Liam Hendrikse

LEGAL CONTEXT: CAITLIN PAKOSH

A. OVERVIEW

The forensic discipline of firearms and ballistics is broad and complex, but the core methodologies employed by experts in the field are not tremendously different today than when first developed.[1] The basis of any forensic investigation is the ability to ask the right questions. Depending on counsel's specific line of enquiry, the knowledge base needed to effectively address forensic firearms issues can range from very basic to highly technical. Having a good understanding of the fundamentals of how different types of firearms work, what the components of ammunition consist of, and the proper use of nomenclature when discussing these issues can ensure that the "right questions" are conveyed properly to an expert and discussed appropriately in a court of law.

Firearms, ballistics, and the role of the firearms expert can be divided into three general categories: theory, casework, and testimony. Each of these can be further divided into three distinct areas that can be presented as evidence for counsel to consider. These are scene of crime work,

1 This is partly due to the fact that the design and use of firearms has not changed substantially since the Victorian era and the American Frontier. The development of "modern" firearms and ammunition began to take place in the middle of the 19th century. The Smith & Wesson Model 1 .22-inch calibre revolver, with its employment of a fully self-contained metallic cartridge, marked a pivotal point in the development of handguns. Such ammunition is still in use today and the semi-automatic pistol has not changed substantially in design over the last 100 years.

analysis at a post-mortem examination, and laboratory analyses and tests. A complete forensic firearms investigation into a homicide, suicide, or suspicious death can involve all three areas.

Counsel should have a good understanding of the principles of firearms, what they are capable of doing, what types of evidence they can produce, and how a firearms expert processes evidence. This understanding is useful when trying to assess whether or not specific questions—or forensic "propositions"—have merit (an expert can, of course, assist in this regard). These propositions can be established in different ways by counsel or by the expert involved in the case. For example, what types of specific situations—or propositions—could produce the physical evidence presented? Conversely, given a hypothetical situation or proposition, what type of physical evidence might one expect as a result?[2]

When these propositions are investigated by both the Crown and the defence, a different, and potentially more balanced, picture of the incident at issue takes form. Defence counsel has the opportunity to see the initial report(s) and explore numerous alternative propositions based on further information given to them by the client(s), by additional witnesses or evidence, or by a qualified expert. The use of a firearms expert can also reveal additional evidence that counsel may not have been aware of in the first instance.

B. THE SCIENCE OF BALLISTICS AND FIREARMS IDENTIFICATION

1) Basic Principles

Two essential questions asked on a regular basis by counsel are "what type of gun is this?" and "how does this gun work?" Understanding how firearms work on a general level can help in understanding the physical evidence encountered in firearms-related casework.

The type of weapon used in a crime will often be dictated by the type of crime itself. The dramatic increase in drug-related crime has led to a corresponding increase in the use of handguns, which are easy to conceal and are often trafficked along with drugs. The use of "long arms" in the form of rifles or shotguns can be found predominantly in domestic or hunting incidents, in addition to some accidental deaths, suicides and mass shootings. Military incidents also involve the use of rifles, assault rifles, and weapons such as machine guns and sub-machine guns. Nevertheless, the

2 R. Cook et al., "A Model for Case Assessment and Interpretation" (1998) 38:3 *Science & Justice* 151.

general function and purpose of each type of conventional firearm remains the same—to use the energy from propellant contained within a round of ammunition to discharge one or more projectiles with lethal effect.

Confusion in the courtroom occurs when different people use different terminology to refer to the same object. For example, the term "casing" has been used in courts to describe a bullet, a cartridge case, and a live round of ammunition. It is therefore easy to appreciate how quickly confusion can arise in court when presenting or discussing firearms-related evidence. There is basic nomenclature that should be used. Some of the most common terms can be found in the glossary to this book.

a) Ammunition

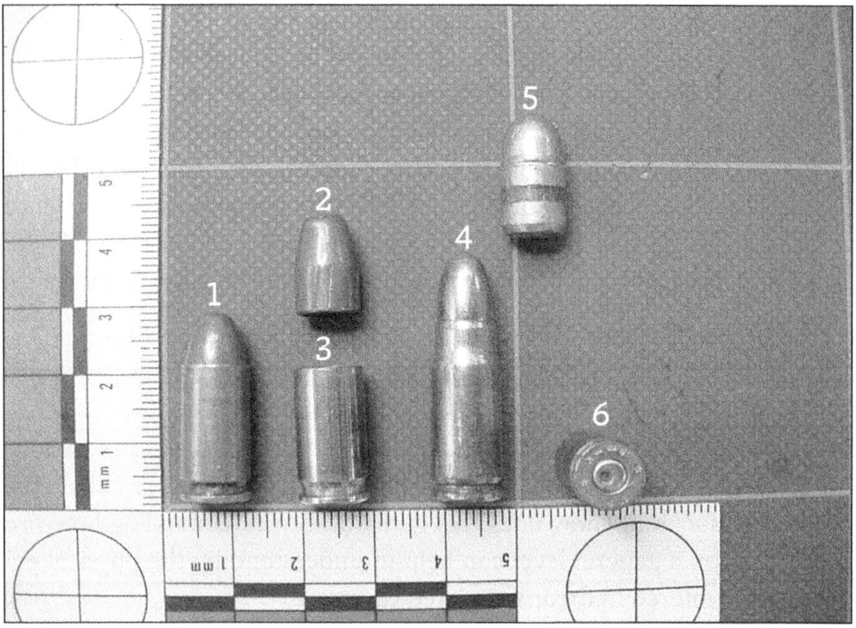

FIGURE 9.1. Ammunition and its component parts.

In Figure 9.1, items 1 and 4 show rounds of live, or unfired, ammunition (sometimes referred to as cartridges) of different calibre and style. Items 2, 3, 5, and 6 show the component parts of the cartridge, with 2 and 5 being the actual bullets and 3 and 6 being the cartridge cases/casings). The bullet is typically one of two types: a "metal jacketed bullet," which has a thin layer of metal over what is typically a lead core fitted to a brass or metal cartridge case (shown in items 1–4); or a solid lead bullet (shown by item 5), which is more commonly found in ammunition for revolvers. The cartridge case contains propellant (i.e., gunpowder) and the bottom of the cartridge case (see item 6) is fitted with a metal disc called the primer. The gun's firing pin impacts and detonates the primer, the primer ignites the main propellant charge, creating heat, pressure, and energy to force the bullet down and out of the barrel and, in the case of semi-automatic handguns, "cycles the action" to extract and eject the fired cartridge case, cock the gun, and chamber the next round of ammunition for firing.

b) Handguns

Handguns generally fall into two categories: revolvers and semi-automatics. Both are considered pistols, but they have clear differences in design and function.

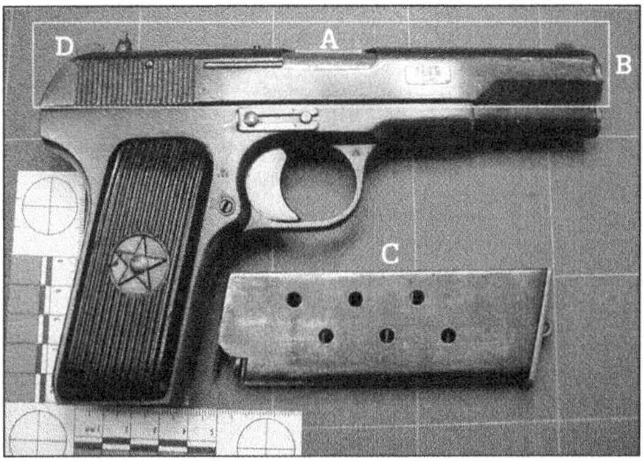

FIGURE 9.2(A). Exemplary semi-automatic pistol with the slide forward and the action closed.

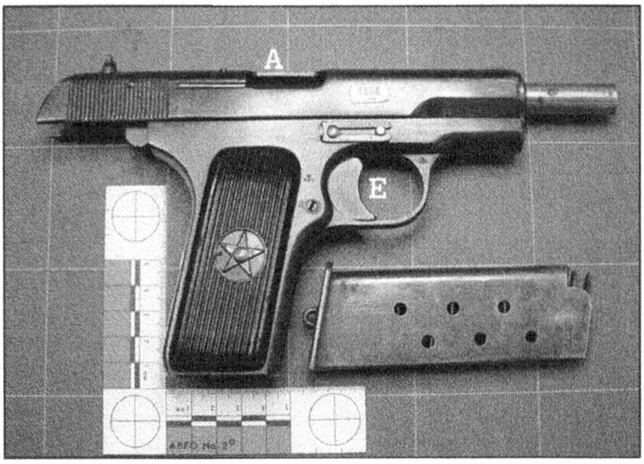

FIGURE 9.2(B). Semi-automatic pistol with the slide back and the breech and chamber exposed.

Figures 9.2(a) and (b) show a semi-automatic pistol. The make, model, calibre, and other information can typically be found stamped on the "slide" (B) and the "chamber" of the barrel (A). The magazine (C) holds the live ammunition. This is fitted into the bottom of the grip. It can be removed by pushing a release button or catch. The partially exposed hammer (D) can also be seen. Not all semi-automatic pistols employ a hammer. Some use an internal striker, which cannot be seen unless the slide is removed from the frame.

The slide (B) can be pulled back manually or forced back automatically by the forces involved in firing a round of ammunition. The latter method ejects the fired cartridge case during the normal course of firing, and then moves forward under spring tension to take a round of ammunition from the magazine and place it in the chamber. This rearward motion of the slide also cocks the weapon. Pulling the trigger (E) again will fire the next round of ammunition and the cycle repeats. Generally, when the magazine is empty and the last shot is fired, the slide is held in the rear/open position by the slide catch. This enables the shooter to demonstrate that the chamber and magazine are empty. This should also be done when a semi-automatic pistol is recovered by an investigation. Ammunition and ammunition components should be securely packaged separate from the firearm, in a non-abrasive container so that any potential toolmarks or individual characteristics are not altered by movement and impact against the packaging.

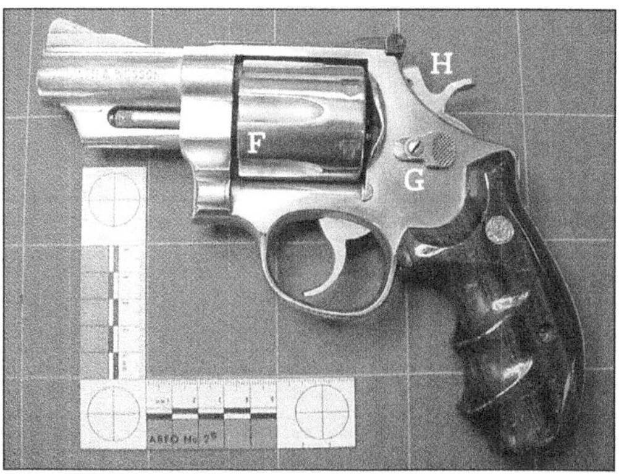

FIGURE 9.3(A). Exemplary revolver, cylinder closed and locked.

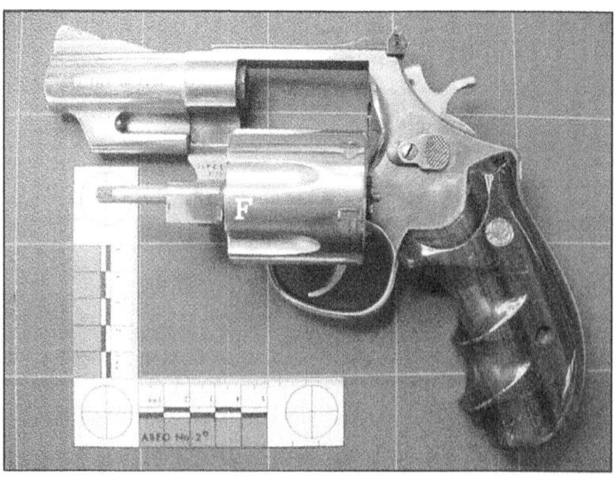

FIGURE 9.3(B). Exemplary revolver, cylinder unlocked and open.

Figures 9.3(a) and (b) show a revolver. The revolver has always been the simpler of the two designs of handgun. The cylinder (F) is unlocked (usually with a button, G) to expose the chambers (Figure 9.3(b)). Ammunition is loaded into these chambers, the cylinder is then closed and locked. The cylinder rotates on its axis. Depending on the specific design, the revolver can be fired in single-action or double-action mode. In single-action mode, the hammer (H) is manually pulled back to a cocked and locked position; a short pull on the trigger then drops the hammer to facilitate firing. Pulling back the hammer also rotates the cylinder so that the next unfired round of ammunition is aligned properly with the barrel. In double-action mode, a longer, heavier pull on the trigger pulls back the hammer and releases it, while at the same time rotating the cylinder. Most modern revolvers can be fired in either mode. Not every revolver has the same type of "swing out" cylinder as pictured above.

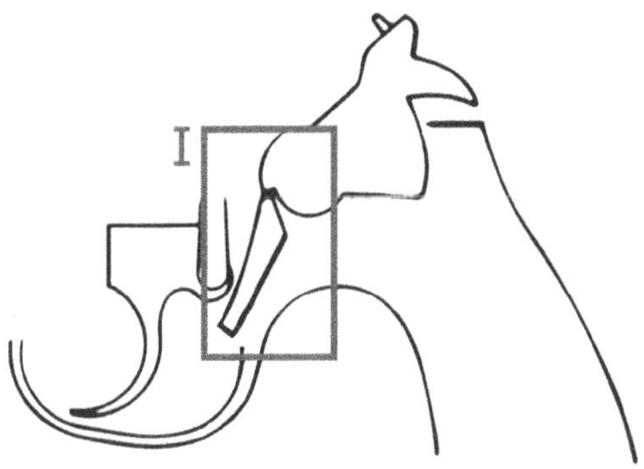

FIGURE 9.4. Internal components of action, sear/notch engagement.

In single-action mode, the hammer is locked back under spring tension when a metal catch referred to as the "sear" engages with a notch in the hammer (Figure 9.4, I). Pulling the trigger releases this engagement so that the hammer falls forward with force. Although marginally more complex, the trigger mechanism on a semi-automatic pistol operates in a similar fashion.

These small, internal parts can be compromised due to the quality of manufacture as well as wear and tear over time. This should always be considered where a gun has been recovered after an alleged discharge, as it relates to the potential for a gun to accidentally discharge.

Unlike a semi-automatic pistol that is designed to automatically extract and eject fired cartridge cases, the cartridge cases fired by a revolver need to be manually removed from the chambers of the cylinder. This has relevance when assessing the type of physical evidence encountered at crime scenes. The absence of fired cartridge cases along with the identification of one or more revolver-style bullets at the scene of the shooting can add a level of information to the investigation about what type of gun(s) may have been used.

c) Internal Ballistics

Internal ballistics is the study of the projectile(s) and related phenomena from the time the primer is struck, discharging the cartridge, to the time the projectile(s) leaves the barrel. During this stage, physical evidence is created in the form of a fired cartridge case and fired bullet, each bearing numerous marks from different parts of the firearm. The combustion of the propellant creates additional physical evidence in the form of firearms discharge residues (FDRs), which become more relevant when dealing with external and terminal ballistics.

Evidence that a gun has been discharged can be quickly determined by a visual inspection of the bore or by conducting a "bore wipe" with a patch of cloth. Fouling in the form of soot, partially burnt and unburnt propellant particles, and additional residue can confirm firing. Importantly, the presence of this type of residue cannot be used to determine when a gun was last fired.

d) External Ballistics

FIGURE 9.5. Exemplary fired bullet (R) along with firearms discharge residues.

External ballistics is primarily concerned with the study of the projectile in flight, after it leaves the muzzle of the barrel. It also incorporates FDRs that initially leave the barrel at velocities similar to that of the projectile. Since FDRs are much lighter than projectiles, they typically do not travel more than a few feet. This has relevance when investigating muzzle-to-target distances as the pattern that these residues produce varies at different ranges from the target.

i) Ammunition

Ammunition comes in different calibres, from different manufacturers, with different sizes and shapes of projectiles, and different types and amounts of propellant. These factors can all affect the patterns of FDRs, the velocity and energy imparted to projectiles, and also the amount of felt recoil that acts in the direction opposite to that of the projectile. Recoil and the travel of a firearm can have relevance when shots are fired in rapid succession by a person unfamiliar with firearms. The final "point of aim" may be markedly different from where it was originally.

Different calibres can also contribute to different sound levels, or perceived loudness, by bystanders, which is a common focal point for counsel in addition to the presence or absence of a muzzle flash. The latter has relevance when reviewing video footage and, again, differences can be seen in this phenomenon across a broad spectrum of calibres. The proximity and resolution of video has a direct bearing on what inferences may be drawn from a possible muzzle flash, or what can be said about any potential firearm and firearms-related evidence observed on-camera.

ii) The Bullet

A bullet is not spherical, so it needs to be stabilized in flight by spinning ("spin-stabilized") for it to travel straight. This spin is facilitated by "rifling," a series of twisting grooves carved into the inside of the gun barrel. As the bullet passes through the barrel, class characteristics in the form of a rifling profile—lands and grooves on the surface of a bullet—are imparted to the bullet (potentially along with individual characteristics), allowing a firearms examiner to offer an opinion on the different makes and models of firearms that could have fired that bullet.

iii) Straight Line Approximation

A straight line approximation is employed when dealing with trajectory analysis over shorter ranges, but this is more general than specific in its approach. One factor that can affect the reliability of the straight line approximation is the presence of intermediary targets. An intermediary target can destabilize the bullet and, depending on the angle of impact and hardness of the target, can cause the bullet to ricochet. This is not always obvious from an analysis of the shooting scene. Subsequent analysis of bullet damage can demonstrate that a ricochet has occurred, but the analysis can be complicated by the target medium and the state of the intermediary target (stationary or moving). The expert should consider these variables when asked to draw an opinion from photographs alone. Additional evidence from the scene may be necessary for a thorough review.

iv) Intermediary Targets

Intermediary targets can have energy imparted to them by the bullet, which can create secondary projectiles that can cause injury or damage. This can be observed by the expert and distinguished from similarly sized evidence such as FDRs. A chemical test for the presence of lead in FDRs can be employed for this purpose; however, this is not always possible when the target medium is the human body. The expert may decide to conduct a confirmatory test on suspect "stippling" or "powder tattooing." When conducted post-mortem, a confirmatory test may be conducted by a firearms expert, the attending pathologist, or another qualified party such as a member of the police forensic identification services.

e) Terminal/Wound Ballistics

Terminal/wound ballistics is the study of projectile(s) upon impact with a target medium. Impact patterns can be seen in the first instance by those attending and analyzing a crime scene where shots have been discharged. The firearms expert has unique expertise with regard to this area and can offer value to this type of investigation. Wound ballistics is also the province of the pathologist, so departments should establish protocols between pathologists and firearms experts to ensure consistency and accuracy when ballistics evidence is discussed.

The documentation and analysis of terminal ballistic effects at crime scenes is predominantly performed by trained members of a Forensic Identification Unit (FIU/FIS/FIB or other). This is separate from input by a forensic firearms and ballistics expert, although the latter is often asked to consider evidence generated by other investigators and is responsible for conducting forensic examinations of clothing.

FIGURE 9.6. Ballistic gelatin and additional tissue simulant, bullet entry at left, bullet's unstable exit at right.

Many of the principles that apply to terminal ballistics have already been covered in the discussions on intermediary targets and ricochet. See Section B(1)(c), above in this chapter, for details of the principles discussed here. A spin-stabilized bullet begins to destabilize upon impacting a denser medium. The loss of spin may lead it to deviate from the straight-line path. It also transfers its energy to the surrounding medium, causing damage. The angle of impact and the hardness of the target can contribute to deflection, ricochet, and fragmentation of a bullet. Entry and exit sites typically have characteristic appearances, and can be distinguished from one another in most cases. A bullet can leave a "bullet wipe" around the margins of an entry site, which can be visually identified and/or subjected to testing for further evidential support. At close range, FDRs can also be deposited around an entry site, and sometimes stippling or powder tattooing can be seen; this is the result of FDRs embedding in a target medium.

2) Considerations for Counsel

a) Identifying Areas of Interest

What are the important factors to consider when reviewing gunshot damage and additional crime-scene related evidence? At the outset, counsel should be provided with the contemporaneous notes of the qualified scene examiner (typically a forensic identification specialist), documenting both the general and specific locations of firearms-related evidence such as: bullet strikes, bullet and cartridge case locations (where applicable), and any other firearms-related phenomena such as ricochet marks. Each article of evidence should be photographed with a scale in proper fashion to allow for the subsequent assessment of such evidence in the context of specific questions that counsel may have. This means that any potential bullet damage should be photographed perpendicular to the vertical and azimuth planes.

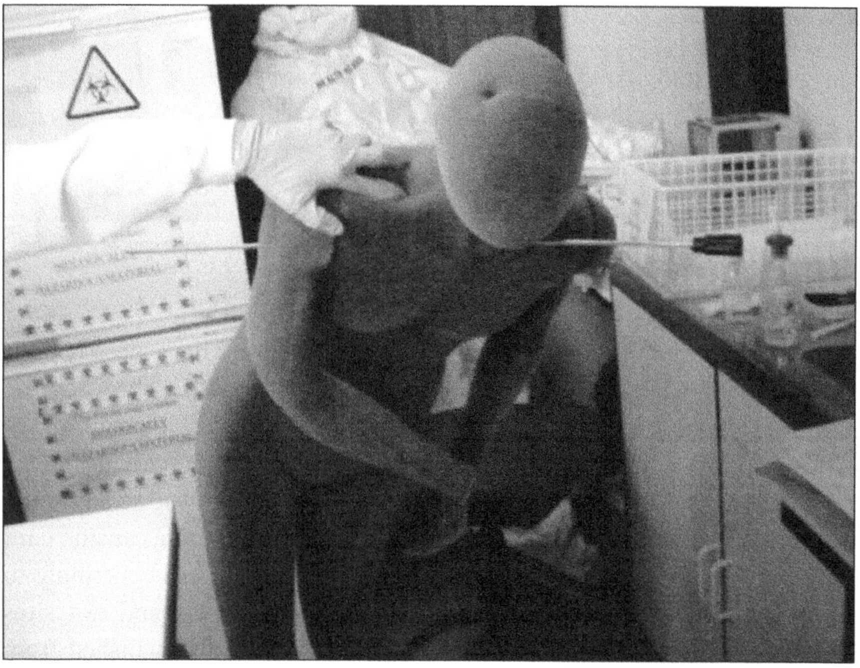

FIGURE 9.7. The use of trajectory rods as part of reconstruction, photographed to present the possible position of the deceased party.

Bullet strikes can also be photographed with "trajectory rods" properly inserted into them to allow counsel to evaluate trajectory (see Figure 9.7). This may be expressed as simply upward/downward or left-to-right/right-to-left. In some cases, however, an actual angle will be measured to give a more specific trajectory. These measurements allow for the theoretical extrapolation of a bullet's trajectory in a rearward direction to offer possible location(s) of the shooter. A number of factors may affect the reliability of the trajectory determination: the type and thickness of the medium that the bullet struck, possible movement of the trajectory rod after insertion into a suspect bullet hole, or any deviation from the approximate straight-line path that may not be accounted for. The term "straight line approximation" is used because it is an approximation, and the information presented as the result of a crime scene analysis or reconstruction has traditionally presented a general picture only. These are not novel concepts, and have been examined more thoroughly elsewhere.[3]

It is sometimes possible to provide greater specificity to an opinion addressing what happened and it is sometimes possible for counsel to rule out propositions that are presented to the expert. For example, a single bullet strike considered along with a single cartridge case may present a very broad range of possibilities for crime scene reconstruction, particularly if a trajectory rod cannot be properly employed. There are a number of possible circumstances causing a single cartridge to be found at a location other than where it was ejected from the gun. In addition, ejection patterns from the same firearm may vary, making it difficult to draw conclusions about what happened at the crime scene.[4] In contrast, several bullet strikes considered along with several fired cartridge cases found in one or more distinct, physical groupings may offer greater certainty regarding the previous course of events in terms of the location of the shooter(s). With the variability of crime scenes, there is no formulaic approach to crime scene analysis. Relevant firearms and ballistics principles and analyses should be applied on a case-by-case basis.

Chemical tests are seldom employed on suspected bullet entry holes or impact sites at crime scenes. When used, however, they are typically presumptive tests to detect the presence of lead, which can provide additional support for the proposition that damage is or is not the result of a bullet strike. Better practice would be for broader use of this type of presumptive testing as there can never be too much forensic documentation and analysis of a crime scene, but there can be too little. Experts rarely get the opportunity to go back and reanalyze a crime scene after a certain length of time has passed. The quality of the work done initially impacts the value of the evidence presented at trial and may ultimately impact the ability to appropriately review historical, or cold, cases.

---

3 M. Haag, "The Accuracy and Precision of Trajectory Measurements" (2008) 40:2 *AFTE Journal* 145.

4 W. Lewinski et al., "Fired Cartridge Case Ejection Patterns from Semi-Automatic Firearms" (2010) 2:3 *Investigative Sciences Journal* 1.

3) Improvements in the Field and Their Application to Historical Cases

The review of old cases is not uncommon, particularly in the United States, where the appeal process is different than in Canada. The practices and methodology in the field of firearms and ballistics have changed little over time because the function and design of firearms has similarly remained largely the same. However, the way in which practitioners collaborate and share information has changed, as has the understanding of the science.

Today, there is a better understanding of the limitations of the field and this is, or should be, reflected in expert report writing and testimony. Standardized testing, guidelines, and protocols have been established to evaluate practitioners and harmonize working practices. The latter has focused on the level of detail required when conducting a physical examination. To improve transparency and encourage thoroughness, examination notes are more descriptive than they once were. This allows the findings to be effectively peer reviewed by a second examiner. Examination notes should also be informative enough, when reviewed in conjunction with contextual information surrounding the case, to allow counsel to draw some inferences from them. Not every possible observation, however, will be made and documented in examination notes.

The establishment of scientific groups such as the National Institute of Standards and Technology, the Scientific Working Group for Firearms and Toolmarks (SWGGUN), and Collaborative Testing Services (CTS) have all contributed to identifying potential areas for improvement in the field, addressing how these improvements should come about, testing of practitioners, and sharing information in a public forum. The Association of Firearm and Toolmark Examiners (AFTE) and the European Network of Forensic Science groups (ENFSI) continually share experiences, knowledge, and new techniques in formal settings. Casework, including specific requests from counsel to conduct a non-routine examination that may assist in clarifying a matter or line of enquiry, also contributes to the growing understanding of firearms and the science of ballistics.

Despite these improvements and the ongoing efforts to standardize the discipline, the quality of individual experts varies depending on their level of experience and the type of firearms-related crimes they are exposed to in their work. This variation in expertise is particularly pronounced in the context of analyses involving crime scenes and post-mortems. This again stresses the need for sharing information and experiences to enhance the familiarity of experts to certain phenomena, particularly when conducting static tests. The quality of the expertise directly ties into the reliability of findings relevant to (1) whether or not a proposition is possible; (2) whether or not the proposition is supported and capable of demonstration in a static environment; and (3) why a phenomenon may have occurred in any given particular incident.

C. THE ROLE OF THE FIREARMS EXPERT IN CRIMINAL CASES

In any firearms laboratory, there is a standard set of general questions that experts ask and they will typically be the only questions asked. This is why the opinion of the expert should include a general disclaimer such as, "I am prepared to review my opinions in light of new information or if the circumstances as stated are found to be incorrect." Of course, any reappraisal by an expert will be more effective if performed before trial, where the expert will have the opportunity to fully consider the new evidence.

The report prepared by a government firearms expert should be accurate within the general parameters of the questions and tests. All significant findings in a report are typically reviewed by a peer. The aim of the expert is to use their extensive knowledge, experience, and ability to conduct tests to answer the following general questions (not every case will implicate every question, and more complex questions can also arise):

1) Is this a firearm?
2) What fired this bullet or cartridge case?
3) Did this weapon fire this bullet or cartridge case?
4) Where are the entry and exit sites in the victim, clothing, or other item(s)?
5) What is the range of firing (i.e., muzzle-to-target distance)?
6) Could the weapon have fired accidentally?

1) The Examination and Significance of Common Questions

a) Is This a Firearm?

When dealing with conventional guns, answering this question is a straightforward process of examining and identifying the submitted item and assessing its mechanical condition before test-firing it to demonstrate that it is in working order. The device may then be classified as a "firearm." For a device to qualify as a firearm, it must be able to discharge a projectile that is capable of causing serious bodily injury or death to a person. If it is, then the next determination is whether it is a restricted, prohibited, or non-restricted firearm.

While it is unlikely that the prosecution and defence will disagree on the classification of a conventional gun, there can be a difference of opinion with guns that have been adapted or modified. There are many modifications and adaptations to a device that might be ineffective in enabling it to satisfy the definition of a "firearm." For example, the most common modification currently encountered is the converted blank-firing/signalling pistol. Removal of the barrel obstruction on a gun intended to fire 9-mm calibre blanks so that it can discharge a conventional round of 9-mm ammunition may prove ineffective due to an undersized or irregular bore. Misalignment between the bore of the barrel and the chamber, or actual damage to the bore, can change the performance of such guns by reducing the velocities and energies of fired projectiles. Because the discharged projectile must be capable of lethal effect or of causing a "serious bodily injury,"[5] this gun might not be classifiable as a firearm. An opinion on this type of gun may be supported through tests to determine muzzle velocity and the kinetic energy of fired projectiles, as well as penetration tests. In the absence of a definition of "serious bodily injury" within the *Criminal Code*, this is an area where a close review of a gun's performance and its comparison to technical data needs to be considered.

The issue of what constitutes a serious bodily injury also has current relevance in the criminal use of air guns. Many of these are legal to buy in stores, but due to their performance in the much-discussed "pig's eye" test and related papers, they are presented as firearms.[6,7] Although the pig's eye test has become generally accepted as a source of data, the question of whether or not it is an absolute test for all types of air guns or converted guns is unclear. Some may consider a database of known injury types collected from casework, or a threshold velocity for consistent penetration of an eye to be a more absolute "test" than a 50/50 test where projectiles fired from a gun may or may not cause such an injury.

---

5 *Criminal Code*, R.S.C. 1985, c C-46, online: laws.justice.gc.ca/en/C-46/index.html.

6 D. Powley et al., "Velocity Necessary for a BB to Penetrate the Eye: An Experimental Study Using Pig Eyes" (2004) 25:4 *American Journal of Forensic Medicine and Pathology* 273.

7 J. Marshall, D. Dahlstrom, & K. Powley, "Minimum Velocity Necessary for Nonconventional Projectiles to Penetrate the Eye: An Experimental Study Using Pig Eyes" (2011) 32:2 *American Journal of Forensic Medicine and Pathology* 100.

The status of guns with missing parts is also an area that should be better understood. What is the gun capable of doing in its current condition, and what is required to restore it to working order? Consideration should be given to the specific make, model, and era of the gun, the specific part that is missing, its availability through legitimate sources, and the level of expertise that would be needed to restore the gun to working order. These are surprisingly complex issues that can be addressed by consulting with a qualified expert.

b) What Fired This Bullet or Cartridge Case?

It is usually quite difficult to determine a specific make and model of a gun from a fired bullet or cartridge case. Different gun manufacturers share similar rifling profiles and leave similar markings and class characteristic(s) on cartridge cases. While the firearms expert should attempt to include every possible make in their report, it is not possible to determine whether or not one make of gun on the list is more likely than another to have been used.

There is no scientific method to determine whether or not a given bullet originated from a specific cartridge case. Microscopic examinations apply only to the comparison of fired bullets to one another, fired cartridge cases to one another, or fired bullets/cartridge cases against test-fires generated from an actual firearm.

When the firearm used at the scene of an incident is not recovered, but the fired bullets and cartridge cases are, the expert will only be able to make observations related to the class characteristics between the fired bullets and cartridge cases at the scene. If the calibre of the recovered bullets, for example, are the same as the recovered cartridge cases, then the expert may conclude that: (1) the bullets were fired from the same gun that fired the cartridge cases; or (2) the bullets were fired from a different gun than the one that fired the cartridge cases. Without recovering the firearm in question, it is not possible to conduct comparison tests on individual characteristics that could link the discharged projectiles or cartridge cases to a specific, individual firearm.

This is a good example of an area where a forensic interpretation of the evidence—in this case, whether or not fired bullets and cartridge cases of the same calibre were fired from the same gun in the absence of a gun—is limited by the tests that can be done. In other words, it is a question of fact that should be addressed by the court based on information provided by the expert and supported by an established test.

c) Did This Weapon Fire This Bullet or Cartridge Case?

When a suspect gun, fired bullet(s) and/or cartridge case(s) are submitted for comparison, the firearms expert fires the gun to obtain control bullets and cartridges cases. Controls are compared using a comparison microscope to determine which areas contain reproducible individual characteristics. Those individual characteristics are compared to the evidential bullet(s) and/or cartridge case(s). Any conclusions drawn are reviewed by a peer. This is the discipline of firearms identification.

Firearms identification relies on the principle that the individual characteristics of a gun are consistent, leaving the same sets of impressions and/or striations on a bullet or cartridge case. On occasion, the tool that creates or finishes a gun part can place the same individual characteristic on consecutively manufactured parts (this is elaborated on below). In its most basic form, firearms identification can be described as "pattern matching."

While the defence does not ordinarily challenge these conclusions, there have been instances where a defence expert has disagreed with the original findings. This may happen with weapons that leave very few reproducible marks on bullets and/or cartridge cases. Comparison microscopy and its principles are always discussed across the forensic community. As the analysis involves a certain amount of subjectivity, complicated by some variability in the quality of the microscopes used, quality assurance trials involving the same test sets of comparison samples can demonstrate different results across the field. In other words, the firearms expert, following proper protocols, may produce an "incorrect" result in a declared test.[8,9]

Subclass characteristics are microscopic marks found on various working parts of a firearm that can be imparted to a fired bullet or cartridge case and can be mistaken for individual characteristics. They are important because the characteristics can be found on more than one firearm, as the manufacturing tool imparts the same fracture(s) to a group of firearms. Subclass characteristics have thus far been found only within the groove impression on fired bullets. This is why comparison and individualization analysis focuses on the land impression. However, subclass characteristics

---

8 Collaborative Testing Services Inc, *Firearms Examination Test No. 10-526 Summary Report*, online: www.ctsforensics.com/assets/news/3026_Web.pdf.

9 European Network of Forensic Science Institutes, *FAID 2005* (2005) [unpublished, on file with author].

on cartridge cases have been documented in published articles[10,11] and collaborative tests. This is why the broader community of firearms examiners has stressed the importance of finding sufficient agreement between marks on fired cartridge cases that were not manufactured by the same tool.[12]

Every expert should be prepared to qualify the opinion of an identification when asked about the possibility of subclass characteristics and also when explaining the meaning of "sufficient agreement" in the case at issue. Photomicrographs—photographs of microscopic comparisons and the agreement found—can be very useful in court. Given the high quality of modern equipment, the use of photomicrographs as demonstrative evidence is very effective, and is becoming a more common practice.

d) Where Are the Entry and Exit Sites in the Victim, Clothing, or Other Item(s)?

The appearance of entry and exit sites can vary with projectile velocity and shape, the condition of the gun barrel, and other phenomena, including intermediary targets. It is important to identify these sites correctly because erroneous entry and exit conclusions will impact the accuracy and reliability of the reconstruction. Identifying the entry and exit sites in a victim post-mortem is not always straightforward. Sometimes the victim's clothing requires forensic examination to confirm which wound represents an entry and which an exit. The attending physician or pathologist is not qualified to conduct forensic examinations into clothing damage. It requires the expertise of a qualified firearms expert.

What happens if debris that resembles firearms discharge residues is found within the wound track by the pathologist and the opinion is given that the muzzle was in close proximity to the deceased at the time of firing, but the clothing worn by the deceased is examined by the firearms expert and there is no evidence of a close-range gunshot? What if that clothing was never submitted for examination? Bullets, particularly those of hollow-point design, can tear fabric from clothing and then deposit that same material in varying amounts along any bullet track. In the absence of further, more

---

10 P. Lardizabal, "Cartridge Case Study of the Heckler & Koch USP" (January 1995) 27:1 *AFTE Journal* 49.

11 G. Rivera, "Subclass Characteristics in Smith & Wesson SW40VE Sigma Pistols" (Summer 2007) 39:3 *AFTE Journal* 247.

12 M.S. Bonfanti & J. De Kinder, "The Influence of Manufacturing Processes on the Identification of Bullets and Cartridge Cases—A Review of the Literature" (1999) 39:1 *Science & Justice* 3.

specific tests, the expert should offer only a provisional opinion. These considerations reinforce the importance of discussion between experts.

The interaction between a bullet and the human body can be unpredictable. A simple straight line trajectory between the entry and exit sites can produce erroneous results as the different densities and shapes of the various components of the human body can cause the bullet to destabilize and change trajectory. Body parts can also twist, turn, and move. In addition, intermediary targets such as heavy clothing, items located within pockets, or other targets between the gun and the victim, can alter both the trajectory of the bullet and the appearance of an entry wound.

To give an example of potential conflicting evidence in a fatal shooting incident, the deceased in a case in North London had what appeared to be a symmetrical bullet entry wound to the middle of the back. The wound was identified at the post-mortem examination and X-rays were taken in an attempt to locate the bullet inside the body. No bullet was found. Based on a provisional observation of the entry wound only, a report at that point might have opined that the bullet was fired roughly perpendicular to the deceased's back, with the deceased in the normal anatomical position. If this wound were presented as a photograph to an expert in court and discussion revolved around deflection or ricochet, the expert may state, "based on the calibre, I would not expect significant deflection or ricochet." Is this a fair statement, and what does it really mean? If the only piece of evidence available is the picture of what is thought to be an entry wound, then it may not be proper to provide a response more specific than that deflection or ricochet "may or may not" be expected.

In the absence of a thorough analysis, the expert needs to be aware of the type of language used when answering a question containing a logical proposition. In the case above, the bullet did appear to enter perpendicularly, but then followed the track of the spine of the deceased upward. The pathologist determined that the bullet had exited out of the end of the deceased's tongue. The bullet was later located in a pool of blood on the street where the deceased fell. This is a good example of what might be considered a random event, one that may never be supported by static tests, and why a proposition based on logic should always be considered by an expert. Framing language, such as "it would be unusual," or "I would not expect," or "not always" is inappropriate because this type of "experiential opinion" often does not apply to specific situations. A proposition is either possible or it is not possible. It is known that a spin-stabilized bullet becomes destabilized when it strikes a medium that is denser than air. Destabilization can lead to a change in trajectory. Striking a harder target, particularly at certain angles or near the edge of the target, can produce both deflection and ricochet. Relying on research or static tests can be applicable and reliable only to the point where they directly relate and apply to the specific situation being addressed.

e) What Is the Range of Firing (i.e., Muzzle-to-Target Distance)?

Firearms Discharge Residues have been previously discussed, but it is important to point out that they are different from microscopic gunshot residue particles (GSR), which are the domain of the firearms chemist. At short ranges, FDRs are deposited on a target and their pattern or distribution varies with range and even from shot-to-shot at the same range. Two shots fired from the same gun using the same ammunition, but at different distances, will produce different residue patterns, while shots fired from the same distance will produce similar patterns. The intensity of the pattern is greater at closer ranges, diminishing at greater ranges until it eventually ceases.

In an ideal situation, the firearms expert will have the gun and ammunition used in the incident and will conduct a series of firing tests to reproduce what was seen on the victim, clothing, or other item, to determine the range of firing. However, the incident gun is often not recovered and it is sometimes not possible to determine the exact make of ammunition used.

While the tests performed are well-established, a number of factors can affect the appearance, and therefore the assessment, of residue patterns. Counsel should be mindful of them. They are:

1) the make of gun and barrel length;
2) the condition of gun;
3) the make and condition of ammunition;
4) the clothing/fabric type;
5) the presence of blood on the victim or clothing, surgical procedures on the victim;
6) incomplete pellet patterns for shotguns; and
7) additional phenomena.

Given the numerous factors that can affect the appearance of residue patterns, range of firing can be a complex issue.

f) Could the Weapon Have Fired Accidentally?

Accidental discharge and trigger pull tests determine whether a gun could fire accidentally without pulling the trigger or if a trigger pull is exceptionally light. The assessment of a gun's safety mechanisms also needs to be done.

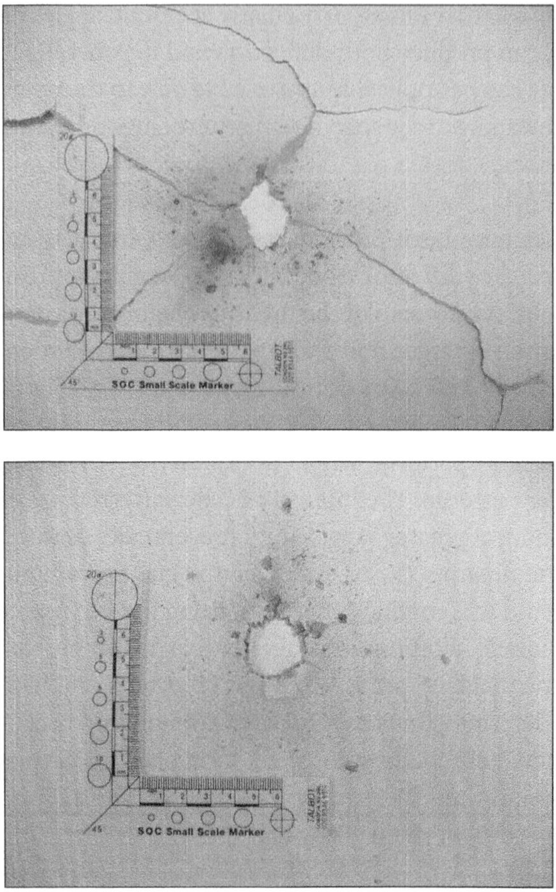

FIGURE 9.8. Exemplary range of firing tests using the same shotgun and ammunition type, at different distances from the target.

Revolvers are generally safer to handle than semi-automatic pistols, even though most do not have a manually operated safety catch. The hammer must be manually cocked or the trigger pulled with considerable force to facilitate firing. Older revolvers can be fired if the back of an uncocked hammer is subjected to an external force, but many modern revolvers have an internal safety block between the hammer and the frame. This means that a device called a "transfer bar" moves into the correct position to transfer the force of the falling hammer to the firing pin only when the trigger is pulled. If the condition of a revolver has been compromised by faulty parts, the removal of certain parts, or the replacement of parts, then even a modern revolver can be susceptible to accidental discharge. These same principles and dangers can exist with semi-automatic pistols.

When the hammer of a revolver is in the cocked position, the most obvious potential for accidental discharge is an attempted de-cocking. An external force on the back of the exposed hammer could also lead to accidental discharge. The potential for accidental discharge increases if the revolver in question does not have an internal safety device such as the transfer bar, or if it has been compromised as previously described. This can be difficult to determine from an external examination as these are internal parts. Again, these same principles can exist with semi-automatic pistols.

Sometimes, "street level" handguns are not in pristine condition. Many of them are the comparatively cheap, less robust metal alloy handguns also known as Saturday Night Specials. Several companies have produced millions of these inexpensive handguns, which appear to be more susceptible to wear and tear of components that are designed to prevent accidental discharge. This susceptibility can lead to these guns being fitted with replacement or ad hoc parts. All of this compromises the overall condition and safety of these handguns, potentially leaving them more susceptible to accidental discharge. If the cocked hammer or striker is not engaging properly, then an external force can cause the hammer or striker to release and fire a chambered round of ammunition. Generally, the safety mechanisms in these cheaper handguns are more rudimentary when compared to their higher quality counterparts.

Accidental discharge tests are conducted on firearms using the general Sporting Arms and Ammunition Manufacturers Institute (SAAMI) method. This method consists of a series of drop tests with the safety (if it has one) on and the firearm in the cocked and ready state. One limitation of the test, particularly with lower quality metal alloy guns or guns in poor condition, is that the test itself may damage or break the gun. This changes the evidence and does not allow for any further testing. With this limitation in mind, if the gun is in poor condition or has had replacement parts fitted to it, then less robust accidental discharge should be performed.

Contextual information can play a key role in determining the appropriateness of the accidental discharge tests. The mechanical condition of the gun should be thoroughly assessed prior to any testing. For instance, in semi-automatic pistols, the hammer/striker is contained within the slide; the sear or catch is contained within the frame. Pulling the trigger moves the catch downward, releasing the hammer/striker. A poor connection between the catch and the notch of the hammer/striker can be uncovered by moving the slide upward to separate the catch from the hammer/striker. This can typically only be done if there is an issue with the quality of fit between the slide and the frame proper. However, whatever the condition, the handgun would need to be subjected to some form of external force for it to accidentally discharge.

The firearms expert typically measures the trigger pull using an electronic gauge, which measures the effort required to pull the trigger in units of pounds or kilograms. There can be variance in opinion on what is considered to be a light- or "hair-trigger," and there is always a difference in the effort required to fire a revolver in single-action versus double-action. Numerous circumstantial factors can bring more scrutiny to the issue of trigger pulls. These factors predominantly relate to the sequence of events or actions of parties during a shooting incident.

D. A CASE STUDY

A male was allegedly shot at in the living room of a residence. The scene was attended by police and physical evidence was recovered and submitted for forensic examination. Standard questions were addressed by a forensic firearms expert.[13] The physical evidence submitted consisted of two fired, slightly impact-damaged bullets and the shirt worn by the individual who was allegedly shot at. No firearm was recovered. The presence of two fired bullets indicated that two shots had been fired, assuming that no other fired bullets were missed during the examination of the scene.

Bullets were identified as "lead round-nosed," which is often seen abbreviated as PbRN in examination notes. Calibre was nominal .38 inch. The type of bullet, in conjunction with an absence of fired cartridge cases, indicated that one or two revolvers had been used to fire them.

Both bullets shared the same class characteristics—their calibre was the same, they appeared to be the same make and style of bullet, and they shared the same rifling profile, which consisted of a number of lands and grooves along with a direction of twist and width. The rifling profile was visually identified and then measured using a micrometer to try to determine the specific make and model of firearm used. In this case, several manufacturers of .38 calibre firearms shared the rifling profile found on the two bullets. It was not possible to provide the investigation with any specific information on the make and model of firearm used. This is not uncommon. The two bullets were then microscopically compared to each other and the individual characteristics found within the rifling impressions were in agreement with one another. The expert opinion was that the two bullets had been fired by the same unknown .38 calibre revolver.

---

13 See Section C, above in this chapter.

Examination of the shirt revealed that there were four holes in it. These were located at the front and back of the left side of the chest and the front and back of the left sleeve. No injuries were sustained by this individual. The holes were confirmed as resulting from fired bullets. Presumptive chemical tests for lead were conducted and lead was found within the margins of two of the holes. These were the holes on the front of the shirt, and the front of the sleeve. This indicated the direction of fire—front to back—and no close-range FDR effects were seen, so the muzzle-to-target range was not close. It appeared that the damage was the result of two separate gunshots.

The firearms expert called by the defence reviewed the case and was also provided with additional information in the form of bullet strike locations within the apartment. The two bullet strike marks were found to be in very different locations—one was in the upper section of a sofa. This introduced a plausible scenario that could be supported by the physical evidence. That is, the damage to the victim's clothing resulted from a single shot while the victim was sitting on the sofa. It could be demonstrated that the fabric of the left sleeve could extend to a position directly behind the entry/exit pair in the left side of the chest area.

This allowed the investigation to consider two possibilities, which is not unusual in a shooting incident. It also demonstrated the importance of sharing information—access to different information can result in different opinions between experts.

E. CONCLUSION

Physical evidence does not exist in a vacuum. It has context. The way a laboratory's analysis of physical evidence relates to information obtained at the crime scene is an important area for counsel's focus. In some jurisdictions, it is not uncommon for the firearms and ballistics expert to attend the crime scene and post-mortem examination and to conduct the relevant analyses. The physical evidence identified during these events can be re-examined in greater detail in the laboratory, where further testing can be conducted if necessary. In this way, a single firearms expert can have ownership over a complex case and be in a better position to address questions or propositions presented in court. Having access to all the pieces of the ballistics puzzle is better than having just a few.

No two cases are ever exactly the same. Random events occur in the field. These events may relate to the manufacture and potential individualization of a firearm, the way a bullet interacts with a target medium; the deposition of firearm discharge residue; and the ejection pattern of fired cartridge cases from a semi-automatic pistol. The constant challenge for a firearms expert is to consider the physical evidence in light of different propositions, to assess the level of certainty behind an opinion, to consider exceptions to the rule, to know when to call for further analysis, and to provide that analysis.

Quite often, the physical evidence combined with theory, research, and experience can support more than one proposition. As a result, two experts might look at the same evidence and express two different opinions. There are multiple reasons for this. Different observations may be made, some interpretations are subjective, knowledge and experience levels can vary, and question(s) or lines of inquiry posed by counsel may be different. These can all contribute to differences in opinions. Many times, there is no one right answer, but rather a broad spectrum of possibilities to explain the physical evidence in a case.

F. LEGAL CONTEXT

> In this Act, 'firearm' means a barrelled weapon[14] from which any shot, bullet or other projectile can be discharged and that is capable of causing serious bodily injury or death to a person, and includes any frame or receiver of such a barrelled weapon and anything that can be adapted for use as a firearm.[15]

The *Criminal Code*'s definition of "firearm" leaves room for interpretation, requiring firearms experts to assist the court in determining whether the device at issue is indeed a firearm and, if it is, the appropriate category of classification: non-restricted, restricted, or prohibited.[16] To this end, a firearms expert may be qualified to testify with respect to issues pertaining

14 *Criminal Code*, above note 4, s. 2. "[W]eapon" means any thing used, designed to be used or intended for use (a) in causing death or injury to any person, or (b) for the purpose of threatening or intimidating any person and, without restricting the generality of the foregoing, includes a firearm and, for the purposes of sections 88, 267 and 272, any thing used, designed to be used or intended for use in binding or tying up a person against their will."

15 *Ibid.*

16 As described in Canada's *Firearms Act*, S.C. 1995, c. 39 and Part III of the *Criminal Code* (ss. 84–117.15). See section 84(1) of the *Criminal Code* for the specifications required of each firearm category. See also *Regulations Prescribing Certain Firearms and Other Weapons, Components and Parts of Weapons, Accessories, Cartridge Magazines, Ammunition and Projectiles as Prohibited, Restricted or Non-Restricted*, SOR/98-462.

to the identification, condition (including damaged or missing parts), manufacture, operation, adaptability to become operative, use and safe handling, and availability of guns and replacement parts. A firearms expert may also provide opinion evidence about ammunition, projectiles, and cartridge magazines, including the ammunition capacity of the firearm in question and the markings on ammunition. The firearms expert may provide testimony addressing the analysis of firearm discharge residue as well.

Criminal Code offences involving firearms relate to use (sections 85–87), possession (sections 88–98.1), trafficking (sections 99–101), assembling (section 102), export and import (sections 103–104), and lost, destroyed, or defaced weapons (sections 105–108). To successfully make out the above offences, the device in question must meet the definition of "firearm" under s. 2 of the *Criminal Code*. Section 84(3) of the *Criminal Code* exempts certain weapons from being deemed firearms.

1) Determining if the Object in Question Is a Firearm

In *R. v. Covin*,[17] a firearms expert testified that fourteen parts of a CO_2 air pistol used in the commission of an armed robbery were either missing or damaged and, of those parts, seven were required for operation. The parts could, however, be replaced in ten to fifteen minutes by an experienced person.[18] Justice Lamer clarified that an operable but unloaded pistol qualifies as a firearm because it can be loaded and fired to cause bodily injury during the commission of the offence. If the pistol is inoperative, the Crown has the burden of proving it is a firearm:

> [I]t is a firearm if, given the nature of the repairs or modifications required and the availability of the parts on the scene, whatever was used could, during the commission of the offence, have been adapted by an ordinary person or by the accused if possessing special skills so as to be capable of firing and of causing serious injury.[19]

The Court applied a purposive approach to section 85 (then section 83)—which addresses the use of a firearm during the commission of an indictable offence—and dismissed the appeal. The Court held that the pistol was not a firearm because it was not operable and could not become operable through repair or adaptation to have the capacity to discharge a

---

17 [1983] 1 S.C.R. 725.

18 *Ibid.* at 727.

19 *Ibid.* at 730.

projectile and to cause serious injury at the time of the offence or during the flight thereafter.[20]

In *R. v. Hasselwander*,[21] the Court held that the application of a purposive approach is equally appropriate when determining the meaning of "capable" as it appears in the definition of "prohibited weapon" in section 84(1) of the *Criminal Code*, stating that the purpose of Canada's prohibited weapons legislation is "to protect the public from these dangerous weapons that are designed specifically to kill or maim people."[22] The interpretation of "capable" extends beyond immediate capacity and includes the potential to be converted to an automatic weapon "in a relatively short period of time with relative ease."[23] The Court restored the forfeiture order relating to the Mini-Uzi submachine gun in question, which was readily convertible from being semi-automatic to fully automatic.[24] The degree of difficulty in altering a weapon to demonstrate prohibited features is often the issue on which post-*Hasselwander* cases turn.[25]

In *R. v. Grant*,[26] both the Crown and defence called firearms experts to testify to the issue of whether the device at issue—a Browning Citori 525 Sporting shotgun receiver, missing its barrel and forestock—was a firearm. The specific question was whether it could be adapted to fire ammunition.[27] In assessing whether the gun was readily adaptable to firing, the court reiterated the test set out in *R. v. Cook*:[28] "is there evidence 'from which it can be reasonably inferred that [the accused] had the capacity by himself or with the assistance of others and within a reasonable time to activate the gun for firing'?"[29] The court preferred and accepted the evidence of the expert called by the defence over the expert called by the Crown since the expert called by the defence was found to be a more knowledgeable and reliable witness on the basis of his experience and the

20 *Ibid.* at 730–31.
21 [1993] 2 S.C.R. 398.
22 *Ibid.* at paras. 35–40 and 46. "Capable" here is seen in the context of the phrase "capable of firing bullets in rapid succession during one pressure of the trigger."
23 *Ibid.* at para. 39.
24 *Ibid.* at para. 47.
25 *R. v. Cancade*, 2008 BCPC 336 at para. 18; conviction appeal dismissed in *R. v. Cancade*, 2011 BCCA 105. See, for example, *R. v. Sinclair*, 2005 ABCA 443; *R. v. Sinclair*, 2006 ABQB 605.
26 [2006] O.T.C. 214 at para. 19 (S.C.J.) [*Grant*].
27 *Ibid.* at paras. 1–9 and 26–29.
28 *R. v. Cook* (1989), 48 C.C.C. (3d) 61 (Man. C.A.).
29 *Grant*, above note 26 at para. 19.

direct inquiries he made into the gun in question.[30] The expert called by the Crown made no specific inquiries into the gun in question and was "prepared to speculate that he could locate the necessary part to make the 525 operational, but he had no idea how long it would take."[31] The court found that the barrel for the 525 could not be purchased commercially but could be obtained from the manufacturer only with "considerable time, difficulty and effort."[32] Ultimately, the court held that Grant did not have the capacity to activate the gun for firing within a reasonable time by himself or with the assistance of others and, as a result, the device was not a firearm.[33]

2) Determining if the Object in Question Must Be Considered a "Weapon" to Be a "Firearm"

In the context of pellet or air guns, expert evidence has assisted the courts in addressing the question, does the device in question need to meet the definition of a "weapon" to be considered a "firearm"? In *R. v. McManus*,[34] the court allowed an appeal from conviction with respect to carrying a concealed weapon contrary to section 90(2) of the *Criminal Code*.[35] The court found that the trial judge erred in finding that the pellet gun at issue was a firearm without first considering whether it was a weapon. The court held that the pellet gun was not a weapon on the basis of the trial record and the trial judge's finding that it was not used to endanger the public peace.[36] The court set aside the conviction and entered an acquittal.

In *R. v. Dunn*,[37] the Crown appealed Alder J.'s acquittal of Dunn for various firearm charges, arguing that the decision in *R. v. McManus*[38] was wrongly decided and failed to consider *R. v. Felawka*, where the majority of the Supreme Court of Canada held that a firearm is always a weapon regardless of the intention of the person carrying the gun.[39] The case turned on the interpretation of the correlative statutory definitions of "firearm" and "weapon."[40] The object at issue was a commercially purchased airgun, complete with a

---

30 *Ibid.* at para. 32.
31 *Ibid.* at para. 33.
32 *Ibid.* at paras. 33–35.
33 *Ibid.* at paras. 35–37.
34 2006 CanLII 26568 (Ont. C.A.) [*McManus*].
35 *Ibid.* at para. 1.
36 *Ibid.* at para. 5.
37 2013 ONCA 539 [*Dunn*].
38 *McManus*, above note 34.
39 [1993] 4 S.C.R. 199.
40 *Dunn*, above note 37 at paras. 1–2.

warning that it was not a toy and its misuse could cause fatal injury.[41] The only issue before the court was whether an object that falls within the section 2 definition of "firearm" also meets the definition of "weapon" in the same section.[42] In considering this question, the court noted that:

> A firearms examiner who gave expert evidence agreed in cross-examination that this type of airgun can be purchased without the purchaser's having to produce any documentation, as long as the muzzle velocity does not exceed 500 feet per second ("ft./s."). The respondent's airgun had an average velocity of 261.41 ft./s.
>
> The expert gave evidence about a scientific study done to determine the velocity needed for a BB to penetrate the human eye—the so-called pig's eye study, which used pig's eyes because of their similar size and composition to the human eye. According to the study's findings, any shot exceeding 214 ft./s. was capable of causing serious injury. A BB shot travelling at this speed would penetrate the eye of a 10-month old pig some of the time. A BB travelling at 246 ft./s. would penetrate the eye 50 percent of the time. The respondent's airgun thus exceeded both thresholds.[43]

The pig's eye test is a threshold standard used to reflect the velocity of a steel BB that might be reasonably capable of causing serious bodily injury.[44] It is important to note that it is not an absolute test and that the data is not gleaned from studying human eyes. In this case, the object in question could create sufficient velocity to meet the "V50 standard"—the speed required of a projectile to penetrate an eye 50 percent of the time.[45] The legislative scheme with respect to firearms was applied by the court by categorizing barrelled objects into three distinct groups according to their ability to shoot a projectile at a certain velocity.[46]

The court stated that "weapon" is a descriptor of "firearm," instead of a formal element of the "firearm" definition, and that to find otherwise would frustrate the parliamentary intention to treat firearms as a distinct, inherently dangerous subset of weapons subject to stricter regulation.[47] Accordingly, when taking into account the legislative history as well as its context and scheme, the court concluded that barrelled objects meeting

---

41 *Ibid.* at paras. 5–6.
42 *Ibid.* at para. 14.
43 *Ibid.* at paras. 7–8.
44 Marshall et al., above note 7.
45 *Dunn*, above note 37 at para. 40.
46 *Ibid.* at paras. 43–46.
47 *Ibid.* at paras. 60–61.

the definition of "firearm" in section 2 do not also need to meet the definition of "weapon" to be considered firearms.[48] The appeal was allowed and three of the four acquittals were set aside. A new trial was ordered on those charges.[49] In 2014, the Supreme Court of Canada dismissed the appeal from the decision of the Court of Appeal on the basis of Justice Rosenberg's reasons, upholding the order for a new trial.[50] In effect, regardless of the use or intended purpose of pellet guns, they can be sufficiently powerful to be considered a firearm. It is unclear if the pig's eye test to determine serious bodily harm will be challenged at the new trial, requiring further expert involvement.

3) Determining if the Firearm Was Discharged Intentionally or Accidentally

In contrast to cases addressing the issue of whether the object in question meets the definition of firearm, cases involving gunshot wounds causing injury or death focus on the issue of whether discharging the firearm was intentional or accidental. In this context, firearms experts may be asked to offer their opinion on the amount of pressure required to discharge the firearm, the distance from which a shot was fired, and whether the firearm could have discharged accidentally (for example, if dropped). With respect to inferring intention from the distance from which the shot is fired, shooting at a person's vital organs at close range suggests an intention to kill.[51] The expert opinion is offered as part of a larger body of available evidence and may be used to support or refute the version of events relayed to the court by witnesses.

In *R. v. Williams*,[52] the court rejected the accused's evidence that the gun discharged accidentally,[53] finding that the evidence of the firearms expert was more consistent with the events described by an eyewitness on key points: (1) there was tattooing[54] or stippling around the deceased's

---

48 *Ibid.* at para. 66.
49 *Ibid.* at para. 67.
50 *R. v. Dunn*, 2014 SCC 69.
51 See *R. v. Baines*, [1985] O.J. No. 41 (C.A.).
52 [2012] O.J. No. 4666 at para. 216 (S.C.J.).
53 *Ibid.* at paras. 204–29 and 274–76.
54 *Ibid.* at para. 82:

> The [firearms expert] witness was familiar with the expression tattooing which he also referred to as stippling. His evidence was it describes phenomena around a bullet wound in instances where the firearm is fired in relatively close proximity

wound, suggesting the firearm discharged approximately three feet away from the deceased and was not in contact with the deceased;[55] and (2) the undischarged bullets on the floor at the scene were more consistent with the firearms expert's explanation of the gun being racked[56] after shooting, than of the accused's explanation that the bullets were ejected after the magazine fell from the gun.[57] The expert testified to the limits of his evidence, explaining that since the firearm in question was destroyed, it was not available for test firing so he could not associate cartridge marks to a particular process or weapon, nor could he draw conclusions about the condition of the firearm, including its safety features.[58]

Similarly, in *R. v. Jaw*,[59] the key issue at trial was whether the decedent, a police officer, was shot intentionally or accidentally.[60] At the time, the officer was responding to a 911 call from the accused's wife in relation to a domestic dispute. A verdict of manslaughter would be appropriate if the killing were accidental, and a verdict of murder would be appropriate if the killing were intentional. The defence argued that the shotgun discharged accidentally during a struggle between the accused and the officer, and that the accused lacked the intention to kill. The Crown relied on forensic pathology and firearms expert testimony addressing the distance from which the shot was fired to argue the killing was intentional. The forensic pathologist estimated that the shot was fired from at least three feet away, likely four to eight feet, on the basis of his analysis of the victim's body.[61] The firearms expert estimated that the shot was likely fired from two to five feet away on the basis

---

to the target surface or skin. He explained [that] the burnt and unburnt gun powder is discharged with a bullet. It can imbed itself in the skin and cause abrasions or burns. This is called tattooing.

55 *Ibid.* at para. 253. The court left open the possibility that this evidence may also be consistent with the version of events described by the accused as he did not describe the distance between the gun and the injured party when the gun was discharged.

56 *Ibid.* at para. 255. The court describes "racking" in the following manner: "[t]he evidence of Mr. Van Drunen [the firearms expert] was that the shell casings would be ejected after the gun was discharged. Undischarged bullets would be ejected by moving the slide backward and forward. This was referred to through the trial as racking."

57 *Ibid.* at paras. 253–56.

58 *Ibid.* at paras. 94–98

59 2009 SCC 42. The issue appealed did not involve the forensic evidence offered at trial but instead involved determining whether the judge's jury charge with respect to post-offence conduct was flawed and whether a new trial was warranted. The Supreme Court of Canada ultimately dismissed the appeal, holding that there was no error in the charge to the jury.

60 *Ibid.* at paras. 6–9.

61 *Ibid.* at para. 8.

of his gunshot residue analysis of the victim's parka and a parka of similar make and style, further testifying that the gun did not discharge by accident. The defence objected to the firearms expert's conclusions, citing the manner of transporting the parka and the order of the chemical tests performed by the expert. The expert admitted that these considerations may have impacted his ability to conclusively form opinions.[62] The expert evidence called by the Crown also contradicted the eyewitness testimony that the accused was holding the butt of the shotgun and the officer was holding the barrel when it fired.[63] On all the available evidence, including the accused having retrieved the shotgun from a closet after being pepper-sprayed, the Crown secured a first-degree murder conviction.

4) The Impact of Identifying a Firearm as the Murder Weapon

As seen in *R. v. Jaw,* forensic pathologists and firearms experts may cross paths in the courtroom. Both have been qualified to provide opinion evidence on the number of times a decedent has been shot. In *R. v. Cain*, for example, the number of times the decedent was shot was at issue—a firearms expert called by the defence at trial was of the opinion that the victim was shot five times, while the pathologist called by the Crown was of the opinion that the victim was shot seven times. The firearms expert testified that the conflicting opinions were the result of the pathologist identifying two wounds as entrance wounds when they were actually exit wounds. A pathologist called by the defence supported the position of the firearms expert.[64]

In an ongoing murder investigation, the identification of a specific firearm as the murder weapon can direct the development of a police investigation and subsequent prosecution, sometimes with harmful consequences. In the malicious prosecution case of Jason Dix, another suspect, Ted Adams, was eliminated based on police intuition and a "fixation" held by police and prosecutors that their location of the apparent murder weapon was connected to Dix, when there was objective evidence contrary to excluding Adams.[65] The police and prosecution viewed the weapon as indicative of guilt, but a firearms expert testified at Dix's preliminary hearing and criminal trial that the weapon had an 80 to 95 percent likelihood of being the murder weapon and Ritter J. explained in his judgment that:

62 *Ibid.*

63 *Ibid.* at para. 57.

64 *R. v. Cain*, [1996] O.J. No. 1588 at paras. 1 & 2 (C.A.).

65 *Dix v. Canada* (AG), 2002 ABQB 580 at paras. 408–9.

> He [the firearms expert] was not able to state that the weapon was for certain the murder weapon. At this trial, the expert went back and forth between saying in his opinion the weapon was the murder weapon but that on a scientific basis he was not able to say that.[66]

During the police investigation, the expert stated to police that they did not need to look for the murder weapon any further since they had found it. Neither the police nor the prosecution reviewed the expert's report, which expressed less certainty, and neither the police nor the prosecution asked the expert for clarification as to why his oral statement during the investigation was more certain than the conclusion in his report.[67] The connection between the murder weapon and Dix was tenuous. Significant, although equally tenuous, evidence pointed to other potential suspects connected to the gun, and the court found that "this should have raised red investigatory flags with the police."[68] Justice Ritter awarded Dix nearly $765,000 in compensation, including damages related to the finding of liability for malicious prosecution and false imprisonment.[69] This case serves as a lesson to investigating authorities and the prosecution to be cognizant of their own bias when conducting an investigation and prosecution, respectively, particularly if it is marked by a problematic expert opinion and weak inculpatory evidence.

5) The Role of the Judiciary: Protecting Trial Fairness

The trial judge plays an important role in keeping trial proceedings fair by deciding the admissibility of evidence and delivering jury instructions that are accurate to the evidence. The case of *R. v. Belic*,[70] an appeal from conviction of second-degree murder and two counts of aggravated assault, addresses an instance where the trial judge excluded evidence relating to the muzzle flash of a gun on the basis that defence counsel "juiced" up the testimony of a firearms expert. The conviction rested on a range of inculpatory evidence,[71]

---

66 *Ibid.* at para. 413.

67 *Ibid.* at para. 412.

68 *Ibid.* at para. 422.

69 *Ibid.* at paras. 619–48.

70 *R. v. Belic*, 2011 ONCA 671.

71 *Ibid.* at paras. 3–6. This evidence included the appellant's behaviour, including the appellant showing a friend his handgun, evidence suggesting he provoked the fight that ended in the shooting, and forensic evidence linking the appellant to the handgun and ammunition that killed the deceased.

as well as witness testimony that a muzzle flash was seen near the area of the appellant at the time shots were fired.[72] The issue of the admissibility of the expert's evidence with respect to the muzzle flash and the trial judge's jury charge respecting that evidence became the focal ground of the appeal.

At trial, the defence advanced the theory that seeing the muzzle flash would not allow a witness to identify the shooter in a group of people.[73] Although the firearms expert agreed that identifying one person in a group on the basis of the muzzle flash would be difficult, he testified that the flash itself is an area beyond his expertise and that he was not comfortable commenting on witnesses' perceptions of the flash.[74] Despite this, the defence closing address relied heavily on the expert's evidence and essentially equated the expert's unwillingness to comment on the significance of the flash to the existence of reasonable doubt in the case:

> He [the firearms expert] will not attribute who the shooter is in terms of the muzzle flash. That is the firearms expert. Whose evidence are we going to rely on? Eye-witnesses in a bar who probably have never seen a flash of a gun before in their lives, [or] a guy whose life is dedicated to that science. That's reasonable doubt.[75]

The trial judge read to the jury the summaries written by the Crown and the defence of their respective positions verbatim, even including the position of the defence that the expert was "'adamant' that a muzzle flash near a person did not necessarily mean that person was the shooter." This would put into question the location of the shooter based on witness testimony.[76] The trial judge then added:

> With respect to that, I would add the following; I note that Mr. Staniek [the expert] was not qualified as an expert regarding muzzle flash establishing the location of the shooter. Rather, Mr. Staniek was allowed to provide expert opinion evidence as a firearms and tool marks examiner. The issue of a muzzle flash and the location of the shooter in relation to the muzzle flash, is not part of his expert testimony. Rather, that determination does not require expert opinion and may be determined by you the jurors, as part of your common sense interpretation of the evidence before you.[77]

---

72 *Ibid.* at para. 3.
73 *Ibid.* at para. 7.
74 *Ibid.* at para. 8.
75 *Ibid.* at para. 9.
76 *Ibid.* at para. 10.
77 *Ibid.* at para. 11.

Defence counsel objected to the trial judge's commentary but the trial judge then stated:

> With Mr. Staniek, it would appear to me that you were trying to take evidence that isn't part of what he was qualified to give expert opinion evidence about, and juice it up into being expert opinion evidence. So I'm going to correct it.[78]

The appellant argued that the trial judge erred in his jury instruction respecting the muzzle flash evidence by ruling it as inadmissible expert opinion evidence. Further, the appellant argued that the trial judge undermined the defence's closing position because the trial judge did not inform the defence of this admissibility ruling in a timely fashion.[79] The Court of Appeal held that there was no error in ruling that identifying the shooter by means of the muzzle flash was beyond Staniek's expertise because it was clear that the trial judge was surprised by the position of defence counsel and, in light of how the defence's position with respect to this evidence developed, there was no error on the part of the trial judge for failing to make the ruling earlier or to warn of the nature of the instruction.[80]

6) Summary

Overall, the evidence provided by firearms experts is varied, complex, and relevant to a number of matters at issue, depending on the individual circumstances of the case. The above cases illustrate the importance of knowledgeable and reliable experts to the effective and just functioning of the criminal justice system, while underscoring the importance of clear communication between the expert and all agents of the system. The significance and limits of the evidence must be understood and respected by police, the prosecution, and the defence. When these parties go beyond their role to investigate, prosecute, and advocate, respectively, then it is up to the trial judge to remind these parties of their roles and to direct the necessary action to ensure the trial process is fair. The complexity of firearms expert evidence and the law surrounding firearms more generally, demands a commitment to detail and accuracy from both the scientific and legal communities.

---

78 *Ibid.* at para. 16.

79 *Ibid.* at para. 12.

80 *Ibid.* at paras. 13–14 and 17.

CHAPTER 10

Fire Investigation

Vladimir (Val) Chlistovsky

LEGAL CONTEXT: CAITLIN PAKOSH

A. OVERVIEW

1) Introduction

According to the National Fire Protection Association's *Guide for Fire and Explosion Investigations* (*NFPA*[1] *921*), fire investigation is "[t]he process of determining the origin, cause, and development of a fire or explosion."[2] More broadly, fire investigation involves collecting and analyzing information from a fire scene to determine where the fire originated, what caused it, and the circumstances that contributed to the ignition and subsequent fire spread.

In the public sector, results from fire investigations are used to assess and monitor trends as well as to inform the development of codes and standards designed to reduce the incidence of fires and related injuries. In the private sector, insurance companies will rely on fire investigators to determine if the cause of a fire falls within a covered category and, in

1 Online: www.nfpa.org. The National Fire Protection Association (NFPA) is a non-profit organization established in 1896 and headquartered in Quincy, MA. Its mission is to "reduce the worldwide burden of fire and other hazards on the quality of life by providing and advocating for scientifically based consensus codes and standards, research, training and education."

2 Technical Committee on Fire Investigations, *NFPA 921: Guide for Fire and Explosion Investigations, 2014 Edition* (Quincy, MA: National Fire Protection Association, 2013) s. 3.3.67 [*NFPA 921*]. Unless stated otherwise, the facts, processes, and methodology for fire investigations discussed in this chapter apply equally to explosion investigations.

subrogated claims (suits to recover costs from a responsible third party), to determine liability or negligence. Fire investigations are also conducted to determine if a fire was intentionally set, assisting the court in establishing if the evidence is sufficient to meet the required burden of proof.

Practitioners in the field of fire investigation should have the skills, experience, and knowledge of several scientific disciplines. In terms of basic methodology, a fire investigator must systematically gather factual data relevant to the fire scene to conduct an analysis that is detailed and accurate. The data collection and analysis ". . . should be accomplished objectively, truthfully, and without expectation bias, preconception, or prejudice."[3] The purpose of a fire investigation is typically to determine, in order: (1) the fire's origin(s); and (2) the fire's cause. To create (i.e., to cause) a fire, three key elements must be present: an ignition source, fuel, and oxidant (e.g., air or oxygen).[4] As part of the investigation, the fire investigator should consider the "circumstances, conditions, or agencies" that could have brought together these basic elements.[5]

2) History

In North America (and many other parts of the world) the premier resource and guide for fire investigators is *NFPA 921*, the *Guide for Fire and Explosion Investigations*,[6] which was first published in 1992. Prior to the release of this guide, ad hoc and scientifically untested approaches were employed by fire investigators to attempt to determine fire causes.[7] Historically, many fire investigators relied on the process of elimination alone to exclude all reasonable ignition sources for a fire. If all reasonable ignitions sources were successfully excluded, the investigator would conclude

---

3 *Ibid.*, s. 4.1.

4 *Ibid.*, ss. 3.3.64 and 4.1.

5 *Ibid.*, s. 4.1.

6 *Ibid.* at 1 & 2. For other reputable and well-accepted resource materials used by the fire investigation community, see John D. DeHann & David J. Icove, *Kirk's Fire Investigation*, 7th ed. (Upper Saddle River, NJ: Pearson, 2012); Vytenis Babrauskas, *Ignition Handbook: Principles and Applications to Fire Safety Engineering, Fire Investigation, Risk Management and Forensic Science* (Issaquah, WA: Fire Science Publishers, 2003); John J. Lentini, *Scientific Protocols for Fire Investigation*, 2d ed. (Boca Raton, FL: CRC Press, 2013) [Lentini, *Scientific Protocols*].

7 See Section B(1)(f), below in this chapter.

that the fire must have been set intentionally. This method, referred to as *negative corpus*,[8] is a clear violation of the scientific method.[9]

In the words of internationally renowned fire scientist John Lentini:

> One thing that *NFPA 921* has accomplished is to make it easier to distinguish between credible investigative results and those based on hunches and feelings or discredited mythology. The guide provides the investigator with the tools to do his or her job, but demands that conclusions be justified with data, sound science, and clear reasoning. This is a good result. Based on my 35 years of studying fires, including more than 2,000 actual fire scene inspections (about 800 of which I determined to be arson) I learned two important things: most fires are accidents, and most arson fires are obvious. Surely there are exceptions, but if a fire investigator over and over again reports an incendiary determination that seems difficult to understand, chances are this investigator needs to find another line of work in which the consequences of error are not as serious."[10]

After *Daubert v. Merrell Dow Pharmaceuticals* in 1993,[11] U.S. courts began referring to *NFPA 921* as the "standard of care" for evaluating expert testimony regarding fire investigations. Canadian courts, guided by the expert evidence admissibility criteria set out in *R v. Mohan*,[12] have followed suit. If successfully qualified as an expert witness, the fire investigator will provide the court with an opinion as to whether the fire in issue should be classified as accidental, natural, incendiary, or undetermined.[13]

NFPA 921, a consensus, peer-reviewed document, has evolved over the years and continues to evolve with each new edition. For instance, earlier versions of *NFPA 921* allowed for the classification of a fire as incendiary if a precise point of origin was determined, even in the absence of evidence of

---

8 *NFPA 921*, above note 2, ss. 19.6.5–19.6.5.1.

9 *Ibid.*, s. 4.3. "The Scientific Method is a principle of inquiry that forms a basis for legitimate scientific and engineering processes, including fire investigation." It is applied by following a set of steps, as explained in Figure 4.3 of the *NFPA 921*, *ibid.*: "Recognize the need (identify the problem), define the problem, collect data, analyze the data, develop a hypothesis (inductive reasoning), test the hypothesis (deductive reasoning), select final hypothesis."

10 John J. Lentini, "The Evolution of Fire Investigation and Its Impact on Arson Cases" (2012) 27 *Criminal Justice* 12 [Lentini, "Evolution of Fire"].

11 509 US 579 (1993).

12 [1994] 2 SCR 9 [*Mohan*]. See Chapter 3 and its discussion of *R. v. J.-L.J.*, 2000 SCC 51.

13 *NFPA 921*, above note 2, s. 20.1.

an ignition source at that location.[14] When the fire investigation community recognized and began to understand the phenomenon of flashover, the traditional rules of fire damage interpretation changed. Flashover typically occurs in structure (indoor) fires and refers to the "transition from 'a fire in a room' to 'a room on fire.'" After flashover, the fire has involved all of the available fuel in the room and is able to grow further only with sufficient ventilation.[15] Flashover marks the transition from a fuel-controlled fire to one that is ventilation-controlled.[16] After flashover occurs (post-flashover fire), a precise point of origin is difficult to determine since full room involvement will obscure the majority of the fire patterns which may have originally indicated a fire origin. Understanding the effects of ventilation is vital in accurately interpreting post-flashover fires.

The difficulty of identifying origin by fire patterns alone in post-flashover fires was demonstrated in 2005 by the U.S. Bureau of Alcohol, Tobacco and Firearms (ATF).[17] In the experiment, two identical fourteen-foot by twelve-foot bedrooms with standard doorways were set on fire and allowed to burn for seven minutes, which was two minutes past flashover. The investigators then asked a group of fifty-three experienced fire investigators to walk through the two burned out rooms and provide their opinion on what quadrant the fire originated in each room. In the first room, only three of the fifty-three participants correctly identified the quadrant of origin. The results were the same for the second room (although no investigator correctly identified the quadrant of origin for both rooms). This study indicated that the "lowest burn and deepest char" methods—the idea that the greatest charring will be present where the fire burned the longest—does not reliably locate the point of origin in post-flashover fires.[18]

---

14 *Ibid.* at 1 & 2.

15 Lentini, "Evolution of Fire," above note 10 at 4.

16 *Ibid.*

17 Steven W. Carman, *Improving the Understanding of Post-Flashover Fire Behavior*, International Symposium on Fire Investigation Science and Technology (May 2008), online: www.nacdl.org/uploadedFiles/files/resource_center/topics/post_conviction/ATF_SA_Carman_Post_Flashover_Fires_ISFI_08.pdf.

18 Lentini, "Evolution of Fire," above note 10 at 4–6. Similar tests, like the undocumented tests at the Federal Law Enforcement Training Center in Glynco, Georgia, have indicated that only 8 to 10 percent of participants correctly identified the fires' quadrant of origin.

B. THE SCIENCE OF FIRE INVESTIGATION

1) Basic Principles

As noted above, fire investigation is a two-step process to determine the fire's origin (i.e., where the fire started) and its cause.[19] In almost all cases, the origin must be determined first, but due to the destructive nature of a fire, this can sometimes be a difficult task. Similarly, investigations into product or structural failures (which may intersect with fire investigations) require that the origin of the failure be determined first, followed by the determination of the cause for that failure.

a) Origin Determination

NFPA 921 defines the area of origin as "a structure, part of a structure, or general geographic location within a fire scene, in which the '*point of origin*' of a fire or explosion is reasonably believed to be located. The *point of origin* is the exact physical location within the area of origin where a heat source and the fuel interact, resulting in a fire or explosion."[20] The determination of the origin of the fire is the most important step in a fire investigation. "[G]enerally, a fire cause determination can be considered reliable only if the origin has been correctly determined."[21]

NFPA 921 defines four sources of information to assist in the determination of the fire origin:

1) *Witness Information.* The analysis of observations reported by persons who witnessed the fire or were aware of conditions present at the time of the fire.
2) *Fire Patterns.* The analysis of the effects and patterns left by the fire.
3) *Arc Mapping.* The analysis of the locations where electrical arcing has caused damage and the documentation of the involved electrical circuits.
4) *Fire Dynamics.* The analysis of the fire dynamics, that is, the physics and chemistry of fire initiation and growth, and the interaction between the fire and the building's systems.[22]

The investigator should consider all four sources of information in his origin determination. If one or more are not considered, the investigator

---

19 *NFPA 921*, above note 2, ss. 3.3.64 and 4.1.
20 *Ibid.*, s. 18.1.
21 *Ibid.*, s. 19.1
22 *Ibid.*, s. 18.1.2 [internal citations omitted].

should be able to explain why. The investigator should use the scientific method in the determination of the origin and cause of the fire by following a stepwise methodology that includes "recognizing and defining the problem to be solved, collecting data, analyzing the data, developing a hypothesis or hypotheses, and most importantly, testing the hypothesis or hypotheses."[23] Through the application of the scientific method to the data collected, the investigator will develop at least one working hypothesis (called the "working hypothesis") that will then be rigorously tested until a final hypothesis is reached that is supported by all of the data and explains the data better than any other hypothesis.[24]

Testing an origin hypothesis requires skill in understanding the ignition properties of materials, fire growth, and fire spread throughout a structure. Focusing narrowly on only the ignition source and the first item ignited may lead the investigator to miss important information that may support a superior fire origin hypothesis. Inexperienced investigators often identify an ignition source and conclude that as being the fire origin, instead of first identifying the origin of the fire and then the ignition sources.[25]

Fire spread analysis helps the investigator determine the validity of a hypothesized ignition sequence and whether the expected fire damage is consistent with the actual results of the fire. For example, a cigarette placed in a waste paper basket is data for the ignition source and first fuel ignited. However, the damage and fire spread will be very different if that waste paper basket is isolated in a corner of a room than if it is in close proximity to a foam cushion mattress. Although both hypotheses suggest the same first fuel and ignition source, the outcomes will be markedly different. An origin hypothesis should be rejected if it is not consistent with the rate of growth and spread of the fire.[26]

In some situations, such as the total burn of a structure, it may not be possible to identify a point of origin of a fire. It may, however, still be useful for the investigator to identify an area of origin as it may still support a credible hypothesis on the origin and cause of a fire.[27]

23 *Ibid.*, s. 18.2.
24 *Ibid.*
25 *Ibid.*, s. 18.2.1.
26 *Ibid.*, s. 18.2.1.1.
27 *Ibid.*, s. 18.2.1.3.

i) Witness Information

When a fire investigator interviews a witness, it is typically for information gathering to assist in the fire origin determination. Information from witnesses may include observations of the fire during its incipient stages and of the conditions prior to, during, and after the fire. It may also include the location of site contents and potential heat and ignition sources, peculiar sounds, smells, noises, or perceptions of heat prior to the fire. The information from witnesses may be used along with data obtained from physical evidence to support or refute the dependability of the witness information. If the physical evidence does not agree with the information from witnesses, each source of information should be evaluated separately.[28]

When other evidence, such as fire patterns, is not available due to heavy fire consumption or building collapse, the investigator may give the witness observations greater weight in determining where the fire started, but the investigator must guard against bias when obtaining information from witnesses. The investigator who has systematically investigated the fire and considered all the evidence is less likely to be biased by information received from witnesses.

Sometimes witnesses are not available to the investigator for direct interviews, but there may be statements taken by insurance adjusters immediately after a fire, or by the investigating police or fire department personnel. There may also be surveillance video or audio recordings to assist the investigator in origin determination.

ii) Fire Pattern Analysis[29]

At the scene of a fire, the fire investigator collects physical evidence regarding the effects of the fire, fire dynamics, and fire pattern development. The investigator must be able to competently recognize and analyze the various fire pattern evidence to assist in developing a correct hypothesis on the origin of a fire.

Although fire patterns are the most commonly available data for origin determination, they are created sequentially. One pattern may mask an earlier pattern, and early fire extinguishment or post-flashover full-room involvement will affect the fire pattern generation and what patterns remain after the fire. If there is a rekindle of a fire after initial extinguish-

28 *Ibid.*, s. 18.3.3.15.

29 For a more extensive discussion of fire patterns, see *NFPA 921*, *ibid.*, c. 6.

ment by a fire department, the sequence of fire patterns or interpretation of how the fire spread may become difficult.[30]

As stated in the *NFPA 921*, "[t]he investigator should not assume that the fire at the origin burned the longest and therefore fire patterns showing the greatest damage must be at the area of origin."[31] Other factors may cause greater damage in areas outside of the fire origin area, including the location and orientation of fuel packages (combustible contents), ventilation (typically influenced by open windows and doors), and firefighting tactics, which may push the fire in a direction away from the origin.[32]

During a fire, ventilation[33] has a large impact on the intensity and heat release rate of the fire, resulting in different amounts of observable fire damage. The fire investigator must therefore consider the effects of ventilation on the fire patterns and resultant damage. By definition, a ventilation-controlled fire is "[a] fire in which the heat release rate or growth is controlled by the amount of air available to the fire."[34] The generation of fire patterns is influenced by ventilation. For instance, fires will burn more intensely near open windows or doors and, as a result, produce greater damage than may be seen in other areas of the structure. Post-flashover fires can cause changes and mask fire patterns that developed during the earlier fuel-controlled phase of the fire.[35] Under these conditions, it is more difficult to identify the patterns that were generated by the first fuel ignited at the point of origin.[36]

iii) Arc Surveys/Arc Mapping

When energized electrical circuits, such as conventional house wiring or wiring in appliances or vehicles, are attacked by a spreading fire, they may leave behind evidence of electrical arcing activity. This will be in the form

---

30 *Ibid.*, ss. 18.4.1–18.4.1.2.

31 *Ibid.*, s. 18.4.1.3.

32 *Ibid.*

33 Ventilation in this context refers to the introduction of oxygen-rich fresh air to the fire through openings in the structure, including an open or breached window, door, or a burned-through roof. If there is ventilation, the heat release rate will be greater in the area where the ventilation is provided.

34 *NFPA 921*, above note 2, s. 3.3.188.

35 *Ibid.*, s. 3.3.88. A fuel-controlled fire (as opposed to the ventilation-controlled fire) is "[a] fire in which the heat release rate and growth rate are controlled by characteristics of the fuel, such as quantity and geometry, and in which adequate air for combustion is available."

36 *Ibid.*, s. 18.4.1.4.

of localized melting of copper or aluminum conductors, localized melting of an adjacent steel enclosure from electrical arcing, arc-severed[37] conductors, and arc splatter.[38] Arc surveys, or arc mapping, is a method used by fire investigators to document and analyze the locations of electrical arcing sites relative to each other and to the source of the power supply.

The methodology is based on predictable behaviour. Typically, the plastic insulation on the conductors for the section of the wiring first attacked by the fire will char, which will make the insulation semi-conductive. Electricity flowing through the charred insulation will generate heat. The heat will cause localized melting, or arcing, on the conductors (most fires are not hot enough to melt the copper conductors). Eventually, the circuit protection, a fuse or a breaker at the source of the circuit, will trip, or open, stopping the flow of electricity and any electrical arcing, leaving behind the recognizable evidence of the electrical arc sites where the fire attacked the wiring.[39]

Data on electrical arcing sites in a compartment can be used in the same manner as a fire pattern in narrowing down the origin of the fire, but there are limits to this technique.[40] Data may be compromised in a fire that burned too long, causing fragmentation of the copper wiring, as well as in fires with a heavy fuel load, where the fire may burn hot enough to melt and mask the area of arc sites. The data may also be corrupted by additional arcing when electrical circuits are accidentally reenergized after a fire. Finally, arcing will occur only where there are electrical conductors, limiting the portions of the room available to provide data.[41] Recognition of arc damage on electrical circuits is a vital skill that is best learned in the field through training and practice. Some of the arc sites may be so small that they require the use of magnification to distinguish arcing from other damage to the copper conductors, such as damage from collapse, eutectic melting (i.e., alloying of metals[42]) and other mechanical damage. Incorrect

---

37 Arc-severing occurs on energized electrical circuits when a fault or short-circuit causes the conductor to separate or sever due to overload from high current (i.e., high electrical energy imposed on the conductor), with the result that the ends of the severed conductors will have smooth globules left on them.

38 *NFPA 921*, above note 2, s. 18.4.5.

39 *Ibid.*, s. 18.4.5.

40 *Ibid.*, s. 18.4.5.6.

41 *Ibid.*, s. 18.4.5.

42 *Ibid.*, s. 6.2.8.6. *NFPA 921* notes that "[a]lloying should be considered when analyzing post-fire metal specimens. The melting of certain metals may not always be caused by fire temperatures higher than the metals' stated melting point; it may be caused

identification of the damage to wiring, such as identifying mechanical or fire damage as an arc site, will result in faulty data and incorrect hypotheses on the origin of the fire. If there is doubt as to the cause of damage on the electrical conductors, the damaged locations may be documented and the wiring collected for further analysis under lab conditions.[43]

Arc mapping works best where the wiring of the branch circuits is exposed, such as in open ceilings in basements, or in a vehicle engine compartment or dash, or on energized appliance cords. Where wiring is within a wall cavity with finishes such as drywall, circuits may fail prior to any arcing caused by the fire. It may also be difficult to determine which wall finish failed first and exposed the electrical wiring to the fire.[44]

If used correctly by a competent fire investigator, arc mapping is an excellent alternate source of data for origin determination independent of, and complementary to, fire pattern analysis.

iv) Fire Dynamics

Fire dynamics is the study of how chemistry, physics, fluid dynamics, heat transfer, and other areas of fire science affect the growth and the spread of the fire.[45] The fundamentals of fire dynamics include the analysis of the various forms of heat transfer (i.e., the movement of heat from one location to another) through mechanisms of heat transfer such as radiant, convective, and conductive. All three heat transfer mechanisms must be understood as they all play a role in fire spread and how various materials are affected by fire.[46]

Another important property to understand is the thermal inertia of a material, which is the measure of how rapidly a material's surface temperature increases when it is exposed to heat.[47] Thermal inertia is a function of thermal conductivity, the density of the material, and its heat capacity. Other fundamentals, such as ventilation, the configuration and geometry of the compartment (including volume and ceiling height), and the ambient conditions, should be evaluated to determine how all of these factors

---

by alloying. Alloying refers to the mixing of, generally, two or more metals in which one or more of the metals is in a liquefied state, resulting in an alloy. Metals such as copper and iron (steel) can be affected by alloying with lower melting point metals such as aluminum, zinc, and lead."

43 *Ibid.*, s. 18.4.5.6.

44 *Ibid.*, s. 18.4.5.

45 *Ibid.*, s. 3.3.65.

46 *Ibid.*, s. 5.5.1.3.

47 *Ibid.*, s. 5.5.2.3.

work together to affect the development and spread of a fire. The analysis of fire dynamics data is used to aid in the development of origin hypotheses and to complement other origin determination techniques.[48]

v) Analysis of Sequential Events

Data collected through the above methodologies may be used to develop a timeline of the various events during a fire to assist in origin identification. Witness information (when available) may be the most useful in developing timelines, but witness information is subjective. The investigator will still have to conduct a thorough investigation to find evidence supporting or undermining the witness information. The analysis may identify gaps or inconsistencies in the information and may assist in formulating additional questions for witnesses. It will also assist in the reconstruction of the fire scene for origin hypothesis development.[49] If the physical evidence is contrary to the witness evidence, the investigator may choose to disregard the witness on that single point or on the entire statement. If the investigator uses information provided in a statement that is inconsistent with the physical evidence, the investigator should be prepared to address and explain the reasoning behind the decision.

vi) Fire Modeling

Fire modeling to test hypotheses regarding a fire origin can be as simple as running algebraic equations or it can require more complex computer models using the fundamentals of fire dynamics. Fire modeling uses data specific to the fire site to predict fire development and spread within the compartment. The results can then be compared to the physical and eyewitness evidence to test an origin hypothesis. Fire modeling can test different conditions related to fire development and fire spread and may be used to predict if injury narratives related to the fire are realistic; the time to flashover; the smoke concentrations; the temperatures of the walls, ceiling, and floor; the time of activation of smoke and heat detectors; and the effects of ventilation and other physical events.[50]

Computer models are complex and require accurate information inputs regarding the three-dimensional properties of the structure, sources of ventilation, location and contents of fuel packages, and many other

---

48 *Ibid.*, s. 18.4.7.

49 *Ibid.*, s. 18.4.6.

50 *Ibid.*, ss. 18.6.2.2. and 22.4.8.

variables for the data used to build the models. The models are run based on assumptions of the pre-fire conditions and the results are used to compare to the actual post-fire damage of the incident fire. The models cannot be run backwards from the post-fire conditions to test hypotheses. A small change in any of the input data variables at any point in the timeline of a model will skew the results of the final outcome. Fire modeling is simply a tool and should be used only in support of an already well-established hypothesis; it cannot by itself determine either the origin or cause of a fire.[51]

vii) Case File Review

It is almost certain that any significant fire investigation will involve more than one party and more than one fire investigator. Sometimes the investigator will find the fire scene altered by a prior investigation, a restoration contractor, or a municipal building department (often for safety reasons). Where the cause is a prior investigation and the first investigator completed a thorough investigation, and took detailed notes and photographs illustrating the systematic narrowing down of the origin area, then the second investigator should be able to use the data collected by the first investigator to draw a reliable conclusion. There may be differences in the opinions of the investigators. In most cases, this can be attributed to the weight each investigator gives to any particular finding, or to their assessments of the fire dynamics within the fire scene.[52]

b) Fire Cause Determination

Once a fire's origin is determined, the investigator can then determine the cause of the fire. The fire cause is determined by "identifying the first fuel ignited, the ignition source, the oxidizing agent, and the circumstances that resulted in the fire."[53] Some public service agencies refer to the entire process as "origin, cause, and circumstances."

The investigator should identify all factors, including human actions and inactions as well as product or appliance failure, that were necessary to start the fire. Unattended cooking is an example of a human action that may ultimately cause a fire. In this example, the contributing factors may include filling a pot with a potential fuel (e.g., oil), placing it near combustible tea towels, and leaving the heated pot unattended. The fire

---

51 Lentini, "Evolution of Fire," above note 10 at 5.

52 *Ibid.*, s. 18.7.3.

53 *Ibid.*, s. 19.1. The oxidizing agent, or oxidant, involved in most fires is the oxygen in the earth's atmosphere. See Section B(1)(b)(iii), below in this chapter.

could have been prevented by removing any of these factors.[54] Witness interviews may provide information about potential ignition sources in the area of origin (the stovetop heating element), competent fuels that were present and in what configuration (oil and tea towels), and recent activities around the area of origin (leaving the pot unattended). Other information that may assist in determining the contributing factors includes the recent purchase or service of appliances, whether they were new or used, how they were used prior to the fire, recent renovation activities and construction details of the scene, and information about any new items that were being used in the area of origin.[55]

i) First Fuel Ignited

All potential fuels in the area of origin at the time of ignition should be identified, as one of these fuels will likely be the first fuel ignited.[56] The investigator should identify the types of fuels, quantities, and the specific locations of content and structural fuels.[57] The first fuel may have been consumed in the fire, but portions of the fuel may have survived. Most building materials are not susceptible to ignition from exposure to low energy, low temperature ignition sources under short durations. For example, a structural support such as a wooden beam, or a kitchen cupboard or carpet will not ignite unless exposed to a high energy heat source. In most cases, a match will not be sufficient. However, in many cases, there will be easily ignitable items present, which, once ignited, are capable of igniting other combustibles. These easier to ignite items should be included, where appropriate, in the sequence of fuels ignited.[58]

Gas vapours and flammable dusts may be the first fuel ignited. These items may complicate the determination of the fire origin since they tend to fill an area, rather than remain in the location where they were first released. As a result, fire spread from the ignition of gaseous fuels or dusts may occur a considerable distance from the ignition source.[59]

---

54 *Ibid.*, s. 19.1.1.

55 *Ibid.*, ss. 19.3.1.6–19.3.3.

56 The first fuel ignited is "that which first sustains combustion beyond the ignition source. For example, the wood of the match would not be the first fuel ignited, but paper, ignitable liquid, or draperies would be, if the match were used to ignite them." *Ibid.*, s. 19.1.2. See also s. 3.3.73.

57 *Ibid.*, s. 19.3.1.

58 *Ibid.*, s. 19.3.1.1.

59 *Ibid.*, s. 19.3.1.5.

ii) Ignition Source

Except in the case of gaseous fuels and flammable dusts (as noted above), the ignition source should be within or close to the point of origin of the fire. After the fire, the ignition source may still be present in recognizable form, but it may be altered, transformed, or completely destroyed. All potential ignition sources must be identified for a cause to be hypothesized.[60] This includes identification and documentation of all heat producing devices in the area of origin, including appliances, motors, electrical devices of building infrastructure, and self-heating and reactive materials. Non-heat producing devices should also be identified and documented if they can produce heat due to malfunction, misuse, or alteration.[61]

Sometimes there is no direct evidence of an ignition source left behind. In these cases, an ignition source may still be hypothesized if it is supported by other evidence.[62] For instance, an improperly extinguished cigarette may be fully consumed in the fire that it ignited. However, a hypothesis that smoking was a potential ignition source may be supported through evidence of other smoking material in the area and witness information that smoking took place within a reasonable timeline of fire discovery. When drawing such inferences, the investigator should be aware that smoldering ignition sources such as cigarettes[63] are not typically competent ignition sources for gasses, vapours, or dusts. Potential ignition sources for these materials include open flame, arcs from operation of switches and motors, standing pilot flames, and static electricity.[64]

iii) Oxidant

The oxidant involved in most fires is the oxygen readily available in the air.[65] Extra consideration should be given to medical oxygen, either stored in oxygen cylinders or generated by oxygen concentrators.[66] Various industrial

---

60 *Ibid.*, s. 19.1.3.

61 *Ibid.*, s. 19.3.2.

62 *Ibid.*, s. 19.1.3.

63 See also *ibid.*, s. 27.4.5. "Modern vehicle upholstery fabrics and materials are generally difficult to ignite with a lighted cigarette. Ignition may occur if a lighted cigarette is buried in paper, tissue, and/or other combustible debris, or if the seat material comes into contact with an open flame. Urethane foam, typical seat cushion material, burns readily once ignited with a flame, and adds substantially to the intensity of a vehicle fire."

64 *Ibid.*, s. 19.3.2.1.

65 *Ibid.*, s. 19.4.3.

66 *Ibid.*, s. 19.1.4.

chemicals may act to supply greater concentrations of oxygen than in the air, and thus play a greater role in enhancing or supporting combustion reactions. There are common chemicals other than molecular oxygen (e.g., pool sanitizers), which are also oxidizers. These chemicals may react with other chemicals or, when they burn, supply their own oxygen to enhance the combustion reaction.[67]

No special documentation is required when the oxidizer is natural oxygen from the air; however, other oxidants should be identified and documented when they are in or near the area of origin. Laboratory testing of residues left by the oxidant at the fire scene may be required.[68]

iv) Ignition Sequence

The ignition sequence of a fire event is "the succession of events and conditions that allow the source of ignition, the fuel, and the oxidant to interact in the appropriate quantities and circumstances for combustion to begin."[69] Identifying the presence of an ignition source, a readily ignitable fuel, and an oxidant, does not automatically pinpoint a fire's cause. The sequence of events, including the ignition source and a fuel in sufficient quantity and configuration to be ignited, and the specific circumstances or events that brought them together, must be identified and documented when establishing the cause of the fire.[70] It is important to understand the temperature of various ignition sources and the temperature required to ignite the hypothesized fuels. The difference between flash point[71] and autoignition[72] temperatures must also be understood. Most building components, such as wood floors, structural wood framing, cabinetry, and carpets are not readily ignited by ignition sources of low energy, low temperature, and short duration. These items must be exposed to an ignition source with sufficient heat energy and duration of exposure to raise them to their ignition temperature.[73] The following factors should be evaluated and included in an explanation of the ignition sequence:

---

67 *Ibid.*, s. 19.3.4.2.

68 *Ibid.*, s. 19.4.3.1.

69 *Ibid.*, s. 19.4.4.1.

70 *Ibid.*, ss. 19.4.4.1–19.4.4.2.1.

71 *Ibid.*, s. 3.3.82. The flash point of a liquid is "the lowest temperature of a liquid, as determined by specific laboratory tests, at which the liquid gives off vapors at a sufficient rate to support a momentary flame across its surface."

72 *Ibid.*, s. 3.3. 15. The autoignition temperature is "the lowest temperature at which a combustible material ignites in air without a spark or flame."

73 *Ibid.*, s. 19.4.1.2.

1) How and sequentially when the first fuel ignited came to be present in the appropriate shape, phase, configuration, and condition to be capable of being ignited (a competent fuel);
2) How and sequentially when the oxidant came to be present in the right form and quantity to interact with the first fuel ignited and ignition source to allow the combustion reaction;
3) How and sequentially when the competent ignition source came to be present and interact with the fuel;
4) How and sequentially when the competent ignition source transferred its heat energy to the fuel, causing ignition;
5) How safety devices and features designed to prevent fire from occurring operated or failed to operate;
6) How and sequentially when any acts, omissions, outside agencies, or conditions brought the fuel, oxidant, and competent ignition source together at the time and place for ignition to occur;
7) How the first fuel subsequently ignited any secondary, tertiary, and successive fuels, which resulted in any fire spread.[74]

Since the 2011 edition, *NFPA 921* has changed its view on cause hypothesis development based on the lack of evidence of an ignition source, referred to as the "*negative corpus*" (see Section (B)(1)(b)(v), below in this chapter):

> There are times when there is no physical evidence of the ignition source found at the origin, but where an ignition sequence can logically be inferred using other data. Any determination of fire cause should be based on evidence rather than on the absence of evidence; however, there are limited circumstances when the ignition source cannot be identified, but the ignition sequence can logically be inferred. This inference may be arrived at through the testing of alternate hypotheses involving potential ignition sequences, provided that the conclusion regarding the remaining ignition sequence is consistent with all known facts. The following are examples of situations that lend themselves to formulating an ignition scenario when the ignition source is not found during the examination of the fire scene. The list is not exclusive and the fire investigator is cautioned not to hypothesize an ignition sequence without data that logically supports the hypothesis.

---

74 *Ibid.*, s. 19.4.4.2.1.

(A) Diffuse fuel explosions and flash fires.
(B) When an ignitable liquid residue (confirmed by laboratory analysis) is found at one or more locations within the fire scene and its presence at that location(s) does not have an innocent explanation.
(C) When there are multiple fires.
(D) When trailers[75] are observed.
(E) The fire was observed or recorded at or near the time of inception or before it spread to a secondary fuel.[76]

v) Negative Corpus

The elimination of hypotheses is done through testing and consideration of all the facts. It is "an integral part of the scientific method" but the process of elimination can be misused.[77] In cases where all known or suspected ignition sources at the point of origin are eliminated, the investigator may be tempted to theorize a fire cause based on the absence of evidence supporting an ignition source. This is referred to in the fire investigation community as the *negative corpus* approach (because the lack of evidence is treated as evidence). This approach goes against the scientific method because the hypothesis cannot be tested, thereby rendering it unreliable and speculative. Conclusions must be based only on the analysis of the evidence, observations, experiments, and the body of scientific knowledge.[78] If there are no hypotheses supported by the evidence, the cause should be classified as undetermined.

vi) Establishing the Cause

After the investigator has considered all of the hypotheses and eliminated any that do not agree with the available evidence, there may be only one hypothesis remaining. Even in these cases, the hypothesis still needs to be tested in a thorough investigation to support a conclusion of the correct fire cause. The investigator must document all of the evidence that supports the cause hypothesis, to the exclusion of all other reasonable causes. If there are two or more possible causes but only one cause is probable while the others are only possible, then the investigator can conclude with

75 *Ibid.*, s. 3.3.181. A trailer is "solid or liquid fuel used to intentionally spread or accelerate the spread of a fire from one area to another."
76 *Ibid.*, s. 19.4.4.3 [internal references omitted].
77 *Ibid.*, ss. 19.6.2–19.6.5.
78 *Ibid.*, s. 19.6.5.

the probable cause. But if more than one cause are equally likely, then the investigator must classify the fire as undetermined.[79]

The cause should be described in terms of a competent ignition source capable of providing sufficient heat to ignite the first fuel, the agencies and circumstances that brought them together, and how the fire then spread to other fuels within the structure. If the ignition source was a device or appliance failure, the investigator will need to account for the failure of safety devices that should have acted to prevent the fire.[80]

vii) Undetermined Fire Cause

If the level of certainty on the fire cause is only "possible" or "suspected," then the fire should be classified as "undetermined."[81] The determination of certainty ultimately rests with the investigator. "Undetermined" should be the default finding in the absence of a level of certainty greater than 50 percent. With levels of certainty below 50 percent, the cause is only "possible." Conclusions of "probable" or "likely" should only be made where the level of certainty is above 50 percent. Most investigators will conclude that there is a specific defined cause only where the certainty level is considerably higher than 50 percent. Ultimately, the level of certainty is a judgment call that is to some extent subjective.

c) Classification of Fire Cause

Determination of the origin and cause of a fire is a separate process from classifying the cause of a fire. There are several reasons the fire investigator will classify a fire cause—assigning responsibility, reporting, and for compilation of statistics.[82] Once the origin and cause of the fire has been investigated and a determination made, the investigator should classify the cause as one of the following: accidental, natural, incendiary, or undetermined.[83] "Suspicious" is not a classification and should be avoided because it does not provide an acceptable level of certainty for accurately describing the cause of a fire. Where the level of certainty does not support a conclusion stronger than possible or suspected, the fire should be classified as undetermined. *NFPA 921* defines the four classifications of fire cause as follows:

---

79 *Ibid.*, s. 19.6.5.1–19.7.2 and 19.7.4.

80 *Ibid.*, ss. 19.7.1 and 19.7.3.

81 *Ibid.*, s. 19.7.4.

82 *Ibid.*, s. 20.1.

83 *Ibid.*

i) *Accidental*

Accidental fires involve all those for which the proven cause does not involve an intentional human act to ignite or spread fire into an area where the fire should not be. When the intent of the person's action cannot be determined or proven to an acceptable level of certainty, the correct classification is undetermined. In most cases, this classification will be clear, but some deliberately ignited fires can still be accidental. For example, in a legal setting, a trash fire might be spread by a sudden gust of wind. The spread of fire was accidental even though the initial fire was deliberate.[84]

ii) *Natural*

Natural fire causes involve fires caused without direct human intervention or action, such as fires resulting from lightning, earthquake, wind, and flood.[85]

iii) *Incendiary*

An incendiary fire is a fire that is deliberately set with the intent to cause a fire to occur in an area where the fire should not be.[86]

iv) *Undetermined*

Whenever the cause cannot be proven to an acceptable level of certainty, the proper classification is undetermined as follows:

(A) Undetermined fire causes include those fires that have not yet been investigated or those that have been investigated, or are under investigation, and have insufficient information to classify further. However, the fire might still be under investigation and the cause may be determined later with the introduction or discovery of new information.

(B) In the instance in which the investigator fails to identify the ignition source, the fire need not always be classified as undetermined. If the evidence established one factor, such as the use of an accelerant, that evidence may be sufficient to establish an incendiary fire cause classification even where other factors such as ignition source cannot be identified.[87]

---

84 *Ibid.*, s. 20.1.1.
85 *Ibid.*, s. 20.1.2.
86 *Ibid.*, s. 20.1.3.
87 *Ibid.*, s. 20.1.4.

d) Responsibility for Fire[88]

The fire investigator's assignment is typically broader than simply investigating the origin, cause, and development of a fire, and may also include the assignment of responsibility for the fire. Accurate assignment of responsibility may contribute to public safety by informing the development of building codes and standards, and supporting civil litigation or criminal prosecution.[89] In the public sector, where, for example, the fire may be investigated by the Office of the Fire Marshal, the fire investigator does not assign responsibility in criminal matters—that is the responsibility of the justice system.

Responsibility for a fire may stem from an act or omission that created the conditions that allowed the fire to happen. For instance, where an unsafe condition was not corrected, or when intended safeties failed or were too easily defeated. The act or omission may be intentional or accidental. Typically, "[r]esponsibility may be attributed to the accountable person or other entity because of negligence, reckless conduct, product liability, arson, violations of codes or standards, or other means."[90]

Responsibility for a fire or explosion may be assigned even where the classification of the fire is undetermined.[91] Consider a fire that occurs in the bedroom of an apartment. The tenant is a smoker who regularly smokes in bed. On the night of the fire, the tenant was also burning a candle in the bedroom. The investigator was able to eliminate items within the building's electrical and mechanical infrastructure, but because of the level of fire damage in the bedroom, the investigator was not able to determine whether the fire was ignited by the candle or through the inappropriate use or disposal of smoking materials. The classification of the fire cause may be undetermined, but responsibility for the fire lies with the tenant because both possible causes were within his control.

e) Incendiary Fires

"An incendiary fire is a fire that is deliberately set with the intent to cause the fire to occur in an area where the fire should not be."[92] There are several indicators, or indicia, regarding fire origin or spread that may be considered

---

88 *Ibid.*, s. 21.5.2. "'Responsibility' for a fire or explosion incident is the accountability of a person or other entity for the event or sequence of events that caused the fire or explosion, spread of the fire, bodily injuries, loss of life, or property damage."

89 *Ibid.*, s. 21.5.

90 *Ibid.*, s. 21.5.1.

91 *Ibid.*

92 *Ibid.*, s. 24.1.

evidence that the fire is incendiary.[93] Indicia of arson can include both potential indicators directly related to combustion and indicators not directly related to combustion. The following sections outline the more common indicators as listed in *NFPA 921*.

i) Multiple Fires

A thorough examination of the fire scene, not just the room or area of origin, may uncover additional fire sets or points of origin of multiple fires—"two or more separate, nonrelated, simultaneously burning fires."[94] The investigator must show that the additional fires are not simply the spread or outgrowth of the initial fire to conclude that there is more than one fire origin. Examples include fires in different rooms, fires on different stories, and separate fires inside and outside the building.[95]

Separate fires that are not caused by multiple deliberate ignitions can result from the following:

1) Fire spread by conduction, convection, or radiation
2) Fire spread by flying brands[96]
3) Fire spread by direct flame impingement
4) Fire spread by falling flaming materials (i.e., drop down) such as curtains
5) Fire spread through shafts, such as pipe chases or air conditioning ducts
6) Fire spread within wall or floor cavities within "balloon construction"[97]
7) Overloaded electrical wiring
8) Utility system failures
9) Lightning
10) Rupture and launching of aerosol containers[98]

---

93 *Ibid.*, s. 24.2.

94 *Ibid.*, s. 24.2.1.

95 *Ibid.*, s. 24.2.1.1.

96 Flying brands are portions of burning building materials that break off or separate from the building during a fire and are carried either by convection or winds, spreading the fire to other building materials or combustibles some distance away from the original fire.

97 Balloon wood framing was an older style of framing, dating from the mid-1800s to the early 1900s that used wall studs that extended across floor levels. Wood floor joists were supported on ribbon or ledger boards nailed to the face of the studs, or in pockets in structural masonry. This type of framing was replaced by platform framing, in use today, which involves wall studs that extend to the underside of the upper level floor joists, which then rest on top of the studs. One common problem with balloon framing is that fire can easily spread upwards in the stud cavity to involve multiple levels as there is no "break" in the cavity. See *NFPA 921*, above note 2, ss. 7.3.2.2–7.3.2.2.2.

98 *Ibid.*, s. 24.2.1.2.

The quicker a fire is extinguished, the easier it is to identify multiple fire sets.[99] Common fire progression such as building collapse, continued burning to full room involvement, and overhaul by the fire department may make the finding of multiple fire sets difficult. Additionally, "[i]f there has been a previous fire in the building, care should be taken not to confuse earlier damage with a multiple fire situation."[100] When multiple fires are indeed suspected, fire scene reconstruction takes on an increasingly important role in the fire investigation as a whole.[101]

ii) Trailers

A trailer is "a deliberately introduced fuel or manipulation of existing fuel(s) used to aid the spread of a fire from one area to another."[102] Trailers (e.g., ignitable liquids, ignitable solids like paper or straw, or a combination of both) may be used to spread a fire from one area to another, or as a fuse to ignite a fire from a safe distance.[103] It is possible for some of the trailer to survive the fire.

Investigators will often clear floor areas of debris and find long, wide, and relatively straight patterns of extensive heat damage, bordered on each side by undamaged or less damaged areas.[104] In the past, investigators would often interpret these patterns as trailers, but the presence of furniture, clothing, carpets, or other items, as well as disparate fire impact on worn floor areas, may also cause this pattern. Protection patterns from clothing, bedding, and other content items may also be misinterpreted as trailers.[105] If an inaccurate conclusion is drawn about the presence of a trailer, then an inaccurate classification of fire cause—incendiary—may also result.

iii) Exotic Accelerants

Exotic accelerants[106] are typically a mixture of exotic fuels and oxidizers that create extremely hot fires. Depending on the conditions, some oxidizers

99 *Ibid.*, ss. 24.2.1.3–24.2.1.4.
100 *Ibid.*, s. 24.2.1.5.
101 *Ibid.*, s. 24.2.1.6.
102 *Ibid.*, s. 24.2.2.
103 *Ibid.*, ss. 24.2.2–24.2.2.2.
104 *Ibid.*, s. 24.2.2.4.
105 *Ibid.*
106 Exotic accelerants in this context are the less-easy to obtain compounds and chemicals that burn with extreme intensity when ignited. These are distinguished in this case from the easily obtainable accelerants/ignitable liquids such as gasoline, fuel oil, turpentine, alcohol, etc.

can self-ignite and cause very rapid fire growth. Thermite[107] mixtures also produce extremely hot fires and may be used as accelerants. A thorough examination of the area may reveal residues left behind by exotic accelerants that can be identified visually or by laboratory analysis.[108] Evidence for the use of exotic accelerants includes very rapid fire growth, bright flares, and melted steel or concrete.

Exotic accelerants are also referred to as high temperature accelerants (HTAs), and have been hypothesized as having been used to start or accelerate fires.[109] However, "[a] study of 25 fires suspected of being associated with HTAs during the 1981–1991 period revealed that there was no conclusive scientific proof of the use of such HTA."[110]

When a fire investigator concludes that the fire was incendiary based on a hypothesis of extremely rapid fire growth and the use of exotic accelerants, other reasons for the rapid growth should also be investigated, including "ventilation, fire suppression tactics, and the type and configuration of the fuels."[111]

iv) Lack of Expected Fuel Load or Ignition Sources

The fire investigator should make note of unexpected fire or burn patterns. "When the fire damage at the origin is inconsistent with the known or reported fuel load, limited rates of heat release, or limited potentially accidental ignition sources, the fire may be incendiary."[112] Areas with typically limited fuel loads include corridors, empty rooms, and stairways. Areas with limited ignition sources include closets, crawlspaces, and attics.[113]

When there is an unusually large fuel load in an area of origin that typically does not contain a large fuel load, or the fuel is in an

---

107 Thermite is a composition of a metal powder and a metal oxide. When ignited by heat, thermite undergoes an exothermic reduction-oxidation (redox) reaction—the combustion process supplies its own oxidizer. Most varieties are not explosive, but can create brief bursts of high temperature in a small area. Its reaction is similar to that of other fuel-oxidizer mixtures, such as black powder. The reaction is used for thermite welding, often used to join rail tracks. Thermites have also been used in metal refining, demolition of munitions, and in incendiary weapons.

108 *NFPA 921*, above note 2, s. 24.2.4.

109 *Ibid.*, s. 24.2.4.1.

110 Steven W. Carman, *High Temperature Accelerants, A Study of HTA Fires Reported in the United States and Canada between January 1981 and August 1991* (Washington, DC: Dept. of the Treasury, Bureau of Alcohol, Tobacco and Firearms, 1994).

111 *NFPA 921*, above note 2, s. 24.2.4.2.

112 *Ibid.*, s. 24.2.3.

113 *Ibid.*

unusual configuration, the fire may be incendiary. An example of an unusual fuel load is the stacking of furniture or other contents to encourage rapid fire growth, or the piling of paper waste, cardboard, or other combustible debris at a location or in a space that would encourage rapid fire development.[114]

v) Burn Injuries

The extent, location, and severity of fire-related injuries may provide information on whether the injuries were sustained in the setting of the fire, during an attempt to extinguish an accidental fire, or in an attempt to rescue a victim. The fire investigator should determine whether they are consistent with the fire cause and fire spread hypothesis.[115]

vi) Incendiary Devices

A variety of mechanisms may be used to ignite an incendiary fire. In many cases, more than one incendiary device is employed in the setting of a fire, and one or more may have failed to operate. Remains of the fuel are often found with the ignition device after a fire.[116] Incendiary devices and the evidence that may be relied upon to determine the use or presence of such devices include:

1) Books of paper matches and cigarettes from which the striker from the matchbook, cigarette filters, remaining cigarette ash, and the combustible materials ignited by the matches or cigarettes may be found in the area of origin.
2) Candles from which their wax and the remains of any combustible material ignited by the candles may be found in the area of origin.
3) Wiring systems or electric heating appliances to initiate a fire (which may be evidenced by indications of tampering or modification of the wiring system, by the movement or arrangement of heat-producing appliances to locations near combustible materials, or by evidence of combustible materials being placed on or near heat-producing appliances).
4) Fire bombs, commonly called Molotov cocktails (which leave evidence in the form of the ignitable liquid, chemicals, or compounds used within them, the broken or intact containers, and wicks).

---

114 *Ibid.*, s. 24.2.5.
115 *Ibid.*, s. 24.2.6.
116 *Ibid.*, s. 24.2.7.

5) Paraffin wax–sawdust incendiary device [which can be evidenced by remains of wax impregnated with sawdust (e.g., artificial fire logs)].[117]

vii) Delay Devices

Delay devices or timers are sometimes used to provide the fire setter with time to leave the scene without being spotted or sustaining an injury, or to provide an alibi prior to the ignition of the fire. Examples of delay devices include cigarettes, candles, and various mechanical or electrical timers.[118]

viii) Ignitable Liquids in the Area of Origin

The term "liquid accelerant" refers to an ignitable liquid at the area of origin of an incendiary fire.[119] Ignitable liquids found in areas where they are not typically expected may be evidence of an incendiary fire and should be thoroughly investigated. For instance, a container of ignitable liquid (e.g., gasoline) will commonly be found in the garage; its presence there would not be suspicious. But if it is found in an unexpected location, like a bedroom, the fire investigator should consider an incendiary cause. Such a finding requires a thorough investigation.[120]

ix) Assessment of Fire Growth and Fire Damage

The fire investigator may subjectively conclude that the rate of fire growth or the extent of damage at the scene is unusual based on the amount and configuration of fuels present as compared to a "typical" or "normal" fire. However, there are no typical fires—fire growth and damage are dependent on a wide array of factors, making every fire in some way unique. When investigating a fire, the investigator will make assumptions based on training and experience. The investigator should not use subjective language such as "excessive," "unnatural," or "abnormal" in the assessment without supporting explanations of why this language is consistent with the fire under investigation.[121] The investigator should carefully consider the effects of ventilation, fuel configuration, and the geometry of the space when determining the significance of unusual data,[122] and "[t]he investigator is

---

117 *Ibid.*, s. 24.2.7.1.
118 *Ibid.*, s. 24.2.7.2.
119 *Ibid.*, s. 24.2.7.3.
120 *Ibid.*, s. 24.2.7.3.1.
121 *Ibid.*, s. 24.2.8.
122 *Ibid.*, s. 24.2.8.1.

strongly cautioned against using subjective opinions to support an incendiary cause determination in the absence of physical evidence."[123]

x) *Potential Indicators Not Directly Related to Combustion*

Indicia not directly related to the combustion of the fire may be used by the investigator to develop ignition hypotheses, to select witnesses to interview, to help develop suspects, and to provide additional data for further investigation.[124] Noncombustion-related indicators include fires in locations that are blocked or obscured from view; fires near service equipment and appliances; alterations to a scene or removal of personal items prior to a fire; blocked or obstructed entryways; prior damage to the structure, the fire protection system, or to fire resistive assemblies; and windows or doors opened to increase ventilation to a fire.[125]

xi) *Other Evidentiary Factors*

After the investigator has concluded that the fire is incendiary, other evidentiary factors may be considered. Such factors may include evidence of other crimes and crime concealment, indications of financial stress of the property owner, a history of code violations, fires at other properties of the owner, overinsurance, timed opportunity, fires during severe natural conditions, fires during civil unrest, and fires occurring when the fire department is unavailable.[126] Such factors may assist in suspect development and identification and may provide information regarding the motive or opportunity for the fire. The investigator, however, is strongly cautioned against using these factors as the basis for concluding that the fire was incendiary.[127]

With respect to timed opportunity, the investigator should be very careful before providing any opinion on the issue of fire development as it pertains to the passage of time. Taking a position that if the fire has developed to *x* stage, then *y* amount of time has passed, is a dangerous opinion to offer and is likely of little or no value to the court. In fact, such an opinion may mislead the court, particularly if the case turns on the investigator's findings.

---

123 *Ibid.*, s. 24.2.8.2.
124 *Ibid.*, s. 24.3.
125 *Ibid.*, ss. 24.3.1–24.3.6.
126 *Ibid.*, s. 24.4.4–24.4.8.3.
127 *Ibid.*, s. 24.4.1–24.4.1.2.

f) Common Mythologies and Misconceptions of Arson Investigations

Prior to *NFPA 921*, it was believed that a fire that was "too hot" or that burned at a rapid rate must have been an accelerated (i.e., incendiary) fire. Evidence of a too-hot or too-rapid fire included crazed glass, spalling of concrete, shiny alligator blisters on wood, sagged furniture springs, and indicators drawn from the depth and location of char as well as lines of demarcation. This is subjective evidence of speed of fire spread, not scientific evidence.

i) Crazed Glass

Patterns of cracks in glass resembling a complex road map was once thought to be indicative of rapid buildup of heat at some point during the fire. Laboratory tests have since shown that crazing, like cratering (pitting of the surface in small circular defects), is caused by water hitting a window already heated by fire exposure, usually during fire suppression.[128]

ii) Spalling

Spalling is the breaking off of pieces of the surface of concrete or brick by intense heat or other factors related to the quality and makeup of the masonry, including freezing, chemicals, abrasions, mechanical movement, shock, force, or fatigue. As recently as the late 1990s, many publications on fire investigation advised that spalling was physical evidence that the fire was incendiary. *NFPA 921* has, since its inception, warned against misinterpreting spalling. The importance of spalling to the fire investigator depends on the documentation and analysis of the heat source.[129] Since spalling is not necessarily fire-related, the investigator should determine if the spalling was present prior to the fire.[130]

iii) Shiny Alligator Blisters

This term describes the shape of the char that forms on wood exposed to heat or fire. The appearance of char and blisters on wood has in the past been used to make determinations that are not supported in controlled laboratory testing. The presence of alligator char, or large shiny blisters, is not evidence of rapid fire spread or growth, or that a liquid accelerant was

---

128 John J. Lentini, "Behaviour of Glass at Elevated Temperatures" (1992) 37 *Journal of Forensic Sciences* 1358. *NFPA 921*, above note 2, s. 6.2.13.1.4.

129 John J. Lentini, "The Mythology of Arson Investigation" [Lentini, "Mythology of Arson Investigation"] in Lentini, *Scientific Protocols*, above note 6.

130 See, generally, *NFPA 921*, above note 2, ss. 3.3.163, 6.2.5–6.2.5.3, and 28.6.11.

present during the fire. Such a conclusion is not scientifically justified as alligator blisters are found in many different fires.[131]

iv) Sagged or Collapsed Furniture Springs

Sagged or collapsed furniture springs have been interpreted to indicate that a flammable liquid created heat intense enough to cause the springs to sag. Laboratory scientists have subjected furniture springs, both loaded and unloaded (i.e., with and without weights on them), to different fire conditions, and concluded that the condition of the springs is of little probative value in fire investigation.[132] Instead, tests indicate that springs are annealed in typical fires, resulting in the loss of tensile strength, and in eventual collapse once weight is applied.[133]

> The value of analyzing the furniture springs is in comparing the differences in the springs to other areas of the mattress, cushion, or frame. Comparative analysis of the springs can assist the investigator in developing hypotheses concerning the relative exposure to a particular heat source. For example, if at one end of the cushion or mattress the springs have lost their strength, and at the other end they have not, then hypotheses may be developed concerning the location of the heat source.[134]

v) Depth and Location of Char

The depth and location of char may be used as reliable physical evidence for the direction of the spread of fire. The fire investigator can assess fire spread by measuring and comparing the depth of char from point to point. Areas with shallower charring are typically further away from the heat source; however, the effect of ventilation and fuel placement should be considered as it may cause greater char in an area outside the fire origin.[135]

Publications have in the past reported typical rates of burning of various woods and this information has been used to conclude that a fire burned too intensely and must have been accelerated (i.e., incendiary). However, these guidelines did not consider the influence of ventilation on fire intensity or that fire burns in three dimensions and will consume wood from more than one direction, making it seem that the wood was

---

131 *Ibid.*, ss. 6.2.4.3–6.2.4.3.1.
132 Lentini, "Mythology of Arson Investigation," above note 129.
133 *NFPA 921*, above note 2, ss. 6.2.14–6.2.14.1.
134 *Ibid.*, s. 6.2.14.1.
135 *Ibid.*, s. 6.2.4.5.

consumed faster than anticipated using these guidelines.[136] Fire investigators understand today that the depth of char analysis should not be used for evaluation of the duration or intensity of a fire.

vi) Lines of Demarcation

Lines of demarcation are the visible separations between different intensities of burning on materials. These lines may be used by the fire investigator to evaluate the direction of fire spread and may indicate the borders of protection patterns made on items that were protected or partially protected from the flames by other items. Such protective items may include clothing and furniture, or pieces of drywall or ceiling tile that collapsed during the fire. Lines of demarcation may also indicate a border where flames were extinguished as a result of insufficient energy to maintain combustion. Historically, sharp lines of demarcation on floors have been used to indicate the presence of accelerants, where the accelerant caused more intense burning on the material where it was poured. However, a study on burn patterns caused by pools of gasoline and kerosene demonstrated that the edges of the patterns produced on wood and vinyl floors were not necessarily sharp.[137] A conclusion of accelerant use should be supported by laboratory testing of samples from the postulated area, as traces of these substances will typically remain after the fire.

2) Cold Cases

In the past, many investigators did not use a systematic approach to their scene investigation and there was little in the way of an established process for conducting a fire investigation. Today, it is generally accepted that an investigation should take a systematic approach to ensure that all relevant data is found, recorded, and considered. With the trend towards a more evidence-based (as opposed to experiential) approach, it may be useful to review old or cold cases with a view to ensuring that investigative conclusions were not flawed or faulty.

Many investigators develop a consistent methodology. This usually takes the form of a "least to most" process, where an investigation begins with the areas of least damage and progresses towards the area with the most damage.

---

136 Lentini, "Mythology of Arson Investigation," above note 129. See, generally, *NFPA 921*, above note 2, ss. 18.4.2.3–18.4.3.5 and 28.6.10.

137 Anthony D. Putorti, Jr., *Flammable and Combustible Liquid Spill/Burn Patterns: NIJ Report 604-00* (Washington, DC: National Institute of Justice, 2001).

Other investigators use an "outside to inside" system, working from the outside of a structure towards the inside. While there is no one best approach, any investigation should follow a systematic approach. The absence of a systematic approach may result in physical evidence being missed.

Proper use of the scientific method ensures that all data identified during the investigation is considered, analyzed, and used in the formation of an opinion with regards to the origin and cause of a fire. When an investigator fails to use the scientific method, the resulting opinion may be flawed for any number of reasons. In some cases, the investigator intentionally or inadvertently fails to consider evidence. Faulty application of scientific principles may lead to flawed theories with regards to ignition of the first fuel, fire spread, and fire dynamics, leading ultimately to a flawed opinion on the origin and cause of the fire. If the theory being considered is not subjected to rigorous testing, the results may be flawed by bias, either intentionally or unintentionally.

C. THE ROLE OF THE FIRE INVESTIGATOR IN CRIMINAL CASES

Within the criminal justice system in Canada, fire investigation experts can generally be categorized as coming from two areas—private industry experts (who are relied upon by defence counsel) and experts from a ministry of the provincial government, such as the Office of the Fire Marshal in Ontario (who are relied upon by the Crown). In some provinces, such as Ontario, there is a distinct separation between the police and the agency tasked with investigating fires and providing expert opinions to the Crown. In other provinces, there may not be so clear a distinction.

An investigation and the resulting expert opinion should be neutral and unbiased. Where there is little or no separation between the fire investigator, who is likely to be an expert witness in court, and the police and the Crown, the likelihood of bias increases. That investigator may feel pressured by peers, coworkers, other investigators, and even prosecutors to provide a particular opinion or to support a particular avenue of the investigation or prosecution. In contrast, an investigator from an agency independent of the police and prosecutor enjoys some protection from undue pressure to provide improper or unsupported opinions.

1) Fire Investigator Qualifications

Fire investigation in North America is an unregulated profession. The National Association of Fire Investigators (NAFI) provides courses and a CFEI (Certified Fire and Explosion Investigator) designation upon successful completion of a test based on *NFPA 921* course material. The International Association of Arson Investigators (IAAI) also provides courses in fire investigation and grants a CFI (Certified Fire Investigator) certification based on education, training, experience, and application approval by a reviewing committee. In Canada, the Canadian Association of Fire Investigators (CAFI) also provides courses and seminars in fire investigation and their CCFI-C (Canadian Certified Fire Investigator—C-level) designation after the successful completion of a test based on *NFPA 921*. These organizations provide very good introductory courses for fire science, fire investigation, and the process of defining an origin. They also provide various levels of course material on fire cause determination.

Public sector fire investigators may obtain their training at a public sector college such as the Ontario Fire College in Gravenhurst, Ontario, or at the Justice Institute of British Columbia (JIBC). After completing their education, public sector investigators are accredited by the International Fire Service Accreditation Congress (IFSAC) or the National Board on Fire Service Professional Qualification (ProBoard).

Both public sector and private sector investigators receive their classroom training through courses given by their respective organizations. The majority of fire investigator experience and expertise is then accumulated through in-the-field training on actual fire investigations.

a) Law-Enforcement Background Versus Engineering Background

Fire investigators come from many walks of life. In Ontario, fire investigators with the Office of the Fire Marshal generally have a law-enforcement background. Private sector fire investigators will generally have a science background and many possess an engineering degree. Great importance is placed on the fire investigators' skills of reasoning, knowledge (including of chemistry and physics as related to combustion), and familiarity with building systems, mechanical systems, electricity and wiring, and the consistent application of a systematic method.

There are varying opinions within the fire investigation community and within the legal community as to whether a fire investigator should be an engineer. At present, there is no requirement that fire investigators/experts be engineers. Engineers are regulated through the association of Professional Engineers of Ontario (PEO), suggesting that if fire investigators were only engineers, then they would be regulated by the PEO. The opposing position is that people other than engineers make good investigators and that good investigators can learn about fire. An ex-police detective or ex-fire prevention officer from the fire service may make a good fire investigator.

Engineers possess technical knowledge that may be beneficial to an investigation. But they may not possess knowledge regarding scene continuity, interview techniques for witnesses, handling of evidence, or proper note taking. Non-engineers may possess these skills but lack the technical knowledge of an engineer. Many organizations marry the two backgrounds, employing both engineers and non-engineers and using the strengths of each to overcome any shortcomings.

In the end, it is the role of the court to determine whether a proposed expert is qualified to provide expert opinion evidence in any particular case. There have been numerous decisions by the courts providing direction and guidance on this issue. The report of the *Inquiry into Pediatric Forensic Pathology in Ontario*[138] also provides comments and recommendations applicable to expert evidence in any profession.

b) Professional Qualifications for Fire Investigators

To assist the court in qualifying the fire investigator expert, *NFPA 1033, The Standard for Professional Qualifications for Fire Investigator*, may be used. The first edition of *NFPA 1033* was published by the NFPA in June 1987. In 1990, the NFPA Standards Council established the Technical Committee on Fire Investigator Professional Qualifications to address the need for specific expertise in the area of fire investigation with the task of reviewing and revising the existing document.

The committee completed a job task analysis and developed specific job performance requirements (JPRs) for fire investigators; these JPRs represent the standard skills and knowledge that should be possessed by the fire investigator, whether working within the public or private sphere. The *NFPA 1033* requires that the fire investigator apply the scientific method as the guiding analytical process throughout the investigation and while drawing conclusions. The fire investigator is expected to remain current on a series of topics through formal education courses, workshops, seminars, and by following professional publications and journals.[139]

---

138 Ontario, Ministry of the Attorney General, *Inquiry into Pediatric Forensic Pathology in Ontario* by the Honourable Stephen T. Goudge, Commissioner, online: www.attorneygeneral.jus.gov.on.ca/inquiries/goudge/report/v1_en_pdf/Vol_1_Eng.pdf.

139 Technical Committee on Fire Investigator Professional Qualifications & Technical Correlating Committee on Professional Qualifications, *NFPA 1033: Standard for*

The investigator *shall* have and maintain at a *minimum* an up-to-date basic knowledge of the following topics beyond the high school level at a post-secondary education level:

1) Fire science
2) Fire chemistry
3) Thermodynamics
4) Thermometry
5) Fire dynamics
6) Explosion dynamics
7) Computer fire modeling
8) Fire investigation
9) Fire analysis
10) Fire investigation methodology
11) Fire investigation technology
12) Hazardous materials
13) Failure analysis and analytical tools
14) Fire protection systems
15) Evidence documentation, collection, and preservation
16) Electricity and electrical systems[140]

Unfortunately, there are currently practicing fire investigators in the field who claim to have the skills and experience to conduct thorough fire investigations, however, many of these investigators are not up to the task. Generalists who practice in multiple areas of forensics (for example, some may specialize in structural engineering, materials engineering, and collision reconstruction, and then dabble in fire investigation), may not possess sufficient fire investigation experience. There are limited advanced courses in fire investigation, which means that most fire investigation experience must be gained on the job.

2) Fire Investigators Called by the Crown

Where a fire investigation leads to criminal charges, the investigator is usually involved in the early stages of the investigation—sometimes even before the police become involved. The fire investigator may identify

---

Professional Qualifications for Fire Investigator, 2014 Edition (2013) at 1, online: www.nfpa.org/codes-and-standards/document-information-pages?mode=code&code=1033 [*NFPA 1033*].

140 *Ibid.*, s. 1.3.7.

evidence that leads to police interest, transforming the fire investigation into a criminal one. There may also be ongoing consultations with police investigators to help both investigators focus their efforts and resources. Care must be taken by the fire investigator during this process not to become or appear to become "part of the team."

In most criminal cases, the overall police investigation will begin during the fire investigation. The police investigation may involve one or two officers, or a larger team. As the investigation unfolds and the case begins to take shape, the police will often make a pre-determination that the fire is incendiary in nature, even though it is the responsibility of the fire investigator to make this determination. The police may identify evidence that leads to a suspect, that points to motive on the part of the suspect, or that identifies opportunity for the suspect to have committed the crime, all before the fire investigator determines that the fire is classified as incendiary.

If the fire investigator becomes aware of the police developing such evidence, the investigator may begin to feel pressure to conclude that the fire is incendiary. If the fire investigator identifies too closely with the police investigators, that pressure will intensify. This pressure may be subtle or even self-induced, but it may also be more overt and even intentionally applied by police investigators. Young or inexperienced police investigators are particularly at risk of such behaviour, especially if they fall into the trap of tunnel vision. They may begin to seek out evidence to support the case, rather than conducting a full investigation heedless of the outcome.

Fire investigators must weigh the ongoing need to understand the progress of the police investigation and the responsibility to share the progress of the fire investigation against the possibility of becoming biased. It may be of value for fire investigators to attend any briefings during the investigation, share relevant findings, and then excuse themselves. They may need to seek other avenues of securing relevant information from the police investigation. In these cases, fire investigators should be careful to avoid exposure to information that may bias their portion of the investigation. For instance, the fire investigator should remain ignorant of any information about a possible suspect, including the existence and identity of a suspect, the suspect's position in the community, the motive, any past criminal record, information on bail, whether the suspect has retained counsel, and who that counsel is. There is a strong case to be made that this is not information a fire investigator needs in order to conduct a thorough investigation. In addition, these are factors that may influence the investigator and introduce bias into the fire investigator's ultimate determination and opinion.

The fire investigator will likely remain involved in the ongoing criminal process. This may include continuing consultations with the police and/or the Crown prosecutor. It will likely also include meetings with the Crown prosecutor prior to preliminary hearing and/or trial.

a) Managing Potential Bias

At all stages of the process, the fire investigator must be cognizant of the risk of bias and take measures to prevent it. Where there is evidence of the fire investigator participating on an ongoing basis in the police investigation prior to the laying of charges, it may be wise for defence counsel to use the cross examination to explore the role played by the investigator, what information was given to and received from the police, and whether this interaction may have biased the fire investigation. Where an agency has several fire investigators available, the choice of lead investigator is important. The lead investigator should be someone who has the experience, self-confidence, and personality to be able to withstand pressure from the police investigators. This is the person who will most likely be aware of, and able to avoid, the danger of bias, including bias that is self-induced.

The investigator may be involved in consultations with Crown counsel prior to the laying of charges. This may be to determine if grounds exist to lay and prosecute charges or to assist in identifying the appropriate charges. Investigators should guard against advocating, or being seen as advocates. Their role is to assist Crown counsel by providing the information necessary for counsel to make the appropriate decision.

In some cases, biasing information comes to a fire investigator unintentionally. It may be as simple as a uniform police officer saying, "hey, did you hear we arrested the mayor's kid for this fire?" The fire investigator should be willing to acknowledge the potential effect of the information. Future testimony and reporting should include a description of the actions taken to protect against bias from this knowledge.

Even the perception of bias may become an issue. When, by their speech and conduct, fire investigators appear to be "part of the team" or to have lost their objectivity, defence counsel may attempt to portray the investigation as biased. To guard against the undermining of their objectivity, investigators should always be cognizant of how they gather their information and how that information is relevant to determining the origin and cause of the fire under investigation. They should conduct themselves in a professional manner and always be guarded in their comments. Any suggestion that they have reached a final opinion on the origin and cause of a fire before they have gathered all relevant information is a strong indicator that not only have they not applied the scientific method to reach their findings, but that their findings may be biased, in whole or in part.

Fire investigators must always be aware of their role, which is to determine the origin and cause of a fire or explosion. They should apply the scientific method to the gathering and analysis of relevant information. Irrelevant information serves no purpose and, if used, may raise the issue of bias in the investigation. Other investigators who are unfamiliar with the process may be unaware of the potential pitfalls of sharing irrelevant information. Therefore, fire investigators bear ultimate responsibility for guarding against the effects of irrelevant information. They should put measures in place to protect themselves from not only the possibility of bias but the perception of bias.

3) Fire Investigators Called by the Defence

An expert retained by defence counsel is usually not involved in the process until after the laying of criminal charges. Usually, defence counsel contacts an expert from private industry to review the disclosure provided by the Crown. This may be to determine whether appropriate charges have been laid or to evaluate the strength of the Crown's case, and especially the strength of the Crown expert's investigation. The results of this review may impact decisions regarding the plea arrangement. It may also influence financial decisions related to the cost of proceeding to trial and continuing to retain the assistance of the expert (the financial cost for an expert for the defence is borne by the defendant).

4) The Shared Role of Both Experts

The expectations for expert witnesses for the Crown and for the defence are the same—to assist the court. In 1994, *R. v. Mohan*[141] established a four-part test that requires the proposed expert evidence to meet the following criteria to be admitted: it must (1) be relevant, (2) be necessary to the trier of fact, (3) not be otherwise subject to an exclusionary rule, and (4) be given by a properly qualified expert. Additionally, experts for both sides

141 *Mohan*, above note 12. See also Chapter 3 in this book.

are expected to provide neutral, unbiased opinions to the court. In this sense, the nature of the charges has no effect on the expectations of the expert. An expert testifying in a murder trial is under the same expectation to provide a neutral, unbiased opinion as an expert testifying in an arson involving a back alley recycling box that caused property damage.

The investigator's role is not to identify the person responsible for the crime alleged. Similarly, advancing opinions of motive and opportunity are not within the investigator's purview. Investigators should be careful not to stray in their evidence, especially when led by counsel to areas outside their expertise. While the investigator may conduct interviews with witnesses to assist in the investigation, those interviews should not become hostile interrogations. The interview is intended only to provide the investigator with information and an understanding of:

1) Pre-fire conditions
2) Fire and smoke development
3) Fuel packages and their location and orientation
4) Victims' activities before, during, and after discovery of the fire
5) Actions taken by survivors resulting in their survival; that is, escape or take refuge
6) Decisions made by survivors and reasons for those decisions
7) Critical fire events such as flashover, structural failure, window breakage, alarm sounding, first observation of smoke, first observation of flame, fire department arrival, and contact with others in the building[142]

Experts for both Crown and defence assist the court in interpreting the evidence. Despite their neutral role, experts should be prepared to undergo rigorous cross-examination by counsel for the opposing side. Canada has an adversarial criminal justice system, and cross-examination is a crucial part of that system. The expert is expected to remain calm and to answer questions from counsel. Opinions should be founded in fact and science without regard to the outcome of the case.

5) The Significance of the Fire Investigator Expert at Trial

When a fire investigation has resulted in criminal charges, the experts called by both the Crown and defence should be able to provide answers

142 *NFPA 921*, above note 2, s. 11.8.5.

to a variety of questions, ranging from the process used to conduct the investigation to the manner in which the final hypothesis of the origin and cause of the fire was reached.

Experts should be able to articulate how they conducted their examination, beginning with whether or not they attended the scene. The expert for the Crown in all likelihood attended the scene and carried out an investigation. The examination should include documentation of the scene through the use of photographs, notes, and/or diagrams. The expert should be able to articulate how they applied a systematic approach to the investigation of the scene. If they deviated from that approach, they should be able to explain why. It may be that portions of the scene were unstable and unsafe to access. The investigator should be able to explain why such a conclusion was made and what measures were attempted to mitigate the danger so the area could be accessed. For example, if the investigator was not able to access a basement because it was full of water, was an attempt made to clear the water or otherwise gain access? Consideration should then be given to what impact this had on the investigation and any opinions reached.

Experts called by defence counsel may have access only to photographs of the scene rather than the scene itself. They may rightfully be challenged on their ability to provide an opinion without having attended the scene. However, under the *NFPA 921*, as long as the data collection and documentation has been performed by a qualified fire investigator, it is not necessary for the testifying expert to have personally performed a scene investigation:

> In any incident scene investigation, it is necessary for at least one individual/organization to conduct an examination of the incident scene for the purpose of data collection and documentation. While it is preferable that all subsequent investigators have the opportunity to conduct an independent examination of the incident scene, in practice, not every scene is available at the time of the assignment. The use of previously collected data from a properly documented scene can be used successfully in an analysis of the incident to reach valid conclusions through the appropriate use of the scientific method. Thus, the reliance on previously collected data and scene documentation should not be inherently considered a limitation in the ability to successfully investigate the incident.[143]

143 *Ibid.*, s. 4.4.3.3.

The investigator/expert should be able to articulate the steps set out in the scientific method and how those steps were applied in the investigation. It is not enough to simply close their eyes and recite the steps in the scientific method. It is how those steps apply to their investigation that is the true test of the accuracy of the investigation and resulting opinion. The opinion of the investigator/expert should include opinions on origin of the fire, the ignition source for the fire, the fuel first ignited, and the circumstances that brought the fuel and the ignition source together with an oxidizer (usually oxygen from the air). The investigator should be able to answer questions relating to the analysis of fire patterns that led to identification of the area of origin and the means by which the fire spread from that area as well as give an opinion on ventilation and its effect on the determination of the area of origin. Lines of inquiry for counsel to consider may include:

- Did the investigator use arc mapping and did the results support the fire patterns in determination of the area of origin?
- If the investigator's theory involves multiple areas of origin, what consideration was given to the possibility of fire spread as opposed to multiple areas of origin?
- How did the investigator identify potential ignition sources within the area(s) of origin? (This often involves excavation of the fire debris, by hand in small scenes or using heavy equipment in large scenes.)
- Who carried out examination of the debris? What instructions were they given and what qualifications did they have?
- If ignition sources were identified and eliminated, how were they eliminated? Were other investigators involved in this process? What were their qualifications?
- What did the investigator do to identify potential fuel packages within the area of origin? (This is often done simultaneously with the identification of ignition sources during excavation of the scene.)
- Who identified the fuel packages? What instructions were they given and what qualifications did they have? If fuel packages were identified by means of statements of occupants or diagrams provided by the occupants, have those statements and diagrams been disclosed?

The investigator/expert should be able to explain why the ignition source identified is a competent ignition source for the fuel first ignited. This includes answering questions pertaining to the ignition temperature of the fuel first ignited and the temperature of the ignition source. For example, if the theory is that a range top element, set on high, ignited a pan with oil on a range top, the investigator should be able to cite the highest temperature that the range element can produce, and provide the auto-ignition temperature of cooking oil.

In the end, it is the role of the trier of fact, either judge or jury, to weigh all of the available evidence and render a verdict. During evidence-in-chief, it is the role of counsel to ask the investigator about the steps taken to guard against bias during the investigation. The investigator should be able to show that their investigation was not unduly focused on information that could have otherwise affected the investigator's conclusions. The investigator should be able to show that the investigation was neutral and unbiased and that all potential theories were considered with regards to area of origin, ignition source, and the fuel first ignited. Theories that are merely "consistent with" the information gathered is speculation and does not reflect the scientific method. The investigator should be prepared to accept that the background information provided to them may be intentionally or unintentionally wrong.

D. A CASE STUDY

A thirty-year-old man purchased a delicatessen that was a going concern (i.e., an existing, ongoing business that is profitable for which there is no reason to burn to receive an insurance settlement). During the first week of possession, shortly after the end of the working day when no one was present, a fire broke out in the basement that ultimately destroyed much of the three-storey facility. A fire investigator was called to examine the scene and the police ultimately charged the owner with arson. At the time of this fire, *NFPA 921* still allowed an incendiary fire conclusion to be drawn using a process of elimination based upon the determination of a precise point of origin and a lack of evidence for an ignition source at that location. The fire investigator suspected that an accelerant had been used because he felt that the fire had spread "too fast" to be a normal fire. The fire investigator took multiple fire debris samples and had them analyzed by a lab for the presence of a volatile combustible liquid (a potential accelerant). At trial, it became evident that the fire investigator:

- had not credibly determined a point of origin for the fire and could not accurately locate his point of origin on a plot plan of the basement,

- had not credibly eliminated two electrical distribution panel installations as potential areas of origin and ignition source,
- was not aware of electrical extension cords and lights that were in his concluded area of origin and may have provided an ignition source, and
- had a very poor timeline for the fire ignition and development and no scientific basis for claiming the fire had spread "too fast" to have been accidental,
- but still maintained that an accelerant had been employed even though the laboratory analyses of all his fire debris samples were reported negative.

When challenged about the accelerant used, the fire investigator identified the accelerant as cardboard boxes. The facts in evidence included that prior to the fire, employees had restocked the shelves and tossed the cardboard shipping boxes down the stairs into the basement. This was standard procedure. Every few days, the boxes were consolidated and put into a dumpster. During the fire, a fraction of the cardboard boxes burned, in the location where they had been tossed by the employees, in the usual manner that cardboard burns. There was no evidentiary basis for the fire investigator's testimony on the use of an accelerant.

The jury quickly returned a verdict of not guilty.

E. CONCLUSION

The results of a fire investigation may be used to support the conviction of a suspected arsonist, deny an insurance claim, or deny a negligence claim when product failure is suspected. To ensure a proper investigation, the fire investigator/expert must be properly qualified, possess adequate knowledge and experience to investigate fires, use a systematic approach, and use the scientific method. *NFPA 1033, the Standard for Professional Qualifications for Fire Investigator*, may be used to qualify the fire investigator. Experts should be able to demonstrate experience with the methodology in *NFPA 921, the Guide for Fire and Explosion Investigations.*

The proper methodology requires that the origin of the fire be properly defined before the investigator opines on the cause of the fire. "Generally, if the origin cannot be determined, the cause cannot be determined, and generally, if the correct origin is not identified, the subsequent cause determination will also be incorrect."[144] The problem with determining

144 *NFPA 921*, above note 2, s. 18.1.

the wrong area of origin is that the ignition source for the fire will not be found there.

It is inappropriate for investigators to allow their understanding of the science of fire investigation to become outdated. To reduce the likelihood of a miscarriage of justice, the fire investigators' methodology, investigation, and report should be closely scrutinized by counsel. The fire investigator should employ the scientific method and guard against bias throughout his investigation.

F. LEGAL CONTEXT[145]

> Other than shaken baby syndrome, the most prominent current example of shifted science [when scientific testimony that led to a conviction is later proved to have been completely invalid] potentially calling into question hundreds or thousands of convictions that occurred over the past few decades is the science of arson investigation. A fairly diffuse field, arson investigation focuses on finding a number of indicators at a fire scene that a qualified investigator may interpret as evidence of an intentionally set fire. Over the decades, however, a series of myths crept into the fire investigation profession and undermined the generally scientific nature of a successful arson investigation.[146]

Fire science has experienced a dramatic shift away from unvalidated conclusions on issues such as fire origin and cause towards the use of systematic scene investigation and analysis based in the scientific method. This reconceived understanding of the reliability of fire science evidence has renounced traditionally held myths and misconceptions from the fire investigator's toolkit, particularly since the publishing of the *NFPA 921, Guide for Fire and Explosion Investigations* in 1992.[147] In 2000, *NFPA 921* was acknowledged by the United States Department of Justice as a "benchmark" for fire investigation experts and was adopted by the International

---

145 Adjunct Professor Tamara Levy, Director of the University of British Columbia Innocence Project at the Allard School of Law, provided valuable feedback to Caitlin Pakosh in refining this chapter's legal context section. Her peer review of this section is greatly appreciated.

146 Caitlin Plummer & Imran Syed, "'Shifted Science' and Post-Conviction Relief" (2012) 8 *Stanford Journal of Civil Rights and Civil Liberties* 259 at 271. The definition of shifted science provided in brackets is quoted from page 263 of the same article.

147 *Ibid.* at 274. See also Gregory E. Gorbett et al., "Use of Damage in Fire Investigation: A Review of Fire Patterns Analysis, Research and Future Direction" (2015) 4 *Fire Science Reviews* 1.

Association of Arson Investigators (IAAI).[148] Relying on the scientific method, modern fire investigators should approach fire origin and cause determinations with caution. They should avoid trying to "recognize arson," as was once the focus of investigator training.[149] Depending on the circumstances of the case, chemists, explosives experts, and electrical engineers may also provide opinion evidence in arson cases.[150]

The fire investigation community's recognition of the phenomenon of post-flashover fires in partially enclosed or enclosed areas, and the resulting changes in fire pattern interpretation knowledge, is in large part responsible for the shift towards the application of the scientific method in fire investigations.[151] Fire patterns remain a key tool used by investigators to determine a fire's origin and necessarily result in "consistent with" opinions. This may create tension when the fire examiner provides his opinion in court since, historically, "consistent with" evidence has drawn a great deal of criticism from the legal community for having the potential to mislead.[152] In 2009, the National Academy of Sciences issued a report considering the scientific foundation of many forensic disciplines, including fire debris analysis. It stated that continued research into burn pattern interpretation is needed to account for variability, damage characteristics, and the presence or absence of accelerants in order to draw scientifically valid conclusions:

> By contrast [to explosion analysis], much more research is needed on the natural variability of burn patterns and damage characteristics and how they are affected by the presence of various accelerants. Despite the paucity of research, some arson investigators continue to make determinations about whether or not a particular fire was set. However, according to testimony presented to the committee, many of the rules of thumb that are typically assumed to indicate that an accelerant was used

148 Lentini, "Evolution of Fire," above note 10 at 3 & 4.

149 *Ibid.* at 4.

150 See, for example, *R. v. Young*, [1996] N.B.J. No. 445 (Prov. Ct.) and *R. v. Reid*, [2000] N.J. No. 347 (S.C.T.D.).

151 For U.S. cases that critically analyze the evolution of fire science, see *Han Tak Lee v. Franklin J. Tennis* (2014), United States District Court for the Middle District of Pennsylvania, Civil No. 4:08-CV-1972, and *Kristine Bunch v. State of Indiana* (2012), Court of Appeals of Indiana, No. 16A05-1007-PC-439 [*Han Tak Lee* and *Kristine Bunch* cases].

152 See, for example, Alan D. Gold. *Expert Evidence in Criminal Law: The Scientific Approach*, 2d ed. (Toronto: Irwin Law, 2009) at 227. For a case involving a fire origin and cause determination based in part on fire pattern evidence, see, for example, *R. v. Fournel*, 2012 ONSC 375 at paras. 61–71, 90, 95–107, and 204. See also *R. v. Goulding*, [1997] N.J. No. 282 at para. 36, point (vi) (S.C.T.D.).

(e.g., "alligatoring" of wood, specific char patterns) have been shown not to be true. Experiments should be designed to put arson investigations on a more solid scientific footing.[153]

1) Fire Science and Miscarriages of Justice

With the application of the scientific method to fire investigation, the United States has seen a number of arson convictions transformed into high-profile miscarriages of justice.[154] One of the most infamous is the case of Cameron Todd Willingham. A fire swept through Willingham's home on 23 December 1991, killing his three young daughters. Willingham testified that he was asleep and his wife was out buying Christmas presents when the fire started. He maintained his innocence but was convicted by a jury in 1992 and sentenced to death on the strength of fire expert testimony and an alleged confession made to a jailhouse informant,[155] Johnny Webb (who recanted his testimony in 2000 and explained that he lied in exchange for a reduced sentence).[156] Willingham refused to plead guilty in exchange for a commutation of his death sentence.[157]

On 17 February 2004, Willingham was executed despite state officials having received a new scientific report by a renowned fire expert, the late Dr. Gerald Hurst, who concluded that "there is not a single item of physical evidence in this case which supports a finding of arson."[158] In response to a request made by the Innocence Project in 2006, the Texas Forensic Science Commission began its investigation into the case in 2008.[159] A state consultant, Dr. Craig L. Beyler, submitted a report to the Commission addressing the faulty fire investigation methods and procedures employed in

153 National Research Council, Committee on Identifying the Needs of the Forensic Sciences Community, *Strengthening Forensic Science in the United States: A Path Forward* (Washington, DC: The National Academies Press, 2009) at 173, online: www.ncjrs.gov/pdffiles1/nij/grants/228091.pdf [footnotes omitted].

154 See, for example, *Han Tak Lee* and *Kristine Bunch* cases, above note 151.

155 See, generally, *The State of Texas v. Cameron Todd Willingham*, Trial Transcript Vol. 15, online: www.innocenceproject.org/files/imported/willinghamv15.pdf.

156 Tom Dart, "Texas Prosecutor Accused of Misconduct for Role in Famous Execution Case" *The Guardian* (19 March 2015), online: www.theguardian.com/us-news/2015/mar/19/texas-prosecutor-accused-misconduct-execution-case.

157 "Cameron Todd Willingham" *The Texas Tribune*, online: www.texastribune.org/tribpedia/cameron-todd-willingham [*Texas Tribune*, "Willingham"].

158 Innocence Project, "Cameron Todd Willingham: Wrongfully Convicted and Executed in Texas" (13 September 2010), online: www.innocenceproject.org/news-events-exonerations/cameron-todd-willingham-wrongfully-convicted-and-executed-in-texas [Innocence Project, "Willingham"]. Quote from *Texas Tribune*, "Willingham," *ibid.*

159 Innocence Project, "Willingham," *ibid.*

the case. Dr. Beyler concluded that arson could not be found based upon either the modern understanding of fire science (articulated in *NFPA 921*) or fire investigation papers from 1980–1992.[160] Dr. Beyler characterized the expert testimony of Manuel Vasquez, a fire investigator from the state fire marshal's office, as reflecting a predisposition to find arson and, further:

> His [Vasquez's] quotations that "[t]he fire tells a story, I am just the interpreter," and "the fire does not lie, it tells me the truth," are hardly consistent with a scientific mindset and is more characteristic of mystics or psychics. The quotes separate the findings from his own judgment and seek to make him not responsible for his own interpretation. It seems to deny the role of rational reasoning. It is an expression of fire investigation as a mystical art rather than an application of science and reason.[161]

The Commission released its final report on 15 April 2011, with an addendum on 28 October 2011, that recognized the role of invalid fire science in Willingham's case and advanced a series of recommendations for future arson cases, committing to the review of existing arson convictions.[162] The Commission also investigated the arson conviction of Ernest Ray Willis, whose charges were dismissed in 2012 after he spent seventeen years in prison. He received compensation from the State of Texas in the amount of $777,943.[163]

The extent of any Canadian wrongful convictions based on invalid fire science is currently unknown.[164] That question is beyond the scope of this guide, but a systemic evaluation of past arson cases, similar to the one in Texas, could potentially be an appropriate recommendation depending on the results of any future research efforts directed to understanding the

---

160 Craig L. Beyler, "Analysis of the Fire Investigation Methods and Procedures Used in the Criminal Arson Cases Against Ernest Ray Willis and Cameron Todd Willingham" (17 August 2009) at 51, online: camerontoddwillingham.com/?page_id=79. The report also addressed the case of Ernest Ray Willis.

161 *Ibid.* at 48 & 49. See also Lentini, "Evolution of Fire," above note 10 at 1.

162 Texas Forensic Science Commission, "Report of The Texas Forensic Science Commission: Willingham/Willis Investigation" (15 April 2011), online: www.fsc.state.tx.us/documents/FINAL.pdf. Texas Forensic Science Commission, "Addendum to The April 15, 2011 Report of the Texas Forensic Science Commission" (28 October 2011) online: www.innocenceproject.org/files/imported/willingham_willis_addendum_2011-4.pdf.

163 The National Registry of Exonerations, "Ernest Ray Willis," online: www.law.umich.edu/special/exoneration/Pages/casedetail.aspx?caseid=3755.

164 Adjunct Professor Tamara Levy hypothesizes that a wave of wrongful convictions involving fire science have not been identified and documented in Canada because there are very few people and organizations looking into innocence claims involving fire-related offences, as compared ot the United States.

issue in the Canadian context. Further study is required and, beyond logistics, the issue is complex for two reasons: (1) fire science has evolved over time, requiring a multi-disciplinary analysis that intersects science and the law; and (2) wrongful convictions are often the result of a series of systemic problems, rather than a single failure. Although the second-degree murder conviction of Leon Walchuk involved fire science and was alleged to be a wrongful conviction by the Innocence Project at Osgoode Hall, the Federal Minister of Justice (in answering a ministerial review application submitted by the Project in 2009) ultimately concluded that there was no reasonable basis to conclude that a miscarriage of justice likely occurred. The Project's application for judicial review of the Minister's decision was refused in 2013 by the Federal Court,[165] a decision which was upheld in 2015.[166]

To provide a brief summary of *R. v. Walchuk*, Leon Walchuk and his wife separated in 1994 and, by 1998, were involved in divorce proceedings marked by a long fight over financial matters. On 30 March 1998, Mrs. Walchuk was at the family farm to pick up their two children, but the children were with Mr. Walchuk's parents at their farm.[167] Mr. and Mrs. Walchuk fought and, at some point, Mrs. Walchuk's car drove through the family home and a fire engulfed the house. Although neighbours and the Walchuk children quickly arrived at the scene, Mr. Walchuk—distraught and with a bloody face[168]—did not tell anyone that Mrs. Walchuk was still in the house until after the fire department arrived. Mrs. Walchuk, who was in the basement, died from smoke inhalation, but she also had severe brain injuries caused by Mr. Walchuk hitting her with a hockey stick, likely resulting in her loss of consciousness before the fire.

Mr. Walchuk was charged with first-degree murder. Forensic pathologists called by the Crown and the defence agreed that Mrs. Walchuk would have survived her head injuries with medical treatment.[169] As detailed by Manson J. in his decision at the Federal Court:

---

165 *Walchuk v. Canada (Minister of Justice)*, 2013 FC 958 [*Walchuk* 2013].

166 *Walchuk v. Canada (Minister of Justice)*, 2015 FCA 85 [*Walchuk* 2015].

167 *R. v. Walchuk*, 2000 SKQB 275 at paras. 1–14 [*Walchuk* 2000].

168 *Walchuk* 2000, *ibid.* at para. 8.

169 *Walchuk* 2013, above note 165 at para. 3. Forensic pathology expertise is necessary in cases involving decedents found at a fire scene to determine whether the deceased died before or after the fire. For another example, see *R. v. Butler*, 2005 BCSC 1890 at para. 35, where the pathologist concluded that the deceased died before the fire started on the basis of "... the lack of soot in the deceased['s] trachea and the lack of carbon monoxide in his blood ...." A similar conclusion was reached at para. 22 of *R. v. Minor*, 2013 ONCA 557, which will be discussed later in this section.

> The trial judge adopted the prosecution's theory that the Applicant had severely beaten the Victim with a hockey stick, left her in the basement, poured some gasoline on the stairs and a landing, and ignited it with a match, intentionally killing her. As part of this conclusion, the trial judge agreed, at para 26 of his decision, that an accelerant was present, and at para 16, that an electrical fire as a result of the car crash was not the cause of the fire. At trial, various expert witnesses were called. Among them were James Fairbank, who testified that an accelerant was used to start the fire; Wayne Davies, who testified that an electrical source was not the cause of the fire; and Arthur Hunter, who testified that the fire was not the result of a vehicle failure.
>
> In addition to this expert evidence, the judge noted other circumstantial evidence pointing towards the Applicant's guilt:
>
> - He had severely beaten the Victim and left her in the basement;
> - He did not immediately tell anyone that she was inside the house;
> - He hid personal items outside the farmhouse, which is a common pre-arson activity;
> - He had plans, but no money, for a new home;
> - He expressed surprise to an undercover police officer that the farmhouse did not "go up";
> - The night of the death was the first time the children had not been at the farm house at 7:00 p.m. for pickup by the Victim;
> - He had made serious threats to the Victim in the past;
> - He made it clear that no one else was welcome on the property that night; and
> - His financial dispute with the Victim may have provided a motive for her murder.
>
> The defence's theory was that the Victim became enraged, drove into the farmhouse in an attempt to kill the Applicant, and proceeded to hit the Applicant with a hockey stick, chasing him into the basement. The Applicant then managed to take the hockey stick from the Victim, and beat her with it. The Applicant then left the basement, noticed there was a fire, attempted to put it out with his jacket, and failed. He heard the Victim screaming, but by that point, there was nothing he could do to help her.[170]

Walchuk was convicted of second degree murder in 2000. His ministerial review application was based on three new expert opinions, which conclud-

---

170 *Walchuk* 2013, *ibid.* at paras. 4–6.

ed that an accelerant was not used and that the fire may have been caused by an electrical problem, weakening the Crown's theory of the fire being intentionally set using an accelerant.[171] The Criminal Conviction Review Group (CCRG) retained an arson expert, who also concluded that no accelerant was used and that damage at the scene correlated with an electrical cause originating from the vehicle or the house, but who cautioned, in part, that, "[t]here is ample circumstantial evidence that is unexplained to warrant consideration of an incendiary fire."[172] The Minister ultimately concluded that there was sufficient other evidence supporting the conclusion that Mr. Walchuk intentionally killed Mrs. Walchuk, finding that there was not a reasonable basis to conclude that a miscarriage of justice likely occurred.[173]

2) The Importance of Circumstantial Evidence in Cases of Alleged Arson

Arson cases are frequently based on circumstantial evidence and are therefore heavily fact-driven and the testimony of the fire expert (directed by the scientific method) is necessarily considered in the context of the case as a whole. In older cases, where the outdated and unreliable *negative corpus*[174] approach was used by the fire investigator, legal and procedural safeguards seemingly added the requirement to consider every hypothesis before classifying a fire as incendiary, years before the transition to the scientific method took hold in the fire investigation community.[175] For example, in *R. v. Monteleone*, a fire started in the basement of Monteleone's clothing store, destroying the three-storey building, which also contained a jewellery store and residential apartments.[176] The fire inspector seems to have applied the *negative corpus* approach, concluding that the fire was incendiary because no accidental cause was determined, and he could not determine the actual cause of the fire.[177] The Crown's case "rested entirely on circumstantial evi-

171 *Walchuk* 2015, above note 166 at para. 12.

172 *Ibid.* at para. 13.

173 *Ibid.* at paras. 15–18.

174 This is a method in which the investigator determines the incendiary nature of the fire by eliminating all reasonable ignition sources for the fire in the absence of other supportive evidence. See Section A(2), above in this chapter.

175 This is a general observation based on a review of the caselaw. It does not preclude the possibility that in some cases legal and procedural safeguards did not protect the accused from an incorrect expert conclusion borne out by the *negative corpus* approach to fire investigation, particularly prior to 1992.

176 *R. v. Monteleone*, [1987] 2 S.C.R. 154 at para. 2 [*Monteleone*].

177 *Ibid.* at para. 3.

dence."[178] The trial judge directed that the jury return a verdict of not guilty on the basis that the evidence as a whole gave rise only to suspicion against the accused, not an inference of guilt.[179] The Crown's appeal against the acquittal was allowed, with the Court of Appeal finding that the trial judge usurped the role of the jury by weighing the evidence himself.[180] The case was heard by the Supreme Court of Canada, which stated that, "[o]ur sole concern is to inquire whether there was a case made by the Crown at trial which ought to have been left to the jury for that determination."[181]

The Supreme Court of Canada highlighted the words of Lacourcière J.A.,[182] which recognized that the fire inspector's evidence alone was not sufficient to find the fire was unlawfully set in this case, noting the value of circumstantial evidence in prosecuting arson cases:

> Lacourcière J.A. acknowledged that the expert evidence of the fire inspector alone did not afford evidence of the unlawful setting of a fire. He said: "taken by themselves, the findings of Inspector MacLean [*sic*] could at best support the conclusion that the origin of the fire was unexplained." However, later he said:
>
> > In most prosecutions for arson, the Crown must depend on circumstantial evidence. The circumstances must be sufficient to exclude every reasonable hypothesis other than a wilful and intentional burning in order to rebut the presumption that the burning was of accidental or natural origin. However, the facts and circumstances which tend to prove the incendiary origin of a fire are often interwoven, as in the present case, with other facts and circumstances which tend to connect the accused with the crime such as the presence of a motive, and the clear opportunity of the accused together with his subsequent incriminatory statements.[183]

The court recognized that the act constituting the crime—the *corpus delicti*—can be proved on the basis of circumstantial evidence and it is not necessary for the act to be proved by direct and positive evidence.[184] The Court,

---

178 *Ibid.* at para. 5.
179 *Ibid.*
180 *Ibid.* at para. 6.
181 *Ibid.* at para. 7.
182 See *R. v. Monteleone* (1983), 38 O.R. (2d) 651 (C.A.).
183 *Monteleone*, above note 176 at para. 10 [internal references omitted].
184 *Ibid.* at para. 13. It is also important to note that a fire expert may be unable to rule out accidental ignition, but the court may nonetheless find that a fire was deliberately ignited on the basis of other evidence, including eyewitness accounts. This does not

quoting from *R. v. Girvin*, explained how this idea applies to arson. "Fires occurring accidentally are common, and any given fire must be assumed to have been accidental until evidence is adduced of intention. . . . No doubt, the evidence of the *corpus delicti* and the evidence of the guilt of an accused may often be more or less inseparable, and that is quite properly suggested as the case here."[185] The Supreme Court of Canada found that there was evidence at trial that met the *Shephard* test and that the weighing of the evidence should have been left to the jury, confirming the order for a new trial.[186]

In cases where the trial judge leaves the evidence to the jury's determination, the trial judge should be mindful of the need to provide an independent review of the evidence in providing instruction to and answering questions from the jury. In *R. v. Minor*,[187] the accused successfully appealed her conviction for the second degree murder of her husband ". . . on the ground that the trial judge failed to conduct an independent review of the evidence in the course of his jury instructions."[188] The accused's husband was discovered deceased when firefighters responded to a call from the accused reporting that she saw soot and black smoke rising from her house when she arrived home from work. Her husband's death was caused by a puncture wound to the chest. Defensive cuts and bruises on his body indicated that he was involved in a struggle.[189] Ten experts testified at trial, including three experts from the Office of the Fire Marshal who concluded that three locations within the house were intentionally set on fire.[190] The Crown theorized, relying on ten timepieces that were

---

necessarily mean, however, that the accused will be convicted. A case-by-case analysis is required. For example, see *R. v. Keller*, 2003 SKPC 171, where the court found that the fire was not accidental but dismissed the charge of arson since the Crown failed to prove that the two accused formed a common intention to commit arson.

185 *Ibid.*, quoting from *R. v. Girvin* (1911), 3 Alta. L.R. 387 at 398 (S.C. *en banc*). The quote is provided only in part in this text.

186 *Monteleone*, above note 176 at para. 8. The Court described the *Shephard* test as follows: "[w]here there is before the court any admissible evidence, whether direct or circumstantial, which, if believed by a properly charged jury acting reasonably, would justify a conviction, the trial judge is not justified in directing a verdict of acquittal. It is not the function of the trial judge to weigh the evidence, to test its quality or reliability once a determination of its admissibility has been made. It is not for the trial judge to draw inferences of fact from the evidence before him. These functions are for the trier of fact, the jury." See para. 17 for a summary of the Court's conclusion.

187 *R. v. Minor*, above note 169.

188 *Ibid.* at para. 1.

189 *Ibid.* at para. 3.

190 *Ibid.* at paras. 19 & 20.

found stopped in the home,[191] that the accused had exclusive opportunity to set the fire. The defence argued that the case represented a "break and enter gone wrong."[192] In providing his instructions to the jury, "[a]part from listing the names of the experts and their areas of expertise, the trial judge did not review any of the expert evidence. Nor did he review any of the numerous exhibits filed at trial, which included over 200 photographs of the crime scene."[193] As a result, Laskin J.A. held that, "[b]y failing to conduct an independent review of the evidence, the trial judge inadvertently downplayed the defence theory and gave disproportionate weight to the Crown's theory."[194] Justice Laskin found the verdict unreliable and ordered a new trial, finding that the trial judge erred by focusing on a single piece of evidence—the stopped timepieces—which misdirected the jury to apply the reasonable doubt standard to a single piece of evidence and caused a real risk that the jury would jump to the conclusion of guilt.[195]

a) Coincidence and Credibility

The trial judgment of *R. v. Nguyen* (involving six arson-related counts with regard to a fire at the accused's nail salon business) drives home the central role of circumstantial evidence in arson cases and the importance of evaluating these circumstances as a whole. The defence conceded that the fire was deliberately set, making the only issue at trial whether the accused set it.[196] The Crown conceded that its case against the accused was entirely circumstantial, but argued that guilt was the only conclusion available on the whole of the evidence.[197] The defence acknowledged that the circumstantial evidence may be consistent with guilt but argued that it is not the only, or even best, explanation.[198] Justice A.H. Silverman concluded that coincidence is impossible under a two-pronged analysis considering whether there is

---

191 *Ibid.* at paras. 16–18.

192 *Ibid.* at paras. 30 & 31.

193 *Ibid.* at para. 45.

194 *Ibid.* at para. 94.

195 *Ibid.* at paras. 100–2. At para. 100, the court cited *R. v. Morin*, [1988] 2 S.C.R. 345 at 354: "it is a misdirection to instruct the jury to apply the standard of reasonable doubt to individual pieces of evidence." At para. 101, the court cited *R. v. White*, [1998] 2 S.C.R. 72 at para. 49, explaining that ". . . such an instruction runs the risk of 'confusing the jury and inviting them to short-circuit their deliberations.'"

196 *R. v. Nguyen*, 2014 BCSC 297 at para. 8.

197 *Ibid.* at para. 9.

198 *Ibid.* at para. 10.

any other rational explanation for the evidence and whether the circumstances "[establish] the accused's guilt as the only rational explanation."[199]

> Coincidences do occur, and certainly there are examples where acquittals have occurred as a result of coincidences and, of greater concern, there are examples in many jurisdictions of wrongful convictions which have occurred as a result of failing to recognize that coincidences may have occurred. . . . Here, in my view, the timing and the number of circumstances in this case make coincidence an impossibility.[200]

Justice Silverman noted the coincidences the defence asked the jury to accept, including the defendant recently purchasing an insurance policy, which took effect only six days before the fire. Three days before the fire, the defendant purchased gasoline in an amount similar to what was found at the scene. And on the day of the fire, she was seen (1) putting boxes in her car four hours before the fire, (2) at the premises three hours before the fire, and (3) her car was seen sitting at the premises two hours before the fire. Justice Silverman continued:

> I ask myself next if these circumstances, when taken together and considered as a whole, could suggest even the mildest reasonable possibility that some person other than the accused committed this crime, and the answer is clearly no. The accused's suggestions to the contrary call for speculation, which I am not permitted to indulge in. That two others had keys is not evidence that they might have committed this crime, in the absence of some evidence, even circumstantial evidence, that one or the other of them was there and had used the key at some relevant time. There is no evidence whatsoever, circumstantial or direct, of that.[201]

In other cases where the only issue at trial is the identity of the perpetrator,[202] the court may be required to conduct an in-depth credibility analysis. The case of *R. v. Bos*, for example, involved charges of arson with disregard for human life and wilfully damaging property,[203] with the critical

---

199 *Ibid.* at para. 62.

200 *Ibid.* at paras. 63 & 64.

201 *Ibid.* at para. 65. In *R. v. Nguyen*, 2016 BCCA 133, the appellant argued that the trial judge erred by "wrongly dismissing possible innocent explanations for circumstantial evidence as 'speculative.'" The Court of Appeal dismissed the appeal, holding that the judge properly assessed the evidence and that the verdict was not unreasonable.

202 For another example, see *R. v. G.A.D.G.*, 2002 BCPC 247.

203 Contrary to sections 433(a) and 430(4) of the *Criminal Code*, R.S.C. 1985, c. C-46, respectively.

question being the identity of the person who set the complainant's house on fire. The personal histories and relationships involved in the case were complex. The Crown theory was that the accused set fire to her fiancée's (the complainant's) home as a diversion, which risked his life, to ensure a real estate transaction for another property did not close. This was done in an effort to conceal her double life—she had told her fiancée that she was a widow who had inherited money from her late husband. In reality, she was still married and was using money from accounts shared with her husband.[204] The defence theory was that the complainant had set the fire because he stood to benefit financially. The property was held in his name, he was having trouble selling it and did not have enough money to invest in another property with the accused, and he had the perfect opportunity to set a fire in the garage.[205]

Jeffrey Post, the expert in "fire scene assessment and examinations related to the origin of fire, sources of ignition, and factors affecting the development and spread of a fire,"[206] was called by the Crown and testified to employing the scientific method by testing the following hypotheses to arrive at the conclusion that the fire was incendiary:

1) Was the fire of an incendiary nature—that is was it intentionally set?
2) Was the fire accidental—caused by human error or a breakdown in equipment?
3) Was the fire caused by a natural source—i.e. lightning?
4) Is the source of the fire undetermined in that it cannot be isolated in terms of origin, or there are conflicting ignition sources?[207]

The expert's opinion that the fire was intentionally set was well received by the court, which found that the expert's unchallenged opinion was well reasoned and supported by the scientific method, excluding all other possibilities.[208] If the fire was intentionally set, then either the complainant or the accused must have caused the fire.[209] Considering the fact-finding assessment heavily depended on the credibility of the complainant's testimony as well as the reliability of the expert's evidence, the court applied the

---

204 *R. v. Bos*, 2012 ONSC 3835 at paras. 185–96.
205 *Ibid.* at para. 207.
206 *Ibid.* at para. 168.
207 *Ibid.* at para. 169.
208 *Ibid.* at para. 256.
209 *Ibid.* at para. 265.

R. v. W.(D.) analysis to the essential elements of the offence.[210] The court explained the application of the principles in *R. v. W.(D.)* and the necessary analytical steps as follows:

> 1. If I believe the exculpatory evidence advanced by the defence, there must be an acquittal;
> 2. If in light of the conflicting testimony, reasonable doubt exists as to exactly where the truth of the matter lies, there must be an acquittal;
> 3. If I accept the Crown's inculpatory account beyond a reasonable doubt, there shall be a conviction.
>
> . . .
>
> When the jury is applying the first two prongs of the three pronged test in W.(D.) they are deciding whether they can accept the accused's version of events or whether it leaves them with a reasonable doubt. Clearly they can only do that by assessing the accused's evidence and the other evidence that favours the accused in the context of all the evidence.[211]

The court found that the defence argument that the complainant sought to "frame" the accused made no sense as he thought he was engaged to her, had no motive, and did not report the fire to police.[212] The court did not accept the accused's testimony denying she committed the offences, finding further that she was in fact living a double life.[213] With respect to the *W.(D.)* analysis, the court found that the exculpatory evidence was not persuasive and the defence theories were speculative, such that the court was satisfied beyond a reasonable doubt that the accused ". . . intentionally set a fire in the wall of the basement stairwell by applying an open flame to a combustible material, namely paper towel."[214]

b) Conflicting Expert Evidence

A detailed assessment of the circumstantial evidence is critical in cases that present with opposing expert theories to explain a fire's origin and cause. In *R. v. Reid*, for example, the accused was charged with intent to defraud his insurance company by causing damage by fire to his guitar business, contrary to section 435(1) of the *Criminal Code*.[215] The fire experts called

---

210 *Ibid.* at para. 250.
211 *Ibid.* at para. 254–55 [internal references omitted].
212 *Ibid.* at para. 268.
213 *Ibid.* at para. 270.
214 *Ibid.* at para. 276.
215 *R. v. Reid*, above note 150 at para. 1.

by the Crown theorized that the fire was incendiary on the basis of finding two points of origin.[216] The Crown also called a chemistry expert who concluded that charred wood at the scene contained "a medium petroleum distillate."[217] The fire expert called by the defence, however, theorized that the fire was accidental, caused by the accused discarding smoking materials (specifically a cigarette) while working.[218] Although Schwartz J. considered the fire highly suspicious, he was not satisfied beyond a reasonable doubt of the accused's guilt and entered an acquittal, reasoning that the court must first determine that the cause was arson before considering the motive and opportunity of the accused.

> In this particular matter no one saw a fire being lit. There are two different theories as provided by the experts. Upon thorough examination of the experts' opinions I am satisfied that one theory is as highly probable to have been the cause of the fire as the other. It is difficult to differentiate one expert's theory from the other. I am also not satisfied from the evidence that there was sufficient motive for the Accused to destroy his business premises based on the accounting that was placed before the Court.[219]

3) Summary

Fire science has made significant advancements in recent years and the underlying reasoning of fire expert conclusions has evolved over time, requiring lawyers to understand the nuances of how knowledge in this discipline has changed. An enduring cornerstone of arson cases is the need for Crown and defence counsel to thoroughly explore the related circumstantial evidence. Such circumstantial evidence may support or oppose the opinion presented by fire experts, who have their own responsibility to be unbiased and considerate of all possibilities, in accordance with the scientific method. Throughout the litigation of such factually and scientifically complex cases, the judiciary plays an important role in ensuring that the trial process is fair and that the presumption of innocence is protected.

---

216 *Ibid.* at paras. 15–20.
217 *Ibid.* at para. 24.
218 *Ibid.* at paras. 21–23.
219 *Ibid.* at para. 31.

CHAPTER 11

Forensic Anthropology

Tracy Rogers

LEGAL CONTEXT: CAITLIN PAKOSH

A. OVERVIEW OF THE DISCIPLINE: FORENSIC ANTHROPOLOGY

The definition of forensic anthropology has changed over the years to reflect its maturation from a specialized branch of biological anthropology, focusing primarily on the identification of anonymous human remains, to an independent subfield with its own body of theory, research paradigms, and goals.[1] Depending on the source, the country of origin, and the year of the publication, forensic anthropology will be variously defined with an emphasis on: (1) the skeleton; (2) identification; and, most recently, (3) the life, death, and post-life history of an individual, reconstructed from analyzing their skeletal remains and the context in which they are located.[2] The latter definition is less concrete, but is more inclusive and better reflects the Canadian experience.

In practice, forensic anthropologists work with police to search for bodies, body parts, and graves in forensic contexts. They recover human remains from a wide variety of scenes in which the condition of the body and the process of extraction could result in damage or loss of evidence if not recovered using specific protocols (e.g., from fires, burials, wells, septic tanks, culverts). Once the remains are recovered, forensic anthropologists con-

1 Debra Komar & Jane Buikstra, *Forensic Anthropology: Contemporary Theory and Practice* (New York: Oxford University Press, 2008).

2 Dennis C. Dirkmaat et al., "New Perspectives in Forensic Anthropology" (2008) 51 *American Journal of Physical Anthropology* 33.

duct a skeletal examination to determine who the person was (the biological profile), the circumstances of death (the trauma analysis), and the sequence of events surrounding and subsequent to the death (the taphonomy).

Although forensic anthropologists obtain information from the skeleton and its context, there are two caveats to the above definition:

1) The person being examined may still be alive. Computerized tomography (CT) scans or other imaging modalities can be used to visualize the skeleton, allowing a forensic anthropologist to estimate the age of the individual. Such situations occur when formal documentation is missing due to war, disaster, political circumstances, and so on.
2) In the case of deceased persons, the body may not be skeletonized when recovered, but may instead be unrecognizable as a result of decomposition, burial practices, or damage. The body will be examined through CT or radiographic imaging, followed by removal of the soft tissues to facilitate skeletal analysis.

The scope of a forensic anthropological case can include one individual, a mass fatality (e.g., train derailment and fire, as in Lac-Mégantic), or serial murders (e.g., the Pickton case). The importance of context to the interpretation of the skeletal analysis, the continuity of evidence, and the need for specialized knowledge during field search and recovery means that, in Canada and the United States, scene work, including excavation, is completed by the forensic anthropologist. There is no separate discipline of "forensic archaeology" because continuity from scene to morgue is highly valued from both an interpretative and evidentiary perspective.

When called to court, the two most common subjects of forensic anthropological testimony are identity and trauma analysis (e.g., injury number, type, pattern, potential causes, weapon type). An examination of forensic anthropological testimony in the United States[3] indicates that, of the 367 instances of forensic anthropological expert testimony listed, 40% related to trauma, 19% related to biological profile or victim identification, and 11% related to the post-mortem interval. In the United States, there were ninety-nine cases between 2010 and 2013 in which the issuing judge referenced forensic anthropological testimony.[4] Since the 1993

3 This examination was conducted using LexisNexis Academic proprietary legal database and Daubert Tracker, a fee-based expert witness database.

4 Kate M. Lesciotto, "The Impact of *Daubert* on the Admissibility of Forensic Anthropology Expert Testimony" (2015) 60 *Journal of Forensic Sciences* 549.

Daubert[5] decision, there have been at least sixteen cases in the United States in which the admissibility of forensic anthropological testimony was questioned. All but one was deemed admissible. Such data is not readily available in Canada, although Skinner and colleagues provide a table of self-reported casework (as of June 2006) in which nine forensic anthropologists state they have appeared in court anywhere from one to thirteen times.[6] An additional sixteen others report doing casework, but do not specify court appearances.

Lesciotto concludes that an attorney's failure to comprehend forensic anthropological testimony and its scientific validity may explain why there have been so few challenges, despite the increased amount of forensic anthropological testimony in the courtroom.[7] An alternate interpretation of the data relates to developments in the field itself. Since 2000, forensic anthropologists have made a concerted effort to be proactive in standardizing and validating their methodology in accordance with the *Daubert*[8] decision in the United States and the *Mohan*[9] ruling in Canada in order to prevent rulings of inadmissibility. The goal of this chapter is to ensure that low rates of *Mohan* challenges to forensic anthropological evidence in the future will be the result of high-quality forensic anthropological analyses, rather than failure on the part of lawyers to understand this field.

B. THE SCIENCE OF FORENSIC ANTHROPOLOGY

There are many scientific principles incorporated into a forensic anthropological analysis depending on how, and in what state, the body has been discovered. Police may involve a forensic anthropologist in an investigation when searching for bodies or graves, and recovering bodies from graves (and wells, fires, etc.). The coroner, medical examiner, or pathologist may call upon the forensic anthropologist to examine the body itself.

A case may begin with a tip to police that someone was murdered and dumped in the woods, followed by the police contacting a forensic anthropologist requesting assistance in the search for a body or grave. In the

---

5 *Daubert v. Merrell Dow Pharmaceuticals, Inc.*, 509 U.S. 579 (1993) [*Daubert*].

6 Mark Skinner & Kristina Bowie, "Forensic Anthropology: Canadian Content and Contributions" in Soren Blau and Douglas Ubelaker, eds., *Handbook of Forensic Anthropology and Archaeology* (Walnut Creek, CA: Left Coast Press, 2009) 87.

7 Lesciotto, above note 4.

8 *Daubert*, above note 5.

9 *R. v. Mohan*, [1994] 2 S.C.R. 9.

absence of a tip, the same case could begin with hikers finding a bone in the woods and bringing it to the police station. The police might email a picture of the bone to a forensic anthropologist for an initial assessment to determine if it is human. If human, the forensic anthropologist will make arrangements with the police to search for the rest of the body, along with any combination of coroner or medical examiner (each province has one or the other) and pathologist to conduct an analysis of the remains. In other cases, a decomposing body found indoors might be examined at the scene by a coroner (or medical examiner, depending on the province) and moved to the morgue for autopsy. The examining pathologist could request a forensic anthropologist to assist with an age, sex, ancestry, or trauma analysis.

Due to the broad scope of forensic anthropological involvement in a case, this chapter will focus on the three primary reasons a forensic anthropologist is requested to testify in a court: (1) to address issues of the victim's identity; (2) to explain the results of a trauma/toolmark analysis; and (3) to determine the post-mortem interval (PMI).

1) Identification: The Biological Profile

The legal identification of the deceased is the responsibility of the coroner or medical examiner based on several factors, including: investigative information relating to the circumstances and context of the death scene; witness statements; and scientific comparisons between physical characteristics of the deceased (post-mortem data) and equivalent data recorded for individuals during their lifetime (antemortem data). DNA and fingerprints recovered from personal effects in the home of a missing person and radiographs of their medical records are all examples of antemortem data. DNA from close relatives of a missing person can be used in a similar fashion to antemortem DNA to assist with identification.[10] A DNA sample will be sought immediately from personal effects or relatives if there is some indication of the identity of the deceased from the beginning of the investigation (e.g., if the body is associated with a driver's licence), but, if the context and effects with the body do not indicate who to sample for identification, a skeletal analysis will be undertaken by a forensic anthropologist. The forensic anthropologist will determine the biological characteristics of the deceased, including age, sex, ancestry,

10 See Chapter 12 of this book for an explanation of DNA identification.

stature, weight, and potentially distinctive medical conditions or visible disorders (e.g., scoliosis or curvature of the spine), forming what is known as the "biological profile" of the deceased. The biological profile will then be compared to missing persons files.

Missing people who are similar to the biological profile will be given highest priority in the investigation. Depending on the population density of the area included in the search (the region, province, country, etc.), many potential matches could result. For example, if a forensic anthropologist indicated the deceased was a female, age between twenty and forty years, of European/White ancestry, in British Columbia, then, in 1999, that profile would have matched 105 of the 1,755 missing people.[11]

The biological profile narrows the scope of the investigation; in the above example, only 105 people would need to be investigated of the total group of 1,755 missing persons. Each file that is similar to the biological profile will have different types of antemortem records available for comparison to the body, including dental records, DNA samples, medical records, radiographs, or CT scans. In some jurisdictions, forensic anthropologists routinely conduct the initial comparisons of found remains and missing persons data to further narrow the search by excluding individuals who exhibit characteristics that are not consistent with the found body. For example, the missing individual may match the age, sex, and ancestry of the body, but the missing person's X-ray might show extreme arthritis in the vertebrae, which are not present in the remains. By excluding such individuals, the forensic anthropologist reduces the number of genetic comparisons required to make an identification.

The following sections briefly address the science behind each of the three primary components of the biological profile—sex, age, and ancestry.

a) Biological Profile: Sex Assessment

Sex is a biological term that refers to a person's genotype (sex chromosomes are XX for female and XY for male), which is mediated by hormones and expressed in the physical appearance of a person, including the presence of particular sex organs, the distribution of body fat, the thickness and robustness of bones, and so on. Because sex differences in the body result from the interaction between genes, hormones, and the environment, it is possible to be one genetic sex yet have the appearance of the other, or to appear indistinct, or a combination of the two (intersex).

11 R. Lamb, RCMP, personal communication, in person (1999 October).

Although Western society often treats biological sex as a dichotomy of male/female based on genotype, sex can be considered a continuum of biological expression when phenotype (the physical manifestation of the gene—that is, how a person looks) is being examined. This normal distribution of male and female physical characteristics ranges from large, muscular hyper-masculine to petite curvaceous hyper-feminine, with significant overlap in between.

i) Sex versus Gender

In contrast to sex, gender is a cultural term that reflects one's identity as a woman, man, or other in a society. It may be self-ascribed, or defined by others in the community. Just as biological sex can be expressed along a continuum, gender is experienced in different ways in different cultures. Some recognize two genders, others three, and still others recognize several. Biological sex and cultural gender do not necessarily reflect one another as Western culture expects, with male sex = man and female sex = woman. Transgender individuals, for example, are born as one genetic sex with the associated sex organs, but feel as though they are members of a different gender and therefore may choose to undergo medical interventions in order for their external bodies to better reflect their internal gender. Forensic anthropologists almost exclusively evaluate skeletal sex, not gender (although circumstantial evidence such as clothing and hairstyle, or evidence of sex alignment surgery, may suggest a person's chosen gender).

ii) The Science of Sex Assessment

Because males and females have different sex chromosomes, there are skeletal differences between them from birth. Such differences are generally detectable only on large samples of juvenile skeletons using statistics to differentiate the two groups, and are not consistently evident when examining an individual child's skeleton.[12] Several techniques of assessing the sex of children's skeletons have been proposed, but none have been shown to be accurate for both sexes when tested by independent observers.[13] Throughout childhood and into adolescence, both male and female skulls appear to be female, while male and female pelves both appear male.

---

12 Louise Scheuer & Sue Black, *Developmental Juvenile Osteology* (San Diego: Academic Press, 2000).

13 Tracy L. Rogers, "Sex Determination of Adolescent Skeletons Using the Distal Humerus" (2009) 140 *American Journal of Physical Anthropology* 143 [Rogers, "Sex Determination"].

As a result, a young male skull is easily confused for a young female one and, similarly, a young female pelvis is easily mistaken for a young male.

If a forensic anthropologist conducts a sex assessment of anyone less than eleven years of age, it should be used as an investigative tool only, not as the basis of identification. DNA is required to confirm the sex of juvenile (or subadult) skeletal remains.

At puberty, hormones trigger secondary sex characteristics and sexual differentiation becomes more marked. Forensic anthropologists use the differences in male and female growth rates, duration, and pattern in order to assess the sex of a skeleton. Males typically grow faster, for a longer period, and, in some parts of the skeleton (most notably the pelvis), the pattern of growth is distinct from females. The overall result is that male bones tend to be larger in length, thicker in width, and characterized by rougher muscle attachment sites on most parts of the skeleton. Such differences can be assessed through measurements (metric analyses) and shape-based assessments (morphological analyses). The two approaches are complementary as each has its advantages and disadvantages. Metrics, for example, are usually only taken on complete bones. If bones are damaged and fragmentary, measurements are not appropriate. Morphology (shape) can be assessed on fragmented bone, but there are fewer sites on the skeleton that exhibit shape differences; therefore, only certain bones, like the skull, pelvis, and humerus are suitable for these analyses.

iii) Measures of Reliability: Accuracy and Precision

Accuracy measures how often the correct result is achieved when a technique is applied to large sample. If men always exhibited 100% "male" traits and women exclusively exhibited "female" traits, methods of skeletal sex assessment would achieve close to complete accuracy. Since there is an overlap between male and female size and muscularity, it is biologically impossible to separate 100% of males and females on the basis of skeletal differences. For this reason, methods of skeletal sex assessment can never be completely accurate. This problem is simply a biological reality, not a failure of methods used to assess skeletal sex. To evaluate the reliability of techniques for skeletal sex assessment, a different measure of reliability is needed. A more realistic threshold of accuracy is 80% because it allows for variation in the normal range of skeletal expression, yet it is statistically significantly higher than can be expected by chance alone (50%).

The second measure of reliability—precision—is the observer's ability to obtain the same result each time the same object is examined (regardless if it is correct). Precision is calculated as the percentage of intra-observer error (such as when one person examines the same bone at two different times and gets two different results) and/or inter-observer error (such as when two people examine the same bone and get two different results). An intra- and/or inter-observer error of less than 10% is considered acceptable, because this threshold recognizes that most skeletal traits begin as relatively undifferentiated bone that gradually grow and develop more defined features with age. Such changes are incremental, occurring along a continuum. It is therefore difficult to consistently recognize and score one stage in that process exactly the same way every time. If the error exceeds 10%, the variation is considered too great to be used reliably.

Depending on which bones are found, it may not always be possible to use a technique that is 80% accurate with less than 10% intra-observer error. In such cases, several methods may be used to provide multiple lines of evidence. If all of the methods indicate the same sex, the assessment is bolstered. If contradictory results occur, a conclusion of "indeterminate" should be made.

A forensic anthropological report should always indicate which techniques were used in the assessment, along with their accuracy and precision.

iv) Metric Analysis: Using Measurements to Assess Sex

Size is not usually the best determinant of sex, because almost 95% of size distributions between men and women overlap. Depending on the bone, the mean (the average) differences in size between males and females may be only a few millimetres. Generally, the more measurements taken, the more accurate the result will be. Depending on the bone and the number of measurements taken, the accuracy of metric techniques can exceed the level typically reported for morphological methods of the skull (which has an accuracy rate of 85%–89%).[14] Most metric methods of sex assessment use multiple measurements in a formula to evaluate sex. Such formulae should be developed on modern skeletal collections where sex is known from death records; there are many such research collections around the world. The formula must then be tested on a second, independent collection to confirm its accuracy. Sometimes, a cut-off point is used for a single measurement, where individuals measuring above the cut-off are male, and those measuring smaller than the cut-off are female. There is usually a large

---

14 Brenda A. Williams & Tracy L. Rogers, "Evaluating the Accuracy and Precision of Cranial Morphological Traits for Sex Determination" (2006) 51 *Journal of Forensic Sciences* 729; M.K. Spradley & R.L. Jantz, "Sex Estimation in Forensic Anthropology: Skull Versus Postcranial Elements" (2011) 56 *Journal of Forensic Sciences* 289.

indeterminate range between these cut-off points. Such single measure techniques may be problematic and often result in indeterminate results.

The degree of overlap in size between the sexes varies between populations (some have an overlap of greater than 95%, and some a bit lower), and the average sizes of males and females also differ between populations. For this reason, methods of sex assessment that rely on measurements may be population specific, or may only work well on related populations (that is, the technique only works for individuals of the same ancestry). One alternative to the problem of population specificity is to use a metric technique that was developed on a very large sample containing individuals from diverse populations—some that are tall with wider bones (e.g., Aboriginal people of Canada) and some that are small (e.g., South Asian). Capturing a large range of diversity produces formulae that are expected to be suitable for any population. Tests of a formula derived from a combined sample of Greek people, South African White people, and South African Black people, for example, show that it was only 2% less accurate than formulae that were made specifically for each population.[15] It remains to be seen how effective these formulae are on populations with smaller or larger body sizes than those used to generate the formulae.

Bone size and the use of metric techniques are also less useful in situations where the bone may be compromised. For example, bones shrink when exposed to fire. *Measurements taken on burned bone will underestimate the true size. Since most female bones are smaller than male bones, a measurement of burned bone that results in an assessment of "female" is suspect. In contrast, a bone shrunk by burning that still produces a "male" result would only have been larger before burning and therefore does not pose a problem.*

v) Morphological Analysis: Using Shape to Assess Sex

The alternative to metric analysis is morphological (shape-based) analysis, which is assessed by scoring features of the skeleton that differ in males and females as a result of differences in growth patterns or growth rates. Because of the physical requirements of giving birth, growth-based shape differences are most pronounced in the female pelvis. Female pelvic bones begin changing at puberty to increase the width of the pubic basin to better accommodate childbirth. Shape differences can also be observed in the skull, although these are the result of the pattern of bone growth extending and

15 M. Steyn & M.L. Patriquin, "Osteometric Sex Determination from the Pelvis: Does Population Specificity Matter?" (2009) 191 *Forensic Science International* 113.

occurring more rapidly for males compared to females, due to the longer and more intense male adolescent growth period. The only bone outside of the pelvis and skull that has been demonstrated to exhibit morphological variation is the humerus (the bone of the upper arm).[16]

A variety of traits can be examined for the pelvis, skull, and humerus, and practitioners sometimes have their own preferences, but the selection of traits should be based on reported accuracy and precision.[17] Population differences do not seem to affect morphological methods drastically; the performance of a single trait might be slightly better or slightly worse in one population versus another, but the overall accuracy of sex assessment when using the traits with the highest reported accuracies is generally 80% for the humerus,[18] 89% –96% for the skull,[19] and 95% or higher for the pelvis.[20]

Once traits with the highest accuracy and precision are scored, the forensic anthropologist examines the results to determine which sex is indicated. Since trait expression overlaps between sexes, it is common for several traits to signify one sex, a few to be indeterminate, and one or two to indicate the opposite sex. In this case, more is not always better. Adding information from features that are not very accurate will only confuse the interpretation.

Traits included in the analysis should meet the criteria of 80% accuracy and less than 10% intra-observer error. When examining the results of all the appropriate traits, the number of indeterminate traits is important, and greatest weight should be given to the traits with the highest accuracy when reaching a conclusion.

vi) Reaching a Conclusion

The final assessment of sex may be based on a combination of metric and morphological analyses. The number and type of analyses that are conducted will depend on the bones that are recovered, their condition, and their proximity.

---

16 Tracy L. Rogers, "A Visual Method of Determining the Sex of Skeletal Remains Using the Distal Humerus" (1999) 44 *Journal of Forensic Sciences* 57 [Rogers, "Visual Method"].

17 T.L. Rogers & S. Saunders, "Accuracy of Sex Determination using Morphological Traits of the Human Pelvis" (1994) 39 *Journal of Forensic Sciences* 1047 [Rogers & Saunders, "Accuracy of Sex Determination"]; B.A. Williams & T.L. Rogers, "Evaluating the Accuracy and Precision of Cranial Morphological Traits to Determine the Sex of Unknown Skeletal Remains" (2006) 51 *Journal of Forensic Sciences* 729; Tracy L. Rogers, "Determining the Sex of Human Remains through Cranial Morphology" (2005) 50 *Journal of Forensic Sciences* 493 [Rogers, "Cranial Morphology"].

18 Rogers, "Visual Method," above note 16; Rogers, "Sex Determination," above note 13.

19 Rogers, "Cranial Morphology," above note 17; Williams & Rogers, above note 14.

20 Rogers & Saunders, above note 17.

If the body is found with tissues linking all the bones (that is, it is evident that this is a single individual), it may be possible to conduct only a morphological analysis of the pelvis (which has an accuracy rate of over 95%). Pelvic traits that consistently score as one sex provide the clearest, most reliable results that can be obtained, which means further testing using less accurate methods will only confuse the results.

In another example, if only a few bones in poor condition are found scattered over a large scene, it is generally necessary to conduct a sex assessment of each bone as one step in determining if they are from the same individual, and to obtain enough information about the sex of the individual to draw a conclusion. It may be difficult to obtain 80% accuracy for a fragmentary bone using a single measurement. Many different lines of evidence (multiple results from multiple bones) will be required to provide enough evidence to reach a decision.

Some reports may state "possible male" or "possible female." This result indicates that there is some difficulty with the assessment: either the technique does not meet the required levels of accuracy and precision, or the features that were assessed look only slightly male or female. "Probable male" or "probable female" generally means that most of the techniques support one sex, but not all methods are in agreement.

vii) Methods

There are innumerable techniques of skeletal sex assessment. Choosing which combination to use depends on the bones recovered and their condition. Rather than address the benefits and limitations of each, the main concerns that should be considered when reviewing an anthropological analysis of sex are highlighted below for easy reference:

- The accuracy and precision of every method should be within the accepted standard of 80% or higher accuracy and less than 10% intra- and inter-observer error, or an explanation should be provided if this is not possible.
- The methods used must have originally been devised and tested on individuals of documented sex, not individuals whose sex was estimated using a different skeletal method, as is sometimes done in bioarchaeology.
- When metric techniques are used, the individual being examined must belong to the same or a closely related population to the one for which the formula was created.

b) Biological Profile: Estimating Age

Skeletal age-at-death estimation is a complicated issue because many factors can influence aging in life. Some people look old for their age, while others appear young due to genetics, nutrition, health, activity levels, and many other environmental factors. For this reason, age-at-death is always estimated as a range (e.g., 20–32 years old).

Age-at-death is never given as a single age point (e.g., 27 years)—no skeletal method is capable of that level of precision or accuracy.

There are different methods of age estimation depending on whether the individual is a child, adolescent, or adult. As a general rule, conducting multiple analyses on different parts of the skeleton will improve the age estimate, although only methods that have been validated should be used. Techniques for estimating age can be broadly divided into those that provide actual age ranges (e.g., 32–67 years old) and those that indicate only a general age category (e.g., young adult, middle-age, elderly).

i) Measures of Reliability

Regardless of the specific methods used or the manner of combining the results, the important consideration for skeletal age estimation is the reliability of the final age estimate. Reliability can be assessed in terms of prediction interval (the age range that produces a particular percentage of correct estimations), the posterior probability (the likelihood that a person is a given age, based on a sample with similar characteristics), the inaccuracy (the average number of years difference between the estimated and actual age), and/or the bias (the average number of years older or younger the estimated age is compared to the actual age, so bias will indicate whether the method typically overestimates or underestimates age).

Prediction intervals are usually set at 90%–95% and are useful because they indicate how often the resulting age range encompasses the actual age. Inaccuracy and bias are useful in helping the analyst decide if a particular technique is reliable for a given age cohort (bias and inaccuracy are usually reported by decade). When considered together, the forensic anthropologist can select the most reliable methods for the individual they are examining, and report the results in a manner meaningful for court.

ii) The Science of Skeletal Age-at-Death Estimation

a. Children

The best method of age-at-death estimation for children is dental development, which is under fairly rigorous genetic control. Although dental formation and eruption occur at approximately the same age for most people, both vary from person to person and from population to population within a two- to three-year range. If dentition is not available, bone growth can be used to estimate age. Each long bone (e.g., femur/thigh bone) has three centres of growth: one that forms the shaft or length of the bone, and one at each end. Long bones grow in length by depositing new bone along the edge of the shaft (diaphysis), where it meets the end of the bone (epiphysis). These edges are held together by cartilage (the growth plate or metaphysis) while a child is still growing. On an X-ray, the bone appears white and the cartilage appears dark, indicating that growth is not complete. The length of the bone shaft is a general indication of the age of a child, although growth can be accelerated or delayed due to factors such as health and nutrition. There are also individual and population growth trajectories. For these reasons, age estimates based on the size of children's long bones will result in larger age ranges than estimates based on dentition.

b. Adolescents

After the adolescent growth spurt, cartilage in the metaphysis is gradually replaced by bone through a process known as epiphyseal fusion or union. No additional height gain is possible once the cartilaginous growth plate is replaced by bone. On an X-ray, the end of the bone will appear almost completely white at this stage, although a thin dark line may remain indefinitely indicating the position of the growth plate. Different bones undergo this process at different times, and each end of every long bone completes its growth at different ages. By examining which bones and ends of bones are growing and which are finished, it is possible to estimate the age of adolescent skeletons. Most skeletal development is completed in adolescence, with a few bones continuing to fuse into an individual's early twenties (e.g., the iliac crest of the pelvis).

c. Living Individuals

When forensic anthropologists estimate the age of living individuals who lack documentation, it is often in an effort to determine their legal status as adult or child (e.g., in cases of refugees, asylum seekers, perpetrators or victims of human trafficking, and targets of child pornography).[21] Forensic anthropologists, odontologists, and radiologists rely on a variety of

---

21 Andreas Schmeling & Sue Black, "An Introduction to the History of Age Estimation in the Living" in Sue Black, Anil Aggarwal, & Jason Payne-James, eds., *Age Estimation in the Living: The Practitioners Guide* (Hoboken, NJ: Wiley, 2011) 1 [Black et al., *Age Estimation*].

modalities (most commonly radiographs and CT scans) and growth indicators (e.g., dentition, epiphyseal union, facial measurements) to reach an assessment of age.[22]

d. Adults

For adults, aging is a degenerative process. Bone tissue gets replaced (a process visible at the microscopic level), bones become worn, joint surfaces become rough and pitted, and diseases such as osteoarthritis and osteoporosis become more common. Estimating age from such modifications produces age ranges that become less precise with each decade. The increasing magnitude of the age range is a reflection of the amount of variation that can accumulate over time, depending on a combination of genetics, environment, and whether or not people take care of their bodies. When estimating skeletal age, it is more important that the actual age of the deceased fall within the estimated range so that investigators are considering the correct people, than that the estimated range be small. Individual methods, such as the pubic symphysis, produce ranges such as 19–34 years for individuals with relatively few changes to the bone (younger individuals), and considerably larger ranges, such as 34–86 years, for individuals whose bones are highly altered (older individuals). No single macroscopic (visual) or microscopic method produces reliable, yet small, age ranges for all stages of life.

iii) Reaching a Conclusion

Combining multiple methods will produce smaller, more useful age ranges than any single method on its own, providing the techniques have been validated. The challenge is in knowing how to combine age ranges resulting from different methods. Studies show that averaging the low end of the ranges to produce a combined lower age limit and averaging the high end of each range to produce a combined upper limit results in classification rates equal to more complex methods of combining results.[23] The only problem with this relatively simple method of combining results is that the accuracy will vary depending on the methods that are combined, and not every combination of methods has been extensively tested. To address this issue,

---

22 One of the most comprehensive texts on this subject is Black et al., *Age Estimation, ibid.*, which recommends a four-pillar approach that combines social and psychological evaluation, external physical estimation of age, skeletal estimation of age, and dental estimate of age.

23 Rogers & Saunders, "Accuracy of Sex Determination," above note 17.

various statistical solutions have been sought. The explanations are somewhat involved, utilizing either Bayesian statistics or regression analysis.[24]

Depending on the research group or academic institution a practitioner is affiliated with, that individual will prefer a different combination of methods and even different means of combining the data.[25] This is not a problem if the process is made transparent.

A forensic anthropological assessment of age that uses multiple techniques should clearly indicate which methods were used, as well as which approach was used to combine the results into a final age estimate.

iv) Chemical and Elemental Analysis

Due to the variability of degenerative changes, other methods of estimating skeletal age have been examined, but these tend to be costly, take longer to complete, and require specialized equipment. Such issues should not be prohibitive, provided that the methods are fully validated and produce significantly more precise and accurate results than existing methods. At this point, testing is ongoing for several such techniques, and many have shown promise, including amino acid racemization,[26] with a standard error of estimation +/- 1.26 years; levels of radioactive carbon retained in bone (bomb carbon), with a reported mean error of 1.9 years,[27] or 1.9 ± 1.4 years prior to the bomb spike (1955–63), and 1.3 ± 1 year after the bomb peak;[28] and a formula produced using biomechanical and analytical analyses that use wet and dry apparent density, porosity, organic/mineral/water fractions, collagen thermal degradation properties, ash content, Ca/P ratios, and osteonal and matrix microhardness of bone sections to produce an age estimate within ± 1 year.[29] For a more detailed explanation of bomb carbon, see Section B(4) below.

---

24 For detailed explanations, see Krista E. Latham & J. Michael Finnegan, *Age Estimation of the Human Skeleton* (Springfield, IL: Charles C. Thomas, 2010).

25 Eugénia Cunha et al., "The Problem of Aging Human Remains and Living Individuals: A Review" (2009) 193 *Forensic Science International* 1.

26 Mohamed A. Elfawal, Sahib I. Algattan & Noha A. Ghallab, "Racemization of Aspartic Acid in Root Dentin as a Tool for Age Estimation in a Kuwaiti Population" (2015) 55 *Medicine, Science, and the Law* 22.

27 N. Wang et al., "Improved Application of Bomb Carbon in Teeth for Forensic Investigation" (2011) 52 *Radiocarbon* 706.

28 Kanar Alkass et al., "Analysis of 14C and 13C in Teeth Provides Precise Birth Dating and Clues to Geographical Origin" (2011) 209 *Forensic Science International* 34.

29 P. Zioupos et al., "Determining 'Age at Death' for Forensic Purposes using Human Bone by a Laboratory-based Biomechanical Analytical Method" (2014) 33 *Journal of the Mechanical Behavior of Biomedical Materials* 109.

v) *Methods*

a. Children

Dental development is the best age indicator for children because it is less affected by environmental factors than bone growth. There are several different types of dental charts (diagrams of stages of tooth development for each age) that could potentially be used to estimate age. Tests have demonstrated that the most accurate charts are those developed specifically for age estimation,[30] rather than those developed from growth studies in the 1950s,[31] or those developed on archaeological populations.[32] Many bone growth and epiphyseal fusion references are also available, but studies have demonstrated that growth rates have changed over time due to nutrition, access to medical care, and so on. For this reason, only recent growth and fusion data should be used to estimate age in forensic cases.[33]

b. Adults

There are a number of adult skeletal age estimation techniques commonly used by forensic anthropologists because they have been widely tested and have established prediction intervals and/or error rates. Most of these methods evaluate changes to one of three specific joint surfaces:

1) *The pubic symphysis*: This is where the two pubic bones meet at the front on the body. Specific techniques include Suchey-Brooks[34] and Katz and Suchey,[35] which provide 95% confidence intervals. There are older versions of the pubic symphysis method, but they suffer from several biases and are no longer in common use. There are also recent modifications to the Suchey-Brooks methods that are intended to better estimate the

---

30 See, for example, S.J. AlQahtani, M.P. Hector, & H.M. Liversidge, "Brief Communication: The London Atlas of Human Tooth Development and Eruption" (2010) 142 *American Journal of Physical Anthropology* 481.

31 See, for example, Marion Maresh, "Linear Growth of Long Bones of Extremities from Infancy through Adolescence" (1955) 89 *American Journal of Diseases of Children* 725.

32 See, for example, Douglas H. Ubelaker, *Human Skeletal Remains: Excavation, Analysis, Interpretation*, 2d ed (Washington, DC: Taraxacum, 1989).

33 Scheuer & Black, above note 12.

34 S. Brooks & J.M. Suchey, "Skeletal Age Determination Based on the Os Pubis: A Comparison of the Acsadi-Nemeskeri & Suchey-Brooks Methods" (1990) 5 *Human Evolution* 227.

35 Darryl Katz & Judy M. Suchey, "Age Determination of the Male Os Pubis" (1986) 69 *American Journal of Physical Anthropology* 427.

age of those over sixty years, but they have produced mixed success when tested by independent observers.[36]

2) *The auricular surface*: This is where the base of the spinal column (sacrum) meets the pelvis. Specific techniques include the original Lovejoy and colleagues[37] method, which uses ten-year age ranges but suffers from high inaccuracy; and the more recent modification by Buckberry and Chamberlain[38] that includes larger ranges, along with the associated probability that the person's actual age falls within that range, based on the phase or score achieved (e.g., an individual with a score of VI has a 0.46 probability of being 85–94 years old). Osborne and colleagues[39] also introduced a modification, reducing the original eight phases to six, and providing descriptive statistics to help forensic anthropologists assess the reliability of their estimates.
3) *The rib ends:* This is where the ribs meet the breastbone (sternum). Two main methods are used, the original fourth-rib methods of Iscan and colleagues,[40] and the first-rib method of Kunos and colleagues.[41] Again, modifications have been proposed, but none have produced consistently better results than the original methods.

All of the above techniques depend upon changes to stable joint surfaces that occur with age and have been independently tested. Their error rates are available as accuracy, inaccuracy, bias, prediction interval, and/or probability of being a given age.

---

36 Catherine E. Merritt, "A Test of Hartnett's Revisions to the Pubic Symphysis and Fourth Rib Methods on a Modern Sample" (2014) 59 *Journal of Forensic Sciences* 703.

37 C. Owen Lovejoy et al., "Chronological Metamorphosis of the Auricular Surface of the Ilium: A New Method for the Determination of Adult Skeletal Age at Death" (1985) 68 *American Journal of Physical Anthropology* 15.

38 J.L. Buckberry & A.T. Chamberlain, "Age Estimation from the Auricular Surface of the Ilium: A Revised Method" (2002) 119 *American Journal of Physical Anthropology* 231.

39 Daniel L. Osborne, Tal L. Simmons, & Stephen P. Nawrocki, "Reconsidering the Auricular Surface as an Indicator of Age at Death" (2004) 49 *Journal of Forensic Sciences* 905.

40 Mehmet Y. Iscan, Susan R. Loth, & Ronald K. Wright, "Age Estimation from the Rib by Phase Analysis: White Males" (1984) 29 *Journal of Forensic Sciences* 1094; Mehmet Y. Iscan, Susan R. Loth, & Ronald K. Wright, "Age Estimation from the Rib by Phase Analysis: White Females" (1985) 30 *Journal of Forensic Sciences* 853.

41 Charles A. Kunos et al., "First Rib Metamorphosis: Its Possible Utility for Human Age-at-Death Estimation" (1999) 110 *American Journal of Physical Anthropology* 303.

vi) Histology (Microscopically Examining Tissues)

Histological analyses involve cutting out a small piece of bone, grinding it until it is paper thin, and examining the bone tissue structures under the microscope. It can be used on any forensic case, but is particularly useful when the usual techniques will not work—for example, if only a few bones or bone fragments are located. Histological age estimates are based on the microscopic changes to bone as a person ages—cracks are repaired, blood vessels are moved, and so on. This process is known as bone remodelling. Microscopic amounts of tissue are removed, leaving a circular tunnel. New bone tissue is then deposited around the edges of the tunnel, gradually filling it in, leaving only a central opening for a blood vessel. When a long bone is cut in cross-section, these circular structures, known as secondary osteons, are visible using a microscope. The number of secondary osteons increases with age, eventually overlapping as almost all of the original bone is replaced. Age is estimated by counting the number of osteons, fragments of osteons, and other similar features located within a given region of the bone and in a specific-sized area. The counts are entered into formulae and an estimate is produced.

Histological methods of skeletal age estimation are theoretically available for every bone, although each bone has a slightly different relationship to age because of the biomechanical forces it is exposed to during life. The most common bones used in histological analysis are the femur and the ribs. There are several techniques that vary in terms of the number of samples taken, how and where the samples are taken, and how the osteons are examined; most result in similar levels of accuracy and bias. They also tend to produce age estimates with similar or slightly smaller age ranges than macroscopic methods. Once again, as long as the accuracy, prediction interval, and some other measure of error rate are provided, the specific technique used is rarely an issue. An excellent step-by-step explanation of preparing histological samples and estimating age-at-death from the sixth rib can be found in Crowder et al.[42]

vii) Lamendin Dental Method

The dental method introduced by Lamendin and colleagues uses the height of gum resorption visible on the tooth root and the height of tooth

---

42 Christian Crowder, Jarred Heinrich, & Sam D. Stout, "Rib Histomorphometry for Adult Age Estimation" in Lynne S. Bell, ed., *Forensic Microscopy for Skeletal Tissues: Methods and Protocols* (New York: Humana Press; Springer, 2012) 109.

root transparency in a formula to estimate age-at-death.[43] The technique has been tested many times and several revisions have been suggested, including Prince and Ubelaker's.[44] The method has been favourably received, although recent evidence suggests that the inaccuracy is larger for remains that have been buried than those found on the surface.[45]

viii) Summary of Age Estimation

There are many different methods of skeletal age-at-death estimation. Techniques used to estimate the age of children tend to be more precise and accurate than those available for adults, because skeletal and dental development are strongly influenced by genetic factors, while adult skeletal degeneration is a highly variable process. A forensic anthropologist's decision to use a particular technique should be based on (1) the bones available and (2) a quantifiable measure of the technique's success that has been verified by an independent researcher (e.g., inaccuracy, bias, prediction interval). Age-at-death estimates typically improve by using multiple methods to generate the predicted age range, provided that both the techniques and the approach used to combine the results have been validated.

c) Biological Profile: Evaluating Ancestry

One of the challenges of assessing ancestry and conveying the results is the confusion that arises between the terms "ancestry," "race," and "ethnicity." People tend to use these words interchangeably, making it difficult to know what is actually intended. For the sake of clarity, forensic anthropologists have formalized the definitions in a functional manner.

- *"Ancestry"* is used to denote biological heritage. Ancestry is the portion of a person's genetic makeup that relates to their family's origins. Intermarriage, migration, shared life and death experiences, and other factors that have a familial link alter the frequencies of genes in a collective gene pool (all the genes in a particular group). Based on the pattern of human evolution and migration, and the

---

43 H. Lamendin et al., "A Simple Technique for Age Estimation in Adult Corpses: The Two Criteria Dental Method" (1992) 37 *Journal of Forensic Sciences* 1373.

44 Debra A. Price & Douglas Ubelaker, "Application of Lamendin's Adult Dental Aging Technique to a Diverse Skeletal Sample" (2002) 47 *Journal of Forensic Sciences* 107.

45 Danilo De Angelis et al., "The Applicability of the Lamendin Method to Skeletal Remains Buried for a 16-year Period: A Cautionary Note" (2015) 60 Suppl 1 *Journal of Forensic Sciences* S177.

fact that it has not been possible for distant groups to meet and interbreed, gene frequencies have a geographic distribution.

Gene frequencies can vary by trait over space, meaning that they are not all linked together. They peak and ebb over the landscape, with some traits overlapping to some degree and others appearing as alternate forms. Those living closest to one another, or who are on trade routes, will likely have similar gene frequencies because of the opportunities for intermarriage and sharing of genes. As one moves farther away, the differences in gene frequencies tend to get larger. Some genes code for physical characteristics such as brown eyes, straight hair, pronounced nose. Others might code for particular enzymes, proteins, and so on that predispose members of the group to particular illnesses. Some code for traits that are expressed on the skeleton, for example, differences in nasal bone shape and the presence of extra foramina (holes) that transmit nerves and blood vessels. These are clearly biological features. Sometimes the term "biogeographical origin" is used interchangeably with "ancestry" to reflect a shared biological heritage that initially had a geographical focus.

- "*Race*" is a cultural construct that reflects beliefs and attitudes about different groups of people; often associated with specific physical characteristics (e.g., skin colour, behaviours). Such categorization of people is not done consistently using the same criteria. Instead, outsiders and insiders tend to view one another differently and use different principles when determining who is, or is not, a member. The word "race" has been used and misused over the years to such a degree that it means different things to different people. Because it refers to aspects of an individual's socio-political or cultural identity, race cannot be assessed from the skeleton.
- "*Ethnicity*" refers to groups of people who identify with one another on the basis of language, religion, or other cultural characteristics (e.g., Hispanic, Jewish). There may be a multitude of biological subgroups within a cultural ethnic group.

i) Expressing Ancestry in Racial Terms

Although forensic anthropologists assess ancestry, not race, race can become a concern for forensic anthropologists during the process of identification because the biological assessment of the skeleton (ancestry) often has to be matched to cultural descriptors of missing people, reported in racial terms. In order to make an assessment of biological variation practical for the purposes of identification, forensic anthropologists must translate the biological observations into culturally meaningful terms. In practice, this may mean conducting a skeletal ancestry assessment and stating the result (e.g., European ancestry), along with a statement that helps the reader understand which groups of people are typically included within this large geographic designator (e.g., European ancestry includes most people who could be considered racially "White," as well as Mediterranean and Middle Eastern peoples, and unless specifically tested for, the people of South Asia, like India and Pakistan).

ii) Limitations of Ancestry Assessment

Ancestry assessment is problematic in several ways. First, only broad geographic groupings are generally recognized (unless one works in specific regions where other groups are common) and these do not cover all the possible geographic groups in the world. Second, people are no longer geographically distinct. Inter-population marriage has become more common, causing gene frequencies to shift. Third, skeletal traits and other physical features might not appear consistent with one another. For example, someone could have all the skeletal traits commonly observed in people of European ancestry, but could also have brown skin as a result of diverse ancestry. If the body is completely skeletonized when discovered, the person would likely be assessed as having been European. Based on skin colour and other cultural factors, in life, the person might have been seen as, or self-identified as, African-American or Black.

iii) Why Bother?

Despite these difficulties, ancestry is used in forensic anthropology because it can provide one more piece of information to help direct the efforts of identification. It is first and foremost a description of the skeleton, in that certain traits are present or absent on that individual. Based on the features that are present, those that are absent, and how they group, it might be possible to characterize the general appearance of the individual as belonging to a particular ancestral group. This type of characterization can be compared to information on missing persons databases, which may report "race" or "ethnicity" or something similar. It can also be used in news releases when information is being sought. Ancestry assessment is primarily an investigative tool, intended to provide focus to the efforts of identifying human remains. It should not be used as a fundamental criterion in making the identification.

Therefore, an ancestry assessment of "European" can be used to narrow the initial search for a potential matching missing person during the investigation, but it cannot be used to confirm the identification once a potential match is found. It is also risky to use ancestry on its own to exclude potential matches, due to the issues noted above. For example, if the biological profile is European female, age twenty-four to thirty-two, and no one of that description has been reported missing, the search should be expanded to all females, age twenty-four to thirty-two. Ancestry assessments are strengthened when multiple lines of evidence are used; both morphology and metric methods should be routinely included.

Ancestry assessment provides the most likely population affiliation. If no match is made on the basis of ancestry, the search should be expanded. Ancestry is arguably the least accurate of the three parameters of the biological profile.

iv) Methods

a. Morphological Analyses

Researchers have documented the frequencies of specific skeletal features in different geographic groups (e.g., Asian, African, European, First Nations). By examining the traits that are present or absent in a particular set of human remains, and considering the frequencies with which they occur in various populations, it is possible to make an assessment of the likely ancestry of that individual. In cases where traits are not following a consistent pattern, it is likely that the person was either: (1) of mixed heritage, or (2) a member of an ancestral group not represented by the reference data and traits being examined. These cases are reported as indeterminate.

For most forensic anthropologists, only large geographic distinctions are possible with ancestry. The results of an ancestry assessment are therefore reported in broad geographic terms, such as European, African, or First Nations. Because people still use cultural terms associated with "race," the same results might be reported as White, Black, or Asian, or even the racial classification groups Caucasoid, Negroid, or Mongoloid. The latter designators are out-dated and, due to the confusion of racial terminology, biogeographical terms are always preferred.

The final results of an ancestry assessment should provide an indication of the strength of the evaluation, which may be reported qualitatively (possible/probable—a statement summarizing how many high or low frequency traits from each population were observed in the unknown remains), or sometimes quantitatively (as a measure of accuracy when this approach is tested on independent samples).

b. Metric Analyses

Just as there are specific trait differences that accumulate in populations, there are overall shape- and size-based differences that can be detected using measurements. Researchers have measured every bone in the human body and subjected them to statistical analyses to determine how effectively two or more groups can be distinguished from one another on the basis of these measurements. Some groups can be easily separated using one or two measurements from a single bone, while others (usually those most closely related to one another) may require multiple measurements of more than one bone to differentiate members. The important factors to consider when examining any metric assessment of ancestry include: (1) the probability statement or accuracy of the technique; (2) the scope of the analysis; and (3) whether or not the method has been independently tested.

One of the most versatile and commonly used metric methods of evaluating ancestry involves the software FORDISC, which creates formulae for the user depending on which bones are available for analysis. The formulae are based on the internal database of measurements that have been uploaded by various forensic anthropologists from their cases and research collections, and are included in each new version of FORDISC. The resulting formula is tested on the database, then the formula is applied to the user's data to determine which of a selected number of potential ancestral groups the unknown remains is most closely affiliated with.

FORDISC, however, is a tool. Using it is very much a case of "garbage in, garbage out." The user must know how to run the analysis and interpret the results. Results from FORDISC should include: (1) the comparative groups used in the initial formula; (2) the sample size used to generate the initial formula; (3) the accuracy of the formula when tested on the database; (4) which population has the best typicality and posterior probability scores; (5) the typicality probability for that group; and (6) the posterior probability for that group. Groups with the lowest probability are removed from the analysis in a step-wise fashion and the entire procedure is repeated until only two or three groups remain in the comparison. The same five pieces of information should be recorded for the final assessment.

In addition to accuracy, typicality, and probability, the forensic anthropologist is looking for consistency in the population that is selected during each comparison. If the most likely population changes depending on which groups the unknown individual is being compared to, it is likely that the unknown does not belong to any of the selected ancestral groups. Such results should be interpreted as indeterminate.

v) Lineage Markers

Haplotypes are groups of genes that are inherited together from either one's mother (examined through mitochondrial DNA, or mtDNA) or father (as a short section of repeating nucleotide base pairs on the male Y chromosome, or Y-STR).[46] Because haplotypes are inherited with little change over generations, they can be used to identify groups of related people—lineages. More similar haplotypes means a greater degree of relatedness. Large reference databases are used to determine the frequency of various haplotypes in different groups of people. Using haplotypes to assess ancestry is similar in its approach to the use of skeletal morphological traits. Haplotypes involve looking at the genotype (groups of genes), whereas skeletal traits involve the phenotype (how the genes are expressed on the skeleton), but both depend on the frequencies of the feature (haplotype or morphological trait) in a population. Lineage markers are a relatively new science, thus the standards and protocols change frequently.

Using genes to assess ancestry might seem like an objective process, but sampling and interpreting haplotype data involves several stages during which subjective decisions and bias can influence the outcome. Most importantly, the comparative databases for mtDNA and Y-STR are separate, which means that it is necessary to run two separate tests to examine the ancestry of both a person's mother and father. There is no indication from the haplotype data which parent the deceased looked like. When ancestry is the same for both parents, this is not an issue. If a person had a European mother and an African father, the haplotype information would not indicate whether the person looked European, African, or a combination of the two. Skeletal ancestry assessment, in contrast, reports what a person looked like, which is helpful from the perspective of identification.

d) Biological Profile: Summary

The age, sex, and ancestry of unidentified remains can be assessed by forensic anthropologists using a combination of morphological (shape-based) and metric (measurement-based) techniques. These variables form the

46 See Chapter 12 of this book for an explanation of these terms.

initial search parameters used to highlight potential matches to individuals in the missing persons database. The use of poorly performing methods can derail the investigation, focusing attention on the wrong group of potentially matching individuals. Following established protocols and selecting appropriate methods increases the efficiency of the identification process.

Practitioners who use techniques that have not been validated or have been shown to perform poorly may face challenges to their qualifications and expertise, but using a technique that is 75% accurate versus one that is 82% accurate does not render the expert incompetent. In fact, as noted above, there may be several reasons why the method that is 75% accurate is the better choice (e.g., population differences, poor preservation of bone). The key issues to consider are: (1) which techniques were used; (2) why; and (3) how is the resulting information being used? If the biological profile is being used for investigative purposes, accuracy should approximate 80% in order to ensure the data will contribute useful information to reduce the pool of potential matches. Sometimes even an indication of where to begin can be useful—for example, in a case with highly fragmented remains, it might be possible to observe only a single trait for sex assessment.

If, on the other hand, the biological profile is required to bolster the identification (for example, when DNA is not viable, dental records are not available, and medical records are minimal), then accuracy does become more of an issue. The forensic anthropologist will still be limited by the bones that are recovered and their condition, but in these cases, the selection of techniques, along with their accuracy, precision, and demonstrated reliability, becomes critical.

2) Positive Identification

Several different terms may be used to designate the robustness of an identification. "Tentative," "putative," or "presumptive" identification may be used when there is circumstantial evidence such as clothing or documentation that suggests a person's identity, but no biological/physical evidence exists to corroborate it.[47]

- Probable identification indicates all the available evidence supports an identification, nothing refutes it, but there is no biological/physical evidence distinctive enough to rule out other possible matches.

---

47 Angi M. Christensen, Nicholas V. Passalacqua, & Eric J. Bartelink, *Forensic Anthropology: Current Methods and Practice* (Oxford: Academic Press, 2014) at 380.

- Positive identification is reserved for situations in which the coroner/medical examiner is satisfied that the correct identification has been made. Typically, this will include agreement between distinctive antemortem (AM) biological/physical characteristics of the missing person and post-mortem (PM) biological/physical features of the found remains, which result from unique developmental environments (e.g., fingerprints), or occur in such low frequencies the possibility of two people sharing the exact same data is minuscule (e.g., DNA).

Whenever possible, identification should be quantified in terms of probabilities or likelihood ratios. Both measures depend on knowing: (1) the frequency of a biological trait in a population; (2) whether or not the features being examined are correlated; and (3) whether the identification universe (the group the body is being compared to) is open (could be anyone), closed (e.g., people who boarded a specific plane that crashed), or related (e.g., family members killed in a house fire).

a) Methods

Although people have used many different skeletal features to make preliminary matches or exclusions between found remains and AM radio graphs or CT scans, the only skeletal methods that should be used for positive identification are those that either: (1) quantify the probability that unknown remains match a missing person;[48] or (2) have been demonstrated to be unique, capable of distinguishing even identical twins. There are only two skeletal techniques that fit the latter category—frontal sinus patterns and cranial suture patterns.

i) Probability-Based Methods

Rogers and Allard and Christensen[49] point out the problems inherent in using so-called unusual observations on radiographs to make a match between unidentified remains and a missing person. A forensic anthropologist who simply states that a feature is "rare" without being able to

---

48 See, for example, Lelia Watamaniuk & Tracy Rogers, "Positive Personal Identification of Human Remains Based on Thoracic Vertebral Margin Morphology" (2010) 55 *Journal of Forensic Sciences* 1162.

49 Tracy L. Rogers & Travis T. Allard, "Expert Testimony and Positive Identification of Human Remains through Cranial Suture Patterns" (2004) 49 *Journal of Forensic Sciences* 203; Angi M. Christensen, "The Impact of Daubert: Implications for Testimony and Research in Forensic Anthropology (and the Use of Frontal Sinuses in Personal Identification" (2004) 49 *Journal of Forensic Sciences* 427.

substantiate that claim is using an experiential approach. Since every person's experience is different, a trait might seem rare to one person, but be very common in another person's experience. Frequency-based or probability-based methods provide independent evidence of the rarity of a trait, giving the coroner/medical examiner, jurors, and other interested parties a measure and a means of evaluating the strength of an identification.

Various trait frequencies have been observed and documented, and some techniques have been specifically designed to address the problem of positive identification using radiographs. Watamaniuk and Rogers is an example of how a frequency-based method can be developed, tested, and validated.[50] Lawyers with a case in which identification is contentious should ensure that the method used to establish a positive identification incorporated the following minimum requirements during its development:

- Large sample sizes are needed to determine the frequency of a trait. Minimally, 100 individuals should be assessed.
- A second subsample should be examined to ensure that the frequencies observed in the first sample were not simply the result of sampling bias; again, 100 individuals should be assessed.
- If multiple traits are going to be used in combination to bolster the identification, they must first be tested to determine whether or not they are correlated. Related groups of traits must be treated as a single trait.
- A method of using the traits to determine positive identification should be tested on a separate sample for which there is not always a match; this helps reduce the bias of knowing that every test case will have a match.
- Results should be presented in terms of the frequency with which such a combination of traits can be expected to occur in a population. For example, given a sample size of 100 people for the comparative group (e.g., all the missing people in a region, or on a plane), the mathematical level of acceptance for a positive identification is a frequency equal to or less than 1/100 or 0.01. If the combined frequencies of the traits examined exceed 0.01, then it is possible for more than one person in the sample to have the same trait frequencies. Such a result means that a positive identification has not been reached. More features can be included in the analysis, providing

50 Watamaniuk & Rogers, above note 48.

the frequency of each trait is known. When the frequency falls below the critical level of 1 in the comparative group's size, a positive identification can be made.

ii) Frontal Sinus

The frontal sinuses are spaces in the bone of the forehead (frontal bone) that begin to develop during childhood and are largely fixed by adulthood. They vary in shape and complexity. Although they are usually paired, some people never develop them and others have unilateral ones. The frontal sinuses can be seen on radiographs or CT scans, and can be used for positive identification if the missing person had a head X-ray or CT scan taken in life. The unique nature of frontal sinuses has been tested by comparing identical twins;[51] examining possible combinations of traits to determine the number of potential variations;[52] examining the frequencies of particular trait expressions;[53] calculating the likelihood ratio and posterior probabilities of a given sinus variant;[54] and determining if two or more people can share similar sinus patterns, and the accuracy with which the sinuses can be used to match two sets of radiographs from one person.[55] All have confirmed the unique nature of frontal sinuses, with the caveats that this approach cannot be used to make a positive identification for individuals with no frontal sinuses (although the absence of a sinus in AM radiographs of a missing person and the presence of sinuses in PM radiographs of the deceased can be used to exclude a match), and that single, simple sinuses are rarely distinctive enough to confirm identification.

Frontal sinus identification techniques can be classified in several ways. Some depend on metric analysis, while others are morphological (shape-based). One of the most important distinctions between the different types of methods relates to the functionality of the technique. Some are based

---

51 I. Kjaer, C. Pallisgaard, & M.T. Brock-Jacobsen, "Front Sinus Dimensions Can Differ Significantly Between Individuals Within a Monozygotic Twin Pair, Indicating Environmental Influence on Sinus Sizes" (2012) 132 *Acta Otolaryngol* 988.

52 Mineo Yoshino et al., "Classification System of Frontal Sinus Patterns by Radiography. Its Application to Identification of Unknown Skeletal Remains" (1987) 34 *Forensic Science International* 289.

53 Joanna L. Besana & Tracy L. Rogers, "Personal Identification Using the Frontal Sinus" (2010) 55 *Journal of Forensic Sciences* 584.

54 Angi M. Christensen, "Testing the Reliability of Frontal Sinuses in Positive Identification" (2005) 50 *Journal of Forensic Sciences* 18.

55 Neha Patil et al., "Uniqueness of Radiographic Patterns of the Frontal Sinus for Personal Identification" (2012) 42 *Imaging Science in Dentistry* 213.

on coding the frontal sinus features of every radiograph for all unknown remains and missing persons in order to build a database to automate and expedite potential matches or exclusions.[56] This type of technique often produces multiple individuals with the same code, but a visual comparison can then be used to refine the assessment. This type of technique should only be used as a screening tool. The second technique allows users to make a positive identification using an outline, superimposition, or tracing approach. The AM and PM radiographs are superimposed to trace the pattern of the frontal sinuses and determine if there is a match between the two radiographs.[57] The utility of this technique is self-evident to the jury because they can easily see that the AM and PM radiographs are exactly the same. The expert is needed to speak to the uniqueness of frontal sinuses, confirming that even identical twins exhibit different sinus patterns.

iii) Cranial Suture Patterns

The cranial sutures are spaces between the bones of the skull that are unique to the individual; not even identical twins share the same pattern. In infants, the cranial bones are widely spaced with membranous tissue (known as "soft spots") between them. The spaces diminish with age as the bones grow closer together, eventually resulting in interlocking fingers of bone along their borders. As a person enters middle adulthood, the bones can fuse together, eventually leaving only remnants of sutures in old age. The specific pattern of peaks, plateaus, and valleys along a suture is a result of both genetic and environmental factors, which is why each person's sutural pattern is unique.[58] With age, the bones may fuse and the sutures may disappear, but for any suture that is still visible, the pattern of peaks, plateaus, and valleys will not change once adulthood is reached.[59] Due to the unique nature of cranial sutures, a positive identification is made when the AM radiographs of a missing person are superimposed on the PM radiographs of the deceased and they align without discrepancies. While it is theoretically possible to calculate the likelihood of a particular

---

56 Yoshino et al., above note 52. K. Reichs & R. Dorion, "The Use of Computed Tomography (CT) Scans in Comparison of Frontal Sinus Configurations" (1992) 25 *Canadian Society of Forensic Sciences* 1.

57 Victoria A. Smith, Angi M. Christensen, & Sarah W. Myers, "The Reliability of Visually Comparing Small Frontal Sinuses" (2010) 55 *Journal of Forensic Sciences* 1413.

58 Rogers & Allard, above note 49.

59 P.T. Jayaprakash & G.J. Srinivasan, "Skull Sutures: Changing Morphology during Preadolescent Growth and its Implications in Forensic Identification" (2013) 229 *Forensic Science International* 166.e1.

sutural configuration occurring in a population, the obvious complexity of a suture pattern and the fact that even identical twins have different patterns is more convincing to juries than theoretical probabilities.[60]

b) Identification Summary

Identification of skeletal remains is a two-step process involving an analysis of the primary biological parameters (age, sex, ancestry) followed by a detailed comparison of traits that are unique to the individual (e.g., cranial sutures and frontal sinuses), or are associated with frequency data from which a calculation of individuality can be made (e.g., thoracic vertebrae).[61] In contrast to the few techniques capable of confirming identity, there are many different skeletal features that can be used in an exclusionary capacity. For example, a bifurcated (naturally divided) rib viewed on AM radiographs can exclude a match with a body that does not exhibit bifurcated ribs. Randomly selected bony features (such as a bifurcated rib) visible in a radiograph should not be used to establish positive identification unless frequency data can be obtained. Without data to indicate the frequency of a trait in a population, there is no way to independently and objectively assess its discriminatory power.

3) Trauma Analysis

Trauma analysis is based on the scientific principles of bone biomechanics, which involves the interaction of energy with the physical properties of bone.[62] There are three main types of trauma analyses undertaken by forensic anthropologists: (1) determining the nature of the injury—blunt force, sharp force, or projectile; (2) determining the sequence and number of injury events; and (3) determining class or individualizing characteristics of the weapon(s) used.

a) Nature of Injury

Interpreting injury patterns is based upon knowing how energy affects bone. The three primary factors that influence the type of injury produced are: (1) the amount of energy applied; (2) the size of the area the energy impacts; and (3) the speed at which the energy is applied. Typically, the greater

---

60 Rogers & Allard, above note 49.

61 Watamaniuk & Rogers, above note 48.

62 For a detailed explanation, see Christensen, Passalacqua, & Bartelink, above note 47.

the energy applied, the more damage is done. Similarly, energy applied to a small area—for example, being hit with a hammer—causes more penetrating damage (i.e., there is a greater chance of damaging organs that are protected by bone) than the same amount of energy dispersed over a wide area (e.g., being hit with a shovel). Finally, if energy is applied slowly over time, bone can bend because it has both an organic (osteoid) and inorganic (calcium phosphate) component. The osteoid gives bone flexibility, while the minerals provide strength. Because of these properties, bone can bend and return to its natural shape (elastic phase) if the force applied is below its yielding point. If the force slowly continues until it exceeds the yield point, bone will warp and fracture (plastic phase). When force is applied quickly, bone breaks without warping. Low force applied quickly produces incomplete bone fractures (hinges), while high force applied quickly results in significant breakage, producing many pieces (comminuted). Forensic anthropologists observe the results of the damage to figure out how the injury must have been caused, considering issues such as whether the bone is warped, how many pieces are produced, and whether the fractures are incomplete.

Distinguishing blunt force from sharp force and projectile force is done on the basis of wound characteristics and bone biomechanics. Sharp force injuries are inflicted with edged weapons that produce incisions, stabs, or chop marks when they encounter bone. They are typically low velocity applied to a small area. Blunt force injuries are made with the flat surface of an object, including hands and even the floor. Blunt force injuries inflicted by people are often low velocity and may be applied to a small or large area. Sometimes a single weapon can be used to inflict an injury that has both blunt force (axe handle) and sharp force (axe blade) components. Projectile injuries, such as bullet and slingshot wounds, are inflicted by objects that are propelled by weapons, (e.g., a gun, or slingshot) and are usually high velocity, although there are exceptions (e.g., a rock at the end of its flight path, a Minie ball from a musket).

b) Sequence and Number of Injuries

Determining the number and sequence of injuries is done on the basis of fracture pattern analysis. When an object such as a skull is hit, energy is transferred from the person wielding the weapon to the victim. Energy will cause the bone to fracture, producing indentations at the point of impact and fracture lines extending away from (radiating) and surrounding (concentric) the point of impact. The fracture lines will extend without wavering where the energy is strongest (at the point of impact) and will begin to wander as the energy dissipates. Fracture lines can curve around strong areas of bone, for example, the brow ridges of the forehead. Fracture lines will continue to propagate (move through the bone) until they lose their energy, or the energy is dissipated along a pre-existing opening of some form (e.g., it reaches the eye socket, a suture, or a previously inflicted fracture line). By examining which fracture lines dissipate naturally and which ones terminate in other fracture lines, it is possible to work out which fracture was present first. In order to determine the sequence of multiple wounds, the fracture lines must intersect at some point.

The number of injuries is a simple count of the number of wounds observed, but there are two issues that a forensic anthropologist must consider when stating the final result. First, it is possible for a single injury to produce what may appear to be multiple marks. For example, a long blade could cut the bone of the upper orbit (eye socket) and the lower orbit (eye socket) in a single strike, but since there is no bone in the centre of the eye to show the passage of the blade, the cut marks appear to be two separate injuries. Once the angles of the apparently separate injuries are compared and a line drawn between the two, it becomes obvious that they resulted from a single cut. In this way, the number of injuries can be overestimated. Second, not all injuries leave a mark on bone, thus the number of wounds observed on bone is usually considered the minimum number.

c) Class and Individualizing Characteristics

Class and individualizing characteristics can only be assessed from bone if a weapon leaves an imprint. Different types of saws, for example, produce different striation patterns because the blades pass through objects at different angles and speeds, and the blades themselves are different shapes and sizes. Individualizing features are typically those produced through random wear (e.g., chips along a blade at particular intervals). The challenge with individualization is in demonstrating that the particular constellation of incidental marks observed on the bone that correspond to imperfections on the putative weapon occurs in such low frequencies that it is unlikely an entirely different weapon could have developed the same suite of imperfections.

4) Taphonomy, the Post-mortem Interval, and the Timing of Bone Fractures

Taphonomy is the study of everything that happens to a body from the time of death to the point at which it is examined. It includes natural changes such as decomposition and bone weathering, as well as alterations inflicted by animals (e.g., scavenging, moving) and people (e.g., dismemberment, burning). The condition of a bone when it is discovered provides a record of what has happened to it over time. Taphonomy can be used to verify or refute a witness's account of events. For example, if a witness claimed that a shovel was used to smash and stir bones when a body was being burned in an outdoor fire, taphonomic evidence of shovel blade damage, fracturing due to smashing with a flat surface like the back of a shovel, and discolouration (brown, black, grey, white) due to burning are all taphonomic observations that support the witness's statement. In contrast, extreme fragmentation without discolouration might suggest use of a wood chipper to destroy the body, refuting the witness's account.

Taphonomy can also be used during a search for a grave or scattered body parts to determine the location of other bones. For example, if the bones that were initially found show evidence of coyote gnawing, the rest of the bones will likely be distributed across the landscape in a particular pattern specific to coyotes. The condition of the bone might also indicate to a forensic anthropologist that there is another scene—the current scene being a secondary location (e.g., if the bones show evidence of being in water, but the site where they were found is not near water). Taphonomy can be used to help estimate the post-mortem interval (PMI) in order to: (1) address the question of forensic significance, and (2) assist with the process of identification. Taphonomic analyses are also undertaken in order to determine if bone fractures occurred perimortem or post-mortem.

a) The Post-mortem Interval

The police and coroner are interested in modern cases, thus an important component of determining the PMI is simply to establish if the case is recent. Human remains are not considered forensically relevant, or forensically significant, if the individual did not die within the last seventy-five years. This boundary can be extended back in time—the definitive issue being whether or not there *could* be anyone still alive to prosecute for the wrongful death of the deceased. In Ontario, historic skeletal remains (dating from the arrival of Europeans to the modern era) and archaeological skeletal remains (dating prior to European contact, encompassing First Nation and Inuit communities) are the responsibility of the Registrar of Cemeteries, who ensures the appropriate stakeholders are contacted and consulted. If the site is to be excavated, it must be done following a site disposition agreement by a licensed archaeologist who reports to the

Ministry of Tourism, Culture, and Sport. Similar processes exist for other provinces. It is the forensic anthropologist who determines the forensic significance of the remains based on taphonomic indicators, context, and presence of artifacts.

The second aspect of PMI is to aid identification of the deceased by narrowing the relevant time frame of potential missing person matches. For example, if the PMI is between five and ten years, someone missing for two years does not fit the time frame. Although a PMI that is recent and limited (e.g., 2–6 hours since death) is desirable because it can be used to eliminate or focus attention on potential suspects, such time frames are outside the scope of forensic anthropology. Forensic anthropologists use the environment in which the remains were found, the season, and the weather to estimate the approximate amount of time required for a body to decompose to the observed condition. Numerous studies have been undertaken to quantify aspects of this process (e.g., length of time from death to skeletonization in various environments, or length of time for bone to become stained after skeletonization).

The issue that prevents the development or implementation of standardized, quantified approaches to estimating the PMI is that there are many variables that influence the timing of decomposition, including but not limited to soil pH; temperature; moisture levels; body size, including the body fat to muscle ratio of the victim; how deep a body is buried; whether the body is covered; and if the body is exposed to sunlight or under tree cover. Due to the complexity of interactions that influence decomposition (including conditions that delay decomposition—for example, dampness changing body fat into a soap-like substance called adipocere, or arid conditions causing mummification), experience estimating PMI in a particular region can be more useful than depending on published data, particularly if the published data is for environments different from where the forensic case exists.

i) PMI and Bomb Carbon

The number of variables influencing decomposition and bone alteration mean that PMI is always reported as a range—often a fairly large one, depending on the stage of decomposition when the body is found. One technique that can be used to generate a much narrower PMI is bomb carbon. In brief, radioactive isotopes such as carbon 14 (^{14}C) decay and, in doing so, lose protons and neutrons, changing into other elements, at predictable rates. Organisms incorporate ^{14}C into their bodies as they eat plants and other animals that contain ^{14}C. Living organisms maintain their level of ^{14}C because as ^{14}C decays into ^{14}N, new ^{14}C is eaten to replace it. After death, no new ^{14}C is being incorporated, which means the ^{14}C will decay and the original level will continue to drop in a predictable manner over time. By assessing the amount of ^{14}C remaining in the body, the year of death can be calculated. This methodology has been utilized for decades in archaeology to date ancient carbon-based materials, but until recently the technology could not be applied to modern samples because the associated measurement error of the technique was larger than the annual decay rate or reduction of ^{14}C.[63]

Worldwide quantities of ^{14}C have now been documented and scientists discovered that the levels increased drastically during the nuclear bomb testing that began in 1945, and decreased when partial banning of this testing occurred in 1963.[64] These levels have been graphed by year, forming a rough bell curve that increases to peak in 1963 and decreases to current levels. The elevated levels of ^{14}C can be used to estimate the date of birth and date of death for people who were born or who died after 1950, by comparing the level of ^{14}C in their body to the graph. Body tissues are routinely replaced during life, incorporating ^{14}C on a regular basis, but this turnover of new tissue can vary from a few months to many years depending on the tissue. For example, blood incorporates ^{14}C in about a year, whereas dental enamel is fixed during formation and does not turnover. Tissues with high turnover will be the best indication of the person's level of ^{14}C at death (i.e., it will be the most up-to-date value, which can be plotted on the ^{14}C curve to find the date of death).

Since most testing was done in the northern hemisphere, most data is available for that region. Tests of individuals born in the southern hemisphere have demonstrated some success,[65] *but validation of the technique is still required.*

Bomb carbon can also be used to estimate the year of birth, or age at death. Dental enamel does not incorporate new carbon after it is formed, so the ^{14}C levels detected in dental enamel are representative of the year the tooth enamel was formed. In order to determine if the individual was born

---

63 Gordon T. Cook & Angus B. MacKenzie, "Radioactive Isotope Analyses of Skeletal Materials in Forensic Science: A Review of Uses and Potential Uses" (2014) 128 *International Journal of Legal Medicine* 685.

64 *Ibid.*

65 D.H. Ubelaker & R.C. Parra, "Radiocarbon Analysis of Dental Enamel and Bone to Evaluate Date of Birth and Death: Perspective from the Southern Hemisphere" (2011) 208 *Forensic Science International* 103.

before or after 1963, two teeth can be sampled to determine the ^{14}C levels on sequentially developing teeth. If the levels increase between the formation of the early developing tooth and the later developing tooth, the person was born leading up to 1963. If the levels decrease between the early and later forming teeth, the person was born on the down-slope of the curve, after 1963 when the partial banning of nuclear bomb testing occurred.[66]

Despite the fact that studies report error rates in the range of +/- 1 year, there are several factors that can increase the expected error rate (e.g., the turnover rate of the tissue that is sampled, differences in tooth development rate, and the age of the individual). Ubelaker cautions that bone turnover slows with age, which means that if the unidentified individual is older than the people used to generate the bomb carbon calibration curve, the year of death could be considerably underestimated.[67]

ii) Distinguishing Post-mortem Damage from Perimortem Trauma

There are a number of factors that are considered when attempting to determine the timing of damage to bone. Bone surface colour versus fractured edge colour, condition of the bone, fracture morphology (outline and angle), and texture of the fracture surface are important considerations.[68] After death, bone begins to lose its elastic properties, becoming more brittle. Rather than following the more organic lines of living bone, fractures in dry bone tend to be angular. The problem with relying on such differences to assess the timing of fractures (post-mortem damage versus perimortem injury) is that bone elasticity is not lost immediately after death, but rather deteriorates along with the decomposition of the organic components of bone. Thus, it is not always possible to determine if an injury occurred when the person was alive, or if damage was inflicted on the remains within a few months of death. The exact amount of time required for bone to lose its elastic properties varies depending on environmental conditions (e.g., moisture levels). Forensic anthropologists refer to this as "perimortem"—the period around death when fracture timing cannot be

---

66 Kanar Alkass et al., "Analysis of Radiocarbon, Stable Isotopes and DNA in Teeth to Facilitate Identification of Unknown Decedents" (2013) 8 *PLoS One* doi: http://dx.doi.org/10.1371/journal.pone.0069597.

67 Douglas H. Ubelaker, "Radiocarbon Analysis of Human Remains: A Review of Forensic Applications" (2014) 59 *Journal of Forensic Sciences* 1466.

68 Steven A. Symes et al., "Taphonomy and the Timing of Bone Fractures in Trauma Analysis" in James Pokines & Steven A. Symes, eds., *Manual of Forensic Taphonomy* (Boca Raton, FL: CRC Press, 2013) 341.

assessed conclusively. This is in contrast to pathologists' use of the term "perimortem" to refer to injuries received at or in relation to the time of death. If the term "perimortem" is used by a forensic anthropologist, it should be made clear which definition is intended.

5) The Evolution of Forensic Anthropology: Cold Cases

Forensic anthropology is a relatively new field, established as a section of the American Academy of Forensic Sciences in 1972. Over the last forty years, there have been many advances and developments in forensic anthropology, especially with respect to field recovery, crime scene interpretation, and trauma analysis. Significant improvements have also been made in establishing the biological profile and personal identification. Cold cases never examined by a forensic anthropologist can benefit from a complete re-evaluation, particularly if the skeletal remains have been retained. If the body has been returned to the family or buried by the province, exhumation may be worthwhile. It may even be possible for forensic anthropologists to provide new insight into cases where the remains are no longer available, based on an examination of scene photographs, maps, autopsy photographs, autopsy reports, and other information. If a forensic anthropologist examined the case within the last ten years, it would be worth contacting that person to discuss potential technical developments that could produce new leads. If it has been more than ten years since a forensic anthropologist examined the case, a re-evaluation can provide insight into aspects of the case that were not part of standard analyses in the past. The only way to determine if a forensic anthropological examination could lead to new evidence is to contact an experienced forensic anthropologist to discuss the nature of the case and the issues that remain unresolved.

C. THE ROLE OF THE FORENSIC ANTHROPOLOGIST IN CRIMINAL CASES

1) Qualifications

There is no Canadian forensic anthropology accrediting body. For those interested in accreditation, the American Board of Forensic Anthropology (ABFA)[69] certifies forensic anthropologists by testing theoretical and prac-

69 See, generally, ABFA, online: www.theabfa.org.

tical knowledge. ABFA is accredited by the Forensic Specialties Accreditation Board and is open to Canadian forensic anthropologists. American accreditation may not be practical for most Canadian forensic anthropologists because it is not required and therefore not worth the expense and time needed to take the exam and pay the annual fees, particularly for those with relatively low caseloads.

While Canadian forensic anthropology is more flexible in terms of qualifications, it lacks standardization. Individuals with different skill sets may claim knowledge of this field and even identify themselves as forensic anthropologists, which can be challenging for lawyers seeking an expert witness. In the absence of accreditation, lawyers may want to consider the following three options: (1) the American Academy of Forensic Science (AAFS) Expert Witness Database; (2) the academic degree, research interests, and training of the expert witness; and (3) the *Mohan* and *Daubert* criteria for accepting expert witness testimony.

1) The most relevant North American organization for forensic anthropologists is the AAFS. The AAFS maintains a list of experts who are willing to provide information and guidance, and conduct casework in their specialization. Lawyers can contact the membership co ordinator from the AAFS website[70] for a list of experts in any forensic specialty. If the prospective forensic anthropological consultant is not listed on the AAFS expert witness list, his or her credentials should be carefully examined.
2) A Canadian forensic anthropology expert witness should have qualifications similar to those required by the ABFA. For example, forensic anthropologists in North America are expected to have completed or be completing a Ph.D. in anthropology with a research focus in forensic anthropology or bioarchaeology (the study of past peoples based on their skeletal remains and burial context), providing the bioarchaeological topic has a potential forensic application. They must also have completed specialized training in forensic anthropological casework, typically through mentoring by their Ph.D. supervisor. Additional professional development is often undertaken to broaden the scope of the novice. For example, the New York City chief medical examiner's office offers a month-long visiting scientist internship for

70 American Academy of Forensic Sciences, online: www.aafs.org/about/staff-directory.

individuals completing a Ph.D. Additional training should be at a level significantly more advanced than a workshop or field school.

3) The *Daubert* criteria are useful in helping to establish the credentials of a potential expert as they provide specific measures to evaluate a potential expert's curriculum vitae (e.g., having published on that topic in a peer-reviewed journal).

In order to mediate the varied education and training of consultants in Ontario, the Ontario Forensic Pathology Service uses a peer-review process for homicide cases in keeping with the recommendations of the Goudge Inquiry,[71] thereby ensuring the quality of both the forensic anthropologist's and forensic pathologist's analyses and reports. Once the forensic anthropology report is reviewed, issues are addressed, and points are clarified, the report is submitted to the forensic pathologist for inclusion in the final pathology report.

2) The Difference between Forensic Anthropologists and Bioarchaeologists

One of the most serious mistakes made by police, coroners, and lawyers with respect to forensic anthropological evidence is in thinking that all anthropologists are equivalent, or that all biological/physical/bioarchaeological anthropologists who work with bones can "do" a forensic case. A bioarchaeologist or biological anthropologist with an "interest in forensic anthropology" is not the same thing as a forensic anthropologist.

There are at least six significant differences between the expertise of a forensic anthropologist and a bioarchaeologist, including knowledge of the following: (1) error rates, standardization, validation, and issues of admissibility in court; (2) evidence handling, chain of custody, and concerns relating to trace evidence on bodies; (3) biohazard and safety concerns working with the recently deceased; (4) crime scene protocols, proper documentation, excavation, and recovery of recently deceased; (5) the differences between dry bone (archaeological) and fresh bone (modern) that can affect observations and interpretations; and (6) ancestry analysis, identification, and aspects of trauma analysis, which are not a focus of

---

71 Ontario, Ministry of the Attorney General, *Inquiry into Pediatric Forensic Pathology in Ontario* by Stephen T. Goudge, Commissioner (2008), online: www.attorneygeneral.jus.gov.on.ca/inquiries/goudge/report.

bioarchaeology (and, consequently, bioarchaeologists have little training or experience in these areas).

Bioarchaeologists gain knowledge and skills relating to the analysis of past populations. They examine skeletons to obtain data on age, sex, and health, but their priorities are very different from forensic anthropologists and therefore their selection and implementation of methodologies also differ. Bioarchaeologists want to extract as much potential information about an individual or population as they can to help build a picture of the community. Thus, a technique might be chosen because it has the *potential* to add new information, rather than because it is known to be highly accurate. In contrast, forensic anthropologists are concerned with the error rates, standardization, and validation of techniques to ensure the admissibility of their testimony in court.

Similarly, forensic anthropologists specialize in the application of anthropological skills and knowledge in a legal context, meaning that they study and practise everything from evidence handling to proper crime scene processing, and have experience with mock crimes scenes and mock trials during their training. Because bioarchaeologists work with people of the past, they are not trained in the legal aspects of anthropology, nor are they experienced in working with modern human remains. Bioarchaeologists analyze dry bone, while forensic anthropologists examine bone in a variety of stages of decomposition—from fresh to dry, burnt with burnt flesh attached, and bone corroded from household solvents. Fresh bone is very different from dry bone in terms of texture, greasiness, colour, presences of adhering soft tissues, and so on—so much so that techniques a bioarchaeologist would be confident conducting on dry bone can be extremely challenging when applied to fresh bone.

3) Testimony and Admissibility

Most Canadian forensic anthropologists are involved in both research and casework, with one informing the other. Forensic anthropologists may be asked to testify to a number of issues relating to the case. Because a forensic anthropologist is required to determine if bone is animal or human, and if human bone is of recent forensic interest, they are often involved in the investigation from the beginning. The information they provide helps direct the focus of inquiry. The investigators and prosecutors build their case based on the evidence that is found and the interpretations of that evidence by various experts. As a result, the investigating forensic anthropologist is typically called to testify by the Crown. The defence can subpoena the forensic anthropologist of record, or may choose to hire its own consultant.

In my experience as a forensic anthropologist, criminal defence lawyers rarely retain their own forensic anthropologist. One high-profile exception was the Pickton case in British Columbia.[72] The lack of forensic anthropologists called by the defence may be explained by the fact that some forensic anthropological analyses (e.g., biological profile and identification) are subsequently verified (or refuted) by DNA, and it is the DNA analysis that is subjected to intense scrutiny in the courts. Forensic anthropological evidence relates primarily to the victim, except in situations where the injuries or activities relating to the crime scene are reported by a witness and can be confirmed or refuted by trauma or taphonomic analyses (e.g., the way in which the victim's body was disposed).

Forensic anthropologists rarely have direct evidence that can identify a perpetrator, but due to their work in recovering and analyzing the remains, they might find and collect trace evidence that can be linked to the accused. Defence lawyers allocating resources may not consider forensic anthropological evidence associated with the victim to be as relevant as evidence relating to the activities of the accused, and as a result do not hire their own consultants. This could be a serious oversight. A forensic anthropologist reviewing the client's case might, for example, find evidence that the body was disposed of in a manner quite different from what a "witness" claims occurred.

The role of a forensic anthropologist hired by a defence lawyer is to review the work of the investigating forensic anthropologist in order to determine if there are any points of contention, incorrect interpretations of evidence, and so on, and to assess whether or not additional analyses could provide information useful to the defence's case. If so, the defence's forensic anthropologist would undertake those examinations and/or obtain samples for additional lab analysis (e.g., bomb carbon for age estimation or PMI). Working from second-hand information and documentation, however, will decrease the likelihood that the consulting forensic anthropologist will be able to learn anything new or useful for the defence. Potential consultants should be contacted as soon as possible. The consulting forensic anthropologist could also sit in the courtroom during the investigating forensic anthropologist's testimony to help defence formulate relevant questions for cross-examination.

72 See the legal context section of this chapter.

a) Common Questions Asked of the Forensic Anthropologists

Given the variety of circumstances in which a body could be discovered, the possible events surrounding death and disposal, and the potential condition of the remains when found, there are thousands of conceivable questions a forensic anthropologist might be able to answer, many of which a lawyer might not think to ask. Posing a series of questions is an excellent way to start a consultation, but ultimately it may prove more useful to tell the forensic anthropologist what you want to know, rather than to ask specific questions—begin with generalities, then work toward specifics.

For example, telling the forensic anthropologist that you want to know anything related to how the victim died lets the forensic anthropologist approach the problem from several different directions. If there is a potential weapon of interest to the case, a follow-up question might be, "Could an axe have inflicted these injuries?" The general question will help avoid tunnel vision and will prevent accusations of biasing the witness. Once the initial analysis is done, focusing on whether a particular weapon or weapon class was used to inflict the injury can be accomplished without losing other potentially relevant information (e.g., that the victim was likely hit by a car around the same time the other injuries were inflicted).

Forensic anthropologists should conduct a complete analysis, not one that is truncated or defined by questions someone is interested in at the time. If a complete analysis was not initially undertaken, there might not be enough information to address follow-up questions that could arise.

Sometimes a consultant might not realize that a lawyer has not grasped—or may have misinterpreted the significance of—something stated in a report or said on the stand. One way to ascertain that the evidence is consistent with the theory of the case is for the lawyer to state the point they want to make (this injury was not caused by falling down, it was inflicted by someone) and indicate which evidence they want to use to support that statement (the striations on the damaged bone show an edged weapon created the injury). The forensic anthropologist can then explain why the evidence does or does not support the theory in the way that the lawyer expected. This type of discussion will help avoid surprises on the stand.

With those caveats in mind, below is a list of issues and questions a forensic anthropologist may be able to address:

- *Was the disposal method premeditated?* Environmental conditions at the scene may be used to provide insight into this question. If the victim was buried, toolmarks might be present in the grave wall, and it may be possible to find evidence of more than one person digging the grave.

- *What was the sequence of events that took place at the scene?* A combination of environmental conditions, the position of the body/bones, and the condition of the remains (forensic taphonomy) can be used to address this question.
- *Is this a primary or secondary scene?* A combination of the bones' location, their position, and their condition (forensic taphonomy) can be used to address this question.
- *Can you tell the difference between recent and old cemetery/archaeological bone?* A combination of bone condition, context, and artifacts can be used to ascertain the nature of the remains; when uncertain, bomb carbon can prove useful.
- *Is it possible to determine if bone fragments are human, even if DNA cannot be extracted?* Bone fragments can be examined microscopically to assess whether or not they are human.
- *Can DNA be extracted from burned bone?* It depends on the degree of burning. If the bone is entirely calcined (white all the way through), DNA cannot be extracted; if bone is not uniformly burned to this degree, it may be possible to obtain DNA.
- *Can a body be completely destroyed by fire?* There is often skeletal evidence recovered from fires, even those burning at high temperatures (e.g., incinerators).
- *Is it possible to distinguish injuries inflicted by a weapon from damage caused by animal scavenging, ploughs, or anything else post-mortem?* Animal scavenging produces distinctive, recognizable marks that can be distinguished from perimortem trauma. Bone damage inflicted months after death can easily be distinguished from perimortem injuries. Some early period post-mortem damage can be distinguished from perimortem injuries, depending on the resulting marks.
- *What instrument was used to inflict damage on the victim?* It may be possible to determine the class of weapon (e.g., knife), or in some cases, even link the injuries to specific weapons on the basis of specific use-wear patterns; other times the shape of the object can be described, but no particular weapon can be identified—in the latter case, it may be possible to demonstrate a particular object in question can or can't be eliminated as a potential weapon.
- *How much force was used to create this injury?* This is a problematic question. Some bones are more sturdy and dense than others

and can withstand more force. There are tables with information providing guidelines on the amount of force required to fracture specific bones, but these numbers will vary depending on the age, health, weight/height ratio, and so on, of the victim. It is possible to indicate whether a bone is one of the stronger (occipital at the back of the skull) or weaker ones (sphenoid at the temple), and whether or not a bone is frequently the site of accidental injuries.

- *What is the sequence of injuries? What was the position of the attacker relative to the victim?* Depending on the interaction of fracture lines and other injuries on the bone, it may be possible to determine the order in which the injuries were inflicted. Similarly, the position of the attacker relative to the victim may be evident from the placement of injuries on the body (e.g., front versus back).
- *Is it possible to confirm or refute a particular scenario relating to the death of the victim?* The prosecution might have a theory of the crime they want to test against the evidence, or the defence might plead to a lesser crime (e.g., indignity to a body—claiming the victim was already deceased when the accused moved the body, and the body was damaged in the process). Depending on the scenario, it may be possible to refute or confirm a particular scenario using the condition of the bone, position of body when discovered, location of remains, and so on.

b) Reviewing the Record and Ensuring Full Disclosure

There is no standard requirement regarding work product and best practices with respect to full disclosure in forensic anthropology. Having said that, forensic anthropologists are usually contracted by police or coroner/medical examiner offices that have specific guidelines regarding disclosure. Forensic anthropologists at the scene usually work closely with identification officers. Often the latter will take a series of photographs at the request of the forensic anthropologist. These are subsequently disclosed along with all the other scene photographs, maps, and so on. If a forensic anthropologist takes supplemental photographs, or her own series of photographs, copies are forwarded to either the identification officer, or the investigator in charge of the case. Identification officers also attend the autopsy and will similarly take all the required photographs, or will receive copies of supplementary photographs taken by the forensic anthropologist. Case notes are photocopied and submitted to the Crown when it is confirmed that the forensic anthropologist will be called to testify. Raw data will be included in the case notes, but unless there is a forensic anthropologist for the opposing side, the raw data will not be particularly useful to anyone.

c) Forensic Anthropological Reports

Forensic anthropologists typically produce a report for the police, relating to work conducted at the scene, and/or the coroner/medical examiner, relating to the recovery of the body and analysis of the remains. The scope, depth, and format of reports vary considerably by jurisdiction, generally reflecting the needs and preferences of the requesting agency. Some prefer detailed explanations of methodologies and references to support interpretations, while others favour brief summaries. Regardless of the style of report the agency requests, the forensic anthropologist should have all the pertinent information regarding references, accuracy, and so on in his notes. Ultimately, the report will be used as the foundation for questions and information that are discussed in court. Forensic anthropologists must be able to navigate their reports effectively in the courtroom to respond to questions. It is therefore sometimes necessary for a consulting forensic anthropologist to stand firm on aspects of the report she knows they will require in court (e.g., the inclusion of specific photographs, information reported in a table), regardless of the preferences of the requesting agency.

Forensic anthropologists might choose to use PowerPoint presentations, three-dimensional animations, three-dimensional prints (replicas/models) of bones, and so on in order to effectively convey their analyses and interpretations to the jury. If so, they should discuss their preferences for using demonstrative evidence with the requesting lawyer in order to determine in advance if there is likely to be a problem with admissibility, and how many copies of each item should be made for disclosure.

d) Ethics

Forensic anthropologists in Canada are members of various professional organizations, such as the Canadian Society for Forensic Science, the American Academy of Forensic Sciences, and the Canadian Association for Physical Anthropology. All of these organizations have ethical guidelines for their members that address professional practice, including respect and proper care for the people, artifacts, animals, and places with which they work, including issues of privacy and confidentiality; responsibility to clients, including confidentiality; research and dissemination of information; teaching; and the importance of ethical practice. Such guidelines address issues relating to work products and the proper dissemination of information, along with client rights, proper representation of credentials, and so on.

D. CONCLUSION

The current scope of forensic anthropology is much broader than in the past, which means that lawyers who have not worked with a forensic anthropologist in the last ten years will benefit from refreshing their knowledge of this field. The breadth of the discipline may also contribute to some of the challenges lawyers face when hiring a forensic anthropology consultant, or reading a forensic anthropology report. With origins in anthropology and ties to archaeology and forensic sciences, forensic anthropology draws on all three subject matters. As a result, forensic anthropologists in Canada can have very diverse academic backgrounds, making it difficult for lawyers to compare the relative strengths of a potential consultant. In the United States, the use of accreditation eliminates the problem of ensuring the consultant is qualified, but in Canada, criteria such as publications, subjects taught, number and type of cases examined in the past, and number of times that individual has testified can be used to help gauge the qualifications of a potential consultant as well as to compare the experience of one expert relative to another.

The remit of forensic anthropology is diverse enough that individual practitioners will have professional competency in most of the subject matter discussed above, but will also have particular expertise in one area (e.g., identification, taphonomy, trauma) that is usually the focus of their primary research. In this sense, "expertise" in one subject indicates that the person has a more nuanced understanding of this subject than colleagues specializing in another topic, and may be able to conduct analyses at a more detailed level. Such additional expertise does not render other consultants incompetent in that subject area, nor does it mean that if two consultants disagree, the one with the specialized knowledge will always be correct. Instead, it means that if culpability depends largely on one particular piece of forensic anthropological evidence (e.g., victim identification, PMI, saw mark analysis), then it befits a lawyer to locate a forensic anthropologist who can provide the fullest, most detailed analysis possible.

Finally, the variety of circumstances in which human remains are located and the variable condition of the bones means that "standardization" in forensic anthropology may be different from what is expected in other disciplines. There is no "one method fits all cases" solution in forensic anthropology. The bones that are found and the condition they are in will constrain the options for analysis. Thus, while every technique must be tested and validated, and only reliable methods should be used, the appropriateness of employing a particular technique will depend on the circumstances of the case, environment of the scene, condition of the bone, and qualities inherent to the deceased (e.g., adult versus child, ancestry). It is consequently the approach to a case that must be standardized in forensic anthropology, including: (1) providing a rationale for using each technique; (2) selecting techniques with a measure of reliability that can be evaluated and debated by independent observers; (3) selecting techniques that are appropriate for the ancestry of the individual, or using methods that have been developed on a sample incorporating population diversity; and (4) understanding the underlying scientific principles of a method in order to correctly interpret results, particularly in cases where results might be ambiguous.

E. LEGAL CONTEXT

Archaeology and physical anthropology have been applied to forensic contexts in Canada since at least 1977, but its foundations as a discipline trace back to the turn of the century.[73,74] Over time, forensic anthropology emerged as a specialty of biological anthropology and the forensic anthropologist, once a marginalized specialist, is today a valued member of the death investigation team who assists in the recovery of human remains and observes toolmarks associated with the grave's construction for the purpose of assisting in crime scene reconstruction, in addition to analyzing the skeleton.[75]

---

73 Michael S. Pollanen et al., eds., "Forensic Science in Canada: A Report of Multidisciplinary Discussion" (4–5 May 2012), online: Centre for Forensic Science & Medicine at the University of Toronto www.forensics.utoronto.ca/Assets/LMPF+Digital+Assets/Forensic+Science+in+Canada.pdf [CFSM, "Multidisciplinary Discussion Report"].

74 Mark F. Skinner, "Applied Archaeology and Physical Anthropology in a Forensic Context: A Review of Twelve Years of Forensic Anthropology in British Columbia" (1989) 22 *Canadian Society of Forensic Science Journal* 83; Douglas H. Ubelaker, ed., *Forensic Science: Current Issues, Future Directions* (Hoboken, NJ: Wiley-Blackwell, 2013) at 132–33 [Ubelaker, *Forensic Science*].

75 Mark F. Skinner et al., "Taking the Pulse of Forensic Anthropology in Canada" (2010) 43 *Canadian Society of Forensic Science Journal* 191 at 193 [Skinner et al., "Taking the Pulse"]; CFSM, Multidisciplinary Discussion Report, above note 73 at 22–24.

Forensic anthropological evidence have been pivotal in several Canadian cases, particularly with respect to interpreting events around the time of death. In the context of the discipline's application to criminal cases, forensic anthropology evidence has addressed the following three broad areas:

1) *Identification, excavation, and evidence collection.* Forensic anthropologists play a key role in identifying, excavating, and recovering human remains in a manner consistent with protecting evidence continuity.

   In the recent Tim Bosma murder trial, for example, Dr. Tracy Rogers recovered bones from a livestock incinerator on the property of Dellen Millard (accused of first-degree murder with Mark Smich). Dr. Rogers testified that the bones were indeed human, of an adult male likely under forty years old and did not represent a complete body (i.e., the incinerator had been cleaned out). The Crown argued that Tim Bosma's remains were burned in the incinerator after he was shot and killed by Millard and Smich. After a four-and-a-half months–long criminal trial, both men were found guilty of first-degree murder in June 2016. Bosma was thirty-two years old.[76]

   Forensic anthropologists have also proven valuable in excavating items of evidentiary value that are not human remains. For example, in the Bandidos case, Dr. Michael Spence's team excavated cell phones, in addition to other valuable physical evidence.[77]

2) *Trauma analysis: Type, cause, and number of injuries.* A forensic anthropologist may be able to identify injuries and to provide an opinion as to what might have caused them; in the reasons for sentencing judgment of *R. v. Dennis*,[78] Justice Veale noted that a forensic anthropologist identified a single gunshot wound to the head of the victim, who was burned beyond recognition.[79] In *R. v. Boutilier*,[80] where Glithero J. dismissed an application to quash the applicants' committal to stand trial for first-degree murder, it was noted that a forensic anthropologist examined the body after an exhumation in 2011 and concluded that at least two and probably three or more impacts were needed to

76 Adrian Humphreys, "Forensic Science Expert at Bosma Murder Trial Climbed Inside 'The Eliminator' to Find Human Remains" (18 February 2016) online: *National Post* natpo.st/1VqZvdA. See also, Adam Carter, "Tim Bosma Trial: Millard and Smich Guilty of 1st-Degree Murder" (17 June 2016), online: *CBC News* www.cbc.ca/1.3634213.

77 Skinner et al., "Taking the Pulse," above note 75 at 195.

78 2014 YKSC 14.

79 *Ibid.* at para. 13.

80 2012 ONSC 1060.

cause the injuries seen to the skull. Further, the injuries on the right side of the body were consistent with the deceased being struck by a train, but it could not be ascertained whether the deceased was hit by a rock or kicked—a significant issue given the testimony at the preliminary inquiry which described the deceased as having suffered beatings prior to death.[81]

Justice Glithero concluded that the findings of the committing judge were "beyond controversy," specifically, "that there was direct evidence of the severe beating at the hands of the three accused, that it occurred at or near the position on the railway tracks where the deceased was struck by the train, and there was evidence that the train was the instrument of death."[82]

3) *Taphonomic analysis: Effects on the body after death.* Forensic anthropologists may be able to provide an opinion addressing what forces and effects have acted on a body after death. For example, forensic anthropologists may opine on whether remains have been subjected to animal activity. Distinguishing between bone damage caused by animal activity compared to perimortem trauma can provide the court with a more in-depth understanding of the extent to which human involvement contributed to the appearance of the remains. Generally, the value of taphonomy from a legal perspective is to discredit or reinforce the report of an eyewitness or suspect, affecting the theory of the case. For example, in *R. v. Hamilton*,[83] police investigated a missing persons case by targeting the appellant in an undercover operation. The appellant told the undercover officer that he shot the individual in question, killing him, and disposed of the body. Based on this information, a burn pit was later discovered by police near the appellant's residence. A forensic anthropologist identified charred human and dog bone fragments in the burn pit, confirming the details the appellant provided to the undercover officers about how he disposed of the body. The appellant had admitted that the body had not completely burned and, based on details he provided to the officer, a search of an area twenty kilometres from the appellant's residence revealed thirteen human bones.[84] This evi-

81 *Ibid.* at paras. 20–21. These paragraphs set out the evidence of the forensic anthropologist in detail.

82 *Ibid.* at para. 32.

83 2003 BCCA 490.

84 *Ibid.* at paras. 20–22 and 29. Correspondence with Dr. Tracy Rogers in May 2016.

dence corroborated key features of the appellant's narrative, leaving the key matter in issue: whether the appellant had acted in self-defence.[85]

In some cases, forensic anthropologists may be able to apply their expertise to areas beyond the traditional application of their discipline (but still within the scope of their expertise). In such instances, the court must determine, first and foremost, whether such evidence is admissible. For example, the case of *R. v. Brown*[86] involved a defence application seeking the admission of photoanthropometric testimony from forensic anthropologist Dr. Iscan, in relation to video evidence depicting the perpetrators of a fatal shooting:

> ... The testimony, as preferred, consists of a description of the morphological traits of a black man, the photoanthropometric analysis of the images of the man in the toque and the man in the black hood compared to Mr. Francis and Mr. Grant [the applicants], respectively, and the superimposition of known photographs onto the images on the videotape alleged to be them. Reference [was] made to the frequency of specified morphological traits in black men and the need to be cautious in accepting them as reliable identifiers. The defence [had] no present intention of eliciting from Dr. Iscan an opinion excluding the applicants as perpetrators. The thrust of the application [was] a request to prove anthropological methodology unknown to lay persons and to apply it to the videotapes of the perpetrators without eliciting an opinion on the ultimate issue to be determined by the jury.[87]

Justice Trafford described the ultimate issue as being "the identity of the man in the toque as Mr. Francis, and the man in the black hood as Mr. Grant."[88] The Crown's case rested heavily on the videos of the shooting at the Just Desserts Café. The frailties of Dr. Iscan's methodology were discussed by Trafford J.; specifically, the difficulties in applying traditional three-dimensional forensic anthropology examinations to two-dimen-

---

85 *Ibid.* at paras. 5 and 23–30.

86 *R. v. Brown [Admissibility of Dr. Iscan Testimony]*, [1999] O.J. No. 4869 (S.C.J.). The crime itself became known as the "Just Desserts shooting" because the 1994 murder occurred in the course of a robbery at the Just Desserts Café in Toronto. See, generally, "Two of Three Convicted in Just Desserts Shooting," *CBC News* (13 December 1999) online: www.cbc.ca/news/canada/two-of-three-convicted-in-just-desserts-shooting-1.179172.

87 *Ibid.* at para. 1.

88 *Ibid.* at para. 8.

sional video and photograph examinations.[89] Despite these frailties, the methodology had been published in peer-reviewed journals with no negative feedback, used to some extent internationally, and was likely respected by Dr. Iscan's peers, even though it may not be completely accepted in the scientific community.[90]

Justice Trafford therefore held that the testimony met the admissibility criteria of expert opinion evidence. The frailties were "not so significant in the circumstances of this case to render the evidence inadmissible."[91] The frailties could be addressed during cross-examination and the charge to the jury could prevent the jury from being overwhelmed by the expert evidence. Justice Trafford remained mindful of maintaining the quality of the administration of justice in the case, as it relates to assessing the reliability of the videos, stating:

> The videotapes are the foundation of the prosecution. Without them, the Crown has no case against Mr. Francis and Mr. Grant. These defendants deny any involvement in the shooting of Ms. Leimonis. The controversy in the field of anthropology relating to the methodology of Dr. Iscan can be assessed by the jury in determining the probative value of the opinion and the other evidence tending to incriminate or exculpate Mr. Francis and Mr. Grant. The right to make full answer and defence and the importance of a verdict being based upon reliable evidence to the public confidence in the administration of justice lead me to admit this evidence despite the potential frailty of the methodology.[92]

Increasingly complex forensic anthropological evidence may be met with similarly complex legal issues, particularly in high-profile cases. Perhaps the most infamous criminal case involving forensic anthropology is that of serial murderer Robert Pickton, as the investigation involved an unprecedented 21-month-long excavation of his property for the remains of missing women from Vancouver's Downtown Eastside.[93] The excavation ended in November 2003, and he was charged with twenty-seven counts of first-degree murder, but since pre-trial rulings quashed one count and severed twenty others, the trial proceeded on six counts of first-degree murder. On 9 December 2007,

---

89 *Ibid.*

90 *Ibid.*

91 *Ibid.*

92 *Ibid.* at para. 9.

93 "Timeline: Key Dates in the Pickton Case" *The Globe and Mail* (17 December 2012), online: http://fw.to/yBIquYl.

Pickton was found guilty of six counts of second-degree murder. His appeal was rejected by the Court of Appeal for British Columbia in 2009, and in 2010, the Supreme Court of Canada upheld his convictions.[94]

At the trial of Robert Pickton, which involved 129 witnesses and 1.3 million pages of documents between the Crown and the defence,[95] the Crown sought to tender the bones of "Jane Doe" as similar fact evidence as it related to the identity of the person responsible for murdering the six women listed in the indictment. The bones consisted of a left heel bone and left rib found on Pickton's property that matched the DNA profile of a partial skull found near Mission, B.C. The statements of Pickton's friend, Gina Houston, were to the effect that this area in Mission was a dumping ground for Pickton. The trial judge found that Houston's evidence did not link Pickton and Jane Doe's skull and the trial judge ultimately did not rely upon Houston's testimony with respect to Pickton travelling to Mission at a time near the time of the skull's deposition at that site.[96]

The saw marks on the skull of Jane Doe arguably linked Pickton's butchering methods and tools as a pig farmer and butcher to identifying him as the perpetrator.[97] The Jane Doe evidence was ruled to be admissible by Williams J. and the Crown led the evidence at trial.[98] After the conclusion of the Crown's case and before commencing itself, the defence applied for a reconsideration of the judgment relating to the Jane Doe evidence on the basis that the facts that grounded the ruling were different than presented at trial.[99] Justice Williams concluded that the jury would be instructed to disregard the entirety of the Jane Doe bone evidence because it "failed to provide 'some evidence' linking Mr. Pickton to the similar act."[100]

On appeal, Finch C.J.B.C., writing for the court, found that the trial judge placed excessive emphasis on Houston's evidence and the time at which Pickton obtained a power reciprocating saw for his butchering practice; the skull was discovered in February 1995 while Pickton obtained a power saw much later, in 1999.[101]

---

94 *Ibid.*

95 *Ibid.*

96 *R. v. Pickton*, 2009 BCCA 300 at paras. 129–34 [*Pickton*, 2009 BCCA] at paras. 129–34. See para. 134 for the court quoting the trial judge's finding.

97 *Ibid.* at para. 130.

98 *R. v. Pickton*, 2006 BCSC 1477 [*Pickton*, 2006 BCSC].

99 See *R. v. Pickton*, 2007 BCSC 1293 [*Pickton*, 2007 BCSC].

100 *Pickton*, 2009 BCCA, above note 96 at paras. 131–33. See also *Pickton*, 2007 BCSC, above note 99 at paras. 29–34.

101 *Pickton*, 2009 BCCA, above note 96 at paras. 129–39.

Chief Justice Finch held that the trial judge erred in his analysis of the Jane Doe evidence and held that "there was clearly some evidence linking Mr. Pickton to the Jane Doe bones,"[102] stating:

> In my respectful view, the learned trial judge erred in his analysis of this issue by focusing unduly on the evidence of Houston and the question of when Mr. Pickton acquired a power reciprocating saw. On the question of whether there was *some* evidence linking Mr. Pickton to the Jane Doe evidence, the obvious starting point was the location of the Jane Doe heel and rib bones found in close proximity to Mr. Pickton's residential trailer, and the slaughterhouse, and in close proximity to the butchered remains of the six victims named in the Indictment. It was only the discovery of those heel and rib bones in that location that made the Jane Doe skull in any way relevant. But for the heel and rib bones, any link between the Jane Doe skull and Mr. Pickton would have been tenuous at best.
>
> . . .
>
> When the location of the Jane Doe heel and rib bones, and their DNA match to the partial skull are considered with the rest of the evidence in the Crown's case, it is my view that the link to Mr. Pickton clearly surpassed the "some evidence" test.[103]

Other anthropological evidence at issue in this case involved the admissibility of proposed similar fact evidence consisting of, in part, a piece of long bone recovered from a manure cistern on Pickton's property that was linked by DNA to Wendy Crawford; the bone was located near Pickton's residential trailer and towards the end of a demolished piggery on the property.[104] After examination by a forensic anthropologist and police toolmark examiner, the bone was ground into powder by a forensic odontologist to facilitate the DNA testing that linked the bone to Crawford. The Crown applied to have the Crawford evidence, along with evidence pertaining to Cynthia Feliks and Inga Hall, admitted as similar fact evidence at trial,[105] submitting that the three women were murdered and butchered

102 *Ibid.* at para. 140.

103 *Ibid.* at paras. 139 and 141.

104 *R. v. Pickton*, 2006 BCSC 1601 at paras. 16 and 70–71 [*Pickton*, 2006 BCSC 1601].

105 For the purposes of this book and the focus of this chapter, the details of the evidence pertaining to Feliks and Hall will not be elaborated upon here, other than to say that portions of both women's remains were found in freezers on Pickton's property and both were drug-dependent sex-trade workers in Vancouver's Downtown Eastside. Refer to *Pickton*, 2006 BCSC 1601, *ibid.*, for further details. The trial judge held that the evidence pertaining to these two women was inadmissible. At

in circumstances similar to the six women in the indictment for six counts of first-degree murder.[106] Specifically, the Crown argued that this evidence included the fact that all three women disappeared, shared similar personal profiles with the deceased women already on the indictment, and shared the circumstance of having their DNA found in remains consistent with butchering practices within the same location as the remains of women already on the indictment who had been clearly murdered and butchered.[107] In the words of the Williams J.:

> The Crown identifies two issues with respect to which it says this proposed similar fact evidence is relevant: the identity of the individual responsible for the murders of the six women named in the Indictment and the truthfulness of Mr. Pickton's statement to Andrew Bellwood. Mr. Bellwood testified at the preliminary hearing that Mr. Pickton had told him, in effect, that he killed drug dependent sex trade workers and dismembered them in his barn.[108]

The trial judge went on to quote Bellwood's testimony that Pickton told him the human remains would be fed to pigs and any uneaten remains would be put into barrels to be delivered to a waste plant.[109]

A *Charter* application brought by the defence earlier in the proceedings against Pickton argued that the defence expert was deprived of the chance to analyze the bone, compromising Pickton's ability to make full answer and defence to the Crown theory that the bone represented the remains of Crawford.[110] On this application, the defence also led evidence addressing contamination of the teeth of two other women, which were similarly ground for the purpose of DNA analysis.[111] The forensic anthropologist called by the defence concluded, based on photographs of the bone, that the bone had been worked into a point that could be used for probing or piercing if attached to a wood shaft and was therefore representative of an aboriginal artifact contaminated with Crawford's DNA.

---

para. 163 in *Pickton*, 2009 BCCA, above note 96, Finch C.J.B.C. found that the trial judge did not apply the correct "some evidence" admissibility test for the evidence pertaining to Feliks and Hall.

106 See *Pickton*, 2006 BCSC 1601, above note 104 at paras. 3–8 for a description of each count of first-degree murder.

107 *Ibid.* at para. 18.

108 *Ibid.* at para. 19.

109 *Ibid.*

110 *Ibid.* at paras. 16–17.

111 *Ibid.* at para. 17.

The forensic anthropologist called by the defence further opined that approximately 140 aboriginal artifacts were found as a result of the search of the Pickton property.[112]

With respect to the proposed similar fact evidence, the defence argued that the Crawford evidence did not meet the admissibility test on the identification issue as (1) the Crown failed to establish that the bone represented Crawford's remains, (2) it was not sufficient evidence to allow a reasonable jury to conclude Pickton murdered Crawford, and (3) it introduced "considerable moral prejudice." The defence further argued that the bone was consistent with the creation of a hunting tool rather than butchery. Trial fairness was also identified as an issue since the defence position was that Pickton's ability to respond to the evidence was "significantly undermined" by the bone's destruction as there was not adequate record-keeping of the bone's "unusual attributes."[113]

The trial judge held that the Crawford bone evidence was inadmissible as similar fact evidence because there was insufficient evidence to link Pickton and Crawford.[114] Bellwood's evidence could link Pickton to Crawford if a reasonable inference could be drawn that the bone's discovery in the cistern was the result of her dismembered remains being fed to pigs. The trial judge found that this inference could not be drawn based upon considerations relating to the geography of the remains, the butchery practices of Pickton, and the admissions made by Pickton to two witnesses—Hiscox and Bellwood. Similar to Bellwood, Hiscox's evidence was that Pickton suggested that, if Hiscox ever needed to get rid of a body, he could throw it in the piggery. The trial judge found this to be a general comment that did not advance a linkage between Pickton and the similar acts since there was no evidence to suggest that Feliks and Hall were fed to pigs and, as a result, the statement could not be attributed any weight to establish such a link.[115]

In short, the trial judge found that: (1) the location of the remains on Pickton's property did not sufficiently link Pickton to Crawford's death

---

112 *Ibid.*

113 *Ibid.* at paras. 16–17 and 30–33. At para. 30, the position of the forensic anthropologist called by the defence (that the bone represented an aboriginal artifact) is characterized by the court as "unchallenged evidence," implying that this particular position was not put to the forensic anthropologist called by the Crown for an opinion.

114 *Pickton*, 2009 BCCA, above note 96 at para. 156, citing *Pickton*, 2006 BCSC 1601, above note 104 at paras. 66 and 69–75.

115 *Pickton*, 2006 BCSC 1601, *ibid.* at paras. 48–49.

and/or dismemberment; (2) the "modified appearance" of the bone did not sufficiently connect to a butchering practice unique to Pickton or a specific tool accessible to him; and (3) Hiscox's evidence did not sufficiently link Pickton to the similar acts of the crimes alleged and, although Bellwood's evidence was compelling, it was insufficient to link Pickton to Crawford without evidence specifying the time that Pickton kept pigs in the piggery and, specifically, whether the piggery was in use in late 1999 when Crawford disappeared.[116]

Further, the trial judge held that the potential prejudice that may be caused by the evidence outweighed its probative value, particularly in light of the "unique prejudice" resulting from the inability of the defence experts to examine the bone, preventing the defence from making full answer and defence by advancing its argument that the bone was an aboriginal artifact contaminated by Crawford's DNA.[117]

On appeal, the Crown advanced an argument similar to that respecting the evidence of Jane Doe's bones: the trial judge's standard to establish a link between the evidence and Pickton was too high, the judge erred by applying the wrong test with respect to similar fact evidence, the judge erred in his prejudicial effect and probative value assessment, and the conclusion that no link was established was unreasonable.[118] The appeal was allowed and the court held that the "trial judge erred in law in holding that the evidence concerning Feliks, Hall and Crawford was inadmissible,"[119] finding that "ample" evidence linked Pickton to the similar fact evidence and that the judge applied a more stringent test than the "some evidence" standard:

> In effect, the trial judge assumed the role of the jury in examining and assessing this evidence. He went well beyond his role as a gatekeeper in ensuring that the evidence met not only the test for similarity, but also met the requirement of "some evidence" to show a link to the accused.
>
> . . .
>
> I think this error may also be said to be a *Morin* error [where the trial judge employed a piecemeal approach to the evidence] because of the defence position that the destruction of the Crawford bone impaired its

116 *Pickton*, 2009 BCCA, above note 96 at para. 156, where the reasons of the trial judge are quoted; see paras. 69–75 of *Pickton*, 2006 BCSC 1601, above note 104.

117 *Pickton*, 2006 BCSC 1601, *ibid.* at paras. 81–86. See also *Pickton*, 2009 BCCA, above note 96 at paras. 158–59.

118 *Pickton*, 2009 BCCA, *ibid.* at paras. 160–61.

119 *Ibid.* at para. 169.

> ability to make full answer and defence. The defence disputed that the bone found in the cistern was part of the remains of Ms. Crawford. What was not disputed was that Ms. Crawford's DNA was on that bone. At a minimum, the trial judge ought to have permitted the Crown to lead evidence that Wendy Crawford's DNA was found in the cistern at the end of the pig trough. The order excluding any reference to the fact of her DNA being found in connection with that bone goes further than was required to protect Mr. Pickton's fair trial interests.[120]

The Pickton case is a particularly complex example of the use of forensic anthropological evidence in a criminal proceeding, where challenges were mounted to both the forensic evidence itself as well as the legal arguments at issue, as advanced by both the Crown and the defence. The interpretations to be gleaned from the recovered bones were challenged at length, contributing to an extensive procedural history that reflected the monumental effort involved in processing the largest crime scene in Canadian history, requiring investigators to search the equivalent of 148 Olympic-sized pools of earth.[121]

In conclusion, forensic anthropological evidence has been used in Canadian courts for almost forty years. With expertise in the recovery and analysis of human remains, forensic anthropologists provide evidence on a variety of issues, from the events occurring around the time of death, to the disposal and any subsequent disturbance of the remains. Forensic anthropological evidence has proven useful in high-profile cases, cold cases, and cases in which bodies were destroyed by fire. The role of the forensic anthropologist in the courtroom is to adhere to an ethos of education, teaching the trier of fact about the discipline and its limitations in the context of the specific case under consideration. The role of the lawyer in cases involving forensic anthropological evidence, whether Crown or defence, is to critically assess the value and limitations of the discipline (including the possibility of bias)[122] for the purpose of presenting an argument that is not only compelling, but accurate to the evidence.

---

120 *Ibid.* at paras. 166 and 168. See, generally, *R. v. Morin*, [1988] 2 S.C.R. 345.

121 Ethan Baron, "Combing Canada's Largest Crime Scene" *The Vancouver Province* (10 December 2007), online: www.canada.com/theprovince/news/story.html?id=57f180ce-02b0-4925-b363-d986a902a2ee.

122 Sherry Nakhaeizadeh, Itiel E. Dror, & Ruth M. Morgan, "Cognitive Bias in Forensic Anthropology: Visual Assessment of Skeletal Remains Is Susceptible to Confirmation Bias" (2014) 54 *Science & Justice* 208.

CHAPTER 12

Forensic Biology and DNA

Cecilia Hageman

LEGAL CONTEXT: CAITLIN PAKOSH AND SARAH HARLAND-LOGAN

A. OVERVIEW OF THE DISCIPLINE: FORENSIC BIOLOGY AND DNA

Forensic biology incorporates the related areas of body fluid identification (also called serology) and deoxyribonucleic acid (DNA) analysis. Serological techniques are used to screen evidence items for the presence and type of body fluid deposition. At its most fundamental level, forensic DNA analysis, like many other forensic tests, is simply a comparison technique that addresses the question of attribution—can two things, be they two fingerprints, hairs, fibres, glass, paint fragments, or in this chapter's case, DNA-containing body tissue cells, be excluded as originating from the same source? If not, the two exhibits either came from the same source or from different sources that, by coincidence, happen to share the same physical or, for DNA evidence, biological attributes. Compared to other forms of forensic evidence, DNA analysis offers the clearest statistical picture of the alternative hypothesis—the probability of a coincidental DNA profile match is accurately determined using well-established principles of probability, statistics, and genetics.

Serological analyses target the biochemicals and cells that define the distinctive functional characteristics of different body fluids, such as hemoglobin in blood and spermatozoa in semen. The targets of interest in forensic DNA analysis are microscopic strands of deoxyribonucleic acid, located in almost every cell in a biological organism. Within long, linear arrays called chromosomes, DNA contains the molecular instructions to build and operate a biological organism, be it a microbe, plant, or animal.

All humans share mostly the same DNA information, but display minor variations at some locations, or "loci," along the chromosomes. Forensic DNA analysis takes advantage of, and tests for, some of these minor DNA differences to compare and distinguish biological evidence samples.

In 1985, Alec Jeffreys and his colleagues at the University of Leicester and the United Kingdom Home Office Forensic Science Service fundamentally changed forensic biology with the introduction of the first forensic DNA technique, restriction fragment length polymorphisms (RFLPs), into the analysis of criminal case evidence.[1] While forensic biology techniques have progressed far beyond RFLP over the last three decades, they all work in the same general fashion: isolating the DNA from samples of biological evidence, targeting known areas of DNA exhibiting minor differences, and visualizing these differences in the form of DNA profiles. The evolution in forensic DNA technology has come from the many technical improvements in targeting and visualizing DNA differences, as well as from significant gains in standardization, sensitivity, discrimination potential, and efficiency. Today, for most criminal and civil casework applications, the majority of forensic DNA laboratories worldwide offer a technology known as short tandem repeat (STR) analysis. This chapter will focus primarily on describing and explaining the STR approach to the forensic analysis of biological evidence samples.

Effectively prosecuting or defending a forensic DNA case, or reviewing an old case with a view to DNA retesting, requires at least a rudimentary, and sometimes greater, understanding of the processes underlying the production and interpretation of profiles, and the role that quality assurance plays in assessing and ensuring the reliability of results. Of equal importance is an appreciation of the statistics surrounding "match" results, as well as an understanding of the probative value of the presence or absence of DNA evidence within the context of particular case circumstances. This chapter will delve into all of these subjects.

B. THE SCIENCE OF FORENSIC BIOLOGY AND DNA

1) Introduction: From Crime Scene to DNA Profile

In the laboratory, a forensic DNA analysis starts with a sample of biological evidence—a blood stain on clothing, a swab of a beer bottle to gather

1 Peter Gill, Alec J. Jeffreys, & David J. Werrett, "Forensic Application of DNA 'Fingerprints'" (1985) 318 *Nature* 577 [Gill].

lip and cheek cells of the drinker, or a cutout of the inside of a baseball cap to sample forehead skin cells of the wearer, to name just a few examples. Typical cell types encountered in forensic criminal casework include blood, semen, saliva (containing the buccal cells from the inside cheeks), nasal secretions, tooth and bone marrow, vaginal cells, skin cells, and the roots of hairs.[2] The laboratory analysis ends with a profile picture—a graphical representation of the DNA variants derived from these cells. This profile is interpreted and compared to other similarly produced profiles.

The final forensic DNA profile is most simply viewed as a set of numbers representing the DNA variants at target locations. These DNA locations are known as "loci" and are the genetic equivalents of addresses or postal codes. Genetic differences at loci are variants, or "alleles." A person's Short Tandem Repeat (STR)-based DNA profile will look something like the following example in Table 12.1, where there is a pair of numbers associated with each genetic address. Each number within a pair represents a DNA variant (allele) inherited from one of the donor's two parents. The Xs represent two X sex chromosomes, denoting a female source.[3]

TABLE 12.1. Short tandem repeat profile produced from a PowerPlex®16[4] analysis of a blood sample of a female donor.[5] PowerPlex®16 analyzes sixteen genetic addresses on the human genome, fifteen from chromosome pairs 1 through 22, and one address from the sex chromosomes. Each number in the pair of results is an allele, a DNA variant.[6]

Genetic address	DNA STR alleles	Genetic address	DNA STR alleles	Genetic address	DNA STR alleles	Genetic address	DNA STR alleles
D3S1358	12, 16	Penta E	10, 15	D16S539	13, 13	vWA	16, 17
TH01	9.3, 9.3	D5S818	12, 13	CSF1PO	10, 11	D8S1179	10, 13
D21S11	28, 29	D13S317	12, 12	Penta D	10, 12	TPOX	8, 8
D18S51	12, 16	D7S820	10, 11	Amelogenin	X, X	FGA	21, 24

2 Urine and feces may contain DNA from cells that line the bladder and intestines, respectively, but are considered to be relatively poor sources for forensic DNA typing purposes.

3 A male donor would display an X and a Y in his DNA profile.

4 PowerPlex®16, a product of Promega Corporation (Madison, WI), is one of a number of commercial kits available to analyze DNA variants for forensic purposes. Identifiler®Plus from Life Technologies (Foster City, CA) also tests fifteen STR locations plus amelogenin.

5 See Figure 12.1 for the laboratory results from which this interpretation was derived.

6 This is the profile of the author of this chapter, Cecilia Hageman.

Between sampling the biological evidence and creating a final forensic DNA profile, there is a multistep laboratory procedure that removes and purifies the DNA in a sample, measures how much DNA there is, zeroes in on and makes easy-to-see copies of the STR areas of interest, separates out and visualizes these copies of DNA, and then assigns STR size designations (the final numbers) to the DNA variants. The whole set of allele number pairs is the DNA profile of the sample, which may be compared to other similarly produced profiles in a case or to a data bank of stored DNA profiles. A disclosure of the contents of a forensic DNA case file will include documentation from each of these laboratory steps, as well as from the interpretation and comparison of profiles. Case file documentation tends to be highly technical and will almost invariably require the assistance of a forensic biologist to review and decipher. While not intended as a substitute for such assistance, what follows is a description of each of these steps as well as some points of advice for reviewing case file disclosure documents. This is preceded by a short description of some basic principles of genetics, the study of inheritance.

2) What Is DNA?

Deoxyribonucleic acid is a molecule found in almost all human[7] cells. It contains the instructional code for building a human being, starting from his or her origins as a single fertilized egg to running the biochemical processes necessary for growing and maintaining that human throughout his or her life. The DNA in each human cell is organized into forty-six structures known as chromosomes, the "chapters" of this genetic manual. If a chromosome were to be completely unraveled and stretched out, it would reveal a seemingly simple structure—a single line of many millions of "bases" in a row, like pearls on a very long string. These bases are the letters of the genetic alphabet, and there are only four of them: Adenine, Guanine, Thymine, and Cytosine. A tiny stretch of a chromosome may look like, for example, - - A A T T T A G G A C - -. A single "gene," a mere sentence in the informational manual, contains the code for making a particular molecule associated with life, such as insulin, and might be just a few hundred bases long. The human genome[8] is comprised of approximately 6.6 billion bases/

7 And, of course, any living thing. This chapter will focus on forensic DNA typing in human samples.

8 A genome is the total genetic content of an organism.

letters in sequence combinations using just these four letters. As human DNA contains about 30,000 genes, most of the 6.6 billion letters do not "code" for known molecules. Different animal, plant, and microbial species also are each defined by their own chromosome numbers and sequence combinations using just these four bases.

DNA is found in a stable double-stranded structure, the "double helix," where two strands come together lengthwise, and the base pairs line up like steps in a twisted ladder. In this ladder, A and T pair only with each other, while G and C pair likewise only with each other (the "base-pairing rule"). The tiny portion of the chromosome described above would be a part of a double strand, *complemented* by a second strand, following the base-pairing rule:

A - T
A - T
T - A
T - A
T - A
A - T
G - C
G - C
A - T
C - G

This simple pairing rule allows chromosomes to replicate themselves to produce new cells, all with the same full set of chromosomes, in a process called mitosis. Replication is accomplished by the double helix opening, the strands separating, and *each strand acting as a template for remaking the complementary strand*:

A T
A T
T A
T A
T A
A T
G C
G C
A T
C G

Every time this happens, the DNA replicates. From one cell, two arise, each with a full complement of genetic material, and growth and cell regeneration can occur:

A-T A-T
A-T A-T
T-A T-A
T-A T-A
T-A T-A
A-T A-T
G-C G-C
G-C G-C
A-T A-T
C-G C-G

The base-pairing rule is exploited at the analytical level, where the key to finding any particular known stretch of DNA, such as a location of interest to the forensic scientist, is to simply open up the double helices of the chromosomes[9] and add a small (a few dozen bases long) piece of "finder" DNA, called a probe or primer, which *finds and binds to only its individual complementary target sequence*. This is the basis for almost all forensic DNA protocols, and indeed many medical, agricultural, and other biological applications.

All humans begin their development as a single cell that arises from the union of a sperm and an egg. The sperm contains twenty-three chromosomes from the father, and the egg contains twenty-three chromosomes from the mother. The fertilized egg therefore contains twenty-three pairs of chromosomes.[10] As the fertilized egg divides again and again to develop into a multi-celled organism, the full set of forty-six chromosomes is copied each time a cell divides in two and is therefore present in almost every human cell.[11] This means that a DNA profile from a person's blood is the same as that from his or her skin, saliva, hair roots, and other body cell types. This also means that humans have a pair of alleles at each genetic location of his or her STR profile, as seen in the Table 12.1 data. Humans display genetic differences in less than 1 percent of their total genome and

9 This is accomplished by cycles of heating and cooling.

10 Labeled Pair One to Pair Twenty-Two, inclusive, and a pair of sex chromosomes, X and Y.

11 Human red blood cells do not have a nucleus with chromosomes. Forensic DNA profiles from blood originate primarily from nucleated white blood cells.

it is from a tiny part of this 1 percent that forensic scientists produce DNA profiles that forensically distinguish human beings. Genetic differences take one of two general forms:

- *Sequence variations*: A single base at a particular genetic location may differ among persons. This is a sequence variation or single nucleotide[12] polymorphism (SNP, pronounced "snip"). For example, a small stretch of DNA at a SNP address might take two forms, Allele 1: AAATTAATT**G**AAATAC and Allele 2: AAATTAATT**C**AAATAC. A human could carry two allele 1s, two allele 2s, or one of each. Millions of SNPs are found throughout the human genome and are the basis of a number of new forensic, as well as many medical and ancestry,[13] tests.
- *Length variations*: Imagine the DNA sequence "AATG", repeated, end-to-end, a number of times. The more times it is repeated, the longer that particular stretch of DNA. This is an example of an STR, a short piece of DNA that is repeated over and over again, in tandem. Tens of thousands of short tandem repeats are scattered throughout the human genome.[14] For example, a person may inherit an allele size "5," AATGAATGAATGAATGAATG, at an STR location from one parent, and an allele size "6," AATGAATGAATGAATGAATGAATG, at this same location from the other parent. This person's STR type for this location would be "5, 6."

The numbers in Table 12.1 represent STRs of particular tandem number sizes at fifteen chromosomal addresses, along with test results from the sex chromosomes. Genetic address D3S1358, found on the third pair of chromosomes, for example, exhibits many different variants in humans, from about nine tandem repetitions of a four-letter sequence to twenty such repetitions. In the Table 12.1 example, the source is STR type 12, 16; she inherited an STR allele twelve repeats long from one parent and sixteen repeats long from her other parent. Because of the large number

12 A nucleotide is a molecule that contains the base.

13 For example, National Geographic's Genographic Project, online: genographic.nationalgeographic.com/about.

14 These locations have sometimes been labelled as "junk" DNA, because they do not appear to code for particular biological necessities of life. However, scientists have all but abandoned that inaccurate description, as these genetic addresses may have functions other than specific coding for biological molecules. See The ENCODE Project: ENCyclopedia of DNA Elements (NIH National Human Genome Research Institute), online: www.genome.gov/encode.

of different STR alleles found at many of these STR addresses and the resulting high discrimination potential, as well as ease of analysis, STR length variations are the basis of most forensic DNA kits used in criminal casework as well as forensic DNA data banks.

2) Inside the Laboratory: Developing an STR Profile from a Biological Sample

a) Examination of Items for Body Fluids and Sampling for DNA

Before forensic DNA analysis can proceed, biological evidence must first be located and sampled. Case circumstances dictate pre-DNA analysis strategies, with some cases requiring testing to find and distinguish body fluid types. Sexual assault cases may necessitate testing evidence items for the presence of semen or saliva, while aggravated assault cases typically require testing for blood. Other samples require no body fluid pre-screening, and sampling decisions are based on expectations for potential DNA transfer through handling and skin friction. Sampling clothing for the wearer's skin cells targets fabric areas in close frictional or body fluid contact, while sampling eating and drinking implements target areas in normal contact with the mouth. Sampling for DNA involves swabbing off or cutting out a small portion of biological material and placing this subsample into a small plastic tube or well.[15] Case notes should indicate the size of the biological sample removed, where it was sampled on an evidence item, and whether any biological sample remains for further testing.

Many current tests for the presence of blood, semen, and saliva are the same as those used for decades, with some improvements.[16] Saliva is usually located with the detection of amylase, a digestive enzyme produced in the mouth to break down food starch. Tests such as Phadebas®[17] target amylase to indicate the potential presence of saliva, especially if a large amount of amylase is found, but cannot confirm its presence because am-

---

15 Samples destined for robotic analysis in the next step will be placed in individual wells of special plastic plates that contain ninety-six such wells. These samples will then be identified in the case notes by their place in the plate; for example, Row E, Column 2 would be sample E02.

16 A detailed description of many of these tests can be found in many general forensics and criminalistics textbooks, and also in Kimberley A. Johnston & Cecilia Hageman, "Blood and Bodily Substances" in G.M. Chayko, E.D. Gulliver, & D.V. Macdougall, eds., *Forensic Evidence in Canada* (Aurora, ON: Canada Law Book Inc, 1991).

17 Magle AB, Lund, Sweden; other test options include Saligae® (Abacus Diagnostics, West Hills, CA) and RSID™ (Independent Forensics, Lombard, IL).

ylase is also found in other body fluids, although to a lesser degree. Semen is presumptively indicated by the presence of acid phosphatase, a ubiquitous enzyme in numerous body fluids but found in relatively large amounts in seminal fluid. Semen is conclusively identified by the additional presence of spermatozoa (sperm cells), by prostate specific antigen (PSA or p30, a protein secreted by the prostate gland),[18] or by DNA results that indicate the presence of spermatozoa-derived DNA in an extraction procedure that specifically targets sperm cells. There are many tests for the presence of blood that target hemoglobin,[19] with varying specificities and sensitivities. While more specific tests for the presence of human blood are available,[20] they are usually redundant when samples are already destined for human-specific DNA analysis.

New approaches to body fluid identification are poised to revolutionize forensic serology, although the relatively quick, sensitive, and inexpensive presumptive chemical techniques are expected to remain in general use, especially for the initial screening of exhibits for body fluid evidence. The new techniques improve upon either or both the sensitivity and specificity of the current screening techniques by targeting forensically novel cell-specific attributes, with the potential to effectively distinguish more forensically relevant cell types, including skin, nasal, and vaginal cells, all of which are largely undistinguishable by current serological methodologies.[21]

b) Extraction: Getting the DNA Out

There are many ways to remove and purify DNA from a biological sample, all relatively equal in their ability to perform these functions. Organic chemical extractions with phenol and chloroform were used extensively in the earlier days of forensic DNA analysis, and are still performed by hand on individual samples today. For the last ten to fifteen years, most of the larger forensic laboratories have implemented robotic technology to perform the extraction function efficiently for large batches of samples, although some samples may still be individually processed through

---

18 ABAcard®p30, Abacus Diagnostics, West Hills, CA.

19 Including Kastle-Meyer, Hemastix™, Luminol, and Bluestar®.

20 ABAcard®HemaTrace®, Abacus Diagnostics (West Hills, CA).

21 Jong-Lyul Park et al., "Identification of Body Fluid-Specific DNA Methylation Markers for Use in Forensic Science" (2014) 13 *Forensic Science International: Genetics* 147; Sarah S. Silva et al., "Forensic miRNA: Potential Biomarker for Body Fluids?" (2015) 14 *Forensic Science International: Genetics* 1.

a chemical extraction to assist in the removal of contaminants. Robotic protocols use "solid-phase" technologies[22] that open biological cells, selectively bind DNA to magnetic beads, and then wash off the non-DNA components, leaving the purified DNA for further analysis. The keys to all these different chemistries are maximizing the yield of DNA from a sample, cleaning the sample of biological and environmental impurities, maintaining a chain of custody, and avoiding sample-to-sample contamination.[23] For each sample, the end result of the extraction process is a small tube or well of liquid containing DNA in a few microliters (μl) of buffer solution.[24] That tube contains "genomic" DNA, meaning this DNA has not undergone any further analytical process—it is pure DNA, released from cells, protected in a liquid environment. If a reanalysis of a sample is required for retesting or for independent testing, the scientist should be asked to review the laboratory case notes to determine how much, if any, of this genomic DNA remains in storage at the laboratory or with investigators.[25]

If a sample contains spermatozoa, a special "differential" extraction of DNA is usually performed in order to separate, as much as possible, male sperm cell DNA from any other (usually female-sourced) DNA. From such a sample, two DNA profiles are obtained—one primarily from sperm cells (the "sperm fraction"), and the second from other cell types (the "female fraction" or "epithelial fraction").

c) Quantitation: Measuring the DNA Yield

A tiny portion of the genomic DNA liquid extraction of a sample is sacrificed to determine if any DNA is even present and, if so, how much. This is important for a number of reasons. If there is no DNA, or if there is an insufficient amount to develop a DNA profile, then the analysis usually stops. The final report will alert the reader to the fact that no DNA or insufficient DNA was obtained. Each forensic DNA laboratory establishes, through validation testing, its own threshold quantity of DNA required to produce a reliable forensic DNA profile for interpretation and also the optimal amount of DNA to proceed in the subsequent steps of the process. In addition, the

---

22 For example, DNA IQ™ (Promega, Madison, WI).

23 Each batch of extractions will also contain positive and negative controls, the latter acting as a check on contamination.

24 A microlitre is a millionth of a litre—it corresponds to the volume of a small drop of liquid. A buffer is a liquid that preserves a sample.

25 Genomic DNA may be stored as frozen liquid or dried onto filter paper and stored at room temperature.

interpretation of DNA profiles by a reporting scientist is performed with a consideration of the quality and quantity of the underlying DNA sample.

Modern techniques for quantitation involve real-time quantitative polymerase chain reaction (RT-qPCR). They are based on a procedure that measures the time it takes to make copies of a human specific DNA sequence. The more starting DNA there is, the faster copies are made. The copying times are compared to times obtained for known quantities of DNA, resulting in estimates of starting DNA for all samples. Commercial kits[26] are sensitive enough to detect DNA from only one or a few cells. The RT-qPCR technology and case file documentation are quite complicated, but the end results are relatively straightforward. For each sample, the case notes will describe the volume of the original extraction extract (usually about 15 to 25 μl), how much of that volume was sacrificed for RT-qPCR quantitation (usually about 1 or 2 μl), and how much DNA was obtained in that sacrificed subsample. From that estimate, the total amount of DNA is calculated for the remaining extract. DNA quantities are typically presented as nanograms (ng) or picograms (pg).[27] Most techniques measure both the total human DNA in a sample extract (called the "auto"[28] estimate), and the proportion of that DNA that is associated only with the male Y sex chromosome (the "Y" quantitation estimate). In a sample from one or more females, this "Y" quantitation estimate would be zero. The separate quantitation of male DNA is useful to highlight those samples in cases that have male DNA, where male cells are actually the ones of probative value. It also assists in alerting scientists to those samples with many female cells mixed with few male cells (for example, under the fingernails of female victims of male assaults, or vaginal swabs containing semen from a vasectomized male). This finding may lead the scientist to attempt other special testing, such as Y-STR testing.

d) Amplification: Targeting and Replicating Short Tandem Repeats

Amplification is the critical point in forensic DNA typing. It is where the process zeroes in on the genetic STR addresses of interest and ignores all the other DNA sequences of a sample. As described previously,

---

26 For example, Plexor® HY QPCR® kit (Promega, Madison, WI) and Quantifiler® Duo DNA Quantification Kit (Life Technologies, Foster City, CA).

27 A nanogram is a billionth of a gram, and a picogram is a thousandth of a nanogram. A single human cell will contain approximately 6 to 7 picograms of DNA.

28 "Auto" stands for "autosomal," a description of the twenty-two chromosomes that are not sex chromosomes.

complementary strands of DNA act as templates for the replication of chromosomes, allowing for cells to divide and proliferate and for organisms to grow. Amplification is just DNA replication on a much smaller scale. It is the replication not of whole chromosomes, but of small portions of the DNA at particular STR addresses.[29]

Amplification is accomplished by taking a measured portion of a sample DNA extract[30] and adding it to a mix that contains all the necessities[31] to make copies of the STR sequences. This mix contains "primers," small pieces of DNA that bind close along the chromosome strand to the STR addresses of interest because they are complementary to, and therefore target, those particular sequences. Strands of DNA containing the STRs, *just at those STR locations*, are then copied many times over, resulting in millions of target copies for further analysis.[32] Thinking back to the concept of the DNA as an instructional manual, consider amplification to be a form of "molecular photocopying" of that manual, but only for a few select pages. The copies of DNA are called "amplicons," and are DNA strands containing the sequences of the STR attached to the primer. They are typically between about 100 and 400 bases long. The more repeat units in the STR, the longer the amplicon. Because the primers are labelled with dyes, the amplicons can be detected in the next part of the procedure.

Amplification is accomplished using commercial kits containing the ingredients necessary to amplify samples at a number of STR locations all at once. These kits are "multiplexes," and the number of target STR loci in multiplexes has increased from a just few in the mid-1990s,[33] to nine or thirteen[34] in the late 1990s, and currently sits at about sixteen[35] or more, providing increased discrimination potential with the addition of each test location. Different commercial kits share common STR test locations nec-

29 Or any DNA sequence of interest—amplification is a basic tool in myriad biotechnology protocols.

30 For most kits, this is optimized to about 1 or 2 nanograms, representing about 150 cells to 300 cells.

31 This mix contains the bases and also an enzyme that adds the bases to the growing string of DNA.

32 The case notes will contain complex technical notes describing the DNA replication process, better known as the polymerase chain reaction (PCR). Briefly, the samples are subjected to multiple rounds of heating and cooling in a device known as a thermocycler, with a duplication of DNA product with each round.

33 Quadruplex, Forensic Science Service, Reading, UK.

34 ProflierPlus™ and CoFiler™ (Applied Biosystems, Foster City, CA).

35 PowerPlex16 (Promega, Madison, WI) and Identifiler®Plus (Life Technologies/Applied Biosystems, Foster City, CA).

essary for inter-laboratory comparisons (the thirteen COmbined DNA Index System (CODIS) loci[36] are the lingua franca of the forensic STR world) and data bank uploads, but may differ in other STR target addresses.

e) Separation and Profile Production

Amplification results in millions of strands ("amplicons") of each STR locus tested, and the next step is to detect them and measure strand lengths. Each sample is subjected to a process called electrophoresis where the amplicons travel through a column containing a gel; the longer the piece of DNA, the more time it takes to move through the gel. As the amplicon strands emerge from the gel—smallest, first, to largest, last—each length is captured by a camera that detects the attached dye. The time at which the camera captures the dye is correlated to the size of the strand, which is then compared to known size standards.[37] The final product is a picture of the profile, an "electropherogram,"[38] where each peak in the picture signifies the camera's timed capture of a particular amplicon length, and therefore allele, at each genetic address.

The Table 12.1 results were interpreted from the Figure 12.1 electropherogram. The designations in grey background are the genetic STR locations. Peaks, the little skinny "hills," signify STR results. Each STR allele is a peak, representing the camera's capture of the dye attached to the strands of copied DNA. The peak height reflects the number of amplicons copied—if a person has two different alleles at one test location, *the peaks should be of roughly similar heights, as the copying process should not significantly favour one target over another*. To interpret the results, observe the numbers in boxes under each peak:

- The first number is the allele designation, the length of the STR.
- The second number is the peak height, a measure of how many copies were made of that STR.

---

36 CODIS is the FBI's software for DNA data banks. There are currently thirteen CODIS STR locations, but this number will increase to accommodate significant growth in data bank sizes in the United States and other jurisdictions.

37 Special software (e.g., GeneMapper, Life Technologies/Applied Biosystems, Foster City, CA) is used to perform measurements and comparisons to standards. These data are commonly kept on a digital file at the laboratory, and are usually not part of the hard copy disclosure of case file documents.

38 Case notes will typically provide electropherograms for all successful amplifications, as well as for positive and negative controls. Allele peaks in the negative control may signify contamination, which could affect the interpretation of other samples in the same batch.

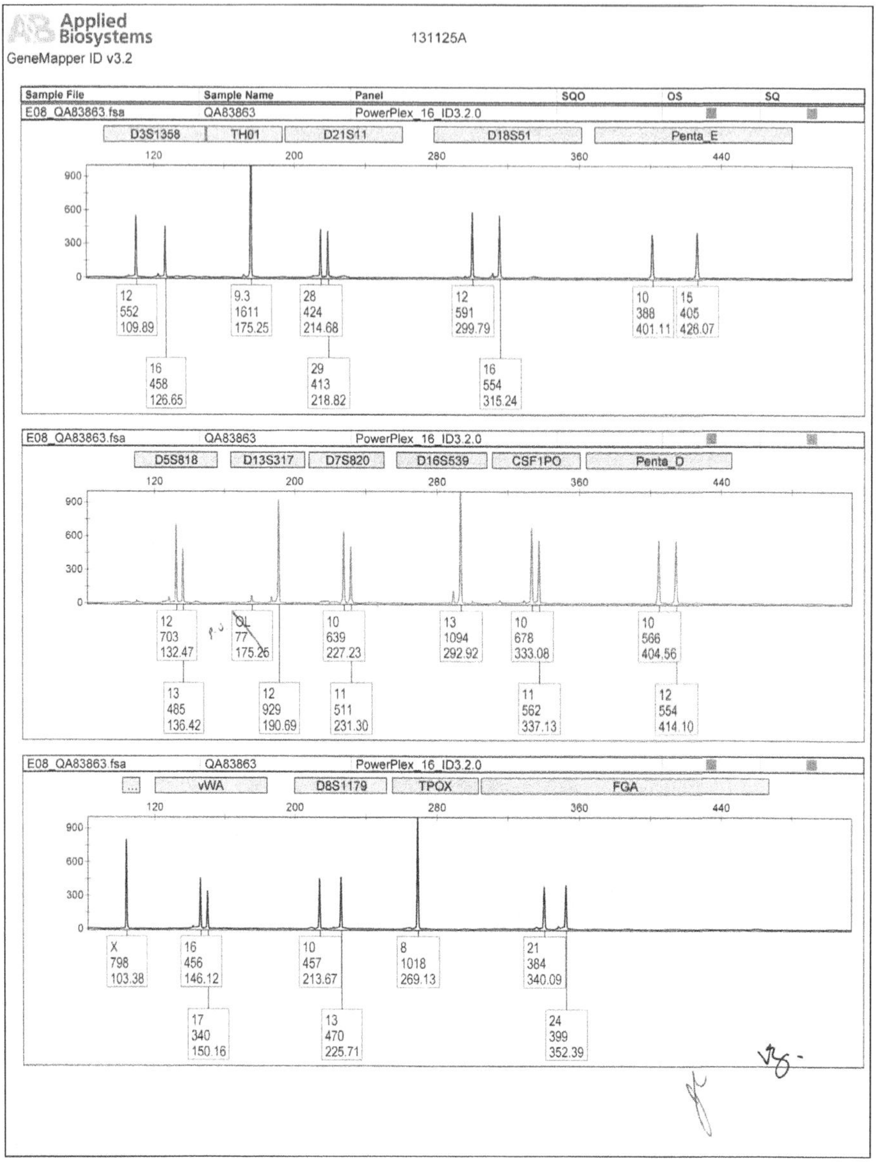

FIGURE 12.1. Electropherogram, or the picture of the DNA profile, of the author, Cecilia Hageman. Courtesy of the Wyndham Forensic Group Inc., Guelph, Ontario.

For example, at the first location (D3S1358), the contributing source is STR type 12, 16—this is because there are two peaks, one of STR repeat length 12 and the other of repeat length 16. The roughly similar peak heights of 552 and 458, respectively, are as expected for a single source that has equal quantities of each type. Moving down this line, there is one peak under the next genetic address, TH01. The contributing source inherited the same STR size from both parents, allele size 9.3.[39] This analysis is done for all sixteen genetic locations, resulting in the interpretation originally described in Table 12.1.

3) Profile Interpretation

The scientist is tasked with the interpretation of electropherograms, which involves addressing and answering key questions: Which peaks signify true STR alleles? Are any of the peaks artifacts of the technical process (that is, are any of the peaks just background noise)? Does the profile come from one or more than one source? In a mixture profile (that is, from a profile of DNA from two or more contributors), what are the relative contributions of each source? Does the profile appear degraded, with the possibility of missing data peaks? Is there a genetic anomaly that must be considered?[40] This interpretation is accomplished with a knowledge of the results of the laboratory's internal validation process, where, through experimentation, the laboratory evaluates the technology with a view to establishing reliability and limitations over a range of casework conditions.[41]

Validation assesses the technology's sensitivity, specificity, accuracy, and reproducibility, and its ability to produce reliable results from mixtures as well as limited and degraded samples.[42] For example, validation will set expectations for allele peak heights. Recall that the technique is an amplification, a copying of target STR sequences. The peak height is a reflection of the underlying DNA quantity—the more DNA, the more amplicons copied, and the greater the peak height. If a person has two alleles at one STR

39 When there is a decimal point in an allele name, the STR allele does not conform to the simple repeat unit number—the fraction denotes either a single base that is missing (.3), two bases that are missing (.2), or three bases that are missing (.1). In the TH01 9.3 allele, one of the STR repeat units is missing a single base, resulting in the 9.3 fraction designation.

40 For example, some people display three genetic variants at a single address. These patterns are "tri-allelic," and are due to a mutation—a duplication of genetic information along a chromosome.

41 Once completed, validation provides the basis for interpretation guidelines, a typical disclosure request for counsel who wish to delve into technical and interpretive details.

42 For a full description of validation criteria, see the FBI's *Scientific Working Group on DNA Analysis Methods (SWGDAM) Validation Guidelines for DNA Analysis Methods* (approved December 2012), online: SWGDAM media.wix.com/ugd/4344b0_cbc27d16dcb64fd88cb36ab2a2a25e4c.pdf.

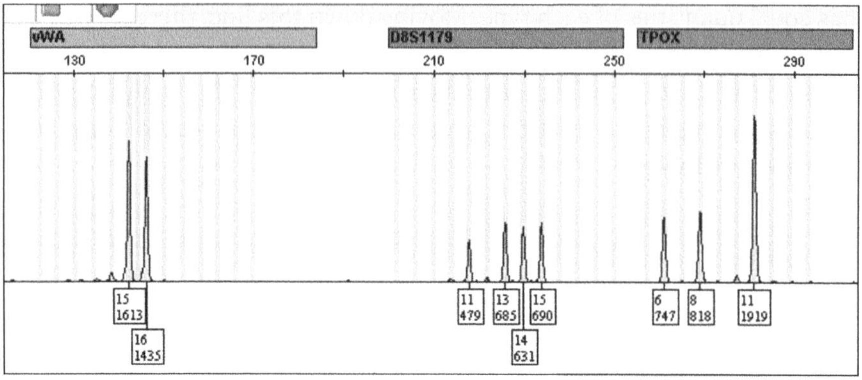

FIGURE 12.2. This figure shows a portion of a mixture profile from equal DNA contributions of two persons. Courtesy of the Centre of Forensic Sciences, Toronto, Ontario.

location, these alleles should be equally targeted and copied, resulting in roughly equal peak heights for allele pairs, as seen throughout Figure 12.1. If the peak heights are significantly different within an address, this could signify the presence of two (or more) unequal contributors to the profile. Validation results will also set expectations for artifacts. The current STR technology tends to produce small peaks that do not actually represent true STR alleles. In Figure 12.1, there are numerous instances of a tiny peak just to the left of a large peak. These are "stutter" peaks, not true alleles, and a well-known artifact of STR amplification. The peak marked "p" is another artifact, called "pull up," caused by a slight misreading of the dye colour by the camera and associated software.

The electropherogram in Figure 12.1 was obtained from a sample from one person, and the interpretation is relatively straightforward. What happens when there are two or more contributors to a sample? Multi-source mixture profiles are a common occurrence in criminal casework. Figure 12.2 shows a portion of a mixture profile from equal DNA contributions of two persons.

The presence of more than one contributor is obvious—there are four peaks at location D8S1179, and a single person cannot have four parents. Taking into account the number of peaks as well as peak heights, there are different ways that this profile could logically come about, and the interpretation and subsequent comparisons must take into account all such possibilities. At the vWA location, there are two equal peaks, at alleles 15 and 16; assuming a dual source (two contributors), either persons with types 15, 15 and 16, 16 contributed DNA, or two type 15, 16s contributed

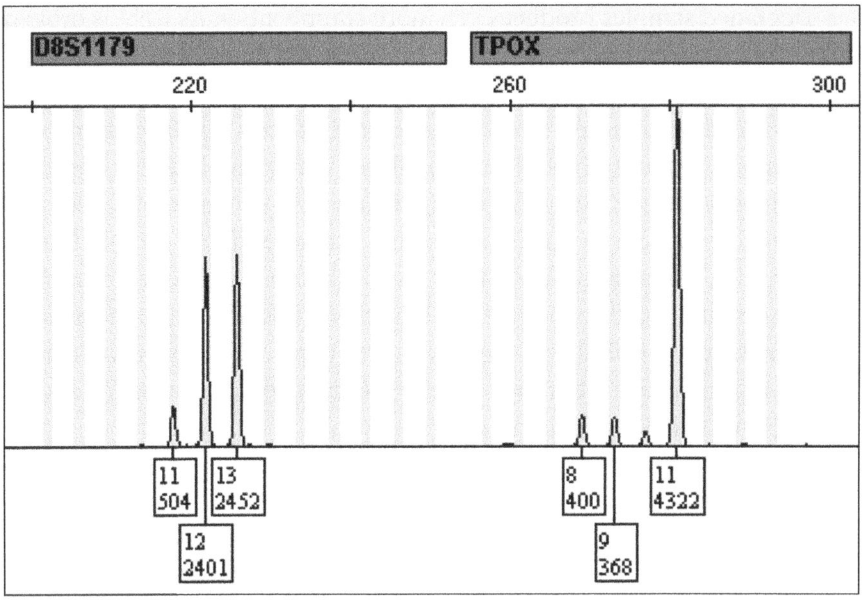

FIGURE 12.3. This figure shows a portion of a mixture profile from two contributors, a major one and a minor one. Courtesy of the Centre of Forensic Sciences, Toronto, Ontario.

DNA. At D8S1179, there are three ways to explain the results: the combination of a type 11, 13 with a 14, 15, or an 11, 14 with a 13, 15, or an 11, 15 with a 13, 14. At the TPOX address, either the contributors were a 6, 8 plus an 11, 11, or a 6, 11 with an 8, 11. The TPOX results cannot be explained by, for example, equal contributions of a 6, 6, and an 8, 11, because the peak height imbalances would not allow for this interpretation—the "8" and the "11" peaks are too dissimilar in height, so do not belong together.

In mixtures where there is more DNA from one contributor than another, the minor contributor's smaller peaks can sometimes be obscured by the major contributor's larger ones, as well as by small artifacts. Figure 12.3 shows a portion of a mixture profile from two contributors, a major one and a minor one.

At the TPOX locus, the major contributor is clearly an 11, 11, while the minor contributor, represented by the small peaks, is a type 8, 9. At the D8S1179 locus, the major is a type 12, 13. The minor profile is not clear-cut. The size 11 peak is too large to be entirely an artifact, but a portion of it could be. The minor profile would have to include the 11 peak, but could be partially masked by the major profile, and could therefore be an 11, 11; an 11, 12; or an 11, 13.

Degraded samples produce even more complexities. As DNA is broken down into smaller pieces by heat or moisture, STR peaks may disappear, especially those representing the longer strands of DNA (at the right-hand side of the electropherogram). Added complications occur when prohibitively small amounts of DNA are analyzed—the amplification process sometimes favours copying one variant at an address over another, known as a "stochastic" effect.[43] This means, for example, that a sample that is truly type 10, 11 may appear as a type 10, with the 11 allele peak either missing or so much smaller as to be attributed to another source in the sample. It is the responsibility of the scientist to apply the relevant validation findings to recognize situations where STR data could be missing, and to account for this in the final interpretation.

Complex STR profiles, due to any or all of the phenomena of mixtures, degradation, and uneven amplification, provide DNA analysts with the greatest challenges in interpretation and, in some cases, reliable interpretations cannot be made. It may not be possible to completely, or even partially, deconvolute a complex profile, meaning that the analyst cannot reliably separate out some or all the potential contributors to the mixture. There are a number of expert software packages that can assist in such interpretations that are especially useful when analyzing mixtures from more than two contributors.[44] These expert systems have been used in criminal cases in the United States[45] and New Zealand,[46] and are examples of "probabilistic genotyping," a means to extract potentially useful data from complex mixture profiles that otherwise might be discarded as uninterpretable. Results are presented as a set of potential solutions with different likelihoods of occurrence.

---

43 How small is prohibitively small? The laboratory's validation process will determine the threshold amount of DNA needed to generally ensure a reliable result. This is the amplification threshold, and in most laboratories will be around a quarter of a nanogram, representing about thirty cells.

44 For example, STRMix™ (strmix.esr.cri.nz) and TrueAllele® (www.cybgen.com/services/index.shtml).

45 "TrueAllele Casework Ruled Admissible in Ohio Daubert Challenge" (22 October 2014), online: *Business Wire* www.businesswire.com/news/home/20141022005529/en/TrueAllele-Casework-ruled-admissible-Ohio-Daubert-challenge#.VhaPe32rGzk.

46 Ian Steward, "New Kiwi Crime Tool Unravels Mixed DNA" (5 January 2014), online: www.stuff.co.nz/science/9577038/New-Kiwi-crime-tool-unravels-mixed-DNA.

4) Comparing Profiles and Calculating the Random Match Probability

When an STR profile from an evidence sample is qualitatively different from that of a reference sample, that reference person is excluded as the source of the evidence sample. In this situation, at one or more STR locations tested, the two profiles show different alleles. No statistics are necessary to clarify or elaborate upon this finding. For example, if a single source evidence DNA profile contained the alleles 13 and 16 for the genetic location D3S1358, the source of the profile in Table 12.1, type 12, 16, would be excluded as the source of the evidence profile.

When there are no qualitative differences between two STR profiles, these two profiles cannot be excluded as originating from the same source. A few further words of clarification are necessary here. A "match" may occur between two profiles where there are no missing data, where there is a partial profile (with some data missing), and also where there is ambiguity in a profile interpretation (where there is more than one interpretation that can account for the findings). Consider again results at one locus of the Table 12.1 reference profile, type 12, 16 at D3S1358. At just this locus, the reference would not be excluded as the source of the following evidence profiles:

- "Type 12, 16"—The presence of two alleles, with no ambiguity.
- "Type 12, *"—There is a 12 allele in the evidence sample, but the analyst cannot reliably determine the second allele of the pair. The asterisk signifies the possibility of that undetermined second allele as being *any* other allele, which could be, in theory, a 16 allele.
- "Type 12, 16 or Type 12, 12"—There is ambiguity in the interpretation, and the analyst has determined that there is more than one potential explanation for the evidence profile results. Because one of those possibilities is a 12,16, the Table 12.1 profile source cannot be excluded.

A significant part of the profile interpretation process, especially for mixture and degraded samples, is to determine when STR data might be missing or obscured, and to account for this in comparisons and statistical computations.

There are two explanations for a DNA profile match result: the reference sample donor is the source of the evidence sample or she is not; for the latter case, the DNA profile match is due to coincidence. The random match probability, or RMP, is the estimate of the coincidental match probability, and theoretically reduces to a very basic question: What is the probability of going into the population at large, picking one person at random, and that person having the target DNA profile? It might seem easiest to attack this probability problem by simply going into a population, sampling many people, and counting how many times the target STR profile is seen. This approach is neither scientifically valid nor feasible. Any forensic STR profile developed with one of the current multi-locus kits is extremely rare. If a thousand or even hundreds of thousands or millions of persons were tested, the STR profile in question would not likely be observed.

However, a knowledge of the rarity of each of the *individual components* of the profile, the STR alleles, allows for an estimation of the probability that a particular set of STR variants at each genetic location, and then at all locations tested, would come together all at once. This estimate is based on an understanding of genetics and human mating habits—to the extent that humans choose their mates *randomly*, their children will have, at each of the tested STR locations, pairs of alleles that come together *randomly*. The random match probability calculation is performed as follows:

- Databases allow the analyst to determine the frequency of occurrence of each STR allele in the geographic region of interest. STR allele databases are constructed by sampling about a hundred to a few hundred random individuals in a population, producing STR profiles for all of them, and then counting how many times each individual STR allele is observed. The database is then compiled which provides a frequency of occurrence of each allele. Due to slight differences in STR allele frequencies among races, databases are compiled for different races in a population.[47]
- The chance of finding the pair of STR results at each genetic location is calculated in one of two ways, depending upon whether the same allele is inherited from each parent (homozygote) or different alleles are inherited (heterozygote):
  - The Table 12.1 profile contains STR type 8, 8 at genetic address TPOX. According to a database of TPOX allele frequencies in On-

47 Many STR allele databases are accessible to the public. See, for example, OmniPop, available at "Published Population Data from a Variety of STR Systems," online: National Institute of Standards and Technology (NIST) www.cstl.nist.gov/strbase/populationdata.htm. Of course, race is not an absolute characteristic, and contributors to a database are usually asked to self identify to a racial group.

tario,[48] the type 8 allele is found 54.3 percent of the time compared to seven other TPOX alleles. The chance of a person inheriting two type 8 alleles is simply the chance of that allele's individual probability multiplied by itself: 0.543 × 0.543 = 0.295 or 29.5 percent.

- » The Table 12.1 profile describes the STR type 10, 13 at genetic address D8S1179. According to the Ontario database, eleven different allele types are commonly found, with allele 10 appearing 8.5 percent of the time, and allele 13, 31.6 percent. The chance of a person inheriting this particular pair of alleles is simply their individual probabilities multiplied together (and then multiplied by two, because there are two ways for the combination to come together[49]): 2 × (0.085 × 0.316) = 0.054, or 5.4 percent.

- The assumption of random mating in humans is largely true but not entirely accurate. A small correction factor is applied to account for the small degree of non-random mating in human populations. This has the effect of very slightly increasing the frequency estimates.[50]
- The chance of finding the *whole* genetic profile at all of the STR locations tested is simply the product of multiplying together the chances at each and every genetic address. For just the two genetic locations calculated above, that would be 0.295 × 0.054 = 0.016 (1.6 percent, or about one in every 62 persons). The final RMP, especially for profiles at nine or fifteen STR locations, is exceedingly small, typically in the order of one in trillions or rarer.

5) Special Applications of Forensic STR Analysis

a) Y-STR Analysis

The X and Y chromosomes are the human sex chromosomes. A female inherits an X chromosome from both parents, resulting in an "X, X" type. A

48 From the Caucasian database compiled by the Ontario Centre of Forensic Sciences, Ministry of Community Safety and Correctional Services, Ontario. Other allelic databases include Asian, East Indian, African-Canadian, and Northern Ontario Native (Royal Canadian Mounted Police).

49 The 10 and 13 alleles came from the mother and father, respectively, or vice versa.

50 The "DNA wars" are essentially over. In the first decade of forensic DNA analysis, there were significant disagreements on the population genetics models and statistics that form the basis of random match probability calculations. The application of correction factors accounts for the slight amount of inbreeding and population substructure (differences in subpopulations) in humans: National Research Council Committee on DNA Forensic Science, *The Evaluation of Forensic DNA Evidence* (Washington, DC: National Academy Press, 1996).

male inherits a Y chromosome from his father and an X chromosome from his mother, resulting in an "X, Y" type. The Y can be used to target and analyze DNA variations unique to males. The procedure for developing Y-STR profiles is the same as that described above for conventional STR typing. The difference is in the final profile—the male only displays one allele type for each genetic location.[51]

Calculating a random match probability in the case of a Y-STR profile match is not the same as for profile matches involving STRs on the other twenty-two pairs of chromosomes. The Y chromosome is inherited as a *single* package through male lines, meaning that it is inherited directly from son to son to son, and so on. There is no random "coming together" of Y-STR alleles from two parents. The determination of the random match probability is therefore different, and calculated by the simpler counting method. This involves tallying the number of times the whole profile is seen in a special Y-STR database, and then applying statistics to estimate the chance of seeing that profile in a particular case. The US Y-STR Database[52] is accessible to the public and contains Y-STR data primarily from American males. Y-STR alleles from an evidence sample are entered using a drop down menu. The software then provides the user with an observation of how many times the full Y-STR profile has been seen and then calculates the RMP. Typical RMPs for Y-STR profiles are usually much less discriminating than for conventional profiles, as the discrimination potential is directly linked to the size of the Y-STR databases.

Forensic Y-STR analysis is best suited to special case circumstances, in particular:

- When a biological sample contains only a few male cells in a large quantity of female cells. Conventional STR analysis may not pick up the small amount of male DNA in such a mixture, where the female DNA essentially obscures the male DNA. Y-STR analysis allows the male DNA to be specifically targeted, like picking a few needles out of a haystack.
- When a sexual assault allegation involves multiple male suspects. Y-STR analysis assists in determining the number of assailants con-

51 There are occasions where two alleles are found, due to duplications and mutations in the Y chromosome.

52 With profiles from over 35,000 males: US Y-STR Database, online: www.usystrdatabase.org.

tributing to, for example, an evidence semen sample obtained from an intimate swab from the female complainant.

- When a reference sample from a male is not available, but a sample from a paternal male relative, such as a father or son, is. The sample from this male relative may be used as a "proxy" DNA reference sample.

b) Paternity Analysis

Consider the following parental types at one STR genetic address: Mother—STR type 8, 9 and Father—STR type 10, 11. A biological child of these parents could be any of STR types 8, 10; 9, 10; 8, 11; or 9, 11. If the mother is STR type 8, 8 and the father is type 9, 9, then there is only one possibility for the child, that of type 8, 9. These are just two of a number of family "trio" possibilities for STR allele inheritance. They all derive from the fundamental principle of inheritance that a person's genetic makeup is derived from *random* contributions from both parents.

While most paternity cases involving forensic STR analysis are civil matters, paternity analysis is also a tool in some criminal cases, many times addressing the same type of question: In a sexual assault allegation, could the accused male be the father of the child?[53] This question is answered by reference to the STR profile of the child, the mother (if available), and the alleged father(s). Consider the following profile results at just three STR locations:

TABLE 12.2. Profile results for three STR locations for mother, child, and three alleged fathers.

STR test location	Mother	Child	Alleged Father #1	Alleged Father #2	Alleged Father #3
D8S1179	7,9	**8**,9	8,9	7,7	8,9
D5S818	10,10	10,**12**	11,12	15,15	11,13
vWA	15,16	16,**18**	18,20	14,14	18,20

If maternity is not at issue, the mother must account for one of the child's alleles at each locus, as underlined in the table. The child must therefore have inherited the STR size 8 allele of D8S1179, the size 12 allele of D5S818, and the size 18 allele of vWA from his father. Alleged father #1 cannot be excluded as the biological father, as he has all these "obligate"

53 Or product of conception.

alleles. The next part of the analysis would be to calculate the statistical likelihood of paternity, known as the paternity index, with the alternative hypothesis being paternity by a random man.[54] This calculation is performed using the same allelic databases as those described above. Alleged father #2 is clearly excluded as the biological father of the child as he has none of the obligate alleles. Alleged father #3 is only excluded at one of the genetic addresses, D5S818, because he does not have the size 12 allele to pass on to the child. However, this is where another principle of genetics must be considered: mutation. Short tandem repeat locations are known to mutate in the development of spermatozoa and egg cells. This means that a man can father a child who does not actually have one of his "obligate" alleles, because the spermatozoa that fertilized the egg was made with a mutation that changed the STR allele size. Therefore, mutation rates must be considered where the alleged father does not possess the obligate allele at one, or even more than one, STR location(s).[55]

There are, of course, myriad paternity and other kinship situations that can be addressed using STR analysis, and a more detailed description of the use of STR in these situations can be found in numerous texts and other resources.[56]

c) Non-Human STR Analysis

There is nothing special about human DNA. The same techniques used to produce human STR profiles can be applied to non-human samples. If the animal source of a biological sample at a crime scene is at issue, then commercial kits are available to target STR variations in, and population allelic databases are available for, horses, dogs, cats, bovines, and other species.[57]

---

54 The alternate hypothesis may change, according to case circumstances. If the alternate hypothesis is that a brother of the accused man is the true father of the child, then a different statistic, known as the "avuncular index," applies.

55 The number of possible mutations depends on the number of STR alleles tested and the mutation rates of the locations. Mutation rates for consideration in paternity testing can be found at "Apparent Mutations Observed at STR Loci in the Course of Paternity Testing," online: NIST www.cstl.nist.gov/strbase/mutation.htm.

56 See, for example, Dr. Charles Brenner's Forensic Mathematics website, online: dna-view.com.

57 For more details, see Short Tandem Repeat DNA Internet DataBase, online: NIST www.cstl.nist.gov/strbase.

d) Beyond STRs: Analyzing DNA Sequence Variations

Forensic STR technology is expected to remain the favoured approach in criminal casework for the foreseeable future. It is very sensitive, highly discriminating, and forms the basis of DNA profile data banks worldwide. However, forensic STR analysis cannot address every potential forensic biology question in a criminal case. Sequence variations, mostly in the form of SNPs (single nucleotide polymorphisms), may be applicable in particular forensic scenarios. Methods for detecting sequence differences are numerous and varied, but the output is similar—a determination of the presence of a particular base (A, T, G, or C) at targeted or random DNA locations. The forensic use of sequence differences has mostly been applied in mitochondrial DNA analysis to date, but is poised to expand.

- *How can mitochondrial DNA assist in forensic investigations?* Human cells contain a nucleus that houses forty-six chromosomes surrounded by cytoplasm, a solution containing the biological machinery necessary to maintain cell function and life. A part of this machinery consists of tiny structures called mitochondria, responsible for energy production in cells and containing their own small chromosomes. A portion of the mitochondrial DNA known to contain sequence variations is typically targeted by forensic scientists. Mitochondrial DNA analysis is rarely performed compared to conventional forensic STR analysis. It is used when hair samples do not contain enough nuclear DNA in their roots—mitochondrial DNA analysis can be applied to the remaining hair shafts. When bone and other samples are heavily degraded, mitochondrial DNA may be the only viable option.
- *Can identical twins be distinguished by DNA analysis?* Twins originating from a single fertilized egg will share the same STR pattern, because they share the same initial set of twenty-three chromosome pairs. Tiny sequence differences, due to rare mutations, may occur at the early embryological stages and can serve to distinguish identical twins. This is accomplished analytically by deep genome sequencing techniques that seek to find and identify the individual bases by canvassing almost the entire genome.[58, 59]

---

58 Jacqueline Weber-Lehmann et al., "Finding the Needle in the Haystack: Differentiating 'Identical' Twins in Paternity Testing and Forensics by Ultra Deep Next Generation Sequencing" (2014) 9 *Forensic Science International: Genetics* 42.

59 Jess Bidgood, "New DNA Test Sought in Identical Twin's Rape Case" *New York Times* (15 September 2015) A17.

- *Can the ethnicity or physical traits of a biological evidence source be determined by forensic DNA profiling?* Investigators may wish to have information regarding the physical traits of a biological evidence source in order to narrow investigations and create new leads. Aside from whether a profile comes from a male or a female, STR profiles do not provide a reliable basis from which these types of inferences can be made. There are, however, single nucleotide polymorphisms throughout the genome that do provide such information. These SNPs are targeted in forensic test protocols for various physical traits, including eye colour,[60] hair colour,[61] and ethnicity.[62]

C. THE ROLE OF THE FORENSIC BIOLOGIST IN CRIMINAL CASES

Most forensic biologists in Canada are government employees[63] with most criminal casework performed at public laboratories at the request of official investigative agencies. Private laboratories also provide forensic biology services for civil and criminal matters. Whether acting in the capacity of a government laboratory employee or on a private contract, forensic biologists share the same professional and ethical duties to perform analyses and interpretations, to report findings, to alert users to the limitations of the findings, and to communicate with justice system participants in a clear, competent, complete, and unbiased manner.[64] Other than situations for which procedural rules may differentiate the responsibilities of opposing parties (such as with disclosure obligations), the role of forensic biologists, whether private or public, includes the following responsibilities:

---

60 Gina M. Dembinski & Christine J. Picard, "Evaluation of the IrisPlex DNA-based Eye Color Prediction Using a United States Population" (2014) 9 *Forensic Science International: Genetics* 111.

61 Susan Walsh et al., "Developmental Validation of the HIrisPlex System: DNA-based Eye and Hair Colour Prediction for Forensic and Anthropological Usage" (2014) 9 *Forensic Science International: Genetics* 150.

62 Katherine Butler Gettings et al., "A 50-SNP Assay for Biogeographic Ancestry and Phenotype Prediction in the U.S. Population" (2014) 8 *Forensic Science International: Genetics* 101.

63 At the Centre of Forensic Sciences, Ontario; the Laboratoire de sciences judiciaires et de médicine légale, Quebec; or the Royal Canadian Mounted Police Forensic Laboratory Services.

64 See, for example, the *Code of Conduct of the Canadian Society of Forensic Science: Rules of Professional Conduct*, online: Canadian Society of Forensic Science www.csfs.ca/code-of-conduct.html; and the *ASCLD/LAB Guiding Principles of Professional Responsibility for Crime Laboratories and Forensic Scientists*, online: American Society of Crime Laboratory Directors www.ascld-lab.org/guiding-principles.

1) Disclose, Upon Request, Relevant Case File Documentation

The forensic biologist will issue a case report describing the evidence examined, the methods employed, the results obtained, and conclusions drawn. The case file contents upon which the report is based will generally include the following documents, any or all of which may be included in a list of disclosure requests:

- Chain of custody information for all evidence items and samples. In many of the larger forensic facilities, this will be downloaded from a laboratory information management system that tracks item and sample transfers through the use of barcodes and secure personal identification numbers;
- requests for analysis from submitting agencies;
- communications (emails, letters, phone call notes, etc.);
- screening notes and photographs (if any) documenting body fluid analysis and sampling;
- technical notes from DNA analysis steps, including extraction, quantification, amplification, separation, and data analysis. In most laboratories, much of this work is performed and documented by technical staff, not by the reporting scientist;
- electropherograms, including results from positive and negative control samples;
- interpretations;
- random match probability calculations;
- technical review of report(s); and
- quality incident reports, if any.

2) Provide Clarity to the Meaning of the Random Match Probability Estimate

A DNA profile from an evidence sample matches that of a known reference sample. Either that known reference is the source of the biological sample or the profile match result is a coincidence. The random match probability (RMP) is an estimate of the probability of this alternate hypothesis of coincidental match. Based on models of genetic inheritance, the random match probability is the chance, in theory, that a person, sampled at random from the population, would have the target DNA profile.

The RMP is a conditional probability. It is the probability of a DNA profile match, *given that* the known reference is not the actual source. The RMP is *not* the probability that the known reference is not the source, given the fact of a profile match result. At first, this may seem to be a subtle difference in wording, but it is a mistake to confuse the RMP by flipping, or transposing,[65] this condition (the "given"). A non-DNA example may help to clarify. Consider the following statement: "There is a very high probability that an animal has four legs *if* that animal is a cat." This is a proper and logical conditional probability statement, measuring the probability of a four-legged animal on the condition that animal is a cat. Now, "flip" this condition and restate the probability: "There is a very high probability that an animal is a cat *if* it has four legs." Obviously, this statement is wrong—switching the condition to "if it has four legs" clearly makes the statement erroneous. Returning to DNA match evidence, the condition of "if the reference is not the source" cannot be flipped in such a way that it now becomes a probability of the reference actually being, or not being, the source. This turns the RMP into a probability of guilt or innocence, and is wrong. It is not unusual for a forensic biologist to be asked a question that incorporates a statistical mistake, and the forensic biologist has the responsibility to provide an answer that corrects the questioner or restates the question in a statistically proper fashion. For example, the expert may be asked:

- *What is the chance that someone else deposited the DNA at the scene?* This chance does not equate to RMP. It is incorrect to say that the likelihood that the DNA profile came from an unrelated person is the RMP; it is, however, correct to say that the RMP describes the probability of the profile if it were from a randomly sampled unrelated person. The likelihood that the DNA donor in this case was, in fact, someone else, requires a consideration of all the evidence in a case, not just the DNA evidence.
- *What is the chance that there is someone (not just an identical twin) walking the earth, right now, who also has the target DNA profile?* Again, this is not the RMP. There may well be someone walking the earth with that profile, but you will never be able to find him or her without testing almost everyone!

There are other case situations where the forensic biologist might need to further clarify the meaning of an RMP. An evidence sample DNA profile may match (or "cold hit") a reference profile on a DNA data bank of convicted offender profiles, such as the Convicted Offender Index of

65 Ian W. Evett, "Avoiding the Transposed Conditional" (1995) 35 *Science and Justice* 127.

Canada's National DNA Data Bank.[66] The United States National Research Council recommended that when a suspect is found by a DNA data bank search, a new match probability should be calculated by multiplying the RMP by the number of persons in that data bank[67]—so, the larger the data bank, the greater the adjustment. For example, if John Doe is linked to a crime scene DNA sample due to his presence on a convicted offender index containing a million offender samples, an RMP of one in 1 trillion would translate to a data bank match probability (DMP) of one in 1 million. DNA evidence is not statistically weaker when it results from a data bank search. The RMP and DMP answer different questions—for the DMP, it is, "What is the probability of finding the target profile in this data bank?" It has also been argued that in such a data bank search, all other non-matching individuals are excluded, providing even stronger evidence that John Doe is indeed the true source.[68]

The hypothesis involving a random person is not always the most appropriate—or even the only alternative—hypothesis. For example, an accused person asserts that he is not the source of an evidentiary DNA profile, but case information suggests that his biological brother could be. In such a case, the alternate hypothesis should change from the potential involvement of a random man to that of a related one. The forensic biologist needs to apply special formulae for this RMP calculation to account for the new alternate hypothesis.[69] The biologist must be ready to answer questions such as: What were your hypotheses, and how did you set them? What case facts did you use for setting the hypotheses?

Another situation for statistical clarification revolves around the issue of a "felon-to-felon match." What is the chance of two persons in a data bank of convicted offender profiles sharing many or all STR test results? In fact, for large data banks, the chances are quite good. This was demonstrated in a study of the Arizona data bank,[70] where two unrelated offenders were found to share STR results at nine of thirteen STR locations tested.

---

66 National DNA Data Bank, online: Royal Canadian Mounted Police www.rcmp-grc.gc.ca/nddb-bndg/index-accueil-eng.htm.

67 *The Evaluation of Forensic DNA Evidence*, above note 50, Recommendation 5.1.

68 David J. Balding, "The DNA Database Controversy" (2002) 58 *Biometrics* 241; David J. Balding & Peter Donnelly, "Evaluating DNA Profile Evidence When the Suspect Is Identified Through a Database Search" (1996) 41 *Journal of Forensic Sciences* 603.

69 *The Evaluation of Forensic DNA Evidence*, above note 50, Recommendations 4.8 & 4.9.

70 Kathryn Troyer, Theresa Gilboy, & Brian Koeneman, "A Nine STR Locus Match Between Two Apparently Unrelated Individuals Using AmpFlSTR®Profiler Plus™ and CoFiler™" in *Genetic Identity Conference Proceedings, 12th International Symposium on*

This felon-to-felon profile comparison finding does not reflect on the general reliability of RMP estimates; in fact, it has no bearing on it whatsoever. The difference between an RMP estimate and a felon-to-felon match is the difference of asking, respectively, "what is the chance of finding this *one target* profile in the population in a randomly sampled person?" compared to "what is the chance of finding *any* two persons in a data bank that share *a* profile, whatever that profile may be?" As DNA data banks continue to grow, some exceeding 10 million profiles, and with increased international co-operation and information sharing, the number of common CODIS loci will increase, enabling increased discrimination power and the reduction of adventitious matches.[71]

3) Clearly Communicate Details and Relevance of the Quality Assurance System

The forensic biologist must disclose, as applicable, the accreditation status of his or her laboratory. Accreditation is the process by which a laboratory demonstrates adherence to standards. ISO/IEC 17025[72] is the general standard that applies to testing laboratories, with forensic laboratories also held to additional standards set forth by accrediting bodies such as the Standards Council of Canada[73] and the Laboratory Accreditation Board of the American Society of Crime Laboratory Directors.[74] Accredited forensic DNA laboratories are also audited against specific requirements set out by the Scientific Working Group on DNA Analysis Methods (SWGDAM).[75] Questions for the forensic biologist involving the quality system might include:

Human Identification, online: Promega www.promega.com/~/media/files/resources/conference%20proceedings/ishi%2012/poster%20abstracts/troyer.pdf.

71 New STR kits, such as PowerPlex® Fusion (Promega) and GlobalFiler® (Life Technologies), will allow typing of over twenty STRs at once.

72 International Organization for Standardization, *ISO/IEC 17025: General Requirements for the Competence of Testing and Calibration Laboratories* (International Organization for Standardization, 2005).

73 Standards Council of Canada, online: www.scc.ca/en/forensic.

74 Laboratory Accreditation Board of the American Society of Crime Laboratory Directors, online: www.ascld-lab.org.

75 "Quality Assurance Standards for Forensic DNA Testing Laboratories," online: Federal Bureau of Investigation www.fbi.gov/about-us/lab/biometric-analysis/codis/qas_testlab.pdf; "Quality Assurance Standards for Convicted Offender DNA Databasing Laboratories," online: Federal Bureau of Investigation www.fbi.gov/about-us/lab/biometric-analysis/codis/stds_offlabs.

- Is the laboratory in which you work accredited? Does the scope of this accreditation cover the type of forensic work performed in this case?
- When did you last perform a proficiency test, and what were the results?
- Were there any quality incident reports in the case? If so, what occurred, and how was the incident dealt with?
- Were there any instances of sample contamination, including results from negative control samples? If so, what was the contamination, and how was this finding dealt with?
- Were there any deviations from standard protocol in this case, and if so, why? For example, if the laboratory attempted an analysis using a sub-threshold quantity of DNA, please explain why this was done and how it could affect the interpretation of the profile.

4) Clearly Communicate All Assumptions Made in the DNA Profile Interpretation Process

Can forensic biologists work within a contextual vacuum? It has been argued that, to avoid contextual bias effects, a forensic biologist might be given case information only as necessary in some sort of sequential manner, and would therefore be blind to case facts that might adversely influence decision making.[76] In reality, forensic biologists are aware of, and must consider, non-scientific case data, including police summaries, to determine what questions need to be addressed and what scientific tests are appropriate. In any case, the forensic biologist must clearly state all assumptions made in the strategic and interpretive processes.

Assumptions may be based on the scientific results, including the number and relative contributions of DNA donors to a mixture profile, or non-scientific data (for example, the contribution of DNA on clothing from the wearer of that clothing). An assumption of DNA attribution in an intimate evidence sample may be made to "tease out" a DNA source from a mixture profile to better discern the remaining, probative parts of that profile. For example, an assumption of the presence of a female assault victim's DNA in her internal vaginal swab or under her fingernail may be

76 Dan E. Krane et al., "Sequential Unmasking: A Means of Minimizing Observer Effects in Forensic DNA Interpretation" (letter) (2008) 53 *Journal of Forensic Science* 1006.

made to more clearly determine what probative DNA is left in the profile. Questions for the forensic biologist may include:

- What assumptions did you make in the profile interpretation, and what were the bases for these assumptions?
- Were any of the profiles complex mixtures? If so, are there alternative interpretations?

5) Use a Scientific Approach to Questions Relating to the Transfer and Persistence of DNA

What is the probative value of finding (or not finding) a DNA profile in a case? A DNA profile may come from biological cells deposited during a criminal episode, or from cells deposited in an unrelated event before or after that episode. The tremendous sensitivity of forensic DNA analysis comes with a price—it can also detect instances of DNA from the sea of innocuous trace DNA that exists throughout the environment. It is not unusual to detect STR alleles that are unsourced—that is, they cannot be attributed to any reference in a case—and these alleles may or may not be necessarily related to a case.[77]

Deriving reliable inferences from forensic DNA evidence depends on a thorough consideration of case details, scientific results, and relevant scientific literature. This is especially important in cases involving the transfer of (mostly) invisible skin cells by handling, touching, or wearing evidence. The role of the forensic scientist in interpreting and contextualizing the transfer and persistence of DNA in a case is best described by Peter Gill[78] to include presenting an account that incorporates all possibilities that may explain how and when DNA evidence may have been transferred, and ensuring that any opinion is firmly based on the experimental evidence. It is beyond the resources of this chapter to describe the multitude of case scenarios involving aspects of DNA transfer and persistence, and the reader is encouraged to consult Professor Gill's text for a comprehensive treatment of the subject. What follows are just three examples of DNA transfer and persistence questions typically put to a forensic biologist:

---

77 Eleanor Alison, May Graham, & Guy Nathan Rutty, "Investigation into 'Normal' Background DNA on Adult Necks: Implications for DNA Profiling of Manual Strangulation Victims" (2008) 53 *Journal of Forensic Sciences* 1074; Christophe Champod, "DNA Transfer: Informed Judgment or Mere Guesswork?" (2013) 4 *Frontiers in Genetics* 300.

78 Peter Gill, *Misleading DNA Evidence: Reasons for Miscarriages of Justice* (London: Academic Press, 2014).

1) *Under what circumstances can DNA be transferred by handling, touching, or wearing?*

   There are many factors that determine whether skin or other cells are transferred in a handling or wearing episode, including the propensity of the handler to shed skin cells,[79] the ability of the target surface to accept and retain cells, and the intensity and time of handling or wearing. The time between purported handling or wearing and laboratory examination will influence the retention or loss of cells, and the laboratory sampling efficiency will also have an effect on DNA yield. The forensic biologist draws upon data from relevant experimental research, including peer-reviewed literature and casework experience, to provide an opinion within a particular scenario. Reflecting the growing importance of this aspect of DNA casework, peer-reviewed articles in the area of DNA transfer and persistence are increasingly found in forensic journals, including descriptions of experiments involving fingernails,[80] the handling of firearms,[81] the loss of DNA on items due to subsequent handling,[82] and other forensically relevant situations.

2) *No DNA was detected on an item purportedly handled by a suspect. What are the possible explanations?*

   Usually, little to no probative value can be ascribed to a negative finding. It may be explained in a number of ways. For example, the item not having been handled by the suspect; the item handled by the suspect with no DNA transferred; or the item handled by the suspect, DNA transferred, and then subsequently removed.

3) *Can DNA be transferred by indirect means?*

   Yes. Indirect transfer of DNA occurs when cells initially deposited on one evidence item are then transferred to another evidence item,

---

79 Alex Lowe et al., "The Propensity of Individuals to Deposit DNA and Secondary Transfer of Low Level DNA from Individuals to Inert Surfaces" (2002) 129 *Forensic Science International* 25.

80 Melinda Matte et al., "Prevalence and Persistence of Foreign DNA Beneath Fingernails" (2012) 6 *Forensic Science International: Genetics* 236.

81 Katie M. Horsman-Hall et al., "Development of STR Profiles from Firearms and Fired Cartridge Cases" (2009) 3 *Forensic Science International: Genetics* 242; Diana Polley et al., "Investigation of DNA Recovery from Firearms and Cartridge Cases" (2006) 39 *Canadian Society of Forensic Science Journal* 317.

82 Roland A.H. van Oorschot, Genna Glavich, & R. John Mitchell, "Persistence of DNA Deposited by the Original User on Objects After Subsequent Use by a Second Person" (2014) 8 *Forensic Science International: Genetics* 219.

with no direct physical contact between the original depositor and the final evidence surface.[83] The likelihood of transferring DNA tends to decrease with each indirect transfer, and is highly dependent on the amount and moisture content of the initial DNA deposit as well as the degree of contact between transferring and receiving surfaces. Successful DNA transfer is also affected by the surface features of both the transferring and retaining media, where porous materials tend to retain cells well but transfer relatively few of them, and non-porous materials transfer cells relatively well but do not retain many cells.

One example of an indirect transfer of DNA occurred in the California case of Lukis Anderson,[84] where paramedics apparently facilitated the transfer of Anderson's DNA to the fingernails of their next patient, a homicide victim.

D. CONCLUSION

Forensic biology has unceasingly evolved over the past thirty years, and this area of forensic science is beginning to benefit from yet another impressive array of innovations, including the potential introduction of microchip arrays to quickly link DNA variations with the physical characteristics of suspects; expert software systems to assist in the analysis of complex DNA mixture profiles; completely automated rapid DNA analysis equipment to quickly produce DNA profiles for direct data bank uploads;[85] and new tests for body fluid identification. With improvements in computing power may come new statistical approaches to evaluating DNA evidence in conjunction with other case evidence.[86]

Non-scientists in the criminal justice system may feel overwhelmed by the pace of progress. While it is important for justice system participants to keep up with and to understand forensic DNA technologies, the technical details should not sway the user from addressing what may be the key question in a forensic DNA case—that of context, and considering

83 Mariya Goray et al., "Secondary DNA Transfer of Biological Substances Under Varying Test Conditions" (2010) 4 *Forensic Science International: Genetics* 62.

84 Osagie K. Obasogie, "High Tech, High Risk Forensics" *New York Times* (24 July 2013) A27.

85 Federal Bureau of Investigation, "Rapid DNA or Rapid DNA Analysis," online: www.fbi.gov/about-us/lab/biometric-analysis/codis/rapid-dna-analysis.

86 A. Biedermann & F. Taroni, "Bayesian Networks for Evaluating Forensic DNA Profiling Evidence: A Review and Guide to Literature" (2012) 6 *Forensic Science International: Genetics* 147.

the meaning of finding or not finding a forensic DNA profile in a particular case circumstance.

E. THE LEGAL CONTEXT

1) Introduction

> There is no question that DNA evidence has revolutionized the way many crimes are investigated and prosecuted. The use of this new technology has not only led to the successful identification and prosecution of many dangerous criminals, it has served to exonerate many persons who were wrongfully suspected or convicted. The importance of this forensic development to the administration of justice can hardly be overstated.[87]

The revolutionary power of DNA evidence, as described by Charron J. in *R. v. Rodgers*,[88] was foreseen two decades earlier by Sir Alec Jeffreys, the geneticist credited with applying the science of DNA to the forensic context. In his 1985 article "Forensic Application of DNA 'Fingerprints,'" Sir Jeffreys explained that DNA could be used to identify the perpetrator of a crime. The authors correctly envisioned that DNA fingerprinting, subsequently dubbed "The Genetic Witness,"[89] would "revolutionize forensic biology particularly with regard to the identification of rape suspects."[90]

Though the application of DNA analysis to criminal investigations initially focused on violent or sexual offences, DNA evidence has since been used in the investigation and prosecution of a broader array of offences.[91] Canadian investigative agencies have been using DNA evidence in criminal cases since 1986,[92] generating caselaw aimed at resolving the controversies

---

87 *R. v. Rodgers*, 2006 SCC 15 at para. 4 [*Rodgers*].

88 *Ibid.*

89 See, for example, Ricardo G. Federico, "'The Genetic Witness': DNA Evidence and Canada's Criminal Law" (1990–91) 33 *Criminal Law Quarterly* 204 at 226; Douglas M. Smith, "Genetic Witness: By Thy DNA So Shall Ye Be Known" (1993) 1 *Health Law Journal* 207; Jay D. Aronson, *Genetic Witness: Science, Law, and Controversy in the Making of DNA Profiling* (New Brunswick, NJ: Rutgers University Press, 2007); Michael Lynch et al., *Truth Machine: The Contentious History of DNA Fingerprinting* (Chicago: The University of Chicago Press, 2008).

90 Gill, above note 1 at 577.

91 Amelia Bellamy-Royds & Sonya Norris, "New Frontiers in Forensic DNA Analysis: International Practices and Implications for Canada" (3 March 2009) Parliamentary Information and Research Service, Library of Parliament, online: www.parl.gc.ca/content/lop/researchpublications/prb0829-e.htm at 1.

92 *Ibid.*

surrounding its use. Concerns raised early in the application of DNA evidence to criminal cases involved determining the scientific validity of "matches" and "non-matches," the reliability of DNA analyses, and the reproducibility of results.[93] In 1992, the National Research Council (NRC) advised that potential problems pertaining to contamination, degradation, and statistical interpretation must be considered when using DNA in forensic casework.[94]

2) Admissibility of DNA Evidence

The 1988 case *R. v. Parent*[95] was the first case in Canada in which the court relied on DNA evidence. Though the Crown introduced the evidence in question, it was used (with, unsurprisingly, defence counsel's consent) to exclude the accused as the perpetrator of a string of sexual assaults.[96]

R. v. McNally,[97] in 1989, was the first Canadian case in which: (1) DNA evidence was used to implicate an accused; and (2) the admissibility of this type of evidence was challenged. The RCMP had used DNA evidence to support a victim's identification of McNally as the perpetrator. McNally maintained his innocence. The novel DNA evidence was admitted and, upon being faced with the inculpatory DNA analysis results, the accused pled guilty.[98]

In 1998, the Ontario Court of Appeal considered the admissibility of DNA evidence in *R. v. Terceira* (subsequently upheld by the Supreme Court of Canada).[99] The appellant submitted that DNA analysis was a "novel sci-

---

93 National Academy of Sciences, *Strengthening Forensic Science in the United States: A Path Forward* (Washington, DC: National Academies Press, 2009) at 40–41.

94 *Ibid.*

95 *R. v. Parent* (1988), 46 C.C.C. (3d) 414 (Alta. Q.B.). N.B.: We are indebted to Ron M. Fourney, et al., "Chapter 8: Forensic Biology" in Michael S. Pollanen et al., eds., *Forensic Science in Canada: A Report of Multidisciplinary Discussion* [Hart House Report] (Toronto: Centre for Forensic Science & Medicine, University of Toronto, 2013) at 82–84, online: www.forensics.utoronto.ca/Assets/LMPF+Digital+Assets/Forensic+Science+in+Canada.pdf, for supplying the framework for the discussion that follows.

96 It appears that the testing was conducted during the course of the trial, so the Crown advanced the similar fact evidence argument without knowledge of the exculpatory DNA results.

97 *R. v. McNally*, [1989] O.J. No. 2630 (Dist. Ct.).

98 Royal Canadian Mounted Police, *The National DNA Data Bank of Canada Annual Report 2010–2011* at 6 [*DNA Data Bank Annual Report 2010–2011*].

99 *R. v. Terceira* (1998), 123 C.C.C. (3d) 1 (Ont. C.A.) [*Terceira*], aff'd [1999] 3 S.C.R. 866.

entific technique" at the time that it was conducted in this case (1990–91),[100] and interpreted *R. v. Mohan*—which called for "special scrutiny" in regards to such techniques[101]—to require the trial judge to admit DNA evidence only where satisfied of its reliability beyond a reasonable doubt.[102] The appellant submitted that this safeguard was needed due to the "overwhelmingly compelling"[103] nature of DNA evidence and its commensurate propensity to create an aura of "'mystic infallibility' . . . in the eyes of the jury."[104]

Justice Finlayson rejected these submissions, finding that *Mohan* did not introduce a new standard of proof for the admissibility of expert opinion evidence relating to a novel scientific theory or technique.[105] Rather, the trial judge is merely required to determine on a balance of probabilities whether the evidence meets a threshold of reliability.[106] Justice Finlayson concluded that there was "no justification for imposing a special burden of proof" for DNA evidence, since it is simply a form of identification evidence (much like fingerprints, dental impressions, or hair samples).[107] Instead, the jury instruction should be formulated so as to combat the risk that the jurors will treat the DNA evidence as infallible. The judge should instruct the jury to refrain from becoming overwhelmed by this evidence and to rely on their common sense in assessing it.[108]

3) Collection Issues: Constitutionality, Discarded DNA, and Concepts of Privacy and Abandonment

Despite the possibility for error, DNA evidence is considered by many to be the "gold standard" of science in forensic investigations.[109] In the criminal

---

100 *Ibid.* at para. 16 (Ont. C.A.).

101 *R. v. Mohan*, [1994] 2 S.C.R. 9 at 255 [*Mohan*].

102 *Terceira*, above note 99 at para. 19.

103 *Ibid.* at para. 49.

104 *Ibid.* at para. 55.

105 *Ibid.* at para. 20.

106 *Ibid.* at para. 45.

107 *Ibid.* at para. 47.

108 *Ibid.* at para. 65. See also *R. v. Prosser*, 2015 NBCA 7, which takes a broad view of the question of how precisely this jury instruction must be formulated in order to be acceptable.

109 See, for example, Dan Frumkin et al., "Authentication of Forensic DNA Samples" (2010) 4 *Forensic Science International: Genetics* 95; William C. Thompson, "The Potential for Error in Forensic DNA Testing," online: Council for Responsible Genetics www.councilforresponsiblegenetics.org/GeneWatch/GeneWatchPage.aspx?pageId=57#;

context, a reference sample from a potential suspect is required to be compared to a sample collected from the scene and/or the victim.[110] In the course of an investigation, authorities may collect a suspect's DNA by: (1) seeking a DNA warrant; (2) obtaining informed consent to collect a voluntary sample; or (3) collecting "discarded" or "abandoned" DNA.

a) DNA Warrant Provisions

In Canada, two statutes govern the authorized collection of DNA samples in the forensic context. The *Criminal Code* permits the issuance of DNA warrants for investigative purposes (as per sections 487.04–487.09), and, after conviction, permits the collection of DNA samples for the National DNA Data Bank (NDDB) (as per sections 487.051–487.058, 487.071, and 487.091). The DNA Data Bank provisions of the *Criminal Code* are to be read in conjunction with the *DNA Identification Act*,[111] which governs NDDB collection orders. The NDDB is comprised of two separate databases: (1) the convicted offenders index (COI), which contains DNA profiles of convicted offenders; and (2) the crime scene index (CSI), which contains DNA profiles collected from crime scenes.[112]

NDDB collection orders are made after sentencing, on the principle that DNA profiles can assist in the early detection, arrest, and conviction of offenders.[113] By contrast, the DNA warrant provisions of the *Criminal Code* allow for the collection of reference samples during investigation for certain designated offences.[114] In *R. v. S.A.B.*, the Supreme Court of Canada

---

Kirk Makin, "The Dark Side of DNA" *The Globe and Mail* (13 March 2010), online: www.theglobeandmail.com/technology/science/the-dark-side-of-dna/article4310360; Andrew Pollack, "DNA Evidence Can Be Fabricated, Scientists Show" *New York Times* (17 August 2009) D3, online: www.nytimes.com/2009/08/18/science/18dna.html.

110 Section 487.04 of the *Criminal Code*, R.S.C. 1985, c. C-46 defines the term "forensic DNA analysis"; the key to this definition is the comparative aspect of the analysis between the seized bodily substance and the existing sample.

111 The NDDB has been operating since 30 June 2000 (see *DNA Data Bank Annual Report 2010–2011*, above note 98 at 6). Note that the NDDB became operational after Bill C-3 (*DNA Identification Act*, S.C. 1998 c. 37) and Bill S-10 (*An Act to Amend the National Defence Act, the DNA Identification Act and the Criminal Code*, S.C. 2000, c. 10) were proclaimed.

112 Royal Canadian Mounted Police, *The National DNA Data Bank of Canada Annual Report 2012–2013* at 3–8.

113 *DNA Identification Act*, above note 111, s. 4(a); Bellamy-Royds & Norris, above note 91 at 2.

114 Set out in section 487.04 of the *Criminal Code*, above note 110, applying to both the DNA warrant provisions and the DNA data bank scheme.

held that the DNA warrant provisions do not violate section 8 of the *Charter of Rights and Freedoms*, and that the standard of "reasonable grounds" is sufficient for DNA warrants.[115] Similarly, in *R. v. Rodgers*,[116] the Supreme Court of Canada held that it is reasonable to collect DNA samples from designated convicted offenders for the NDDB, and that the collection procedures set out in section 487.055(1) of the *Criminal Code* do not violate the offender's section 7 and section 8 *Charter* rights.

b) Collection of Discarded DNA

i) R. v. Stillman

In *R. v. Stillman*,[117] police collected DNA samples from the appellant (a young person suspected of the rape and murder of a fourteen-year-old girl) while he was in custody following his arrest.[118] The youth initially refused to provide bodily samples, but submitted when police threatened to use force against him; hair samples and dental impressions were then obtained from him.[119] Police also obtained the appellant's DNA from a mucous sample taken from a tissue that he had discarded.[120] The appellant was rearrested several months later, and further hair samples and dental impressions, as well as buccal swabs, were taken without his consent.[121] The appellant was convicted of first-degree murder, and the Court of Appeal upheld his conviction.[122]

At the Supreme Court of Canada, Cory J. (writing for the five-judge majority) held that the appellant's section 7 and 8 *Charter* rights were seriously infringed when the bodily samples were taken.[123] Characterizing the invasion of bodily integrity as "the ultimate invasion of personal dignity and privacy,"[124] he held that the common law power of search and seizure incident to arrest could not be so broad as to allow officers to seize bodily samples.[125] Justice Cory also found that admitting compelled bodily samples into evidence would generally render a trial unfair, as it violated the

115 *R. v. S.A.B.*, 2003 SCC 60 at paras. 55 and 61 [*S.A.B.*].
116 *Rodgers*, above note 87.
117 *R. v. Stillman*, [1997] 1 S.C.R. 607 [*Stillman*].
118 *Ibid.* at paras. 2 and 5.
119 *Ibid.* at paras. 5–6.
120 *Ibid.* at para. 7.
121 *Ibid.* at para. 9.
122 *Ibid.* at para. 11.
123 *Ibid.* at paras. 91 and 123.
124 *Ibid.* at para. 87.
125 *Ibid.* at para. 49.

principle against self-incrimination and thus the section 7 right to security of the person.[126] The Court excluded the samples from evidence as per section 24(2) of the *Charter*, holding that it would shock the conscience of the community "that the police rode roughshod over a young offender's refusal to provide his bodily samples."[127]

Regarding the mucous sample obtained from the discarded tissue, Cory J. found that this seizure also constituted a *Charter* violation.[128] However, the majority and dissenting judges agreed that the DNA evidence obtained from the tissue should be admitted.[129] The majority held that this *Charter* violation was not serious, since the sample was not obtained by force and its seizure did not interfere with the appellant's dignity or bodily integrity, and concluded that its admission would not bring the administration of justice into disrepute.[130] Ultimately, the Court ordered a new trial, in which the bodily samples of the appellant's hair, saliva, and dental evidence would be excluded, while the mucous sample from the tissue would be admitted.[131]

*ii) Post-*Stillman *Caselaw Regarding Warrantless Collection of Discarded DNA*

Canadian caselaw post-*Stillman* has generally favoured admission of DNA samples obtained from objects discarded by the accused.[132] The taking of this type of sample is usually *Charter*-compliant, excepting certain circumstances where the accused was in police custody. As summarized in John Burchill's helpful article on this topic, section 8 *Charter* challenges regarding DNA obtained from abandoned items rarely succeed because

126 *Ibid.* at paras. 86 and 89.

127 *Ibid.* at para. 127.

128 *Ibid.* at para. 128.

129 *Ibid.* at paras. 128–29, 172, and 193.

130 *Ibid.* at para. 128.

131 *Ibid.* at para. 129.

132 In addition, some caselaw has supported the admissibility of complainant DNA samples taken via genital swab from suspects in sexual assault cases. See, for example, *R. v. Saeed*, 2014 ABCA 238 (Watson and Bielby JJ.A.), finding that the procedure violated s. 8 of the *Charter*, but admitting the evidence under s. 24(2); *R. v. Amey*, 2013 ONSC 5108 and *R. v. Harasemow*, 2014 BCSC 2287, holding that the taking of penile swabs did not violate ss. 7 or 8 of the *Charter* due to the exigent circumstances at play (though the resulting DNA samples were nonetheless excluded in *Amey* due to a s. 10(b) violation). Recently the Supreme Court of Canada weighed in on the issue, dismissing the appeal in the *Saeed* case with the majority finding (at para. 7) that the appellant's "s. 8 *Charter* rights were not breached, and that the evidence of the complainant's DNA obtained from the swabbing was properly admitted." For details, see *R. v. Saeed*, 2016 SCC 24.

the collection of discarded DNA evidence is not usually seen as a seizure and there is generally "no reasonable expectation of privacy in a person's garbage."[133] Specifically, courts have addressed the admissibility of warrantless DNA evidence in the following circumstances:

1) *Where the suspect is not in police custody (i.e., not detained)*: Police may safely collect and test items discarded by a suspect in a public place.[134] In *R. v. Delaa*, for example, an undercover officer induced the accused to provide a DNA sample by asking him to participate in a fictitious chewing gum survey.[135] The accused chewed four pieces of gum and spit them out into a Dixie cup provided by the officer.[136] The court held that this ruse did not violate Delaa's *Charter* rights, since he had no reasonable expectation of privacy in the gum that he discarded in a public place following his free choice to participate in the survey.[137]
2) *Where the suspect is not in police custody but is under some degree of police control (i.e., not detained)*: The Alberta Court of Appeal held in *R. v. Fash* that police can constitutionally retrieve discarded DNA samples that were obtained while the accused was on police property, but not in police custody.[138] In *Fash*, police obtained DNA samples from three cigarcttc butts discarded by the appellant in the course of a police interview in which he voluntarily agreed to participate (i.e., he was not detained).[139] During this interview, the appellant refused to provide bodily samples for DNA analysis.[140] The court found that the seizure of the appellant's discarded cigarette butts was not in violation of section 8 of the *Charter*, since he had no reasonable expectation of privacy in relation to them, and could have chosen not to smoke or to take the cigarette butts with him when he left.[141] The court upheld the trial judge's decision to admit the DNA evidence.[142]

---

133 The following examples are presented in: John Burchill, "Mr. Stillman, DNA and Discarded Evidence in Criminal Cases" (2008) 32 *Manitoba Law Journal* 5 at para. 3, PDF online: robsonhall.ca/mlj/sites/default/files/articles/burchill.pdf. It is recommended that this article be read in full for further discussion and caselaw on this topic.

134 *Stillman*, above note 117 at para. 38.

135 *R. v. Delaa*, [2006] A.J. No 948 (Q.B.).

136 *Ibid.* at paras. 26–27.

137 *Ibid.* at paras. 123–25.

138 *R. v. Fash*, 1999 ABCA 267 [*Fash*].

139 *Ibid.* at paras. 19–29 and 47.

140 *Ibid.* at paras. 43–44.

141 *Ibid.* at paras. 68–69.

142 *Ibid.* at paras. 70.

More recently, Clark J. of the Ontario Superior Court found in *R. v. Marini* that the seizure of the accused's DNA from two ginger ale cans that he had discarded in the courthouse during pre-trial motions did not violate his section 8 *Charter* rights.[143] The court found that the accused did not have a subjective expectation of privacy in the discarded cans, nor would such an expectation have been objectively reasonable.[144] The court rejected defence counsel's submission that there was a "coercive aspect"[145] to the accused's situation because he was required to attend at the courthouse throughout the pre-trial motions.[146] The accused did not have to drink any beverages at the courthouse (he was permitted to leave during recesses) or to discard the cans.[147] The court concluded that this case resembled not *Stillman* but *Fash*.[148] However, the court found that a reasonable expectation of privacy might attach to discarded DNA evidence where the accused had demonstrated that expectation by seeking to frustrate potential attempts to secure a DNA sample (e.g., by rinsing the cans before throwing them away).[149]

3) *Where the suspect is in police custody*: The caselaw generally favours admission of DNA evidence obtained from a suspect who is in custody at the time that the sample is discarded, even where the court finds a violation of the accused's *Charter* rights (as with the mucous sample in *Stillman*). In *R. v. Nguyen*, for example, police devised a plan to obtain a DNA sample from the appellant so as to circumvent his refusal to provide bodily samples.[150] Police offered the appellant a piece of gum while he was being transported to and from the courthouse; two DNA samples were obtained from the chewed gum that he discarded.[151] The Ontario Court of Appeal found that his section 8 rights were breached, because in these circumstances the appellant did not relinquish his privacy interest in the gum by discarding it.[152] The court admitted the evidence under section 24(2), because the officers were acting in good

143 *R. v. Marini*, [2005] O.J. No. 6197 at paras. 7, 21–22, and 34 (S.C.J.).
144 *Ibid.* at paras. 33–34.
145 *Ibid.* at para. 11.
146 *Ibid.* at paras. 11 and 52.
147 *Ibid.* at paras. 24 and 26.
148 *Ibid.* at paras. 27–28.
149 *Ibid.* at paras. 30 and 33.
150 *R. v. Nguyen* (2002), 161 C.C.C. (3d) 433 at para. 11 (Ont. C.A.) [*Nguyen*].
151 *Ibid.* at paras. 11–12.
152 *Ibid.* at paras. 15 and 21.

faith;[153] the evidence was non-conscriptive and discoverable; the seizure did not interfere with the appellant's dignity or bodily integrity; and considering the seriousness of the offence (first-degree murder) and the importance of this evidence, its exclusion would bring the administration of justice into disrepute.[154] The court agreed with the trial judge that the ruse was unobjectionable in that it was "entirely passive"[155]—the police had merely created an opportunity, the outcome of which depended on the voluntary actions of the accused.[156]

A contrasting example is *R. v. Johnson*, where the Manitoba Court of Queen's Bench found that obtaining a DNA sample from a cigar discarded by the accused while in police custody was not in violation of his section 8 *Charter* rights.[157] In *Johnson*, though the accused was "technically in custody,"[158] he was merely awaiting the completion of his bail paperwork; "his freedom was not restricted except for the fact that he could not leave without the documentation being completed."[159] Thus, he was free to step outside to smoke, and to abandon the cigar in the ashtray.[160] The trial judge concluded that the seizure of the cigar was constitutional, and admitted the DNA evidence.[161]

4) DNA Analysis Interpretation: Potential Problems Posed by Sample Contamination and Secondary Transference

In the words of Jerome Kennedy, Q.C., "as long as human beings are involved in the collection, testing and interpretation of DNA evidence and its presentation in Court there is the possibility of mistake."[162] Poor handling of samples by technicians and analysts, as well as a lack of understanding of the science behind DNA analysis by justice system participants, can give rise to dangerous errors in interpretation, generating wrongful convictions.

---

153 Note that this ruse was carried out prior to *Stillman*, above note 117.
154 *Nguyen*, above note 150 at paras. 1, 12, and 21.
155 *Ibid.* at para. 19.
156 *Ibid.* at paras. 19–20.
157 *R. v. Johnson*, 2004 MBQB 63 at para. 19.
158 *Ibid.* at para. 18.
159 *Ibid.*
160 *Ibid.*
161 *Ibid.* at para. 19.
162 Jerome Kennedy, "DNA Evidence—Do Not Be Afraid" (Paper delivered at the LSUC Seminar—Forensic Science and the Criminal Law, Toronto, 22 February 2014) at 1.

It is easy to make such mistakes of analysis or interpretation because DNA can be transferred by touch, either directly (e.g., when an offender touches a victim) or indirectly (e.g., when a laboratory technician touches a DNA sample and then touches an unrelated object). "Touch DNA" (the term for DNA left behind when a person touches or otherwise comes in contact with an object) typically features smaller deposits of DNA than are found in bodily fluid samples, but the same laboratory methods are employed for both types.[163]

Touch DNA analysis can be a powerful tool for identifying and prosecuting perpetrators, but also raises concerns regarding (1) contamination; and (2) incorrect inferences as to how an accused person's DNA ended up in the location where it was found.[164] When assessing the DNA evidence in court, the relationship, if any, between the victim and the accused must be taken into account to address the possibility of innocent DNA transfer. This is particularly true in family or cohabiting situations, since "[t]ouch DNA can easily be transferred throughout the household via day-to-day interactions, contact with furniture items/bedding, or through the laundry."[165]

a) DNA Sample Contamination

i) Human Error and Phantom Killers

Accidental DNA transfer between one DNA sample and another is a common problem that can produce false "matches."[166] In the *Turner* case, for instance,[167] the only evidence linking the accused to the victim was a small amount of her DNA found on a gold ring belonging to Turner.[168] The jury ultimately acquitted Turner; but, as he later explained to *Globe and Mail* justice reporter Kirk Makin, in view of this seemingly highly probative evidence, he had "feared he was bound for life in prison."[169]

The DNA testing in his case, however, had been far from perfect. Prior to the trial, Turner's defence counsel requested the DNA profiles of the RCMP laboratory personnel who had performed the DNA tests. He discovered that a lab technician had contaminated two of the exhibits with

---

163 Angela L. Williamson, "Touch DNA: Forensic Collection and Application to Investigations" (2012) 18 *Journal of the Association for Crime Scene Reconstruction* 1 at 1–2.

164 *Ibid.* at 4–5.

165 *Ibid.* at 3.

166 Thompson, above note 109.

167 *Ibid.* at 6, referencing *R. v. Turner*, [2001] N.J. No. 104 (S.C.T.D.) [*Turner*].

168 *Turner, ibid.* at paras. 1–2 and 11; Kennedy, above note 162 at 6; Makin, above note 109.

169 Makin, *ibid.*

her own DNA, mixing it with that of the victim. Moreover, this same technician had worked on Turner's ring at the same time that she was working on DNA from the complainant's fingernails; the two exhibits were only inches apart, raising the issue of possible cross-contamination.[170] The defence was then permitted to lead evidence of this possible contamination, alerting the jury to this problem and leading to an acquittal.[171]

Turner's circumstances, while unusual, are not unique; similar instances of DNA contamination adversely affecting an investigation have been documented in other jurisdictions. For example, Lukis Anderson of San Jose, California, was wrongly implicated in the murder of a Silicon Valley millionaire in a robbery in 2012.[172] Anderson was arrested after his DNA was found under the victim's fingernail. It emerged, however, that the DNA transfer from accused to victim was the result of contamination, rather than criminal activity: paramedics had clipped an oxygen-monitoring device onto Anderson's finger when he was brought to the hospital; later, the same implement was clipped to the victim's finger. Prosecutors dropped the charges against Anderson after defence counsel brought these events to their attention.[173]

A particularly infamous case of DNA contamination is "the Phantom of Heilbronn," the case of an elusive serial killer who left the same female DNA profile on objects retrieved from forty crime scenes, including fourteen murders. Investigators described this phantom killer as Germany's "most dangerous woman."[174] Eventually, police realized that this DNA profile originated from a factory worker—not a criminal mastermind—who had manufactured the cotton swabs used by police to take DNA samples at each of the crime scenes. The "Phantom" was aptly named; police had been searching for a prolific killer who did not in fact exist.[175]

Since it is not possible to determine how a given DNA sample arrived at the location where it was found, it is generally not possible to conclusively

---

170 *Ibid*; *Turner*, above note 167 at paras. 30–32 and 66; Kennedy, above note 162 at 6.

171 *Turner*, above note 167 at paras. 64 and 66; "RCMP Defends Murder Investigation" *CBC News* (29 May 2003), online: www.cbc.ca/news/canada/newfoundland-labrador/rcmp-defends-murder-investigation-1.411466.

172 Tracey Kaplan, "Monte Sereno Murder Case Casts Doubt on DNA Evidence" *San Jose Mercury News* (28 June 2014), online: www.mercurynews.com/crime-courts/ci_26055401/san-jose-case-casts-doubts-dna-evidence; Obasogie, above note 84.

173 *Ibid.*

174 Makin, above note 109; "'DNA Bungle' Haunts German Police" *BBC News* (28 March 2009), online: http://news.bbc.co.uk/2/hi/europe/7966641.stm.

175 *Ibid.*; Obasogie, above note 84.

prove that DNA found on a piece of evidence arrived there via cross-contamination rather than direct contact, unless the DNA profile in question belongs to a third party.[176] For this reason, the impact of evidence concerning the possibility or likelihood of DNA sample contamination must be assessed on a case-by-case basis.

For example, in *R. v. Doan*, the British Columbia Court of Appeal upheld the trial judge's finding that the possibility of secondary DNA transference among various objects retrieved from the crime scene did not raise a reasonable doubt as to the appellant's guilt.[177] Doan and his co-accused were convicted of various offences pertaining to the kidnapping of three complainants.[178] In finding that the complainants had been bound and their mouths duct-taped shut, the trial judge relied heavily on the presence of two complainants' DNA on duct tape retrieved from the crime scene.[179] He reached this conclusion despite the questionable methodology of the officers who searched the scene: they wore the same pair of gloves throughout, and emptied numerous bags of evidence "onto one large plastic sheet."[180]

On appeal, Doan argued that the trial judge misapprehended the expert evidence that the DNA samples could have been cross-contaminated by the officers.[181] The Crown and defence experts had agreed that the DNA evidence found on the duct tape could theoretically have been transferred "from other personal items in the garbage or the gloves worn in the search."[182] However, the court saw no reason to interfere with the trial judge's rejection of this explanation,[183] noting that (1) several different DNA transfers would have had to occur, thereby (2) coincidentally producing the DNA pattern that one would expect "from duct tape that had covered a mouth."[184]

ii) Secondary DNA Transference between Parts of the Complainant's Body

Secondary transference of the accused's DNA from one location on the complainant's body to another may occur and is an issue that may be relevant to counsel's argument. In the Ontario Court of Appeal case *R. v. M.C.*,

---

176 *R. v. Abdelhamid*, 2015 MBCA 35 at paras. 26 and 30 [*Abdelhamid*]; Kennedy, above note 162 at 6; Makin, above note 109.

177 *R. v. Doan*, 2013 BCCA 123 at paras. 38–39.

178 *Ibid.* at paras. 1–2.

179 *Ibid.* at paras. 9–11.

180 *Ibid.* at para. 14.

181 *Ibid.* at para. 5.

182 *Ibid.* at paras. 17, 22, and 27.

183 *Ibid.* at para. 38.

184 *Ibid.* at para. 21.

for example,[185] the five-year-old complainant had testified that M.C. had digitally penetrated and performed oral sex on her while playing games described as "tickle monster" and "zerbert monster."[186] Justice LaForme (writing for the court) found that the trial judge had "critically misapprehended the forensic evidence"[187] that she relied on to convict the appellant. The trial judge had incorrectly held that the 322-nanogram deposit of DNA retrieved from the front panel area of the complainant's underwear—which she incorrectly stated was from the crotch area—was comprised solely of the appellant's DNA, meaning that the sample was too large to have been the result of secondary DNA transference.[188] In fact, the DNA expert had testified that this sample included DNA from both the complainant and the appellant.[189] The expert had testified that she "could not rule out secondary transference onto the underwear from saliva that was deposited on [the complainant's] ... hand or stomach"[190] when he gave her "zerberts" in these areas. Justice LaForme found that these errors had impacted the trial judge's credibility and reliability assessment.[191] He allowed the appeal and ordered a new trial.[192]

By contrast, in *R. v. Abdelhamid*, the Manitoba Court of Appeal upheld the appellant's conviction for the sexual assault of his patient notwithstanding the theoretical possibility of secondary transference of his DNA from one part of the patient's body to another.[193] The appellant's DNA was found on the complainant's genital area.[194] The trial judge rejected the defence submission "that a secondary transfer of DNA had ... resulted from the skin-to-skin examination"[195] of the complainant by the appellant—which the DNA experts agreed was a possibility[196]—finding instead that the DNA evidence was better explained by a sexual assault.[197] Justice Monnin (writing for the appellate court) found that this conclusion was

---

185 *R. v. M.C.*, 2014 ONCA 307 [*M.C.*].
186 *Ibid.* at paras. 1–2.
187 *Ibid.* at para. 29.
188 *Ibid.* at paras. 30, 36–41, 54, and 58.
189 *Ibid.* at para. 39.
190 *Ibid.* at para. 19.
191 *Ibid.* at para. 44.
192 *Ibid.* at paras. 29 and 66.
193 *Abdelhamid*, above note 176 at paras. 1 and 4.
194 *Ibid.* at para. 30.
195 *Ibid.* at para. 31.
196 *Ibid.* at paras. 29–31.
197 *Ibid.* at paras. 31–32.

open to the trial judge,[198] and moreover that the DNA evidence was secondary to the trial judge's reasoning and was "not the sort of material evidence that would bring about the type of evidentiary misapprehension that is referred to in *M.C.*"[199]

5) Interpretation Issues: Scope of Expert Testimony, Use of Statistics, and Contextual Bias

The persuasive power of DNA evidence derives from its use of probability statistics, which express the likelihood of two randomly selected individuals in a population having "matching" genetic profiles by chance.[200] It is common for both juries and legal actors to be confused about how statistics relate to the probative value of the DNA evidence, and, as a result, it is easy to commit logical fallacies in interpreting this evidence.[201] Statistical interpretation in criminal trials remains controversial, as it is widely agreed that jurors usually apply statistics incorrectly to decision making and may commit either prosecution-friendly or defence-friendly errors.[202]

In early Canadian caselaw treating DNA evidence, the courts considered how to handle the presentation of statistics in the context of DNA analysis, given the ability of these data to overwhelm the jury and the need for them to be presented by a qualified expert. In two unrelated judgments from 1991, *R. v. Baptiste* and *R. v. Bourguignon*, the court rejected the use of statistical evidence but allowed the experts to qualitatively describe probability as "remote," "extremely remote," and "rare."[203] In *Bourguignon*, the statistical evidence was not admitted due to the realistic fear that the jury would commit the "prosecutor's fallacy"—defined in *Terceira* as "equating the probability of a random match with the probability of the appellant's innocence."[204]

---

198 *Ibid.* at para. 32.

199 *Ibid.* at para. 33.

200 Soren Frederiksen, "The National Academy of Sciences, Canadian DNA Jurisprudence and Changing Forensic Practice" (2011) 35 *Manitoba Law Journal* 111 at 126.

201 Ron C. Michaelis, Robert G. Flanders, Jr., & Paula H. Wuff, *A Litigator's Guide to DNA: From the Laboratory to the Courtroom* (Burlington, MA: Elsevier, 2008) at 91.

202 *Ibid.* at 241.

203 Frederiksen, above note 200 at 130–33, referencing *R. v. Baptiste*, [1991] B.C.J. No. 3945 (S.C.); *R. v. Baptiste* (1994), 88 C.C.C. (3d) 211 (B.C.C.A.); and *R. v. Bourguignon*, [1990] O.J. No. 1205 (Prov. Ct.).

204 *Ibid.*; *Terceira*, above note 99 at para. 58.

In the 1992 case of *R. v. Johnston*, statistics expressing the likelihood of a random match were also found to be inadmissible, due to the imprecise and subjective components of the process used to generate them.[205] Conversely, Vertes J.S.C. took the opposite view in the roughly contemporaneous case of *R. v. Lafferty*,[206] where he found that there is no subjective judgment involved in performing the probability calculations pertaining to the DNA analysis, guarding against the potential abuse of such evidence and requiring contrary expert evidence to attack the underlying assumptions of population genetics.[207]

In the wake of *Mohan*, defence counsel have continued to challenge the admissibility of probability statistics in the context of DNA evidence, particularly in view of the potentially overwhelming impact of these statistics on the jury. Courts have generally held, however, that these concerns should go to weight, rather than admissibility. In 1996, the court in *R. v. Beamish*[208] denied the accused's request that the expert giving testimony on the DNA analysis at issue "be restricted from expressing any opinion on the probability estimates in numerical or statistical terms,"[209] finding that the use of qualitative adjectives alone would "not convey the full evidence to the jury."[210] Subsequently, the courts in *Terceira*[211] and *Eatman*[212] upheld the decision of the respective trial judges to admit statistical evidence regarding DNA analysis. In *Eatman*, Larlee J.A.—relying on *Terceira*—held that the admission of statistical evidence should be left to the trial judge's discretion because:

> [T]he concern over the effects that these probability statistics may have on a jury is a matter of weight, not admissibility. These statistics are clearly relevant and any concerns over the potential prejudicial effects of the evidence can be extinguished with a proper instruction by the trial judge.[213]

A striking example of a defence challenge to the presentation of DNA statistical evidence is found in Larry Fisher's 2003 appeal.[214] After David

---

205 *R. v. Johnston* (1992), 69 C.C.C. (3d) 395 at para. 133 (Ont. Ct. Gen. Div.).
206 *R. v. Lafferty* (1993), 80 C.C.C. (3d) 150 (N.W.T.S.C.).
207 *Ibid.*
208 *R. v. Beamish* (1996), 144 Nfld. & P.E.I.R. 310 (P.E.I.S.C.T.D.) [*Beamish*].
209 *Ibid.* at para. 22.
210 *Ibid.* at para. 26.
211 *Terceira*, above note 99.
212 *R. v. Eatman* (1999), 222 N.B.R. (2d) 120 (C.A.) [*Eatman*].
213 *Ibid.* at para. 19, citing *Terceira*, above note 99 at para. 43.
214 *R. v. Fisher*, 2003 SKCA 90 at para. 4 [*Fisher*].

Milgaard spent twenty-three years in prison for a murder that he did not commit, DNA testing in 1997 showed that Larry Fisher, a serial rapist, was the true perpetrator.[215] In 1998, Fisher was convicted on the basis of this DNA evidence, similar fact evidence of three other rapes that he committed, and additional circumstantial evidence.[216] Fisher appealed, arguing that the random match probability statistic—estimated by the expert to be one in 950 trillion[217]—should have been determined by a population geneticist or population biologist, rather than a forensic DNA analyst.[218] The court rejected this argument, holding that the forensic DNA analyst was qualified to present the statistical likelihood of a random match, and that deficiencies in the witness's knowledge should go to weight, rather than admissibility.[219] The court also rejected Fisher's argument that the probability of a random match was such an overwhelming number that it would mislead the jury and result in an unfair trial,[220] holding that the assessment of the statistic's probative value and prejudicial effect should be left to the trial judge, and that there was no reason to interfere with the decision to admit this evidence.[221] The court concluded that a jury instruction addressing the limitations of the expert and statistical evidence should be sufficient to guard against potential prejudice to the accused.[222]

6) Can Courts Establish a Perpetrator's Identity on DNA Evidence Alone?

In view of the interpretive dangers posed by secondary transference and cross-contamination, most Canadian courts appear reluctant to found a conviction on DNA evidence alone. Courts do, however, appear generally willing to convict individuals whose DNA is found at the scene where: (1) there is at least one additional significant piece of evidence; and/or (2) it

215 Sarah Harland-Logan, "Historical Cases: David Milgaard," online: Innocence Canada www.aidwyc.org/cases/historical/david-milgaard.

216 *Fisher*, above note 214 at para. 4.

217 *Ibid.* at para. 22.

218 *Ibid.* at paras. 8–9.

219 *Ibid.* at para. 19; such deficiencies include "lack of more training in statistics, personal knowledge of the compilation of the database, and reliance upon the studies of others" (*ibid.*).

220 *Ibid.* at para. 22.

221 *Ibid.* at paras. 26–29.

222 *Ibid.* at para. 29.

is clear that the DNA evidence was deposited contemporaneously with the offence in question.

In *R. v. Wills*,[223] for example, the appellant's DNA, along with that of other unidentified persons, was found on two bandanas used in a robbery.[224] In addition, one complainant described a weapon carried by one of the robbers that resembled a metal baton seized from the appellant's closet.[225] Justice Doherty (writing for the majority) found that the DNA evidence, though important, could not alone support the inference that the appellant was one of the burglars since there was no indication as to when the appellant's DNA had been deposited on the bandanas.[226] The reasonableness of the appellant's conviction was therefore dependent on the probative value of the evidence of the baton found in the appellant's closet.[227] Justice Doherty described this case as a "close call,"[228] but was satisfied that the combined force of the DNA and baton evidence was sufficient to render the jury's verdict reasonable.[229]

DNA evidence played a still larger role in *R. v. Mufuta*, where the appellant had been convicted of voyeurism.[230] The Crown's key piece of evidence was a sample of the appellant's DNA obtained from a pop bottle that had been left in the bathroom stall where the voyeuristic act took place.[231] Despite finding that the rest of the Crown's identification evidence was "completely neutral,"[232] the trial judge held that "the only rational conclusion . . . was that the appellant was guilty."[233] The appellant submitted that this verdict was unreasonable.[234] Justice Cronk (writing for the court) dismissed this argument and upheld the conviction.[235] She

---

223 *R. v. Wills*, 2014 ONCA 178 at paras. 1–2 and 86 [*Wills*].
224 *Ibid.* at paras. 2–3 and 14–17.
225 *Ibid.* at paras. 19–21.
226 *Ibid.* at paras. 18, 34, and 36.
227 *Ibid.* at para. 42.
228 *Ibid.* at para. 44.
229 *Ibid.* The case was appealed to the Supreme Court of Canada: *R. v. Wills*, 2014 SCC 73. The majority, in a 3:2 split, dismissed the appeal for the reasons set out by Doherty J.A.
230 *R. v. Mufuta*, 2015 ONCA 50 [*Mufuta*].
231 *Ibid.* at para. 7.
232 *Ibid.* at para. 10.
233 *Ibid.* at paras. 10 and 13.
234 *Ibid.* at para. 14.
235 *Ibid.* at paras. 42 and 50.

distinguished the case from *R. v. Mars*[236] and *R. v. Wills*,[237] finding that the DNA obtained from the pop bottle was "a powerful piece of evidence linking the appellant to the scene of the crime,"[238] particularly since (in contrast to *Wills*) the appellant was the sole contributor to the DNA sample.[239] Moreover, unlike in *Mars* and *Wills*, other evidence established a timeline for the deposition of the DNA evidence on the bottle, tying this event to the time of the offence.[240]

The general principle articulated in *Mufuta* and *Wills*—that, in addition to the DNA evidence, some further supporting evidence will be required to found a conviction[241]—has not, however, been universally adopted. In *R. v. McLeod*, for example, the only evidence presented at trial came from two DNA experts called by the Crown. [242] There was no evidence that McLeod "knew the [murder] victim or even that he was in the same neighbourhood or same city at the time of the offence. The Crown's entire case ultimately rested on the results of the DNA testing"[243] of a cucumber, a paring knife, and a pair of underwear found near the victim's body.[244] The appellant could not be excluded as a contributor of DNA found on all three items.[245]

The Saskatchewan Court of Appeal dismissed all three of McLeod's grounds of appeal. First, the court dismissed the appellant's argument that an accused person's identity "cannot be proven by DNA evidence alone in the absence of an 'attribution statement,'"[246] that is, a DNA expert's

---

236 In *R. v. Mars* (2006), 205 C.C.C. (3d) 376 (Ont. C.A.), the court held that the fingerprint evidence at issue was not by itself sufficient to prove the appellant's guilt. (See further discussion in Chapter 8.)

237 *Wills*, above note 223.

238 *Mufuta*, above note 230 at para. 24.

239 *Ibid.* at paras. 24, 27, and 32–34, referencing *Wills*, above note 223 at paras. 14–17.

240 *Ibid.* at para. 41.

241 See also *R. v. Ibrahim*, 2014 ONCA 157 (upholding the appellant's robbery conviction based on deposits of his DNA obtained from a balaclava and toy gun retrieved within forty-five minutes of the offence from a nearby garbage bin).

242 *R. v. McLeod*, 2010 SKCA 43 at paras. 6 and 16 [*McLeod*]. (See also *R. v. Johnson*, 2010 ABCA 230, upholding the appellant's sexual assault conviction based solely on the DNA evidence, various inferences deriving therefrom, and a vague description in the victim's statement.)

243 *McLeod*, above note 242 at para. 16.

244 *Ibid.* at paras. 3–4.

245 *Ibid.* at paras. 9–11. Regarding the sample taken from the underwear, the probability of randomly selecting an unrelated individual whose DNA profile matched the perpetrator's was one in 8.5 trillion (Canadian Caucasian population) or one in 140 billion (First Nations population): at para. 9.

246 *Ibid.* at para. 17.

statement that the DNA sample came from the accused, to 99.9 percent certainty.[247] The court found that the "beyond a reasonable doubt" standard does not equate to this high certainty threshold,[248] and upheld the trial judge's finding that though this threshold had not been met in this case, there was no reasonable doubt as to the appellant's guilt.[249] The trial judge had correctly understood the limits of the DNA evidence, including that it did not "serve as a direct answer to the question"[250] of the appellant's guilt.[251] Second, the court dismissed McLeod's argument that "the trial judge failed to take proper account of the impact of 'related populations' on random match probabilities,"[252] since there was no evidence that any of his relatives were suspects.[253] Finally, the court rejected the argument that the underwear, which was discovered later than the other two items, had been planted at the scene.[254] The conviction was upheld,[255] and the Supreme Court of Canada dismissed McLeod's application for leave to appeal.[256]

7) DNA Canvassing in Small Communities

Familial or kinship DNA searching—that is, searching a DNA data bank for a "profile that has a high probability of belonging to a close relative of the person who left the crime scene evidence"[257] (rather than to that specific person)—is not authorized under the *DNA Identification Act*.[258] However, this method can be used in the context of police performing mass-testing of groups of people without warrants under the auspices of a request for

247 *Ibid.* at para. 19.
248 *Ibid.* at para. 22.
249 *Ibid.* at paras. 13–15 and 21–24.
250 *Ibid.* at para. 24.
251 *Ibid.* at paras. 23–24.
252 *Ibid.* at para. 17; see also paras. 25–32.
253 *Ibid.* at paras. 30–31.
254 *Ibid.* at para. 34.
255 *Ibid.* at para. 35.
256 *R. v. McLeod*, [2010] S.C.C.A. No. 158.
257 Bellamy-Royds & Norris, above note 91 at 10.
258 *Ibid.* at 12; *DNA Identification Act*, above note 111. For a case example, see *R. v. Karas*, 2007 ABCA 362, leave to appeal to S.C.C. refused, [2008] S.C.C.A. No. 22. This judgment considers the question of whether or not Karas provided his DNA sample voluntarily, rather than addressing the constitutionality of the investigative practice of familial DNA searching. The court held that "the principles governing the voluntariness of confessions are applicable when considering whether [the accused] . . . voluntarily gave his blood sample" (see para. 32, referencing *R. v. Oickle*, 2000 SCC 38 at paras. 68 and 71).

community members to voluntarily provide samples to aid in an investigation. This technique, termed a "DNA dragnet"[259] or "DNA canvass,"[260] may identify suspects through familial DNA recorded in the data bank when their own DNA is not present in that data bank.[261]

One such DNA canvass was performed in the case of *R. v. Osmond*, where the defendant was convicted (at his second trial) of the first-degree murder of a thirteen-year-old girl.[262] Police performed a DNA canvass, collecting approximately twelve DNA samples from young men in the victim's community in Zeballos, British Columbia, population approximately 750.[263] Osmond's profile matched the suspect DNA found on the victim's fingernail clippings and on her sister's bed (where she would often sleep).[264] The defence argued that the DNA evidence obtained through the community canvass was inadmissible.[265] Analogizing this technique to the "random virtue testing" disapproved of in *R. v. Swan*,[266] Osmond submitted that the canvass had "almost Orwellian overtones"[267] and offended the presumption of innocence.[268] The trial judge rejected these arguments, finding that the use of the DNA canvass in this case did not violate any of the accused's *Charter* rights.[269] The British Columbia Court of Appeal upheld this judgment, holding that this investigation was "much more focussed" than the

---

259 Vincenzo Rondinelli, "The DNA Dragnet: A Modern Day Salem Witch Hunt?" (2003) 10 *Criminal Reports* (6th) 16; Jonathan Will, "Comment: DNA as Property: Implications on the Constitutionality of DNA Dragnets" (2003) 65 *University of Pittsburgh Law Review* 129; Sepideh Esmaili, "Search for a Needle in a Haystack: The Constitutionality of Police DNA Dragnets" (2007) 82 *Chicago-Kent Law Review* 495.

260 *R. v. Osmond*, 2012 BCCA 382 at paras. 8, 16, and 22 [*Osmond* BCCA]. This case was considered in *R. v. Leung*, 2013 BCSC 412, but not in the context of a DNA canvass. See also the court's discussion of informed consent in *R. v. Swite*, 2012 BCSC 1518.

261 Bellamy-Royds & Norris, above note 91 at 10 and 13.

262 *R. v. Osmond*, 2009 BCSC 1713 at paras. 1 and 22–30.

263 *Ibid.* at paras. 1, 5; *R. v. Osmond*, 2009 BCSC 550 at para. 12 [*Osmond voir dire*]; *Osmond* BCCA, above note 260 at para. 6.

264 *Osmond* BCCA, *ibid.* at para. 10.

265 *Ibid* at paras. 7–9. (N.B.: The *voir dire* where the defence first made this argument was conducted before Garson J., who was unable to complete the trial but whose reasons were adopted in full by the trial judge.)

266 *Osmond voir dire*, above note 263 at para. 24; *Osmond* BCCA, *ibid.* at paras. 16–18, citing *R. v. Swan*, 2009 BCCA 142 at para. 29. In *Swan*, police cold-called various numbers, absent any basis for reasonable suspicion, in hopes of discovering "dial-a-dope operations" (paras. 10, 25, and 29); the court found that this behaviour constituted entrapment and ordered a stay of proceedings (paras. 44 and 49).

267 *Osmond voir dire*, above note 263 at para. 24.

268 *Ibid.*

269 *Ibid.* at paras. 57–58; *Osmond* BCCA, above note 260 at paras. 9–10.

one in *Swan* and was a permissible process in the circumstances.[270] Leave to appeal to the Supreme Court of Canada was refused, affirming the use of warrantless DNA canvassing.[271]

The officer who supervised the investigation in *Osmond* testified that police chose to perform a DNA canvass since they had no suspects for whom they could seek DNA warrants.[272] He went on to testify that "it might mean something if a person refused"[273] to be sampled for the DNA canvass (implying that anyone who refused could be considered a suspect for that reason). Consider, in this context, Russell J.A.'s salient observation in the earlier DNA warrant case of *R. v. S.A.B.*:

> It must be acknowledged that it cannot be assumed that the innocent will voluntarily submit to DNA testing. There may be any number of reasons for an innocent person to refuse . . . including fear or distrust of those in authority, or fear of inculpation with respect to another crime.[274]

The Supreme Court of Canada has yet to hear a case addressing the overarching policy implications of DNA canvassing—a wide-reaching, non-target-specific technique that intrudes upon the privacy interests of third parties. The approach taken by Arbour J. in *R. v. S.A.B.* (at the Supreme Court level) may indicate that the Court will one day find that warrantless DNA canvassing generally casts too wide a net, and that such non-target-specific, intrusive searches must be judicially authorized as an investigative tool of last resort, similar to wiretap authorizations.[275]

---

270 *Ibid.* at paras. 22 and 24.
271 *R. v. Osmond*, [2013] S.C.C.A. No. 40.
272 *Osmond voir dire*, above note 263 at para. 51.
273 *Ibid.*
274 *R. v S.A.B.*, 2001 ABCA 235 at para. 88 (affirmed in *S.A.B.*, above note 115).
275 *S.A.B.*, above note 115 at paras. 53–54.

CHAPTER 13

Forensic Botany

Rolf W. Mathewes

LEGAL CONTEXT: CAITLIN PAKOSH

A. OVERVIEW

> Forensic botany is the study of plants and how they can relate to law and legal matters.[1]

In a broad sense, all definitions of forensic botany refer to the scientific use of plants and plant parts in legal cases. Several books and publications have showcased the discipline as a useful investigative tool across a variety of cases.[2] In addition to criminal investigations and court proceedings, forensic botanical evidence may also be useful in cases involving Aboriginal land claims, as described in Section F, below. Botany's possible forensic applications rely on a broad range of studies involving plant anatomy, growth patterns (i.e., growth rings in wood), phenology (i.e., timing of flowering, pollination, fruiting, and leaf fall), taxonomy (i.e., identifica-

---

1 David W. Hall, "Introduction to Forensic Botany" in D.W. Hall & J.H. Byrd, eds., *Forensic Botany: A Practical Guide* (West Sussex, UK: Wiley-Blackwell, 2012) at 1 [Hall, "Introduction to Forensic Botany"].

2 *Ibid*; Heather Miller Coyle, ed., *Forensic Botany, Principles and Applications to Criminal Casework* (Boca Raton, FL: CRC Press, 2005) [Coyle, ed., *Forensic Botany Applications*] (a particularly good summary of various sub-disciplines of forensic botany); Shirley Graham, "Crime Solving Plants" (Fall 2006) 52 *Plant Science Bulletin* 78 [Graham, "Crime Solving Plants"]; A.G. Brown, "The Use of Forensic Botany and Geology in War Crimes Investigations in NE Bosnia" (2006) 163 *Forensic Science International* 204 [Brown, "Forensic Botany in NE Bosnia"].

tion), ecology, and other aspects, including the use of plant DNA to confirm identifications or establish links of investigative interest.

Forensic botany has a long history in several jurisdictions globally and has been successfully used and accepted in court proceedings in the United States, Great Britain, New Zealand, and Australia, among others. Published information and legal decisions involving forensic botany are rare in Canada, suggesting that forensic botany is an underused forensic tool.[3] The reasons for this underuse are many, including a general lack of knowledge about plants by police investigators, relatively few specialists in plant science who conduct forensic investigations and testify in court, and educational systems that de-emphasize classical whole-plant botanical studies in favour of new molecular approaches. Current trends are clearly towards the use of plant DNA and palynology as key tools in forensic botany.[4]

The 1935 Lindbergh kidnapping case in New Jersey is a particularly well-known and instructive landmark case involving forensic botany in North America. The investigation and court proceedings relied heavily on testimony by Arthur Koehler, an expert in wood anatomy and identification, whose findings ultimately contributed to the conviction of Bruno Richard Hauptmann, who was later executed.[5] Two pieces of wood played a key role in the trial. One was part of a rail from the homemade ladder used in the abduction. The other was from a cut floorboard in the attic of Hauptmann's residence in the Bronx, discovered after he was arrested for passing marked money from the ransom. Koehler's analysis made a convincing match of wood species, growth rings, tool marks, and nail holes that showed the ladder was constructed, in part, from wood in Hauptmann's attic and fashioned by Hauptmann's plane.

A host of other case applications in the United States have followed the Lindbergh case, notably through the work of Dr. V.M. Bryant, Jr. and his co-workers in Texas, using the relatively new techniques of palynology.[6]

---

3 Jane H. Bock & David O. Norris, "Forensic Botany: An Under-Utilized Resource" (1997) 42 *Journal of Forensic Science* 364; Heather Miller Coyle et al., "Forensic Botany: Using Plant Evidence to Aid in Forensic Death Investigation" (2005) 46 *Croatian Medical Journal* 606 [Coyle et al., "Death Investigation"].

4 Coyle et al., "Death Investigation," *ibid.*

5 Hall, "Introduction to Forensic Botany," above note 1; Graham, "Crime Solving Plants," above note 2.

6 D.C. Mildenhall, P.E.J. Wiltshire, & V.M. Bryant, "Forensic Palynology: Why Do It and How It Works" (2006) 163 *Forensic Science International* 163 [Mildenhall et al., "Why Forensic Palynology"].

In Canada, forensic botany in general and palynology in particular have a limited history in court proceedings[7] and, although botany has been successfully applied as an investigative tool in many homicide and other investigations, the discipline is not typically featured in trial judgments.

Macroscopic plant parts, like seeds and leaves, as well as microscopic pollen and spores associated with crime scenes are useful trace evidence, but perhaps not surprisingly, they are generally viewed as less definitive than other types of evidence, like DNA analysis. Nevertheless, in some Canadian homicide and other investigations, forensic botany has proven an important investigative tool.[8]

B. THE SCIENCE OF FORENSIC BOTANY

1) Basic Principles of Investigation

In all cases, investigations using forensic botany rely on the experience of the investigating botanist backed by a solid training in botany, plant ecology, plant anatomy, taxonomy, and other basic plant science knowledge. The principles of investigation must be tailored to the specific circumstances of the case under investigation, and depend on local circumstances regarding the quality of the preserved evidence (the condition of the sample) as well as the environmental context. Training and experience can be applied in a variety of ways to interpret evidence from a crime scene, and naturally varies among forensic botanists.

If the investigation involves fieldwork by the botanist, such as visiting a crime scene or searching for a clandestine grave, then careful field notes, samples, and camera documentation of local vegetation composition and conditions are crucial for later analysis and support for expert testimony in court. The principles of investigation using plants or plant parts can be grouped into four categories:

1) *Macroscopic plant materials*: Identification, quantification, and interpretation of scattered leaves, seeds, whole mosses, other plants, wood or wood fragments, and other plant parts that can be seen with the

---

7 Rolf W. Mathewes, "Forensic Palynology in Canada: An Overview with Emphasis on Archaeology and Anthropology" (2006) 163 *Forensic Science International* 198 [Mathewes, "Forensic Palynology in Canada"].

8 The author has personally submitted over twenty casework reports to various police departments or coroners, including the Royal Canadian Mounted Police Serious Crimes Unit, but only once to defence counsel.

naked eye. Since visible materials are sometimes noticed during police investigations, they may be collected at the scene or during an autopsy and later sent to botanists for identification and interpretation. The ideal, however, is to include a botanist early in an investigation to collect, prepare, and preserve the samples that might later be presented as evidence in court proceedings.

2) *Microscopic remains*: Identification, quantification, and interpretation of pollen, spores of plants and fungi, and other microscopic organic remains that can be recovered from soil, air filters, or a wide range of other materials, such as carpets, packing materials, drugs, fabrics, hair, stomach contents, and any other surfaces where dust can accumulate (including automobile or window glass, walls, floors, etc.). The forensic value of these potential information sources lies in the fact that they are present during the commission of crimes but not visible to the naked eye of individuals committing crimes, who can carry contact traces with them on their person or in vehicles. They are also not visible to investigators, which makes collecting and using microscopic evidence difficult in practice unless a specialist can attend to the collection of samples.

   Pollen specifically has been valuable in the forensic context and has helped to:

   - Link offenders or their belongings to places and other objects.
   - Predict the location of places associated with suspects or their belongings.
   - Estimate the length of time human remains or objects have lain *in situ*.
   - Differentiate between murder sites and body deposition sites.
   - Provide information on perimortem events affecting the deceased.
   - Provide limited temporal information on the post-mortem interval through gut analysis.
   - Provide information concerning food intake prior to death through gut analysis.[9]

---

9 Patricia E.J. Wiltshire, "Consideration of Some Taphonomic Variables of Relevance to Forensic Palynological Investigation in the United Kingdom" (2006) 163 *Forensic Science International* 173 [Wiltshire, "Taphonomic Variables"]; Eleanor White et al., "Microsatellite Markers for Individual Tree Genotyping: Application in Forest Crime Prosecutions" (2000) 75 *Journal of Chemical Technology and Biotechnology* 923 [White et al., "Microsatellite Markers"].

Forensic pathology considers time of death estimates based on stomach contents to be unreliable. As a result, estimates of the post-mortem interval based on forensic botany evidence involving gut analysis should be viewed with caution and limits to such evidence should be thoroughly canvassed by counsel.[10]

3) *Plant DNA*: Plants produce three kinds of DNA (nuclear, mitochondrial, and chloroplast) that can be analyzed and used to identify plant fragments to the species level. Techniques to identify plants through chloroplast DNA barcoding show promise.[11] In some cases, databases exist or can be constructed to link plant fragments to a specific location and even an individual source plant.
4) *Phenological and taphonomic considerations*: Phenology is the study of the timing and seasonality of plants, such as germination, growth rates, flowering and fruiting, and leaf drop. Taphonomy is the study of processes that transport, preserve, decompose, or otherwise alter plant remains at a location. Such information can help to establish timelines and alternate explanations for the presence of plant evidence at a crime scene.

Most investigations need to incorporate identification and quantification of plant material into their investigation prior to interpretation and reporting of what these data may mean. Proper preservation and storage of plant evidence in a secure lockup is vital in case it is needed for follow-up studies or court proceedings.

2) Methods and Applications

a) Macroscopic Plant Materials

Fragmentary plant parts, such as leaves, flower parts, seeds and fruits, woody stems, twigs, and roots, or whole small plants such as mosses, liverworts, lichens, and fungi, are often encountered during an investigation. These plant materials are sometimes collected as potential evidence by police and sent to a forensic botanist for identification and interpretation. On occasion, fresh plant material is collected by

---

10 For more information about forensic pathology and the use of stomach contents in determining time of death, specifically in the Steven Truscott case, see Chapter 18.

11 P.D.N. Hebert et al., "Biological Identifications through DNA Barcodes" (2003) 270 *Proceedings of the Royal Society B: Biological Sciences* 313 [Hebert et al., "Biological Identifications"].

investigators. Anyone collecting specimens as potential evidence should take care not to collect the plant material in sealed, plastic evidence bags because mold can develop quickly in such conditions, degrading the plant material and interfering with subsequent analysis. Samples are best collected dried in a paper bag or frozen until analysis. Rehydrating and pressing and drying the plant material for long-term preservation are best done by a botanist.

Depending on what material is present and how well it is preserved, identification of common plants is relatively straightforward using a dissecting microscope, standard reference manuals (either in book form or online), and electronic databases such as the eFlora of British Columbia. Specimens can also be checked against reference collections of preserved plants in university or provincial herbaria, ideally through on-site visits or through online collections of images. Important evidence should be documented using macrophotography or digital photography under a dissecting microscope.

If detailed identifications of plant material need to be made or confirmed, the forensic botanist may need to seek the advice of taxonomic specialists. In rare cases, a scanning electron microscope may be needed to examine surface details of small seeds or other plant parts.

It is often necessary during identification to section plant parts (i.e., to cut into thin slices) to help identify tissues or to determine plant age based on growth rings. Where the material is well preserved, it is usually sufficient to "hand-section" a specimen using a single-edged razor blade. Embedding the specimen in wax is sometimes necessary before sectioning, but this requires special equipment and is time-consuming. Sections may also be stained with various dyes to highlight specific tissues before mounting on microscope slides for examination. Plant specimens, slides, photographs, and notes must be retained and securely stored, as required for all forensic evidence.

b) Microscopic Remains

Palynology, or pollen analysis, is mostly concerned with the recovery and study of pollen grains, spores, and other small organic plant material. The techniques used to analyze these microscopic plant remains have an extensive history in archaeology, geology, forest history, climatology, and other scientific areas, but they were not applied forensically until 1959, when they were used in a homicide case in Austria. Since then, forensic palynology has been successfully applied to many types of criminal investigations and court cases in Great Britain,[12] New Zealand,[13] Australia,[14] and the United States.[15] As mentioned above, pollen analysis is rarely used in Canada.

The methods used to collect and identify pollen and spores in a forensic context are well described,[16] including constraints and limitations of data and interpretation.[17]

The methods of palynology are founded on the following basic principles:

1) Most pollen types are variable in size, shape, and surface ornamentation. They can be readily assigned to a family, genus, and, sometimes, species based on morphological features.
2) The outer wall of spores and pollen is readily preserved for long periods, particularly in continuously dry or wet conditions, due to the chemical sporopollenin.
3) Pollen is often produced in very large numbers, especially in wind pollinated plants, including many trees, shrubs, grasses, and herbs, and is therefore present almost everywhere. Even though pollen is not visible, it exists as "dust" and coats surfaces. Plants pollinated by insects or other animals also produce significant quantities of pollen that can be easily transferred to clothing or shoes by direct contact. Pollen from insect pollinated plants, which do not distribute pollen far from their source, is particularly useful in linking suspects to crime scenes.
4) Since different geographic regions tend to have different pollen signatures based on which plant species dominate or are locally present in a region, accumulated pollen in soils and sediments can be used as a geotracking tool. Surface samples of pollen have been used for comparison with forensic samples to see if items of interest, such as drugs, vehicles, or persons, have been transported from one region or ecological zone to another.

---

12 Wiltshire, "Taphonomic Variables," above note 9.

13 Dallas C. Mildenhall, "Forensic Palynology in New Zealand" (1990) 64 *Review of Palaeobotany and Palynology* 227.

14 Lynne Milne, *A Grain of Truth: How Pollen Brought a Murderer to Justice* (Frenchs Forest, N.S.W.: New Holland, 2005).

15 Vaughn M. Bryant Jr., John G. Jones, & Dallas C. Mildenhall, "Forensic Palynology in the United States of America" (1990) 14 *Palynology* 193.

16 Lynne A. Milne, Vaughn M. Bryant Jr., & Dallas C. Mildenhall, "Forensic Palynology" in Coyle, ed., *Forensic Botany Applications*, above note 2, 217.

17 Wiltshire, "Taphonomic Variables," above note 9.

Forensic palynology primarily uses the above principles to determine the likelihood of establishing associative trace evidence in a particular case.[18] The "pollen and spore profile" of any specific site is likely to be similar to other sites. A large number of samples are typically required to establish that a certain pollen assemblage is distinctive enough to "match" evidence found on a suspect.

Palynological information is an important and useful tool for investigators, but it rarely appears in court, either in Canada or abroad.[19] Kevan Walsh and Mark Horrocks have assessed the position of palynology in the field of forensic science and they concluded that fundamental studies and experiments are still needed in this area for the discipline to withstand the intensive scrutiny of the courtroom environment. Some research is being done for specific types of botanical investigation, including document analyses,[20] but more is needed. There is also a need to implement independent proficiency testing of forensic botanists.

c) Plant DNA

Plants produce three kinds of DNA: nuclear, mitochondrial, and chloroplast. The latter is not found in animal cells. Plant DNA analysis can be used to identify species or to link evidence samples with possible source locations or even individual source plants. The first published homicide investigation using plant DNA is the famous case, *State of Arizona v. Mark Alan Bogan*.[21] Investigators linked DNA from the seed pods of a tree at the crime scene (where the deceased woman's body was found) to two pods of the same *palo verde* tree recovered from a suspect's truck.[22] The importance of this case lies in the use of plant DNA to identify not just the species, but also the individual tree.

Identification of plants can now be done by barcoding—sequencing part of a mitochondrial DNA gene from an evidence sample and then comparing it to DNA from the main source of interest using a comparative DNA

---

18 Mark Horrocks & Kevan A.J. Walsh, "Forensic Palynology: Assessing the Value of the Evidence" (1998) 103 *Review of Palaeobotany and Palynology* 69.

19 Kevan A.J. Walsh & Mark Horrocks, "Palynology: Its Position in the Field of Forensic Science" (2008) 53 *Journal of Forensic Science* 1053.

20 R.M. Morgan et al., "The Recovery of Pollen Evidence from Documents and Its Forensic Implications" (2013) 53 *Science and Justice* 375 [Morgan et al., "Recovery of Pollen Evidence"].

21 (11 April 1995), No. 1 CA-CR 93-0453 (Court of Appeals of Arizona. Division 1, Department C).

22 C.K. Yoon, "Botanical Witness for the Prosecution" (1993) 260 *Science* 894.

database or genomic library.[23] DNA barcoding can automate the process of obtaining species identifications. The process is similar to human forensic DNA analysis techniques in that a standardized battery of genetic markers is used to identify unknown samples. The Canadian Centre for DNA Barcoding (CCDB)[24] is the information hub for these procedures in Canada, where the "International Barcode of Life" database contains genetic information on over 200,000 plants, animals, and fungi.

An obvious limitation of plant DNA analysis is that, unlike human DNA analysis, there are insufficient DNA databases for most plant species to allow identification of individual plants within a species with a high degree of probability. That being said, however, local population data for a species can be generated to identify the likely source area of plant evidence. In Canada, for example, the Western Red Cedar (*Thuja plicata*) is a large and valuable tree that is often illegally harvested and sold. The DNA of various populations has been analyzed and two genomic libraries have been created and tested for identification purposes using microsatellite markers. With this information, it is possible to match DNA in cut stumps of Western Red Cedar with stolen wood.[25]

In one case from Vancouver, Environment Canada seized imported plant material thought to represent stems of a medicinal *Dendrobium* orchid species protected under the *Convention on International Trade of Endangered Species* (CITES).[26] The defence was able to establish that the DNA barcoding did not support an orchid source, and only identified apple and pine DNA. Several non-orchid plant groups could be represented in the seized samples. This conclusion was supported by the anatomy of the seized plant tissues and an analysis of reporting errors in documentation. The charge was withdrawn. In other cases, the identification of marijuana plant parts or residues is routinely and successfully done both by biochemical tests for the active ingredient THC, or by a variety of standardized DNA analyses.[27]

---

23 Hebert et al., "Biological Identifications," above note 11.

24 Online: http://ccdb.ca.

25 White et al., "Microsatellite Markers," above note 9.

26 *Convention on International Trade in Endangered Species of Wild Fauna and Flora*, online: www.cites.org. The author was engaged by the defence as a consulting expert.

27 Heather Miller Coyle et al., "An Overview of DNA Methods for the Identification and Individualization of Marijuana" (2003) 44 *Croatian Medical Journal* 315.

It is clear that the future of forensic botany is going to increasingly depend on the availability of plant DNA techniques as well as the findings and testimony of molecular geneticists.

d) Phenological and Taphonomic Considerations

The field of phenology relates to the timing of life history events by plants, such as flowering, fruiting, leaf drop, or seasonal differences in growth rates. An understanding of this area may help to answer questions like the age of a gravesite, the timing of leaf drops, or the rate at which covered grass loses its colour. These questions, in turn, can assist in developing a timeline for a crime, which may support or challenge other evidence. Each case has its own unique characteristics and research requirements, but phenological information can be very useful as part of an investigation.

Taphonomic issues present theoretical problems and are important where human bodies or other physical evidence have been moved from one locality to another, such as in cases involving the exhumation and reburial of war crime victims in an attempt to conceal the size and severity of the mass atrocity.[28]

A well-known case study used pollen recovered from the nasal cavities of thirty-two male skulls from a mass grave in Magdeburg, Germany, to show that they were executed in summer, rather than spring.[29] Twenty-one skulls were analyzed and seven contained abundant pollen from plants such as ribwort plantain, which sheds its pollen in summer, rather than spring. This timeline supported the hypothesis that Soviet secret police executed Soviet soldiers who refused to put down a local revolt in June 1953, rather than an alternate hypothesis that the murders were carried out by the Gestapo in the spring of 1945.

Depending on whether pollen and spores are relatively abundant and mobile (mostly wind-pollinated plants) or locally restricted (insect- and self-pollinated plants), different taphonomic features (i.e., how plant deposits were formed or altered) may determine the significance of these pollen and spores to an investigation. Determining which pollen types are present, in what quantities, and how definitively they can be interpreted are complex questions and the subject of debate among palynologists. For example, most pollen types can be reliably identified to genus level (e.g., pines, birches, alders, etc.), but determining the species of many plants

---

28 Brown, "Forensic Botany in NE Bosnia," above note 2.

29 R. Szibor et al., "Pollen Analysis Reveals Murder Season" (1998) 395 *Nature* 449.

(e.g., Lodgepole pine versus Ponderosa pine) using pollen is often difficult and sometimes impossible. There are also uncertainties when comparing pollen assemblages (proportions of different pollen types from a sample) from a crime scene or from drugs found on a suspect or in his vehicle to establish associations relevant to the matter at issue. Successful associations have been made, however, when the pollen of plants is identified in quantities that are not typical of surrounding areas, as determined from comparison with control samples.[30] The introduction of forensic botany evidence to support an association invites debate in the courtroom. Judges, lawyers, and juries may question the palynology evidence presented at trial when considering the admissibility, legal strategy, or weight of such evidence, respectively.

3) Investigating a Cold Case

Since the development of new DNA techniques, many police forces have reopened unsolved cases from years or even decades ago. Forensic botany can be used in conjunction with DNA investigations in such cases. An example is a Canadian homicide investigation which occurred after the 1992 discovery of a fifteen-year-old girl's body in a remote forest area of southern interior British Columbia. A suspect was identified; the suspect was also under investigation in the murders of other teen victims in other provinces. The botanical connection arises from a pile of branches found on top of the remains: could it have formed naturally through branches falling from surrounding Douglas fir trees, or was it deliberately placed there to hide the body?

The botanical review began in 2003 with a visit to the site where the human remains were found. The investigator[31] made various field observations and took photographs of tree cover, plant species, litterfall, slopes, and other ground conditions. Since the original brush pile was no longer present, photographs and videotape taken by police during their original investigation, dubbed "Project Ekor," were relied upon. Based on the predominant north-south orientation of the branches, the thick layering, and the presence of a dead sapling (which could not have fallen there naturally), the clear conclusion was that the brush pile was deliberately placed. The trial did not proceed as the suspect was found dead from a suicide in March 2005.[32]

30 Wiltshire, "Taphonomic Variables," above note 9.

31 The author served as investigator in this case.

32 Suzanne Wilton & Emma Poole, "Suspect in Several Murders Found Dead of Apparent Suicide" *Vancouver Sun* (29 March 2005).

C. THE ROLE OF THE FORENSIC BOTANIST IN CRIMINAL CASES

As mentioned earlier, forensic botany in Canada has little published information on its role at trial. Its value is clearer when used to assist police investigations, such as by narrowing searches for clandestine graves, making connections between vehicles, places, and people, establishing possible time since death, and providing other time and location information. A forensic botany assessment can be used to support other types of evidence and to support or refute alibis and suspect statements. Botany reports that are sent to investigators for evaluation may or may not end up in court, and they may or may not be specifically cited in judicial decisions if they are presented at trial.

To be qualified as an expert at trial, the forensic botanist must meet the requirements set out by *R. v. Mohan*.[33] This typically involves an assessment by the court of the botanist's education, academic background and credentials, and experience in the specific field of inquiry being presented. A master of science or doctorate degree in botany or plant science is usually needed for expert qualification in forensic botany for trial purposes.

The lack of an understanding of the underlying principles of forensic botany often leads counsel to pose general questions at trial, addressing the accuracy of plant identifications, the possibility of contamination of a sample (especially for microscopic plant remains) and sample transport, as well as handling and storage as it relates to continuity of the chain of custody. Questions rarely address the technical issues surrounding plant science itself, but questions about the level of certainty in an expert's interpretation of the data do frequently arise. Conflicting opinions among expert witnesses over the scientific merits of a finding are rare.

D. A CASE STUDY

The disappearance of ten-year-old Heather Thomas on 1 October 2000 in Cloverdale, B.C., led to a massive search by more than 1,200 volunteers and forty assigned police officers, without any result. Three weeks later, her body was found floating at the shore of Alouette Lake in Golden Ears Park. A twenty-three-year-old man, Shane Ertmoed, a resident in the housing complex where Heather disappeared, was identified as a suspect based on

---

33 *R. v. Mohan*, [1994] 2 S.C.R. 9.

his distinctive vehicle being noticed in Golden Ears Park around the time of her disappearance. Media coverage was extensive throughout this case.

Ertmoed was arrested on 3 November 2000 and, under police questioning, made a detailed confession where he described the murder occurring during an attempted sexual assault and detailed the specific actions he undertook to hide the body in the aftermath. He admitted to putting Heather's body in a large sports bag, carrying it to his car, and driving to Golden Ears Park, where he hid the bag with her body in the forest, covering it with plant material. He marked the location by spinning his tires on the soft road shoulder. The next day, he returned to recover the bag and body, drove to a boat launch, inflated a small boat, and took it some distance out onto Alouette Lake where he sank the bag and the body. The bag had a faulty zipper in the main compartment, which allowed the body to float loose. It was recovered some time after.

Forensic botany became involved when police divers recovered the sports bag on the bottom of Alouette Lake. The bag contained clothing belonging to the victim, as well as a variety of plant material. A forensic botanist was summoned by police to inspect the plants in the sports bag to determine if they were aquatic or terrestrial in origin. Following confirmation of a terrestrial source, the investigator analyzed all the plant materials from the main compartment of the bag and all four side pockets and compared it to an area of interest in Golden Ears Park to look for possible connections to the plants in the bag.

Twelve kinds of plant parts were identified, including needles of common conifer trees, mosses, fern fragments, a birch twig, wood and charcoal fragments, and leaves and broken stems of salmonberry bushes. The broken salmonberry stems were unusual in the manner of breakage, suggesting possible human interference. These plants are all native to Golden Ears Park and similar areas of coastal British Columbia. Two small foliage fragments of a non-native juniper bush were also recovered from the main compartment and a side pocket of the sports bag, and several also from the trunk of the suspect's car.

Further botanical investigation was requested by the police, primarily to find the location where the bag containing Heather's body was originally hidden in the forest near the roadside—the tire-track site marked by the suspect at the time of the murder. The spot was found with a high degree of subjective confidence since all the native plant materials found in the sports bag, including the relatively uncommon birch twig, were present in a small area, including a fallen rotten log with a burned charcoal section.

Most telling were the broken stems of salmonberry bushes that were consistent with two similarly broken twigs found in the main compartment of the sports bag. In addition, some of the unusually torn swordfern fragments that were found in the bag were also present in the hair of Heather Thomas.

The botanical evidence helped to link the body to the main compartment of the sports bag, and the bag to the specific location in the forest, and to Ertmoed's confession. The small fragments of juniper foliage from the sports bag and trunk of Ertmoed's car were consistent with a non-native Chinese juniper that was densely planted beside the suspect's parking area, located at the housing complex shared by him and the victim. The link was suggestive but, without DNA evidence, it could not be confirmed that the juniper pieces were definitively from the housing complex.

A preliminary hearing was held in the Surrey Provincial Court of British Columbia in 2001, where the forensic botanist gave testimony on the botanical findings.[34] The transcript of botanical evidence spans fifty-eight pages, beginning with discussions of the qualifications of the forensic botanist among the judge, Crown prosecutor, and defence counsel before accepting him as an expert witness. Details of the botanical findings and their potential significance in a jury trial were presented in detail and cross-examined by defence counsel.

After an extensive *voir dire* wherein Ertmoed's confession was ruled admissible, the jury trial began in May 2002. Ertmoed recanted the confession but in the ensuing trial he was convicted of first-degree murder. He received the mandatory twenty-five-year sentence with no chance of parole. An appeal of the verdict was filed in 2006 in the Court of Appeal for British Columbia, based on claims of ineffective assistance of counsel. The appeal was unanimously dismissed and Shane Ertmoed continues to serve his sentence. In the appeal decision,[35] the court makes a final botanical note, stating that the appellant's confession was consistent with many known facts, which included, "his description of concealing the bag with branches and brush."[36]

E. CONCLUSION

A general lack of knowledge by police, prosecutors, defence lawyers, and judges regarding how plants can be used in the forensic context has

34 *R. v. Ertmoed* (28 February and 1 March 2001), Surrey 115166-2c (B.C. Prov. Ct.).

35 *R. v. Ertmoed*, 2006 BCCA 365 [*Ertmoed*].

36 *Ibid.* at para. 20.

contributed to a situation where, even in jurisdictions where forensic botany has been used successfully, it is still an underused resource. An exception to this general finding is with respect to *Cannabis* investigations, where DNA and other analyses are well-established. The relatively few professional botanists who could theoretically expand the resources of investigators are generally academics for whom forensic work is a sideline. Many others appear to be reluctant to get involved in criminal court proceedings.

The usefulness of forensic botany appears to be greatest at the investigative stage, rather than at trial. Findings are often treated like other trace evidence, filling in part of a puzzle, but inconclusive on their own. The resulting reports may go largely unchallenged by defence counsel, especially in cases where other types of evidence, such as DNA, fingerprints, or eyewitness testimony, may be more damaging to their client's case. These other types of evidence are also more familiar to defence counsel, making it comparatively easier to address and potentially dispatch them in cross-examination.

In many investigations, the forensic botanist is not involved early on and, as a result, is limited to identifying plant parts or soil samples collected by police. This is not ideal. Having the forensic botanist collect samples and make observations directly in the field is always preferable since a trained botanist may recognize potential evidence that other investigators may miss.

Forensic botany as a field of inquiry is still establishing a formal set of methodologies and operational principles. Experience from other jurisdictions has demonstrated the usefulness of forensic botany in many types of investigations, including homicide, rape, and drug smuggling. Certain sub-disciplines, including palynology, are poised to become important tools. Plant DNA analysis especially could become more widely applied as genomic libraries and reference databases expand. In particular, the identification of individual source plants that can be matched to plants collected in evidence would allow for major advances in investigative procedures.

F. LEGAL CONTEXT

> Palynological analysis is shown from published and unpublished Canadian examples to be a useful tool in forensic investigation, although the technique is almost unknown and therefore under-utilized by forensic investigators. The techniques of pollen and spore identification and

interpretation are continually improving, indicating that the potential for forensic applications is real.[37]

Environmental profiling combines techniques from the fields of geology and botany, such as mineralogy and palynology,[38] respectively, to reduce the possibility of falsely matching an object or individual to a site in question.[39] Forensic botany applies the study of plant and plant materials to legal investigations and, in the criminal context, can be particularly useful in circumstantial cases lacking DNA and eyewitness evidence.[40] The discipline can be applied to both outdoor and indoor investigations and may be used in cases involving deceased or living victims.

1) Forensic Botany in Criminal Cases

Published case studies have shown forensic botany—specifically forensic palynology—to be useful in a variety of criminal cases, including those involving charges of forgery,[41] rape,[42] homicide, genocide, terrorism, drug dealing, assault and robbery, arson, hit-and-run, counterfeiting, and illegal importation.[43] For example, in one case study, sexual intercourse was an agreed fact but consent was at issue; the couple engaged in consensual sexual activity earlier that day so DNA would not have been of assistance. But the individuals gave different accounts of where intercourse took place. Forensic palynology and mycology (i.e., pollen and fungi) evidence supported the complainant's version of events with respect to the location and, when confronted with this evidence, the defendant confessed. The case study recommended that vaginal swabs be routinely examined for pollen in suspected rape cases.[44]

---

37 Mathewes, "Forensic Palynology in Canada," above note 7 at 198.

38 Mildenhall et al., "Why Forensic Palynology," above note 6 at 163: "Forensic palynology is the study of modern and fossil spores, pollen and other acid resistant micro-plant remains in a legal context."

39 Brown, "Forensic Botany in NE Bosnia," above note 2 at 204.

40 Maple Ridge-Pitt Meadows Times, "Botanist Featured in Series" *CanWest MediaWorks Publication Inc.* (16 May 2008), online: www.canada.com/story.html?id=abeec2d2-6727-4cf7-9c4f-00156f32860b ["Botanist Featured in Series"].

41 Morgan et al., "Recovery of Pollen Evidence," above note 20.

42 Patricia E.J. Wiltshire et al., "Palynology and Mycology Provide Separate Classes of Probative Evidence from the Same Forensic Samples: A Rape Case from Southern England" (2014) 244 *Forensic Science International* 186 [Wiltshire et al., "Palynology Case Study"].

43 See, for example, Mildenhall et al., "Why Forensic Palynology," above note 6 at 163. This article provides a list of how palynology can be used in the forensic context.

44 Wiltshire et al., "Palynology Case Study," above note 42 at 194.

Forensic palynology has been used since at least the 1950s and has been admitted as evidence in criminal trials in various jurisdictions internationally, including Australia, New Zealand, and the United Kingdom.[45] The discipline, however, has not been fully accepted in other jurisdictions, including Canada, and few of the palynologists practicing in Canada apply their work to the forensic realm.[46] Canadian caselaw addressing the use of forensic botany as evidence in criminal cases is sparse at best, reflecting that this type of analysis is indeed underused in this country. Further, in cases where forensic botany has been used, the evidence may not have been relied upon or, if relied upon, was not detailed in the reported judgment, making it difficult to assess the role of the evidence in the court's decision.

The first-degree murder trial of *R. v. Lowe*[47] is an example of a case where forensic botany testimony had been heard but the opinion evidence was not relied upon by the Crown. The court made a finding of guilt based primarily on the inculpatory statements made by Lowe during the course of a Mr. Big sting. The court accepted Dr. Rolf Mathewes as a forensic botanist qualified to provide opinion evidence, but his opinion with respect to how long the remains had been at the scene was inconsistent with other evidence:

> I accepted Dr. Mathewes as qualified to give evidence in forensic botany. On September 18, 1996, at the request of the coroner he attended at the site where the remains were found. He testified that there were some indications from the botanical evidence that the remains had been there since 1989–90, but other indications that they had been there since 1993. Since there was overwhelming evidence that William Rudy was alive until at least February 21, 1994, the Crown did not rely on Dr. Mathewes's opinion evidence.
>
> The Crown did rely on Dr. Mathewes's description of the scene. He testified about the area where the large amount of black plastic sheeting with duct tape attached and a shoe were found. He stated that the area was in the lower part of a natural depression, flanked by a fallen log, shrubs, swordferns and several young tree saplings. There was forest debris on top of the plastic. He testified that insect pupae were found beneath the plastic after it was moved, suggesting that human remains could have been there for some time.[48]

45 Mildenhall et al., "Why Forensic Palynology," above note 6.
46 Mathewes, "Forensic Palynology in Canada," above note 7 at 198.
47 *R. v. Lowe*, 2004 BCSC 1104.
48 *Ibid.* at paras. 158–59.

In another criminal case, forensic botany was used to support Shane Ertmoed's confession to the murder of ten-year-old Heather Thomas. The defence argued at trial that the confession was false. As discussed in Section D, above in this chapter, Thomas went missing on 1 October 2000.[49] Hikers found her body floating in Alouette Lake in the Golden Ears Provincial Park of Maple Ridge on 22 October 2000.[50] Ertmoed was arrested and, during the course of a police interview, confessed to killing Thomas and disposing of her body.[51] A jury found Ertmoed guilty of first-degree murder and Ertmoed appealed. In 2006, the Court of Appeal dismissed Ertmoed's appeal and described his confession to the interviewing officer, Cpl. Bishop, as follows:

> The appellant [Ertmoed] described to Cpl. Bishop how he had used his black football bag to carry her body to his car, along with her clothing, and how he drove to Golden Ears Park that same afternoon because it was near to where he worked. He said he hid the bag in dense forest adjacent to the park's roadway concealing it with branches and brush. He told Cpl. Bishop he returned the next morning, 2 October, on his way to work, driving slowly along the park's roadway and eventually finding the location where he had concealed the bag by finding the tire tracks his car had left the day before on the road shoulder. He left the car unattended with its hood open while he went to find the bag, but he left the bag undisturbed because he was in a hurry to get to work on time. He left work early on the pretext of being ill, returned to the park, recovered the bag, parked at the park's boat launch, inflated a small dinghy and dropped the bag into the lake about 500 metres to the left of the boat launch.[52]

At trial, Ertmoed testified that the confession was false, stating that he did not kill Thomas and dispose of her body. He further testified that the bag, found by police on the lake bed and containing Thomas' pants and underpants, was not his and that he had never been to Golden Ears Park.[53]

The case was reported in the local news, with journalists focusing on the value that forensic botany brought to the case in supporting the truth of Ertmoed's confession. It was reported that, by analyzing the plant fragments found in the black duffel bag used to transport Thomas' body,

49 *Ertmoed*, above note 35 at para. 9.
50 *Ibid.* at paras. 1–10.
51 *Ibid.* at para. 17.
52 *Ibid.* at para. 19.
53 *Ibid.* at paras. 11 and 25.

Dr. Mathewes confirmed that the bag and body had been in Golden Ears Provincial Park and that swordfern and salmonberry branches were used to conceal it. This supported the truthfulness of Ertmoed's confession, which was also consistent with other known facts of the case.[54]

2) Forensic Botany in *Delgamuukw v. British Columbia*

Although not a criminal case, the historical Aboriginal rights and land title claim case so familiar to the legal community, *Delgamuukw v. British Columbia*,[55] involved forensic botanical expert testimony at trial to support the oral histories ("adaawk") and the spiritual performances ("kungax") of the Gitksan and Wet'suwet'en hereditary chiefs, respectively, who were claiming Aboriginal rights and title to approximately 58,000 km^2 of land in northwestern British Columbia.[56] The trial began in 1987, lasted 374 days, and concluded in 1990, with Chief Justice Allan McEachern of the Supreme Court of British Columbia providing his Reasons for Judgment on 8 March 1991.[57] On days 143 and 144, Dr. Rolf Mathewes testified as an expert in paleobotany, specifically pollen analysis and environmental reconstruction.[58] This was followed by testimony from Dr. Allen Gottesfeld, an expert in geomorphology (i.e., the study of existing land forms and the processes that created them),[59] who addressed the debris flow and torrent history of the mountains in the area.[60] Testimony from geology, archaeology, and anthropology experts was also heard in this case, described as the "largest, most expensive, and important land claims trial in Canadian history."[61]

Forensic botanical evidence was specifically used by the plaintiffs to support the "Men of Medeek" *adaawk*. In the Medeek *adaawk*, a giant grizzly bear came down the mountain valley and destroyed the forest, disturbing the land with great force and leaving behind it a clear path of destruction.[62] In his own article years after the trial, Dr. Mathewes explained that it is

---

54 "Botanist Featured in Series," above note 40; Burnaby Now, "Botanist Helps Solve Crimes" *CanWest MediaWorks Publications Inc.* (24 May 2008) online: www.canada.com/burnabynow/news/community/story.html?id=cd99536e-836d-4275-b935-9b3313b17948; *Ertmoed*, above note 35 at para. 20.

55 *Delgamuukw v. British Columbia* (1997), 3 S.C.R 1010 [*Delgamuukw SCC*].

56 *Ibid.* at para. 13; Mathewes, "Forensic Palynology in Canada," above note 7 at 200.

57 *Delgamuukw v. The Queen*, 1991 CanLII 2372 (BCSC) [*Delgamuukw BCSC*].

58 *Ibid.* at 167–68. Mathewes, "Forensic Palynology in Canada," above note 7 at 200.

59 *Delgamuukw BCSC*, above note 57 at 163.

60 Mathewes, "Forensic Palynology in Canada," above note 7 at 200.

61 *Ibid.*

62 *Ibid.*

reasonable that Aboriginal oral histories would have remembered a destructive debris flow as a supernatural, giant grizzly bear—Europeans have similarly perceived the noise created by debris flows and torrents as "raging giants and infuriated dragons."[63] This reasoning links the giant grizzly bear of the Medeek *adaawk* to the real events of the Chicago Creek debris flow and the rise of Seeley Lake. The plaintiffs asked the court to infer from the evidence, including but not limited to the forensic botany evidence, that the Gitksan lived in the Chicago Creek area since at least the time of the slide, strengthening their claim to the land.

Dr. Mathewes testified that carbon dating of macrofossils and pollen samples from a clay band taken from the Seeley Lake bed established that the samples were 3,380 years old, plus or minus ninety years, and could be explained as being attributable to a sudden rise in Seeley Lake's water levels. A sudden increase in the concentration of birch seeds and pollen in the clay band was also described by Dr. Mathewes as being caused by rising water levels, as the water would have swept up the seeds from the forest floor, depositing them on the lake bed. The large concentration of macrofossil remains of a water plant, *Ceratophylum*, above the clay band was considered to be consistent with a landslide disturbing the water. Alternative theories, including fires, storms, and beaver activities, were considered and rejected by Dr. Mathewes.[64]

Although the court had difficulty equating a landslide to a grizzly bear, the court stated that, "the appearance of a bear in the course of such a slide may be understandable post hoc reasoning which does not affect the dating of the event."[65] Chief Justice Allan McEachern could not infer more than human presence if the *adaawk* stood alone. Using other evidence, particularly archaeology, linguistic, and genealogical evidence, the court inferred the long-term presence of the Gitksan and Wet'suwet'en in the Chicago Creek area, without deciding if the Men of Medeek *adaawk* described the landslide identified by scientists.[66] The court found it unnecessary to rely on the "possible connection between the landslide and Gitksan presence" but, at the same time, did not reject the possible connection.[67]

---

63 *Ibid.* at 200, citing G.H. Eisbacher & J.J. Clague, *Destructive Mass Movements in High Mountains: Hazard and Management, Paper 84-16* (Ottawa: Geological Survey of Canada, 1984) at 74.

64 *Delgamuukw BCSC*, above note 57 at 169–70.

65 *Ibid.* at 171.

66 *Ibid.* at 173–74.

67 *Ibid.* at 174.

Ultimately, the Supreme Court of Canada denied the land claim but found that Aboriginal oral histories must be accepted in the future by courts as a key aspect of establishing land claims. It was also held that the development of ancestral lands must be done in consultation with Aboriginal peoples.[68] Other, unrelated instances have similarly shown such oral histories to be a strong source of historical knowledge. Inuit oral histories, for example, contributed to the 2014 discovery of one of the ships of the Franklin expedition, lost in 1846 to the waters of Nunavut.[69]

3) Summary

Although forensic botany has proven to be a useful tool in the criminal context internationally, experts in Canada are few in number and have largely been excluded from the investigative process. Research advancements in the field and in combination with other disciplines may entice investigators and lawyers alike to seek novel approaches to advancing their case by, for example, seeking forensic expert opinions with respect to soil DNA analysis,[70] individual tree DNA profiling,[71] mycological trace evidence,[72] and diatom transferability.[73] Increasing awareness of the discipline's existence might increase the demand for this type of evidence in court proceedings and, in turn, may eventually lead to an improved appreciation for including the discipline in the investigative process.

---

68 Mathewes, "Forensic Palynology in Canada," above note 7, at 202.

69 Louie Kamookak, "Franklin Find Proves 'Inuit Oral History Is Strong'" *CBC News* (10 September 2014) online: www.cbc.ca/news/canada/north/franklin-find-proves-inuit-oral-history-is-strong-louie-kamookak-1.2761362.

70 Jennifer M. Young et al., "Limitations and Recommendations for Successful DNA Extraction from Forensic Soil Samples: A Review" (2014) 54 *Science and Justice* 238.

71 White et al., "Microsatellite Markers," above note 9.

72 David L. Hawksworth & Patricia E.J. Wiltshire, "Forensic Mycology: The Use of Fungi in Criminal Investigations" (2011) 206 *Forensic Science International* 1.

73 Kirstie R. Scott et al., "The Transferability of Diatoms to Clothing and the Methods Appropriate for the Collection and Analysis in Forensic Geoscience" (2014) 241 *Forensic Science International* 127.

CHAPTER 14

Forensic Document Examination

Dan C. Purdy

LEGAL CONTEXT: CAITLIN PAKOSH

A. OVERVIEW

Forensic document examination is "the application of science to the analysis, recognition and interpretation of any evidence in the form of a document for legal and/or regulatory purposes."[1] Such a broad definition encompasses a variety of analyses and examinations that include, but are not limited to, comparing handwriting samples, associating office equipment with the documents they produce, detecting alterations and/or additions to documents, restoring impressions in paper, deciphering obliterated or faded inscriptions, and dating documents through their physical or chemical properties, to name just a few.

Under a common definition used by forensic specialists, a document is "any material which [*sic*] contains marks, symbols, or signs either visible, partially visible, or invisible that may presently or ultimately convey a meaning or message to someone."[2] This broad definition includes material not normally thought of as documents, such as graffiti on a brick wall, inscriptions on survey stakes, some tattoos, and even coded marks on the backs of playing cards. These materials and many others that surface during a criminal or civil investigation are often submitted to a forensic laboratory for analysis.

1 Jane A. Lewis, *Forensic Document Examination—Fundamentals and Current Trends* (Oxford: Academic Press, 2014) at 37.

2 Ordway Hilton, *Scientific Examination of Questioned Documents* (Chicago: Callaghan, 1956) at 1.

Forensic document examiners (FDEs) are called upon to examine documents for various reasons. Solutions to the complex problems outlined above require special knowledge, skills, and abilities that only qualified experts can provide. In Canada, the examination of disputed documents can be traced back to the early twentieth century. Eugene John O'Sullivan and Herbert J. Walter, both from Winnipeg, examined disputed handwritten documents and, on several occasions during the early 1900s, gave expert testimony addressing whether the documents in question were legitimate or fraudulent. John J. Lomax, a court reporter in Montreal, was also recognized by the courts as a qualified handwriting expert during those early years.

The first scientific laboratory to operate in Canada was l'Institut de Médecine Légale et de Police Scientifique, which opened in Montreal, under the direction of Dr. Wilfrid Derome, in July of 1914. J. Edgar Hoover reportedly visited this laboratory twice before establishing the FBI Laboratory in Washington, D.C. In 1932, the deputy attorney general of Ontario organized a medicolegal laboratory in Toronto to carry out forensic analyses, primarily for the province's police agencies.[3] This laboratory, which became the Attorney General's Laboratory in 1951, was renamed the Centre of Forensic Sciences in 1966. The laboratory was transferred to the new Ministry of the Solicitor General in 1972 and then to the Ministry of Community Safety and Correctional Services in 2002. In 1992, Ontario's Northern Regional Laboratory opened to deliver services in northern Ontario.

In December 1936, Dr. Maurice Powers was hired by the Royal Canadian Mounted Police who sent him to The New York University College of Medicine and the Office of the Chief Medical Examiner to be trained in serology, microscopy, toxicology, photography, ballistics, and pathology. After returning to Canada, he opened the RCMP's first scientific laboratory in Regina on 22 September 1937. Corporal Stephen Lett was the agency's first document examiner and he received most of his training from O.B. Stanton of Toronto and from the FBI at their Washington, D.C., facility.

Once the potential value of physical evidence in the form of a document became recognized, provincial and federal government laboratories were created in several regions of the country. By the 1930s, most of these laboratories employed document examiners who provided scientific services to police departments, government agencies, and courts throughout Canada.

---

3 D.M. Lucas, "North of 49—The Development of Forensic Science in Canada" (1997) 37 *Science & Justice* 47.

Rapid expansion took place during the following decades as the RCMP opened full service laboratories in Ottawa (1942), Sackville (1957), Vancouver (1960), Edmonton (1968), Winnipeg (1970), Montreal (1979), and Halifax (1979). All of these federal laboratories employed forensic document examiners to analyze documents submitted by municipal, provincial, and federal government agencies throughout their jurisdictions.

The vast number of analyses performed by forensic document examiners underscores the versatility of the discipline, which includes the following: comparing handwriting samples; associating printed or typed documents with the office equipment that produced them; determining the age of documents; identifying dating anachronisms; analyzing writing inks, paper, and other types of media; detecting document alterations; restoring indented writing; determining writing sequence; and recovering entries on erased, charred, or obliterated documents. These types of analyses are described in the following section.

B. THE SCIENCE OF FORENSIC DOCUMENT EXAMINATION

1) Types of Analyses

a) Handwriting Comparisons

During the early 1900s, document examiners were often known as "handwriting experts" because most of their work involved the examination and comparison of handwriting, including hand printing and signatures. Today, the majority of cases submitted to document laboratories still involve the examination of handwritten entries, but, since these specialists perform many other kinds of analyses, they are more commonly referred to as forensic document examiners.

The comparison of a disputed handwritten document usually begins with an inspection of the suspect signature, initials, hand printing, or handwriting. During this stage, the line quality of the writing is carefully assessed to determine if the entry appears to be freely and naturally executed. Variable pen pressure, smooth curved strokes, connected letters, and tapered initial/terminal strokes are all trademarks of genuine handwriting (see Figure 14.1).

FIGURE 14.1. Rapidly executed pen strokes, variable pen pressure, and smooth curved strokes all contribute to the natural appearance of this signature. (All figures taken from author's files unless otherwise noted.)

There are two methods that forgers use to produce a signature that closely resembles a genuine signature. The first method is referred to as a freehand simulation. Freehand simulation involves either the copying of a genuine signature that is on hand for the forger to replicate or, alternatively, attempting to recreate another's signature from memory. The second method is referred to as a traced forgery. These signatures are produced by following the outline of a genuine signature with a writing instrument. For instance, carbon paper may be used to trace a faint outline of the signature onto the suspect document. The faint outline is then overwritten with pen and ink to produce the final version. A traced forgery may also be created by placing the suspect document atop a genuine signature. A light may then be shone through both documents from the other side, creating a visible signature on the suspect document, which is then traced with pen and ink.

The line quality of a disputed entry can be indicative of an attempt to falsely replicate the signature or handwriting of another person. In such cases, careful retouching, blunt stroke endings, hesitations, tremor, or faint guidelines often occur. A suspect signature may appear similar in form to the genuine signature of a known writer, but these common elements typically pertain to gross or obvious elements such as the size, shape, and form of letters. Subtle features and inconspicuous structural elements often expose the forger's failed attempt to produce a convincing copy.

In most cases, forged signatures are written much more slowly than a genuine signature. This is due to the forger's attempt to carefully draw characteristics of the genuine signatures that are believed to be important. Whether traced directly from a genuine model or replicated from memory, the forged signature usually contains other telltale signs associated with forged signatures, such as careful retouching, blunt terminal and initial strokes, hesitations, and tremor (see Figure 14.2).

FIGURE 14.2. Evidence of: (1) tremor; (2) hesitations; (3) pen lifts; (4) irregularities; and (5) blunt terminal/initial strokes in this suspect signature arouse suspicion concerning its genuineness.

Most writers develop their signatures through repetition and practice over many years. Despite attempts to produce a consistent version, no two signatures will ever be exactly alike. This is referred to as natural variation, an attribute of all genuine writing. It is the reason why several examples are needed to fully represent the characteristics that can reliably identify a person's signature or handwriting. The number of specimens needed to fully capture a writer's signature habits varies from one person to another and is dependent on the complexity of the signature, the range of variation, and the number of significant writing features it contains.

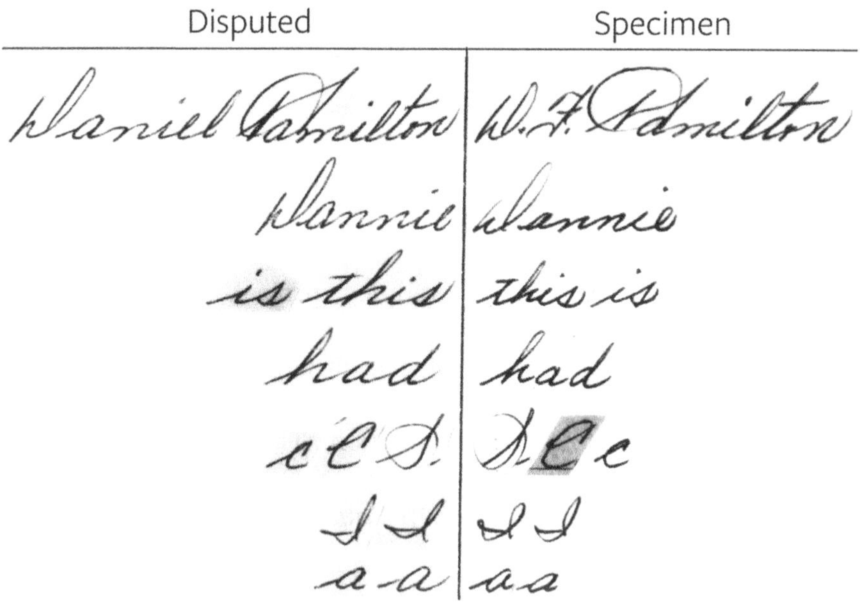

FIGURE 14.3. The disputed and genuine handwriting samples depicted in this chart are sufficient to support a conclusion that they are all the product of one writer. Experts often use these charts to support the findings expressed in their reports or while giving expert testimony.

Figure 14.3 shows a signature and several handwritten entries from a disputed document, juxtaposed with specimen signatures and handwriting of the alleged writer. The suspect and specimen writing have several significant features in common. The significance or weight assigned to any handwriting characteristic is ultimately determined by two factors. The first factor is the commonality of that feature in the general population of writers—unusual letter formations are assigned more significance than formations that are frequently encountered in the general population.

The second factor concerns the frequency of a feature within a group of specimens by the writer. A handwriting characteristic that is found repeatedly in writing samples produced by an individual is given more weight than other features that only appear intermittently.

Every area of scientific study has uncertainty, making it impossible for any field to claim a zero error rate. For example, a handwriting study[4] conducted by Dr. Sargur Srihari and others from the Center of Excellence for Document Analysis and Recognition (CEDAR) at the University at Buffalo, involving 1,500 male and female writers of different ages and ethnicities in the United States, captured various structural elements of writing (e.g., word and line spacing, margins, line skew, the position of letters at the beginning, middle, and terminal position of a word, as well as various letter and number combinations). CEDAR-FOX, a computer software program, was developed by the researchers to extract quantifiable macrofeatures (e.g., slant, word proportion, pen pressure, writing movement, and stroke formation) and microfeatures (e.g., gradient, structure, and concavity features) of each handwritten document. This study confirmed that the writer of a particular sample can be identified with a 98 percent level of confidence. Dr. Srihari's group divided the population of writers into a pre-determined number of subpopulations, or strata. Independent probability samples were drawn from each stratum and then pooled to obtain overall population estimates based on 1996 U.S. census projections. The results suggested that writer identification over the entire U.S. population could be established with a 96 percent level of confidence. Dr. Srihari further suggested that, "by considering finer features, we should be able to make this conclusion with a near 100 percent confidence."[5] Note, however, that even a claim of "near 100 percent confidence" does not preclude the possibility of error.

An additional study[6] conducted by Dr. Srihari and colleagues further supports the principle of handwriting individuality. Writing samples were obtained from 206 pairs of twins from 150 different cities and seven different countries, as well as 412 individuals (not twins) from the general population of the United States. This research included four areas of study: (1) comparing the performance of the handwriting of twins with that of the general population, (2) determining the performance when the textual content of the suspect and specimen handwriting is different, (3) comparing

4 S.N. Srihari et al., "Individuality of Handwriting" (2002) 47 *Journal of Forensic Sciences* 1.

5 *Ibid.* at 16.

6 S.N. Srihari et al., "On the Discriminability of the Handwriting of Twins" (2008) 53 *Journal of Forensic Sciences* 430.

the performance of fraternal and identical twins, and (4) comparing the performance of the CEDAR-FOX system to that of laypersons in the general population and that of trained forensic document examiners. The results indicated that document examiners who participated in the study found it more difficult to distinguish the writing of twins than the writing of non-twins, and that they found it more difficult to distinguish the writing of identical twins than the writing of fraternal twins. The CEDAR-FOX verification error rate for twins was higher than that for non-twins, which means that the software encountered more difficulties distinguishing the writing of twins than samples produced by non-twins. Most importantly, the study established that the CEDAR-FOX system performed better than laypersons, but that it was unable to reach the performance level of qualified experts.

Forged signatures usually exhibit a certain degree of similarity to the genuine signatures they attempt to imitate. As noted previously, the signatures of an experienced writer invariably contain some natural variation. On occasion, a disputed signature will resemble a genuine signature in virtually every detail. Since no two genuine signatures are exactly the same, this striking similarity combined with other structural defects, such as tremor, blunt stroke endings, the presence of a guideline, pen lifts, hesitations, or careful retouching, usually provides sufficient proof to declare the questioned signature a traced forgery. The degree to which a traced signature resembles the genuine model from which it was traced is easily demonstrated by overlaying the two signatures (see Figure 14.4). The absence of sufficient variation between these two signatures should alert the experienced document examiner to examine the signatures for signs of manipulation, tracing, or simulation. In this instance, a further inspection of the genuine signature with oblique light revealed indentations produced during the tracing process (see Figure 14.5).

i) Disguised Writing

Occasionally, writers will make a deliberate attempt to remove, conceal, or modify some or all of their normal writing habits. In the majority of cases, these efforts affect only the pictorial appearance of the writing. Subtle distinguishing handwriting characteristics are rarely affected. In a study involving 135 writers, Edwin Alford discovered that subjects employed various methods (e.g., use of the awkward hand; change of slope and size or use of modified letter forms; altering upper and lower extensions; deceptive spelling; changes to initial/terminal strokes) to alter or hide their normal handwriting habits. It was found that the elements most often changed are

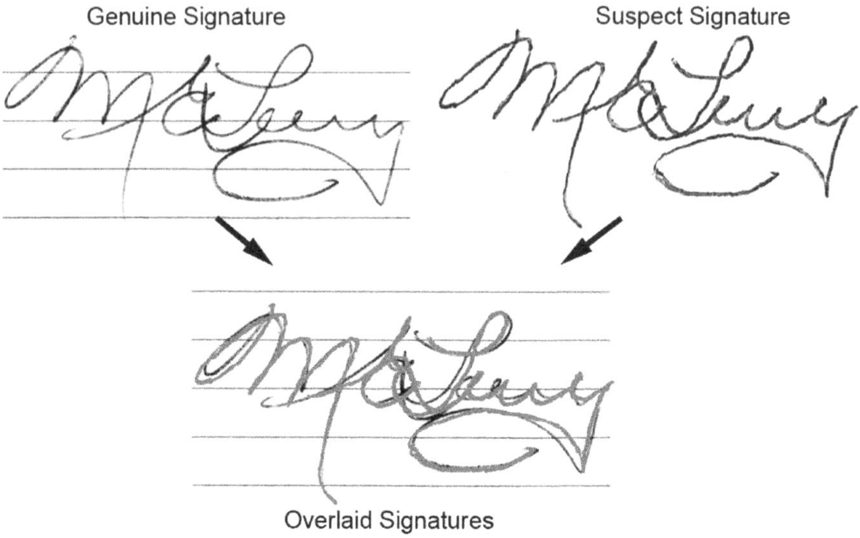

FIGURE 14.4. When the two signatures at top are overlaid, the suspect signature (in red) superimposes very closely with the genuine signature (in black). This strongly suggests it was traced from the genuine model.

FIGURE 14.5. Indented impressions near the genuine signature confirm that it was the model used to trace the suspect signature.

those that most drastically affect the pictorial appearance of the writing, but most attempts at disguise are neither consistent nor successful.[7]

Another study concurred with the findings of Alford, reporting that "[m]ost subjects tended to disguise letter shapes, angle of slant and other foreground aspects, whereas characteristics of the finer structure remained unchanged. It is rarely difficult or impossible to discriminate between disguised and forged signatures, the most common difficulties arise where the disguised signature is very unexpressive or if it is copied slowly in the manner of a forgery."[8]

When dealing with questioned signatures, only a limited sample of writing has been disguised or duplicated. Isolated signatures that do not contain many letters consequently offer few opportunities to detect features associated with disguise. Signatures normally produced by illiterate or infirm writers often have a clumsy appearance due to hesitations, tremor, or pen lifts, which are also frequently observed in disguised signatures. As a result, difficulties are often encountered when attempting to categorically identify the disputed signatures of an unskilled and/or aged writer. In cases of simulated or traced signatures, the document examiner may be able to opine that a questioned signature is not genuine, but forgers can rarely be identified through comparison with samples of their writing. These fake signatures contain few, if any, natural writing habits of the forger.

ii) Handwriting Specimens

The outcome of any handwriting comparison is dependent on the quantity and quality of specimen material. When the writer's handwriting does not vary to any great extent, only a few samples are usually needed to support a categorical conclusion. However, in most instances, a more robust collection of specimen material is needed to fully represent the handwriting habits of the writer. Handwriting specimens fall into one of two general groups—collected samples and requested samples.

a. Collected Samples

Collected samples consist of documents that were written, signed, or initialed during the normal conduct of the writer's personal or business affairs. These specimens are usually naturally written and free from any evidence

---

7 Edwin F. Alford, Jr., "Disguised Handwriting—A Statistical Survey of How Handwriting Is Most Frequently Disguised" (1970) 15 *Journal of Forensic Sciences* 476.

8 L. Michel, "Disguised Signatures" (1978) 18 *Journal of the Forensic Science Society* 25.

that the writer was attempting to alter or disguise his handwriting characteristics. It is often possible to locate collected samples that are contemporaneous with the alleged date of the disputed document. Despite these benefits, there are also disadvantages associated with these specimens in that it may be difficult to duplicate the word or letter combinations that appear in the questioned text, especially if the text consists of the names, signatures, or addresses of other individuals. Difficulties can also be encountered when proving the authorship of collected writing samples to the satisfaction of the courts.

b. Requested Samples

Requested samples are those prepared for the sole purpose of conducting a handwriting comparison. The advantage of this type of specimen writing is that it is possible to duplicate the same sentences, words, and letter combinations that appear in the disputed document. Since requested handwriting samples are always witnessed, the proof of authorship is much easier to prove. Unfortunately, some requested samples may be written in an unnatural fashion due either to a deliberate attempt by the writer to alter her handwriting or by the nervous state of the writer when creating the writing sample.

Handwriting samples should be made with a writing instrument similar to that used to prepare the suspected writing. The paper used to prepare these samples should also be similar in nature to the questioned document (e.g., thickness, finish, size, and the presence of rulings). When asking an individual to provide signature samples, each signature should be written on a separate slip of paper.

Extended handwriting samples should include repetitions of the same words that appear in the disputed document. It might not be possible or advisable to dictate the actual text of a threatening letter or obscene note. In such cases, a suitable text should be prepared in advance and dictated to the writer. If the physical position of the writer of the original document is known (e.g., sitting at a desk, standing at a counter, standing while holding the paper against a vertical surface), the requested writing samples should be produced under similar conditions.

b) Office Equipment Impressions

Most office equipment (typewriters, computer printers, photocopiers, facsimile machines, rubber stamps, staple machines, and marking devices, etc.) acquire defects through use and abuse that affect the quality of the documents they produce. These defects, which are also referred to as acquired characteristics, can associate a questioned document with the particular machine that produced it. If it is suspected that a document originated from a particular office, contemporaneous samples produced by all the equipment at that location could be sufficient to express an opinion that it was produced elsewhere. For instance, office equipment examinations can reveal that: (1) a disputed document was produced by a particular make and model machine, (2) portions of a typed document were produced by more than one machine, (3) some pages of a multi-page document were produced by different photocopiers, (4) the header in the top margin of a faxed document was not produced by a suspect fax machine, or (5) that a dating anachronism exists (i.e., that defects present in a disputed document did not exist when the document was allegedly produced).

i) Typewriting

For more than 100 years, typewriters have been used to prepare both official and personal correspondence. Today, nearly all documents are created by computer printers, but typewritten documents do occasionally surface and are brought to the attention of a forensic document examiner. Most of the questioned documents purport to be produced decades ago, but sometimes a typewriter stored in a garage or basement will be used to prepare an anonymous letter by someone unaware that the machine produces unique defects.

The two basic types of examination are typewriter classification and typewriter identification. Typewriter classification attempts to establish the make and model of the typewriter or type element used to prepare the document in question. Typewriter identification attempts to establish the specific typewriter or type element. The make and/or model of the machine used to produce a document is ascertained by examining the typed document microscopically in an effort to determine if it was produced by an older typebar machine, an electric typewriter, or a more modern system consisting of a typewriter equipped with an interchangeable type element. The size, spacing, and style of letters are all class characteristics that identify the typewriter manufacturer. The search results can also be narrowed through identification of the kind of ribbon (e.g., fabric, bi-colour, film) used and whether the machine was equipped with a correcting ribbon. Once all the class characteristics have been studied, these parameters are used to search large collections of typewriter standards to identify machines that have the same distinctive elements. This method is employed when attempting to identify the source of a typed anonymous letter. A fraudulent document is quickly exposed if the make/model of typewriter that produced it was not released to the market until later.

Typing defects are very helpful when identifying the specific typewriter or typing system that produced a questioned document. Most defects are acquired through wear and tear to a typewriter's components. These defects include bent typebars, broken typefaces, worn bearings, dirty typefaces, and damage to the typewriter's paper advance mechanism. In addition to identifying the work of a specific typewriter, these defects can be used to identify the approximate time when a suspect document was produced. With enough information about the suspect typewriter, the appearance or disappearance of defects can identify the period when a particular document was produced. This method relies on a chronological study of a machine's defects over an extended period. Typewriter defects are rarely acquired during a short period of time. Instead, they surface gradually over months or years according to the quality of the machine, its schedule of maintenance, the care of its operator(s), and the use of the typewriter.

If a typewriter is used without frequent cleaning, its typefaces can become filled with dirt. Recesses in the loops of letters such as the "o," "e," and "g" may become clogged with a combination of dirt, paper components, and ribbon residue. The body of the digit "6," for example, can become a solid black circle. If some characters in a disputed document are degraded in this fashion while the same characters strike clearly in other areas of the document, the two passages are likely to have been typed at a significantly different time (see Figure 14.6).

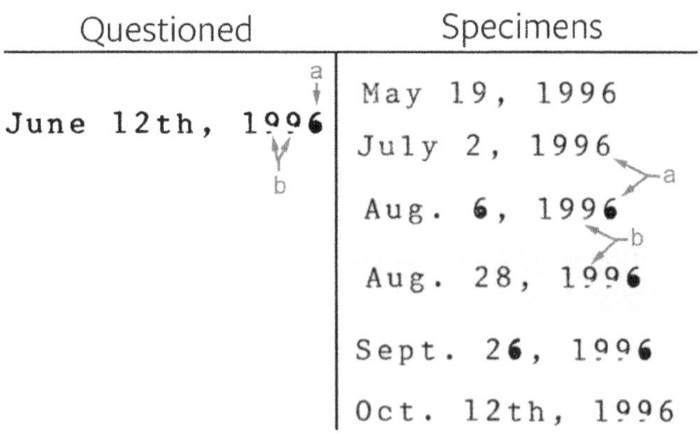

FIGURE 14.6. Damage to the "9" and dirt in the oval of the "6" are inconsistent with the dates when these defects appeared on the specimen documents and confirm that the questioned document was not typed on 12 June 1996.

There are also instances where the condition of a typewriter's ribbon can provide evidence of a dating anachronism. This type of analysis relies on the availability of chronological specimens from the typewriter suspected of producing the questioned document. The contents of documents are sometimes instrumental in challenging the purported creation date. This is why the temporal significance of a company address, phone number, postal code, printed letterhead, and even the typist's initials can expose a backdated document.

ii) Computer Printer Identification

Despite a common interest among businesses to replace paper records with digitally stored media, hundreds of thousands of documents are produced on a daily basis by photocopiers and computer printers in offices across Canada. Occasionally, the legitimacy of documents produced by office printers and copiers are challenged. In these situations, the expert must determine if a photocopied reproduction exhibits the same distinctive flaws associated with the photocopier or printer that allegedly produced the document. Three major issues typically surround the origin of photocopied documents. The first is whether two or more documents originate from the same printer or photocopier. The second is whether a printed or photocopied document was produced by a particular machine. The third and most challenging issue is establishing when a printed or photocopied document was produced.

Computer printer identification has been a subject of extensive research by forensic document examiners since these devices came on the market. Problems related to the recognition of computer printed documents are significantly more complex than those associated with typewriter identification. Recent decades have seen the emergence of several different printing technologies, including the daisy wheel, dot-matrix, inkjet, bubblejet, thermal, and laser printers. As with typewriters, printers produce documents that possess characteristics related to the type or class of printer. Worn or defective printer components produce imperfections in a printed document that can enable identification of the specific machine that produced it. These defects must be carefully evaluated to establish if they are sufficient in both number and significance to identify the source of a disputed document.

a. The Daisy Wheel Printer

The daisy wheel printer is an early type of impact printer invented in 1969 by David S. Lee, an engineer who worked at Diablo Data Systems. These printers use an interchangeable pre-formed metal or plastic disk that typically contains ninety-six characters or "glyphs" that produce high-quality printing equivalent to that produced by premium typewriters, such as the IBM Selectric. Consequently, documents produced by daisy wheel printers have the outward appearance of documents prepared on electric typewriters. The operation of the printer is controlled by a logic board that receives instructions from the computer. This board performs many functions, including the selection of characters and the activation of the hammer that strikes the typeface against the ribbon. The board also advances the disk to the appropriate space and rotates the platen or roller before producing the next line of type. The daisy wheel is capable of rotating either clockwise or counter-clockwise and its characters can incur damage, such as bent/broken spokes or flattened typefaces, that can be used to identify the printed documents it produces. Minor imperfections in the surfaces of daisy wheels produced by some manufacturers can also form the basis of an association between a document and a make of daisy wheel. By the mid-1980s, daisy wheel technology was being replaced by a growing array of affordable dot matrix, laser, and inkjet printers.

b. The Dot Matrix Printer

Dot matrix is another impact printing technology that employs a printhead that moves across a sheet of paper to produce printed letters by striking an ink-impregnated ribbon. The first dot matrix printer was introduced by the Japanese manufacturer OKI in 1968. Metal pins in the printhead are activated by instructions received from a computer to produce different styles of printed characters or "fonts" in addition to graphic designs. Defects in documents produced by matrix printers usually pertain to the alignment and structure of printed characters. These imperfections can result from excessive wear to the printhead that causes pins in the matrix to strike the paper out of their normal position. Pins can become bent, broken, or misshapen, causing misalignment problems or gaps in the outline of printed characters. Excessive wear to the paper advance and ribbon feed mechanisms may introduce other flaws that can form the basis of an association between a document and a particular dot matrix printer.

Dot matrix printers were gradually phased out during the late 1970s due to the improved quality, speed, and generally quiet operation of inkjet and laser printers. Dot matrix technology is still used in cash registers, automatic teller machines, and other point-of-sale terminals.

c. The Inkjet Printer

Inkjet printers became quite popular during the late 1970s. These printers use a high pressure pump to force specially formulated ink through a series of nozzles in the printhead towards the paper. The ink droplets emitted from the nozzles pass through an electrostatic field that causes each drop to strike the paper at a precise location. The printhead of an inkjet printer is part of the ink cartridge. Any defect attributable to the printhead will be untraceable after the cartridge is replaced.

Most defects are the result of imperfections in the inkjet printer's cartridge. Such defects may occur over time due to mechanical and thermal stresses. Other defects are caused by faults in the printer's operation. A horizontal white line through a printed area of a document is usually the result of a faulty electrical connection or a blocked nozzle in the printhead. Banding within solid colour areas of a document can also occur when the machine is printing in bi-directional mode.[9] Isolated ink drops surrounding a printed character are referred to as spatter. The amount of spatter can vary from machine to machine, as can the shape of comet-like tails that extend from isolated ink drops or "satellites" on a printed document.

The appearance of letters on an inkjet-printed document depends on the quality of ink in the cartridge as well as the surface characteristics of the paper itself. It is often difficult, in many cases impossible, to identify the source of an inkjet-printed document, but specimens produced by the suspect printer immediately before and after the date when the questioned document was purportedly produced can be helpful in reaching a meaningful conclusion.

Bubblejet and inkjet printers differ in that the former do not use mechanical pressure to force ink from a printhead towards the paper. Instead, bubblejet printers use a solvent-based ink that is rapidly heated in the printhead nozzle. This causes a bubble to form near the heating elements which fires a small drop of ink towards the paper. Despite differences in the formulation of their inks and how ink is directed towards the paper, bubblejet printing is similar in many respects to printing produced by inkjet printers.

d. The Laser Printer

Laser printers are similar to direct electrostatic photocopiers in that they use a photosensitive print drum to transfer a latent image of a document

---

9 In bi-direction mode, the printhead alternates between forward and reverse passes while applying ink to the document.

from the drum to a blank sheet of paper. The photosensitive drum is first given an electrostatic charge that is dissipated in specific areas by a laser to form an image of the document on the drum's surface. Oppositely charged toner applied to the drum clings only to the charged areas. The toner is transferred to a sheet of paper as it is passed over the drum's surface. The toner is then fused to the paper by heat and/or pressure. When viewed microscopically, laser printed characters consist of tiny particles fused to the surface of the printed document.

iii) Facsimile-Transmitted Documents

The fact that a document has been transmitted by a facsimile machine (faxed) may be a cause for concern in a criminal investigation or civil litigation if it arouses suspicion concerning the manner in which it was allegedly produced. Facsimile machines consist of three principle components: a scanner that produces a digital image of the document to be transmitted, a modem that transmits the digitized information over a telephone line, and a receiving fax machine that converts the electronic signal into a recognizable image and prints the transmitted document.

The edges of printed characters and handwritten pen strokes have a saw-tooth appearance in facsimile-transmitted documents. These jagged edges are created by the sending machine as it scans the original document one line at a time as it advances through the machine. This effect is more prominent with older thermal machines, but it also exists in documents transmitted by more modern machines designed to provide a higher quality product.[10]

Faxed documents often contain a line of printed information at the top (and occasionally at the bottom) of each page that contains information about the sending and/or the receiving fax machine. Text that corresponds to the sending machine is referred to as the transmitting terminal identifier or TTI header. The TTI header usually includes the sender's name, date, time, and page number, as well as the sender's fax number. The receiving fax machine can be programmed to produce receiving terminal identifier or RTI information at the top or bottom of each printed page.

At the time of writing, all fax machines are capable of printing a header in the upper margin of all received documents. A collection of fax fonts

---

10 M. Casey Owens, "A Look into Facsimile Transmission" (1990) 35 *Journal of Forensic Sciences* 112.

has been produced that can be used by document examiners as an aid in identifying the make and model of a fax document from its TTI or RTI.[11]

iv) Photocopier Identification

It is difficult to categorically state that a photocopied document originates from a particular office copier, but source can be indicated through a unique pattern of trash marks caused by dust or dirt particles adhering to the photocopier's internal components or the surface of its glass platen. Other defects on a photocopy can be attributed to rollers or other mechanical components of the copier that direct the paper through the machine. Before using these defects to associate a document with a particular copier, the document examiner must consider if the questioned document is a first-generation copy or if it was produced by two or more machines. Trash marks from the first-generation copy will be reproduced on subsequent copies.

The quality of copies produced by any copier will vary over time. Trash marks may disappear when the platen glass is cleaned or when the machine is serviced by a technician. Worn mechanical components responsible for defects in photocopied documents tend to be more permanent and are usually present until the defective components are replaced.

When dealing with colour photocopies, many people are unaware of the repeated pattern of yellow dots that are produced by photocopier manufacturers such as Xerox and Canon. This pattern or matrix of dots is embedded within every copy produced by a particular machine and it corresponds to the make, model, and serial number of the copier that produced them. Their arrangement in some copiers can also show when a document was produced. These yellow dots are usually too pale to be seen by the naked eye but they can be observed by viewing the colour photocopy with a VideoSpectral Comparator (see Figure 14.7).

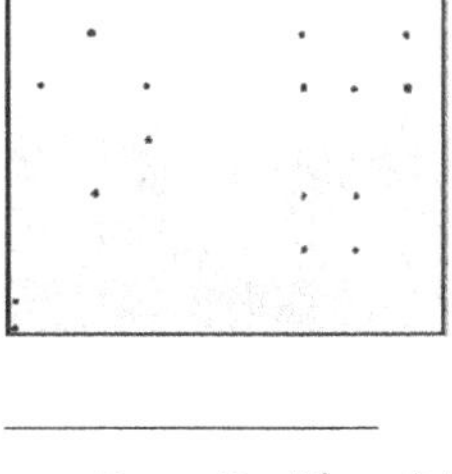

FIGURE 14.7. This pattern of dots appears in the background of every colour copy produced by the author's Ricoh Aficio colour copier. The yellow colour was changed to black to improve visibility in this photograph.

11 James Davidson & Diane K. Tolliver, "A Collection of Fax Fonts" (Paper delivered at the annual meeting of the American Society of Questioned Document Examiners, Milwaukee, WI, 1992).

c) Indented Writing Examinations

When documents are written while resting atop other papers, impressions of the writing are often transferred to the underlying sheets as indented writing impressions that may or may not be visible with oblique lighting. The heavier the pen pressure, the deeper and more visible are the impressions. When normal or light pen pressure is used, the indentations are typically too weak to be seen and a more sensitive technique is needed to decipher these faint impressions.

Documents suspected of containing decipherable indented writing impressions may be tested in a laboratory using an Electro-Static Detection Apparatus or ESDA (see Figure 14.8). The suspect document is placed on the ESDA's platen and covered with a thin sheet of Mylar film. A corona wire passed over the film distributes an electrostatic charge on its surface. This charge becomes concentrated in regions of the Mylar that are located directly above impressions in the paper. Black toner powder is then distributed over the charged film to render visible the faint indented writing impressions on a page (see Figure 14.9).

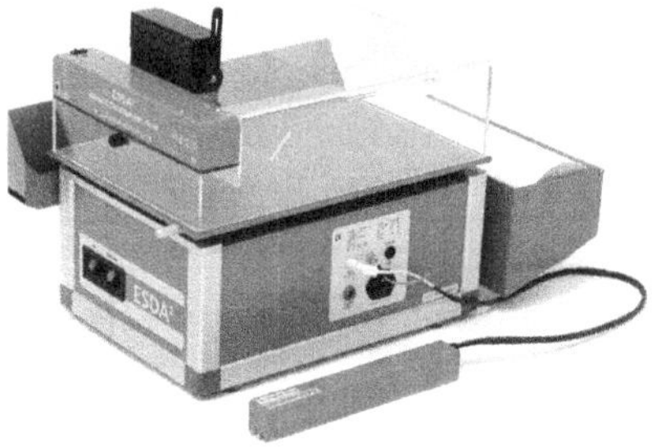

FIGURE 14.8. The ESDA is designed to restore indented writing impressions on suspect documents.

(Permission to use this image was obtained from Foster & Freeman, 46030 Manekin Plaza, Suite 170, Sterling, VA.)

d) Examination of Writing Media

The forensic document examiner may be called upon to examine and compare the materials used to prepare a suspect document. Most experts are qualified to compare writing inks and identify entries made with different pens. Laboratory equipment used for this purpose includes binocular and stereoscopic microscopes, as well as video comparators that analyze the optical properties (e.g., infrared luminescence, infrared reflectance, and ultraviolet fluorescence) and physical characteristics (e.g., stroke width, colour, opacity) of the ink. Some experts are equipped to conduct tests that determine the chemical composition of inks. These tests require the removal of a small amount of ink from the document in question and are therefore destructive methods that affect both the appearance and the condition of the document.

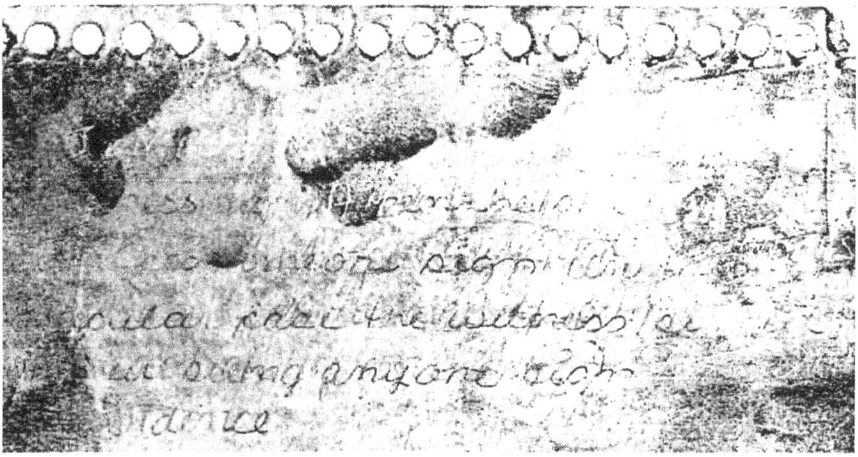

FIGURE 14.9. This photograph shows an acetate sheet with faint indented writing impressions recovered from a suspect document using an ESDA.

Few document laboratories are able to determine when a signature or entry was written on a suspect document. Ink dating can be approached in two ways. The first dating method involves extracting a sample of ink and separating it into its various components, primarily pigments, dyes, volatile components, and additives that enhance the properties of the ink. Once separated in this manner, the results are compared to a large collection of writing inks to identify the manufacturer, which can indicate the date when the ink formulation was first used. The second dating method involves the quantitative analysis of volatile components in an ink sample using gas chromatography mass spectrometry (GC-MS) to determine its dynamic or aging properties. Only a few laboratories in North America have the equipment and expertise to provide this service.

Document examiners can also provide information concerning the sequence of entries on a document, such as whether a signature was written before or after the body of the document was printed or typed. The results of such tests can expose insertions, additions, or deletions that took place after a document was executed.

e) Physical Matching

Reconstructing documents does not require a great deal of technical ability or knowledge. The basic procedure is to compare the edges of torn or perforated pieces of paper to determine if their edges physically match, taking into account the surface properties, contours, and the printed information of each piece. This type of examination is requested by clients who want to know if a sheet of paper was torn from a book, if a postage stamp was at one time attached to other stamps from a known source, or whether shredded paper can be reassembled into its original form.

2) Hierarchy of Conclusions

The wording used and the number (or levels) of opinions forensic document examiners use to describe the results of their analyses have long been subjects of controversy. During the 1970s, FBI examiners approached the problem by limiting their opinions to only three levels of opinions: identify, eliminate, and inconclusive. Today, some examiners utilize seven different conclusion levels to express their findings while other examiners employ only five levels. Categorical conclusions are easily understood, but problems have surfaced when experts' results are not definitive. Beyond the controversy over conclusion levels, some document examiners create further confusion by expressing conclusions cloaked in enigmatic, evasive language that hinders clarity and diminishes the credibility of their evidence.

During the 1990s, a committee organized by the document section of the American Academy of Forensic Science (AAFS) was given the task of reaching a consensus regarding the number of conclusions used to express a document examiner's findings and establishing standards with respect to the wording. In 2004, ASTM International released *E 1658 Standard Terminology for Expressing Conclusions of Forensic Document Examiners*,[12] which was developed to make conclusions readily understandable to clients, investigators, attorneys, judges, and jury members. It was eventually adopted by the Scientific Working Group for Documents (SWGDOC).[13]

In October 2014, the Organization of Scientific Area Committees (OSAC) was mandated by the National Institute of Standards and Technology (NIST) to "create a sustainable organizational infrastructure dedicated to identifying and fostering the development of technically sound, consensus-based documentary standards and guidelines for widespread adoption

---

12 Online: www.astm.org/Standards/E1658.htm.

13 Scientific Working Group for Forensic Document Examination, "SWGDOC Standard Terminology for Expressing Conclusions of Forensic Document Examiners," online: www.swgdoc.org/images/documents/standards/SWGDOC%20Standard%20Terminology%20for%20Expressing%20Conclusions%20of%20Forensic%20Document%20Examiners%20150114.pdf.

throughout the forensic science community."[14] With OSAC replacing SWGDOC (see Chapter 1 for further information), many forensic document examiners continue to use a nine-point opinion scale to express the likelihood that two or more items are related until the Forensic Document Examination Subcommittee's recommendations are made available. The following conclusions apply to handwriting comparisons made according to the nine-point opinion scale. Wording can be modified to include other analyses described in this chapter.

1) IDENTIFICATION: *The writer of the specimen handwriting on item K-1 has been identified as having written the questioned handwriting on item Q-1.*

   This is the upper limit of confidence that document examiners use to identify the writer of an unknown document. Although prohibited from using the word "fact," the document examiner is virtually certain that the writer of the known material wrote the writing in question.

2) HIGHLY PROBABLE (IDENTIFICATION): *It is highly probable that the writer of the specimen writing on item K-1 wrote the questioned writing on item Q-1.*

   The evidence is very persuasive, yet some feature or quality of the questioned writing may be missing, so an opinion of identification is not justified. The questioned writing may be limited in amount, it may lack individuality, or the photocopied nature of the document may conceal certain handwriting features that exist in the original writing. Alternatively, the available specimens may not fully represent the person's writing habits. Whatever the cause, the document examiner is quite confident that the questioned and known writings were written by the same individual.

3) PROBABLE (IDENTIFICATION): *The writer of the specimen writing on item K-1 probably wrote the questioned writing on item Q-1.*

   This opinion is used in cases where the evidence is strong but certain features within the questioned writing are not represented in the specimens. Other limitations include instances where the writing lacks individuality, where the questioned or specimen writing are disguised, where the writing covers a wide range of variation, where original documents are unavailable, or where the specimen material is unsuitable.

14 Mark Stolorow & Jeremy Triplett, "Organization of Scientific Area Committees (OSAC) for Forensic Science: Status Update" (Paper delivered at the American Society of Crime Lab Directors meeting, Washington, DC, 28 April 2015).

4) INDICATIONS (IDENTIFICATION): *There is some evidence that suggests the writer of the specimen writing on item K-1 could have written the questioned writing on item Q-1.*

This opinion is appropriate when the evidence falls short of a "probable" degree of confidence. Certain writing habits appear in both the questioned and specimen writing, but other elements of the questioned writing are not accounted for. Any divergences that are present must be attributed to a particular cause or otherwise be reconciled. Inadequate specimens, lack of individuality within the writing, poor quality reproductions (carbons, photocopies, faxes, etc.), limited questioned material, and simple letter forms are all reasons why this conclusion may be expressed.

5) INCONCLUSIVE: *The writer of the specimen writing on item K-1 has not been identified or eliminated as having written the questioned writing on item Q-1.*

This conclusion marks the zero point on the confidence scale and is used when important limiting factors, such as evidence of disguise in the questioned or known writings, are present. Other restrictions may also be responsible, but the degree to which they influence the comparison is more severe. Document examiners render this conclusion when they cannot say if the suspect writer wrote the questioned handwriting or not.

6) INDICATIONS (NEGATIVE): *There is some evidence that suggests the writer of the specimen writing on item K-1 may not have written the questioned writing on item Q-1.*

This opinion carries the same weight as (4) Indications (Identification). The few differences present suggest the suspect writer may not be the person who wrote the questioned document.

7) PROBABLE (NEGATIVE): *The writer of the specimen writing on item K-1 probably did not write the questioned writing on item Q-1.*

This opinion carries the same weight as (3) Probability (Identification). Although differences in the writing point away from the suspect writer, this opinion falls short of the highly probable (i.e., virtually certain) category.

8) HIGHLY PROBABLE (NEGATIVE): *It is highly probable that the writer of the specimen writing on item K-1 did not write the questioned writing on item Q-1.*

This conclusion carries the same weight as the (2) Strong Probability (Identification). The document examiner is virtually certain that the questioned and known writings were not written by the same person.

9) ELIMINATION: *The writer of the specimen writing on item K-1 did not write the questioned writing on item Q-1.*

This opinion represents the highest degree of confidence that a writer did not write a contested document. The document examiner is virtually certain that the questioned and known writers are different people. The expert must be satisfied that at no time did the writer have the ability to incorporate into his handwriting the same combination of qualities and features that exist in the questioned writing. Document examiners are rarely able to express this opinion unless another person has been identified as authoring the questioned writing. Generally, the quantity of specimen material needed to eliminate a writer is greater than that required for identification. To support a categorical elimination, the specimens provided must represent the full range of the writer's skill, graphic maturity, and variability.

The above conclusions must be supported by significant handwriting features noted by the expert during the course of a handwriting comparison. The ratio of similarities and differences will vary from one case to another but Figure 14.10 illustrates, in a general fashion, the relationship between these ratios and the conclusions they support.

FIGURE 14.10. The relationship between conclusions used by many document examiners to express examination results are shown. This does not represent the actual number or significance of similarities and differences observed during the course of an examination.

The reasoning employed by the forensic document examiner is both subjective and intuitive. Even DNA profiling, considered by many to be the most exacting method of identification, is exposed to subjectivity when scientists visually inspect test results and formulate their interpretation of those results. When conducting a handwriting comparison, the document examiner relies on training and experience to establish the significance of critical features that are observed during the course of the examination. Generally, more experienced experts are able to more accurately assess the significance of handwriting characteristics than those with more limited experience.

Handwriting analysis has thus far resisted attempts to establish a more defensive probabilistic and empirical foundation. In addition to interpersonal and intrapersonal variability, specific examples of handwriting may be affected by known and unknown circumstances. The heterogeneity of people with respect to ethnicity, handedness, writing system, and physical and mental condition, as well as the writer's physical positioning, visual acuity, writing instrument, and the influence of both prescription and nonprescription drugs, can alter the appearance of handwriting.

The National Academy of Sciences (NAS) stated in 2009 that,

> [t]he scientific basis for handwriting comparisons needs to be strengthened. Recent studies have increased our understanding of the individuality and consistency of handwriting and computer studies and suggest that there may be a scientific basis for handwriting comparison, at least in the absence of intentional obfuscation or forgery. Although there has been only limited research to quantify the reliability and replicability of the practices used by trained document examiners, the committee agrees that there may be some value in handwriting analysis.[15]

Recommendations in the 2009 NAS Report have prompted researchers to undertake a number of studies that should more firmly establish a scientific basis for handwriting identification.

Some projects currently underway include: (1) measuring pen stroke dynamics to differentiate between genuine, disguised, and simulated handwriting; (2) establishing a list of statistical frequencies for numerous handwriting and hand printing features that will demonstrate their level of uniqueness; and (3) developing a Bayesian methodology to quantitatively assess handwriting evidence by means of a likelihood ratio (LR) described for multivariate data. It is expected that these and other research projects will support decision making in casework by providing a more objective framework for examinations.

C. THE ROLE OF THE FORENSIC DOCUMENT EXAMINER IN CRIMINAL CASES

Forensic document examiners face the same challenges regardless of whether the documents examined relate to criminal charges, civil litigation,

---

15 National Research Council Committee on Identifying the Needs of the Forensic Sciences Community, *Strengthening Forensic Science in the United States: A Path Forward* (Washington, DC: National Academies Press, 2009) at 166–67, online: www.ncjrs.gov/pdffiles1/nij/grants/228091.pdf [2009 NAS Report].

or regulatory matters referred to boards of enquiry. Any opinion or conclusion reached must be rendered strictly in accordance with the physical evidence contained in the documents examined. All statements made in reports and during testimony should be supported by evidence and free from any misleading or inaccurate claims.

Experts should be impartial and base their findings only on features observed during the course of the investigation. Lawyers should use the following questions when deposing opposing experts:

- What do you perceive as your purpose and function in this case?
- Assuming that your opinion is wrong or invalid, what steps would you go through to analyze and assess the opinion to find your error?
- What further work do you intend to do and what further work have you been asked to do for this case?
- Do you have any criticism of the police or of my expert(s) in this case in terms of their methodology or techniques?
- Have you made any credibility judgments or assumptions as part of your analysis in this case?[16]

These questions may not apply to every case, but they can help indicate when an expert's approach to an examination was in any way prejudicial or biased.

Recent changes to the Rules of Civil Procedure adopted by many provinces have had a positive influence on the content and purpose of expert reports. Previously, some experts provided very little information concerning the methods used or the features that were observed during the course of their examinations. The requirement that expert reports include a description of the salient features supporting the opinion and any factual assumptions upon which it is based should help eliminate testimony by unqualified, partisan witnesses.

1) Locating a Qualified Expert

Just as the qualified forensic document examiner can assist a client in establishing the provenance of a questioned document, an incompetent or unethical expert can cause irreparable damage to what would otherwise be a successful outcome. Document experts must make full use of their

16 Christa Zevitas, "Five 'Silver Bullet' Questions for Opposing Experts" *Lawyers Weekly USA* (6 September 1999) at 99.

education, training, and experience to overcome the challenges that they face when determining the facts surrounding the preparation of a questioned document. The search for a competent expert should therefore begin with close inspection of the expert's curriculum vitae for evidence of the following qualities.

a) Academic Qualifications

An undergraduate degree from an accredited university is considered the minimum educational requirement for entering the profession. The document examiner will find a strong foundation in chemistry and physics useful when analyzing writing inks, stationary products, adhesives, and opaquing fluids. A baccalaureate degree is also a requirement for holding membership in most forensic societies (e.g., the Canadian Society of Forensic Science, the American Academy of Forensic Science, the American Society of Questioned Document Examiners). Those seeking certification from the American Board of Forensic Document Examiners or the Chartered Society of Forensic Sciences also must possess a baccalaureate degree from an academic institution or from an institution or higher education program whose degrees would be considered equivalent to an earned baccalaureate degree.

b) Professional Training

There is no substitute for sound theoretical and practical training. The widely accepted minimum standard for training in forensic document examination is two years of full-time study under the direction and supervision of a qualified instructor. In Canada, most qualified document examiners are trained at and employed by provincial or federal government agencies, which include the Laboratoire de Sciences Judiciaires et de Médecine Légale in Montréal, the Centre of Forensic Sciences in Toronto and Sudbury, the laboratories of the Royal Canadian Mounted Police, or Canada Revenue Agency's laboratory in Ottawa. The courses include theoretical principles of forensic document examination, as well as their application to practical problems. The topics covered by courses at these agencies vary somewhat, but typically include such core areas as handwriting identification, the restoration of indented writing, alterations to documents, identifying documents produced by printers, typewriters, and other types of office equipment, document dating, and expert testimony, to name just a few. Written examinations, practical problems, and mock trials are administered periodically and at the end of these programs to ensure all training objectives have been met.

c) Certification

The oldest and most recognized certification program for document examiners in North America is the American Board of Forensic Document Examiners (ABFDE), which was established in 1977. Certified forensic document examiners must successfully complete a series of written, practical, and oral examinations based on a broad range of problems frequently encountered in document examination. These problems may include questions concerning the authorship of handwriting; the authenticity or spuriousness of a signature; the source of typed or computer printed documents; the presence of alterations, additions, or deletions on documents; the comparison of inks, papers, and writing instruments; or similar questions as promulgated by the ABFDE.

Candidates who successfully complete the testing program are recognized as Diplomates of the American Board of Forensic Document Examiners. The certification status of diplomates is reviewed every five years to ensure they continue to meet the high professional standards set by this certifying body.

A certification program similar in nature to that offered by the ABFDE was established by the Chartered Society of Forensic Sciences during the 1980s. This body awards a diploma in Document Examination to applicants who are professional members of the Chartered Society of Forensic Sciences and who satisfactorily complete written, practical, and oral examinations.

d) Continuing Education

The need to acquire knowledge and skills does not cease once a document examiner has completed the initial period of training. Forensic document examiners, like all scientists, must make a concerted effort to keep abreast of recent developments in the profession, which includes learning about new analytical methods, recent research results, and the latest developments by scientific equipment manufacturers.

e) Memberships in Professional Organizations

Memberships in professional organizations provide document examiners with an opportunity to promote professionalism, improve their knowledge, and share information with their peers. Several North American societies organize annual conferences where members and invited guests can attend plenary sessions, seminars, and workshops to improve their qualifications and take advantage of invaluable learning opportunities. Those claiming to be qualified forensic document examiners should be asked if they are members in good standing of any of the following organizations, and if so, to confirm their level of membership: the American Society of Forensic Document Examiners, the Southeastern Association of Forensic Document Examiners, the Midwestern Associations of Forensic Document Examiners, the Southwestern Association of Forensic Document Examiners, the Canadian Society of Forensic Science, and the American Academy of Forensic Sciences.

2) Before Consulting a Forensic Document Examiner

Prior to contacting a forensic document examiner, lawyers should be able to provide the following information: the names of all parties involved, as well as the names of their lawyers; the circumstances surrounding the production of the questioned document (i.e., when it surfaced, who produced it, where it was stored, etc.); the nature of the questioned document (i.e., whether it is an original or a copy of an original document); the number of original and photocopied documents bearing specimen material; whether the originals of any document reproductions can be made available at a later date; whether the reproductions are first-generation or multiple generation copies; the number of documents bearing specimen material and the nature of the material; the number of documents bearing specimen material that are contemporaneous with the alleged date of the disputed document; and any deadlines that must be met with respect to completing the analyses, producing a forensic report, or giving expert testimony. If the matter involves a disputed signature or handwriting, the document examiner will also need to know the age, mental state, and physical condition of the writer at the time the disputed document was purportedly produced.

D. A CASE STUDY

The manager of a local business reported that an anonymous hand printed note (Figure 14.11) was left on the desk of one of his employees. The incident has negatively affected the morale and productivity of the entire office.

The manager asked if a document examiner could determine whether the printed note was made by one of his fourteen employees. Specimen hand printing from each employee was provided for comparison purposes.

A preliminary inspection of the questioned note revealed features (i.e., block hand printing, distorted letters, blunt stroke endings, tremor, alternate forms of the same letter, and slow writing movements) that suggested the writer was attempting to alter or disguise his or her writing

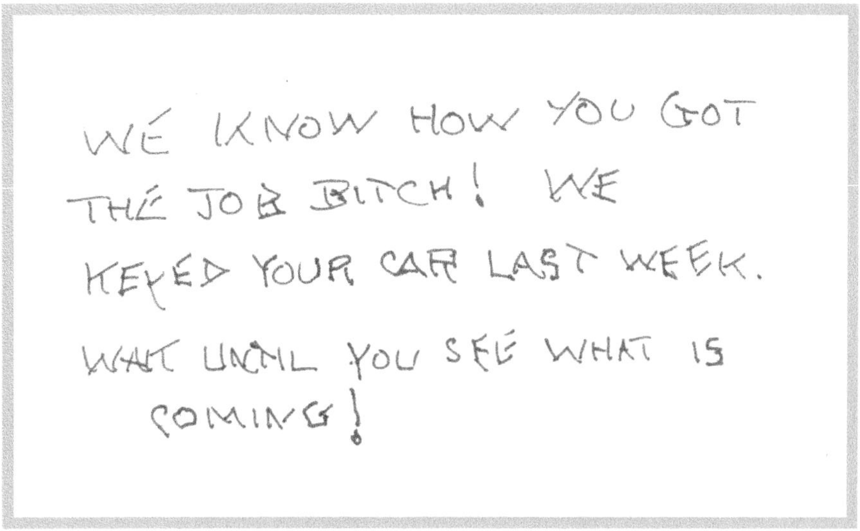
WE KNOW HOW YOU GOT
THE JOB BITCH! WE
KEYED YOUR CAR LAST WEEK.
WAIT UNTIL YOU SEE WHAT IS
COMING!

FIGURE 14.11. Anonymous note received by an office employee.

habits. The document examiner stated that a comparison of the distorted printing with freely executed specimens from the fourteen employees would likely not produce meaningful results.

When an individual writes or draws on a document, the paper is compressed in the process and impressions are transferred through the sheet and onto the underlying surfaces. A microscopic examination of the edges of the note revealed traces of adhesive along one edge, which indicated it was likely a sheet torn from a notepad. An examination of the note using an ESDA to reveal indented writing uncovered the following impressions: "John, I mailed the attached contract to our client last Tuesday. Do you know if there is a deadline for shipping the products? Steph" (see Figure 14.12).

A comparison of the restored handwritten impressions with specimen handwriting from one of the employees disclosed a combination of significant handwriting characteristics with no apparent differences (see Figure 14.13). These similarities were sufficient to identify the writer.

When interviewed by the manager, "Steph" confessed to writing the hand printed note and placing it on a colleague's desk.

Indented writings are perhaps the most overlooked form of document evidence. This case illustrates that writing impressions recovered on threatening messages, anonymous letters, hold-up notes, suspicious suicide notes, or pages torn from journals can yield valuable information concerning the origin and history of a disputed document.

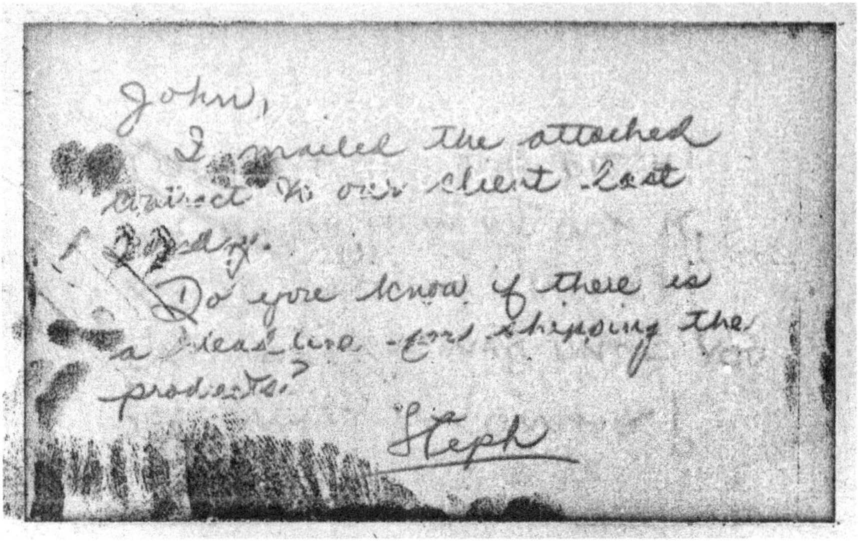

FIGURE 14.12. Cursive handwritten impressions restored with an ESDA.

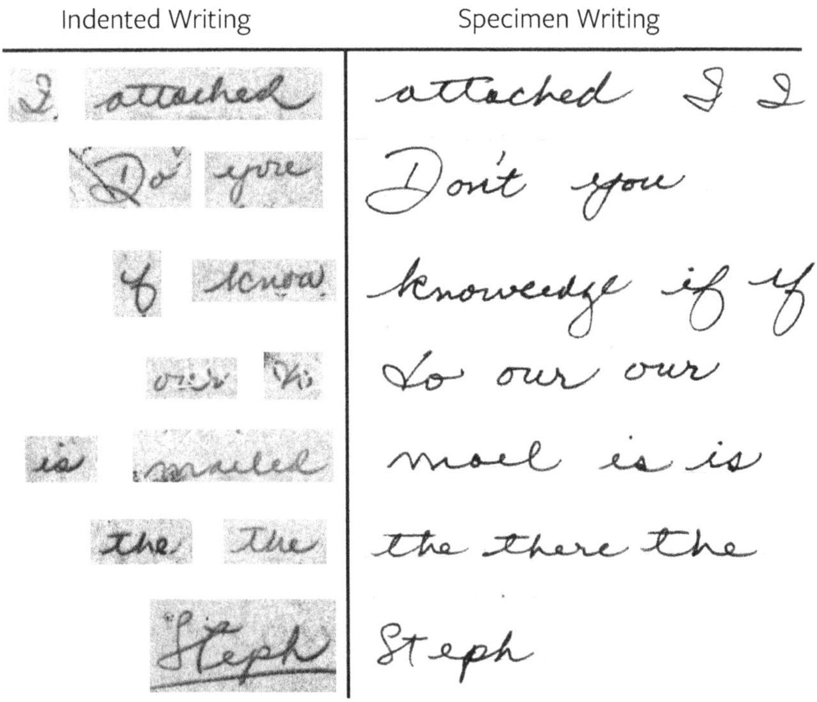

FIGURE 14.13. Several similar handwriting features appear in both the writing impressions restored on the anonymous note and specimen handwriting from one of the employees.

E. CONCLUSION

The field of questioned document examination today is broader and more complex than it was fifty years ago. Forensic document examiners work primarily in office settings and laboratories, providing information concerning the genuine or fraudulent nature of disputed documents to corporations, police departments, government regulatory agencies, the general public, law firms, and the courts. Basic problems of handwriting and signatures are still a principal focus of document examiners, but their work also involves other analyses related to the materials and equipment used to prepare a suspect document.

As science and technology have advanced, so too has the profession. Forensic document examiners make use of computers, micro analysis, and other technology to assist in examining documents to determine their authenticity. This chapter explores the many analyses performed in a forensic document examiner's laboratory. This information will provide some guidance to anyone seeking to have a disputed document examined. Experience has shown that when lawyers clearly understand the expert's requirements, the quality of submitted material improves and examination results can be presented with greater certainty.

F. LEGAL CONTEXT

> Questioned document examination involves the comparison and analysis of documents and printing and writing instruments in order to identify or eliminate persons as the source of the handwriting; to reveal alterations, additions, or deletions; or to identify or eliminate the source of typewriting or other impression marks. Questions about documents arise in business, finance, and civil and criminal trials, and in any matter affected by the integrity of written communications and records.[17]

The term "documents" is given a broad definition to include both traditional written documents and modern electronic documents,[18] but this section will focus on the former, with an emphasis on the caselaw involving handwriting.[19] In cases involving criminal charges, forensic document examiners are most commonly called upon to speak to the authorship of

---

17 2009 NAS Report, above note 15 at 163.

18 Alan W. Bryant, Sidney N. Lederman, & Michelle K. Fuerst, *Sopinka, Lederman & Bryant: The Law of Evidence in Canada*, 3d ed. (Markham, ON: LexisNexis, 2009) at 1213 & 214 [*Law of Evidence in Canada*].

19 See Chapter 7 for a discussion of electronic documents.

a document in question and, to that end, will speak to whether the document is authentic and genuine. A wide variety of cases may benefit from the opinion of a forensic document examiner, including those involving forgery, fraud,[20] counterfeiting, suicide, homicide, kidnapping, and extortion.[21]

1) False Documents and Determining Authorship

A "false document" is "any document that is false in some material particular."[22] A false document may, for example, include a photocopy of an altered cheque,[23] or a document bearing a forged signature.[24] Relying on the meaning of "false documents" as defined in section 321 of the *Criminal Code*,[25] the offence of forgery is made out under section 366(1):

> **366.** (1) Every one commits forgery who makes a false document, knowing it to be false, with intent
> (a) that it should in any way be used or acted on as genuine, to the prejudice of any one whether within Canada or not; or
> (b) that a person should be induced, by the belief that it is genuine, to do or to refrain from doing anything, whether within Canada or not.[26]

As stated in *R. v. Cunsolo*,[27] a mortgage fraud case in which the accused was convicted under section 380(1)(a) of the *Criminal Code*, the accused may admit or agree that the writing in question was made by him or, if authorship is disputed, the Crown may establish the accused's authorship through:

---

20 For the elements of the offence of "fraud," see: *R. v. Théroux*, [1993] 2 S.C.R. 5; *R. v. Zlatic*, [1993] 2 S.C.R. 29. See also "false pretence" under s. 361(1) of the *Criminal Code*, R.S.C. 1985, c. C-46 [*Criminal Code*].

21 National Forensic Science Technology Center, "A Simplified Guide to Forensic Document Examination" (2009) at 2 & 3, online: www.crime-scene-investigator.net/SimplifiedGuideQuestionedDocuments.pdf. For an interesting case involving document examination in the extradition context, see *France v. Diab*, 2014 ONCA 374. France sought to extradite Diab for his alleged role in a bombing that occurred outside a Paris synagogue in 1980.

22 *R. v. Gaysek*, [1971] S.C.R. 888 at 891.

23 *R. v. Nuosci*, [1991] O.J. No. 2232 (C.A.).

24 *R. c. Ogilvie*, 1993 CanLII 3510 (Que. C.A.).

25 For details, see *Criminal Code*, above note 20, s. 321.

26 *Ibid.*, s. 366(1). See also *R. v. McMillan*, 2003 CanLII 52178 (Ont. C.A.).

27 2011 ONSC 1349 [*Cunsolo*]. We are indebted to Justice Hill for his excellent explanation of document examination in this case and have relied heavily on his framework of analysis for this chapter. The Court of Appeal affirmed his decision, finding that Justice Hill did not err by relying on his own comparison of the handwriting evidence as his conclusions were justified by detailed reasons and his approach did not result in unfairness; see paras. 40–44 of *R. v. Cunsolo*, 2014 ONCA 364.

(1) a witness acquainted with the accused's writing,
(2) expert evidence, or
(3) comparative evaluation by the trier of fact without the testimony of a witness.[28]

The handwriting or signature in question may also be proved by "a witness who saw the document being written or signed."[29] As stated in *R. v. Meer*, the trier of fact can conduct handwriting analysis in the absence of expert evidence:

> The appellant argues, however, that the three modes of proof mentioned in *Cunsolo* are given in "order of preference." That may be so. It may be that expert evidence is the better evidence. But there is nothing in *Cunsolo* to support the proposition that handwriting analysis by the trier of fact is only permissible if it is supplementary to expert evidence on that subject.[30]

Depending on the case, the authorship of a document may provide key circumstantial evidence reflecting the author's familiarity with the connected subject matter, active participation in the transaction in question,[31] state of mind,[32] or, in some cases, identity as the perpetrator.[33] This is well articulated by the documents in possession doctrine, which speaks to the admissibility of documents found in a party's possession:

> Documents which are, or have been, in the possession of a party will, as we have seen, generally be admissible against him as *original (circumstantial) evidence* to show his knowledge of their contents, his connection with, or complicity in, the transactions to which they relate, or his state of mind with reference thereto. They will further be receivable against

---

28 *Ibid.* at para. 243.
29 *Law of Evidence in Canada*, above note 18 at 1247.
30 2015 ABCA 141 at para. 86, citing *Cunsolo*, above note 27 at para. 246. The appeal as of right to the Supreme Court of Canada was dismissed, *R. v. Meer*, 2016 SCC 5. The appeal as of right arose from Berger J.A.'s dissent that the appellant did not receive a fair trial by virtue of the "woefully incompetent" conduct of his trial counsel; see para. 153 of *R. v. Meer*, 2015 ABCA 141.
31 *Cunsolo*, above note 27 at para. 242.
32 *R. v. M.K.*, 2012 ONSC 1765 at para. 37 [*M.K.*].
33 See *Law of Evidence in Canada*, above note 18 at 1248 for a discussion of *R. v. Voisin*, [1918] 1 K.B. 531, [1918–19] All E.R. Rep. 491 (C.C.A.). This murder charge involved the finding of part of a woman's body in a parcel with a handwritten note reading "Bladie Belgiam" coupled with the defendant making the same spelling error when asked to write "Bloody Belgian" by police. See also the discussion below of *R. v. Ward*, 2003 CanLII 26255 (ON SC) [*Ward*].

> him as *admissions* (i.e. exceptions to the hearsay rule) to prove the *truth* of their contents if he has in any way *recognized*, *adopted* or *acted* upon them.[34]

Even if documentary evidence is not found in a party's possession, such evidence may still be helpful in cases where the evidence adduced by the Crown is entirely circumstantial. For example, in *R. v. Ward*,[35] the accused was charged with committing aggravated assault against his girlfriend. The victim's injuries were, in the words of the court, "severe and disfiguring," leaving no doubt that the offence occurred. The only issue was whether the requisite elements were proven by the Crown and that the accused was the perpetrator.[36] The defence called no evidence, there were no witnesses to the assault, and the victim had no memory of the assault.[37] The victim had been discovered in her bedroom by her grandmother; she was naked and unconscious and the scene was bloody.[38] The Crown conceded that blood, DNA, and fingerprint analyses failed to link the accused with the crime scene.[39]

Investigating police officers found a note on the victim's bedroom dresser, next to keys belonging to the accused that could open the victim's apartment and building.[40] When the victim and the accused left her apartment earlier that night, the note and the keys had not been there.[41] A qualified expert in handwriting analysis examined the note and, after receiving additional samples of the accused's handwriting, ultimately concluded in his second report that the accused wrote his name on the dresser note and that the accused probably wrote the remaining questioned writing on the note.[42] Justice G.P. Smith noted that:

> The contents of the note are significant. It reads:
>
> > If you survive, it's because I let you
> > I'm done with head games.
> > Yes pig these are my keys.
> > I told you to quit drinking[43]

---

34 Sidney L. Phipson & Michael Howard, *Phipson on Evidence*, 15th ed. (London: Sweet & Maxwell, 2000) at 30-10, as cited in *Cunsolo*, above note 27 at para. 260 [footnotes omitted; emphasis in original].

35 *Ward*, above note 33 at para. 4.

36 *Ibid.* at para. 3.

37 *Ibid.*

38 *Ibid.* at para. 10.

39 *Ibid.* at para. 28.

40 *Ibid.* at para. 13 & 14.

41 *Ibid.* at para. 14.

42 *Ibid.* at paras. 16–21.

43 *Ibid.* at para. 19.

The victim testified that the accused, who frequently expressed his concern over her drinking, often used the term "head games."[44] In analyzing the evidence, the court found that the argument of a third party committing the crime was speculative[45] and similarly rejected the argument that "the note may have been written at different times or by different people."[46] The court ultimately found the accused guilty as charged, holding that this conclusion was the only reasonable inference from the evidence as a whole.[47]

2) Handwriting Comparisons by the Trier of Fact

Both common law and section 8 of the *Canada Evidence Act* allow the trier of fact to conduct handwriting comparisons between an unknown or disputed writing and a known writing properly admitted into evidence without assistance from an expert witness.[48] In *R. v. Abdi*,[49] the appellant appealed against his convictions for trafficking heroin and possession of heroin for the purpose of trafficking. The appellant was observed by a police officer selling heroin, which was "packaged in white paper with blue ink scribbling on it."[50] The purchaser also identified the appellant as the seller.[51] Police seized twenty packets of heroin from the appellant's apartment, eighteen of which were similarly packaged in white paper with blue scribblings. Two address books, one brown and one red, were also seized. The red book primarily contained Persian handwriting known to be the appellant's (i.e., the genuine writing) and he admitted that the book was his. The brown book contained a list of names and telephone numbers, including that of the purchaser.[52] The appellant denied that the brown book (i.e., the disputed writing) was his, further stating that he did not know the purchaser or his phone number, did not sell heroin at the time in question, and "had no knowledge of the heroin found in his apartment."[53] The only issue on appeal was "whether the trial judge erred in permitting the jury to compare the handwriting in the address books, or alternatively, in not cautioning the jury adequately as to the dangers of making such comparisons."[54]

---

44 *Ibid.* at para. 22.
45 *Ibid.* at paras. 46 and 54.
46 *Ibid.* at para. 53. This quote is in the words of the court.
47 *Ibid.* at paras. 59–61.
48 *Cunsolo*, above note 27 at para. 246, and *R. v. Abdi*, [1997] O.J. No. 2651 (C.A.) [*Abdi*].
49 *Ibid.* See also *R. v. Malvoisin*, 2006 CanLII 33304 at para. 4 (Ont. C.A.) [*Malvoisin*].
50 *Abdi*, above note 48 at para. 2.
51 *Ibid.*
52 *Ibid.*
53 *Ibid.* at para. 7. This quote is in the words of the court
54 *Ibid.* at para. 12.

The Court of Appeal dismissed the appeal, finding that the trial judge did not err on the issue of the handwriting comparison conducted by the jury because the jury was reminded that no expert evidence was introduced and they were appropriately instructed to use their common sense in assessing the address books.[55] Further, other "ample" evidence addressing identity pointed to the appellant.[56] The Court of Appeal did state, however, that, although "a more complete instruction would not have affected the result," the trial judge should have clarified that a cautionary approach should be taken by the unassisted jury, particularly since most of the writings were in a Persian dialect unfamiliar to the jury, which "would obviously make it more difficult to assess the similarities and differences between the documents."[57] The Court of Appeal highlighted the potential dangers of a trier of fact conducting an unassisted document comparison and the role of the trial judge's charge to mitigate this issue:

> There is, of course, a potential danger in making unassisted comparisons and the judge's charge should reflect this danger. The jury should be reminded that it has no expert or other evidence relating to the writings and directed as to the care to be exercised in making the comparison. Any difficulties that a comparison may reasonably present in the light of the circumstances of a given case should be brought to the jury's attention. As well, the jury may require instruction on the quality of the handwriting exemplar, whether it is of sufficient length and clarity for comparison purposes and, depending on the nature of the facts and the charge, on other matters going to the weight that may be placed upon such a comparison. In cases where forgery or the like is alleged, expert evidence may well be essential.[58]

As held in *R. v. G.T.*,[59] if a trial takes place before a judge sitting without a jury, then it is preferable for the judge to "explicitly caution himself about the care to be taken in unassisted comparisons of handwriting," but it is not a reversible error on appeal if such a caution is not made.

---

55 *Ibid.* at para. 10.

56 *Ibid.* at para. 31. For contrast, see *R. v. Botha*, 2011 ONCJ 326. In that case, a proper signature comparison was not possible and Botha could not be identified or eliminated. Botha was acquitted on the basis of "doubt as to the identity of the individual depicted in the surveillance video utilizing the card [connected to the loan alleged to be fraudulent]" (see para. 35).

57 *Abdi*, above note 48 at para. 29. A cautionary approach to handwriting comparisons conducted without the benefit of expert witness testimony was similarly approved of in *R. v. C.F.*, 2010 ONCA 424.

58 *Abdi*, above note 48 at para. 27.

59 2015 ONCA 221 at para. 5. See also *Malvoisin*, above note 49.

In *Cunsolo*,[60] Hill J. set out important reasons why the trier of fact should adopt a cautionary approach when comparing handwriting:

> The trier of fact must therefore exercise caution in performing comparative handwriting analysis for any number of reasons including:
>
> (1) weakness of proof respecting the known sample of the accused's writing
>
> (2) the lack of expertise and experience in performing the task
>
> (3) lack of access to special equipment utilized by experts and laboratories
>
> (4) the quality of the handwriting exemplar, including consideration of length and clarity
>
> (5) the deficits occasioned to the process by photocopies
>
> (6) the natural variation in everyone's handwriting (intrasource variation)
>
> (7) given that different individuals may well have similar handwriting, the necessity of separating out class master patterns from identifying significant individuality of features and habitual repetition of same supporting the view that the samples are the product of a single writer
>
> (8) deciding how many features or attributes of similarity are required to move beyond resemblance to identification of a writer
>
> (9) identification of not superficial, but persistent and fundamental, differences in the relevant samples detracting from the probative force of discerned similarities[61]

A comparison done by the trier of fact should be done with notice to defence counsel in order to provide an opportunity for the defence to make full answer and defence by introducing evidence and presenting an argument on the issue. In *R. v. Anderson*,[62] the handwriting in question—photographs of handwriting on a calendar that appeared to be a watering and feeding schedule for marijuana plants in a grow operation—and the known writing of the appellant on a cheque, were marked as exhibits at trial. "Neither counsel made any reference to the cheque or the calendar in their closing submissions; nor did the trial judge draw attention to the documents, the similarity of the handwriting or his intention to make a comparison in his consideration of the case."[63] The conviction, however, resulted from the trial judge's handwriting comparison.[64] On appeal, Donald J.A. found that conducting this comparison without notice to the parties denied the defence the

---

60 *Cunsolo*, above note 27.

61 *Ibid.* at para. 253 [citations omitted].

62 2005 BCCA 143.

63 *Ibid.* at para. 8.

64 *Ibid.* at para. 9.

opportunity to make full answer and defence, creating procedural unfairness that could only be resolved by allowing the appeal and ordering a new trial.[65]

3) Handwriting Comparisons by the Expert

Although the trier of fact is able to engage in document comparison without the assistance of an expert, the accuracy of the comparison may arguably be improved if expert evidence is admitted at trial. In the *voir dire* of *R. v. Guilbride—Trial Ruling No. 26*,[66] the Crown sought to qualify a civil RCMP member, Gregory Dale Smith, as an expert in forensic document examination to testify to the authorship of handwriting found in various exhibits.[67] Defence counsel raised questions about the weight of the evidence, instead of questioning Smith's expertise as a forensic document examiner. The issues to be decided by E.A. Arnold P.C.J. were: (1) should Smith's evidence "be characterized as expert or non-expert opinion evidence?" and (2) is Smith's testimony necessary to assist the trier of fact?[68]

With respect to the first issue, Smith was found to be "a properly qualified expert,"[69] and, although the court recognized that a "wide variety of people"[70] can conduct handwriting comparisons, this does not preclude an expert from making such a comparison using protocols that may increase the accuracy of the comparison. This does not translate to 100 percent accuracy on the part of the forensic document examiner and does not preclude the possibility of error, but his expertise and training will likely improve the accuracy of his opinion.[71] The court explained that, "[a]s pointed out by the Crown, s. 8 of the *Canada Evidence Act* does not distinguish between the expert and the non-expert witness . . . ."[72]

With respect to the necessity of Smith's testimony in assisting the trier of fact, the court found that the testimony was necessary since ". . .

---

65 *Ibid.* at paras. 11–16. For a discussion of ethical considerations for counsel involving tactical decisions, specifically with respect to whether to call one's client and his wife, in the context of critical handwriting evidence tendered without notice at trial, see *Meer*, above note 30.

66 2003 BCPC 270 [*Guilbride*].

67 *Ibid.* at para. 1.

68 *Ibid.* at para. 2.

69 *Ibid.* at para. 10. For an example of a case that considers whether a document analyst meets the *Mohan* criterion of being a properly qualified expert, see *R. v. Williams*, 2013 ONSC 1079 [*Williams*].

70 *Guilbride*, above note 66 at para. 11.

71 *Ibid.* at para. 12.

72 *Ibid.* at para. 13.

there is literally more to handwriting comparison and analysis than first meets the eye."[73] In arriving at this finding, E.A. Arnold P.C.J. explained that the scientific part of the forensic document examiner's work rests in the ability, "by virtue of his or her training and experience, to distinguish letters or techniques of word formation that a lay person would be unable to observe."[74] The court further stated that:

> The question of what features are significant, and what may be inferred from them, relate to the expert's judgment, assessment and opinion. I reject the submission of [defence counsel] Mr. Lanning that Mr. Smith is simply doing what we all could do, if we paid sufficient attention to the task at hand.[75]

Beyond identifying or excluding a person as the author of the document in question, the examiner may speak to when the document was created, what materials were used in creating it, and whether the original writing was modified—modifications may be latent (i.e., invisible to the naked eye) or patent (i.e., visible to the naked eye).[76] For example, in the sexual assault case of *R. v. M.K.*,[77] the complainant wrote in her mathematics textbook, "if anything happens to me, it's because of my step-dad," adding "see page 111," where the writing on that page had been erased.[78] The forensic document examiner, Gregory Boyd, testified to the words he was able to identify in the erased writings: "I mean if I die or . . . ing . . . it's . . . T.R. [the complainant's initials]"[79] T.R.'s teacher also recognized her handwriting.[80] When read together, the notes reflected the complainant's fear for her life at the hands of her stepfather and spoke to her state of mind at the time. The timing of the writing is significant because it made the defence suggestion of collusion between T.R. and her brother to advance false allegations of sexual touching against the accused to be, in the words of the court, "highly unlikely," as the "notes would have been written before T. [her brother] visited her in Canada."[81] The court did not

---

73 *Ibid.* at para. 21.

74 *Ibid.* at para. 18.

75 *Ibid.* To read about how this documentary evidence fit into the case as a whole and to view the trial judge's discussion of its weight, see *R. v. Guilbride*, 2004 BCPC 101 at paras. 63–82.

76 *Simplified Guide to Forensic Document Examination*, above note 21 at 2 & 3.

77 M.K., above note 32.

78 *Ibid.* at para. 35.

79 *Ibid.* at para. 36.

80 *Ibid.* at para. 37.

81 *Ibid.* at para. 38.

believe the testimony of T.R.'s mother and younger brother that they did not recognize the writing in the textbook as the complainant's.[82] The court found T.R. to be "extremely credible and trustworthy"[83] and accepted her evidence, finding that the accused sexually touched T.R.[84]

With respect to the weight of an expert's report in the face of an accused's testimony denying authorship, documentary and *viva voce* evidence should not be pitted against one another in a credibility contest.[85] To that end, "where the expert's report concludes one writer authored certain documents without identifying the writer, it is accepted for the truth of its contents with minimal defence submissions as to weight as the defence submits that the prosecution has failed to establish that the accused is that writer."[86] Further, differences between systems of document examination, specifically whether one is inferior to the other, goes to weight, rather than admissibility.[87]

In *R. v. Williams*,[88] a case addressing a gang shooting, there was "no evidence as to when the writings in question were created and, thus, no temporal nexus to the crime with which the accused stand [sic] charged." Based on the caselaw, Clark J. found that this "lack of direct evidence as to when the documents were created, or by whom, goes to weight and not admissibility."[89] Justice Clark also rejected the defence argument that the documents in question, which showed hostility to the gang to which the deceased belonged,[90] should not be admissible. If attributed to the accused by the jury, the documents would represent bad character evidence that invites propensity reasoning.[91] Since the documents were probative to an issue at trial, specifically motive, the documents were admissible, notwithstanding their demonstration of bad character.[92] Ultimately, it remained within the jurisdiction of the jury to decide if the writings reflected motive, as argued by the Crown, or the accused's efforts as an aspiring rap artist, as argued by the defence.[93]

---

82 *Ibid.* at para. 39.
83 *Ibid.* at para. 59.
84 *Ibid.* at para. 84.
85 *Cunsolo*, above note 27 at para. 245, citing *R. v. Coburn* (1982), 66 C.C.C. (2d) 463 (Ont. C.A.).
86 *Ibid.*
87 *Williams*, above note 69 at para. 22.
88 2013 ONSC 3100 at para. 32.
89 *Ibid.* at para. 36.
90 *Ibid.* at para. 62.
91 *Ibid.* at paras. 37 and 40.
92 *Ibid.* at para. 40.
93 *Ibid.* at paras. 62–68.

In *R. v. Bath*,[94] a fraud and money laundering case, the subjective nature of handwriting analyses and the potential for bias were canvassed at length by the court. The handwriting examiner, Mr. Tanaka, concluded that there was a "strong probability" that Bath's co-accused, Khangura, authored the handwriting found on deposit slips and GST refund cheques fraudulently claimed in the name of two sham companies.[95] Mr. Tanaka agreed on cross-examination that handwriting identification is primarily a subjective analysis, where examiners try to be as objective as possible and it is possible that error may result from unintended bias.[96] The court found that Mr. Tanaka understood that the Canada Revenue Agency (CRA) investigation focused on implicating certain individuals and that his conversations with CRA investigators may have been more extensive than he was able to recall.[97] The court found that the relationship between the CRA and Mr. Tanaka did not discredit his expertise or invalidate his opinions, but that it did "require caution in placing any heavy reliance on those opinions, because of the possibility that Mr. Tanaka may have been subjected to influence that he himself was unable to detect."[98]

The court also addressed what weight should be given to non-conclusive or qualified handwriting opinions, where the handwriting analysis scale reflects different levels of the examiner's certainty in his identification:

> Mr. Tanaka explained that the scale reflects different levels of certainty, but emphasized that the relationship among those levels cannot be numerically represented. He testified that he arrives at a qualified conclusion when a conclusive determination cannot be given because of a "technical limitation" such as poor copy quality, the absence of a feature that appears in the known writings, or the presence of a feature that does not so appear.[99]

Although Mr. Tanaka's opinions of "strong probability" provided some evidence of Khangura's authorship of the writings, the court provided them limited weight; the opinions did not establish Khangura's involvement on their own.[100] Mr. Tanaka failed to explain the features and factors

---

94 2011 BCSC 1726, aff'd 2014 BCCA 89 [*Bath*].
95 *Ibid.* at paras. 231, 353, and 419 (SC).
96 *Ibid.* at para. 340.
97 *Ibid.* at para. 343.
98 *Ibid.* at para. 344.
99 *Ibid.* at para. 352.
100 *Ibid.* at para. 359.

of the samples that formed the basis of his opinion, making it difficult to assess his opinions.[101] The court also rejected the Crown's submission that the peer review process guaranteed the reliability of Mr. Tanaka's opinions, finding that the peer review process may have improved the quality and reliability of Mr. Tanaka's approach but that his opinion's reliability "cannot be bolstered by reference to hearsay peer opinions unidentified as to source or precise content."[102] Since, however, the opinions were part of a "network of surrounding inculpatory circumstances" that connected Khangura with two of the sham companies in question, the court found that the opinions carried "some weight."[103]

4) Summary

Overall, forensic document examiners provide opinions in a variety of cases, often focusing on determining a document's authorship and authenticity. Although research is underway to strengthen the scientific basis for handwriting comparisons, document examination remains recognized as a valuable field of opinion evidence based on the expertise, training, and subjective analyses of the document examiner. The examiner should be able to identify and explain the features in the sample writing that caused him to arrive at his conclusion, explaining the limits of the discipline and the related opinion. Although triers of fact may conduct their own handwriting comparisons, the specialized knowledge of the document examiner should positively impact on the accuracy of their conclusions. If unassisted by an expert witness in the discipline, the trier of fact should approach the task of conducting a handwriting comparison with caution. Most importantly, the trier of fact must remember that any document examination conclusion should be evaluated in the larger context of the case as a whole on the totality of the evidence.

---

101 *Ibid.* at paras. 345, 356, & 357. The court refers at para. 356 to *R. v. Rockwood*, 2004 NLSCTD 66, where Adams J. "concluded that to give the opinion weight would be unsafe, because the expert did not explain the foundation for her opinion, which the Court therefore could not meaningfully assess, and stated that as such the opinion approached the ultimate issue."

102 *Bath*, above note 94 at para. 347 (SC). The court relied on *R. v. Ranger* (2003), 67 O.R. (3d) 1 at para. 65 (C.A.).

103 *Bath*, above note 94 at para. 419.

CHAPTER 15

Forensic Entomology

Gail S. Anderson and Sherah L. VanLaerhoven

LEGAL CONTEXT: CAITLIN PAKOSH

A. OVERVIEW

Forensic or, more correctly, medicolegal entomology is the study of the carrion insects associated with a dead body. The primary aim of forensic entomology is to estimate the minimum colonization time of insects on a dead body in order to infer a minimum elapsed time since death (the post-mortem interval). The principles of forensic entomology can also be applied to a live person in cases of abuse or neglect. Insects may indicate whether a body has been moved from one site to another, whether it has been disturbed after death, and the presence or position of wound sites that are no longer visible due to decomposition. Insects can be used as alternate toxicological specimens when more traditional samples are no longer available and, because they feed on the host, the victim's DNA can sometimes be extracted from insects left behind when the body has been removed. Hence insects are extremely valuable evidence in criminal investigations.[1]

Forensic entomology is one of the oldest forensic sciences, being first reported in a murder investigation in tenth-century China.[2] Modern use

1 Although the principles of forensic entomomlogy are primarily used to assist investigations into human deaths, carrion insects are attracted to any dead animal and so it is equally valuable in criminal cases involving animals, such as in wildlife or animal cruelty crimes.

2 Bernard Greenberg & John C. Kunich, *Entomology and the Law: Flies as Forensic Indicators* (Cambridge: Cambridge University Press, 2002).

began in mid-nineteenth-century France and it became established in South America and Europe in the early part of the twentieth century. Its first use in Canada did not come until the 1960s, and then only in a very unusual manner. A suspect in a murder case was picked up by police with Canadian banknotes in his possession. The notes had strange hair-like material stuck to them with dried blood. Similar material was found in the pocket of the victim and in the drawer in which he was known to keep his money. The RCMP took this material to entomologists at the Entomology Research Institute, Canada Department of Agriculture, in Ottawa, where they were identified as the plumose hairs of a bumblebee. The police re-investigated the drawer in which the decedent kept his money and found the remains of a dead bumblebee. This information was instrumental in the conviction of the suspect.[3]

Forensic entomology became more widely adopted in North America in the 1970s, and research in this area has grown exponentially in the last twenty to thirty years. Today, it is a well-recognized, well-researched, and highly valuable tool in criminal investigations. Its value has been accepted by academics, police, and the criminal justice system. Where previously forensic entomologists would have been brought into a case only to provide an estimate of the elapsed time since death, today they offer insights into many other areas, including evidence of body relocation, pet animal and wildlife crime, and abuse.

1) Application in Canadian Criminal Courts

As noted above, the forensic entomologist appearing in court will typically testify to the length of time insects have been associated with the remains, which informs an estimate of the minimum elapsed time since death. But before a case goes to court, and often prior to the identification of a suspect, the forensic entomologist will submit a report to the requesting agency. The report may be accepted into evidence on its own by the court, other times the forensic entomologist will be called to testify to explain the scientific reasoning behind the report's conclusions. An explanation would likely include a description of how insects colonize remains, how they develop through their life cycle, and how each stage and species can be identified. From this, the entomologist can explain how the age of an

3 H.F. Howden, "The Mercure Trial: A Sideline of Entomology" (1964) 96 *The Canadian Entomologist* 121.

insect is estimated and from that the age of the insect colony on the victim. For example, the forensic entomologist might explain that, based on the stage, size, and species of the insects on the body, together with an understanding of local weather conditions, the oldest insects on the remains are at least seven days old. Therefore, the deceased was colonized at least seven days before discovery, hence this individual died at least seven days before the insects were collected.

2) Objectives

Forensic entomology is considered one of the most accurate methods for estimating the time elapsed since death in the later post-mortem interval.[4] It is also generally of interest to jurors and, when presented correctly, is not difficult to understand. But despite the ability of forensic entomology to aid in several areas of investigation, it is often underused due to a lack of understanding of its potential. This chapter will explain the basic premises of forensic entomology, as well as the challenges and advances in the discipline so that lawyers will be able to understand its worth and lead or challenge such evidence accurately.

B. THE SCIENCE OF FORENSIC ENTOMOLOGY

The basic premise of forensic entomology is that insects are usually the first witnesses to a death, arriving on a body within minutes or seconds if the conditions are suitable.[5] A body begins to decompose immediately after death and goes through a sequence of rapid biological, chemical, and physical changes. Each of these changes attracts and repels different species of insects. For instance, some insects are attracted and able to feed only when the tissue is fresh, others when it is undergoing protein breakdown, still others when it is undergoing fat breakdown or is dry.

The vast majority of insects do not feed and live on carrion. Only very specific groups and species of insects are attracted to a dead body. This

---

4 V.K. Kashyap & V.V. Pillai, "Efficacy of Entomological Method in Estimation of Post-mortem Interval: A Comparative Analysis" (1989) 40 *Forensic Science International* 245.

5 Gail S. Anderson & Sherah L. VanLaerhoven, "Initial Studies on Insect Succession on Carrion in Southwestern British Columbia" (1996) 41 *Journal of Forensic Sciences* 617; P. Nuorteva, "Sarcosaprophagous Insects as Forensic Indicators" in Cesare G. Tedeschi, William G. Eckert, & Luke G. Tedeschi, eds., *Forensic Medicine: A Study in Trauma and Environmental Hazards* (Philadelphia: W.B. Saunders, 1977) 1072.

means that when carrion insects (insects that feed on dead bodies) are recovered from a scene, they arrived to colonize the body specifically and were not just naturally endemic to the area. The most valuable carrion insects in a forensic case are those that feed exclusively on carrion for at least a part of their life cycle.

Although the colonization of a body is a continuous process, forensic entomologists divide it into two main areas of analysis. The first area of analysis is insect development, which focuses on the blow fly life cycle. These insects feed on fresh tissue. Blow fly colonization of the body begins immediately after death and lasts three to four weeks, until the first blow flies have completed their life cycle. Therefore, blow fly development can be used to infer minimum elapsed time for up to four weeks after death. The second area of analysis is successional ecology, which focuses on the sequence of insects that colonize the remains over time. This method is valuable until there are no nutrients left—a year or more after death.

1) Estimating Length of Time of Insect Colonization

a) Fly Development

In the first few hours, days, and weeks after death, the forensic entomologist will analyze the immature stages of the blow flies. Blow flies are true flies (family Calliphoridae in the order Diptera) and are usually the first colonizers. Calliphoridae are present globally and, although the particular species colonizing the body will vary based on geography, members of this family are invariably the first to arrive (in some regions, flesh flies or Sarcophagidae, another family of true flies, are the first to arrive). Blow flies are bright, metallic, large flies that can be seen buzzing around garbage in summer. They are frequently very bright blue or green, although some are darker and duller.

The host body is not a food source for themselves, it is a nursery for their offspring. Adult blow flies feed on sugar and protein, so they feed primarily on plant nectar and protein sources such as feces or carrion, but their offspring feed only on carrion. The adult female can locate a body rapidly even over great distances. Having found a body, she will explore it for a few minutes, tasting it with taste receptors on her feet until she locates a suitable place to lay her eggs. The most attractive egg laying site is a wound where there is liquid protein for the first hatched larvae or maggots to feed. Absent a wound, the female will choose a moist, easily accessible area. Orifices, which are lined with a mucosal layer, are also easier for the very tiny larvae to pierce and the moisture prevents desiccation. Once a suitable egg-laying, or oviposition, site is located, the female will lay a clump of eggs. Usually, many females are attracted at the same time so many thousands of eggs may be laid in the same area.

i) Blow Fly Life Cycle

An understanding of the blow fly life cycle is important because it will allow a calculation of the minimum length of time that the person has been deceased. Adult blow flies are of little value because they may have developed from the body but equally may have just arrived minutes earlier. The immature stages, however, are inextricably associated with the corpse.

The first stage, or first instar larvae, begins when the eggs hatch, only a few hours after being laid. The larvae, very tiny maggots only about one to two millimetres in length, are very vulnerable to predation and desiccation. They also have very tiny mouthparts and are not able to penetrate dry adult human skin. This is why the female parent takes such care in locating a suitable site. Because survival of her offspring depends on this, female blow flies have evolved to locate even the smallest wound.

The second stage, or second instar, begins when the larvae moult. The larvae in this stage are a little bigger, with larger mouthparts that can break human skin. They feed for a period of time and then moult again. At this second stage, the larvae feed voraciously, removing a tremendous amount of tissue. They often form large aggregations called "maggot masses." When larvae feed, they store food in an organ called a crop at the front of the gut, or foregut. In the early instars, the crop can be quite small, although large compared with the rest of the animal.

In the third stage, or third instar, the crop becomes very obviously visible as a large dark red or brown oval area occupying a third to two-thirds of the larval body. This is the larva's food reserve. The third instar includes two morphologically similar but physiologically and behaviourally different stages. The early part of the third instar involves the frenetic feeding activity just described, but, after a set period of time, the larvae enter a non-feeding stage referred to as the prepuparial, prepupal, or wandering stage. At this point, the larvae leave the food source in search of a dry safe place in which to metamorphose to the adult stage. During this wandering stage, they subsist on the reserved food in the crop, which shrinks correspondingly. Although externally similar to the feeding stage of the third instar, a larva in the wandering stage can be identified by the reduction in the size of the crop, its position relative to the food source, and its lack of interest in feeding. Larvae are vulnerable to predation by birds, so the insect's usual choice of pupation site is in the loose soil around the corpse, a few centimetres under the surface. They may also be under or in clothing, hair, carpets, or appliances. They are usually only centimetres to metres away from the corpse.

After the successful location of a pupation site, the larva becomes shorter, more opaque, and more oval shaped. It forms a hard outer puparial case. Inside this case it metamorphoses into an adult fly. When the adult fly emerges from the puparial case, it is damp, crumpled, and unable to fly. It will expand its wings and dry over the next few hours. In this stage it is called a teneral adult. Although teneral flies are technically adults, the fact that they cannot yet fly indicates that they too have emerged from the body and their presence indicates that an entire life cycle has been completed on the body. Once the teneral fly has dried its exoskeleton and is capable of flight it will leave the area and seek out a food source, a mate, and eventually its own oviposition source. The fly will not usually return to the original corpse as by this time the body will have decomposed to a level that is no longer attractive to blow flies. The empty puparial case is left behind as evidence that the cycle has been completed.

Only the oldest immature blow flies are of value as they will indicate the minimum time since death of the body. It is common for several species of blow fly to be attracted; the forensic entomologist will assess the immature insects on the body to determine the oldest stage of each species. This will indicate the first insects to colonize and will therefore infer the minimum elapsed time since death.

ii) Estimating the Age of the Insects

Insects are cold blooded so their metabolism and development are based on ambient temperature. Insects develop more rapidly when temperature increases and more slowly when it decreases and, within optimum temperatures, this relationship is linear, making it predictable. Therefore, the length of time that a species spends in each developmental stage is predictable, based on temperature and species. Each species will develop at a slightly different rate; therefore, it is imperative that the insects on the body are correctly identified. To estimate the age of the oldest immature blow flies on the body, the forensic entomologist requires four main pieces of information:

1) *The oldest stage of immature insect on, or associated with, the body.* This is determined by a careful examination of the insects on the body and

in the surrounding area; therefore, it is always best if the person collecting the insects at the scene is a forensic entomologist. If an entomologist is not available, a death investigator can perform the collection, but must be trained in entomological collections. Immature insects collected at the scene should be divided into two samples. One sample is preserved immediately at the scene to prevent further development, and the other is kept alive and reared to adulthood. It is also important to collect at the scene rather than at the morgue, as insects that have moved away from the body will be missed. If insect collection is not done at the scene (this is still possible for some time after removal of the body), the final estimate may underestimate the elapsed time since death.

2) *The species of insects present.* This is determined by morphological examination of the specimens under a microscope and the use of appropriate dichotomous keys.[6] Adult insects are much easier to identify than immatures as they possess many more diagnostic features. This is the purpose of collecting a second sample of insects to be reared to adulthood. However, larger larvae can also be identified. In cold cases or when only extremely young or damaged specimens are collected, DNA may be used for identification.
3) *The temperature of the crime scene.* This is determined using weather station data generated by Environment Canada[7] or other sources. In some cases, the scene may be a considerable distance from the nearest weather station, in which case a datalogger can be placed at the scene to record temperatures for a period of time after the remains have been removed. These data can then be compared with data from the weather station using linear regression analyses to first ensure that the weather station is correlated with temperatures at the crime scene and to develop an equation that allows the prediction of crime scene temperatures based on the weather station temperatures.
4) *The published developmental data for each species.* Many publications describe developmental data for carrion insects.

---

6 Dichotomous insect keys are used to identify any species of insect. First developed by Carl Linnaeus, the father of taxonomy, these keys are a technique to identify a species through a series of questions about its characteristics. For example: "Are there wings or are there no wings?" When the reader chooses one of the two options, another question is asked. The procedure continues until only one species meets the criteria.

7 Online: www.climate.weather.gc.ca.

With these four pieces of data the forensic entomologist can estimate the minimum number of days required to reach the stage collected, the minimum number of days insects have been on the body, and, therefore, the minimum number of days the decedent has been dead (this method only reveals the minimum number of days, it cannot determine a maximum, as the exact period between death and the first egg-laying event is unknown).

iii) Analysis of a Case

To estimate the age of the insects, certain calculations are required. Environment Canada weather stations will provide weather data either as daily highs and lows or as hourly temperatures. These data can be downloaded from the Environment Canada website and, if required, can be certified by a meteorologist. Microclimate must also be considered. Maggots in a maggot mass generate heat primarily by friction and metabolism and can raise the temperature of the mass by more than 20°C.[8] However, only certain stages are impacted by this heat, such as feeding third instar larvae, as well as subsequent younger larvae. Very early stages, as well as post-feeding larvae and pupae are unaffected as they are not part of the mass. This must also be taken into consideration.

The identification of the oldest stage of the insects associated with the remains should be relatively straightforward, especially as there are several new and excellent insect keys available.[9] Once the species of blow flies present are identified, then the question is simply: "how long does it take this species to reach this stage, under these temperature conditions?"

Just a few years ago, limited data on blow fly development rates were available, but the number of publications has grown exponentially so that now there are many datasets available for most species. Datasets provide information on the length of time a given species spends in each developmental stage at specific temperatures. For example, a dataset may provide information on the development of a species at 15°C, 20°C, 25°C, and 30°C. However, this requires further interpretation as it is probable that the death

8 D. Charabidze, B. Bourel, & D. Gosset, "Larval-Mass Effect: Characterisation of Heat Emission by Necrophageous Blowflies (Diptera: Calliphoridae) Larval Aggregates" (2011) 211 *Forensic Science International* 61.

9 Terry Whitworth, "Keys to the Genera and Species of Blow Flies (Diptera: Calliphoridae) of America North of Mexico" (2006) 108 *Proceedings of the Entomological Society of Washington* 689; S.A. Marshall, T. Whitworth, & L. Roscoe, "Blow Flies (Diptera; Calliphoridae) of Eastern Canada with a Key to Calliphoridae Subfamilies and Genera of Eastern North America, and a Key to the Eastern Canadian Species of Calliphorinae, Luciliinae and Chrysomyiinae" (2011) 11 *Canadian Journal of Arthropod Identification* 1.

scene temperatures may fall between these temperatures. It is also important to remember that temperatures fluctuate over the course of a day. At optimum temperatures (a range that varies by species), the relationship between temperature and development is relatively linear, so when development at several temperatures is known, this information can be interpolated to predict development at other temperatures along this straight line.

To estimate the development rate based on the temperatures determined to exist at the crime scene, data generated at other temperatures can be converted to thermal units known as "degree days." Degree days are calculated by multiplying the length of time that the insect takes to reach a given stage at a given temperature. This calculation is then compared to the weather records to determine how many thermal units were available at the crime scene. The number of accumulated degree days are based on a simple reverse summation process, beginning when the insects were collected and preserved at the scene and counting backwards to reach the required degree days. If the data are generated in hours, then degree hours can be determined by the same process.

Temperatures below or above which insects cannot develop are known as developmental thresholds. These are barriers beyond which insect development slows and eventually ceases. The lower threshold is typically the barrier faced by the forensic entomologist trying to determine the time required for insect development. The lower threshold, when known, is subtracted from both sides of the equation. For example, if the lower threshold below which the species does not develop is known to be 4°C, then 4 is subtracted from the temperature each day and the temperature at which the data were generated. In reality, thresholds are difficult to determine as many insects continue to develop, albeit very slowly, at very low temperatures,[10] and insects in Canada seem to have evolved to develop at lower temperatures than their conspecifics in warmer climates. Therefore, practically, a threshold of 0°C is frequently used.

This calculation is best illustrated using a hypothetical example. A gunshot victim is found at 7 a.m. on 28 August, with fly eggs in the wound area. A few of these eggs have just started to hatch into first instar larvae. Insects are collected, with half preserved immediately and half reared to adulthood

---

10 L. Davies & G.G. Ratcliffe, "Development Rates of Some Pre-Adult Stages in Blowflies with Reference to Low Temperatures" (1994) 8 *Medical and Veterinary Entomology* 245; C. Ames & B. Turner, "Low Temperature Episodes in Development of Blowflies: Implications for Postmortem Interval Estimation" (2003) 17 *Medical and Veterinary Entomology* 178.

for identification. The flies are identified as *Calliphora vicina* R.-D. Therefore, the oldest insects on the body are first instar *C. vicina*. Published, peer-reviewed research shows that this species takes a minimum of twenty-one hours to reach the start of this stage at a constant temperature of 23.3°C.[11] Therefore, this species requires a minimum of 489.3 degree hours (temperature, 23.3°C, multiplied by the number of hours, twenty-one) to reach this stage. Table 15.1 shows hypothetical weather data for the crime scene.

TABLE 15.1. Hypothetical Weather Data and Accumulated Degree Hours (ADH) Summation.

Date	Time	Temperature (°C)	ADH	Comments
27 August	9 a.m.	27	544	
27 August	10 a.m.	28	517	Death occurred at or before this time.
27 August	11 a.m.	28	490	Minimum thermal units acquired.
27 August	12 p.m.	29	462	
27 August	1 p.m.	30	433	
27 August	2 p.m.	28	403	
27 August	3 p.m.	26	375	
27 August	4 p.m.	29	349	
27 August	5 p.m.	28	320	
27 August	6 p.m.	26	292	
27 August	7 p.m.	24	266	
27 August	8 p.m.	22	242	
27 August	9 p.m.	18	220	
27 August	10 p.m.	18	202	
27 August	11 p.m.	17	184	
27 August	12 a.m.	18	167	
28 August	1 a.m.	17	149	
28 August	2 a.m.	18	132	
28 August	3 a.m.	19	114	
28 August	4 a.m.	23	95	
18 August	5 a.m.	23	72	
28 August	6 a.m.	24	49	
28 August	7 a.m.	25	25	Discovery, first instar just hatching.

Note: The insect takes twenty-one hours to reach the first instar at 23.3°C. If the temperature is very cool at the scene, it will take much longer to accumulate 489.3 ADH. Conversely, if it is warmer, it takes less time. Looking at the table, start at the time the insects were collected and known to be already in the first instar (the bottom of the table, 7 a.m. on 28 August) and accumulate ADH every hour by reverse summation. By 11 a.m. on 27 August, 490 ADH have been accumulated.

11 G.S. Anderson, "Minimum and Maximum Developmental Rates of Some Forensically Significant Calliphoridae (Diptera)" (2000) 45 *Journal of Forensic Sciences* 824.

In this example, counting back from when the first instar *C. vicina* larvae were collected at the scene on 28 August, 489.3 ADH are acquired by 11 a.m. on 27 August. Since the eggs must have been laid no later than 11 a.m. of the day prior to discovery of the body, death must have occurred by that time.

b) Insect Succession

For bodies discovered after completion of the blow fly life cycle, time since death is estimated based on insect succession. A dead body, human or animal, supports a rapidly changing ecosystem. As the body decomposes, it goes through a series of rapid biological, chemical, and physical changes. As it goes through these changes, it becomes more attractive to some insect species as a food source and less attractive, even repellent, to others. While this sequence of colonization of the body over time is predictable, it is geographically and seasonally specific and can be impacted by a number of factors such as habitat, exposure, burial, confinement, burning, and scavenging.[12] In particular, it is vital to use geographically appropriate databases for insect times of arrival as well because species composition can vary greatly between regions. If local databases are available, then the forensic entomologist will look at the composition of species on the remains and compare them with the local database to estimate the window of time within which the death took place.

For example, local databases indicate that species A, B, and C are all first found on carcasses two, four, and six weeks after death, respectively, but are no longer present eight weeks after death. Meanwhile, species D and E are first found six and ten weeks after death, respectively. If species D and E are found alive and feeding on the remains, but only past evidence of species A, B, and C are recovered, then the remains are past the state of attraction to A, B, and C, but are still attractive to D and E, indicating a minimum elapsed time since death of ten weeks or more. Unless combined with species' developmental information, this method can typically establish only a broad window of time. It is also dependent on the availability and reliability of local databases, as such information cannot be interpolated from other regions at our current level of knowledge.

---

12 G.S. Anderson, "Factors that Influence Insect Succession on Carrion" in Jason Byrd & James Castner, eds., *Forensic Entomology: The Utility of Arthropods in Legal Investigations*, 2d ed. (Boca Raton, FL: CRC Press, 2009) 201.

2) What Else Can a Forensic Entomologist Determine in a Death Investigation?

In almost all cases, the forensic entomologist is asked to provide an estimate of the elapsed time since death. However, in some situations, entomologists may also be able to provide further information about the death scenario.[13]

a) Body Relocation

It is not uncommon for a murder victim to be moved by the killer (or an accomplice) in an attempt to prevent discovery of the body. Some carrion insects are ubiquitous, but others are very habitat or geographically specific. Therefore, if a body is discovered with species A, which is common to that habitat, and species B, which is found in an entirely different habitat, it suggests that the remains have lain for a period of time in the habitat of species B before being moved to the habitat of species A. The presence of species B may help to indicate the original location of the body (though not necessarily the scene of the crime, as the body may have been moved more than once). Molecular techniques are currently being developed to indicate relatedness of flies to help indicate movement of the remains after death.[14]

b) Body Disturbance

It is not uncommon for a killer to disturb the body some time after death, perhaps to recover incriminating evidence or merely to check on the remains. If the insects are disturbed as well, the timing of the disturbance may be estimated. For example, if the victim is buried a few hours after death and it was exposed during the intervening time, flies may have laid eggs. The subsequent burial may limit further insect access to the remains. Therefore, the eggs laid on the remains would continue to develop but no further eggs would be laid. If the body was exposed again at a later time and then reburied, flies may lay eggs during the exposure, but there would again be no further access. Upon ultimate discovery of

---

13 Because carrion insects feed on any dead animal, with no preference for humans, all the above are equally applicable to animal cases.

14 K.J. Faulds, J.D. Wells, & C.J. Picard, "Verification of AFLP Kinship Methods of Entomological Evidence by Sequencing" (2014) 245C *Forensic Science International* 58; C.J. Picard & J.D. Wells, "A Test for Carrion Fly Full Siblings: A Tool for Detecting Postmortem Relocation of a Corpse" (2012) 57 *Journal of Forensic Sciences* 535.

the body, a forensic entomologist may be able to estimate the timing of the two periods of exposure based on the two distinct cohorts of insects on the remains, indicating minimum time since death and time of disturbance.

c) Wound Location

Blow flies are preferentially attracted to wound sites because they provide excellent oviposition sites. However, decomposition can often obscure wound sites and, if wounds are in the soft tissue, they may be missed. If wounds are not present, insects would be expected to colonize the orifices preferentially. When remains are discovered, larval activity most pronounced in non-orifice areas such as the stomach or back is suggestive of the presence of wounds. It is not up to the entomologist to indicate the presence of a wound; this is the responsibility of the forensic pathologist. However, the entomologist can explain why such an area is unlikely to be colonized normally, as well as conduct a more extensive examination of the area to provide the pathologist with information about a potential wound. Some wounds may also help to explain a scenario, such as the presence of defensive wounds. For instance, the palms of the hands are covered in tough skin and are not normally colonized by insects. If insects are present in the palms of the hands, it may be indicative of wound sites in these areas.

d) Artifacts

Where a forensic pathologist may conclude that a wound was likely caused by a knife or bullet, an entomologist may determine that the damage was likely caused by insects. Therefore, the forensic pathologist and forensic entomologist should work together to determine wound causation.

e) Neglect and Abuse

Blow flies feed on dead organic matter, but living people can have dead organic matter on them, such as gangrenous or highly infected tissue. In some cases, blow fly larvae will develop in such areas, feeding on the dead tissue. This is termed cutaneous myiasis. In such cases, the forensic entomologist uses traditional methods to estimate the length of time the insects have been feeding on the person. Working with a forensic pathologist who can determine the timing of tissue necrosis, this technique will allow an estimate of the minimum length of time that the person has been neglected.

f) Drug Use

Estimations of the age of insects can be impacted by drugs or other chemical compounds present in the host body. When insects feed on tissue, they bioaccumulate any toxins in the food source, and these toxins can be detected in the larvae and pupae. Drugs can impact insect development—speeding it up or slowing it down, depending on the drug involved and the developmental stage of the insect—or can cause an age-dependent mortality that kills the oldest specimens. A forensic toxicologist can process the larvae as toxicological specimens when the decedent is too decomposed to allow for the collection of normal toxicological specimens. The forensic entomologist should, therefore, be informed of the results of the toxicological analysis and the presence of other chemicals on or around the decedent.

g) DNA Source

The crop of the larva contains host tissue that can be extracted and profiled to indicate the identity of the victim, see Section B(1)(a)(i), above in this chapter. This is valuable when the victim is no longer present, such as when a body has been removed from a site and not recovered by investigating authorities. The presence of the victim's DNA in the foregut of maggots indicates that they have been feeding on that person and strongly suggests their death.

3) The Evolution of Forensic Entomology: Identifying Red Flags

Although forensic entomology is a very old science, its use in modern criminal investigations is only a few decades old. In that short time, its contributions have become so highly valued that the number of researchers in the field and the consequent increase in knowledge and publications has increased exponentially. This has resulted in a much greater understanding of carrion ecology and its proper application in court.

A few years ago, developmental data existed for only a few insect species, and geographical and seasonal databases were almost non-existent. Today, large datasets have been developed for many species, and geographical databases have been established globally. There is, however, a need for more databases in some areas. In the last two decades, several forensic entomology scholarly associations have been formed, including the North American Forensic Entomology Association,[15] the European As-

15 Online: www.nafea.net.

sociation of Forensic Entomology,[16] and the American Board of Forensic Entomology,[17] which is the certifying board for forensic entomologists in North America.

a) What Do We Mean by Time of Death?

When the entomologist states that death occurred, for example, on or before the 6th of May, it is common for the court to misunderstand this statement to mean that death occurred on the 6th of May. But forensic entomologists do not give the time of death of the decedent. Instead, they calculate the minimum length of time that insects have colonized a body, which in turn infers the minimum length of time that the person has been dead. There are several reasons why only a minimum time can be given.

First, although insects usually colonize a body shortly after death, there are a number of factors that can delay this colonization. Insects are only active when temperatures are above their activity temperature thresholds. This means, for example, that a person dying in temperatures below 0°C will not be colonized until it is warmer. Another delaying factor is time of day—blow flies are active only during the day, so a person dying at night will not be colonized until the next morning. Insect colonization may also be delayed if the death occurs inside a house or vehicle, during very heavy rain, or if the body is wrapped or buried immediately upon death.

Second, when using insect developmental records, forensic entomologists look primarily at the minimum length of time it takes an insect species to reach each stage, erring on the side of caution. They determine the time the insect entered a certain developmental stage, but they cannot determine how long the insect has been in it. For example, the third instar lasts several days, but it is difficult to determine reliably whether the insect has just entered this stage or has been in it for some time. The entomologist should exercise caution and only say that the oldest stage was third instar and estimate minimum time based on how long the insect species requires to reach this stage. Recent research is helping to narrow down the range.

Third, even if there was no impediment to access, the forensic entomologist usually does not know what happened between the time of death and the time of colonization. Although a general estimate can be made based on scientific experimentation, the unique circumstances of every case prevents this estimate from informing the entomologist's conclusions.

---

16 Online: www.eafe.org.

17 Online: www.forensicentomologist.org.

For example, replicated scientific experiments suggest egg laying is rapid if the remains are found with open wounds in an open exposed area during mid-summer, but the forensic entomologist cannot be certain whether this set of circumstances applied fully between the time of death and the time of discovery by authorities. They can only work with the known facts, which are the presence, age, and development of the insects on the body.

b) Qualifying Factors

There are many different factors that can impact our estimates, some of which can be ameliorated while others are still unknowns. The forensic entomologist should disclose all limitations in the report.

Insect development is temperature dependent, so knowing the temperature of the death scene is imperative. Since no one has been murdered right beside a weather station (so far), weather conditions must be estimated based on data from the nearest station, see Section B(1)(a)(ii), above in this chapter.

Crime scenes inside residences or vehicles also pose problems because weather station data are unlikely to be applicable, although research does exist to provide vehicular internal temperatures under various conditions. If an air conditioner or heater is operating at the crime scene, then it is important to learn how the equipment was operating.

Insect development is relatively linear at optimum temperatures, but it becomes nonlinear and less predictable at temperature extremes. See Section B(1)(a)(iii), above in this chapter. Accumulated Degree Day calculations are only accurate during the linear portion, so it is always best to use developmental data that were generated at a temperature closest to that of the crime scene.[18] If the mean crime scene temperature is 17°C, and there are published data at 16°C, 23°C, and 26°C, then the best dataset is generated at 16°C.

When successional insects are being analyzed, geographically local databases are required for an analysis since considerable differences in species composition and tenure on remains have been shown to exist between different regions. Developmental data, on the other hand, are based on temperature and such data are generally considered valid for that species globally. Recent research, however, has shown that developmental differences can exist between geographically distinct populations

---

18 Anderson, above note 11.

of the same species.[19] These may be genuine genetic differences.[20] Like all species, insects adapt to their environment and it is logical to assume that a species in a primarily cooler environment will adapt to a different set of pressures than the same species in a much warmer climate, although research in this area is relatively recent.[21] Either way, this highlights the need to use local developmental data, or at least data developed from similar regions, when available. The forensic entomologist's report should indicate which databases are being used in the analysis.

4) Cold Cases

Cold cases are problematic in forensic entomology as a full analysis requires insect evidence from the time of discovery of the body. If its value was not recognized at the time, then invariably the evidence will have been destroyed long ago. When a case is reopened, it is common for an entomologist to be called in case they are able to provide assistance, but at this stage of the case, where the only crime scene evidence is usually photographic, there is generally little service they can provide.

In the case of Steven Truscott, who was accused and convicted in the 1959 rape and murder of his school mate, Lynne Harper, entomological evidence was collected, correctly reared, and identified, but was, unfortunately, never used in the original court proceedings. Instead, unreliable stomach contents analysis was used to provide an unrealistically narrow window of the time of death, during which Truscott was seen giving a bike ride to Ms. Harper. This window was accepted by the jury. But Truscott was well alibied for the forty-three hours from the closing of this window to the time her body was discovered. Based on the strength of the time of death window, Steven Truscott, at the age of fourteen, was convicted of murder and sentenced to hang. His sentence was later commuted to life

---

19 Stacy A. Boatright & Jeffery K. Tomberlin, "Effects of Temperature and Tissue Type on the Development of *Cochliomyia Macellaria* (Diptera: Calliphoridae)" (2010) 47 *Journal of Medical Entomology* 917; M.R. Gallagher, S. Sandhu, & R. Kimsey, "Variation in Developmental Time for Geographically Distinct Populations of the Common Green Bottle Fly, *Lucilia Sericata* (Meigen)" (2010) 55 *Journal of Forensic Sciences* 438.

20 A.M. Tarone et al., "Population and Temperature Effects on *Lucilia Sericata* (Diptera: Calliphoridae) Body Size and Minimum Development Time" (2011) 48 *Journal of Medical Entomology* 1062.

21 A.M. Tarone & D.R. Foran, "Components of Developmental Plasticity in a Michigan Population of *Lucilia Sericata* (Diptera: Calliphoridae)" (2006) 43 *Journal of Medical Entomology* 1023.

and he was released on parole after serving ten years. Once free, Mr. Truscott led an exemplary life. Almost fifty years after the murder, the case was re-examined and, importantly, this time the entomological evidence was included. Due in no small part to the examination of the entomological evidence, which showed that the time of death may have been later than the jury originally concluded based on the stomach contents evidence, the Ontario Court of Appeal unanimously overturned the original conviction in 2007.[22]

C. THE ROLE OF THE FORENSIC ENTOMOLOGIST IN CRIMINAL CASES

1) Comparing the Role of the Investigating Expert With the Defence Expert

Although establishing a time of death is important in all cases, forensic entomologists are usually only consulted when the death is believed to have resulted from foul play. Accidental and suicidal deaths are sometimes also investigated. In any case where a forensic entomologist is needed, it is paramount that one be called to the scene as soon as possible after discovery of the body. The collection of live insects from the body, preferably at the scene, before the body is moved, is vital. Hence, a forensic entomologist should be involved even before the police determine whether the death is a homicide, and long before charges are laid.

From the point of view of the expert witness, there is no difference between testifying for the prosecution or the defence. The role is simply to interpret the entomological evidence for the judge or jury. The real difference is the timing of the arrival of the forensic entomologist in the case. The defence expert will virtually always be engaged too late to collect insects at the scene, before they have been disturbed by the removal of the body, or at autopsy. Once the autopsy is complete, the body is washed and any insect evidence will be irrecoverably lost. Hence, collection and initial analysis, if any, will be done by the forensic entomologist called in by police, the coroner, or medical examiner. A report of the analysis will be submitted to the investigating agency very early in the investigation, often before a suspect is identified. The report should always be an unbiased interpretation of the entomological evidence.

---

22 *R. v. Truscott*, 2007 ONCA 575 [*Truscott*].

Forensic entomologists usually testify for the defence as rebuttal witnesses. Their analysis is limited to an evaluation of the report and any photographs. The latter are extremely problematic, as it is often very difficult to make any conclusions based on photographs. Insects need to be examined under a microscope to determine the species, a vital step in reliably estimating the minimum time elapsed since death.

2) Common Questions at Trial

1) *Can a forensic entomologist determine an absolute time of death?* No, the forensic entomologist can tell the court the length of time that insects have been colonizing the body. This provides a minimum, rather than absolute, elapsed time since death.
2) *Can a forensic entomologist determine the maximum time of death?* No. A forensic entomologist may make statements regarding the condition of the scene and its effect on insect development. For instance, if the body were in full sun with no restriction of access during insect season, then rapid colonization of the remains would be expected. However, despite these ideal conditions, the time to colonization remains unknown. The body may have been in another location or another condition for some indeterminate time prior to being exposed.
3) *How does the accuracy of the weather measurements affect the accuracy of the entomologist's time of death estimates?* Since insect development depends on temperature, accurate temperature measurements are vital. To establish the most accurate weather measurements for the analysis, a temperature datalogger can be placed at the scene to measure temperature over several weeks. See Section B(1)(a)(ii), above in this chapter.
4) *Can the age of an insect be estimated from a photograph?* This depends on various factors. If it is a teneral or freshly emerged adult and can be identified to species, then developmental and temperature records will enable an estimate of the insect's age. With immature larval insects, the required morphological characteristics that indicate the specific stage or species are rarely visible. If a ruler is present in the photograph, then an estimate of stage may be possible based on the size of the larva. Identification, except in rare species which are morphologically distinctive without the use of a microscope, cannot usually be made from a photograph, but it may be possible to determine the species present in the area and then estimate a range of ages, based on those species.

3) Reviewing the Record and Ensuring Full Disclosure

At the time of writing, there are only three or four forensic entomologists in Canada, so standards are usually discussed across North America. The major publication in the area of best practices was developed by the European Association of Forensic Entomology, with major consultation with forensic entomologists around the world.[23] In North America, the American Board of Forensic Entomology (ABFE)[24] certifies forensic entomologists. It has established guidelines for entomology case reports to ensure that they contain all of the information required for the investigating agency and counsels, as well as being thorough enough to allow an entomologist for the defence to re-evaluate the case. The ABFE also provides guidelines on insect collection, scene observations, and weather data collection. Board certification ensures that members and diplomates adhere to strict ethical guidelines and meet minimum qualification requirements.

The ABFE recommends that the following be included in all reports: contact information of requesting police officer and agency; time and dates of consultation; detailed information, usually tabulated, of the insect evidence received or collected, including where and when collected (i.e., site on body or at scene, stage collected, number preserved, number reared to adulthood, emergence rate, and identification); a summary of the case as it pertains to the insect evidence and question being asked; background information on the species recovered with appropriate literature citations; explanation of how the analysis was performed and the conclusions reached; and full name, address, and signature of the forensic entomologist. Copies of all materials related to continuity of evidence, such as courier receipts, all field and lab notes, references, and meteorological data, should also always be available on request.

The complete report should:

- Explain how all calculations were made and reference the appropriate literature.
- Point out any caveats in the analysis and explain how conclusions were reached.
- Identify the weather station from which weather data were collected.
- Include links to weather data and full citations of all references.
- Note the secure location of all insect specimens.

---

23 J. Amendt et al., "Best Practice in Forensic Entomology—Standards and Guidelines" (2007) 121 *International Journal of Legal Medicine* 90.

24 Above note 17.

D. A CASE STUDY

A man was found murdered several blocks from the Las Vegas strip on 8 July 2001, at about 10 a.m. He had suffered numerous injuries, including stab and slash wounds. His penis had been cut off and his rectal area was injured. The time since death was estimated medically as having occurred within twelve hours of discovery of the body. Ms. Kirsten Blaise Lobato, eighteen years old, was identified as a possible suspect but had an accepted, unbreakable alibi: she was at her home three hours away from Las Vegas that morning from 11:30 a.m., effectively proving she could not have committed the murder. However, at trial, the medical estimate of the time since death changed from up to twelve hours to between ten and eighteen hours before discovery of the body; this new estimate extended four-and-a-half hours beyond the time of her accepted alibi.

In 2002, Ms. Lobato was convicted of first-degree murder and sexual penetration of a dead body. In 2004, the conviction was overturned due to multiple trial court errors. She was retried in 2006. During the second trial, the medical estimate of the time of death was again up to eighteen hours prior to discovery of the body. Ms. Lobato was convicted of voluntary manslaughter and sexual penetration of a dead body and was sentenced to thirteen to thirty-five years in prison. At no point in either trial was entomological evidence considered.

The entomological evidence, or in this case the lack of entomological evidence, is extremely important. Although the body was lying in a very accessible area, in a virtual blood bath at the height of summer, and offered multiple attractive sites for blow fly egg laying, no eggs were present on the body when it was discovered. Blow fly eggs are laid in clumps and so are very visible. Close examination of the photos of the victim and crime scene indicate that, despite gaping bloody wounds, no eggs had been laid on the body. In late 2009, the case was brought to the attention of a forensic entomologist, who examined the photographs and other evidence.

The only explanation for the lack of eggs is that the victim must have died in the evening when blow flies are not active. On the night of the murder, sunset occurred at 8:01 p.m., with civil twilight occurring at 8:31 p.m., and nautical twilight occurring at 9:08 p.m. Therefore, entomological evidence indicated that, to a reasonable scientific certainty, the victim must have died after sunset and probably after nautical twilight. The body could not have been at the crime scene during the day without acquiring insect eggs. The expertise of a forensic pathologist also corroborated this time frame.

A *habeas corpus* petition in 2010 brought forward twenty-one grounds of new evidence, with the forensic entomology evidence as ground one. This was denied in 2011. As of fall 2014, Ms. Lobato's appeal is submitted for decision after oral argument in the Nevada Supreme Court.

Ms. Lobato remains in prison.

E. CONCLUSION

Forensic entomology is an underused forensic science. A better understanding of its principles and potential by law enforcement and the criminal justice system should increase its use in death investigations. All forensic entomologists in Canada and a majority worldwide are employed as professors at universities who take forensic entomology cases on contract. Consequently, they do not work for police agencies and can be unbiased in their work. Their interest is in explaining the details of insect colonization and how this can be used to infer minimum elapsed time since death to the trier of fact. As impartial witnesses, forensic entomologists are usually willing to speak to both counsels before trial to make the evidence as clear as possible.

F. LEGAL CONTEXT

> The premise of this area of expertise, in a nutshell, is that if one knows the life cycle of particular insects that tend to colonize dead bodies, as well as the other variables that can affect their life cycle, then an examination of the age and remnants of insect body life on or near a dead body can provide the minimum time that it has been dead.[25]

The first Canadian forensic entomology study occurred in 1897 in Quebec, but it was not until the 1970s that growing police interest in the field prompted its increased use in casework. Today, forensic entomology is typically applied to death investigations to assist in estimating the minimum length of time a person has been dead, assisting in the development of a timeline that may focus police efforts and either strengthen or weaken a suspect's alibi. The reliability of time of death estimates depends on a number of factors, including: local temperature and weather conditions, whether the body is in a terrestrial or aquatic environment, whether the body is shaded or covered in a terrestrial environment, whether the body is floating or touching sediment

---

25 *R. v. Hosack*, 2013 BCSC 2504 at para. 74 [*Hosack*]. See paras. 74–80 for a review of relevant forensic entomology principles.

in an aquatic environment, and whether the body is naked or clothed.[26] The discipline can also be used to discern information about a body after death, including whether a body has been moved, disturbed, or wounded.[27]

Forensic entomology has been applied to cold cases, as well as more current cases involving serial murder, dismemberment, and identification of the remains of previously missing persons. In the infamous case of serial murderer Robert Pickton, for example, forensic entomology was used to provide: (1) an estimate of the amount of time between death and the freezing of the remains of two victims, and (2) an opinion on the time of year when the women died.[28] Forensic entomology was also used to establish a time of death in the case of one of Canada's youngest serial killers, Cody Legebokoff, who was convicted of four counts of first-degree murder in September 2014.[29]

Forensic entomology is, in the words of Schultes J. in *R. v. Hosack*, "useful evidence in the right circumstances."[30] The *Hosack* case was complex, involving the dismemberment and hiding of various body parts, with the earliest discovery of some parts being approximately one month after death. Dr. Gail Anderson, a forensic entomologist, explained in cross-examination that the linear relationship between temperature and insect development breaks down at higher temperatures, limiting her ability to calculate the effect of higher temperatures on the time of death estimate.[31] As a result of the complications in the case, the court did not rely on the forensic entomology evidence:

> Dr. Anderson is clearly an eminent authority in her field, and the dating of time of death based on insect colonization could be useful evidence

---

26 G.S. Anderson, "Forensic Entomology in British Columbia: A Brief History" (2001) 98 *Journal of the Entomological Society of British Columbia* 127 at 130–33.

27 *Ibid.* at 127–29. The first Canadian research project in the twentieth century began in 1992 in British Columbia, led by Dr. Gail Anderson.

28 *R. v. Pickton*, 2007 BCSC 102 at para. 10. The CBC reported that the Pickton case was "the largest serial killer investigation in Canadian history." Pickton was convicted in December 2007 of murdering six women. See "Pickton Trial Timeline" *CBC News* (30 July 2010), online: www.cbc.ca/1.927418.

29 "Cody Legebokoff Sentenced to Life on 4 Counts of 1st-Degree Murder" *CBC News* (16 September 2014), online: www.cbc.ca/1.2768118. Mark Nielsen, "Officer Details Discovery of Woman's Body" *The Prince George Citizen* (17 June 2014), online www.princegeorgecitizen.com/news/legebokoff-trial/officer-details-discovery-of-woman-s-body-1.1132687. See also *R. v. Legebokoff*, 2014 BCSC 1636 at para. 18.

30 *Hosack*, above note 25 at para. 129.

31 *Ibid.* at paras. 83–85.

> in the right circumstances. In this case, though, I find that the temperatures, the species involved, and the complications introduced by the hiding of the body render her opinion too imprecise and too prone to influence by factors that I cannot measure for me to rely on it. In particular, the fact that one of the species involved would have had a start date at a time when Mr. Falardeau was still alive speaks to the unpredictable influence of the higher temperatures that must have been present in the suite, and the unsuitability of the airport temperature to this particular analysis. I accept that higher temperatures speed up the process and that bags or other impediments to the flies' access to the body can slow it, but the non-linear nature of those relationships, particularly the one based on increasing temperature, remains too significant a wild card.[32]

The limits of forensic entomology must be understood by the courts. The courts, in turn, must be ready to set entomological evidence aside where the estimate is likely to be imprecise due to the effect of any number of variables.

Perhaps the most famous use of forensic entomology in Canadian history was in the quashing of the 1959 wrongful murder conviction of Steven Truscott as a miscarriage of justice. In 2007, forensic entomology evidence pertaining to time of death was admitted as fresh evidence in the interests of justice and under section 683(1) of the *Criminal Code*.[33] This fresh evidence supported new forensic pathology and gastroenterology evidence that led the court to conclude that the forensic pathology evidence originally presented at trial was "scientifically untenable."[34] The forensic entomology method used to establish time of death was not commonly used in 1959 and involved two families of flies: Sarcophagidae (flesh flies, which deposit larvae after death) and Calliphoridae (blow flies, which deposit eggs after death).[35]

Truscott was seen giving his classmate, Lynne Harper, a ride on his bicycle between 7 p.m. and 7:30 p.m. on 9 June 1959. She was found sexually assaulted and strangled on 11 June 1959 in a wooded area known by locals

---

32 *Ibid* at para. 129.

33 *Criminal Code*, R.S.C. 1985, c. C-46.

34 *Truscott*, above note 22 at paras. 3, 8, 307, and 777–78. Archival documents were also relied upon by the appellant to raise concerns about the credibility and reliability of the time of death estimate provided at trial by the attending pathologist, Dr. Penistan. For further information about the new forensic pathology and gastroenterology evidence in the Truscott case, refer to Chapter 18 in this book.

35 *Ibid.* at paras. 307 and 322.

as Lawson's Bush, close to the route she and Truscott travelled on County Road.[36] Truscott became the prime suspect early in the investigation and was arrested the next day, on 12 June.[37]

At trial, the Crown relied upon the evidence of attending pathologist Dr. Penistan that Harper died between 7 p.m. and 7:45 p.m. on 9 June 1959, based on his observations of her stomach contents, *rigor mortis*, and body decomposition.[38] The crucial importance of the time of death evidence was that, if the jury accepted Dr. Penistan's evidence, then they could conclude that Harper died before 8 p.m. and that Truscott had exclusive opportunity to kill her.[39]

In its 2007 decision, the Ontario Court of Appeal concluded that Truscott's acquittal would be the likely result if a hypothetical new trial proceeded on the basis of the entirety of the fresh evidence.[40] Of five entomologists called at this reference—two for the Crown and three for the defence—four agreed that the time of death window was much wider than what was proposed at trial, and included the entire next day, 10 June. Dr. Anderson, one of the four entomology experts who agreed that the time of death window was wider than that proposed at trial, had been called by the Crown. Her analysis did not support the position of the prosecution.[41]

In contrast, Dr. Neal Haskell, the other entomology expert called by the Crown, concluded that the original timeline was sound and that Harper died before 8 p.m. on 9 June. In discussing the credibility of these experts, the court concluded that Dr. Haskell was dogmatic and adversarial in his approach to casework—in short, his conclusions were based on bias, rather than empirical science. In finding that Dr. Haskell's opinion could potentially be excluded by the trial judge of a hypothetical new trial, the court highlighted the importance of experts providing nonbiased, objective testimony based on a foundation of replicable and relevant factual data:

> Dr. Sherah VanLaerhoven and Dr. Richard Merritt, who testified for the appellant, gave evidence in a careful and measured way. Their evidence

---

36 *Ibid.* at paras. 4–5. Lawson's Bush is near Clinton, Ontario.

37 *Ibid.* at n 25.

38 *Ibid.* at para. 29. At para. 304, the judgment outlines the four key factual pillars relied upon by the Crown: (1) the time of death, (2) "the County Road evidence," (3) Truscott's post-offence conduct, and (4) evidence relating to lesions on Truscott's penis.

39 *Ibid.* at para. 306.

40 *Ibid.* at para. 3.

41 Dr. Anderson was not called to testify as it was a reference, not a trial. Only those who were to be cross-examined were called to testify.

> was indicative of an objective consideration of the relevant factual data. The same cannot be said for Dr. Haskell. Despite what would appear to be impressive credentials, Dr. Haskell tended to overstate the effect of his opinion. He was dogmatic and reluctant to admit obvious errors. He assumed an adversarial position as revealed in correspondence with the Crown that Crown counsel disclosed to the appellant's counsel. Several critical elements of his opinion were based on nothing more than his purported experience, which could not be verified and was not supported by any empirical work. He was unable to demonstrate that his experience had been replicated by other scientists.
>
> At a hypothetical new trial, the absence of evidentiary support for the factual assumptions on which Dr. Haskell's opinion are based could potentially lead to the exclusion of his opinion by the trial judge. Even if the trial judge were to find that his opinion cleared the admissibility hurdle, we think it is unlikely that a reasonable jury would place any reliance on his opinion.[42]

The court then considered the forensic entomology evidence itself, providing a summation of the methods used to estimate time of death and detailing that the identification of the insect type and development stage is crucial to determining the "post-mortem interval" (PMI), which was defined by the court as "the interval between the time of death and the collection of insect specimens from the body."[43] The PMI is estimated to a range of time when insects likely deposited eggs or larvae.[44] None of the experts claimed to be able to pinpoint the PMI.[45] The court explained that the most accurate PMI estimates are based on identifying the oldest larvae since they have been on the body for the longest period of time, but cautioned that the oldest larvae are not necessarily the largest.[46] The experts calculated PMI based on both blow fly and flesh fly larvae.

The size of the blow fly maggots in the nose and mouth areas was probably the most important factual assumption made by the appellant's

42 *Truscott*, above note 22 at paras. 313–14.

43 *Ibid.* at para. 315.

44 *Ibid.* at paras. 315–80. At para. 321, it is noted that: "[e]ntomologists cannot pinpoint with absolute precision the PMI. Rather, they provide a range of time during which the insects likely deposited their eggs or larvae."

45 *Ibid.* at para. 361.

46 *Ibid.* at paras. 316 and 358. Since flesh flies deposit larvae, they may be larger than the larvae that hatch from blow fly eggs, even though the flesh fly larvae may have colonized the body at the same time or later than blow flies.

experts. Dr. VanLaerhoven testified that the blow flies collected from the face and abdomen were deposited during daylight, sometime after 11 a.m. on 10 June. Although she could not exclude the possibility that eggs were deposited before sunset on 9 June, she testified that the possibility was unlikely because the maggots would have been larger than 2 mm if given the opportunity to feed overnight.[47] Dr. Merritt's opinion was that the blow fly eggs were likely deposited after 2 a.m. on 10 June. Since blow flies are active only during the day, this meant sometime after sunrise.[48] The opinion was based on Kamal data; the accuracy of this method was criticized by Dr. Anderson, but the court stated that the criticism was compensated for by error terms Dr. Merritt provided for his calculations. Overall, Dr. Anderson agreed with the opinions provided by Dr. VanLaerhoven and Dr. Merritt.[49]

The court noted two concerns with the appellant's expert opinions: (1) if the maggots had "a slight increase in size, of about a millimeter,"[50] this would change the classification of the development stage, increasing the likelihood of egg deposition prior to the sunset on 9 June, if using Kamal's developmental data;[51] and (2) if the appellant's experts' assumptions with respect to the species of blue bottle fly were incorrect, then the resulting PMI could be wrong.[52] The court found that a reasonable jury would find the opinions offered by Dr. VanLaerhoven and Dr. Merritt to be reliable and was satisfied that sufficient evidence existed for these opinions that the jury could be tasked with determining the weight of the evidence.[53]

Dr. Haskell opined that the blow flies colonized the body before sunset on 9 June based on his finding that the larvae found in the vaginal area were blow flies, and therefore were the oldest larvae. Dr. Haskell's theory that trauma in the vaginal area caused blow flies to be preferentially attracted to that area over the mucous membranes in the face was without scientific basis. To account for the difference in maggot size between the vaginal and facial areas, the blow flies would have needed to colonize the vaginal area first, then delay colonization of the facial area for one day. Dr. Merritt's testimony that he could not provide any reason for the order of coloniza-

47 *Ibid.* at para. 363–64. The maggots were 2 mm at the time of autopsy.

48 *Ibid.* at paras. 320 and 366.

49 *Ibid.* at paras. 366–67.

50 *Ibid.* at para. 368.

51 The time of death estimate is dependent on the reliability of the larval length recorded decades earlier.

52 *Truscott*, above note 22 at paras. 368–69. The court was satisfied that the appellant's experts' species assumptions "do not undermine the value of their opinion."

53 *Ibid.* at paras. 362–66 and 379.

tion proposed by Dr. Haskell would be preferred by a reasonable jury. The court concluded that a reasonable jury would likely reject Dr. Haskell's opinion that the maggots in the vaginal area were blow flies and that it was instead reasonable to assume these maggots were flesh flies, as was the opinion of the appellant's experts.[54] The flesh fly identification agreed with the findings made by Mr. Elgin Brown on 7 July 1959. Mr. Brown worked at the laboratory of the Attorney General and had been trained in entomology at the Ontario Agricultural College in Guelph.[55]

With respect to the flesh fly PMI, Dr. Haskell theorized that flesh flies will wait a minimum of twelve to twenty-four hours after death to deposit larvae once arriving on a body. Based on this theory, Dr. Haskell calculated that death occurred at least twelve to twenty-four hours before the mid-afternoon of 10 June, when he believed flesh flies deposited larvae on the body. The court concluded that this "fly-by" theory would likely be given no weight by a reasonable jury, noting that the scientific literature offered little support, the appellant's experts contradicted the theory, and Dr. Haskell himself provided the opposite opinion in a 1992 Ontario first-degree murder case. If Dr. Haskell's opinion were admitted, the court concluded that a reasonable jury could find that his flesh fly PMI supports the time of death proposed by the appellant's experts: the morning of 10 June. The experts, however, seemed to agree that flesh flies might colonize a body later than blow flies. Because of this uncertainty in the timing of initial colonization, the court concluded a reasonable jury would most likely find that flesh flies offer a less compelling basis for time of death estimations compared to blow flies.[56]

With respect to the forensic entomology evidence, the court ultimately concluded that:

> The entomology evidence that could well be received at a new trial further undermines the Crown's claim that Lynne Harper died before 8 p.m. [on 9 June]. While the evidence is subject to certain frailties, if it were admitted and if it were accepted by a jury, it could go so far as to exclude the appellant as the killer and would, at a minimum, cast further doubt on the Crown's claim that Lynne died before 8 p.m.[57]

---

54 *Ibid.* at paras. 347–57. The appellant's experts did have slightly different opinions on the development stage of the flesh flies found in the vaginal area.

55 *Ibid.* at paras. 337–39. As discussed earlier in this chapter, this entomological evidence was collected, correctly reared, and identified, but was, unfortunately, never used in the original court proceedings.

56 *Ibid.* at paras. 371–77.

57 *Ibid.* at para. 778.

CHAPTER 16

Forensic Nursing

Sheila Early

LEGAL CONTEXT: CAITLIN PAKOSH

A. OVERVIEW OF THE DISCIPLINE: FORENSIC NURSING

Forensic nursing is one of the more recent nursing specialties in North America, having emerged as a formal entity in the early 1990s. Many definitions have been set forth over the last two decades, but each has evolved from the original definition as described by Virginia Lynch in 1986. Lynch has since further refined her definition of forensic nursing as:

> The application of the forensic aspects of healthcare that are combined with the bio/psycho/social/spiritual education of the registered nurse in the scientific investigation and the treatment of trauma, and/or death of victims and perpetrators of violence, criminal activity and traumatic accidents. The forensic nurse provides direct services to individual clients, consultation services to nursing, medical and law-related agencies, as well as providing expert court testimony in areas dealing with questioned death investigation processes, adequacy of services, delivery and specialized diagnosis of specific conditions as related to nursing.[1]

The most current—and considerably less detailed—definition is from the International Association of Forensic Nurses (IAFN): "Forensic nursing is defined as the global practice of nursing that results when healthcare

1 Virginia A. Lynch, *Forensic Nursing* (St. Louis, MO: Elsevier Mosby, 2006) at 3.

and legal systems intersect."[2] Prior to the formalization of the discipline, registered nurses (RNs), rather than Forensic Nurses (FNs), testified in criminal cases, often as medical fact witnesses who could not provide opinion evidence.

Gradually, as nurse examiners testified more frequently, the role became recognized for its expertise and nurse examiners were qualified as experts in both provincial and Supreme courts. Today, the nurse examiner in sexual assault cases is routinely deemed an expert by the courts. A key area of testimony for nurse examiners involves their expertise in documenting the physical findings at the time of examination of a patient. The systematic, organized, and objective examination of the patient (with the patient's consent) can provide physical findings that may corroborate or refute the patient's version of events.[3]

Forensic nursing in Canada has its roots in Calgary, Alberta. In 1975, Dr. John Butt, the Interim Chief Medical Examiner for the City of Calgary at the time, hired RNs to become the medical examiners' investigators in his department.[4] Dr. Butt conducted a five-year study into the practice, concluding, "that it was the registered nurse who provided the qualities and professionalism essential to a scientific, social and cultural investigation of death."[5]

Since 1975, forensic nursing science has been a slowly evolving entity in Canada. This slow evolution can be attributed to a number of factors, including:

- lack of awareness of the emerging specialty of forensic nursing by the healthcare system;
- lack of educational opportunities for specialized forensic nursing education and advanced practice;
- lack of recognition by mainstream nursing for the contributions made by FNs in providing healthcare to victims of violence, trauma, and crime;
- lack of funding for forensic nursing positions within acute healthcare; and
- the variety of roles that fit the definition of forensic nursing, each expanding and developing mostly in isolation to each other.

---

2 International Association of Forensic Nurses, "What is Forensic Nursing?" online: www.forensicnurses.org/?page=whatisfn.

3 For example, see *R. v. Ruddick*, [1998] O.J. No. 6208 at paras. 25–26 (Ct. J.) [*Ruddick*].

4 Lynch, above note 1 at 371.

5 *Ibid.*

Further, since forensic nursing has only been recognized as a subspecialty in nursing by the Canadian Nurses' Association since 2007, mainstream nursing has not embraced forensic nursing as a whole. As a result, funding for the education of FNs is not part of the general healthcare funding for other specialties, such as emergency nursing, critical care nursing, or pediatric nursing. The International Association of Forensic Nurses, however, provides Canadian forensic educators in forensic nursing education with documents that are global in nature and require very little adaptation for Canadian purposes.[6]

The FN of today has developed the specialized body of knowledge and skills that differentiates forensic nursing from other specialities and subspecialties of nursing. A forensic nursing curriculum includes: "nursing science, forensic science, law, healthcare and associated legal issues regarding patient care."[7] Unlike most nursing specialties, forensic nursing is made up of different subspecialties of nursing practice often identified by the populations served, including:

- clinical forensic nursing, focusing on victims of interpersonal violence;
- forensic correctional nurses, focusing on offenders in federal or provincial institutions or those in secure environments, such as pre-trial detention centres;
- forensic nurse examiners and, specifically, sexual assault nurse examiners, focusing on child, adolescent, and adult post-sexual-violence incidents;
- forensic nurse death investigators, focusing on decedents; and
- forensic geriatric or pediatric nurses, focusing on geriatric or pediatric victims of abuse and neglect.[8]

6 See, generally, International Association of Forensic Nurses, "Sexual Assault Nurse Examiner Education Guidelines, Adult and Pediatric" (2015), online: iafn.site-ym.com/?2015EdGuidelines; International Association of Forensic Nurses, "Forensic Nurse Death Investigator Education Guidelines" (2013), online: c.ymcdn.com/sites/iafn.site-ym.com/resource/resmgr/Education/Nurse_Death_Investigator_Edu.pdf; International Association of Forensic Nurses, "Intimate Partner Violence Nurse Examiner Education Guidelines" (2013), online: c.ymcdn.com/sites/iafn.site-ym.com/resource/resmgr/Education/Nurse_Death_Investigator_Edu.pdf; International Association of Forensic Nurses, "Core Competencies for Advanced Practice Forensic Nursing" (2004), online: c.ymcdn.com/sites/iafn.site-ym.com/resource/resmgr/Education/APN_Core_Curriculum_Document.pdf.

7 Donna Garbacz Bader & Sue Gabriel, *Forensic Nursing: A Concise Manual* (Boca Raton, FL: CRC Press, 2010) at 18.

8 Virginia A. Lynch & Janet Barber Duval, *Forensic Nursing Science*, 2d ed. (St. Louis, MO: Elsevier Mosby, 2011) at 20.

There is always the question of how to balance the competing interests of advocacy and objectivity when moving between the roles of registered nurse (RN) and FN. The RN is a patient advocate for the health and medical care of the individual patient, maintaining objectivity within the bounds of a nurse-patient relationship. In contrast, an FN must examine the patient and report results in an objective fashion; as an expert, the FN must be careful not to advocate for the patient, as doing so will introduce bias that may result in the expression of inaccuracies and negatively impact criminal proceedings. Further, before the nurse examiner even enters the courtroom, he or she must maintain objectivity when conducting an exam to ensure all evidence relevant to the case has been explored, providing informed consent is obtained to collect such evidence. For example, a nurse examiner should not deliberately choose to not collect toxicology screening samples because the results might be harmful to the patient's stated history of the presenting event.

Overall, this chapter will provide an overview of forensic nursing in Canada, mainly focusing on the clearly defined roles of the forensic nurse examiner, sexual assault/abuse nurse examiner, nurse coroner/death investigator, and legal nurse consultant. Basic principles of forensic nursing will be discussed and guidelines will be provided for lawyer-expert relationships in regards to testimony. Future trends for forensic nursing will be explored, with the hope that the legal community will increasingly rely upon the expertise of FNs, particularly in cases of sexual assault.

B. THE SCIENCE OF FORENSIC NURSING

1) Basic Principles of Forensic Nursing

The FN must be prepared to handle a variety of situations and patients, as the expertise of the FN may be helpful in the investigation of a range of offences, including sexual abuse, intimate partner violence, and human trafficking. In order to be an asset to the criminal justice system, the FN must perform examinations using a few key basic principles, discussed below.

Like many other forensic sciences, Locard's Exchange Principle is key to forensic nursing science and sets out that "whenever two objects come in contact with one another, a transfer of material will occur. The transfer may be tenuous but will certainly occur."[9] Forensic nursing science

9 Stuart H. James & Jon J. Nordby, eds., *Forensic Science: An Introduction to Scientific and Investigative Techniques* (Boca Raton, FL: CRC Press, 2003) at 172.

is more specifically based on evidence-based practice, which is described as a "problem-solving approach to clinical decision making within the health-care organization that integrates the best available scientific evidence with the best available experiential (patient and practitioner) evidence."[10] Thus, as forensic science changes, so does the evidence-based practice of FNs.

Historically, in medical healthcare, providers rely on the ability of a patient to provide informed consent for whatever intervention or treatments is to be provided. This is based on the principle that competent, informed adults[11] must provide consent for care in order to legally protect the care provider. If the patient does not have the capability to provide informed consent, then an alternate individual can be named as the decision maker for healthcare decisions. Consent is not needed in life-threatening, emergency situations when any delay will result in loss of life or limb. Informed consent "compromises four parts. First, the risks of the procedure or treatment must be explained. Second, the patient should be told about the benefits; third, the patient should be informed of any alternatives to the recommended treatment. Finally, the patient needs to be told the consequences if the treatment or procedure is not performed."[12]

In medical forensic care, patient consent is often a challenge because the individual may not be capable of providing informed consent, may not be of the age of consent, or simply may decline to allow evidence collection. The situation affecting the patient is often emotionally charged and the patient may feel that an examination is a further invasion of her body. When an FN is caring for a patient in a forensic context, the need for informed consent is paramount. The FN may be asking the patient for permission to identify, collect, and preserve forensic evidence that is on or inside the patient's body. Unconscious or unresponsive patients pose a significant challenge to consent issues. Some forensic nursing services and sexual assault nurse examiner (SANE) programs have partially addressed this matter by developing protocols that allow forensic evidence samples to be collected and held in storage until such a time that the patient is

---

10 K. Eldredge, E. Huggins, & L.C. Pugh, "Alternate Light Source in Sexual Assault Examinations: An Evidence-based Practice Project" (2012) 8 *Journal of Forensic Nursing* 39.

11 The age of who qualifies as an adult varies between provinces and territories.

12 Lynch & Barber Duval, above note 8 at 541.

either able to provide consent (or not) for the collection or a warrant is obtained for the evidence in criminal investigations.[13]

When informed consent for care is obtained, the FN may proceed with an examination of the patient. Throughout an examination, an FN must practise patient-centred care by "providing care that is respectful and responsive to the individual patient's preferences, needs and values and ensures that patient values guide all clinical decisions."[14] The key difference between an FN and other healthcare providers is that the FN is responsible for maintaining the chain of custody (also known as the continuity of evidence). The chain of custody is defined as "involving a witnessed, written record of all the individuals who maintained uninterrupted control over items of evidence."[15] The FN is specially educated in the process of collecting, preserving, and documenting forensic evidence from the time it is identified until it is provided to law enforcement or the judicial system. An unbroken chain of custody is essential to the determination of the validity of the evidence and what forensic science is able to determine from the evidence.

From the beginning of the FN's interaction with the patient to their final role in testifying at a criminal trial, it is important that the FN is objective and focused on the truth, as supported by evidence found upon examination. A forensic nurse must be "unbiased and value neutral in all matters" when caring for the forensic patient population in any setting.[16] Objectivity and neutrality are essential values of the FN.[17] That being said, however, the FN must provide the patient with trauma-informed care, which refers to:

> trauma-informed systems and organizations [that] provide for everyone within that system or organization by having a basic understanding of the psychological, neurological, biological, social and spiritual impact that trauma and violence can have on individuals seeking support.

---

13 See, for example, Ontario Network of Sexual Assault/Domestic Violence Treatment Centres, "Guidelines for the Collection of Forensic Evidence from the Person who is Unable to Provide Consent" (June 2010), online: www.satcontario.com/files/Guidelines_for_Collection___unable_to_consent.pdf ["Guidelines re Person Unable to Provide Consent"].

14 Committee on Quality Healthcare in America, Institute of Medicine, *Crossing the Quality Chasm: A New Health System for the 21st Century* (Washington, DC: National Academy Press, 2001).

15 Bader & Gabriel, above note 7 at 95.

16 Lynch & Barber Duval, above note 8 at 11.

17 *Ibid.*

> Trauma-informed services recognize that the core of any service is genuine, authentic and compassionate relationships.[18]

Although the FN is expected to provide compassionate care to the patient, the role of the FN as an expert witness is to assist the court, not to be an advocate for the patient. In this manner, the FN must respect the scope of her role in the criminal justice system.

It is important for the FN to operate using a perspective based in gender neutrality, which avoids discrimination based on a person's sex or gender. Sexual violence can affect males, females, and transgendered persons, regardless of sexual orientation. A male person seeking an FN examination should not be turned away on the basis of outdated and incorrect ideas that sexual assaults only affect women, although there are a number of centres that only provide services to female patients. That being said, however, a woman-centred approach to health has furthered the understanding of health boards that "women and men are affected differently by health policies and programs."[19]

The FN assimilates all the described concepts and puts them into practice during the clinical assessment, intervention, and evaluation of the patient who has undergone violence or trauma. Thus, the FN must be non-judgmental, treat all patients with dignity and respect, adhere to ethical standards, and provide options for care to include the patient in the decision-making process. Since sexual violence affects all genders, objectivity and a non-judgmental attitude must be part of the FN's makeup. Even the use of terminology comes into play here in that the term "alleged," for example, has a negative connotation that implies the patient may not be telling the truth. This term is never used to describe someone presenting with chest pain or abdominal pain, yet it is often applied to those presenting for care post sexual violence. The term "refused" also has a negative connotation of not wanting to co-operate. When options for care are provided, the individual can then make a choice; declining one course of treatment and choosing another does not amount to a refusal or a failure to co-operate—the patient is simply exercising choices as part of their care.

---

18 Klinic Community Health Centre, *Trauma-Informed: The Trauma Toolkit*, 2d ed. (2013), online: trauma-informed.ca/wp-content/uploads/2013/10/Trauma-informed_Toolkit.pdf at 16.

19 Vancouver/Richmond Health Board, "A Framework for Women-Centred Health" (June 2001), online: www.atira.bc.ca/AdvancingHealthCareWorkshop/womenframework.pdf at 8.

2) Subspecialties of Forensic Nursing

a) Clinical Forensic Nursing[20]

The clinical FN "provides care for the survivors of crime and liability related injury and death."[21] This nurse needs to ensure that a patient's legal rights are met by collecting forensic evidence correctly as well as documenting it appropriately. This role is not clearly defined in Canada and often overlaps with the other roles listed below. The clinical FN's area of practice is likely the emergency departments of acute care hospitals in major city centres.

Canada has yet to establish the position of clinical FN as a specific role. Sexual assault nurse examiners have been gradually expanding their scope of practice beyond sexual assault, whether in the emergency department or other designated facilities. However, the clinical FN is often limited by the mandate of that particular program and may not, for example, address potential forensic patient populations from vehicular incidents, interpersonal violence, workplace injury incidents, post-intimate partner violence, or domestic violence.

This role has the potential to be of considerable value as facilities move to recognize the expertise of an FN to identify gunshot wounds, stab wounds, blunt force trauma, and other injuries, and collect and preserve forensic evidence related to these injuries. Their documentation skills alone may be crucial to the forensic and legal needs of the patient population.

b) Forensic Correctional, Institutional, or Custodial Nurse

This nurse specializes in "the care, treatment and rehabilitation of persons who have been sentenced to prisons or jails for violation of criminal statutes and require medical assessment and intervention,"[22] and to that, Lynch and Barber Duval add, "detainees held in specific circumstances."[23] "Specific circumstances" may include individuals detained as refugees or terrorism suspects.

Forensic correctional nurses may not identify themselves specifically as FNs in Canada. The Correctional Service of Canada health services oper-

---

20 Rita M. Hammer, Barbara Moynihan, & Elaine M. Pagliaro, eds., *Forensic Nursing: A Handbook for Practice* (Sudbury, MA: Jones and Bartlett, 2006) at 12–13; Lynch, above note 1 at 25–26.

21 Lynch, *ibid.* at 25.

22 Hammer, Moynihan, & Pagliaro, above note 20 at 13.

23 Lynch & Barber Duval, above note 8 at 16.

ations provide primary healthcare for federal offenders, employing 700 nurses.[24] Each province and territory also provides similar health services in correctional facilities, with nurses being the largest component of healthcare professionals.

c) Forensic Nurse Examiners and Sexual Assault Nurse Examiners

The forensic nurse examiner provides "an incisive analysis of physical and psychological trauma, questioned deaths, or psychopathological evaluations related to forensic cases that involved interpersonal violence (child abuse, domestic violence, elder abuse, sexual assault, or injury resulting from lethal weapons, torture, police brutality, etc.)."[25] The patient may be living or dead.[26] Thus, it is entirely possible for a forensic nurse examiner to also be a forensic nurse investigator.

Forensic nurse examiners working in situations involving patients who suffered sexual violence first became known as sexual assault nurse examiners some time in late 1992 or early 1993 in Winnipeg, Manitoba, and Surrey, British Columbia. The sexual assault nurse examiner is "a registered nurse specially trained to provide forensic/medical examination and evaluation of sexual trauma while maximizing the collection of biological, trace, and physical evidence and minimizing the patient's emotional trauma."[27] In Canada, the first documented sexual assault nurse examiner testimony in a *Criminal Code* case was in 23 August 1994 in British Columbia.[28]

Until 1995, the Winnipeg and Surrey programs remained the only nurse-based services for sexually assaulted adolescents and adults in Canada. Large urban centres, such as Vancouver and Toronto, had physician-based programs. In other areas, care was dependent on the physician-based care found in emergency departments, health facilities, or clinics. Over time, physician-based programs added nurse examiners to their services, combining the use of physicians and specially trained nurse examiners.

Currently, all provinces except Quebec and Prince Edward Island have at least one forensic nurse examiner or SANE program. Yukon Territory also has RNs trained as sexual assault nurse examiners. The Ontario Network of Sexual Assault/Domestic Violence Treatment Centres has since

---

24 Correctional Service Canada, "Nurse," online: www.csc-scc.gc.ca/careers/003001-1301-eng.shtml.

25 Lynch & Barber Duval, above note 8 at 16.

26 *Ibid.*

27 *Ibid.*

28 Personal knowledge of Sheila Early, the author of this chapter.

expanded to thirty-five centres throughout Ontario and now includes interdisciplinary, skilled care for women, men, and children for sexual assault/abuse, domestic violence/intimate partner violence, and interpersonal violence. New Brunswick has a provincial network of three nurse examiner programs based in the three urban centres. The rest of the provinces and territories do not have a provincial network at this time.

d) Forensic Nurse Investigator

The forensic nurse investigator is "employed by a medical examiner/coroner jurisdiction and represents the decedent's right to social justice through scientific investigation of the scene and circumstances of death."[29] The first Canadian nurse death investigator role was created in 1975, within the medical examiner's office in Calgary, Alberta.[30] Other provinces with a medical examiner's service include Manitoba, Nova Scotia, and Newfoundland and Labrador.

Provinces which have a coroner's system of death investigation (British Columbia, Saskatchewan, Quebec, New Brunswick) and the territories (Yukon, North West Territories, and Nunavut) frequently have RNs on staff either as coroners or death investigators.[31] The chief coroner of Saskatchewan, for example, is R. Kent Stewart, a Diploma nurse, appointed to this position in 2004.[32] The provinces of Ontario and Prince Edward Island have coroner's systems for the investigation of deaths but, to date, they have not hired RNs into the role and instead fill the coroner positions with medical physicians.

e) Forensic Psychiatric Nurse

The forensic psychiatric nurse specializes in "the assessment and intervention of criminal defendants and patients in legal custody who have been accused of a crime or have been court mandated for psychiatric evaluation."[33] Forensic psychiatric nurses do not necessarily identify themselves as part of the forensic nursing subspecialty in Canada. Their roles in forensic

---

29 Hammer, Moynihan, & Pagliaro, above note 20.

30 Personal correspondence, 22 June 2015.

31 Colin Harris, *Introduction to Forensic Health Sciences* (Paper presented at British Columbia Institute of Technology, Burnaby, B.C., 2012).

32 Government of Saskatchewan, News Release, "New Chief Coroner Appointed" (18 June 2004), online: www.saskatchewan.ca/government/news-and-media/2004/june/18/new-chief-coroner-appointed.

33 Hammer, Moynihan, & Pagliaro, above note 20 at 12.

mental health and forensic facilities predate many of the current roles and their education may come from educational services within their scope of practice. In Western Canada (British Columbia, Alberta, Saskatchewan, and Manitoba), the education of the registered psychiatric nurse (RPN) is separate from the education of the RN and the forensic layer of education is added onto the RPN's or RN's education when they are employed in a forensic facility or institution. There are approximately 5,600 registered psychiatric nurses in Canada.[34]

f) Legal Nurse Consultant

The legal nurse consultant provides:

> consultation and education to judicial, criminal justice, and healthcare professionals in areas such as personal injury, product liability, and malpractice, among other legal issues related to civil and criminal cases; investigates questioned documents such as medical records, health histories, or medical instructions pertaining to abuse, neglect, maltreatment, or death; recovers evidence from the context of such documents rather than from the scene of the crime or the body.[35]

Legal nurse consultants in Canada are recognized as a professional specialty by the Canadian Nurses Association. There are approximately eighty current members in the Legal Nurse Consultant Association of Canada (LNCAC) at this time and there are additional legal nurse consultants in Canada who are not members of LNCAC.[36]

Legal nurse consultants may not identify as FNs, and vice versa. Often, the legal nurse consultant is most likely engaged in civil matters, whereas FNs are most likely to be engaged in criminal matters. The similarities are that both interact with Canadian legal systems, both have specialized skills that enable them to provide expert opinion in specific cases, both are skilled professionals with shared nursing standards of practice and ethics, and both are often skilled witnesses. However, the difference is that the FN has a clinical role with a patient as their primary focus and the legal nurse consultant is not in a practising clinical role with the patient at any time.

---

34 Registered Psychiatric Nurse Regulators of Canada, "About Us," online: www.rpnc.ca/about-us.

35 Lynch & Barber Duval, above note 8 at 16.

36 Angela Sibbald, President, Legal Nurse Consultants Association of Canada, personal correspondence, 3 March 2015.

g) Nurse Attorney

A nurse attorney is an RN who also holds a law degree and practises as an attorney-at-law in either civil or criminal cases as a nurse attorney. Often, they work exclusively in health-related cases. The nurse attorney role is very limited in Canada, with very few individuals practising both as an RN and as an attorney. The author found one such individual practising in Calgary, Alberta. In the United States, there is a larger group of nurse attorneys, as evidence of the formation of the American Association of Nurse Attorneys in 1990.

h) Nurse Coroner

A nurse coroner is an RN who is able to officiate a death and can also investigate and certify a questioned death—that is, can determine the cause and manner of death. The nurse coroner is also able to determine the decedent's identity and provide the notification of the next of kin. In Canada, this position is always an employee of a particular coroner's service, whereas in the United States, the position is an elected one depending on jurisdiction.

Nurse coroners have a significant role in death investigations in Canada depending on the province or territory. The following provinces and territories have RN roles as death investigators and/or coroners: British Columbia, Alberta, Saskatchewan, Manitoba, New Brunswick, Nova Scotia, Yukon, North West Territories, and Nunavut. Newfoundland and Labrador, Prince Edward Island, Quebec, and Ontario do not have RNs in the death investigation role. The current chief coroner of Saskatchewan is a former nurse, while Nunavut has a nurse coroner, as does North West Territories.[37]

3) Methods in Forensic Nursing

Forensic nurses employ a concept called the "nursing process" when conducting their work and this process is defined as "a scientific method that nurses use to provide care, beginning with an initial patient assessment and the establishment of a nursing diagnosis. Planning, intervention and

---

37 Michael S. Pollanen et al., eds., "Forensic Science in Canada: A Report of Multidisciplinary Discussion" (4–5 May 2012), online: Centre for Forensic Science & Medicine at the University of Toronto www.forensics.utoronto.ca/Assets/LMPF+Digital+Assets/Forensic+Science+in+Canada.pdf [CFSM, "Multidisciplinary Discussion Report"].

evaluation activities complete the nursing process."[38] When applied to forensic nursing, each of the aspects of the nursing process can be broken down into the following distinct steps: assessment; planning; intervention; evaluation; and documentation (using standardized forms, body maps, forensic photography, and forensic videography).

a) Assessment

Assessment includes both objective physical findings in the form of a head-to-toe examination and subjective information based on the patient's responses to specific history-taking practices. Subjective information collection may be based on specific standardized forms with standardized questions, which are posed to the patient, with their responses being recorded by the FN. The subjective information will include both medical and forensic components and is the beginning basis for the head-to-toe physical examination. The patient's presenting concern is only one factor and it is the role of a skilled FN to "note problems that might otherwise be missed."[39]

Theoretically, the subjective data is collected first unless there is an immediate or urgent medical need that must be addressed to ensure that the patient is not put at further risk. For example, an immediate medical need might be severe vaginal bleeding in a patient presenting for examination post stated sexual assault.

The head-to-toe physical examination is literally an examination of the patient from the top of their head to their toes. Palpation involves the use of the hands to examine the body while looking for injury, illness, or disease. Oftentimes, a patient will not be aware that a particular injury is present until that location is palpated and a response of pain or discomfort is registered by the patient.[40]

Based on the subjective and objective data, the FN formulates a nursing diagnosis upon which to base patient care. The nursing diagnosis is a "clinical judgement about individual, family or community responses to actual or potential health problems/life processes."[41] Nurses make nursing diagnoses based on the human response to a real or potential health problem, the clinical skills of the nurse, and the collected data/patient information. In contrast, physicians make medical diagnoses based on a

---

38 Lynch & Barber Duval, above note 8 at 6.

39 *Ibid.*

40 *Ibid.*

41 *Ibid.* at 7.

disease process or medical condition. Medical diagnoses are listed in the International Classification of Diseases.[42]

b) Planning

The FN must plan for both short- and long-term interventions that will ensure that the short- and long-term goals for patient care are met. For example, a protocol for patient safety when they present for immediate healthcare is a short-term intervention, whereas having a specialized program for the ongoing care of an individual who has been trafficked is a long-term intervention.

c) Intervention

Forensic nurses are often advanced practice nurses and they have formal policies, procedures, and processes to guide their practice. The FN performs interventions, and then assesses their outcome based on patient responses, then modifies, changes, and revises the interventions accordingly. Interventions are actions that a nurse performs based on their assessment and nursing diagnosis. An intervention might be a treatment, a procedure, or simply a communication with a patient that alters the course of their care. These interventions are then evaluated based on patient responses, which may indicate that more interventions should be initiated. The desired outcome is that "the ideal forensic examination is carefully implemented to decrease emotional trauma while increasing optimal forensic evidence recovery."[43]

d) Evaluation

The FN evaluates results of the nurse-patient interactions in order to determine the positive and negative effects of the interventions performed. If an intervention has not produced the desired outcome, the FN must look at different means to address the patient's needs in order to facilitate a different, and more positive, outcome. Formal evaluation methods can be used, as well as similar presentations, which may have similar goals and outcomes.

---

42 World Health Organization, "International Classification of Diseases (ICD)," online: www.who.int/classifications/icd/en/.

43 Lynch & Barber Duval, above note 8 at 6.

e) Documentation

Documentation is the principal tool used by the FN as it is a permanent record of all observations, interactions, and outcomes between the FN and the patient. As Bader states, "Accurate and complete documentation is the legal responsibility of every forensic nurse or nurse."[44] Bader also describes contributing factors such as documenting all care, using quotation marks for patient statements, documenting behaviours, using correct forms, not leaving spaces on the forms, and signing every entry with one's legal name and credentials. Both physical and emotional conditions of the patient are vital and any inaccuracies or omissions in documentation may adversely affect a legal outcome. Documentation may be recorded by way of standardized forms, body maps, forensic photography, and forensic videography. Overall, the FN relies upon this documentation to produce a final, concise, and unbiased medical-legal report (also known as a legal report or a forensic report).

i) Standardized Forms

The use of standardized forms developed for a specific forensic patient population is common practice in many areas, including those involving sexual violence, child abuse, death, forensic psychiatry, and corrections. The forms are based on what is current best practice for any given situation and are reviewed on a regular basis to ensure they meet the most current guidelines for forensic nursing practice. One common form is the sexual assault record, which is used by nurse examiners to document the most important aspects of the medical forensic examination. Another example is a forensic evidence record, used to document the collection and preservation of forensic evidence and the chain of custody associated with the forensic evidence.

Informed consent from the patient is paramount for the FN in sexual violence care and, as a result, it is important to document the patient's informed choice by using consent and release forms. The patient will normally have two options available to them: (1) consent to an examination and report the incident to law enforcement; or (2) consent to an examination, without reporting the incident to law enforcement. If the choice of examination, collection, and storage of forensic samples is available to the patient, this too must be clearly documented. If the incident initially goes unreported but the patient then decides to report the incident, then a new

44 Bader & Gabriel, above note 7 at 133.

release or consent form for transferring forensic samples to law enforcement is needed. Programs vary in the length of time of sample storage for unreported cases, ranging from three months to one year.

ii) Body Maps

Also known as traumagrams, body maps aid the FN in documenting the extent and location of all identified injuries on a patient's body. This is especially important when there are multiple injuries and findings on many parts of the body. For example, the use of a body map, such as the BALDSTEP guide (which is attached at the end of this chapter), aids the FN in decreasing the time required to document all findings. The BALDSTEP mnemonic was developed in 2011 by Catherine Carter Snell, a Canadian FN, to facilitate the documentation of injuries during a head-to-toe assessment.[45] Shorthand references in the BALDSTEP mnemonic are used to indicate the type of injury observed by the FN:

- B: bruise (BR), bleeding (BL), bitemark (BI), burn (BU)
- A: abrasion (AB), avulsion (AV)
- L: laceration (LA)
- D: deformity (acute) (DE)
- S: swelling (SW), stain (ST) (+ FL if fluorescent)
- T: tenderness to palpation (TE), trace evidence (describe) (TR)
- E: erythema (indicate area) (ER)
- P: patterned injury (draw shape) (PA), petechiae (PT), penetrating injury (+ I incised, S stab) (PE), puncture (P), known gunshot (G)

Another example of a body map is a specific chart that enables the documentation of a patient's burns and the calculation of the percentage of the body's surface area that has been burned.

Body maps or traumagrams enable the examiner to pinpoint the location of any findings in an organized and concise manner. They are in addition to photographs and thus can be compared to photographs to provide a second verification of the FN's findings.

iii) Forensic Photography

Photography as a forensic nursing tool is becoming available in specialized nurse examiner programs throughout Canadian urban centres. The thirty-

---

45 Cathy Carter Snell, "Injury Documentation: Using the BALDSTEP Mnemonic and the RCMP Sexual Assault Kit" (2011) 34 *Outlook* 15.

five Sexual Assault/Domestic Violence Treatment Centres in Ontario conduct external and genital photography.[46] Centres vary in their protocols as to what is photographed. For example, pediatric patients may not have genital findings due to the time interval between incident and examination and, therefore, genital photos may not be needed. In adult patients, the physical external findings are often still visible at the time of examination, while genital findings may not be.

Over the last decade, FNs in the subspecialties of forensic nursing, such as sexual violence, child maltreatment, elder maltreatment, and intimate partner violence, have taken forensic photography courses in order to digitally record and document injuries and findings. Some nurse examiner programs have implemented specific policies and procedures, while others are still struggling to include forensic photography in their education. The value of photography lies in its ability to record what injuries are (and are not) present at the time. The photographs can also be used for peer review, as well as for education, with the patient's consent. Informed consent from the patient is needed in order for the FN to photograph such findings. Forensic images can be stored indefinitely, making them available for assessment when needed by the justice system.

iv) Forensic Videography

Currently, the use of forensic videography is limited to video recording forensic medical interviews and examinations in child maltreatment cases when healthcare and FNs are involved in the care of the child. It is not routinely used during adolescent and adult forensic medical interviews and examinations at this time. Other subspecialties, such as forensic psychiatric nursing and forensic correctional nursing, may also utilize videography within a clinical situation. Again, informed consent from a parent or guardian is required when handling pediatric and adolescent cases.

v) Differentiating between the Medical Record and the Forensic Record

Since it is most likely that a patient who self-reports an event of non-consensual intercourse is cared for in a healthcare facility, two types of documentation are generated: the medical record and the forensic record.

---

46 Sheila MacDonald, Provincial Coordinator of the Ontario Network of Sexual Assault/ Domestic Violence Treatment Centres, personal correspondence, 22 February 2015.

The routine records for any patient in a healthcare facility, such as an emergency department, form the medical record and include the:

- emergency record
- nursing history and assessment
- nurse's interdisciplinary notes or progress notes
- physician's orders and progress notes
- results of any tests/procedures performed in the facility, such as laboratory or radiology procedures and operative reports
- discharge instructions/teaching

The medical record is not part of the forensic record and has to be subpoenaed in any legal proceedings. It may take up to thirty days to become available to the party requesting the medical records. The medical records may prove to be helpful in cases where, for example, a medical alcohol and toxicology screening was done but a forensic screen was not done—a patient may not have consented to a forensic screen, but a medical screen does not need patient consent.

f) The Forensic ABCDs of Trauma Care

Unique to Canadian forensic nursing is the mnemonic developed by Linda McCracken, a nurse clinician in the emergency department of Foothills Medical Centre, in Calgary, Alberta. The forensic ABCDs of trauma care refers to the concept that "any patient admitted to the emergency room with potential liability-related injuries, whether victim or victimizer, living or dead, is considered a clinical forensic patient."[47] McCracken developed the mnemonic in the 1990s to represent the additional layer of care a forensic patient needs in the emergency department:

A *Assessment* of/*advocate* for the victim/victimizer
B *Bridge* the gap—liaison with outside agencies (police, medical examiner, etc.)
C *Chain* of custody—know the methods of evidence collection, establish continuity of evidence possession, and disposition of the evidence
D *Documentation* of findings (including diagrams)
E *Evidence*—physical /potential evidence (gross, trace, informational)
F *Families*—remember them, keep them informed

---

47 Virginia A. Lynch, "Clinic Forensic Nursing: A New Perspective in the Management of Crime Victims from Trauma to Trial" (1995) 7 *Critical Care Nursing Clinics of North America* 489 at 490.

G *Go* to court—be prepared for written or verbal testimony
H *Hospital* (other institutional) policies—know them and know where to access their guidelines
I *Index* of suspicion—keep it high, be cognizant of symptoms of abuse (child, elder) and domestic violence[48]

4) Key Concepts Addressed by Forensic Nurse Examiners

a) Consensual Versus Non-consensual Genital Injuries

Nurse examiners document external and internal findings within the genital area of a patient during a forensic medical examination. The resulting question from the legal community is: "Has a sexual assault occurred?" First, it is important to remember that sexual assault is not a medical condition or a diagnosis; it is an offence under the *Criminal Code*.

Second, current research and literature in forensic nursing has documented evidence that differentiation between consensual versus non-consensual sexual activity cannot be determined scientifically. In one study, Crane identified predictors of injury associated with rape (i.e., sexual assault), rather than specific injuries.[49] She measured both victim and forensic characteristics in a sample of 620 females, aged 13 to 87 years old. The majority of subjects were examined by forensically trained care providers within twenty-four hours of the reported incident. Data analysis revealed that 88.7 percent of the sample group had injuries, where 53.9 percent had both body and genital injuries, 20.5 percent had genital injuries only, and 14.4 percent had body injuries only.[50] Further, 11.3 percent had ***no*** injuries at the time of examination. Crane states that "only 15% of women in this study had injury documented when their examination was > [i.e., longer than] 72 hours after the rape."[51]

The *Color Atlas of Sexual Assault* by Girardin, Faugno, Seneski, Slaughter, and Whelan, published in 1997, was the first forensic nursing text to document research by Slaughter and Brown showing that "genital injury may or may not be present in sexually assaulted patients, even when

48 Linda McCracken, "Living Forensics: A Natural Evolution in Emergency Care" (1999) 7 *Accident and Emergency Nursing* 211.
49 Patricia A. Crane, "Predictors of Injury Associated with Rape" (2006) 2 *Journal of Forensic Nursing* 75.
50 *Ibid.* at 79.
51 *Ibid.* at 81.

examined within 48 hours."[52] Slaughter's research identified the "posterior fourchette, labia minora, hymen and fossa navicularis as most common sites of injury in penile vaginal penetration."[53] Jones, Rossman, Hartman, and Alexander's study of 523 adolescents, aged 13 to 17 years old, found that "the localized pattern, severity and extent of injuries in rape victims appear to differ from changes after CSI" (consensual sexual intercourse), with 73 percent of adolescents studied who had consensual intercourse having documented anogenital injuries, compared to 85 percent of victims of sexual assault (i.e., non-consensual sexual intercourse) who had anogenital injuries.[54] They also conclude "anogenital injury is not an inevitable consequence of sexual assault—the lack of genital injury does not imply consent by the victim or lack of penetration by the assailant."[55]

b) Blunt Force Trauma Versus Sharp Force Trauma

Forensic examiners are well versed in the difference between injuries caused by blunt force trauma versus sharp force trauma. Blunt force trauma is defined as an "injury incurred by the crushing impact of, or when a moving body strikes, a blunt object."[56] Examples of blunt force trauma include abrasions, contusions or bruises, lacerations, and fractures. Sharp force trauma comes in many forms, which can be categorized as incised wounds (e.g., cuts and slashes) or puncture wounds (e.g., stab wounds).[57]

Sharp trauma is often mislabelled as blunt trauma when a cut (which is sharp trauma) is documented as a laceration (which is blunt trauma). Lacerations may well be the most incorrectly documented injury recorded by healthcare providers without forensic education. The importance of identifying a laceration as blunt force is most pronounced when the mechanism of injury conflicts with the injury found. For example, a round smooth-surfaced stick will cause a laceration, whereas a sharp piece of glass will cause a cut. If a weapon is used in the commission of a crime, labelling a cut as a laceration may cause confusion in identifying the weapon in question.

---

52 Barbara Girardin et al., *Color Atlas of Sexual Assault* (St. Louis, MO: Mosby, 1997) at 22.

53 *Ibid.* at 23.

54 J.S. Jones et al., "Anogenital Injuries in Adolescents after Consensual Sexual Intercourse" (2003) 10 *Academic Emergency Medicine* 1378 at 1380.

55 *Ibid.*

56 Lynch, above note 1 at 694.

57 *Ibid.* at 343.

c) Medical Consent Versus Forensic Medical Consent

Medical consent should not be confused with forensic medical consent. Medical consent is for medical treatments, procedures, and medical care only, and does not give the forensic examiner the ability to collect and preserve forensic evidence. In emergency situations where life and limb are threatened, healthcare providers are covered legally for treatment without verbal or written consent, but that is not the case for forensic medical examinations conducted by FNs. Therefore, consent must be informed and written for a forensic medical examination to take place when the patient is a competent adult (or adolescent, depending on the jurisdiction). Exceptions include children and adults deemed not competent to direct their own care by law. In some instances, an alternate or substitute decision maker has been appointed for them, but not necessarily for forensic medical examinations.

Another exception in Canada is a forensic medical examination performed on an unconscious patient in which there is a high likelihood that a sexual assault has been committed. The Ontario Network of Sexual Assault/Domestic Violence Treatment Centres has developed a protocol for such cases.[58] Other nurse examiner programs in Canada are debating the issue. Some have chosen to conduct examinations only under certain circumstances. An example of such a circumstance is if a physician needs to do a vaginal speculum examination for medical reasons. If this occurs, then the nurse examiner will collect forensic samples, or will collect external body evidence and store it as an unreported case. Once the patient is able to provide informed consent, then that evidence is transferred from being stored as an unreported case to a case under investigation by law enforcement.

d) Light Source Instruments Used to Detect Injuries

i) Ultraviolet Lights (Such as a Wood's Lamp)

The first nurse examiners in Canada used an instrument known as the Wood's lamp, which is an ultraviolet light source with a wavelength of 280 to 360 nanometers (nms) to detect materials (such as semen) on clothing or on a patient's body. Without the light source, these foreign materials may not be visible to the naked eye of the examiner. The instrument, however, has been less than reliable and Eldridge et al. recommended that "the Wood's lamp be eliminated from sexual assault examinations."[59] Unfortunately, not

58 "Guidelines re Person Unable to Provide Consent," above note 13.

59 Eldredge, Huggins, & Pugh, above note 10 at 43.

all healthcare providers are aware of the unreliability of the Wood's lamp and it may well still be in use in facilities in Canada.

Currently, sexual assault/forensic nursing programs have gradually made the move to alternate light sources, with wavelengths in the range of 400 to 600 nms. These instruments are more sensitive and specific to the identification of semen. Specific wavelengths have been determined to detect specific materials. For example, a wavelength of 470 nms is appropriate to detect DNA.[60]

ii) Alternate Light Sources Used to Detect Bruising

Anecdotally, some examiners felt they could visualize underlying bruises beneath the skin of patients with an alternate light source. However, science has yet to prove this can be done reliably and it has been stated that "[f]luorescence under [an alternate light source] is not sufficient to accurately or responsibly diagnose subclinical bruising."[61]

C. THE ROLE OF THE FORENSIC NURSE IN CRIMINAL CASES

The role of the forensic nurse in criminal cases in Canada depends on the area of practice. Since the majority of roles for FNs remain in corrections, forensic psychiatry, forensic mental health, sexual violence across the life span, and death investigation, some FNs regularly appear in court proceedings while others will never testify in court. Since the role of the FN as an expert witness is relatively new, it is still evolving and being defined differently from jurisdiction to jurisdiction. In some Canadian jurisdictions, the concept of a nurse testifying in place of a physician is unfathomable, while in other jurisdictions, such as Surrey, British Columbia, the forensic nurse examiner testifying as an expert in sexual violence routinely provides opinion evidence in criminal cases involving children, adolescents, and adults.

1) The Forensic Nurse as an Expert Witness

The FN becomes involved in criminal cases when they have cared for an individual who has potentially been the victim of a crime or has possibly been accused of a crime. Outside of forensic psychiatry and correctional nursing,

---

60 *Ibid.*

61 M. Lombardi et al., "Is Fluorescence Under an Alternate Light Source Sufficient to Accurately Diagnose Subclinical Bruising?" (2015) 60 *Journal of Forensic Sciences* 444 at 444.

the FN may not know they are actually caring for such an individual. As a result, the FN must consider that any patient may become the subject of a criminal investigation. Not all FNs are qualified as experts, especially at the beginning of their careers. They progress to being an expert as they gain experience, education, knowledge, and skills. They will build upon their courtroom skills testifying as fact witnesses, when necessary in their given role.

Forensic nurses are not often aware that charges have been laid in criminal cases until they are notified by the Crown that they are required to testify. Occasionally, an investigating officer may contact the FN to clarify points in the report or the circumstances reported by the patient. If a case has not been reported to law enforcement at the time of examination, the patient may report the case at a later date. The FN is then contacted for any forensic samples that were collected and stored as well as any documentation related to the examination. The patient must provide a written consent for the forensic samples and documentation to be released to law enforcement. Even though documentation is stored indefinitely, most programs are, unfortunately, unable to store forensic samples beyond a year.

Historically, the FN is called as a witness by the Crown, but it is not unheard of for the FN to be either consulted by the defence or to be called as a witness by the defence. In either situation, the FN has the same guide lines for testimony: to provide the best possible information that will assist the court in deciding the matter at hand. The FN examiner typically testifies in cases involving sexual violence. There is a lack of research in Canada addressing the differences between having a nurse examiner involved in a criminal case versus a medical physician or a nurse practitioner. International research, however, indicates that care providers who have specialized education and knowledge in forensic aspects of patient care are better prepared to assess, intervene, and evaluate patients who may be victims or perpetrators of crimes. Du Mont and White state that,

> The collection and processing of medico-legal evidence involves a number of professional groups, including those who administer medical forensic examinations, the police to whom the findings may be submitted and the forensic scientists who analyse and interpret them. The availability of these professionals and the nature of their training can have an impact on the collection, quality and use of medico-legal evidence.[62]

62 Janice Du Mont & Deborah White, "The Uses and Impact of Medico-Legal Evidence in Sexual Assault Cases: A Global Review" (2007), online: World Health Organization (WHO) www.svri.org/medico.pdf at 41.

Significantly, "some data suggest that this expertise has led to better-collected and more viable medico-legal evidence."[63]

2) The Qualifications of a Registered Nurse and, Specifically, a Nurse Examiner

Traditionally, RNs testified in criminal cases, most commonly as fact witnesses discussing the circumstances surrounding the nursing care provided to the complainant or the accused. The evolution of the RN as an expert witness became identifiable in the criminal justice system with the advent of the sexual assault nurse examiner role in 1993. With this new role, the courts had to face the dilemma of having an RN as the primary care provider in cases of sexual assault rather than a medical physician (as was the previous situation in modern medicine and healthcare).

The courts had to be convinced that an RN could be a credible witness based on her education, specialized skills, and experience. Registered nurses in Canada vary in their basic and advanced education curricula but professional standards of practice govern all licensed RNs practising within each province or territory. Between 1994 and 1995, the first sexual assault nurse examiners started to appear as witnesses in sexual assault cases as a result of specialized programs based in Winnipeg, Manitoba, and Surrey, B.C.

a) Education

Registered nurses have two to four years of basic nursing education. The nursing profession was undergoing transition at the time, and the basic nursing course was moving from two years, to three, and, eventually, four years of basic education. Many nurses also had nursing degrees at the baccalaureate level (B.S.N or B.Sc.N), which added additional years to their education depending on their educational institution.

b) Professionalism

Registered nurses belong to a professional body that governs their practice as care providers. The Standards of Nursing Practice and Code of Ethics clearly define the roles and responsibilities of the RN in delivering patient care. Most provinces and territories require continuing education to be documented throughout the RN's career. Registered nurses are subject to criminal record checks as well.

---

63 *Ibid.* at 43.

c) Specialized Training

The original nurse examiners underwent a minimum of forty hours of specialized training, involving interdisciplinary educators from the forensic sciences, criminal justice system, law enforcement, physicians, and nurse educators. All of this training was specific to the field of performing sexual assault examinations for adolescents and adults. The training was followed by a preceptorship, providing experience in the clinical skills needed to perform as a nurse examiner. The preceptorship included completing a specific number of vaginal speculum examinations on "well women" (i.e., women who are not presenting for a specific reason, including sexual assault, infections, and disease processes), learning forensic evidence collection techniques, documenting sexual assault cases using specific forms, and certifying their ability to perform vaginal speculum examinations competently.

d) Experience

The first sexual assault nurse examiners were often skilled emergency nurses with excellent assessment skills. Many had decades of emergency nursing experience and this proved to be a significant asset to their additional roles as nurse examiners. Other nurse examiners hailed from other specialties, including obstetrical nurses and operating room nurses.

e) Preparation for Court

Since testifying as a witness is not taught in nursing education, the forensic sciences and criminal justice experts assisted the nurse examiners in creating a plan for court preparation. This included:

- developing a curriculum vitae for court purposes;
- conducting interviews with Crown counsel to review documentation;
- observing trials before appearing in court;
- understanding appropriate dress and demeanour; and
- undertaking continuing education in the field.

3) The Significance of the Forensic Nurse at Trial: Common Questions

Once admitted as an expert witness by the court, the forensic nurse examiner is commonly faced with a variety of issues that they must be prepared to address in order to be of value to the court. Most commonly, legal actors seek to address three key issues by engaging with an FN: (1) determining whether the sexual activity was consensual or non-consensual; (2) determining the significance, if any, of not finding genital injury in cases involving a complaint of sexual assault; and (3) explaining the causes or possible causes of the findings made upon examination.

a) Determining Whether the Sexual Activity Was Consensual or Non-consensual

The forensic nurse expert will probably be asked to differentiate between consensual and non-consensual sexual activity, as it is often the primary issue before the court in addressing charges of sexual assault. The reality is that the expert cannot make this differentiation using objective criteria, like injury presentation, as consensual and non-consensual findings may appear very similar at any given time. The expert can give an opinion based on their own experiences as an examiner and the current research addressing physical and genital findings in this context. However, a definitive answer of, "this is/is not non-consensual sexual activity" is not scientifically possible as "existing research regarding injury following consensual sex is fraught with limitations, so drawing a firm conclusion is difficult."[64]

b) Determining the Significance, if Any, of Not Finding Genital Injury in Cases Involving a Complaint of Sexual Assault

The FNE expert may be asked to explain why there are no genital findings in the case in question. The simple answer is that patients who experience non-consensual sexual activity may not exhibit genital injury. For example, the 2006 Crane research, discussed earlier, found that approximately 20.5 percent of patients reporting non-consensual activity had genital injury alone.[65] Other literature has made similar research results.

c) Explaining the Causes or Possible Causes of the Findings Made Upon Examination

The FNE expert may be asked to explain the causes or possible causes of the findings made upon examination. In doing so, the FNE expert will need to address the significance of such causes. For example, an abrasion is blunt trauma and a cut is sharp trauma, so differentiating blunt from

---

64 J. Markowitz & J. Pierce-Weeks, "Consensual Sex Injury" in International Association of Forensic Nurses & Tara Henry, eds., *Atlas of Sexual Violence* (St. Louis, MO: Mosby, 2013) c 5 at 90.

65 Crane, above note 49 at 80.

sharp trauma can be very important, particularly when considering the details of the case before the court. The expert is often given a hypothetical example of what might have caused a particular finding. One example commonly asked is if the finding in question can be due to "rough sex." The expert then should respond by asking counsel to clarify their definition of "rough sex." Some hypothetical examples are in the realm of possibility and the expert must weigh each question carefully to determine if it is a legitimate possibility, basing their response on experience, research, and the circumstances provided. It is important for the FNE expert to be mindful of bias and, as a result, the FNE expert should be considerate of all possibilities that could explain a finding made upon examination.

d) Addressing Typical Questions Presented by Legal Counsel

Beyond the above three key issues, the FNE expert is typically asked certain questions and, for the benefit of the lawyer-reader, examples of such questions are addressed below. The questions and responses are examples only and it is important to keep in mind that responses may vary between examiners and between jurisdictions.

i) What Are Your Qualifications?

The FNE should state their qualifications as outlined in their curriculum vitae, elaborating on details to provide the court with sufficient information to determine their specific area of expertise, allowing the FNE to be qualified and admitted as an expert. Forensic nurse examiners might, for example, testify to their years of experience as an RN, educational background, and previous and current professional roles. Forensic nurse examiners should describe the length of time that they have been a sexual assault nurse examiner and provide a summary of their clinical experiences in caring for both female and male patients within that length of time. Forensic nurse examiners should also speak to their previous court experience as either a fact or expert witness.

Any additional certifications should be described. It is important to note that forensic nurses in Canada do not have their own certification process and, therefore, FNEs can choose to voluntarily obtain certification in two areas from the International Association of Forensic Nurses: Sexual Assault Nurse Examiner-Adolescent/Adult (SANE-A©) or Sexual Assault Nurse Examiner-Pediatric (SANE-P©). Certification is obtained via an online examination held twice a year. Once obtained, these certifications can be maintained via continuing education for three-year intervals. Another certification is available for Canadian death investigators, as they can obtain certification via the American Board of Medicolegal Death Investigators on two levels: Registry Certification (basic) and Board Certification (advanced) by examination processes. Again, for death investigators, no Canadian certification is available to them. For the FN, being certified by a professional association increases their likelihood of being deemed an expert in the courts, whether criminal or civil.

ii) What Does Your Training Program as a Forensic Nurse Examiner Involve?

The FNE expert should describe their initial educational course and the length of their course. The FNE should list topics or, ideally, provide the court with copies of the course content. Continuing education is an important criterion for being deemed an expert and should be detailed in an FNE's *curriculum vitae*, as should additional classroom, online, and conference educational events relating to forensic nursing and sexual assault care specifically. Individuals seeking to be qualified as an expert should keep a current list of their educational activities, presentations, and publications.

iii) Did You Make Note of the Patient's Demeanour?

This question is one of the most frequently asked questions of the FNE expert. The expert should describe the behaviours observed during the assessment, treatment, and follow-up with the patient. The expert should describe such observations as, for example, whether the patient was crying (along with physical indicators, like swollen, red eyes), whether the patient presented with a dishevelled appearance (e.g., torn shirt, no shoes, matted down hair, etc.), whether the patient was able to focus on responding to the examiner's questions (e.g., did the examiner have to repeat her questions), and whether the patient explicitly expressed her thoughts at the time (e.g., the patient stating, "I cannot believe this happened to me").

Since demeanour is subjective, experts should only speak to what they observed, framing it using objective data rather than documenting judgmental characterizations, such as whether the patient was anxious, upset, distraught, drunk, under the influence of drugs, angry, or calm. All are subjective terms and are difficult to explain since individuals vary so greatly. What may appear as an angry individual to one examiner may appear to be an agitated individual to another.

The FNE expert may be asked if the demeanour of the individual was consistent with someone who had recently been sexually assaulted. This question should be responded to in a manner that allows for any behaviours or specific demeanour exhibited by an individual to be a response to sexual violence, as behaviours cannot be predicted or evaluated as normal or abnormal behaviour in this context. The most calm, co-operative, and responsive individual can be very traumatized emotionally from the event.

iv) Did You See Any Signs of Intoxication?

The FNE must be able to articulate why an informed consent was obtainable in order to do the medical forensic examination in the first place. Unless the FNE expert had access to drug and alcohol medical toxicology screening results, the expert should confine responses to patient behaviours observed during the course of the time spent with the patient, often over an extended time (such as four to five hours).

If an informed consent cannot be obtained, the examination process must be delayed until such a time one can be obtained. The FNE documents all signs and symptoms, which might include talkativeness, muscular incoordination, memory impairment, slowed reaction times as evidenced by delay in responding to questions, decreased alertness, vital signs outside normal limits, or signs of drug ingestion. To respond to this question, the expert must be familiar with the effects of both alcohol and common drugs, whether prescribed or not.

v) What Did You Find on Examination?

The FNE expert responds to this question by describing the examination process according to the procedures and protocols of their program or facility. This may include describing the head-to-toe and genital/vaginal/anal examinations with a listing of the objective data obtained during these procedures. The appearance of the patient's clothing (if worn during the incident) would also be described. For example, the FNE expert may describe the clothes as follows: "right strap on bra not attached to bra, shirt has tear at right side of neck opening, front zipper of blue denim jeans has links missing, stains present on clothing." The expert may then be asked to explain the significance of these findings, whereas a fact witness would not.

Listing the physical findings in an organized, brief, and consistent manner is helpful in allowing the expert to readily describe each finding precisely. Findings should be detailed with respect to type, size, shape, location, and colour. For example, a finding may be recorded as: "Purple-red circular bruise, 1.5 cm in diameter on left side of face, 2.0 cm below left eye midline." Correlating the description of the physical findings to the trauma map will assist the court to visualize exactly where the finding is located on the patient. In describing genital injuries, it may also be helpful to use landmarks or analogies, such as the twelve-hour clock face to assist in describing location. Without being specifically asked, the FNE expert should also define any terms used when describing genital findings.

vi) You Did Collect Samples? How Did You Collect Them?

The FNE expert again follows established forensic science and forensic nursing science procedures according to the relevant program and jurisdiction. The procedures reinforce the chain or continuity of custody for all samples. Each sample collection may need to be described. The FNE may also need to address questions relating to cross-contamination. Describing regular procedures may assist in answering such questions; for example, the cleaning of examination rooms, equipment, changing of lab coats, changing of gloves, and checking for intactness of sample containers before use may be described. It is good practice to have responses based on the most current procedures used by the FNE.

vii) Were You Able to Estimate the Time Frame When These Injuries Would Have Been Made?

The FNE expert should respond to this question very carefully since the mechanism of injury for any blunt or sharp trauma can easily be misinterpreted. Bruises, for example, should not be given a definitive time frame due to the substantial number of variables that affect their appearance in individuals. The experienced FNE expert knows that the time frame for bruise formation is so imprecise that to say a bruise is twenty-four hours old is setting oneself up for a defence expert to contradict the testimony. Dating a bruise is one of the questions that the FNE expert is not able to answer beyond a shadow of doubt. In contrast, it may be easier to provide a time frame for a cut—if the cut is actively bleeding, it can be determined to be "recent," as opposed to "not recent" (i.e., when the healing process has begun). The FNE expert must be aware of the body's healing processes to explain to the court why a certain finding cannot be estimated based on skin integrity.

viii) Can You Give the Court Any Opinion as to the Cause of Your Findings?

The FNE expert is able to provide opinion evidence as long as it remains within the scope of their qualified expertise. It is up to the expert to ensure that they only respond to questions that fit within this specific area. When in doubt, the expert should communicate their doubt to the judge in order to obtain direction on whether a question can be responded to or not, regardless of whether the question is being asked by the Crown or the defence. It is inappropriate for an FNE to respond to questions not included in their area of expertise.

ix) What is the Significance of the Absence of Sperm?

The FNE expert may be asked why spermatozoa were not identified when vaginal/oral/anal-penile intercourse was said to have taken place. The expert should respond with the factors relating to the recovery of spermatozoa in the first place, which is not always part of the forensic collection process.

In the 1990s, vaginal pool washings were done in order to obtain vaginal fluids and slides were prepared from the washings, to be examined by an FNE before being submitted as evidence. The identification of spermatozoa was used as a guideline to suggest that sexual intercourse indeed had taken place. The examiner was not always skilled at this laboratory procedure, thus the credibility of the finding was frequently in question. A lack of expertise on the part of the examiner in identifying spermatozoa often led to misidentification, which would be contradicted by forensic scientists. The use of a barrier during intercourse (e.g., a condom) and the time interval between the incident and the examination also contributed to difficulties in successfully identifying spermatozoa.

Much has changed since that time and, today, advances in DNA technology have meant that swabs are collected and submitted for DNA analysis. In most jurisdictions, the identification of spermatozoa by an examiner is no longer necessary.

x) Have You Examined Women after Consensual Intercourse?

As part of their clinical experience, the FNE expert normally examines females seeking healthcare in situations not involving non-consensual intercourse. A variety of settings may provide the FNE expert with the opportunity to potentially examine women who have recently engaged in consensual intercourse, including general practitioner offices, obstetrician/gynecologist offices, youth clinics, and sexually transmitted infections clinics. A nurse practitioner or a youth clinic nurse in particular may perform "well women" examinations routinely in a role other than their FNE role. Emergency nurses who are also FNEs normally assist physicians in gynecological examinations within the emergency department and have opportunities to observe normal genital and vaginal appearances.

For male and female patients, the insertion of a Foley urinary catheter into the bladder for continuous urine drainage during the course of medical interventions also offers the FNE experience in visualizing and assessing genital structures. Since nurses generally care for patients in all circumstances of life, the appearance of both male and female genitalia after sexual activity allows for normal versus abnormal assessments.

xi) Questions on "Rough Sex"

The FNE expert needs to be prepared to respond to questions addressing the issue of whether a particular finding might be the result of consensual "rough sex." Since there are many definitions of rough sex, the expert should ask for clarification on what exactly the questioner means by the term. Oftentimes, a clear definition is not provided and, as a result, the question is then broken down into specifics that the FNE expert can respond to appropriately. Since similar findings can be present in both consensual and non-consensual sexual activity, this question comes back to the issue of consent between the individuals. The FNE expert may provide a comparison of findings normally found in consensual as compared to non-consensual instances of sexual activity based on current literature, research, and their clinical experience.[66]

4) Common Myths and Misconceptions

An important part of the FNE's role in a criminal case is to help the trier of fact identify and navigate common myths and misconceptions, since such perspectives may influence the trier of fact and specifically their assessment of witnesses.

TABLE 16.1. Table depicting myths and misconceptions, paired with their respective realities. "SA" stands for "sexual assault." This table is the result of research literature over two decades from a variety of sources. It is by no means meant to be exhaustive.

Myth	Reality
1. The primary motive for SA is sexual. People who commit SA do not have any other outlet for their sexual needs.	Major motives for SA are: • Power and control (to overpower and control another person) • Anger • Dominance SA is not about sex. It is sexualized violence, not violent sex. Myth allows shifting of blame for SA from offender to victim.

66 *Atlas of Sexual Violence*, above note 64 at 91.

Myth	Reality
2. The victim can provoke an SA.	Someone's actions or dress cannot send a message "asking" for SA. Majority of SAs are planned in advance, making the patient's demeanour or dress at the time of the SA irrelevant. The known risks of pregnancy, sexually transmitted infections, physical injury, and death in a physical attack make this myth less than credible.
3. SA is an impulsive act.	In the majority of cases, offender has made plans to commit SA on a person or a specific person. Often, offender will take advantage of a person in a vulnerable situation, such as alcohol intoxication.
4. SA occurs only among strangers.	Majority of SA cases involve acquaintances, friends, or family members, not strangers, according to Canadian, British, and American studies.
5. Anyone can prevent an SA if they really want to.	Vulnerability of women is increased as the majority of women are not physically aggressive and physically are not as strong as men.
6. Offenders are "perverts."	Assumes only "sick" or "insane" people are offenders and that their primary motive is sex. Expectation is that the offender has recognizable characteristics, which is not true. There is no classic profile of an abuser.*
7. Women frequently make false accusations of SA.	In Canada, only a minority of all sexual assaults reported are false, which means that most of reports are true. False accusations of rape happen no more often than false reports of other types of crime. Of every 100 incidents of sexual assault, only six are reported to the police. Acquaintance sexual assault is the most under-reported crime in Canada.**
8. It cannot happen to me.	Anyone can be sexually assaulted. Victims are from every racial, ethnic, religious, economic, and social background. Age is from newborns to elderly. Females, males, any sexual orientation, and people with physical and mental disabilities have all been assaulted.
9. Sexual assault is not common.	Statistics indicate that the true number of SAs is so under-reported that real knowledge of the number of SAs happening yearly is unrealistic.
10. It is only an SA if weapons are used.	A weapon and visible physical injuries do not have to be present for the event to be an SA. SA is based on lack of consent according to *Criminal Code*.
11. Women cannot be sexually assaulted by their boyfriends or husbands.	Legally, a woman can say "no" to any form of sexual contact. Each partner must give consent for each sexual encounter.

* Angelo P. Giardino et al., *Quick Reference: Sexual Assault for Healthcare, Social Services and Law Enforcement Professionals* (St. Louis, MO: GW Medical Publishing, 2003) at 5.

** Women against Violence against Women Rape Crisis Centre, "Rape Myths," online: www.wavaw.ca/mythbusting/rape-myths.

Myth	Reality
12. When a woman is drunk or "passed out," it is okay to have sex with her.	If any person is unconscious or has impaired judgment for any reason (e.g., drugs, alcohol, medical condition, etc.), legally, they cannot give consent.
13. Only young women are sexually assaulted.	Sexual assault occurs across the lifespan from infants to elderly.
14. You can tell if a person has been sexually assaulted by the way she/he acts.	There are many reactions to SA including fear, anger, guilt, shame, sadness, shock, disbelief, and denial. Every person has a unique and different reaction to SA based on his or her own personal response system to the circumstances of the incident.
15. Once someone has said "yes" to sex, they cannot change their mind.	Every person can change his or her mind at any time during a sexual encounter. A person can consent to one form of sexual contact and not consent to another form of sexual contact.
16. A woman can avoid being sexually assaulted if she avoids being alone at night in the dark, or in deserted places such as alleys or parking lots.	Most assaults occur in a private home (60%) and up to 38% occur in the victim's own home.[†]
17. Unless she is physically harmed, a victim will not suffer any long-term effects.	"Violence against women continues to be a significant and persistent social and economic problem in Canada with serious impacts on our health, justice, and social services systems."[††]
18. Men who rape other men are gay.	Often perpetrators identify as heterosexual. They rape other men as part of an act of violence and the need to dominate.
19. Sexual assault is an act of sex, committed by sexually starved men.	SA is a crime of violence, committed by "ordinary" men.
20. Women who don't fight back haven't been raped.	SA occurs when one is forced to have sex against their will, regardless of whether or not the person has decided to fight back.
21. Women who say "no" can really mean "yes."	This assumption is based on rigid and outdated sexual stereotypes.
22. Carrying some form of protection can prevent an SA.	Maybe; maybe not. A weapon (could be pepper spray, knife, or other object) may actually be used against the individual by the perpetrator if the perpetrator does not already have a weapon.
23. Certain types of women are "unrapeable."	Regardless of a woman's profession or sexual practices, she can still be sexually assaulted. If consent is not given willingly, it is a crime.
24. It will not happen to me.	National statistics report that 1 in 3 females and 1 in 6 males will experience sexual assault at some point in their life.[‡]

† *Ibid.*

†† Federal-Provincial-Territorial Ministers responsible for the Status of Women, "Assessing Violence against Women: A Statistical Profile," online: www2.gnb.ca/content/dam/gnb/Departments/eco-bce/WI-DQF/pdf/en/Statusofwomen.pdf at 2.

‡ University of Alberta Sexual Assault Centre, "Understanding Sexual Assault," online: uofa.ualberta.ca/current-students/sexual-assault-centre/understanding-sexual-assault, citing Statistics Canada 2006 figures.

5) Standards of Practice

Forensic nurses are RNs, registered nurse practitioners, or registered psychiatric nurses (unique to Western Canada) before specializing as FNs. With this in mind, the RN is governed by standards of practice, which come from their registering body, such as, for example, the College of Registered Nurses of British Columbia, the College of Nurses of Ontario, and the Registered Nurses Association of Northwest Territories and Nunavut. The standards may include professional standards, practice standards, best practice guidelines, clinical practice guidelines, and position statements. For example, there are practice standards regarding consent, documentation, administering medications, and ethics. Practice standards differ from practice guidelines in that the standards are in place to provide for patient safety, while guidelines address a specific issue related to clinical practice. The provinces and territories of Canada have very similar standards, guidelines, and scope of practice for RNs, nurse practitioners, and registered psychiatric nurses. For example, the Code of Ethics (2008) of the Canadian Nurses Association is used by the majority of the provinces and territories as their standard of ethical practice.[67]

Each of the twenty nursing specialties recognized by the Canadian Nurses Association have certification examinations based on the specialized body of knowledge that their practice entails. Currently, forensic nursing does not have a Canadian certification process and, as a result, the majority of Canadian FNs look to the IAFN for guidance on best practices. Since the IAFN has global membership, with Canadian nurses being the second highest membership group, the standards can very readily be adapted for use in Canada.

Currently, standards for forensic nursing practice do not exist in Canada. The Canadian Nurses Association recognizes the Forensic Nurses Society of Canada[68] as an emerging subspecialty of nursing. The move towards forensic nursing being recognized as a full specialty is necessary to establish forensic nursing as a viable career option for FNs in Canada. In contrast, the American Nurses Association recognized forensic nursing as a specialty in 1995.

---

67 Canadian Nurses Association, "Nursing Ethics," online: www.cna-aiic.ca/en/on-the-issues/best-nursing/nursing-ethics.

68 Founded in 2007 by Cathy Carter Snell, Janet Calnan, Kathleen Soltys, and Sheila Early.

a) Best Practices

Best practices originate from research upon which a specialized body of knowledge can be created. Forensic nursing best practices depend on research from a multitude of disciplines, including those that address nursing science, forensic sciences, evidence collection, and neurobiology of violence and trauma. It is therefore not a simple task to develop and keep current best practices. The IAFN is the main source of best practice guidelines globally, but the practices have to be modified for Canadian nurses in accordance with the healthcare and criminal justice systems in place (which are different compared to the United States).

Ontario was the first province to develop provincial standards in sexual assault care with the inception of the Ontario Network of Sexual Assault/Domestic Violence Treatment Centres in 1993. The Ministry of Health and Long-Term Care established the network, which has since grown to include thirty-five centres. In British Columbia, two health authorities (Fraser Health and Vancouver Island) have recently joined programs within their respective regions. New Brunswick has followed Ontario's lead and has established its own provincial standards—the Provincial Network for Sexual Assault Nurse Examiners. These efforts to develop best practice guidelines and to standardize the role of the sexual assault nurse examiner are stepping stones towards furthering the forensic nursing specialty in Canada.

D. A CASE STUDY

Maria Elena is a twenty-three-year-old Mexican student attending a Canadian university. She is in the third year of her studies to become a social worker. Her goal is to become a social worker and return to her home country. She is the first of her family to attend a university and is in Canada on a scholarship.

Maria Elena needed to move from one apartment to another. She asked several of her friends to assist her with the move and promised them a chicken dinner and beer for assisting her. The move went well. Most of her friends left, and only one male friend, Rolando, remained behind to help her clean up the dishes. Rolando had been Maria Elena's friend since she arrived from Mexico to start her studies; he was in his fourth year of university and is also from Mexico. There had never been any romantic or intimate relationship between the two.

Rolando started to kiss Maria Elena in the kitchen as they were doing dishes. She emphatically said she did not want to be kissed and said he should leave now. He said he wanted to have sex with her; she refused and tried to get him out of the kitchen. Maria Elena was wearing a white T-shirt, jeans, panties, and a bra. She also had her menstrual period at this time. Rolando pushed her up against a wall and tried to pull her jeans off her. She fought and the zipper of the jeans became ripped and gaping. Rolando then put his hand inside her jeans and panties and penetrated her vagina with three fingers. Maria Elena continued to resist, then Rolando withdrew his fingers from her vagina and wiped his fingers across her white T-shirt, leaving smears across it. He left, slamming the door.

Maria Elena immediately called police and they arrived shortly after her call. After a short interview, the attending officer escorted Maria Elena to the SANE program, which provides specialized care to individuals reporting non-consensual sexual events. Another officer immediately went to find Rolando as Maria Elena gave them his name, address, and the make of the car that he drove.

The nurse examiner on call arrived at the local emergency department to conduct a medical forensic examination, as requested by Maria Elena. After obtaining informed consent, the nurse examiner first had Maria Elena remove each piece of clothing separately and place it in a paper bag:

1) White T-shirt with brown coloured stains across the front in diagonal linear pattern.
2) White bra with left strap unattached to main body of bra at back (posterior).
3) Dark blue denim jeans with front zipper not intact, three zipper teeth missing on left side of zipper. The front metal button at the waistband is hanging from the fabric and is not attached to fabric in several places.
4) Black panties with brown coloured stains on front of the panties.

With respect to injuries, the nurse examiner noted:

- Three blue bruises on left upper anterior (front) arm, circular in shape. First bruise is 1.3 cm in diameter, second is 1.0 cm in diameter, and third is 0.9 cm in diameter.
- One red linear horizontal abrasion, measuring 3.5 cm long and .3 cm wide beginning at left nose to left ear. There are multiple areas of dried red fluid along the length of the abrasion indicating this is a recent injury.

On vaginal examination, using a lighted vaginal speculum to visualize the internal structures, a circular red abrasion was visualized at the position of three o'clock on the cervix. Dark brown fluid is present in the vagina and is seen coming from the cervical os (the internal female genital structure that is the opening to the uterus). Maria Elena was treated and discharged following standardized protocols following her examination.

Rolando had fled back to Mexico before he could be apprehended by police and the extradition process took two-and-a-half years before he was returned to Canada to stand trial for sexual assault under the *Criminal Code*.

The nurse examiner testified to the condition of Maria Elena's clothing, the results of the medical forensic examination, and Maria Elena's demeanour during the examination process. The external findings of three bruises and one abrasion, plus the internal abrasion on the cervix, were consistent with blunt trauma to the areas involved.

Following the nurse examiner's testimony, the attending police officer testified and presented the stained T-shirt, bra, panties, and jeans to the court as evidence. A forensic laboratory scientist testified that the brown stains on Maria Elena's T-shirt were bloodstains that matched the DNA of Maria Elena.

Rolando was convicted of sexual assault and sentenced to one year in provincial custody.

E. CONCLUSION

Forensic nursing experts have an invaluable role in the criminal justice system because of their expertise in both healthcare and forensic nursing science. Forensic nursing is still emerging as an entity within Canada's nursing specialties, as well as within the criminal justice system. It is no longer a novelty for FNs to be deemed experts in a court of law and to testify in their area of expertise.

The Canadian history of forensic nursing started in 1975 and, in forty years, it has made tremendous advancements—not only in the healthcare of forensic patient populations, but in the judgments of the courts that consider the testimony of FNs. With so many subspecialties and such broad areas of practice, there will be constant changes over the next several decades as forensic nursing moves to the forefront of the healthcare response to violence and violence prevention. Forensic nurses have changed the healthcare response to sexual violence in particular and are expanding their role to include providing care to individuals who have been subjected to physical violence, spanning from birth to (and including) death. Other subspecialties, such as forensic psychiatry, forensic mental health, and forensic corrections, are also becoming recognized within the healthcare system.

Until all jurisdictions in Canada recognize FNs as being experts in their own right, FNs will continue to be compared to physicians, especially in cases of sexual violence. In Canada, the forensic science aspect of forensic nursing would benefit from the use of a standardized forensic evidence kit for the collection of forensic samples, also known as a sexual assault evidence kit. Currently, Ontario is the only province in Canada to use a standardized forensic evidence collection kit. The RCMP Forensic Laboratory Service is working towards a national standardized forensic evidence kit that would be available to all provinces and territories for use. Even with the vastness of the country, it is entirely feasible to have such a kit available. It would benefit not only forensic science, but also the forensic examiners who perform the actual sample collection.

Forensic nursing research needs be expanded greatly in Canada so that there is a clear body of knowledge deemed Canadian for the FN to draw on as standards of practice and best practice guidelines are further developed and revised. Forensic nurses have an obligation to maintain their own expertise and knowledge through continuing education. Educational facilities need to provide learning opportunities relevant to all areas of the forensic nursing practice. The end result of these initiatives will be that the court will have even better FN experts available to assist them in coming to just decisions.

F. LEGAL CONTEXT

Forensic nursing is "the integration of forensic-science knowledge and principles with nursing knowledge in the clinical investigation of trauma and the recovery of medical evidence."[69] The responsibilities of the FN include identifying, evaluating, and documenting trauma, disease, and death, while preserving evidence and providing direct services to a variety of parties, including victims, suspects, perpetrators, and witnesses of violence.[70] Not surprisingly, the majority of criminal cases involving forensic nursing pertain to allegations of sexual assault and domestic violence. Interestingly, *Forensic Science in Canada: A Report of Multidisciplinary Discussion* (colloquially referred to as the "Hart House Report," published in 2012) identified

69 CFSM, "Multidisciplinary Discussion Report," above note 37 at 41.

70 *Ibid.* at 41–42.

the major scientific controversy in forensic nursing as its utilization in cases of sexual assault and domestic violence.[71] This paradox may exist because differentiating between consensual and non-consensual sexual activity cannot be determined scientifically (see Section B(4)(a)). In contrast to the Hart House Report, the 2009 National Academy of Sciences Report in the United States,[72] which heavily criticized a number of the forensic sciences, speaks only to forensic nurses needing to be certified in order to practice and is silent on the specifics of the nursing subspecialty.

Sexual assault examination evidence may address a variety of issues, serving as a piece of a larger body of evidence during a criminal trial that may:

- represent "opinion evidence on the assessment and mechanism of injury as it relates to a complaint of sexual assault," often paired with an explanation of the importance of obtaining informed consent before a SANE explanation;[73]
- assist in the determination of whether sexual intercourse occurred and, if so, whether sex was consensual or non-consensual;
- corroborate the complainant's evidence, such as in trial judgments of *R. v. J.G.E.S.*,[74] *R. v. McNabb*,[75] *R. v. Reiss*,[76] *R. v. Kennedy*,[77] and *R. v. Lally*;[78]
- support the demeanour evidence, cognitive state, and capacity of the complainant after the stated sexual assault, such as in the trial judgment of *R. v. Adbelhamid*;[79]
- result in "consistent with" conclusions[80] that may assist the court in evaluating the narrative offered at trial;[81]

---

71 *Ibid.* at 111, "Appendix F: Major Scientific Controversies by Forensic Discipline.

72 See Chapter 5 of this book for a more detailed explanation of this report.

73 *R. v. Ryder*, 2011 BCSC 133 at para. 53 [*Ryder*].

74 *R. v. J.G.E.S.*, 2005 BCSC 1916. Note that this case involved three different counts of sexual assault using a weapon involving three different complainants. The issue in all counts was consent. The court considered the expert opinion evidence to be weak with respect to the first two complainants and did not give those opinions much weight. With respect to the third complainant, K.P., the court found substantial corroboration, including the forensic nurse's observations, that the complainant was sexually assaulted.

75 *R. v. McNabb*, 2010 SKQB 169.

76 *R. v. Reis*, 2010 BCSC 1775.

77 *R. v. Kennedy*, 2012 NLTD(G) 101 [*Kennedy*].

78 *R. v. Lally*, 2012 ONCJ 397.

79 *R. v. Abdelhamid*, 2013 MBQB 119 [*Abdelhamid*].

80 *Ruddick*, above note 3.

81 *R. v. Rohani*, 2003 BCPC 551 [*Rohani*].

- lead to an acquittal or stay of proceedings, such as in the case of *R. v. T.K.*,[82] where a novice police officer conducted an improper police investigation when investigating an allegation of sexual assault by acting on an uncorroborated complaint. If the officer had read the sexual assault nurse examiner's report or interviewed the nurse, then he would have discovered that the complainant's report differed from what she had told him. The court granted a judicial stay of proceedings.[83]

Typically, sexual assault nurse examiners who are qualified as experts in court provide opinion evidence addressing whether the observations noted during examinations are consistent with sexual activity and, specifically, consensual or non-consensual sexual intercourse. This involves the FN testifying to her examination of the complainant, the observations made during examination, and the conclusions drawn with respect to those observations. Conclusions are usually expressed using "consistent with" terminology, with varying levels of qualification. Historically, "consistent with" evidence has drawn a great deal of criticism from the legal community.[84] The use of such terminology makes the discipline vulnerable to challenge on the basis of its potential to mislead, particularly if an expert expresses a dogmatic, unqualified, or unscientific conclusion. On the other hand, if the opinion evidence is qualified (as it should be), then criminal courts are often only able to rely on the evidence to support or refute the consistency of the narrative before the court, rather than rely on the evidence as proof of a fact in issue. For example, in *R. v. Rohani*, Steinberg Prov. Ct. J. states:

> Her [Nurse Sheila Early's] summary is as follows: the inner labia reddened areas at eleven o'clock, the tear at six o'clock, and the redness at twelve o'clock in the anal sphincter are all consistent with recent blunt force trauma to those areas. She, in examination, said that that would also be consistent simply with pressure to those areas. Her next set of conclusions were highly qualified, I find. I quote again, "The posterior pharynx reddening *could be* indicative of pressure or blunt force trauma to that area. The purple-red bruise on the upper right anterior thigh and the faint purple bruise on the upper right lateral thigh *can be* recent."

82 *R. v. T.K.*, [1999] B.C.J. No. 3170 (S.C.).

83 *Ibid.* at para. 47.

84 See, for example, Alan D. Gold. *Expert Evidence in Criminal Law: The Scientific Approach*, 2d ed. (Toronto: Irwin Law, 2009) at 227.

> *Those qualifications of "could be" and "can be" are, in a criminal trial, not to be used as proof, but simply as indicative as to whether or not there is a consistency with a narrative.*[85]

The existence and corroborative power of DNA may assist the court in finding the accused guilty or not guilty, if that verdict is indeed appropriate on the totality of the evidence.[86]

1) The Law Relating to Sexual Assault

Sexual assault contravenes section 71, and is indirectly defined in section 265(1) of the *Criminal Code*[87] as an assault "committed in circumstances of a sexual nature, such that the sexual integrity of the victim is violated."[88] In cases involving allegations of sexual assault, the issue at trial is often consent, which is defined in the context of sexual offences as "the voluntary agreement of the complainant to engage in the sexual activity in question."[89] Only two conclusions are available to the trier of fact on this issue: either the complainant consented or did not. Implied consent is not a defence in Canada.[90] Rather, there is a positive, ongoing obligation to take reasonable steps to determine whether or not there is consent.[91] This obligation is proportionate to the circumstances of the case.[92]

The elements of the *actus reus* and *mens rea* of sexual assault are described by the Supreme Court of Canada in *R. v. Ewanchuk*:[93]

> *The* actus reus *of sexual assault is established by the proof of three elements: (i) touching, (ii) the sexual nature of the contact, and (iii) the absence of consent. The first two of these elements are objective.* It is sufficient for the Crown to prove that the accused's actions were voluntary. The sexual nature of the assault is determined objectively; the Crown need not prove

85 *Rohani*, above note 81 at para. 22 [emphasis added].
86 A good example of this can be found in *Abdelhamid*, above note 79.
87 *Criminal Code*, R.S.C. 1985, c. C-46.
88 *R. v. Ewanchuk*, [1999] 1 S.C.R. 330 at para. 24 [*Ewanchuk*]. This is in the words of the court and does not represent a quote from s. 265(1). See also *R. v. S.(P.L.)*, [1991] 1 S.C.R. 909.
89 *Criminal Code*, above note 87, s. 273.1.
90 *Ewanchuk*, above note 88 at para. 31.
91 *R. v. A.J.*, 2011 SCC 28 at para. 42.
92 *R v. G.(R.)* (1994), 38 C.R. (4th) 123 at para. 29 (B.C.C.A.); followed in *R v. Cornejo* (2003), 181 C.C.C. (3d) 206 at para 23 (Ont. C.A.), leave to appeal to S.C.C. refused, [2004] S.C.C.A. No. 32.
93 *Ewanchuk*, above note 88.

> that the accused had any *mens rea* with respect to the sexual nature of his or her behaviour: see *R. v. Litchfield*, [1993] 4 S.C.R. 333, and *R. v. Chase*, [1987] 2 S.C.R. 293.
>
> The absence of consent, however, is subjective and determined by reference to the complainant's subjective internal state of mind towards the touching, at the time it occurred: see *R. v. Jensen* (1996), 106 C.C.C. (3d) 430 (Ont. C.A.), at pp. 437–38, aff'd [1997] 1 S.C.R. 304, *R. v. Park*, [1995] 2 S.C.R. 836, at p. 850, per L'Heureux-Dubé J., and D. Stuart, *Canadian Criminal Law* (3rd ed. 1995), at p. 513.[94]
>
> . . .
>
> However, since sexual assault only becomes a crime in the absence of the complainant's consent, the common law recognizes a defence of mistake of fact which removes culpability for those who honestly but mistakenly believed that they had consent to touch the complainant. To do otherwise would result in the injustice of convicting individuals who are morally innocent: see *R. v. Creighton*, 1993 CanLII 61 (SCC), [1993] 3 S.C.R. 3. As such, *the* mens rea *of sexual assault contains two elements: intention to touch and knowing of, or being reckless of or wilfully blind to, a lack of consent on the part of the person touched*. See *Park*, *supra*, at para. 39.[95]

When determining credibility, the trier of fact should consider the honesty and reliability of the evidence presented by the witnesses, which includes an evaluation of "external factors such as ability to observe, remember, or relate accurately."[96] The proceedings should not become a credibility contest between the complainant and the defendant and, without shifting the onus to the accused, it must be determined whether the Crown met its onus to prove the charges beyond a reasonable doubt.[97]

In determining credibility, the trier of fact should approach the analysis from a common sense perspective, rather than one based on outdated stereotypes.[98] In *R. v. W.(R.)*,[99] a case involving sexual offence convictions

---

94 *Ibid.* at paras. 25–26 [emphasis added]. At para. 27, the Court continues: ". . . for the purposes of determining the absence of consent as an element of the *actus reus*, the actual state of mind of the complainant is determinative. At this point, the trier of fact is only concerned with the complainant's perspective. The approach is purely subjective." The testimony of the complainant must be considered in light of all evidence.

95 *Ibid.* at para. 42 [emphasis added].

96 *R. v. H.C.*, 2009 ONCA 56 at para. 43.

97 *R. v. W.(D.)*, [1991] 1 S.C.R. 742.

98 See Section C(4), above in this chapter.

99 [1992] 2 S.C.R. 122.

based on the testimony of child complainants, Chief Justice McLachlin took issue with the stereotype that victims of sexual assault will report the assault in a timely manner:

> Finally, the Court of Appeal relied on the fact that neither of the older children was "aware or concerned that anything untoward occurred which is really the best test of the quality of the acts." This reference reveals reliance on the stereotypical but suspect view that the victims of sexual aggression are likely to report the acts, a stereotype which found expression in the now discounted doctrine of recent complaint. In fact, the literature suggests the converse may be true; victims of abuse often in fact do not disclose it, and if they do, it may not be until a substantial length of time has passed. In any event, the Court of Appeal erred in concluding that there was no complaint. In fact the two older girls did complain to their mother; S.W. about the respondent getting into bed with her, and both M.W. and S.W., it would seem, about the way in which he wrestled with them.
>
> In summary, the Court of Appeal was right to be concerned about the quality of the evidence and correct in entering upon a re-examination and reweighing, to some extent, of the evidence. It went too far, however, in finding lacunae in the evidence which did not exist and in applying too critical an approach to the evidence, an approach which appears to have placed insufficient weight on the trial judge's findings of credibility, influenced as the Court of Appeal appears to have been by the old stereotypes relating to the inherent unreliability of children's evidence and the "normal" behaviour of victims of sexual abuse.[100]

As found by the Supreme Court of Canada in *R. v. D.D.*,[101] "The significance of the complainant's failure to make a timely complaint *must not* be the subject of any presumptive adverse inference based upon now rejected stereotypical assumptions of how persons (particularly children) react to acts of sexual abuse."[102] In the context of a jury trial, a trial judge should recognize and address the potential effect of such stereotypes on the jury's assessment of the complainant's credibility by ensuring the issue forms part of the charge to the jury:

---

100 *Ibid.* at 136.

101 2000 SCC 43.

102 *Ibid.* at para. 63 [Citations relied upon by the court removed, emphasis in original].

> A trial judge should recognize and so instruct a jury that there is no inviolable rule on how people who are the victims of trauma like a sexual assault will behave. Some will make an immediate complaint, some will delay in disclosing the abuse, while some will never disclose the abuse. Reasons for delay are many and at least include embarrassment, fear, guilt, or a lack of understanding and knowledge. In assessing the credibility of a complainant, the timing of the complaint is simply one circumstance to consider in the factual mosaic of a particular case. A delay in disclosure, standing alone, will never give rise to an adverse inference against the credibility of the complainant.[103]

2) Criminal Cases Involving Forensic Nursing Evidence

In criminal proceedings, nurses have routinely testified as witnesses after examining a patient, but, like other experts, they must be appropriately qualified under the *Mohan* criteria to provide opinion evidence. The *voir dire* of *R. v. Thomas*[104] turned on the final *Mohan* criteria—a properly qualified expert—with respect to the Crown seeking to qualify an FN, Michele McIntosh, as an expert in determining whether the observed injuries are more consistent with non-consensual sexual activity compared to consensual sexual activity. The defence agreed that the first three criteria were met.[105] The court held that the nurse should not be qualified as an expert and contrasted her qualifications to the qualifications of Dr. Parker in *Quashie*[106] and *Liu*[107] throughout the judgment to "highlight the deficiencies" in her qualifications.[108] In arriving at its decision, T. Ducharme J. found a series of areas where the nurse lacked qualifications to provide opinion evidence and, as an example, stated the following with respect to her knowledge of the literature:

> I am astonished that a proposed expert witness is unable to discuss the literature relevant to her supposed field of expertise with any greater precision. Incredibly, Ms. McIntosh was unable to cite specifically a single relevant study, author or article. While she did make reference to certain journals relevant to sexual assault generally and an unnamed text from

103 *Ibid.* at para. 65.
104 *R. v. Thomas*, [2006] O.J. No. 153 (S.C.J.) [*Thomas*].
105 *Ibid.* at paras. 1–4.
106 *R. v. Quashie* (2005), 198 C.C.C. (3d) 337 (Ont. C.A.).
107 *R. v. Liu* (2004), 190 C.C.C. (3d) 233 (Ont. C.A.).
108 *Thomas*, above note 104 at para. 18.

> the University of Alberta—she was unable to refer to any articles dealing with the particular topic of distinguishing injuries caused by consensual sex from injuries caused by non-consensual sex . . . .[109]

In the unrelated judgment of *R. v. Dueck*,[110] in which the appellant was seeking to appeal his sexual assault conviction, it was argued that the inadvertent disclosure of a nurse's curriculum vitae to the jury should have resulted in a mistrial.[111] Like *Thomas*, the nurse was not qualified as an expert on *voir dire*. Her testimony was restricted to her sexual assault examination observations as a fact witness.[112] The nurse's curriculum vitae was not in evidence at trial, and, when the disclosure to the jury was discovered at trial, the jury was immediately instructed by the trial judge to disregard it.[113] On appeal, the defence argued that the curriculum vitae would cause the jury to view the nurse as a "quasi-expert" and to conclude that sexual intercourse with the appellant was the only explanation for the complainant's vaginal injuries.[114] The court did not find the defence argument convincing, further stating: "One might think that, if anything, Ms. Carlson's curriculum vitae would have led the jury to wonder why, if the complainant had in fact been sexually assaulted, Ms. Carlson had nothing to say about the matter."[115] The court dismissed the appeal against conviction.

Sexual assault nurse examinations are key to recording the observations and collecting the forensic evidence necessary to determine whether the available physical evidence supports the finding that a sexual assault did or did not occur, as stated by the complainant. Even in cases where the nurse is a qualified and impressive expert witness, however, these observations alone are not sufficiently probative to allow the court to arrive at a final conclusion with respect to consent and, as a result, the evidence must be considered on the totality of the evidence at trial. For example, in *R. v. Ryder*,[116] the extreme intoxication of the complainant and her active hallucinations

---

109 *Ibid.* at para 17.

110 *R. v. Dueck*, 2011 SKCA 45.

111 *Ibid.* at para. 2. Note that this is only one of the five grounds of appeal raised in this case.

112 *Ibid.* at para. 35.

113 *Ibid.* at para. 37.

114 *Ibid.* at para. 38.

115 *Ibid.* at para. 39.

116 *Ryder*, above note 73.

at the time of the alleged sexual assault resulted in Arnold-Bailey J. rejecting her evidence alleging a lack of consent. Justice Arnold-Bailey commented that the nurse's opinion evidence alone could not prove a lack of consent:

> Ms. Harder impressed the Court as a well-trained sexual assault nurse examiner and a person who made careful observations and notes. She was professional and non-partisan. Her observations as to the body of E.K. are consistent with the complainant and the accused engaging in sexual intercourse, and perhaps with less than gentle sexual contact depending on the origin of the bruises and abrasions. However, in and of themselves, I do not regard the observations to prove a lack of consent on the part of the complainant to intercourse with the accused.[117]

For obvious reasons, the condition of the genital area is most frequently described by FNs in cases of sexual assault, but FNs may also testify to the condition of other areas of the body, as observed during the course of a head-to-toe examination. For example, in *R. v. J.W.S.*, a trial judgment involving various charges including sexual assault, it was noted by the trial judge that the sexual assault nurse examiner testified to a complainant's body bruises being consistent with bitemarks.[118] In some cases, a blacklight (also known as a Wood's lamp, discussed earlier) may be used by the nurse to visually detect and illuminate fluids and bruises on the complainant that cannot yet be seen by the naked eye.[119] As noted earlier in this chapter, however, FNs have since moved on to using other, more specific technologies.

In the case of *R. v. J.F.*,[120] the dissent of Deschamps J. reviewed the trial evidence pertaining to the development of a timeline of bruising, as it related to a four-year-old foster child who died from multiple blunt force trauma to his head at the hands of his foster mother. The foster mother had pled guilty to manslaughter and the issue before the Supreme Court of Canada was whether the verdicts relating to the foster father were

---

117 *Ibid.* at para. 57.

118 *R. v. J.W.S.*, 2012 NSPC 102. This was only briefly mentioned in the judgment and the nurse's testimony to this effect was not in issue or discussed further. See Chapter 17 of this book for further information about bitemarks.

119 For example, the use of this tool is mentioned in the cases of *Kennedy*, above note 77 and *Ryder*, above note 73. The tool's use was mentioned only in passing and a defence challenge to its use and the observations arising therefrom is not apparent in either judgment.

120 *R. v. J.F.*, 2008 SCC 60.

inconsistent.[121] At trial, a nurse and doctors opined on the suspected age of the extensive bruising, with varying conclusions ranging from being over twenty-four hours old, to being only able to delineate between "recent" and "old" bruises, to advising that aging a "recent" bruise is not possible by simply visualizing it.[122] One doctor cautioned that aging soft tissue injuries is not, in the words of the trial judge, a "precise science," that aging bruising is non-specific, and that it is possible for two different people to interpret the colouring of the same injury differently.[123] According to the trial judge's summary, reproduced in part in this judgment, the accuracy of the photographs on which each expert called by the Crown relied upon was also contentious.[124] Although the timeline itself was not the issue in this judgment, it remains an interesting case study in varying expert opinions with respect to aging bruises, particularly given the cautions earlier in this chapter that bruises should not be given a definitive time frame due to the substantial number of variables that affect their appearance in individuals.

Lastly, it is important to remember that FNs must assess the evidence before them—embodied in the complainant—by assessing the complainant physically and emotionally in order to conduct a global assessment of the situation presented to them. There is an understandable—but troubling—potential for the expert to uncritically accept the complainant's story, in light of the emotionally shattering personal violation inherent in sexual assaults and the role of the nurse as a patient advocate. Although this bias is understandable, it endangers the objectivity of the FN as an expert witness and may result in less weight being attributed to his or her opinion, as was the case in *R. v. Samuel*,[125] where Feldman J. stated:

> Ms. Bainbridge [the forensic nurse] formed the opinion, based on the physical and emotional condition of the complainant, that she [the complainant] was forced to have intercourse, and that there was no other possible explanation. What was somewhat troubling to the Court was that this impressive witness was not offering her firm conclusion in the traditional expert's context of it being more consistent with one position than

121 *Ibid.* at paras. 38–39; the Court held that the verdicts at trial were inconsistent, must be quashed, and that a new trial would not be ordered.

122 *Ibid.* at paras. 78–85.

123 *Ibid.* at para. 79.

124 *Ibid.* at paras. 79–80.

125 *R. v. Samuel*, [2001] O.J. No. 895 (Ct. J.).

another. Rather, *she advocated an unqualified conclusion that would have the effect of usurping the function of the Court on the ultimate issue. Ms. Bainbridge concedes she is less than entirely objective.* She describes the mandate of the Centre as believing its clients and providing them with unconditional support, a laudable and understandable approach. *She admits to a certain bias in her attitude in analyzing what she sees on the basis of what the client tells her. Her function is to gather evidence supporting sexual assault.* I accept that this honest witness offers what she considers to be objective observations of the patient's physical state. An expert can offer strong objective opinions. But I am concerned that, both in perception and substance, the neutrality of this expert's conclusions is, to a degree, diminished. She appeared, in her analysis of the injuries, to downplay the significance of the physical confrontation which occurred after the sexual relations, in linking those injuries to coerced sex. Her discussion of alternative explanations for her findings in relation to the genitalia were offered, for the most part, reluctantly or as an afterthought. *Her strong conclusions bordered on advocacy, perhaps in response to the recanting nature of her patient's testimony. That is not the role of a neutral expert.* However much I respect the qualifications and experience of this witness, I place somewhat reduced weight on her opinion of the significance of her observations.[126]

3) Summary

Grim history has taught both the forensic and legal communities that if a forensic expert witness sees him- or herself as having the function to gather evidence supportive of a conviction, then there is a real risk of wrongful conviction, even with the best intentions. The role of the FN in both assessing and caring for the complainant must be a difficult role to navigate but, to ensure the proper functioning of the criminal justice system as a whole, it is important for all experts, including FNs, to remind themselves that their opinion will be afforded the greatest possible weight if it is non-partisan.

126 *Ibid.* at para. 23 [emphasis added].

CHAPTER 17

Forensic Odontology

David Sweet O.C.

LEGAL CONTEXT: CAITLIN PAKOSH

A. OVERVIEW OF THE DISCIPLINE: FORENSIC ODONTOLOGY

On a damp, dark evening in mid-October, a young woman was grabbed as she left a bar and was walking to her car. After the unknown man forced her to drive to the edge of the city, he dragged her from the car and assaulted her. Later, she could not be visually identified because of the beating. However, the police needed to identify her before they could start to piece the bits of evidence together. Once it was determined who she was, they could then focus on the teeth impressions the murderer left behind.

Cases of sexual homicide similar to the one described above are difficult to solve and raise many questions. Who do the police call to help them jump-start the investigation? Who is it that can assist investigators to identify the victim so the search can begin for where she was last seen, whose company she was in, what circumstances led to her disappearance, and much more? Who can potentially identify the perpetrator by analyzing the bitemark left on her body? The forensic odontologist is the expert that the police call for specialized help to answer these crucial questions.

Forensic odontology (dentistry) is the area of intersection and overlap between the dental and legal professions. The discipline involves proper recognition, collection, examination, and evaluation of dental evidence on behalf of a legal authority. Dental evidence may be found in the teeth and various oro-facial structures, including the tissues and bones of the face (used for age estimation and person identification) or in the impressions and marks left by teeth on relatively soft substrates (used for bite-mark investigation).

There are two ways that forensic dental evidence can be applied to criminal cases: (1) the identification of living or deceased persons using the characteristics of their teeth and jaws compared to pre-existing dental or medical records, and (2) the linkage of one person to another or of a person to a place through the identification and comparison of atypical physical features of the teeth to subsequent impressions or marks from the same teeth. Conversely, forensic dental evidence can operate for exclusionary purposes.

Historically, interest in forensic dentistry in North America increased when the first formal instructional program was presented at the Armed Forces Institute of Pathology in Bethesda, Maryland, in the 1960s. Since then, many formal courses have been presented in Canada and the United States, and several organizations have been established to foster the education and development of dentists with an interest in providing expertise to the civil and criminal bar.[1] The number of cases reported has continued to increase to a point in Canada where assistance is readily available for cases involving dental evidence.[2]

B. PERSON IDENTIFICATION

Conclusions from forensic dentists after comparing the post-mortem dental records of a deceased victim and the antemortem dental records of a missing person can answer important questions at trial. Answering, "Who was it that died?" is obviously an important legal question in a homicide trial. In countries like Canada, where accurate, precise, and readily available dental records exist, the identification of the deceased victim can be accomplished in an efficient, inexpensive, and expeditious way compared to other identification methods. Community-based forensic dentists consult with coroners, medical examiners, and police agencies with jurisdiction in any given case to employ dental records for these purposes. Identification of deceased persons in Canada is a coroner or medical examiner's responsibility depending on the region within the country, and police

1 L. Luntz, "History of Forensic Dentistry" (1977) 21 *The Dental Clinics of North America* 7 at 13–14.

2 S.L. Kogon, "Dental Evidence" in Gary M. Chayko & Edward D. Gulliver, eds., *Forensic Evidence in Canada*, 2d ed. (Aurora, ON: Canada Law Book, 1999) 361.

investigations often occur in parallel. Dental identification conclusions have been shown to be sound, scientifically based, and reliable; however, personal interpretation of changes in a person's dental status over time by dentists of varying experience and the fact that there is no method to measure the uniqueness of the traits that forensic dentists consistently rely on are inherent problems.

1) The Science of Forensic Odontology: Person Identification

Given various ambient conditions, such as heat, moisture, ultraviolet light, and animal predation, the human body will decay, decompose, and disintegrate after death. Teeth can survive these conditions well and thus can provide important evidence. In Canada, dental traits allow effective identification of a person because of the availability of high-quality dental records from the person's dentist. Clinical dentists store a record of natural plus acquired traits of a person's teeth and authorities can seize these records when the person goes missing. Forensic dentists can complete comparisons of these records to similar traits in a found body. If the natural and other traits acquired through previous treatments are determined to be the same and no unexplainable discrepancies exist, the body can be identified as the missing person from whom the dental records are obtained.[3]

This comparison of before- and after-death dental records is referred to as comparative dental identification. It is different than reconstructive identification, in which the odontologist attempts to profile the deceased person (e.g., estimate age at death, ethnicity, socio-economic status). These estimates are subjective opinions that are based on the dentist's knowledge and previous dealings with large numbers of patients from various ages and populations.[4]

Only *original* dental records should be seized from a dentist's office for identification purposes. Copies of various records are very problematic. For example, duplicated film-based radiographs have no left-right laterality markers, and the colours present on written dental charts that depict cavities and various traits or treatments are lost in black-and-white photocopies. Most practising clinicians believe that their original records should

3 I.A. Pretty & D. Sweet, "A Look at Forensic Dentistry—Part 1: The Role of Teeth in the Determination of Human Identity" (2001) 190 *British Dental Journal* 359.

4 *Ibid.*

not be released from the practice; however, identification of missing persons is an acceptable reason to do so. The dentist can copy the original records prior to releasing them to authorities and then the copy can be stored in the dental office. Following use, the original records can be released back to the originating source.

The scope of dental disease in Canada today for young people is much different than it was for adults growing up in previous generations. Both the amount of decay and the need for dental treatment occurs far less frequently today. The absence of dental restorations (fillings, crowns, etc.) means that, for relatively young victims, a forensic dentist must depend on morphological traits (e.g., forms, shapes, sizes, structures, contours) for comparisons. Examples of useful dental morphological traits include curvatures of tooth roots, bone trabecular patterns (micro trusses and girders that give the bone its strength), unusual shapes of the nerve canals inside a tooth's crown and roots, supernumerary (extra) teeth, pulp stones, and so on. These have become increasingly important for person identification when dental treatments are absent.[5]

Clinic- or hospital-specific abbreviations in the records of persons from other locations can present interpretation problems for forensic dentists. Most countries in the world, including Canada, use a tooth nomenclature system referred to as the Fédération Dentaire Internationale (FDI) system, but a different system (the Universal numbering system) is used in the United States. Notations in other languages have also presented challenges. Any poor quality dental records and data that are difficult to interpret may result in interpretation errors. In extreme cases, this can lead to misidentification unless the forensic dentist is diligent. In the post-mortem situation, all of the teeth may not be recovered because of loosening or trauma and subsequent loss. Fire can cause irreversible damage to restorations and teeth. Despite these problems, teeth and dental records provide invaluable, reliable identification parameters.[6]

Comparison of the available forensic data is simple, but interpretation can be complex. The protocol is similar to the examination steps used by clinical dentists treating patients in their offices. In the dental office, comparisons of traits from previous appointments to current traits are used to determine any changes in dental status over a period of time. These

---

5 D. Sweet, "Forensic Dental Identification" (2010) 201 *Forensic Science International* 3 [Sweet].

6 *Ibid.*

previous data are analogous to antemortem forensic records and the current data are analogous to post-mortem records for the forensic dentist. Dental traits are compared between the seized records from the decedent's dentist and the records produced at autopsy. Discrepancies in wear and various natural or treatment changes can be revealed through the detailed comparison of one set of traits to the other, but these discrepancies can be explained by the passage of time.[7] If the discrepancies present cannot be explained by time passing, additional treatments, or in other ways, then the forensic dentist must conclude that the records are not from the same person.

Dental data are typically available for missing persons in developed countries because of the relatively high quality of dentistry. The absence of such data—either because patients do not seek care or because dental care is not available—is the main reason why bodies are not identifiable by dental means. Additionally, some decedents can remain unidentified because of the lack of suitable antemortem data, including poor quality records from the treating dentist, even in Canada.[8]

The availability of stored records is an issue, especially for cold cases. A dentist's records may be unavailable if the victim of a homicide remains unfound for many years. The length of time that dentists must store diagnosis and treatment records for patients varies from province to province. Examples of the ultimate limitation period for dental records storage in Canada include: British Columbia, fifteen years; Saskatchewan, six years; Manitoba, ten years; Ontario, ten years; Quebec, five years; and Nova Scotia, ten years.[9]

2) Methods in Person Identification

In Canada, depending on provincial jurisdiction, either a coroner or medical examiner makes the request for a forensic dentist to join in on the casework. When a person has died, these authorities are mandated to investigate the "who," "why," "where," and "under what circumstances" of the death. A forensic dentist works on behalf of the coroner or medical examiner as a consultant and, following data interpretation and analysis, reports conclusions to them. This information can be valuable to police

7 D. Sweet, "Why a Dentist for Identification?" (2001) 45 *Dental Clinics of North America* 237.

8 Sweet, above note 5.

9 Dental Provincial Regulatory Agencies as of February 2015.

investigators if the person has died as a result of murder. The dentist responds to such casework on behalf of, and reports her conclusions to, the requesting coroner or medical examiner. Subsequently, the coroner or medical examiner may share the conclusions with the police.

The forensic dentist conducts a dental autopsy to assess and document the dental and oro-facial status of the decedent. The dentist attends the morgue typically after the forensic pathologist has completed his examination and medicolegal autopsy so as not to interfere with or potentially contaminate any evidence on, in, or associated with the body. Because forensic dentists are often dentists in private practice, their attendance at the morgue is usually after hours and may or may not involve an assistant.

In many cases, a tentative (putative) identity for the decedent has been established using circumstantial evidence from the scene or the context of the death. The coroner or medical examiner will use this information to seek out and obtain antemortem dental records for this person. These will be made available to the forensic dentist at the time of the dental autopsy for comparison purposes in an attempt to confirm investigative suspicions. Since a putative identification has been established, the forensic dentist is usually confirming or refuting a preliminary conclusion that has been developed by others.

If the decedent has been missing for a period of time, it is typical that a missing person report will have been filed with the local police detachment. Police will customarily obtain antemortem dental (and possibly medical) records for this missing person, enter them on a provincial[10] and national database (e.g., Canadian Police Information Centre), and store the dental records in the detachment. Interestingly, when a body is discovered and there is a need for comparison of post-mortem data to the records stored in police missing-person files, the coroner or medical examiner must request that the police release them to the forensic dentist for use on behalf of the coroner or medical examiner.

During the dental autopsy, the forensic dentist conducts a full and complete examination of the decedent's teeth, jaws, and facial region. Photographs and radiographs are exposed to document the structures under examination and comprehensive notes are recorded along with a chart of the various natural and acquired defects (e.g., fractures, fillings

10 British Columbia and Ontario currently have missing person dental databases jointly operated by police and the Office of the Chief Coroner in each jurisdiction. Other provinces are being encouraged to adopt this model given its success.

and other treatments, crowding, missing teeth). As with any forensic comparison, the unknown dental data are compared to the known dental data. This is to reduce and hopefully eliminate any perception of bias that the evidence from the known source is being fitted to the evidence from the unknown source. To this end, the forensic dentist in the morgue does not examine the supplied antemortem dental data from the missing person until after completing a full examination and dental chart for the decedent. Only after this comprehensive chart is recorded from the decedent is the antemortem record from the known person unsealed and used for comparison purposes.

In a stepwise fashion, the individual traits and characteristics depicted in both the antemortem and post-mortem records are evaluated, interpreted, and assessed. Any discrepancies may be explained by the passage of time and/or subsequent treatment, deterioration, and so on. Forensic dentists must ask themselves, based on their experience and given the number of records that they have personally examined in their career, plus their knowledge of the frequency of occurrence of certain characteristics in the population at large, if there could be any other person that would possess the pattern of natural and acquired features seen in the current case. If the answer to this question is "no," then the two records must originate from the same source and the body of the decedent can be identified positively as being that of the person represented by the dental record obtained from the treating dentist's office.

The coroner or medical examiner's request is specifically for person identification. However, there may be other features of the teeth and oro-facial structures that the forensic dentist is asked to comment on by police investigators. For example, trauma to the teeth and/or facial bones can sometimes be interpreted by the dentist with respect to the amount of force required to cause a fracture and/or the direction of such force, given the fracture pattern. These conclusions are typically reported to police directly and separately from the person identification aspects that are reported to the coroner or medical examiner.

The forensic dentist's report on person identification includes the following:

- case details and summary of circumstances, with associated file numbers;
- date and time of dental autopsy, persons present, and records obtained;

- summary of antemortem records supplied and from whom, patient's name, and date of birth;
- type of antemortem records supplied, date and time of acceptance, and by whom; and
- conclusions, date and time reached, printed name, and signature.

Since the forensic dentist was not present at the time the antemortem dental records were produced for the missing person, she cannot verify the exact origin of these supplied records. Thus, it is necessary for the forensic dentist to state that the records "are purported to be of a person known as . . ." since they cannot categorically state that the records are those of a particular person.

Given that the forensic dentist has produced a comprehensive record from the teeth and oro-facial structures of the decedent, and that antemortem dental data are made available for a missing person that is thought to be the same person as the decedent, there are potentially four conclusions available in person identification cases.[11] These are:

1) *Positive identification*: The decedent and the missing person are one and the same. There are no irreconcilable discrepancies present between the records; they originate from the same individual.
2) *Possible identification*: The decedent cannot be excluded as being the missing person. There are consistent features, but due to the quality or extent of the records it is not possible to establish identification via dental means.
3) *Insufficient evidence*: Based on the available evidence, no conclusion can be reached.
4) *Negative identification*: Exclusion. The antemortem and post-mortem data are inconsistent. The decedent and missing person are not the same individual.

3) The Evolution of Person Identification

Use of dental means to identify a deceased person is widely accepted as one of the most reliable, accurate, and cost effective methods that can be used for single victims (e.g., a victim of homicide) or for multiple victims (e.g., victims of disasters, or a mass murder). The International Criminal

11 ABFO Guidelines 2015, online: www.abfo.org/resources/abfo-manual.

Police Organization (INTERPOL) accepts three primary identifiers for human cadavers: dental traits, fingerprints, and DNA profiling.[12]

No minimum number of identification points exists so each forensic dentist's threshold for identification is necessarily based on their experience and knowledge of the frequency of occurrence of the traits being compared. No statistical inferences about an identification conclusion can be expressed because the individuality or uniqueness of most dental traits has not been established. The incidence of some traits included in the dental pattern being compared for identification purposes are known, such as the frequency of occurrence for a supernumerary tooth in the midline of the upper jaw or the absence at birth of an upper incisor. Identification conclusions are customarily established using large numbers of dental traits, such as the number of absent teeth, curvature of the roots of various teeth, presence or absence of a pulp stone in the nerve chamber of a tooth, outline of dental restorations, enamel thickness, migration and tipping of teeth, and wear on the biting surfaces of the front or back teeth. This large data set and the concomitant frequency of occurrence of each trait are considerations that the individual forensic dentist uses in reaching an opinion.

A variety of radiographic views can be produced to visualize the structures of the teeth and oro-facial complex. This includes radiographic films or sensors that can be placed inside the mouth and exposed, as well as extra-oral films or sensors that produce large panoramic or regional views. The most accurate of these radiographic views are the ones produced inside the mouth since the film or sensor is relatively close to the structures of interest. The intra-oral radiographs from the antemortem record can be compared to intra-oral radiographs from the post-mortem record. However, in some cases the only available antemortem radiograph that can be obtained is an extra-oral panoramic radiographic. Although many macro structures are visible on both types of images and it is possible for gross comparisons to be completed, a forensic dentist must be introspective and cautious about drawing high-level conclusions that are based on comparisons between extra-oral antemortem and intra-oral post-mortem radiographs. Added to this problem with differing accuracy between the two image types is the associated problem of the angle of the central X-ray beam that is used to expose an extra-oral versus an intra-oral radiograph. The comparison of traits within radiographic images that are taken from

12 INTERPOL Disaster Victim Identification Guide 2013, online: www.interpol.int/INTERPOL-expertise/Forensics/DVI-Pages/DVI-guide.

different directions automatically reduces the reliability of the conclusions reached about shapes and relative sizes of oral structures, such as root curvature, filling outlines, bone patterns, and so on. This is because no direct measurements from each image can be used since the relative sizes of the structures in the two images are different.

4) A Case Study: Person Identification

The body of a deceased adult woman was discovered buried under approximately four feet of soil and rock in remote parkland. The clothing, backpack, and personal effects found in the grave led the coroner to believe the decedent was a missing person named Jane SMITH (DOB: 22 May 1963). SMITH had been missing for seventeen years. The consultant forensic dentist responded to produce a post-mortem dental record of the skeletal human remains. The coroner approached the municipal police's missing persons unit to request release of the antemortem dental records on file there for Jane SMITH.

Figure 17.1 shows one of the antemortem dental radiographs contained in SMITH's record from her previous dentist. This illustrates the presence of a small metal filling in a lower premolar tooth and a porcelain-metal crown on a second lower premolar tooth (along with two retentive pins under the crown). Evidence of an infection is seen at the tip of the root of this tooth. A large metal filling is present on a lower molar tooth. Notes by the dentist that completed these restorations were present in the record; they confirmed the materials used and dates of treatment.

Figure 17.2 shows one of the post-mortem dental radiographs exposed by the forensic dentist on the body recovered from the park and transported to the morgue for autopsy. It is not directly superimposable over the radiograph shown in Figure 17.1 without discrepancy. Nevertheless, the forensic dentist concluded that the body found buried in the park was that of Jane SMITH.

The tooth with the porcelain-metal crown that was infected at its root tip was extracted on a date after the radiograph in Figure 17.1 was taken. Treatment was completed after the diagnosis of the infection was made from that diagnostic radiograph. The presence of the small metal filling in the remaining lower premolar tooth is confirmed as is the presence, size, and shape of the large metal filling in the lower molar tooth. There is a shadow on the radiograph in Figure 17.2 that is the healing site from where the infected tooth was extracted.

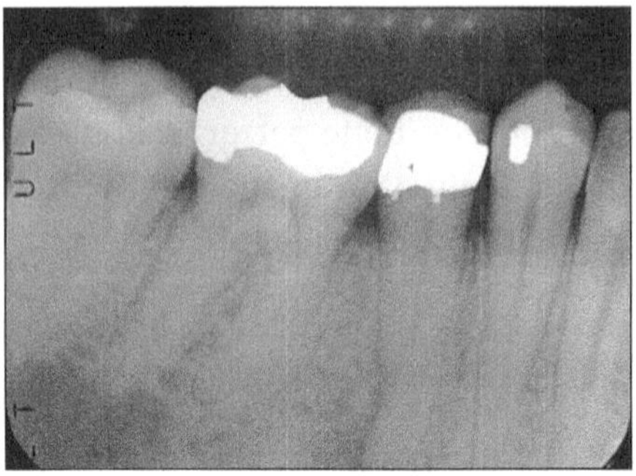

FIGURE 17.1. Antemortem radiograph.

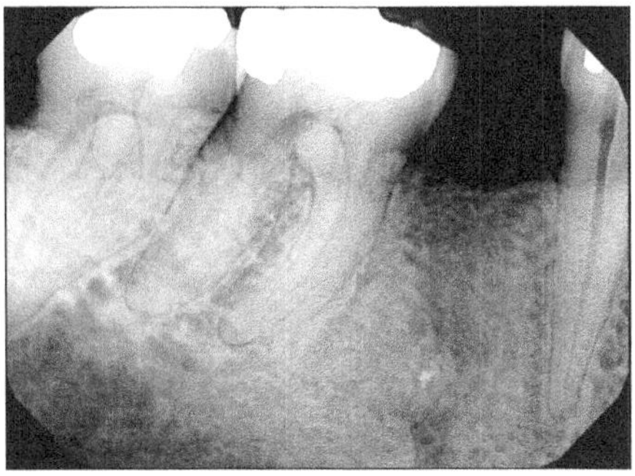

FIGURE 17.2. Post-mortem radiograph.

5) The Role of the Forensic Odontologist in Criminal Cases Involving Person Identification

In most cases of dental identification of a deceased person, the forensic dentist is working on behalf of authorities that are investigating the circumstances of the death. The conclusions that the forensic dentist supplies to the coroner or medical examiner are subsequently shared with the police investigators and become part of the framework of attempts made by police to prosecute the accused for murder. The role of the forensic dentist in court will not assist in identifying a perpetrator, but it will assist the court in establishing who it was that died.

6) The Significance of the Forensic Odontologist in Criminal Cases Involving Person Identification

Through other investigative means, if a suspect is apprehended and charges proceed, the forensic dentist is most commonly called to give evidence on behalf of the Crown. The dentist must be qualified by the court as an expert to give opinion evidence based on his skill, knowledge, training, and experience, and with respect to the relevance of the evidence to the specific case under consideration. The identification of the victim is not often contested, but when it is, defence counsel can use either rigorous cross-examination methods or employ their own defence expert to assess the veracity of the conclusions put forward by the expert called by the Crown.

In order to be qualified to give expert opinion evidence, the dentist must convince the court that she has experience in producing, examining, interpreting, and comparing the dental records of specific and different persons. These are, of course, the skills and techniques that are used in forensic identification cases using dental records. It should be noted that these skills are distinct from the ones that provide the necessary expertise to analyze, interpret, and draw conclusions about bite-mark evidence, which is covered in Section C. For person identification, it is not necessary for a forensic dentist to be a specialist, only to have a moderate to high level of experience as a general dentist who has examined a relatively large number of patients, has dealt with many and varied dental treatment techniques, and is up-to-date with the latest in modern biomaterials and techniques that are common to all dental disciplines.

To lead dental evidence, the Crown will ask the dentist questions about who requested his involvement, what the request entailed, when and where he responded, what steps he completed, and what conclusions he reached from his analysis. When the dentist expresses his conclusions, the Crown will ask about the meaning of the terms used and the dentist's level of certainty. This is often difficult for the dentist to describe because no numerical example or statistical inference can be made to answer the question, "How certain are you [the dentist] that no other person could have this pattern of dental traits?"

Defence counsel will typically focus on issues addressing the acceptability of the methods as viewed within the discipline itself, the "general acceptance" of the methods by the courts (i.e., precedents), and the reliability of the expert's conclusions in the specific case before the court. Reliability is an important issue to address when cross-examining a dentist about her conclusions. Would the dentist reach the same conclusion if she looked at the same evidence again some time later after a suitable washout period? Importantly, would another dentist with the same skill, knowledge, training, and experience who examines and analyzes the same evidence reach the same conclusion?

An expert called by the defence could provide counsel with a series of questions to ask the investigating expert and could provide expert testimony about technical matters that arise. For example, this could involve the comparison of extra-oral antemortem radiographs to intra-oral post-mortem radiographs, as mentioned previously. Another technical question may involve asking if the radiographs were viewed in a darkened room on a view box for film radiographs or on a high-resolution medical monitor for digital radiographs. Did the dentist use magnification or enlarge the radiographic images in any way to enhance his ability to see details?

It is not possible for the forensic dentist to be definitive about sex or ethnicity based on examination of a person's teeth, although this is sometimes thought to be possible. Some clues to determining these classifications are present in the shape and size of the jaw and the robustness of muscle attachments, but they are not present in the teeth per se. Such examinations and conclusions are best left to a forensic anthropologist. Wear of the teeth and the presence and degree of periodontal (gum) disease can be a marker for age, but chronological age can only be estimated by dentists, and wide tolerances must be included (e.g., 45 years old ± 10 years). Specific conclusions about the amount of force necessary to cause damage, such as fracture to teeth and jawbones and the direction of such force, is not often the purview of forensic dentists unless they have considerable experience with such trauma. These conclusions are often left to the forensic pathologist who routinely deals with fractures in hard tissues from blunt force trauma, or to oral and maxillofacial surgeons with similar experience.

7) Reviewing the Record and Full Disclosure in Cases Involving Person Identification

In the morgue and in all aspects of casework, forensic dentists should keep detailed notes about who initially contacted them to request involvement, as well as when and under what circumstances. Notes about similar case management details should be kept as the case unfolds.

Details such as when the dentist arrived at the morgue and subsequently departed, what was completed, who was present, and whether these attendees assisted in or simply observed the process should all be documented. It is also important to note details of interactions with coroners, medical examiners, police investigators, and, potentially, with the dentists supplying the antemortem records when a forensic dentist is in search of additional dental data. These interactions can take the form of telephone conversations, email threads, and so on, and become part of the case materials. The dentist typically retains these in their custody and customarily only releases a brief narrative report that is submitted to the original requestor (e.g., the coroner or medical examiner). However, at the time of disclosure, if this case goes to trial, all materials, notes, documents, and antemortem and post-mortem records must be disclosed.

The original dental records and these other documents mentioned above are not typically disclosed. Instead, high-resolution digital copies saved as PDF files are disclosed through Crown counsel. Occasionally, photocopies will be disclosed but these are usually of inferior quality. If a defence expert has been retained, then disclosure of the original radiographs and other original dental records to that expert by the Crown is reasonable, given that it is important for the defence expert to examine the same specific data and materials that were used by the investigating expert to reach her conclusions.

In rare cases in Canada, the investigating expert and the defence expert have talked about the case materials, techniques, and methods in an attempt to co-operate to determine if best practices have been followed and to ensure that all materials are provided. However, this is the exception and not the rule.

There are no standards or guidelines that have been agreed upon by practising forensic odontologists in Canada, so most active odontologists follow the standards and guidelines for body identification set out by the American Board of Forensic Odontology.[13]

C. BITE-MARK EVIDENCE

In struggles, combat situations, and life-and-death fights, teeth can be and are used as weapons. Perpetrators of violence can use their teeth to inflict pain and damage to the skin of victims. Victims of assault can use their teeth, hands, fingernails, and anything else available to them to try to defend themselves. Thus, dental evidence from scenes of struggles, combat, and fights includes patterned injuries from teeth on skin that are potentially found both on the victim and on the perpetrator. During sexual assaults, such as rape, sexual homicide, and child abuse, perpetrators bite their victims to express rage, dominance, or animalistic behaviour.[14]

---

13 ABFO Guidelines 2015, above note 11.

14 D.A. Webb, I.A. Pretty, & D. Sweet, "Bitemarks: A Psychological Approach" (2000) 6 *Proceedings of the American Academy of Forensic Sciences Reno, NV* 147.

The first case in Canada that included bite-mark evidence was *Regina v. Wayne Clifford Boden*.[15] Boden was convicted of four murders (Shirley Audette, 20; Marielle Archambault, 20; Jean Wray, 24; and Elizabeth Pourteous, 33) and sentenced to four life sentences on 16 February 1972. He had left bitemarks on the breasts of all four victims and, because of this, he became known as the Vampire Rapist. It was alleged that he also assaulted and bit the breast of a fifth victim, Norma Vaillancourt, 21. Since Boden's case predated the American case of notorious serial killer Ted Bundy, which also included bite-mark evidence, it was the first conviction in a serial crime involving bite evidence in North America.

The link between two people that are present at a crime scene, such as the perpetrator and victim, can obviously be very important evidence at trial. This is the primary application of human bite-mark evidence. The secondary—but also powerful—conclusion that can be drawn by the trier of fact from this evidence is the degree and severity of the bite injuries. Almost all people have experienced a bitemark during their lifetime, often at play with children or young peers. Thus, the trier of fact, through evidentiary photographs, can appreciate the pain and damage that is associated with the forceful application of teeth to skin. The prosecution commonly uses this to illustrate the aggressive and violent nature of an attack. Forensic odontologists are often requested to comment on the severity of such injuries and the amount of damage to the skin, including abrasion, bruising, cutting, and avulsion (removal) of part or all of the bitten skin. This line of questioning is, however, usually beyond the scope of the odontologist's expertise. Conclusions based on damage to skin should be left to the forensic pathologist. Historically, the original presentation of bite-mark evidence at trial was to draw a linkage between certain people and, today, this continues to be the primary reason it is presented.

1) The Science of Forensic Odontology: Bite-Mark Identification

Bite-mark evidence is accepted by the courts in North America and in several jurisdictions around the world but, in recent years, it has come under increased scrutiny. This is due to a perception that its reliability and validity are in question. The 2009 National Academy of Sciences (NAS) report in the United States was critical of bite-mark evidence, stating that the

15 Lee Mellor, *Cold North Killers: Canadian Serial Murder* (Toronto: Dundurn, 2012) at 368.

uniqueness of the human dentition has not been scientifically established. Additionally, the ability of the dentition to transfer a unique pattern to human skin, and the ability for the skin to maintain that uniqueness, had also not been scientifically established. Physical distortion of the injuries on skin from the dentition because of the skin's elasticity, and one's ability to analyze and interpret the degree of this distortion, are also seen as limitations. NAS stated that a standard for the type, quality, and number of individual characteristics required to reach a threshold of evidentiary value has not been established, leading many to conclude that the scientific basis of bite-mark evidence is insufficient.[16]

Enormous controversy currently exists both inside and outside the discipline about the value, scientific basis, and rigour of bite-mark examinations, analyses, and conclusions. In a 2015 peer-reviewed manuscript, Dr. Gregory Golden states:

> As a result of a desire to "do the right thing" on the part of a few forensic dentists, coupled with bungled police work, misidentification from mistaken or bought eyewitnesses, coerced false confessions, tunnel vision by investigators, unethical or incompetent lawyers, uninformed judges and phony science, the most unspeakable of outcomes occurred. Innocent people were sentenced to prison. Some 30 to 40 years after the innocent person has been vindicated and the true perpetrator identified, a review of how the damage was done is varied, including all those reasons listed above for the original convictions plus more . . . .
>
> As for bite-mark injuries, considering that the majority of them are evaluated from an elastic medium such as human skin and are typically delivered under dynamic, variable conditions, one would expect to see certain inherent distortions in the victim's injury. This hypothesis has proven itself true. One would think that information alone would persuade forensic odontologists to use extreme caution when attempting to identify the perpetrator of a bite-mark injury, particularly when their opinion may cause a significant impact on an individual's freedom.[17]

---

16 National Academy of Sciences, *Strengthening Forensic Science in the United States: A Path Forward* (Washington, DC: National Academies Press, 2009) at 7, 42, 86, 173, and 175 [2009 NAS Report].

17 G.S. Golden, "Bite-Mark and Patterned Injury Analysis: A Brief Status Overview" (2015) 43 *Journal of the California Dental Association* 309.

The main focus of the controversy is the profound nature of the conclusions often developed by odontologists given the elasticity of skin, the three-dimensional aspects of the teeth and jaws, the two-dimensional depiction of the resulting bite using photographic evidence, and the diffuse nature of many bruises caused by teeth on skin. In the past, odontologists have concluded that no other person could have made a given bitemark when the quality and amount of evidence is seen by some to be lacking. Today, odontologists are required to limit their conclusions in open, undefined populations and reduce the level of and confidence in their opinions when the quality of the evidence available to them is lacking.

The controversy over bite-mark identification evidence is divided into two camps: the prosecutors, along with forensic dentists, that support bite-mark evidence while recognizing its limitations because of subjective interpretation, and then, on the other hand, the disbelievers that consider any subjective, human-based analysis methods and opinions, especially bite-mark evidence and its conclusions, to be unreliable. Both sides appear to recognize that egregious errors have been committed in a small number of the total bite-mark cases adjudicated. Currently, there is a large movement, particularly in the United States by the Innocence Project, to target bite-mark analysis to bring its dependability into question in each case in which this evidence has appeared.[18]

Odontologists that work with bite-mark evidence are now starting to follow the suggestions and recommendations of organizations of subject matter experts, such as the American Board of Forensic Odontology (ABFO), to avoid high-level identification conclusions in favour of a more reflective, cautioned approach. What can actually be concluded based on this evidence found on soft, pliable, distortable, curved skin? This is the burning question in all cases involving bite-mark evidence. Odontologists are encouraged—and may soon be required by their certifying body—to critically evaluate the evidence first for its forensic significance and then to understand that the confidence that can be expressed in available conclusions is reduced when the highest evidentiary value is not present. If few teeth appear in the bite, or if the dentist is uncertain if the injury is caused by teeth, or if the photographic evidence is poor, and so on, then the conclusions available in the case will be necessarily reduced from the highest level to a level appropriate to the evidence. The odontologist's

18 *Ibid.*

confidence in his conclusions must be supported by the available evidence, which ideally shows well-defined features of a large number of teeth in a clearly detailed photograph. Odontologists should advise the court when the bitemark is not sufficiently detailed or clear to support a conclusion that connects the accused to the crime.

a) American Board of Forensic Odontology (ABFO)

The ABFO is the certification body located in Colorado Springs, Colorado, that conducts assessments of dentists seeking specialty status in North America in forensic odontology. The objective of the ABFO is to establish, enhance, and revise standards of qualification for those practising forensic odontology. The assessment and certification of specialist members (referred to as diplomates of the ABFO) includes initial examination of the specialists to determine if they reach a given threshold of knowledge, training, and skill, plus ongoing assessment of the member's proficiency every five years.[19]

In addition to its examination and credentialing role, the ABFO has developed guidelines and standards for its specialist members to follow. These guidelines have become the main criteria by which all forensic dentists function in daily casework throughout North America. This is now true even for those dentists that are not board certified by the ABFO, since they must use these same guidelines and standards to maintain the standard of practice for the discipline. All diplomates of the ABFO are responsible for being familiar with and using appropriate analytical methods according to the guidelines. All evidence received or collected must be reviewed, and the analyses performed, as well as the results obtained, must be included in the odontologist's final report. The ABFO attempts to be proactive in improving standards of practice. For example, it dictates that new analytical methods that are developed and proposed for use should be scientifically sound and verifiable and that these new methods should be used in addition to existing accepted techniques specified in the ABFO guidelines until they are generally accepted.

One of the main roles that the ABFO has assumed under its parent organization, the American Academy of Forensic Sciences, is the consolidation and definition of standards for forensic odontology terminology and nom-

19 ABFO Qualifications, online: www.abfo.org/apply.

enclature, in particular for bitemarks. Terms assuring "unconditional identification" of a perpetrator or "identification without doubt" are not sanctioned as final conclusions in an open population of suspects. Terms used in a manner different from the ABFO guidelines should be explained in the body of a report or in testimony, but it is recommended that terms be used in accordance with ABFO guidelines.

2) Methods in Bite-Mark Identification

a) Preliminary Examination

The following is a description of the steps taken by a forensic odontologist to assess and determine the evidentiary value (forensic significance) of patterned injury evidence to determine if the patterned injury is a bitemark.

Photographs of the patterned injury are submitted to the forensic odontologist so it can be determined if the injury: (1) was caused by human or animal teeth; (2) has a high degree of significance (i.e., represents a large number of teeth); and (3) has sufficient detail recorded in the substrate (often human skin, which is not a good impression medium) to make determinations about the size, shape, pattern, position, and characteristics of individual teeth that comprise the overall injury. Occasionally, impressions of the bitten skin have been taken and casts produced from them, but these are not as useful in most cases as good quality photographic evidence.

i) Quality of the Bitemark

If there is a high number of teeth depicted in the injury and the injury includes abrasions (scratches) or lacerations (cuts), then the bitemark may be considered to have high evidentiary value, allowing it to potentially be used for origin determination (comparison to the suspect's teeth) and interpretation of the situation that caused the mark. Abrasions and cuts to the skin impart details that mimic the physical characteristics of the teeth that caused them and so are useful for interpretation and comparison. In contrast, simple redness in the skin (erythema) and diffuse bruises (contusions) that result from the application of lesser forces may reflect trauma, but generally do not provide an accurate copy of the teeth that caused the trauma. Tissue that is removed by biting (avulsed tissue) results in distortion to such a large degree that little interpretation of the physical traits of the causative teeth is possible.

TABLE 17.1. The Human Bite Mark Severity and Significance Scale, as developed by I.A. Pretty.[20]

Component Injury Type	Injury Severity	Forensic Significance
Class 1—Mild bruises, no individual tooth marks visible, diffuse arch shapes.	Very low	Low
Class 2—Moderate bruises with discrete areas of damage from individual teeth, intact skin.	Low	Moderate
Class 3—Very obvious bruising plus lacerations from specific teeth; assessed as a definite bitemark.	Moderate	High
Class 4—Lacerations with bruising, skin is disrupted; unlikely to be confused with cause other than teeth.	Moderately high	High
Class 5—Lacerations present with partial avulsion of tissue.	Severe	Moderate
Class 6—Complete avulsion of tissue with or without scalloping of the edges from incision and tearing.	Extreme	Low

Other important questions that the forensic odontologist must answer with respect to the quality of the bitemark include, "Can the marks from the upper and/or lower teeth be determined?" and "Can the right side of the biter's mouth be distinguished from the left side of the biter's mouth?" Further, the forensic odontologist must answer questions like: "Are irregularities that are unusual, rare, or unique present in the marks?" and "Do they depict the shape, pattern, position, and size of the teeth causing the injury(ies)?"

Skin is not a good impression medium due to its elasticity and, because skin is relatively soft, it distorts when pressure is applied to it. Thus, any damage to the skin's surface resulting from trauma inflicted by the biting edges of the front teeth must necessarily be considered by the forensic odontologist to be distorted when interpreting two-dimensional photographic images of the three-dimensional patterned injury. This distortion may limit the odontologist's findings and, consequently, must limit his testimony in court to broad, non-specific findings.

Three conclusions are available to the odontologist for reporting her preliminary examination findings, with respect to whether the patterned injury is a bitemark caused by human teeth: (1) the injury is a bitemark; (2) the

20 I.A. Pretty, "Development and Validation of a Human Bite Mark Severity and Significance Scale" (2007) 52 *Journal of Forensic Science* 687.

injury is suggestive of a bitemark; and (3) the injury is not a bitemark.[21] Injuries on skin that are caused by interactions with objects other than teeth are often confusing in the absence of sufficient information supplied to the odontologist. Examples of various objects that have caused such artefacts include: bottle caps and jar lids; gear sprockets; circular burn patterns from the end of a hair curling iron; trauma from the end of a stick, tree limb, or bat; and bruises or abrasions from adhesive disks used by emergency personnel, such as EKG leads, that were placed when the victim was alive but are then removed at autopsy and create a circular patterned injury.

Attempts have been made by the ABFO Bitemark Committee in recent years to establish a protocol for odontologists to follow in an attempt to standardize the approach to, and interpretation of, bites. In 2014, these efforts resulted in the development of a decision tree by the ABFO to guide the expert through the preliminary phase of evidence appraisal to determine if sufficient detail and evidence existed to warrant comparisons, as well as through the subsequent phase of comparison to a suspect's teeth.

This decision tree has not been widely implemented yet, since it is pending further assessment and validation.[22] By using the decision tree, the odontologist can determine the best next steps, given varying levels of recorded detail on the skin, the quality of photographs, the number of teeth depicted in the injury, and so on. If an injury is known to not be a bitemark and if an injury is only suggestive of being caused by teeth, then no further action should be taken, especially with respect to comparison with a suspect's teeth. Therefore, in these circumstances, the odontologist should conclude that the injury is: (1) not a bitemark; or (2) is only suggestive of a bitemark and, therefore, does not warrant further investigation or comparisons according to current recommended approaches to casework.

ii) Quality of the Photographic Evidence

Forensic odontologists depend on and must have access to excellent evidentiary photographs depicting the bitemark. Without such images, they are unable to interpret the marks from individual teeth within the injury and are therefore unable to attempt to determine the characteristics present in the biter's teeth or to compare the injuries to the teeth

21 ABFO Guidelines 2015, above note 11.

22 See, generally: ABFO, "ABFO Bitemark Analysis and Comparison Decision Tree," online: www.abfo.org/wp-content/uploads/2012/08/ABFO-Dec-Tree-2-17-2014-2.pdf.

of suspects. In addition to the photographs being adequately exposed, of high resolution, uncompressed (the photos need to be RAW and/or TIFF images), and sharply focused, forensic photographers capturing images of bite-mark injuries must consider the following:

1) Orientation, medium close-up, and close-up images depicting the general site on the body, plus details of the specific site and components of the bitemark caused by various teeth.
2) Images must be perfectly perpendicular to the plane of the skin on which the bitemark is located to avoid perspective distortion of the pattern of the injury when it is depicted in two dimensions. The long axis of the camera lens must be perpendicular to this plane. Another way to think of this is that the camera back, and therefore its digital sensor, must be in precisely the same plane as the bite-mark injury.
3) A reference scale of known size must be present in the image so that accurate measurements within the image are possible. Forensic odontologists developed the ABFO No. 2 Reference Scale for this purpose and now it is also widely used by other forensic sciences to photograph evidence. This reference scale has several important features: (1) 18 percent grey-scale for exposure adjustment; (2) three circles that allow the forensic photographer to determine if the camera was exactly perpendicular to the scale; and (3) millimetre rulers on two axes that allow accurate enlargement to life-size or twice life-size of the bitemark during analysis. Please see Figures 17.3 and 17.4, opposite.

b) Suspects with Access and Opportunity

An important consideration by the odontologist is the number of persons that had access and opportunity to cause the injury (or injuries) to the victim. The odontologist must answer the question, "Is the population open or closed?" In other words, is the population of potential suspects that could have caused this injury undefined and thus open to include all persons? Or, alternatively, are the potential suspects defined by a relatively small number of persons that had access to the victim? For example, a child victim's mother, father, grandmother, and babysitter form a defined population of suspects. Because of the absence of scientific data to support the supposition that exists that the pattern of each person's dentition is unique in the world, forensic odontologists should not attempt to identify one individual to the exclusion of all other persons in an undefined population. In a defined population of suspects, opportunities

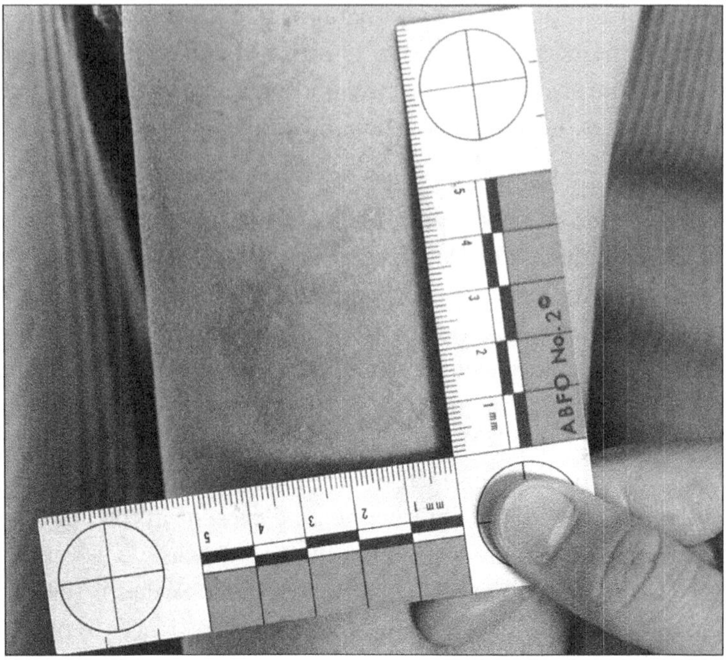

FIGURES 17.3 AND 17.4. The ABFO No. 2 Reference Scale. Above is an example of a human bite-mark reference scale near the patterned injury, where the camera is not exactly perpendicular to scale. Below is an example of a human bite-mark reference scale where the camera is perpendicular to scale.

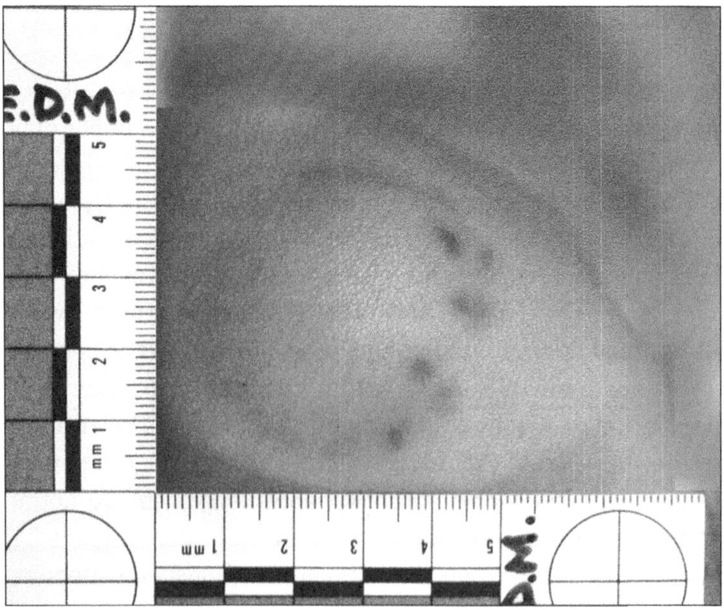

exist for more confidence in bite-mark conclusions because it is possible to exclude certain suspects that could not have caused the injury (e.g., the tooth that caused a mark is not present in the suspect's mouth), potentially only leaving one person in the set of suspects that could have caused the injury. In short, bite-mark evidence must be considered in the context of the population relevant to the specific circumstances of the case and the odontologist's conclusions are limited by the relevant population of the case.

c) Avoiding Bias in Comparisons

It is of paramount importance that the odontologist attempt to avoid confirmation bias from police investigators. Investigators often obtain a large amount of evidence implicating a particular suspect as the perpetrator of a crime. This is done —and conclusions with respect to the suspect's suitability as the perpetrator are made—prior to police requesting the odontologist to compare the suspect's teeth to the photographs of a bitemark. From the police officer's point of view, the odontologist is confirming a long list of other evidence that points to the suspect; therefore, unfortunately, police can intentionally or unintentionally influence the bite-mark expert through discussions that release their pre-existing conclusions.

One way to neutralize this bias is for the odontologist to request that the police place the suspect's dental casts in a sequential series (e.g., five to six sets of upper and lower dental casts) that include foils not associated with the case. Alternatively, the dental casts of each person with access or opportunity in a defined population can be provided for the purpose of including or excluding these persons based on their dentition. For a sequential series, the police would have to keep a master list of the persons who contributed casts and mark the sets of upper and lower casts with a number or letter, rather than using a contributor's name, so that the odontologist will not know which of the casts are from the suspect in question. Blind tests like this can effectively remove bias from the odontologist's findings.

Another important consideration for the odontologist is external validation of her conclusions. Following the comparison of the photographic images from the bitemark to the series of dental casts and the development of final conclusions, the ABFO recommends that the odontologist then hand off all of the evidence that was used to reach his conclusions to another odontologist with the same skill, training, and experience. The second odontologist is asked to complete her comprehensive examination and comparison as well, and to reach her own conclusions to independently verify or reject the conclusions by the first expert.[23]

d) Analysis Methods

Human and animal bites are considered to be examples of forensic physical evidence that is similar to ballistics, toolmarks, fingerprints, and shoe and tire impressions. Gross, class, and accidental characteristics of hard objects (e.g., tools) that cause the marks (impressions) on substrates are compared to individuate the origin of the marks. Dynamic striations and static impressions can be found in bitemarks just like they can be found in other toolmark or impression evidence and, as a result, odontologists use similar analysis methods to compare suspect tools (i.e., traits depicted on a suspect's dental casts) to photographs of impressions (bite injuries).

The pattern of the biting edges of the suspect's front teeth is captured and compared to the marks comprising the injury on the victim's skin. Due to the presumption of innocence, most odontologists approach a case by first attempting to exclude the dental casts as the cause of the bitemarks. If a person's teeth cannot be excluded, then an interpretation of the relative rarity of the dental traits is estimated by the odontologist based on his knowledge and experience. From this estimation, the odontologist attempts to establish a level of confidence in the conclusion that these dental casts represent the person's teeth that are the cause of this bitemark.

The biting edges of the teeth can be transferred from the actual dental casts to a clear sheet of acetate. This is a life-sized representation of the pattern of the bite that would be caused by these dental casts. Using the reference scale depicted within the evidentiary photos of the bitemark, it is possible to enlarge the image to life-size to enable a direct physical comparison of the pattern on the acetate to the enlarged photo of the bitemark. The image of the reference scale depicted on the acetate overlay and the image of the reference scale depicted in the life-sized photograph can be compared to assure the two are enlarged accurately to the same degree. The odontologist reverses the acetate and then superimposes it over the bite photograph in order to view the pattern of the suspect's teeth from the same vantage point that the biter would approach the skin of the victim.

---

23 ABFO Guidelines 2015, above note 11.

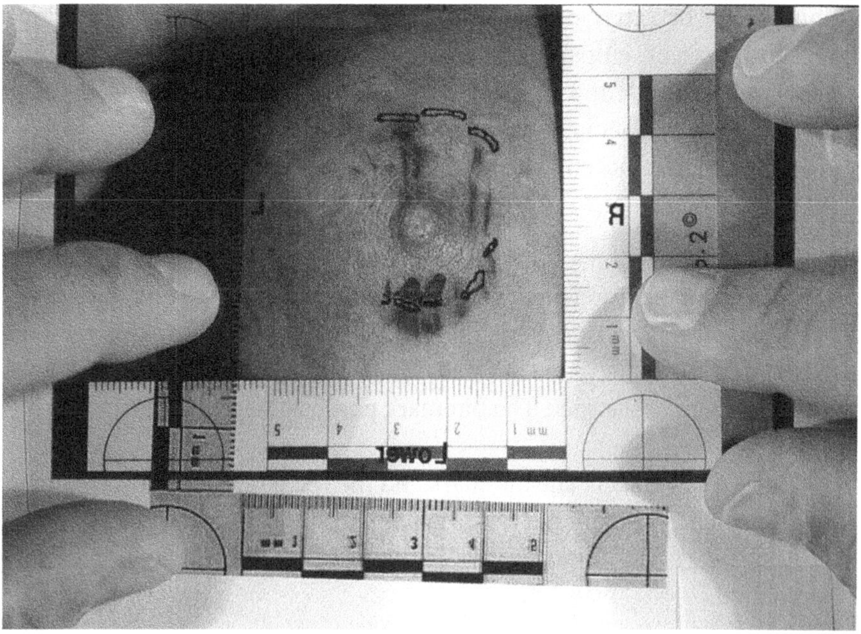

FIGURE 17.5. Comparison of a transparent acetate overlay depicting biting edges of the front teeth to a bitemark on skin.

Typically, the odontologist prints the acetate transparencies from the computer and conducts the physical comparison of it to the photographs by hand.[24] More recently, methods have been developed to conduct this comparison within a computer using high-resolution images and then printing the final images to illustrate the conclusions.[25]

e) Conclusions

No minimum number of matching comparison points exists for the odontologist to establish identification in bite-mark cases. Instead, each odontologist conducts an analysis to recognize and record the concordant traits and characteristics between the dental exemplars of the suspect and the bitemark. The identification threshold is based on the expert's experience and her associated knowledge of the incidence, frequency, or occurrence of the traits being compared. Given the expert's knowledge of the relative

24 D.J. Sweet, M. Parhar, & R.E. Wood, "Computer-based Production of Bite Mark Comparison Overlays" (1998) 43 *Journal of Forensic Science* 1050 [Sweet, Parhar, & Wood].

25 Raymond J. Johansen & C. Michael Bowers, *Digital Analysis of Bite Mark Evidence Using Adobe Photoshop*, 2d ed. (Santa Barbara. CA: Forensic Imaging Services, 2000).

commonality or rarity of characteristics like tooth positions, rotations, interdental spaces, chips, fractures, wear, and many other acquired traits categorized as accidental (i.e., acquired) dental characteristics, a degree of confidence in the conclusion is determined.

There are five potential conclusions available in bite-mark physical comparison cases:

1) *The biter*: The bitemark originates from this person's teeth. There are no irreconcilable discrepancies present between the injury and the teeth.
2) *The probable biter*: The bitemark most likely originates from this person's teeth.
3) *Not excluded as the biter*: The bitemark possibly originated from this person's teeth.
4) *Excluded as the biter*: The bitemark and the teeth of the person are inconsistent. The bitemark did not originate from this person's teeth.
5) *Inconclusive*: Based on the available evidence, no conclusion can be reached.[26]

It is important to note that no statistical inferences about the above potential conclusions can be expressed because, similar to person identification cases, the individuality or uniqueness of most comparison traits in bitemarks has not been established. The incidence of some traits that are found in the dental pattern are known, such as the frequency of occurrence for a congenitally misshapen lateral incisor (e.g., a peg-shaped lateral), but much research is underway to attempt to draw inferences from the incidence of other traits. Identification conclusions are customarily established using large numbers of matching characteristics that develop and occur independently from each other. This includes examples such as spaces between the front teeth; slight, moderate, or severe rotations from the tooth's normal position; longer or shorter teeth from wear, fracture, or growth; and changes to the tooth's crown from customized fillings, veneers, or prosthetic crowns. This large dataset and the expert's knowledge of how often these typically occur in a given population of patients are considerations that the forensic odontologist must use in reaching an opinion; however, it is important for lawyers to understand the limits of the conclusions presented by the testifying odontologist.

26 ABFO Guidelines 2015, above note 11.

3) The Evolution of Bite-Mark Identification

Changes and improvements to the bite-mark aspects of forensic odontology fall into two main categories: (1) the evolution of comparison methods; and (2) the presentation of demonstrative evidence at trial.

Odontologists have continued to search for comparison methods that allow them to visualize what is happening at the biting edge of the front teeth when these edges interact with a substrate during the application of force. Originally, dentists took the casts of a suspect's teeth and superimposed them in real time over the actual bitemark to attempt to assess the interaction and to compare the two patterns to assess the degree of match. However, it is very difficult—if not impossible—to see the biting edges of all front teeth during this interaction because the cast is in the way; the odontologist's vision is obstructed. Initially, odontologists solved this by applying ink to the teeth on the casts and then pressing them to a non-bitten area of skin to assess the mark left there compared to the injury near it. Use of this "test bite" was beneficial because it allowed the odontologist to see if they could reproduce the marks seen in the bite through manipulation of the casts in different directions and with more or less pressure applied. Subsequently, odontologists pressed un-inked dental casts to a wafer of wax so that depressions from the biting edges were recorded in the surface. The pattern of these depressions could then be assessed for similarity to the bitemark on soft skin.

Eventually, the expert's approach to comparison evolved to a point where only the pattern of the teeth was the investigative focus because of the realization of the importance of the different positions and different shapes of the biting edges, in combination with the variety of teeth present at the front of a suspect's mouth (central incisors, lateral incisors, canines, premolars). The depressions and/or the amount of force were still significant, but were no longer the focus of the expert's approach. Rather, the positions, shapes, sizes, and relative contours of the pattern became paramount.

A technique called *hollow volume overlays* to transfer the contours of the teeth on to a transparent acetate sheet was developed to visualize the comparisons; because the overlays were drawn by hand, the technique has since become outdated and is no longer used. The technique involves a number of steps. The upper and lower dental casts are placed with the biting edges in contact with the platen of a photocopier and an image is produced. The paper output with the image is turned over on a light source and the teeth are traced by hand with a fine pen on the backside of the paper to produce an outline of the biting edges. Then, a sheet of clear acetate is fed into the photocopier and the traced contours of the teeth are transferred from the paper to the acetate to produce a transparent comparison overlay.[27]

Because the tooth contours were traced by hand, the accuracy of this method was worrisome. Thus, subsequently, a method to digitize the tooth contours using a flatbed scanner, and a computer application to produce the transparent overlay, was developed and implemented.[28] This method, called digital transparent overlays, became widely accepted for its accuracy. Use of Adobe Photoshop® is now the standard within the discipline, not only for producing transparent overlays for physical comparison, but also to enable digital comparison of the suspect's teeth to the bite-mark photographs.[29]

Odontologists testifying at trial have used a variety of methods to illustrate the active process of comparing a suspect's dentition to photographs of a bitemark using transparent overlays. Some methods, such as PowerPoint presentations or booklets of still photographs with superimposed transparent overlays, have proven beneficial to depict the degree and extent of concordance between the patterns of the teeth and the bitemark impression. However, movement of the teeth over the wounds to illustrate the dynamics of biting behaviour (e.g., striations, scratches, and/or abrasions) is not possible with these methods. Recently, odontologists have chosen to show video clips to illustrate this movement or they have demonstrated the movement using real-time overhead projection while they demonstrate the dynamic interaction between the teeth depicted on the overlay and the impression depicted in the photographs. Courtrooms that are equipped with computer monitors have enabled such demonstrations, if the technology is supported locally.

---

27 J.C. Dailey, "Practical Technique for Fabrication of Transparent Bite Mark Overlays" (1991) 36 *Journal of Forensic Science* 565.

28 Sweet, Parhar, & Wood, above note 24.

29 Johansen & Bowers, above note 25.

4) The Role of the Forensic Odontologist in Criminal Cases Involving Bite-Mark Evidence

a) The Law Enforcement's Use of the Forensic Odontologist

In the majority of cases, the forensic odontologist plays a role for the police investigators and, subsequently, for the prosecution at trial. Forensic identification specialists from the police agency at the crime scene or forensic pathologists at autopsy recognize or suspect that an injury on a person's body could be a bitemark and then request the involvement of an odontologist.

The odontologist reviews the case and offers advice about the injury's evidentiary value, the level of conclusion that can be reached, and what best-practice options exist. The police officers and the forensic pathologist may have little or no prior experience with bitemarks and so, generally speaking, they are unfamiliar with the proper collection and handling of this evidence from the scene and from the victim's body. Additionally, later, if police identify a prime suspect, they will be unfamiliar in seizing dental exemplars from the suspect for comparison purposes. In these cases, the odontologist must be proactive to instruct the police about the standards and guidelines that exist to collect, handle, preserve, and transfer such evidence. Importantly, any problems leading to a loss of quality with the bite-mark evidence will result in subsequent reduction in the potential for high-level conclusions to be reached from any comparisons. Similarly, it is important for the odontologist to recommend that any patterned injury that does not meet certain minimum threshold criteria not be taken forward for evaluation and comparison to the suspect's teeth. These criteria have been described earlier in this chapter.

Early in the case, the odontologist instructs the police about what photographic evidence is needed for analysis. Then, the police expose numerous photos with available, flash, and alternative light sources. Additional follow-up photographs are exposed each day over a period of forty-eight to seventy-two hours to record the various developmental stages of bruises that occur. This is particularly true for a living victim with an active healing response, but it is also necessary for a deceased victim since changes to the skin's surface and colour also occur in injuries in the absence of a healing response. High-resolution RAW and TIFF images should be taken of the site(s) and, as described previously, each image must be well-exposed and sharply focused, while also including a reference scale for measurement and enlargement purposes.

It is important for the odontologist who is working with the police to keep in mind that he is an independent expert searching for the truth and is not working on behalf of the police to assist in obtaining a conviction. At the time of comparison of the suspect's dental casts to the injuries, a recommended best-practice approach is for the odontologist to assume that the suspect is innocent and, in doing so, attempt to exclude the suspect's teeth as the cause of the injuries. Exclusion is a conclusion that is reached with certainty. If the odontologist cannot exclude a given suspect, then she must determine her level of confidence[30] with respect to how certain she is that a suspect must be included as the cause of the bitemark. This is where the available conclusions listed above are used to express a degree of certainty that ranges from high (positive identification) to low (possible identification).

b) The Prosecution's Use of the Forensic Odontologist

If charges against the suspect are brought and the odontologist is called to give evidence at trial, then his role is to assist in the presentation of his conclusions in the clearest, most understandable way. The odontologist should continue to be mindful that he is acting independently as a subject matter expert and is not concerned with the outcome of the case or the final verdict. The odontologist should attempt to reduce or eliminate confusion and potential misunderstandings related to terminology. Clear, concise definitions should be provided not only at the time of report writing, but also (especially) when giving evidence at trial.

The expert called by the prosecution should be even-tempered and should faithfully answer questions that are presented to inform the trier of fact. However, conclusions are necessarily subjective and establishing certainty is complex and often problematic. Any injuries on soft, distortable, and elastic skin are fraught with interpretative risks. It must be kept in mind that there are self-imposed limitations from the discipline on what can be determined from this evidence.[31] Prosecution experts must be cautious in establishing a positive identification relying on a particular set of teeth as the cause of a bitemark, especially in open, undefined suspect pools. In the absence of statistical inferences available to other forensic disciplines, odontologists rely only on subjective opinions.

---

30 Conclusions of certainty for bite-mark cases are not yet drawn on statistical inference. Statistics are not used in any calculations.

31 ABFO Guidelines 2015, above note 11.

c) The Defence's Use of the Forensic Odontologist

The role of the dental expert called by the defence includes being familiar with the discipline's guidelines and standards as well as assessing if these guidelines and standards were followed by the expert called by the prosecution. The expert called by the defence will provide her opinion on whether the conclusions generated by the expert called by the prosecution use accepted and current methods and techniques.

Today, much to the chagrin of the trier of fact, there is often a very large amount of information that comes forward from defence lawyers about the minutiae of a case, with the focus on materials used, the labelling of exhibits, evidence continuity, and so on. Due to a focus on these details, some lawyers fail to ask the defence expert's opinion about whether these details could have altered the potential outcome of the bite-mark analysis or could have played a role in changing the conclusions that were reached by the expert called by the prosecution. It must be remembered both by experts called by the defence and the prosecution that the roles played by each involves a search for truth. If the final conclusion about any potential bite-mark linkage between the complainant and the accused is the same on both sides, then this should be the focus of the comments made by the expert called by defence counsel, as opposed to focusing on comments about minutiae, for example, if JPEG images were used instead of TIFF images, or if a hard copy of a computer overlay was used instead of a digital comparison using a computer. These details have been the focus of recent bite-mark cases in Canada.[32]

With the assistance of the expert called by the defence, defence counsel should focus on issues with the acceptability of the methods employed; that is, if they are generally accepted methods. Are the methods used reliable and scientifically valid?[33] Do they have sufficient *sensitivity* to avoid false negatives (i.e., to avoid false exclusions of suspects) and do they have sufficient *specificity* to avoid false positives (i.e., to avoid false identifications)? Reliability is an important issue to address when cross-examining the expert about his conclusions. Would the dentist reach the same conclusion if he looked at the same evidence again some time later after a suitable washout period? Importantly, would another dentist with the same skills, knowledge, training, and experience, who evaluates the exact

---

32 *R. v. Kines*, 2012 MBCA 97 [*Kines*].

33 *Validity and Reliability of Measurements*, University of Ottawa, online: www.med.uottawa.ca/sim/data/Measurement_validity.htm.

same evidence, reach the same conclusion? Were the conclusions in this case externally validated through an independent verification process?

5) The Significance of the Bite-Mark Expert at Trial

As with testimony in cases of person identification using dental records, the odontologist must be qualified as an expert by the court based on her skills, knowledge, training, and experience to proffer bite-mark opinion evidence. In bite-mark cases, these are highly specialized skills and knowledge and so the courts must keep the complex nature of bite-mark cases in mind during a potential expert's *voir dire* for qualification. A general dentist can be allowed to give opinion evidence about a dental identification because the skills are those of a general dentist; however, a general dentist often does not have sufficient skills and training to adequately and appropriately deal with bite-mark cases, especially with respect to comprehensive knowledge that can assist the court about skin, injuries, and toolmark evidence.

The expert who is allowed to give evidence about bite injuries and the cause of these injuries can answer questions about which aspects of the injury are caused by upper, lower, right, and left teeth, as well as which classes of teeth (e.g., incisors, canines) caused certain injuries, how many teeth are represented within a given bitemark, and other related interpretations. From this, the odontologist can indicate if these teeth were present in the accused's mouth at the time of the offence and if the shapes, sizes, and overall pattern of the teeth are the same as or similar to the bitemark.

Of extreme importance is if any distortion is present in the photographic depiction of the injuries or in the dental exemplars. From any distortion that might be present, do any discrepancies exist between the two patterns when they are superimposed? If discrepancies exist between the patterns, then are these explainable? Reasonable explanations include disparities that arise through movement of the teeth or skin at the time of injury, skin elasticity and/or the contours of the skin's surface, and any perspective distortion that is present in the photographs of the injury. Despite such discrepancies, the accused's teeth may still be the cause of the injury. Defence lawyers should ascertain if the expert has made any errors that could compound to result in an incorrect conclusion. Most significant is the degree of confidence that the expert assigns to her conclusion. Given that distortion is present and discrepancies between the two patterns exist, how certain is the expert that the accused's teeth are the actual cause of the bitemark?

The odontologist is not typically able to answer questions about the timing of a bitemark. The skin goes through changes from healing in a living victim that commence almost immediately (redness and possible bleeding), leading to bruising with associated changes in colour over time and changes in contour through swelling. There are also changes to the skin at an injury site in a deceased person, although the changes are not as dramatic or rapid. It is generally beyond the odontologist's scope of practice and expertise to answer questions about the timing of a bite from only an assessment of its appearance and, in particular, in relation to the time of death.

Similarly, the odontologist is typically unable to answer questions about the amount of force that is needed to cause a certain degree of injury. Such questions are more within the expertise of the forensic pathologist. However, the odontologist is able to formulate an opinion about the status of a suspect's dental health and if the teeth and supporting tissues for the teeth (gums, bones of the jaw below the gums, etc.) are sufficiently strong for a particular suspect to generate the needed forces to cause a given injury.[34]

6) Reviewing the Record and Full Disclosure in Cases Involving Bite-Mark Evidence

As with disclosure for person identification casework, in all bite-mark identification cases, the forensic dentist keeps detailed notes about his requested involvement, what specifically was requested, case management details, what was completed, who was present, methods used, data observed and recorded, what conclusions were reached, and so on. Notes and records from telephone, email threads, and other conversations are retained, and at the time of disclosure, all of these materials, notes, documents, and records must be disclosed. Demonstrative evidence that is planned for use in court to illustrate methods and conclusions is also disclosed.

If an expert has been retained by the defence, then disclosure of the suspect's dental casts and the bite-mark photographs will be disclosed through the Crown because it is important for the expert called by the defence to

34 At the time of seizing (with a warrant) the dental exemplars from the suspect, a dentist will have assessed the periodontal status of the teeth and their supporting structures.

examine the same specific key materials that were used by the expert called by the prosecution to reach her conclusions.

There are no standards or guidelines that have been agreed upon by practising forensic odontologists in Canada, so most active odontologists follow the standards and guidelines for bite-mark evidence set out by the American Board of Forensic Odontology.[35]

D. CONCLUSION

This chapter describes the use of forensic odontology evidence in Canada, including for cases of person identification through dental records and bite-mark identification. Many Canadian dentists from private practice and universities have contributed to forensic odontology casework since the 1970s. Certification as a specialist in forensic odontology has been allowed in many countries; however, the Royal College of Dentists of Canada has not recognized this discipline. Therefore, a handful of forensic dentists in Canada have sought board certification by the American Board of Forensic Odontology in the United States; these specialists work and mentor others in Canada.

Two postgraduate training programs exist at universities in Vancouver and Montreal, but there are no academic or professional societies to support the specialty, and no funding is available for research and development, so progress has been slow. There is a relatively strong literature base and gradual improvements are being made; additionally, there is renewed interest in forensic odontology among younger dentists, bringing promise to the future development of the discipline in Canada.[36]

E. LEGAL CONTEXT

On 17 September 1949, in Toronto, the S.S. *Noronic* was engulfed in a fire that spread suddenly and quickly, killing 118 of its over-700 passengers. The intensity of the fire meant that dental records would be the only way to identify the victims. This tragedy marked the first significant application of dental identification to mass disasters in Canadian history. Forensic

35 ABFO Resources, online: www.abfo.org/resources.

36 Michael S. Pollanen et al., eds., "Forensic Science in Canada: A Report of Multidisciplinary Discussion" (4–5 May 2012), online: Centre for Forensic Science & Medicine at the University of Toronto www.forensics.utoronto.ca/Assets/LMPF+Digital+Assets/Forensic+Science+in+Canada.pdf [Hart House Report].

odontology literature addressing mass disaster identification procedures followed shortly thereafter.[37]

Today, forensic odontology is typically used to: (1) identify skeletonized, decomposed, burnt, or fragmented human remains, where visual identification or identification through fingerprints and DNA is not possible;[38] (2) determine whether a mark in question is a bite and, if so, whether the bite is animal or human;[39] and (3) identify or exclude a person as causing the bite in question. In general, the application of forensic odontology can be divided into two broad categories: person identification and bite-mark analysis. This information can be applied to a wide range of cases, including those involving missing or unidentified persons, murders, mass disasters, family abuse or neglect,[40] and sexual violence.

In contrast to person identification, the interpretations arising from analyzing bitemarks—seen most frequently in homicide, sexual assault, and child abuse cases—remain controversial and bite-mark analysis has been subject to recent criticism over its value and scientific validity, despite its recognized ability in sometimes reliably excluding suspects.[41] The accuracy of bite-mark analysis results may be limited by the changing features of the bitemark on skin over time (attributed to skin elasticity, surface unevenness, swelling, and healing), as well as practical problems, including photographic distortion and changes over time in a suspect's dentition.[42] On a more fundamental level, science has not established that human dentition is unique.[43] In 2009, the National Academy of Sciences (NAS) in the United States released a report that highlighted the problems and potential for bias that follows forensic odontology, specifically bite-mark analysis, as an experience-based forensic method:

> There is no science on the reproducibility of the different methods of analysis that lead to conclusions about the probability of a match. This includes reproducibility between experts and with the same expert over time. Even when using the guidelines, different experts provide widely

37 Summarized from George E. Burgman, "A History of Forensic Odontology in Canada" (1987) 8 *American Journal of Forensic Medicine and Pathology* 39.

38 Forensic odontology was, for example, used to identify the victim described in *R. v. Pilotte*, [2002] O.J. No. 866 at para. 72 (CA).

39 See the below discussion of the Louise Reynolds case.

40 See, for example, *R. v. Turner*, [1995] N.B.J. No. 333 (Q.B.).

41 2009 NAS Report, above note 16 at 173–76.

42 *Ibid.* at 173–74.

43 *Ibid.* at 175.

> differing results and a high percentage of false positive matches of bite marks using controlled comparison studies.
>
> No thorough study has been conducted of large populations to establish the uniqueness of bite marks; theoretical studies promoting the uniqueness theory include more teeth than are seen in most bite marks submitted for comparison. There is no central repository of bite marks and patterns. Most comparisons are made between the bite mark and dental casts of an individual or individuals of interest. Rarely are comparisons made between the bite mark and a number of models from other individuals in addition to those of the individual in question. If a bite mark is compared to a dental cast using the guidelines of the ABFO, and the suspect providing the dental cast cannot be eliminated as a person who could have made the bite, there is no established science indicating what percentage of the population or subgroup of the population could also have produced the bite.[44]

In 2015, the assistant director of the White House Office of Science and Technology Policy, Jo Handelsman, called for bite-mark evidence to be "eradicated from forensic science."[45] The Innocence Project in New York characterized Handelsman's statements as "unprecedented."[46] These recent developments hark back to previous injustices taken on by the Innocence Project, specifically the case of Kennedy Brewer, who was convicted in 1995 of murdering a three-year-old girl on the strength of the questionable bite-mark evidence presented at trial. He was sentenced to death but, in 2001, post-conviction DNA testing excluded Brewer and implicated one of the original suspects in the crime. Brewer was exonerated on 15 February 2008.[47] Several forensic odontologists[48] working with the Innocence Project post-conviction determined that the original odontologist called by the prosecution had made grave errors of interpretation.[49] More recently, in 2016, the Texas Forensic Science Commission recommended that bite-mark identification evidence should not be admitted in criminal trials.[50]

---

44 *Ibid.* at 174.

45 Radley Balko, "A High-Ranking Obama Official Just Called For the 'Eradication' of Bite Mark Evidence" (22 July 2015), online: The Washington Post http://wpo.st/2_AE1.

46 *Ibid.*

47 The National Registry of Exonerations, "Kennedy Brewer" (11 August 2015), online: www.law.umich.edu/special/exoneration/Pages/casedetail.aspx?caseid=3047.

48 Drs. David Senn, Iain Pretty, and David Sweet.

49 Caitlin Pakosh's correspondence with Dr. David Sweet (August 2015).

50 Erik Eckholm, "Texas Panel Calls for an End to Criminal IDs via Bite Mark" (12 February 2016), online: The New York Times http://nyti.ms/1R12tnG.

In the Canadian context, *Forensic Science in Canada: A Report of Multidisciplinary Discussion* (colloquially referred to as the "Hart House Report") identified three problems relating to bite-mark cases arising from Ontario: police personnel sometimes offered opinions about bite-mark identification; unapproved forensic dentists undertook bite-mark examinations; and approved forensic dentists feared civil litigation, particularly in cases involving living victims, making them reluctant to offer an opinion.[51] Although this report has recognized the frailties of bite-mark identification evidence, it has not gone nearly as far as its American counterparts, but the reason for this is clear: the committee writing the Hart House Report did not view it as within its expertise to direct how its observations should be used by criminal justice system stakeholders, including the courts.[52]

Although the value of bite-mark analysis for *identification* purposes has been sharply called into question recently, bite-mark analysis may be of value as an *exclusionary* tool, if done correctly and if conducted in an investigative environment that is considerate of all possibilities. Like other types of impression evidence (e.g., fingerprints, toolmarks, firearms identification), bite-mark analysis evidence is expert *opinion* evidence and must be considered on the totality of the evidence before the court. To provide a balanced perspective of the controversy over bite-mark analysis, this section will explore a variety of Canadian cases.

1) Determining if the Mark Is a Bite

The initial determination any forensic odontologist must make in a case involves concluding whether the injury under review has indeed been caused by teeth and, if so, concluding whether the bite is human or non-human.

The infamous murder of Gail Miller in Saskatoon in 1969, for which David Milgaard was wrongly convicted (and for which he subsequently spent twenty-three years in prison)[53] was finally solved with the help of DNA evidence—the true perpetrator, Larry Fisher, was convicted for Miller's murder on 22 November 1999.[54] An often-forgotten detail of the

---

51 Hart House Report, above note 36 at 34.

52 *Ibid.* at 10.

53 Sarah Harland-Logan, "Historical Cases: David Milgaard," online: Innocence Canada www.aidwyc.org/cases/historical/david-milgaard.

54 Saskatchewan, Commission of Inquiry into the Wrongful Conviction of David Milgaard, *Report* by Edward P. MacCallum, Commissioner (Saskatoon: Commission of Inquiry into the Wrongful Conviction of David Milgaard, 2008) Appendix A: Master Chronology of Events at 884, online: www.justice.gov.sk.ca/milgaard/DMfinal.shtml.

case is that the Featherstone Project, initiated on 29 July 1997 (four days after Fisher's arrest for the murder), sought to assist the attorney general in its prosecution by following up on a number of tasks, including the preparation of a brief which, in part, consisted of a dental impression warrant and a *Criminal Code* warrant for Fisher's dental records; dental impressions were obtained from Fisher.[55] Although an expert called by the Crown, Dr. David Sweet, identified a previously undetected, probable human bitemark, the autopsy photos reviewed to reach this conclusion were not suitable for comparison to Fisher's dentition.[56] The opinion of a dental expert called by the defence concluded that the lacking class and individual characteristics of the mark, as well as a small intercanine measurement (less than normal for an adult white male and less than Fisher's measurement specifically) indicated that it was not a bitemark. Ultimately, the inculpatory DNA results were admitted while the contradictory bite-mark evidence was not.[57]

Devastating consequences may flow from incorrect conclusions that a mark is or is not representative of a bite, particularly if such an incorrect determination is supported by flawed forensic pathology evidence. The case of Louise Reynolds is an example of a case where forensic pathology and odontology evidence *incorrectly* excluded dog bites as the cause of injury. In 1997, Louise Reynolds was charged with killing her seven-year-old daughter, Sharon, on the basis of forensic pathology and forensic odontology opinions that concluded Sharon's injuries represented "more than eighty stab wounds to her body made by a knife or a pair of scissors,"[58] not dog bites. This finding was made despite the smell of animal urine and feces being present in Reynolds's basement, where Sharon's body was discovered.[59]

The family's small dog was found in the same basement at the time and subsequent police investigation determined that a neighbour's pit bull was also in the basement on the day of Sharon's death.[60] It was determined

55 RCMP, "Update 98-02-05 Briefing Note, Re: Miller Task Force," online: www.justice.gov.sk.ca/milgaard/pubdocs/11282005/Rick%20Pearson/082069.pdf.

56 *R. v. Fisher*, 1999 SKQB 88 at para. 32.

57 Robert B.J. Dorion, *Bitemark Evidence: A Color Atlas and Text*, 2d ed. (Boca Raton: CRC Press, 2011) at 272–73.

58 *Reynolds v. Kingston (City) Police Services Board*, 2007 ONCA 166 at para. 2 [*Reynolds* civil suit].

59 Inquiry into Pediatric Forensic Pathology in Ontario, *Report* by Stephen T. Goudge, Commissioner (Toronto: Inquiry into Pediatric Forensic Pathology in Ontario, 2008) vol. 2 at 22, online: www.attorneygeneral.jus.gov.on.ca/inquiries/goudge/report/v2_en_pdf/V2_Eng_2.pdf.

60 *Ibid.*

that, on the night of Sharon's death, the pit bull had a red substance on its chest and paws, blood was present on its collar and hair, and blonde hairs may have been present in its feces in the days after Sharon's death. The dog was euthanized and its head was destroyed in 1997 for an unrelated biting incident.[61]

Reynolds was charged on the strength of the assertion of the forensic pathologist, Dr. Charles Smith, that the wounds did not represent dog bites. In response to the defence argument and a coroner's recommendation, the Crown obtained the opinion of a forensic odontologist, Dr. Robert Wood, who concluded in his 1998 consultation report that the wounds were "without equivocation" not representative of dog bites.[62] The forensic odontologist retained by the defence, Dr. Robert Dorion, completely contradicted Dr. Wood's report. Dr. Dorion reported that there were over twenty bitemarks on Sharon's body and that these marks were most likely caused by a dog.[63]

At Reynolds's preliminary hearing, Dr. Wood did not testify,[64] but Dr. Smith did and he again dismissed the idea that the wounds were caused by a dog, stating: "As absurd as it is to think that a polar bear attacked Sharon, so is it equally absurd that it's a dog wound."[65] Dr. Smith, whose name is today synonymous with a number of wrongful convictions, overstated his expertise in bite-mark analysis, stating to the court:

> I've seen dog wounds, I've seen coyote wounds, I've seen wolf wounds. I recently went to the archipelago of islands owned by another country up near the North Pole and had occasion to study osteology and look at patterns of wounding from polar bears.[66]

At the end of the preliminary hearing, Reynolds was committed to stand trial for second-degree murder.[67] In 1999, Dr. Cairns and Dr. Young of the Office of the Chief Coroner for Ontario attended a meeting of the American Academy of Forensic Sciences, where they learned that four prominent experts (including Dr. Dorion) were concerned that the Reynolds case may represent a miscarriage of justice. The experts believed a

---

61 *Ibid.*
62 *Ibid.* at 23.
63 *Ibid.*
64 *Ibid.*
65 *Ibid.* at 26.
66 *Ibid.* at 181.
67 *Ibid.* at 23.

dog killed Sharon. Although both Dr. Smith and Dr. Wood continued to assert that the wounds were not dog bites, it was agreed that Sharon's body would be exhumed for a second autopsy to rule out the possibility once and for all.[68]

A second autopsy after exhumation resulted in conflicting expert opinions, but all agreed that most, if not all, of Sharon's injuries were caused by dog bites, contrary to Dr. Smith's preliminary hearing evidence.[69] The false charges against Reynolds were then dropped, after she spent two years in pre-trial custody. Reynolds then launched a civil suit against the City of Kingston Police Services Board, six police officers, Dr. Smith, and the forensic odontologist.[70] Dr. Smith was stripped of his medical license in February 2011. On 14 March 2011, it was reported that Reynolds had accepted a settlement of a confidential amount.[71]

2) Admitting and Relying Upon Human Bite-Mark Evidence

Considering the complexity, controversy, and miscarriages of justice attributed to bite-mark analyses, it may be difficult for trial judges to avoid venturing into weighing related expert evidence when considering the admissibility of bite-mark analyses in the context of a jury trial. For example, in *R. v. Kines*,[72] the Crown sought to appeal the trial judge's acquittal of the accused, after a motion for a directed verdict, for charges of first-degree murder, aggravated sexual assault, and sexual interference involving a three-year-old girl.[73] The Manitoba Court of Appeal summarized the testimony of the forensic odontologist as follows:

> The autopsy revealed that the cause of death was multiple blunt force injuries resulting from non-accidental trauma. The victim had a combination of lacerations, bruises and human bite marks all over her body. Her vagina had been torn and bite marks were found just above her vagina. A forensic odontologist testified that the accused had a "very highly unusual" dentition that lined up with most of the bite marks on the body.

---

68 *Ibid.* at 23–24.

69 *Ibid.* at 26.

70 *Reynolds* civil suit, above note 58.

71 Harold Levy, "Charles Smith; Compensation Up-Date; Part Two; Settlements To Date (And Related Issues); Louise Reynolds" (24 July 2011), *The Charles Smith Blog*, online: smithforensic.blogspot.ca/2011/07/charles-smith-compensation_24.html.

72 *Kines*, above note 32.

73 *Ibid.* at para. 1.

> He definitively excluded the other members of the household as being the biter for all but one bite mark. The expert testified that the accused was "most likely" the biter. He also said that he was "very confident" in his identification of the accused and explained that "probable" identification was as definite a designation as his discipline allowed, except in rare circumstances.[74]

The trial judge withdrew the case from the jury on the basis that the bite-mark identification evidence implicating the accused did not amount to proof beyond a reasonable doubt, holding that the identification was insufficient to support convicting the accused since it was only "probable," according to the expert.[75] The Court of Appeal set aside the acquittals put in place by the trial judge and ordered a new trial because the judge conflated the Crown's *evidentiary* burden on a directed verdict test with the Crown's burden of *proof* beyond a reasonable doubt.[76] The trial judge's failure to differentiate these burdens caused him to weigh evidence that properly fell within the jurisdiction of the jury.[77] The court agreed with the Crown's argument that the trial judge failed to consider the totality of the circumstantial evidence in this case and found that there was some evidence that the accused was the perpetrator.[78]

The admission of problematic expert testimony may negatively affect the result at trial and the fairness of the proceedings, but so too could failing to admit a credible forensic opinion significant to the case before the court. In the case of *R. v. J.A.A.*,[79] the defence sought to introduce forensic odontology evidence as fresh evidence after J.A.A.'s convictions for sexual assault and sexual assault with a weapon.[80] At trial, the central issue was whether the sexual relations between J.A.A. and his wife were consensual. At the time of the alleged confrontation, they were living in different areas of the same house and were in the process of separating.[81] The complainant

74 *Ibid.* at para. 3.

75 *Ibid.*

76 *Ibid.* at para. 7. The court cites *R. v. Fontaine*, 2004 SCC 27 at para. 11 to explain that, "'[The evidentiary burden] determines whether an issue should be left to the trier of fact,' while the burden of proof 'determines how the issue should be decided.' The first is for the judge; the second is for the jury."

77 *Ibid.* at para. 8.

78 *Ibid.* at para. 8. At para. 7, the case cited "some evidence" as the proper test for a directed verdict, as established in *R. v. Litchfield*, [1993] 4 S.C.R. 333 at 362.

79 *R. v. J.A.A.*, 2011 SCC 17 [*J.A.A.*].

80 *Ibid.* at para. 1.

81 *Ibid.* at para. 18.

had testified that, in the course of J.A.A. covering her mouth to prevent her from screaming, she bit his finger "as hard as [she] could."[82] The police officer responsible for interviewing J.A.A. after the alleged confrontation testified at trial that a cut on one of J.A.A.'s fingers looked like a bitemark. Although the defence did not object to the admission of the officer's statements, cross-examination addressed the officer's lack of expertise as well as the failure to consult with a dental mark expert.[83] J.A.A. denied that the complainant bit him and also denied sexually assaulting her, stating that the relations were consensual. The trial judge twice referred to the bitemark on J.A.A.'s finger when instructing himself, regarding it as corroborative evidence that proved useful in determining credibility.[84]

J.A.A. was ultimately convicted and appealed his conviction to the Ontario Court of Appeal, arguing, among other issues, that the trial judge erred in considering the bitemark as corroborative evidence of the complainant's testimony, considering the inadmissibility of the officer's lay opinion. J.A.A. also sought to introduce fresh evidence in the form of the opinion of a forensic dentist, Dr. Robert Wood, that the mark on the complainant was not a bitemark. Dr. Wood concluded that he would have expected J.A.A. to have a bitemark, given the complainant's testimony. Although it was argued that this new evidence undermined the judge's reasons as well as the verdict itself, the majority dismissed the appeal and rejected the application to introduce fresh evidence on the basis that Dr. Wood's evidence could not reasonably be expected to have affected the result at trial, even if it were believed.[85]

As of right, J.A.A. appealed to the Supreme Court of Canada, which allowed the fresh evidence application after analyzing whether this new evidence met the *Palmer* criteria for admission.[86] The case turned on

---

82 *Ibid.* at para. 28.

83 *Ibid.* at para. 2.

84 *Ibid.* at paras. 10–12.

85 *Ibid.* at paras. 4–5. See, generally, the Court of Appeal judgment, *R. v. J.A.A.*, 2010 ONCA 491.

86 *J.A.A.*, above note 79 at para. 7:

> The criteria for admissibility of fresh evidence, established in *Palmer v. The Queen*, [1980] 1 S.C.R. 759, are well known: (1) the evidence should generally not be admitted if, by due diligence, it could have been adduced at trial; (2) the evidence must be relevant in the sense that it bears upon a decisive or potentially decisive issue in the trial; (3) the evidence must be credible in the sense that it is reasonably capable of belief; and (4) it must be such that if believed it could reasonably, when taken with the other evidence adduced at trial, be expected to have affected the result.

whether the new evidence, if believed, could reasonably be expected to affect the result at trial when considered with the other evidence adduced at trial.[87] The court analyzed the significance of the fresh evidence and ordered a new trial:

> The fresh evidence now reveals that reliance on this evidence [of injury to J.A.A.'s finger] is misplaced. Dr. Wood's evidence, if accepted, not only vitiates one of the bases for the trial judge's reliance on the complainant's testimony and his rejection of the appellant's version of events, but it also arguably undermines the credibility of S.A.'s testimony that she bit down on J.A.A.'s finger "as hard as [she] could". While the officer was qualified to describe the injury he saw, his evidence arguably exceeded the proper boundaries of lay opinion evidence. As the appellant fairly concedes in his factum, "If the opinion stood unchallenged, the error may have been of little consequence." However, in light of Dr. Wood's direct refutation of the officer's opinion, "the prejudicial effect of its erroneous admission is brought into sharp focus" (A.F., at para. 43). It is not necessary to decide on this application to what extent the officer's testimony may have been inadmissible. For our purposes, it suffices to say that it appears to have been clearly wrong. Thus, the trial judge's reliance on this item of evidence is of much concern.[88]

The introduction of bite-mark evidence at trial by a police officer in the case of *J.A.A.* is a lesson in ensuring that the court must only admit expert opinion evidence from a properly qualified expert[89] and, if no such expert is produced, then the court should refrain from making findings that properly lie within the scope of a forensic odontologist's expertise.[90] Similarly, in *R. v. Chirimar*,[91] a case of long-term domestic violence, Trotter J. stated in footnote 1 of his judgment that he had observed the photos

---

This case turned on criterion #4 since the defence conceded criterion #1 could not be met, while the Crown conceded that criteria #2 and #3 were met.

87 This represents the fourth criterion for the admission of fresh evidence established in *Palmer v. The Queen*, [1980] 1 S.C.R. 759.

88 *J.A.A.*, above note 79 at para. 11.

89 *R. v. Mohan*, [1994] 2 S.C.R. 9.

90 For two judgments addressing the *Mohan* criteria of a "properly qualified expert" with respect to forensic odontology, see, for example, *R. v. Weir*, 2013 ONSC 7394 and *R. v. Weir*, 2013 ONSC 7390. These cases do not address bite-mark analysis but instead address the need to have expert assistance in determining if the complainant's jaw fracture was caused by a punch or a fall.

91 *R. v. Chirimar*, 2007 ONCJ 385.

of the victim but, without expert testimony to assist him, he could not find that the victim, Chirimar's wife, had been bitten. Further, Chirimar's guilty plea to two counts of assault causing bodily harm did not include an admission that he bit his wife. Justice Trotter's assessment of the case underscores the importance of the legal and expert communities respecting their individual roles in the criminal justice system.

Perhaps the most frequently cited Canadian case involving problematic forensic odontology evidence is that of *R. v. Taillefer; R. v. Duguay*,[92] where the first-degree murder and manslaughter convictions of Taillefer and Duguay, repectively, were quashed by the Supreme Court of Canada in favour of a new trial and a stay of proceedings, respectively, as a result of fresh evidence from the Commission d'enquête chargée de faire enquête sur la Sûreté du Québec (Poitras Commission). The Commission revealed a substantial failure on the part of the police and the Crown to disclose important evidence to the defence at the time of trial.[93] In 2003, the Court described the fresh evidence as several documents related to the police investigation that, if disclosed at the time of trial, could have significantly assisted the defence in making full answer and defence:

> The fresh evidence essentially consisted of the oral and written statements of various witnesses gathered by the police during their investigation, investigation notes taken by police officers in the course of questioning the accused, and the information sworn by a police officer for the purpose of obtaining a search warrant. As we shall see later, when more details are added, some of the undisclosed evidence was relevant for the defence's purposes. A considerable part of it could have been used to impeach the credibility of certain prosecution witnesses. Other evidence raised serious doubts as to the credibility of the theory put forward by the Crown. Finally, the defence could have used some of that evidence to explore or discover new avenues of investigation.[94]

Both Taillefer and Duguay were convicted of first-degree murder on 1 February 1991.[95] At trial, a pathologist called by the Crown testified to observing bitemarks on the deceased and a forensic odontologist, Dr. Robert Dorion, identified Duguay as the biter.[96] Dr. Dorion testified that the mean-

92 *R. v. Taillefer; R. v. Duguay*, 2003 SCC 70.
93 *Ibid* at paras. 2, 29, and 134–35.
94 *Ibid.* at para. 29.
95 *Ibid.* at para. 21.
96 *Ibid.* at para. 17.

ing of the word "consistent" was that the identification was "beyond a reasonable doubt."[97] The defence called two of their own experts to dispute the validity and reliability of Dr. Dorion's methods, expressing doubt that the marks even represented bites.[98] It is unclear from the judgment if Dr. Dorion's comment in French could be translated to "reasonable medical certainty," which was the term used by the ABFO guidelines at the time. Although the Court of Appeal upheld Taillefer's conviction, Duguay's conviction was quashed and a new trial was ordered on a second-degree murder charge. Duguay pled guilty in exchange for the reduced charge of manslaughter.

Years later, the Poitras Commission would reveal that the undisclosed 12 April 1990 information sworn by a police officer for the purpose of obtaining a search warrant was directed at obtaining a mould of Taillefer's lower teeth. The information relayed Dr. Dorion's opinion at the time that the marks on the deceased's body were consistent with *Taillefer's* upper teeth. This was in direct opposition to Dr. Dorion's testimony at trial, where he identified *Duguay* as the biter. The newly disclosed evidence put the credibility of Dr. Dorion's opinion into question.

Upon learning of this fresh evidence from the commission in 1999, Duguay filed an affidavit supporting his leave to appeal application to the Court of Appeal, proclaiming his innocence and stating that he had no participation in the murder. His lawyers supported his claims to innocence and one of his lawyers, Stéphane Painchaud, explained that Duguay only pled guilty because "he no longer felt capable either of holding up through a second trial or of running the risk of a murder conviction."[99] Both Taillefer and Duguay successfully secured the opportunity to appeal a second time to the Court of Appeal.[100]

Ultimately, the Court of Appeal upheld both convictions after conducting an item-by-item analysis of the fresh evidence.[101] Of note is that Biron J.A. conceded that the newly disclosed information about Dr.

97 *Ibid.* at para. 36 [translation].

98 *Ibid.* at para. 20.

99 *Ibid.* at para. 110.

100 *Ibid.* at paras. 26–29. Note that Taillefer's second appeal to the Court of Appeal was a result of his case being referred to that court by the Federal Minister of Justice under s. 690 (now s. 696.1) of the *Criminal Code* on the basis of fresh evidence. Duguay's second appeal to the Court of Appeal was the result of his applications to the Court of Appeal being allowed (i.e., applications for an extension of time, for leave to appeal, and to introduce fresh evidence).

101 *Ibid.* at para. 51.

Dorion's opinion was problematic, but Biron J.A. concluded that the credibility problem was apparent at trial and the fresh evidence could not be used to further impeach his testimony. Dr. Dorion seemingly sought to qualify his previous testimony at trial by stating that, in his mind, "*compatible*" [consistent] did not equate to stating his identification was "beyond a reasonable doubt."[102]

The Supreme Court of Canada held that the Court of Appeal erred by assessing the fresh evidence as individual parts, rather than assessing the impact of the evidence as a whole.[103] The disclosure rights of both men were seriously infringed.[104] Accordingly, Taillefer's conviction was quashed and a new trial ordered. Taking into account the context of Duguay's case and section 24(1) of the *Charter*, the Supreme Court of Canada granted leave to withdraw the guilty plea, quashed the conviction, and directed a stay of proceedings.[105]

3) Determining Whether Complex and Controversial Bite-Mark Evidence Is Helpful

In terms of providing help to the court, bite-mark analysis has assisted in a range of cases, including those involving false confessions (such as those obtained during the course of a "Mr. Big sting," which is an undercover police operation directed at eliciting a confession from a target/suspect), serious and/or long-term child abuse, and murders. Even if bitemarks cannot be identified to a particular person, they may be helpful as corroborative evidence in supporting or refuting a witness's version of events, speaking to the credibility of the witness and perhaps even a perpetrator's *modus operandi*. For example, in the case of the "Abbotsford killer" (Terry Driver), information pertaining to a bitemark on the right nipple of one of his victims was withheld from the media. In taunting the police and the public as an unidentified killer who was looking to strike again, Driver stated in one of his calls to police that the victim's "right nipple tasted pretty good." This information presumably only could have been known by someone directly involved in the murder.[106]

---

102 *Ibid.* at para. 46.
103 *Ibid.* at para. 91.
104 *Ibid.* at para. 3.
105 *Ibid.* at paras. 134–35.
106 *R. v. Driver*, 2001 BCCA 70 at para. 10.

In the case of *R. v. Kyle Wayne Unger*, Unger had been convicted of first-degree murder in 1992 following the sexual assault and murder of a sixteen-year-old girl who, in 1990, attended the same rock concert as him and his co-accused, Timothy Lawrence Houlahan.[107] Although the case has since become recognized as a wrongful conviction based on erroneous hair microscopy evidence and a false confession obtained during the course of a Mr. Big sting,[108] it is important to note that the three bitemarks on the deceased were not made by Unger—a forensic odontologist testified to this effect and, interestingly, Houlahan declined to provide a dental specimen for comparison.[109] The Crown advanced the argument that the bitemark, though a minor injury, was indicative of Houlahan's consensual interaction with the victim escalating to sexual assault and, relying on other evidence which would later be recognized as erroneous, the Crown further argued that the assault then intensified and escalated to murder by Unger's involvement.[110] As stated by the Court of Appeal in 1993, when evaluating the opening remarks of Unger's counsel at trial, it is inflammatory, speculative, and prejudicial to suggest that Houlahan would need to explain the origins of the bitemark.[111] That being said, however, the bite-mark analysis that excluded Unger hinted at the wrongful conviction that would be uncovered in the years to come. In October 2009, after Unger spent fourteen years in jail, the charges against him were withdrawn and Manitoba's deputy attorney general requested that Unger be acquitted, after determining that mitochondrial DNA evidence excluded Unger as the source of the hair on the victim's sweatshirt.[112]

In a more recent, post-*Hart*[113] Mr. Big case, the bite-mark evidence in *R. v. Streiling* excluded the accused and assisted the court in finding an ac-

107 CBC News, "Hair Evidence in Manitoba Murder Trials under Scrutiny Again" (15 September 2004) online: CBC News www.cbc.ca/news/canada/hair-evidence-in-manitoba-murder-trials-under-scrutiny-again-1.489632.

108 See Chapter 5 in this book for further information about this case. See also Innocence Canada, "Historical Cases: Kyle Unger," online: Innocence Canada www.aidwyc.org/cases/historical/kyle-unger [Innocence Canada, Unger]. Note that in *R. v. Hart*, 2014 SCC 52 at para. 62, the Supreme Court of Canada comments on the Unger case but takes the position that, "To date, there are no established wrongful convictions stemming from its [Mr. Big stings] use."

109 *R. v. Unger*, [1993] M.J. No. 363 at paras. 9 and 149 (C.A.).

110 *Ibid.* at para. 152.

111 *Ibid.* at para. 128.

112 Innocence Canada, Unger, above note 108. See Chapter 12 of this book for an explanation of the uses of mitochondrial DNA, or "mtDNA" in criminal investigations.

113 See, generally, *R. v. Hart*, 2014 SCC 52. In this case, the Supreme Court of Canada held that confessions obtained during the course of Mr. Big stings are presumptively inadmissible unless it meets the framework set out by the court.

quittal at trial. The charge was for the second-degree murder of Streiling's almost two-year-old stepson, Noah, who had died of a "massive head injury" on 9 April 2008.[114] Streiling had told his girlfriend (Noah's mother), Meadow Dykes (who testified that Noah was accident prone),[115] as well as police officers attending the scene, that Noah had accidentally fallen from the bathtub, hit his head on the floor, and, shortly thereafter, said he was "okay" despite a bruise forming on his forehead.[116] After Streiling sent Noah to his room to pick the clothes he wanted to change into, Streiling heard a crash and, upon checking on Noah, saw him seizuring; Noah then became unconscious and never woke again.[117] In contrast, Streiling's confession to "Mr. Big" was that Noah went unconscious after Streiling hit Noah's head against the floor a few times.[118]

Dykes testified that she shared custody of her four children, including Noah, with their biological father and his wife. Four to six weeks prior to Noah's death, Dykes noticed that Noah "seemed dizzy, slept a lot, and ate little."[119] Dykes began keeping a diary of Noah's symptoms because he always seemed tired after coming back from his father's house and she noticed he would be returned to her with injuries, including bruises and bitemarks. The bitemarks found on Noah at the time of his death—two suspected bites (one on his left cheek and one on the back of his left thigh) and one confirmed bite on his left shoulder[120]—could suggest that someone other than Streiling was abusing Noah at the time of the incident.[121] The forensic odontologist, Dr. David Sweet, testified that the confirmed bitemark was made by a person who was at least fourteen years old. Dr. Sweet's analysis excluded Noah's mother, father, and Streiling as possible biters, but did not exclude the wife of Noah's father.[122]

The Crown called medical evidence supporting a cause of death, cranial trauma, which was consistent with Streiling's confession. The experts presenting this evidence concluded that the abusive, non-accidental head

114 *R. v. Streiling*, 2015 BCSC 1044 at paras. 1–3 [*Streiling*]. The court said that Noah was effectively Streiling's stepson as Streiling was living with Noah's mother and assisted in taking care of the children.

115 *Ibid.* at para. 26.

116 *Ibid.* at paras. 6 and 57.

117 *Ibid.* at para. 57.

118 *Ibid.* at para. 4.

119 *Ibid.* at para. 18. This quote is in the words of the court.

120 *Ibid.* at para. 66.

121 *Ibid.* at para. 24.

122 *Ibid.* at para. 66.

injury[123] suffered by Noah was inconsistent with an accidental short fall from a bathtub.[124] The Crown did, however, concede that they did not have a case without Streiling's confession.[125] The defence called medical expert witnesses who concluded that the injuries could be from a fall from a bathtub and, further, that Noah had a pre-existing subdural hematoma that would have increased his tendency to bleed and would have therefore increased his susceptibility to suffer from a catastrophic cascade effect, where subsequent minor trauma might cause significant bleeding in the brain.[126] Considering the Crown's weak case, in conjunction with the exculpatory bite-mark evidence, the trial judge was not satisfied that Streiling's confession was true and acquitted him.

4) Summary

Although the sub-discipline of bite-mark analysis is currently embroiled in controversy, the above cases show that this type of analysis is perhaps more reliably used as a tool for exclusion, rather than identification. This fact has become clear to the forensic odontology community and is now filtering into the justice system. Bite-mark analysis may also be used to support or refute events surrounding the incident in question, providing that the resulting conclusions are viewed in the context of the case as a whole. When the limits of this sub-discipline are fully understood, it is possible to ensure that only the most accurate and up-to-date testimony is presented in court.

The recent criticisms directed at bite-mark analysis do not damage the reliability of forensic odontology as a whole, however, since the discipline is most often used for person identification. In this respect, forensic odontology has a long history of success in identifying missing persons, otherwise unidentifiable victims of homicide, and individuals who have died during the course of mass disasters or human rights atrocities.

---

123 See Chapter 18 of this book to review other cases addressing pediatric forensic pathology as well as specific issues related to non-accidental abusive head trauma.

124 *Streiling*, above note 114 at paras. 43–44.

125 *Ibid.* at para. 9.

126 *Ibid.* at paras. 50–51.

CHAPTER 18

Forensic Pathology

Forensic Pathologists of the Provincial Forensic Pathology Unit in Toronto[*]

LEGAL CONTEXT: CAITLIN PAKOSH

A. OVERVIEW

1) Qualifications of the Forensic Pathologist

Forensic pathology is the specialty of medicine that underlies the medico-legal investigation of death. The forensic pathologist, then, is a specialist in death investigation, a physician who uses the tools of science and medicine to discover the truth behind a person's death. Forensic pathologists undertake five years of postgraduate training in anatomical (i.e., hospital) pathology, followed by an additional year of training in forensic pathology. Their training in both pathology and forensic pathology is recognized through certification from the Royal College of Physicians and Surgeons of Canada (Royal College) after meeting the college's requirements and passing examinations.

Forensic pathology has been a subspecialty of the Royal College for only a few years. Prior to this, many forensic pathologists in Canada obtained their training and certification in other jurisdictions. Some forensic pathologists currently working in Ontario (and elsewhere in Canada) have been "grandparented" into the speciality based on long experience and recog-

* In alphabetical order: Maggie Bellis, MB, BCh, BAO, FRCP; Kristopher Cunningham, MD, PhD, FRCPC; Anita Lal, MD, D-ABP, FCAP; Jayantha Herath, MD, DLM, MD (Forensic), FCAP, FRCPC (AP & FP); Michael Pickup, MSc, MD, FRCPC; Michael S. Pollanen, MD, PhD, FRCP, DMJ (Path) FRCPC Founder; Ashwyn Rajagopalan, MD, FRCPC; Toby H. Rose, MD, FRCPC. For further biographical information, please refer to the Contributors section of this book.

nized expertise in the criminal justice system. In Ontario, any pathologist or forensic pathologist who wishes to perform medicolegal autopsies must be on the register of pathologists of the Ontario Forensic Pathology Service.

Provincial and territorial medicolegal death investigation systems may be headed by a medical examiner or by a coroner. Medical examiners are always forensic pathologists. Depending on the province, coroners may be medical or nonmedical. At the time of this writing, no chief coroner in Canada is a forensic pathologist.

2) Practice of Forensic Pathology

Sudden and unexpected deaths are investigated to determine the cause and manner of death. The manner of death is sometimes described as "by what means" the death occurred. In Ontario, the possible manners of death are: natural, accidental, suicide, homicide, and undetermined. In medical examiner systems, the medical examiner certifies the cause and manner of death (i.e., fills out the medical certificate of death) and submits it to the registrar general or other official. In coroner systems, the coroner is responsible for certification. In both types of death investigation systems, forensic pathologists are the medical specialists who perform autopsies and testify about them in court.

Less than twenty percent of the typical forensic pathologists' work involves the criminal justice system. The remainder is spent dealing with other types of sudden death, including those resulting from accident, suicide, and natural causes.

B. THE SCIENCE OF FORENSIC PATHOLOGY

1) The Medicolegal Autopsy (Post-mortem Examination)

An autopsy, or post-mortem examination, is the examination of a body after death. An important function of any autopsy is the conclusive identification of the body. During the autopsy, the forensic pathologist observes, documents, and interprets any findings. Objective findings establish the facts underlying the death and lead to an expert opinion on the meaning of those findings (expert opinions usually relate to the cause of death). However, deciding the cause of death may be only the beginning in most cases, since the medicolegal issues may be subtler than just the cause of death. The process of the medicolegal autopsy is divided into five steps:

1) *Consideration of the scene and circumstances around the death.* This step includes the transmission of historical information from police, coroners, or other investigators or medical experts and the review of the scene by inspecting digital images. Forensic pathologists may visit the scene to make first-hand observations that may be relevant in the ultimate interpretation of the autopsy.
2) *External examination of the body in the autopsy room.* In this step, the body is examined both clothed and unclothed from head to toe and photographs, samples, physical exhibits, and observations are made and recorded. A detailed examination is made of injuries and changes due to natural disease. This will often include the creation of diagrams or written descriptions with both qualitative and quantitative data. Evidence of post-mortem changes and injuries (i.e., post-mortem artifacts) are recorded, along with evidence of attempted resuscitation or surgical/medical treatment. In some cases, such as stabbings or shootings, X-ray images are obtained to check for projectiles or other metal foreign bodies, such as knife tips, in the body.
3) *Internal examination of the body.* Routine dissections include the head, neck, chest, abdomen, and pelvis, with a detailed examination of injuries and changes due to natural disease, as above.

   Additional dissections are performed as required, including dissection of the tissue layers of the face and anterior neck, the back, and the extremities. In some cases, such as potential sexual assault, the external genitalia and pelvic organs may be further dissected. Photographs are made, and tissue samples are obtained for microscopic examination.

   This step may require consultation with other experts to examine specific tissues or organs. A neuropathologist can give an expert opinion on the brain in cases of head injury and a forensic anthropologist may be consulted to give an expert opinion on injuries to bones and assistance with identification of the body, particularly where the remains are skeletonized, burned, decomposed, mutilated, or otherwise unrecognizable.
4) *Special laboratory tests (ancillary tests).* Some tests are performed by a pathologist and some by other experts. The most frequent tests are toxicology (i.e., examination of body fluids for drugs and poisons) and histology (i.e., microscopic examination of tissues for abnormalities and injuries). Other ancillary tests may be performed according to the specific requirements of the case.
5) *Creation of an expert opinion.* The final product is a written report of post-mortem examination, including the pathologist's determination

of the cause of death and an opinion on the surrounding facts. In many homicides, the cause of death is straightforward as the fatal injuries are noncontroversial. However, a forensic pathologist's expert opinion can be quite complicated.

The forensic pathologist's courtroom testimony can be viewed as the conclusion of the post-mortem examination. By observing, documenting, and interpreting the changes to a body in criminally suspicious cases, forensic pathologists can contribute vital fact and opinion evidence. Forensic pathologists sometimes determine that an initially suspicious death was the result of disease, accident, or suicide. Alternatively, they may find that a nonsuspicious death was in fact a homicide.

2) Causal Issues in Forensic Pathology

Multiple medicolegal opinions may flow from a forensic post-mortem examination. Among them, the identity of the decedent, the nature and timing of injuries, the type of weapon(s) that may have been used, an estimation of the post-mortem interval, and an itemization of relevant contributing factors in the death.

The most important opinion is often the cause of death (COD). The COD statement is usually a succinct determination of why an individual died, which typically links events around the time of death to disease, trauma (i.e., injury), or toxicological considerations. Usually the COD is a straightforward inference drawn from the circumstances of the death in combination with the pathological findings at autopsy (e.g., beaten, stabbed, shot, strangled). It should be as etiologically specific as possible and should contain the most important elements contributing to the death. In addition, the COD statement should convey what the pathologist believes to be true and can be reasonably supported through evidence derived from the steps of the post-mortem examination. Like all medicolegal opinions provided by forensic pathologists, the COD statement should represent a balanced interpretation of all the information available.

The cause of death can be viewed as the injury or disease that initiates a chain of events that ultimately leads to death, such as a gunshot wound to the chest. The mechanism of death, however, typically encompasses the aberrant pathophysiological chain of events that follows from the cause of death (e.g., hemorrhage and physiological shock). The immediate cause of death may be considered as the cause that directly preceded death in time, while the underlying cause of death may be a cause that occurred in the more distant past, but led to the immediate cause of death. For example:

- An acute infection (i.e., the immediate COD) that was directly caused or made inevitable by a traumatic event (the underlying COD) that occurred earlier, such as a spinal cord injury causing quadriplegia.
- Death from a recognized complication of a surgical procedure that was undertaken to treat an inflicted injury would be an indirect cause because of the intervening actions of the surgeon.

There are several possible constructions for a COD statement after a post-mortem examination:

1) The relevant factors may be linked through a direct causal chain: A caused B, which caused C.
2) The relevant factors are not etiologically linked, but are all determined to play a significant contributory role in an individual's death: A led to death in a person with B and C.
3) There are multiple significant, interrelated factors that contribute to an individual's death that cannot be easily unified into a single conclusion or diagnosis. The latter may require a more descriptive COD statement.

Whatever form the COD statement uses to convey the factors thought to be most important in explaining the death, the opinion section of the post-mortem report should explicitly outline which facts were relied on to formulate the COD (or any other medicolegal opinions proffered), as well as any limitations to those opinions. Finally, the COD may occasionally be given as "unascertained," "undetermined," or "no anatomical or toxicological cause of death." These statements are largely interchangeable and can reflect different outcomes of a death investigation:

- There is insufficient data available to ascertain the cause of death. For instance, some forms of asphyxial death (i.e., death from a lack of oxygen) leave minimal historical and pathological evidence.
- There is insufficient information about the circumstances of the death coupled with relatively non-specific pathological findings. For instance, an individual may be found in a dumpster showing evidence of wrist restraint and nonlethal blunt trauma, but a clear cause of death cannot be identified at autopsy.

- The circumstances of death have been obscured by environmental factors such as fire, water, or decomposition. Post-mortem alteration or interference by people, carnivores, or insects can also obscure pathological findings relevant to a death investigation.
- "Unascertained" may be used when two equal but competing causes of death are encountered with no way of determining which was more significant given the information available. Such scenarios are rare and may be amenable to a more refined and clear characterization of the COD if the forensic pathologist is made aware of further investigative information that was not available at the time of the post-mortem examination.

A careful outline of all possibly relevant factors should be included in the post-mortem report.

3) Blunt Force Trauma

Blunt force trauma is caused by the direct application of force against tissue, causing deformation of the tissue beyond its tensile strength, with disruption of the tissue as well as hemorrhage. There are four types of blunt force trauma injuries: contusions (i.e., bruises), abrasions (i.e., scrapes, scratches, superficial gouges), lacerations (i.e., cuts), and fractures. Blunt force injuries may occur in isolation, or any combination can occur as part of the same injury.

Blunt force trauma may be caused by an individual striking a firm surface or a firm surface striking an individual. While the precise etiology of the injuries may not be determined from the post-mortem examination alone, some inflicted injuries show typical features that suggest how those injuries were caused (e.g., tire-tread marks, footwear impressions, "tram-track" contusions). These injuries are referred to as "patterned injuries." Patterned injuries typically reveal the nature of the object that caused them, but not the specific tool or weapon.

The severity or extent of a blunt force injury may not be apparent during external examination of the body, particularly in cases of head and abdominal trauma. Depending on the mechanism of injury (e.g., high velocity vehicular collisions or a fall from a great height followed by striking a firm surface), blunt force trauma can be combined with acute deceleration trauma, typically characterized by extensive tearing of internal tissues. Furthermore, some forms of penetrating injuries and chop injuries may show additional signs of blunt force injury.

Death from blunt trauma may occur through multiple mechanisms. The most common types include:

- intracranial hemorrhage with mass effect that compresses the brain;
- disruption of brain tissue;
- cervical spinal (i.e., spinal cord) injury;
- flail chest (with numerous rib fractures)/pneumothorax;
- external trauma (typically lacerations), leading to exsanguination and shock;
- visceral trauma resulting in internal hemorrhage and shock (especially injury to the lungs, heart, liver, and spleen);
- visceral or soft tissue trauma leading to delayed death through hemorrhage (e.g., spleen), infection (e.g., peritonitis), or inflammation (e.g., pancreatitis); and
- extensive bony and soft tissue trauma, leading to multifocal soft tissue hemorrhages and fat embolism syndrome and/or rhabdomyolysis (i.e., muscle breakdown with renal failure).

Important forensic issues to consider:

- Was there sufficient blunt impact injury to cause death?
- If not, did the blunt impact trauma contribute to the cause of death?
- What was the mechanism of injury?
- What was the timing of injury relative to the time of death?
- Were the injuries likely inflicted or not? (Were they intentional or accidental?)
- If the trauma was inflicted, was an implement used? If so, what type of implement may have caused the injuries?
- What was the minimum number of impacts?

4) Sharp Force Injuries

Sharp force injuries are wounds produced by a sharp-edged weapon, such as a knife or broken glass. Sharp force injuries usually cause death from bleeding, either externally (injuries resulting in visible blood loss) or internally (typically from damage to the heart or major internal blood vessel). Suicide attempts by sharp force are usually in "sites of election" such as the front of the wrists or the sides of the neck. Accidental incised wounds are rare, but can occur, for instance, through contact with shards of glass.

Most sharp force injuries are caused by knives. Knife wounds will differ depending on whether the knife is single- or double-edged, with a smooth or serrated surface. Sharp-edged weapons leave three types of wounds on the body: (1) stab wounds, where the wound extends deeper into the tissues than the length of the cut on the skin; (2) incised wounds (i.e., incisions), where the length of the cut on the skin is longer than the depth of the wound into the tissues; and (3) chop wounds. Chop wounds result from a heavy sharp-edged weapon such as an axe. Each type of object may leave its own pattern of injury. For example:

- A stab wound from a single-edged knife may reflect the shape of the blade with one pointed and one squared-off end.
- A stab wound from a double-edged knife may have two pointed ends.
- Serrated blades may cause stab wounds and cuts which are indistinguishable from wounds produced with ordinary knives, but if the blade scrapes the skin surface sideways, the serrations may appear as sharp, parallel, linear scratches.
- A plus sign (+) may suggest a Phillips-head screwdriver.
- Two round puncture wounds may suggest a barbeque fork.
- Four round puncture wounds with consistent spacing may suggest a kitchen fork.
- Scissors tend to produce linear wounds if closed, but paired perforations if open.

An autopsy performed by the forensic pathologist will attempt to determine by X-ray whether a broken knife tip is present in the body; identify, examine, and describe sharp force injuries, including the pathway in the body; determine the number and special features of sharp force injuries; and interpret delayed deaths after sharp force injuries. In addition, the forensic pathologist may be able to determine the depth of a stab wound, which does not depend on the length of the blade alone due to the elasticity and compressibility of the body. Similarly, since stab wounds are often a combination of stabbing and cutting, the length of the wound in the skin does not necessarily correlate with the width of the blade. The only definitive measurement of the size of a stab wound is made by using the distance between two fixed points, such as bone to bone. The autopsy may enable the forensic pathologist to give an opinion as to the type of weapon and correlate the wounds with weapons found at the scene. It may also inform an opinion on volitional activities (i.e., the ability to move after sustaining injury), based on scientific evidence.

Some factors that should be considered when investigating sharp force injuries are:

- The gaping of a sharp force injury, which results from the tension or relaxation of the skin and Langer's lines (i.e., lines of skin tension).
- Bones, teeth, and cartilage are the hardest tissues in the body and are the most difficult to penetrate. The skin is the next hardest tissue to penetrate, but once the skin is perforated, only minimal force is needed to penetrate internal organs.
- Hesitation marks are commonly found in suicides, with incised wounds of the neck or wrists. The cuts are usually multiple, very superficial, and parallel to each other. Similar wounds may be found in homicides if the victim tries to pull away from the assailant or the assailant hesitates in cutting the throat.
- Defensive (or defensive-type) wounds are usually caused when the victim attempts to protect the head and torso from injury. They are commonly found on the forearms and hands.
- Chop wounds are associated with a groove or cut in the underlying bone. If the edge is dull, there may be blunt force components to the wound.

5) Gunshot Wounds

Forensic pathologists are experts in the appearance and interpretation of gunshot wounds. There are five types of gun, each of which leaves its own signature wound: (1) handguns, (2) rifles, (3) shotguns, (4) submachine guns, and (5) machine guns. In Canada, the most commonly used guns are handguns (i.e., revolvers and automatic loading pistols), rifles, and shotguns. Shotguns fire cartridges (i.e., shells), which contain multiple pellets (or a single slug), primer, gunpowder, and a wad (the paper or plastic that holds the pellets). All other types of gun cartridges contain a bullet, primer, and gunpowder. When a gun is fired, the muzzle end of the gun becomes heated and can cause burns. The exiting bullet/shotgun pellets are accompanied by a jet of flame, a cloud of gas, vaporized metals, and gunpowder that is burnt, burning, and unburnt. All of these substances can contribute to the appearance of the entrance wound.

The projectile in a perforating gunshot wound enters and exits the body. In a penetrating gunshot wound, the projectile enters the body, but does not exit. Bullets and large calibre shotgun ammunition (i.e., buckshot) remaining in the body should be recovered and submitted to investigating police. Small calibre ammunition (i.e., birdshot) may result in numerous pellets present in the body. Some pellets should be recovered and submitted.

The objective of an autopsy on a gunshot victim is to (1) identify and describe the wounds; (2) interpret the number of entrance and exit wounds; (3) determine the number of gunshot wounds to the body; (4) recover retained projectiles and submit them to investigating police; (5) interpret any special features of the gunshot wounds; (6) interpret the pathological range; (7) describe the bullet track and path of injury; (8) distinguish between antemortem and post-mortem wounding; (9) identify and describe other types of wounds; (10) determine cause, mechanism, and manner of death; (11) interpret volitional activities (i.e., movement after injury); and (12) interpret timing of death after wounding.

a) Typical Entrance Wounds

The appearance of the entrance wound is dependent on the type of gun, the range of fire, and the region of the body involved.

i) Features of Typical Entrance Wounds Caused by Handguns

The characteristic feature of a handgun entrance wound is the marginal abrasion (i.e., abrasion collar) caused by the bullet scraping the skin before it enters. Entrance wounds of the chest, abdomen, or extremities are usually circular. Other features of handgun entrance wounds that may assist forensic pathologists in determining the muzzle-to-target distance:

- With contact and close wounds, there is burning and soot deposition dependent on the muzzle-to-target distance. With contact wounds (hard or loose contact), the muzzle-to-target distance is near zero. Skin splits around the central defect (i.e., the central injury) in hard contact wounds. With close wounds, there is less burning and soot deposition.
- At intermediate range, stippling (i.e., powder tattooing) is present, caused by gunpowder penetrating the skin around the central defect.
- Indeterminate range (previously referred to as distant range) leaves an entrance wound that is round to oval with a marginal abrasion (i.e., abrasion collar).
- Entry and exit wounds in the skull cause beveling of the bone, which indicates the direction of the bullet.

ii) Features of Typical Entrance Wounds Caused by Shotguns

Entrance wounds are usually larger than those created by handguns, and contact wounds can be explosive in nature. The spread of shotgun pellets is dependent on the muzzle-to-target distance. At close range, the entrance wound is circular. As the distance increases, the central defect takes on a scalloped border with satellite pellet marks. Ultimately, the central defect disappears and only individual pellet marks are seen in distant wounds. Injuries caused by the wad also vary with distance.

iii) Factors Affecting the Appearance of Entrance Wounds

Additional features of the entrance wound may provide valuable information to the forensic pathologist during autopsy. The end of the muzzle may cause a muzzle imprint, indicating a contact wound. The flame and/or hot gases may cause burning of the skin, also indicating close or hard contact. The wound path may show evidence of cavitation. Shotgun wads may cause additional injury.

b) Typical Exit Wounds

The typical exit wound caused by a handgun will generally be larger than the entrance wound and will be irregular in shape, stellate, or slit-like. Where the wound is caused by a shotgun at intermediate or distant range, there is usually no exit wound. Pellets exit the body more often when the wound is contact or close range or the pellets are larger calibre.

c) Factors to be Aware of During Autopsy of a Gunshot Victim

The body should be X-rayed to detect retained projectiles, and clothing should be examined. Most suicidal gunshot wounds are contact and typically involve a "site of election," such as the temple, forehead, inside of the mouth, under the chin, or the central chest. Gunshot residue may also be collected from skin and clothing for analysis by an expert in chemistry.

The examiner should be mindful of the fact that the size of the entrance wound does not correspond to the calibre of a bullet. The skin is second only to bone in its resistance to the entrance of a bullet. When a bullet passes through an intermediary target or ricochets, the entrance wound will be atypical and is usually larger with an atypical abrasion collar as well. Exit wounds can have a marginal abrasion collar if the skin is constrained by a supportive object, such as tight clothing or the ground ("shored exit wound"). Forensic pathologists determine only the pathological range. The exact range may be concluded through test firing by a firearms expert.

6) Asphyxia and Strangulation

The term "asphyxia" refers to the inadequate oxygenation of tissues and, in general, results from a failure of oxygen to reach the brain for any of a number of reasons. Asphyxial deaths fall into three general categories: chemical asphyxia, suffocation, and strangulation. The Goudge Inquiry[1] recommended that forensic pathologists should be clear in their testimony as to how they are using the term "asphyxia" (i.e., to reflect either its benign medical meaning or an associated category of death that may be considered inculpatory).

a) Chemical Asphyxia

Some gases, such as carbon monoxide, hydrogen cyanide, and hydrogen sulphide, prevent the body's cells from using oxygen. Poisoning by these substances is usually accidental or suicidal.

b) Suffocation

There are five different types of suffocation.

- Environmental suffocation is caused by inadequate oxygen in the atmosphere due to an environmental condition (e.g., being locked in an airtight refrigerator).
- Smothering is caused by a mechanical obstruction of the nose and mouth (e.g., a plastic bag).
- Choking is caused by the blockage of internal airways (e.g., choking on food).
- Mechanical (traumatic/crush) asphyxia is caused by pressure on the chest and abdomen that restricts breathing, such as a heavy weight that has fallen on the victim.
- Strangulation results from external pressure on the neck causing constriction of the blood vessels in the neck. The mechanism of death is lack of oxygen supply to the brain due to the interruption of blood flow. The three types of strangulation are hanging, ligature strangulation, and manual strangulation.

i) A Brief Anatomy of the Neck

The important anatomical structures include two carotid arteries, two jugular veins, two vertebral arteries, the larynx (i.e., voice box), esophagus,

1 Ontario, Ministry of the Attorney General, *Inquiry into Pediatric Forensic Pathology in Ontario* by the Honourable Stephen T. Goudge, Commissioner, online: www.attorneygeneral.jus.gov.on.ca/inquiries/goudge/report/index.html at 33 and 43 [Goudge Inquiry Report].

vertebral column (i.e., spine), and nerves. Skin covers the neck, which also contains the thyroid gland, parathyroid glands, and strap muscles. The larynx is composed of cartilages connected by soft tissue. The U-shaped hyoid bone is located just above the larynx.

In a healthy person, occlusion of both carotid arteries will produce a loss of consciousness in fifteen to twenty seconds. However, death can be caused by occlusion of the jugular veins only, which requires less pressure. It is not necessary to fracture the spine or cut off the air supply through the airway. In hanging, the carotid arteries are usually occluded and thus the face is pale. In strangulation, there is intermittent or insufficient pressure to completely obstruct blood flow through the carotid arteries and jugular veins, resulting in a congested face and numerous petechial hemorrhages on the face and conjunctivae (i.e., the lining of the eyes and eyelids).

Petechiae are almost always seen in strangulation. However, they are a non-specific finding. Petechiae are commonly seen in other types of death, particularly sudden death from heart disease.

ii) Post-mortem Findings in Strangulation

Different patterns of post-mortem findings are seen in hanging, ligature strangulation, and manual strangulation. Forensic pathologists must do a thorough external and internal examination, including a layered anterior neck dissection ("dry neck"), to demonstrate these findings.

a. Hanging

In hanging, a ligature (or "noose") is tightened around the neck by the weight of the body. The resulting ligature mark is situated at or above the Adam's apple at the front of the neck, and rises on the sides of the neck in an inverted "V" shape to the point of suspension. The ligature may have a slip-type knot or a more elaborate knot. Scene photographs should be viewed, and the ligature should be examined by the forensic pathologist. Internal injuries, such as hemorrhages in strap muscles and fractures of thyroid cartilages and the hyoid bone, may be seen in hanging. The presence of petechiae depends on whether the body is completely or incompletely suspended.

b. Ligature Strangulation

Pressure is applied to the neck by a ligature that is tightened by pressure other than the body weight, usually by the hands of an assailant. The manner of death is usually homicidal. Accidents and suicides are rare. The ligature mark is usually horizontal and lies at or below the Adam's apple, and numerous petechial hemorrhages are present on the conjunctivae (i.e., the membrane covering the eye) and face. The face is congested. Internal injuries, such as hemorrhages in strap muscles and fractures of laryngeal cartilages and/or hyoid bone, are usually seen.

c. Manual Strangulation

Pressure on the neck is applied by the hands or forearm. Almost all cases are homicidal and manual strangulation may accompany rape-murders and elder abuse. Common findings in manual strangulation are: (1) numerous petechiae on the face, including the cheeks, forehead, conjunctivae, and on the mucosal surface (i.e., lining) of the mouth and lips, as well as larger hemorrhages; (2) crescent-shaped abrasions and discoid bruises on the skin of the neck caused by fingernails and fingertips (of the assailant or victim); (3) injuries to deeper layers of the neck, including strap muscle hemorrhages; and (4) fractures of laryngeal cartilages and hyoid bone.

7) Drugs and Alcohol in Homicide Cases

In most jurisdictions, toxicologic analysis is performed in all homicides and criminally suspicious cases. This analysis is typically performed for the sake of completeness and does not substantively alter the investigation or influence the subsequent criminal proceeding. The forensic pathologist, legal counsel (both prosecution and defence), and the trier of fact must be able to assess when toxicology findings are relevant.

a) Toxicologic Samples

Blood and urine samples are collected at the time of autopsy. Because blood does not circulate after death or become mixed by the heart's pumping, these samples can be used to estimate the concentration of a particular substance in the body around the time of death. When analyzing the specimens, the toxicologist should consider the anatomical locations in the body from which the samples were taken (likewise, the forensic pathologist should consider this when analyzing the reports). Otherwise, post-mortem redistribution or leaching from sites, such as the stomach, can lead to under- or overestimation of the actual perimortem concentration.

Typical post-mortem samples include heart blood, peripheral blood, and urine. Heart blood may be screened first to direct specific quantitative assays on peripheral blood. Peripheral blood (often from the femoral vein or artery in the leg) is best to estimate the quantity of a drug in the body around the time of death. Urine can be used to determine which drugs were in the body but were being eliminated in the urine before death. For instance, 6-monoacetyl-morphine (6-MAM), a metabolite of diacetylmorphine (heroin) is principally excreted in the urine and can indicate heroin overdose.

Other samples that can be sent for toxicological testing include:

- Vitreous fluid from the eyes, which can be used for rapid (i.e., STAT) ethanol quantification. Vitreous fluid provides a good estimate of the perimortem blood ethanol concentration.
- Stomach contents, which can detect ingested (i.e., swallowed) drugs, but not the concentration of drugs in the body, which must first reach the bloodstream. Quantification (i.e., measuring the quantity) of substances in the stomach might have probative value in some cases (e.g., when the decedent is unable to self-administer drugs or medications due to developmental stage or physical impairment).
- Liver samples, particularly when no blood is available for collection, allow interpretation in a binary fashion (i.e., substances are either present or absent). These should be interpreted with caution since determination of drug levels in the liver is unreliable.

When there is a period of survival in hospital after an incident that leads to death, the post-mortem blood sample may be irrelevant. The hospital admission blood samples are usually of greater importance; hospitals may have admission blood samples in their clinical laboratories (e.g., biochemistry and hematology laboratories) for several days after a patient's death. If a person recovering from a criminal or criminally suspicious incident dies suddenly, the post-mortem sample may become more relevant. Both admission and post-mortem samples can be tested, if available.

b) Toxicologically Significant Drugs

There are many thousands of prescription drugs on the market, few of which are toxicologically significant. In addition, there are a growing number of available illicit substances, most of which are toxicologically significant. In general, toxicologically significant substances can be classified as stimulants or depressants. Stimulant drugs include cocaine, methamphetamine, and methylphenidate (Ritalin). They can result in sudden death by triggering an irregular heart rhythm and/or narrowing of a coronary artery by atherosclerotic plaque rupture, spasm, or clot formation (i.e., thrombosis). Depressant drugs include ethanol, heroin, oxycodone, and fentanyl.

An overdose results in gradual loss of consciousness and respiratory depression, sometimes leading to death.

Other drugs that are not usually considered toxicologically significant can be significant in certain cases. For example, minor head trauma could lead to significant intracranial hemorrhage in a person taking warfarin, a blood thinner.

c) Toxicology and Homicide

In most jurisdictions, most homicides are committed through beating, shooting, stabbing, or strangulation. Intentional poisoning that directly results in death is less common. However, drugs and alcohol are frequently detected in the blood and urine samples of homicide victims. The forensic pathologist must determine whether the detected substances played a significant role in the death.

The toxicologic analysis never stands alone in any death investigation, criminal or otherwise. Data acquired from the scene, positive and negative findings from the post-mortem examination, and overall pathologic assessment are always considered when determining the relative contribution of toxicologic substances to the death. The goal of this holistic assessment is to give an opinion as to whether the detected substances played a role in the death, impaired timely access to medical treatment after an otherwise nonlethal injury, resulted in impairment and therefore may have facilitated the homicide, directly contributed to death, or directly caused the death.

In many cases, the detected illicit substances or prescription drugs are incidental and irrelevant to the circumstances leading to death or the cause of death (physiologically—this is separate from the question of poor decision making as a contributing factor). For instance, it would be very difficult to link any concentration of cocaine, heroin, or alcohol to a lethal injury such as a gunshot wound through the heart or brainstem.

In some cases, drugs or alcohol may contribute to death by impairing timely access to medical treatment for an otherwise sub-lethal injury. For instance, in the case of a minor head injury with a bleeding scalp laceration in a victim with decreased level of consciousness or impaired judgement from an intoxicating substance, the victim may choose not to seek medical attention or become unconscious before seeking help. Since the scalp is highly vascular, slow bleeding over several hours can cause death.

Physical impairment from drugs or alcohol may also prevent possibly life-saving self-help. For example, in the case of homicidal suspension (i.e., hanging), drowning, or mechanical asphyxia (i.e., smothering or strangulation), a fully alert victim may be able to escape lethal injury. In some cases, detection of sedating substances in the post-mortem blood can speak to a form of confinement and can be important to the trier of fact.

Injury and toxicology play contributory roles in alcohol-concussion syndrome, in which sub-lethal head injury combines with sub-lethal concentrations of a sedating substance to result in neurorespiratory depression and death. Other drugs interfere with clotting mechanisms (e.g., blood thinners).

In addition to these scenarios where drugs and alcohol can be contributory factors, toxicity sometimes directly results in death. In a situation where a complete autopsy reveals no anatomical cause of death (i.e., no evidence of significant injury or natural disease) and toxicologic analysis confirms potentially lethal concentrations of a substance, the most balanced and reasonable cause of death would be toxicologic in nature. Information as to whether the toxicologic death resulted from criminal activity would depend on police investigation with possible corroborative evidence from the autopsy.

d) Limitations of Forensic Pathology

Drugs and alcohol can be self-administered, administered by another individual with or without consent, or covertly administered by another individual. The purpose of such administration varies, but may include assisting with recreational drug use, inflicting intoxication for the purpose of temporary incapacitation, or committing murder. Clarification of the circumstances leading to intoxication can have probative value to the courts; however, the precise circumstances leading to intoxication can rarely, if ever, be answered by the forensic pathologist. Recently, homicide and manslaughter charges have been laid against drug suppliers in toxicologic deaths, even when the drug is self-administered. The question of who supplied the lethal drug is outside the scope of the forensic pathologist.

Intentional poisoning is the covert administration of a substance that independently leads to death. While the autopsy may assist with route of administration (e.g., oral, intravenous), the issue of who administered the substance remains within the purview of the police investigation. Post-mortem findings might indicate that an individual was physically incapable of self-administering the substance.

e) Toxicology and Physical Restraint

Restraint, particularly prone restraint and choke holds, when combined with stimulant drug use, carries an increased risk of sudden death. This is thought to be due to the combined effects of *hypoxia* related to mechanical asphyxia and exertion, and stimulant effects on the heart leading to the development of fatal cardiac arrhythmias. The majority of the reports in the literature describe sudden death in young individuals under the influence of stimulant drugs (such as cocaine or methamphetamine) during prone restraint by police. The autopsy typically shows no structural abnormality in the heart, and toxicologic analysis is positive for stimulant drugs.

8) Fatal Child Abuse and Neglect

Child abuse encompasses four major forms: physical, sexual, psychological, and neglect. "Child abuse syndrome" (i.e., "battered baby" or non-accidental injury in childhood) exists when an infant or child suffers repetitive physical injuries inflicted by a parent or guardian in circumstances that exclude accident. The syndrome may also include psychological and sexual abuse, but the physical abuse leads to death. This section will focus on fatal physical child abuse (also referred to simply as child abuse) and neglect.

Fatal child abuse is characterized by injuries distributed in time and space that indicate repeated episodes of injury. At autopsy, children have various injuries of different ages in addition to a recent fatal injury that is the immediate cause of death. While older injuries are healed or healing and do not directly contribute to the immediate cause of death, their presence indicates a pattern of physical abuse or neglect. Inflicted injuries can include blunt force, sharp force, and thermal injuries. The majority of deaths are caused by hitting or beating with the hands or an object, throwing or dropping the child, or less often by burning or suffocation.

Neglect is defined as the failure of a caregiver to adequately provide safety, food, clothing, shelter, education, protection, medical care, and/or supervision for a child. It is an uncommon but important cause of child mortality. The most common cause of death by neglect is malnutrition or starvation with or without dehydration. There are three possible explanations for a child presenting this way: criminal neglect, parental ignorance of the care and feeding of a child, or organic causes including a myriad of chronic illnesses.

a) Scene and Circumstances

In cases of fatal child abuse, there are usually significant discrepancies between the history given by the parents or caregivers and the post-mortem findings. The most common discrepancies are (1) the degree and type of injury do not fit with the history given; and (2) the reported activities of the child do not match the child's age or developmental stage or the scene findings. It is also common that (1) the explanation as to how injury occurred is vague (e.g., multiple bruises are explained as the child "bruises easily" or is "always falling"); and (2) a delay in bringing an unresponsive child to the hospital is characterized by parents as resulting from their failure to realize the child was so ill. However, the presence of these features in the given history does not equate to a finding of child abuse. Forensic pathologists may only conclude that the case represents child abuse on the totality of their observations and findings.

It is not the role of the forensic pathologist to advocate for the guilt of the parent or caregiver. Forensic pathologists should take care to restrict their testimony to the medical finding of child abuse, not the legal finding of guilt. It is the role of the forensic pathologist to be aware of the history from all caregivers and witnesses, and obtain the child's medical records, birth history, and the parents'/caregivers' social histories. Medical records may reveal evaluations at well-baby visits, or the lack thereof, and document signs of possible chronic illness. The forensic pathologist should visit the scene or view digital photographs, noting the level of cleanliness, presence of food supplies, possible insect infestation, and so on.

Commonly recognized risk factors for fatal child abuse or neglect include: children living with an adult with no biological relationship to them, maternal youth, substance abuse, depression, and poverty. It should not be assumed, however, that the presence of any of these risk factors is determinative of child abuse in the absence of other evidence. As discussed in the Goudge Inquiry Report,[2] forensic pathologists should "think truth" in child death cases by using an evidence-based approach instead of "thinking dirty"—treating child death cases with a high degree of suspicion of child abuse. The "thinking dirty" approach was rejected by Commissioner Goudge. Forensic pathologists should objectively evaluate the available evidence, rather than making child abuse a default diagnosis in the absence of an alternative explanation for the child's death.

b) Post-mortem Findings in Fatal Child Abuse Cases

Although many abused children show hallmark external signs of trauma, infants and young children may have devastating internal injuries with no

2 *Ibid.*

external signs. Layered dissections may demonstrate subcutaneous (i.e., under the skin) or intramuscular (i.e., within the muscle) hemorrhage that is not visible on the surface.

i) Bruises

Bruises, which can be seen anywhere on the body, are the most common injury. Battered babies especially often show multiple bruises of various ages. Sites of predilection (i.e., sites of preference for certain conditions or injuries) strengthen the diagnosis of abuse. Typical injuries children get while playing tend to be on the lower legs or forearms, but battered children tend to have injuries on the head, face, chest, back, buttocks, ankles, and wrists. Injuries may be patterned; for instance, round lesions on a child's chest/back may result from fingers grabbing the torso, or injuries may resemble the outline of a belt buckle or coat hanger.

ii) Fractures

Limb fractures characteristic of abuse involve the ends of long bones (i.e., metaphyseal fractures) and are caused by swinging, dragging, or violently pulling the child by the limbs. Other important fracture characteristics indicative of abuse include breaks located in the shafts of the long bones and rib fractures, often multiple and of varying ages (i.e., acute and healing), most commonly in a posterior location. It may be impossible to differentiate an isolated skull fracture caused by an accidental fall from one inflicted during abuse. Forensic pathologists should be careful to rule out the "brittle bone diseases" that cause abnormal skeletal fragility, but only a small minority of infants have such abnormalities.

iii) Other Injuries

When examining a body for signs of fatal child abuse, the forensic pathologist should note evidence of blows to the face, which may cause injuries to the inner surface of the lips or the frenulum (i.e., the cord that attaches the inside of the lip to the gums); scalds, cigarette, or other types of burns; and genital or anal injuries suggestive of sexual abuse. The examination should also note internal injuries, such as tears or ruptures in the abdominal organs and injury to the central nervous system (e.g., intracranial hemorrhages and retinal hemorrhages may be associated with abuse). This evidence should be interpreted carefully after consideration of the circumstances, including accidents, natural disease, and birth trauma, but with an understanding of the limits of alternative explanations—studies show that rib fractures and intra-abdominal injuries are rarely caused in children by chest compressions performed through CPR.

Forensic pathologists performing autopsies should photograph all injuries. Bitemarks on skin should be swabbed for DNA, and consultation with a forensic odontologist should be requested.

iv) Causes of Death

The most common cause of death in cases of fatal child abuse is head trauma, including intracranial hemorrhage with or without a skull fracture. Additional common causes include injuries to the abdomen, asphyxia, and poisoning (which may show no findings at autopsy).

v) Dating of Injuries

Dating of injuries by microscopic examination is of paramount importance in child abuse cases because injuries of differing ages indicate episodes of injury at different times, a hallmark of child abuse. The age of the fatal injury may help to confirm or refute the history given by a parent or caregiver. Dating of injuries may also help include or exclude potential perpetrators.

c) Post-mortem Findings in Fatal Child Neglect Cases

Neglected children may show no evidence of physical abuse, but may have signs of failure to thrive. Externally, they may show a poor general state of health, including evidence of malnourishment or overall emaciation or dehydration. They may also show poor hygiene, with or without severe diaper rash. Internally, an autopsy may reveal a lack of subcutaneous fat and visceral fat or a lack of foodstuff in the stomach and intestines. There may be muscle wasting or bony disease in the form of osteopenia (i.e., reduced bone mass), rickets, or some variation. Before drawing any conclusions from such findings, it is important to establish that there is no evidence of natural disease that would prevent adequate digestion or absorption of food.

d) Autopsy in Fatal Child Abuse and Neglect Cases

The investigation of fatal child abuse and neglect is multidisciplinary in nature and requires the input of various agencies and experts. The forensic pathologist's role is to perform a comprehensive post-mortem examination to determine the most reasonable cause of death and rule out any competing causes. The following steps should be undertaken at autopsy (with modifications as required) in cases of suspected child abuse or neglect.

External examination:

- Photograph (including a scale marker) all positive and negative findings.
- Make an alternate light source examination of the body for the detection of body fluids, if appropriate.
- Assess the hygiene and nutritional status of the body at time of death.
- Note the location of livor mortis on the body and how it relates to the position in which the body was found.
- Document growth parameters and any dysmorphic features.
- Document all injuries in detail.
- Examine all body orifices for injury.
- Preserve samples of injuries for microscopy and timing.

Internal examination:

- Photograph (including a scale marker) all positive and negative findings.
- Make layered dissections of anterior neck and face, anterior and posterior torso, including posterior neck, buttocks, and limbs (if appropriate). Examine testes, middle ears, globes of the eyes, and optic nerves *in situ* (with or without removal), spinal cord, and perform a pelvic exenteration (if appropriate).
- Preserve samples of all organs and tissues for microscopy.

Ancillary tests:

- Radiographs (conducted prior to autopsy), including a full skeletal survey (results to be formally reported by radiologist). CT and MRI, if possible.
- Submit blood samples for toxicology and metabolic screening.
- Bacterial and viral cultures from blood, nasopharynx, lungs, stool, urine, and elsewhere, as appropriate.
- Vitreous fluid for biochemistry.

Other tests to consider:

- Cerebrospinal fluid for culture and cell count.
- Bile for metabolic screening.
- DNA from trace samples and from decedent.
- Fibroblast cultures and cytogenetic testing.

9) Fatal Elder Abuse and Neglect

The very young and the very old are in similar situations. They generally have limited ability to care for themselves and are dependent on others. As a result, they are more susceptible to being abused. Elder abuse is an act or omission that results in harm or threatened harm to the health or welfare of an elderly person. It encompasses physical, sexual, psychological, and financial abuse, as well as neglect, but forensic pathologists are concerned with the physical aspects of elder abuse and neglect. Like child abuse, elder abuse is often under-reported due to under-recognition by healthcare workers or family members, but also because of denial or the inability of the victim to verbalize the abuse. Older persons who have difficulty performing the activities of daily living or have dementia or other physical impairments have a higher risk of becoming victims of abuse and neglect.

Suspected elder abuse requires a thorough medicolegal death investigation, including scene and history investigation, autopsy, and ancillary studies, to properly determine the cause and manner of death and to support or refute claims of abuse. Abuse or neglect may occur at home, where the responsible caregiver(s) are usually family members, or in institutions, such as nursing homes.

a) The Aging Process

The normal aging process and the changes that go along with it may mimic injury or maltreatment and may be misinterpreted as evidence of injury. Natural disease processes also cause changes in an elderly person's body that may be misinterpreted as maltreatment. An aging person's physical condition may be compromised by weakness, instability, or immobility. As they age, people often become increasingly dependent on others. Common changes seen in old age include easy bruising, fragile skin that is more prone to tearing, decreased body fat, muscle atrophy, and fecal and urinary incontinence. The elderly are more prone to falls, which can produce injuries that may be mistaken for abuse. Therefore, physical injuries must not be interpreted in a vacuum. In most cases, death is from a natural disease, but elder abuse and neglect may have played a significant role.

b) Physical Elder Abuse

Common forms of elder abuse include the use of physical force resulting in bodily injury, pain, or impairment; blunt force trauma that causes bruises, lacerations, fractures, or head injuries; and marks from burns, bites, and restraint. Repeated abuse will often show a pattern of injury of different ages on different areas of the body, as well as injuries that cannot be otherwise reasonably explained.

c) Neglect

The category of neglect includes the intentional or unintentional failure of a caregiver to meet the needs of a person; the failure to provide adequate food, hydration, clothing, shelter, hygiene, social stimulation, or medical treatment. There is also the possibility of self-neglect, where a person becomes unable to care for him- or herself. Neglect may manifest in dehydration, starvation, malnutrition, poor hygiene, unsafe living conditions, and undiagnosed disease.

d) Scene and Circumstances

Living conditions that reveal signs of neglect include disarray, dirty clothes and linens, improper temperature control, infestation, poor sanitation, human and pet excrement, and an inadequate supply of food. Examination of the scene should look for signs of confinement or restraint, as well as the presence of other hazards.

An examination of the overall health of the decedent at the time of death should include a full medical history including a list of medications, a review of medical reports of any recent hospitalization, the psychiatric and social history, and level of independence and competency of the individual.

e) Post-mortem Findings in Fatal Elder Abuse and Neglect

Blunt force injuries are indicated by bruises of various ages on various sites of the body. Of particular note are bruises or abrasions around the ankles and wrists, which may indicate restraint, and bone fractures and intracranial hemorrhages (whether the skull is fractured or not). Features that indicate neglect include poor hygiene, such as unkempt hair and nails, encrusted dirt on the skin, poor anogenital cleanliness, and poor dental hygiene. Malnutrition, starvation, and dehydration manifest in the elderly in a manner similar to that in children.

In the elderly, weight loss and organ atrophy are natural to the aging process, but atrophy is more profound in chronic starvation. Lack of contents in the stomach and bowels, and presence of impacted stool indicate chronic starvation or dehydration. Chronic natural disease is also common in the elderly and must be ruled out as a cause for low body mass index (BMI) before the forensic pathologist concludes that it is due to malnutrition. Anatomical, histological, and biochemical investigations must rule out other conditions, such as cancer, that may lead to wasting.

Contractures and pressure sores are also commonly seen in the elderly. Contractures are abnormal, often permanent, bending and fixation of a limb, caused by the atrophy of a muscle and its replacement by scar tissue. Contractures arise from prolonged disuse and indicate inadequate exercise of the joints. Pressure sores, also known as bedsores or decubitus ulcers, arise from prolonged pressure over bony prominences in persons who are bedridden and are not moved regularly. Pressure sores may also be caused by malnutrition and some natural diseases. Deep pressure sores may become infected, with further spread of infection into the bloodstream, sometimes leading to death. Multiple sites and sores that extend deep into bone may indicate neglect, but even with exemplary care, a person's state of health and nutrition may result in pressure ulcers.

f) The Autopsy in Fatal Elderly Abuse and Neglect

To reach a final conclusion about the cause and manner of death where elder abuse or neglect is suspected, forensic pathologists require detailed history and background information to inform a meticulous autopsy that documents and accounts for changes from disease or general aging, evidence of physical injury, and features of neglect. The following steps are routinely undertaken at autopsy in cases of suspected elder abuse, with modifications on a case-by-case basis.

External examination:

- Collect trace evidence, including through sex swabs.
- Make an alternate light source examination of the body for the detection of body fluids, if appropriate.

Internal examination:

- Photograph (including a scale marker) all positive and negative findings.
- Make layered dissections of anterior neck and face, anterior and posterior torso, including posterior neck, buttocks, and limbs (if appropriate). Examine testes and spinal cord, and perform a pelvic exenteration (if appropriate).
- Preserve samples of tissues for microscopy and other studies.
- Consider neuropathological consultation for dementia studies.

Ancillary tests:

- Full body X-ray.
- Preserve a blood sample for toxicology.
- Bacterial and viral cultures from blood, nasopharynx, lungs, stool, urine, and elsewhere, if infection is suspected.
- Vitreous fluid for biochemistry.
- DNA from trace swabs.
- Microscopy of all sampled tissues and injuries.
- Sample injuries or other findings (e.g., pressure sores) for microscopic and microbiological examination.

The forensic pathologist performing the autopsy should carefully document the subject's general physical condition, including length and weight, age-related changes, cleanliness of skin, hair, and nails, and clothing. In addition, note should be made of nutritional status, level of hydration, and injuries, including any at body orifices.

C. THE ROLE OF THE FORENSIC PATHOLOGIST IN CRIMINAL CASES

The forensic pathologist testifies in court as an expert witness, having been granted the privilege of providing opinion evidence based on special medical knowledge. In Canada, expertise is most often established through a combination of formal training, certification, and experience in the field. Regardless of whether they are called by the prosecution or the defence, the duty of the forensic pathologist is to the court and to the public.

1) Direct Examination

The forensic pathologist is typically called as an expert witness by the prosecution in criminally suspicious cases. Even in seemingly simple cases, a pre-trial meeting between the Crown attorney and the forensic pathologist is advisable. This will allow for discussion of any additional relevant information, including the autopsy report, and structuring of the direct examination. The pathologist will expect to testify on the autopsy findings and the cause, manner, and mechanism of death. If additional issues are of interest to the court, they can be communicated at this time.

The direct examination usually follows the natural flow of the medicolegal autopsy: (1) history and scene information, (2) external findings, (3) internal findings, (4) ancillary testing, and (5) summary and opinion. The opinion on cause of death can be presented at both the beginning and the end of the testimony. Most forensic pathologists are comfortable presenting a narrative in this order and should require only limited direction. Photographs, diagrams, and other techniques (e.g., X-rays) can be used to illustrate key findings. Medical jargon should be kept to a minimum. Any necessary technical terms should be "translated" into plain language as they come up.

In most cases, the forensic pathologist's opinions will develop in an obvious, logical, and unambiguous way from the facts (e.g., a shotgun wound to the head as the cause of death). More complex opinions may derive from multiple facts, medical knowledge, or exclusionary evidence. The reasoning behind a complex opinion should be clearly explained to the court. While numerical answers regarding possibility and probability (typically, percentage estimates) are seldom provided, forensic pathologists should be able to support the facts and opinions they offer by documentation from the autopsy and reference to the medical literature.

Any limitations to the pathologist's opinion should be made clear. This most commonly occurs when an opinion is based (at least in part) on information provided by another source, rather than independent autopsy findings. Forensic pathologists should also make clear what information is derived from their knowledge of forensic pathology and what is derived from general medical knowledge. While a pathologist may be able to provide an opinion on a general medical issue, an opinion should be sought from an expert in that field if it is critical to the case.

2) Cross-Examination

A pretrial meeting may be invaluable for defence counsel. Discussion of key issues prior to trial can lead to more relevant questions in court. When the difference between fact and opinion is made clear, it becomes easier to judge the merits of an alternative explanation or scenario. The forensic pathologist should be prepared to discuss alternative scenarios during the cross-examination. Claims based on experience should also be carefully scrutinized.

3) Common Practical Issues at Trial

There are a few recurrent issues in murder trials involving forensic pathology evidence. Most of these issues are not complex and can be anticipated.

One of the most common omissions in a murder trial is the failure of the prosecution and defence lawyers to meet with the forensic pathologist before the preliminary inquiry or trial. This is a missed opportunity to understand how to elicit evidence in direct examination and relevant concessions in cross-examination. This failure to fully explore the content of the forensic pathologist's findings and opinions may also hamper witness preparation.

Visual aids, such as autopsy photographs or other presentation material, are often helpful in making an argument or scenario understandable. However, there may be a challenge from opposing counsel regarding the admissibility of visual aids. Absent the application of specific rules of admissibility, the judge will rule by balancing the probative value against the prejudicial effect of the images. This can sometimes be resolved in a *voir dire.* In general, pathologists should be expected to decide how to present their evidence most effectively.

It is important that the Crown prosecutor, defence attorney, judge, and witness pay close attention to the use of terminology that may be vague or misleading. "Consistent with" may be equated in the minds of jurors with "evidence of." "Consistent with" is a more specialized term, usually referring only to a possibility, or the inability to exclude an assertion. Pathologists ought to pay particular attention to the use of language that communicates an accurate level of certainty about their expert opinions, particularly opinions that will be crucial to the outcome of the case. On this basis, direct and cross-examination that is focused on eliciting balanced and plain language about an expert's opinion is vital. Otherwise, there is the real risk of the jury misunderstanding the meaning of the opinion, or the strength with which the opinion is held.

D. CONCLUSION

Forensic pathology is a body of medical knowledge that can assist the legal system in discovering the direct or indirect causes of death and injury. It can be a powerful tool in documenting observable fact (e.g., wounds) and interpreting the significance of observations (e.g., determining how the wounds occurred) as a first step towards attaining justice. The science of forensic pathology is predicated on our ability to apply medical and scientific knowledge in a logical framework that leads to valid or reliable expert opinions. This is both the strength and the weakness of expert evidence. It is a strength because the explanatory powers of modern medical science are unprecedented. The weakness of expert opinion is that knowledge is incomplete. There will always be gaps or insufficiencies that prevent a perfect understanding of the events that led to the death or injury in question. This may not hamper the typical murder trial that relies on well understood and settled medical knowledge (e.g., the clearly fatal wound that was clearly caused by a gunshot), but occasionally the expert opinion will be discordant or will delve into areas of forensic medicine that lack consensus or hard data to back it up. The criminal justice system and the forensic pathology system have developed four main tools or concepts to deal with these issues.

First, it is important to have a properly qualified forensic pathologist who functions in an evidence-based framework. Second, it is essential that the state provide a quality assurance program for forensic pathology expert opinions that can be relied upon by the court. This is typically achieved by institutionalized peer review. Third, the judge must act as gatekeeper, determining admissibility and threshold reliability. Finally, controversial expert evidence must be tested by effective cross-examination.

Biomedical science and the law are linked by their commitment to the search for truth. When harnessed properly, forensic pathology can ensure that medical knowledge helps the court resolve certain questions of fact and opinion in a fair and reliable manner.

E. LEGAL CONTEXT

> The criminal justice system values finality. However, forensic pathology is an evolving science in which controversies exist, and where findings and opinions often require interpretation [creating tension between forensic pathology and the criminal justice system] . . . . Moreover, the evolution of scientific knowledge will often be accompanied by controversy—as pathologists debate whether the existing scientific knowledge permits certain opinions to be reasonably formed, and whether new scientific knowledge casts doubt on previously expressed opinions or, at the very least, modifies the levels of confidence with which those opinions can be reasonably expressed.
>
> The reliability of forensic pathology opinions matters a great deal to the criminal justice system. In cases in which there are important issues of pathology, as often occurs in pediatric death cases, flawed pathology can lead to tragic outcomes.[3]

Forensic pathology is "the application of pathology to legal issues involving deaths that society has an interest in examining for the good of pub-

3 Goudge Inquiry Report, *ibid.* at 9 & 10.

lic health."[4] Forensic pathologists may investigate sudden and unexpected deaths, unnatural or suspicious deaths, and deaths occurring in-custody or in prison.[5] It falls to the forensic pathologist to "examine the dead to identify specific classes of injury, collect medical evidence, determine the presence or absence of natural disease, and determine the physiological cause of death."[6] Forensic pathologists may also describe the manner of death, which can be categorized as natural, accidental, suicide, homicide, or undetermined.[7] Information is gathered at autopsy. Other analyses, like microscopic tissue analysis (i.e., histological analysis), will also be performed when necessary.

Forensic pathology evidence is a key part of the death investigation narrative presented to the trier of fact in cases of alleged murder, manslaughter, and infanticide. When forensic pathologists give conflicting opinions on the cause of death, the trier of fact must determine what weight to give each opinion.[8] Forensic pathology evidence in court has, at a minimum, addressed the following five broad areas:

- *Key considerations relevant to a fact at issue.* The principles of forensic pathology have been used to establish the leakage of semen from the vagina due to gravity, with the resulting semen staying on the body and staining clothing;[9] the position of the deceased in a vehicle at the time of a motor vehicle accident;[10] and the time elapsed from a shooting to the arrival of police on the scene based on blood loss as well as the changes in the blood's colour and consistency.[11]

---

4 Michael S. Pollanen et al., eds., "Forensic Science in Canada: A Report of Multidisciplinary Discussion" (4–5 May 2012) at 11 [Hart House Report], online: www.forensics.utoronto.ca/Assets/LMPF+Digital+Assets/Forensic+Science+in+Canada.pdf.

5 *Ibid.* See also *Coroners Act*, R.S.O. 1990, c. C.37, s. 10(1).

6 National Research Council Committee on Identifying the Needs of the Forensic Sciences Community, *Strengthening Forensic Science in the United States: A Path Forward* (Washington, DC: National Academies Press, 2009) at 257, online: www.ncjrs.gov/pdffiles1/nij/grants/228091.pdf [2009 NAS Report].

7 *Ibid.*

8 *R. v. MacLeod*, 2014 NSCA 63 at para. 46. The majority quashed the second-degree murder conviction and ordered a new trial. The Supreme Court of Canada dismissed the appeal, finding that the trial judge erred by not charging the jury on manslaughter. See *R. v. MacLeod*, 2014 SCC 76.

9 *R. v. Hall*, 2010 ONCA 724 at paras. 64–70.

10 *R. v. Gallant*, 2007 NBCA 36. The central issue was determining who drove the vehicle at the time of the accident. The pathologist's opinion relevant to the position of the deceased in the vehicle, however, was not disclosed prior to trial and, for that reason, the Court of Appeal unanimously decided to quash the conviction and order a new trial.

11 *R. v. Perlett* (2006), 82 O.R. (3d) 89 (C.A.), leave to appeal to S.C.C. refused, [2007] S.C.C.A. No. 96. See also Glenn R. Anderson, *Expert Evidence*, 3d ed. (Markham, ON: LexisNexis, 2014) at 405 [Anderson].

- *Wound causation and weapon identification.* Forensic pathology can be used to determine the estimated distance from which a gun was fired;[12] whether pattern injuries are consistent with being inflicted by certain objects and items;[13] and the types of instruments capable of inflicting a particular wound.[14]
- *The significance of health considerations to injury determination.* Forensic pathologists are able to make observations of apparent injuries—for example, where pregnancy cannot be eliminated as a factor producing the injury.[15]
- *The importance of analyses after autopsy to assess a case with confidence.*[16] Microscopic tissue examination (i.e., histological analysis), for example, is used to confidently determine cause of death.
- *Scientific theories beyond the knowledge of the court.*

The variety of issues requiring forensic pathology expertise, however, does not equate to such evidence being unfettered by judicial gatekeeping. In the *voir dire* of *R. v. Taylor*,[17] the forensic pathologist called by the Crown opined definitively that "all the wounds were inflicted from behind" and "were consistent with an attack from behind."[18] Justice Henderson held that the opinion was inadmissible as it failed to meet the threshold level of reliability required by *Mohan*.[19] Further, the forensic pathologist referred to characteristics of "homicidal attacks" and, since the term "homicidal" prejudged an issue before the jury, the court held that the term should not be used in evidence.[20] Overall, Henderson J. held that the opinion was inadmissible since it was beyond the scope of the expert's expertise and, alternatively, did not meet the reliability threshold for admission since the forensic pathologist provided "no real exposition" on how he arrived at the opinion.[21]

---

12 *R. v. Jaw*, 2009 SCC 42.

13 *R. v. Butorac*, 2010 BCSC 877. See also Anderson, above note 11 at 409.

14 *R. v. R.D.*, 2014 ONCA 302.

15 *R. v. Panghali*, 2010 BCSC 1836. The uncertainty arose with respect to the cause, not the presence of the hematoma. In *R. v. Panghali*, 2012 BCCA 407, the Court of Appeal found that the forensic pathologist's evidence of the hematoma's presence fell into the realm of fact, not opinion. See also Anderson, above note 11 at 409.

16 See, generally, *R. v. Dorsay*, 2003 BCSC 894. The defence application on *voir dire* for a stay of proceedings was refused.

17 *R. v. Taylor*, 2001 BCSC 1025.

18 *Ibid.* at para. 9.

19 *Ibid.* at paras. 9–11. If the expert had limited himself to the more modest "consistent with" opinion, however, it would have been admissible.

20 *Ibid.* at para. 12.

21 *Ibid.* at para. 16.

The professionalization of forensic pathology has become a focus of the field in recent years, catalyzed in large part by the Goudge Inquiry, which highlighted the tragedies that can be caused by flawed forensic pathology evidence. The importance of forensic pathology to the criminal justice system is perhaps best appreciated by examining the wrongful convictions that the discipline both contributed to and assisted in correcting. The following cases taken on by Innocence Canada (formerly known as the Association in Defence of the Wrongly Convicted [AIDWYC]) exemplify such tragedies. Those wrongful convictions stemmed from the flawed pediatric forensic pathology evidence and once eminent reputation of Charles Smith, a pathologist who was later stripped of his medical licence in 2011.[22]

1) William Mullins-Johnson[23]

On 26 June 1993, William Mullins-Johnson was babysitting Valin, his four-year-old niece, and her siblings. The twenty-two-year-old checked on

22 The Canadian Press, "Disgraced Pathologist Charles Smith Stripped of Medical Licence" *Globe and Mail* (1 February 2011), online: http://fw.to/Sxc7XNF. We are indebted to Innocence Canada for providing on their website the case information for the discussion that follows. The summaries of these cases in this book have been constructed relying on the more detailed overview provided on the Innocence Canada website. For a more extensive overview of each of the cases discussed, visit Innocence Canada's website directly at: www.aidwyc.org. Maria Shepherd's recent acquittal underscores the damage Smith caused and the continuing efforts to rectify miscarriages of justice stemming from his involvement in criminal cases. On 29 February 2016, Maria Shepherd's 1992 manslaughter conviction in relation to the death of her three-year-old stepdaughter, Kasandra, was quashed by the Court of Appeal for Ontario. New forensic expert evidence concluded that Kasandra died from natural causes (specifically, seizures or a related disorder) and that Dr. Smith's opinion—that Kasandra was abused, and killed by a blow(s) that left a watch-shaped impression on her head—was without scientific basis. The Crown agreed that Dr. Smith's evidence was flawed and that an acquittal was appropriate. Decades earlier, Ms. Shepherd had pled guilty mid-trial based on her lawyer's advice, who cautioned her of Dr. Smith's eminent reputation. Ms. Shepherd was also deeply concerned about protecting her children as much as possible in the situation; the risk of continuing with a trial involving Dr. Smith was too high. See, Wendy Gillis, "Woman Acquitted in Stepdaughter's 1991 Death" (29 February 2016) online: Toronto Star http://on.thestar.com/1T46UBP.

23 Sarah Harland-Logan, "Historical Cases: William Mullins-Johnson," online: Innocence Canada www.aidwyc.org/cases/historical/william-mullins-johnson. For a discussion of the details of the forensic pathology involved in this case, readers are encouraged to read M.S. Pollanen, "Forensic Pathology and the Miscarriage of Justice" (2012) 8 *Forensic Science, Medicine, and Pathology* 285. See also *R. v. Mullins-Johnson*, 1996 CanLII 1214 (ON CA), appeal dismissed in *R. v. Mullins-Johnson*, [1998] 1 S.C.R. 977; acquittal entered on basis of fresh evidence in *R. v. Mullins-Johnson*, 2007 ONCA 720.

Valin after she had gone to bed and found her sleeping soundly. The next morning, Valin's mother discovered that Valin had died during the night.

Smith and a team of two other doctors concluded that Valin was strangled between 8 p.m. and 10 p.m., when Mullins-Johnson was babysitting the children alone. The team also concluded that Valin was the victim of chronic sexual abuse. The next day, 27 June 1993, Mullins-Johnson was arrested for the first-degree murder and aggravated sexual assault of Valin.

At trial, what were thought to be bruises on Valin's chest, neck, and head—which were later determined to have resulted from her head-down position—were relied upon by Smith and other expert witnesses to conclude that Valin was abused and then suffocated. Despite a lack of physical evidence connecting Mullins-Johnson to Valin's death, he was convicted of first degree murder in 1994. In 1996, the Ontario Court of Appeal dismissed the appeal, although Justice Borens dissented and would have ordered a new trial on the basis of the lack of forensic evidence connecting Valin and Mullins-Johnson. In 1998, the Supreme Court of Canada dismissed Mullins-Johnson's appeal.

Innocence Canada took up the case in February 2003. A request for Valin's samples for independent review by Dr. Bernard Knight was stonewalled by Smith. The Goudge Inquiry Report later found that, "Dr. Smith actively misled those who might have engaged in meaningful oversight of his work."[24] Dr. Michael Pollanen, who had become the chief forensic pathologist for Ontario, reviewed the case, including the microscope slides, and concluded that Smith's conclusions were wrong and that, specifically, the dilated anus to which Smith alone testified to as being indicative of abuse, was a normal post-mortem artifact. Dr. Pollanen concluded that there was no evidence indicating that Valin was the victim of sexual abuse or murder. Dr. Knight agreed that Valin's death was natural.

On the basis of Innocence Canada's section 696.1 application, the Federal Minister of Justice remanded the case to the Ontario Court of Appeal, which acknowledged the case as a miscarriage of justice and acquitted Mullins-Johnson on 15 October 2007. Chris Bentley, the attorney general of Ontario at the time of the acquittal, apologized on behalf of the Ontario government to Mullins-Johnson and his family. Mullins-Johnson was compensated with $4.25 million after serving thirteen years in prison.

---

24 Goudge Inquiry Report, above note 1 at 19.

2) Tammy Marquardt[25]

On 18 May 1991, Tammy Marquardt's son, Kenneth, was born. He had a number of health problems, including asthma, pneumonia, and epilepsy. He was hospitalized on several occasions because of the frequency and severity of his seizures. On 9 October 1993, Kenneth was discovered by Marquardt tangled in bed sheets, struggling for air. He was revived at hospital but died shortly thereafter.

Dr. Smith conducted Kenneth's autopsy and concluded that the cause of death was asphyxia caused by strangulation or smothering. Marquardt was arrested and charged with the second degree murder of her son on 23 November 1993. At trial, Smith was the key witness for the Crown, which theorized that Marquardt suffocated Kenneth in frustration. The defence argued that Kenneth's death was the result of an epileptic seizure, but called no expert. Marquardt testified in her own defence, but was convicted in 1995. Her appeal was unanimously dismissed in 1998.

In 2004, Marquardt applied to Innocence Canada and her case was reviewed by experts as part of the chief coroner's review, preceding the Goudge Inquiry. A 2007 report concluded that Smith's finding was "against scientific evidence-based reasoning" and that the conclusion was inappropriately based on non-specific findings. The cause of death should have been unascertained. In 2008, a second expert review concluded that Kenneth may have died while suffering an epileptic seizure or from other natural causes.

In 2009, the Supreme Court of Canada remanded the case to the Ontario Court of Appeal to consider this new evidence. In 2011, the Court of Appeal quashed the conviction and ordered a new trial, indicating that sudden unexpected death in epilepsy (SUDEP) could not be excluded as a cause of death. The Crown withdrew the charges.

3) Richard Brant[26]

Richard Brant discovered his nine-week-old son, Dustin, motionless in his carriage while taking him out for a walk. Although revived momentarily at hospital, Dustin died on 18 November 1992. Dr. Sukrita Nag performed the

25 Sarah Harland-Logan, "Historical Cases: Tammy Marquardt," online: Innocence Canada www.aidwyc.org/cases/historical/tammy-marquardt. *R. v. Marquardt*, 1998 CanLII 3527 (ON CA), appeal dismissed; fresh evidence admitted, conviction quashed and new trial ordered in *R. v. Marquardt*, 2011 ONCA 281.

26 Sarah Harland-Logan, "Historical Cases: Richard Brant," online: Innocence Canada www.aidwyc.org/cases/historical/richard-brant. See *R. v. Brant*, 2011 ONCA 362.

autopsy and concluded that the death resulted from pneumonia complications (shortly before death, Dustin had a respiratory infection). Without any evidence implicating Brant in his son's death, police believed Brant killed his son. They asked for a second opinion from Smith, who concluded that Dustin died of shaken baby syndrome. Charged with manslaughter, Brant pled guilty to a reduced charge of aggravated assault and was sentenced to six months in prison. He felt he had no other option since he faced up to fifteen years in prison and, at the time, he had a new baby on the way.

The case was reviewed as part of the chief coroner's review leading up to the Goudge Inquiry and, in 2007, reviewing experts agreed that no evidence supported Smith's conclusion. Instead, pneumonia might have been involved. A joint request to acquit Brant was put forward by his Innocence Canada lawyers and the Crown. In 2009, Brant's application for leave to appeal to the Court of Appeal was allowed. On 4 May 2011, the Court of Appeal set aside the guilty plea and entered an acquittal.

4) Dinesh Kumar[27]

In 1991, Kumar immigrated to Canada with his wife and their son, Saurob. On 11 February 1992, the family had a second son, Gaurov. On 18 March 1992, Gaurov stopped breathing. Kumar performed CPR, but could not revive Gaurov, who was rushed to hospital but died on 20 March 1992. Smith performed Gaurov's autopsy and concluded that the injuries were consistent with shaken baby syndrome. On 26 June 1992, Kumar was arrested and charged with second degree murder. Informed by his lawyer of Smith's esteemed reputation, Kumar knew he would be unable to support his family if imprisoned and might face deportation back to India. The Crown offered a plea bargain: if Kumar pled guilty to criminal negligence causing death, he would serve ninety days of jail time on weekends and police would not report him to the immigration authorities. In 1992, Kumar pled guilty even though he privately maintained his innocence.

The case was reviewed as part of the chief coroner's review leading up to the Goudge Inquiry and, in 2007, experts opined that they had serious disagreements with Smith's findings in the case. Kumar's application for leave to appeal to the Ontario Court of Appeal was allowed. Experts opined that the cause of death was undetermined and that there was no

---

27 Sarah Harland-Logan, "Historical Cases: Dinesh Kumar," online: Innocence Canada www.aidwyc.org/cases/historical/dinesh-kumar. See *R. v. Kumar*, 2011 ONCA 120.

evidence suggesting Kumar injured his son. Instead, it was possible that Gaurov's death may have been caused by a head injury sustained at birth. On 20 January 2011,the Court of Appeal set aside Kumar's guilty plea and entered an acquittal.

5) Sherry Sherret-Robinson[28]

Sherry Sherret-Robinson found her four-month-old son, Joshua, face down in his playpen and not breathing on 22 January 1996. He could not be revived at hospital and the twenty-year-old mother was advised by doctors that her son had died. Dr. Smith concluded that the death was a result of smothering. Sherret-Robinson's other son was removed from her care on 7 March and put up for adoption. She was arrested and charged with Joshua's murder on 27 March 1996. The Crown offered to withdraw the murder charge and replace it with a charge of infanticide, which carried a far shorter prison term. In exchange, Sherret-Robinson would agree to not challenge the Crown's argument that she smothered her son. Feeling that she had no choice, Sherret-Robinson accepted the offer. She was found guilty on 2 June 1999 and sentenced to one year in prison.

In 2006, Sherret-Robinson read about the Goudge Inquiry and contacted Innocence Canada, which recommended she contact the Office of the Chief Coroner for Ontario and request the inclusion of her case in the investigation. Investigating experts concluded Joshua had not been smothered, but instead probably asphyxiated accidentally in his playpen's blankets. Smith's conclusions were reached in error and his own autopsy procedures created hemorrhages in Joshua's neck tissues. These "injuries" were relied upon by Smith in his conclusions. The Crown agreed with Innocence Canada lawyers that Sherret-Robinson should be acquitted. In 2009, the Ontario Court of Appeal entered an acquittal.

★ ★ ★

The Goudge Inquiry and the cases connected to the flawed evidence of Smith highlight the importance of training experts and professionalizing the discipline, improving oversight and accountability within the system, ensuring effective communication with the criminal justice system, and educating criminal justice stakeholders about their respective roles.

---

28 Sarah Harland-Logan, "Historical Cases: Sherry Sherret-Robinson," online: Innocence Canada www.aidwyc.org/cases/historical/sherry-sherrett-robinson. See *R. v. Sherret-Robinson*, 2009 ONCA 886.

Beyond individual and systemic flaws, there are controversial areas in forensic pathology itself that demand the greatest level of attention to detail by all parties in the criminal justice system. As outlined in the Hart House Report,[29] current scientific controversies relate to time since death estimates, post-mortem artifacts, shaken or abused infants, negative autopsies, and deaths in police custody.[30] Of these controversies, shaken baby syndrome (SBS) in particular has been the subject of growing concerns over its scientific foundations, with questions arising as to whether or not the phenomenon even exists.[31]

The constellation of injuries ("the triad") used to diagnosis SBS is now being applied in association with abusive head trauma (AHT, also known as non-accidental abusive head trauma) and for that reason should, perhaps, also be added to the above list of current scientific controversies. The triad consists of three non-specific findings: brain edema, subdural and subarachnoid hemorrhaging, and retinal hemorrhaging.[32] In *R. v. Laverdiere*,[33] the triad was found at the autopsy of a twenty-month-old foster child who suddenly collapsed and stopped breathing while in the care of his foster mother, who had performed CPR without success.

Both the Crown and the defence called forensic pathology expert witnesses. The expert called by the Crown opined that the triad can be created in certain accidents but that, in this case, the cranial trauma was non-accidental because there was no "good" story explaining its presence.[34] The expert explained that a good story might be a motor vehicle accident with sudden braking, a fall from more than five feet, or a fall down stairs in a walker. Stories that were not good were falling from standing or sitting, or dropping from a parent's arms.[35] In contrast, the expert called by the defence opined that the physical findings resulted exclusively from lack of oxygen after cardiac arrest associated with seizures and an airway blocked by vomit. There were no bruises to the brain, scalp, or skull, no tearing in the brain, no evidence of impact, and no traumatic injury to the brain. The expert opined that a conclusion of violence is not proper if there is

29 Above note 4 at 111 (Appendix F).

30 *Ibid.* at 111 (Appendix F). A negative autopsy is one in which no anatomical, toxicological, or biochemical cause of death is established after a detailed examination.

31 *R. v. Schoenthal*, 2007 SKCA 80 at para. 141.

32 In other words, brain swelling, brain bleeding, and retinal (i.e., eye retina) bleeding.

33 *R. v. Laverdiere*, 2014 ABQB 161.

34 *Ibid.* at paras. 88 and 104.

35 *Ibid.* at para. 90.

no evidence of trauma.[36] The defence expert also questioned the scientific validity of diagnosing abuse as a default in the absence of an alternate explanation. Such an approach fails to answer the question, "On what basis did you determine that it was abuse?"[37]

The defence argued that approaching causation by using AHT as a default diagnosis based on the triad's presence in the absence of a valid explanation for the child's injuries comes close to reversing the burden of proof and usurping the role of the trier of fact. Counsel referred to "warnings from the Goudge Inquiry that the absence of a credible explanation is not a substitute for a proper diagnosis."[38] In considering the evidence as a whole, M.T. Moreau J. found the accused not guilty of manslaughter.[39]

Individual, systemic, and scientific issues deserve consideration when forensic pathology evidence is presented in court, but it is also important to critically analyze caselaw, because it may not reflect current scientific knowledge. The evolving nature of forensic pathology and its clash with the finality of the law is perhaps best exemplified by the case of Steven Truscott, whose 1959 murder conviction was quashed in 2007 as a miscarriage of justice on the basis of new forensic pathology and gastroenterology evidence. The time of death estimate presented at trial was seriously undermined by a challenge to outdated wisdom that considered stomach contents and external decomposition evidence as reliable indicators of time of death. Archival documents also put the reliability and credibility of the attending pathologist's time of death estimate into question. This evidence, supported by new forensic entomology evidence, led the Ontario Court of Appeal to conclude that the forensic pathology evidence originally presented at trial was "scientifically untenable."[40]

Truscott was seen giving his classmate, Lynne Harper, a ride on his bicycle between 7 p.m. and 7:30 p.m. on 9 June 1959. He returned to the school grounds no later than 8:15 p.m.[41] Harper was found sexually assaulted and strangled on 11 June in a wooded area known by locals as Lawson's

---

36 *Ibid.* at paras. 113 & 114.

37 *Ibid.* at para. 134.

38 *Ibid.* at para. 140. This quote is in the words of the court.

39 *Ibid.* at paras. 202 & 203.

40 *R. v. Truscott*, 2007 ONCA 575 at paras. 3, 8, 307, and 777 [*Truscott*]. See Chapter 15, Section F for a discussion of the forensic entomology evidence. Note that Innocence Canada submitted a ministerial review application in 2001, which resulted in the minister of justice referring the case to the Court of Appeal.

41 *Ibid.* at para. 213. This was on the Crown's submission at trial.

Bush, close to the route she and Truscott travelled on County Road.[42] The attending pathologist, Dr. John L. Penistan conducted the autopsy on 11 June.[43] Truscott became the prime suspect early in the investigation and was arrested the next day.[44] Although the cause of death was never an issue, the time of death evidence was crucial since, according to the Crown's theory, Truscott had exclusive opportunity to kill Harper if she died before 8 p.m. on 9 June. The Crown argued that Truscott must have murdered Harper before returning to the school grounds.[45] At trial, the Crown relied upon the evidence of Dr. Penistan that Harper died between 7 p.m. and 7:45 p.m. based on his observations of her stomach contents, *rigor mortis*, and body decomposition.[46] Dr. Penistan testified that, under normal conditions, digestion and stomach emptying is completed within two hours—Harper's mother testified that Harper finished her last known meal at 5:45 p.m.[47] Dr. Penistan testified in chief "that *rigor mortis* was still, although only just, demonstrable" and that "the state of the body suggested that death had occurred some two days previously," which he viewed as separate but compatible with the time of death estimate based on his stomach contents observations.[48] It is important to note that the defence failed to ask Dr. Penistan if a time of death after 8 p.m. was compatible with his findings.[49] The complex and conflicting witness testimony in the case, referred to as the "County Road evidence," was filtered through this time of death opinion.

The 1966 Reference focused on whether stomach contents could fix a limited time of death window, with the majority of the Supreme Court of Canada concluding that it could be used in such a manner.[50] The time frame stood despite concerns raised by experts about Dr. Penistan's method. All experts agreed that Dr. Penistan's time frame could not be excluded as a possibility but could also not be expressed so narrowly if relying upon stomach contents and *rigor mortis*.[51] Finally, in its 2007 decision, the Ontario Court of Appeal concluded that Truscott's acquittal would be the likely re-

42 *Ibid.* at paras. 4 & 5. Lawson's Bush is near Clinton, Ontario.

43 *Ibid.* at para. 128.

44 *Ibid.* at fn 25.

45 *Ibid.* at paras. 126, 213, and 306.

46 *Ibid.* at para. 29. Also see para. 304, where the judgment outlines the four key factual pillars relied upon by the Crown: (1) the time of death, (2) the County Road evidence, (3) Truscott's post-offence conduct, and (4) evidence relating to lesions on Truscott's penis.

47 *Ibid.* at para. 134.

48 *Ibid.* at para. 135. This is quoted from Dr. Penistan's testimony at trial.

49 *Ibid.* at para. 155.

50 *Ibid.* at para. 129. See *Reference re: Truscott*, [1967] S.C.R. 309.

51 *Ibid.* at paras. 147–50.

sult if a hypothetical new trial proceeded on the basis of the entirety of the fresh evidence, necessitating the quashing of the conviction.[52] The appellant called upon the pathology evidence of Dr. Michael Pollanen and Dr. Bernard Knight to discredit Dr. Penistan's opinion that Harper was dead by 7:45 p.m. on 9 June, as well as archival documents that brought into question the reliability and credibility of Dr. Penistan's time of death opinion.[53]

The Crown called upon Dr. Werner Spitz and Dr. Nicholas Diamant, a forensic pathologist and gastroenterologist, respectively.[54] The court rejected the evidence of Dr. Spitz because of his dogmatic conclusions that lacked scientific grounding in an evidence-based approach:[55]

> Before we summarize this evidence, we must comment on the evidence of the Crown's expert, Dr. Spitz, who has been a forensic pathologist for more than fifty years. Dr. Spitz provided the opinion that Dr. Penistan's determination that Lynne Harper died by 7:45 p.m. is "admirably accurate" and rests on "solid scientific foundation." *It became abundantly clear during cross-examination, however, that the only basis for Dr. Spitz's opinion was his own experience* in conducting autopsies and his belief arising from this experience that if stomach contents are readily identifiable at autopsy, then death must have occurred within two hours of the last meal.
>
> Dr. Spitz was unable to cite any recent scientific literature that would support this view. He refused to acknowledge obvious shortcomings in his opinion when these were pointed out to him in cross-examination. *He refused to concede that his opinion rested on faulty assumptions and misperceptions of the available primary evidence in this case.* These shortcomings could well explain why the Crown does not ask us to rely on his evidence other than in a few very minor respects. *In the result, we have not placed any reliance on his evidence and we give it no further mention.*[56]

According to Dr. Pollanen, Dr. Penistan's narrow time of death estimate was scientifically unsound. Dr. Pollanen highlighted the importance of (1) asking the right question to determine a matter in issue, and (2) considering

52 *Ibid.* at paras. 3 and 215.

53 *Ibid.* at para. 307.

54 *Ibid.* at para. 164.

55 See, generally, Jeffrey A. Claridge & Timothy C. Fabian, "History and Development of Evidence-Based Medicine" (2005) 29 *World Journal of Surgery* 547. According to this article, the evidence-based approach in medicine began taking its modern form in the 1970s and became increasingly formalized and accepted in the 1990s.

56 *Truscott,* above note 40 at paras. 165 & 166 [emphasis added].

all of the available evidence in arriving at a particular conclusion.[57] With respect to stomach contents, Dr. Pollanen explained that the volume and appearance of the stomach contents indicate that the material was in the lag phase of the stomach-emptying process, which is less predictable in duration compared to the second stage of the two-stage process, the emptying phase. External variables such as stress, and intrinsic factors, such as the size and nature of the meal, may extend one or both phases. With respect to decomposition, such changes were less than what would be expected over a two-day post-mortem interval, given the environmental conditions.[58] It was therefore equally true that Harper could have been killed during or after the time frame identified by Dr. Penistan.[59] Dr. Pollanen supported the latter and he concluded that time of death could not be specified to Dr. Penistan's narrow forty-five minute window. Dr. Pollanen cautioned that:

> If there is no specific evidential basis to choose which end [of the available temporal window] is more valid, then the choice is reduced to speculation, or the postmortem interval must be estimated as a widely inclusive time frame.[60]

The evidence of both Dr. Knight and Dr. Diamant supported Dr. Pollanen's overall conclusion, with Dr. Knight going so far as to state that a time of death estimate based on stomach contents and its state of digestion "should never be used as probative evidence."[61] Dr. Diamant opined that stomach contents cannot be used to determine a precise time of death. Although a rough estimate of stomach emptying under "normal circumstances" could be made, Dr. Penistan could not use Harper's stomach contents to limit the time of death period to one to two hours after her last meal.[62] Further, modern research not available in 1959 or in 1966 showed that stomach emptying of a solid meal may last up to six hours or more, undermining the traditional wisdom that the stomach typically empties in three to four hours.[63]

The decomposition evidence also went further than previously heard, addressing the state of internal decomposition for the first time by considering the significance of histology (i.e., microscopic tissue examination)

---

57 *Ibid.* at paras. 171–74.
58 *Ibid.* at para. 176.
59 *Ibid.* at paras. 171 & 172.
60 *Ibid.* at para. 181.
61 *Ibid.* at para. 184.
62 *Ibid.* at paras. 191 & 192.
63 *Ibid.* at paras. 196–204.

as an independent indicator of the degree of changes to the body after death. Both Dr. Pollanen and Dr. Knight found the absence of widespread autolytic or putrefactive changes in the tissue surprising given the hot and humid weather during the time between Harper's disappearance and discovery. Together, the external and internal decomposition evidence pointed to a time of death closer to the day or night of 10 June. No autopsy evidence corroborated Dr. Penistan's narrow time of death estimate.[64]

Three archival documents further questioned the reliability and credibility of Dr. Penistan's time of death evidence: two unofficial or preliminary versions of the autopsy report and a memorandum reviewing the pathology findings at autopsy, the so-called agonizing reappraisal, which was prepared in 1966 by Dr. Penistan at the request of the Crown prior to the 1966 Reference.[65] One unofficial autopsy report obtained in 2005 was likely prepared during autopsy. It provided an estimated time of death of about 12:45 a.m. on June 10—a time when Truscott had an unchallenged alibi.[66] This report described the stomach contents as having "*no* obvious meat."[67] A second unofficial autopsy report found in 2002 provided an estimated time of death between 4:45 a.m. and 10:45 a.m. on 10 June—yet another time of death estimate impossible to reconcile with the Crown's theory.[68] This second report described the stomach contents as having only "a few shreds of apparent meat."[69] This variation in the description of meat in the stomach contents was explained by Dr. Penistan in his agonizing reappraisal as his wanting to "avoid an unjustifiably dogmatic statement that meat was in fact present when further examination was required to establish this with certainty."[70]

With respect to the agonizing reappraisal, Dr. Penistan wrote the report to clarify his earlier work and advised that the review did not change his conclusions.[71] The Court of Appeal found that the memo contradicted or, at a minimum, cast doubt on many of Dr. Penistan's assertions at trial and suggested that his evolving descriptions of the stomach contents indicated

64 *Ibid.* at paras. 206 & 207.

65 *Ibid.* at paras. 216 and 225. The formal title of the "agonizing reappraisal" is: "Regina v. Truscott: Autopsy on the body of Lynne Harper—a review of the pathological findings." It was marked "Draft."

66 *Ibid.* at paras. 219 & 220.

67 *Ibid.* at para. 221 [emphasis in original].

68 *Ibid.* at para. 222.

69 *Ibid.* at para. 224.

70 *Ibid.* at para. 228.

71 *Ibid.* at para. 225.

that he was making his evidence consistent with the Crown's time of death theory.[72] The memo further clarifies that the state of decomposition and *rigor mortis* was compatible with death having occurred both forty-eight hours prior to autopsy as well as a day before or after; Dr. Penistan noted that it was only stated in evidence and confirmed in cross-examination that these two factors were compatible with death having occurred two days before autopsy, implicitly highlighting the significance of defence counsel not asking at trial if his findings were compatible with death after that time.[73]

The agonizing reappraisal also acknowledged a discrepancy in the volume of stomach contents between a report and Dr. Penistan's evidence at trial, which was explained by Dr. Penistan's assumption that some of the stomach contents went uncollected.[74] The report's final conclusion with respect to time of death was that all of the findings were compatible with death having occurred within two hours of Harper's last meal, yet were not incompatible with death having occurred later, "up to 12 hours or even longer."[75] Significantly, the cautious agonizing reappraisal does not share the definitive tone that Dr. Penistan adopted at trial when he opined that Harper died between 7 p.m. and 7:45 p.m on 9 June.[76]

The Court of Appeal found it unnecessary to draw conclusions as to why Dr. Penistan changed his time of death opinion in the reports and why the doctor insisted he had not changed his opinion in his agonizing reappraisal. Instead, it was the potential impact of these documents that was significant. If the documents had been available for cross-examination, Dr. Penistan may have qualified or retracted his definitive time of death opinion and, even if this did not occur, it is possible that a reasonable jury would not accept Dr. Penistan's evidence in light of the documents.[77] Forty-eight years after conviction, Truscott's name was finally cleared. In 2008, the attorney general of Ontario apologized to Truscott and the province compensated him with $6.5 million to recognize the miscarriage of justice.[78]

---

72 *Ibid.* at paras. 233 & 234.
73 *Ibid.* at para. 226.
74 *Ibid.* at para. 227.
75 *Ibid.* at para. 230.
76 *Ibid.* at para. 236.
77 *Ibid.* at para. 239–41.
78 Sarah Harland-Logan, "Historical Cases: Steven Truscott," online: Innocence Canada www.aidwyc.org/cases/historical/steven-truscott/#_ftn18.

CHAPTER 19

Forensic Psychiatry[1]

Hy Bloom and Richard D. Schneider

A. OVERVIEW

Forensic psychiatry is a subspecialty within the field of psychiatry that addresses mental health issues that may arise in a criminal or civil law context. The discipline subsumes correctional psychiatry and often overlaps with occupational and organizational psychiatry, as forensic assessment skills are generally an asset in conducting assessments in workplace contexts. The creation of forensic psychiatry in Canada was brought about by necessity. Courts, lawyers, and agencies turned to psychiatrists interested in the application of psychiatry to legal scenarios for specific expertise in conducting a variety of assessments, including those relating to criminal responsibility, violence risk, sexual offences, and malingering.

In the Canadian context, Court et al. reference the important early role played by Dr. Joseph Workman in providing forensic psychiatric expertise to the courts as superintendent of the newly established Provincial Lunatic Asylum, which was established in 1850.[2] Dr. Workman and his successor asylum heads were among the first physicians to venture outside their

1 This chapter is a modified and updated version of a previous writing on similar subject matter. See Alan Gold & Hy Bloom, "Giving Evidence as an Expert Witness" in Hy Bloom & Richard D. Schneider, eds., *Law and Mental Disorder: A Comprehensive and Practical Approach* (Toronto: Irwin Law, 2013) 59.

2 John P.M. Court et al., "Contesting Mad versus Bad: The Evolution of Forensic Mental Health Services and Law at Toronto" (2014) 21 *Psychiatry, Psychology and Law* 918.

traditional institutional and treatment roles, and provided forensic psychiatric expertise in the courtroom decades before forensic psychiatry became an area of clinical and academic interest at university-based departments of medicine and psychiatry, and more than 150 years before forensic psychiatry was officially recognized as a distinct subspecialty in Canada.[3]

In reviewing the evolution of forensic psychiatry in Toronto, Court et al. go on to describe the writings of Professor Daniel Clark who, in his first-ever Canadian psychiatric textbook for medical students, included four chapters on topics within forensic psychiatry;[4] the content is remarkably similar to subjects covered in current forensic psychiatry textbooks.

By the early twentieth century, the Province of Ontario recognized its responsibilities for patients found either unfit to stand trial or not guilty by reason of insanity (as it was then called) held under Lieutenant Governor's Warrants and, by 1926, clinicians at the new Toronto Psychiatric Hospital's (TPH) Forensic Clinic were assessing criminally accused persons pursuant to court-ordered remands.[5]

Along with the establishment of a dedicated forensic psychiatric assessment program at the TPH and later, at Metropolitan Forensic Service (METFORS), program directors recognized the need for assiduous gathering of demographic information and research. Academic and clinical interest in areas of social concern (e.g., poverty and criminality) became the focus of considerable attention in the second half of the twentieth century. This spawned research into sexual behaviour and offending, assessment and treatment of offenders, dangerousness and violence risk assessment, criminal responsibility, fitness to stand trial, and malingering, to name a few areas. Research in these areas has been maintained to the present day. METFORS and the University of Toronto established relationships with forensic programs at the Pinel Institute in Montreal and the Forensic Psychiatric Services Commission in British Columbia. Efforts were undertaken in Ontario to create collaborative relationships between professionals working in courts, corrections, and academia (e.g., the criminology program at the University of Toronto).[6]

---

3 Forensic psychiatry was officially recognized as a designated subspecialty within psychiatry by the Royal College of Physicians and Surgeons of Canada in September 2013.

4 Daniel Clark, *Mental Diseases: A Synopsis of Twelve Lectures* (Toronto: William Briggs, 1895).

5 *Ibid.*

6 *Ibid.*

A detailed review of the history of forensic psychiatry in Canada is well beyond both the scope and purpose of this chapter. Suffice it to say that the field has grown considerably, owing in part to legislative changes that have made it easier for accused to extricate themselves from the jurisdiction of provincial or territorial review boards.[7] The field has also grown as result of necessity and creativity, creating an ever-expanding list of uses for mental health expertise in both the criminal and civil law arenas. The Royal College of Physicians and Surgeons of Canada only recently approved forensic psychiatry as a subspecialty within psychiatry in September 2013. At present, there are approximately 140 to 150 designated forensic psychiatrists in Canada.

This chapter deals with the nature, role, and pitfalls of the psychiatrist in the expert role, both as a consultant to lawyers and in court. This chapter will focus on what psychiatric experts working principally within the criminal context need to do to ensure the quality of their assessment and the integrity of their opinions. Among other things, this involves a thorough approach, guided by adherence to medical and psychiatric guidelines and ethics, a solid grasp of the legal issues and context, and a healthy level of skepticism about the veracity and potentially self-serving nature of the evaluee's information.[8] Experts must also be ever-mindful and self-aware of the potential for bias (as should lawyers) and take deliberate steps to manage it from the inception of the case to its conclusion.

B. THE SCIENCE OF FORENSIC PSYCHIATRY

1) Forensic Psychiatric Expertise in Criminal Proceedings

The last twenty to thirty years has seen a considerable evolution of jurisprudence touching on topics within the forensic psychiatry sphere (e.g., criminal responsibility, dangerousness, and the limits of psychiatric expertise)

---

7 *R. v. Swain*, [1991] 1 S.C.R. 933, played a pivotal role in modifying the justice system's view of mentally disordered offenders and, more importantly, led to Bill C-30 (*An Act to amend the Criminal Code (mental disorder) and to amend the National Defence Act and the Young Offenders Act in consequence thereof*, S.C. 1991, c. 43) which resulted in severing changes to the *Criminal Code*, R.S.C. 1985, c. C-46), namely Part XX.1 of the *Criminal Code*, which sets out the rules governing detention of mentally ill accused found unfit or not criminally responsible, the test for their release and derestriction, and procedural safeguards in their management.

8 Hy Bloom, "Insuring the Integrity of Psychiatric Assessments" (26 April 2013) *The Lawyers Weekly* 15–16.

and to an expanding awareness of the multiple applications of mental health expertise within both criminal and civil law. The various uses of psychiatric consultation in criminal proceedings relate to issues including:

- voluntariness of statements
- suitability for diversion
- fitness to stand trial
- sentencing and rehabilitation
- suitability for bail
- testimonial capacity
- criminal responsibility, which may include making assessments related to:
  - automatism
  - diminished responsibility
  - intoxication
  - provocation, duress, and self-defence
  - dangerousness
  - the paraphilias
  - dangerous offenders and long-term offenders
  - treatability

Expert psychiatric reports need to be "comprehensive, detailed, precise, clearly written, and well substantiated"[9] and should also be the vehicle for conveying the accused's narrative—how his life history, relationships, biological and genetic determinants, and so on, resulted in him not only becoming the person he became, but how he came to do what resulted in his current dilemma. Ideally, reports should be readable and interesting, but at the same time, should be as objective and unbiased as possible. Some of the more common problems and pitfalls in forensic psychiatric reports include:

- failure to identify sources of information
- failure to rely on a recognized diagnostic scheme
- fringe theories and diagnoses
- failure to consider alternate hypotheses
- failure to correctly characterize and address the psycholegal issues

9 Robert M. Wettstein, "The Forensic Evaluation and Report" in Robert I. Simon & Liza H. Gold, eds., *The American Psychiatric Publishing Textbook of Forensic Psychiatry*, 2d ed. (Washington, DC: American Psychiatric Publishing, 2010) 175.

- failure to consider relevant information
- failure to pursue relevant data (e.g., collaterals)
- inconsistencies and contradictory information
- ignoring information that runs contrary to expert's opinion
- failure to reflect significant changes made to a previous draft at the retaining lawyer's request
- editorial comments suggesting bias
- diagnostic myopia (failure to hypothesize malingering and manipulation, and to deal with them)
- failure to show facts relied on and reasoning behind opinions and conclusions

In Canada, there are no specific professional credentials required for a clinician to give an expert opinion in court, provided the psychiatrist or other mental health professional holds a medical or other relevant licence and a higher qualification in the specialty of psychiatry or psychology. Indeed, "expert" is a designation conferred by the court on a case-by-case basis. As such, expertise in specific areas such as domestic violence or sexual offending, in which there are no formal qualifications, will be assessed by the court on a case-by-case basis relying on such criteria as training, professional experience, and publication in the area. As a result of this process, expert witnesses are in the uniquely vulnerable position of having to demonstrate their core knowledge on the witness stand.

Forensic psychiatrists must have a detailed understanding of the key psychiatric disorders implicated in common medicolegal scenarios and "a well-ordered, well-digested comprehensive knowledge of mental phenomena, in a sound as well as unsound state."[10] Forensic psychiatric practice requires a measure of psychological flexibility—allowing the forensic psychiatrist to manage moving between clinical considerations and legal paradigms. Wills characterizes the forensic psychiatrists' ability to function at either end of the bridge between the two disciplines as professional "(ambidex[terity])."[11]

10 Isaac Ray, *A Treatise on the Medical Jurisprudence of Insanity* (Boston: Charles C. Little and James Brown, 1838).

11 Cheryl D. Wills, "The Psychiatric Report" (2013) 38 *American Academy of Psychiatry and the Law Newsletter* 1 at 1.

2) Evidence-Based Forensic Psychiatry

Evidence-based medicine (EBM) has become as much a battle cry in forensic psychiatry as it is in most other fields of medicine, as it should be. Eddy and Billings are often credited for their impactful 1988 article addressing the importance of analyzing evidence of the effectiveness and risk of various medical practices through scrupulous attention to the quality of the evidence.[12] Eddy introduced the term "evidence-based" in 1990 and expanded the concept over the ensuing decade.[13]

Canada's preeminent role in advancing the EBM discussion cannot be overstated, particularly because of the work of Guyatt, Sackett, and colleagues, who animated the discussion by introducing epidemiological methods and critical appraisal of scientific/medical evidence into the then-fledgling medical curriculum at McMaster University.[14] According to Sackett et al., "[e]vidence-based medicine is the conscientious, explicit and judicious use of current best evidence in making decisions about the care of individuals."[15] This approach entails combining the best available external evidence, acquired by sound inquiry (usually extrapolated from studies of large populations) and clinical experience, applied to the specific context at hand.

Unlike other branches of medicine, forensic psychiatry and its methods of assessment and communication of findings (e.g., through reports and testimony) have not yet been subjected to rigorous scientific scrutiny. Forensic psychiatrists have more science to draw on when their focus is psychiatric diagnosis and treatment, but are likely to find themselves on shakier ground when asked to opine on key areas within the field, such as criminal responsibility, violence risk, and dangerousness. For example, the Cochrane Collaboration—a gold standard method of critical appraisal of scientific/medical literature (through systematic reviews of published research studies)—has few subject areas specific to forensic psychiatry.[16]

---

12 David M. Eddy & John Billings, "Quality of Medical Evidence: Implications for Quality Care" (1988) 7 *Health Affairs* 19.

13 David M. Eddy, "Practice Policies: Where Do They Come From" (1990) 263 *The Journal of the American Medical Association* 1265.

14 See David L. Sackett et al., "Evidence-Based Medicine: What It Is and What It Isn't" (1996) 312 *The BMJ* 71, and Kathryn J. Bennett et al., "A Controlled Trial of Teaching Critical Appraisal of Clinical Literature to Medical Students" (1987) 257 *The Journal of the American Medical Association* 2451.

15 Sackett et al., above note 14.

16 Cochrane, online: www.cochrane.org/about-us.

The EBM standard can nevertheless be targeted and achieved in forensic psychiatry by infusing as much science into the forensic psychiatric assessment process as possible. This would accord with the *Daubert*[17] standards adopted into Canadian caselaw,[18] but this goal is inherently difficult to attain in a field in which blood and metabolic analyses, microscopy, and medical imaging are usually less useful. In this latter regard, Knoll and Resnick[19] observe that the recent trend in the United States of using neuroimaging (e.g., positron emission tomography (PET) scans and MRIs—tendered to show that the metabolic functioning of murderers' prefrontal cortices are different from controls) to bolster psychiatric opinions given in respect of an evaluee's insanity defence is premature and insufficiently grounded in science. Morse has playfully referred to this use of neuroscientific expertise to diminish or eliminate criminal responsibility as "brain overclaim syndrome." [20]

Endorsement of the evidence-based approach, according to Professor Paciocco,[21] was endorsed in the *R. v. Mohan* case,[22] but operationalized in practice by the Goudge Inquiry Report,[23] which made a "real [and] enduring contribution" to the way in which expert evidence should be tendered and received in court. As Professor Paciocco[24] points out, the Goudge Inquiry Report,[25] in its reflections on darker moments in the use of psychiatric and psychological expertise, offers a passing and disapproving nod in

---

17 *Daubert v. Merrell Dow Pharmaceuticals, Inc.*, 509 U.S. 579 (1993).

18 *R. v. J.-L.J.*, 2000 SCC 51.

19 James L. Knoll IV & Phillip J. Resnick, "Insanity Defense Evaluations: Toward a Model for Evidence-Based Practice" (2008) 8 *Brief Treatment and Crisis Intervention* 92.

20 Stephen J. Morse, "Brain Overclaim Syndrome and Criminal Responsibility: A Diagnostic Note" (2006) 3 *Ohio State Journal of Criminal Law* 297. But see also Lisa Claydon, "Are There Lessons to be Learned from a More Scientific Approach to Mental Condition Defences?" (2012) 35 *International Journal of Law and Psychiatry* 88, where the author suggests that judicious use of scientific data, including neuroimaging, has a role to play in criminal cases, and that to ignore such evidence could be scientifically disingenuous and inconsistent with the needs of justice.

21 David Paciocco, "Taking a 'Goudge' out of Bluster & Blarney: An 'Evidence-Based Approach' to Expert Testimony" (2009) 13 *Canadian Criminal Law Review* 135 at 135.

22 [1994] 2 S.C.R. 9.

23 See the Executive Summary in Ontario, Ministry of the Attorney General, *Inquiry into Pediatric Forensic Pathology in Ontario* by the Honourable Stephen T. Goudge, Commissioner (Ontario: Ministry of the Attorney General, 2008) [Goudge Inquiry Report].

24 Paciocco, above note 21.

25 Goudge Inquiry Report, above note 23.

the direction of now debunked syndromes, like false memory syndrome[26] or child sexual abuse accommodation syndrome.[27]

Above all, the expert should avoid incursion into the exclusive domain of the judge and jury by offering opinions, for example, about the credibility of a witness or complainant, or about ultimate issues, like fitness to stand trial, criminal responsibility, and whether an accused is a dangerous offender. The expert's observations and opinions inform but do not dispose of these issues.

3) The Distinction between Therapeutic and Forensic Psychiatric Assessments

The scope of a therapeutic or clinical assessment is wide: it is concerned with diagnosis, personality function, and management. Within the therapeutic context, the patient is the client. Clinicians can therefore permit the patient to drive the process, occasionally steering the material and interaction to allow for a therapeutic outcome. The clinician will work to understand the patient's perspective, generally accepting information from her at face value. Trust and the development of a therapeutic alliance require the clinician to allow the relationship to unfold somewhat organically.

In contrast, the forensic assessment is more focused. The forensic psychiatrist is retained to address specific questions and provide a psychiatric opinion on issues of particular concern to the court or the party retaining him. This assessment is highly structured and the information gathering process can be laborious. The forensic evaluation routinely requires consideration of multiple sources of information (e.g., criminal, medical, insurance, school, and occupational records) as well as interviews with family members, co-workers, employers, friends, police officers, and eyewitnesses. The evaluation may include observing the evaluee in the home, the workplace, the courtroom, and other non-clinical settings.[28] The forensic

---

26 The scientifically untenable idea that memories of childhood sexual abuse can be buried, as it were, in the mind and subsequently retrieved by a triggering event or (dubious) therapeutic acumen. See Gold & Bloom, above note 1. See, generally, Chapter 21 in this book, about memory in the criminal courts.

27 A debunked but long-held theory that certain behaviours children performed (subsequently demonstrated as generic for many types of problems or events) supported the view that the child must have been abused and the accused must have been the perpetrator. See *R. v. Olscamp* (1994), 95 C.C.C. (3d) 466 (Ont. Ct. Gen. Div.).

28 Larry H. Strasburger et al., "On Wearing Two Hats: Role Conflict in Serving as Both Psychotherapist and Expert Witness" (1997) 154 *American Journal of Psychiatry* 448.

clinician is required by the mandate given to her to retain more objectivity with respect to the individual being assessed. The purpose of the assessment is not clinical improvement; it is to provide a coherent assessment of the specific aspects of the individual relevant to the court proceedings. Importantly, the "patient" is not the assessor's client—the client is the lawyer or retaining agency.

In the forensic context, there is a high risk of conscious or intentional distortion of information, as evaluees have a significant non-therapeutic interest (e.g., liberty, money) in the outcome of the evaluation. Moreover, shame or embarrassment may contribute to a person distorting the facts of the situation. In the therapeutic context, the risk of manipulation of information is considerably less, and the implications of such manipulation are likely of less significance, although there is always a risk of unconscious distortion of information.

Therapeutic clinicians deliberately foster trust through an empathic relationship developed for the purpose of advancing the patient's interests. Forensic examiners should not be perceived in this type of helping role. Indeed, the nature of the relationship should be made explicit at the outset. A measure of distance is required not only to serve all of the interests involved, but to maintain the degree of objectivity that is at the core of the exercise.

A brief summary of the key distinctions between an assessor in a typical diagnostic and therapeutic consultative role and a clinician in a medicolegal (forensic) role are set out in Table 19.1 below.

TABLE 19.1. Differences between Therapeutic Assessment and Medicolegal Assessment.

Therapeutic	Medicolegal
• Agenda: Symptom relief (patient's agenda)	• Agenda: Exoneration, liberty, financial or other benefit (examiner's agenda)
• Confidentiality expected	• Confidentiality not possible
• Attitude: Accepting	• Attitude: Skeptical
• Doctor–patient relationship	• No doctor-patient relationship
• Information (mostly) accepted at face value	• High index of suspicion about quality of information
• Information from patient (and occasionally family member)	• Multiple sources of information
• Truth not challenged	• Untruthfulness and impression management a major concern

Therapeutic	Medicolegal
• Diagnosis and differential diagnosis	• Diagnosis, differential diagnosis, and malingering
• Advocate for patient	• Competing theories for behaviour/symptom/etc.
	• Impartial consultant
• Empathetic	• Respectful, but investigative

4) Forensic Psychiatric Assessments

Thoroughness defines forensic psychiatric assessments and reports, particularly because of the impact psychiatric expertise could have on both the accused's and the public's interests. There is presently no mandated format that clinicians are required to follow to carry out a forensic psychiatric assessment and draft a forensic psychiatric report. That being said, quality assessments and reports often speak for themselves in that they reflect that care and attention has been paid to information gathering, analysis, and communication (e.g., in a report and oral testimony).

The American Academy of Psychiatry and the Law (AAPL) has recently published a practice guideline [29] that provides consensus-based guidance, garnered from available literature, setting out the information to be gathered when conducting various types of civil and criminal forensic psychiatric assessments. There are, as well, a number of American[30] and British[31] textbooks with chapters on subjects relevant to the function of a psychiatric assessor, and a recent Canadian textbook[32] with chapters on assessment, the expert witness, and medicolegal report writing.

C. THE ROLE OF THE FORENSIC PSYCHIATRIST IN CRIMINAL CASES

Experts can offer courts inferences drawn from facts and opinions. This comes with the "responsibility of maintaining an attitude of strict inde-

29 Graham Glancy et al., "AAPL Practice Guideline for the Forensic Assessment" (2015) 43 *Journal of the American Academy of Psychiatry and Law* S3.

30 Simon & Gold, eds., above note 9.

31 John Gunn & Pamela J. Taylor, eds., *Forensic Psychiatry: Clinical, Legal and Ethical Issues*, 2d ed. (Boca Raton, FL: Taylor & Francis, 2014).

32 Bloom & Schneider, above note 1.

pendence and impartiality."[33] The primary task of the behavioural sciences expert witness is to inform the court of matters within the expert's knowledge; that is, to diagnose a mental disorder, to define psychological variables that may be at play in a case, and, above all, to educate the court (and lawyers and retaining agencies) on matters about which the court knows little. The expert always owes the court the duty of good faith and truthfulness.

1) The Expert–Lawyer Relationship

Negotiating the expert–lawyer relationship depends on developing a strong relationship based on communication, while avoiding common pitfalls that may negatively impact both the relationship itself and the case as a whole. It is important that the lawyer and expert confer periodically over the course of the evaluation as doing so limits the risk of misunderstanding the needs and views of the other.

Lawyers should be extremely careful about either intentionally or unintentionally withholding relevant or critical information from an expert because that information is likely to influence the expert's opinion in an unfavourable way.[34] Not only is this an unethical practice, but it is at high risk for backfiring if the opposing lawyer brings forward the withheld information during cross-examination, in an attempt to impugn the expert's credibility.[35] It is not possible, however, for the expert to know whether all relevant information has been disclosed to her. For this reason, the information upon which an opinion is based should be stated explicitly at the outset of the expert's report.[36] Similarly, a mental health expert should not withhold information from a report or during verbal testimony.

With the above in mind, lawyers and referring agencies should still be very cautious about the nature and scope of the information provided to the expert. Reading or reviewing superfluous information is not only costly but may provide excessive information that obfuscates, rather than clarifies, the issues on which the expert has been asked to focus. At a minimum, in a criminal prosecution, the expert should be provided with relevant Crown disclosure, including: witness statements; inculpatory or

33 *Bedford v. Canada* (AG), 2010 ONSC 4264 at para. 101 [*Bedford*].

34 Ralph Slovenko, "The Lawyer and the Forensic Expert: Boundaries of Ethical Practice" (1987) 5 *Behavioral Sciences & the Law* 119.

35 Bruce Gross, "Private Defense Evaluations" (2006) 15 *Forensic Examiner* 57.

36 Bloom & Schneider, above note 1 at 39.

exculpatory statements by the accused; audio recordings and videos; and medical, psychiatric, probation, parole, and other documentation relevant to the accused, including his criminal history. Some cases, both civil and criminal, require expanding the inquiry to include interviewing previous or current teachers, previous or current employers, family members, and current and previous romantic partners. In addition, obtaining documentation such as school records, work records, and military records may be required. The general rule is that an expert needs to be provided with a sufficient fund of information to support the opinion he provides. The greater the reliability of the facts underpinning the opinion, the greater the weight to be attached to that opinion. Put another way, an expert opinion is only as strong as the factual foundation that supports it.

A common pitfall involves the clinician's failure to be clear about who the client is. Is it the person being examined, a referring lawyer, or a court or agency? Or is there a duty to society at large, as is the case where public protection is the issue?[37] The clinician should clarify who the client is from the very beginning of the expert–lawyer relationship (and well before evaluating the accused) to avoid misunderstandings and ethical problems.

Even if it is clear who the client is, the expert–lawyer relationship may need to take positive steps to resolve ethical and professional issues that arise during the evaluation of an accused person, particularly where the well-being and safety of the evaluee or public is at risk. For example, the expert's conclusions may be adverse to the evaluee's legal interests and, as a result, the lawyer may advise the expert that her report (and testimony) is not required. The expert may nonetheless continue to be concerned about the evaluee's well-being absent intervention. In cases like this, the expert should communicate her concerns to counsel, consider offering some recommendations to address the evaluee's needs, and carefully document the discussion and advice given. In situations in which the expert has, as a result of the assessment, developed concerns about the evaluee's risk to members of the public, then concerted steps may have to be taken. In this regard, a psychiatric examiner who concludes that an evaluee is at imminent risk of committing serious physical or psychological harm to an identifiable victim or pool of victims should take just those steps necessary

37 The duty to warn or at least alert the authorities when a psychiatrist has reason to believe an evaluee is at risk for imminent serious physical or psychological harm to an identifiable victim or group of victims: see *Smith v. Jones*, [1999] 1 S.C.R. 455 [*Smith v. Jones* SCC].

to avert the harm.[38] This disclosure, which could represent a significant breach of confidentiality, applies even in circumstances where the clinician has learned about the potential harm through an examination carried out at the behest of a lawyer. Although assessments of this kind would ordinarily come under the umbrella of solicitor–client privilege, the duty supersedes the privilege. This would usually entail alerting the authorities.

At trial of the issue, the British Columbia Supreme Court concluded that disclosure in such circumstances was *mandatory*,[39] but the British Columbia Court of Appeal found the trial judge had erred on this point, and ruled that disclosure was *permissible*.[40] The Supreme Court of Canada's decision about this obviously important distinction was unfortunately unclear.[41]

Similarly, positive steps must be taken by the expert as part of his obligation to report child abuse. For example, if a middle-aged man is being assessed for a first-time charge of sexual victimization of a minor, then it would be reasonable for the examiner to forewarn the lawyer that other victims, potentially unknown to the authorities, will be enquired about (although the examiner may caution the evaluee about not providing identifying data that might crystallize the reporting obligation).

To maintain the integrity of the expert lawyer relationship and to avoid ethical and professional pitfalls, communication is key. Mutual expectations and obligations should be explored prior to conducting an evaluation. The expert should forewarn both the lawyer and the evaluee about his various reporting obligations prior to and at the outset of the assessment.

2) Bias, Perception, and Expectation

As a clinician/expert retained by a party (e.g., defence, prosecution, plaintiff, defendant, management, union), the expert's principal role is to serve as consultant to that party—usually legal counsel—to assess an accused or litigant, review documents, and critically appraise the report of an opposing expert. As much as the expert's involvement and role is party-driv-

---

38 *Ibid.*

39 *Smith v. Jones*, [1997] B.C.J. No. 3136 at para. 35 (S.C.).

40 *Smith v. Jones* (1998), 62 B.C.L.R (3d) 198 at 208 (C.A.).

41 *Smith v. Jones*, SCC, above note 37.

en, professional and ethical obligations, particularly self-monitoring for bias, are always in the background.[42]

According to the American Academy of Psychiatry and Law, the expert is to testify "honestly and striv[e] for objectivity." The most significant threat to practicing in accordance with this ideal is the possibility of unchecked bias, which in many instances, the expert may not be aware of, deriving from a multitude of sources. Awareness of these possibilities is the best armament against them.[43]

a) Public and Judicial Perception of Psychiatric Experts

Public perception — or more often, misperception — can contribute to the challenges of being an expert, can threaten the needed appearance of solemnity in serious legal proceedings, and can shake the public's trust in both the courts and medicine. For reasons well beyond the scope of our discussion in this chapter, psychiatry, and its historical and scientific foundations, draws more fire, and often much more attention, than other expertise in the courtroom. Perhaps this has to do with how readily the pop-psychology–saturated media and culture are prepared both to proffer and to attack opinions that they would be hesitant and even self-conscious about articulating if the expertise were that of another medical discipline or another discipline altogether (e.g., forensic accounting or forensic engineering). Further complicating the matter, the facts and issues in which psychiatry may play a role in the criminal arena are unusually close to home for most people, involving their security, well-being, and integrity, and that of their families. As well, the types of cases that the media report — murders, sexual assaults, terrorism — can both stimulate the public's curiosity, gratify its prurient interests, and create scapegoats identified as evil-doers.

It should be pointed out that the public's views of psychiatry are not just the result of seeing and hearing about psychiatrists (usually forensic psychiatrists) who testify at publicized trials. The problem runs deep and is connected to a more pervasive erosion of the public's confidence in physicians — a trend that has been occurring over the last two decades, owing in part to negative publicity, especially in relation to boundary transgressions by physicians, most notably, psychiatrist–patient sexual violations. Psych-

42 Bloom & Schneider, above note 1 at 1271.

43 Thomas G. Gutheil & Robert I. Simon, "Avoiding Bias in Expert Testimony: The General Practice Clinician Stepping into the Arena of Forensic Psychiatry Must Take Care to Maintain Objectivity" (2004) 34 *Psychiatric Annals* 260.

iatrists' honesty and ethics are poorly regarded by the public, compared to those of other health-care professionals, and of other professionals more generally.[44]

The portrayal of psychiatrists in the cinema (450 films by 1999[45]), particularly of psychiatrists in court, is rather unflattering and films often depict them as evil and exploitative, as professorial and aloof, as mercenary hired guns, or as too involved with the person about whom they are testifying to provide the court with an accurate and truthful picture. With respect to hired guns, Cooper and Neuhaus report on several studies they conducted on the factors mock jurors considered in appraising the credibility of expert scientific testimony.[46] Highly paid experts who testify frequently are perceived as "hired guns," and are neither liked nor believed. Complex testimony that was difficult for jurors to understand heightened their negative views of the expert.

Typical criticisms the public may harbour about psychiatric experts are myths and include the following:

- Psychiatrists never agree with each other.
- Psychiatrists attempt to supplant the facts in a case with psychological explanations.
- Compared to their medical colleagues, psychiatrists are substandard physicians.
- Psychiatrists distort the line between madness and badness, thereby excusing evil.
- Psychiatrists in court offer little more than bafflegab.
- As hired character assassins, psychiatrists do the bidding of the side that has retained them.

The fact is that lawyers as a group, and judges in particular, are not especially knowledgeable about mental illness, and have relatively few

44 Rebecca Riffkin, "Americans Rate Nurses Highest on Honesty, Ethical Standards" *Social Issues* (18 December 2014), online: www.gallup.com/poll/180260/americans-rate-nurses-highest-honesty-ethical-standards.aspx. Gallup, "Honesty/Ethics in Professions," online: www.gallup.com/poll/1654/honesty-ethics-professions.aspx.

45 Glen O. Gabbard & Krin Gabbard, *Psychiatry and the Cinema* (Washington, DC: American Psychiatric Press, 1999).

46 Joel Cooper & Isaac M. Neuhaus, "The 'Hired Gun' Effect: Assessing the Effect of Pay, Frequency of Testifying, and Credentials on the Perception of Expert Testimony" (2000) 24 *Law and Human Behavior* 149.

opportunities to deal with and delve deeply into psychiatric defences like not criminally responsible (NCR) or automatism.[47]

From the earliest times until relatively recently, criminal trials were opportunities for the public to witness evil being dealt a hard blow through highly public displays of punishment. Against this historic landscape, the role of explainers and mitigators of evil acts is fairly recent and arose intertwined with the court's distrust of forensic psychiatry as a whole.

b) Nature, Sources, and Dynamics of Bias

Dr. Bernard Diamond, a pioneer of modern forensic psychiatry, insisted that the honest forensic psychiatrist should admit that impartiality and objectivity are impossible ideals.[48] Experts, he wrote, cannot be completely impartial, as they, like most everyone else, invariably cannot keep their biases and backgrounds out of their professional work. The issue is not to eliminate bias but to recognize and adjust one's perspective and approach, which to a great extent is achieved through self-awareness.[49] Nonetheless, it is essential that these potential prejudices not contaminate the evaluation process. Diamond suggested that honesty is the characteristic that separates the expert who has integrity from the "hired gun."[50]

Frank Datillo, in his tribute to another highly respected forensic psychiatrist, Dr. Robert Sadoff, similarly comments that as much as honesty and integrity—"best defined as being scrupulously truthful with oneself and others"—are moral and professional goals people strive to achieve, few actualize living their lives on the foundation of these values (and even fewer achieve becoming exemplars of these values for others).[51] Datillo notes parenthetically that this degree of openness and transparency is an inevitable challenge for forensic sciences experts in that it can compel them to disclose and face shortcomings.

---

47 See the recent study of limitations in both the North Carolina bench's and bar's knowledge of mental disorder and mental health defences, in Richard L. Frierson et al., "Mental Illness and Mental Health Defenses: Perceptions of the Criminal Bar" (2015) 43 *Journal of the American Academy of Psychiatry and Law* 483.

48 Bernard Diamond, "The Fallacy of the Impartial Expert" (1959) 3 *Archives of Criminal Psychodynamics* 221.

49 Gutheil & Simon, above note 43.

50 Diamond, above note 48.

51 Frank M. Datillio, "On Honesty and Integrity in Forensic Science: A Snapshot of Robert L. Sadoff" (2012) 40 *Journal of Psychiatry & Law* 117 at 117.

Mitchell and Mandhane note a trend towards greater scrutiny by courts of expert independence and impartiality.[52] They define *independence* through an objective lens: "[I]t concerns a person's status or relationship to others," whereas *impartiality*, "is primarily subjective, it concerns a person's state of mind or attitude in relation to the issues and the parties."[53] Expressed differently, "impartiality concerns how the expert acts, while independence concerns who the expert is."[54]

Mitchell and Mandhane see the cases of *R. v. Mohan*[55] and *R. v. J-L.J*[56] as foundational in the "evolution of an overarching duty on the part of the expert witness to the court."[57] They further note the impact of the *Ikarian Reefer* case, an English decision now widely accepted in Canadian courts, on setting out the expert's duties in civil cases.[58] The impact of this case was similarly recognized by the court in *Bedford*.[59] The *Ikarian Reefer* duties are paraphrased and summarized below:

- The appearance of bias is important. Expert evidence should not only be, but be seen to be, the expert's independent product, uninfluenced as to content or form by the needs and circumstances of the litigation.
- An expert should never assume the role of advocate, but should provide a court with objective unbiased opinions.
- An expert should be clear about what facts his opinion is based on, and not omit from consideration facts that detract from that opinion.
- An expert should concede when a question or issue is beyond her expertise.
- Experts should characterize their opinions as provisional if they lack data to be conclusive, and openly acknowledge any qualifications in reaching an opinion.

---

52 Paul Mitchell & Renu Mandhane, "The Uncertain Duty of the Expert Witness" (2005) 42 *Alberta Law Review* 635 at 638.

53 *Ibid.*

54 *Ibid.* at 639.

55 Above note 22.

56 Above note 18.

57 Mitchell & Mandhane, above note 52 at 641.

58 *National Justice Compania Naviera S.A. v. Prudential Assurance (The Ikarian Reefer)*, [1993] 2 Lloyd's Rep 68 (C.A.) [*Ikarian Reefer*].

59 Above note 33 at para. 100.

- If an expert's opinion on a material issue changes following an exchange of expert reports, then this expert should acknowledge it and communicate the change.
- The materials an expert has relied upon in arriving at his conclusions should be disclosed to opposing counsel at the same time the reports are exchanged.[60]

While psychiatric evaluations may be solicited by the defence, prosecution, plaintiff, defendant, or the court, there is a tendency to view court-referred cases as less inclined toward bias. That being said, the suggestion that the court-appointed expert is necessarily neutral is a misconception. Non-party appointment may simply mask an expert's inevitable personal biases. Moreover, court appointment does not render the expert immune to vigorous cross-examination by experienced counsel seeking to undermine the expert's opinions.

Experts may sometimes appear biased solely as an artifact of being repeatedly retained by one side or the other. This circumstance, which often has nothing to do with the expert's ideology or other leanings, may be solely a function of accepting a retainer. Many, if not most, experts try to accept retainers from either side, depending on which side asks first. As much as this may be an expert's goal, the reality is that trends outside of an expert's control can develop. For example, consulting on a succession of cases for a management-employment law firm may suggest to union counsel that the psychiatric expert is biased in favour of management. This may be union counsel's first line of attack on cross-examination, although cross-examiners often, if not invariably, gain little from this approach, since it is the quality of examination, the report, and expert testimony that will disclose whether bias is present—not who retained the expert.

There is no single unitary cause for expert bias. The factors motivating experts to lean in one direction or another are complex and likely represent a composite of life and professional experience, personality strengths and deficits, adequacy or inadequacy of training and experience, identification with (good and bad) instructors and role models, personal, religious, political and ideological beliefs, self-misdirection, a need to be in the "limelight," a need to be liked or loved, financial considerations, exigencies in the dyadic relationships with legal counsel (including pressure by counsel), or with the evaluee(s), and so on.[61] Motivation for bias can be

---

60 *Ikarian Reefer*, above note 58 at 642–43.

61 Gutheil & Simon, above note 43; see discussion at 261–69.

conscious, unconscious, or a combination of both. The below table sets out a non-exhaustive list of potential conscious and unconscious sources of bias.

TABLE 19.2. Potential conscious and unconscious sources of bias.

MOTIVATION/BIAS IS CONSCIOUS		
"Hired-Gun" Zone	Well-Intended Zone	
• Money motivated/mercenary • Political/ideological agenda • Personal agenda (grudge/misgiving/ cause) • Desperate for work	• Therapist-advocate • Misguided loyalty • Pressure to espouse the ideology of clinical centres or universities	
MOTIVATION/BIAS IS UNCONSCIOUS		
Personality Pathology Zone	Countertransference Zone	Learning Curve Zone
• Self-aggrandizement/ narcissism • Paranoid • Masochistic – need to be mocked and devalued • Sadistic/punitive (solely prosecution oriented) • Proneness to boundary violations	• Need for love, admiration/approval • Personal agenda, e.g. past trauma • Forensic identification • Insecurity • Competitive feelings	• Suggestible and impressionable • Novice/lacks experience • Difficulty shifting from therapeutic role to expert • Alignment with ideals or views of outside influence

Reprinted with permission of Hy Bloom (2012)

Likely, the source(s) and motivation(s) for the expert's bias may not be easily discernible. This is not generally of particular concern to courts, although it may be inferred from critical comments of an expert in a judgment. This occurred in the recent Ontario civil case of *Frazer v. Haukioja*, in which a psychiatric expert's evidence was rejected because he was "[c]herry picking facts that supported a diagnosis that just happens to support the cause of the client . . . and fail[ed] to include the facts that hurt the cause, whether those latter facts are capable of explanation and elimination in the course of the development of the expert's analysis and opinion or not."[62]

c) The Lawyer's Contribution to the Problem of Expert Bias

Some lawyers, especially those with particular experience working with experts, may search for an expert they expect or feel certain will be sympathetic to their client's case. They vet an expert's views in reconnaissance-type

62 *Frazer v. Haukioja*, 2008 CanLII 42207 at para. 154 (Ont. S.C.J.), aff'd 2010 ONCA 249.

calls before a retainer is formalized. Their research may have suggested that the "leanings"—however subtle—of an expert in past cases are ripe for exploitation. Greater or lesser involvement with one side or the other is more often than not the result of happenstance. Experts often accept any work, provided it fits their expertise, schedule, and so forth. Which side calls more often has little or nothing to do with the expert's leanings. What may appear to be ideologically driven bias (e.g., favouring the prosecution, presumptively in order to punish badness and not excuse madness) may more simply represent an expert's unconscious inclination towards and advocacy for the side that retained her because the retainer represents approval and respect.

Clinicians are certainly vulnerable to the influences of agency (i.e., the referral source). Zusman and Simon reviewed psychiatric opinions given about mental damages sustained by victims of the 1972 collapse of the Buffalo Creek Dam.[63] They found a marked difference in agreement between experts retained by the adversarial parties. All the assessors were university-based and there was no evident financial incentive to provide biased views. Differences in some opinions were thought to be attributable not only to factors such as the interview setting and the examiner's training or orientation, but also to "forensic identification"—an unintentional (or unconscious) process whereby the clinician adopts the theory of the lawyer who retained him. Some lawyers are consciously or unconsciously aware of this identification and may develop personal relationships with experts, so that even if the expert has initially come to an opinion inconsistent with the lawyer's needs in the case, she will be reluctant to disappoint a friend.

Most lawyers understand that their clients will be best served by an expert who presents his evidence in an objective manner. Only under-informed, naïve, or unscrupulous lawyers will hire an expert they know to be biased, or fail to deal with bias in an expert they did not know or expect to become a "cheerleader" for their side. The point was driven home in *Bailey v. Barbour*, where Healey J. ordered a lawyer to pay $98,000 of $490,000 of costs because the lawyer knowingly used a biased expert (who was eventually ejected from the case) and wasted court time.[64]

---

63 Jack Zusman & Jesse Simon, "Differences in Repeated Psychiatric Examinations of Litigants to a Lawsuit" (1983) 140 *American Journal of Psychiatry* 1300.

64 *Bailey v. Barbour*, 2014 ONSC 3698.

A change to expert reports is another area rife with risk for concerns about bias. This issue was recently addressed in *Moore v. Getahun*,[65] where the Ontario Court of Appeal rejected the trial judge's stern view that the practice of consultation between counsel and experts about draft reports needed to end, period.[66] The trial judge also suggested stringent rules around disclosure of drafts, work memos, and correspondence and notes reflecting communication between counsel and an expert, which the Court of Appeal also did not agree with. Writing for the court, Sharpe J. stated that

> Absent a factual foundation to support a reasonable suspicion that counsel improperly influenced the expert, a party should not be allowed to demand production of draft reports or notes of interactions between counsel and an expert witness . . . .[67]

The point is that while the above case allows the practice of lawyers conferring with experts to continue, it emphasizes the importance of everything being above board and consistent with both medical and legal ethics.[68] No such similar guidance exists around drafts and consultations between expert and defence counsel in a criminal matter. It seems prudent, however, to follow the civil law trend. Experts should hold onto drafts, memos, notes, and so on, especially if discussions with criminal defence counsel have resulted in substantive changes.

d) Managing Concerns about Bias

Managing bias should ideally be part of the curriculum and early training for becoming either an expert or a lawyer. Lawyers should ensure that their experts get *all* the data needed to consider *all sides* of the case, particularly information running contrary to the retaining lawyer's client's interests.

Early steps that lawyers can take to manage bias include having clear and detailed conversations with their clients about what to expect in the

---

65 *Moore v. Getahun*, 2015 ONCA 55 [*Moore*].

66 *Moore v. Getahun*, 2014 ONSC 237.

67 *Moore*, above note 65 at para. 78.

68 See *Carmen Alfano Family Trust (Trustee of) v. Persanti*, 2012 ONCA 297. See also Principle 3 of: The Advocates' Society, "Principles Governing Communication with Testifying Experts" (June 2014) at 6, online: www.advocates.ca/assets/files/pdf/The_Advocates_Society-Principles_Governing_Communications_with_Testifying_Experts_3_sep18.pdf.

assessment while highlighting the importance of honesty, clarity, and openness. This would be the time for lawyers to disabuse their clients of any beliefs they might have or myths they might subscribe to about the expert's objectivity. Lawyers should also be mindful of the conflict inherent in retaining an accused's treating psychiatrist to write a psychiatric report for court, and then testify.[69]

After all the preparatory work has been done, lawyers can also take pre-emptive steps during examination-in-chief to neutralize the risk of all-out accusations or suggestions of bias during cross-examination. This approach has been referred to as expert "inoculation."[70] It is based on the view that lawyers appear more trustworthy and experts appear more credible when weaknesses in the expert's assessment—limitations in the database, lack of clarity in diagnosis, muddled science in the area, and alternate hypotheses to the expert's opinions—are exposed and dealt with in examination-in-chief, leaving little wind within the sails of cross-examination.[71]

The most basic, expected role for the mental health expert is as a consultant/educator and it is in this capacity that the expert will likely feel most comfortable and will best be able to avoid the suggestion of bias. The advent of dedicated forensic psychiatric training programs and the Royal College of Physicians and Surgeons of Canada's forensic psychiatric subspecialty designation has brought with it the requirement for knowledge of ethical and professional obligations, including the need to guard against bias.

Lessons about bias that clinicians inadequately learn or exemplify, for whatever reason, may be instilled more forcefully by court decisions that chastise the expert and criticize her testimony, with potential implications for her image, self-esteem, and even livelihood.

Experts can deal with bias by recognizing influences that may be at play in a case—due to party dynamics—or because they have insight into their attitude about the subject matter and/or the parties. Seasoned experts are likely to have considered unconscious variables that may be at play.[72]

---

69 Gutheil & Simon, above note 43 at 261.

70 Mitchell H. Ziemke & Stanley L. Brodsky, "Unloading the Hired Gun: Inoculation Effects in Expert Witness Testimony" (2015) 42–43 *International Journal of Law and Psychiatry* 91 at 92.

71 Kipling D. Williams et al., "The Effects of Stealing Thunder in Criminal and Civil Trials" (1993) 17 *Law and Human Behavior* 597.

72 For example, transference, a mental process whereby a person transfers feelings, expectations, and behaviours previously experienced with important figures earlier in life, onto another. In the legal scenario, judges, lawyers, and experts may be seen as beneficent or punitive fathers or mothers, or as saviours. Counter-transference

Simopoulos and Cohen recently conceded that complete impartiality was difficult for an expert to achieve, given the psychologically evocative nature of many offences. They argued, however, that knowledge of unconscious and conscious processes could "bolster the intellectual integrity of the clinical assessment," and help keep bias in check.[73] Experts should, to use the vernacular, take their "bias temperature" for all cases and discuss any concerns in that area with counsel before the retainer proceeds any further.

Since bias often emanates from relational dynamics, experts should ensure that close attention is paid to that dynamic—to overtures and subtle influences encouraging (or even demanding) that the expert be on board. The expert's feelings about an opposing side's expert can be another area of unconscious dynamics influencing the expert. He may view the opposing expert as either someone to be idealized and agreed with, or antithetically, as a contemptible charlatan who should be defeated and taught a lesson. In a similar vein, opposing-side experts who are unconsciously admired and/or feared could evoke competitive and rivalrous feelings[74] in an expert, whose focus on the case has now become compromised by hitherto unrecognized and inadequately dealt with personal psychological baggage.

Fraternizing with lawyers over a lengthy career may be difficult for experts to avoid. The point is not so much abject avoidance as it is insuring that problematic dynamics are closely monitored and undue influences are guarded against. A social relationship, for example, should not impact the expert's need to ensure that the retaining lawyer has provided the expert with all the information needed, and that the lawyer has not been selective (or even devious) about it; that could be a formula for disaster for the expert, lawyer, and evaluee.

D. CONCLUSION

Unlike many other forensic sciences, forensic psychiatry does not have the same array of objective recordable measures and calculations and laboratory tests clinicians can draw on to arrive at their opinions. Psychiatry

---

is the *reciprocal* phenomenon for the practitioner (whether judge, lawyer, or expert), and can result in loss of objectivity.

73 Eugene F. Simopoulos & Bruce Cohen, "Application and Utility of Psychodynamic Principles in Forensic Assessment" (2015) 43 *American Journal of Psychiatry and the Law* 428 at 428.

74 Gutheil & Simon, above note 43 at 267.

necessarily relies on considerably greater subjectively interpreted data and observations. However, whatever forensic psychiatry lacks in hard science (and that landscape is changing, in any event), it makes up for in a well-grounded tradition and practice that centres on scrupulous attention to detail; in-depth knowledge about mental illness and psychological phenomenology; and above all, a curious, probing, detail-oriented, and skeptical mindset.

Forensic psychiatry has fully embraced the evidence-based approach, which has strong roots in Canadian research and innovation. This approach dictates:

- thoroughness
- reliance on the best theories, applications, and practices
- open-mindedness and receptiveness to alternate theories
- transparency in the gathering and use of information
- objective, fair, and clear presentation of opinions and conclusions that sets out the underlying reasoning behind those opinions and conclusions[75]

Careful inquiry and equally careful analysis of the data (including attention to shortcomings in the information relied on) hardly immunizes the expert against the risk of an attack on his integrity and method, but it goes some way towards protecting his credibility. In forensic psychiatric expert practice, the elephant in the room is bias. Although the finger-pointing claiming partisan participation is usually in the direction of the expert, managing bias is the collective job of experts, lawyers, and courts. Early and ongoing consistent efforts in training and education are the central pillars to managing such bias and ensuring the related legal process is as fair and accurate as possible.

The use of psychiatric expertise in the legal process clearly involves challenges but, notwithstanding occasional criticism and pushback, its need and uses are expanding. To discount the value of psychiatric expertise in key areas courts are concerned about, like criminal responsibility and dangerousness, would be akin to uninventing the wheel.[76]

---

75 Paciocco, above note 21.

76 *Barefoot v. Estelle*, 463 US 880 (1983), White J. for the majority.

E. LEGAL CONTEXT

Reviewing the psychiatric expert's approach to the many uses of psychiatric evidence in criminal cases is not possible here. Consequently, the sections below highlight a few of the best known areas of expert psychiatric involvement in the criminal arena, focusing on what amounts to a well-done or flawed assessment and/or report.

1) Fitness to Stand Trial

The most common psycholegal issue for which psychiatric evidence is called into play is the assessment of fitness to stand trial. In Canada, the rules pertaining to fitness to stand trial, originally developed at common law, were codified in 1992 and are contained in section 2 of the *Criminal Code*:

> "[U]nfit to stand trial" means unable on account of mental disorder to conduct a defence at any stage of the proceedings before a verdict is rendered or to instruct counsel to do so, and, in particular, unable on account of mental disorder to
> (a) understand the nature or object of the proceedings
> (b) understand the possible consequences of the proceedings, or
> (c) communicate with counsel [. . . .][77]

The procedures for dealing with the issue of unfitness to stand trial, and mental disorder in general, are set out in Part XX.1 of the *Criminal Code*.

Fitness to stand trial has to do with the accused's present state of mind (at the time of trial) as contrasted with assessments of criminal responsibility (see below), which deal with the accused's state of mind at the time of an alleged criminal act. The fitness rules evolved at common law in order to protect a mentally ill accused from the prosecution of the state while unable, on account of the mental disorder, to either conduct his own defence or instruct counsel to do so. The necessary but not sufficient underlying condition is "mental disorder" which is also defined in section 2 of the *Criminal Code* and means "a disease of the mind," a broad concept where:

> In summary, one might say that in a legal sense "disease of the mind" embraces any illness, disorder or abnormal condition which impairs the human mind and its functioning, *excluding however, self-induced states*

77 *Criminal Code*, above note 7, s. 2.

> *caused by alcohol or drugs*, as well as transitory mental states such as hysteria or concussion.[78]

Fitness to stand trial is presumed and must be displaced by a party asserting "unfitness" on a balance of probabilities (section 672.22 of the *Criminal Code*). As set out in section 672.23, if the court believes on reasonable grounds that the accused is unfit to stand trial at any stage of the proceedings, the court may direct a trial of the issue upon its own motion or, upon application of one of the parties. Assessment orders can be made by the court to assist with the determination pursuant to the provisions of section 672.11(a).

As stated by Blair J.A. in *R. v. Morrissey*, "Meaningful presence and meaningful participation at the trial, therefore, are the touchstones of the inquiry into fitness."[79] Of importance, however, is that testimonial competence "is not a condition precedent to the accused being declared fit to stand trial."[80] The goal of testimonial capacity is to meet "minimum standards of reliability and trustworthiness" and these goals are different than the ones underpinning the fitness requirement, making it unnecessary to combine the two concepts.[81]

In *R. v. Taylor*, the only issue with respect to the fitness criteria set out in section 2 of the *Criminal Code* was determining "the proper test to be applied in determining the accused's ability to communicate with counsel."[82] The accused (a former lawyer) met the first two criteria since he understood the nature and object of the proceedings, as well as its possible consequences. At trial, however, two psychiatrists testified as to the accused's mental state, specifically that he suffered from paranoid schizophrenia and that he suffered from delusions involving the justice system and its participants conspiring against him. In the opinion of both doctors, the accused was unfit to stand trial. The trial judge agreed with the psychiatrists and commented that the accused's delusions were "pervasive" and "irrational" before finding that the accused was not fit to stand trial because he was not able to act in his own best interests (i.e., the accused did not meet the analytic capacity test for fitness to stand trial). The Court of

---

78 *R. v. Bouchard-Lebrun*, 2011 SCC 58 at para. 39, quoting and adding emphasis to a passage from *Cooper v. The Queen*, [1980] 1 S.C.R. 1149 at 1159.

79 2007 ONCA 770 at para. 36.

80 *Ibid.* at para. 25.

81 *Ibid.* at para. 37.

82 [1992] O.J. No. 2394 at para. 42 (C.A.) [*Taylor*]. To review earlier proceedings related to this case see, generally, *R. v. Taylor*, 1991 CanLII 7317 (Ont. C.A.).

Appeal found that the trial judge and the Ontario Review Board imposed too high a threshold by using the analytic capacity test and that the proper test with respect to determining the accused's ability to communicate with counsel is the limited cognitive capacity test:

> Under the "limited cognitive capacity" test propounded by the *amicus curiae*, the presence of delusions do not vitiate the accused's fitness to stand trial unless the delusion distorts the accused's rudimentary understanding of the judicial process. It is submitted that under this test, a court's assessment of an accused's ability to conduct a defence and to communicate and instruct counsel is limited to an inquiry into whether an accused can recount to his/her counsel the necessary facts relating to the offence in such a way that counsel can then properly present a defence. It is not relevant to the fitness determination to consider whether the accused and counsel have an amicable and trusting relationship, whether the accused has been cooperating with counsel, or whether the accused ultimately makes decisions that are in his/her best interests. The *amicus curiae* relies on this court's decision in *Reference re R. v. Gorecki (No. 1)* (1976), 1976 CanLII 833 (ON CA), 14 O.R. (2d) 212, 32 C.C.C. (2d) 129, and *R. v. Trecroce, supra.*
>
> . . .
>
> The "limited cognitive capacity" test strikes an effective balance between the objectives of the fitness rules and the constitutional right of the accused to choose his own defence and to have a trial within a reasonable time.
>
> In asking the court to require that the accused be able to act in his own best interests, the respondent is asking this court to adopt the higher threshold "analytic capacity" test for determining the accused's fitness to stand trial. This test has clearly been rejected by the courts.[83]

Justice Lacourcière, writing for the Court of Appeal, allowed the appeal in part, quashed the disposition of the Ontario Review Board and the trial judge's finding of unfitness, and ordered a new trial.

In *R. v. Whittle*, the limited cognitive capacity test approved of in *Taylor* was adopted by the Supreme Court of Canada in the context of the vol-

---

83 *Taylor*, above note 82 at paras. 44, 52, & 53. The court went on to state at para. 46: "I have considered this court's decisions in *Reference re R. v. Gorecki (No. 1)* and *R. v. Trecroce*, relied upon by both counsel. In my opinion, these cases set out the appropriate test at common law for unfitness."

untariness of inculpatory statements made by the accused.[84] The accused was charged with first-degree murder after detailing his involvement in a murder—he had been cautioned of his right to counsel and his counsel advised him to remain silent but, nonetheless, he waived his right to silence and spoke to police about the crime to stop the voices in his head: the accused suffered from schizophrenia. As stated by Sopinka J., who delivered the judgment of the Court, "The question that I must deal with is whether there is any justification for requiring a higher standard of cognitive capacity in making the choices inherent in the confessions rule, the right to silence and the right to counsel than in respect to fitness to stand trial." The Court found that the statements made by the accused were voluntary and admissible. The accused possessed the limited degree of cognitive capacity needed to meet the operating mind test. The accused understood what he was saying, understood the court process, and was fit to instruct counsel but, "because of the voices that were telling him to unburden himself, he did not care about the consequences." This cannot amount to the exclusion of his statements and, as explained by the Court, "[I]nner compulsion, due to conscience or otherwise, cannot displace the finding of an operating mind unless, in combination with conduct of a person in authority, a statement is found to be involuntary."[85]

There has been some debate as to whether the limited cognitive capacity test requires too little of the mentally ill accused and that the test is therefore set too low. Justice Trotter in *R. v. Adam* takes a broad view of "meaningful participation" as an essential ingredient in a finding of fitness, and he takes a view of fitness which, of necessity, requires a modicum of "rationality" in order for the test to comport with the broad intention of the fitness requirement; that is, to protect individuals from the state's prosecution where they are not equipped to respond.[86] It is submitted that the view taken by Trotter J. in *Adam* may be signalling a shift in more formally recognizing what the courts have, in practice, been applying for some time.

The psychiatric assessment will be focused upon the accused's current mental state, the presence of any mental disorder as defined by the *Criminal Code*, a description of the accused's "inabilities" caused by the men-

---

84 [1994] 2 S.C.R. 914.

85 *Ibid.* at para. 54.

86 *R. v. Adam*, 2013 ONSC 373 at para. 29 [*Adam*].

tal disorder, and whether or not these would preclude the accused from either representing himself or instructing counsel to do so.

2) Criminal Responsibility Assessments

"Insanity," as it was known for centuries, pertains to the accused's mental state at the time of the otherwise criminal act. With Bill C-30, in 1992, the terminology was modernized to "not criminally responsible on account of mental disorder" (NCR). The test is set out in section 16 of the *Criminal Code*. The caselaw pertaining to criminal responsibility is voluminous and will not be covered in this chapter.

> 16. (1) No person is criminally responsible for an act committed or an omission made while suffering from a mental disorder that rendered the person incapable of appreciating the nature and quality of the act or omission or of knowing that it was wrong.
>
> (2) Every person is presumed not to suffer from a mental disorder so as to be exempt from criminal responsibility by virtue of subsection (1), until the contrary is proved on the balance of probabilities.
>
> (3) The burden of proof that an accused was suffering from a mental disorder so as to be exempt from criminal responsibility is on the party that raises the issue.

The first discussion lawyers need to have with clients who are prospective candidates for a defence of NCR is not so much about eligibility as it is about whether or not an NCR defence favours the accused's legal and social interests. The assumption here is that, given the choice, most if not all accused would opt for the fastest route to liberty as the outcome of their criminal trial. NCR defences are rarely raised and are often unsuccessful when raised. Contested NCR defences are uncommon.

An accused who might be successful in her bid for an NCR defence could be at risk of stepping into supervisory quicksand if her history demonstrates poor prognostic features, like a severe illness that responds insufficiently to medication and other treatment, medication non-compliance, poor insight, substance abuse, personality pathology, anger dysregulation, and a history of injurious acting-out behaviour, including violence. Such an accused's course through progressive derestriction (from higher- to lower-intensity secure psychiatric hospitals, to being monitored in the community, and to ultimately complete freedom by way of an absolute discharge from the jurisdiction of a provincial or territorial review board) could occur at a snail's pace, if at all. An accused person could be looking at potentially indeterminate detention for an offence that would have yielded a low-to-modest period of incarceration. A forensic psychiatrist, following a file review, and ideally, a face-to-face meeting with the accused, could offer a critically important experience-based forecast concerning how the accused will fare during observation and evaluation and how long and under what circumstances her liberty may be curtailed.

Multiple factors are usually at play in violent crime and only the most naïve, inexperienced, or misguided expert would say that a particular behaviour is 100 percent driven by psychosis. Even if psychosis played a central role in directing the accused's behaviour, various motivational threads may have been involved in bringing about the event at issue before the courts.

For a psychiatric expert, the premise going into the assessment involves a dual thought process characterized by both objectivity and a high index of suspicion—the accused is either genuine in his recitation of the events and the reporting of his symptoms, or is providing a self-serving account that involves exaggerated or malingered symptoms. An open-minded and scientific approach to uncovering what the accused was thinking and feeling entails considering, among other factors, the context of the offence, the nature of the relationship between perpetrator and victim (and, in particular, pre-existing animus between them), "similar fact" types of behaviours or episodes of deranged mental functioning in his past (e.g., history of anger dysregulation, impulsivity, violent action, and fantasies), as well as detailed knowledge of an accused's affective state and potential motive(s) at the critical time. Other personal details, as well as family histories, may also be relevant.

The clinician/expert knows that an accused's mental state at the time of an event cannot be known and must be surmised from all the information the clinician/expert has fastidiously pursued. The more cogent information a clinician/expert has about the accused's mental state at the time of the offence, the better and more solidly anchored the opinion will likely be. Records specific to this task generally include:

- the prosecution brief, including synopses, witness and police officer statements and notes, relevant video and audio recordings, and information about the victim
- the accused's statement and videos of the same, if a statement was given

- crime scene photographs, videos, and forensic reports
- the accused's criminal record and probation and parole records
- medical, psychiatric, and substance abuse records
- academic, military, and employment records (where relevant)

The clinical portion of the assessment of the accused proceeds along the lines of a standard medical/psychiatric consultation, with a special focus on the accused's mental state prior to, immediately after, and, most importantly, at the time of the offence. Care must be taken to distinguish between what the accused remembers and what he has learned from other sources (e.g., a witness).

Given that some form of psychotic disorder is likely to be postulated as the basis for the contemplated NCR defence, the examiner should do her utmost to elicit symptoms in her mental examination of the accused that support or refute the symptoms that will be relied upon for the NCR defence, even though those symptoms may have dissipated, disappeared, or (less commonly) increased by the time of the assessment.

Experts often pick a point in time when the accused's mental state was notably distinguishable from his alleged mental state at the time of the offence(s), whether that is minutes, hours, days, weeks, or months before. The minimum here is twenty-four hours and the examiner will be looking closely at what, if anything, changed in the accused's thoughts, perceptions, and/or feelings, and what induced the changes.

Under section 16(2) of the *Criminal Code*, it is presumed that every person does not suffer from a mental disorder that exempts them from criminal responsibility; the existence of such a disorder must be proved on the balance of probabilities and, under section 16(3), the burden of proof is on the party who raises the issue. Assessing whether the accused "appreciated the nature and quality" of his act(s)—the first branch of the NCR test in section 16(1) of the *Criminal Code*[87]—entails first allowing the accused to unfold the story, followed by close questioning of the accused about all relevant aspects of the incident and his experience. As gruesome as the event(s) may be, a play-by-play review of them, with special emphasis on what the accused felt, saw, and understood moment-by-moment is unavoidable.[88]

---

87 Above note 7.

88 For a detailed discussion of questions that might be asked to elicit this information, see Hy Bloom, "Not Criminally Responsible on Account of Mental Disorder (NCRMD)," in Bloom & Schneider, above note 1 at 263.

Asking what the accused knew and understood about the legal and moral appropriateness of his actions—the second branch of the NCR test—generally involves a more direct inquiry into why the accused chose the particular course of action and forfeited other options. The goal is to obtain insight into the accused's awareness in the instant of the moral and legal soundness of her actions. Many accused find it hard to retrospectively put themselves back in the moment and often claim some degree of memory impairment. Amnesia is raised frequently in violent crime. Seasoned experts are unlikely to attach too much significance to it; they know that apart from being in a psychotic state—a relatively uncommon reason for violence in its own right—the intense emotional state most individuals are in before they commit violence can impede the laying down and retrieval of memory, as does alcohol and drug use (which themselves have a very high correlation with violent crime). A conscious and/or unconscious wish not to acknowledge reprehensible and shameful behaviour is yet another potent factor pushing the retrieval of details of the crime to the back burner of memory.

Reports addressing criminal responsibility are often divided into two subsections: the prosecution's version of the events and the accused's version. To be useful to lawyers and the courts, the NCR assessment report must provide a recitation of the relevant information and data, followed by a cogent analysis. Forensic assessments and reports could and should "connect the dots" for the reader; the clearer the connections are, the more the parties and the court will feel that loose ends have been tied off; the need to testify may even be obviated by the high quality of the report.[89]

The logic path between the diagnosed mental illness and its impact on exemption from criminal responsibility is helpfully set out in *R. v. Noyes*.[90] This path is illustrated below as a five-step process, in the context of a psychotic accused who committed a violent act.

89 Hy Bloom, "Medico-legal Report Writing" in Bloom & Schneider, above note 1 at 39.

90 *R. v. Noyes*, 2010 BCSC 1240.

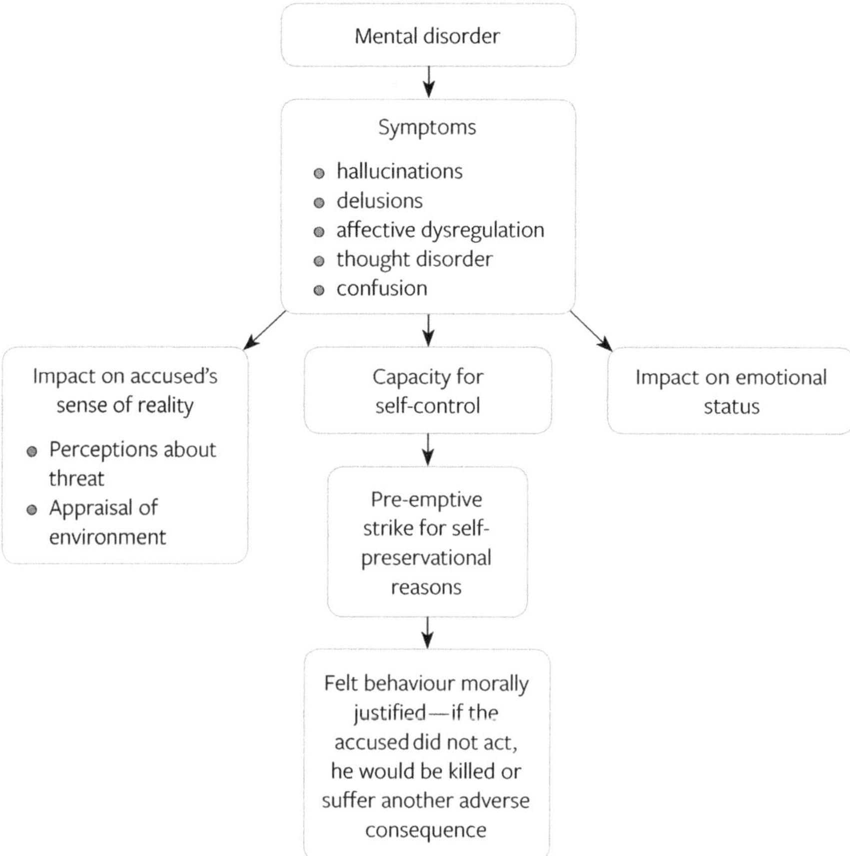

Reprinted with permission of Hy Bloom ©.

FIGURE 19.1. Elements and Flow of an NCR Defence.

Forensic psychiatrists expect to be cross-examined on their reports. They are invariably at risk in all forensic cases, whether civil or criminal, of being cross-examined about issues like bias, the thoroughness of their evaluation, and whether they have addressed the issue of malingering. Other areas a cross-examiner might target include any deficits in the expert's knowledge and understanding of relevant legislation (i.e., section 16 of the *Criminal Code*) and caselaw on point.[91]

91 The need to understand important caselaw that addresses the legal standard involved and/or the way psychiatric evidence may or may not be useful is yet another way in which general and forensic psychiatry are distinguishable.

Psychiatric experts can also botch an NCR assessment and be targeted in cross-examination as a result. This may occur when psychiatric experts fail to consider other hypotheses, when they assume a mental disorder is synonymous with absent criminal responsibility, and when they fail (in scenarios involving multiple charges) to consider the accused's mental state for each offence and erroneously assume that the same deficits in appreciation and knowledge exist for every separate event.

While the provisions of section 16 dealing with the NCR create a supervening defence which will very often incidentally defeat the requisite *mens rea*, mental disorder may also operate so as to defeat the requisite *actus reus*. The common law defence of automatism results where an intervening force negates the required voluntariness of the act.[92] Where the intervening force is a "mental disorder," the accused obtaining the verdict will be treated as if they were found to be NCR within the ambit of section 16 and will be subject to the relevant provisions of Part XX.1 of the *Criminal Code*.

3) Violence Risk Assessment

Assessing an accused's risk for violence has become one of the most common forensic psychiatric tasks in criminal proceedings. Violence risk assessment is a complex process of thorough information gathering focused on being able to make informed decisions about an individual's risk for violence (i.e., sexual recidivism or other untoward behaviours) and managing that risk. Psychiatrists appraise risk on a day-to-day basis, perhaps without even thinking about it as such, when they assess a patient's candidacy for civil commitment. Formal risk assessments are most often undertaken in the context of sentencing, particularly dangerous offender and long-term offender (DO/LTO) proceedings, and judicial interim release.

Risk assessments answer the question: which perpetrator will commit which actions by what means towards whom within what timeframe? Although the evaluee is clearly the focus of the assessment, expert assessors appreciate that violence does not generally occur in a vacuum. It is interactional and almost always depends on the presence of and friction between two or more variables, including susceptible perpetrators and victims, environmental factors, and an event or stressor that serves as an accelerant for the conflagration of violence. In any violence risk assessment, examiners should develop a theory about from where and whence the violence derives.

92 *R. v. Parks*, [1992] 2 S.C.R. 871; *R. v. Stone*, [1999] 2 S.C.R. 290.

Violence risk assessment is a new science with a thirty- to forty-year history of research and writings about what makes people violent, the association between mental illness and violence, and, importantly, how to rate violence risk with any level of accuracy; this latter area tends to receive the most attention in court, when a disposition depends on quantifying an accused's risk and his amenability to treatment and risk reduction measures.

The violence risk assessment process is equally (if not more) entailed than assessing criminal responsibility, as the information-gathering process in risk assessment penetrates even further into the evaluee's life and is not as dependent on a point in time when an illness set in. Childhood oppositional, defiant, and conduct disorder behaviours are important and are often accessed by interviewing others and obtaining school records. Not only is the accused's criminal record important, but so are the minute details of his offences and their circumstances, and the accused's psychological state at the time. Information in respect of how he met his legal obligations and abided by terms of bail and probation has predictive value in respect of whether and how he will manage legal obligations in the future.

The database created by the forensic psychiatrist should also include information gathered from the accused, collateral informants, and from records (to the extent available) about behaviour, attitude, and performance at school and work. This information should address institutional and social realms and provide information about key domains of functioning that are often implicated in violence risk (e.g., mental health and addictions history, brain injury, capacity to form meaningful relationships, and management of emotions, particularly anger and impulsivity). Management of stress, loss, and shame are important, as is information about peer associations, usual or historic victim choice, insight, viability of future plans, and attitude towards receiving help.

a) Sentencing

Risk assessment tools have become a standard part of the assessment process and courts hear much about them, especially in DO/LTO proceedings. A review of the science behind them and the debate (more historic than current) concerning which style tool—actuarial[93] or structured professional judgment (SPJ)[94]—is better, is beyond the scope of this chapter. Both of the observational tools include an item that rates an evaluee for the

93 This method relies on differently weighted historical (static) factors alone, demonstrated through research to have predictive value.

94 SPJ melds historical and dynamic (clinical and risk management) factors.

presence of personality pathology, the most important of which relevant to risk would be antisocial personality disorder or psychopathy.[95] The latter is most commonly rated using the *Hare Psychopathy Checklist*.[96] Although the latter tool was created to measure whether an individual manifests psychopathic to a diagnostic threshold, it has over the years proven valuable in assessing multiple kinds of risks for criminal, violent, and sexual recidivism; institution adjustment; and amenability to treatment. Importantly, although the presence of psychopathic personality is a potent factor in the calculation of violence risk, there are other tools (only a few of which have been referenced in this chapter) more specific to this purpose.[97]

Best known among the various violence risk appraisal tools are (1) the *Violence Risk Appraisal Guide* (VRAG)[98] and (2) the *Historical, Clinical, and Risk Management-20* (HCR-20).[99] These tools represent the actuarial approach and the SPJ approach, respectively.[100] The VRAG, which is based on a sample of 618 maximum security psychiatric hospital male adult offenders with histories of mental disorder and violence, is a twelve-item tool that relies on static (i.e., unchangeable) factors vetted as most valuable from a considerably longer list of static factors associated with future violence. In comparison, the HCR-20 strives for a more balanced approach by considering several domains of information—historical risk factors, clinical factors, and future risk management factors. The twenty empirically supported risk factors were drawn from research and clinical experience.

---

95 In the case of the HCR-20, it is the presence or absence of "personality disorder" and in the case of the VRAG, the (heavily weighted) item rates the presence and depth of psychopathic traits.

96 Robert D. Hare, *Hare Psychopathy Checklist-Revised* (PCL-R) *Technical Manual*, 2d ed. (Toronto: Multi-Health Systems, Inc, 2004).

97 Michael Brook, "The Role of Psychopathic and Antisocial Personality Traits in Violence Risk Assessment: Implications for Forensic Practice" (2015) 45 *Psychiatric Annals* 175.

98 Grant T. Harris et al., *Violent Offenders: Appraising and Managing Risk*, 3d ed. (Washington, DC: American Psychological Association, 2015).

99 Christopher Webster et al., *HCR-20: Assessing Risk for Violence* (*Version 2*) (Burnaby, BC: Mental Health, Law, and Policy Institute, Simon Fraser University, 1997); Kevin S. Douglas et al., *HCR-20V3 Assessing Risk of Violence User Guide* (Burnaby, BC: Mental Health, Law, and Policy Institute, Simon Fraser University, 2013).

100 For research that prefers the SPJ approach, see R.K. Otto, "Assessing and Managing Violence Risk in Outpatient Settings" (2000) 56 *Journal of Clinical Psychology* 1239; D.A. Pinals, C.E. Tillbrook, & D.L. Mumley, "Violence Risk Assessment" in Fabian M. Saleh et al., *Sex Offenders: Identification, Risk Assessment, Treatment, and Legal Issues* (New York: Oxford University Press, 2009) [Saleh et al., *Sex Offenders*] ch 5; Dean R. Cauley, "Risk Assessment of Civilly Committed Sexually Violent Predators: Static Versus Dynamic Orientations" (2007) 16 *Forensic Examiner* 18.

Neither style of tool (actuarial or SPJ) is capable of accurately pinning down exactly what an evaluee will do, how severe his future actions will be, who the actions will be directed to, and when these actions may occur. Lawyers should be wary of experts proffering purportedly accurate forecasts of what an individual will do, regardless of the method used. There is an evolving literature precisely on this point that criticizes claims by the proponents of the actuarial method for overreaching. Authors like Mossman, Buchanan et al., and Hart et al. argue that extrapolations assessing what a *specific* individual will do based on what *groups* tend to do are fraught with statistical error.[101] Such erroneous extrapolations are dangerous when a person's liberty is at stake.

The two approaches recently clashed in *Ewert v. Canada (Correctional Service)*, a case in which a psychology expert on behalf of the plaintiff (Dr. Stephen Hart) opposed a proponent of the actuarial method (Dr. Marnie Rice) on the basis that the actuarial tools used to rate Ewert's risk lacked cross-cultural sensitivity and validation.[102] Ewert was an Aboriginal federal inmate and Dr. Hart concluded that the actuarial tests were "not sufficiently predictably reliable for Aboriginals because of the cultural variance or bias of the tests."[103] Dr. Rice's zealous and uncompromising approach in support of the accuracy of the actuarial tools in characterizing Ewert as an "undue risk to society" resulted in stern criticism from the court and the discounting of her evidence, except where it was consistent with Dr. Hart.[104] The court concluded that the actuarial assessment tools were not "responsive to the special needs of Aboriginal people"[105] and further use breaches section 24(1) of the *Corrections and Conditional Release Act*, which requires the Correctional Service of Canada to "take all reasonable steps to ensure that any information about an offender that it uses is as accurate,

101 See Douglas Mossman, "Another Look at Interpreting Risk Categories" (2006) 18 *Sexual Abuse* 41; Alec Buchanan et al., "Resource Document on Psychiatric Violence Risk Assessment" (2012) 169 *American Journal of Psychiatry* 1, data supplement; and Stephen D. Hart, Christine Mitchie, & David J. Cooke, "Precision of Actuarial Risk Assessment Instruments: Evaluating the 'Margins of Error' of Group versus Individual Prediction of Violence" (2007) 190 (suppl. 49) *British Journal of Psychiatry* 60.

102 2015 FC 1093 [*Ewert*].

103 *Ibid.* at para. 41.

104 See *ibid.* at para. 52. See Douglas Mossman, "From Group Data to Useful Probabilities: The Relevance of Actuarial Risk Assessment in Individual Instances" (2015) 43 *Journal of the American Academy of Psychiatry and the Law* 93, where the author argues that notwithstanding its pitfalls, when considered in context, actuarial statements about an individual's risk drawn from group data improves decision making.

105 *Ewert*, above note 102 at para. 113.

up to date and complete as possible."[106] The court held that Ewert's section 7 *Charter* rights were violated without justification under section 1.[107]

Experts should bring a degree of humility to the task of risk assessment and be prepared to acknowledge its various limitations. At the same time, however, experts should not throw up their hands and disclaim any ability whatsoever in the area.

b) Dispositions

Expert psychiatric opinion is also typically called in order to determine whether an accused who has obtained a verdict of NCR is a "significant threat to the safety of the public." The *Criminal Code* states:

> 672.5401 For the purposes of section 672.54, a significant threat to the safety of the public means a risk of serious physical or psychological harm to members of the public—including any victim of or witness to the offence, or any person under the age of 18 years—resulting from conduct that is criminal in nature but not necessarily violent.

Psychiatric evidence is typically necessary to determine whether the accused is a significant threat and, if so, for what type of behaviour within what window of time. This evidence will then inform the review board as to what sorts of measures need to be included in the accused's disposition to mitigate the risk he poses.

In *Winko v. British Columbia (Forensic Psychiatric Institute)*,[108] the Supreme Court of Canada indicated that "significant threat" means a real risk of physical or psychological harm (with Bill C-14, now section 672.5401, significant threat has been redefined as "a risk of physical or psychological harm"):

1) there is to be no presumption that the mentally disordered accused poses a significant threat to the safety of the public;
2) the accused is never in a position of having to disprove dangerousness—the accused is therefore relieved of any legal or evidentiary burden—the accused need do nothing (unless, of course, dangerousness is otherwise established);[109]
3) this tactical incentive to adduce evidence is not properly described as a shifting of the legal or evidentiary burden to the accused;

---

106 S.C. 1992, c. 20, s. 24(1).
107 *Ewert*, above note 102 at para. 113.
108 [1999] 2 S.C.R. 625.
109 *Re Marzec*, 2015 ONCA 658 at paras. 29–33.

4) if the court or review board is unable to conclude that the accused constitutes a significant threat to the safety of the public, the accused must be absolutely discharged;
5) jurisdiction over the accused cannot be maintained where there is doubt regarding dangerousness, continued jurisdiction requires an affirmative finding of significant threat;
6) the threat posed must be more than speculative in nature; it must be supported by the evidence;
7) the threat must also be "significant," both in the sense that there must be a real risk of physical or psychological harm occurring to individuals in the community and in the sense that this potential harm be serious. A miniscule risk of a grave harm will not suffice. Similarly, a high risk of trivial harm will not meet the threshold;
8) the conduct or activity creating the harm must be criminal in nature;[110] and
9) finally, it is up to the court or review board to ensure that it has sufficient information in order to make the determination.

"Significant threat" clearly contemplates a prospective inquiry. The least onerous and least restrictive (necessary and appropriate) standard must be applied to not only the type of disposition imposed (that is, discharge, discharge subject to conditions, or detention subject to conditions) but to the particular conditions themselves.[111]

The least onerous and least restrictive test is applied in a way that is commensurate with the level of threat posed by the accused. Levels of security and potential privileges are matched to that threat,[112] but they are to be in no way connected with any notion of punishment.[113] The appropriate level of security and accompanying terms which constitute the least onerous and least restrictive disposition are determined through consideration of terms including:

1) recommendations of the clinical team and hospital at which the accused is detained or reporting to,
2) the nature and circumstances of the index offence,
3) the accused's level of insight,
4) the availability of necessary treatment opportunities,

110 See *Chambers v. British Columbia (Attorney General)*, 1997 CanLII 2978 (B.C.C.A.).
111 *Penetanguishene Mental Health Centre v. Ontario* (AG), 2004 SCC 20 [*Tulikorpi*].
112 *Pinet v. St. Thomas Psychiatric Hospital*, 2004 SCC 21.
113 *R. v. Owen*, 2003 SCC 33.

5) the need to protect the public from dangerous persons.[114]

4) Assessment of Sexual Offenders

For psychiatrists who assess accused facing criminal charges, evaluating sex offenders is likely a common task in their day-to-day professional activities. It appears that deviant sexual behaviour and sexual offending has increasingly come to the public's attention, not only because of the media, but likely also because of our expanding awareness of the phenomenon of sexual victimization and the concomitant realization that sexual offences occur more frequently than we seem to suspect.

The proliferation of Internet pornography—a boon to both normal and deviant erotica consumers—is also a factor. Accessibility, low cost, nature, magnitude, and diversity of erotica, as well as presumptive anonymity of Internet use are a few key factors behind the phenomenon.[115] The Internet has allowed for circumstances in which pedohebephilic individuals (i.e., persons whose erotic interests centre on prepubescent and/or pubescent children)—hitherto skilled in the avoidance of acting out in public—fly into the radar and become tripped up in one of many local and international police initiatives to catch Internet child pornography perpetrators. The sexual violence recidivism assessment tools discussed below were conceived of and constructed with contact offences in mind, and are consequently not specific or appropriate for evaluating risk in an Internet child pornography offender, except in so far as they may provide a useful (albeit non-exhaustive) grid for information gathering.[116]

Assessing an accused for a sexual charge(s), whether at the behest of Crown or defence counsel, generally involves looking at three domains: (1) motivation for the offence (which in large part directs diagnosis), (2) risk for recidivism, and (3) recommended risk reduction or risk management recommendations; this latter category subsumes treatment.

As regards motivation, it is sometimes too easy for lawyers, judges, law enforcement personnel, and the general public to conflate the social/legal

---

114 *Beauchamp v. Penetanguishene Mental Health Centre* (1999), 138 C.C.C. (3d) 172 at para. 29 (Ont. C.A.).

115 L. Alvin Malesky, Jr. et al., "Child Pornography and the Internet" in Saleh et al., *Sex Offenders*, above note 100, ch 22.

116 A model for assessing risk in this group has been proposed by Ward and Beech. See Tony Ward & Anthony R. Beech, "The Etiology of Risk: A Preliminary Model" (2004) 16 *Sexual Abuse* 271.

designation of "sex offender" with its potential diagnostic counterpart (e.g., pedophilia, when the victim is a minor). This is particularly important in the area of child Internet pornography, where the knee-jerk assumption about anyone found in possession of child pornography is that he must be pedophilic.[117] That said, considering the availability of every sort of erotica available on the Internet, choosing to collect child pornography is diagnostically significant[118] but not dispositive of the issue. Diagnoses are best made drawing on the foundation provided by the three-layer medical model: history, examination, and investigations. In forensic contexts, the model necessarily relies on multiple sources and collateral information to ensure the truth is exposed.

From a motivational and diagnostic perspective, sex offenders are a heterogeneous group that includes accused with paraphilias (e.g., pedophilia, exhibitionism, sexual sadism); sexually addicted and compulsive individuals whose relentless pursuit of novelty and variety at increasingly higher thresholds of erotic titillation may lead them to forbidden and illegal Internet pursuits; and accused who are socially and developmentally challenged (e.g., with an autism spectrum disorder condition, or congenital or acquired cognitive impairment, respectively). The group also includes personality disordered (particularly antisocial, psychopathic, and narcissistic) men with one or more of the following characteristics: a strong sense of entitlement; poor impulse control; anger dysregulation; indifference to the suffering of others; an underdeveloped conscience and capacity for remorse; uncaring attitude towards people, society, and its laws; and a negative (if not misogynistic) view of women. When personality disordered offenders commit sexual crimes, alcohol and/or drugs may often be involved.

Major mental disorders (i.e., psychotic disorders like schizophrenia or delusional disorder, or bipolar disorder) are infrequent causes of sexual offending. While the most common reason to have a sexual offender assessed is for sentencing purposes, the occasional sexual offender engages in the behaviour that resulted in his charge(s) for psychotic reasons. For example, the offender may hear voices that commanded him to commit an act and/or his misapprehensions about the victim or the act reached

117 See Hy Bloom, "Internet Child Pornography Consumers Aren't Always Pedophiles" (27 February 2009) 28 *The Lawyers Weekly*.

118 Michael C. Seto et al., "Child Pornography Offenses Are a Valid Diagnostic Indicator of Pedophilia" (2006) 115 *Journal of Abnormal Psychology* 610.

delusional proportions. The focus of the assessment in these exceptional cases would be on his eligibility for an NCR defense.

Similar to other types of assessments, the need for thoroughness is a key aspect of assessing sexual offenders. There are, however, several areas of assessment/investigation unique to the evaluation of sex offenders to discuss. The first concerns the need for particular kinds of collateral information, namely from current and past intimate partners, given the offence category. Evaluees and/or defence counsel are sometimes surprised and even put off by the potential intrusiveness of such a request and some evaluees are afraid that a current or former partner will disclose information injurious to their case. Evaluees and counsel in scenarios like this need to be reassured that bypassing information from current and former intimate partners in sexual offence cases (as is also the case in domestic violence risk assessment cases) is for the most part professionally untenable. Cross-examiners could easily and compellingly suggest that failing to interview current and past intimate partners reflects expert bias since the expert would necessarily have to place undue reliance on the evaluee's history and self-characterization of his sexual interests and practices. Experts should not accept any history or characterization at face value, including that collected from the accused; experts should critically analyze all information provided to them, regardless of source.

The second area of assessment unique to the evaluation of sex offenders includes the potential need for blood tests or other investigations like a CT scan or MRI of the brain.[119] Penile plethysmography, commonly referred to as phallometric testing (a physiologic measure of sexual arousal) is an indispensible adjunctive diagnostic test in the assessment of two categories of sexual offenders—child offenders, including child pornography offenders, and men who have committed a sexual assault against an adult female.[120] This latter category, especially when it involves a female previously unknown to the accused, associates diagnostically with sexual sadism or an interest in or preference for coercive sex. Use of phallometric testing to evaluate men charged with "rape-context" offences is controversial, however, because men who fall into this category of sexual offending are inherently more heterogeneous than men who offend against children, and because the preponderance of men who sexually assault women do

119 Hormone dysregulation, i.e., a disturbance in an evaluee's hypothalamic-pituitary-gonadal axis, is an infrequent to rare cause of deviant sexual behaviour, as is a genetic/chromosomal anomaly, or a structural abnormality in the brain.

120 This is the opinion of Dr. Hy Bloom.

not have paraphilia.[121] Phallometric testing is more often than not available at university-based forensic psychiatry departments; the latter often have sexual offender treatment programs. There are a handful of private phallometric labs across Canada.

There are appropriate and inappropriate uses of phallometric testing.[122] Foremost amongst its appropriate uses is enhancing diagnostic acuity, measuring treatment progress, and confronting evaluees whose continuing denial of certain paraphilic interests in the face of strong evidence to the contrary is inconsistent with both their legal and therapeutic interests. The foremost inappropriate use of phallometric testing is to bolster an accused's claim to innocence or to establish his guilt. These are ultimate issues for a judge and/or jury to decide.[123] Manipulation of the test results (i.e., "faking") by an evaluee[124] is a significant concern that has been addressed in the literature.[125]

Although there is reasonable consensus within the field concerning the diagnostic utility of phallometric testing, standardization of equipment used,[126] stimuli presented to test subjects,[127] and the types of paraphilias

121 See Michael C. Seto & Howard E. Barbaree, "Victim Blame and Sexual Arousal to Rape Cues in Rapists and Non-Offenders" (1993) 6 *Annals of Sex Research* 167; Vernon L. Quinsey & Terry C. Chaplin, "Stimulus Control of Rapists' and Non-Sex Offenders' Arousal" (1984) 6 *Behavioural Assessment* 169; Martin L. Lalumière et al., "Are Rapists Differentially Aroused by Coercive Sex in Phallometric Assessments?" (2003) 989 *Annals of the New York Academy of Science* 211.

122 The most efficacious uses for phallometric testing are to determine an evaluee's gender preference, i.e., for adult females (gynephilic) or adult males (androphilic) and age preference, i.e., adults or minors. Use of phallometric testing to diagnose paraphilias, like exhibitionism or voyeurism, is controversial.

123 See *R. v. J.-L.J.*, above note 18, where at trial, an expert who carried out phallometric testing of the accused was tendered to show that the accused lacked the sexual proclivities perpetrators of the sexual offence in question were likely to have, a view which, if ultimately accepted, would have usurped the trier of fact's role. See also D. Richard Laws, "Penile Plethysmography: Will We Ever Get It Right?" in Tony Ward et al., *Sexual Deviance: Issues and Controversies* (Thousand Oaks, CA: Sage Publications, 2003) ch 1.

124 Through conscious suppression of responses to stimuli the evaluee knows or surmises will disclose sexual deviancy, aversion of eye contact, or attempting to reduce penile responses by masturbation or substance use before the test.

125 See Laws, above note 124; see Kurt Freund et al., "Signs of Feigning the Phallometric Test" (1988) 26 *Behaviour Research and Therapy* 105; J. Paul Fedoroff et al., "Laboratory Measurement of Penile Response in the Assessment of Sexual Interests" in Saleh et al., *Sex Offenders*, above note 100, ch 7.

126 The circumferential method relies on changes in penile girth measured by a strain gauge, whereas the volumetric method measures penile response by displacement of air within an enclosed space.

127 Laboratories use visual (photos and videos) and audio materials that in part depend on the types of erotica an individual (or institution) is allowed to be in possession of in the jurisdiction they are in.

the test can diagnose, considerable variation occurs between one laboratory and another. Significantly, the efficacy of the test (i.e., its ability to diagnose a paraphilia) also varies from one laboratory to another. Among the very few laboratories that have published results, the Centre for Addiction and Mental Health (CAMH) and one of its predecessor facilities, the Clarke Institute, have published extensively about various aspects of the test, including its limitations.

CAMH's laboratory describes itself as having taken a deliberately conservative approach in its use of phallometric testing to diagnose pedohebephilia in order to diminish the social, legal, and penal risks misdiagnosis could have for an accused undergoing evaluation.[128] Incest offenders (i.e., fathers and stepfathers who sexually molest a prepubescent or pubescent daughters or stepdaughters) are less likely than men who molest minor female strangers to be diagnosed with pedohebephilia. Motivation for offending in the incest-context often has more to do with intrafamilial dynamics.[129]

Use of both actuarial and SPJ tools to assess risk for sexual offence recidivism has become common practice. Once again, the idea is to gather a wealth of relevant data about the evaluee and then analyze the data having regard to some sensible rating structure or scheme that is itself based on the soundest science and clinical wisdom available, for the purpose of identifying risk factors extant in the case at hand, quantifying level of risk (e.g., low, moderate, and high), and making meaningful risk reduction recommendations.

---

128 In its phallometric reports, CAMH describes its method as:

> purposefully biased in favor of the client and in labeling results as "not indicative" of pedophilia or hebephilia. In the case of our tests for a sexual preference for pubescent or prepubescent children, if the test results are "indicative", we can be more than 95% certain of the conclusion (i.e., the specificity of the test is 96%). To achieve that degree of certainty, however, the test sacrifices some of its ability to identify the largest number of individuals with a sexual preference for children (i.e., if 100 individuals who had a history of behaviour clearly indicating that they sexually prefer children to adults, only approximately 60 [i.e., its sensitivity] would generate a result of "indicative" on the test. That is, a significant minority of all individuals with this preference are "missed" on phallometric testing, in order to be more conservative in concluding that someone sexually prefers children to adults.

129 The incest context/dynamic refers to sexual violation of, or boundary transgression with, female minors. Intrafamilial sexual assaults against male minors are more likely the act of a pedophile.

Among the most commonly used actuarial style tools, the Rapid Risk Assessment of Sex Offender Risk (RRASOR)[130] and Static-99[131] (and its more recent and purportedly improved iteration, the Static-2002),[132] have relatively few risk factors (four, ten, and thirteen, respectively) and are fairly easy to score. The SVR-20 is probably the best-known SPJ-style tool to assess risk in individuals charged with or convicted of a sexually violent offence.[133] Its twenty risk factors fall under three headings—psychological adjustment, history of sexual offences, and future plans. Since actuarial and SPJ approaches rely on different (though somewhat overlapping) information gathering, and use different timeframes for manifestation of risk (i.e., re-offence), clinicians are likely to do best when they draw on information and scores obtained from both types of tools.[134]

5) Assessment of Malingering

Malingering refers to the deliberate feigning or exaggeration of symptoms for a discernible and tangible purpose that usually involves avoiding legal ramifications, punishment, work, or military conscription, to name a few. Regardless of the specific reason behind this behaviour, a malingerer seeks to obtain some material gain or benefit. Malingering—which is categorized in the *Diagnostic and Statistical Manual of Mental Disorders* (5th edition)[135] as a condition not considered a mental disorder, but which may nevertheless be a focus of clinical attention—is full or pure malingering when the individual feigns a non-existent disorder. Partial malingering is posited when there is a pre-existing mental condition, but the evaluee has distorted or embellished it for gain or benefit. False imputation refers to a scenario in which an evaluee consciously imputes her symptoms to an event that she knows is not the source of the symptoms/problem.

---

130 R. Karl Hanson, *The Development of a Brief Actuarial Risk Scale for Sexual Offense Recidivism* (User Report 1997-04) (Ottawa: Solicitor General Canada, 1997).

131 R. Karl Hanson & David Thornton, *Static-99: Improving Actuarial Risk Assessments for Sex Offenders* (User Report 1999-02) (Ottawa: Solicitor General Canada, 1999).

132 R. Karl Hanson & David Thornton, *Notes of the Development of Static-2002* (User Report 2003-01) (Ottawa: Solicitor General Canada, 2003).

133 Douglas P. Boer et al., *Manual for The Sexual Violence Risk-20* (Vancouver: British Columbia Institute against Family Violence, 1997).

134 Cauley, above note 100.

135 American Psychiatric Association, *Diagnostic and Statistical Manual of Mental Disorders: DSM-5*, 5th ed. (Washington, DC: American Psychiatric Press, 2013).

Malingering is distinguishable from defensiveness, which comes up more in the civil arena and involves the conscious or unconscious concealment of symptoms predating the event in question as a strategy to avoid devaluing the claim. The term "dissimulation" is used to describe efforts by evaluees to provide false, misleading, or confusing information to keep the examiner from the truth. Like malingering, defensive evaluees and those who dissimulate, come across as guarded and evasive.

Although a fair amount has been written about the phenomenology and detection of malingering, limited scientific research is available about its prevalence. It seems clear, however, that the numbers are considerably higher in forensic contexts.[136] In the United States, about 15 to 20 percent of accused persons undergoing assessments in criminal matters (e.g., fitness to stand trial and criminal responsibility assessments) feign or exaggerate a mental disorder.[137]

Malingering is also a potential concern in correctional contexts where inmate access to psychiatric services often falls into three motivational categories: (1) to get medication an inmate can get high on or prefers to what he has been prescribed (or can trade with); (2) to secure or avoid transfer to a better or less desirable environment, respectively; or (3) to avoid duties. The malingering rate in penal environments is thought to be fairly high—somewhere between 20 and 65 percent of referrals to healthcare (which are often self-referrals by inmates).[138]

In criminal contexts, an accused will most commonly feign or exaggerate psychosis, amnesia for critical events, and/or cognitive impairment. Self-preservation and optimization of prospects for liberty have

---

136 Barbara E. McDermott, "Psychological Testing and the Assessment of Malingering" (2012) 35 *Psychiatric Clinics of North America* 885.

137 See Richard Rogers et al., "A Comparison of Forensic and Non-Forensic Malingerers: A Prototypical Analysis of Explanatory Models" (1998) 22 *Law and Human Behaviour* 353; Richard Rogers et al., "Assessment of Criminal Responsibility: Initial Validation of the R-CRAS with the M'Naghten and GBMI Standards" (1986) 9 *International Journal of Law and Psychiatry* 67; and Barbara E. McDermott et al., "Triaging the IST Patient: A Brief Screen to Reduce LOS" (Paper delivered at 2009 American Academy of Psychiatry and the Law Annual Meeting, Baltimore, MD, 29 October–1 November 2009).

138 See Glenn D. Walters et al., "Use of the MMPI to Identify Malingering and Exaggeration of Psychiatric Symptomatology in Male Prison Inmates" (1988) 56 *Journal of Consulting and Clinical Psychology* 111; Richard Rogers et al., "Convergent Validity of the Personality Assessment Inventory: A Study of Emergency Referrals In a Correctional Setting" (1998) 5 *Assessment* 3; and Barbara E. McDermott & Gregory Sokolov, "Malingering in a Correctional Setting: The Use of the Structural Interview of Reported Symptoms in a Jail Sample" (2009) 27 *Behavioural Sciences and Law* 753.

also spawned the inspired, resourceful, and creative to try to harness the power of mental illness/psychological disturbance in the interest of exoneration or mitigation. Feigned battered woman's syndrome evidently allowed Karla Homolka[139] to negotiate a favourable plea bargain based on the idea that she was a powerless and frightened victim and conscript of an abusive spouse's sadistic machinations.[140] Details disclosed after the plea bargain was sealed showed her to be an active and autonomously motivated co-collaborator.[141] The hoped-for benefit of feigning psychosis is almost invariably avoidance of criminal responsibility, but again, as described earlier, psychotic mental disorders (e.g., schizophrenia) have highly specific signs and symptoms which trained clinical eyes can identify.

Mental illness is not that easy to feign. Evaluees understandably look to and draw on stereotypical portrayals of mental illness in movies and on television. Like other bad actors, however, they rarely get it right. Evaluees may, for example, claim disturbing voices and beliefs but unrealistically present these symptoms without the emotional distress that almost always accompanies inherently disturbing symptoms. As Appelbaum and Gutheil put it, evaluees who malinger may "know the words [to psychosis] but not the music."[142] It is also very difficult for malingerers to fake disordered thought and speech—another cardinal symptom of psychotic disorders, like schizophrenia.

As much as malingering may be difficult for the evaluee to fake, it can also be difficult for the assessor to spot, particularly if she is not looking for it (as an assessor always should). Malingerers have "tells"—the most commonly encountered of which are set out below:

- They are more likely to present their symptoms in a melodramatic or theatrical fashion.
- They are more likely to have court-ordered psychiatric assessments (versus inpatient psychiatric treatment).

---

139 Homolka and her then husband, Paul Bernardo, are among Canada's most notorious sadistic rapists and serial murderers.

140 Battered woman's syndrome, however, might be relevant to raising a defence of self-defence. See, generally, *R. v. Lavallee*, [1990] 1 S.C.R. 852. For information about the case and the resulting review by Justice Lynn Ratushny, *Self Defence Review: Final Report* (Ottawa: Department of Justice, 1997), see Chapter 5 in this book.

141 Anne McGillivray, "'A Moral Vacuity in Her Which Is Difficult if Not Impossible to Explain': Law, Psychiatry and the Remaking of Karla Homolka" (1998) 5 *International Journal of the Legal Profession* 255; see also *R. v. Bernardo*, 2000 CanLII 5678 (Ont. C.A.).

142 Paul S. Appelbaum & Thomas G. Gutheil, *Clinical Handbook of Psychiatry and the Law*, 2d ed. (Baltimore: Williams & Wilkins, 1991) at 303.

- They are more likely to have a personality disorder diagnosis.
- They are more likely to have a history of substance abuse.
- They are more likely to claim sudden onset and/or cessation of symptoms, i.e., "temporary insanity." Psychopathological processes neither onset nor remit in this way.
- They present only the symptoms more commonly known to the lay public (like voices), as opposed to thought disorder or negative symptoms of schizophrenia (e.g., flat affect, apathy).
- They display improbable or preposterous symptoms.
- They give vague and evasive answers, as opposed to just saying "I don't know," or approximating when asked to by the examiner (antithetically, however, saying "I don't know" in response to questions about pedestrian issues is also suggestive of malingering).
- They are unwilling to co-operate.
- They repeat questions (creating more time to think).
- They are hostile, particularly when confronted about a response or expected fact.
- They use a pattern of speech that suggests careful and deliberate steps by the evaluee to avoid a misstep, like hesitation, slow rate of speech, or hedging through use of qualifiers.

Claimed amnesia is also common, particularly in violent crime where alcohol or drug use and the highly charged emotional state[143] of the accused immediately prior to (and at) the time of the offence provide legitimate reasons for trouble laying down or retrieving memories of the event. A conscious or unconscious need to distance oneself from the behaviour is a complicating variable. Claims to amnesia based on organic neuropsychiatric diseases and syndromes, like delirium, dementia, and head injury, are looked upon with less skepticism than claims to amnesia based on psychological mechanisms like rage and dissociation.

Genuine and feigned amnesia can also be raised in support of an NCR defence. That being said, however, the inability to remember (whether claimed or real) the events says little to nothing about an accused's capacity to form the requisite intent for the offence, nor does it speak directly to his wherewithal about the nature, impact, legality, or morality of his actions (unless the memory disturbance is a component of larger-scale cognitive

---

143 Gayla Swihart et al. have referred to this as a "red-out." See Gayla Swihart et al., "The Role of State-Dependent Memory in 'Red-Outs'" (1999) 22 *International Journal of Law and Psychiatry* 199.

impairment, sufficient enough to affect awareness of one's actions; psychosis; or a disturbance in consciousness or volition, as in dissociation—a disconnection between consciousness and behaviour).

Memory problems and other cognitive deficits (i.e., in attention and concentration, orientation, and judgment) are more likely to come up in fitness to stand trial proceedings. The idea here is that some cognitive defect(s) have rendered the accused unable to conduct a defence or instruct defence counsel.[144] The inability to recall events, however, has yet to result in a finding of unfitness in Canada, the United States, the United Kingdom, or Australia.[145] In *R. v. Sabourin*, the accused went as far as being admitted to a facility for patients with dementia and attending Alzheimer Society meetings in order to be seen as unfit (for sentencing) in the hope of avoiding a penitentiary sentence for multiple frauds and tax evasion.[146] The accused's attempts to malinger memory and other cognitive deficits were uncovered by a detailed evaluation which disclosed numerous inconsistencies and fabrications. As amorphous as amnesia may appear to the untrained eye, the phenomenon, like psychosis, follows certain rules. Accused who feign amnesia often do so by claiming focal retrograde amnesia for the circumscribed timeframe of the crime. That, together with evidence of pre-offence planning, is highly suggestive of malingering.[147]

As in all forensic assessments, addressing a concern about malingering requires an extensive database that includes:

- a clinical assessment, in which the examiner is careful not to disclose his suspicions;
- access to extensive data about the evaluee's medical, criminal, legal, educational, and employment histories;
- interviews of collateral informants; and
- psychological testing, which allows for a multidisciplinary assessment (the ideal approach when malingering is a live issue).

There are a number of special forensic context tests useful in the assessment of malingering. The Structured Interview of Reported Symptoms[148]

---

144 See *Criminal Code*, above note 7, s. 2.

145 See *R. v. Morrissey*, [2003] O.J. No. 5960 (S.C.J.); *R. v. Morrissey*, above note 79; *R. v. Eisnor*, 2015 NSCA 64.

146 *R. v. Sabourin* (2009), File No. 03-G30181 (Ont S.C.J.).

147 Charles L. Scott, "Evaluating Amnesia for Criminal Behaviour: A Guide to Remember" (2012) 35 *Psychiatric Clinics of North America* 797.

148 Richard Rogers et al., *Structured Interview of Reported Symptoms (SIRS-2) and Professional Manual* (Lutz, FL: Psychological Assessment Resources, 2010).

and the Miller Forensic Assessment of Symptoms Test[149] are industry standards to test for feigned psychiatric (particularly, psychotic) illness and impairment, whereas the Test of Malingered Memory[150] assists in evaluating claimed memory problems and cognitive impairment. Personality inventories like the Minnesota Multiphasic Personality Inventory[151] and Personality Assessment Inventory[152] have validity scales that are also helpful in detecting over-reporting and/or under-reporting of symptoms.

F. ADMISSIBILITY

While the forensic psychiatrist might have important contributions to make at several junctures within the prosecutorial process, admissibility will be determined by the court as set out in Chapter 3 of this book. The concluding comments of that chapter are equally applicable in the present context. Expert opinions can enable a court to decide matters that would otherwise be insoluble. Expert opinions can provide the trier of fact with knowledge that can break through a fact-finding impasse, but despite the importance of expert opinions to the resolution of many cases, courts must manage the expert opinion vigilantly, and use it sparingly and only when necessary. To ensure the opinion serves its proper function and does not usurp the role of the trier of fact through exaggerated influence or otherwise unduly sway the court's conclusions, certain safeguards must be in place. Providers of expert opinion must be scrutinized to ensure that they are indeed qualified to offer the opinions sought. They must be willing and able to provide a fair, non-partisan, and objective opinion. The trier of fact must carefully examine the factual foundation upon which any expert opinion rests. And, finally, the opinion must be independent and impartial; only then can the opinion evidence be safely introduced into court and into the record.

---

149 Holly A. Miller, *M-FAST: Miller Forensic Assessment of Symptoms Test* (Lutz, FL: Psychological Assessment Resources, 2001).

150 Tom N. Tombaugh, *Test of Memory Malingering: TOMM* (Toronto: Multi-Health Systems, 1996).

151 Starke R. Hathaway et al., *The Minnesota Multiphasic Personality Inventory Manual* (New York: Psychological Corporation, 1951).

152 Leslie C. Morey, *Personality Assessment Inventory (PAI)* (Lutz, FL: Psychological Assessment Resources, 1991).

CHAPTER 20

Forensic Toxicology—Alcohol and Drugs

James Wigmore[*] *and James Watterson*[**]

LEGAL CONTEXT: CAITLIN PAKOSH AND SARAH HARLAND-LOGAN

A. OVERVIEW: FORENSIC ALCOHOL AND DRUG TOXICOLOGY[1]

Forensic toxicology is the science of drugs and poisons (i.e., toxins) and their adverse effects on the human body as applied to the medicolegal context. Forensic toxicology has been generally divided into two main sections—(1) alcohol, and (2) other drugs—and, as such, this chapter has been divided between the two to explore the various aspects of alcohol and drugs in criminal cases.

Forensic alcohol toxicology focuses solely on the adverse effects of ethyl alcohol in the human body and is one of the oldest of the forensic sciences. The discipline's long history is shown in Table 20.1.[2]

---

* Forensic Alcohol Toxicology.

** Forensic Drug Toxicology.

1 This overview section was written collaboratively by James Wigmore and James Watterson.

2 A.W. Jones, "Measuring Alcohol in Blood and Breath for Forensic Purposes—A Historical Review" (1996) 8 *Forensic Science Review* 13; D.M. Lucas, "Alcohol and Driving: The Development of Law Enforcement Countermeasures in Canada" (2009) 42 *Canadian Society of Forensic Science Journal* 237.

TABLE 20.1. Key Historical Developments in Forensic Alcohol Toxicology

Year	Development
1803	Henry's Law is published. This law determines a fixed ratio between a volatile in air and a liquid. It is the basis of breath alcohol testing.
1867	Breath alcohol concentrations are first determined in England by F.E. Anstie, who uses an acid dichromate solution. This is the method of detection used by the Breathalyzer when it is first developed in 1954.
1914	E.M.P. Widmark develops a method for analyzing blood and urine alcohol by using an acid dichromate solution for medicolegal cases in Sweden.
1927	E. Bogen first describes the use of breath alcohol testing for medicolegal cases in the United States.
1954	R.F. Borkenstein at Indiana University develops the Breathalyzer, the most successful and widely used breath alcohol testing instrument for police enforcement of drinking and driving laws. Approximately 30,000 Breathalyzers are manufactured worldwide until production ceases in 1997.
1956	The Breathalyzer is first used in Canada by H.W. Smith of the Centre of Forensic Sciences in Toronto. The Breathalyzer is used in Canada until 2010 but is then replaced by the Intoxilyzer, which is introduced in 1994.
1958	First use of Gas Chromatography for alcohol analysis in a forensic laboratory in Canada at the Centre of Forensic Sciences in Toronto.
1967	The Alcohol Test Committee of the Canadian Society of Forensic Science is formed "to study scientific, technical and law enforcement aspects of breath tests for alcohol."*
1969	Mandatory breath alcohol testing and "over 80" laws are first enacted in Canada.
1976	Mandatory roadside alcohol screening is introduced in Canada.
1994	J.G. Wigmore and J. Patrick first introduce the Intoxilyzer in Toronto to replace the Breathalyzer. The Intoxilyzer employs infrared (IR) light to detect alcohol and becomes the most common method for evidential breath alcohol testing by the police in Canada.

* Canadian Society of Forensic Science, "Canadian Society of Forensic Science Alcohol Test Committee Recommended Best Practices for a Breath Alcohol Testing Program" (4 May 2014) at 1, online: www.csfs.ca/uploads/3/2/2/1/3221058/2014_05_04_best_practices.pdf.

Forensic drug toxicology also has a lengthy history but focuses on a variety of drugs and toxins, unlike forensic alcohol toxicology. This discipline may be subdivided into three general areas: post-mortem toxicology, human performance toxicology, and forensic drug testing.

- *Post-mortem toxicology* involves the analysis of biological samples derived from a decedent as part of a death investigation and the interpretation of those analyses to determine whether drugs (including alcohol) were causative of, or contributive to, death. Various sample types may be analyzed, but blood, urine, and visceral tissues are the most common samples analyzed in post-mortem toxicology. The goal of post-mortem toxicology is to use these analyses of biological samples to assess the degree of toxicity experienced by the decedent.

- *Human performance toxicology* involves the analysis of biological samples derived from a subject as part of an investigation that has the goal of determining whether the subject was impaired with respect to the performance of a specific task. Very often, the task in question is the operation of a motor vehicle, but the approach may be extended to cases involving allegations of sexual assault where there is evidence of voluntary or involuntary exposure to drugs and wherein the complainant's state of intoxication is relevant to the case. Analysis of biological samples (typically urine) for performance-enhancing drugs also falls under the category of human performance toxicology.
- *Forensic drug testing*, in this context, refers to any toxicological analysis wherein the goal is simply to assess whether the subject has been exposed to drugs in the recent past. The sample types analyzed in these scenarios are often urine or hair, since those sample types are associated with longer time windows of detection.

The case types encountered in forensic toxicology can vary considerably. In post-mortem toxicology, the death investigation (which requires forensic toxicology analyses) may include criminal homicide investigations. A very large portion of forensic toxicology casework is related to allegations of impaired driving, where the vast majority of such cases focus on the role of alcohol as the impairing substance. In cases where the role of alcohol can be ruled out, further analysis of biological samples for the presence of drugs may be undertaken where the attending officer can establish grounds. In such cases, the subject may undertake standardized field sobriety tests and subsequent examination by a drug recognition expert (DRE) for the collection of physiological measurements (e.g., pupil size, reactivity to light, pulse, blood pressure). Where these examinations provide indications of impairment, the Canadian *Criminal Code* provides for officers to make a demand for biological samples (i.e., blood, urine, or oral fluid). Toxicological analysis is then used to verify drug exposure, and is interpreted in terms of whether the analytical results are consistent with the DRE observations. Other criminal case types encountered include sexual assault and administration of a noxious substance.

B. FORENSIC ALCOHOL TOXICOLOGY

1) The Science of Forensic Alcohol Toxicology

Alcohol is the most common drug detected in various types of criminal cases, but particularly in drinking and driving offences. As breath alcohol testing will be by far the most frequent method of determining blood alcohol concentration (BAC) encountered by the criminal lawyer, it will be described in the most detail. Blood and urine alcohol testing in hospitals and forensic laboratories will also be discussed.

a) Breath Alcohol Testing

Several million breath alcohol tests are conducted annually by various police agencies globally, mainly to enforce various drinking and driving laws. Breath alcohol testing is widely used because of its many advantages over blood and urine alcohol testing, and they are described below:

- *Breath alcohol testing is noninvasive.* Unlike blood samples, no needles are required, eliminating the possibility of injury or transmission of disease.
- *Breath results are known immediately.* The police immediately know what charges to lay and whether medical treatment may be required for the arrested driver (e.g., for alcohol poisoning). In comparison, it takes several weeks for blood alcohol to be reported by forensic laboratories.
- *There are no chain of custody or continuity or storage and transportation issues.* The breath sample is provided directly into the breath testing instrument. Special blood tubes, swabs, identity seals, biohazard refrigeration, and special transportation are not required, as would be for blood samples.
- *Neither special medical staff nor phlebotomists are required for breath alcohol testing, which may be conducted by trained police officers.* This results in fewer problems (such as the availability of medical staff to testify) in criminal courts.
- *No problems arise with real or alleged blood or needle phobias of the drinking driver.*

i) Principles of Breath Alcohol Testing

Alcohol is a unique drug in that it is a small, volatile, simple molecule that is totally soluble in water. This is important since the human body is composed mainly of water. Once alcohol is consumed orally, it passes rapidly through the stomach and small intestines and appears in the blood within minutes. The blood containing alcohol is pumped by the heart to the lungs and then to the rest of the body and distributed to the various tissues (including the brain) according to their water content.

When the blood (containing alcohol) passes through the lungs, there is a rapid exchange between the volatile alcohol in the blood and the air in the lungs. The lungs are specially adapted for rapid and efficient gas exchange between the blood and breath as they contain approximately 250 million small sacs known as alveoli, creating a large surface area of approximately 55 square metres.

The diffusion of alcohol from the blood to the breath is based on Henry's Law, which determined a fixed ratio between a volatile in air and a liquid. The blood breath alcohol ratio (BBR) for alcohol for breath testing instruments used in Canada is 2100:1. That is, 2100 millilitres (mL) of breath contains the same amount of alcohol as 1 mL of blood. It has been known for over fifty years that using a BBR of 2100:1 will *underestimate* the actual BAC by approximately 10 percent as the actual BBR in humans is closer to 2300:1.[3] Hence, breath alcohol testing of drinking drivers will tend to underestimate the BAC and give a "benefit of the doubt" to the person being tested.

The two main limitations of breath alcohol testing are: (1) the mouth alcohol effect; and (2) poor breath samples, which results from the subject failing to co-operate with testing.

a. Mouth Alcohol Effect

Alcohol in the oral cavity from a recent drink or the use of an alcohol-containing compound (such as mouthwash) can falsely elevate the breath alcohol test results as the residual alcohol in the mouth can be added to the alcohol exhaled from the lungs. This effect lasts for approximately ten to fifteen minutes and can be avoided by having a deprivation/observation period of that duration, and by conducting a second breath test which would not be as affected by mouth alcohol. In addition, the evidential instruments that use infrared light have a mouth alcohol detector.

---

3 A.W. Jones, "Variability of the Blood:Breath Alcohol Ratio in Vivo" (1978) 39 *Journal of Studies on Alcohol* 1931.

b. Poor Breath Samples and the Failure of the Subject to Co-operate with Testing

Another limitation of breath alcohol testing is that co-operation of the subject is required. If the subject does not provide a full exhalation as requested by a qualified breath technician, the measured BAC can be lowered by 20 to 40 percent.[4] Good coaching and positive encouragement by the qualified technician can assist in obtaining a proper breath sample. In Canada, it needs to be determined if the inability to provide proper breath testing is reasonable or not. Criminal charges may be laid if the subject refuses or fails to provide a breath sample.

ii) Methods of Breath Alcohol Analysis

The main methods used by the police in Canada to detect the alcohol concentration of breath are infrared (IR) light; fuel cell or electrochemical (EC) detection; or a combination of IR and EC.

a. Infrared Light

IR light is light that cannot be seen by human eyes as it is at a wavelength that is longer than visible red light. The alcohol molecule (C_2H_5OH) absorbs alcohol maximally at 3.4 and 9.4 micrometers (um). Evidential breath alcohol instruments employed by the police use IR light at these wavelengths to detect alcohol and to increase specificity. The basic design of these instruments consists of a heated sample chamber into which the subject exhales via a mouthpiece. IR light is passed through the sample chamber and any alcohol in the exhaled breath of the sample will absorb IR light, causing a decrease in the brightness or intensity of the IR light received at the IR detector. This decrease in intensity is measured electronically and can be expressed mathematically by the Lambert-Beer law as follows:

$$I = I_0 e^{-abc}$$

Where:

- **I** = final intensity of IR light (at the detector)
- **I_0** = initial intensity of IR light (before breath sample provided)
- **e** = mathematical constant (2.71)
- **a** = absorption coefficient of alcohol
- **b** = path length (distance the IR light travels through sample chamber)
- **c** = concentration of alcohol in breath sample

---

4 S.C. Bishop et al., "Manual Versus Automatic Sampling Variations of a Preliminary Alcohol Screening Device" (2009) 33 *Journal of Analytical Toxicology* 521.

Examples of instruments using this type of detector are the Intoxilyzer 5000C, the Intoxilyzer 8000C, the BAC Datamaster C, and the DataMaster DMT-C.

b. Electrochemical (EC) Detector

Electrochemical (EC) detectors oxidize the alcohol in the breath sample and also produce a direct electrical current that is directly proportional to the alcohol concentration as follows:

$$CH_3CH_2OH + 3H_2O \rightarrow 2CO_2 + 12H^+ + 12e^-$$

The alcohol is oxidized to carbon dioxide (CO_2), hydrogen (H^+), and electrons (e^-), respectively.

The disadvantage of EC detector instruments is that they only analyze alcohol at a single point in the exhalation of breath and not the entire exhalation curve, as is permitted by IR instruments. Thus, breath instruments using EC detectors cannot detect mouth alcohol and could incorrectly interpret the mouth alcohol effect as breath alcohol shortly after alcohol was consumed. An example of these types of instruments is the Alco-Sensor IV/RBT IV.

c. Dual EC/IR

This type of breath testing instrument incorporates both the IR and EC methods. Typically, the IR is used to monitor the breath sample and check for mouth alcohol. The last part of the forced exhalation is then analyzed by the EC to determine the alcohol concentration. Examples of dual EC/IR instruments are the Alcotest 7110 Mk II Dual C and the Intox EC/IR. This type of instrument generally has more specificity, as two independent methods are used to analyze alcohol in the breath.

iii) The Alcohol Test Committee

The Alcohol Test Committee (ATC) of the Canadian Society of Forensic Sciences has been the principle scientific advisor to the Minister of Justice on breath and blood alcohol testing for nearly fifty years. The ATC is composed of the top forensic alcohol toxicologists from across Canada and usually has an international member. The ATC evaluates approved instruments and screening devices according to strict standards and uses two independent laboratories (usually forensic laboratories in Canada) to conduct testing. The ATC also regularly publishes and updates its recommendations and procedures for the training of qualified technicians and proper breath and blood alcohol testing. The latest updates can be obtained at: www.csfs.ca.

a. Approved Screening Devices

It is often difficult for the police to determine at the roadside whether a driver has a BAC greater than 80 milligrams of alcohol in 100 millilitres of blood (80 mg/100 mL) by physical observation alone. One study in Alberta found that police officers were only able to identify 8 percent of the drivers who had a BAC greater than 80 mg/100 mL.[5] Even medical doctors examining patients in emergency rooms have trouble identifying patients with BACs in excess of 300 mg/100 mL.[6]

This inability to visually detect impairment is due in part to the development of higher levels of tolerance to the obvious physical effects of alcohol by heavy drinkers or alcohol-dependent individuals. These individuals can have high BACs without exhibiting obvious physical symptoms, such as a staggering gait and slurred speech. Convicted drunken drivers are even more difficult to visually identify as they are more often alcoholics (69 percent of first-time offenders) compared to individuals found in the general population (5–7 percent).[7] Chronic heavy drinkers or alcoholics may not show physical symptoms of intoxication to as great a degree as average drinkers.

Approved screening devices are small, portable, battery-operated devices that use EC detectors to detect BAC. They are simple to use and can be operated with minimal training. The breath results are usually given in a range of BACs. BACs less than 50 mg/100 mL will be expressed as a numerical result in order to enforce provincial graduated licensing provisions. A BAC greater than 50 mg/100 mL and less than 100 mg/100 mL will result in a WARN indicator, which usually results in the temporary provincial suspension of licence. A BAC of 100 mg/100 mL or greater will cause a FAIL indicator, which will result in an arrest and additional evidential breath alcohol testing, usually at the police station.

The ATC has published the following recommended operational procedures for the approved screening device:

---

5 W.R. Picton, "Legislation to Allow the Safe Release of Potentially Unsafe Drinking Drivers" (1978) 40 *Criminal Reports (New Series)* 30.

6 T. Urso, J.S. Gavler, & D.H. Van Thiel, "Blood Ethanol Levels in Sober Users Seen in an Emergency Room" (1981) 28 *Life Sciences* 1053.

7 R.D. Yoder & R.A. Moore, "Characteristics of Convicted Drunken Drivers" (1973) 34 *Quarterly Journal of Studies on Alcohol* 927.

1. The calibration of the Approved Screening Device shall be checked by a Screening Device Calibration Technician with an alcohol standard at least every 31 days.
   a. Where a simulator is used for the calibration check, the temperature of the alcohol standard shall be within the range of 33.8 to 34.2°C to produce a target value of 100 mg/100 mL. The use of a portion of a batch/lot of alcohol standard in a simulator shall not exceed seven days or sixteen calibration checks, whichever occurs first.
   b. Where a dry gas alcohol standard is used for a calibration check, the cylinder shall be kept at ambient room temperature and used only within the acceptable temperature range specified by the manufacturer. The dry gas standard shall not be used below a pressure specified by the manufacturer. An accessory device shall be used to determine the target value from the stated value in mg/100 mL, based on barometric pressure or the Approved Screening Device itself shall be capable of determining a target value.
   c. Any alcohol standard, aqueous or gaseous shall not be used past its expiry date.
   d. During the calibration check, the results shall give a reading within +/-5 mg/100 mL of the target value of the alcohol standard. If the result falls outside of this range, the Approved Screening Device must be recalibrated.
2. Appropriate steps shall be taken to restrict access to the calibration adjustment by anyone other than a Screening Device Calibration Technician.
3. The results of the calibration checks shall be documented.
4. Units with rechargeable batteries shall be charged according to the manufacturer's recommendations.
5. If the Approved Screening Device is battery operated, a battery check shall be part of the test procedure.
6. A test on a subject shall not be conducted until the Approved Screening Device is verified that it is ready to receive a sample.
7. A test on a subject shall not be conducted until at least fifteen minutes after the time the subject states that alcohol has been last consumed.
8. The Approved Screening Device shall be operated according to the manufacturer's recommendations.[8]

8 CSFS Alcohol Test Committee, "Recommended Standards and Procedures of the Canadian Society of Forensic Science Alcohol Test Committee" (2013) 42 *Canadian Society of Forensic Science Journal* 1 at 12.

b. Approved Instruments

In Canada, evidential breath alcohol testing instruments are called "approved instruments" and are listed in the *Approved Breath Analysis Instruments Order*, SI/85-201. Approved instruments used in Canada are mainly based on IR detectors or EC/IR combination and are more accurate, precise, and specific than approved screening devices. They are also operated by qualified technicians who are trained under the guidance of a forensic laboratory, such as the Centre of Forensic Sciences in Toronto.

The operational procedures for approved instruments are recommended by the ATC as follows:

1. The subject shall not have consumed or placed alcohol (or any other substance that may interfere with the test) in the mouth for at least fifteen minutes prior to the collection of a breath sample.
2. A system blank test shall be conducted and shall give a reading not greater than 10 mg/100 mL.
3. A system calibration check shall be conducted within the range of 50 to 150 mg/100 mL and shall give a reading within 10% of the target value of the alcohol standard. The alcohol standard shall be certified by a designated analyst.
    a. When a simulator is used for the calibration check, the temperature of the alcohol standard shall be within the range of 33.8°C to 34.2°C to produce a target value of 100 mg/100 mL. The use of a portion of a batch/lot of alcohol standard in a simulator with a non-recirculating system shall not exceed seven days or sixteen calibration checks whichever occurs first. For a simulator with a recirculating system, use shall not exceed fifteen days or 50 calibration checks—whichever occurs first.
    b. Where a dry gas alcohol standard is used for a calibration check, the cylinder shall be kept at ambient room temperature and used only within the acceptable temperature range specified by the manufacturer. The dry gas alcohol standard shall not be used below a pressure specified by the manufacturer. The dry gas alcohol standard shall only be used with Approved Instruments that are capable of determining the target value.
    c. Any alcohol standard, aqueous or gaseous, shall not be used past its expiry date.
4. Readings for the blank and calibration checks shall be recorded to the nearest milligram and shall not be truncated.

5. Two samples of deep lung breath collected at least fifteen minutes apart shall be tested.
   a. Readings of breath tests shall be truncated before being reported.
   b. If the reported result of two tests differ by more than 20 mg/100 mL, a third sample shall be collected and tested.
   c. If more than two samples of breath are necessary for a proper analysis as specified in the Criminal Code, a certificate of a Qualified Technician should not be tendered into evidence, the Qualified Technician should present viva voce testimony.[9]

The typical sequence of evidential breath alcohol testing for arrested drinking drivers is summarized in Table 20.2.

TABLE 20.2. An example of an evidential breath alcohol testing sequence.

Sequence
Fifteen- to twenty-minute observation/deprivation period
Air blank
Calibration check
Air blank
First breath alcohol test
Air blank
Second breath alcohol test
Air blank
Results are automatically printed

Air blanks are conducted to ensure the instrument retains no alcohol vapour from the previous test and that there is nothing in the room's air to give a false result. A calibration check is conducted to ensure the instrument's accuracy using an external simulator containing a certified alcohol solution. Two breath tests are conducted to increase the reliability of the results and to provide a safeguard against the mouth alcohol effect.

9 *Ibid.* at 13.

b) Blood Alcohol Analysis

The next most common method of determining the BAC in criminal cases is by a blood alcohol analysis, which is conducted in the clinical setting of a hospital or a forensic laboratory.

i) Hospital Analysis

Blood samples are routinely collected at hospitals from trauma victims at the emergency department. An alcohol analysis is usually conducted as part of the screening of the blood sample to assist in the clinical assessment of the patient. A high BAC of the patient may mask the pain of injuries and have an adverse reaction with drugs administered at the hospital.

Alcohol analysis at the hospital is usually conducted on serum/plasma instead of blood and so a conversion factor is required as serum/plasma contains more water than whole blood and thus will contain more alcohol.[10]

Alcohol is typically analysed at the hospital using an enzymatic method in which the alcohol in the serum/plasma is converted into acetaldehyde by an enzyme, alcohol dehydrogenase (ADH), and a cofactor (NAD+, or the oxidized form of nicotinamide adenine dinucleotide). The amount of NADH (the reduced form of nicotinamide adenine dinucleotide) generated in this enzymatic reaction is related to the alcohol concentration of the sample and is measured to determine the serum/plasma alcohol concentration.

The hospital results are usually reported as ETOH or ETHANOL, and in the units of millimoles per litre (mmol/L). To convert a serum/plasma alcohol concentration into a BAC in the units of the *Criminal Code* (mg/100 mL), the results just have to be multiplied by four as shown below:

$$\text{mmol/L} \times 4 = \text{mg/100 mL}$$

For example, a hospital result of 50 mmol/L is equivalent to a blood alcohol concentration of 200 mg/100 mL. A hospital result of 35 mmol/L is equivalent to 140 mg/100 mL.

ii) Forensic Laboratory

Blood analysis at the forensic laboratory may be conducted on seized hospital blood samples or on blood that is collected under a police demand using a blood collection kit with two approved blood containers (see Table

---

10 B.T. Hodgson & N.K. Shajani, "Distribution of Ethanol: Plasma to Whole Blood Ratios" (1985) 18 *Canadian Society of Forensic Science Journal* 73.

20.3). The method of alcohol analysis is usually headspace gas chromatography instead of the enzymatic method employed in the clinical setting.

TABLE 20.3. Typical contents of a police blood collection kit.

Typical contents
Two approved blood containers
Non-alcoholic swab
Disposable sterile syringe and double-ended needle
Security seals for blood containers
Mailing container

This method involves pipetting a measured volume of sample (usually 0.1 to 0. 5 mL) into two glass vials. An internal standard such as t-butanol is added to ensure greater reliability and accuracy; since t-butanol does not exist in the blood, adding a known amount to the blood sample allows for the forensic alcohol toxicologist to determine if the instrument is working correctly (the presence of this internal standard shows that the instrument is working). The vials are then sealed. The sealed vials are placed on a heated computerized tray and are heated to a temperature of 40°C to 50°C for a fixed period of time. Heat causes the alcohol to form a vapour above the sample, which is then sampled by the gas chromatograph by the automatic injection of a sampling needle. The vapour then passes through two different columns, which separates the vapour from the sample into the different alcohols and other volatile compounds such as methanol, ethanol, isopropanol, and acetaldehyde, as shown in Figure 20.1.

For each blood sample analysed, there are usually four results printed since the samples are analysed in duplicate on two separate columns. Typically, the mean or average BAC is reported. External and internal alcohol standards are also evaluated throughout the analysis of the case samples to ensure the accuracy of the run.

If the blood sample from the drinking driver is in an approved container and is analyzed by a designated analyst, and the blood sample is collected within two hours of the person having driven, then the forensic alcohol toxicologist will not be required in court to "back-calculate" the BAC. If the analysis was conducted on a hospital sample or not in an approved blood container, or the sample was collected more than two hours from the time of driving, a forensic alcohol toxicologist will be required to back-calculate the BAC to the time of driving.

FIGURE 20.1. Gas Chromatogram of a mixed alcohol standard.[11]

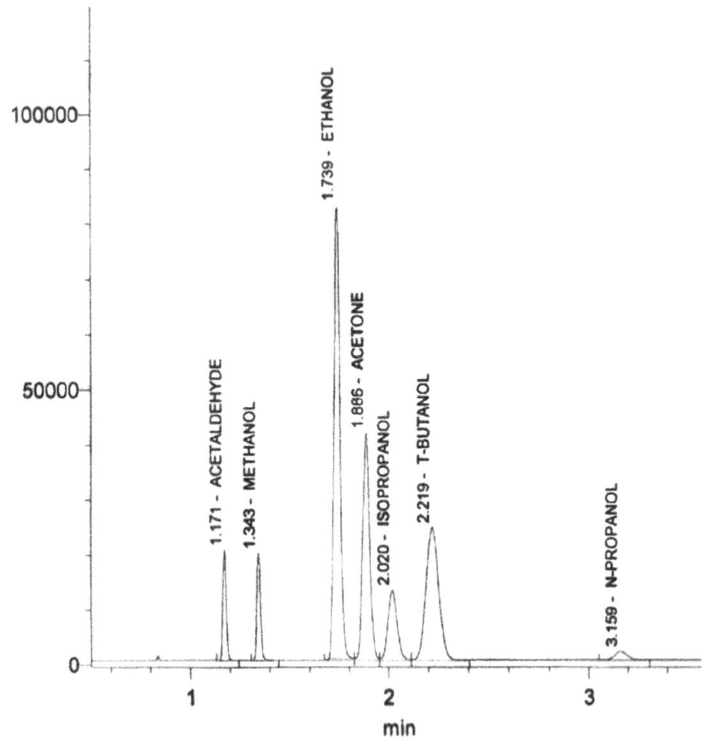

c) The Effects of Alcohol on Driving Ability

The effects of alcohol on driving ability have been well summarized by the American Medical Association as follows:

> Alcohol impairs driving skills by its effects on the central nervous system, acting like a general anesthetic. It renders slower and less efficient both information acquisition and information processing, making divided attention tasks such as steering and braking more difficult to carry out without error. The influence of alcohol on emotions and attitudes may be a crash risk factor related to driving style in addition to driving skill.[12]

---

11 Figure by James Wigmore.

12 Council on Scientific Affairs, "Alcohol and the Driver" (1986) 235 *Journal of the American Medical Association* 522 at 522.

For nearly the past 100 years, numerous scientific studies on the effect of alcohol on driving ability have shown that impairment of driving ability in all individuals occurs at a BAC of 50 mg/100 mL and above.[13] Although the current *Criminal Code* limit is 80 mg/100 mL, enforcement of the lower limit occurs with provincial legislation with a temporary suspension of driver's licences at BACs in excess of 50 mg/100 mL.

Younger, novice drivers have been found to have greater impairment of driving ability at lower BACs than older, more experienced drivers, as they have a lower tolerance to alcohol and do not have long-established driving habits.[14] In Ontario and other provinces, the licences of these Graduated Licensing Class drivers is suspended at a BAC of 10 mg/100 mL and above.

d) Blackouts

A blackout is another type of impairment due to alcohol that has a major impact on criminal cases, especially sexual assaults where consent may be the only issue. Blackouts are total memory loss, or "anterograde amnesia," which occurs at relatively high BACs caused by rapid drinking. Blackouts are simply a loss of long-term memory recording that can occur with high levels of alcohol intoxication. This type of impairment does not involve any change in behaviour, such as automatism, which may occur with other drug intoxication.

As one of the leading researchers in alcoholic blackouts, D.W. Goodwin, has stated:

> Our findings had legal implications. Blackouts have rarely been held in extenuation for crimes but lawyers continually try. I receive calls; when I tell lawyers what we found, they usually do not call back. What we found was that remote memory was intact but that people had trouble with short term memory, which meant that during a blackout, a person would be able to recite the Ten Commandments and know the consequences of robbing a bank, it was simply that he would not remember these things for 30 minutes later or the next day. He knew right from wrong at the time of the act and this appears to be the crucial fact as far as the law is concerned.[15]

---

13 T.L. Martin et al., "A Review of Alcohol-Impaired Driving: The Role of Blood Alcohol Concentration and Complexity of the Driving Task" (2013) 58 *Journal of Forensic Sciences* 1238.

14 R.C. Peck et al., "The Relationship between Blood Alcohol Concentration (BAC), Age, and Crash Risk" (2008) 39 *Journal of Safety Research* 311.

15 D.W. Goodwin, "Alcohol Amnesia" (1995) 90 *Addiction* 315.

On average, ten to fourteen drinks are consumed prior to a blackout and the average BAC at which a blackout occurs is approximately 220 mg/100 mL.[16] The factors which increase the likelihood of suffering from an alcoholic blackout are:

- consuming both liquor and beer, rather than just beer alone;
- gulping drinks, especially on an empty stomach; and
- engaging in binge drinking behaviour, where college students are therefore one of the groups that are most prone to alcoholic blackouts.[17]

Many persons who have experienced blackouts have to rely on others to provide details of what occurred during the blackout and often have a sense of dread or apprehension about what occurred. This is a particularly difficult situation if an alleged criminal act occurred during a blackout.

2) The Role of the Forensic Alcohol Toxicologist in Criminal Cases

The main role of the forensic alcohol toxicologist, whether called by the Crown or the defence, is to ensure that the blood alcohol concentrations reported to court are accurate. This is done by the investigating toxicologist (called by the Crown) ensuring that all of the quality control/quality assurance measures were applied properly and by the toxicologist called by the defence examining the records of the alcohol analysis to ensure no mistake or human error was missed. Both toxicologists ensure the accuracy of breath alcohol testing by examining the printed outputs of the evidential breath alcohol testing instruments. The toxicologists can also calculate how much the individual had to consume to obtain the recorded BAC, which can be used to impeach the witness's statements of alcohol consumption.

The toxicologist can advise the court about the impairing effects of alcohol on driving ability at certain BACs as well as the increased risk of a motor vehicle collision with increasing BAC. The toxicologist may further advise on alcoholic blackouts and alcohol's effect on memory.

The most common "toxicological" defence currently relied upon in over eighty cases is "the last drink" or "the drink after" defence, in which the driver has recently consumed alcohol or consumed alcohol after the incident and may still be on the rising BAC phase. The blood or breath

16 J.G. Wigmore, *Wigmore on Alcohol: Courtroom Alcohol Toxicology for the Medicolegal Professional* (Toronto: Irwin Law, 2011) at 268–74.

17 *Ibid.*

alcohol results are not questioned, but the defence raises the possibility that the driver may be below 80 mg/100 mL at the time of driving but has a breath/blood result of over 80 mg/100 mL later, at the time of the breath tests or blood sampling. The toxicologist may calculate how much alcohol is required for the person to be below 80 mg/100 mL. Typically, this type of defence is for drivers with BACs around 100 mg/100 mL and are of a lighter body weight; it is a more viable defence for individuals of this profile, compared to individuals with a heavier body weight.

The toxicologist can also assist is determining whether an arrested driver should be physically able to provide a breath sample. This assessment is done by examining the driver's lung function tests, especially forced vital capacity and forced expired volume in one second.

3) A Case Study

A forty-five-year-old man (5′11″ in height and weighing 170 pounds) had a minor collision with a parked car in his apartment building parking lot. He left a detailed note on the damaged car giving his name, address, and phone number, and then went to his apartment. One hour later, the police knocked on his door, as the owner of the damaged car had phoned the police and demanded a full investigation. In the intervening hour, the driver had consumed two regular bottles of beer (12 fl oz/bottle, 5% v/v alcohol) in his apartment as he was unaware of a potential police investigation. The empty bottles were on the kitchen table.

The police had a suspicion that the driver had alcohol in his system and demanded a breath test using an approved screening device, which registered a FAIL. He was arrested and one-half hour later provided two breath samples into an Intoxilyzer 8000C (an approved instrument). The results were 100 milligrams of alcohol in 100 millilitres of blood (100 mg/100 mL). He was charged with an "over 80" offence.

At the trial, the police had no record of whether they had waited at least ten minutes from the time of the driver's last consumption of beer and so the FAIL may have been due to a mouth alcohol effect. The Intoxilyzer 8000C tests were not contested, however, the consumption of two beers after the minor collision could have contributed up to 50 mg/100 mL to the breath test results for someone of his physical description. Thus, at the time of the collision, the driver could have had a BAC below 80 mg/100 mL. As the evidence of post-accident drinking was credible and not unreasonable, the driver was acquitted of the "over 80" charge.

4) Conclusion

A general knowledge of forensic alcohol toxicology is important for the criminal lawyer, as that drug is the most frequently encountered drug in all criminal matters; however, knowledge of the strength and weaknesses of blood and alcohol breath testing are important in assessing the various potential defences. Alcohol-induced blackouts, or memory loss, can be a serious issue, especially in assault and sexual assault cases.

C. FORENSIC DRUG TOXICOLOGY

1) The Science of Forensic Drug Toxicology

a) A Primer on Basic Pharmacological Concepts

In order to better understand how toxicological measurements are interpreted, an appreciation of basic pharmacological concepts is required. Pharmacology may be defined as the study of the effects of xenobiotics (i.e., any chemical, exclusive of a normal diet, that can alter the body's physiology) on the body. Pharmacology may be divided into two broad sub-disciplines: pharmacokinetics and pharmacodynamics.

Pharmacokinetics is the study of the various processes that influence the time course of a drug and its metabolites within the body. These processes include *absorption* (the means and rate by which the drug enters the bloodstream), *distribution* (how, and to what extent, the drug is distributed to various tissue groups within the body), *metabolism* (the various chemical reactions that transform the drug into by-products, also called metabolites), and *elimination* (the processes by which the drugs/metabolites are removed from the body). Taken together, these processes determine the drug and metabolite concentrations reached in the blood following a given dose, the rate at which maximum blood concentrations are achieved, the rate at which the blood concentrations decline, and the time window over which drugs and metabolites may be detectable in the blood and urine.

The route of administration is also an important parameter, as it determines the efficiency with which the drug is absorbed in the blood stream. For example, drugs that are taken orally must pass through the chemically harsh environment of the stomach, followed by passage into the small intestine. In both of these environments, drugs diffuse across the tissue and blood vessel walls and into blood circulation. The rate of this process depends on the dose, the pH (i.e., acidity) of the local tissue environment, the acid-base characteristics of the drug, and structural features of the tissues themselves. Conversely, when a drug is smoked, it is inhaled into the thin sacs in the lungs (alveoli), which allows for very rapid transport into the blood stream. Since metabolism begins immediately upon drug arrival into the blood as it is passes through the liver (the predominant site of metabolism for most drugs), smoking a given dose often results in a larger maximum blood concentration than would be observed with an equivalent dose taken orally. Variability in absorption by the smoking route is introduced by variations in smoking technique and the extent to which the drug undergoes chemical decomposition by heat (pyrolysis). When a drug is injected intravenously, there is no need to cross tissue membranes and the dose enters the blood stream instantly, as one large volume.

Once the drug has been absorbed into the blood stream, it is carried throughout the body systems where it may interact with the various tissue types. Some tissue types are highly vascularized, such as the lungs and the liver, and drugs generally distribute extensively into these tissues. Those drugs that are more fat-soluble may partition more extensively into tissues than those that are more polar (i.e., water-soluble). Such drugs may also be more rapidly and extensively delivered to the brain, as they are better able to travel across the tissue barrier between the blood stream and the central nervous system (i.e., the blood-brain barrier). Examples of such drugs are delta-9-tetrahydrocannabinol (THC) and heroin.

As the drug circulates through the body, metabolism occurs by a variety of mechanisms. A dominant mode of metabolism is hepatic metabolism, which occurs in the liver. Enzymes (protein molecules that catalyze specific chemical reactions) in the liver facilitate the chemical alteration of the drugs (also known as biotransformation) such that the newly formed metabolites may be more easily removed from the body. These reactions may occur in a number of steps, and metabolites formed may be further metabolized before being eliminated from the body. While the liver is the major site of drug metabolism, the majority of metabolizing enzymes are also located in other areas of the anatomy, including the gut and, for some drugs, the blood plasma. Metabolism occurs to different extents for different drugs; some drugs are extensively metabolized (e.g., cocaine) and some are eliminated substantially unchanged from the body via the kidneys (e.g., amphetamine). A drug and its suite of metabolites may be eliminated from the body in the urine, feces, breath, and sweat.

An important parameter that arises from drug metabolism is the half-life ($t_{1/2}$), which is defined as the time required for the drug concentration to be reduced by 50 percent. Based on this definition, the general rule of thumb is that five to six half-lives are required for a drug to be essentially cleared from the body (i.e., the drug concentration is reduced to roughly 3 percent or less of the maximum concentration achieved), regardless of dose. It must be noted that this is an approximation and does not apply to all drugs. The half-life of a drug is determined by the rate of its metabolism, which in turn may be influenced by genetic factors affecting the level and activity of metabolizing enzymes, drug interactions, and other biological parameters. The practical consequence of this is that the half-life of a given drug can vary considerably between and even within individuals. For example, a common reference text[18] explains that the half-life of cocaine in the blood can vary from roughly thirty to ninety minutes. Conversely, the half-life of methylenedioxymethamphetamine (MDMA) can vary from five to eleven hours. The half-life of lorazepam (Ativan®) can vary from eight to twenty-five hours.

Importantly, some very common drugs (e.g., alcohol and gamma-hydroxybutyrate [GHB]) do not display this property. Those particular drugs are metabolized at a constant rate, which means that the larger the dose, the longer it takes for metabolism to reduce the drug concentration to undetectable levels.

Pharmacodynamics may be loosely described as the study of the effects of drugs on the body. An important concept in pharmacodynamics is that of drug-receptor binding. Receptors are proteins in the body that have sites where a drug may bind, with varying degrees of specificity. In some cases, drug receptor binding triggers a cascade of biochemical reactions that leads to a measurable physiological effect (such a drug is termed an agonist at that receptor). In other cases, drug receptor binding may not yield any effect other than to block another chemical (sometimes naturally occurring) from binding to that receptor and preventing its effects from manifesting (such a drug is termed an antagonist at that receptor).

A critical feature of these ideas is that all compounds theoretically bind to all receptors, albeit with potentially vastly different affinities (some bind so weakly that it appears that they do not bind at all). Another important consideration is that the effect of a given drug, felt by the body, is the result of the sum of all of the biochemical effects of its binding to all receptors throughout the body. The effects, colloquially referred to as "side effects," are the result of the drug interacting with receptors in addition to the desired target receptor.

---

18 R.G. Baselt, *Disposition of Toxic Biomedical Drugs and Chemicals in Man*, 7th ed. (Foster City, CA: Biomedical Publications, 2004).

b) The Process of Forensic Toxicological Analysis

i) Sampling and the Importance of a Sample Matrix

The information required from a toxicological analysis depends upon the type of case under investigation. In death investigations (i.e., post-mortem toxicology), the concentration of the drug(s) in the blood, along with consideration of other factors—such as which part of the body the blood was drawn from, the history of drug use of the decedent, and chemical properties of the drug (such as stability in post-mortem tissues)—are used to determine whether toxicity was causative or contributory to death.

The information that may be derived from a toxicological analysis of a biological sample is very much dependent upon the type of sample being analyzed.

a. Blood

Blood may be considered to be the "gold standard" sample type, as toxic effect is typically best correlated with blood drug concentrations. In post-mortem toxicology, blood samples may be taken from a variety of anatomic sites, which may be divided into two groups: central and peripheral sites. Central sites are those situated within, or very close to, the torso. Examples of central sites include the heart and aorta. Conversely, peripheral sites are those more closely associated with limbs. A very common source for peripheral blood is the femoral vein.

b. Urine

Urine drug concentrations are of much lower value in terms of interpreting toxicity, as they vary dramatically within and between individuals. Drugs and their metabolic by-products are distributed differently between blood and urine. The blood is continuously filtered through the kidneys, producing urine that is collected, over time, in the bladder. Because of this continuous pooling of urine in the bladder, measured urine drug concentrations represent an average of the concentrations experienced over time between urination.

Drugs and, more often, metabolites concentrate in the urine at concentration ratios that may differ substantially from those seen in the blood. Often, drug metabolites are present in greater concentration than parent drugs in the urine.

c. Hair

Drugs and metabolites enter the hair via the cellular material that are exposed to the blood supply for nutrients in the hair follicle, through sweat and sebum (an oily secretion from sebaceous glands in the skin), or by external contamination. Hair grows from that cellular material as a non-living by-product as the cells within the follicle become dehydrated and are keratinized (i.e., transformed into a dead, thorny, or scaly tissue), which implies that the hair shaft will contain chemicals that had been incorporated into the cells in the follicle. The hair shaft is pushed upward by the cell division within the follicle, which in turn implies that the concentration of those chemicals may vary along the length of the shaft as a function of changing blood concentration over time. This phenomenon is the reason that it may be possible to establish an estimated drug use timeline by means of segmental analysis (i.e., analysis of different segments of the sampled hair). This also requires some knowledge of hair growth rate, which has been reported to average roughly one centimetre per month, with substantial variability between individuals (0.6–2 cm/month).[19]

Hair samples may be derived from various anatomic sites, but are commonly collected from a tied sample at the rear of the head, known as the posterior vertex or the occipital region. Care is taken to tie the hair sample near the base prior to any attempts at segmentation to minimize the shifting of hairs relative to each other, which would impact the interpretive value of attempts to establish a timeline of drug exposure.

d. Oral Fluid

Oral fluid is a complex mixture of fluids formed within the salivary glands and other minor glands, in combination with gingival fluid, epithelial cell material, and various particulates. It exists in equilibrium with blood plasma, which implies that there is transport of chemical compounds between the oral fluid and the blood plasma and, as a result, drug concentrations in oral fluid are related to those in blood, and are more reflective than urine drug concentrations of the drug profile in circulation in the blood at a given time.

Oral fluid is generated in significant quantities, on the order of litres per day. The relationship between drug and metabolite concentrations in oral fluid and those in blood depends on the salivary flow rate (which in turn is affected by drug effects and physiological state), the acid-base characteristics of the drug, the extent to which the drug is bound to plasma proteins, and so on.

---

19 M.A. LeBeau, M.A. Montgomery, & J.D. Brewer, "The Role of Variation in Growth Rate and Sample Collection on Interpretation of Segmental Analysis of Hair" (2011) 210 *Forensic Science International* 110.

e. Miscellaneous Tissues

These tissues may be taken at autopsy, and can include a variety of different tissues, including those from the liver, kidney, spleen, brain, and others. In post-mortem cases where severe decomposition has precluded the collection of conventional samples, such as blood, urine, or even visceral tissues, the only tissues remaining for analysis may be hair, dry muscle, or skeletal tissues (i.e., bone marrow and/or bone). The liver is, perhaps, the most commonly collected visceral tissue at autopsy.

TABLE 20.4. Sample types commonly analyzed in forensic toxicology and the associated time window of detection (approximate) following drug exposure.

Sample Type	Typical Detection Time*	Predominant Analyte(s)**	Relative Predictive Value for Toxic Effect***
Blood	Hours to days	Parent drug	High
Urine	Days	Metabolites	Low
Liver	Hours to days	Parent drug and metabolites	Moderate
Oral fluid	Hours	Parent drug	Moderate
Hair	Weeks to months*	Parent drug	Low

* Dependent on various factors, including growth rate, nature of the hair (e.g., pigment levels), and hair treatment practices (e.g., dyeing/colouring).

** In many cases, both parent drug and metabolites are detectable in any given matrix. The relative amount of parent drug and metabolites is observed as a complex function of exposure pattern, the time expired since exposure, the nature of the matrix, and the metabolism of the drug.

*** Relative predictive value is drug dependent, with the reliability of predictive effect varying between drugs due to phenomena including tolerance, redistribution, and stability.

ii) Sample Handling, Storage, and Analysis

a. Submission/Triage

Typically, all samples are submitted to a laboratory's central receiving office. From there, the individual seal numbers present on the evidentiary seals affixed on the sample container by the submitter are catalogued in the laboratory information management system, which tracks chain of custody for all samples submitted in a given case. At this triage point, the laboratory for various reasons may refuse some samples. For example, this may be done if the analyses requested cannot provide information of forensic value.

iii) Analytical Processes

Before commencing a discussion of the analytical processes used in the forensic toxicology laboratory, it is important to define some terms with respect to the type of analysis done. Presumptive analyses are those that are simple tests used to indicate the presence or absence of a particular drug or drug class. Positive presumptive tests are not conclusive and the identity of the drug contained in samples yielding such a result must be confirmed by methods with greater sensitivity and selectivity.[20]

In many forensic toxicology laboratories, presumptive testing is largely done by immunoassay. Immunoassay makes use of antibodies (proteins used by the body to bind foreign substances) that have been raised to bind specific drug targets or drug classes. The amount of drug in a sample is estimated by measuring the extent of drug-antibody binding, which is typically achieved by allowing the drug in the sample to compete for antibody-binding sites with a form of the drug that has been chemically altered to contain a label that may be measured by a variety of techniques. Thus, by measuring the amount of labelled drug that is bound to the antibody, one can obtain an indirect measurement of the amount of drug present in the sample.

Unfortunately, this approach is actually measuring the amount of antibody-binding by substances other than the labelled drug. While antibodies are generally quite specific with respect to the chemical structure that they will bind, substances that bear similar chemical structures to the drug of interest may also bind to the antibody to a greater or lesser extent. This property is termed "cross-reactivity."

Once biological samples are received and catalogued by the laboratory triage system, they are stored under refrigeration until the scientific staff has reviewed the case file contents. Based on the specific type of investigation (e.g., motor vehicle accident, death investigation, sexual assault) and the specific details of the case history (which are used to assist with the choice of analyses performed and with the interpretation of the results), various analyses of one or more of the submitted samples is undertaken. The exact combination and sequence of those analyses also depends on the amount of each sample type available.

a. Presumptive versus Confirmatory Analyses

Presumptive and confirmatory tests differ in terms of their reliability for identification of the substance present. A presumptive test that is "positive" may be interpreted as "the substance is likely present, but that must

20 Refer to Chapter 5 in this book for a discussion of the review into The Hospital for Sick Children's Motherisk program in this context.

be confirmed by a more rigorous method." Ideally, a presumptive test can be used to quite reliably exclude the presence of a particular drug.

Confirmatory tests are more sophisticated techniques that typically involve some preparation of the sample at hand, followed by a separation and identification of the constituents in the prepared sample. Sample preparation is done to remove the constituents of a sample that would impede its analysis by the technique. Techniques used in sample preparation may include precipitation (i.e., addition of a chemical that causes some constituents to come out of solution and form a solid, so that the remaining liquid sample can be further prepared), centrifugation (i.e., rapid spinning of the sample to cause solids to collect at the bottom of the container), and dilution. The primary technique used in most applications is extraction, which first involves adjusting the sample chemistry through changes in pH and salt content, followed by mixing the sample with an immiscible solvent (liquid-liquid extraction) or passing the sample through a bed of material that is designed to selectively remove chemical compounds with particular properties (solid-phase extraction). The end result of a successful extraction is a much "cleaner" sample (although it remains a mixture of multiple constituents) that is amenable to the next step, which typically involves separating extracted constituents by gas chromatography (GC) or liquid chromatography (LC).

Both forms of chromatography inject a portion of the extracted mixture into a column, where the sample constituents are carried via a fluid (the mobile phase) flowing through the column. During transit, the constituents interact with a stationary phase, and through chemical interactions, are slowed in their movement through the column. Differences in the degree of slowing or retention between constituents result in their exiting the column at different times (i.e., retention times). The retention time of a chemical compound under a given set of chromatographic conditions is one descriptor used in identifying the compound. GC differs from LC in that a portion of the sample is heated to evaporation and is carried through the column by a carrier gas (e.g., helium). The need to evaporate the sample prior to introduction onto the column may be problematic for those substances that are not readily volatile or those that decompose at higher temperatures. Conversely, LC uses a liquid mobile phase, and the composition of that liquid mobile phase may vary to optimize the separation. LC is a more versatile technique, as the absence of the evaporation step implies that a wider range of compounds may be analyzed by this method.

Once a given constituent (e.g., a drug) of the extracted mixture exits (or is eluted from) the column, it is then passed through a detector. Detectors generate a response that is dependent on the mass of sample passed through them, implying that they may be used to estimate the quantity (i.e., the concentration) of each substance detected. The most common form of detector used in forensic drug toxicology is a mass spectrometer (MS) or a tandem mass spectrometer (MS/MS). These instruments charge and fragment each molecule, separate the fragments, and measure the mass and intensity (a measure of quantity) of each fragment. When done under controlled conditions, each chemical compound will fragment in a reproducible manner, and in a pattern that is characteristic of that compound, generating a mass spectrum. The mass spectrum is then used as another descriptor of a compound, and when combined with a retention time, one can obtain a reliable set of descriptors for substance identification. In general, forensic drug toxicology standards of practice require that a substance be identified through at least two independent descriptors of sufficient reliability for confirmation of its presence in a sample. For example, in the case of GC-MS, a compound is identified as a given drug only if that compound has the same retention time (within accepted tolerance limits) as a pure version of that drug, and the same mass spectrum (within accepted tolerance limits).

TABLE 20.5. Various analytical techniques used in toxicological analysis for the presence of drugs, typical sample types employed, and suitability for quantitative versus qualitative analysis.

Technique	Presumptive (P) vs. Confirmatory (C)	Quantitative (qN) vs. Qualitative (qL)
Colour Test	P	qL
Immunoassay	P	qL*
UV-Vis Absorbance	P**	qN or qL**
FTIR	P**	qN or qL**
GC (no MS)***	P/C***	qL or qN
LC-PDA***	C	qL or qN
GC-MS(/MS)	C	qL or qN
LC-MS(/MS)	C	qL or qN

* While immunoassay is often interpreted as being only a qualitative analysis, it is typically used in a semi-quantitative fashion, wherein the data is used to determine whether the drug(s) being tested for may be present above a threshold (cut-off) value.

** UV-Vis Absorbance and Fourier Transform Infrared (FTIR) spectroscopy are used as presumptive tests in most drug toxicology applications, but are capable of providing some information about concentration under certain conditions.

*** GC may also be done with simple detectors that provide no information about the structure of a given compound. In those cases, retention times using two different columns with different stationary phase chemistries must be used to support compound identification. The GC response may still be concentration dependent, allowing for quantitative analysis.

b. Analytical Caveats

Limitations in Analytical Sensitivity: Limits of Detection

When measuring the quantity of a substance, the limit of detection is the smallest quantity (expressed as a mass or a concentration) that can be statistically differentiated from the background signal. This means that non-detection of a drug *by a given method* does not imply that the drug is not present in the sample. *It implies that the drug (or compound targeted by the test) is either absent or is present at a quantity below the method's limit of detection.*

Therefore, when a biological sample is analyzed and the compound of interest is not detected, it does not mean that the person was not exposed to the substance. It is possible that the person was exposed to a very low dose or that a sufficient period of time expired since exposure, so that the drug was metabolized and eliminated from the body to such an extent as to render it undetectable by the methods used. In this sense, it is important to use methods that are sufficiently sensitive to measure concentrations of a given drug that are relevant to the question at hand. A potent drug may be present at very low blood concentrations that are, nonetheless, toxicologically significant. Methods with higher limits of detection (i.e., those that are less sensitive and unable to detect concentrations at very low levels) also suffer from shorter time windows over which a drug can be detected after a given exposure.

Limitations in Analytical Precision

Analytical precision refers to the reproducibility of the measurements reported, and is reported as the relative standard deviation of replicate measurements. In most forensic drug toxicology applications, such precision typically falls within 20 percent of the mean measured value. Precision is assessed when analytical methods are validated to ensure that it is acceptable for use in casework and is further checked within a given set of analyses to ensure that the precision remains acceptable over time for all analysts. Analysis of complex sample types (e.g., decomposed tissues) may be associated with less precision than analyses of less complex sample types (e.g., plasma or vitreous humor), and precision may vary between different methods based on the steps involved in sample preparation.

Limitations in the Analytical Accuracy

Analytical accuracy refers to the ability of the method to generate a true result, or to the closeness of the measured result to the actual value. Accuracy is assessed by blind analysis (where the analyst is given a sample wherein a pure standard version of a drug or set of drugs has been added to a known concentration, without knowledge of that concentration), and determination of the bias (i.e., the relative difference in measured and accurate values, expressed as a percentage).

$$\text{Bias} = \frac{\text{Measured Value} - \text{Actual Value}}{\text{Actual Value}} \times 100\%$$

The level of acceptable bias may vary between applications (e.g., workplace drug testing versus post-mortem toxicology), and is generally 20 percent or less in many applications.

c. Interpretive Caveats

A number of factors influence the ability of the toxicologist to interpret the toxicological significance of a measured drug level in a given sample and some of those caveats are dependent on the type of biological sample being analyzed.

Blood Testing Caveats

In post-mortem toxicology, where the goal is to estimate toxicity based on blood concentration, these factors include post-mortem redistribution, drug tolerance, drug interactions, drug stability, post-mortem/post-sampling synthesis, and the route of administration.

POST-MORTEM REDISTRIBUTION

Post-mortem redistribution is the process by which drugs that have accumulated in tissues diffuse out of those tissues and into the surrounding blood after death. Since many drugs accumulate extensively in the visceral organs, the heart, and the lungs, blood drawn from the heart or elsewhere in the thoracic region often has significantly greater levels of some drugs than would be found in blood drawn from sites peripheral to (i.e., distant from) the thoracic region (e.g., the femoral vein). Even in blood drawn from the peripheral sites, there may be some variation in measured drug levels from the time of death. In general, interpretation of toxicological analyses of post-mortem blood is best done using measurements made from peripheral blood samples.

DRUG TOLERANCE

After repeated exposures to a given drug, there may be a reduction in an individual's response to a given dose, with higher doses being required to reach an expected effect. This phenomenon is known as drug tolerance. Tolerance interferes with the interpretation of measured drug concentrations with respect to the estimation of toxic effect. The opiates are one class of drug whose effects are well-known to be susceptible to tolerance. Accordingly, for the opiates, the range of blood concentrations associated with fatal toxicity typically overlaps with the range of blood drug concentrations where death was incidental to drug use. For example, a study by Martin et al.[21] reported fentanyl concentrations in femoral blood in fatalities in the following circumstances:

- when attributed to fentanyl toxicity alone (3–383 ng/mL; mean: 25 ng/mL);
- in cases of fatal mixed drug toxicity (4.8–119 ng/mL; mean: 21 ng/mL);
- in fatalities attributed to mixed fentanyl and alcohol toxicity (6.4–37 ng/mL; mean: 16 ng/mL);
- in deaths due to natural causes (2.7–33 ng/mL; mean: 12 ng/mL); and
- in cases where death was incidental to fentanyl use (3.1–14 ng/mL; mean: 6.8 ng/mL).

DRUG INTERACTIONS

As described above, a given drug can affect numerous different receptor systems in the body, leading to various physiological and psychological effects. Unfortunately, polypharmacy (i.e., the consumption of multiple drugs simultaneously) is very common. In such cases, the consumption of multiple drugs that share a particular effect can result in enhanced drug effects, and consequently, toxicity at lower blood drug concentrations. One example of such a drug interaction would be the combined ingestion of alcohol and an opiate, such as oxycodone. Both drugs depress the central nervous system and lead to respiratory depression. Combined ingestion of both drugs may lead to an additive respiratory depression, which can then lead to death at a lower oxycodone concentration than what may have otherwise been survivable. A study by Cone et al.[22] suggested that blood oxycodone concentrations in fatalities involving mixed drug toxicity were significantly lower than those in fatalities where oxycodone was the only drug detected.

---

21 T.L. Martin, K.L. Woodall, & B.A. McLellan, "Fentanyl-Related Deaths in Ontario, Canada: Toxicological Findings and Circumstances of Death in 112 Cases (2002–2004)" (2006) 30 *Journal of Analytical Toxicology* 603.

22 E.J. Cone et al., "Oxycodone Involvement in Drug Abuse Deaths. II. Evidence for Toxic Multiple Drug-Drug Interactions" (2004) 28 *Journal of Analytical Toxicology* 616.

DRUG INSTABILITY

Certain drugs decompose in biological samples, in either the post-mortem or post-sampling environments. One of the most notorious examples of such drugs is cocaine, which can be converted to its pharmacologically inactive metabolite (benzoylecgonine) in blood, in the absence of proper preservation.[23] It is important to consider that, in this case, cocaine may undergo some conversion to its metabolites in the body post-mortem, even if such transformations are effectively halted by preservation after sample collection at autopsy. Overall, even though blood samples drawn post-mortem are stored in the appropriate chemical preservative, the interval between death and sample collection may have involved some conversion of cocaine to benzoylecgonine.

ENDOGENOUS PRESENCE AND/OR SYNTHESIS OF DRUG

Certain drugs occur endogenously (i.e., are naturally formed within the body) and may appear, or become elevated, in biological samples after death or sample collection as a result of biological processes (e.g., putrefaction). This can occur with alcohol, as well as with gamma-hydroxybutyrate (GHB). In the case of GHB, the compound occurs naturally and is also abused exogenously.

ROUTE OF ADMINISTRATION

The route of administration is an important determinant of drug effect, as it determines the rate at which the drug enters circulation and reaches the various sites of action. In turn, this influences the maximum blood drug concentration that will be reached for a given dose. As a result, a given dose taken intravenously will reach a higher maximum blood drug concentration, and more quickly, than the same dose taken orally.

Urine Drug Testing Caveats

In urine drug testing, the primary interpretive concerns may be endogenous synthesis (i.e., a compound that has formed within the body as opposed to having arisen from external exposure to it), instability, and adulteration (i.e., the process by which urine samples are deliberately altered in an attempt to avoid drug detection).

GHB, a drug of abuse that has been implicated in cases involving drug-facilitated sexual assaults, exists endogenously in the body and is

---

23 D.S. Isenschmid, B.S. Levine, & Y.H. Caplan, "A Comprehensive Study of the Stability of Cocaine and its Metabolites" (1989) 13 *Journal of Analytical Toxicology* 250.

detectable in the urine. A number of studies have been done to determine the level of GHB in the urine that can be attributed to endogenous production. To date, these studies appear to be in agreement that a urine GHB concentration in excess of 10 mg/L is consistent with exogenous exposure to GHB. The primary challenge with measuring GHB in biological samples is the complex elimination kinetics. To detect a GHB exposure via urine measurements, sampling must occur within roughly twelve hours.

Adulteration of urine samples to avoid drug detection has included dilution of urine to render drugs or metabolites undetectable; addition of chemicals to dilute or render the presumptive tests ineffective through destruction of their required reagents; and substitution of urine from another person for that of the subject of interest.[24] In cases involving urine drug testing, an obvious concern is ensuring the integrity of the collected urine sample. In the strictest practice, this involves third party observation of sample collection and continuity. In addition, some jurisdictions have implemented a variety of measures that have been put in place to assess whether the urine sample displays indicia of adulteration. Measurements of pH, specific gravity, and creatinine levels are used to determine whether they are consistent with untampered urine.

Oral Fluid Drug Testing Caveats

Oral fluid is in direct equilibrium with the blood plasma, implying that drugs or metabolites present in the blood will partition into the oral fluid. An important factor in interpreting oral fluid drug concentrations is the extent to which drugs and metabolites partition from the blood into oral fluid, measured as the oral fluid-blood concentration ratio. This ratio varies substantially across different drugs.

Hair Testing Caveats

Hair testing has been used to identify drug use that occurred weeks to months prior to sample collection. A variety of factors influence the observed drug levels in hair.

Estimates of the timeline of drug exposure are possible, provided that the hair sampled is long enough. Hair growth rates vary between individuals.

---

24 W.B. Jaffee et al., "Is This Urine Really Negative? A Systematic Review of Tampering Methods in Urine Drug Screening and Testing" (2007) 33 *Journal of Substance Abuse and Treatment* 33.

iv) Drug Classes

a. Types of Classification

A number of means of drug classification are used. Drugs may be classified on the basis of how they are formed or manufactured (i.e., synthetic versus semi-synthetic versus naturally occurring), although this is not a terribly useful means. Examples of naturally occurring drugs are THC (in cannabis products), morphine, and cocaine. A semi-synthetic drug is one that is formed through the chemical reaction of a naturally occurring drug to form a new product. A common semi-synthetic drug is heroin, formed through the treatment of morphine in a process called acetylation. Synthetic drugs are prepared entirely in the laboratory. Examples of synthetic drugs include methamphetamine and phencyclidine (PCP).

Drugs may also be classified in terms of their effect (e.g., sedative, stimulant, hallucinogen). This is a more useful means of classification as it provides a way to estimate the types of effect associated with a given drug. The limitation of this approach is that drugs with different effect profiles may be included in a given classification. For example, diphenhydramine is an antihistamine that is found in Benedryl® and various over the counter sleep aids (e.g., Nytol®) and is well-known to cause sedation. Its pharmacological profile differs from other drugs that are known to cause sedation, such as trazodone (an antidepressant drug) and lorazepam (an anti-anxiety drug). Similarly, drugs are classified according to their desired pharmaceutical use (e.g., antidepressant, anticonvulsant, analgesic, anti-inflammatory, etc.). In this case, too, a given drug may fit into more than one group.

b. Effects of Selected Drug Classes (and Example Drugs) of Forensic Interest

Stimulants are drugs that involve stimulation of the central and/or peripheral nervous systems. Central nervous system stimulants typically cause euphoria, excitement/agitation, heightened energy, and pupil dilation, as well as elevations in heart rate and blood pressure. Elevated doses, overuse, or abuse can lead to paranoia, delusions and hallucinations, cardiovascular damage, and seizures. Some central nervous system stimulants are habit-forming and may be subject to tolerance. Examples include amphetamine, methamphetamine, cocaine, and cathinone-related drugs (the "bath salts," including methylone, mephedrone, and MDPV). The effects of many stimulants are subject to tolerance.

Drugs that depress the central nervous system, leading to sedation, drowsiness, and reductions in respiratory rates, may be grouped under the term "depressants." Such a class may be further subdivided into other classes according to pharmacological effects. Sedative-hypnotics are drugs that cause somnolence and reduce anxiety. Such drugs may be used to treat insomnia or anxiety disorders, and, in some cases, seizure disorders. Examples of sedative-hypnotics are benzodiazepines (e.g., temazepam, diazepam, lorazepam), zolpidem, zopiclone, and barbiturates (e.g., phenobarbital, secobarbital, butalbital). Generally, these drugs cause sedation, somnolence, dizziness, impairments to balance, confusion, and disorientation. Narcotic analgesics are drugs that are sleep-inducing, but also display a substantial analgesic efficacy. Effects include euphoria, pupil constriction, sweating, itchiness, sedation, drowsiness, and mental cloudiness. Included in this class are the various opioid drugs, such as morphine, heroin, oxycodone, fentanyl, hydrocodone, codeine, hydromorphone, and methadone. Other depressant drugs include muscle relaxants and alcohol. The effects of many depressants are subject to tolerance.

Hallucinogens

Hallucinogens are a class of chemicals that can cause significant distortions in the perception of time, space, colour, and sound. A variety of such drugs are abused, including lysergic acid diethylamide (LSD), psilocybin (found in hallucinogenic mushrooms), mescaline, the NBOMe drugs (substituted 2C phenethylamines), and the tryptamine drugs (e.g., dimethyltryptamine, DMT). In addition to the various forms of perceptual distortion, these drugs typically cause pupil dilation as well as disorganized thought and speech. In some cases, perceptual distortions may be described as being pleasant, with users reporting an enhanced sense of well-being and empathy. In other cases, perceptual distortions may be very severe, and other effects may include agitation and anxiety. In some cases with NBOMe drugs, substantial elevations in heart rate (tachycardia) and blood pressure (hypertension) may ensue, progressing to seizures and organ failure. The duration of drug effects may vary considerably, as some drugs are short-acting (e.g., DMT, with duration of effects of roughly one hour), some are long-acting (e.g., LSD with duration of effects lasting up to roughly ten to twelve hours), and there are examples with duration of action lying between these extremes (e.g., psilocybin). A subclass of the stimulant drugs sometimes referred to as the hallucinogenic amines (which includes drugs such as MDMA and MDA) display stimulant properties as well as perceptual distortions and enhanced feelings of closeness and empathy. Toxic effects may include tachycardia, hypertension, hyperpyrexia (i.e., dangerous elevation in body temperature), which can be worsened by environmental factors, leading to seizures and organ failure. The effects of many hallucinogens are subject to tolerance.

Cannabis and Cannabis Products

Cannabis is perhaps the most widely abused illicit drug. In a recent study[25] of Ontario students (grades 7–12), 23 percent reported using cannabis at least once during the twelve months before the survey. As may be expected with such pervasive use, cannabis is often cited as perhaps the most frequently encountered illicit drug in drug-facilitated sexual assault and drug-impaired driving cases.

Cannabis products are typically taken through smoking (including vaporizing) or orally (through direct ingestion, or cooking foods infused with cannabis or cannabis oil). The effects of THC include euphoria; relaxation; altered temporal perception; impairments to concentration, coordination, learning, and memory; alterations to mood (e.g., panic, anxiety); alterations in blood pressure (increase or decrease); tachycardia; reddening of the eyes; dryness of the mouth and throat; and increased appetite. Some users report a beneficial effect in reducing nausea and efficacy in reducing seizure activity.

Maximum THC effect does not coincide with the maximum blood THC concentration when cannabis is smoked. Blood THC concentrations are maximal very close to the cessation of smoking, while maximal effects are felt some time (twenty to thirty minutes) later. In oral cannabis ingestion, maximum blood THC concentrations occur much longer after ingestion, often after a few hours. In those cases, maximal effects are also often delayed by a similar scale. The duration of THC effects is roughly three to four hours when smoked, but can be substantially longer when ingested orally. One feature of THC is its propensity to accumulate in fatty tissue following exposure, followed by a slow release back into circulation. This results in the potential for measurable concentrations of THC and metabolites to appear in blood and urine for an extended period of time following use, and after the abatement of drug effect. The magnitude of the residual THC and metabolite concentrations and the time over which the residual concentrations fall to undetectable levels can vary considerably among users, related in part to the frequency of their cannabis use. This phenomenon must be

25 Centre for Addiction and Mental Health, "Ontario Student Drug Use and Health Survey: 2015" online: www.camh.ca/en/research/news_and_publications/ontario-student-drug-use-and-health-survey/Pages/default.aspx.

considered closely in cases of suspected THC-related impairment, where blood THC concentrations associated with recent use may be very close to those associated with the "baseline" THC levels in regular users.

v) *Drug-Induced Impairment*

a. Forensic Relevance of Impairment

As is the case with alcohol, drug effects can impair the ability of an individual to perform a variety of tasks, including motor vehicle operation. Drug-induced impairment has forensic relevance beyond safely driving a car and includes operating other motor vehicles (e.g., boats, planes, snow machines). It is also relevant in workplace accidents (see also, the *Coroner's Act, Ontario*), cases of sexual assault, and assessments of witness credibility.

It is valuable to note the difference between intoxication and impairment: "intoxication" refers to the observable physiological drug effects (e.g., pupil dilation or constriction, elevated heart rate), whereas "impairment" refers to a drug-induced decrement in the ability to perform a given task. Most day-to-day tasks, especially the safe operation of a motor vehicle, require the simultaneous execution of a number of tasks. In particular, driving is a complex task that has been termed one of the most overlearned tasks that we undertake within our society. Safe driving requires the simultaneous performance of a number of tasks, including maintaining a safe speed and distance from neighbouring vehicles, scanning the direct and peripheral fields of view for potential hazards, and keeping the vehicle within the lane markings. Drugs that affect cognition, risk tolerance, and/or psychomotor control may impair one or more of the faculties required for the safe operation of a motor vehicle.

In cases of suspected drug-impaired driving, the accused may undergo physical coordination tests by a drug recognition expert (DRE),[26] who is an officer with specialized training in conducting standardized field sobriety tests as well as some other physical/clinical examinations (e.g., measurement of pulse, blood pressure, and temperature, as well as pupil size and reactivity to light). The DRE uses the totality of these observations, as well as the DRE Symptomology Matrix (a reference chart that describes the types of responses to each test that may be expected from a given class of drugs). In cases where the DRE forms the opinion that an individual is under the influence of a particular class of drug, upon completion of the

26 Royal Canadian Mounted Police, "Drug Recognition Expert Evaluations" online: www.rcmp-grc.gc.ca/ts-sr/dree-eert-eng.htm.

test the suspect is required to provide a sample of blood, urine, or oral fluid which will undergo toxicological analysis in the laboratory. If a drug detected in the biological sample is of the same class that was identified as part of the battery of tests done by the DRE, then such a finding provides further support for the allegation of impairment.

As discussed above, the choice of biological sample is important. These sample types have different time windows of detection and implications with respect to drug effect. For example, urine drug measurements are less valuable than blood drug measurements in terms of estimation of toxic effect. Further, drugs and metabolites may remain in the urine for an extended period of time, implying that the individual may have been exposed to the drug some time before the incident, but that the drug may have been cleared from the blood by the time of the incident. While blood sample collection is invasive and requires a trained phlebotomist for collection, oral fluid provides a less invasive alternative that is more reflective of the suite of drugs in circulation at the time of sampling.

b. Evidence of Impairment: How Is Impairment Studied by Experts?

Impairment by drugs or alcohol may be studied in a variety of ways. Forensic toxicologists examine a range of different studies on a given drug (including alcohol) to assess the extent to which the drug may impair task performance under a variety of conditions including dose, route of administration, and drug combinations. Studies of the impairing effects of a drug may include laboratory studies of psychomotor performance, studies that use task simulators (driving simulators may be the most common type), studies of actual task performance (including operation of a motor vehicle, either on a closed course or on-road), and epidemiological studies, which examine toxicological findings associated with a given type of negative event (e.g., fatal motor vehicle accident) over an extended period of time and within particular geographical boundaries.

Laboratory Studies

A number of laboratory studies are used in the assessment of impairment. They generally either examine cognitive impairment or psychomotor impairment. Psychomotor and cognitive tests include:

- Balance/body sway
- Simple reaction time
- Choice reaction time (the time required to respond correctly to a specific stimulus)

- Tracking (the ability to maintain a moving object within a set of boundaries—in practice, this is related to maintaining a car within a particular lane)
- Critical tracking
- Divided attention (the ability to divide one's attention between two or more tasks)
- Smooth pursuit
- Pursuit rotor
- Vigilance (i.e., sustained attention)
- Digit symbol substitution
- Number recall
- Risk-taking
- Visual search/Letter cancellation

Simple reaction time may be defined as the time taken by a subject for a response to a stimulus (typically, auditory or visual), usually by means of actuation of a switch or signal (i.e., press a button or a foot pedal). Choice reaction time may be defined as the time taken by a subject to respond to a selected stimulus from a series of stimuli and to respond in a particular manner (e.g., the action of stepping on the brake pedal when the brake lights of the car ahead are actuated). Choice reaction time is certainly more important than simple reaction time in assessing the impairing effects of a given drug. In measurements of choice reaction time, both accuracy (i.e., correct response to the correct stimulus) and reaction time are measured.

Driving Simulator Studies

Driving simulator studies involve the use of a simulated driving system complete with hand (i.e., steering wheel) and foot controls and a video display, intended to simulate driving conditions.

Scoring the performance may be based on a wide range of factors, including positional errors (e.g., Standard Deviation of Lateral Position [SDLP—a measure of "weaving" along the trajectory], crossing of the line marking the lane boundary, collisions with objects), reaction time and associated errors in response to a stimulus, and time required for completing the driving course.

Actual Driving Studies

Actual driving studies involve the operation of an actual vehicle on a closed course, or on public roads under supervised conditions (i.e., in a training car). As with simulator studies, scoring the performance may be based on various factors, including those mentioned in the previous paragraph.

Epidemiological Studies

Epidemiological studies attempt to correlate accident risk and/or accident severity with the presence/concentration of drugs/alcohol within the body. Those studies may focus on one or more drugs, on a particular subset of the population, or on a particular geographic region.

c. Important Considerations in Experimental Evaluations of Drug-Induced Impairment

Unfortunately, not all studies of the effects of drugs on task performance are suitable for forensic applications. A number of questions should be asked about a given study when considering its applicability to forensic casework:

1) *Are the dose levels used relevant to normal/expected consumption patterns or to the specific case at hand?*

   Many drugs of abuse are used in high doses, with repeated exposures (e.g., binge use). In controlled studies of drug effects, ethical constraints may limit the dose of the drug being administered, or the route by which it is administered. For pharmaceutical drugs that are being abused (e.g., oxycodone), tablets may be crushed and insufflated or dissolved and injected. Since the route of administration can be a critical factor in the blood drug concentration reached, laboratory studies may not reflect the blood drug concentrations and time course that is encountered by many users. An important example is cocaine, which is often abused in the form of smoked crack cocaine, or as insufflation of hydrochloride salt. Cocaine is often used in a binge-like fashion, where numerous doses are taken over a period of hours or even days. Such dosing is unlikely to ever be approved for use in research, although it may be common amongst regular users.

2) *How is the study designed?*

   Studies may take a number of designs, and some are better than others. Ideally, a study will be a double-blind, cross-over study using different doses of the drug and measuring the blood drug concentrations (as opposed to using dose as the variable) to correlate with any observed impairment. In a double-blind study, neither the researchers nor the subjects know whether they are receiving the drug or a placebo (this information is held by a third party). In a cross-over design, all subjects receive all treatments, preferably in randomized order (as opposed to comparing one group of subjects receiving a placebo with a different group of subjects receiving the drug). In a cross-over design, it is possible to see how the task performance (or symptomology) for each individual changes when the drug dosage is changed. It is also important to examine the task performance over a period of time following dosing. This is relevant because it provides a measure of the duration of impairment, and may also allow for differentiation of the degree of impairment during the various pharmacokinetic phases (i.e., rising phase, plateau phase, or declining phase).

3) *Are the tasks being analyzed the best choice for the case at hand?*

   Different drugs influence the various faculties differently, and some faculties are more sensitive to the effects of drugs than others. *Generally, impairment is more significant as the complexity of the task is increased.*

4) *Has the study accounted for "learning effects"?*

   All task performance laboratory studies have a learning component, wherein the subjects display improved performance as they repeat the test a few times (this is akin to learning how to play a video game). All good studies allow the subjects to attempt the tasks for a period before the study begins, in order to eliminate the influence of learning effects on the measurements.

5) *Considering the distribution of drugs/alcohol in the blood of accident victims, is it possible to establish a relationship between drug findings and accident causality?*

   One difficult aspect in epidemiological studies of drug/alcohol influence on accident risk is the inclusion of a proper control group.

   For example, a group of accident victims may be assessed in terms of presence/concentration of drugs and/or alcohol in the blood. We may find that there is a greater number of subjects who are drug positive in that group than subjects who have no drugs detected. However, without knowing the proportion of drug-positive drivers not involved in accidents, the conclusions that can be drawn from that result may be skewed. This has been addressed in epidemiological studies by employing random roadside screening, and through an analysis of patient groups not involved in accidents (e.g., those in the hospital for treatment of trauma).

d. Impairment by Selected Drug Types

Cannabis (THC)

Psychomotor and driving (simulator and on-road) tests have shown that THC impairs various faculties required for driving, including divided attention[27] and temporal perception,[28] as well as measured SDLP, both on road[29] and in driving simulators.[30] The magnitude of impairment in these faculties appears to be dependent upon dose and the tolerance of the subject, although correlation of symptoms of impairment with plasma THC concentration may be somewhat misleading because of distribution effects and tolerance. Some authors have attributed the variability in effect to both tolerance and to the inconsistent efficiency of drug delivery through smoking.

Various studies have noted a significant interaction in the impairing effects of alcohol and THC, wherein the combination of low doses of THC and alcohol have resulted in substantial impairment. Thus, examination of the impairing effects of THC must consider the presence of other drugs as well.

Cocaine

Cocaine and other stimulants (i.e., amphetamines) have been examined in a number of laboratory studies of performance. Some studies actually show enhancement of task performance. However, these studies have generally used single, relatively low drug doses; recall that the typical pattern of cocaine use is multiple dosing or "binge" use. It often occurs over the course of an evening or multiple days—higher cocaine concentrations may be reached and the potential for a "crash" phase exists. Depression, extreme fatigue, "drifting" in and out of sleep, and/or prolonged, unrousable sleep characterize the "crash" phase. Thus, the impairment in this phase may be very similar to the impairment caused by extreme fatigue. Recall that the effects of cocaine include euphoria, heightened energy, and

---

27 D.F. Marks & M.G. MacAvoy, "Divided Attention Performance in Cannabis Users and Non-users Following Alcohol and Cannabis Separately and in Combination" (1989) 99 *Journal of Psychopharmacology* 397.

28 R.A. Sewell et al., "Acute Effects of THC on Time Perception in Frequent and Infrequent Cannabis Users" (2013) 226 *Journal of Psychopharmacology* 401.

29 J.G. Ramaekers, H.W.J. Robbe, & J.F. O'Hanlon, "Marijuana, Alcohol and Actual Driving Performance" (2000) 15 *Human Psychopharmacology Clinical and Experimental Journal* 551.

30 R.L. Hartman et al., "Cannabis Effects on Driving Lateral Control with and without Alcohol" (2015) 154 *Drug and Alcohol Dependence* 25.

pupillary dilation. With repeated, high doses, the effects of cocaine may progress to hallucinations and paranoia.

The euphoria and stimulation (as well as the hallucinations and paranoia) associated with cocaine use may also be associated with increased risk-taking (e.g., perceptions of being chased, or feelings of fearlessness or extreme strength). The dilation of pupils may cause elevated light sensitivity, which raises concerns of impaired glare recovery during nighttime driving. The delusions and paranoia may be reasonably expected to be distracting, which can serve to impair the ability to divide attention between the tasks required for safe driving.

Opiates

Acute opiate intoxication is characterized by depressed mental status, drowsiness, respiratory depression, and often (but not in all cases), constriction of pupils. Depression of mental status and drowsiness are potentially impairing, as is the case with fatigue. However, these effects can be highly subject to tolerance. Consequently, various studies have examined the effects of opiate drugs on sufferers of chronic pain who use opiates regularly for analgesia and have shown no significant impairing effects before versus after drug exposure.

2) The Role of the Forensic Drug Toxicologist in Criminal Cases

The forensic drug toxicologist is involved with the analysis of biological (and occasionally, non-biological) samples for the presence of drugs, alcohol, or other toxins; the toxicological interpretation of the results of those analyses in the context of the case at hand; and the communication of those results and interpretations to the court via written report and/or viva voce testimony. The context of the case is important as it determines the question the toxicologist is being asked: a case involving allegations of homicide may require the toxicologist to provide an opinion on whether a detected substance was present in sufficient quantity to cause death, while a case involving allegations of impaired driving would require the toxicologist to provide an opinion on whether a detected substance was present in sufficient quantity to impair one's ability to safely operate a motor vehicle. The role of the forensic drug toxicologist is to provide expert scientific opinion to the trier of fact on the measured results and limitations of their reliability, and the toxicological implications of those measurements, along with the limitations of those interpretations.

Interpretation of the toxicological implications of a given measurement will vary and depend upon various factors, including the sample type analyzed; the pharmacological properties of the drug, the potential drug interactions, the details with respect to the timing of the incident and sample collection; the instability of the drugs in question; and the potential for drug presence that is toxicologically incidental to the case (e.g., low levels of cannabinoids in occasional users of cannabis).

3) Conclusion

Forensic drug toxicology is a complex science that draws upon a variety of scientific disciplines in its application, including analytical chemistry and pharmacology. The type of case determines the forensic questions being asked of the toxicologist. Those questions inform the decision about what samples are best for the analysis, since the type of sample analyzed (e.g., blood versus urine) determines the toxicological information that may be gleaned (e.g., evidence of toxic effect versus evidence of exposure). Drug effects and toxicity are quite variable depending on a variety of factors including dose, route of administration, drug interactions, and the health and drug use history of the individual. Notwithstanding the development of well-validated, precise analytical methods, interpretation of drug concentrations in biological samples requires consideration of a variety of factors and extensive review of the scientific literature.

D. LEGAL CONTEXT

Forensic toxicology applies toxicology (i.e., the study of "adverse effects of chemicals on living organisms"[31]) to medicolegal investigations that pertain to the detection of drugs in living or deceased persons, and the interpretation of these results.[32] Forensic toxicologists analyze drugs, alcohol, and poisons in order to provide expert opinions about the presence and effects of these substances in the human body. Forensic testing to determine whether alcohol or other drugs played a role in an alleged offence

31 National Forensic Science Technology Center, "A Simplified Guide to Forensic Toxicology" (2013) at 2, online: Forensic Sciences Simplified www.forensicsciencesimplified.org/tox/Toxicology.pdf.

32 *Ibid.*

must be conducted by an accredited laboratory.[33] Forensic toxicologists rarely attend crime scenes or autopsies, though their presence may be helpful when police discover and process clandestine drug laboratories, as officers may need assistance to identify evidence or safety hazards.[34]

Forensic toxicologists are called upon to provide opinions based on the results of testing and analysis of bodily samples in many types of cases, including impaired driving and drug-facilitated sexual assaults and homicides.[35] In these contexts, forensic toxicologists may assist the court by:[36] providing an opinion as to a driver's blood alcohol concentration at the time of a vehicle collision,[37] "taking into account the effects of absorption, metabolism and elimination"[38] over the time period in question (further discussed below); performing blood and urine tests for the presence of a date rape drug;[39] or determining a deceased person's alcohol consumption and degree of impairment in the hours leading up to his death.[40]

The procedural and technical features of cases involving forensic toxicology evidence can be quite complex, and a comprehensive treatment of each of these features would far exceed the scope of this section. The authors recommend that litigators working in this area seek out additional resources exclusively treating the particular topic that they wish to

33 There are three primary forensic toxicology service providers in Canada: (1) Laboratoire de sciences judiciaires et de médecine légale (LSJML), in Montreal; (2) Centre of Forensic Sciences (CFS), based in Toronto, with an additional laboratory in Sault Ste. Marie; and (3) the Royal Canadian Mounted Police (RCMP). Additional toxicology services are operated in association with various Chief Medical Examiner and Public Health offices: Michael S. Pollanen et al., eds., "Forensic Science in Canada: A Report of Multidisciplinary Discussion" (4–5 May 2012) at 74 [Hart House Report], online: www.forensics.utoronto.ca/Assets/LMPF+Digital+Assets/Forensic+Science+in+Canada.pdf.

34 Gail S. Anderson, "All You Ever Wanted to Know about Forensic Science in Canada but Didn't Know Who to Ask!" at 21, online: British Columbia Institute of Technology www.bcit.ca/files/cas/forensics/pdf/forensic_science_anderson.pdf.

35 Hart House Report, above note 32 at 74.

36 The authors wish to express gratitude to Glenn R. Anderson and to recommend his textbook from which this list of examples is derived: Glenn R. Anderson, *Expert Evidence*, 3d ed. (Markham, ON: LexisNexis, 2014) at 415–16 and 428.

37 *Ibid.* See, for example, *R. v. Peters*, 2010 ABPC 110. Anderson notes at 416: "The opinion was based on unproved assumptions and given little weight."

38 *Ibid.*, Anderson, *Expert Evidence*. See, for example, *R. v. Finlayson*, 2002 NSPC 34 at para. 12.

39 *Ibid.*, Anderson, *Expert Evidence*. See, for example, *R. v. Alouache*, [2003] O.J. No. 5280 (S.C.J.).

40 *Ibid.*, Anderson, *Expert Evidence*. See, for example, *R. v. Wallbanks*, [2001] O.J. No. 3906 (S.C.J.).

explore—and, further, that they be particularly cognizant of the probable need for expert evidence to be presented in these cases.[41]

In view of the frequency with which impaired driving offences are prosecuted, this section will focus primarily on that topic.[42]

1) Toxicology and Impaired Driving

a) Statutory Framework

The *Criminal Code*, the *Controlled Drugs and Substances Act* (*CDSA*), and provincial *Highway Traffic Act* legislation[43] are the key statutes that pertain to offences where forensic toxicology expertise may be required in court.

b) Prevalence of Impaired Driving Offences

Impaired driving is the most frequently occurring type of case in the Canadian criminal justice system, comprising 9.2 percent of all charges (or 106,835 charges of a national total of 1,161,018) and 11 percent of all adult court cases (or 45,068 of a national total of 392,907).[44] The rate of impaired driving offences is 223 incidents per 100,000 population.[45] Alcohol (rather than other drugs) is most frequently involved in impaired driving incidents: in 2013, police-reported crime statistics indicated that alcohol is involved in 97 percent of impaired driving incidents, while other drugs are only involved in 3 percent of cases.[46] With respect to *CDSA* offences,

---

41 The authors wish to recommend Alan D. Gold, *Defending Drinking and Driving Cases* (Toronto: Carswell, 2015), and also to express their gratitude to Mr. Gold, whose work has been of great assistance in the preparation of the "Legal Context" section of this chapter.

42 Note: concepts relating to post-mortem toxicology (rather than to the investigation of living persons in criminal proceedings) are reviewed in Chapter 18; and that wrongful conviction concerns arising from flawed forensic drug toxicology are addressed in Chapter 5, particularly in Section M, "The Motherisk Hair Analysis Independent Review."

43 *Criminal Code*, R.S.C. 1985, c. C-46; *Controlled Drugs and Substances Act*, S.C. 1996, c. 19; and see, for example, the Ontario *Highway Traffic Act*, R.S.O. 1990, c. H.8.

44 Jennifer Thomas, "Five Offences Represent Half of Caseload" in *Adult Criminal Court Statistics, 2008/2009*, online: Statistics Canada www.statcan.gc.ca/pub/85-002-x/2010002/article/11293-eng.htm#a24 and *Table 1: Charges and Cases in Adult Criminal Court, Canada, 2008/2009*, online: Statistics Canada www.statcan.gc.ca/pub/85-002-x/2010002/article/11293/tbl/tbl1-eng.htm.

45 Jillian Boyce, Adam Cotter, & Samuel Perreault, "Police-Reported Impaired Driving Rates Decrease for Second Consecutive Year" in *Police-Reported Crime Statistics in Canada, 2013*, online: Statistics Canada, www.statcan.gc.ca/pub/85-002-x/2014001/article/14040-eng.htm.

46 *Ibid.*

about two-thirds (67 percent) of these offences pertained to cannabis, most commonly possession.[47] The rate of *CDSA* offences in 2013 was 310 incidents per 100,000 population.[48]

2) Toxicology and Impaired Driving: Alcohol

Several *Criminal Code* provisions govern the collection of breath or blood samples in the context of impaired driving offences. The following provisions allow the taking of breath or blood samples to enable an analysis determining the concentration, if any, of alcohol or drugs in the sample.[49]

a) Breath Screening Demand (*Criminal Code*, section 254(2)(b))

A police officer is empowered to make a breath screening demand where there are "reasonable grounds to *suspect* that a person has alcohol or a drug in their body and that the person has, within the preceding three hours, operated a motor vehicle" (or other type of vehicle, as detailed in the statute).[50] If this standard is met, the officer may demand that a breath sample be provided forthwith into an approved screening device.[51] The officer may also demand that the person perform physical coordination tests.[52] According to the *Evaluation of Impaired Operations (Drugs and Alcohol) Regulations*, there are three standard field sobriety tests: (a) the horizontal gaze nystagmus test; (b) the walk-and-turn test; and (c) the one-leg stand test.[53]

---

47 Jillian Boyce, Adam Cotter, & Samuel Perreault, "Police-Reported Drug Offences Decrease in 2013, but Remain Higher Than a Decade Earlier" in *Police-Reported Crime Statistics in Canada, 2013*, above note 45.

48 *Ibid.*

49 See, generally, Steven Penney, Vincenzo Rondinelli, & James Stribopoulos, *Criminal Procedure in Canada* (Markham: LexisNexis Canada, 2011) at 234–37.

50 *Criminal Code*, above note 43, s. 254(2) [emphasis added]. See the statute for the full text.

51 *Ibid.*, s. 254(2)(b). For the purposes of s. 254, the following are considered to be approved screening devices: (a) Alcolmeter S-L2; (b) Alco-Sûr; (c) Alcotest® 7410 PA3; (d) Alcotest® 7410 GLC; (e) Alco-Sensor IV DWF; (f) Alco-Sensor IV PWF; (g) Intoxilyzer 400D; (h) Alco-Sensor FST; and (i) Dräger Alcotest 6810 (Approved Screening Devices Order, SI/85-200, s. 2). New breath-testing instruments must meet the standards published by the Alcohol Test Committee (ATC) of the Canadian Society of Forensic Science (CSFS) before their use is deemed acceptable for law enforcement agencies. The ATC does not, however, oversee Canadian breath-testing programs; instead, various government and policing agencies operate their own programs. See Hart House Report, above note 33 at 77.

52 *Criminal Code*, above note 43, s. 254(2)(a).

53 *Evaluation of Impaired Operation (Drugs and Alcohol) Regulations*, SOR/2008-196, s. 2.

b) Breathalyzer Demand (*Criminal Code*, section 254(3)(a)(i))

Where there are "reasonable grounds to *believe* that a person is committing, or at any time within the preceding three hours has committed, an *offence* under section 253 as a result of the consumption of alcohol," the officer may demand that the person provide, as soon as is practicable, "samples of breath that, in a qualified technician's opinion, will enable a proper analysis to be made to determine the concentration, if any, of alcohol in [their] . . . blood" (i.e., to provide breathalyzer samples).[54]

In *R. v. Bernshaw*, the Supreme Court of Canada held that an officer's subjective belief that a drinking and driving offence has been committed must be supported by objective reasonable grounds. In short, "[t]he existence of reasonable and probable grounds entails both an objective and a subjective component."[55]

c) Blood Sample Demand (*Criminal Code*, section 254(3)(a)(ii))

If a police officer has reasonable and probable grounds to believe that the driver has committed a drinking and driving offence and is incapable of providing breath samples due to his or her physical condition, or that it would be impracticable to obtain a breath sample, then the officer may demand that a blood sample be taken as soon as practicable.[56]

In *R. v. Salmon*, the British Columbia Court of Appeal held that there must be both subjective and objective reasonable and probable grounds to support a blood sample demand.[57]

d) Blood Sample Warrant (*Criminal Code*, section 256)

A justice may issue a warrant requiring a qualified medical practitioner to take a blood sample where there are reasonable grounds to believe that: (1) the person (a) has committed an offence under section 253 within the preceding four hours as a result of alcohol or drug consumption, and (b) "was involved in an accident resulting in the death of another person or in bodily harm to himself or herself" or others;[58] and (2) in the opinion of a qualified medical practitioner, (a) the person cannot consent to the taking

---

54 *Criminal Code*, above note 43, s. 254(3)(a)(i) [emphasis added].

55 *R. v. Bernshaw*, [1995] 1 S.C.R. 254 at para. 48. See, generally, Penney, Rondinelli, & Stribopolous, above note 49 at 235 for their explanation of relevant principles.

56 *Criminal Code*, above note 43, s. 254(3)(a)(ii).

57 *R. v. Salmon*, 1999 BCCA 740, leave to appeal to S.C.C. refused, [2000] S.C.C.A. No. 510. See also Penney, Rondinelli, & Stribopolous, above note 49 at 235.

58 *Criminal Code*, above note 43, s. 256(1)(a).

of blood samples because of his or her physical or mental condition, which resulted from consuming alcohol or a drug, the accident, "or any other occurrence related to or resulting from the accident," and (b) the taking of such samples would not endanger the person's health or life.[59]

e) Refusal to Provide a Sample (*Criminal Code*, sections 254(5), 258(3))

Refusing to provide a breath or blood sample is a criminal offence.[60] Further, evidence of a refusal without reasonable explanation is admissible, and the court may draw an adverse inference from this evidence.[61]

f) Statutory Presumption (*Criminal Code*, sections 258(1)(c), (d), (d.01), (d.1))

Where breath and blood samples are taken in accordance with the procedural requirements set out in these subsections (notably, that the sample be: taken as soon as practicable after the time of the alleged offence, and not later than two hours after that time; received directly from the accused into an approved container or instrument; and analysed by a qualified person), "the evidence of the results of the analyses so made is conclusive proof that the concentration of alcohol in the accused's blood both at the time when the analyses were made and at the time when the offence was alleged to have been committed was . . . the concentration determined by the analyses," in the absence of evidence tending to show that the testing instrument "was malfunctioning or was operated improperly."[62]

However, it remains open to the defence to lead evidence showing that the accused consumed alcohol in a manner that was consistent with *both*: (1) a blood alcohol concentration that did not exceed the "over 80" threshold at the time of the alleged offence; and (2) the blood alcohol concentration determined by the breath or blood sample testing (further discussed at "Potential Defences," below).[63]

---

59 *Ibid.*, s. 256(1)(b).

60 *Ibid.*, s. 254(5).

61 *Ibid.*, s. 258(3).

62 *Ibid.*, ss. 258(1)(c) & 258(1)(d)). See also s. 258(1)(d.01), clarifying that evidence of instrument malfunction or misuse incorrectly yielding an "over 80" result does *not* include evidence to the effect that the accused's alcohol consumption was incommensurate with the test results (and therefore the testing must have been conducted improperly).

63 *Ibid.*, s. 258(1)(d.1).

In *R. v. St-Onge Lamoureux*,[64] the Supreme Court of Canada held that the statutory presumption that breath testing results are conclusive proof of the accused's blood alcohol concentration at the time of the alleged offence violates section 11(d) of the *Charter*, but is saved by section 1. However, the Court struck down the two further requirements listed in s. 258(1)(c) that purport to require the accused—in addition to establishing that the breathalyzer was malfunctioning or was used improperly—to demonstrate that this problem resulted in the determination that the accused's blood alcohol concentration was "over 80" at the time of the alleged offence, and that this determination was incorrect.[65]

The recent Ontario Court of Appeal decision *R. v. Jackson*[66] placed new limits on the types of records that defence counsel may draw upon in seeking to rebut the statutory presumption. The defendant, who had been charged with impaired and "over 80" operation, had requested an order requiring additional disclosure, specifically, of the Intoxilyzer's service records; usage and calibration records; and results of breath tests preceding and following his breath tests.[67] The trial judge found these records to be first-party records governed by *Stinchcombe* and ordered their disclosure.[68] This decision was upheld by a motions judge of the Superior Court.[69] The Crown and the Ottawa Police Service (the holder of the records in question) appealed to the Ontario Court of Appeal.[70]

The court allowed the appeal and quashed the disclosure order.[71] The court found that the records sought were third party records governed by the *O'Connor* regime, rather than first party records governed by *Stinchcombe*.[72] Citing the Supreme Court decisions of *Quesnelle* and *McNeil*, the court concluded that the Ottawa Police Service was a third party for the

---

64 *R. v. St-Onge Lamoureux*, 2012 SCC 57 [*St-Onge Lamoureux*].

65 *Ibid.*; *Criminal Code*, above note 43, s. 258(1)(c).

66 *R. v. Jackson*, 2015 ONCA 832 [*Jackson*].

67 *Ibid.* at paras. 2, 13, and 62.

68 *Ibid.* at paras. 13, 15, and 64, referencing *R. v. Stinchcombe*, [1991] 3 S.C.R. 326 [*Stinchcombe*].

69 *Jackson*, above note 66 at paras. 4, 16–17, and 65.

70 *Ibid.* at paras. 14 and 19. The court elected to hear the appeal despite its mootness (the records had already been disclosed to the defence in accordance with the trial judge's ruling) (paras. 19 and 54). The court observed that the issues raised in this case "are of common occurrence in the prosecution of alcohol-driving offences" (para. 55) and that "the conflicting decisions of trial courts afford[ed] no assistance to the record-holders . . . [who were thus] left to the vagaries of judicial assignment" (para. 57).

71 *Ibid.* at para. 140.

72 *Ibid.* at para. 90, referencing *R. v. O'Connor*, [1995] 4 S.C.R. 411 [*O'Connor*].

purpose of disclosure,[73] and observed that "[a]part from the police duty to supply the prosecuting Crown with the fruits of the investigation, records in the hands of third parties, including the police . . . are generally *not* subject to the *Stinchcombe* disclosure rules."[74] The court held that the records sought had "no association with the offence"[75] in question and thus did not constitute "fruits of the investigation" subject to *Stinchcombe* disclosure.[76] The court found this result to be consistent with *St-Onge Lamoureux*—notwithstanding Deschamps J.'s statements (for the majority) that the breath testing instrument and the people who maintain and operate it are under the Crown's control[77]—taking the view that "*St-Onge Lamoureux* was not about disclosure"[78] and, moreover, "referred to *O'Connor*, the progenitor of the third party production regime, as the procedure to invoke to obtain remedies for non-disclosure."[79]

The court then considered the question of whether or not the records sought would meet the "likely relevant" standard required to pass the first stage of the *O'Connor* test; it held that they would not.[80] The court concluded with a post-script proposing "a principled approach to the issue, akin to that enacted in . . . s. 278.3(4) of the *Criminal Code*,"[81] that could assist trial judges in discouraging what the court characterized as "unmeritorious third party records applications that devour limited resources."[82]

---

73 *Jackson*, above note 66 at paras. 96 and 98.

74 *Ibid.* at para. 80 [emphasis in original], citing *R. v. Quesnelle*, 2014 SCC 46 at para. 11 and *R. v. McNeil*, 2009 SCC 3 at para. 25.

75 *Jackson*, above note 66 at para. 95. More specifically, the court observed that "[t]he information was not created, produced or even located during the investigation of the respondent and his alleged offences" and "played no role in the acquisition of any evidence available for proffer in the prosecution . . . . Indeed, much of it originate[d] in the investigation of others" for unrelated offences (*ibid.*).

76 *Ibid.* at para. 94.

77 *Ibid.* at paras. 99 and 102, citing *St-Onge Lamoureux*, above note 64 at para. 48.

78 *Jackson*, above note 66 at para. 100. That is, though the Supreme Court did consider "the availability of additional disclosure about the reliability of the approved instrument as a relevant factor in its constitutional analysis" of the new provisions, "the court eschewed consideration of the nature and scope of evidence that might be considered in rebuttal [of the statutory presumption] and thus could be the subject of a disclosure request" (*ibid.*).

79 *Ibid.* at para. 105, citing *St-Onge Lamoureux*, above note 64 at para. 78.

80 *Jackson*, above note 66 at paras. 107, 117, 126, 129–30, and 134.

81 *Ibid.* at para. 139, citing the *Criminal Code*, above note 43, s. 278.3(4) (listing claims that do not, without more, meet the "likely relevant" standard).

82 *Jackson*, above note 66.

The scope of impact of *R. v. Jackson* on accused persons' ability to make full answer and defence in impaired driving cases remains to be seen.

3) Toxicology and Impaired Driving: Other Drugs

a) Drug Evaluation by DRE Officer (*Criminal Code*, s. 254(3.1))

Where there are reasonable grounds to believe that a person is committing, or has at any time within the past three hours committed, an impaired driving offence "as a result of the consumption of a drug or of a combination of alcohol and a drug," an officer may demand that the person be evaluated, as soon as is practicable, by a drug evaluation officer (or DRE),[83] who must be certified and accredited by the International Association of Chiefs of Police.[84] The DRE may conduct a number of tests including: evaluation of pupil size and eye tracking; tests of balance and coordination; taking the person's pulse, blood pressure, and temperature; and examination of exposed extremities for evidence of injection sites.[85]

b) Bodily Sample Demand (*Criminal Code*, s. 254(3.4))

If, following the preliminary evaluation, the DRE has reasonable grounds to believe that the person is indeed impaired by a drug or by a combination of alcohol and a drug, the officer may require the person to provide a bodily sample (e.g., blood, saliva, or urine) as soon as is practicable, such that a proper determination can be made as to whether the person is using a drug.[86]

4) Use of Forensic Toxicology Evidence in Defending Impaired Driving Cases

Typically, both Crown and defence counsel will need to work with a forensic toxicologist in order to properly prepare for impaired driving or "over 80" cases. The forensic toxicologist will provide an opinion as to the accused's blood alcohol concentration at the time of the alleged offence (i.e., the "blood alcohol extrapolation"), of which the court is not permitted to take judicial notice.[87] In his recent book addressing the defence of drinking

83 *Criminal Code*, above note 43, s. 254(3.1).
84 *Evaluation of Impaired Operation (Drugs and Alcohol) Regulations*, above note 53, s. 1.3.
85 *Ibid.*, s. 3.
86 *Criminal Code*, above note 43, s. 254(3.4).
87 *Dennis v. British Columbia (Superintendent of Motor Vehicles)*, 2000 BCCA 653.

and driving cases, Alan D. Gold recommends that defence counsel provide the forensic toxicologist with "an outline based upon [the] . . . client's evidence regarding the amount [of alcohol] consumed and the timing of consumption,"[88] and to "include references to any medicines that the client was taking that impact on his condition."[89] Gold further notes that toxicologists can also assist in examining videotapes of the client's booking and breath testing procedures "to see if any issues are apparent regarding the testing procedures involved, or the client's apparent condition."[90]

a) Admissibility

Generally speaking, forensic toxicology evidence, as a species of expert evidence, must meet the *Mohan* admissibility criteria (that is, it must be relevant, necessary to assist the trier of fact, not subject to any exclusionary rule, and presented by a properly qualified expert) in order to be received.[91] For this reason, the opinion evidence of DRE (drug evaluation) officers as to impairment has not historically been viewed as admissible for any purpose other than establishing grounds for making a bodily sample demand (per s. 254(3.4) of the *Criminal Code*), unless their evidence meets the *Mohan* criteria.[92] Disquietingly, however, the Ontario Court of Appeal recently held, in *R. v. Bingley*, that DRE officers' evidence as to im pairment *is* admissible as expert testimony, without the need for a *Mohan voir dire*.[93] The Supreme Court granted leave to appeal in January 2016.[94] The case had not yet been heard at the time of writing.

b) Disclosure

Defence counsel will wish to ensure that they have requested and received the full complement of disclosure that is available in cases where approved screening device and/or breathalyzer evidence is at play, including the following components: the police officers' notes and will say statements; the calibration records of the approved screening device and/or repair records of the breathalyzer machine used in the investigation; and

88 Gold, above note 41 at 18.
89 *Ibid.*
90 *Ibid.*
91 *R. v. Mohan*, [1994] 2 S.C.R. 9.
92 See, for example, *R. v. Tonelli*, 2011 ONCJ 542 [*Tonelli*]; *R. v. Bright*, 2011 ONCJ 333; *R. v. Wakewich*, 2010 ONCJ 86.
93 *R. v. Bingley*, 2015 ONCA 439 [*Bingley*].
94 [2015] S.C.C.A. No. 361.

any video recordings that were made of the client (e.g., recordings of the breath testing procedure or as part of the parade procedure).[95]

c) Potential Defences

i) Defeating the Statutory Presumption

As seen above, it remains open to the accused person to rebut the statutory presumption that an "over 80" breathalyzer result conclusively proves that he or she had a blood alcohol content above this threshold at the time of the alleged offence. For example, defence counsel could suggest that the accused drank a significant quantity of alcohol immediately prior to the police encounter—such that some of the alcohol that the accused consumed (and that was reflected in the testing results) had not yet entered his or her bloodstream at the time of the alleged offence—meaning his or her blood alcohol content might still have been below the legal limit at that point.[96] Along similar lines, defence counsel could argue that the accused consumed additional alcohol *after* the time of the alleged offence.[97]

ii) Charter *Defences*

Another potential approach is to argue that the breath sample evidence was obtained in contravention of the accused's *Charter* rights and should be excluded as per section 24(2). For instance, courts have excluded breathalyzer evidence: where the accused was unlawfully strip searched (in contravention of section 8 of the *Charter*) after being taken into custody upon failing his roadside screening;[98] where the accused was arbitrarily detained following

95 Mr. Gold's recent work (Gold, above note 41 at 18–19 on disclosure) provided the framework for this discussion. Note the potential impact of *R. v. Jackson*, above note 66, on counsel's ability to procure some of this disclosure: see Section D(2)(f), "Statutory Presumption (*Criminal Code*), sections 258(1)(c), (d), (d.01), (d.1))," above.

Note also that it may be possible to successfully advance the argument that an instrument's readings are unreliable if equipped with sufficient records that allow for an expert to conduct a meaningful review of the instrument's history. One case, the acquittal of Gurder Singh, was heavily reported in the news in May 2016 as Justice Elinore Ready accepted the evidence of Ben Joseph (a scientist formerly with the Centre of Forensic Sciences), who testified to the instrument's history of inaccurate results, as well as other failures, and the maintenance records failed to explain the malfunctions or steps taken to address the problems. Justice Ready found that the Intoxilyzer readings were incomplete because the readings were not accompanied by an "uncertainty of measurement" (i.e., an error rate). The Crown has filed an appeal in the case and the case may be one for legal practitioners to watch as it progresses through the criminal justice system.

96 See, for example, *R. v. Carney*, 2015 ONSC 4801; *R. v. Del Riccio*, 2010 ONSC 1.

97 See, for example, *R. v. Turner*, 2014 ONSC 6820; *R. v. Murray*, 2011 ONSC 2739.

98 *R. v. Samuels*, 2008 ONCJ 85.

his breathalyzer testing (in breach of section 9 of the *Charter*);[99] and where the accused's drug evaluation was not carried out as soon as practicable (also breaching his section 9 *Charter* right not to be arbitrarily detained).[100]

5) Other Areas of the Criminal Law where Forensic Toxicology is Often Invoked

a) Determining Criminal *Mens Rea*

Forensic toxicology evidence may assist the court in determining whether the defence of intoxication is available to the accused so as to negate specific intent (and thus, for instance, reduce murder to manslaughter).[101] The recent case of *R. v. Iverson*[102] provides a helpful summary of the current state of this area of the law (as set forth by the Supreme Court of Canada in *R. v. Daley*[103]), as follows:

> [There are] . . . three legally relevant states of intoxication . . . . The first state, "mild" intoxication, arises where alcohol merely induces a state of disinhibition on the part of the intoxicated party. Intoxication to this degree does not negate *mens rea*, nor is it relevant in determining whether the accused possessed the requisite *mens rea*. The third state of intoxication described in Daley involves "extreme intoxication akin to automatism." Such intoxication negatives the voluntariness of the actions of the accused and thereby operates as "a complete defence to criminal responsibility." . . . [A]ny such defence would be rare and, in any event, unavailable for offences that involve "assault or any other interference or threat of interference by a person of the bodily integrity of another," per s. 33(1) of the *Code*. The second state . . . that of advanced intoxication . . . applies where the accused is impaired in his or her foresight of the consequences of his or her actions, such that he or she did not or could not form the specific intent contemplated by the *mens rea* for the offence charged . . . . [W]here death is the "obvious consequence" of the accused's actions, only a particularly advanced degree of intoxication will assist the accused.[104]

---

99 *R. v Simmons*, 2002 BCPC 144.

100 *Tonelli*, above note 92.

101 See, for example, *R. v. Daley*, 2007 SCC 53 (particularly at para. 40) [*Daley*]; *R. v. Bird*, 2013 BCCA 316; *R. v. Iverson*, 2014 BCSC 2400 [*Iverson*].

102 *Iverson*, *ibid.*

103 *Daley*, above note 101.

104 *Iverson*, above note 101 at paras. 45–46 [internal citations omitted], citing *Daley*, above note 101 at paras. 39, 41, and 43, and the *Criminal Code*, above note 43, s. 33(1).

b) Abstention Conditions as Terms of Probation

Another context in which toxicology testing is often employed is as part of an offender's probation conditions. This recent change to the law was catalyzed by the Supreme Court of Canada's finding, in *R. v. Shoker*, that sentencing judges' jurisdiction to craft probation conditions under section 732.1 of the *Criminal Code* does not include the authority to require breath, urine, or blood samples for toxicological analysis in order to monitor compliance with abstention conditions (preventing the probationer from using alcohol or other drugs).[105] There were, at the time, no *Criminal Code* provisions regarding bodily sample demands in this context; the Court concluded that, since Parliament had not provided such a scheme, it was not for the Court to judicially enact one.[106]

In response to *Shoker*, the legislature amended the *Criminal Code* provisions pertaining to probation, conditional sentences, and peace bonds to explicitly authorize courts to require a probationer to provide a bodily sample, on demand or at regular intervals, to either police or probation officers. These amendments (under the title *Response to the Supreme Court of Canada Decision in R. v. Shoker Act*, formerly known as Bill C-30), and the attendant *Samples of Bodily Substances Regulations*, came into force on 31 March 2015.[107]

6) Conclusion

It is essential that counsel who take on cases involving a forensic toxicological component commit to: (1) investing the time required to develop sufficient competency in this oftentimes technically demanding context; and (2) retaining a forensic toxicologist to testify on the many occasions where expert evidence will be indispensible. This commitment could be said to take on especial significance in the impaired driving context, in view both of the high volume of driving offences prosecuted each year in Canada, and of the Ontario Court of Appeal's recent undermining (in *Jackson* and in *Bingley*) of the procedural rights to which these accused persons have been historically entitled.

---

105 *R. v. Shoker*, 2006 SCC 44 at paras. 2–3 and 27.

106 *Ibid.* at paras. 3 and 25–26.

107 *Response to the Supreme Court of Canada Decision in R. v. Shoker Act*, S.C. 2011, c. 7; *Order Fixing the Day that is 90 Days after the Day on which this Order is registered as the Day on which the Act Comes into Force*, SI/2014-105, online: Canada Gazette www.gazette.gc.ca/rp-pr/p2/2014/2014-12-31/html/si-tr105-eng.php; *Samples of Bodily Substances Regulations*, SOR/2014-304.

CHAPTER 21

Memory in the Criminal Courts

Timothy E. Moore, Stephanie Marion, C. Lindsay Fitzsimmons, & Brian Cutler

A. INTRODUCTION

The criminal justice system is heavily reliant on human memory as a source of evidence: a convenience store is robbed at gunpoint and the cashier is asked to identify the suspect from a photo array; the sole witness to a kidnapping tries to remember how the abduction was accomplished; a family doctor is informed by one of his patients of a sexual assault that occurred two decades earlier. Unlike the items on the shelves of the evidence room (e.g., weapons, clothing, documents), memories are intangible. They exist in the witness's head. Their accuracy depends, in part, on how thoroughly the initial perceptions were encoded, how much time has passed, and how those memories were elicited from the witness by investigators. Unlike a video, our memories are reconstructive and selective. We add, delete, and modify information in various ways to make sense of past experiences. Sometimes we suffer from what is known as source amnesia—an inability to distinguish information acquired at the time of an experience from information that may be added later. Sometimes we confuse actual events with imagined ones. While some autobiographical memories may be quite accurate and relatively permanent, research has shown that they are often distorted or embellished, and may be modified over time.

Inaccurate accounts of past experiences can come about because we unwittingly reconstruct an event based on what we think we know, rather than on actual memories. The act of remembering takes place against a backdrop of prior knowledge that influences and filters what gets into memory. We organize and understand new information through associations with what we already know. Cognitive psychologists sometimes refer to this background information as a conceptual framework, or schema. Many aspects of our day-to-day experiences are redundant. For example, restaurants contain tables, chairs, waiters, and menus, and we go to a restaurant with the expectation that we will get food there. Similarly, dentists' offices contain a waiting room, a receptionist, hygienists, and so on. We know what to expect when we visit these places because of our generic knowledge about such situations. Schemas provide a summary of the redundancies and help us interpret and organize our knowledge. Schemas are efficient. They let us interpret, store, and retrieve more information than we could possibly deal with otherwise. This efficiency, however, has costs. Witnesses relying on their memory can make errors; details fade over time. Witnesses may unknowingly compensate for gaps in memory by making inferences. Because these inferences are unconscious, when witnesses produce inaccurate accounts, they may not be lying, they may simply be mistaken.

This should not be taken to imply that memory is routinely capricious and unreliable. In general, our memories are fairly accurate. Many elements of past experiences are usually preserved with good fidelity; however, memory mistakes do occur and they can be large, undetectable, and subjectively compelling. The passage of time provides increasing opportunities for memories to be altered or lost altogether. Even under ideal circumstances, the most conscientiously candid and forthright witness is not going to be completely accurate. In this chapter, we provide an overview of specific aspects of memory that have long-standing forensic significance. Errors in memory do not happen haphazardly. Certain factors are known to compromise memory's reliability. By understanding how memory works, the courts will be in a better position to know when (or when not) to have confidence in a witness's account.

B. EYEWITNESS TESTIMONY

In 1989, Anthony Hanemaayer of Toronto pled guilty to an attempted rape that he did not commit. The victim's mother had identified him as the assailant. She was adamant that he was the person she had seen. Hanemaayer, who was eventually exonerated,[1] later stated that if he had been a juror,

---

1 *R. v. Hanemaayer*, 2008 ONCA 580.

he would have believed the witness who identified him. Eyewitnesses are frequently not just mistaken, they are confidently mistaken, and a confident witness is compelling to jurors. In 2012, the U.S. National Registry of Exonerations summarized 873 DNA exonerations over the previous twenty-three years. In 80 percent of the sexual assault cases and in 81 percent of the robbery cases, mistaken eyewitness identification contributed to the false conviction.[2]

Eyewitnesses identify suspects in a variety of contexts. Some identifications are driven by the eyewitness, rather than the police. For example, an eyewitness might see the suspect in a public place and call the police. Some eyewitnesses conduct an active search for the suspect on social media and may contact the police if they find him or her. In many cases, the police conduct an eyewitness identification procedure, such as a showup (where the police bring the suspect to a place where they expect to find witnesses), a photo array, or a live lineup (although live lineups are rare). In laboratory research on eyewitness identification, the investigator has the important benefit of knowing whether an identification is correct or incorrect, and this knowledge allows the investigator to classify identifications by accuracy. A correct identification occurs when an eyewitness positively identifies the suspect and the suspect is in fact the perpetrator. A false identification occurs when the eyewitness identifies an innocent suspect as the perpetrator. When the eyewitness expresses the belief that the suspect in question is not the perpetrator, this decision is either a correct rejection (i.e., the suspect is in fact not the perpetrator) or a miss (i.e., when the suspect actually is the perpetrator). In photo arrays, an eyewitness might also make a "filler identification." A filler is a photo of a person who is known to not be the perpetrator but has been included in the photo array together with the suspect. Filler identifications are errors but they do not lead to arrests. Classification of identification decisions in this manner allows researchers to examine the influence of various factors on the different types of errors in eyewitness identifications. Research on eyewitness identification does not focus on general identification accuracy rates per se, but rather on the influence of specific factors on identification accuracy.

---

2 Samuel R. Gross & Michael Shaffer, "Exonerations in the United States, 1989–2012" (2012) *The National Registry of Exonerations* 103, online: www.law.umich.edu/special/exoneration/Documents/exonerations_us_1989_2012_full_report.pdf; see also Andrew M. Smith & Brian L. Cutler, "Identification Procedures and Conviction of the Innocent" in Brian L. Cutler, ed., *Reform of Eyewitness Identification Procedures* (Washington, DC: American Psychological Association Press, 2013) 3.

1) General Impairment Factors

General impairment factors refer to conditions at the scene of the crime that can impair identification accuracy. These factors include: (1) the characteristics of the witness (for example, eyewitnesses make more false identifications when identifying members of a different race[3] and children make more false identifications than adults),[4] (2) concealment measures by the perpetrator (for example, eyewitnesses are more likely to make mistakes when the perpetrator makes efforts to disguise or hide facial features),[5] (3) short exposure times,[6] (4) high stress levels during the crime,[7] (5) conspicuous weapons (the "weapon focus effect"),[8] and (6) a prolonged interval between the crime and the identification.[9]

2) Suspect Bias Factors

Suspect bias factors refer to aspects of the identification test itself. They are called suspect bias factors because they bias the witness toward identifying a suspect. Selecting fillers who do not resemble the eyewitness' description of the perpetrator increases the risk that an eyewitness will use deduction, rather than memory, to figure out which photo in the array is the suspect. Selecting fillers based on the witness' description of the perpetrator reduces the risk of false identification.[10] Other procedures that can guard against suspect bias factors include the use of sequential presentation, blind administration procedures, and cautionary instructions to the

---

3 Christian A. Meissner & John C. Brigham, "Thirty Years of Investigating the Own-Race Bias in Memory for Faces: A Meta-Analytic Review" (2001) 7 *Psychology, Public Policy, and Law* 3.

4 Alejo Freire et al., "Lineup Identification by Children: Effects of Clothing Bias" (2004) 28 *Law and Human Behavior* 339.

5 J.K. Mansour et al., "Impact of Disguise on Identification Decisions and Confidence with Simultaneous and Sequential Lineups" (2012) 36 *Law and Human Behavior* 513.

6 Brian H. Bornstein et al., "Effects of Exposure Time and Cognitive Operations on Facial Identification Accuracy: A Meta-Analysis of Two Variables Associated with Initial Memory Strength" (2012) 18 *Psychology, Crime & Law* 473.

7 K.A. Deffenbacher et al., "A Meta-Analytic Review of the Effects of High Stress on Eyewitness Memory" (2004) 28 *Law and Human Behavior* 687.

8 Jonathan M. Fawcett et al., "Of Guns and Geese: A Meta-Analytic Review of the 'Weapon Focus' Literature" (2013) 19 *Psychology, Crime & Law* 35.

9 Peter N. Shapiro & Steve D. Penrod, "Meta-Analysis of Facial Identification Studies" (1986) 100 *Psychological Bulletin* 139.

10 Gary L. Wells, Sheila M. Rydell, & Eric P. Seelau, "The Selection of Distractors for Eyewitness Lineups" (1993) 78 *Journal of Applied Psychology* 835.

eyewitness. Sequential presentation carries a lower risk of false identification relative to simultaneous presentation.[11] Blind administration—where the investigator conducting the photo array does not know the identity of the suspect—obviates the inadvertent communication of the suspect's identity to the eyewitness, thus reducing the risk of false identification.[12] Instructions that explicitly warn the eyewitness that the perpetrator may not be in the photo array reduce the risk of false identification.[13] Many of these research findings have been incorporated into recommended eyewitness identification procedures in Canada.[14]

3) Self-Assessment Factors

The most common self-assessment factor is confidence. Confident eyewitnesses are persuasive. Individuals who express their belief with very high confidence will appear knowledgeable and credible. A considerable body of psychological research shows, however, that even under ideal circumstances, confidence is only moderately related to accuracy.[15] Although highly confident eyewitnesses are more likely to be accurate than less confident eyewitnesses, there is much room for error. Some eyewitnesses will express high levels of confidence in false identifications, as we noted above in *R. v. Hanemaayer*. The association between confidence and accuracy is further attenuated by general impairment factors.[16] Other self-assessment factors include the quality of their original viewing conditions, the strength of memory, and witnesses' beliefs in their ability to identify the perpetrators. Research has shown that these self-assessments

---

11 Nancy K. Steblay, Jennifer E. Dysart, & Gary L. Wells, "Seventy-Two Tests of the Sequential Lineup Superiority Effect: A Meta-Analysis and Policy Discussion" (2011) 17 *Psychology, Public Policy, and Law* 99.

12 S.M. Greathouse & M.B. Kovera, "Instruction Bias and Lineup Presentation Moderate the Effects of Administrator Knowledge on Eyewitness Identification" (2009) 33 *Law and Human Behavior* 70.

13 Nancy K. Steblay, "Lineup Instructions" in Cutler, ed., *Reform of Eyewitness Identification Procedures*, above note 2 at 65.

14 FPT Heads of Prosecution Committee Working Group Report, Public Prosecution Service of Canada, *The Path to Justice: Preventing Wrongful Convictions, Report of the Federal/Provincial/Territorial Heads of Prosecutions Subcommittee on the Prevention of Wrongful Convictions* (2011), online: www.ppsc-sppc.gc.ca/eng/pub/ptj-spj/index.html.

15 Siegfried D. Sporer et al., "Choosing, Confidence, and Accuracy: A Meta-Analysis of the Confidence-Accuracy Relation in Eyewitness Identification Studies" (1995) 118 *Psychological Bulletin* 315.

16 *Ibid.*

are malleable and can be influenced by procedures and information acquired after the identification has been made.[17] For example, when Timothy McVeigh rented the truck he used in the Oklahoma bombing, there were three employees at the rental agency. Two of them thought McVeigh had been alone, but after discussing it with the third witness, they came to believe he had had an accomplice. The social cost of disagreeing with a peer can change people's accounts and change their memories.[18]

Suggestive eyewitness identification procedures can inflate both eyewitness confidence and self-assessment, thus making the identification appear more believable. It is for this reason that modern eyewitness identification practices include the documentation of the eyewitness' confidence rating immediately after the identification has been made and before any feedback is received.[19]

In some cases, suspect identifications are made by an earwitness (identification is made on the basis of the suspect's voice). Research on earwitness identification suggests that voice identification is difficult and accuracy rates are low.[20] As with eyewitnesses, earwitnesses can be influenced by general impairment and suspect bias factors. Earwitness confidence is also not strongly related to accuracy.[21]

C. CHILD WITNESSES

Children often participate in legal proceedings. Sometimes, they are victims of alleged sexual assaults for which there is no physical evidence or other witnesses. The child's report is thus the sole source of information. How reliable are children's memories? There is no simple answer to this question because the age of the child, the nature of the event, the retention interval, and a host of other considerations all factor into reliability.

---

17 Nancy K. Steblay, Gary L. Wells, & Amy B. Douglass, "The Eyewitness Post Identification Feedback Effect 15 Years Later: Theoretical and Policy Implications" (2014) 20 *Psychology, Public Policy, and Law* 1; Gary L. Wells & Deah S. Quinlivan, "Suggestive Eyewitness Identification Procedures and the Supreme Court's Reliability Test in Light of Eyewitness Science: 30 Years Later" (2009) 33 *Law and Human Behavior* 1.

18 Daniel B. Wright et al., "When Eyewitnesses Talk" (2009) 18 *Current Directions in Psychological Science* 174.

19 Andrew M. Smith & Brian L. Cutler, "Identification Test Reforms" in Cutler, ed., *Reform of Eyewitness Identification Procedures*, above note 2 at 203.

20 A. Daniel Yarmey, "Earwitness Speaker Identification" (1995) 1 *Psychology, Public Policy, and Law* 792.

21 *Ibid.*

That said, it is clear that even quite young children (e.g., four years old) are capable of accurately remembering personal experiences over long time periods.[22] The reliability of their reports has more to do with the manner in which they are interviewed than to any inherent shortcomings of their memory capacity. Children are, however, vulnerable to suggestion, coercion, and social pressure. Unless interviews with children are conducted carefully and thoughtfully, the quality of the information obtained may be compromised. In 1992, several children in a family-run day-care centre in Martensville, Saskatchewan, made allegations of sexual and physical abuse against the staff members. Some of the accusations were grotesque and implausible. One boy claimed he had seen a caretaker cut off a boy's nipple and eat it. A few weeks later, the accusations expanded to include police officers who were investigating the earlier accusations. Eventually, all but one of over one hundred charges were dismissed, with the Saskatchewan Court of Appeal noting that:

> [C]oercive or highly suggestive interrogation techniques can create a serious and significant risk that the interrogation will distort the child's recollection of events, thereby undermining the reliability of the statements and subsequent testimony concerning such events.[23]

Similar incidents are chronicled in Ceci and Bruck's groundbreaking work.[24] Prompted partly by these high profile cases, extensive research was conducted to address the psychological factors that affect the reliability of children's reports. This research, which continues, has provided the foundation for the development of evidence-based interviewing practices that minimize the risks of contaminated accounts.[25]

Children can easily be influenced, consciously or otherwise, to develop false memories of experiences that they have only imagined. They

---

22 Carole Peterson, "Children's Autobiographical Memories Across the Years: Forensic Implications of Childhood Amnesia and Eyewitness Memory for Stressful Events" (2012) 32 *Developmental Review* 287.

23 *R. v. Sterling*, [1995] S.J. No. 612 at para. 277 (C.A.).

24 Stephen Ceci & Maggie Bruck, *Jeopardy in the Courtroom* (Washington, DC: American Psychological Association 1995); see also Stephen Ceci & Maggie Bruck, "Suggestibility of the Child Witness: A Historical Review and Synthesis" (1993) 113 *Psychological Bulletin* 403.

25 Deborah Poole & Michael Lamb, *Investigative Interviews of Children* (Washington, DC: American Psychological Association, 1998); see also Michael Lamb et al., *Tell Me What Happened: Structured Investigative Interviews of Child Victims and Witnesses* (Hoboken: Wiley, 2008) [Lamb et al.].

will sincerely believe that they have experienced the events in question. Certain types of questioning may create an especially high risk that child complainants will come to believe they have experienced events that never occurred.[26] As noted in Section A, above in this chapter, both children and adults often suffer from source amnesia, where information that has been overheard or imagined becomes confused with information obtained from actual experience.

Research shows unequivocally that when people are exposed to misinformation or suggestive questioning, they may fabricate an experience and remember it as real. For example, children readily incorporate overheard and fictitious rumours into their own autobiographical memory.[27] This can happen even in the absence of any suggestive questioning, let alone coaching. In the cited study, preschoolers participated in a magic show at their child-care centres. During the show, Mumford the Magician failed at pulling a rabbit out of his hat. Immediately following the show, some of the children overheard a scripted conversation between one of the teachers and another adult in which the adult confederate stated that the magician had failed because the rabbit was loose in the school rather than in the magician's hat. Another group of children were the classmates of those who overheard the rumour. It was expected that some of these children would receive indirect information about the alleged lost rabbit through naturally occurring conversations with their classmates who overheard the conversation. A third group of children (witnesses) saw a live rabbit eating carrots in their classroom. Children who heard the rumour were as likely as those who actually saw a loose rabbit to report having seen it. Those children who heard the rumour from their classmates were as likely to report having seen the rabbit as were those who heard the rumour directly from the adult confederate. The rumour-exposed children's "experiences" were embellished with many elaborative details—more details, in fact, than those who had actually seen the rabbit. This is strong evidence that narrative detail is not an indication of accuracy when children have been exposed to suggestive influences. The findings also demonstrate that envisioning an event can create a belief in its historical authenticity. Through a process called imagination inflation,

26 See, for example, Sena Garven et al., "More than Suggestion: The Effect of Interviewing Techniques from the McMartin Preschool Case" (1998) 83 *Journal of Applied Psychology* 347.

27 Gabrielle F. Principe et al., "Believing Is Seeing: How Rumors Can Engender False Memories in Preschoolers" (2006) 17 *Psychological Science* 243.

an imagined event can take on an aura of subjective reality over time.[28] The "memory" can be vivid and can seem real to the person recounting it. Obviously, the children in the Mumford study could not recall the source of their "memory."

Informed by research conducted at the National Institute of Child Health and Human Development in Bethesda, Maryland, a "best practices" protocol now exists that provides guidance for how to interview child witnesses. The NICHD protocol is in widespread use in North America,[29] the United Kingdom,[30] Israel, Australia, and parts of Europe. Research has repeatedly shown that open-ended prompts are more likely to elicit accurate information than more focused recognition prompts.[31] The protocol provides guidelines for interviewers that specify the types of questions and prompts that are appropriate for children, while limiting potential opportunities for leading questions. The full protocol can be found in Lamb et al.[32]

Recent research in Australia has evaluated the effectiveness of an interactive interviewer training system that provides NICHD protocol training by means of computer-assisted learning activities that train interviewers to elicit important evidential details from child witnesses in a narrative format.[33] Using a pre-test/post-test design, the researchers measured: (1) the proportion of interviewer question types, (2) the proportion of desirable interviewer behaviours, (3) adherence to the interview protocol,

---

28 Maryanne Garry & Devon L. Polaschek, "Imagination and Memory" (2000) 9 *Current Directions in Psychological Science* 6.

29 The NICHD protocol is used in the Toronto Police College's child interviewing course.

30 Great Britain, Home Office, *Achieving Best Evidence in Criminal Proceedings: Guidance for Vulnerable or Intimidated Witnesses, Including Children* (London: Home Office Communication Directorate, 2002).

31 Katja Erdmann, Renata Volbert, & Claudia Böhm, "Children Report Suggested Events Even when Interviewed in a Non-Suggestive Manner: What Are the Implications for Credibility Assessment?" (2004) 18 *Applied Cognitive Psychology* 589; David J. La Rooy, Deirdre Brown, & Michael Lamb, "Suggestibility and Witness Interviewing Using the Cognitive Interview and NICHD Protocol" in Anne M. Ridley, Fiona Gabbert, & David J. La Rooy, eds., *Suggestibility in Legal Contexts: Psychological Research and Forensic Implications* (West Sussex: Wiley, 2013); L. Melnyk, A.M. Crossman, & M.H. Scullin, "The Suggestibility of Children's Memory" in Michael P. Toglia et al., eds., *The Handbook of Eyewitness Psychology, Volume I: Memory for Events* (Mahwah, N.J.: Lawrence Erlbaum Associates, 2007) 473.

32 Lamb et al., above note 25.

33 Mairi S. Benson & Martine B. Powell, "Evaluation of a Comprehensive Interactive Training System for Investigative Interviewers of Children" (2015) 21 *Psychology, Public Policy, and Law* 309.

(4) interview length, and (5) the quality of evidential information sought. They found clear support for the utility of the training system, with some evidence supporting sustained performance one year later.

D. REMEMBERING CONVERSATIONS

The child complainant is sometimes unable to testify in a trial for which the child is the only witness (e.g., a sexual assault case). When this happens, hearsay witnesses (e.g., a parent or a teacher) might testify about the abuse that the child disclosed to them. The adult's testimony is offered in lieu of the child's direct testimony, as in the case of *R. v. Khan*.[34]

Prior to *Khan*, there was a long legal history of rules against admitting hearsay testimony and various reasons for wanting to prohibit it. For example, the defendant cannot confront the witness. False accusations are assumed, by some, to be less likely in the context of face-to-face confrontations. Hearsay obviates cross-examination of the complainant, it denies the jury access to the demeanour of the witness, and it may suggest guilt by implying that the child needs protection from the defendant. There is more room for error in hearsay evidence. The hearsay witness must have accurately heard, interpreted, remembered, and reported the declarant's original statements. These are all legitimate concerns, but there are compelling reasons for making exceptions to the hearsay prohibition. It is difficult to prosecute sexual abuse cases. The act is covert. There are frequently no witnesses and no physical evidence. The case may depend exclusively on the child's disclosure and, for understandable reasons, children may be intimidated, confused, and embarrassed about having to describe sexual events. Also, their memories may have deteriorated. The admissibility of their out-of-court statements may be crucial for a successful prosecution.

Psychological studies help us understand the reliability of hearsay evidence. When a child's disclosure has been obtained during the course of an interview by an investigator, or during an exchange with a parent, we would like to be able to rule out the possibility that the child's report was the consequence of leading questions and/or social pressure. Can hearsay witnesses provide accurate accounts of how the child's statements were elicited? In a study by Lamb and colleagues,[35] forensic interviewers

---

34 *R. v. Khan*, [1990] 2 S.C.R. 531.

35 Michael Lamb et al., "Accuracy of Investigators' Verbatim Notes of Their Forensic Interviews with Alleged Child Abuse Victims" (2000) 24 *Law and Human Behavior* 699.

took verbatim notes while conducting their interviews, and these notes were compared to transcripts of the electronic recordings. There was an under-reporting of both the details provided by the children and of the interviewers' utterances. The notes rarely contradicted the audio recording; however, the interview structure was incorrectly characterized. Details provided by the children were routinely misattributed to more open-ended, rather than focused, questions. The interviewers unconsciously downplayed their own role in extracting the information that was subsequently treated as if it had come unprompted from the children. Warren and Woodall[36] reported similar findings.

Another study addressed mothers' memories of exchanges that they had with their four-year-old children.[37] Mothers were asked to talk with their children about the activities of a play session that the mothers had not attended. Three days later, the mothers were asked to recall the details of their earlier exchanges. The details that were recalled were accurate, albeit incomplete. Most important, however, was that they had trouble remembering whether the children's statements were prompted or spontaneous, and whether utterances were spoken by themselves or by their child.

Cauchi et al.[38] asked experienced child abuse investigators to take notes as they listened to transcripts of interviews that were read aloud at a normal speech rate. Only 61 percent of abuse-related details were recorded in the notes. Furthermore, the note takers clearly gave preference to documenting the answers compared to writing down the interviewers' questions. Questions were less likely to be recorded (or recorded accurately) than were the children's responses.

Such studies demonstrate that hearsay statements, whether from memory or from notes, are likely to obscure the extent of interviewer tainting. Leading and suggestive questions are under-reported. Consequently, reports that may have been contaminated by interviewer effects are likely to be presented as reliable. Not just lay witnesses, but trained professionals as well, are insensitive to the extent to which their own questions may contain

---

36 Amye R. Warren & Cara E. Woodall, "The Reliability of Hearsay Testimony: How Well Do Interviewers Recall their Interviews with Children?" (1999) 5 *Psychology, Public Policy, and Law* 355.

37 Maggie Bruck, Stephen Ceci, & Emmett Francoeur, "The Accuracy of Mothers' Memories of Conversations with their Preschool Children" (1999) 5 *Journal of Experimental Psychology: Applied* 89.

38 Rita T. Cauchi, Martine B. Powell, & Carolyn H. Hughes-Scholes, "A Controlled Analysis of Professionals' Contemporaneous Notes of Interviews about Alleged Child Abuse" (2010) 34 *Child Abuse & Neglect* 318.

the information that is subsequently attributed to the child respondent. These data demonstrate unequivocally the importance of an electronic record of child interviews.

E. MEMORY DISTRUST

The Reid Technique[39] is an interrogation technique in widespread use in North America. The procedure is guilt presumptive. Its purpose is to elicit a confession from a suspect who is purportedly "known" or strongly suspected to be guilty. In the course of eliciting the desired confession, the interrogator may inform the suspect that there is ample proof of his guilt and that his culpability has been determined beyond the shadow of a doubt. These assertions are repeated often, with unwavering confidence on the part of the investigator. It may also be implied that failure to admit guilt will make the consequences of the inevitable conviction worse. In addition to the forceful accusations of guilt, the investigator often claims to have foolproof corroborative evidence by way of witnesses, DNA, or fingerprints. Although the popularity of the Reid Technique may be waning in Canada,[40] thousands of police officers have been trained to use it, thus Reid-induced confessions will not disappear overnight.

The effects of such false or exaggerated "evidence" can have the effect of shaking the witness' confidence in their own memory. They may believe that the "incriminating evidence" is as irrefutable as the interviewers have made it out to be. The ensuing doubts can trigger cognitive dissonance accompanied by a reimagining of what might have happened. As a result of imagination inflation, over time the events that the interviewers have been advocating can take on an aura of subjective authenticity. In other words, the witness' original memory can be altered, possibly permanently.

Increasing concern has been expressed by legal scholars regarding the role of memory distrust in the development of false confessions.[41] Re-

---

39 Fred E. Inbau et al., *Criminal Interrogation and Confessions*, 5th ed. (Burlington, MA: Jones & Bartlett Learning, 2013).

40 Sigrid Forberg, "Conversations over Confessions: Investigative Interviews Focus on Information" (2015) 77 *RCMP Gazette* 26.

41 Miriam S. Gohara, "A Lie for a Lie: False Confessions and the Case for Reconsidering the Legality of Deceptive Interrogation Techniques" (2005) 33 *Fordham Urban Law Journal* 100; Gisli H. Gudjonsson et al., "The Role of Memory Distrust in Cases of Internalised False Confession" (2014) 28 *Applied Cognitive Psychology* 336; see also Richard Ofshe, "Coerced Confessions: The Logic of Seemingly Irrational Action" (1989) 6 *Cultic Studies Journal* 1.

cently, Shaw and Porter[42] attempted to implant false memories of criminal activity in a sample of university students, using suggestive memory-retrieval techniques. Participants were interviewed three times at weekly intervals for approximately forty minutes each time about one true and one false memory from their early teens. The researchers had enlisted the help of the participants' parents or caretakers to establish the legitimacy of the true memory. The false memory events were invented, but the participants were informed that their parents had confirmed their validity. For both true and false memories, some contextual cues were supplied by the researchers (e.g., the city that the participant lived in, the participant's age, the season when the crime took place). Of the criminal false memory group, 70 percent developed memories of having committed a serious crime. Accounts of true and false memories (criminal and non-criminal) were similarly complex, detailed, and multisensory. For example, one girl reported throwing a rock at another girl on the playground and knocking her unconscious because the latter had called her a slut. Another participant described the police coming to his house to investigate a complaint. He recalled that both officers were male, one Caucasian, the other Hispanic. In a third instance, a boy described being frightened by a large brown and black German shepherd dog when walking with his mother. The dog had been standing at the end of a driveway in which a boat had been parked. The dog had brown eyes and was wearing a collar. It had been a windy day. What is remarkable about these recollections is that none of them were true. Beyond informing the students of the nature of the to-be-remembered event (e.g., assault with a weapon, attacked by a dog), the researchers did not provide any details of the events.

When people are encouraged to recall an inaccessible memory, they may try to retrieve it by forming a mental image of the event. Repeatedly imagining a non-experienced event can cause imagination to be confused with reality and, as Shaw & Porter pointed out, ". . . what something *could* have been like can turn into elements of what it *would* have been like, which can become elements of what it *was* like."[43] The memory retrieval techniques used in their study are commonplace in some police interrogation

---

42 Julia Shaw & Stephen Porter, "Constructing Rich False Memories of Committing Crime" (2015) 26 *Psychological Science* 291.

43 Quin M. Chrobak & Maria S. Zaragoza, "When Forced Fabrications Become Truth: Causal Explanations and False Memory Development" (2013) 142 *Journal of Experimental Psychology: General* 827; Shaw & Porter, above note 42 at 298.

procedures.[44] These research findings support the worries of critics who are concerned about the risks of false confessions that can arise from aggressive, deceptive, and confrontational interrogation tactics.

F. MEMORIES FROM THE DISTANT PAST

The 1990s saw an outbreak of sexual abuse allegations made by adults who recalled having been abused years earlier. Because there is no statute of limitations for indictable offences in Canada, charges can be brought against an alleged abuser years (sometimes decades) after the abuse is said to have occurred. In some instances, recovered memories are the only evidence against the accused. Some therapists believe that a patient's distress may be symptomatic of earlier abuse, the memories for which have been "repressed" in response to the trauma. They might ask patients complaining of mood disorders, eating disorders, or interpersonal problems, for example, if they can recall ever having been abused. These therapists might use what we now know to be highly suggestive techniques to help patients "recover" memories of earlier sexual abuse. These techniques can include hypnosis, guided-imagery (where patients shut their eyes and imagine scenarios suggested by the therapist), "journaling" about the abuse and reading it aloud, or interpreting dreams and body memories (interpreting physical symptoms like rashes or gagging as reflections of earlier abuse).[45] Therapists may also recommend group therapy where patients share their abuse histories and offer support to one another.

Some therapists used popular books that lacked scientific rigour as recommended reading for their patients. *Uncovering the Mystery of MPD*[46] is one such example. MPD (Multiple Personality Disorder) diagnoses increased dramatically in the 1990s. In his book, Friesen states that "97% of MPD patients have suffered serious abuse at an early age. Most of them

---

44 Steven Drizin & Richard Leo, "The Problem of False Confessions in the Post-DNA World" (2004) 82 *North Carolina Law Review* 891; Saul M. Kassin et al., "Police-Induced Confessions: Risk Factors and Recommendations" (2010) 34 *Law and Human Behavior* 49.

45 Deborah Davis & Elizabeth F. Loftus, "The Scientific Status of 'Repressed' and 'Recovered' Memories of Sexual Abuse" in Jennifer L. Skeem, Kevin S. Douglas, & Scott O. Lilienfeld, eds., *Psychological Science in the Courtroom: Consensus and Controversy* (New York: Guilford Press, 2009) 55; D. Stephen Lindsay & J. Don Read, "Psychotherapy and Memories of Childhood Sexual Abuse: A Cognitive Perspective" (1994) 8 *Applied Cognitive Psychology* 281.

46 James G. Friesen, *Uncovering the Mystery of MPD* (Eugene, OR: Wipf and Stock, 1997).

have been abused sexually."[47] However, there are no references to indicate the sources of these statistics. *The Courage to Heal: A Guide for Women Survivors of Child Sexual Abuse* was another popular book used as recommended reading by some therapists in the 1990s. It suggested that:

> If you are unable to remember any specific instances . . . but still have a feeling that something abusive happened to you, it probably did. . . . If you think you were abused and your life shows the symptoms, then you were. . . . Writing gives you the opportunity to define your own reality. . . . You [the therapist] must believe your client was sexually abused even if she sometimes doubts it.[48]

Again, no research was cited to support the authors' claims. These types of suggestions pose the risk of encouraging people to recall instances of abuse that may not have occurred. While it is possible that such interventions are useful for people who have been abused, the problem lies in their potential to create vivid, salient, richly detailed, but false memories in people with no history of abuse. Repeatedly imagining a non-experienced event can inflate confidence that the event occurred.[49] Memory researchers were skeptical that people could completely forget traumatic experiences.[50] The evidence suggests that when a person has been traumatized, they are likely to struggle with intrusive, uncontrollable remembering, not forgetting.[51] Thus, a controversy arose. Based on case studies of their patients, many therapists believed that traumatic memories could be repressed, sometimes for years or decades, and recovered

---

47 *Ibid.* at 42.

48 Ellen Bass & Laura Davis, *The Courage to Heal: A Guide for Women Survivors of Child Sexual Abuse* (New York: Perennial Library, 1988).

49 Lyn M. Goff & Henry L. Roediger, "Imagination Inflation for Action Events: Repeated Imaginings Lead to Illusory Recollections" (1998) 26 *Memory & Cognition* 20–33.

50 David S. Holmes, "The Evidence for Repression: An Examination of Sixty Years of Research" in Jerome L. Singer, ed., *Repression and Dissociation: Implications for Personality Theory, Psychopathology, and Health* (Chicago: University of Chicago Press, 1995) 85; J.D. Read, "The Recovered/False Memory Debate: Three Steps Forward, Two Steps Back?" (1999) 7 *Expert Evidence* 1.

51 Deborah Davis & Elizabeth F. Loftus, "Expectancies, Emotion and Memory Reports for Visual Events" in James R. Brockmole, ed., *The Visual World in Memory* (New York: Psychology Press, 2009) 178; Elke Geraerts, "Cognitive Underpinnings of Recovered Memories of Childhood Abuse" in Robert F. Belli, ed., *True and False Recovered Memories: Toward a Reconciliation of the Debate* (New York: Springer, 2012) 175; Mark L. Howe & Lauren M. Knott, "The Fallibility of Memory in Judicial Processes: Lessons from the Past and Their Modern Consequences" (2015) 23 *Memory* 633; Richard J. McNally, "Debunking Myths About Trauma and Memory" (2005) 50 *Canadian Journal of Psychiatry* 817.

through therapeutic intervention.[52] Social scientists, however, wondered if some recovered memories were false memories that had been inadvertently implanted in therapy.[53] Social scientists conducted laboratory investigations to explore the topic further and found that memories could be implanted quite easily, with some people being especially suggestible.[54]

Researchers could not ethically set out to implant memories of abuse in their participants, but they designed studies to determine whether more benign historical memories could be cultivated. In 1995, Loftus and Pickrell[55] sought to implant a memory of being lost in the mall around the age of five, crying, being rescued by an elderly person, and being reunited with parents. Twenty-four people between the ages of eighteen and fifty-three were asked to try to remember four childhood memories (three of which were true, as reported by a parent or close relative of each participant). Two interviews about the four events were conducted over a period of weeks and 25 percent of participants came to recall most or all of the lost in the mall event as true.[56]

Other studies have demonstrated that illusory memories can be induced for having spilled a bowl of punch on the bride's parents at a wedding,[57] being attacked by a vicious dog,[58] and being hospitalized overnight for an ear infection.[59] Such studies typically find that false memories can be implanted in a quarter to a third of participants.[60] Lindsay and colleagues introduced photographs into their study of implanted memories, based on the practice of some therapists who have encouraged their patients to

---

52 J.L. Alpert et al., "Final Conclusions of the American Psychological Association Working Group on Investigation of Memories of Childhood Abuse" (1998) 4 *Psychology, Public Policy, and Law* 933; Richard J. McNally, *Remembering Trauma* (Cambridge: Belknap Press/Harvard University Press, 2003).

53 Howe & Knott, above note 51; Elizabeth F. Loftus, "The Myth of Repressed Memory and the Realities of Science" (1996) 3 *Clinical Psychology: Science and Practice* 356.

54 Read, above note 50.

55 Elizabeth F. Loftus & Jacqueline E. Pickrell, "The Formation of False Memories" (1995) 25 *Psychiatric Annals* 720.

56 *Ibid.*

57 Ira E. Hyman, Troy H. Husband, & F. James Billings, "False Memories of Childhood Experiences" (1995) 9 *Applied Cognitive Psychology* 181.

58 Stephen Porter, John C. Yuille, & Darrin R. Lehman, "The Nature of Real, Implanted, and Fabricated Memories for Emotional Childhood Events: Implications for the Recovered Memory Debate" (1999) 23 *Law and Human Behavior* 517.

59 James Ost, Alan Costall, & Ray Bull, "A Perfect Symmetry? A Study of Retractors' Experiences of Making and then Repudiating Claims of Early Sexual Abuse" (2002) 8 *Psychology, Crime & Law* 155.

60 Davis & Loftus, above note 51.

look at old photographs to assist them in recovering "repressed" memories of childhood sexual abuse.[61] They had participants try to remember three childhood incidents: two true incidents and one false event ("sliming" the teacher's desk in grade one or two). Half were given class photos from the year the events were said to have occurred. Among participants in the non-photo group, almost 50 percent developed partial or complete memories for the false event after the second interview, while the rate was 78 percent for the photo group. The authors speculated that the photograph may have enhanced the credibility of the suggested false event.

The Paul Ingram case in the United States provides a dramatic illustration of how false memories can be created.[62] After repeated, aggressive, suggestive police questioning, as well as hypnosis, Ingram came to believe he had sexually abused his children. The accusations included ritualistic, satanic abuse, and murders (although no bodies were ever found). Richard Ofshe, a prominent researcher in false confessions literature, set out to demonstrate that these memories could have been implanted. He told Ingram about an incident of abuse that was not included in the allegations against him. After thinking and praying over the course of a day, Ingram not only agreed that he had committed the fictitious crime, he provided a richly detailed account of the event.[63]

Trying to evaluate the veracity and accuracy of memories of childhood sexual abuse is a contentious task. We do not want to deny the existence of sexual abuse that did occur, but we do not want to wrongly convict innocent people accused of abuse.[64] Richard McNally and colleagues sought to determine if true and false traumatic memories might be distinguished by the physiological arousal experienced by the people recounting them. To this end, they interviewed a sample of people who reported having been abducted by aliens—a highly improbable traumatic experience. They found that the physiological reactions and emotional self-reports of participants recounting alien abductions were indistinguishable from those accompanying reports of other traumatic experiences (e.g., military combat).[65]

61 D. Stephen Lindsay et al., "True Photographs and False Memories" (2004) 15 *Psychological Science* 149.

62 Lawrence Wright, *Remembering Satan* (New York: Knopf, 1994).

63 Richard Ofshe & Ethan Watters, *Making Monsters: False Memories, Psychotherapy, and Sexual Hysteria* (Berkeley: University of California Press, 1994).

64 Alan D. Gold, *Expert Evidence in Criminal Law: The Scientific Approach*, 2d ed. (Toronto: Irwin Law, 2009).

65 Richard J. McNally et al., "Psychophysiological Responding During Script-Driven Imagery in People Reporting Abduction by Space Aliens" (2004) 15 *Psychological Science* 493.

The weight of the scientific evidence clearly indicates that corroboration is vital in cases of recovered memories of sexual abuse. Both the Canadian Psychological Association[66] and the Canadian Psychiatric Association[67] have policy statements warning of the dangers of convicting someone based solely on memories recovered in therapy.

1) Recommendations

In 1998, several prominent memory researchers collaborated to form the American Psychological Association Working Group on Investigation of Memories of Childhood Abuse. Their conclusions are as follows:[68]

1) Controversies regarding adult recollections should not be allowed to obscure the fact that child sexual abuse is a complex and pervasive problem in America that has historically gone unacknowledged.
2) Most people who were sexually abused as children remember all or part of what happened to them.
3) It is possible for memories of abuse that have been forgotten for a long time to be remembered.
4) It is also possible to construct convincing pseudo-memories for events that never occurred.
5) There are gaps in our knowledge about the processes that lead to accurate and inaccurate recollections of childhood abuse.

Lindsay and Read[69] outlined the factors to be considered when trying to determine the accuracy of recovered-memory reports:

- the presence/absence of converging evidence
- how the memories came about (the less evidence of suggestive memory-recovery work, the greater the confidence)

---

66 Canadian Psychological Association, "Policy Statement: Convictions Based Solely on Recovered Memories" (1998), online: www.cpa.ca/aboutcpa/policystatements/#convictions.

67 Stella Blackshaw et al., "Position Statement of the Canadian Psychiatric Association: Adult Recovered Memories of Childhood Sexual Abuse" (1996) 41 *Canadian Journal of Psychiatry* 305.

68 Alpert et al., above note 52.

69 D. Stephen Lindsay & J. Don Read, "The Recovered Memories Controversy: Where Do We Go from Here?" in Graham Davies & Tim Dalgleish, eds., *Recovered Memories: Seeking the Middle Ground* (New York: Wiley, 2001) 71.

- the nature and clarity of the memories (with more credence given to detailed, integrated recollections than to vague feelings)
- the likelihood of the alleged events being forgotten if they had actually occurred (e.g., when and how often the abuse is said to have occurred, the probability that the person would have encountered reminders, the overall memorability of the alleged events)
- the plausibility of having memories to recover (e.g., less credence given to reports of events said to have occurred before two years of age)
- the base rate of the alleged type of abuse

Claims of recovered memories became much less common after the 1990s. Some people who brought charges against an alleged abuser later retracted their claims.[70] Some people who had been accused of abuse based on memories recovered in therapy brought successful lawsuits against the therapists.[71] Despite great advances in our understanding of recovered memories in recent years, it appears there may still be a split between social scientists and therapeutic practitioners. Recent surveys have revealed that the majority of practitioners: (1) believe that memories are often repressed, and (2) believe that repressed memories can be accurately retrieved through therapeutic intervention.[72] Social scientists would likely consider these claims contentious in view of the findings of memory research conducted over the past thirty years.

G. CONCLUSION

As we mentioned at the outset, our brains are not repositories of the video stream of life. Despite popular beliefs, we do not store our experienced life events as intact replications that can be accessed and replayed on demand. Decades of psychological research on human memory have demonstrated that remembering is very much a reconstructive process. Subjectively, it may seem like we are watching a movie, but the picture that we observe is a creation of our own making. Notwithstanding the scientific evidence, the "memory as video" belief is widespread. In recent

---

70 Ost, Costall, & Bull, above note 59.

71 Jeffrey A. Mullins, "Has Time Rewritten Every Line? Recovered-Memory Therapy and the Potential Expansion of Psychotherapist Liability" (1996) 53 *Washington and Lee Law Review* 763.

72 Howe & Knott, above note 51.

surveys, half (50 percent) of the respondents agreed that "human memory works like a video camera, accurately recording the events we see and hear so that we can review and inspect them later."[73] Commenting on the impact of suggestion on the creation of false memories, Wells and Loftus[74] cautioned that the extant research "should give pause to investigators and others who think that they are extracting recalcitrant, accurate memories from witnesses and suspects by using techniques that resemble the ones that psychologists have studied."

---

73 Daniel J. Simons & Christopher F. Chabris, "What People Believe About How Memory Works: A Representative Survey of the U.S. Population" (2001) 6 *PLoS One* e22757; Daniel J. Simons & Christopher F. Chabris, "Common (Mis)Beliefs About Memory: A Replication and Comparison of Telephone and Mechanical Turk Survey Methods" (2012) 7 *PLoS One* e51876.

74 Gary L. Wells & Elizabeth F. Loftus, "Eyewitness Memory for People and Events" in Randy K. Otto & Irving B. Weiner, eds., *Handbook of Psychology, Vol. 11: Forensic Psychology*, 2d ed. (Hoboken: Wiley, 2013) 617 at 624.

CHAPTER 22

Probability

Alison Weir

A. INTRODUCTION

Statistical analysis assumes one has a sample and asks questions about the populations that could have generated the observed sample. Probability theory assumes everything is known about a population and asks questions about potential samples. Probability is littered with paradoxes and surprising results, including the following examples:

1) *The Birthday Problem*: How many people should you have at a party if you want there to be a 50 percent chance of at least two people sharing the same birthday?

   Answer: Twenty-three.

   Many people find this number surprisingly small, but the question is about pairs of people and twenty-three party-goers allows for 253 different pairings. Enough that there is a 50 percent chance that at least one pair will share a birthday.
2) *The Monty Hall Problem*: In the old television game show *Let's Make a Deal*, a contestant is asked to pick one of three doors. Behind one door is a valuable prize and, behind the other two, a goat. The contestant gets to pick a door, which remains unopened. The host then opens one of the other two doors, revealing a goat. The crux of the contest comes next, when the contestant is asked if he or she wants to keep the original selection or switch to the remaining unopened door. What should the contestant do?

Answer: Switch.

At this point, there are two doors—one has a goat, the other has a car. Intuitively, one may think that each door has a 50 percent chance of having the car behind it. So why is switching the right choice? The key to the answer is that, when the contestant originally chose a door, there was a one in three chance of winning the prize. The door that was opened to reveal a goat was not opened randomly. Instead, the producers of the show made certain to open a door that hid a goat. As a result, the contestant's original one-third chance remains one third. Looking at it another way, the chance of the contestant having made the wrong choice remains two-thirds, and therefore switching doubles the chance of winning.

3) *The Boy-Girl Problem*: Sam has two children. The older child is a girl. What is the probability that both children are girls? Ali has two children. At least one of them is a boy. What is the probability that both children are boys?

   Answer: There is no controversy about the first question—there is a 50 percent chance both of Sam's children are girls. But we cannot answer the second question because there is a subtle paradox arising from the two possible ways to approach the problem of Ali's children.

   - Look at all *families* with two children, one of whom is a boy. The possible outcomes for these families are, by birth order, boy/boy, boy/girl, or girl/boy. The probability that both children are boys is 33 percent.
   - Look at all *boys* with exactly one sibling. The possible outcomes are that the sibling can be either a boy or a girl. The probability that both children are boys is 50 percent.

B. PROBABILITY

Statisticians and mathematicians express probability as a number between 0 and 1 that represents the degree of belief that a particular event will occur. An event with probability 1 is certain to occur, and an event with probability 0 is certain not to occur. Outside of these fields, it is typical to express the number as a percentage. This is largely a formatting issue. Where a statistician might express a confidence level of .33, an economist will be 33 percent confident.

1) Where Does Probability Come From?

P(A) is statistical notation for the probability that event A will occur. There are two primary methods of assigning probability to events:

a) Method 1: Empirical or Relative Frequency Probability

P(A) is determined through sampling—estimating the characteristics of a large population by examining a subset that is intended to be representative. A small sample may have an average probability at large variance from the population average, but as the sample size increases, the sample average will more reliably approximate the population average.[1] When designing a study, statisticians must determine the level of certainty (accuracy) needed.

Empirical or relative frequency is determined through observation of a large number of repeated trials.

Repeat a process many times and tabulate the occurrences of event A.

$$P(A) = \text{The probability of an event } A = \frac{\text{How many times A occurs}}{\text{How many trials}}$$

b) Method 2: Subjective Probability and the Legal Burden of Proof

Subjective probabilities are values assigned by individuals based on how likely they think events are to occur. Subjective probabilities cannot be validated; different experts may give different subjective probabilities.

The standard for burden of proof—beyond a reasonable doubt in criminal law—makes it tempting for triers of fact (a judge or jury, depending on the type of trial) to construct subjective probabilities to draw conclusions. In a criminal trial, an approach by the trier of fact that creates subjective probabilities to arrive at a verdict does not meet the high standard of "reasonable doubt" as enunciated by the Supreme Court of Canada:

> [9] . . . There was misdirection because the trial judge equated "reasonable doubt" with "an ordinary everyday phrase" when in fact it is far from a "perfectly ordinary concept" (p. 234). Scott C.J.M. observed that the standard by which everyday decisions are typically made is "a standard of probability and, often within that, at the low end of the scale" (p. 235) and not a standard of proof "beyond a reasonable doubt."
>
> . . .

1 See "The Law of Large Numbers," Encyclopedia Britannica, online: www.britannica.com/science/law-of-large-numbers.

> [24] Ordinarily even the most important decision [*sic*] of a lifetime are based upon carefully calculated risks. They are made on the assumption that certain events will in all likelihood take place or that certain facts are in all probability true. Yet to invite jurors to apply to a criminal trial the standard of proof used for even the important decisions in life runs the risk of significantly reducing the standard to which the prosecution must be held.
>
> . . .
>
> [33] In the United Kingdom juries are instructed that they may convict if they are "sure" or "certain" of the accused's guilt. Yet, in my view, that instruction standing alone is both insufficient and potentially misleading. Being "certain" is a conclusion which a juror may reach but, it does not indicate the route the juror should take in order to arrive at the conclusion.
>
> [34] It is only *after* proper instructions have been given as to the meaning of the expression "beyond a reasonable doubt" that a jury may be advised that they can convict if they are "certain" or "sure" that the accused is guilty.[2]

In model jury instructions addressing the fundamental principles of the presumption of innocence, burden of proof, and reasonable doubt, it is made clear that a juror's belief in the accused being "probably guilty" or "likely guilty" is insufficient to meet the standard of "beyond a reasonable doubt."[3]

2) The Law of Large Numbers and the Non-existent Law of Averages

Figure 22.1 shows the empirical frequency of "heads" for five simulations of 500 coin tosses. Notice that the probabilities are converging on one half, but they are doing it slowly and unevenly. Even after 500 tosses, none of the simulations resulted in exactly 50 percent heads, with one of simulation consistently showing more than 50 percent heads.

---

2 *R. v. Lifchus*, [1997] 3 S.C.R. 320.

3 National Judicial Institute, "Model Jury Instructions," online: www.nji-inm.ca/index.cfm/publications/model-jury-instructions/preliminary-instructions/fundamental-principles/presumption-of-innocence-burden-of-proof-and-reasonable-doubt.

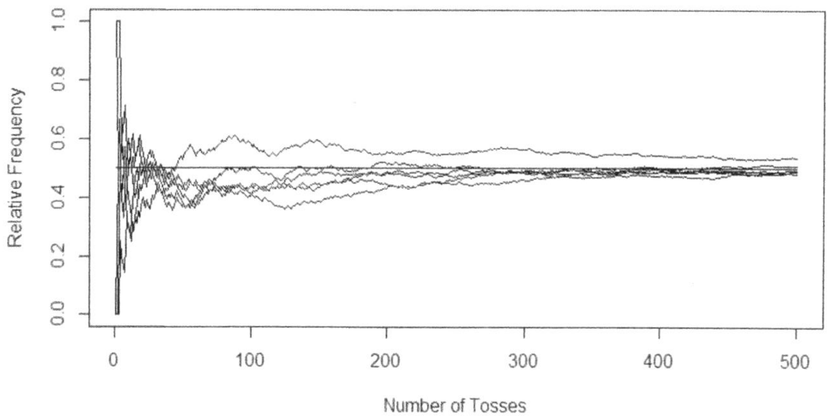

FIGURE 22.1. Graph depicting the empirical frequency of "heads" for five simulations of 500 coin tosses. (All figures and tables have been created by the author unless otherwise stated.)

Many people confuse the law of large numbers with the so-called law of averages. The law of averages is an undefined term that is often used to argue that averages converge to a constant after some, usually small, number of trials. The law of large numbers is a clearly defined mathematical theorem that can be used to argue that averages converge to a constant after a large (possibly huge) number of trials. Figure 22.1 shows that the sequence of averages in the coin tossing experiment definitely do not converge in a short run of fifty trials, and will not necessarily converge in the longer run of 500 trials.

Averages have no predictive power in small samples. For example, suppose that on 17 June, the local television weather reporter says, "It's been a dry month. So far we've had only 10 millimetres of rain. Historically, the average June rainfall is 71.5 millimetres, so by the law of averages, we're due for a lot of rain over the next few weeks." This is wrong. There is no reason that every June must have an average amount of rain. A sample size of one (a single June) is far too small to expect convergence around an average.

a) The Gambler's Fallacy

The gambler's fallacy is another example of the misunderstanding of chance based on the concept of a law of averages. The gambler's fallacy assumes that runs of wins or losses will be "corrected." That each successive heads in a coin flip increases the chances that the next flip will be tails, but every individual flip has a 50 percent chance of being heads (or tails). Past results have no effect on the probable outcome of the next result.

3) Joint, Marginal, and Conditional Probability

Table 22.1 presents data on indictments involving cases of murder in Florida from 1976 to 1987. The data looks at three variables: the defendant's race (black, white), the victim's race (black, white), and the death penalty (yes, no). Joint probabilities assess the impact of all three variables. Marginal probabilities assess one or two variables. Conditional probabilities assess the remaining variable(s) when the other(s) are specified.

TABLE 22.1. Data Studying the Effects of Racial Characteristics of Convicted Murderers, Their Penalties, and Their Victims[4]

		Death Penalty			
Defendant	Victim	Yes	No	Total	Total
White	White	53	414	467	483
	Black	0	16	16	
Black	White	11	37	48	191
	Black	4	139	143	
	Total	68	606	684	674

a) Simpson's Paradox

Tables 22.2–22.4 illustrate Simpson's Paradox, which was named after E.H. Simpson, the researcher credited with identifying the phenomenon in 1951.[5] The paradox states that a trend observed between two variables may reverse when a third variable is introduced to the analysis as a condition: "Simpson's paradox refers to a phenomenon whereby the association between a pair of variables (*X*, *Y*) reverses sign upon conditioning of a third variable, *Z* regardless of the value taken by *Z*."[6]

4 John C. MacAdams, "Racial Disparity and the Death Penalty," (1998) 61 *Law and Contemporary Problems* 153, online: scholarship.law.duke.edu/lcp/vol61/iss4/8. See also David C. Baldus et al., "Racial Discrimination and the Death Penalty in the Post-Furman Era: An Empirical and Legal Overview with Recent Findings from Philadelphia," (1998) 83 *Cornell Law Review* 1638, online: scholarship.law.cornell.edu/clr/vol83/iss6/6.

5 E.H. Simpson, "The Interpretation of Interaction in Contingency Tables" (1951) 13 *Journal of the Royal Statistical Society, Series B* 238.

6 Judea Pearl, "Comment: Understanding Simpson's Paradox" (2014) 68 *The American Statistician* 8 at 8.

TABLE 22.2. Data Studying the Effects of Racial Characteristics of Convicted Murderers, Their Penalties, and Their Victims, Specifically with Respect to Outcome, Type of Probability, and Probability (Represented as a Percentage)

Outcome	Type of Probability	Probability
White defendant, black victim, death penalty	Joint	0÷647=0 or 0%
White defendant	Marginal	483÷674=0.7166 or 71.66%
White defendant, death penalty	Marginal	(53+0)÷647=0.0786 or 7.86%
Death penalty, given that the defendant was white	Conditional	(53+0)÷483=0.1097 or 10.97%
White defendant, given that the death penalty was imposed	Conditional	(53+0)÷68=0.7794 or 77.94%

Conditional probabilities are written:

$$P(\textit{death penalty} \mid \textit{white}) = \frac{53+0}{483} = 0.1097 = \frac{P(\textit{death penalty} \text{ and } \textit{white})}{P(\textit{white})}$$

and

$$P(\textit{white} \mid \textit{death penalty}) = \frac{53+0}{68} = 0.7794 = \frac{P(\textit{white} \text{ and } \textit{death penalty})}{P(\textit{death penalty})}$$

TABLE 22.3. Probability of the Death Penalty, Conditional on the Race of the Defendant

Defendant's Race	Probability of Death Penalty
White	(53+0)÷483=0.1097 *or* 10.97%
Black	(11+4)÷191=0.0785 *or* 7.85%

TABLE 22.4. Probability of the Death Penalty, Conditional on the Race of the Defendant and the Race of the Victim

Defendant's Race	Victim's Race	Probability of Death Penalty
White	White	53÷467=0.1135 *or* 11.35%
	Black	0÷16=0 *or* 0%
Black	White	11÷48=0.2292 *or* 22.92%
	Black	4÷143=0.0284 *or* 2.84%

Tables 22.3 and 22.4 suggest contradictory conclusions. Table 22.3 suggests that a white defendant is more likely to get the death penalty than a black defendant. Table 22.4, by adding the additional factor of race of the victim, suggests that (1) if the victim is white, a black defendant is more likely to get the death penalty than a white defendant; and (2) if the victim is black, a black defendant is more likely to get the death penalty than a

white defendant. This paradoxical result is explained by the small number of murders in the black-on-white and white-on-black categories and the large probability of the death penalty in the black-on-white category. The correct conclusions must come from Table 22.4; death penalty rates are not adequately described by averaging over the victim's race.

i) Graduate School Admissions at UC Berkeley, 1973

In 1973, the University of California-Berkeley was sued for sex discrimination. The numbers looked bad for Berkeley: the graduate schools had accepted 44 percent of male applicants and only 35 percent of female applicants. But when Berkeley's defence team broke down the applications and admissions by department, the direction of discrimination switched. Men more often applied to science departments, while women inclined towards humanities. Science departments accepted a large percentage of a small number of qualified applicants. Humanities departments accepted a small percentage of a large number of qualified applicants.[7] The conclusion is that sexism occurred before Berkeley saw the applications: women were directed by their socialization and education towards the fields of graduate study that are generally more crowded.

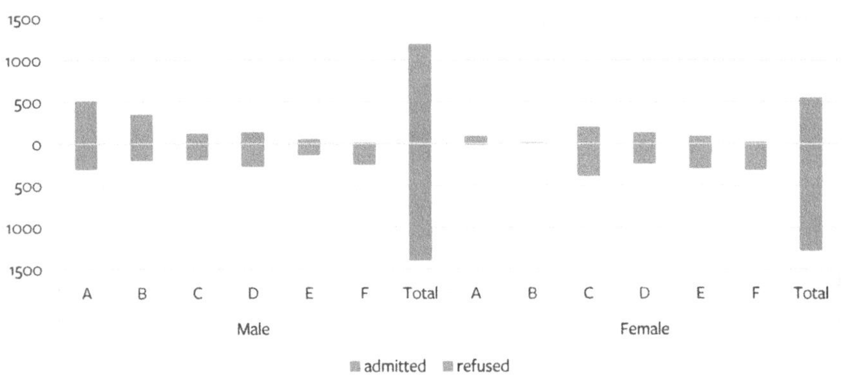

FIGURE 22.2. Application Decision Split by Gender and Department.

The number of admitted applicants are shown as the heights of the upper (blue) rectangles and the number of refused applications are shown as the heights of the lower (orange) rectangles. The seven bars on the left show application status for

7 P.J. Bickel, E.A. Hammel, & J.W. O'Connell, "Sex Bias in Graduate Admissions: Data From Berkeley" (1975) 4175 *Science* 187 at 398–404.

men within each of seven graduate departments (labelled A to F) and their totals. The seven bars on the right are data for female applicants. This data is a subset of all Berkeley graduate application data from fall 1973. The department names themselves are protected but, from the admission numbers, it is reasonable to conclude that departments A and B are science departments, since a large percentage of a small number of qualified applicants were accepted.[8]

Gender				Male			
Department	A	B	C	D	E	F	Total
Applications	825	560	325	417	191	272	2590
Admitted	512	353	120	138	53	16	1192
% Admitted	62%	63%	37%	33%	28%	6%	46%

Gender				Female			
Department	A	B	C	D	E	F	Total
Applications	108	25	593	375	393	341	1835
Admitted	89	17	202	131	94	24	557
% Admitted	82%	68%	34%	35%	24%	7%	30%

C. INDEPENDENCE

Statistically, events are called independent if the probability of occurrence of event A is unrelated to the occurrence (or non-occurrence) of event B. For example, A is the event of a coin landing heads up and B is the event of a die landing with five spots up. There is a 50 percent chance the coin will land heads up regardless of what happens with the die. Two events are considered independent if the probability of A conditional on B, the probability of A conditional on not-B, and the marginal probability of A are all the same. If events A and B are independent, then the probability they both occur equals the product of their individual probabilities:

$$P(A \text{ and } B) = P(A)P(B)$$

Statistically, events are called dependent if the probability of occurrence of event A differs when event B does and does not occur. For example, if we define my carrying an umbrella as event A and the happening of a rainstorm as event B, then event B (rain) is an independent variable of event A, whereas event A is a dependent variable of event B. This is so because the rain will fall or not fall regardless (independent) of whether I am prepared with an umbrella, whereas I am much more likely (dependent) to carry

8 Data from https://en.wikipedia.org/wiki/Simpson's_paradox.

an umbrella if it is raining. Dependent events are not necessarily causal events. They may be necessary conditions that allow but do not motivate or encourage an event; my carrying of an umbrella will not cause a rainstorm.

If event A is dependent on B, then the probability that they both occur equals the product of the probability A occurs, conditional on B having occurred, and the probability B occurs:

$$P(A \text{ and } B) = P(A \mid B)P(B) = P(B \mid A)P(A).$$

1) The Wrongful Conviction of Sally Clark

Sally Clark, an English solicitor, was convicted of murdering her first two children.[9] When Clark's first child died, his death was attributed to Sudden Infant Death Syndrome (SIDS). When her second child died, suspicions were raised about both deaths and she was arrested.

Clark was alone with each child at the time of death. Trial evidence consisted primarily of expert testimony. Sir Roy Meadow, Professor Emeritus of Paediatrics and Child Health at St. James's University Hospital in Leeds, testified using data from his own research. He stated that the probability of a SIDS death, in a household with no SIDS risk factors (as was the case here), was 1 in 8,543. Professor Meadow then stated that the probability of two SIDS deaths in Sally Clark's home was about 1 in 73 million live births:

$$\frac{1}{8{,}543} \times \frac{1}{8{,}543} = \frac{1}{72{,}982{,}849}$$

Clark was convicted of two counts of murder and received two life sentences.

The calculations used to convict Clark, however, were wrong. In the calculation the professor assumed the two deaths were independent. This could only be true if SIDS occurred randomly, without any chance of hidden, unknown causes that would make some families more vulnerable to SIDS than other families. It was improper for Meadow to assume that multiple SIDS deaths in one family are independent events.

In addition to the grave calculation error, new exculpatory evidence was later discovered and, on her second appeal, her convictions were quashed and she was released from prison. In the appellate court's 2003 decision, Lord Justice Kay highlighted that the trial judge tried to divert the attention of the jury from relying on the statistical evidence, re-stating the caution the trial judge provided to the jury:

9 *R. v. Clark*, [2003] EWCA Crim 1020.

> I should . . . just sound a word of caution about the statistics. However compelling you may find them to be, we do not convict people in these courts on statistics. It would be a terrible day if that were so. If there is one SIDS death in a family, it does not mean that there cannot be another one in the same family.[10]

Sadly, the whole experience had broken Clark and she died a few years later of acute alcohol poisoning.

2) Likely and Unlikely Events

A fair coin is tossed ten consecutive times. Which of the following outcomes is most likely?

Choice #1:	H	H	T	H	T	H	T	T	H	T
Choice #2:	T	T	T	T	T	T	T	T	T	T

Our natural reaction might be to focus on the unlikelihood of ten identical results and pick choice #1 as the most likely because it looks more like what we would expect to get from ten coin tosses. This is a fallacy. The key to the solution is that each is a specific sequence. The first result is no more random that the second and, therefore, the two sequences are equally likely. They both have probability:

$$\left(\frac{1}{2}\right)^{12} = \frac{1}{1{,}024}\ .$$

a) The Ecological Fallacy

The ecological fallacy confuses the specific with the general. The probability of any particular mother giving birth this year to her eighth child, all of whom are boys, is indeed very low. But the probability of this happening in this year to at least one mother in the world is very high.

3) Combining Probabilities

Evidence is often the totality of a combination of components. The evidence may be "he was left-handed and bald" or "either event A or event B occurred." To attach a probability to such evidentiary statements, it is often necessary to combine the probabilities of its components.

---

10 *Ibid.* at para. 104.

- If two events, A and B, are independent, then the probability of A and B both occurring is the product of their individual probabilities.

$$P(A \text{ and } B) = P(A)P(B) \leftrightarrow A \text{ and } B \text{ are independent}$$

- If two events, A and B, are dependent, then the probability of A and B both occurring is the product of (1) the probability of A occurring and (2) the probability of B occurring, conditional on A having occurred.

$$P(A \text{ or } B) = P(A) + P(B)P(B) - P(A \text{ and } B)$$

- If two events, A and B, are mutually exclusive (meaning A cannot occur at the same time as B occurs), then the probability of either A or B occurring is the sum of their individual probabilities.

$$P(A \text{ or } B) = P(A) + P(B) \leftrightarrow A \text{ and } B \text{ are mutually exclusive}$$

- If two events, A and B, are not mutually exclusive (meaning it is possible that A and B occur at the same time), then the probability of wither A or B (or both of them) occurring is the sum of their individual probabilities minus the probability of both A and B occurring.

$$P(A \text{ or } B) = P(A) + P(B) - P(A \text{ and } B)$$

- The probability of at least one event occurring out of multiple events is equal to one minus the probability of none of the events occurring.

$$P(\text{not } A) = 1 - P(A) \qquad P(\text{neither } A \text{ nor } B) = 1 - P(A \text{ or } B)$$

4) The Use of Mathematical Probability Evidence by the Prosecution

In 1964, a robbery was committed when an elderly woman stooped to pick up her dropped groceries as she walked home from the shops. As she was bending down, she was shoved from behind; when she looked up all she saw was a woman running away. A witness, who did not see the robbery but did see two people making a ruckus, described a blonde pony-tailed woman and a black man with a moustache and beard running into a car, part of which was yellow. A husband and wife, Malcolm Ricardo Collins and Janet Louise Collins, matched this description and were arrested. During their trial,[11] a mathematician called by the prosecution provided the table of probabilities seen in Table 22.5.

11 *People v. Collins*, 68 Cal. 2d 319 (1968).

TABLE 22.5. Table of Probabilities Presented at Trial[12]

Event	Probability
Yellow car	1 in 10
Man with moustache	1 in 4
Girl with pony tail	1 in 10
Girl with blonde hair	1 in 3
Negro man with beard	1 in 10
Interracial couple in a car	1 in 1,000

The expert multiplied the six probabilities, and stated that the probability of all six events occurring was 1 in 12,000,000. The Collinses were convicted. They appealed and were released. On appeal, the court held that the expert's probability technique could not be used in this case as the related testimony caused a fatal error and distorted the jury's fact-finding role. Justice Sullivan stated:

> Mathematics, a veritable sorcerer in our computerized society, while assisting the trier of fact in the search for truth must not cast a spell over him. We conclude that on the record before us defendant should not have had his guilt determined by the odds and that he is entitled to a new trial. We reverse the judgment.

The mathematician was not an expert in probability or statistics and there were a number of problems not only with his evidence, but with how his evidence was used by the prosecution:

1) All six probabilities were subjective; the expert and his office staff made them up.
2) The six events are not independent, so the joint probability is not the product of the marginal probabilities.
3) The prosecutors used the prosecutor's fallacy (see Section E(1), below, in this chapter) to gain a conviction.

The court held that the case was prejudiced by two errors resulting from the prosecution's introduction and use of statistics:

> (1) The testimony itself lacked an adequate foundation both in evidence and in statistical theory; and (2) the testimony and the manner in which the prosecution used it distracted the jury from its proper and requisite function of weighing the evidence on the issue of guilt, encouraged the jurors to

12 *Ibid.* at 320.

> rely upon an engaging but logically irrelevant expert demonstration, foreclosed the possibility of an effective defence by an attorney apparently unschooled in mathematical refinements, and placed the jurors and defence counsel at a disadvantage in sifting relevant fact from inapplicable theory.[13]

5) The Conjunction Fallacy

The following example of the conjunction fallacy shows how easy it is to fall into a probability trap:

Linda is thirty-one years old, single, outspoken, and very bright. She majored in philosophy. As a student, she was deeply concerned with issues of discrimination and social justice, and also participated in anti-nuclear demonstrations. Which is more probable?

1) *Linda is a bank teller.*
2) *Linda is a bank teller and is active in the feminist movement.*

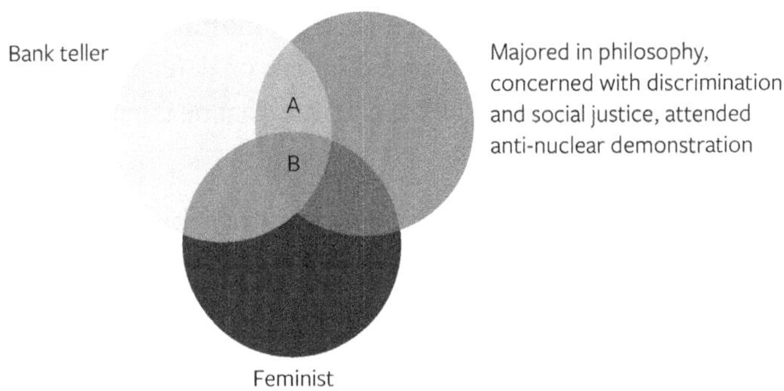

FIGURE 22.3. Diagram depicting all of the various combinations that are possible given the above scenario.

No data is needed to answer this question. Every person fits into exactly one of the seven regions in the Venn diagram. A feminist, philosophy major with a social conscience, who is also a bank teller fits into region B, for example.

Linda is in the green circle since she majored in philosophy and has a social conscience. If Linda is a bank teller and also a feminist, she must be in region B. Since region B is smaller than the region formed by joining A and B, there are fewer people in region B than there are in the region formed by joining A and B. Thus, Linda is less likely to be in region B than

13 *Ibid.* at 327.

she is to be in the region formed by joining A and B. Whenever a new event is created by applying a conjunction to an original event, the probability of the new event cannot be larger than the probability of the original event. Almost always the probability of the new event is smaller than the probability of the original event.

D. UPDATING PROBABILITIES USING BAYES' THEOREM

Bayes' theorem provides a useful method for updating probabilities of events by a three-step process.

1) *Prior probability.* The initial estimate of the probability that event A has occurred is called the prior probability. Of necessity, prior probabilities are often subjective. In a criminal investigation, event A is usually that the suspect is guilty and, assuming prior ignorance regarding the investigation, P(A) = ½ may be assumed to be the prior probability of guilt.
2) *Observed data and information.* Next, some information relevant to the probability that A has occurred is collected. In a criminal investigation, the observed data is the evidence (DNA, admission of guilt, fingerprints, eyewitness identification, etc.).
3) *Posterior probability.* Every piece of evidence causes a revision to the probability of guilt. The prior probability and the observed information are woven together using conditional probability to update the probability that event A has occurred. The final calculation of the probabilities is called the posterior probability.

Bayes' theorem is usually presented using one of many formulas, all of which are intimidating to the uninitiated. The formulas are avoided in the example that follows. The following question was used in a study to assess physicians' statistical knowledge.[14] One percent of women at age forty who participate in routine screening have breast cancer. Eight percent of women with breast cancer will get positive mammographies and 9.6 percent of women without breast cancer will also get mammographies. A woman in this age group had a positive mammography in a routine screening. What is the probability that she actually has breast cancer?

---

14 David M. Eddy, "Probabilistic Reasoning in Clinical Medicine: Problems and Opportunities" in Daniel Kahneman, Paul Slovic, & Amos Tversky, eds., *Judgment Under Uncertainty: Heuristics and Biases* (Cambridge: Cambridge University Press, 1982) at 249.

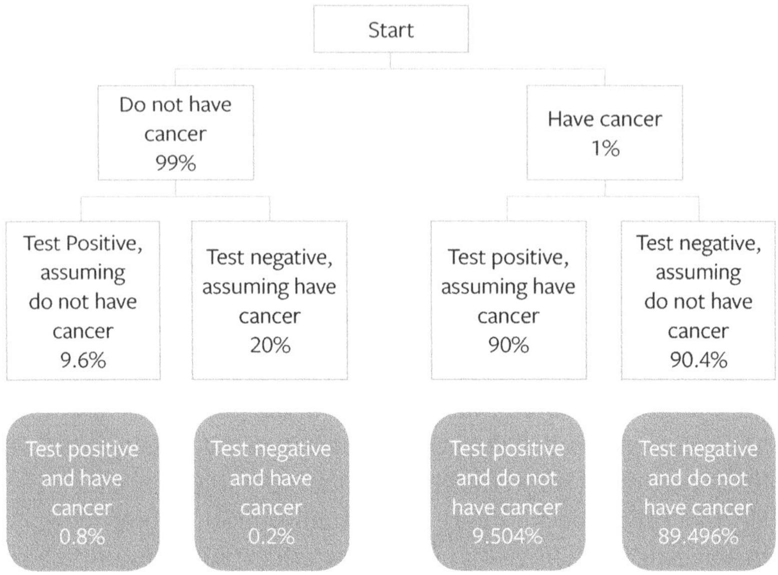

FIGURE 22.4. Tree diagram depicting the above scenario.

Amazingly, only about 15 percent of the respondents gave the correct answer. Most estimated the probability to be between 70 and 80 percent, which is wildly incorrect. Suppose that, for illustrative purposes only, the population consists of 1 million 40-year-old women. Of those 1 million women, about 1 percent (about 10,000 women) will have breast cancer. The rest (about 990,000) will not. The above mammography statistics generate the following outcomes:

1) Of the 10,000 women who have breast cancer, about 80 percent (8,000 women) will test positive and about 20 percent will test negative.
2) Of the 990,000 women who do not have breast cancer, about 9.6 percent (95,040 women) will test positive, and about 90.4 percent will test negative.

Therefore, in a population of 1 million women, about 103,040 women will test positive for breast cancer and about 95,040 of those will be false positives. The probability that a woman with a positive mammography test has breast cancer is calculated as:

$$P(\textit{has cancer} \mid \textit{test positive}) = \frac{\#\ \text{who } \textit{have cancer} \text{ and } \textit{test positive}}{\#\ \textit{who test positive}} = \frac{8{,}000}{10{,}040} = \begin{matrix}0.07764 \text{ or}\\ 7.764\%\end{matrix}$$

The physicians in the original study who estimated the probability to be between 70 and 80 percent committed what is known as the base rate fallacy. They ignored the impact of the low breast cancer rate in 40-year-old women when they estimated the probability of having cancer, given a positive mammography result.

The Royal Statistical Society has advised legal professionals in the United Kingdom to avoid Bayes' formula in presentations to a jury. They recommend the use of a tree diagram, as shown in Figure 22.4.

E. BAYES' THEOREM IN THE COURTROOM

Prior probabilities and conditional probabilities are necessary for Bayes' theorem to apply. In many applications, theoretical results or historical data can be used to construct sensible prior and conditional probabilities. That was the case in the cancer example above.

1) *Prior Probabilities*, P(G) and P(not G). In a criminal trial, there is no reliable way to create justifiable prior probabilities of guilt. The presumption of innocence suggests that the prior probability of guilt always equals zero, but a prior probability of zero cannot be accommodated in Bayes' theorem. The accused's criminal history could help quantify prior probability of current guilt, but it is unethical and unacceptable by the rules of evidence to provide juries with this information. It is possible to use the national census and other demographic data to create a prior probability of guilt, but that too is unethical. Some proponents of Bayes' theorem suggest using prior ignorance to define the prior probabilities (probability of guilt = probability of innocence = ½), but this is no less arbitrary than any other subjective probability. These probabilities are not probabilities of legal findings, they are subjective probabilities representing "strength of belief" in guilt or innocence.
2) *Conditional Probabilities of Evidence*, P(E|G), P(E|not G), P(not E|G), and P(not E|not G). Many of these probabilities have been investigated and quantified in academic research. Care must be taken in combining these probabilities since they are almost certainly not independent events.
3) *Posterior Probabilities*, P(G|E) and P(not G|E). These can be calculated as described in Sections D(1) to D(3), above, in this chapter.

Blair and Rossmo used academic research data to determine the minimum level of pretrial belief (prior probability) in a defendant's guilt.[15] They found that some level of prior probability of guilt is necessary to generate a post-trial belief in a defendant's guilt (the posterior probability of guilt). Blair and Rossmo determined the necessary prior probabilities for seven combinations of three types of evidence: eyewitness identification, confession, and fingerprint. They showed that the level of pretrial belief in a defendant's guilt that is required to reach a level of post-trial belief in a defendant's guilt sufficient for conviction can be very low. The findings are presented in Table 22.6.

TABLE 22.6. Minimum Level of Pretrial Belief in a Defendant's Guilt Necessary to Find Guilt at Trial.*[16]

			Level of pretrial belief of guilt (prior probability of guilt) necessary to ensure:	
Eyewitness Identification	Confession	Fingerprint	Level of post-trial belief of guilt (posterior probability of guilt) >50%	Level of post-trial belief of guilt (posterior probability of guilt) >95%
+	+	+	<1%	<1%
+	-	+	1%	3%
-	+	+	1%	5%
+	+	-	4%	33%
-	-	+	7%	57%
-	+	-	57%	97%
+	-	-	46%	94%

* + indicates evidence in favour of guilt; - indicates evidence in favour of innocence.

According to this table:

- A juror who is originally only 1 percent convinced of the defendant's guilt will become more than 50 percent convinced of guilt after being presented with incriminating fingerprint and eyewitness evidence.
- A juror who is originally only 5 percent convinced of the defendant's guilt will become more than 95 percent convinced of guilt after being presented with incriminating fingerprint evidence and a confession.

15 J. Pete Blair and D. Kim Rossmo, "Evidence in Context: Bayes' Theorem and Investigations" (2010) 13 *Police Quarterly* 123.

16 *Ibid.*, bibliography.

1) The Prosecutor's Fallacy

Suppose a crime has been committed in the era prior to DNA analysis and the perpetrator left some of their blood at the scene. The blood type is rare, only one in every thousand people has this type. A suspect, Joe, who has this blood type, is put on trial. The prosecutor states that the probability an innocent person has the matching blood type is 0.001, or one in a thousand. Therefore, the probability that Joe is innocent is one in a thousand.

The prosecutor's fallacy wrongly equates two probabilities: the probability of finding the evidence (DNA, hair, etc.), where the probability is calculated on the condition that the defendant is innocent, and the probability the defendant is innocent, where the probability is calculated on the condition that the evidence was found. In statistical terms, $P(E|not\ G) = P(not\ G|E)$, where G represents the event that the defendant is guilty and E represents the event that an adult male has a blood type matching that found at the crime scene.

Bayes' theorem must be applied to correctly determine the probability of innocence given the evidence. Returning to the above example, suppose that the crime could only have been committed by an adult male and there are 100,000 adult males in the local population. We would expect about 100 to have the matching blood type. If there is no evidence to link Joe to the crime, then Joe is no more likely than any of the other ninety-nine matching men to have committed the crime. This means that the probability that Joe is innocent is 99 in 100, or 0.99, not the 0.001 claimed by the prosecutor.

The jury needs to know P(not G|E), but they have been presented with $P(E|not\ G)$. They have been presented with the fallacious argument that these two probabilities are the same. Bayes' theorem as applied in Figure 22.5 sorts this out.

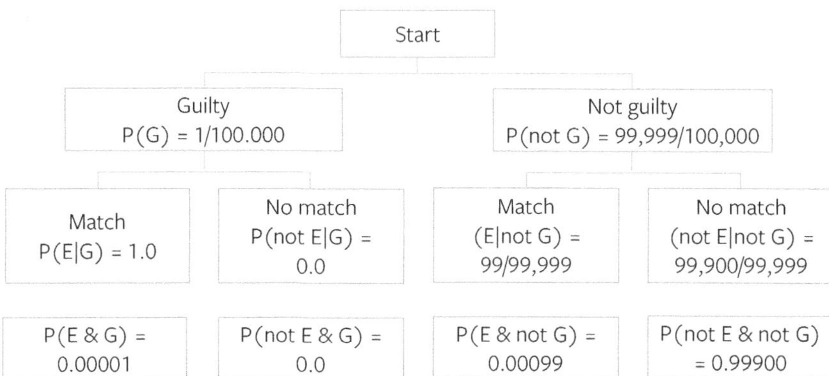

FIGURE 22.5. Tree diagram depicting the above scenario.

The following cases illustrate some instances of the prosecutor's fallacy.

1) *The Sally Clark Case: United Kingdom.* When Sally Clark was convicted in 1999 of smothering her two children, jurors and judges believed the assertion that the probability of two siblings dying of SIDS was too unlikely for her to be innocent. In fact, it is likely rarer for a mother to kill both her children. (See Section C(1), above, in this chapter.)
2) *The Lucia de Berk Case: Netherlands.* Investigators looked into a series of suspicious deaths in hospital wards where Lucia de Berk had worked as a nurse from 1999 to 2001. They found that she had been present when many of the deaths took place. An expert calculated (incorrectly, as it turned out) that the probability that this was simply coincidence was one in 342 million. The prosecutor argued that the probability of her innocence, conditional on her presence at the deaths, was one in 342 million. Lucia de Berk was convicted of seven counts of murder.

   Statistician Richard Gill of the University of Leiden did a statistical analysis and he concluded that a more accurate probability is approximately one in fifty and that it could be as low as one in five. Based on this evidence, Berk was freed on appeal in 2010, after spending six years in prison.
3) *The Malcolm Ricardo and Janet Louise Collins Cases: United States.* In 1964, a robbery was committed. Witnesses suggested a pair of suspects: a blond pony-tailed woman and a black man with a moustache and beard, using a partially yellow car. Malcolm and Janet Collins matched this description and were arrested. During their trial, a mathematical "expert" stated that the probability of such a couple in the general population was one in 12,000,000. The Collins' were convicted. They appealed and were later released. (See Section C(4), above, in this chapter.)

2) The Defence Attorney's Fallacy

The defence attorney's fallacy makes the assumption that everyone with the same physical traits is equally likely to have perpetrated the crime. Probability should be put into perspective using motive, access to the crime scene, and legitimate alibis. The probability should always be stated correctly, for example: "The probability of randomly selecting the observed physical trait from a population of unrelated individuals is one in 10,000."

F. CONCLUSION

Probability quantifies the likelihood, or degree of belief, that a specific event has already occurred when the actual outcome is unknown. A suspect is either guilty or not guilty of an offence. Any attempt to form a subjective probability of guilt lacks precision and, even though a trier of fact may be tempted to base a verdict on a belief that an accused is "probably guilty" or "likely guilty," this is too low a threshold to convict under Canadian law. American jury studies, however, provide insight into the practical realities of the decision-making process of the jury and may serve to inform Canadian criminal lawyers of the potential for success in the case before the court.

All probabilities are either implicitly or explicitly conditional probabilities. Probabilities related to physical characteristics, such as those testified to by forensic scientists, are implicitly conditional on a subset of the general population, such as adult males or adult Caucasian females, where the subset contains only biologically unrelated individuals who have the relevant physical characteristic. The most subtle, and arguably the most important, aspect of the implicit condition in these probabilities is the fact that the population subset does not contain the individual who is actually on trial. All statements of explicitly conditional probability contain implicit conditions like this.

Together, statistics and probability form a specialized discipline, apart from any other, but used by many others. Probability is rife with pitfalls for the unwary. There are many logical fallacies that can trap people unfamiliar with the field. There are many surprising results and many popularly held, yet erroneous, beliefs. Any interpretation or testimony regarding facts or theories touching on probability should be analyzed by a qualified statistician. Statistical experts can be consulted through the statistics department of any Canadian university.

CHAPTER 23

Statistics

Alison Weir

A. INTRODUCTION

Statistics is the analysis of data. Statisticians assist other professionals in the production of trustworthy data by analyzing and modelling data to make the meaning clear so that practical conclusions can be drawn from the information. The role of statistics is to provide mechanisms for the extrapolation of information in sample data to the real world, as well as to develop measures of reliability for all such extrapolations. These measures of reliability are particularly important in law when the trier of fact, whether judge or jury, is tasked with weighing the evidence presented at trial.

All disciplines use statistics:

- Medical researchers use statistically designed experiments.
- Global warming researchers use statistical predictive models with missing data.
- Many industrial decisions are based on statistical systems that have replaced hunches and guesswork.
- Government statistical agencies investigate issues to guide public policy.

A lack of understanding of the basic principles of statistics among the general public has led to significant statistical misinformation being presented in the media and on the Internet. Questionable statistical applications are easy to find even in the research literature of many disciplines. Care should always be taken to use statistical information from proper sources. When in doubt, ask a statistician.

B. WHAT IS DATA?

Data in its most basic form (known as raw data) is a collection of individual pieces of information. Datum can be a number, word, measurement, categorization, even description. Data, correctly analyzed, increases knowledge and informs decisions.

1) Data Can Be Categorical or Interval

Categorical data places subjects into categories. For example: gender (M/F). Interval data is measured or counted. For example: number of siblings, or height.

a) Categorical Data Can Be Nominal or Ordinal

Nominal data has no proper order. For example, gender could be presented (M/F) or (F/M). Ordinal data has an order, but the order is not truly numeric. For example, Likert scales, where respondents rate statements on a scale of 1-to-7, with 1 being "strongly disagree" and 7 "strongly agree," are ordinal data.

b) Interval Data Can Be Continuous or Discrete

Continuous data are real numbers. Practically speaking, any number from any type of measurement is a real number. For example, length, area, and volume are all continuous. Discrete data are numbers from any finite set of numbers. Countable data (for instance, the sequence 2, 4, 6, . . .) and categorical data are also discrete.

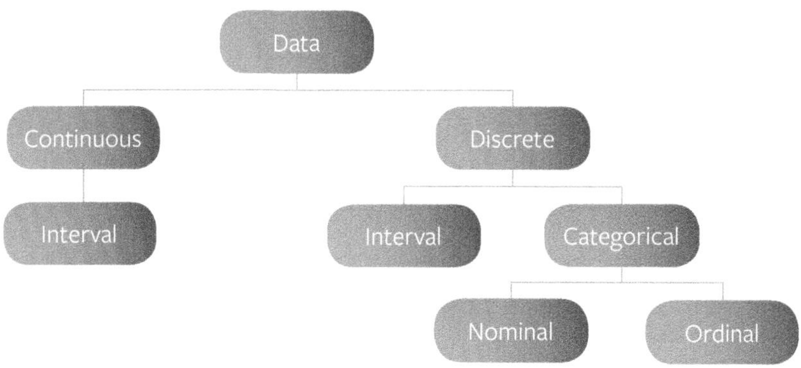

FIGURE 23.1. Types of data. (All figures and tables have been created by the author, unless otherwise stated.)

C. WHERE DOES DATA COME FROM?

Quantitative research relies heavily on two mechanisms for data production and/or collection: designed experiments and observational studies. A third mechanism, the quasi-experiment, is a combination of a designed experiment and an observational study.

1) Designed Experiments

A designed experiment is the optimal method for research data collection. The relevant factors can be isolated, the process can be replicated, and the conclusions can be confirmed or rejected. In a designed experiment, various conditions are applied to individuals according to two principles: (1) randomization, which removes selection bias by using a random mechanism to assign subjects a test status (control group or test group); and (2) control, which removes possible alternative influences so that the outcome may be ascribed to the condition being tested. For example, a weight-loss study may first randomly divide participants into two groups—one receiving the diet under study (the test group) and the other maintaining a normal diet (the control group). Then the test group may be monitored to ensure they are following the diet.

Designed experiments inform the conclusions of chemistry, biology, and psychology.

It is not always possible to place the needed controls on the subjects. In this case, the other influences that may affect the results are measured and accounted for in the modelling and conclusions.

2) Observational Studies

Observational data is neither controlled nor manipulated by an experimenter. There is no randomization or control, usually due to ethical issues. Researchers observe real world scenarios and attempt to quantify their observations. Economics and sociology rely primarily on observational studies.

3) Quasi-experiments

In a quasi-experiment, some influences are controlled, but randomization is not used to assign one of the various conditions to each subject in the experiment. The lack of randomization is usually due to ethical issues. Medical and educational research often rely on quasi-experiments.

a) Data Collection

i) Samples, Populations, and Statistical Inference

The population is the entire group of something—people, animals, cars, sediments, pollution concentrations, sales, temperatures, and so on—that you want to draw conclusions about. Where a population is too large to study in its entirety, a sample is selected to represent the larger group. The more representative the sample is of the population (the more closely the attributes of the sample match the attributes of the population), the more reliable the conclusions will be. One way we try to ensure that the sample is representative of the population is by randomly selecting the individual units included in the sample. Another method is to take as large a sample as practicable.

Statistical inference makes use of information from a sample to draw conclusions (i.e., to make inferences) about the population from which the sample was taken. Because a sample is only a subset of the population, this technique necessarily introduces uncertainty.

ii) Sampling Error

For each population, there are many possible samples and many possible methodologies for collecting a sample. In this section, assume that a good sampling technique is used and all members of the population have equal chance of being included in the sample. If the population is infinite, there are an infinite number of possible samples. Some samples are "good," in that they are representative of the population. Patterns and relationships in good samples have a high likelihood of being similar to the patterns and relationships in the population as a whole. But some samples are "bad." Patterns and relationships in bad samples do not have a high likelihood of being similar to the patterns and relationships in the population as a whole. The difference between the sample and the population is called sampling error, which cannot be controlled by the researcher.

iii) Non-sampling Errors

There are many different types of non-sampling errors. Non-sampling errors occur when a poor sampling methodology has been employed and members of the population do not have equal chances of being included in the sample. Such errors arise when:

- Specific groups in the population are excluded or underrepresented
- Participants select themselves for inclusion in the survey
- There is a low (less than 50 percent) response rate (i.e., too small a proportion of the sample takes part)
- Surveys include poorly worded, ambiguous, or leading questions

Most non-sampling errors introduce bias by under- or over-representing sectors of the population and should be addressed by the researcher.

D. WHAT IS STATISTICS?

The goal of statistics is to draw rational conclusions from data. Statisticians collect, analyse, and interpret data, generally through the extrapolation of information in sample data to the real world. As part of this process, they develop measures of reliability for the extrapolations.

1) Statistics Can Be Inferential or Descriptive

Inferential statistics are used to assess the validity of extrapolating any patterns, relationships, trends, and so on, from an observed data set to a population larger than the observed data. For instance, economists typically estimate inflation in the economy as a whole by tracking price fluctuations in a standard set of goods. Descriptive statistics summarize a dataset. Information obtained by descriptive statistics cannot be extrapolated beyond the observed data. For instance, the box scores of the sports page summarize yesterday's games, but that information cannot be used to inform decisions not related to the sports covered.

a) Inferential Statistics Can Assess either Association or Causality

i) Association

Association allows us to make statements such as, "if A is increasing, then so is B"; it does not allow us to infer a causal relationship between A and B. Association can be concluded from an observational study or a quasi-experiment.

The following observational study would assess the association between cigarette smoking and lung capacity:

1) Find 100 women, of whom fifty are smokers and fifty are not.
2) Record the women's ages.

3) Record how much each smoker smokes and how long each smoker has smoked.
4) Measure the lung capacity of each of the 100 women.

The age of the women and the number of cigarettes smoked by those women are not controlled. Smoking (yes or no) is not randomized (the women choose for themselves whether they will be in the smoking or the non-smoking group). From the observed data, statisticians would be able to determine whether there is an association between cigarette smoking and lowered lung capacity in women.

The following quasi-experiment would assess the association between cigarette smoking and lung capacity:

1) Find 100 thirty-year-old women, of whom fifty have been smoking a pack of cigarettes a day for the last ten years and fifty have not smoked.
2) Measure the lung capacity of each of the one hundred women.

The age of the women and the number of cigarettes they smoked are controlled. Smoking (yes or no) is not randomized (the women are already found to be in one category or the other). From the observed data, statisticians would be able to determine whether there is an association between smoking a pack of cigarettes a day for ten years and lowered lung capacity in thirty-year-old women.

ii) Causality

Causality allows us to talk about A causing B. Causality can be concluded only from a designed experiment. For instance, the following designed experiment would assess the impact of smoking on lung capacity:

1) One hundred twenty-year-old women take part in a study. They do not currently smoke.
2) Fifty of the 100 women are assigned to the smoking treatment and the other fifty are assigned to the non-smoking treatment.
3) Those in the smoking group smoke one pack of cigarettes each day for ten years, while those in the control group remain smoke-free for ten years.
4) After the ten-year study period, researchers measure the lung capacity of each participant.

The age of the women and number of cigarettes they smoke are controlled. Smoking (yes or no) is randomized (the women are randomly assigned to the smoking or non-smoking group). From the observed data, statisticians would be able to draw conclusions regarding the effect of smoking a pack of cigarettes a day for ten years on the lung capacity of thirty-year-old women.

b) Descriptive Statistics Describe or Summarize a Set of Data

Descriptive statistics explain the meaning in data. They may show patterns or tendencies; they are exploratory, often suggesting directions for further substantive analysis.

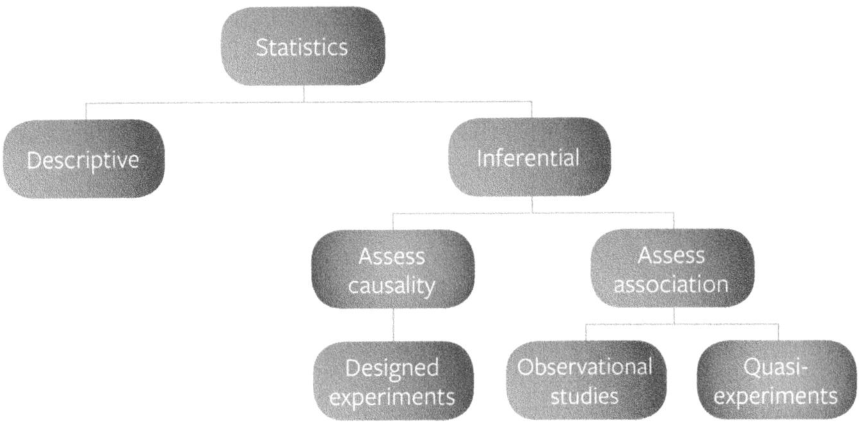

FIGURE 23.2. Functional chart showing relationship between types of statistics.

2) Numeric Summaries

a) Measures of Location

The measure of location is a number representing the typical or central value that best describes the data. The same data can have more than one location, depending on the needs of the statistician. Table 23.1 looks at three ways of determining the measure of location.

TABLE 23.1. Type of Statistic, Type of Data, and Explanatory Description

Statistic	Type of Data	Description
Mean ($\bar{x}$)	Interval	Average
Median	Interval	Middle (half above/half below)
Mode	Categorical	Most commonly occurring category

If a dataset is symmetric, the median and the mean will be virtually the same. If a dataset is skewed, with a few outliers having a large influence on the average value, then the mean and the median may differ substantially. The mean is pulled in the direction of the skew.

Figure 23.3 shows the annual salaries of all players on Canadian National Hockey League teams for the 2014–2015 fiscal year. The mean (average) is skewed, with a long tail to the right, due to the effects of a small number of highly paid players.

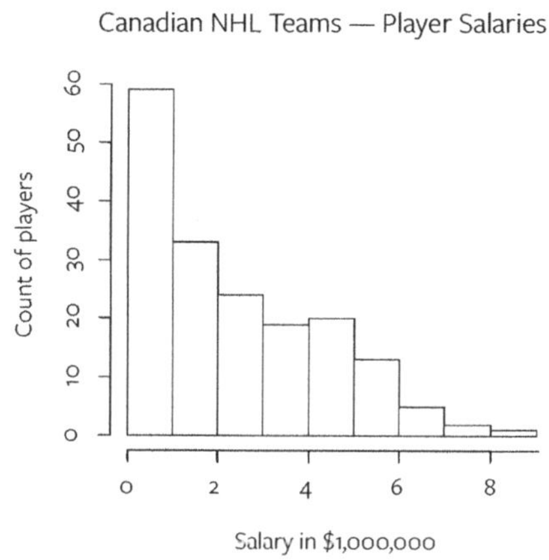

FIGURE 23.3. Figure depicting data for the annual salaries of all players on Canadian NHL teams in the 2014–2015 fiscal year (Source: www.spotrac.com/nhl/rankings/2014).

In a salary dispute, the union, whose interests lie in portraying NHL players as undercompensated would use the median, $1.9 million, as the measure of location. Management, whose interests lie in portraying the players as adequately compensated, would use the mean of $2,556,519.

b) Measures of Spread

A measure of spread is a number summarizing the "dispersion" of the numbers in the dataset. Measures of spread are only applicable to interval data, such as number of siblings or height.

TABLE 23.2. Type of Statistic and Explanatory Description.

Statistic	Description
Range (*R*)	Largest observation minus smallest observation
Standard deviation (*s*)	Approximate average distance between each observation and the mean
Variance (s^2)	Average squared distance between each observation and the mean

The range of hockey players' salaries is $8.45 million, a useful measure for the union to argue for higher salaries for their players because higher salaries are indeed available. The standard deviation of the salaries is $1,918,023. Management might argue that while the salaries of each player do differ, the overall variation is not so great as the range suggests.

c) Measures of Association

Pearson's product-moment correlation coefficient, informally referred to as "correlation," is the most commonly used measure of association.

- Correlation measures the "strength" of the linear (i.e., straight line) relationship between two variables. For example, Chapter 15 shows how forensic entomologists rely on linear relationships between temperature and insect development to provide estimates of the minimum length of time a person has been deceased.
- Correlations are calculated to fall between -1 or +1, with a strong correlation falling close to one of these extremes. It is possible, although rare, to have a strong correlation where no relationship exists. A correlation of 0 indicates no linear relationship exists between the variables.
- Correlations between two variables are shown graphically on a chart where one variable is plotted on the x axis and the other variable on the y axis. Positive or negative correlation is determined by looking at the resulting placement of the data points. If y increases linearly as x increases, there is a positive correlation. If y decreases linearly as x increases, there is a negative correlation.
- Correlations do not imply causality.
- Correlations may be spurious (i.e., coincidental). Two variables, x and y, may seem to be correlated, when in fact the association is between each of the two variables with a third variable, z. Apparent correlations may also be coincidental.

To convert the correlation into a percentage relationship, square the correlation and then multiply the result by 100. The resulting number quantifies the proportion of variability in one variable that is explained by the other variable. For example, suppose the correlation between test mark (x) and time studied for the test (y) is 0.63. This says that $100 \times (0.63)^2$ of the differences between test marks is attributable to the differences in the hours studied for the test. The remaining 60.31 percent of the differences between test marks is attributable to other influences (e.g., sleep, general approach to the class, aptitude).

d) Graphical Summaries

TABLE 23.3. Type of Graph, Type of Data, and Explanatory Comments.

Graph	Type of Data	Comments
Bar graph	Categorical	Bars not joined
Histogram	Interval	Bars joined
Pie chart	Categorical	Hard to read
Scatterplot	Interval	Look for relationship
Time series plot	Interval	Look for evolution over time

i) Graphs: The Good, the Bad, and the Ugly

Graphical presentations can be a bit like online dating profiles. They likely contain some truth, but with differing degrees of distortion. And bits of the truth might be omitted altogether. Honest statisticians learn to avoid misrepresentations. Figure 23.4 shows plots demonstrating some different ways of presenting the same data.

The good: It's simple and clear.

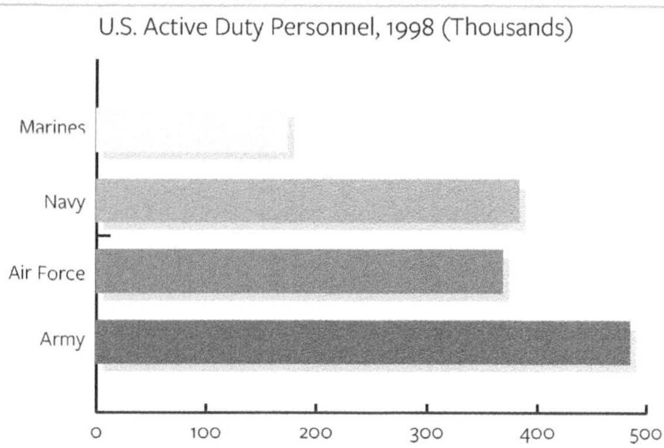

The bad: Percentages in a pie chart are areas of the pie. Although most people can compare lengths, many have difficulty comparing areas.

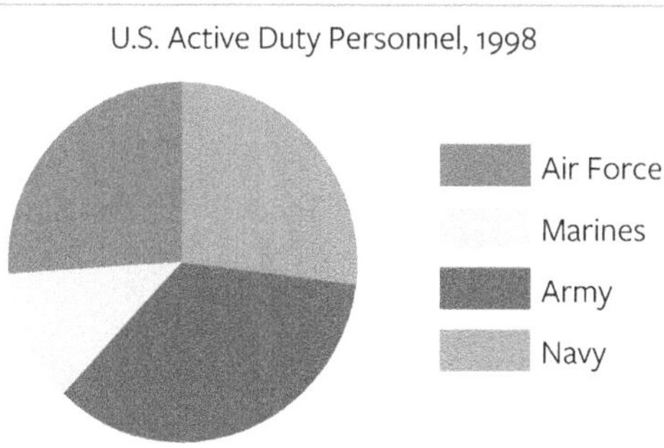

The bad: Counts in this 3D bar graph can only be read by extrapolating from the top of the boxes to the horizontal lines on the back of the graph, and then following that line around to the misleadingly placed heights on the vertical axis.

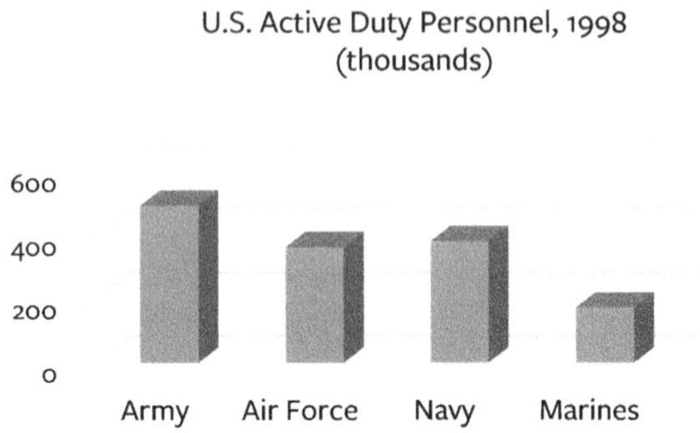

The ugly: Information in this graph is too splintered to be easily deciphered.

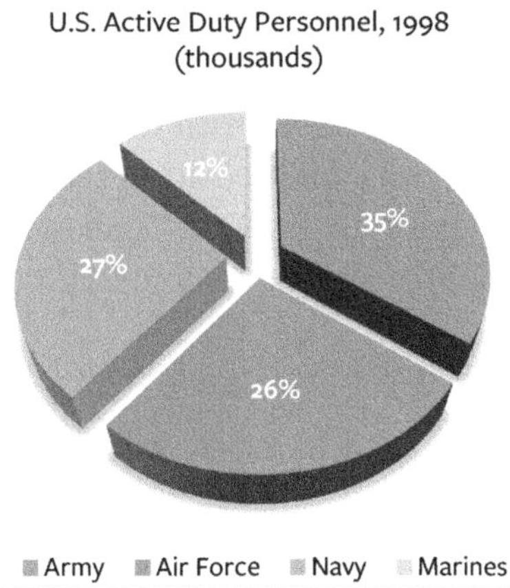

FIGURE 23.4. Counts of American active duty personnel, in 1998, in four branches of the military: army, navy, air force, and marines (Source: U.S. Department of Defense).

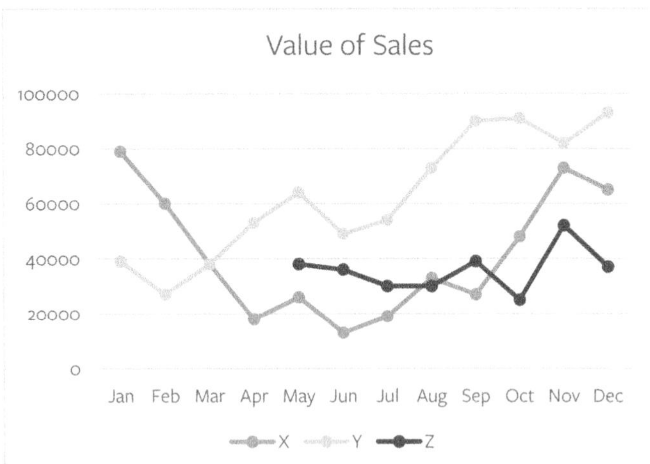

FIGURE 23.5. Time series plot showing the revenue from sales of three products. The y-axis shows revenue in dollars and the x-axis shows time in months.

Correlations do not imply causality and may be completely coincidental (see section D(2)(c), above, in this chapter). Further, readers should be mindful of how chart axes are numbered as poor numbering of axes may lead the casual reader to draw erroneous conclusions. The key to reading any chart and drawing conclusions from it is employing critical thinking.

E. STATISTICAL INFERENCE: HYPOTHESIS TESTING

1) The Structural Similarities between Criminal Trials and Statistical Hypothesis Tests

A statistical hypothesis test is a decision rule between two competing hypotheses:

1) The null hypothesis (H_0). The null hypothesis is the hypothesis the researcher is trying to disprove (or nullify). A common null hypothesis is the current popularly held belief about the issue under investigation. For example, in testing for global warming, the null hypothesis might be that the earth's atmosphere is warming at a rate of 7°C every 1,000 years. If there is no currently held belief, the null hypothesis would be that there is no correlation. For example, in testing a new drug for its ability to reduce high blood pressure, the null hypothesis would be that the new drug has no effect.
2) The alternative, or research, hypothesis (H_a). The alternative, or research, hypothesis is the negation of the null hypothesis. For example, an alternative hypothesis regarding the acceleration of global warming may be that the earth's atmosphere is warming at a rate greater than 7°C every 1,000 years. An alternative hypothesis regarding the efficacy of a new drug for the reduction of high blood pressure would be that the new drug lowers blood pressure. The alternative hypothesis is not a statement of any specific belief about the issue at hand, but researchers usually hope to find support for this hypothesis.

There are similarities and differences between criminal trials and statistical hypothesis tests. Both start with a presumption that is rejected only after a standard threshold is met. In a murder trial, defendants are presumed innocent until proven guilty beyond a reasonable doubt. In a statistical hypothesis test, the null hypothesis is assumed true until it can be shown that it is very unlikely to actually be true.

Consider this scenario: Rob is on trial for murder.

- H_0: Rob is innocent
- H_a: Rob is guilty

The prosecutor will try to show the trier of fact (whether jury or judge) that Rob is guilty beyond a reasonable doubt. The prosecutor's job is to provide enough evidence to reject the null hypothesis (i.e., the presumption that Rob is innocent). If there is insufficient evidence to reject the presumption of innocence and find guilt, Rob will be acquitted (i.e., the null hypothesis stands).

Just as with a criminal trial, a statistical hypothesis test is a proof by contradiction. The researcher is looking for evidence to prove beyond a reasonable doubt (the statistical equivalent of "beyond a reasonable doubt" differs from that used in the courtroom) that the assumed truth of the null hypothesis (i.e., innocence) is actually an incorrect assumption. The researcher's evidence is a test statistic, a number that is calculated using data.

TABLE 23.4. Possible Outcomes of a Criminal Trial and a Statistical Hypothesis Test.

		Truth	
		H_0 false	H_0 true
Test conclusion	**Fail to reject H_0**	Type II error: acquit a guilty defendant	Correct: acquit an innocent defendant
	Reject H_0	Correct: convict a guilty defendant	Type I error: convict an innocent defendant

In Rob's murder trial, if Rob is innocent but he is convicted, a Type I error has been committed. If instead Rob was guilty, but he is acquitted, then a Type II error has been committed. Since our legal system is based on the presumption of innocent until proven guilty, the system operates on the principle that it is worse to convict an innocent person than to acquit a guilty person. In a trial, making a Type I error is worse than making a Type II error.

Type I and Type II errors in a statistical hypothesis test have the same relative consequences as those in a criminal trial. If a Type I error is committed, the null hypothesis is incorrectly rejected. A researcher, having incorrectly rejected the null hypothesis, recommends unnecessary changes be made to existing structures or procedures. These changes may be costly in time and money, and thus this error is considered serious. If a Type II error is committed, the null hypothesis is incorrectly retained. Since the world is currently functioning under the assumption that the null hypothesis is true, no serious error has usually been made.

Since a Type I error is usually more serious, we want to ensure there is a small probability of making one. In a statistical hypothesis test, the probability of making a Type I error, $P(\text{reject } H_0 \mid H_0 \text{ is true})$, is called the level of significance. It is the maximum acceptable probability of making a Type I error. Prior to testing, it is set at a small value, usually $P(\text{reject } H_0 \mid H_0 \text{ is true}) = 0.05$ is used.[1] In a criminal trial, the probability of a Type I error is $P(\text{found guilty} \mid \text{really is innocent})$. There is no legal principle defining suitable values for this probability.

A criminal trial does not set out to prove a defendant is innocent; this is assumed from the outset. The prosecutor's job is to contradict this assumption. A defendant found not guilty is not proven to be innocent in truth—there is just not enough evidence to contradict the assumption of innocence. The same holds for a statistical hypothesis test. We do not set out to prove the null hypothesis is true; this is assumed from the outset. If a statistical test does not reject the null hypothesis, this does not prove the null hypothesis is true—there is just not enough evidence to contradict the assumption of its truth.

2) The *p*-Value

The conclusion to a statistical hypothesis test is made using a *p*-value. The *p*-value quantifies the strength of the evidence against the null hypothesis and in favour of the alternative hypothesis. Specifically, the *p*-value is the probability of obtaining the observed sample (how likely is it?), or another sample with even less support for the null hypothesis, assuming that the null hypothesis is true. The *p*-value is not the significance level, which is the probability of a Type I error. The *p*-value ranges from 0 to 1. The following are some illustrative examples:

- If the *p*-value is "large-ish," say $p = 0.634$, then there is a 63.4 percent chance of obtaining the observed sample, or another sample with less support for the null hypothesis, if the null hypothesis is true. In this example, the probability is quite high—63 times out of 100. There is insufficient evidence to disprove the null hypothesis.

---

1 This somewhat arbitrary number was determined by Sir Ronald Fisher, a statistician of some magnitude, who replied "once in twenty" when he was asked to define his idea of an unlikely probability.

- If the p-value is small, say $p = 0.002$, then there is a 0.2 percent chance of obtaining the observed sample, or one with even less support for the null hypothesis, if the null hypothesis is true. One, or the other, of two things must have occurred. The null hypothesis may be true and we have a rare sample, but the far more likely explanation is that the null hypothesis is false. The common convention is that p-values smaller than 0.05 provide enough evidence for rejection of the null hypothesis. If the first option is actually the truth about what happened, then a Type I error will be made.

TABLE 23.5. Summarizing Conclusions for Various p-Values.

p-Value	Conclusion
$p > 0.1$	Insufficient evidence to reject the null hypothesis. The data appear to be consistent with the null hypothesis.
$0.05 < p \le 0.1$	Weak evidence against the null hypothesis in favour of the alternative.
$0.01 < p \le 0.05$	Evidence against the null hypothesis in favour of the alternative.
$0.001 < p \le 0.01$	Strong evidence against the null hypothesis in favour of the alternative.
$p \le 0.001$	Very strong evidence against the null hypothesis in favour of the alternative.

Sometimes a p-value less than 0.05 is described as statistical proof.

The p-value is often incorrectly interpreted as the probability that the null hypothesis is true. This is a mistake. We can only say of a $p > 0.05$ that we have failed to disprove the null hypothesis. In a frequentist interpretation of probability (i.e., the probability of an event is determined by its relative frequency, as seen within a large number of trials), there is nothing random about whether the hypothesis is true (it is either true or not true); all randomness is in the process of collecting the data.

a) The Kristen Gilbert Case: Massachusetts

In the 1990s, Kristen Gilbert was a nurse at a veteran's hospital in Massachusetts. Other nurses noticed that there appeared to be an increased number of deaths and other patient crises when she was on duty. She was accused of killing several patients by giving them fatal doses of a heart stimulant. The defence and the prosecution both retained a statistical expert. The experts conducted the same test:

- H_0: the death rate while Gilbert is on duty is the same as the death rate when she is not.
- H_a: the death rate while Gilbert is on duty is higher than the death rate when she is not.

The experts reached the same conclusion: very strong evidence against the null hypothesis ($p = 0$). The judge did not admit the statistical evidence. On the basis of other evidence, Gilbert was convicted of three first-degree murders, one second-degree murder, and two attempted murders.

3) The Appeal to Ignorance Fallacy

If a null hypothesis is not rejected, nothing has been proven. Failing to reject the null hypothesis does not imply that the null hypothesis is true. The "appeal to ignorance" fallacy is the logical error of assuming that a null hypothesis is true based on a non-rejection.

a) The Guy Paul Morin Case: Ontario

Guy Paul Morin was charged with the 1984 murder of a nine-year-old girl, Christine Jessop, who was his next door neighbour. On 22 April 1985, Morin, twenty-five years old at the time, was arrested despite repeatedly claiming innocence. During his first trial in 1986, the Crown theorized that the crime occurred in a span of seventy-five minutes: Morin abducted Christine when he arrived in Queensville at 4:15 p.m. and drove her to the site where he sexually assaulted and killed her. He then drove back to Queensville, where he destroyed evidence of blood on his clothes, body, and car before arriving home at 5:30 p.m. with groceries.[2] The prosecution viewed Morin's descriptions of his activities and the supporting evidence of his parents as a false alibi.[3] At his first trial in 1986, a jury found Morin not guilty. A second trial was ordered by the Ontario Court of Appeal, a decision which was affirmed by the Supreme Court of Canada. On 30 July 1992, Morin was convicted of first degree murder.[4] He spent eighteen months in jail.[5]

There were many errors that led to his wrongful conviction, one of which related to a single hair found entangled in Jessop's necklace. The

---

2 Dawn Anderson & Barrie Anderson, *Manufacturing Guilt: Wrongful Convictions in Canada*, 2d ed. (Halifax: Fernwood, 2009) at 73.

3 Ontario, Ministry of the Attorney General, *Report of the Kaufman Commission on Proceedings Involving Guy Paul Morin* (Toronto: Queen's Printer for Ontario, 1998) at 34–35, online: www.attorneygeneral.jus.gov.on.ca/english/about/pubs/morin/morin_recom.pdf [*Morin Inquiry*].

4 *Ibid* at 1; Sarah Harland-Logan, "Historical Cases: Guy Paul Morin," online: Innocence Canada www.aidwyc.org/cases/historical/guy-paul-morin.

5 Peter Edwards, "Guy Paul Morin and the Christine Jessop Killing: 10 Things Learned from the Case" *Toronto Star* (2 October 2014), online: www.thestar.com/news/gta/2014/10/02/christine_jessop_killing_10_things_that_were_learned_from_the_case.html.

hair was assumed to have belonged to the perpetrator. A forensic scientist, relying on hair microscopy, tested the null hypothesis that the necklace hair had no differences from Morin's hairs. She failed to reject the null hypothesis and concluded that the hair belonged to Morin, falling into the trap of the appeal to ignorance fallacy. This error was presented as fact by the prosecution. Today, it is now understood that hair microscopy cannot individualize a hair to a specific individual (see Chapter 5).

Morin was acquitted ten years later, on 23 January 1995, by the Court of Appeal on the basis that new DNA evidence proved that the semen on Jessop's underpants did not belong to him.[6] On 24 January 1997, Morin was provided $1.25 million in compensation for his wrongful conviction.[7] To this day, the case remains unsolved and the true perpetrator is unknown.[8]

4) Statistical Power

The statistical power of a hypothesis test is the probability that the null hypothesis is correctly rejected. Symbolically, power is expressed as P (reject H_0 | H_0 is not true). Statistical power is always greater than the significance level of the test, but it is not constant.

- If a popular belief is close to the truth, then a random sample from "the truth" could easily look like a random sample from the popular belief. It is unlikely that sample data could convince anyone that the popular belief is wrong. Statistically speaking, if the truth is close to H_0, power is low.
- If a popular belief is far from the truth, then a random sample from "the truth" is unlikely to look like a random sample from the popular belief. It is likely that sample data will convince almost everyone that the popular belief is wrong. Statistically speaking, if the truth is far from H_0, power is high.

a) The Labelling rbST Milk Products Case: Ohio

A synthetic form of a natural bovine protein, called recombinant bovine somatotropin (rbST or rbGH), can increase milk production by 10 to 40 percent, but its use can cause udder infections and mastitis. These conditions add pus and antibiotics (used to treat the infections) to the milk. The

6 *R. v. Morin*, 1995 CanLII 8944 at paras. 1–2 and 10 (ON CA).
7 Anderson & Anderson, above note 3 at 80.
8 Edwards, above note 6.

FDA approved rbST in the United States in 1985. Many consumer and environmental groups believe the FDA got it wrong and that milk produced using rbST poses health risks to humans. At the very least, these advocacy groups want milk products produced by cows given rbST to be labelled as such. Since 1993, Ohio milk producers who did not use rbST were banned, by law, from labelling their product as such, but in 2010, an Ohio court ruled that this law be repealed. The use of rbST is banned in Canada.

When new drugs are tested for negative side effects, the null hypothesis is that negative side effects do not exist. The alternative hypothesis is that side effects do exist. If a null hypothesis is not rejected, this does not prove that the null hypothesis is true. Testing for negative side effects of rbST, and all other new drugs, is problematic. Failure to reject the null hypothesis does not prove that there are no negative side effects. The null hypothesis was not rejected for most tests regarding negative side effects of rbST. The manufacturers of rbST (e.g., Monsanto and Eli Lilly) argue that failing to find evidence of negative side effects proves they do not exist, while the advocacy groups argue that although negative side effects were not found, this does not prove they do not exist.

5) Combining Hypothesis Tests and *p*-Values

When multiple hypothesis tests are conducted using variables that are known or presumed to be interconnected, it is usually desirable to synthesize the individual test conclusions into an overall conclusion. There are various methodologies for combining *p*-values, each with strengths and weaknesses, and each optimal in different circumstances.

Incorrect synthesizing of hypothesis tests is a widespread problem, even at the advanced level. Of the 120 cellular and molecular articles in *Nature Neuroscience* from 2009 and 2010, there were twenty-five studies that combined test conclusions. None of these twenty-five studies correctly combined the conclusions.[9]

a) The Lucia de Berk Case: Netherlands

Investigators examined a series of suspicious deaths in hospital wards where Nurse Lucia de Berk had worked from 1999 to 2001. They found

9 Sander Nieuwenhuis, Birte U. Forstmann, & Eric-Jan Wagenmakers, "Erroneous Analyses of Interactions in Neuroscience: A Problem of Significance" (2011) 14:9 *Nature Neuroscience* 1105.

that she had been present when many of them took place. A law professor giving expert testimony calculated that the probability that this could be simple coincidence is 1 in 342 million. The expert arrived at this figure by multiplying the *p*-values of the individual hypotheses that made up his analysis. This was an incorrect approach. The true probability is about 1 in 7.

F. PRACTICAL VERSUS STATISTICAL SIGNIFICANCE

There is a huge difference between practical significance and statistical significance:

- Statistical significance is attained if a hypothesis test's *p*-value is less than 0.05.
- Practical significance is attained if a statistically significant result is also useful in the real world.

For example, it has been statistically proven ($p < 0.05$) that if you take vitamin P daily, you will have a 99 percent chance of never getting another cold. But vitamin P costs $1,000 per pill. Although the result is statistically significant, and it is proven to work, it has no practical significance to those unwilling or unable to pay $1,000 per day to ward off the common cold. Prior to using or publishing statistically significant results, the results should be assessed for practical significance.

1) Statistical Inference: Confidence Intervals

Suppose a researcher is interested in finding the proportion of all living Canadian adult male convicted felons who are currently alcoholics. It is easy to estimate this proportion by taking a sample of all convicted felons and determining the proportion of these who are currently alcoholics. This is called a point estimate. If the sample is large, the point estimate will likely be a good estimate of the true proportion. If the sample is not large, the estimate may, or may not, be a good estimate of the true proportion.

A 95 percent confidence interval is a different kind of estimate. It consists of two calculated numbers, one smaller than the other. These two numbers enclose an interval of numbers. This interval is called a confidence interval: 95 percent of all possible samples will yield intervals that contain the true proportion, and 5 percent will not. The researcher has one sample (large or small) and it generates one confidence interval. The sample is randomly selected. We hope our sample was one of the good samples (one of the 95 percent) and that the true proportion is included in the calculated confidence interval.

For example, suppose we sampled twenty-five convicted felons and found that six of them were currently alcoholics. This data gives (0.044, 0.436) or (4.4%, 43.6%) as the 95 percent confidence interval. This does not mean that there is 95 percent chance that the true proportion of convicted felons who are currently alcoholics is somewhere between 4.4 percent and 43.6 percent. It means that 95 percent of all samples of convicted felons will yield an interval that contains the true proportion of those that are currently alcoholics. Hopefully our sample is one of the "good" 95 percent and thus the true proportion is in the interval (4.4%, 43.6%) and not one of the "bad" 5 percent and thus the true proportion is not in the interval (4.4%, 43.6%).

Notes about confidence intervals:

- Confidence intervals can be constructed for means, medians, standard deviations, correlations, etc.
- Narrow confidence intervals are better than wide ones. I have a much better idea how to dress tomorrow if the confidence interval for the high temperature is (18, 22) than I would be if it is (-20, 40).
- Increasing the sample size will (virtually always) result in narrower confidence intervals. By taking a large enough sample, it is possible to construct an arbitrarily narrow confidence interval.

A confidence interval is often interpreted as an interval that with 95 percent probability captures the truth. This is a mistake. In a frequentist interpretation of probability, there is nothing random about the truth, the randomness is in the process generating the data.

2) Statistical Inference: Modelling and Case Examples Including Racial Bias

Applied statisticians create mathematical models that describe the relationships among a group of variables. While statistical modelling often requires advanced mathematics and programming skills, some models are used by everybody. The simplest summary model is the average, or sample mean. Statistical models require techniques that range from relatively straightforward to quite complex. A statistical expert should validate all but the most basic of these.

3) Statistical Models

All statistical models describe interconnections within a group of variables. The overall form of a statistical model is based on existing knowledge and other suspected relationships. In addition to the overall form, all statistical models contain an intrinsically random component that is attributable to all other variables not included in the model. Statistical models are really hypotheses about the nature of the interconnections between variables in a population, and they can be written as partially specified mathematical expressions. In a predictive model, there is typically one main variable of interest. For example, the relationship between the height of a shrub, the amount of bacteria in the soil, and the hours of exposure to the sun may be expressed as:

$$\textit{height} = A + B \times \textit{bacteria} + C \times \textit{sun} + D \times \textit{bacteria} \times \textit{sun} + \textit{random}$$

where A, B, C, and D are numbers (to be estimated using data) and the random term contains everything else that affects the height of a shrub (amount of water, nitrogen in the soil, humidity level, air temperature, etc.).

Another example describes the evolution of wine sales over time using the model:

$$\text{January 2016 sales} = A + B \times \text{December 2015 sales} + A + C \times \text{January 2015 sales} + \text{random}$$

where A, B, C, and D are numbers (to be estimated using data) and the random term contains everything else that affects wine sales (population growth, price of wine, wine advertising, unemployment rates, etc.).

a) Statistical Models in Forensic Science

The academic research that supports much of the material covered in other chapters of this book is based, at least in part, on many different types of statistical models.

- Forensic biology relies on Bayesian methods, logistic regression, and stochastic processes.
- Forensic toxicology relies on linear regression, designed experiments, and time series analysis.
- Forensic anthropology relies on generalized linear models and discriminant analysis.
- Memory research relies on designed experiments, linear and logistic regressions, and generalized linear models.

b) Statistical Models in the Law

i) The Brink's Parking Meter Thefts: New York City

Between March 1978 and March 1980, Brink's was contracted to collect coins from all parking meters in New York City. During that period, City officials received a tip that the collected money was not all being delivered to the city. The City began an investigation using "salted" coins (i.e., coins treated with a fluorescent substance and inserted into specific meters) and surveillance cameras. Five Brink's employees were arrested, found with $4,500 in coins stolen from that day's collection, and convicted of grand larceny. Brink's contract was terminated and a new collection agency, CDC, was awarded the contract.

The City of New York filed a civil suit against Brink's. The City was seeking reimbursement from Brink's for their lost revenue. Brink's was found guilty. Lawyers for the City used a linear model to demonstrate that: (1) CDC's collections were greater than Brink's, and (2) CDC's collections had a different trend than that for Brink's. The City was able to argue successfully that these findings were not attributable to anything other than the change of collection company.

ii) McCleskey v. Kemp[10]

Warren McCleskey, a black man, was convicted of two counts of armed robbery and one count of murder in the death of a white police officer in Fulton County, Georgia. At the sentencing hearing, it was found that two aggravating circumstances existed: the murder was committed during the course of an armed robbery, and the murder was committed upon a police officer engaged in the performance of his duties. A finding of either of these aggravating circumstances was sufficient for the death penalty. McCleskey received a sentence of death.

On appeal, the defence argued that Georgia's capital sentencing process was racially biased. This claim was based on a publication by Baldus,[11] and supported in court by a statistician. Baldus, a law professor, studied 2,500 murder cases in Georgia. Baldus's study concluded that anyone convicted of murdering a white person is far more likely to receive the death penalty. One of his logistic regression models concluded that, even after taking account of thirty-nine non-racial variables, defendants charged

---

10 *McCleskey v. Kemp*, 481 U.S. 279 (1987).

11 David C. Baldus et al., "Racial Discrimination and the Death Penalty in the Post-Furman Era: An Empirical and Legal Overview with Recent Findings from Philadelphia" (1998) 83 *Cornell Law Review* 1638.

with killing white victims were 4.3 times more likely to receive a death sentence than defendants charged with killing black victims. The court determined that the Baldus study was not substantial evidence and did not revoke the death penalty.

iii) State v. Soto[12]

The public defender's office, acting on behalf of seventeen black defendants on charges of transporting drugs (drugs found during stops on the New Jersey Turnpike), conducted two experiments to investigate discrimination on the part of the police with regard to stopping black and non-black drivers. They used logistic regression to show that on the New Jersey Turnpike black drivers were (estimated to be) 4.85 times more likely to be stopped by police than were non-black drivers. The judge determined that the defence established a *prima facie* case of selective enforcement that the State failed to rebut, requiring suppression of all contraband and evidence seized. All charges of transporting drugs were dropped.

G. CONCLUSION

Statistics and probability form a specialized discipline, apart from, but used by, many others. It is rife with pitfalls and logical fallacies waiting to trap the unwary. There are surprising results and erroneous yet popularly held beliefs. The language of statistics gives narrow and precise definitions to popular and broadly defined words such as "correlated," "significant," and "confident," which only adds to confusion in the courtroom.

Any statistical or probabilistic issue arising in court requires a response from a qualified statistician. Experts can be contacted through the statistics department of any Canadian university. Many of these departments provide formal consulting services, but all have at least one faculty member who is available for private consultation.

12 *State v. Soto*, 734 A. 2d 350 (N.J. Super. Ct. App. Div. 1996).

Glossary

NOTE:

* *Reproduced from the Medical Glossary used in the Goudge Inquiry Report, as licensed.*

† *Reproduced from the publicly available terminology of SWGSTAIN (Scientific Working Group on Bloodstain Pattern Analysis), "Recommended Terminology" online: www.swgstain.org/resources.*

AAFS. American Academy of Forensic Sciences

AAPL. American Academy of Psychiatry and the Law

ABFA. American Board of Forensic Anthropology

ABFDE. American Board of Forensic Document Examiners

ABFE. American Board of Forensic Entomology

ABFO. American Board of Forensic Odontology

ABMDI. American Board of Medicolegal Death Investigators

abrasion.* Superficial damage to the skin, generally not deeper than the *epidermis* (the outermost layer of the skin). A scrape or scratch.[1]

accompanying drop.† A small blood drop produced as a by-product of drop formation.

1 "A scrape or scratch" has been added to the existing definition provided from the Medical Glossary used in the Goudge Inquiry Report.

accreditation. The process by which a laboratory demonstrates adherence to standards.

accuracy. A measure of scientific reliability. Accuracy measures how often the correct result is achieved when a technique is applied to a large sample set.

acetaldehyde. A metabolite of alcohol produced by the liver, which causes facial flushing, nausea, and dizziness. Occurs at high concentrations in most Asian persons (e.g., Chinese, Japanese, Korean) and in individuals on Antabuse therapy (a therapy used to treat chronic alcoholism).

acetone. A volatile substance produced by the body in uncontrolled diabetics, fasting persons, or due to a high protein/low carbohydrate diet. It does not interfere with current approved instrument or screening devices.

ACE-V method. Analysis, Comparison, Evaluation, and Verification. The steps of the method used to identify, primarily, fingerprints.

acid phosphatase. A ubiquitous enzyme in numerous body fluids but found in relatively large amounts in seminal fluid.

ACP. Automatic Colt pistol. This term is seen with calibres such as .25 ACP, .32 ACP, .380 ACP, and .45 ACP.

action. Refers to the mechanism that operates the firearm, and although there are many different types, the most common that are encountered in casework are:

- *automatic*: This type of firearm feeds cartridges from the magazine to the chamber, and it also fires, extracts, and ejects cartridge cases as long as proper pressure is applied to the trigger, and there are cartridges available in the firearm. Also referred to as fully automatic.
- *bolt action*: This type of firearm has a manually operated breech system whereby the user unlocks the mechanism by rotating the bolt handle upward and to the rear. This extracts and ejects a fired cartridge case, and when returned to the lock position, the bolt feeds a cartridge from the magazine into the chamber and also cocks the firearm. Some bolt action mechanisms involve a straight pull of the bolt only.
- *revolver*: A very common type of handgun, this firearm has a cylinder containing a number of chambers to hold unfired cartridges. The cylinder rotates around an axis, which can be accomplished by a single, long pull of the trigger in double-action mode, or by first manually cocking a hammer in single-action mode before a shorter pull of the trigger is performed.

- *semi-automatic*: The most common type of handgun and firearm encountered in criminal cases, this firearm uses the energy from each discharged cartridge to extract and eject a fired cartridge case, cock the firearm, and feed the next cartridge from the magazine to the chamber. The trigger must be released, then pressed again, to discharge the next cartridge.
- *pump-action*: Typically found on shotguns, this type of firearm employs a forearm that is manually worked forward and backward on the underside of the barrel to chamber an unfired cartridge that is taken from a tubular magazine, and then to extract and eject it after discharge.

actuarial method. Used in *Psychiatric Risk Assessment*, this method relies on differently weighted historical (static) factors alone, demonstrated through research to have predictive value.

acute.* Of recent origin.

ADD (weather; entomology). Accumulated degree days

adenine, guanine, thymine, and cytosine. The four bases of the genetic alphabet.

ADH. Alcohol dehydrogenase, the main enzyme in the liver that metabolizes alcohol. Also used in hospital enzymatic analysis of alcohol.

ADH (weather; entomology). Accumulated degree hours

AFIS. Automated Fingerprint Identification System. AFIS is a searchable database of persons who have been lawfully fingerprinted under the authority of the *Identification of Criminals Act*. It also includes fingerprint impressions collected at crime scenes. In Canada, AFIS is managed by the Royal Canadian Mounted Police (Canadian Criminal Real Time Identification Services—CCRTIS) in Ottawa. Federal, provincial, regional, and municipal police services have access to AFIS through local network users groups. AFIS is not relied upon to confirm or exclude identity. It is simply used to narrow the potential search down to fingerprints with similar features (e.g., pattern type and minutiae). Identifications remain the task of qualified fingerprint examiners and are subsequently and independently verified by another qualified examiner.

air gun. A gun that employs some form of compressed air or gas to discharge a projectile. The type of projectile can vary depending on the gun, as can the type of air or gas. Performances and wounding capabilities can vary greatly, sometimes introducing difficulties with regards to whether or not a particular air gun constitutes a "firearm."

alleles. Genetic differences or variants at DNA locations.

alloying (eutectic melting). "Alloying refers to the mixing of, generally, two or more metals in which one or more of the metals is in a liquefied state, resulting in an alloy. Metals such as copper and iron (steel) can be affected by alloying with lower melting point metals such as aluminum, zinc, and lead."[2]

ALS. Alternate Light Source. These instruments, with wavelengths in the range of 400 to 600 nanometres (nm), are sensitive and specific to the identification of semen. Although this wavelength range is used to detect semen, different wavelength options are available for different uses and the type of instrument used will cause other bodily fluids and other types of trace evidence to fluoresce. Some ALS instruments, for example, may use ultraviolet (UV) and infrared (IR) wavelengths. It has not yet been shown that visualizing bruises underneath the skin can be done reliably with this instrument.

altered stain.[†] A bloodstain with characteristics that indicate a physical change has occurred.

ammunition. A single round of ammunition can also be referred to as an *unfired cartridge* or *live ammunition* and it consists of a cartridge case fitted with a primer, the case containing propellant/gunpowder, with one or more projectiles inserted into the open end.

amplicons. Copies of DNA made during amplification.

amplification (of DNA). DNA replication on a small scale. It is the replication not of whole chromosomes, but only of small portions of the DNA at particular *STR* addresses. See also **STR**.

amylase. A digestive enzyme produced in the mouth to break down food starch, the detection of which is used to locate saliva.

analytical precision (toxicology). The reproducibility of the measurements reported, and is reported as the relative standard deviation of replicate measurements.

anatomical pathology.[*] A medical specialty concerned with the diagnosis of disease and gaining additional medical information based on the examination of organs, tissues, and cells.

ancestry. Used to denote biological heritage. Ancestry is the portion of a person's genetic makeup that relates to their family's origins.

---

2 See Technical Committee on Fire Investigations, *NFPA 921: Guide for Fire and Explosion Investigations, 2014 Edition* (Quincy, MA: National Fire Protection Association, 2013) s. 6.2.8.6 [*NFPA 921*].

angle of convergence.[†] The area containing the intersections generated by lines drawn through the long axes of individual stains that indicates in two dimensions the location of the blood source.

angle of impact.[†] The acute angle (alpha), relative to the plane of a target, at which a blood drop strikes the target.

anogenital. Relating to the anus and the external genitals.[3]

anthropology.* The scientific study of humans; includes the investigation of human origin and the development of physical, cultural, religious, and social attributes.

anthropometry. Also known as *bertillonage*, an identification technique that involves the use of anatomical measurements, such as arm length and head circumference (among others), and physical characteristics, such as eye and hair colour. The technique has been criticized for inaccuracy and the inability to individualize.

antibodies. Proteins used by the body to bind foreign substances.

apocrine sweat glands. Sweat glands that are primarily found in the underarm and genital areas.

approved instrument. An evidential breath alcohol instrument used by the police, typically at a police station, to determine the *BAC* of the arrested drinking driver.

arc mapping. Also called *arc surveys*. A method to analyze the locations where electrical arcing has caused damage, and the documentation of the electrical circuits which were involved.

arc surveys. See **arc mapping.**

arch pattern, plain. A fingerprint pattern type in which the friction ridges enter on one side of the impression and flow, or tend to flow, out the other side with a rise or wave in the centre.

arch pattern, tented. A fingerprint pattern type that possesses either an angle, an upthrust, or two of the three basic characteristics of the loop.

arc-severing. Occurs on energized electrical circuits when a fault or short-circuit causes the conductor to separate or sever due to overload from high current (i.e., high electrical energy imposed on the conductor), with the result that the ends of

---

3 "External" has been added to the existing definition provided from the Medical Glossary used in the Goudge Inquiry Report.

the severed conductors will have smooth globules left on them. The presence of these smooth globules indicate that the conductors arc severed.[4]

area of origin (fire investigation). "[A] structure, part of a structure, or general geographic location within a fire scene, in which the 'point of origin' of a fire or explosion is reasonably believed to be located."[5]

area of origin† (bloodstain pattern analysis). The three-dimensional location from which spatter originated.

artefact.* Artificial product; in relation to autopsy, a sign or finding imitating pathology, disease, or injury occurring in life.

ASD. Approved screening device. A small portable device to determine a *BAC* range of a suspected drinking driver at the roadside. Usually the device uses the electrochemical (EC) method of detection.

asphyxia.* Sudden death due to lack of oxygen such as what occurs with smothering, suffocation, neck compression (e.g., strangulation), and other modes of interference with oxygen delivery in the body. Asphyxia is a complex and confusing term used in varying ways by different authors. The common notion of asphyxia is that of a mechanical interference of some sort of breathing. *Mechanical asphyxia*, which the common understanding of the term asphyxia, refers to the mechanical interference with breathing, including smothering, choking, throttling (manual strangulation), ligature strangulation, hanging, and severe sustained compression of the chest (and abdomen) termed traumatic asphyxia.

association. Two variables are associated if some of the variability of one can be accounted for by the other. Causality is not implied by an association.

ATC. Alcohol Test Committee

atrophy.* The partial or complete wasting away of a part of the body. Causes of atrophy include poor nourishment, poor circulation, loss of hormonal support to the organ, loss of nerve supply, disuse, disease, or lack of exercise.

auricular surface. Where the base of the spinal column (sacrum) meets the pelvis.

autoignition temperature. "The lowest temperature at which a combustible material ignites in air without a spark of flame."[6]

---

4 *NFPA 921*, above note 2, s. 18.4.5.
5 *Ibid.*, s. 18.1.
6 *Ibid.*, s. 3.3.15.

autopsy.* Post-mortem dissection and examination of the organs and tissues of the deceased to discover disease and injury causing or contributing to death.

average. This term typically refers to the arithmetic mean. The term may also refer to the median, the mode, and various other measures of location.[7]

avulsion. Removal.

axon.* A nerve fibre.

BAC. Blood alcohol concentration

backspatter pattern.† A bloodstain pattern resulting from blood drops that have travelled in the opposite direction of the external force applied; associated with an entrance wound created by a projectile.

ballistics, external. The study of the projectile after it leaves the barrel of a firearm.

ballistics, internal. The study of the projectile and related phenomena from the time the cartridge discharges to the time the projectile leaves the barrel.

ballistics, terminal/wound. The study of the projectile upon impacting a target medium. If the target medium is, for example, a body, the appropriate term would be **wound ballistics** as the impact of the projectile causes wounding. If the target medium is an inanimate material (e.g., wood, metal, etc.) that sustains damage, rather than injury, then the appropriate term would be **terminal ballistics**.

barrel. A roughly cylindrical length of steel through which the bullet or projectile is discharged. The bullet or projectile exits the muzzle end of the barrel. The inside of the barrel (*bore*) can be either rifled or, in the case of shotgun barrels, smooth.

BBR. Blood:breath ratio for alcohol employed to convert a breath alcohol concentration into a blood alcohol concentration. In Canada, the BBR of 2100:1 is used, which underestimates the BAC by approximately 10 percent.

bent. Also known as *sear notch*. A small notch, usually in the hammer of a firearm, in which the sear or trigger is held under tension of the mainspring until the trigger is pulled, or in the case of an accidental discharge, an external force causes the sear or trigger to disengage.

---

7 The definition of this term has been modified from the following statistical glossary: P.B. Stark, "Glossary of Statistical Terms," online: University of California www.stat.berkeley.edu/~stark/SticiGui/Text/gloss.htm#mean [Stark, "Glossary of Statistical Terms"]. It is highly recommended that this online glossary be consulted for further statistical terms.

benzoylecgonine. The pharmacologically inactive metabolite of cocaine.

bertillonage. See anthropometry.

bifurcation. A type of friction ridge path characteristic that is also called a *dividing ridge*. This is the point at which one friction ridge divides into two friction ridges.

bilateral.* Both sides (of the body).

biochemistry (biochemical).* Relating to the chemical substances present in living organisms and the reactions and methods used to identify or characterize them.

biomechanics.* The application of mechanical forces to living organisms and the investigation of the effects of the interaction of force and the body or system; includes forces that arise from within or outside the body.

biopsy.* The removal of a sample of tissue from a living person for laboratory examination.

bivariate. Involving two variables.[8]

blackout. A total loss of memory (but not consciousness) during alcohol intoxication. Usually occurs as the result of gulping drinks and having a high *BAC*.

blank test. A test to ensure that the breath testing instrument is not affected by ambient air and is alcohol-free before the subject's test.

blind experiment. An experiment where the individuals being tested do not know if they are part of the treatment or control (i.e., no treatment) group.[9]

blood clot.† A gelatinous mass formed by a complex mechanism involving red blood cells, fibrinogen, platelets, and other clotting factors. Sometimes used as synonym for *thrombus*.[10]

bloodstain.† A deposit of blood on a surface. See also **altered stain**; **drip stain**; **parent stain**; **satellite stain**; **saturation stain**; **spatter stain**; **transfer stain**.

bloodstain pattern.† A grouping or distribution of bloodstains that indicate through regular or repetitive form, order, or arrangement, the manner in which the pattern was deposited. See also **backspatter pattern**; **cast-off pattern**; **cessation cast-off**

---

8 *Ibid.*

9 *Ibid.*

10 The last sentence of this definition has been added to the existing definition provided from the Medical Glossary used in the Goudge Inquiry Report.

pattern; drip pattern; drip trail; expiration pattern; flow pattern; forward spatter pattern; impact pattern; mist pattern; pool; projected pattern; splash pattern; swipe pattern; wipe pattern.

bloodstain pattern analysis. The study of the shapes, sizes, and locations of bloodstains in order to interpret the physical events that gave rise to their origin.

BLUESTAR® FORENSIC. A test for the presence of blood that targets hemoglobin.

blunt force trauma. Defined as an "injury incurred by the crushing impact of, or when a moving body strikes, a blunt object." Examples of blunt force trauma include abrasions, contusions or bruises, lacerations, and fractures.[11]

bone biomechanics. Scientific principles involving the interaction of energy with the physical properties of bone.

bone trabecular patterns. The patterns of micro-trusses and girders that give the bone its strength.

booting. In digital forensics, "booting" a computer refers to starting the computer.

bootstrap methods. A modern, computer-intensive way of testing hypotheses and building confidence intervals. Bootstrap methods are useful when necessary assumptions for traditional methods are not met.

bore. See **barrel**.

brainstem.* The stem-like part of the brain that connects the cerebral hemispheres with the spinal cord.

breathalyzer. A breath alcohol testing instrument based on the colour change of chemicals in a glass ampoule. It was invented by R.F. Borkenstein in 1954 and was widely used by the police throughout the world. The name "breathalyzer" has become generic for any type of breath alcohol testing instrument.

breech. In modern firearms, the part at the rear of the bore (the end opposite the muzzle of the barrel) where a cartridge is inserted.

breech face. The part of the breech/breech block that supports and presses against the head/bottom of the cartridge case during firing.

---

11 J.S. Jones et al., "Anogenital Injuries in Adolescents after Consensual Sexual Intercourse" (2003) 10 *Academic Emergency Medicine* 1378 at 1380.

breech face marks. A series of impressions of microscopic features from the breech face of the firearm that can be visualized on the head/bottom of a cartridge case after firing. They are more commonly found on the primer, because the primer is softer than the case proper.

bruise, bruising.* Bleeding into tissues from damaged blood vessels, usually as a result of external injury; most commonly understood as a bruise in or under the skin, but can occur in any tissue or organ (e.g., muscle, heart, liver).

bubble ring.† An outline within a bloodstain resulting from air in the blood.

buccal swab. Used to collect DNA from cells inside a person's cheek.

buckshot. Lead shotgun/shotshell pellets ranging in size from .20 inches to .36 inches in diameter. The exact number found in a cartridge depends on the calibre and pellet size.

buffer solution. A liquid that preserves a sample.

bullet. A non-spherical projectile intended to be fired from a rifled barrel. It is fitted into the mouth of a cartridge case. The term "bullet" is often used erroneously to describe an unfired cartridge or live ammunition.

bullet core. The inside portion of a jacketed bullet, and it is usually made of lead. The core and jacket can separate from each other on impact with a hard target, creating two destabilized projectiles.

bullet energy. Also known as *muzzle energy* (if the energy of the bullet is being measured at the point it leaves the muzzle) or *kinetic energy*. A measure that can be derived from the velocity and mass of a projectile, typically expressed in the unit of foot-pounds or joules. Most relevant when assessing the performance and potential of air guns.

bullet jacket. A metal cover over the bullet's core; typically copper or brass.

bullet splash. The fragmentation and spatter of a bullet upon impacting a hard surface.

bullet wipe. The dark area around the margins of a bullet hole that can be useful for identifying an entry site (as opposed to an exit site). Typically caused by lubricant, lead, dirt in the bore, and discharge residues. Can be further confirmed by chemical testing.

burr hole surgery.* A form of surgery in which a hole is drilled into the skull, exposing the dura mater (the outermost layer of membrane surrounding the brain and spinal cord) in order to treat health problems; used to treat epidural and subdural hematomas and to gain surgical access for other procedures, such as intracranial pressure monitoring.[12]

byte. A series of eight digits, or bits, is called a "byte." A byte is the smallest collection of bits that will display onscreen in a human-readable format. In human-readable format, a byte will display as a single character or digit.

calibration check. A test to independently check the calibration or accuracy of the approved instrument, usually by using an Alcohol Standard (which is certified for use by a qualified analyst with the approved instrument to check its calibration; it contains a known amount or quantity of alcohol) heated to 34°C in a simulator. The standard used may also be pressurized dry gas containing alcohol.

calibre. Calibre relates to both firearms and ammunition. For the former, it is the measured diameter of the circle created by the lands of a rifled barrel. For the latter, it is the number found in the cartridge name which indicates a nominal bullet diameter. It may not exactly reflect the diameter of the bullet.

Calliphoridae. Family of flies in the order Diptera. Also known as blow flies.

carbon 14 (14C). A radioactive isotope.

cardiac.* Pertaining to the heart.

cardiorespiratory arrest.* Can mean (1) the cessation of normal circulation of the blood due to failure of the heart, and (2) the cessation of normal breathing.

cartridge. An assembled round of ammunition that consists of the cartridge case fitted with a primer, and loaded with propellant/gunpowder and one or more projectiles.

cartridge case. The metal container that holds all the other components that comprise a cartridge. Typically brass/metal for single projectiles, and plastic/paper for shotgun pellets.

cartridge case extractor groove. A circumferential groove just forward of the head/bottom of a cartridge, to allow the extractor to grip and remove a cartridge or fired cartridge case from the chamber.

cartridge, centre-fire. A round of ammunition where the disc-shaped primer is in the centre of the bottom of the cartridge case.

---

12 "And" prior to "to gain" has been added to the existing definition provided from the Medical Glossary used in the Goudge Inquiry Report.

cartridge, rim-fire. Most commonly found in .22 calibre ammunition, the primer is contained around the circumference of the outer edge of the base of the cartridge case.

cast-off pattern.[†] A bloodstain pattern resulting from blood drops released from an object due to its motion.

central limit theorem. This is a fundamental theorem of probability. In simple terms, the theorem says that if a very large number of independent and identical trials are carried out—say fair coin flips where the number of heads is being tabulated—a count of the number of heads will behave like a single outcome from a normal distribution. The normal distribution is popularly known as the bell curve.

centrifugation (toxicology). Rapid spinning of the sample to cause solids to collect at the bottom of the container.

cerebellum.* The portion of the brain forming the largest segment of the rhombencephalon (hind brain). It is involved in the synergic control of skeletal muscles and plays an important role in the coordination of voluntary movements.

cerebral.* Relating to or located in the hemispheres of the brain (cerebrum).

cerebral contusion.* Traumatic brain injury in the form of bruised brain tissue. Often appearing as multiple microhemorrhages (small blood vessel leaks into brain tissue), they occur primarily under the site of an impact. Contusions can cause increases in intracranial pressure and damage to delicate brain tissue.

cerebral edema.* Accumulation of excessive fluid in the substance of the brain. The brain is especially susceptible to injury from edema, because it is located within a confined space and cannot expand. Also known as brain edema, brain swelling, swelling of the brain, and wet brain.

cerebrum.* The largest part of the brain, consisting of two hemispheres separated by a deep longitudinal fissure.

cessation cast-off pattern.[†] A bloodstain pattern resulting from blood drops released from an object due to its rapid deceleration.

CFS. Centre of Forensic Sciences. The Ontario provincial forensic laboratory; located in Toronto (Centre of Forensic Sciences) and Sault Ste Marie (Northern Regional Forensic Lab).

CSFS. Canadian Society of Forensic Science

CH_3CH_2OH. Alcohol, also known as ethanol or ethyl alcohol.

chain of custody. Also known as *continuity of evidence* or *evidence continuity*. Defined as "involving a witnessed, written record of all the individuals who maintained uninterrupted control over items of evidence."[13]

chamber. The area at the breech end of the barrel bore that has been fashioned to accept a particular cartridge. In a revolver, several chambers are found integral to the cylinder proper.

chamber marks. Individual microscopic marks imparted to the sides of a cartridge case, by the chamber. These can be imparted by a live round moving into the chamber; the expansion of the cartridge case upon firing; and the extraction of a fired cartridge case or live round.

child sexual abuse accommodation syndrome. A debunked but long-held theory that certain child behaviours (subsequently demonstrated as generic for many types of problems or events) supported the view that a child must have been abused and the accused must have been the perpetrator.

Choice Reaction Time (CRT). May be defined as the time taken by a subject to respond to a selected stimulus from a series of stimuli and to respond in a particular manner (e.g., the action of stepping on the brake pedal when the brake lights of thc car ahcad arc actuatcd).

chronograph. A piece of electronic equipment used to determine the velocity of a fired projectile.

class characteristics. General characteristics that define a category of items or objects, but are not alone sufficient enough to define individuality.

clinical.* Relating to patients.

cloud storage. Simply means locating programs or data on remote server computers, which may be located anywhere. For individuals, cloud storage permits access to large amounts of data storage capacity not found on a personal computing device, as well as instant data backup in the case of device loss or replacement.

CO_2. Carbon dioxide

cock. Placing a firing mechanism under spring tension.

CODIS. COmbined DNA Index System. The FBI's software for DNA databanks.

---

13 Donna Garbacz Bader & Sue Gabriel, *Forensic Nursing: A Concise Manual* (Boca Raton, FL: CRC Press, 2010) at 95.

CoFiler™. A commercial DNA analysis kit.

comparison microscope. Two microscopes connected to an optical bridge, which allows the user to observe two like objects for the purposes of firearms identification.

compound file. A single discrete file that is made up of many parts. For example, an Outlook PST email database is a single discrete file, but it can contain many thousands of individual email messages.

computer forensics. See **digital forensics.**

confidence level. The probability a sample gives a confidence interval that captures the truth.

confirmatory testing (toxicology). More sophisticated techniques than presumptive testing, which typically involves some preparation of the sample at hand, followed by a separation and identification of the constituents in the prepared sample.

confounding. When the apparent effect of a treatment may actually be due to some other, unobserved variable. This is a common problem in observational studies.

congenital.* Born with.

congestion.* An excessive amount of blood in an organ or in tissue.

continuity of evidence. See **chain of custody.**

contrecoup injuries.* Contrecoup is damage that may occur approximately to the opposite side of the brain as the brain bounces against the skull. See also **coup injuries.**

control group. The subjects who do not receive any treatment in an experiment.

contusion.* Bruise.

convenience sample. A sample drawn for reason of convenience. Such samples are unlikely to be representative of the population of interest and is not a probability sample.

core. The approximate centre of a fingerprint impression.

coup injuries.* The coup is the damage to the brain just beneath the site of impact. See also **contrecoup injuries.**

craniotomy.* A surgical operation in which part of the skull, called a bone flap, is temporarily removed in order to access the brain.

crazed glass. Patterns of partial thickness cracks resembling a complex road map appearing in glass, caused by a spray of water hitting a window already heated by fire exposure (this usually occurs during fire suppression efforts).[14]

cross-over study. All subjects receive all treatments, preferably in randomized order (as opposed to comparing a *control group* with a different group of subjects who received a drug).

cross-reactivity (toxicology). While antibodies are generally quite specific with respect to the chemical structure to which they will bind, substances that bear a similar chemical structure to the drug of interest may also bind to the antibody to a greater or lesser extent.

cross-sectional study. A cross-sectional study is taken at one point in time, a cross section of time.

CSFS. Canadian Society of Forensic Science

CT (computerized tomography).* CT scanning computes multiple X-ray images to generate cross-sectional and other views of the body's anatomy. It can identify normal and abnormal structures and can be used to guide medical procedures.

cursive. A type of writing in which most of the letters are joined and the writing instrument is not lifted from the paper after most strokes.

cutaneous myiasis. When blowfly larvae feed on dead tissue on a living being.

cyanosis of nailbeds.* Cyanosis of the nailbeds is less serious than central (blue lips and mucous membranes) cyanosis. Post-mortem, this is an *artefact*. See **cyanosis**.

cyanosis.* A bluish colouration of the skin due to the presence of deoxygenated hemoglobin in blood vessels near the skin surface. In life, a sign of oxygen deficiency.

cylinder. The part of a revolver containing a series of chambers and which rotates around an axis.

cytoplasm. A solution containing biological machinery necessary to maintain cell function and life that surrounds chromosomes in the nucleus of human cells.

---

14 See John J. Lentini, "Behaviour of Glass at Elevated Temperatures" (1992) 37 *Journal of Forensic Sciences* 1358. See also *NFPA 921*, above note 2, s. 6.2.13.1.4.

D-ABMDI. Registry certification as a death investigator through the *ABMDI*.

data. Binary information that is digitally recorded and forensically displayed in various forms, such as a series of bits represented by a 1 or a 0, that are converted to a human-readable format.

data, non-volatile. Data (binary information) that is not lost when power is removed from the storage device.

data output, application-generated. Content that an application generates automatically, sometimes unknown to the user, and that can contain some user-created content.

data output, system-generated. Content that a system generates automatically. System-generated content is similar to application-generated content to the extent that the user has little control over what output the system generates.

data output, user-created. Content that a user creates and saves as their work product.

data science. A mix of statistics and statistical modelling, computer science, and math, coupled with business sense, communication skills, and the ability to ask good questions.

data, volatile. Data (binary information) that is lost when power is removed from the storage device. Volatile memory is also known as random access memory (RAM).

database match probability (DMP). The probability of finding the target DNA profile in a certain data bank.

degree days. A unit of measurement that combines temperature and time to develop a timeline of insect development. Usually used in forensic entomology to help estimate the post-mortem interval.

degree hours. Similar to *degree days*, but with hourly data.

delta. The point on a fingerprint ridge at or nearest to the *point of divergence* of two type lines, and located at or directly in front of the point of divergence. Additional features known as *friction ridge path characteristics* (also known as "minutiae" or "Galton Details") are used in the identification process.

dentition. The arrangement of teeth.

deoxyribonucleic acid (DNA). A molecule found in almost all human cells. It contains the instructional code for building a human being.

depressants. Drugs that depress the central nervous system, leading to sedation, drowsiness, and reductions in respiratory rates.

dermis. Also known as the dermal layer. A thick foundation layer of skin.

developmental thresholds. Those temperatures below or above which insects (or other organisms) cannot develop.

DFSA. Drug-facilitated sexual assault

diagnosis.* The term denoting the disease or syndrome a person has or is believed to have.

diaphysis. The shaft of a long bone.

diastasis.* The separation of normally joined parts, such as the separation of adjacent bones without fracture or of certain abdominal muscles during pregnancy. Bones in the skull that have diastasis is a possible indication of cerebral edema.

dichotomous insect keys. Keys used by all scientists to identify a species (this can be applied to anything, not just insects). First developed by Carl Linnaeus, the father of taxonomy, these keys are a technique to identify a species through a series of questions about its characteristics; for example: "Are there wings or are there no wings?" When the reader chooses one of the two options, another question is asked. The procedure continues until only one species meets the criteria.

diffuse axonal injury.* Disruption of the *axons*, not necessarily directly due to trauma.

digital evidence. Latent evidence that can only be seen by the digital examiner when it is displayed in human-readable format. The science of digital evidence can be described as consisting of two basic components: (1) preservation and (2) analysis.

digital forensics. The methodological acquisition, authentication, reconstruction, and examination of digital media using computer software, hardware, and analytical techniques for the purpose of presenting digital evidence at any judicial or quasi-judicial proceeding. "Digital forensics" is used interchangeably with the term *computer forensics*. An additional term that is often used today is *IT forensics*, but this term focuses on a networked environment and deals with a current or previous breach of network security.

digital transparent overlays. A method used in forensic odontology to digitize the tooth contours using a flatbed scanner and a computer application to produce the transparent overlay for comparison.

Diptera. Also known as true flies, an order of flies.

directional angle.[†] The angle (gamma) between the long axis of a spatter stain and a defined reference line on the target.

directionality.[†] The characteristic of a *bloodstain* that indicates the direction blood was moving at the time of deposition.

disconnector. A small internal device to prevent a semi-automatic firearm from firing fully-automatic.

disguised writing. Disguised writing can be defined as any written entry produced by someone who is deliberately attempting to alter or conceal his or her natural handwriting habits.

distance/range of firing. Also known as *muzzle-to-target determination*. The laboratory testing procedure that attempts to replicate firearms discharge residue patterns or shotgun pellet/wadding patterns seen on an evidential target, using the same (or similar) firearm and ammunition combination as identified from a particular incident, where possible.

distribution. A mathematical function giving the probabilities of all possible outcomes to an experiment.

dividing ridge. See **bifurcation**.

DNA canvass. Police mass-testing groups of people without warrants under the auspices of a request for community members to voluntarily provide samples to aid in an investigation. Also known as a *DNA dragnet*.

DNA dragnet. See **DNA canvass**.

DO. Dangerous offender

DOJ. Department of Justice (United States)

double-blind study. Neither the researchers nor the individuals being tested know if they are receiving the drug (treatment group) or placebo (*control group*). This information is held by a third party.[15]

DRE. Drug recognition expert

DRE symptomology matrix. A reference chart that describes the types of responses to each test that may be expected from a given class of drugs.

---

15 Stark, "Glossary of Statistical Terms," above note 7.

drip pattern.† A bloodstain pattern resulting from a liquid that dripped into another liquid, at least one of which was blood.

drip stain.† A bloodstain resulting from a falling drop that formed due to gravity.

drip trail.† A bloodstain pattern resulting from the movement of a source of *drip stains* between two points.

duodenum.* The first part of the small intestine.

e-. Electron

earwitness identification. Identification of an individual based on the sound of his or her voice. Voice identification is difficult and accuracy rates are low. Similar to eyewitnesses, earwitnesses can be influenced by general impairment and suspect bias factors. Confidence in an earwitness identification is not strongly related to accuracy.[16]

EC. Electrochemical. A method of determining breath alcohol by the electrochemical oxidation of alcohol.

EC/IR. Electrochemical/infrared. A combination of two methods of determining breath alcohol that increases the specificity of the analysis.

eccrine sweat glands. Located over the entire body, and the only type of sweat glands located on the *palmar* and *plantar surfaces*.

edema.* An abnormal buildup of fluid between tissue cells.

edge characteristic.† A physical feature of the periphery of a bloodstain.

edgeoscopy. A method of identification through the examination of the unique details and characteristics found along the edges of individual fingerprint ridges.

ejection. The act of removing a cartridge case from a firearm, the location of which may or may not be useful when assessing a crime scene.

ejection port. An opening in the slide or receiver of a firearm that allows for the passage of an extracted and ejected cartridge case. Typically on the right-hand side, it can also be on top of a firearm.

ejector. A metal tool housed inside a firearm, typically at the *breech* end, which ejects a round of ammunition or fired cartridge case from a firearm. Typically a separate

---

16 For an article addressing the reliability of non-expert voice identification evidence, see, generally, Christopher Sherrin, "Earwitness Evidence: The Reliability of Voice Identifications" (2015) *Osgoode Legal Studies Research Paper Series*. Paper 101, online: http://digitalcommons.osgoode.yorku.ca/olsrps/101.

tool, although some firearms use the *firing pin* to both strike the primer and facilitate *ejection.*

electropherogram. The plotted results of a DNA analysis using *electrophoresis.*

electrophoresis. The process during DNA analysis where the *amplicons* travel through a column containing a gel.

en bloc.* As a whole or en masse; used to refer to surgical excision.

enclosure. A type of *friction ridge path characteristic* that is also called a *lake.* This is a single friction ridge that bifurcates and rejoins after a short course and continues as a single friction ridge.

encryption, container. Where one or more files found within the boundaries of a container are encrypted (container can be of various sizes; for example, a 2-GB container may store many files).

encryption, file. Where one or more files are individually encrypted.

encryption, whole disk. Where access to any of the data on the source media is inaccessible until the disc is mounted.

ending ridge. See **ridge ending**.

endogenous. Naturally formed within the body.

entomology.* The study of insects.

epicardium.* The protective outer layer of the wall of the heart.

epidemiology (epidemiological).* The study of the distribution and determinants of health-related states and *events* in populations, and the application of this study to the control of health problems. Epidemiology is concerned with the traditional study of epidemic diseases caused by infectious agents, and with the health-related phenomena including accidents, suicide, climate, toxic agents (such as lead), air pollution, and catastrophes due to ionizing radiation.

epidermis. The epidermal layer; the thin surface or outer layer that is attached atop the dermis by a double row of dermal papillae, or little skin pegs. The epidermis is comprised of several sub-layers of skin. Each of the sub-layers referenced below is in descending order from the outer surface inward, with the basal layer being the bottom (i.e., innermost) layer of the epidermis, adjacent to the dermis:

- stratum corneum (horny)
- stratum lucidum (hyalin/hyaline)

- stratum granulosum (granular)
- stratum spinosum (spinous)
- stratum basal/basale (basal)

epiglottis (epiglottic).* The flap of cartilage lying behind the tongue and in front of the entrance to the larynx (voice box) that keeps food from going into the trachea (windpipe) during swallowing. When it gets infected and inflamed, it can obstruct, or close off, the windpipe. This obstruction may be fatal unless treated quickly.

epiphysis. The end of a long bone.

erythema. Simple redness in the skin.

ethanol. The chemical name of ethyl alcohol, beverage alcohol, or alcohol. This is the most non-toxic of all the alcohols and is made from fermentation and distillation.

ethnicity. Refers to groups of people who identify with one another on the basis of language, religion, or some other cultural characteristics (e.g., Hispanic, Jewish).

etiology.* The cause of a disease or the study of the causes of disease.

event. A collection of outcomes to an experiment.

evidence container. The evidence container is one or more files (sometimes referred to as segments) that "contain" the data from the source media and that must be read by forensic software to enable human interpretation of the forensic evidence.

evidence-based medicine (EBM). "[T]he conscientious, explicit and judicious use of current best evidence in making decisions about the care of individuals."[17]

evidence-based practice. A "problem-solving approach to clinical decision making within the health-care organization that integrates the best available scientific evidence with the best available experiential (patient and practitioner) evidence."[18]

exhumation.* Removal of a dead body from the grave after it has been buried.

experiment. Any process consisting of a number of trials, each of which generates a random outcome. It may not be possible to predict the outcome of each individual trial, but the overall outcome across many trials may be predictable.

---

17 David L. Sackett et al., "Evidence-Based Medicine: What It Is and What It Isn't" (1996) 312 The BMJ 71 [Sackett et al, "Evidence-Based Medicine"].

18 K. Eldredge, E. Huggins, & L.C. Pugh, "Alternate Light Source in Sexual Assault Examinations: An Evidence-Based Practice Project" (2012) 8 *Journal of Forensic Nursing* 39.

expiration pattern.[†] A bloodstain pattern resulting from blood forced by airflow out of the nose, mouth, or a wound.

explanatory variable. In a linear, or generalized linear model, an explanatory variable is one that is used to explain or predict another variable. This term is synonymous with *independent variable.*

exsanguination.* A loss of blood.

extraction (toxicology). First involves adjusting sample chemistry through changes in pH and salt content, which is followed by mixing the sample with an immiscible solvent (liquid-liquid extraction) or the sample passing through a bed of material that is designed to selectively remove chemical compounds with particular properties (solid-phase extraction).

extractor. A small tool for removing the cartridge or cartridge case from the chamber. Typically found integral to the slide near the *ejection port* on a firearm.

extra-oral. Outside the mouth.

F-ABMDI. Advanced certification as a death investigator through the American Board of Medicolegal Death Investigators.

false memory syndrome. The scientifically untenable idea that memories of childhood sexual abuse can be buried in the mind and subsequently retrieved by a triggering event or (dubious) therapeutic acumen.

false power. The probability one will correctly detect that a statistically significant result is too large, and the probability one will miss that a genuine effect is too low. This is caused by incorrect application of statistical methodologies; the most common error is making incorrect assumptions about the distribution of the data.

Faraday bag. An enclosure that prevents devices from receiving or sending radio waves, including those relating to cellular telephones.

Faraday cage. A room specially built to block radio waves, including those relating to cellular telephones.

Fédération Dentaire Internationale (FDI) System. A tooth nomenclature used in most countries of the world, including Canada, but not in the United States.

femur. Thigh bone.

FEV1. Forced expiratory volume of breath exhaled within one second. A measure to determine the health of the lung.

file attributes. File attributes are those attributes that are stored external to the file and within the file system, such as the date a document was created, the date it was last modified, and if the document is hidden or is a system file.

filicide.* The killing of a child by a parent.

filler (in photo array). A photo of a person who is not a suspect but has been included in the photo array together with the suspect.

fingerprint. In Canada, this commonly refers to both the *friction skin* pattern formation found on human skin (found on both the *palmar surface* and the *plantar surface*), as well as the impression or mark left on a surface after having had contact with this type of skin.

fire dynamics. The analysis of "the physics and chemistry of fire initiation and growth, and the interaction between the fire and the building's systems."[19]

fire modeling. An analytical tool to test hypotheses regarding a fire origin. This type of analysis uses fire-site-specific data to predict fire development and fire spread within the location under investigation. Fire modeling is simply a tool and cannot by itself determine either the origin or the cause of a fire.[20]

fire patterns. The analysis of the effects and patterns left by fire.

firearms identification. The scientific method that primarily determines if a fired bullet, fired cartridge case, or other ammunition component was fired by a particular firearm, or if certain parts of a live round of ammunition were marked by a particular firearm.

firearms reference collection. A collection of different firearms that each lab should have in order to assist with:

- determining the make, model, and other relevant characteristics, such as parts, by comparing firearms from the reference collection to evidence firearms.
- repairing evidence firearms that have missing/broken parts.
- training and demonstration purposes.
- firing tests, predominantly muzzle-to-target determinations and other ballistic investigations.

19 *NFPA 921*, above note 2, s. 18.1.2.
20 *Ibid.*, ss. 18.6.2.2. and 22.4.8.

firing pin. The small part of a firearm that strikes the primer of a cartridge to start the process of ignition.

firing pin hole. A hole in the breech face that allows for the movement of the *firing pin* from inside the breech face, to the primer. Can sometimes be visualized as a microscopic toolmark on the primer of a fired cartridge case.

first fuel ignited. In a fire investigation, the fuel that "first sustains combustion beyond the ignition source."[21]

fissure.* A groove, natural division, deep furrow, cleft, or tear in a part of the body.

flash hole (firearms). A hole between the primer pocket of a cartridge case and the main body, which allows the detonated primer to ignite the main propellant charge.

flow pattern.† A bloodstain pattern resulting from the movement of a volume of blood on a surface due to gravity or movement of the target.

FNE. Forensic nurse examiner

FORDISC. Software used in forensic anthropology to evaluate ancestry. The software creates formulae for the user depending on which bones are available for analysis.

forensic botany. Broadly refers to the scientific use of plants and plant parts in application to legal cases.

forensic entomology (medicolegal). The study of the carrion insects associated with a dead body with the primary aim of estimating their minimum colonization time and, from this, to infer minimum elapsed time since death.

forensic nursing. Defined as "the integration of forensic-science knowledge and principles with nursing knowledge in the clinical investigation of trauma and the recovery of medical evidence."[22]

forensic odontology. A branch of forensic medicine that deals with teeth and marks left by teeth (as in identifying criminal suspects or the remains of a dead person). See also **odontology**.

---

21 *Ibid.*, s. 19.1.2. See also s. 3.3.73.

22 Michael S. Pollanen et al., eds., "Forensic Science in Canada: A Report of Multidisciplinary Discussion" (4–5 May 2012) at 41 [Hart House Report], online: www.forensics.utoronto.ca/Assets/LMPF+Digital+Assets/Forensic+Science+in+Canada.pdf.

formalin.* An aqueous solution of 37 percent formaldehyde (a colourless gas with a distinctive smell that, when dissolved in water, gives a solution in which organic specimens are preserved).

forward spatter pattern.† A bloodstain pattern resulting from blood drops that travelled in the same direction as the impact force.

fracture.* A break of a bone.

friction ridge. "A raised portion of the epidermis on the palmar or plantar skin consisting of one or more connected ridge units of friction skin."[23]

friction ridge path characteristics. A feature of the *friction ridge*. Commonly referred to as minutia(e), Galton detail, point, feature, ridge formation, or ridge morphology.

friction skin. Skin that is ridged and furrowed, located on the *palmar* and *plantar surfaces* of the body.

frontal sinuses. Spaces in the bone of the forehead (frontal bone).

fuel-controlled phase of a fire. "A fire in which the heat release rate and growth rate are controlled by characteristics of the fuel, such as quantity and geometry, and in which adequate air for combustion is available."[24] See, for comparison, **ventilation-controlled fire**.

full room involvement. "Condition in a compartment fire [a fire in a compartment or closed room] in which the entire volume is involved in combustion of varying intensities."[25] All combustible material in the compartment is burning.

FVC. Forced vital capacity. The number of litres of breath a person can exhale after a maximum inhalation. A measure of lung capacity; can be employed to determine if a drinking driver could physically provide a suitable breath sample as demanded by the police.

g/100 mL. Grams of alcohol in 100 millilitres of blood, the unit of measurement of *BAC* in the United States. To convert g/100 mL into mg/100 mL, multiply by 1,000.

ganglion.* A mass of nervous tissue composed principally of neuron cell bodies lying outside the brain or spinal cord.

---

23 Scientific Working Group on Friction Ridge Analysis, Study and Technology (SWGFAST), "Glossary," "friction ridge" at 4, online: www.swgfast.org/documents/glossary/090508_Glossary_2.0_Archived.pdf [SWGFAST glossary].

24 *NFPA 921*, above note 2, s. 3.3.88.

25 *Ibid.*, s. 3.3.89.

gas chromatography (GC). A method of analysis of separating volatile compounds (such as alcohol, acetone, and acetaldehyde) depending on their chemical affinity for a column and used mainly in forensic alcohol analysis. Used to separate extracted constituents in toxicology tests.

gender. A cultural term that reflects one's identity as a woman, man, or elsewhere along the gender spectrum in society.

gender neutrality. Avoids discrimination based on a person's sex or gender.

GeneMapper®. Software that provides DNA strand sizing and allele/variant labelling.

general pathology.* The branch of medicine concerned with all aspects of laboratory investigation in health and disease. The discipline incorporates both morphological and non-morphological diagnostic techniques in the areas of anatomical pathology, medical biochemistry, medical microbiology, hematopathology, and transfusion medicine.

general rifling characteristics. The characteristic of a firearm or fired bullet relating to the number, width, and direction of twist of the rifling. The FBI's general rifling characteristics database allows the examiner to narrow down the possible make or model of firearm that fired a particular bullet, based on these measurements.

genome. The total genetic content of an organism.

genotype. A cell's, and therefore an organism's, genetic constitution. The genotype is one factor that determines a cell's, and therefore an organism's, phenotypes (the physical manifestation of a gene). For example, two different individuals may have blue eyes (a phenotype) but each individual might have two different combinations of *alleles* (representing the genotype).

geomorphology. The study of existing land forms and the processes creating them.

GlobalFiler®. Test to analyze DNA variants at twenty-four genetic locations for forensic purposes.

grain. The avoirdupois unit of weight used by firearms examiners when measuring ammunition components; 7000 grains equals one pound.

H^+. Hydrogen

H_2O. Water

half-life ($t_{½}$) (toxicology). The time required for a drug concentration to be reduced by 50 percent.

hallucinogens. A class of chemicals that can cause significant distortions in the perception of time, space, colour, and sound.

haplotypes. Groups of genes that are inherited together from either a person's mother or father. Haplotypes can be used to identify groups of related people.

Hart House Report. Colloquial reference for *Forensic Science in Canada: A Report of Multidisciplinary Discussion*, published in 2012.

hash analysis, digital forensics. The process of passing the entire contents of a file or document through a mathematical algorithm, resulting in a single alpha-numeric output that can be compared to other such output to identify files that are the same.

HCR-20. Historical, Clinical, and Risk Management-20. A tool used for violent risk appraisal.

headstamp. A series of numbers, letters, or symbols stamped onto the bottom/head of a cartridge case or shotgun cartridge that allows the firearms examiner to identify the manufacturer, calibre, and any other additional information.

Hemastix™. Presumptive test for the presence of blood that targets hemoglobin.

hematological pathology.* The domain of laboratory medical practice and science concerned with the study, investigation, diagnosis, and therapeutic monitoring of disorders of blood, blood-forming elements, hemostasis, and immune function in adults and children.

hematoma.* A collection of blood, generally the result of a hemorrhage or internal bleeding; usually resulting from injury (e.g., bruises in skin), but indicative of a more serious injury when located within organs, most critically inside the skull, where hematomas may place pressure on the brain.

hemorrhage.* The loss of blood from a ruptured blood vessel.

Hirschsprung's disease.* The most common cause of lower gastrointestinal obstruction in neonates. Patients with this disease exhibit signs of an extremely dilated colon and accompanying chronic constipation, fecal impaction, and overflow diarrhea.

histology.* The microscopic study of tissue sectioned as a thin slice. Tissues are sliced using a *microtome*.

histopathology.* A branch of pathology concerned with the study of microscopic changes in diseased tissues.

hollow volume overlays. A technique used in *forensic odontology* to transfer the contours of the teeth (i.e., the shape and position of the teeth) on to a transparent acetate sheet, creating an "overlay." The overlay is then superimposed over the photograph of a bitemark to gauge the degree of similarity between the pattern of the teeth and the pattern of the component injuries, allowing the forensic odontologist to conduct a visual comparison. When the hollow volumes were drawn by hand it was determined to be inaccurate and has since become outdated and is no longer used. Today, the hand traced overlays have been replaced by digitally produced overlays generated by a computer that ensures the accuracy of the technique.

humerus. The bone of the upper arm, which extends from shoulder to elbow.

hyperpyrexia. A dangerous elevation in body temperature.

hypertension. A substantial elevation in blood pressure.

hypoxic-ischemic encephalopathy.* Brain damage caused by a lack of oxygen and blood flow to the brain. Brain damage occurs very quickly and, once it occurs, is, effectively, irreversible.

IAFN. International Association of Forensic Nurses

IAI. International Association for Identification

Identifiler®Plus. A test to analyze DNA variants at sixteen genetic locations for forensic purposes.

ignition sequence. "[T]he succession of events and conditions that allow the source of ignition, the fuel, and the oxidant to interact in the appropriate quantities and circumstances for combustion to begin."[26]

ignition source. To cause a fire, three key features must be present: an ignition source, fuel, and an oxidant (e.g., air or oxygen). The ignition source "has sufficient energy and is capable of transferring that energy to the fuel long enough to raise the fuel to its ignition temperature."[27] For example, if a pot is left unattended on a hot stovetop, the heating element may be a potential ignition source.

ignition temperature. Also known as *piloted ignition temperature.* "Minimum temperature a substance should attain in order to ignite under specific test conditions."[28]

---

26 *Ibid.*, s. 19.4.4.1.
27 *Ibid.*, s. 3.3.36.
28 *Ibid.*, s. 3.3.106.

imagination inflation. A process through which an imagined event can take on an aura of subjective reality over time. In such cases, a person will remember having experienced an event that, in reality, they only imagined.

immunoassay testing (toxicology). Uses *antibodies* that have been raised to bind to specific drug targets or drug classes.

impact pattern.[†] A bloodstain pattern resulting from an object striking liquid blood.

impairment. Refers to a drug-induced decrement in the ability to perform a given task.

impression, latent (invisible). The most commonly encountered fingerprint impression at crime scenes. This type of impression is invisible to the naked eye and requires some form of development technique to render it visible. These development techniques can include the use of fingerprint powder, chemical treatment, or a light source. Oblique or grazed lighting techniques can assist in visualizing a latent impression prior to the application of any development technique.

impression, patent (visible). Patent impressions are visible to the naked eye and require minimal or no development. They are generally composed of a combination of natural bodily secretions and foreign material. The foreign material is frequently blood, dirt, ink, or grease.

impression, plastic or mold. These are three-dimensional impressions, created by depressing the finger into soft material. Common occurrences of this type of impression are in chocolate, cheese, putty, caulking, or chewing gum.[29]

impression, take away. An impression that is created when surface contact is made, but instead of a deposit occurring, something (e.g., dust) is removed from the surface. For example, as a hand is removed from a dusty surface, the dust adheres to the *friction skin*, creating a void on the surface. The resulting detail is reversed, in that the dust-free area of the impression is replicating the friction ridges, and the remaining dust, the furrows.

incendiary fire. A deliberately set fire.

indentations. Latent or visible impressions in paper or other media.

independent and identically distributed. Random variables all with the same distribution and all independent.

independent variable. See **explanatory variable.**

---

29 Ross M. Gardner, *Practical Crime Scene Processing and Investigation*, 2d ed. (Boca Raton, FL: CRC Press, 2012).

individual characteristics. Individual characteristics are generally considered to be exceptional characteristics that may establish the uniqueness of an object and support the conclusion that the object in question can be linked to a known object (i.e., both the questioned and known object originated from a common source). For example, marks on various parts of a firearm that come into contact with the bullet/cartridge case may create individual characteristics that are produced by the random imperfections or irregularities on the surfaces of those parts. These individual characteristics are produced incidental to manufacture and/or caused by wear, corrosion, or damage. They are considered to be unique to that tool, but they are not always visualized in sufficient quantity on fired bullets/cartridges.

individualization (fingerprint). The determination by a fingerprint examiner that there is sufficient quality and quantity of detail in agreement to conclude that two friction ridge impressions originated from the same source.

infanticide.* Infanticide is defined in the *Criminal Code*[30] as follows: "A female person commits infanticide when by a wilful act or omission she causes the death of her newly-born child, if at the time of the act or omission she is not fully recovered from the effects of giving birth to the child and by reason thereof or of the effect of lactation consequent on the birth of the child her mind is then disturbed." The term has been used historically in forensic pathology to indicate all forms of homicide of babies around the time of birth.

inflammation.* One mechanism the body uses to protect itself from invasion by foreign organisms and to repair tissue trauma. Its clinical hallmarks are redness, heat, swelling, pain, and loss of function of a body part. It is also marked by the migration of white blood cells into the affected area; this can be seen under the microscope.

informed consent. Informed consent comprises four parts: "First, the risks of the procedure or treatment must be explained. Second, the patient should be told about the benefits; third, the patient should be informed of any alternatives to the recommended treatment. Finally, the patient needs to be told the consequences if the treatment or procedure is not performed."[31]

insect stain.† A bloodstain resulting from insect activity.

instar. A developmental stage of insect life.

---

30 R.S.C. 1985, c. C-46, s. 233.

31 Virginia A. Lynch & Janet Barber Duval, *Forensic Nursing Science*, 2d ed. (St. Louis: Elsevier Mosby, 2011) at 541 [Lynch & Duval, *Forensic Nursing*].

interventions (nursing). Actions that nurses perform based on their assessments and nursing diagnoses.

intoxication. Refers to observable physiological drug effects (e.g., pupil dilation or constriction, elevated heart rate).

intracranial.* Within or introduced into the skull.

intracranial pressure.* Increased intracranial pressure is a serious medical problem because it causes the compression of important brain structures and restricts the blood flow through blood vessels that supply the brain, thereby possibly damaging it. Symptoms in infants include a bulging fontanelle (one of two "soft sports" on an infant's head), lethargy, and vomiting.

intra-oral. Inside the mouth.

intrathoracic.* Within the cavity of the chest.

IP address. Internet Protocol address. This address is used to identify the individual computing devices, often referred to as a "node," that are communicating over a network.

IR. Infrared. Refers to a method of detection of breath alcohol by using infrared light, typically at wavelengths of approximately 3.4 and 9.4 microns.

island. See **short ridge**.

ISO/IEC 17025. The general standard that applies to testing laboratories.

isopropanol. The chemical name of isopropyl alcohol or rubbing alcohol.

IT forensics. See **digital forensics**.

Kastle-Meyer. Presumptive test for the presence of blood that targets hemoglobin.

keratinized. The process of cell transformation into dead, thorny, or scaly tissue (e.g., hair follicles).

kinetic energy. See **bullet energy**.

laceration.* A wound or irregular tear of the flesh caused by blunt impact.

lake. See **enclosure**.

land and groove impression. The negative impressions on the surface of a bullet caused by the rifling in the barrel of the firearm from which it was fired.

larynx (laryngeal).* Also known as the voice box, a structure in the neck involved in sound production and in the protection of the trachea (windpipe).

lesion.* A circumscribed area of pathologically altered tissue, an injury or wound, or a single patch in a skin disease.

line quality. As applied to handwritten documents, line quality is the degree of regularity of pen strokes judged by the sum total of their attributes (e.g. speed, rhythm, pressure, skill).

liquid accelerant. Ignitable liquid.

liquid chromatography (LC). Used to separate extracted constituents in toxicology tests.

live ammunition. See **ammunition**.

liver.* The largest solid organ in the body, situated on the right side below the diaphragm. The liver secretes bile (a fluid) and is the site of numerous metabolic functions.

lividity (post-mortem).* A dark-blue staining of the dependent surface of a cadaver, resulting from the pooling and congestion of blood. Also known as livor mortis.

LNCAC. Legal Nurse Consultants Association of Canada

Locard's exchange principle. The principle underlying many forensic sciences that sets out that "whenever two objects come in contact with one another, a transfer of material will occur. The transfer may be tenuous but will certainly occur."[32]

long rifle. Often a source of confusion for the layperson, it most commonly refers to a particular calibre of .22 rim-fire firearms and ammunition (.22 long rifle calibre).

loop pattern. A fingerprint pattern type in which one or more friction ridges enter upon one side, recurve, touch, or pass an imaginary line between *delta* and *core* and flow out, or tend to flow out, on the same side the friction ridges entered. Types include:

- left slant loops, in which the pattern flows to the left in the impression;
- right slant loops, in which the pattern flows to the right in the impression;

32 Stuart H. James & Jon J. Nordby, eds., *Forensic Science: An Introduction to Scientific and Investigative Techniques* (Boca Raton, FL: CRC Press, 2003) at 172.

- radial loops, in which the pattern flows in the direction of the radius bone of the forearm (i.e., toward the thumb); and
- ulnar loops, in which the pattern flows in the direction of the ulna bone of the forearm (i.e., toward the little finger).

LTO. Long-term offender

luminol. A chemiluminescence test that detects the potential presence of blood by targeting its hemoglobin. The test is not specific to blood and, as a result, other oxidizing agents (e.g., bleach) may result in luminescence when exposed to luminol. Presumptive blood tests, such as *Kastle-Meyer* or *Hemastix*™ tests, should be used if the luminol reacts to a potential sample.

magazine. A container for ammunition that has a spring and a follower to facilitate the feeding of that ammunition from the magazine into the chamber of a firearm. Magazines can be detachable (e.g., semi-automatic pistol) or integral to the firearm (e.g., pump-action shotgun). See **action, semi-automatic** and **action, pump-action.**

mainspring. The spring that provides the energy to operate the striker or hammer of a firearm by virtue of it being compressed and then released.

malignant.* Growing worse; resisting treatment (said of cancerous growths); tending or threatening to produce death.

malingering. Refers to the deliberate feigning or exaggeration of symptoms for a generally discernible and tangible purpose that usually involves avoiding legal ramifications or punishment, work, other duties, or military conscription, or obtaining some material gain or benefit.

mandible (mandibular).* The lower jaw.

margin of error. A measure of the uncertainty in an estimate of a population parameter. This may be a confidence interval, or it may be some other measure.

mass spectrometer. An instrument used in toxicology tests to charge and fragment each molecule, separate the fragments, and measure the mass and intensity (a measure of quantity based on the brightness of the light released) of each fragment. The process itself is called mass spectrometry (MS).

mean. The sum of a list of numbers, divided by the count of the numbers. May refer to a sample or a population. Also known as an *average*.

mechanical asphyxia. See **asphyxia**.

metabolism (toxicology). The various chemical reactions that transform a drug into by-products, also called *metabolites*.

metabolites. By-products of drugs caused by chemical reactions in the body.

metadata. Metadata is "data about the data" and not all files contain metadata. For example, metadata may be the date, time, and GPS coordinates of a photograph included within the digital photograph itself.

metaphysis. The growth plate of a bone.

methanol. The chemical name of methyl alcohol or wood alcohol.

M-FAST. Miller Forensic Assessment of Symptoms Test. Used to test for feigned psychiatric (particularly psychotic) illness and impairment.

mg/100 mL. Milligrams of alcohol in 100 millilitres of blood, the unit of measurement of *BAC* in the *Criminal Code*.

microbiology (microbiological).* The scientific study of micro-organisms.

microliter (µl). One millionth of a litre.

microns. A millionth of a metre, a unit of measurement used to measure the wavelength of infrared light.

microtome. A mechanical instrument used to cut biological specimens into very thin segments for microscopic examination.

mineralogy. The scientific study of minerals.

misfire. In a firearm, the failure of the primer to detonate by the normal striker of a firing pin, or if the propellant/gunpowder does not properly ignite.

mist pattern.† A bloodstain pattern resulting from blood reduced to a spray of microdrops as a result of the force applied.

Mitochondrion (*sing.*; mitochondria, *plur.*). An organelle (i.e., a little organ) found within a cell's cytoplasm (the solution within the cell) that is responsible for energy production in cells and contains its own small chromosomes. Mitochondria are targeted in mitochondrial DNA (mtDNA or mDNA) analysis, which is rarely performed compared to conventional forensic *STR analysis*. Each person's mitochondrial DNA is genetically inherited from their mother.

mmol/L. Millimoles of alcohol in 1 litre of blood, the unit of measurement of *BAC* used in hospitals internationally. To convert mmol/L into mg/100 mL, multiply by four.

MMPI-2. The Minnesota Multiphasic Personality Inventory-2 Restructured Form test.

***Mohan* criteria.** The standard for the admission of expert evidence under *R. v. Mohan*[33] requires four criteria to be met: (1) necessity in assisting the trier of fact; (2) relevance; (3) a qualified expert; and (4) the absence of an applicable exclusionary rule.

morphology. The study of the form and structure of organisms.

mount. Mounting a file system is opening it so that it can be read. The file system has to be "open" or "mounted" before data can be written to a device.

multi-user computing environment. A computing environment consisting of one computer and many users, with no passwords or common password in use.

mutually exclusive events. Events which cannot occur together.

muzzle energy. See **bullet energy**.

mycology. Branch of biology dealing with fungi.

NAD+. Nicotinamide adenine dinucleotide. An enzymatic cofactor in the oxidation of alcohol in the body and for hospital enzymatic alcohol analysis; the reduced form of NAD+ is NADH.

nanogram (ng). One billionth of a gram.

narcotic analgesics. Drugs that are sleep-inducing, but also display a substantial analgesic efficacy. Effects include euphoria, pupil constriction, sweating, itchiness, sedation, drowsiness, and mental clouding.

NAS. National Academy of Sciences (United States)

NDDB. National DNA Data Bank (Canada)

***negative corpus*.** This method to determine fire cause is outdated, should not be used by fire investigators, and is a clear violation of the scientific method. In this approach, the absence of evidence is viewed as evidence. Historically, many fire investigators relied on this method and, in doing so, relied on the process of elimination alone to exclude all reasonable ignition sources for a fire. If the investigator eliminated all reasonable ignitions sources, then the investigator would conclude that the fire must have been set intentionally.

neuropathologist.* A pathologist who specializes in the diagnosis of diseases of the brain and nervous system by microscopic examination of the tissue and other means.

---

33 *R. v. Mohan*, [1994] 2 S.C.R. 9.

NFPA. National Fire Protection Association. A non-profit organization established in 1896 and headquartered in Quincy, Massachusetts. Its mission is to "reduce the worldwide burden of fire and other hazards on the quality of life by providing and advocating for scientifically based consensus codes and standards, research, training and education."[34]

NICHD. National Institute of Child Health and Human Development. Located in Bethesda, Maryland.

NIST. National Institute of Standards and Technology (United States)

noise. In statistics, noise is a term for random error. It is generally used in time series analysis. In data, mining noise refers to messy data with typos, non-standardized entries, and so on.

nursing diagnosis. A "clinical judgement about individual, family or community responses to actual or potential health problems/life processes."[35]

nursing process. Defined as "a scientific method that nurses use to provide care, beginning with an initial patient assessment and the establishment of a nursing diagnosis. Planning, intervention and evaluation activities complete the nursing process."[36]

observation. One unit that has been sampled and measured in a survey or experiment. See also **sample**.

occipital region. The rear of the head.

odontology.* The study of the teeth, jaws, and related structures. A science dealing with the teeth, including their structure, development, and diseases. See also **forensic odontology**.[37]

oral fluid. A complex mixture of fluids formed within the salivary glands and other minor glands, in combination with gingival fluid, epithelial cell material, and various particulates.

oral fluid-blood concentration ratio (OF/B). Measurement of the extent to which drugs and metabolites partition from the blood into the oral fluid.

oro-facial. Relating to the mouth and face.

---

34 From the NFPA website, online: www.nfpa.org.

35 Lynch & Duval, *Forensic Nursing*, above note 31 at 7.

36 *Ibid.* at 6.

37 "The study of the teeth, jaws, and related structures" has been added to the existing definition provided from the Medical Glossary used in the Goudge Inquiry Report.

OSAC. Organization of Scientific Area Committees (United States). The result of the National Commission on Forensic Science, co-chaired by the Department of Justice (DOJ), and the National Institute of Standards and Technology (NIST), to enhance the practice and reliability of the forensic sciences in the United States. The traditional Scientific Working Groups (SWGs) have transitioned to the Organization of Scientific Area Committees (OSACs) to reach consensus on documentation standards and guidelines, as well as to ensure that each forensic discipline has a sufficient scientific basis. Communications and collaborations arising from the SWGs have helped to guide the forensic community in the United States, as well as internationally. Guidelines published by the SWGs remain in place until new guidelines are published by the OSACs.

osteology.* The science concerned with the structure and function of bones.

outlier. An observation that is many standard deviations from the mean. Outliers should only be discarded if it is certain that the value is wrong (typo, faulty equipment, etc.). Wrongly discarding outliers induces false power.

over 80 mg/100 mL. Refers to the criminal charge of driving with a *BAC* in excess of 80. Known colloquially as "over 80."

oviposition. To lay cggs, cspccially with rcspcct to insccts.

PAI (forensic psychology). Personal Assessment Inventory test

palmar surface. The ridged surface located on the palms and the underside of the fingers.

palpation. Involves the use of the hands to examine the body while looking for injury, illness, or disease.

palynology. The study of pollen, including the microscopic analysis of pollen.

pancreas.* A gland located behind the stomach. The secretions of the pancreas consist of powerful enzymes that contribute to the digestion of all food types in the small intestine.

parabellum. A Latin word meaning "for war." Commonly found in the cartridge designation 9mm parabellum (also known as 9mm Luger).

parent stain.† A bloodstain from which a *satellite stain* originated.

parietal bone.* The main bone of the side and top of the skull.

pathologist.* A medical professional trained to examine tissues, cells, and specimens of body fluids for evidence of disease.

pathology.* The study of the nature and cause of disease, which involves changes in structure and function.

patient-centered care. Described as "providing care that is respectful and responsive to the individual patient's preferences, needs and values and ensures that patient values guide all clinical decisions."[38]

PCL-R. Hare Psychopathy Checklist-Revised

pediatrics.* That branch of medicine involving the diagnosis and treatment of illness in children.

pedohebephilic individuals. Persons whose erotic interests centre on prepubescent and/or pubescent children.

peg-shaped lateral. Congenitally misshapen lateral incisor (tooth).

pen lift. An interruption in a stroke that is produced when the writing instrument is lifted from the writing surface.

pen pressure. The force with which the writing instrument contacts the writing surface.

penile plethysmography. See **phallometric testing.**

perimeter stain.† An altered stain that consists of the peripheral characteristics of the original stain.

periodontal disease. Gum disease.

peripheral blood samples. Samples taken from areas of the body that are distant from the thoracic region.

petechial hemorrhage (petechiae).* Pinpoint hemorrhage; tiny purple or red spots that appear on the skin because of small spots of bleeding in the skin.

Phadebas®. Test used to target *amylase* to indicate the potential presence of saliva.

phallometric testing. *Penile plethysmography*, commonly referred to as phallometric testing, is a physiologic measure of sexual arousal.

pharmacodynamics. Loosely described as the study of the effects of drugs on the body.

---

38 Committee on Quality Healthcare in America, Institute of Medicine, *Crossing the Quality Chasm: A New Health System for the 21st Century* (Washington, DC: The National Academy Press, 2001).

pharmacokinetics. The study of the various processes that influence the time course of a drug and its metabolites within the body.

phenology. Refers to aspects of timing and seasonality of plants, such as germination, growth rates, flowering and fruiting, and leaf drop.

phenotype. The physical manifestation of a gene (i.e., how a person looks).

picogram (pg). One thousandth of a nanogram.

piloted ignition temperature. See **ignition temperature**.

plantar surface. The ridged surface located on the soles of the feet and the underside of the toes.

plasma. See **serum**.

point of origin. "[T]he exact physical location within the area of origin where a heat source and the fuel interact, resulting in a fire or explosion."[39]

point of divergence. The point where two *friction ridges*, that have been running parallel or nearly parallel, separate.

polar (toxicology). Water-soluble.

polymerase chain reaction (PCR). The DNA replication process.

polypharmacy. The consumption of multiple drugs simultaneously.

pool.[†] A bloodstain resulting from an accumulation of liquid blood on a surface.

poroscopy. A method of personal identification through the comparison of the impressions of sweat pores, present on friction ridges of palmar and plantar surfaces.

post-mortem interval (PMI). Minimum elapsed time since death.

post-mortem redistribution. The process by which drugs that have accumulated in tissues diffuse out of those tissues and into the surrounding blood after death.

PowerPlex® Fusion. A test to analyze DNA variants from twenty-seven genetic locations for forensic purposes.

PowerPlex® 16. A test to analyze DNA variants at sixteen genetic locations for forensic purposes.

---

39 *NFPA 921*, above note 2, s. 18.1.

precipitation (toxicology). The addition of a chemical that causes some constituents to come out of solution and form a solid, so that the remaining liquid sample can be further prepared.

precision. A measure of scientific reliability. Precision is the observer's ability to obtain the same result each time the same object is examined (regardless of whether or not the result is correct).

prepuparial, prepupal, or wandering stage (forensic entomology). The point at which a larva leaves the food source in search of a dry safe place in which to metamorphose to the adult stage of its life cycle.

presumptive analyses (toxicology). Simple tests used to indicate the presence or absence of a particular drug or drug class.

presumptive testing. As indicated by a presumptive test, the target substance is likely present but that must be confirmed by a more specific method.

primer (firearms). The primer is a disc-shaped piece of metal fitted to the bottom of the cartridge case. It contains a chemical mixture that ignites when struck by the firing pin. This travels through the flash-hole, igniting the main propellant charge.

primer (DNA testing). Small pieces of DNA that bind close along the chromosome strand to the *STR addresses* of interest.

probabilistic genotyping. A means to extract potentially useful data from complex forensic DNA mixture profiles that otherwise might be discarded as uninterpretable.

probability. The chance that an event will occur, expressed as a number between 0 and 1 inclusive. (1) *Empirical Probability*: the fraction of times the event occurs in an infinite number of identical trials, used in all sciences. (2) *Subjective Probability*: personal estimate of probability, reflecting the degree of belief than an event will occur under certain circumstances, only used in Bayesian statistics.

probability sample. A sample such that all individuals in a finite population have the same probability of being included in the sample. Methodologies include simple random sampling, stratified sampling, and cluster sampling. Used to maximize the probability that the sample is representative of population. Non-probability samples include quota samples and systematic samples.

ProflierPlus™. A commercial DNA analysis kit that tests nine genetic locations for forensic purposes.

projected pattern.[†] A bloodstain pattern resulting from the ejection of a volume of blood under pressure.

propellant. The chemical compound found inside a cartridge that generates energy when ignited by the primer. Also known as gunpowder and smokeless powder.

PSA/p30. Prostate-specific antigen. A protein secreted by the prostate gland.

Psychiatric Risk Assessment. See **Violence Risk Assessment**.

pubic symphysis. Where the two pubic bones meet at the front on the body.

pull ups. Peaks in an electropherogram which are not *alleles* but are instead caused by a slight misreading of the dye colour by the camera and associated software.

pulmonary.* Concerning, affecting, or associated with the lungs.

pulmonary congestion.* A condition characterized by the engorgement of the pulmonary vessels.

pulmonary pleura.* The portion of the pleura (the delicate membranous covering of the lungs) that covers the surface of the lungs and dips into the fissures between its lobes.

putrefaction. The process of decay or rotting in organic material.

pyrolysis (toxicology). Chemical decomposition by heat.

race. A cultural construct that reflects beliefs and attitudes about different groups of people.

radial slope. Fingerprint loops that exit towards the thumb.

radiologist.* A physician who uses X-rays or other sources of radiation, sound, or radio-frequencies for diagnosis and treatment.

radiology.* The branch of medicine concerned with radioactive substances, including X-rays, and the application of this information to prevention, diagnosis, and treatment of disease.

random match probability (RMP). The estimate of the coincidental match probability between two or more DNA samples.

RCPSC. Royal College of Physicians and Surgeons of Canada; now abbreviated to **Royal College**.

rebleeding (of a healing subdural hemorrhage).* Refers to the controversy in pediatric forensic pathology about whether a relatively insignificant old or healing subdural hemorrhage can develop into a massive and life-threatening acute subdural hemorrhage as a result of normal handling or minor trauma.

recoil. The rearward movement of a firearm that results from firing.

reload. A cartridge that has been reassembled with a new primer, propellant, and projectile(s). Cartridge cases can have pre-existing toolmarks found on them from the previous firing—but these will not appear on the primer.

retinal hemorrhage.* Bleeding onto the surface of the retina (the light-sensitive membrane in the back of the eye) caused by the rupture of the tiny blood vessels that lie on the surface of the retina. Retinal hemorrhage indicates increased pressure within the skull, possibly resulting from head trauma and bleeding. It was once believed to be pathognomonic (a sign or symptom that is so characteristic of a disease that it makes the diagnosis) of shaken baby syndrome, although this is no longer generally believed to be true.

RFLPs. Restriction fragment length polymorphisms. The first forensic DNA technique.

rib ends. Where the ribs meet the breastbone (sternum).

ridge dot. See **ridge unit**.

ridge ending. Also known as an *ending ridge*. A type of friction ridge path characteristic; it is a single friction ridge that terminates within the friction ridge structure.

ridge unit. Also known as a *ridge dot*. A type of friction ridge path characteristic; it is an isolated ridge unit whose length approximates its width in size.

ridgeology. In fingerprint identification, the study of the uniqueness of friction ridge structures and their use for personal identification.

rigor mortis.* The stiffening of the muscles after death.

Royal College. Royal College of Physicians and Surgeons. Previously known as the **RCPSC**.

RN. Registered Nurse

RPN. Registered Psychiatric Nurse

RRASOR (forensic psychology). Rapid Risk Assessment of Sex Offender Risk. An actuarial-style tool of assessing sexual violence recidivism.

RT-qPCR. Real-time quantitative polymerase chain reaction. The basis for quantitative testing for DNA.

Saligae®. A test used to target *amylase* to indicate the potential presence of saliva.

sample. The collection of all units surveyed. See also **observation**.

sample space. The sample space is the set of all possible outcomes of a given experiment.

SANE. Sexual Assault Nurse Examiner

SANE-A©. Certification as a Sexual Assault Nurse Examiner-Adolescent/Adult. Received through the International Association of Forensic Nurses.

SANE-P©. Certification as a Sexual Assault Nurse Examiner-Pediatric. Received through the International Association of Forensic Nurses.

Sarcophagidae. Family of flies of the order *Diptera*.

satellite stain.† A smaller bloodstain that originated during the formation of the *parent stain* as a result of blood impacting a surface.

saturation stain.† A bloodstain resulting from the accumulation of liquid blood in an absorbent material.

sear. A small internal part of the firearm which holds the hammer or striker in the cocked position until the trigger is pulled.

sear notch. See **bent.**

sebaceous sweat glands. Sweat glands that are found on areas of the body associated with hair follicles.

sebum. Secretions from sebaceous glands, comprised mainly of saturated fats, waxes, and squalene.

secondary projectile. Any fragment—such as shattered glass, wood, or bone—or any other object that becomes a projectile due to the energy imparted to it by a striking bullet.

segments. See **evidence container.**

semi-synthetic drug. A drug that is formed through the chemical reaction of a naturally occurring drug to form a new product.

sequelae. Health conditions that are the result of previous disease or injury.

serology. The scientific study of body fluid identification.

serum stain.† The stain resulting from the liquid portion of blood (*serum*) that separates during coagulation.

serum. Also known as **plasma.** Components of blood without the red blood cells; has an alcohol concentration of approximately 1.16 times that of the blood alcohol concentration.

sex. A biological term that refers to a person's genotype.

SFST. Standardized Field Sobriety Test

shaken baby syndrome (SBS).* Sometimes called shaken infant syndrome; a serious illness characterized by subdural hemorrhage, petechial and other hemorrhages in the retina, and hypoxic-ischemic encephalopathy, usually in circumstances where there is no evidence of blunt impact to the head. Injuries to the neck, such as hemorrhage around cervical spine nerve roots, may also be present.

sharp force trauma. Comes in many forms, which can be categorized as incised wounds (e.g., cuts and slashes) or puncture wounds (e.g., stab wounds).

shiny alligator blisters. The description of the shape of the char that forms on wood exposed to heat or fire.[40]

short ridge. A type of *friction ridge path characteristic* that is also called an island. It is a single friction ridge that begins, travels a short distance, and ends.

signature analysis, digital forensics. The process of matching a file extension, such as .DOC or .XLS, with the file's signature. Typically, the signature is the first several bytes of the file, not visible in the native application, and recognizable by a knowledgeable user with a suitable utility.

simple reaction time (SRT). May be defined as the time taken by a subject to respond to a stimulus (usually auditory or visual), usually by means of actuation of a switch or signal (e.g., press a button or a foot pedal).

SIRS-2. Structured Interview of Reported Symptoms-Version 2. Used to test for feigned psychiatric—particularly psychotic—illness and impairment.

skeletal survey.* A radiological study of the entire skeleton to look for evidence of occult fractures, multiple myeloma, metastatic tumours, or child abuse.

skull sutures.* Also known as *cranial sutures*. The fibrous joints between the bones of the skull that allow a baby's skull to expand with his or her growing brain. The bones continue to grow together until they are separated only by interlocking projections commonly referred to as cranial sutures.[41]

SNP. Single nucleotide polymorphism. A sequence variation in DNA.

---

40 *Ibid.*, ss. 6.2.4.3–6.2.4.3.1.

41 "Also known as cranial sutures" and "The bones continue to grow . . . sutures" has been added to the existing definition provided from the Medical Glossary used in the Goudge Inquiry Report.

source amnesia. An inability to distinguish information acquired at the time of an experience from information that may be added later.

source media. The storage device identified as the media to be copied. This is the data that requires analysis by an investigator trained in conducting forensic digital analyses.

spalling. The breaking off of pieces of the surface of cement or brick due to intense heat or other factors related to the quality and makeup of the masonry, freezing, chemicals, abrasions, mechanical movement, shock, force, or fatigue.[42]

spatter stain.† A bloodstain resulting from a blood drop dispersed through the air due to an external force applied to a source of liquid blood.

spinal cord.* Part of the central nervous system. The spinal cord is an ovoid column of nerve tissues that extends from the medulla to the lumbar vertebrae. It is the pathway for sensory impulses to the brain and motor impulses from the brain.

splash pattern.† A bloodstain pattern resulting from a volume of liquid blood that falls or spills onto a surface.

spleen.* A dark-red, oval lymphoid organ in the upper-left abdominal quadrant, posterior and slightly inferior to the stomach. After birth, the spleen forms lymphocytes (white blood cells responsible for much of the body's immune protection).

Static-2002. An actuarial-style tool of assessing sexual violence recidivism.

Static-99. An actuarial-style tool of assessing sexual violence recidivism.

status epilepticus.* Continuous seizure activity without a pause; that is, without an intervening period of normal brain function.

stimulants. Drugs that involve stimulation of the central and/or peripheral nervous systems, typically causing euphoria, excitement/agitation, and heightened energy, as well as elevations in heart rate and blood pressure, and an increase in pupil diameter.

stochastic effect. Can occur when prohibitively small amounts of DNA are analyzed—the *amplification* process sometimes favours copying one variant at an address over another.

storage device. The medium which stores the digital evidence. The computer itself houses the storage device. The storage device is physical evidence that can be seen, touched, and recorded for continuity of evidence purposes.

---

42 *NFPA 921*, above note 2, s. 6.2.13.1.4.

STR. Short Tandem Repeat DNA. A short piece of DNA that is repeated over and over again, in tandem.

STRMix™. Expert software package for analyzing complex forensic DNA mixture profiles.

Structured professional judgment (SPJ). Used in *Psychiatric Risk Assessment*, this method melds historical and dynamic (clinical and risk management) factors.

stutter peaks. Peaks in an electropherogram which are not *alleles*, produced by the technology used in DNA *amplification*.

subclass characteristics. A phenomenon of firearms identification where microscopic features can appear to be in agreement because the tool that created them on the firearm has not changed appreciably over time. They are produced incidental to being manufactured, they are more restrictive than *class characteristics*, and they can be confused for *individual characteristics*.

subdural hematoma.* Also known as subdural hemorrhage. Caused through the stretching and tearing of small veins in the brain, most often resulting from a head injury. Blood collects between the dura (the outer protective covering of the brain) and the arachnoid (the middle layer of the membranes that envelop the central nervous system), often causing an increase in intracranial pressure and possible damage to delicate brain tissue. Onset of symptoms is slower than other types of hemorrhaging, usually occurring within twenty-four hours, but possibly taking up to two weeks to appear. Signs of subdural hemorrhage may include loss of consciousness or fluctuating levels of consciousness, numbness, disorientation, nausea or vomiting, personality changes, a deviated gaze, and difficulty in speaking and walking.

subgaleal bruise.* Bruising between the galeal aponeurosis, a fibro-muscular layer effectively attaching the scalp to the skull.

substrate. Underlying surface on which a process occurs (e.g., fingerprints are retained on a substrate).

successional ecology. Area of analysis in *forensic entomology* that considers the sequence of insects that colonize the remains over time, beginning with the first colonizers.

Sudden Infant Death Syndrome (SIDS).* The sudden unexpected death of an infant under twelve months of age, with onset of the fatal episode apparently occurring during sleep, which remains unexplained after a thorough investigation, including performance of a complete autopsy and review of the circumstances of the death and clinical history.

Sudden Unexplained Death Syndrome (SUDS).* Also known as sudden unexpected death syndrome, sudden unidentified death syndrome, and sudden unexpected death in infancy (SUDI). This is a broader categorization of deaths in infancy that includes unexplained deaths other than sudden infant death syndrome.

supernumerary. Extra in number (e.g., teeth).

surgical pathology.* The application of pathology procedures and techniques for investigating tissues removed surgically.

SVR-20. Sexual Violence Risk-20. An SPJ (*structured professional judgment*)-style tool of assessing sexual violence recidivism.

SWGDAM. Scientific Working Group on DNA Analysis Methods

SWGFAST. Scientific Working Group on Friction Ridge Analysis, Study and Technology. Closed in 2014, operations moved to the Friction Ridge Subcommittee (FRS) of the Organization of Scientific Area Committees (OSAC).

swipe pattern.† A bloodstain pattern resulting from the transfer of blood from a blood-bearing surface onto another surface, with characteristics that indicate relative motion between the two surfaces.

synthetic drug. Prepared entirely in the laboratory.

tachycardia. Substantial elevation in heart rate.

tandem mass spectrometer (MS/MS). Instrument used in toxicology tests to charge and fragment each molecule, separate the fragments, and measure the mass and intensity (a measure of quantity based on the brightness of the light released) of each fragment.

taphonomy (forensic anthropology). The study of everything that happens to a body from the time of death to the point at which it is examined.

taphonomy (forensic botany). Refers to understanding the processes that transport, preserve, decompose, or otherwise alter plant remains at a location.

target.† A surface onto which blood has been deposited.

t-butanol. The chemical name of tertiary-butyl alcohol. Typically used as an internal standard for headspace gas chromatographic analysis. Also known as **tert-butanol.**

teneral flies. Flies which have just emerged from their pupal case and cannot yet fly.

thermal inertia. The measure of how rapidly a material's surface temperature increases when it is exposed to heat.

thermite. A composition of a metal powder and a metal oxide, used for thermite welding, metal refining, demolition of munitions, and in incendiary weapons. Sometimes found during fire investigations.

thermocycler. A device used in DNA analysis to heat and cool samples in order to target and make copies of DNA sequences.

thoracic.* Involving or located in the chest.

thrombus. See **blood clot**.

thymus.* A small glandular organ situated behind the top of the breast bone, consisting mainly of lymphatic tissue.

TOMM. Test of Malingered Memory. This test assists in evaluating claimed memory problems and cognitive impairment.

touch DNA. The term for the DNA that is left behind when a person touches or otherwise comes in contact with an object.

toxicology.* The division of medical and biological science concerned with toxic substances, their detection, their avoidance, their chemistry and pharmacological actions, and their antidotes and treatment.

trailer. A trailer is "solid or liquid fuel used to intentionally spread or accelerate the spread of a fire from one area to another."[43]

transfer stain.† A bloodstain resulting from contact between a blood-bearing surface and another surface.

trauma informed care. Refers to "trauma-informed systems and organizations [that] provide for everyone within that system or organization by having a basic understanding of the psychological, neurological, biological, social and spiritual impact that trauma and violence can have on individuals seeking support. Trauma informed services recognize that the core of any services is genuine, authentic and compassionate relationships."[44]

---

43 *Ibid.*, s. 3.3.181.

44 Trauma-Informed, "The Trauma Toolkit" (2d ed., 2013) at 16, online: trauma-informed.ca/wp-content/uploads/2013/10/Trauma-informed_Toolkit.pdf.

traumagram. Body map that aids the forensic nurse in documenting the extent and location of all identified injuries on a patient's body.

triage of a computer. Triaging a computer or storage device involves conducting a preliminary review of the digital evidence with the objective of identifying the presence or absence of content that is relevant to the investigation underway.

tri-allelic. A genetic anomaly that results in the display of three genetic variants at a single address in an electropherogram.

TrueAllele®. Expert software package for analyzing complex forensic DNA mixture profiles.

trusted system. A computer system that is controlled by the investigator, has a known configuration and operating behaviour, is clean of viruses, and has installed upon it the necessary forensic software to copy the data from the *source media*.

UAC. Urine alcohol concentration

ulcer; ulceration.* A lesion that often heals poorly on a surface such as skin, a cornea, or a mucous membrane.

ulnar slope (fingerprint). Fingerprint loops that exit towards the little finger. See also **ulnar loop**.

unfired cartridge. See **ammunition**.

ventilation (fire investigation). Refers to the introduction of oxygen-rich fresh air to the fire through openings in the structure, be it an open or breached window, door, or a burned-through roof. If there is ventilation, the heat-release rate will be greater in the area where the ventilation is provided.

ventilation-controlled fire. "A fire in which the heat release rate or growth is controlled by the amount of air available to the fire."[45]

Violence Risk Assessment. Also referred to as **Psychiatric Risk Assessment.** A term of art in the field of psychiatry and forensic psychiatry that refers to a process of thorough information-gathering for the purpose of making informed judgments about an evaluee's risk for committing violence, and to inform risk management. The process generally concludes with the evaluator providing an estimation of the individual's likelihood of committing violence, defining its anticipated nature and severity, the environment and timeframe in which it might occur, who is likely to be a victim, and the conditions that will enable or suppress the prospect of its occurrence.

---

45 *NFPA 921*, above note 2, s. 3.3.188.

virtual machine. A virtual machine permits the examiner to use a copy of the data from the seized device and recreate how the device would have appeared and functioned at the time it was seized. Using what is often referred to as VM software, the examiner can display to the court how the device would have appeared to the user, showing what was visible, what was accessible, and what steps would have been required to access the data in issue.

viscera.* The internal organs of the body, specifically those within the chest (e.g., the heart and lungs) or abdomen (e.g., the liver, pancreas, and intestines).

void.† An absence of blood in an otherwise continuous bloodstain or bloodstain pattern.

volar pad. Area on the fingers and toes where friction ridge patterns will ultimately form. Pressure and tension present on volar pads during fetal development can influence friction ridge pattern formation.

VRAG. Violence Risk Appraisal Guide

whorl pattern. A fingerprint pattern type consisting of the combination of two different types of patterns (excluding the plain arch), with two or more *deltas*. This pattern can be classified into several different types, depending on its characteristics, including: plain, accidental, central pocket loop, and double loop.

Wilms' tumour.* A rapidly developing tumour of the kidney that usually occurs in children.

wipe pattern.† An altered bloodstain pattern resulting from an object moving through a pre-existing wet bloodstain.

xenobiotics. Any chemical, exclusive of a normal diet, that can alter the body's physiology.

Contributors*

Gail S. Anderson, MPM, PhD, is a professor in forensic entomology in the School of Criminology at Simon Fraser University (SFU), co-director of the Centre for Forensic Research, and a forensic consultant to the RCMP and municipal police across Canada; she holds a Burnaby Mountain Endowed Professorship at SFU. She is a fellow of the American Academy of Forensic Sciences and the Canadian Society of Forensic Science. Dr. Anderson has been analyzing forensic entomology cases since 1988 and has testified as an expert witness in court many times. She received the Simon Fraser University Alumni Association Outstanding Alumni Award for Academic Achievement in 1995 and a YWCA Women of Distinction Award for Science and Technology in 1999, and was also a recipient of Canada's Top 40 under 40 Award in 1999. Dr. Anderson was listed in Time magazine as one of the top five innovators in the world, this century, in the field of criminal justice and was featured on the cover. Dr. Anderson was presented with the Derome Award in 2001. She was listed as one of the 100 most influential women in British Columbia by the Vancouver Sun and received a Dean's Medal for Academic Excellence in 2014.

Maggie Bellis, MB, BCh, BAO, FRCP, joined the Provincial Forensic Pathology Unit in Toronto as a forensic pathologist in 2014, following residency training in forensic pathology at the University of Toronto. She completed a bachelor of science degree at Western University and received her medical training at the National University of Ireland, Cork. After completing residency training at the University of Toronto,

* Please note that the views in this book are representative of these individuals only, and not necessarily their employers.

Dr. Bellis received her FRCPC in anatomical pathology in 2013 and in forensic pathology in 2014. She is an investigative coroner for homicides and criminally suspicious deaths in Ontario.

Hy Bloom, BA, LLB, MD, FRCPC, is a forensic psychiatrist and lawyer who assesses individuals whose psychological and emotional states, motivations, or behaviours are of potential relevance in criminal, civil, professional, regulatory, or employment matters. He is a CEO of workplace.calm inc., consultants in workplace conflict and violence prevention and management, and a founding associate of the PSILEX Group, consultants in behavioural sciences and the law. He is also a part-time staff member in the Complex Mental Illness Program at the Centre for Addiction and Mental Health, an assistant professor in the Department of Medicine at the University of Toronto, an assistant clinical professor in the Department of Psychiatry and Behavioural Neurosciences at McMaster University, and adjunct faculty at University of Toronto's Faculty of Law. Dr. Bloom is a psychiatric member and alternate chair on both the Ontario and Nunavut review boards. He has spoken and published extensively on a number of topics in psychiatry and the law. Information about his various books and other publications can be accessed at www.workplace.calm.to.

Vladimir (Val) Chlistovsky, BASc, CFEI, CVFI, PEng, is the practice lead of the fire group at Giffin Koerth Forensic Engineering. He is an internationally certified fire and explosion investigator and an internationally certified vehicle fire investigator. He has investigated over 600 fires, and is well-recognized as a fire investigation and electrical expert. Mr. Chlistovsky is the vice-president of the Canadian Association of Fire Investigators and holds membership with the National Association of Fire Investigators. Mr. Chlistovsky is also a professional engineer and member of the Professional Engineers of Ontario. He actively participates as a technical expert and technical assessor with the Certifying Bodies and Laboratory Accreditation programs with the Standards Council of Canada. In addition to Mr. Chlistovsky's experience in forensics, he has also spent ten years in the insurance industry working for FM Global in heavy machinery and equipment appraisal and seven years in a manufacturing setting as a production and approvals engineer.

Kristopher Cunningham, MD, PhD, FRCPC, is a forensic pathologist and cardiovascular pathologist at the Provincial Forensic Pathology Unit in Toronto and an assistant professor in the Department of Laboratory Medicine and Pathobiology at the University of Toronto. Dr. Cunningham has an interest in the pathology of sudden death, including structural and non-structural causes of sudden cardiac death.

He helped to establish the molecular autopsy laboratory of the Ontario Forensic Pathology Service (OFPS) and create a molecular autopsy program for the OFPS. Dr. Cunningham travelled as a representative of the Federal (with the Department of Foreign Affairs and International Trade) and Ontario governments to assist in disaster victim identification following the earthquake in Haiti in 2010. He is an investigative coroner for homicides and criminally suspicious deaths in Ontario.

Brian L. Cutler, PhD, is professor in the Faculty of Social Science and Humanities at the University of Ontario Institute of Technology in Oshawa, Ontario. Professor Cutler regularly authors and edits books, chapters, and articles on forensic psychology and serves as a consultant and expert witness on eyewitness identification and false confession.

Sheila D. Early, RN, BScN, has four decades of health care experience as a registered nurse, administrator, clinician, and educator in emergency and forensic nursing. Ms. Early co-developed British Columbia's first sexual assault nurse examiner program in 1992. She developed Canada's first classroom-delivered Advanced Specialty Certificate in Forensic Health Sciences at the British Columbia Institute of Technology (2005). Ms. Early performed the first nurse examiner medical forensic examination in British Columbia (1994), remaining a practicing nurse examiner until 2007. Her experiences have provided her with the background to provide education to health care providers and other disciplines in forensic healthcare issues relating to violence, trauma, and crime. She has provided forensic nursing education both nationally and internationally for the past fifteen years. She has received nursing awards, including the British Columbia Institute of Technology Teaching Excellence Award (2014), the University of Saskatchewan College of Nursing Alumni Nurse of Influence Award (2014), the International Association of Forensic Nurses Achievement Award (2010), the B.C. Ministry of Health "One of 150 Outstanding Nurses of BC" (2008), the Registered Nurses Association of B.C. Award of Excellence in Nursing Practice (2002), and the National Emergency Nurses Affiliation Award of Excellence in Emergency Nursing Education (1997). Ms. Early was the first non-American president of the International Association of Forensic Nurses (2014). Sheila and her husband Peter have resided in Surrey, B.C., for twenty-seven years.

Lindsay Fitzsimmons, MA, is currently a doctor of philosophy degree candidate in York University's graduate program in clinical-developmental psychology. She has published in the area of forensic psychology on *Charter* protections and false confessions, and teaches Psychology & Law at York University.

Cecilia Hageman, BSc (Genetics), PhD (Plant Sciences), LLB (Western University), LLM (Osgoode Hall), is an associate member of the Law Society of Upper Canada (called to the bar in 1991) and was employed as a forensic biologist with the Centre of Forensic Sciences (CFS) in Toronto, beginning in 1991. She has been an expert witness in criminal proceedings in Ontario courts in the fields of body fluid identification, forensic DNA analysis, and bloodstain pattern analysis. She was a member of the CFS's biology section management team from 1998 to 2013. In July 2013, she joined the Faculty of Science at the University of Ontario Institute of Technology (UOIT) in Oshawa as an assistant professor in UOIT's forensic science program, where she mentors and supervises student research, and also develops and teaches undergraduate and graduate courses in forensic biology, population genetics, criminalistics, and law. Her publications include C. Hageman, D. Prevett, & W. Murray, *DNA Handbook*, 2d ed. (Oxford: Butterworths, 2008) and K. Johnston & C. Hageman, "Blood and Bodily Substances," in G. Chayko, et al., eds., *Forensic Evidence in Canada*, 2d edition (Toronto: Canada Law Book, 1999).

Sarah Harland-Logan, BA, JD, is an associate at Kapoor Barristers, a criminal defence firm in Toronto, Ontario. She obtained her bachelor of arts degree (magna cum laude) from Harvard University, where she studied English literature and health policy. During her undergraduate years she also served as special assistant to Dr. James Orbinski, past International President, Médecins Sans Frontières. Ms. Harland-Logan earned her juris doctorate at the University of Toronto, graduating in 2014. In law school, she worked in the criminal and university affairs divisions at Downtown Legal Services, examined CSIS practices with regard to security certificates at the David Asper Centre for Constitutional Rights, and prosecuted provincial offences in Toronto and Kenora. Ms. Harland-Logan began volunteering with Innocence Canada (formerly known as the Association in Defence of the Wrongly Convicted [AIDWYC]) in 2012 and is the principal author of the "Historical Cases" section of Innocence Canada's website. After completing her articles at Greenspan Humphrey Lavine, she was called to the Ontario Bar in 2015 and subsequently worked as a sole practitioner focusing on Ontario Review Board disposition appeals. Ms. Harland-Logan is a member of the Criminal Lawyers' Association, the Ontario Bar Association, and the Toronto Lawyers Association.

Liam Hendrikse, BSc (Hons), MSc (ForSci), was born in Nassau, Bahamas, and raised in the Toronto area. He graduated from McMaster University in 1995, with an honours bachelor of science degree in chemistry. In 1998, he graduated from King's College at the University of London, with a master of science degree in forensic science. He was a British Home Office forensic scientist from 1998 until

2006, where he specialized in the examination of firearms, ammunition and related items, and crime scene and post-mortem analyses. During that time, he was a lead reporting officer for Armed Criminality, a lecturer at King's College in forensic science, a representative at the European Network of Forensic Science Institutes and Working Groups, a registered member of the Council for the Registration of Forensic Practitioners, a member of the Forensic Science Society, and a recipient of the first Cambridgeshire High Sheriff's Award for Excellence in Forensic Science. He now resides in Hamilton, acting as a consultant to criminal lawyers on matters relating to firearms and ballistics, in addition to working with the University of Ontario Institute of Technology on expanding, developing, and delivering their forensic science programs and courses. He is also a registered expert in firearms and ballistics both with the International Criminal Court in The Hague and the County of Los Angeles Superior Court in California.

Jayantha Herath, MD, DLM, MD (Forensic), FCAP, FRCPC (AP & FP), is a staff forensic pathologist, the medical director of the Provincial Forensic Pathology Unit (Toronto) of the Ontario Forensic Pathology Service, and an assistant professor in the Department of Laboratory Medicine and Pathobiology at the University of Toronto. He obtained his medical degree and master's degree from the Medical University of Varna, Bulgaria (1993), and a post-graduate diploma in legal medicine and doctor of forensic medicine (2002) from the University of Colombo, Sri Lanka. He completed his residency in anatomical pathology (2010) and a fellowship in Forensic Pathology at the University of Manitoba, and obtained certification in anatomical pathology (2010) and forensic pathology (2012) from the Royal College of Physicians and Surgeons of Canada (FRCPC). Dr. Herath worked as a medical examiner for the Province of Manitoba and as an assistant professor in the Department of Pathology of the University of Manitoba before joining the Ontario Forensic Pathology Service. He worked as a senior lecturer in the Department of Forensic Medicine and Toxicology at the University of Colombo and as a specialist in forensic medicine in Sri Lanka before immigrating to Canada.

Wade Knaap, Toronto Police Service Det. Cst. (Retired), is a part-time faculty member in the forensic science program at the University of Toronto Mississauga where he teaches forensic science and forensic identification-related courses. Prior to this, Mr. Knaap was a detective constable with the Toronto Police Service and a forensic identification specialist in the Forensic Identification Services Unit. Mr. Knaap regularly lectures and conducts workshops at universities, colleges, and conferences throughout Canada and the United States on forensic development techniques and related topics. He is a past president of the Canadian

Identification Society and a former chair of the Ontario Police College Forensic Advisory Board. Mr. Knaap is a serving member of the Forensic Advisory Committee at the University of Ontario Institute of Technology and teaches a course in applied methods of forensic identification at the University of Windsor. He has been published numerous times in the *Journal of Forensic Identification*, *Identification Canada*, and the *RCMP Gazette* regarding forensic identification concepts. Mr. Knaap was also a contributing author in the textbook *Crime and Measurement: Methods in Forensic Investigation* (Durham, NC: Carolina Academic Press, 2011). Since 2012, Mr. Knaap has been the editor of *Identification Canada* (published by the Canadian Identification Society). In 2002–2003, he was the recipient of the Al Waxman Award for Excellence in the Field of Forensic Identification.

Anita Lal, MD, D-ABP, FCAP, became a staff forensic pathologist at the Provincial Forensic Pathology Unit in Toronto in 2013 and is a lecturer in the Department of Laboratory Medicine and Pathobiology at the University of Toronto. She obtained a medical degree at Ross University in the West Indies. She completed her residency training in anatomical and clinical pathology at Wayne State University and a fellowship in forensic pathology at the Wayne County Medical Examiner's Office, both in Detroit, Michigan. Dr. Lal was an assistant chief medical examiner at the Office of the Chief Medical Examiner in Calgary, Alberta, and a clinical assistant professor at the Faculty of Medicine, University of Calgary, before taking her position in Toronto. She has testified as an expert witness in Alberta, Michigan, and Ontario. She is an investigative coroner for homicides and criminally suspicious deaths in Ontario.

Patrick Laturnus, RCMP S/Sgt. (Retired), is an acclaimed forensic crime scene specialist who has been doing this work since 1975, specializing as a Bloodstain Pattern Analyst in 1990. He retired from the Royal Canadian Mounted Police with thirty-one years of service and then became a full-time instructor at the Ontario Police College for six years. He presently works as a private consultant in Ottawa, Ontario, which entails criminal casework as well as teaching on an international basis. Mr. Laturnus was responsible for establishing a training program that has certified people as qualified bloodstain analysts not only in the province of Ontario, but also in other provinces as well as internationally. He has written several bloodstain-related articles and has appeared on radio and television to discuss his work. His international work was recognized when he was designated a Distinguished Visitor by the Government of Singapore. He is the proud recipient of the Amethyst and Ovation awards from the Government of Ontario, as well as the winner of the Foster Award, which is the highest honour bestowed by the Canadian

Identification Society. The ultimate recognition, as a bloodstain analyst, was being awarded the honour of Distinguished Member of the International Association of Bloodstain Pattern Analysts.

Stéphanie B. Marion, MA, PhD, is a SSHRC postdoctoral fellow conducting research at the University of Ontario Institute of Technology in Oshawa, and at CUNY's John Jay College of Criminal Justice in New York. Her research focuses on the factors that influence the accuracy and content of lay witness reports.

Rolf W. Mathewes, BSc, PhD, is currently a full professor of biological sciences, and served as associate dean of Science at Simon Fraser University (SFU) between 2000 and 2011. He received a bachelor of science degree in biology from SFU in 1969 and a doctoral degree in botany from the University of British Columbia in 1973. After a year's postdoctoral research in Cambridge, England, he returned to British Columbia and eventually took up a faculty position in biological sciences at SFU in 1975. He has conducted paleoenvironmental research in Scotland, Western Canada, and Europe, and has researched in Germany as an Alexander von Humboldt Foundation research fellow on three occasions. In his academic career, he has been president of both the Canadian Association of Palynologists and the American Association of Stratigraphic Palynologists, and associate editor of the *Canadian Journal of Botany and Ecoscience*. He has published more than 120 scientific articles and co-edited a book on Haida Gwaii in 2005. He received the 2011 SFU Alumni Association award for academic achievement. As a forensic botanist, he has, since 1986, investigated homicide cases with the RCMP, the Vancouver Police Department, and municipal police forces, as well as non-homicide cases, including Aboriginal land claims issues.

Tim Moore, BA, PhD, is professor of psychology and chair of the Psychology Department at York University's Glendon College, where he teaches Psychology & Law. He has served as a consultant or expert witness in dozens of criminal trials on issues related to witness reliability, investigative practices, and police undercover operations. Dr. Moore is a regular participant in various legal educational programs, including Innocence Canada (formerly known as AIDWYC), the Criminal Lawyers' Association, the Ontario Bar Association, Osgoode's Professional Development series, and the National Judicial Institute.

Caitlin M. Pakosh, HBSc, JD, has been working as case management counsel of Innocence Canada (formerly known as AIDWYC) since 2012 and is responsible for managing the Association's cases across Canada. She obtained her honours bachelor of science degree, specializing in forensic anthropology and earning a minor in biology, from the University of Toronto Mississauga in 2008. Her undergraduate thesis, which examined the decomposition of dismembered pig limbs enclosed in plastic bags and submerged in Lake Ontario, was conducted during her internship with the Toronto Police Service Marine Unit and published in the *Journal of Forensic Sciences* in 2009. Ms. Pakosh obtained her Juris Doctor degree from the University of Calgary in 2011. She has appeared in the Court of Appeal for Ontario and has worked on intervener and appellate cases, appearing at a variety of levels of court, including the Supreme Court of Canada, as well as ministerial review applications. Since 2013, Ms. Pakosh has cross-examined forensic science students in annual mock trials at the University of Toronto Mississauga, where students practise being expert witnesses. She is a member of the Criminal Lawyers' Association and the National Association of Criminal Defense Lawyers. She is also an associate member of the American Academy of Forensic Sciences and the Canadian Society of Forensic Science.

Michael Pickup, MSc, MD, FRCPC, obtained his medical degree and completed residency training in anatomical pathology, followed by subspecialty fellowship training in forensic pathology at the University of Toronto. He holds certification in both anatomical and forensic pathology from the Royal College of Physicians and Surgeons of Canada. Dr. Pickup is currently a staff forensic pathologist at the Provincial Forensic Pathology Unit in Toronto, an assistant professor in the Department of Laboratory Medicine and Pathobiology at the University of Toronto, and an adjunct professor of pathology and laboratory medicine at Western University. He has helped develop a collaborative educational initiative between the University of Toronto's Department of Diagnostic Radiology and Laboratory Medicine and Pathobiology. He is an investigative coroner for homicides and criminally suspicious deaths in Ontario, and a consultant forensic pathologist to Bermuda.

Michael S. Pollanen, MD, PhD, FRCPath, DMJ (Path), FRCPC Founder, forensic pathology, is the chief forensic pathologist of Ontario, a professor of laboratory medicine and pathobiology at the University of Toronto, a founder of the forensic pathology program of the Royal College of Physicians and Surgeons of Canada, and an investigative coroner for homicides and criminally suspicious deaths in Ontario. He oversees the Ontario Forensic Pathology Service, and directs the Centre for Forensic Science and Medicine and the Forensic Pathology Residency/Fellowship training programs at the University of Toronto. Dr. Pollanen has a special interest in capacity development of forensic medicine in low- and middle-income countries to support human rights and the rule of law. Dr. Pollanen has regularly published in the peer-reviewed literature. He provides second opinions on controversial cases (prosecution, defence, and reviews for other jurisdictions). He has conducted over 2,000 medicolegal autopsies, testified over 200 times in court, and has twice testified in the Ontario Court of Appeal, in the cases of *Truscott (Re)*, 2007 ONCA 575 and *R. v. Mullins-Johnson*, 2007 ONCA 720.

Dan C. Purdy, BSc, FSSocDip, FCSFS, D-ABFDE, majored in mathematics and physics at the University of British Columbia and, in 1969, joined the RCMP, completing a two-year training program in forensic document examination. Mr. Purdy joined the Canadian Society of Forensic Science in 1971 and served terms as a chairperson, director, and society treasurer. He transferred to the RCMP's Ottawa laboratory in 1979 where he became head of the RCMP's Document Operational Support Unit and Ottawa Document Section. He received a certificate of qualification in forensic document examination from the American Board of Forensic Document Examiners in 1980 and served as its president from 1993 to 1995. In 1989, Mr. Purdy was appointed the RCMP's chief scientist of Document Services. In 1999, Mr. Purdy commenced work in the private sector. He is a member of the American Society of Questioned Document Examiners (serving as president from 2004 to 2006), the American Academy of Forensic Science, and a fellow of both the Chartered Society of Forensic Science and the CSFS. In 2012, Mr. Purdy was presented with the Albert S. Osborn Award of Excellence by the American Society of Questioned Document Examiners. Mr. Purdy has written over thirty scientific papers; examined over 4,500 cases; and testified as an expert witness in British Columbia, Alberta, Manitoba, Ontario, Quebec, Newfoundland & Labrador, the Yukon Territory, Nunavut, Bermuda, the United States, and Hong Kong. In 2015, he received the American Academy of Forensic Science's Award of Merit.

Ashwyn Rajagopalan, MD, FRCPC, joined the Provincial Forensic Pathology Unit in Toronto as a staff forensic pathologist in 2013, after completing his forensic pathology residency training at the University of Toronto. He graduated from Queen's University with a doctor of medicine degree, and completed his residency in anatomical pathology at McMaster University. Dr. Rajagopalan is a lecturer in the Department of Laboratory Medicine and Pathobiology at the University of Toronto. He has been a consultant to the Cayman Islands and is an investigative coroner for homicides and criminally suspicious deaths in Ontario.

Steve Rogers, EnCE, A+, CNA, formerly worked in law enforcement, having retired from the RCMP in 2003 as staff sergeant in charge of the "O" Division Technological Crime Unit. He began conducting digital forensics in 1994 and was subsequently transferred to the "O" Division Technological Crime Unit. Since retiring from the RCMP, he has continued digital forensics investigations through his private investigation agency, Digital Evidence International Inc., in London, Ontario. Mr. Rogers has conducted or assisted with the examination of thousands of pieces of digital evidence in cases such as murder, fraud, proceeds of crime, theft of intellectual property, copyright, and child pornography. In Mr. Rogers's practice, he provides unbiased and impartial analysis of digital evidence in civil matters as well as criminal matters for both the defence and law enforcement communities. He has provided expert reports, affidavit evidence, and has testified at trial for both civil and criminal matters.

Tracy Rogers, BA, MA, PhD, is the director of the Forensic Science Program at the University of Toronto Mississauga and an associate professor of anthropology. She is a forensic anthropologist who has been actively involved in case work since 1998, and is currently a consultant to the Ontario Forensic Pathology Service. Dr. Rogers has worked on cases in Ontario, Manitoba, and British Columbia, and most notably was the primary forensic anthropologist during the investigation of serial killer Robert Pickton in 2002–2003. She has been qualified as an expert witness in the B.C. Supreme Court, the Court of Queen's Bench of Manitoba, and the Ontario Court of Justice. Her research interests involve the identification of unknown skeletal remains, including methods of estimating the age-at-death of an individual from the skeleton; skeletal sex determination; skeletal techniques for assessing the ancestry/biogeographical origin of the deceased; and positive identification of unidentified human remains. Related topics include factors influencing skeletal health, the study of juvenile skeletons, and trauma analysis. She also researches the application of new technologies to the documentation and analysis of outdoor crime scenes and clandestine graves, including 3D methods of capturing data that are both geospecific and quantifiable.

Toby H. Rose, MD, FRCPC, is the deputy chief forensic pathologist of the Ontario Forensic Pathology Service and works at the Provincial Forensic Pathology Unit in Toronto. Dr. Rose received a bachelor of science degree and a doctor of medicine degree from the University of Saskatchewan, and trained in anatomical pathology at the University of Toronto. She is a fellow of the Royal College of Physicians and Surgeons of Canada in anatomical pathology, a Diplomate of the American Board of Pathology in both Anatomical and Forensic Pathology, and assistant professor of Laboratory Medicine and Pathobiology at the University of Toronto. She has performed more than 5,000 medicolegal autopsies and has given expert testimony in courts in Ontario, Nova Scotia, and Nunavut. Dr. Rose is an investigative coroner for homicides and criminally suspicious deaths in Ontario.

Vincenzo Rondinelli, LLB (Osgoode), LLM (Osgoode), is a criminal defence lawyer in Toronto. He has appeared at all levels of the courts including the Supreme Court of Canada and argues appeals regularly before the Ontario Court of Appeal. He joined the adjunct faculty at Osgoode Hall Law School in 2003 and is currently co-director of the Criminal Intensive Program and co-instructor in the Forensic Science & the Law course. He is certified by the Law Society of Upper Canada as a specialist in criminal law.

Daniel M. Scanlan, BA, LLB, has been with the Criminal Justice Branch since 1999 and is currently assigned to the Prosecution Support Unit where he specializes in issues related to digital evidence, search and seizure, and wiretaps. His litigation practice is focused on cases with cyber crime or electronic evidence issues. He teaches a course on electronic evidence to B.C. Crown counsel and has been responsible for policy on electronic disclosure, electronic evidence, and related issues. Mr. Scanlan acts as a resource person to B.C. police in his fields. He has authored a book entitled *Digital Evidence in Criminal Law* (Toronto: Canada Law Book, 2011). He has in the past prosecuted cases of assault, murder, fraud, and assisted suicide. Mr. Scanlan provided advice to police on investigations regarding child pornography, Internet luring, computer hacking, and wiretap evidence. Prior to joining the Victoria office, he was a prosecutor with the federal Department of Justice from December 1992, and was in private practice prior to that with the firm of Singleton Urquhart in Vancouver.

The Honourable Mr. Justice Richard D. Schneider, BSc, MA, PhD, LLB, LLM, CPsych, of the Ontario Court of Justice (appointed 2000), is chair of the Ontario Review Board and deputy judge of the Territorial Court of the Yukon. He was named honourary president of the Canadian Psychological Association in 2002. He was previously a criminal defence lawyer and certified clinical psychologist, working as counsel to the Ontario Review Board from 1994 to 2000. His private practice was generally limited to the representation of mentally disordered accused. Justice Schneider is certified by the Law Society of Upper Canada as a specialist in criminal litigation. He is also an adjunct professor for the Department of Psychiatry, Faculty of Medicine, and Faculty of Law at the University of Toronto. He has also been appointed as alternate chairman of the Nunavut Review Board. A great deal of his time has been spent presiding at the Mental Health Court in Toronto (www.mentalhealthcourt.ca). Justice Schneider's major research interests are competency and criminal responsibility. He has published extensively in the area of mental disorder and the law. Recent books include: *Mental Disorder and the Law: A primer for legal and mental health professionals* (2006, with H. Bloom); *Mental Health Courts: Decriminalizing the Mentally Ill* (2007, with H. Bloom and

M. Heerema); *Annotated Mental Health Statutes* (2007); *The Lunatic and the Lords* (2009); *Law and Mental Disorder: A Comprehensive and Practical Approach* (2013, with H. Bloom) (all published by Irwin Law www.irwinlaw.com).

Dr. David Sweet, OC, DMD, PhD, DABFO, FICD, FACD, is the associate dean of students and a tenured professor of oral diagnosis and forensic odontology at the University of British Columbia. He is director of the BOLD Forensic Laboratory, a unique resource dedicated to full-time forensic dentistry research, casework, and graduate teaching. This is the place where laboratory discoveries and modern forensic science methods are applied to dental evidence to assist in the resolution of legal issues. Since the laboratory opened in 1996, Dr. Sweet has been involved in over 1,000 high-profile criminal cases. He has developed new techniques that are now used internationally by forensic investigators. In 2008, Dr. Sweet was appointed an officer of the Order of Canada for his work as a forensic scientist, researcher, teacher, and consultant. Dr. Sweet was chief scientist for disaster victim identification at INTERPOL in France from 2005 to 2011 and a forensic advisor to the International Committee of the Red Cross in Switzerland from 2009 to 2012.

Dr. Sherah VanLaerhoven, BSc, MPM, PhD, received her doctor of philosophy degree (2001) from the University of Arkansas in entomology, and master of policy management degree (1997) and bachelor of science degree in biology (1995) from Simon Fraser University, B.C. Dr. VanLaerhoven is an associate professor in the Department of Biology at the University of Windsor. She is a past president of the North American Forensic Entomology Association and currently serves on the board of directors for the Canadian Society of Forensic Science. She has served on the board of directors for the entomological societies of British Columbia and Ontario. She is a Board Certified Entomologist (BCE); a Diplomate of the American Board of Forensic Entomology (D-ABFE); and a consultant and expert witness for police, medical examiners/coroners, and lawyers in Canada and internationally, including the high-profile cases *R. v. Truscott* and *R. v. Baltovitch*. Her research in forensic entomology focuses on causes and mechanisms for variability in arrival patterns of insects on bodies and testing current assumptions regarding the behaviour of forensically relevant insects. Her work has been featured numerous times in different media including Discovery Channel, *Discovery Magazine*, the *Globe and Mail*, NPR, and CBC Radio. She was awarded Canada's Top 40 under 40 (2006) and the C. Gordon Hewitt Medal (2009).

James Watterson, PhD, F-ABFT, is an associate professor in the Department of Forensic Science at Laurentian University. He obtained his bachelor of science degree in chemistry from McGill University and his master of science and doctor of philosophy degrees, both in analytical chemistry, from the University of Toronto. Dr. Watterson worked as a forensic toxicologist at the Centre of Forensic Sciences in Toronto before joining the faculty at Laurentian University. He is a consulting forensic toxicologist and a fellow of the American Board of Forensic Toxicology (F-ABFT). He is cross-appointed to the Department of Chemistry & Biochemistry and the biomolecular sciences program at Laurentian University.

Alison Weir, PhD, is an associate professor, teaching stream statistics at the University of Toronto Mississauga (UTM). She obtained her bachelor of mathematics from the University of Waterloo, her master of science degree in statistics from the University of London, UK, and her doctor of philosophy degree in statistics from the University of Toronto. Her interests include applied statistics, particularly modern non-parametric methodologies. She is also interested in statistical literacy, an increasingly important advantage for professionals operating in today's technological data-heavy world. Dr. Weir designed and implemented a UTM course in statistics for forensic sciences and she has helped numerous forensic science students with their fourth-year projects. Dr. Weir has a passion for assisting lawyers in understanding the statistics underlying the forensic sciences. She enjoys working as a consultant and hopes that her future work with legal professionals will help to strengthen statistical literacy in the court system.

James G. Wigmore, HBSc, worked as a forensic alcohol toxicologist at the Centre of Forensic Sciences in Toronto from 1976 until his retirement in 2005. He obtained his honours bachelor of science degree from the University of Toronto in 1980. He is a designated analyst under section 254(1) of the *Criminal Code* of Canada and was a member of the national advisory board, the Alcohol Test Committee (which advises the federal Department of Justice on breath and blood alcohol testing) from 1993 to 2005. Mr. Wigmore has testified in over 600 criminal trials at various levels of court, as well as in civil and coroner cases, and has published more than fifty articles in the field of forensic alcohol toxicology. In October 2005, he was the recipient of the most prestigious award of the Canadian Society of Forensic Sciences, the Derome Award, which recognizes outstanding contributions to the field of forensic science. Between 2004 and 2012, Mr. Wigmore was a faculty member of the Center for Studies for Law in Action and as such lectured at the Borkenstein Course at Indiana University in Bloomington, Indiana. His recently published book, *Wigmore on Alcohol: Forensic Alcohol Toxicology for the Medicolegal Professional* (Irwin Law, 2011) has received international acclaim.

SPECIAL MENTION

Katherine Linton, BA, JD candidate (2017), began her undergraduate studies at the University of Waterloo in recreation and leisure, intending to pursue a career in fine arts or the sports industry. After her second year, however, her work at a respite facility for children with neurological disorders sparked her strong and continuing interest in psychology and advocacy. Ms. Linton returned to school in the fall with new direction and enthusiasm to help society's most vulnerable persons. She shifted her focus towards the study of law, graduating from the University of Waterloo with a major in psychology and an option in criminology. She is currently a law student at the Bora Laskin Faculty of Law at Lakehead University, interested in pursuing a career in family law. Ms. Linton assisted with this guide by taking the notes of the meeting that formed the basis for Chapter 2, "Forensic Experts in the Criminal Justice System."

Jessica Piekny, HBSc, is a graduate student from the University of Toronto Mississauga. She graduated from the forensic science program with an honours bachelor of science degree specializing in forensic chemistry in June 2014. During her undergraduate studies, Ms. Piekny completed a one-year internship at the Ontario Office of the Fire Marshal in collaboration with the Centre of Forensic Sciences. Her research paper was published in *Identification Canada* in September 2013. Ms. Piekny is also an active member of the Canadian Identification Society, a past member of the conference organizing committee (2014), and a serving member of the editorial review board for *Identification Canada*. Ms. Piekny was a laboratory technician at the University of Windsor for the Forensic Science Field Course during the summer semester of 2014 and the sessional instructional assistant for the Forensic Identification and Advanced Forensic Identification courses at the University of Toronto (2014–2015). Most recently, Ms. Piekny worked at the Centre of Forensic Sciences as a forensic analyst/receiving officer in the Centre Receiving Office. Ms. Piekny aided with this guide by assisting Wade Knaap in conducting research and identifying important issues to address in Chapter 8, "Fingerprint Evidence." In concert with Mr. Knaap, Ms. Piekny also provided feedback to Caitlin Pakosh in refining the legal context section for that same chapter.

Kristy S. Simpson, BA, MI Candidate (2016), is currently a master of information candidate at the University of Toronto's Faculty of Information. She completed her undergraduate degree in criminology and sociology at the University of Toronto and has volunteered with both the Prisoners AIDS/HIV Support Action Network (PASAN) and Innocence Canada (formerly known as AIDWYC). She is currently completing a practicum project in the library at the Centre for Addiction and Mental Health (CAMH). She hopes to find a librarian position in the fields of social justice, health, or education. Ms. Simpson assisted with this guide by formatting and following up with chapter citations. She was also instrumental in formulating the glossary of this book by evaluating each chapter and identifying terms appropriate for inclusion in the glossary; in doing so, Ms. Simpson provided feedback to the editor on the content of various chapters.

In addition to the above contributors and individuals of special mention, the editor would also like to express her gratitude to:

Mr. Michael Dineen of Dawe & Dineen, for peer-reviewing and providing valuable feedback for the chapters and legal context sections written by Caitlin Pakosh.

Dr. Glenn Langenburg of Elite Forensic Sciences, for peer-reviewing and providing valuable feedback for the fingerprint evidence legal context section written by Caitlin Pakosh, particularly as it relates to enhancing the section's coverage of current forensic literature related to fingerprint analysis.

Dr. Robert Langille of the Centre of Forensic Sciences, for peer-reviewing the forensic drug toxicology section written by Dr. James Watterson.

Adjunct Professor Tamara Levy, Director of the University of British Columbia Innocence Project at the Allard School of Law, for providing research materials, peer review, and feedback for the legal context section of Chapter 10, "Fire Investigation."

Table of Cases

Index

NOTES: Entries for the forensic disciplines are listed under the keyword (e.g., anthropology, forensic); glossary page references are shown in boldface; F = figure; N = note; T = table and symbols

Printed and bound by CPI Group (UK) Ltd, Croydon, CR0 4YY
15/09/2026
14962406-0001